T0145102

Lecture Notes in Computer Science   10714

Commenced Publication in 1973
Founding and Former Series Editors:
Gerhard Goos, Juris Hartmanis, and Jan van Leeuwen

More information about this series at http://www.springer.com/series/7409

Adrian David Cheok · Masahiko Inami
Teresa Romão (Eds.)

Advances in Computer Entertainment Technology

14th International Conference, ACE 2017
London, UK, December 14–16, 2017
Proceedings

 Springer

Editors
Adrian David Cheok
City, University of London
London
UK

and

Imagineering Institute
Iskandar Puteri
Malaysia

Masahiko Inami
University of Tokyo
Tokyo
Japan

Teresa Romão
NOVA University of Lisbon
Lisbon
Portugal

ISSN 0302-9743   ISSN 1611-3349   (electronic)
Lecture Notes in Computer Science
ISBN 978-3-319-76269-2   ISBN 978-3-319-76270-8   (eBook)
https://doi.org/10.1007/978-3-319-76270-8

Library of Congress Control Number: 2018934342

LNCS Sublibrary: SL3 – Information Systems and Applications, incl. Internet/Web, and HCI

Printed on acid-free paper

This Springer imprint is published by the registered company Springer International Publishing AG part of Springer Nature
The registered company address is: Gewerbestrasse 11, 6330 Cham, Switzerland

Preface

This book consists of the proceedings of the 14th International Conference on Advances in Computer Entertainment Technology (ACE 2017), held in the vibrant city of London, UK, during December 14–16, 2017. There were a total of 59 paper presentations, including 14 short presentations, and over 100 participants from 21 countries at this annual academic event.

For many years, ACE followed a somewhat traditional conference format in terms of presentation styles, with separate tracks for submissions such as full/short papers, posters, and creative showcases etc. During ACE 2016 in Osaka, keynote speaker Prof. Hirokazu Kato initiated many discussions about the future directions of ACE in computer entertainment research, especially with the emergence of more and more academic conferences in this field over the years. ACE has always aimed to stand out as the leader and one of the best conferences in computer entertainment, and that means we need to fundamentally challenge and change the ways "entertainment" is assessed and presented to our community. The Steering Committee decided that it was time to break the boundaries of the traditional 20th century conference format and truly embrace the value of entertainment by transforming the conference into an inspirational, interactive, and creative playground for researchers.

At ACE 2017, a radical new format was tested out from the paper submissions, to the selection process, to the presentation requirements. First, we eliminated different tracks for submissions and carefully reviewed every paper as a full paper. We also removed previous restrictions and requirements for the presentation of each accepted work. Instead of allocating different sessions for oral presentations and demonstrations, we simply assigned a time slot to each paper during which authors could use any technique or style to present their work. Authors could also display and demonstrate their work during the coffee breaks and lunch breaks to stimulate more discussions. We encouraged presenters "as leaders in computer entertainment to make their presentation as entertaining as possible and not a normal PowerPoint presentation." Besides showing demonstrations, videos, or posters, they could also "recite a poem, do a dance or sing a song etc." Many presenters surprised us with their creativity and effort put into making their presentations fun and innovative. Most notably, one presenter delivered his entire presentation in a poem, another presenter turned his presentation into a realtime quiz in which the audience competed with each other by answering questions related to the paper.

To complement the goal of making radical changes, we invited Dr. David Levy to give a though-provoking keynote speech "Can Robots and Humans Make Babies Together?" Through our choice of the keynote speech, we hope to have conveyed to our participants that not only does ACE look into the conventional research topics, but we also accept and invite discussions of the somewhat controversial topics of computer science.

Lastly, we hope all delegates enjoyed the new experiences at ACE 2017 in one of the world's most exciting cities. We also hope you enjoy reading these proceedings and find the papers helpful in your research.

December 2017   Adrian David Cheok

Organization

Steering Committee

Adrian David Cheok	City, University of London, UK, Imagineering Institute, Malaysia
Masahiko Inami	University of Tokyo, Japan
Teresa Ramão	Universidade NOVA de Lisboa, Portugal

General Chair

Adrian David Cheok	City, University of London, UK, Imagineering Institute, Malaysia

Program Chair

Saša Arsovski	Imagineering Institute, Malaysia

Demo Chair

Masahiko Inami	University of Tokyo, Japan

Organizing Chair

Emma Yann Zhang	Imagineering Institute, Malaysia

Senior Program Committee

Anton Nijholt	University of Twente, The Netherlands
Daisuke Sakamoto	Hokkaido University, Japan
Eduardo Dias	Universidade NOVA de Lisboa, Portugal
Fernando Birra	Universidade NOVA de Lisboa, Portugal
Haruhiro Katayose	Kwansei Gakuin University, Japan
Lindsay Grace	American University, USA
Maic Masuch	University of Duisburg-Essen, Germany
Shoichi Hasegawa	Tokyo Institute of Technology, Japan
Yoram Chisik	Madeira Interactive Technologies Institute, Portugal
Wolfgang Mueller	PH Weingarten, Germany
Ralf Doerner	HS Rhein-Main, Germany

Program Committee

Ali Nassiri	Manuel Fonseca
Antonio Roda	Marc Herrlich
Augusto Sousa	Marcello Gomez-Maureira
Beatriz Sousa Santos	Masahiro Furukawa
Bongkeum Jeong	Mitsuru Minakuchi
Bosede Edwards	Nishikant Deshmukh
Chamari Edirisinghe	Nosiba Khougali
Daniel Rea	Oscar Mealha
Filipe Luz	Patricia Pons
Frank Nack	Patrícia Gouveia
Frutuoso Silva	Pedro A.-Santos
Gavin Sim	Pei-Yi Kuo
Henrik Warpefelt	Phil Lopes
Hiroyuki Kajimoto	Robert Allison
Hiroyuki Mitsuhara	Robert Mcgrath
Holger Reckter	Rui Nóbrega
Ichiroh Kanaya	Sharon Kalu Ufere
Idris Muniru	Simone Kriglstein
Insook Choi	Somaiyeh Vedadi
Jose Danado	Susanne Haake
Jose Luís-Silva	Thomas Laubach
Julian Fietkau	Thomas Klauer
Kaoru Sumi	Tom Vierjahn
Kasun Karunanayaka	Valentina Nisi
Kevin Bielawski	Winyu Chinthammit
Khiet Truong	Yongsoon Choi
Knut Hartmann	Yuichi Itoh
Leonel Morgado	

Sponsoring Institutions

Multimodal Technologies and Interaction Journal

Multimodal Technologies and Interaction
an open access journal by [MDPI]

Can Robots and Humans Make Babies Together?
(Keynote Speech)

David Levy

15 December 2017

This talk gives a guided tour of the advances achieved by researchers in cell biology and biorobotics, which prompted the question whether it is possible for humans and robots to make babies together. Until the birth of the first test tube baby, it was believed that a human baby could only be conceived by the means of sexual intercourse between a man and a woman. A series of breakthroughs in stem cell research, such as the frog experiments done by John Gurdon, the ability to reprogram cells, the creation of embryos from skin cells, as well as the TNT technology, has proven once and again that life can be created by the genetic engineering of human cells. This talk also looks into the genetic robot, created from a set of computerized DNA codes that determine its personality. It is possible for such genetic codes from a robot to be combined with human cells to create a baby that has genetic information from both a human and a robot. The talk concludes by discussing the ethical implications related to the genetic engineering of human embryos.

Contents

Creating Room-Scale Interactive Mixed-Reality Worlds Using
Off-the-Shelf Technologies. 1
   Vlasios Kasapakis, Damianos Gavalas, and Elena Dzardanova

Evaluation of a Mixed Reality Head-Mounted Projection Display
to Support Motion Capture Acting 14
   Daniel Kade, Rikard Lindell, Hakan Ürey, and Oğuzhan Özcan

Step by Step: Evaluating Navigation Styles in Mixed Reality
Entertainment Experience. 32
   Mara Dionísio, Paulo Bala, Valentina Nisi, Ian Oakley, and Nuno Nunes

Increasing Presence in a Mixed Reality Application by Integrating
a Real Time Tracked Full Body Representation 46
   Felix Born and Maic Masuch

An Approach to Basic Emotion Recognition Through Players Body
Pose Using Virtual Reality Devices. 61
   Gabriel Peñas and Federico Peinado

Development and Evaluation of an Interactive Therapy Robot 66
   *Tomoko Kohori, Shiho Hirayama, Takenori Hara, Michiko Muramatsu,
   Hiroyuki Naganuma, Masayuki Yamano, Kazuko Ichikawa,
   Hiroko Matsumoto, and Hiroko Uchiyama*

Lost Puppy: Towards a Playful Intervention for Wandering
Dementia Patients 84
   Yacintha Aakster, Robby van Delden, and Stefan Lentelink

A Dynamic Scenario by Remote Supervision: A Serious Game
in the Museum with a Nao Robot. 103
   Damien Mondou, Armelle Prigent, and Arnaud Revel

Hugvie as a Therapeutic Agent in the Improvement of Interaction Skills
in Children with Developmental Disabilities: An Exploratory Study 117
   *Diana Leonor Garcês Costa, Yoram Chisik,
   and Ana Lucia dos Santos Faria*

A Week Without Plastic Bags: Creating Games and Interactive
Products for Environmental Awareness 128
   *Anna Gardeli, Spyros Vosinakis, Konstantinos Englezos,
   Dimitra Mavroudi, Manolis Stratis, and Modestos Stavrakis*

A Tentative Assumption of Electroacoustic Music as an Enjoyable Music
for Diverse People   139
   Takuro Shibayama, Hidefumi Ohmura, Tatsuji Takahashi,
   and Kiyoshi Furukawa

Voice Animator: Automatic Lip-Synching in Limited
Animation by Audio   153
   Shoichi Furukawa, Tsukasa Fukusato, Shugo Yamaguchi,
   and Shigeo Morishima

Polymorphic Cataloguing and Interactive 3D Visualization for Multiple
Context of Digital Content: MoSaIC   172
   Hiroyo Ishikawa and Kunitake Kaneko

Leveraging Icebreaking Tasks to Facilitate Uptake of Voice
Communication in Multiplayer Games.   187
   Kieran Hicks, Kathrin Gerling, Patrick Dickinson, Conor Linehan,
   and Carl Gowen

Including Non-gamers: A Case Study Comparing Touch and Motion Input
in a 3D Game for Research   202
   Isabelle Kniestedt, Elizabeth Camilleri,
   and Marcello A. Gómez Maureira

Player Adaptivity and Safety in Location-Based Games   219
   João Jacob, Ana Lopes, Rui Nóbrega, Rui Rodrigues,
   and António Coelho

Dreadful Virtualities: A Comparative Case Study of Player Responses
to a Horror Game in Virtual Reality and Flat Screen   239
   Marta Clavero Jiménez, Amanda M. S. James,
   Marcello A. Gómez Maureira, and Isabelle Kniestedt

HapPull: Enhancement of Self-motion by Pulling Clothes   261
   Erika Oishi, Masahiro Koge, Takuto Nakamura, and Hiroyuki Kajimoto

Promoting Short-Term Gains in Physical Exercise Through
Digital Media Creation   272
   Oral Kaplan, Goshiro Yamamoto, Takafumi Taketomi,
   Yasuhide Yoshitake, Alexander Plopski, Christian Sandor,
   and Hirokazu Kato

Towards Player Adaptivity in Mobile Exergames   278
   João Jacob, Ana Lopes, Rui Nóbrega, Rui Rodrigues,
   and António Coelho

A Hybrid Virtual-Augmented Serious Game to Improve Driving
Safety Awareness   293
    Lucía Vera, Jesús Gimeno, Sergio Casas, Inma García-Pereira,
    and Cristina Portalés

Cheer Me!: A Video Game System Using Live Streaming Text Messages . . .   311
    Yu Matsuura and Sachiko Kodama

Exploring the Use of Second Screen Devices During Live Sports
Broadcasts to Promote Social Interaction   318
    Marco Cruz, Teresa Romão, Pedro Centieiro, and A. Eduardo Dias

Picognizer: A JavaScript Library for Detecting and Recognizing
Synthesized Sounds.   339
    Kazutaka Kurihara, Akari Itaya, Aiko Uemura, Tetsuro Kitahara,
    and Katashi Nagao

Towards an Emotion-Driven Adaptive System for Video Game Music.   360
    Manuel López Ibáñez, Nahum Álvarez, and Federico Peinado

Koto Learning Support Method Considering Articulations   368
    Mayuka Doi and Homei Miyashita

Evaluation of the Game Exermon – A Strength Exergame Inspired
by Pokémon Go   384
    Alf Inge Wang, Kristoffer Hagen, Torbjørn Høivik,
    and Gaute Meek Olsen

Photo Curation Practices on Smartphones.   406
    Xenia Zürn, Koen Damen, Fabienne van Leiden, Mendel Broekhuijsen,
    and Panos Markopoulos

The Handling of Personal Information in Mobile Games   415
    Stefan Brückner, Yukiko Sato, Shuichi Kurabayashi, and Ikumi Waragai

A Serious Mobile Game with Visual Feedback for Training
Sibilant Consonants.   430
    Ivo Anjos, Margarida Grilo, Mariana Ascensão, Isabel Guimarães,
    João Magalhães, and Sofia Cavaco

Optimized HMD System for Underwater VR Experience   451
    Hiroyuki Osone, Takatoshi Yoshida, and Yoichi Ochiai

Magnetic Table for Levitating Food for Entertainment.   462
    Kevin Stanley Bielawski, Nur Ellyza Abd Rahman, Azhri Azhar,
    Kasun Karunanayaka, Mohammed Rabea Taleb Banalzwaa,
    Ibrahim Gamal Mahmoud Moteir, and Adrian David Cheok

FunCushion: Fabricating Functional Cushion Interfaces
with Fluorescent-Pattern Displays   470
    Kohei Ikeda, Naoya Koizumi, and Takeshi Naemura

Immersion and Togetherness: How Live Visualization of Audience
Engagement Can Enhance Music Events   488
    Najereh Shirzadian, Judith A. Redi, Thomas Röggla, Alice Panza,
    Frank Nack, and Pablo Cesar

Accuracy Evaluation of Remote Photoplethysmography Estimations
of Heart Rate in Gaming Sessions with Natural Behavior.   508
    Fernando Bevilacqua, Henrik Engström, and Per Backlund

eSport vs irlSport   531
    Christopher McCutcheon, Michael Hitchens, and Anders Drachen

Heritage Hunt: Developing a Role-Playing Game for Heritage Museums   543
    Suzanne de Kock and Marcello A. Gómez Maureira

Words in Freedom: A Manifesto Machine as Critical Design   557
    Simone Ashby, Julian Hanna, Sónia Matos, and Ricardo Rodrigues

Omnidirectional Video in Museums – Authentic, Immersive
and Entertaining   567
    Jaakko Hakulinen, Tuuli Keskinen, Ville Mäkelä, Santeri Saarinen,
    and Markku Turunen

Photographing System Employing a Shoulder-Mounted PTZ Camera for
Capturing the Composition Designated by the User's Hand Gesture   588
    Shunsuke Sugasawara and Yasuyuki Kono

Roulette++: Integrating Physical Lottery Process with Digital Effects   601
    Misturu Minakuchi

Online Communication of eSports Viewers: Topic Modeling Approach   608
    Ksenia Konstantinova, Denis Bulygin, Paul Okopny,
    and Ilya Musabirov

The Development of an Augmented Virtuality for Interactive Face
Makeup System   614
    Bantita Treepong, Panut Wibulpolprasert, Hironori Mitake,
    and Shoichi Hasegawa

UPP (Unreal Prank Painter): Graffiti System Focusing on Entertainment
of Mischievous Play   626
    Shunnosuke Ando and Haruhiro Katayose

Interactive Dance Choreography Assistance   637
   Victor de Boer, Josien Jansen, Ana-Liza Tjon-A-Pauw, and Frank Nack

DanceDJ: A 3D Dance Animation Authoring System
for Live Performance.   653
   Naoya Iwamoto, Takuya Kato, Hubert P. H. Shum, Ryo Kakitsuka,
   Kenta Hara, and Shigeo Morishima

Automatic System for Editing Dance Videos Recorded Using
Multiple Cameras   671
   Shuhei Tsuchida, Satoru Fukayama, and Masataka Goto

Structured Reciprocity for Musical Performance with Swarm Agents
as a Generative Mechanism   689
   Insook Choi

Creating a Theatrical Experience on a Virtual Stage   713
   Joe Geigel

Serious...ly! Just Kidding in Personalised Therapy Through Natural
Interactions with Games.   726
   Rui Neves Madeira, André Antunes, Octavian Postolache,
   and Nuno Correia

Building Virtual World for a Project Management Game – A Case Study . . .   746
   Akash Mohan, Pranalika Arya, and Sandeep Athavale

Timebender: A Multiplayer Game Featuring Bullet Time Mechanics   761
   Christoph Pressler and Helmut Hlavacs

Move, Interact, Learn, Eat – A Toolbox for Educational
Location-Based Games   774
   Leif Oppermann, Steffen Schaal, Manuela Eisenhardt,
   Constantin Brosda, Heike Müller, and Silke Bartsch

Awkward Annie: Game-Based Assessment of English Pragmatic Skills   795
   G. Tanner Jackson, Lindsay Grace, Patricia Inglese, Jennifer Wain,
   and Robert Hone

Using a Serious Game to Assess Spatial Memory in Children and Adults . . .   809
   Mauricio Loachamín-Valencia, M.-Carmen Juan,
   Magdalena Méndez-López, and Elena Pérez-Hernández

Mafia Game Setting Research Using Game Refinement Measurement   830
   Shuo Xiong, Wenlin Li, Xinting Mao, and Hiroyuki Iida

Exploring Patterns of Shared Control in Digital Multiplayer Games.   847
   Philipp Sykownik, Katharina Emmerich, and Maic Masuch

RAIL: A Domain-Specific Language for Generating NPC Behaviors
in Action/Adventure Game.   868
    Meng Zhu and Alf Inge Wang

Speech Emotion Recognition Based on a Recurrent Neural Network
Classification Model   882
    Rubén D. Fonnegra and Gloria M. Díaz

Author Index   893

Creating Room-Scale Interactive Mixed-Reality Worlds Using Off-the-Shelf Technologies

Vlasios Kasapakis[1(✉)], Damianos Gavalas[2], and Elena Dzardanova[2]

[1] Department of Cultural Technology and Communication, University of the Aegean,
Lesvos, Mytilene, Greece
v.kasapakis@aegean.gr
[2] Department of Product and Systems Design Engineering, University of the Aegean,
Syros, Hermoupolis, Greece
{dgavalas,lena}@aegean.gr

Abstract. Mixed-Reality (MR) represents a combination of real and virtual worlds. Off-the-shelf solutions already exist for quite some time which enable the creation of MR worlds where physical and digital objects co-exist and interact in real time. However, little is still known regarding methodological and technical challenges involved in the development of room scale MR worlds with the use of high-end technologies, especially when considering real-object representation. This paper reports hands-on experiences in creating a room-scale MR world, using widespread, off-the-shelf object-tracking technologies and 3D modelling techniques, which enable free user movement, accurate real-object representation in the virtual world, as well as interactivity between real and virtual objects.

Keywords: Mixed reality · Virtual reality · Photogrammetry · 3D scanning
Real-time object tracking

1 Introduction

Virtual Reality (VR) refers to interactive synthetic worlds which often mimic the properties of real-world environments and allow user immersion. Notwithstanding, these synthetic worlds may exceed the limitations of physical reality, since any law, which naturally governs space, time, mechanics, material properties and so on, can be tempered with [1]. A related field of immersive technologies, which involves mixing of real and virtual elements, is referred to as Mixed Reality (MR) [1]. Intensive research has allowed the implementation of MR in fields such us gaming [2], education [3], industrial design [4] and medicine [5].

Recent advances in VR-related technology generated affordable and compact systems, such as Head Mounted Displays (HMDs), resulting to the commercial breach of VR systems since 2015. These developments have triggered various VR and MR expansions, especially by independent developers and small laboratories. According to ongoing research reports, it appears that the use of real objects in MR worlds, has a positive impact on users [6]. However, studies specifically addressing real-object usage in MR are scarce, whereas the techniques used to incorporate real objects in virtual

A. D. Cheok et al. (Eds.): ACE 2017, LNCS 10714, pp. 1–13, 2018.
https://doi.org/10.1007/978-3-319-76270-8_1

worlds do not take advantage of recent technological standards, which greatly increase user comfort and quality of experience.

In this paper, we showcase the design and development of a room-scale MR environment which will provide a testbed for future experiments. More importantly, several critical aspects related to MR implementation are addressed such as free user movement, accurate real-to-virtual object representation in the VR environment, as well as interactivity between real and virtual objects. Therefore, this study supports future developers by providing a detailed report of the steps involved in creating a room-scale MR world with the use of widespread, off-the-shelf technologies. More specifically, in this paper we showcase the development process of a dungeon- themed MR world which incorporates:

- registration of user movement, performed in the real world, into the VR environment,
- accurate representation of texturally rich real objects (i.e. a rock and a wooden stick) in the VR environment,
- registration of accurate user-interaction with real objects into the VR environment, and
- interactivity between real and virtual objects.

The remainder of the paper is structured as follows: Sect. 2 discusses some seminal conceptual issues regarding VR and MR, as well as examples of MR applications; Sect. 3 presents the process followed to generate accurate virtual representations of real objects; Sect. 4 presents the process followed to materialize the MR world along with a number of emerging issues and finally, Sect. 5 concludes our work and draws directions for future research.

2 Related Research

The evident, ascending development growth of VR technologies is in accordance with what has been foretold, even though the pursuit of the "ultimate display" [7] is nowhere near its finish line. In 1995, Slater and Usoh refer to a totality of inputs and the need of total immersion for each sense separately [8] which could only mean the seamless expression of proprioceptive mechanisms, both conscious and non-conscious, to exteroceptive stimuli that at no point disrupt the otherwise naturally occurring environmental and bodily events. This understanding does not equal virtual worlds grounded in realism, as this is not a matter of content, but rather the taming of those realistic elements which would allow the introduction of any implausible content imaginable.

What precedes the ideal immersive virtual experience is a long list of conceptual and technical prerequisites. And, as complicated as those may be, intertwining the real with the virtual, particularly on the right-end side of the reality-virtuality (RV) continuum [9], is an additional, head-on challenge of whichever degree of immersion might have been achieved till that point. The human body and its sensorimotor channels, as the "primordial communication medium", are indeed the perpetual central question [10] and the gravitational pull of an orbital quest. In other words, the simultaneous engagement of virtual and real events, elements and, more importantly for the present study, objects in

MR worlds, deals with challenges on two fronts and by default, presents higher technological challenges as well [11].

Examples of MR, specifically Augmented Reality (AR) applications, can be traced back to Ivan Sutherland and the emergence of prototype, see-through displays projecting 3D graphics [11]. To date, several MR systems have been designed, providing users with high quality immersive experiences [12, 13].

For instance, one of such interactive MR systems is the eXperience Induction Machine (XIM), which is mostly used in psychology and human-artifact interaction related experiments. XIM consists of a physical room equipped with peripherally placed projector screens, a luminous floor, interactive sound systems, and several sensors (e.g. pressure sensors, microphones, cameras), allowing multi-user interaction, with both physical and virtual worlds, in real-time [14].

Another example is MR MOUT (Mixed Reality Military Operations in Urban Terrain), providing training simulation with the use of a video see-through HMD and re-creation of urban landscape. Using a combination of bluescreen technology and occlusion models, MR MOUT allows the trainees to move around a courtyard and hide behind objects, whilst real and virtual players emerge from portals and engage in close-combat battle [15].

Touch-Space is an ubiquitous, tangible, and social MR game-space, which, whilst using the physical and social aspects of traditional game-play, incorporates the real-world environment as an intrinsic and essential game element [16]. Touch-Space provides a full spectrum of game interaction as well as an embodied experience that starts off in the real, physical surroundings (human to human and human to physical world interaction) and gradually transcends through augmented reality (AR) towards the virtual environment [16].

Several other MR systems, developed by widespread technology providers, blend the real world with virtual ones. The accelerating emergence of such systems is indicative of the field's industrial and marketing appeal. Real Virtuality[1] for instance, is a multi-user immersive platform, combining a 3D environment which can be seen and heard through a VR headset, with a real-life stage set. Users are tracked by a motion capture system, whilst being able to see their own bodies, move physically in the virtual environment and interact with physical objects. Whereas, VIRTSIM[2] is a highly immersive virtual reality system which can pit squads of players against each other in a realistic virtual reality combat environment. The system utilizes full-motion body capture, VR headsets, gun props, and even shock-feedback.

Even though MR systems like Real Virtuality and VIRTISM are not yet commercially available, room-scale VR experiences are; Oculus room-scale solution[3] allows users to freely move in a room with the use of Oculus Rift.

Research and development of MR systems, that allow simultaneous interaction with a real object and its virtual representation, a process termed as passive haptics, are already being carried out [17]. Such a case is the creation of a virtual world on top of the physical one with the use of Tango enabled smartphone devices whilst users' full

---

[1] http://www.artanim.ch/blog/tag/siggraph/.

[2] https://www.roadtovr.com/virtsim-virtual-reality-platform/.

[3] https://www.oculus.com/blog/oculus-roomscale-tips-for-setting-up-a-killer-vr-room/.

body locomotion is tracked with Microsoft Kinect sensors allowing free movement. In this MR system real objects and their virtual representations differ in appearance, yet maintain some tactile characteristics (e.g. size and weight), to secure coherence in some sensory feedback. For example, the system allows users to touch two real, paper boxes, assigned with markers, in the physical world and interact with their virtual representations in the virtual world. Again however, boxes are easy to recreate in 3D and the system does not offer solutions for complex objects in regards of texture and morphology.

The technological advances presented above reveal a promising future for MR, where users will be able to freely move around real and virtual spaces simultaneously, while interacting with both real and virtual objects. However, the development of room-scale MR worlds like Real Virtuality and VIRTISM is a challenging process, especially since there are no guidelines in regards of technical setup, cost-effective solutions, or suggested methods of development. In addition, the aforementioned MR systems do not in fact include texturally rich objects and thus, there are no paradigms of complex real-object representations into MR worlds. As already mentioned, when users interact with a real-object's virtual representation, tactile augmentation through touch and grasp increases the realism of the virtual environment in MR systems [6]. Thus, the ability to incorporate any object, regardless of texture and morphology, is critical for MR development.

3   Accurate Real-Object Representations

When designing an interactive MR world, one of the most crucial components is accurate real-to-virtual object representation. Dimensions of the virtual object should of course be identical to the original, but also, its virtual 'physiology', simulated via appropriate textures and materials, should also be in accordance with the original object. Immersed users who are meant to touch a real object, virtually represented in the VR environment, should not experience inconsistencies regarding tactile-to-visual correlating information.

Therefore, realistic correlation of characteristics is a requirement which can be met via conventional 3D modelling methods (e.g. polygonal modelling) only for simple objects, in regards of geometry and texture. Otherwise, the modelling process is strenuous and time consuming, especially for complex objects like the rock used for the present development of a MR experience. To address this issue, the 3D modelling techniques of Photogrammetry and 3D object Scanning were used, using low-cost methods and equipment.

3.1   Photogrammetry

Photogrammetry, with the use of image measurement and interpretation, delivers the form and location of an object by using one or more photographs of that object [18]. Nowadays, various accessible software solutions simplify the process of creating 3D models via photogrammetry. In this work Autodesk Remake[4] was used.

In order to create an interactive 3D object with the use of digital imaging, a sequence of photographs is required, circling the perimeter of the object and alternating the capture

---

[4] https://remake.autodesk.com.

angle at about 5° to 10° between each shot so that the resulting photographic sequence has approximately 70% of overlapping information [19]. Moreover, all photographs need to be sharp and overall capture all possible angles of the object. Finally, the room/ space, where the Photogrammetry process is taking place, needs to have proper lighting conditions to achieve diffused illumination of the object, whilst high contrast, intense shadows and the use of a flash light are prohibited.

For the purposes of the present study the 3D model of a rock was generated using photogrammetry, to be later incorporated in a MR experience within a dungeon themed VR environment. Figure 1a shows the preparation of the room where the sequential photographing of the rock took place. The rock was elevated with the use of a tripod to expose the maximum number of visible angles, whereas artificial lighting ensured diffused lighting conditions.

(a)   (b)

(c)   (d)

Fig. 1. (a) Photoshoot preparation (b) Initial photogrammetry results; (c) Final 3D model; (d) Photos positions.

The resulting sequence of photographs was imported into Autodesk Remake and the primitive 3D model was created. However, 3D objects, modelled via photogrammetry, often require additional tweaking, since surrounding objects may interfere with the extraction of object information through digital imaging (see Fig. 1b). Autodesk Remake offers a set of tools which allow alterations of the object and removal of excess information. The final 3D model representing the rock object is presented in Fig. 1c, while Fig. 1d shows the positions wherefrom the photos of the object were taken.

3.2 3D Scanning

The second method utilized to create 3D models for the purposes of the present study, was the 3D scanning of real objects, with the use of relevant technologies, such as structured light or laser scanners, to create detailed 3D models of real objects [20]. To perform 3D scanning in this work, the low-cost, 3D depth camera-enabled, Microsoft Kinect sensor was used. The Microsoft Kinect sensor is based on an infrared light (IR) projector and an IR camera which allows the capture of changes on an IR pattern (see Fig. 2a). The Microsoft Kinect sensor utilizes the abovementioned process to produce depth images (see Fig. 2b). Finally, an RGB camera allows the capture of color [21].

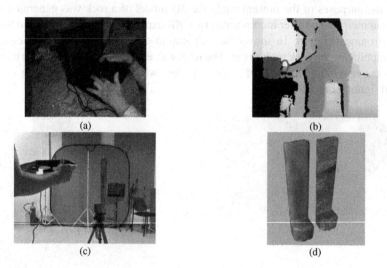

Fig. 2. (a) Microsoft Kinect sensor IR image; (b) Microsoft Kinect Sensor depth image; (c) 3D Scanning of object using Microsoft Kinect sensor; (d) 3D Scanning result (3D model on the left) and texture replacement into Cinema 4D (3D model on the right).

Having installed the Microsoft Kinect sensor using the Kinect SDK[5], the Skanect[6] software has been used to 3D scan objects. The object chosen to be 3D scanned was a wooden stick, also placed on a tripod to ease the scanning process. After feeding the dimensions of the object into Skanect, the 3D scanning process began, moving the Microsoft Kinect sensor around the wooden stick to capture as much geometry as possible (see Fig. 2c). Then, the colorize function of the Skanect software was used to analyze data captured by the RGB camera of the Microsoft Kinect sensor, creating a texture to be applied on the 3D model.

Finally, the 3D model was exported from Skanect to the 3D graphics creation software, Cinema 4D[7], where the additional unwanted geometry caused by surrounding objects was removed, finally producing the desired 3D model. However, the colorize function of Skanect produced low quality textures. Therefore, the wooden stick texture was replaced with one of higher quality, also representing a wood interface, created in Cinema 4D (see Fig. 2d).

---

[5] www.microsoft.com/en-us/kinectforwindows.

[6] http://skanect.occipital.com/.

[7] https://www.maxon.net/en/products/cinema-4d/overview/.

It should be noted that, based on the software available to this study, the 3D models produced with the process of photogrammetry were better suited for a MR experience, in terms of texture quality and lower number of polygons. However, using photogrammetry to create 3D models of objects with slim parts, such as the wooden stick, resulted in inaccurate models, thus dictating 3D scanning as a preferred option.

Therefore, the choice of modelling method depends on various parameters and combination of software is mandatory for accurate real-to-virtual representation of objects, especially for MR worlds.

4   MR World Materialization

4.1   Real Object Registration to the MR World

Vicon's motion capture system, along with its complementary software, Blade, were the crucial components of the present study[8]. The Vicon motion capture system is built upon infrared cameras (see Fig. 3a), commonly placed along the perimeter of a room's ceiling, allowing the tracking of retroreflective markers in real space (see Fig. 3b).

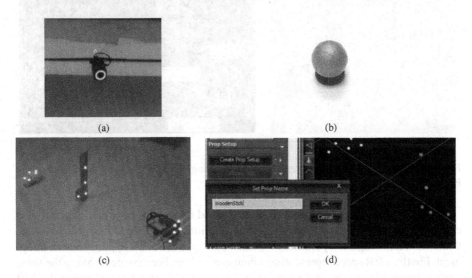

(a)   (b)

(c)   (d)

Fig. 3. (a) Infrared camera; (b) Retroreflective marker; (c) Retroreflective markers assignment; (d) Prop creation in Vicon Blade.

Apart from full-body human motion capture, which is Vicon's main purpose, tracking of prop objects is also possible by placing retroreflective markers around an object. To be able to track the position of the rock and the wooden stick objects in the real space, both were assigned with at least five (5) retroreflective markers (Fig. 3c) to ensure smooth tracking. Moreover, retroreflective markers were also assigned to an

---
[8] https://www.vicon.com/products/software/blade.

Oculus Rift Head Mounted Display (HMD), which was used by the user to navigate and experience the MR world (Fig. 3c).

Following the marker assignment, the objects were placed on the floor and a data sample, including location and rotation of markers, was recorded using Blade. After reconstructing the data sample, the retroreflective markers' positions appear in Blade, wherefrom they can be selected in groups. Finally, each retroreflective markers-group can be converted into a prop object, by assigning a prop name and then calibrating the prop using Blade's built-in prop creation tool (see Fig. 3d).

The process described above allows the real-time registration (i.e. solving) of the position and rotation of the real objects to the props through Blade (see Fig. 4a and b). It must be noted that Blade calculates the position of a prop using a bone object, with the first marker selected during prop creation serving as the root of the bone and the second marker selected to represent the end-point of the bone. Figure 4a, presents the rock item assigned with markers, while Fig. 4b shows the root, end-point and bone of the respective prop in Blade.

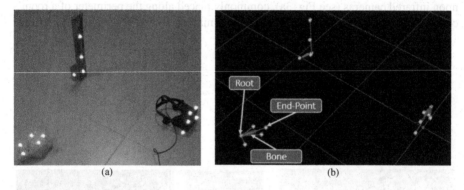

(a)   (b)

Fig. 4. (a) Objects location in the real world; (b) Solving of real object location to the props in Blade.

Next, to successfully materialize the MR world created in this work, the Unity 3D engine has been used[9]. Unity 3D allows the creation of 3D interactive virtual worlds, whilst also allowing incorporation of Oculus Rift supported VR applications development. Firstly, a VR space representing a dungeon cell has been created, having the same square dimensions as the real room where the user was whilst experiencing the MR world. Then, the 3D objects, created using photogrammetry and 3D scanning, have been imported in the VR space (see Fig. 5a). 3D objects are often affected by the software used when creating or processing them. Therefore, once they are imported into Unity 3D, their scale factor may require adjustment to secure proper dimensions in relation to the real objects.

---

[9] https://unity3d.com/.

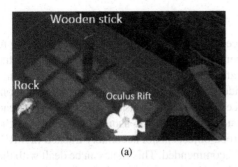 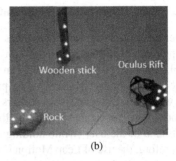

(a)   (b)

Fig. 5. (a) Objects location in the virtual world; (b) Objects location in the real world.

The next step refers to the data flow between Blade and Unity 3D; a process which is typically handled by Vicon's Tracker[10] or the Pegasus[11] software. Since those however were unavailable, a cost-effective solution was implemented using Vicon's Datastream SDK[12], along with a custom script created for Unity 3D. The custom script was based on the script used to enable interaction between Unity 3D and Vicon Pegasus[13]. More specifically, the script collected information sent through Blade's data stream function and used the names of the props to match the 3D objects' and real objects' location and rotation[14].

The Oculus Rift Core Package for Unity 3D[15] allowed preparation and application of the Oculus Rift HMD in the MR world. This package includes tools which enable the integration of Oculus Rift HMD as part of a Unity 3D project, using simple drag and drop functions. Also, the Oculus Rift HMD comes with a separate sensor which tracks the HMD location up to a certain distance. However, the tracking process only works when the HMD is directly in front of the sensor, thus limiting the user's range of movement whilst in the MR world. In addition, whilst trying to track the Oculus Rift prop location and rotation, the Oculus sensor interfered with the ones provided by Vicon, and therefore had to be disabled. Even though Oculus Rift comes with official instructions on how to implement a room scale solution, it is not suitable for real-time object tracking.

The processes described above results to an MR world wherein the user, in real-time, is free to move around, interact with real objects and their accurate virtual representations, and apply interaction/collision between real and virtual objects[16].

---

[10] https://www.vicon.com/products/software/tracker.

[11] https://www.vicon.com/products/software/pegasus.

[12] https://www.vicon.com/products/software/datastream-sdk.

[13] https://docs.vicon.com/display/Pegasus12/Using+Vicon+Pegasus#UsingViconPegasus-UnrealIntegration.

[14] The script used to register 3D objects location and rotation to the virtual space based on the props positions can be found at: http://zarcrash.x10.mx/Program.cs.

[15] https://developer.oculus.com/downloads/unity/.

[16] An example of the MR world created in this work can be found at https://www.youtube.com/watch?v=Hy_wCD1LJYk.

4.2   Real-Time Hand Representation

Even though the above process was successful, several issues emerged when trying to implement hand interaction and subsequently test the accuracy of users' touch with the real objects. First, Leap Motion[17], an infrared sensor allowing precise hand tracking into VR environments was tested, to provide users with real-time hands visualization. However, the retroreflective markers placed on the real objects considerably affect Leap Motion's performance. Figure 6a illustrates the issue while using Leap Motion as the left hand of the user (while holding the rock object) is not accurately tracked in VR[18]. Therefore, the use of Leap Motion is not recommended. This issue can be dealt with the use of alternative solutions for finger and hand movement tracking, which do not use infrared light, such as the ManusVR data glove[19].

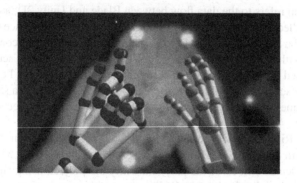

Fig. 6. (a) Leap motion hand tracking and occlusion issue.

4.3   Object Tracking Accuracy Issues

When developing MR worlds with technologies such as the ones proposed in this paper, another issue to consider is proper adjustment of the 3D object's pivot points (the center of the object's rotational system), in order to enable accurate representation of real objects in the virtual world.

The pivot point of every 3D object should be adjusted at the same location as its respective prop's root point, to increase the tracking precision and also avoid incidents such as rotation and location offsets during user interaction with the real objects.

To test the precision of this process we designed (using Cinema 4D) and 3D Printed a 10×10 cube, assigned it with retroreflective markers and finally registered it as a prop in Blade (see Fig. 7a and b). Moreover, the pivot point of the 3D model of the cube was assigned to the root of the prop item (see Fig. 7b and c). Finally, a coded script which acquired the markers positions from Blade and visualized them into Unity 3D, thus

---

[17] https://www.leapmotion.com/.

[18] An example of the LeapMotion performance can be found in https://www.youtube.com/watch?v=MoY7R02_ShE.

[19] https://manus-vr.com/.

testing in detail the prop markers' location both in real and virtual world (see Fig. 7d). This way we could accurately move and rotate the cube object[20] (see Fig. 7e).

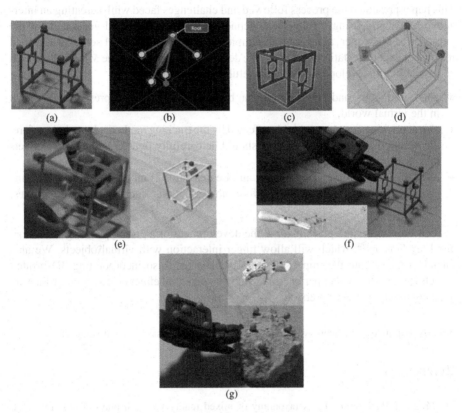

Fig. 7. (a) 3D Printed cube assigned with retroreflective markers; (b) 3D Printed cube prop in Blade; (c) Pivot point adjustment; (d) Markers visualization in Unity 3D; (e) 3D Printed cube registration in VR; (f) Accurate hand interaction with the 3D Printed cube in VR; (g) Accurate hand interaction with the rock object in VR.

To test accuracy of user touch on real objects and their virtual representations, we used a 3D hand model which represented a user's real hand tracked by Blade in the virtual world (see Fig. 7f). The 3D hand had the same dimensions as the user's hand. Tests examining interactivity of the virtual hand with both the cube[21] and the rock[22] object showed successful levels of accuracy, since the user was able to touch each detail of the objects, both in real and virtual world.

---

[20] An example of the interaction between the user and the cube item can be found at https://www.youtube.com/watch?v=p-f7z2oUk7s.

[21] An example of the interaction between the user hand and the cube item can be found at: https://youtu.be/nwnU8BiJX00.

[22] An example of the interaction between the user hand and the rock item can be found at: https://www.youtube.com/watch?v=4b3QDFap2Ok.

5   Conclusion and Future Work

This paper presented the process followed and challenges faced whilst creating an interactive MR world using off-the-shelf technologies. The MR world generated for the purposes of this paper, along with the implementation process, will serve as a testbed for further experimentation. However, the development process of the MR world, which can assist future developers, revealed useful directions such as:

- photogrammetry and 3D Scanning can be used to accurately represent real objects in the virtual world,
- object tracking accuracy is highly affected by the tracking method adopted; therefore, the pivot points and object scaling should be carefully treated as the tiniest offsets may greatly affect user experience,
- hand tracking accuracy is important and Leap Motion is incompatible with systems using retroreflective markers, therefore other solutions, such as ManusVR gloves, should be used.

Our future research plans involve the development of a prototype using Arduino[23] and Flex Sensors[24], which will allow finger interaction with virtual objects. We also intend to investigate the impact of real object usage (also incorporating 3D printed objects) as part of a MR experience and study its potential effect on users' co-ordination and perceived level of immersion.

Acknowledgment. This work was supported by VR First (https://www.vrfirst.com/).

References

1. Milgram, P., Kishino, F.: A taxonomy of mixed reality visual displays. Trans. Inf. Syst. **77**(12), 1321–1329 (1994)
2. Cheok, A.D., Sreekumar, A., Lei, C., Thang, L.N.: Capture the flag: mixed-reality social gaming with smart phones. Pervasive Comput. **5**(2), 62–69 (2006)
3. Pan, Z., Cheok, A.D., Yang, H., Zhu, J., Shi, J.: Virtual reality and mixed reality for virtual learning environments. Comput. Graphics **30**(1), 20–28 (2006)
4. Fiorentino, M., de Amicis, R., Monno, G., Stork, A: Spacedesign: a mixed reality workspace for aesthetic industrial design. In: Proceedings of the 1st International Symposium on Mixed and Augmented Reality, p. 86. IEEE, Darmstadt (2002)
5. Ferrari, V., Megali, G., Troia, E., Pietrabissa, A., Mosca, F.: A 3-D mixed-reality system for stereoscopic visualization of medical dataset. Trans. Biomed. Eng. **56**(11), 2627–2633 (2009)
6. Hoffman, H.G.: Physically touching virtual objects using tactile augmentation enhances the realism of virtual environments. In: Proceedings of the Virtual Reality Annual International Symposium, pp. 59–63. IEEE, Atlanta (1998)
7. Sutherland, I.E.: The ultimate display. Int. Fed. Inf. Process. **2**, 506–508 (1965)
8. Usoh, M., Slater, M.: An exploration of immersive virtual environments. Endeavour **19**(1), 34–38 (1995)

---

[23] https://www.arduino.cc/.
[24] https://learn.sparkfun.com/tutorials/flex-sensor-hookup-guide.

9. Milgram, P., Takemura, H., Utsumi, A., Kishino, F.: Augmented reality: a class of displays on the reality-virtuality continuum. Telemanipulator Telepresence Technol. **2351**, 282–292 (1994)
10. Biocca, F., Levy, M.R.: Communication in the Age of Virtual Reality. Routledge, London (2013)
11. Van Krevelen, D., Poelman, R.: A survey of augmented reality technologies, applications and limitations. Int. J. Virtual Reality **9**(2), 1 (2010)
12. Davies, M., Callaghan., V.: iWorlds: building mixed reality intelligent environments using customisable 3D virtual worlds. In: Proceedings of the 6th International Conference on Intelligent Environments, pp. 311–314. IEEE, Kuala Lumpur (2010)
13. Tecchia, F., Avveduto, G., Brondi, R., Carrozzino, M., Bergamasco, M., Alem, L.: I'm in VR!: using your own hands in a fully immersive MR system. In: Proceedings of the 20th Symposium on Virtual Reality Software and Technology, pp. 73–76. ACM, Edinburg (2014)
14. Bernardet, U., Bermúdez, S., Duff, A., Inderbitzin. M., Groux, S., Manzolli, J., Mathews, Z., Mura, A., Väljamäe, A., Verschure, P.: The eXperience induction machine: a new paradigm for mixed-reality interaction design and psychological experimentation. In: Dubois, E., Gray, P., Nigay, L. (eds.) The Engineering of Mixed Reality Systems. Human-Computer Interaction Series, pp. 357–379. Springer, London (2010). https://doi.org/10.1007/978-1-84882-733-2_18
15. Hughes, C.E., Stapleton, C.B., Hughes, D.E., Smith, E.M.: Mixed reality in education, entertainment, and training. Comput. Graph. Appl. **25**(6), 24–30 (2005)
16. Cheok, A.D., Yang, X., Ying, Z.Z., Billinghurst, M., Kato, H.: Touch-space: mixed reality game space based on ubiquitous, tangible, and social computing. Pers. Ubiquit. Comput. **6**(5–6), 430–442 (2002)
17. Sra, M., Schmandt, S.: Bringing real objects, spaces, actions, and interactions into social VR. In: Proceedings of the 3rd VR International Workshop on Collaborative Virtual Environments, pp. 16–17. IEEE, Greenville (2016)
18. Luhmann, T., Robson, S., Kyle, S.A., Harley, I.A.: Close Range Photogrammetry: Principles, Techniques and Applications. Whittles, Dunbeath (2006)
19. Santagati, C., Inzerillo, L., Di Paola, F.: Image-based modeling techniques for architectural heritage 3D digitalization: limits and potentialities. Int. Arch. Photogrammetry, Remote Sens. Spatial Inf. Sci. **5**(w2), 555–560 (2013)
20. Tong, J., Zhou, J., Liu, L., Pan, Z., Yan, H.: Scanning 3D full human bodies using kinects. Trans. Vis. Comput. Graph. **18**(4), 643–650 (2012)
21. Zhang, Z.: Microsoft kinect sensor and its effect. Multimedia **19**(2), 4–10 (2012)

Evaluation of a Mixed Reality Head-Mounted Projection Display to Support Motion Capture Acting

Daniel Kade[1]([⊠])[iD], Rikard Lindell[1], Hakan Ürey[2], and Oğuzhan Özcan[2]

[1] Mälardalen University, Högskoleplan 1, 72123 Västerås, Sweden
d.kade@web.de, rikard.lindell@mdh.se
[2] Koç University, Rumelifeneri Yolu, 34450 Sariyer/Istanbul, Turkey
{hurey,oozcan}@ku.edu.tr,
http://www.mdh.se,
http://www.ku.edu.tr

Abstract. Motion capture acting is a challenging task, it requires trained and experienced actors who can highly rely on their acting and imagination skills to deliver believable performances. This is especially the case when preparation times are short and scenery needs to be imagined, as it is commonly the case for shoots in the gaming industry. To support actors in such cases, we developed a mixed reality application that allows showing digital scenery and triggering emotions while performing.

In this paper we tested our hypothesis that a mixed reality head-mounted projection display can support motion capture acting through the help of experienced motion capture actors performing short acting scenes common for game productions. We evaluated our prototype with four motion capture actors and four motion capture experts. Both groups considered our application as helpful, especially as a rehearsal tool to prepare performances before capturing the motions in a studio. Actors and experts indicated that our application could reduce the time to prepare performances and supports the set up of physical acting scenery.

Keywords: Motion capture · Mixed reality
Head-mounted projection display · HMPD · MR · Acting

1 Introduction

Acting for virtual environments such as movies, commercial spots or computer games is challenging [1,2]. Actors need to overcome the issues of short preparation times, being able to create a character on the spot, using improvisational acting and having good imagination skills. In previous research, it has been shown that motion capture actors face such challenges and need to be supported when good acting in short time is required [1].

In todays motion capture for smaller productions or for computer games, the performances and the characters to be played are often shaped on the shoot

© Springer International Publishing AG, part of Springer Nature 2018
A. D. Cheok et al. (Eds.): ACE 2017, LNCS 10714, pp. 14–31, 2018.
https://doi.org/10.1007/978-3-319-76270-8_2

day. Repetitions to get the performance right and explanations of scenarios and scenes result in longer recording times, which take away valuable recording time or increase the costs of a motion capture shoot.

In order to support motion capture actors, we further developed a head-mounted projection display (HMPD) usable in a motion capture environment, providing the ability to see virtual scenery and triggering emotions while acting. [3]. We also extend previously performed research with theatre and TV actors [4] by improving digital scenarios, evaluations and by allowing directors to trigger digital events. In this paper we show an improved hardware setup and the evaluation of user tests with end users of our prototype, namely motion capture actors and experts from a professional motion capture studio. Our head-mounted projection display (HMPD) uses a laser projector and a retro-reflective material as screen to display the imagery. A smartphone is used as an image-processing unit and as a sensor platform, detecting head movements. This setup can be seen in Fig. 1.

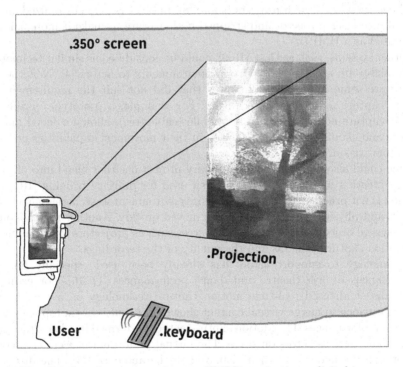

Fig. 1. Visualization of a user wearing our HMPD, projecting a digital scenery onto a retro-reflective screen covering the walls around the user. A connected keyboard allows to interact with the virtual environment.

The aim of this study is to evaluate if acting with our prototype allows supporting motion capture actors, as well as to find out in which ways, if at all, our application is useful for the motion capture industry.

To prove our concept, we evaluated our device and software with 4 experienced motion capture actors and 4 experts of a motion capture studio. In order to evaluate the actors' feedback and performances, we chose several accepted methods in interaction design, namely observation, card sorting [5,6] and semi-structured interviews as means of evaluation. Feedback from motion capture experts was captured and evaluated by using semi-structured interviews.

The contribution of this research lies in, further improvements made to a prototype from previous research [3,4] and the conducted user tests to evaluate if our mixed reality application is useful as motion capture acting support.

2   Related Work

Our prototype uses a head-mounted projection display (HMPD) and a retro-reflective material to enhance the image quality. This technology, as well as the use and evaluation of reflective materials, used as screens, have already been discussed and introduced [7]. Laser projectors, as we use it in our research have also been used in research projects before [8]. In our case, we customized an off-the-self pico laser projector and stripped its hardware to make it more suitable to be used as a HMPD.

Other systems, such as CastAR [9], could be considered as similar technology and possibly be used to show virtual environments to actors [4]. Nonetheless, there were some important differences that did not suit the requirements of motion capture acting, as stated in [3]. For example, a prototype, usable for motion capture acting, needs to be mobile (cable-free), allow for facial motion capture and should not limit the actors in their movement capabilities or block the actors' vision.

One could also imagine using stationary projections that blend into physical objects creating a scenery, as it has been used for military training [10]. This solution is not practical in a motion capture environment as sceneries can change quickly and physical objects need to be moved quickly. Another major issue is that physical objects and strong light sources such as projectors would influence the motion capture cameras and the quality of the recordings.

Technology to support actors has already been used especially for acting rehearsals or live theatre and dance performances [11–16]. For example, Andreadis et al. used real-time motion capture technology on a live theatrical performance to merge virtual content shown on a multi-screen topology with on-stage performances [11]. Motion capture actors performed in a backstage area at the same time as actors on stage. The virtual performances were created by motion capture actors and then displayed to the audience [11]. The displayed scenery and interactions with the on-stage actors were used as a narrative but not directly used to support the actors, as we intend to do.

Motion capture technology was also used in dance performances where dancers steer digital content with their artistic movements [12,13]. The three above-mentioned research projects or similar projects focused on adding artistic expressions that were meant to be perceived by the audience and only to a minor extent allow actors to use the digital content for their act.

Another type of acting support, which was already explored by multiple research projects, is to use virtual environments for acting rehearsals [14–16]. Here, 6 actors and 1 director met in a shared non-immersive virtual environment to rehearse a short play [14]. It was stated that the system was seen as supportive and allowed to create a basis for the live performance, without the actors having to meet in person. Their setup allowed achieving a better result than by only learning the script or using video conferences.

Other shared immersive environments have also been used to explore the rehearsal of plays over distance [15, 16]. One research project used two actors and a director to evaluate their setup which captured movements through motion capture technology and showed the digital content using a head-mounted display or a CAVE system to the actors [15]. These systems supported the actors by using a virtual environment but do not support the actors during the performance, as it is our goal for motion capture acting.

Additionally, another research project found out that training acting performances in an immersive virtual reality environment was more successful compared to using a 2D computer screen [17]. This also encouraged us to test our application during a performance compared to not using any support. Nonetheless, our work differs in the point that we test the usefulness of a mixed-reality application for on-stage acting support and guidance in a motion capture environment.

3 Our Concept of Supporting Motion Capture Acting

Our approach to support motion capture actors with their work in a virtual environment is that we show a digital environment to actors in real-time while acting. In other words, we show a virtual scenery to motion capture actors and allow them to get an understanding of the environment. This also allows to use correct dimensions of the scene and to steer the actors' performance towards correct placement and alignment in the virtual scene. We added animations and sound to the scenes allowing for a better understanding of moods and emotions to be played, as well as to provide triggers that actors can use for their performances. Our application also provides a way of discussing the scene to make it easier to understand the demands of a performance. Furthermore, we want to give the director a way to interact with our application through triggering sounds when pressing buttons on a wireless keyboard, which is connected to our HMPD. We see this additional feature as a starting point to trigger more natural reactions from the actors and a different way to steer the actors through their act.

Discussing the limitations of an acting area, the feel of an environment, locations of actions and events do not need to be imagined, when using our device. Therefore, we believe that the discussions between actors and director will be easier as both can see the scenery and layout of a scene. We see the virtual environment that we built as means to trigger and support the actors' emotions and moods through sounds, animations and the provided atmosphere.

4 Prototype Description

Earlier research already suggested a head-mounted projection display as support for motion capture actors [3,4]. We further developed this concept and software that aimed at showing virtual scenery to actors, triggering emotions and moods for their performance. The prototype in this other research had a smaller field of view, differing virtual environments and we use an improved algorithm for the head rotations. Moreover, we allow interactions with the head-mounted projection display through a Bluetooth keyboard. We see this as an interesting way of exploring interaction from a third person, in our case e.g. a director or motion capture experts with actors while acting.

Our current prototype consists of two Lithium Polymer batteries ($2 \times 3,7$ V $\times 2000$ mAh $= 14,8$ Wh) that are used as power source for the stripped down pico laser projector, SHOWWX+ from Microvision. We constructed 3D printed housings to mount the hardware parts of the projector on an adjustable headband, to protect the electronics from light shocks and from electrostatic discharge when accidentally being touched. A smartphone is connected via a MHL adapter and a HDMI cable to the projector. This setup of our prototype can be seen in Fig. 2. As smartphone, we use a Samsung Galaxy S4+ that runs an app created in Unity 4, which processes the sensor data from the smartphone's in-built gyroscope detecting head movements and rendering the virtual environments.

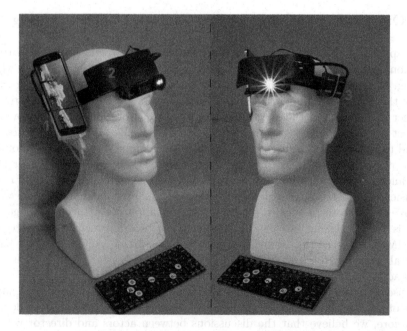

Fig. 2. Picture taken from two angles, showing our HMPD consisting of (1) smartphone, (2) laser projector, (3) battery pack, (4) 180° fish eye lens and (5) Bluetooth keyboard.

The created virtual environments are explained in more detail at a later section below. Moreover, a connected Bluetooth keyboard allows for simple interaction triggering sounds suiting the acting environment and events.

A 180° fish eye lens was mounted in front of the projector to increase the field of view from 44° × 25° to 83.6°× 47.5°.

Our prototype uses a retro-reflective cloth that works as a screen and increases the very low brightness of the laser projector from 15 lumen to a brightly perceived retro-reflected image. Using the reflective cloth no. 6101 from RB Reflektör provides high-quality optical properties and tends to give an impression of having the digital content spatially closer to the user as when only projecting an image to a wall. With this reflective material, we covered a CAVE-like room (3 × 3 × 3 m) with a 350° projection area to create the "acting stage", as shown in Fig. 3. The floor and ceiling were not covered with the reflective cloth.

5   User Tests

For our user tests, we invited 4 experienced motion capture actors (3 male, 1 female). Three actors had more than 11 years of acting experience and one between 6 and 10 years. The actors' motion capture experience ranged from 3, 4, 6 to 15 years of experience. Two actors were between 26 and 35 years old

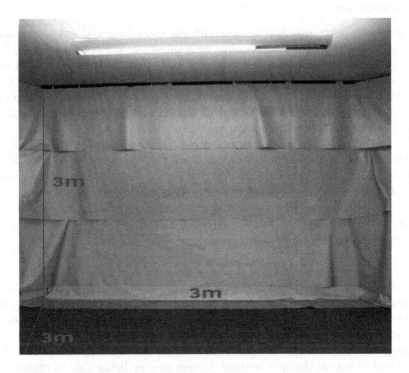

Fig. 3. CAVE-like acting space covered with retro-reflective cloth

and 2 actors older than 35 years. Two out of 4 actors tried a head-mounted display before. All actors were invited individually for a 1-h session to test our prototype and to give feedback on our acting support application. Important in the selection of the actors was that the actors were highly experienced in motion capture acting and show a diverse portfolio of motion capture acting skills. In this respect, some actors had traditional acting education and other had attended acting workshops. Most actors also have experiences in stunts and martial arts or *Improv* (improvisational) acting. After the tests, all actors were compensated for their participation.

On a separate day, we interviewed 4 motion capture experts after showing them recorded outcomes from the actors' performances, letting them try our prototype and having given an introduction to our research project. The experts were between 27 and 33 years old and have worked for the motion capture industry between 5 and 9 years.

A decision to only use 4 experienced actors and 4 motion capture experts was taken because of one main limiting reason. This was that the access to highly trained and experienced motion capture actors for research sessions is challenging and was not achievable for us in higher numbers at that time. Nonetheless, we had access to highly skilled and trained motion capture actors as well as experts who have worked in the field for a long time who were able to give detailed and qualified feedback to evaluate our prototype and hypothesis.

5.1 Procedure

One week before the user test session with the actors, we sent out a very short description of three acting scenes that we wanted the actors to perform. These descriptions briefly described the character and emotions to be played in each scene, as well as a rather short description of the story. There was no script to be learned, as we expected more of an *Improv* performance. The short descriptions and the *Improv* decision were taken, as this is a very common procedure in motion capture acting for computer games and animation.

On the test day, actors were first introduced to the test environment and the idea behind our research in general. Then the actors were reminded about the description of the scene before every scene and were also given small cards for each scene with keywords about the feelings and moods in the scenes. The actors chose themselves to use the examples on the cards for their performances or not. These cards were meant as inspiration and means of communicating how the scenes should be played.

We asked the actors to perform each of the 3 scenes, which were about 2 min long, 2 times; once without and once with our prototype. To avoid getting false measurements by influencing the actors' feedback through showing the virtual environment first, we used a counterbalanced order [18]. Two actors started acting with the device and two without it. All three scenes were performed sequentially either with or without the device. All actors had the chance to ask questions about the scene and their act before the shooting the scenes. The actors had to act on the spot without having seen or being able to explore the virtual environments. As success criteria, we set the goal to complete all six shots playing the character as they see fit according to the instructions and explanations given for each scene, as well as being near the time frame of 2 min. All performances were videotaped for later references and to show the videos for evaluation to motion capture experts. These videos have also been used to reevaluate and spot certain key findings for our evaluations. Occurrences have been counted and compared but do not follow a specific video transcoding method. The video material rather serves as a way to reconfirm notes findings during the user tests, interviews and to discuss events with the motion capture experts.

Thereafter, all actors performed a card sorting task and then a semi-structured interview. For the card sorting task, we used 20 positive and 20 negative words, inspired from a list of product reaction cards [5,6], which could be associated with our prototype. Then we told the actors to choose as many cards as they saw fit. In two cases the actors picked more than 6 cards. We asked the actors to pick those cards that reflect their main thoughts. The actors choose between 3–6 cards which were then used to conduct an interview on the cards, as suggested by others [5]. Then, we conducted a semi-structured interview asking each actor 6 predefined questions about the use and benefit of our prototype for motion capture acting.

Finally, we performed semi-structured interviews with the 4 motion capture experts, were we asked 4 questions about the use usefulness of our head-mounted projection display. Before the interview, we gave the experts the chance to try our device and we showed video clips of the actors' performances. Moreover, information about features and the technology of our setup was given to the motion capture experts.

5.2   Description of Acting Scenes

In motion capture acting, actors need to be able to change moods and emotions quickly between scenes. Therefore, we aimed at providing 3 scenarios that are, in terms of moods, emotions and acting, fairly distinct from each other. The designs of our virtual environments were modeled after scenarios that could occur in motion capture shoots for computer games and animations.

All actors performed the scenes in the same order, starting with a nature environment then a war environment and at last a scary environment.

Nature Scene. The idea for this scene was to provide a nice and friendly nature environment, where the character waits on a roadside to be picked up, enjoying the nature environment. Here, the character to be played had no specific descriptions and the conversation had no predefined script. After a defined time (1:10 min) a car stopped in a distance, honking the horn. This was a signal when the characters mood needed to switch to 'worried' and feeling 'uncertain' about who is driving the car and what is going on. When acting without our device, key elements to trigger actions, like the approaching of the car or honking the horn were signaled by clapping the hands of the researcher supervising the shoot. When using the acting support device, sounds and animation were played through it automatically. After 1:40 min we triggered a gun shot by pressing a button on the wireless keyboard to see how actors react when unexpected sounds were played while using our mixed reality device. This was neglected when acting without the prototype as we assumed that clapping the hands again would have only confused the actors.

War Scene. Here, the actors were given the task to play an experienced soldier in an army camp located in a desert environment. It was explained that the army base is on high alert and will be attacked shortly. The goal for the actors was to act out the tension, alertness and stress before the attack and then command other soldier to get back in line after the attack.

Scary Scene. In this scene, the actor was placed in a night environment, near a cemetery located in a forest. For this scene we provided more detailed information about the story and character. We explained that the character found a hidden cemetery in the woods by chance, after his dog ran away. Then the character finds the dog barking from inside the cemetery. Here, we wanted the actor to play a character that felt scared, spooked and only wants to leave the strange place but pushes himself or herself to overcome the fear of the environment and to get the dog back.

To get a visual understanding of how the scenes looked in the virtual environment, a screenshot of all three environments can be seen in Fig. 4.

Fig. 4. The upper image shows the nature scene, the lower left image shows the scary scene and the lower right image shows the war scene.

The scenes, were modified and adjusted according to feedback from previous research that were performed with trained theatre and TV actors to provide a more supportive acting environment [4].

6   Evaluation Results

In the following, we describe the results of our evaluation from the performed card sorting tasks, observations and interviews of the user tests with motion capture actors and experts.

6.1   Card Sorting

Through the card sorting task we set a basis for the interviews and allowed the actors to express their experiences and feelings when using our device. We provided 20 cards with positive words and 20 cards with negative words that could be associated with our device. The actors picked the cards that they found suitable. The results of this task are shown in Fig. 5 as a word cloud where the size of the words is an indicator of the number of chosen words. All picked cards and descriptive words, reflecting their emotions with the prototype, from the 4 actors are depicted in this figure.

Fig. 5. Word cloud of the results.

After having picked 3–6 cards, actors were asked to explain why they picked the cards. Two actors picked the card 'unconventional' and explained that our approach is new to acting and that the device "is guiding you" and placing the actors "deep into the world". Another actor picked the card 'distracting' and explained that the provided virtual environment would hinder the actor's imagination. Moreover, three actors picked the card 'Useful' and explained that especially the sounds were very helpful to trigger real reactions and emotions and that the device is helpful to understand the environment, as well as that it was useful to get a spatial understanding of the scene. Then the cards 'Frustrating' and 'Hard to use' were selected by another actor. The clarification showed that this was related to the fact that one cannot move physically in the virtual environment with our current prototype. Another actor selected the card 'Engaging' and said that it took him "less effort to get into the scene". He also picked the card 'Convenient' and mentioned that to prepare a shoot, actors usually ask a lot of questions to understand the scene. This would be quicker and would need less explanation when using the device. Furthermore, one actor picked the cards 'Vague' and 'Unrefined' and explained that the faces of animated characters and their emotions were not visible and therefore not usable for his acting. After that, two unexpected cards, 'Contradicting' and 'Awkward', were picked by one actor. Here, the actor explained that there was no feedback or interaction possible with the virtual acting scenery, animated characters in the scene would not react when the actors tried to talk or interact with him.

The results from the card sorting task and the visualized answers in Fig. 5 show that 'Fun', 'Unconventional' and 'Useful' was picked by 2–3 actors. This gave a very first impression that our device could be useful to support motion capture actors. Nonetheless, we see from the feedback that there are suggestions for improvements and the need to ask more directed questions, which we did in the following interviews.

6.2   Interviews

All interviews with the motion capture actors and experts were recorded and then later transcribed and analyzed. Notes were taken during the interviews. Each interview was performed individually and as a semi-structured interview giving the actors and experts the opportunity to express their thoughts on our prototype. At first we describe the outcomes of the interview with the actors and thereafter the outcomes of the interviews with experts from a motion capture studio.

Interviews with Actors. For the interview with 4 motion capture actors, we asked 5 questions and gave the opportunity to add additional comments at the end of the interview. The following list depicts the questions asked to the motion capture actors:

(1) How would you describe your experience when acting with the HMPD in comparison to acting without it?
(2) If you could personalize our motion capture acting support device to your own preferences what would you modify?
(3) How would you see our device to be used in motion capture acting?
(4) What were your experiences when acting with the virtual environment in comparison to imagining it?
(5) When thinking about moods and emotions that you were asked to play what were your experiences with the device?

These questions were meant to get feedback on our acting support application and an understanding if the actors see our prototype as useful. An excerpt of the answers from the 4 actors was grouped according to the questions asked and stated below to provide a better understanding on the actor's thoughts.

Question 1: A general comment that we got from multiple actors was that our tool was useful to get a common understanding of the scene. One actor mentioned that it was "easier to get a geographical idea on what is happening" and "visual aspects make it easier to see where things are" when using the acting support device. Three actors mentioned that using the device would limit their imagination to what is shown to them in terms of virtual content. On the other hand, all actors mentioned that the audible triggers and environmental sounds used in our acting application were very helpful to get into the right acting moods and the actors were able to use them for their acting. Finally, another actor mentioned that there was not a large difference for him when acting with or without the device. Nonetheless, the actor mentioned that when using our prototype, he got into the scenes quicker and added that with less explanation of the scene and the spatial layout was needed.

Question 2: Multiple actors mentioned that they would like to be able to actually move in the virtual environment, when they move in the real world. At the moment, it is only possible to look around in the environment, no direct interactions from the actor, other than using natural head movements to look around in the environment, are possible.

Another point mentioned by one actor was that he would like to have the ceiling and the floor covered with the retro-reflective screen to see content even there. Moreover, he mentioned that motions of animated characters should be more realistic and the opportunity to actually interact with them would be helpful. On the other hand, another actor mentioned that he preferred the nature scene where the virtual environment was focusing on showing scenery and only key triggers to change the act.

Question 3: All actors gave a general consensus when they mentioned that our application gave them a fast and detailed understanding of the acting environment and the events in the scene. The actors saw our application as helpful for preparations and as an inspirational tool to trigger their imagination before the shoot. Two actors mentioned that our device could save "a lot of time on the shooting day" and therefore "make the shoot day less stressful". The actor with 15-years of experience in motion capture acting added that this tool could also help other actors that are not used to motion capture acting or similar acting environments while performing. The application could help those actors to get quicker into the act and to get movements and expressions right so that they look good in the game. This would then in turn help animators to do less post-processing when the actors get the movements and directional turns correct right away. Moreover, this actor stated that our tool could help even experienced actors while performing in situations that are hard to imagine or to recreate. The actor gave an example of standing in front of a huge monster and interacting with it while still having the correct body pose.

Question 4: For this question, three actors mentioned that it was harder to imagine things when they were using the device, as they were more focused on using and interacting with the things that they saw, instead of imagining what could happen in the scene. One actor added, "if you are not used to the device it was easier without it". On the other hand, another actor mentioned that seeing the scenery and the virtual objects helped to guide his acting.

Question 5: Here, the actors mentioned that especially the sound effects helped to trigger their emotions and moods. One actor mentioned that the sound effects were "more of an emotional lift then when just clapping" the hands to give an indication of an event. Another actor added that she liked that the sound adjusted spatially when looking in different directions, it helped to direct the act. One actor stated that for him, especially the scary scene supported him to understand the emotions needed to act for this scene. Finally, another actor stated that seeing the scene and having visual triggers helped him, also during acting.

Interviews with Experts. For the interview with the 4 motion capture experts, we asked 4 questions and also gave the opportunity to add additional comments at the end of the interview. The following list shows the questions asked to the motion capture experts:

(1) How would you see our device to be used in motion capture?
(2) What impacts do you see for the motion capture industry and the process?
(3) For which stages in a motion capture would you use our device?
(4) What features would you change, add or improve if you could?

Question 1: The first answer that all 4 experts gave was that our device could be used as a rehearsal tool and as support to understand the scenes as well as the spatial layout of a scene. It was furthermore mentioned that this could give the actor more information about the environment while the director is giving instructions where to look at and what to do during a shoot. Moreover, another expert mentioned that when less time for the actors to prepare is available and "actors need to jump into the scene", our application could help to trigger natural reactions. Furthermore, it was mentioned by two experts that our prototype could be helpful for virtual production and pre-visualization to setup the scene or giving the director the chance to modify the virtual scenery before a shoot.

Question 2: Two experts mentioned that for the motion capture process, our tool could make it simpler for the actors on the shoot day and give more clarity in terms of directions and how to act in the scenes. It was also mentioned that rehearsals could be made more efficient. When reflecting about the industry impact of our prototype, it was mentioned that using a game engine to render the virtual scenery, as we do it in our application, could be interesting as scenes could be used directly from the game development process.

Question 3: The experts see our tool especially in the preparation phase, before a shoot, as useful. It was mentioned that rehearsals could be performed at the actors' home or another facility and therefore allow for more flexibility for the motion capture studio but also for actors and directors. Moreover, it was mentioned that building props and placing them at the right position would reduce the setup time with the actors before a shoot. Furthermore, the experts see our device as a way of supporting discussions between director and actors to prepare for a shoot.

Question 4: Three experts mentioned that they would like to integrate the prototype into their motion capture systems. This would allow them to use the projected virtual environment to see and match content in real-time from the perspective of the actor. Moreover, the experts mentioned that sending positional data from the motion capture system to our device would allow for very precise tracking and the ability to move around in the virtual environment with high precision. This would also allow the experts to place real objects at precise locations and make the motion capture shoot and the experience with the device even more accurate. Some technical improvements were also mentioned. Two expert said that they would like to have a higher resolution and an even larger field-of-view.

A few general concerns were mentioned by the experts, also in comparison to acting without the device. A common concern among the experts was the battery life. As the battery holds up to 3–4 h and is easily exchangeable it was not an issue for their operation especially considering that the battery holds long enough to be changed in e.g. the lunch break. Another concern was raised that actors should not be confronted with our device for the first time on a shoot day as it could take more time to introduce the actors to the device as wanted in a smooth motion capture procedure. Therefore, the suggestion was to give the device already beforehand to the actors to familiarize with the device and digital scenery.

6.3   Technology and Usability Evaluation

The general technology that we are using was evaluated in other work before [3,4]. Nonetheless, improvements in terms of hardware and software stability, digital scenery and reduced polygons have been made for this research. The software stability did not pose any issues during our user testing sessions but we experienced a delay of about 1 s when triggering sounds or animation via the bluetooth keyboard. As this was noticed early on, we accounted for this during the tests and actors did not notice this issue. Visual and auditory quality was well perceived by the actors and worked without any problems. Actors were able to move quickly and were not disturbed or hindered by the projections or the device itself. When asking the actors about any discomfort or if they feel the weight of the device while acting, no negative comments were given by the actors. Nonetheless, the actors mentioned that the technology was new to them and they had to adjust to the fact when getting to close to the reflective foil leads to a smaller image and not as expected to a larger image. In terms of optic this is a logical phenomenon but from a user perception it is at the beginning unexpected. As we knew about this design restriction we planned for it by placing the reflective cloth a bit further away from the actor. Another way of accounting for this is by steering the actor through spatial happenings in the digital environment. A future improvement that we noticed while testing was that the stripped down pico projector hardware should be embedded in a more rugged housing so that accidentally touching the delicate electronics does not lead to restarting the device. This did not occur during the actors' performances but when fitting the head-mounted projector and can be avoided in the future.

6.4 Observation

In this section, we describe findings from our observations of the acting performances and when analyzing the recordings of these performances. Notes were taken during the performances and video material was then analyzed to evaluate our initial observations.

A key finding that we saw with all 4 actors was that when acting without our device, the performances were more spatially directed towards an audience, which in our case was were the researcher supervising the shoot was placed. This was not the case when using our prototype. The actors then were using the spatial directions where useful content for their performance was located.

What we found as an interesting observation was that especially in the nature scene, three actors chose not to speak and only use body acting when they acted without the device. When using our device, the actors used speech and more body movements during their performance.

In terms of timing and switching to different acting moods demanded in the nature and war scene, actors were more guided than when not using the device. This was even though the triggers were also indicated through clapping the hands when acting without the device. Two actors switched to another acting phase on their own pace, before the indicator came, when acting without the device. In one case, the actor realized this mistake and asked to redo the scene. To even further investigate the differences in acting when performing with or without a head-mounted projection display, we see the use of a motion capture system for future research as an interesting addition to allow for even more data to be compared in a quantitative evaluation.

We also observed that one actor was visibly more engaged in his acting performance and delivered a performance that we saw more fit to the description of the acting scene than when acting without the device.

7   Discussion and Conclusion

Our initial goal when developing our mixed reality application was to support actors while recording performances for motion capture shoots and allowing them to trigger natural emotions and movements. In this research we have evaluated our prototype with experienced motion capture actors and experts from a motion capture studio to find out if our application is useful to support actors performing in a motion capture environment.

Our expected results from this research were that actors find it useful to use our application during the performance and possibly suggest improvements to be made. This expectation was not fully confirmed by the outcomes of our study. Nonetheless, nearly all actors and experts considered our tool as very helpful as a rehearsal tool and to get an understanding of the acting scenario, the events and the demanded performance. One actor mentioned that our application gave a "very good look into the scene" and that he used this for his following performance as inspiration when acting without the device. All actors considered the sound effects that we used as acting triggers and to create the atmosphere as very helpful for their acting.

Using our prototype during acting was perceived with mixed feelings. Three actors mentioned that they would rather use our device before the performance to prepare and then be able to use it as an inspiration and a guideline to fully use their imagination and artistic freedom during the motion capture shoots.

Actors also mentioned contradicting wishes when it comes to realism of the virtual environment. One actor preferred to have a virtual environment that is more realistic with more animation, visuals and interactive human-like virtual characters. Another actor preferred to have a more simplistic environment that only shows the scenery and gives some audible triggers for his acting. Yet another actor said that the projected environment, helped his acting and that he sees a large potential to use it for inexperienced motion capture actors helping them to perform. This shows that actors are very diverse in their preferences but also in how they can be supported during their performance. Sound triggers seemed to work and were appreciated by all actors during the performances.

An observation that we made is that actors seemed to be more directed and guided during their performance and use correct spatial positions to act towards when using our device. In comparison to acting without our prototype, actors performed intuitively towards the camera and where researchers were standing. For the actors this was believed as the direction of the audience. Also less other spatial directions pointing away from the audience were used to act towards.

Using our device to support actors during a motion capture shot has shown that it is possible but relies on the preferences and experiences of the actors. Furthermore, it highly relies on accurate visual and audible presentation of virtual content. Acting triggers should not distract the actors from their performance and the support application should allow them to fully use their imagination and artistic freedom, if this is desired for the shoot.

A common consensus between actors and experts was that our application could safe shooting time and reduce preparation time for the actors. Our research has shown that our application, in its current state, was considered by experienced motion capture actors and experts of a motion capture studio as rehearsal tool, as preparation tool and as a tool to set up the physical scenario in the motion capture studio.

8   Future Work

We are planning to provide a more compact and robust housing for the electronic components, as well as to find more common features that help supporting different actors on stage. Also, we are planning to investigate the use of our system as a rehearsal tool for the actors. Moreover, we consider to integrate our independently working device with a motion capture system to allow a more immersive experience and to use the device for preparing motion capture shoots. This could allow to support the motion capture experts to place and align physical objects with the digital environment and allow for a very precise tracking. Moreover, it would allow for more data from the motion capture system that could be used for evaluation.

References

1. Kade, D., Özcan, O., Lindell, R.: Towards stanislavski-based principles for motion capture acting in animation and computer games. In: Proceedings of CONFIA 2013, International Conference in Illustration and Animation, IPCA, pp. 277–292 (2013)
2. Kade, D., Özcan, O., Lindell, R.: An immersive motion capture environment. In: Proceedings of the ICCGMAT 2013, International Conference on Computer Games, Multimedia and Allied Technology, World Academy of Science, Engineering and Technology, pp. 500–506 (2013)
3. Akşit, K., Kade, D., Özcan, O., Ürey, H.: Head-worn mixed reality projection display application. In: Proceedings of the 11th Conference on Advances in Computer Entertainment Technology, ACE 2014, pp. 11:1–11:9. ACM, New York (2014)
4. Kade, D., Lindell, R., Ürey, H., Özcan, O.: Supporting acting performances through mixed reality and virtual environments. In: Proceedings of SETECEC 2016, Fifth International Conference on Software and Emerging Technologies for Education, Culture, Entertainment, and Commerce, Italy, Blue Herons Editions (2016)
5. Benedek, J., Miner, T.: Measuring desirability: new methods for evaluating desirability in a usability lab setting. Proc. Usability Professionals Assoc. **2003**(8–12), 57 (2002)
6. Travis, D.: Measuring satisfaction: Beyond the usability questionnaire (2008). http://www.userfocus.co.uk/articles/satisfaction.html
7. Hua, H., Gao, C., Rolland, J.P.: Imaging properties of retro-reflective materials used in head-mounted projective displays (HMPDs). In: International Society for Optics and Photonics on AeroSense 2002, pp. 194–201 (2002)
8. Harrison, C., Benko, H., Wilson, A.D.: Omnitouch: wearable multitouch interaction everywhere. In: Proceedings of the 24th Annual ACM Symposium on User Interface Software and Technology, pp. 441–450. ACM (2011)
9. Technical Illusions: Castar (2014). http://technicalillusions.com/castar/
10. University of Southern California: Flatworld Project (2007). http://ict.usc.edu/projects/flatworld. Accessed 24 Apr 2014
11. Andreadis, A., Hemery, A., Antonakakis, A., Gourdoglou, G., Mauridis, P., Christopoulos, D., Karigiannis, J.N.: Real-time motion capture technology on a live theatrical performance with computer generated scenery. In: 2010 14th Panhellenic Conference on Informatics (PCI), pp. 148–152. IEEE (2010)

12. Meador, W.S., Rogers, T.J., O'Neal, K., Kurt, E., Cunningham, C.: Mixing dance realities: collaborative development of live-motion capture in a performing arts environment. Comput. Entertainment (CIE) **2**(2), 12 (2004)
13. James, J., Ingalls, T., Qian, G., Olsen, L., Whiteley, D., Wong, S., Rikakis, T.: Movement-based interactive dance performance. In: Proceedings of the 14th Annual ACM International Conference on Multimedia, pp. 470–480. ACM (2006)
14. Slater, M., Howell, J., Steed, A., Pertaub, D.P., Garau, M.: Acting in virtual reality. In: Proceedings of the Third International Conference on Collaborative Virtual Environments, pp. 103–110. ACM (2000)
15. Normand, J.M., Spanlang, B., Tecchia, F., Carrozzino, M., Swapp, D., Slater, M.: Full body acting rehearsal in a networked virtual environment-a case study. Presence Teleoperators Virtual Environ. **21**(2), 229–243 (2012)
16. Steptoe, W., Normand, J.M., Oyekoya, O., Pece, F., Giannopoulos, E., Tecchia, F., Steed, A., Weyrich, T., Kautz, J., Slater, M.: Acting rehearsal in collaborative multimodal mixed reality environments. Presence **21**(4), 406–422 (2012)
17. Gruzelier, J., Inoue, A., Smart, R., Steed, A., Steffert, T.: Acting performance and flow state enhanced with sensory-motor rhythm neurofeedback comparing ecologically valid immersive VR and training screen scenarios. Neurosci. Lett. **480**(2), 112–116 (2010)
18. MacKenzie, I.S.: Human-computer interaction: an empirical research perspective. Newnes (2012)

Step by Step: Evaluating Navigation Styles in Mixed Reality Entertainment Experience

Mara Dionísio[1(✉)] 🄳, Paulo Bala[1] 🄳, Valentina Nisi[1] 🄳, Ian Oakley[2] 🄳,
and Nuno Nunes[1] 🄳

[1] Madeira-ITI, University of Madeira, Campus da Penteada, 9020-105 Funchal, Portugal
`msgdionisio@gmail.com`
[2] Ulsan National Institute of Science and Technology, Ulsan, Republic of Korea

Abstract. The availability of depth sensing technology in smartphones and tablets adds spatial awareness as an interaction modality to mobile entertainment experiences and showcases the potential of Mixed Reality (MR) for creating immersive and engaging experiences in real world contexts. However, the lack of design knowledge about interactions within MR represents a barrier to creating effective entertainment experiences. Faced with this challenge, we contribute a study of three navigation styles (NS) for MR experiences shown on a handheld device. The navigation styles range from fully virtual, through a mixed style that involves both on-screen and in-world activity, to fully real navigation. Our findings suggest that when designing an MR experience, the navigation style deployed should reflect the context, content and required interactions. For our MR experience, "The Old Pharmacy", with its specific content, context and required interactions, results show that navigation styles relying on in-world activity leads to higher levels of Presence, Immersion and Flow.

Keywords: Mixed reality · Mobiles devices · Depth perception
Navigation style · User experience · User study

1 Introduction

After many years of promising research, virtual and augmented reality systems are becoming mainstream. The next generation of mobile and wearable devices, such as Google's Project Tango [1] and Microsoft's HoloLens [2], combine high-resolution graphics with sophisticated tracking and scanning systems. These devices enable consumers to access rich Mixed Reality (MR) spaces where digital and physical objects can interact in real time in application areas as diverse as gaming [3] education [4] and navigation [5, 6]. They promise advantages and benefits in terms of delivery of contextual information [7] and in supporting increased levels of user presence [8].

However, MR systems are highly diverse, spanning the spectrum of the Reality-Virtuality Continuum (RVC) [9] from entirely virtual to fully real. This diversity presents considerable challenges to designers, as there is a lack of design knowledge relating to how systems at different positions on the RVC spectrum will impact the experiences of their users. While this is true for a wide range of application areas, we believe it is particularly relevant to the domain of entertainment, where experiential

© Springer International Publishing AG, part of Springer Nature 2018
A. D. Cheok et al. (Eds.): ACE 2017, LNCS 10714, pp. 32–45, 2018.
https://doi.org/10.1007/978-3-319-76270-8_3

qualities such as immersion, engagement and fun are foregrounded. We argue that, as MR applications and use cases become more commonplace, it is important to understand how interaction techniques impact user experience and engagement in entertainment focused MR contents and applications.

In this paper, we contribute to advancing the understanding of MR entertainment experiences by studying the impact of Navigational Styles (NS) on the user experience of MR environments. This is valuable as navigating around digital content is a core feature of MR scenarios. Users can navigate MR environments by a range of mechanisms that parallel the RVC itself, from the use of controllers in virtual environment to fully real navigation in the physical world. Different styles result in very different experiences and, we argue, will translate into different entertainment outcomes.

The main contribution of this paper is a systematic study of the influence of navigation styles used in MR experiences supporting a range of on-screen and in-world activities. First, we classify three navigation styles covering the RVC: (i) *Screen* (virtual based), (ii) *Hybrid* (involving on-screen and in-world) and (iii) *Spatial* (in-world). We then contrast these styles in terms of measures of presence, game experience and qualitative comments captured from participants in order to evaluate which navigation style provides a better experience from an entertainment point of view. Our findings reveal that a NS with in-world activity is preferred to a NS with virtual controls when trying to achieve higher levels of Presence, Immersion and Flow. Based on these results, we also contribute a discussion of how content, context and required interactions can inform designers' choice of a NS to better support compelling entertainment experiences.

2   Related Work

Milgram and Kishino's [10] define Mixed Reality within the *"Reality Virtuality Continuum"*, encompassing Physical Reality, Augmented Reality and Virtual Reality. Combining Mixed Reality with a ubiquitous knowledge of the world forms what Dourish calls a *"ubiquitous human media"* [11]. Moreover, Cheok illustrates [12–14], how ubiquitous human media actually pushes people to become fully involved in social, physical and natural interactions [12, 15].

Immersion is a common word widely used to describe the level of involvement or engagement one experiences during activities such as playing games [16, 17]. It is relevant to mobile MR experiences as it may lead to increases in presence [18]. Presence is defined as an emergent property of an immersive system, and refers to the participant's sense of *"being there"* in the virtual world [19]. In a MR experience, participants need to be immersed in the virtual aspects of the experience but also maintain awareness of their surroundings for, at least, reasons such as safety. Due to the nature of MR, participants may never achieve full immersion [10] but greater immersion may lead to a stronger merging of the virtual and real worlds.

How to interact within MR experiences and navigation techniques are a core topic of study within both MR and VR communities. Indeed a substantial body of work can be found in the VR field, where the study of immersive types of input for traditional VR systems and VR Head Mounted Displays (HMDs) have been investigated.

Initially, traditional VR systems restrained the users to their desk and limited their interactions with the virtual environment by enabling navigation through pointing devices, keyboards and game controllers [13]. Studies have demonstrated that the effectiveness of a VE is related with the sense of Presence it evokes; high levels of Presence are therefore seen as desirable [19]. Slater *et al.* showed that interaction techniques in VR play a crucial role in the determination of Presence [18]. These results are corroborated by Templeman *et al.*'s survey summarizing VR interaction techniques [20]. One theme within this research relates to the benefits of using the whole body in VR environments to increase levels of immersion and feelings of presence [21]. For example, numerous user studies concerning immersive travel techniques have been reported in the literature, such as those comparing different travel modes and metaphors for virtual environment applications [22]. Physical motion techniques were also studied, such as the use of a "lean-based" technique [23]. Slater *et al.*'s [24] indicated that naive subjects in an immersive virtual environment experience a higher subjective sense of presence when they locomote by walking-in-place (*"virtual walking"*) than when they push-button-fly (*"along the floor plane"*). Later this study was replicated, adding real walking as a third condition [25] and showing this achieve yet higher scores for the presence. Similarly, Hwang [26] compares perceived field of view (FOV), levels of immersion and presence, task performance and usability among users of various VR platforms including hand-held devices. The results highlight that motion based interaction, a unique characteristic of hand-held platforms, can help presence/immersion and the perceived FOV.

More recently, technologies such as Oculus Rift[1] (with touch controllers), HTC Vive[2] and PrioVR[3] have led to a new range of interaction techniques that seek to facilitate transitions between the physical and virtual worlds. Lopes *et al.* designed and tested mechanical devices targeted at providing electrical muscle stimulations such as stepping onto uneven ground [27] or the haptic sensation of hitting and being hit [28]. The work of Tregillus and Folmer [29, 30], the VR-DROP and VR-STEP prototypes, use a smartphone's inertial sensor to simulate walking in mobile VR demonstrating that walking in place provides an immersive way to achieve virtual locomotion in mobile VR [39, 40]. In fact, research shows that users immersed in VR experiences perform better if it displays the sensory data related to their surroundings [18, 31]. With the incorporation of real world elements, research in VR is converging with MR. However, while trying to bridge virtual and real worlds, some of the above examples rely on complex technologies that require highly specific sensing or actuation setups. As such they are unavailable to current MR designers using commodity technology solutions. To better target this group, the current research focuses on prototyping through technology that is accessible, mobile and self-contained. It seeks to explore how existing mobile technology can bridge between the virtual and real worlds, while still providing natural interaction and high level of immersion.

The release of Project Tango led to a series of experimental concepts embracing the motion control abilities in several domains from games to education. Garden is a MR

---

[1] www.oculus.com.

[2] www.htcvive.com.

[3] www.priovr.com.

experience [3] enabling players to transform their real environment into a virtual garden where they can play in using Project Tango device as a HMD. Ghostly Mansion [32] is a first person story-driven hidden object game for the Project Tango device, where the player explores virtual rooms looking for hidden objects related to the story narrative. Project Tango applications also target commercial scenarios with applications such as Car Visualizer [33] (to view, walk around and interact with 3D representations of purchasable cars) or Home AR Designer [34] (that enables you to superimpose furniture in your home before you buy it, taking into account the real dimensions of the space). Additionally there are sandbox experiences (VRMT: Worldbuilder [35] and Tango Minitown [36]) and Project Tango applications with educational purposes such as Project Tangosaurs [37] or Solar Simulator [38]. These enable users to explore rich virtual content (in this case, dinosaurs and planets) as if they were in a museum setting.

In our work, we identify a gap in the study of interaction techniques applied to MR experiences that seek to entertain their users. We draw inspiration from related work in the VR field, specifically Slater et al.'s study [24], and Hwang's study [26] showing how motion tracking in VR positively affected the users' experience. Accordingly, the study in this paper looks at how different interaction techniques affect the users experience in a MR storytelling experience, with a special attention to the role of motion tracking. We analyse the user experience in terms of Presence and key game experience components such as flow and imaginative immersion. These are particularly relevant as prior literature has posited a link between feelings of Presence and "being in flow" during entertainment experiences [39].

3   MR Experience: "The Old Pharmacy"

"The Old Pharmacy" is an MR story-driven interactive experience where users explore a reconstruction of a 19th century pharmacy on a handheld device (Fig. 1). The user, embodying the character of the proprietor Laura, is asked by a virtual character (a customer) to make a medicinal drink by gathering four objects, spread around the virtual pharmacy. To accomplish this task, the user must navigate and orient themselves in the virtual world and examine the objects within it. The pharmacy is a visually complex environment with many objects distributed around the space both horizontally and vertically (e.g. on furniture). The search task requires the user to move around and explore different viewpoints. The experience features a total of 15 selectable objects. When a user is within reaching distance of one of these, the object is highlighted visually with a glow effect and a user can select it with an on-screen tap. An audio dialogue between the customer and Laura elaborates on the properties of the object. When an object that is part of the set of ingredients needed to make the drink is selected the user receives encouraging on-screen and auditory feedback.

"The Old Pharmacy" experience was built using the Unity 5 game engine [40] for the Project Tango platform. Using depth perception information and computer vision algorithms, Project Tango can reconstruct mathematical models of the real world over time. The system estimates the movement of the device in relation to the real world, allowing for motion tracking (navigation and orientation) of the user holding the device.

Abstracting from the technology behind it, this type of system showcases the potential of using knowledge of the surrounding world as input.

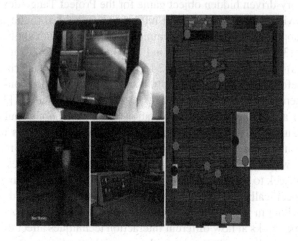

Fig. 1. "The Old Pharmacy" mixed reality experience with room layout (orange dots are selectable objects and green objects are selectable objects that need to be collected). (Color figure online)

4 Study: Navigation Styles in a MR Experience

4.1 Experimental Design

The study used a single independent variable: Navigation Style (NS). Three groups of participants experienced "The Old Pharmacy", each with a different NS (see Fig. 2). We used a between groups design, instead of a more powerful repeated measures design, as completing the experience once reveals the location of the key items and would strongly impact behaviour during subsequent runs through the system. The three NS are: *Screen*, *Hybrid* and *Spatial*. *Screen* is a baseline and interaction within the virtual environment is achieved by the common approach of manipulating two on-screen virtual joysticks, one to look around (view orientation) and one to walk (location). In the second style, *Hybrid*, we used the mobile device's gyroscope and accelerometer to control the user's orientation and a virtual joystick to enable navigation to different locations. Unlike *Screen*, this involves an MR experience, as device sensors translate the real world orientation into the virtual world. Finally, in *Spatial*, interaction relies solely on Project Tango motion tracking for controlling both orientation and translation. By creating a direct mapping between sensory–motor actions in both the real and virtual worlds, we aim to achieve a higher sense of realism and fidelity [41].

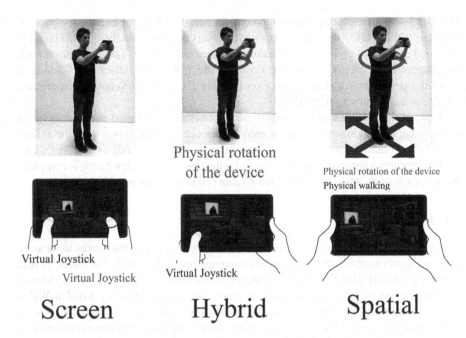

Fig. 2. Interaction techniques for conditions: *Screen*, *Hybrid* and *Spatial*. The green represents navigation actions and red represents looking actions. Objects are selectable by touch in all conditions. (Color figure online)

4.2 Demographics

We recruited 36 users (38.9% females) for the study using the university mailing list. Participants' ages ranged from 18 to 44 years (27.8% were less than 25 years, 63.9% within the 25–34 age range and 8.3% above 34 years old). Participants were randomly assigned among the navigation styles (12 per condition) and demographics captured previous experience with games, VR, HMD and smartphones on seven point Likert items. A Kruskal-Wallis test on this data showed no significant differences across the groups, indicating samples were homogenous.

4.3 Procedure and Measures

The trial was carried out in a controlled environment consisting of a 5 m by 6 m room without furniture. Participants were given a debriefing statement explaining the experiment in detail and signed a consent form. After completing demographics, they were handed a tablet device containing the "The Old Pharmacy" and given a short tutorial on the navigation style they were to use. They then completed the experience. Immediately after the trial, they completed a survey using the core module of the Game Experience Questionnaire (GEQ) [16], and the Igroup Presence Questionnaire (IPQ) [42]. The IPQ [43] features constructs of Spatial Presence, Involvement and Experienced Realism. Using it measures how the experience invoked a sense of Presence in the participants.

The GEQ seeks to capture in-the-moment qualities of a game experience and we expected that the GEQ modules components to vary amongst the three NS. The GEQ core module focuses on in-game experience by measuring Flow, Tension, Sensory and Imaginative Immersion, Competence, Positive Affect, Negative Affect, and Challenge, while the post-game module focuses on Positive Experience, Negative Experience, Tiredness and Returning to Reality.

Next, an experimenter conducted an unstructured interview, based on the observation notes, to capture comments on the overall experience and interaction with the system and content. Finally, participants completed the post-game module of the GEQ. This module captures a participant's opinions and reflections after an experience is complete. In total, each study session took around 45 min (10 min for the actual task).

4.4 Data Analysis

Scoring guidelines for each of the scales were followed to obtain the scores to measure the participants experience according to the navigation style. Due to the nature of data measured (ordinal data from Likert scales) and the small sample size, we performed separate non-parametric tests on each measure. These were one-way Kruskal-Wallis ANOVAs followed by Mann-Whitney *post-hoc* pairwise comparisons. We used an alpha value of $p < 0.05$. Due to the multiple comparisons made, Bonferroni corrections ($p < 0.05/3$) are typically applied. After careful consideration we opted to report the statistics without these corrections since we used non-parametric tests, which are in general more conservative. In the particular case of our study, performing Bonferroni corrections and specially taking into account the small sample size, could inflate type II errors [44]. Furthermore, in the interests of brevity, only significant results are reported.

4.5 Quantitative Data Results

IPQ data are plotted in Fig. 3. Kruskal-Wallis tests showed that the sense of Presence (Total Presence $H(2) = 11.18$, $p = 0.004$) was different depending on the NS. Pairwise comparisons showed differences between *Screen* and *Spatial* conditions ($U = 20.0$, $p = 0.03$, $R = -0.50$) and between *Hybrid* and *Spatial* conditions ($U = 26.0$, $p = 0.008$, $r = -0.45$). We also performed Kruskal-Wallis tests on all three IPQ constructs, only two showed that the NS significantly influenced ratings: Experienced Realism ($H(2) = 6.57$, $p = 0.037$) and Spatial Presence ($H(2) = 7.48$, $p = 0.024$). Pairwise comparisons showed differences between *Screen* and *Spatial* conditions for Spatial Presence ($U = 25.0$, $p = 0.006$, $r = -0.46$). Regarding the Experienced Realism pair wise comparisons revealed that there was a significant difference between *Hybrid* and *Spatial conditions* ($U = 31.50$, $p = 0.019$, $r = -0.003$).

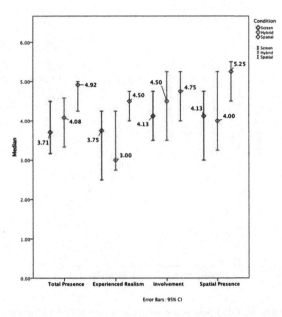

Fig. 3. Median scores of total presence and IPQ components *Experienced Realism, Involvement* and *Spatial Presence*

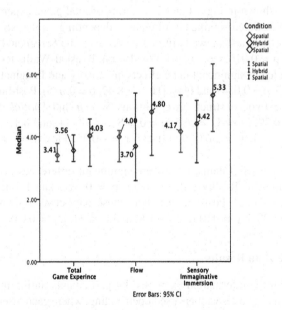

Fig. 4. Median scores for total GEQ and GEQ core module components Flow and Sensory and Imaginative Immersion

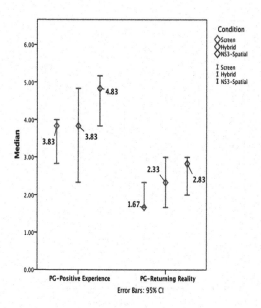

Fig. 5. Median scores for GEQ post-game components Positive Experience and Returning to Reality and error bars representing confidence intervals at the 95% level.

GEQ data are shown in Figs. 4 and 5. In terms of total game experience the Total GEQ scores demonstrated significant differences depending on the NS, $(H(2) = 6.47, p < 0.039)$. A post-hoc test showed differences between the *Screen* and *Spatial* conditions $(U = 27.0, p = 0.016, r = -0.40)$. We also ran Kruskal-Wallis tests on the GEQ constructs which led to significant main effects in Sensory and Imaginative Immersion (SII) $(H(2) = 6.75, p = 0.034)$ and Flow $(H(2) = 8.42, p = 0.015)$. Post-hoc tests showed differences in the two constructs in conditions *Screen* and *Spatial* (SII-$U = 31.0$, $p = 0.018, r = -0.39$; Flow-$U = 26.5, p = 0.008, r = -0.44$) and between *Hybrid* and *Spatial* conditions (SII-$U = 36.0, p = 0.037, r = -0.35$; Flow-$U = 28.5, p = 0.021$, $r = -0.39$).

In the post-game GEQ items, there were significant differences in ratings for the factors of Returning to Reality $(H(2) = 6.93, p = 0.031)$ and Positive Experience $(H(2) = 6.91, p = 0.032)$. Post-hoc tests bore these out between *Screen* and *Spatial* (respectively: $U = 28.5, p = 0.011, r = -0.42$ and $U = 31.5, p = 0.019, r = -0.39$).

4.6 Qualitative Data Results

After gathering all the information expressed by participants during the unstructured interviews, a team of two researchers used open coding, where each researcher selected quotes and created high-level categories. These codes were then reviewed and merged or divided into new categories, as described below. We identify the participants' quotes with the navigation style and their session ID (e.g.: *Screen*-P30 – navigation style *Screen* participant session 30).

Interaction

Most participants in *Screen* agreed that navigation was inadequate, reporting difficulties in adapting to the controls (*Screen*-P30 *"Controls were a surprise [...] I found them to control and to explore the virtual environment"*). Moreover, the need for high cognitive effort to calculate movement in order to achieve accurate navigation was mentioned. In *Hybrid*, the number of users highlighting this problem was reduced, (*Hybrid*-P40 *"I felt that I always had to be calculating my movement and my gaze."*, *Hybrid*-P33 mentioned confusion in the beginning of the experience *"Using both joystick and my arms to pinpoint place and things was a bit confusing in the beginning"*). In *Spatial*, one user expanded on difficulties experienced with the interaction mode (*Spatial*-P21 *"If I wanted to look back, I felt forced to turn my whole body back"*).

In *Screen* and *Hybrid*, fewer participants specifically mentioned the comfortable navigation (no tiredness, stress or pain), than in *Spatial* (*Spatial*-P9 *"Walking around the room was an interesting experience; the control of the movement felt natural."*). However at least 2 participants specifically mentioned the possibility of problems if the experience was longer (*Spatial*-P20 *"If the story was bigger, I would feel very tired, arms mostly, and concerned since the tablet gets hot."*).

Immersion in MR

More participants from *Hybrid* and *Spatial* than from *Screen* reported feeling immersed and experiencing a sense of being in the virtual world (*Spatial*-P15 *"I had the sense that I, as a whole, got sucked into the virtual world. You just need to always keep mindful about where you step"*, *Spatial*-P19 *"I definitely felt part of the game. I walked to places to get my ingredients, I looked up and down to explore and, I was talking to a client."*). However participants from all the conditions explicitly felt like they were adding to the story and content (*Spatial*-P19 *"I enjoyed being able to interact with lots of objects in the VE. It made me feel in control."*, *Screen*-P27 *"I felt like I was building the story through the objects"*). A couple of participants mentioned that the task given was short for them to really feel engaged and immersed. For example, *Hybrid*-P44 said: *"I could not feel any empathy with the characters. I had no time to get to know them and get passionate about their struggles."*

Sense of Body

Across all conditions, several users made remarks regarding their sense of body in the MR environment. Some of the comments touched upon the relationship between the scale of the room and their size within it. Some users reported feeling big while, others felt like they were smaller than their real self. For example, *Screen*-P23 *"I felt both tall and short. When looking up, the ceiling was to close. When looking down I felt too close to the ground."* Or *Hybrid*-P35 *"I felt shorter in the game. The place that I recall I felt this mostly is near the window, as you look to the old lady, you get the sense she is quite tall."* Some users enjoyed this different sensation *Hybrid*-P42 *"[...] I felt quite tall. It was a good sensation"*, *Spatial*-P4 *"I got the feeling I was shorter than I am [...] I found it interesting. It was like being in a hobbit house."*. Participants from *Screen* and *Hybrid* did not mention experiencing differences in relation to how navigation input was mapped to response in the interaction modes. In contrast, in *Spatial* the mapping between navigation in the real world and the virtual world was noticed. *Spatial*-P16 mentioned *"I felt I walked faster in the game than in the real world. It was good, since it would cover more ground on the game without taking too much of my real space."*

Some participants across all conditions also mentioned a desire to see their virtual body represented. They desired to see their hands while choosing the ingredients and their full body when looking down. *Spatial*-P17 *"The thing though, got strange when I first interacted with an object. I was expecting to see a hand picking it up."* Or *Spatial*-P9, *"When I looked down I was expecting to see my feet. I wanted to see myself walking.".*

Awareness of Real Space

Participants in *Spatial* were more aware of the real space; several participants commented about this issue. For example, one participant (*Spatial*-P17) initially thought that the tables in the real world were matching the tables in digital world. Another (*Spatial*-P16) mentioned that the real world space was smaller than the virtual. Awareness of the real space was also came across through comments regarding safety during walking. Some users were at relative ease while interacting (*Spatial*-P20 *"Unless there were holes in the ground, I felt safe playing the game"*; *Spatial*-P15 *"got sucked into the virtual world. You just need to always keep mindful about where you step."*), while others expressed concern (*Spatial*-P16 *"I was worried about tripping in any of the chairs."*; *Spatial*-P17 *"it needs a lot of space, if it's bigger how can I play it safely?"*).

5   Discussion

The results show the *Spatial* condition produces a richer MR experience than the other two conditions in terms of a range of metrics from both the IPQ and GEQ. There are several caveats to this broad conclusion and we discuss the details below.

Interaction: The *Spatial* condition supports higher levels of presence than the baseline *Screen* and the *Hybrid* but in different ways. The first finding ties in with prior research [18] indicating that virtual controls lead to reduced presence compared to more natural navigation styles [8]. However, some aspects of presence were negatively affected by the *Hybrid* condition. Specifically, Experienced Realism dropped against the baseline. We suggest this is because the "hybrid" interaction scheme does not have a direct analogy in the real world - although its natural to control orientation in the scene with similar movements of the device, its challenging to integrate this real world activity with traditional on-screen input to control position. This finding is corroborated by observed user behaviour: participants walked in the *Hybrid* condition, despite the fact this had no impact on the game world. The *Spatial* condition performed uniformly well in terms of the Spatial Presence component. We suggest this is due to participants' actions with their real body being accurately reflected by actions in the virtual world, leading to an increased sense of "being there" [41].

Content: The NS for an experience needs reflect the content in the experience. In our specific case, story content was scaffolded onto an exploration task. The goal was for participants to feel immersed and present in the story, not just the sensory experience.

Results from the questionnaires suggest that the *Spatial* condition supported this goal - the natural body movements facilitated users in role playing the character of Laura as she moved around the virtual space. *Spatial*-P15 stated "I had a sense that I, as a whole, got sucked into the virtual world." However, the kind of mapping we present here would likely be unsuitable for other types of virtual experiences, such as those that involve driving or piloting vehicles. In these cases, the real motions used in the *Spatial* condition might negatively impact presence.

Context: In the experience in this study, the dimensions of the virtual world (the pharmacy) matched the dimensions of the space surrounding the participant (the experimental environment). In many experiences, this correspondence may be undesirable or hard to achieve. For example, to simulate a large virtual environment, a one-to-one mapping to a real space is likely impossible. In such a situation, the *Hybrid* condition described in this article may be more appropriate. Beyond this issue, *Spatial* also raises issues of safety and social acceptability. If applied in a large public space would an AR environment distract its users and therefore, potentially, endanger them? And how would non-participants react and relate to those engaged in the experience? These questions are substantially beyond the scope of work in this paper, but serve to highlight how the issue of NS can have broad reaching implications for the design and deployment of a MR experience.

6   Conclusion and Future Work

In this paper, we report on a study of the impact of navigation styles on mixed reality experiences. The results show that using navigation styles with in-world activity favorably impacts measures such as Flow, Presence and Immersion. Additionally, we identify that factors such as context, content and required interactions need to be considered when selecting a navigation style for a MR experience. For example, when deciding to include in-world activity, safety concerns (in real world situations) and ergonomic concerns (when considering longer experiences) should be considered. These concerns highlight the need for further studies in this area, specifically using similar experiences in real world context, varied contents and with a longer duration.

Acknowledgments. We wish to acknowledge our fellow researchers Rui Trindade, Sandra Câmara, Dina Dionísio and the support of LARSyS (Projeto Estratégico LA 9 - UID/EEA/50009/ 2013), MITIExcell (M1420-01-0145-FEDER-000002) and the Ph.D. Grants: PD/BD/114142/ 2015 and PD/BD/128330/2017.

References

1. Tango. https://get.google.com/tango/
2. Microsoft: Microsoft HoloLens. https://www.microsoft.com/microsoft-hololens/en-us
3. Sing, K.H., Xie, W.: Garden: a mixed reality experience combining virtual reality and 3D reconstruction. In: Proceedings of the 2016 CHI Conference Extended Abstracts on Human Factors in Computing Systems, pp. 180–183. ACM, New York (2016)

4. Zhang, J., Ogan, A., Liu, T.C., Sung, Y.T., Chang, K.E.: The influence of using augmented reality on textbook support for learners of different learning styles. In: 2016 IEEE International Symposium on Mixed and Augmented Reality (ISMAR), pp. 107–114 (2016)
5. Möller, A., Kranz, M., Huitl, R., Diewald, S., Roalter, L.: A mobile indoor navigation system interface adapted to vision-based localization. In: Proceedings of the 11th International Conference on Mobile and Ubiquitous Multimedia, pp. 4:1–4:10. ACM, New York (2012)
6. Rao, Q., Tropper, T., Grünler, C., Hammori, M., Chakraborty, S.: AR-IVI — implementation of in-vehicle augmented reality. In: 2014 IEEE International Symposium on Mixed and Augmented Reality (ISMAR), pp. 3–8 (2014)
7. Grubert, J., Langlotz, T., Zollmann, S., Regenbrecht, H.: Towards pervasive augmented reality: context-awareness in augmented reality. IEEE Trans. Vis. Comput. Graph. 23, 1706–1724 (2016)
8. Waterworth, J.: Human-Experiential Design of Presence in Everyday Blended Reality. Springer, Heidelberg (2016). https://doi.org/10.1007/978-3-319-30334-5
9. Milgram, P., Takemura, H., Utsumi, A., Kishino, F.: Augmented reality: a class of displays on the reality-virtuality continuum. In: Telemanipulator and Telepresence Technologies, pp. 282–293. International Society for Optics and Photonics (1995)
10. Milgram, P., Kishino, F.: A taxonomy of mixed reality visual displays. IEICE Trans. Inf. Syst. 77, 1321–1329 (1994)
11. Dourish, P.: Where the Action Is: The Foundations of Embodied Interaction. MIT Press, Cambridge (2001)
12. Cheok, A.D., Fong, S.W., Goh, K.H., Yang, X., Liu, W., Farzbiz, F.: Human Pacman: a sensing-based mobile entertainment system with ubiquitous computing and tangible interaction. In: Proceedings of the 2nd Workshop on Network and System Support for Games, pp. 106–117. ACM (2003)
13. Cheok, A.D., Yang, X., Ying, Z.Z., Billinghurst, M., Kato, H.: Touch-space: mixed reality game space based on ubiquitous, tangible, and social computing. Pers. Ubiquitous Comput. 6, 430–442 (2002)
14. Farbiz, F., Cheok, A.D., Wei, L., ZhiYing, Z., Ke, X., Prince, S., Billinghurst, M., Kato, H.: Live three-dimensional content for augmented reality. IEEE Trans. Multimed. 7, 514–523 (2005)
15. Bowlby, J.: Attachment and Loss. Basic Books, New York (1983)
16. Ijsselsteijn, W., de Kort, Y., Poels, K.: The game experience questionnaire: development of a self-report measure to assess the psychological impact of digital games. Manuscript in Preparation
17. Ermi, L., Mäyrä, F.: Fundamental components of the gameplay experience: analysing immersion. Worlds Play Int. Perspect. Digit. Games Res. 37, 37–53 (2005)
18. Slater, M., Usoh, M.: Body centred interaction in immersive virtual environments. In: Artificial Life and Virtual Reality, pp. 125–148. Wiley (1994)
19. Witmer, B.G., Singer, M.J.: Measuring presence in virtual environments: a presence questionnaire. Presence Teleoperators Virtual Environ. 7, 225–240 (1998)
20. Templeman, J.N., Denbrook, P.S., Sibert, L.E.: Virtual locomotion: walking in place through virtual environments. Presence Teleoperators Virtual Environ. 8, 598–617 (1999)
21. Brooks Jr., F.P., Airey, J., Alspaugh, J., Bell, A., Brown, R., Hill, C., Nimscheck, U., Rheingans, P., Rohlf, J., Smith, D., et al.: Six generations of building walkthrough: final technical report to the National Science Foundation (1992)
22. Chung, J.C.: A comparison of head-tracked and non-head-tracked steering modes in the targeting of radiotherapy treatment beams. In: Proceedings of the 1992 Symposium on Interactive 3D Graphics, pp. 193–196. ACM, Cambridge (1992)

23. Fairchild, K.M., Lee, B.H., Loo, J., Ng, H., Serra, L.: The heaven and earth virtual reality: designing applications for novice users. In: 1993 IEEE Virtual Reality Annual International Symposium, pp. 47–53 (1993)
24. Slater, M., Usoh, M., Steed, A.: Taking steps: the influence of a walking technique on presence in virtual reality. ACM Trans. Comput. Hum. Interact. **2**, 201–219 (1995)
25. Usoh, M., Arthur, K., Whitton, M.C., Bastos, R., Steed, A., Slater, M., Brooks, F.P.: Walking > Walking-in-place > Flying, in virtual environments. In: Proceedings of the 26th Annual Conference on Computer Graphics and Interactive Techniques, pp. 359–364. ACM Press/Addison-Wesley Publishing Co., New York (1999)
26. Hwang, J., Jung, J., Kim, G.J.: Hand-held virtual reality: a feasibility study. In: Proceedings of the ACM Symposium on Virtual Reality Software and Technology, pp. 356–363. ACM (2006)
27. Lopes, P., Ion, A., Kovacs, R.: Using your own muscles: realistic physical experiences in VR. XRDS **22**, 30–35 (2015)
28. Lopes, P., Ion, A., Baudisch, P.: Impacto: simulating physical impact by combining tactile stimulation with electrical muscle stimulation. In: Proceedings of the 28th Annual ACM Symposium on User Interface Software & Technology, pp. 11–19. ACM (2015)
29. Tregillus, S.: VR-Drop: exploring the use of walking-in-place to create immersive VR games. In: Proceedings of the 2016 CHI Conference Extended Abstracts on Human Factors in Computing Systems, pp. 176–179. ACM, New York (2016)
30. Tregillus, S., Folmer, E.: VR-STEP: walking-in-place using inertial sensing for hands free navigation in mobile VR environments. In: Proceedings of the 2016 CHI Conference on Human Factors in Computing Systems, pp. 1250–1255. ACM, New York (2016)
31. McGill, M., Boland, D., Murray-Smith, R., Brewster, S.: A dose of reality: overcoming usability challenges in VR head-mounted displays. In: Proceedings of the 33rd Annual ACM Conference on Human Factors in Computing Systems, pp. 2143–2152. ACM, New York, NY, USA (2015)
32. Rabbx Inc.: Ghostly Mansion (2015)
33. NVYVE Inc.: Car Visualizer
34. Elementals Studio: Home AR Designer
35. Defective Studios: WorldBuilder
36. Lee, J.: Tango Minitown
37. Project Tango: Project Tangosaurs
38. Angstrom Tech: Solar Simulator
39. Bracken, C.C., Skalski, P.: Immersed in Media: Telepresence in Everyday Life. Routledge, New York (2010)
40. Unity - Game Engine. https://unity3d.com/
41. Heeter, C.: Being there: the subjective experience of presence. Presence Teleoperators Virtual Environ. **1**, 262–271 (1992)
42. Schubert, T.W.: The sense of presence in virtual environments: a three-component scale measuring spatial presence, involvement, and realness. Z. Für Medien. **15**, 69–71 (2003)
43. Turner, P.: The intentional basis of presence. In: Proceedings of the 10th International Workshop on Presence, pp. 127–134. Citeseer (2007)
44. Perneger, T.V.: What's wrong with Bonferroni adjustments. BMJ **316**, 1236–1238 (1998)

Increasing Presence in a Mixed Reality Application by Integrating a Real Time Tracked Full Body Representation

Felix Born[(✉)] and Maic Masuch

Entertainment Computing Group, University of Duisburg-Essen,
Duisburg, Germany
{felix.born,maic.masuch}@uni-due.de

Abstract. Mixed Reality applications create highly immersive experiences by integrating real world objects into the virtual world and thus expanding the virtual experience by a tactile perception. Interaction with mixed reality worlds becomes more natural if the user can interact using only his hands. Hence, the question arises whether the experience in mixed reality applications can be increased if the user's hands and body are integrated and virtually represented as well. Hence, as a proof of concept, we developed a mixed reality application in which every physical object has a respective virtual counterpart. The major concept of the development is to experience height while walking over a wooden plank and to solve an interaction task afterwards. We present an empirical study that examines the effect of a full body vs a hands vs no representation on the experience on presence and the physiological arousal. Results indicate that integrating a virtual body increases the experience of presence as well as the physiological arousal.

Keywords: Virtual reality gaming · Immersion · Presence
Body representation · Real time tracking · Mixed reality
Substitutional reality

1 Introduction

Like no other medium, Virtual Reality (VR)-systems are able to provide simulated stimuli to the human sensory system using Head-Mounted displays (HMD). VR-Systems that use HMDs are capable of shifting the user's perception from the real world to a virtual one by displaying simulated cues. This effect is called sensory immersion and describes the ability of a system to deliver audio-visual and proprioceptive cues that are close to real perceptions [1,33]. Thus, immersion can be defined as an objective quality of a medium. The more senses and

---

We wish to thank C. Kremzow-Tennie, D. Pohl, A. Rygula, and M. Wagner for their participation and commitment in the development and research.

© Springer International Publishing AG, part of Springer Nature 2018
A. D. Cheok et al. (Eds.): ACE 2017, LNCS 10714, pp. 46–60, 2018.
https://doi.org/10.1007/978-3-319-76270-8_4

cognitions of the user are addressed by the system, the higher its level of immersion. A high level of immersion is a prerequisite for a user to feel him/herself present in the virtual world [32], which is often defined as presence or the feeling of "being there" [5]. It is differentiated between different forms of presence like social presence, spatial presence, telepresence and copresence [22]. Within a mixed reality application, the most crucial form of presence is spatial presence, that describes the sense of being physically present in the virtual environment [25]. The occurrence of presence is commonly interpreted as the most significant quality criterion for a VR-system. At least it indicates the extent to which real world perceptions are suppressed by the simulated virtual world. Though suppressing all real world perceptions increases the experience of presence, physical objects of the real world cannot be eliminated. Hence, to sustain the virtual illusion physical objects of the real world can be integrated into the virtual world. This approach is referred to as mixed reality [19], blended reality [10], or substitutional reality [26,30] and allows a tactile exploration of the world. By addressing another human sense, this approach aims at creating a higher level of immersion and thus a greater presence than common VR-systems. One of the most famous companies which creates mixed reality applications is THE VOID[1]. The company is developing high quality mixed reality applications, in which users can explore a virtual world together at the same time. Every physical object in the real world has a virtual counterpart and is embedded in the experience. Plain white walls become doors of an alien ship and a wooden stick appears as a flickering torch. So far, THE VOID has opened four different stores in four different countries and will expand in the next year. The major goal of mixed reality applications, such as the developments of THE VOID, is to create a realistic experience that is similar to the real world. Aiming at a realistic experience by merging physical objects of the real with the virtual world, raises the question whether a virtual representation of the user's body is crucial for a mixed reality application. Considering that physical interactions in the real world are performed with the user's body, the lack of this representation and its movement could lead to a lower realism and thus to a lower experience of presence. Hence, we want to examine whether a mixed reality application benefits from representing a virtual body, whose movements are based on the real movements of the corresponding real world body.

2   Passive Haptics

The integration of natural movement in VR has become easier and more effective when HTC and Valve released the HTC Vive and Facebook released the Oculus Rift. Until then, movement in VR-systems was mostly based on artificial movement like teleporting or flying [31]. When VR became a research subject in the 90s Slater et al. [28] hypothesized that a match between real and virtual movement enhances presence due to the match of proprioceptive information from the user's movements and sensory feedback from the VR-system. They stated out,

---

[1] https://www.thevoid.com/ - 2017/07/28.

that walking in place results in a higher presence score than artificial movement that was controlled by a 3D mouse. In a further study Usoh et al. [31] expanded that hypothesis and discovered that real walking in a VR-system leads to a higher presence than walking in place. However, high presence scores due to the match of elements of the real world and the virtual world are not limited to movement. In virtual environments, the same laws of physics apply as for the real world [12,27]. Thus, the user's interactions with the virtual environment are based on the experience of interactions with the real world. The more the virtual interaction corresponds to an interaction with the real world, the higher the experienced presence is. This circumstance leads to a general problem. Physical objects that are only represented in the virtual world but not in the real world lead to a mismatch of sensory information and can be a presence breaking problem. To provide feedback and create a sensory match Lindemann et al. [15] present the idea of passive haptics. This concept refers to the integration of objects that exist in the real as well as in the virtual world. Hoffmann [9] was one of the first who examined this idea and discovered, that the experienced realism of a virtual world increases, if the user can physically touch a virtual object that has the same properties in the virtual as well as in the real world. Furthermore, Dinh et al. [4] examined the impact of multi-sensory input on the sense of presence in virtual environments. They discovered higher presence scores when tactile and auditive information of the real world were merged with the virtual world. Hence, merging the real world with the virtual world is a promising approach to increase the level of experienced presence. A virtual world, that is merged with the real world is referred to as Mixed Reality [19].

2.1 Mixed Reality

Mixed reality applications are based on the idea of merging sensory information of the real world with the virtual world to increase the experience of presence. If all physical objects in the virtual world have a counterpart in the real world the experience is also called substitutional reality [26,30]. Hettiarachchi and Wigdor [7] examined a further approach they call nnexing reality. Their system scans the user's real-world surrounding and matches physical objects with similar virtual counterparts to create a complete haptic experience. Furthermore, Sra et al. [29] demonstrate an approach which allows a procedural generation of a virtual world that includes virtual counterparts of real-time tracked physical objects. Insko [12] examined the benefits of such a system on the effect of presence. The created virtual world in this study consisted of a wooden ledge on which the users could walk. The real world consisted of an identical counterpart, that was positioned at the same place. Every physical movement in the real world was mapped to the same movement in the virtual world. The virtual ledge was mounted without a handrail above another room, so that the user of the virtual world could look several meters downstairs and thus experience the impression of height. The real ledge was place on the ground. The results of the study indicate significant higher reported presence scores and a higher heart rate when the real ledge was present. The beneficial effects of a mixed reality application are manifold and can be found in several domains. Lindgren et al. [16] examined a positive influence of a mixed reality learning app on the students' learning gains and levels of engagement. Kontranza and Lok [14] discovered a beneficial effect on virtual patient treatment when they integrated a tangible interface into a VR application. Furthermore, Carlin et al. [3] examined a positive effect on the treatment of arachnophobia using a mixed reality approach.

2.2 Controls in Mixed Reality

Though the merging of real world objects with virtual representations is beneficial for the experience of presence, a complex issue arises from this application. In order to experience the match between the physical objects of the real world and their virtual representations, it is necessary to accurately track the user's body movement and adapt the virtual representations accordingly. Touching a physical object in the real world without seeing a virtual hand that behaves the same way leads to a mismatch and to a break of presence. To integrate this possibility, modern VR systems use wireless room-scale controllers that accurately map the movements to the virtual world and are represented accordingly. However, according to [18] interactions in virtual environments are most efficient if they are considered natural. This is one of the reasons why most of the mixed reality applications, that can be found in the literature, are using an interaction design that is based on free hands interaction. There are two different approaches for integrating a free hand interaction. On the one hand, the interactions are tracked with gloves that have special tracking sensors attached [3,9,23,26,34]. On the other hand, modern camera technology like the Microsoft Kinect or Leap Motion facilitate the possibility to accurately track the user's body movement without the need for any other sensors [2,17]. In a mixed reality application, the user's visual and auditive perception is extended by a tactile perception. While a mismatch of visual information can result in motion sickness [8] and thus in a reduction of presence [20] and non-matching sounds also results in a lowered experience of presence [6], a mismatch of the tactile perception is most likely to result in lower presence as well. However, there are studies that examined the impact of a mixed reality application and did not implement a virtual representation of the body, nevertheless they discovered a significant increase in presence [12,14]. These results are surprising since the authors created the possibility for tactile perception but did not consider an appropriate representation in the implemented mixed reality application. This instance raises the question whether an accurate tracking and representation of the user's body is beneficial to the experience of presence in a mixed reality application. Bottone and Johnsen [2] examined the impact of the integration of a virtual representation of the representation of a user's hand on the experience of presence. They tracked the user's hands using a Microsoft Kinect. The user had to play a car race game with a steering wheel as input method. They found out, that when the user's hands were displayed on the steering wheel in the virtual environment, users reported higher presence scores and were able to solve driving tasks faster. However, these results account for a stationary setting in which the user interacts with the virtual world while sitting. If these findings are applied to a non-stationary context, two questions arise. On the one hand, it is interesting to examine to which degree representing the user's hands is beneficial to the user's presence in a mixed reality scenario. In such a system that is based on room-scale VR, the user also interacts with his legs by walking through the created world. Thus, on the other hand, it is interesting to find out whether representing the user's full body within the virtual world has a positive influence on the experience of presence. This question is of particular importance if the physical ground of the real environment is modified and a unique part of the virtual experience, as it was done by Insko [12], who created a wooden ledge on which the users walked and thus ought to feel aroused due to the displayed height.

3   Development of a Mixed Reality Application

Based on the idea to examine the effect of the user's body representation in a mixed reality application we developed a virtual environment in a confined space in which every physical object has a real world counterpart. The fully immersive virtual world was implemented using the game engine Unity. To facilitate the possibility to walk around freely in the real world and in the virtual world at the same time, we used the room-scale VR-system HTC Vive. This system allows the user to move freely in a maximum area of 4.5 m * 4.5 m. We deliberately neglected the interaction via the HTC Vive controllers, instead the user interacts naturally with the virtual world using only his hands. The movement of the hands is tracked using a Leap Motion sensor, which is installed in front of the HMD of the HTC Vive. Within the virtual environment every movement of the user's hand is mapped to a virtual hand model, which is pictured in Fig. 2. The user's body movement is tracked using the Microsoft Kinect sensor. In our installation, the sensor is placed outside the walkable area and thus the player never leaves the visible area of this sensor. All real body movements are mapped to a corresponding virtual representation. The virtual body was created using Makehuman[2]. The virtual hands are taken from the assets of the Leap SDK.

3.1   Setting

Within the virtual world the user experiences the virtual environment in the first-person perspective of a virtual character. The virtual environment consists of different floating islands, that are positioned at different heights. A virtual water surface was used as ground. The floating island, on which the user is located has a distance of 300 m to the water. When the mixed reality application starts, the user is instantly able to assess the displayed height. We used different shaders and implemented birds, which fly beneath the player to create reference points in order to facilitate to assess the height of the floating island. At the edge of the islands no rails or physical borders have been installed to evoke an

---

[2] http://www.makehuman.org/ - 2017/07/31.

Fig. 1. The two floating islands are connected via a wooden plank. The player is walking over the wooden plank to reach the mechanical desk that is installed on the left island. The desk is connected to an Arduino Uno that notices the user's input and transmits the signals to the game engine.

uncomfortable feeling. At the start of the application the user looks at a second island that is floating within a few meters distance to the starting island. Both islands are connected via a wooden plank that is attached at the end of each island. At the end of the plank on the second island, a mechanical control desk is installed. Whereas the height is apparent and a central element while the player is on the first island and on the wooden plank, the user cannot perceive the height on the second island due to its design that limits the view downwards. At several corner points of the islands, balloons are installed, that are not inflated when the application starts.

3.2 Task

We deliberately neglected a tutorial or introduction in order to give the user the opportunity to freely explore the application and to focus on the virtual environment without being biased by instructions. A sign next to the mechanical desk explains how to handle the switches, which are installed on the mechanical desk. In order to get to the desk and complete the given task, the user has to walk over the wooden plank. The wooden plank is 2.4 m long and coated with an anti-slip surface so the users can walk safely to the other side. If the user falls off the plank in the real world, the character of the virtual world starts to fall into the water. Afterwards, the virtual character will be respawned on the player's real world position. To accurately track the users horizontal position on the plank, we build a belt to which the HTC Vive controllers are attached. If both controllers are beside the plank, the user will start to fall down. This technique ensures an exact mapping of the real movement on the plank to the virtual movement of

Fig. 2. In the picture on the left the virtual representation interacts with the switches on the desk. The picture in the middle shows the corresponding interaction of the real user. The picture on the right shows the user's perspective while interacting. Within this task, the user's arms are not displayed to avoid a mismatch of the Kinect and Leap Motion position systems.

the character. At the end of the wooden plank, the mechanical desk is attached to a pillar. On the top side of the desk six metallic switches and a wooden slider are installed. The user's task is to reverse the position of every switch. If the user reverses a switch, one balloon on each side of the islands will start to inflate. To indicate an activated switch, a green light around the switch will appear. If all balloons are inflated, the user can move the slider on the right side of the desk upwards. This will finish the game and allows the user to float away with the island. At the same time, the screen slowly fades to black and the application ends.

4   Evaluation

We conducted a study to investigate whether the integration of a virtual body representation that is based on the real user's body in a mixed reality application helps to increase the experience of presence. We wanted to know whether the representation of the user's body and hands has a greater influence on the user's presence than just representing the user's hands or than showing no virtual representation. We hypothesize that a more realistic and complete virtual representation in a mixed reality application leads to a higher physiological arousal, experienced spatial presence, and sensory immersion.

4.1   Participants

Overall, 54 Participants were recruited online. Exclusion criteria were a history of neurological diseases such as epilepsy. Three participants were excluded from the study because the measured heart rate values for the participants indicate fault measurements for these particular cases. Therefore, only 51 participants were included and considered in the statistical analysis. All participants gave written informed consent before the investigation started and received one hourly credit as a trial subject, which has to be collected in several degree courses. Our study was approved by the ethical review board of our university.

Measurement of Virtual Reality Experience. Data about the sensations, feelings and experiences while playing in the VR game was collected via self-reports. The sense of presence, which is experienced in a virtual world was measured using the igroup presence questionnaire (IPQ) [25]. The IPQ consists of four subscales: *spatial presence, expected realism, involvement,* and a single-item scale for the general experience of presence. Since it is hypothesized that presence is also influenced by traits of the individual, we used the immersive tendencies questionnaire (ITQ) [20] to measure how easily a person becomes cognitively immersed into a several kinds of media. The subscales of the ITQ are *focus, involvement, games,* as well as a *total score.* The game experience was measured using the game experience questionnaire (GEQ) [11]. The GEQ assesses experiential constructs of *immersion, tension, competence, flow, negative affect, positive affect,* and *challenge.* Finally, to assess the effects of simulator sickness, we used the simulator sickness questionnaire (SSQ) [13] which consists of four subscales: *Nausea, Oculomotor, Disorientation,* and a *total score.*

Measurement of Arousal. In our mixed reality application, the suggested height is a central element. To assess an objective construct that refers to the arousal of the experienced height [12], we measured the heart rate for every participant. The heart rate was measured using the Polar H7 pulse belt. The data was continuously gathered via Bluetooth using an additional self-implemented program that is based on the "Bluetooth Generic Attribute Profile" from Microsoft.

Study Design and Methodology. Based on our scientific problem, a 1×3 between-subject design was used to investigate the influence of the body representation (full body and hands, hands, no representation) on the user's presence. Thus, we differentiate between three different groups: the full body and hands are represented (FB), only hands are represented (H) and no representation exists (N). All participants worked on the same procedure but had different body representations while playing in our mixed reality application based on their group which they were randomly assigned to. The participants did not know about the intended purpose of the study. Before the procedure started, the participants gave their consent and had to put on the pulse belt while the instructor waited outside the laboratory. Afterwards all participants filled out demographic data and the ITQ. During this period, the average heart rate was calculated and stored as a baseline measurement (HR1). Because a congruent perception of the in-game self and ideal self leads to higher presence [24], users in the full body group could choose between four different virtual body representation which differed in their gender and body weight. Afterwards the mixed reality application was started. Depending on the group the participant was assigned to, the full body and hands, only hands, or no body representation was shown. Then, the participant had to complete the task within the application. There was no time limit and no case in which a participant needed an exceeding amount of time to complete the task. While the user was in the virtual world, two further heart rate calculations were done. One calculation measured the average heart rate from the start of the mixed reality application to the point where the user left the wooden plank (HR2). The last calculation was done from the point when the user left the wooden plank to the point when he finished the task (HR3). This results in three different values: HR1 represents the baseline measurement, HR2 represents the period that includes the experience of height and the plank, and HR3 refers to the period, in which the user could not directly experience the height and solved the task. Immediately after the VR experience, the IPQ, the GEQ, and the SSQ were used to assess the presence, game experience, and simulator sickness. At the end participants had the possibility to enter comments considering the whole study. The experiment was finished with the complete debriefing and when the participant removed the pulse belt while the instructor waited outside.

4.2 Results

Sociodemographic Variables. 51 students (31 female), aged between 18 and 52 years ($M = 23.06, SD = 7.14$) were included in the statistical analysis.

Heart Rate Measurements. We calculated a mixed-design Anova with a within-subjects factor of the measuring moment of the heart rate (HR1, HR2, HR3) and a between-subject factor of group affiliation (FB, H, N). Mauchly's test indicated that the assumption of sphericity has been violated, $\chi^2(2) = 40.58, p < .001$, therefore degrees of freedom were corrected using Huynh-Feldt estimates of sphericity ($\epsilon = .63$). An effect of heart rate $F(2.53, 64.33) = 46.5, p < .001, \eta_p^2 = .49$ is qualified by an interaction between heart rate and group affiliation, $F(2.68, 64.33) = 2.91, p = 0.47, \eta_p^2 = .11$. Figure 3 shows the corresponding heart rate values for the measuring moments for each of the groups.

Simulator Sickness. Simulator Sickness Scores are extremely low. All symptoms were rated lower than 1, most of them even lower than 0.4 on average. Table 1 reports the weighted scores for the corresponding groups. No significant differences were found between the groups.

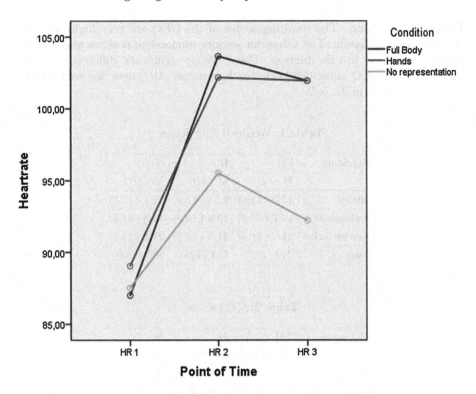

Fig. 3. The diagram shows the average heart rate for every group for the corresponding measuring moments. While the HR is similar for all groups in the baseline, the HR increase after the VR exposition (HR1) and is significantly higher for the groups with virtual representations.

Immersive Tendency, Immersion and Presence. Immersion was measured by the corresponding subscale of the GEQ and is very high in all groups which is shown in Table 2. No significant differences were found between the groups. According to the results of the IPQ, participants perceived very high levels of spatial presence as indicated independent of their group affiliation ($M = 4.05, SD = 0.73$). However, analysis of variance showed a main effect of group affiliation on spatial presence $F(2, 48) = 4.13, p = .02$. Post hoc comparisons using the Bonferoni test indicated the mean score for the FB condition ($M = 4.48, SD = 0.86$) significantly differs ($p = 0.40$) from the H condition ($M = 3.86, SD = 0.65$) and nearly significantly differs ($p = 0.50$) from the N condition ($M = 3.89, SD = 0.60$). No significant difference was found between the H condition and the N condition. Immersive Tendency is distributed normally in the N ($M = 59.1, SD = 13.5$) and H ($M = 58.5, SD = 13.5$) condition but not in the FB group ($M = 59.1, SD = 13.5$). No significant differences were found between the groups.

Game Experience. The resulting scores of the GEQ are very high independent of group affiliation. The values for sensory immersion, positive affect, competence, and flow are the highest. There are no significant differences of the corresponding GEQ subscales between the groups. All values for each of the groups are shown in Table 2.

Table 1. Weighted SSQ Scores

SSQ Score	FB	H	N
	M *(SD)*	M *(SD)*	M *(SD)*
Nausea	14.0 *(13.0)*	9.54 *(11.2)*	12.1 *(15.5)*
Oculomotor	19.7 *(23.2)*	15.6 *(10.9)*	19.5 *(18.4)*
Disorientation	21.3 *(31.2)*	21.3 *(23.1)*	23.4 *(23.7)*
Total	219 *(223)*	173 *(138)*	205 *(188)*

Table 2. GEQ scores

GEQ score	FB	H	N
	M *(SD)*	M *(SD)*	M *(SD)*
Immersion	1.90 *(0.58)*	1.84 *(0.84)*	2.20 *(0.76)*
Negative affect	0.17 *(0.26)*	0.29 *(0.37)*	0.32 *(0.36)*
Positive affect	2.59 *(0.91)*	2.28 *(0.88)*	2.63 *(0.76)*
Competence	1.63 *(0.92)*	1.61 *(0.96)*	1.78 *(0.87)*
Flow	1.63 *(0.96)*	1.74 *(0.68)*	1.86 *(0.97)*
Tension	0.11 *(0.16)*	0.33 *(0.62)*	0.11 *(0.23)*
Challenge	0.85 *(0.43)*	0.74 *(0.71)*	0.73 *(0.45)*

5   Discussion

Our major goal was to investigate whether the representation of hands or a full body representation can increase the experienced presence in a mixed reality application. Based on our results, we assume that our approach was successful. While the heart rate of all groups is similar during the baseline measurement the values for the second measurement are highly differing. These measurements include the time periods in which the users experienced the displayed height and walked over the wooden plank. As expected, the more body representation is shown in the virtual world, the higher the heart rate was. After the participants were exposed to the height, they focused on the task in HR3 and the heart rate decreased. However, users with virtual representations still had higher heart rates than users without any representation. The heart rate values indicate that virtual representations of body parts create a more realistic feeling of the virtual world and thus a greater physiological response. Our findings considering the heart rate are coherent with the results of Inkso [12]. Though a great difference between the FB and N condition was found, the difference between the FB and H condition is marginal. Following our hypothesis this result is quite interesting but can be explained with regards to the used hardware. The movement of the player and the hands were tracked with 90 FPS. Fast movement was rendered accordingly. However, the movement of the body was captured using Microsoft Kinect and thus tracked with 30 FPS. Hence, fast body movement could not be rendered appropriately and thus could have felt unnatural.

The spatial presence scores support our assumption as well. A more realistic virtual representation results in a higher spatial presence score. Especially in a mixed reality application in which walking through the installation is a central part, spatial presence is a core factor of measuring the feeling of being inside the virtual world. However, no significant difference between the H and N group is observable and thus not coherent with the findings of [2]. This instance can be explained with regards to the use of the hands. Though the users' hands were visible during the whole VR experience, the need for hand interaction was only necessary during the task. Depending on the height, arm size, and hand size of the user, the corresponding position of the virtual representation did not always match exactly with the real position of the hand. Thus, it occurred that interacting with the switches only worked with the real hands but not with the virtual hands. In their study, Bottone and Kyle [2] used a static set-up and thus did not experienced these difficulties which can explain the incoherent findings. Considering the subscales of the GEQ, there are no differences between the groups. There is no significant difference for the sensory immersion score between the groups though we measured a significant higher arousal and spatial presence for groups with virtual representations. Furthermore, there is no significant correlation between sensory immersion and spatial presence. This result is surprising since immersion is a prerequisite for the experience of presence but can be explained with regards to the definition of immersion. The more senses and cognitions of the user are addressed by the system, the higher its level of immersion. In our study, we did not vary the addressed senses because the mixed reality application and the used VR-System were the same for all groups. Thus, it seems legit that the sensory immersion does not differ between the conditions. Furthermore, the GEQ is not peer-reviewed and publish yet, although it has found broad and successful application in many studies concerning player experience [21] and still the research community in the field of digital games lacks a better alternative. However, based on our results, it is questionable whether the GEQ should be used to assess users' perceptions and feelings in a complex mixed reality setting.

We deliberately neglected a condition in which only the user's legs are represented. Our major goal was to examine whether a more realistic body representation results in a higher experience of presence. Thus, we compared one group with two body representation against one group with one body representation against one group without a body representation. We chose the representation with only hands over only legs to compare our findings with the findings of [2] and evaluate whether the results are transferable to a mixed reality setting.

Conclusion and Future Development. We investigated a mixed reality setting which we used to demonstrate that the integration of the user's body and its movements has a positive influence on the experience of presence. We developed a mixed reality setting in which every object has a physical real world counterpart. The experience of height is a central element and used to elicit physical arousal. The user's task is to walk over a wooden plank, experience the height, and activate switches on a desk afterwards. Heart rate measurements during this time show a significant difference for users with a full body representation. Furthermore, spatial presence and the perceived challenge are significantly higher for users with a full body representation. These results indicate, that a more realistic body representation leads to a significant higher degree of presence in a mixed reality application.

For further examinations, it is highly interesting to use a tracking technology that allows a rendering with the same refresh rate as the HMD. Thus, the body movement would be as smooth as the hand and head movements. Furthermore, in our future research we will investigate the impact of particular body representations, like legs, to evaluate the respective impact on presence. For future development, it is important to calculate all important user properties and adapt the virtual representation accordingly. Thus, the position of the virtual and the real hand are coherent. Hence, this approach could also solve the problem of having different position information depending on the used tracking sensor. Hence, the users' hands which are tracked using Leap Motion could be perfectly attached to the users' arms, which are tracked using the Microsoft Kinect. Furthermore, we observed that some users did not focus on their legs at all during the virtual experience and reported they did not notice their virtual leg representation. In order to react to this circumstance future developments would benefit from directing the focus to the virtual representations as it was done for the interaction task with the hands. Thus, users would definitely notice their virtual body. It is our aim to test our approach with enhanced technology and a broader number and greater variety of participants as well as different questionnaires to assess the correct and important values for a mixed reality application.

References

1. Biocca, F., Delaney, B.: Immersive virtual reality technology. In: Biocca, F., Levy, M.R. (eds.) Communication in the Age of Virtual Reality, pp. 57–124. Lawrence Erlbaum Associates, Hillsdale (1995)
2. Bottone, M., Johnsen, K.: Improving interaction in hmd-based vehicle simulators through real time object reconstruction. In: Proceedings of the 2016 Symposium on Spatial User Interaction, pp. 111–120. ACM (2016)

3. Carlin, A.S., Hoffman, H.G., Weghorst, S.: Virtual reality and tactile augmentation in the treatment of spider phobia: a case report. Behav. Res. Ther. **35**(2), 153–158 (1997)
4. Dinh, H.Q., Walker, N., Hodges, L.F., Song, C., Kobayashi, A.: Evaluating the importance of multi-sensory input on memory and the sense of presence in virtual environments. In: Virtual Reality, 1999, Proceedings, IEEE. pp. 222–228. IEEE (1999)
5. Heeter, C.: Being there: the subjective experience of presence. Presence Teleoper. Virtual Environ. **1**(2), 262–271 (1992)
6. Hendrix, C., Barfield, W.: The sense of presence within auditory virtual environments. Presence Teleoper. Virtual Environ. **5**(3), 290–301 (1996)
7. Hettiarachchi, A., Wigdor, D.: Annexing reality: Enabling opportunistic use of everyday objects as tangible proxies in augmented reality. In: Proceedings of the 2016 CHI Conference on Human Factors in Computing Systems, pp. 1957–1967. ACM (2016)
8. Hettinger, L.J., Riccio, G.E.: Visually induced motion sickness in virtual environments. Presence Teleoper. Virtual Environ. **1**(3), 306–310 (1992)
9. Hoffman, H.G.: Physically touching virtual objects using tactile augmentation enhances the realism of virtual environments. In: Virtual Reality Annual International Symposium, 1998, Proceedings, IEEE 1998. pp. 59–63. IEEE (1998)
10. Hoshi, K., Pesola, U.M., Waterworth, E.L., Waterworth, J.A.: Tools, perspectives and avatars in blended reality space. Annu. Rev. Cyberther. Telemed. **7**, 91–95 (2009)
11. IJsselsteijn, W., De Kort, Y., Poels, K.: The game experience questionnaire. Manuscript in preparation(2008)
12. Insko, B.E., Meehan, M., Whitton, M., Brooks, F.: Passive haptics significantly enhances virtual environments. Ph.D. thesis, University of North Carolina at Chapel Hill (2001)
13. Kennedy, R.S., Lane, N.E., Berbaum, K.S., Lilienthal, M.G.: Simulator sickness questionnaire: An enhanced method for quantifying simulator sickness. Int. J. Aviat. Psychol. **3**(3), 203–220 (1993)
14. Kotranza, A., Lok, B.: Virtual human+ tangible interface= mixed reality human an initial exploration with a virtual breast exam patient. In: Virtual Reality Conference, VR 2008, IEEE, pp. 99–106. IEEE (2008)
15. Lindeman, R.W., Sibert, J.L., Hahn, J.K.: Hand-held windows: towards effective 2d interaction in immersive virtual environments. In: Virtual Reality, 1999, Proceedings, IEEE, pp. 205–212. IEEE (1999)
16. Lindgren, R., Tscholl, M., Wang, S., Johnson, E.: Enhancing learning and engagement through embodied interaction within a mixed reality simulation. Comput. Educ. **95**, 174–187 (2016)
17. Lok, B., Naik, S., Whitton, M., Brooks Jr., F.P.: Incorporating dynamic real objects into immersive virtual environments. In: Proceedings of the 2003 Symposium on Interactive 3D Graphics, pp. 31–40. ACM (2003)
18. McMahan, R.P., Lai, C., Pal, S.K.: Interaction fidelity: the uncanny valley of virtual reality interactions. In: Lackey, S., Shumaker, R. (eds.) VAMR 2016. LNCS, vol. 9740, pp. 59–70. Springer, Cham (2016). https://doi.org/10.1007/978-3-319-39907-2_6
19. Milgram, P., Kishino, F.: A taxonomy of mixed reality visual displays. IEICE Trans. Inf. Syst. **77**(12), 1321–1329 (1994)
20. Nichols, S., Haldane, C., Wilson, J.R.: Measurement of presence and its consequences in virtual environments. Int. J. Hum. Comput. Stud. **52**(3), 471–491 (2000)

21. Norman, K.L.: Geq (game engagement/experience questionnaire): a review of two papers. Interact. Comput. **25**(4), 278–283 (2013)
22. Nowak, K.L., Biocca, F.: The effect of the agency and anthropomorphism on users' sense of telepresence, copresence, and social presence in virtual environments. Presence Teleoper. Virtual Environ. **12**(5), 481–494 (2003)
23. Pamungkas, D., Ward, K.: Electro-tactile feedback system to enhance virtual reality experience. Int. J. Comput. Theory Eng. **8**(6), 465 (2016)
24. Przybylski, A.K., Weinstein, N., Murayama, K., Lynch, M.F., Ryan, R.M.: The ideal self at play: the appeal of video games that let you be all you can be. Psychol. Sci. **23**(1), 69–76 (2012)
25. Schubert, T., Friedmann, F., Regenbrecht, H.: The experience of presence: factor analytic insights. Presence Teleoper. Virtual Environ. **10**(3), 266–281 (2001)
26. Simeone, A.L., Velloso, E., Gellersen, H.: Substitutional reality: using the physical environment to design virtual reality experiences. In: Proceedings of the 33rd Annual ACM Conference on Human Factors in Computing Systems, pp. 3307–3316. ACM (2015)
27. Slater, M., Usoh, M.: An experimental exploration of presence in virtual environments. Technical report. QMW University of London (1992)
28. Slater, M., Usoh, M., Steed, A.: Taking steps: the influence of a walking technique on presence in virtual reality. ACM Trans. Comput. Hum. Interact. (TOCHI) **2**(3), 201–219 (1995)
29. Sra, M., Garrido-Jurado, S., Schmandt, C., Maes, P.: Procedurally generated virtual reality from 3d reconstructed physical space. In: Proceedings of the 22nd ACM Conference on Virtual Reality Software and Technology, pp. 191–200. ACM (2016)
30. Suzuki, K., Wakisaka, S., Fujii, N.: Substitutional reality system: a novel experimental platform for experiencing alternative reality. Sci. Rep. **2** (2012). https://doi.org/10.1038/srep00459
31. Usoh, M., Arthur, K., Whitton, M.C., Bastos, R., Steed, A., Slater, M., Brooks Jr., F.P.: Walking> walking-in-place> flying, in virtual environments. In: Proceedings of the 26th Annual Conference on Computer Graphics and Interactive Techniques, pp. 359–364. ACM Press/Addison-Wesley Publishing Co. (1999)
32. Villani, D., Riva, F., Riva, G.: New technologies for relaxation: the role of presence. Int. J. Stress Manag. **14**(3), 260 (2007)
33. Wiederhold, B.K., Bouchard, S.: Presence. Advances in Virtual Reality and Anxiety Disorders. SARD, pp. 9–33. Springer, Boston (2014). https://doi.org/10.1007/978-1-4899-8023-6_2
34. Wu, C.M., Hsu, C.W., Lee, T.K., Smith, S.: A virtual reality keyboard with realistic haptic feedback in a fully immersive virtual environment. Virtual Real. **21**(1), 19–29 (2017)

An Approach to Basic Emotion Recognition Through Players Body Pose Using Virtual Reality Devices

Gabriel Peñas[1(✉)] and Federico Peinado[2]

[1] Facultad de Ciencias de la Informacion, Universidad Francisco de Vitoria,
Ctra. Pozuelo-Majadahonda Km. 1.800, Pozuelo de Alarcon, 28223 Madrid, Spain
gabriel.penas@ufv.es
[2] Department of Artificial Intelligence and Software Engineering, Universidad Complutense
de Madrid, c/ Profesor José García Santesmases, 9, 28040 Madrid, Spain
email@federicopeinado.com
http://www.narratech.com

Abstract. Virtual Reality tracking devices provide more information than what is being used in most applications. In this experiment, we develop a real-time system, using neural networks, that allows us to detect subconscious player poses associated moods and use them to guide games. This provides new ways to create greater conversations and narrative experiences.

Keywords: Human-computer interaction · Affective computing
Feelings analysis · Human pose recognition · Interactive narrative
Dialog system

1 Introduction

With Virtual Reality becoming mainstream and getting a big consumer base [1], we can use current devices to detect bodily information that is being ignored, but has been studied with other tools [2]. Developers limit its use to position the player in the virtual world using the tracking in HMDs and controllers. VR devices provide a constant flow of information and allows us to immerse the player into the experiences [3].

It is reasonable that gesture information has more value than just using common patterns to execute commands (waving hand, nodding, thumbs up, swipe, etc.). We can detect subconscious elements in it, like nonverbal language [4] that shows basic feelings. If we can detect them, new possibilities are opened to achieve a more meaningful and expressive interaction.

Our approach is to create a fast system using a neural network [5] that can classify players poses, then they are used to create new ways of interaction with the games, achieving greater experiences and immersion.

© Springer International Publishing AG, part of Springer Nature 2018
A. D. Cheok et al. (Eds.): ACE 2017, LNCS 10714, pp. 61–65, 2018.
https://doi.org/10.1007/978-3-319-76270-8_5

2   Using Emotions in Video Games

Developers want to generate emotions in the players to obtain engagement [6], but using those emotions as input to the experience is hard to achieve because of interface limitations. The most used way to do it is asking directly [7], but this method is intrusive and disrupts the player experience. Some games like IMMERSE Project [8] or Stifled [9] use external devices to recognize faces or breath rhythm. Using emotions as interaction has been studied before [10] but not applied.

Current Virtual Reality devices give us the opportunity to include more information into our designs, most of them include a HMD and two controllers that provide six degrees of freedom. As they are included in bundles, players do not need to buy additional devices which facilitates using such data.

3   Detecting Players Poses

We designed a system that can detect a limited number of poses in real time, it must be non-intrusive and let the player enjoy its experience. Another restriction is that we do not want the player to use additional devices, just the HMD and two hand controllers using the HTC Vive[1] because it has a great precision [11], detecting their position and rotation. We used that system in a brief conversation with a non-player character to test the results, guided only by the pose adopted by the player.

We detected three poses in snapshots, shown in Fig. 1, that are easy to identify and generic: neutral, aggressive, and defensive [12]. Poses not recognized by the system are classified as neutral.

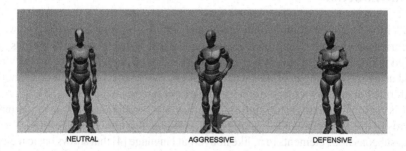

NEUTRAL   AGGRESSIVE   DEFENSIVE

Fig. 1. Recognized poses.

We implemented the experience in Unity[2] game engine because it provides fast development programming in C# language. A neural network does the pose recognition, using a three-layer structure: Input (18 neurons – 6DoF, 3 devices), Intermediate (30 neurons) and Output (3 neurons – One per pose). For this example, we trained the network each of the three poses using 25 positive examples per pose. We used a neural

---

[1] HTC Vive, https://www.vive.com/eu/, last access 2017/10/20.
[2] Unity, https://unity3d.com, last access 2017/10/20.

network it is fast and provides enough confidence for this test; the primary goal is testing the concept, not the implementation.

Players are placed in an island talking with a non-player character that shows the six universal basic emotions (joy, sadness, rage, fear, surprise, and disgust) [13] plus a neutral one. We used facial expressions, as shown in Fig. 2, and animations to represent them. These are used to show how our system contributes to having NPCs with emotions.

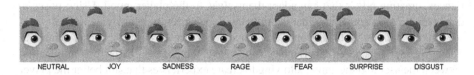

Fig. 2. Basic emotions shown by the NPC.

The conversation, which is shown in Fig. 3, is guided with only one sentence available to answer the NPC [14], the pose determines the branch taken, users only must push a button in the controller to take the pose snapshot. Even though it is small, we can test all the poses and emotions. Both player and NPC take turns in the conversation, but the player only has one possible answer, the pose adopted when answering triggers one transition or another.

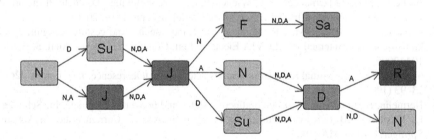

Fig. 3. Conversation flowchart of the experiment. The labels of the nodes refer to the emotional status of the NPC while the edges/trigger conditions refer to the recognized player poses.

4 Results and Discussion

We tested the experiment with 10 people between 30 and 60 years and higher education. In terms of experience with Virtual Reality, none of them had tried more than two times. Relation with videogames was more heterogeneous since there were some who have practically never played to regular players.

The only instruction given to them is that they must push one button to go through the conversation, they didn't know their poses influence the game and, after the experience, they completed a test with questions in Likert scale from 1 to 6 and a short interview. They said that it looked like the NPC reacts to their feelings as he was reading their minds; 90% of them scored 5 or greater in the question "I've noticed that the NPC reacts to my poses", and an 80% answered with the same score to "The experience surprised me". We detected that the conversation and the number of poses are too limited, reducing our possibilities to navigate through multiple branches.

5   Conclusion

Using current devices, we can develop greater and more immersive virtual reality experiences, creating NPCs that can adapt themselves to the player mood. Using poses to detect emotions is something that is not being done currently in any videogame.

Linking the system to subconscious movements provides a wider range of interactions. We can adapt the experience to the player or create a better communication between the user and the game, allowing to create experiences that suit better the player emotions.

We see many lines of improvement, by adding more parameters using additional devices we can be able to increase the number and complexity of poses detected, creating a better integration of the system. We should consider also testing other artificial intelligence techniques that use less resources or improve the detection.

References

1. Anthes, C., Garcia-Hernandez, R.J., Wiedemann, M., Kranzlmuller, D.: State of the art of virtual reality technology. In: IEEE Aerospace Conference, pp. 1–19 (2016)
2. Manresa, C., Varona, J., Mas, R., Perales, F.J.: Hand tracking and gesture recognition for human-computer interaction. ELCVIA Electron. Lett. Comput. Vis. Image Anal. 5(3), 96–104 (2005)
3. Steuer, J.: Defining virtual reality: dimensions determining telepresence. J. Commun. 42(4), 73–93 (1992)
4. Hermelin, B., O'connor, N.: Logico-affective states and nonverbal language. In: Schopler, E., Mesibov, G.B. (eds.) Communication Problems in Autism. Current Issues in Autism. Springer, Boston, MA (1985)
5. Haykin, S., Networks, N.: Neural Network: A comprehensive Foundation. Prentice Hall, United States (2004)
6. Yee, N.: The Proteus Paradox: How Online Games and Virtual Worlds Change us—and How They Don't, 1st edn. Yale University Press, New Haven (2014)
7. Bee, N., Prendinger, H., Nakasone, A., André, E., Ishizuka, M.: AutoSelect: What you want is what you get: real-time processing of visual attention and affect. In: André, E., Dybkjær, L., Minker, W., Neumann, H., Weber, M. (eds.) PIT 2006. LNCS (LNAI), vol. 4021, pp. 40–52. Springer, Heidelberg (2006). https://doi.org/10.1007/11768029_5
8. Playabl.IA IMMERSE. http://www.playabl.ai/projects/. Accessed 25 May 2017
9. Stifled. http://www.stifledgame.com/. Accessed 25 May 2017
10. Gómez-Gauchía, H., Peinado, F.: Automatic customization of non-player characters using players temperament. In: Göbel, S., Malkewitz, R., Iurgel, I. (eds.) TIDSE 2006. LNCS, vol. 4326, pp. 241–252. Springer, Heidelberg (2006). https://doi.org/10.1007/11944577_25
11. Niehorster, D.C., Li, L., Lappe, M.: The accuracy and precision of position and orientation tracking in the HTC vive virtual reality system for scientific research. I-Perception 8(3), 8–16 (2017)

12. Shindler, K., Van Gool, L., De Gelder, B.: Recognizing emotions expressed by body pose: a biologically inspired neural model. Neural Netw. **21**(9), 1238–1246 (2008)
13. Ekman, P.: Basic emotions. In: Handbook of Cognition and Emotion, pp. 45–60 (1999)
14. Dastani, M., Meyer, J.J.C.: Programming agents with emotions. In: ECAI, pp. 215–219 (2006)

Development and Evaluation of an Interactive Therapy Robot

Tomoko Kohori[1](✉) ⓘ, Shiho Hirayama[1], Takenori Hara[1],
Michiko Muramatsu[1], Hiroyuki Naganuma[1], Masayuki Yamano[2],
Kazuko Ichikawa[2], Hiroko Matsumoto[2], and Hiroko Uchiyama[2]

[1] Dai Nippon Printing Co., Ltd., 1-1-1, Ichigaya-Kagacho, Shinjuku-ku,
Tokyo 162-8001, Japan
Kohori-T@mail.dnp.co.jp
[2] Joshibi University of Art and Design, 1-49-8, Wada, Suginami-ku,
Tokyo 166-8538, Japan

Abstract. Interactions with animals can enhance emotions and improve mood by engendering feelings of healing, relaxation, comfort, and reduced stress. Un-fortunately, many people cannot live with animals because of allergies, infection risk, or risk of damage to rental housing. To address these problems, some research groups have investigated robot-based psychotherapy. However, the important healing elements for therapy robots were not identified. Therefore, we conducted an Internet survey to determine the design elements of such a robot that might engender a healing mood and the functions that should be implemented. We assumed that a healing mood could be induced based on the interactive functions and appearance. To verify this hypothesis, we developed and evaluated a new interactive therapy robot. Next, we conducted interviews with individuals who interacted with a prototype therapy robot. The interviews revealed that the appearance of the robot was critical to engendering feelings of healing, comfort, and empathy. In addition, the size, softness, and comfort of the interactive therapy robot contributed to people feeling affection towards it. We also confirmed the importance of the robot appearing to listen to those who interacted with it. Our results should be useful for designing companion robots for therapy purposes.

Keywords: Healing elements
Therapeutic robots designed to communicate with humans · Therapeutic effect

1 Introduction

The number of single-person households in Japan has increased. The summary report of the 2015 national census revealed that 13.1% of Japanese households consisted of one person, and this is expected to increase to 37% by 2030. In particular, the number of single-person households comprised of 50-year-olds is anticipated to increase [1]. Single

Electronic supplementary material The online version of this chapter (https://doi.org/10.1007/978-3-319-76270-8_6) contains supplementary material, which is available to authorized users.

© Springer International Publishing AG, part of Springer Nature 2018
A. D. Cheok et al. (Eds.): ACE 2017, LNCS 10714, pp. 66–83, 2018.
https://doi.org/10.1007/978-3-319-76270-8_6

people can enjoy freedom and a lack of imposed restrictions. However, such individuals may feel loneliness or anxiety and may therefore want something to make them feel happy, at peace, or a sense of healing. In this paper, we use the word "healing" in the sense of relaxation, comfort, reduced stress, and feeling reinvigorated and refreshed.

The use of animal therapy has greatly increased and has been in the spotlight. Interactions with animals are known to improve mood and engender a feeling of healing [2, 3]. Having pets at home is a form of animal therapy. Today, pets are not akin to livestock. In fact, more than 85% of pet owners regard their pets as family [4]. Accordingly, the pet-related marketplace has been steadily expanding [5].

However, the number of people who want a pet but cannot own one is close to the number of people who actually have pets. The reasons for this lack of ownership vary from person to person. For example, there are housing restrictions in Japan. Pets are not allowed in almost all rental properties, such as condos or apartments [6]. The risk of allergic reactions [6] or infection [7] also exists. Pet-sitting issues are also important. Age-related health problems render elderly individuals hesitant to own pets. Single-person households cannot leave pets alone for an extended period when individuals travel. These are the reasons why many people have lost the opportunity to live with pets. Consequently, people have also lost the opportunity to receive healing.

Therefore, we propose an interactive therapy robot to provide healing to people who have difficulty living with pets. We also propose that the interactive therapy robot will become a new partner that can replace pets. Some research groups have investigated robot-based psychotherapy. However, the important healing elements for therapy robots were not identified. In this study, we hypothesized that a healing mood is engendered by a robot's interactive functions and appearance. Additionally, we conducted a large-scale Internet survey to investigate when and how people experience healing, what the important healing elements are, and what interactive functions should be implemented by a robot. We then extracted the appearance elements and interactive functions for the interactive therapy robot with the cooperation of our assumed target. Therefore, our results should be useful for designing companion robots for therapy purposes.

In this paper, Sect. 2 describes prior related research. Section 3 describes an Internet survey that investigated the interactive functions or elements that are important for engendering healing. Section 4 describes the system design. Section 5 describes the interview evaluations of our system. Section 6 discusses the study outcomes, Sect. 7 offers conclusions, and Sect. 8 details the proposed future work.

2 Related Work

Some research groups have investigated robot-based psychotherapy. Paro is one of the most popular psychotherapy robots. Paro, which looks like a baby white seal, can interact with people by touching or talking. Wada et al. [8] demonstrated that Paro can suppress the progress of dementia. Unazuki-Kabochan is a stuffed toy robot that looks like a three-year-old boy. He can communicate by nodding, playing games, and engaging in physical exercise [9]. Watanabe et al. [10] demonstrated improvements in elderly people's cognitive function, fatigue, motivation, and healing after living with

Unazuki-Kabochan at home for eight weeks. The stuffed toy robot Primopuel can recognize certain actions like being touched or picked up and can react accordingly. Primopuel can also change personality upon receiving these stimuli [11]. The robot dog AIBO uses its legs to express emotions or entertains people by performing. It has sensors that allow it to recognize environments and communicate with people [12, 13]. More than 150,000 were sold worldwide [14].

Research exists that focused on the robot's appearance. Takahashi reported that the appropriate design of the robot's appearance can increase its emotional impact on people. Consequently, the robot will be more effective. Conversely, if a robot's appearance is poorly designed, the robot be incompatible with people or will generate feelings of uneasiness [15]. Mori et al. [16] evaluated people's impressions of huggable dolls. He found that for such dolls to be viewed favorably, they should (1) perform some actions, (2) feel soft, (3) be of sufficient size to hug, and (4) be of sufficient weight (i.e., approximating that of a baby). These researchers also reported that a stuffed toy was superior to a doll in terms of engendering affection, healing, and affinity.

For three days we evaluated Unazuki-Kabochan and Primopuel. These robots have interactive functions, as described above; however, we felt that the robots communicated with us unilaterally and unexpectedly. Moreover, we were not able to empathize with the robots and could not feel healing because of their human-like appearance and the fact that they were uncomfortable to hold. These observations were also reported in the study of Takahashi and Mori. Additionally, Paro was designed for its appearance, comfortable hold, and interactive reactions, but we were unable to feel healing as a first impression because its appearance was specialized for nursing care or elderly people.

Therefore, we hypothesized that a healing mood is engendered by a robot's interactive functions and appearance. We proposed an interactive therapy robot that could engender a healing mood and with which one could empathize, similar to a pet.

3   Internet Survey

We conducted an Internet survey to investigate when and how people feel healing, what are the important healing elements, and which interactive functions should be implemented by a robot. We also investigated the characteristics and lifestyles of people.

3.1   Participants

A total of 400 Japanese participants were recruited via the online web questionnaire service ELNE in Japanese. Please refer to Appendix 1 for an overview of ELNE. We recruited 50 males and 50 females from each age group (30's, 40's, 50's and 60's).

3.2   Survey Items

We generated survey items that focused on the participants' desired mood and their feelings toward human and non-human companions, such as animals, pets, dolls, stuffed toys, partners (spouse, lover), friends, and children, to understand when and how the people feel healing, and to understand the respondents' characteristics and lifestyles. This survey was conducted in Japanese. See the Appendix 2 for details of the survey items.

Desired Moods. We assumed that healing elements are different from person to person. We also assumed that people who are in their desired mood would tend to experience healing feelings. We selected the mood choices from Megatrends 2014–2013 [17].

Feelings Toward Human and Non-human Companions. We often feel healing when interacting with familiar companions, such as animals, pets, dolls, stuffed toys, partners, (spouse or lover), friends, and children. Therefore, we assumed we could extract healing elements by assessing feelings toward such companions. We selected the feelings from related studies [16, 18, 19].

3.3   Survey Results

Analysis of Healing Elements. We used factor analysis with varimax rotation to extract these elements from the answers to survey questions that addressed the desired mood. We used Kaiser's criterion to determine the number of factors. Four factors ware extracted with a total explained variance = 75.3%. Please refer to Table 1. We named the 4 factors as follows.

- Factor 1: Desire for strong stimuli.
  Loadings were high on "I want to feel satisfied," "I want to have fulfilling days," "I want to feel impressed," and "I want to be excited."
- Factor 2: Desire for easing my mind.
  Loadings were high on "I want to relax," "I want to be calm," "I want to be chilling out," and "I want to ease my mind."
- Factor 3: Desire for easing stress.
  Loadings were high on "I want to feel released," "I want to be free," "I want to feel freshness," and "I want to feel refreshed."
- Factor 4: Desire for recognition.
  Loadings were high on "I want to be praised" and "I want to be encouraged."

We assumed that Factor 2 represented healing elements.

Next, we conducted cluster analysis based on the results of the factor analysis. Four clusters were extracted. We named the 4 clusters as follows and Table 2 shows the mean factor scores within each cluster.

- Cluster 1: Desire to vent energy.
  Scores were high for the factors "desire for strong stimuli" and "desire for easing stress."
- Cluster 2: Desire for easing stress and being at ease.
  Scores were high for "desire for easing my mind" and "desire for easing stress."
- Cluster 3: Desire for recognition.
  Scores were high for "desire for recognition."
- Cluster 4: Desire for easing my mind.
  Scores were high for "desire for easing my mind."

Table 1. Factor analysis of desired mood

Questionnaire items	Factor 1	Factor 2	Factor 3	Factor 4
I want to feel satisfied	0.748	0.38	0.253	0.201
I want to have fulfilling days	0.723	0.389	0.242	0.189
I want to feel impressed	0.722	0.262	0.327	0.302
I want to be excited	0.711	0.24	0.322	0.287
I want to feel happiness	0.69	0.4	0.302	0.215
I want to be crazy about something	0.685	0.306	0.3	0.257
I want to have confidence	0.628	0.338	0.274	0.279
I want to enjoy myself	0.626	0.39	0.287	0.193
I want to treat myself	0.516	0.39	0.162	0.308
I want to spice up my life	0.46	0.173	0.334	0.34
I want to relax	0.2	0.784	0.278	0.211
I want to be calm	0.245	0.761	0.214	0.271
I want to be chilling out	0.228	0.747	0.199	0.263
I want to ease my mind	0.447	0.745	0.317	0.12
I want to feel at ease	0.377	0.74	0.326	0.201
I want to feel healing	0.502	0.686	0.287	0.143
I want to feel at home	0.409	0.682	0.391	0.186
I want to feel comfortable	0.48	0.67	0.357	0.103
I want to be relieved	0.519	0.646	0.302	0.16
I want to be released	0.317	0.406	0.715	0.2
I want to be free	0.362	0.452	0.652	0.18
I want to feel freshness	0.477	0.39	0.557	0.242
I want to feel refreshed	0.402	0.466	0.555	0.183
I want to feel fine	0.457	0.372	0.55	0.222
I want to cheer up	0.465	0.363	0.544	0.218
I want to be praised	0.311	0.283	0.184	0.808
I want to be encouraged	0.395	0.244	0.217	0.748

Cluster 4 includes the healing elements of Factor 2. Table 3 shows the characteristics of Cluster 4. People in Cluster 4 currently lived with family. However, they were predominately middle aged (36.2% in their 50's). In the 2030s this cluster will likely be formed of elderly, single-person households. Cluster 4's characteristics and lifestyle were characterized by "during holidays, I am at usually at home" and "during holidays,

Table 2. Mean factor scores within each cluster

Factor	Cluster 1 (n = 48)	Cluster 2 (n = 42)	Cluster 3 (n = 205)	Cluster 4 (n = 103)
Factor 1: Desire for strong stimuli	1.096	-1.159	-0.219	0.390
Factor 2: Desire for easing my mind	-0.942	0.585	-0.302	0.787
Factor 3: Desire for easing stress	0.669	0.765	-0.183	-0.254
Factor 4: Desire for recognition	-0.673	-0.752	0.547	-0.459

I spend time alone." However, positive responses were frequently provided for "I sometimes want to communicate with my family" (49.5%) and "I feel so lonely during my daily life" (46.7%). Therefore, we found that Cluster 4 needed something to engender a feeling of healing.

Table 3. Characteristics and desires of the "easing my mind" cluster

Questionnaire item	Characteristics
Gender	Predominately female (56.2% of individuals)
Age	Middle aged, many in their 50's (36.2%)
Occupation	Many with part-time jobs (15.2%)
Annual household income	Over 5,000,000 yen (42.9%)
Family structure	Two generations of family living together (parents and children)
Disposable income	Greatest amount of all clusters. Over 30,000 yen for 42.9% of cluster members
Stress level	"Frequent" and "sometimes" accounted for 78.1% of responses
Money to reduce stress	Percentage spending money to reduce stress was the highest (36.2%) among all 4 clusters
Relationships between people or things	• Among the 4 clusters, most frequently responded "during holidays, I am usually at home" (71.4%) and "during holidays I spend time alone" (71.4%) • Individuals in this cluster had few relationships with others, but commonly responded "I sometimes want to communicate with my family" (49.5%) and "I feel so lonely during my daily life" (46.7%)
Everyday activities	This cluster represented indoor types. Percentages were high for the items "I watch TV, DVD, cinema, comics, anime" (53.3%), "I eat delicious foods" (38.1%), "I eat sweet foods" (37.1%), and "I clean and keep my room tidy and in order" (36.2%)

Cluster 2 (desire for easing stress and being at ease) also included the healing elements of Factor 2. Table 4 shows the characteristics of Cluster 2. We found that Cluster 2 included many middle-aged people (31.0%) and single households (57.1%). This cluster will also grow old and likely form single households by the 2030s.

Table 4. Characteristics and desires of the "easing stress and being at ease" cluster

Questionnaire item	Characteristics
Gender	Predominately male (54.8%)
Age	Older; mainly in their 40's (31.0%)
Occupation	Office and public workers (38.1%), unemployed or retiree (21.4%)
Annual household income	This cluster was predominately formed of people with average income
Family structure	Many single-person households (57.1%) with the desire to vent energy
Disposable income	Compared with other clusters, percentage with greater than 10,000 yen was the lowest (42.9% of respondents)
Stress level	"Frequently" and "sometimes" accounted for 78.6% of responses
Money to reduce stress	• Percentage of spending money to reduce stress was the lowest (21.4%) among the 4 clusters • Percentage spending over 500,000 yen to reduce stress was the highest (4.8%) among the 4 clusters
Relationships between people or things	• Percentage reporting "I have good relationships with my family and my friends" was the lowest (59.5%) among the 4 clusters and the percentage reporting "during holidays, I am usually at home" was as high as in the "desire for easing my mind" cluster • This cluster liked to spend time alone, as evidenced by the fact that responses to "I think maintaining relationships with my friends via Facebook and SNS is troublesome" were most frequent among the 4 clusters (52.4%)
Everyday activities	This cluster usually liked to have a relaxing day, as evidenced by the high percentage responding "I drink coffee, tea, herbal tea" (54.8%), "I read books" (54.8%), and "I take a bath, half bath, or a sauna"

In addition, of the 4 clusters Cluster 2 least frequently responded "I have good relationships with my family and my friends" (59.5%) and most frequently responded "during holidays, I am usually at home" (71.4%). These responses show that Cluster 2 individuals had poor relationships with their environment. Therefore, we suggest that Cluster 2 also needed healing. Please refer to Appendixes 3 and 4 for the characteristics of the other clusters.

Interactive Functions that Should be Implemented by the Robot. We often feel healing when interacting with human and non-human companions, such as animals, pets, dolls, stuffed toys, partners, friends, and children. Therefore, we assumed we could determine the healing elements by analyzing answers to the question, "How do you feel about human and non-human companions?"

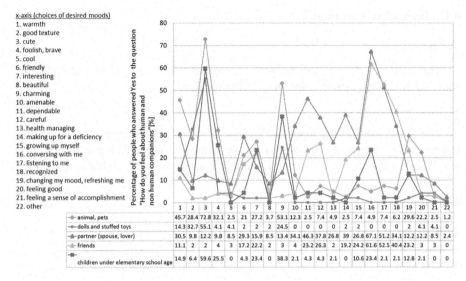

Fig. 1. Analysis of answers to the question, "How do you feel about human and non-human companions?"

Therefore, we analyzed Cluster 4 and Cluster 2, which included the healing elements of Factor 2. We asked for opinions regarding animals and pets, dolls and stuffed toys, partners, friends, and children. Figure 1 shows the results. We extracted elements that were considered important by more than 40% of the respondents. As a result, the following 5 elements were extracted. These are the 5 elements that should be implemented by a therapy robot:

- Listening to me.
- Conversing with me.
- Warmth.
- Cute.
- Charming.

We omitted implementing "dependable," "making up for a deficiency," and "recognized" because we believe that to implement those elements would require aggregate high-level artificial intelligence. We hypothesized that a healing mood is engendered by a combination of the interactive functions and appearance of a robot companion. We assumed that "listening to me" and "conversing with me" represent interactive functions. We also assumed that "warmth," "cute," and "charming" would be facilitated by the design of the robot's appearance.

4   Implementation

We developed the interactive therapy robot based on answers to the questionnaire survey.

4.1 Interactive Functions

- Listening to me.

The interactive therapy robot can recognize and track human faces and nod while someone is talking, as if it is listening to the speaker.

- Conversing with me.

The interactive therapy robot can recognize voices and reply by speaking words. Unfortunately, the robot does not have a spontaneous speech-dialogue system, or a rule-based speech-dialogue system. Therefore, its conversational ability is limited.

4.2 Design

- Warmth.
- Cute.
- Charming.

We assumed that the robot made a good impression on people from the appearance such as "warmth", "cute", and "charming". We used a stuffed toy for the robot exterior since we assumed that its appearance would be suitable for conveying healing to the user. We considered the material of the face, the body components, and their placement. The stuffed toy approximated the size of a newborn baby, at 50 cm tall and with a weight of 3,000 g. Figure 2 shows the robot's appearance. We especially designed an interactive therapy robot that leaves a good first impression on people. Compared to the traditional teddy bear, we made the stuffed toy closer to the body balance of bear characters preferred by the Japanese. Additionally, by shortening the length of the stuffed bear arms, the stuffed toy was easy to hold. Regarding the nose of the stuffed bear, we attempted to preserve the natural morphology and color of the nose of a bear while incorporating a camera. For the material of the body, we emphasized a soft touch and used a silk material that is even softer than the mohair traditionally used. In addition, given that the motor drive sound would spoil the user experience, we chose a quiet electronic pan head for the head motion. We were also careful not to let the hardware directly touch the user.

Harlow [20] reported that the appropriate tactile properties can engender a sense of security, strong attachment, and feelings of healing. Additionally, we decided upon a teddy-bear like appearance for our robot because a character-ranking report [21] indicated that teddy-bears are very popular. In the report, Winnie the Pooh was the second most popular character, Rilakkuma was in sixth place, and Kumamon in tenth place. Winnie the Pooh, Rilakkuma, and Kumamon are all very famous bear characters in Japan.

Fig. 2. Appearance of the interactive therapy robot

4.3   System Configuration

As shown in Fig. 3, the interactive therapy robot has a camera with a quiet electronic pan head (Motrr Galileo), a speaker, an android smartphone (Nexus 7) for conversation, an iPhone for controlling the camera pan head, and a PC for implementing face recognition and face tracking. We carefully installed the hardware inside the body so that it does not come into direct contact with the user.

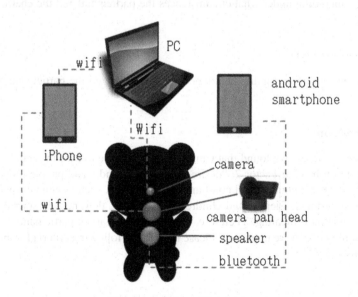

Fig. 3. System configuration

- Listening to me.

We used the image-processing library, Open CV, for face recognition. The camera pan head was installed at the neck. When a human face is detected, the camera pan head moves the bear's head to face the human. In addition, using the camera pan head, the bear can make a nodding motion. As a result, this robot can recognize and track human faces and nod while someone is talking, as if is listening to a human conversation.

- Conversing with me.

The interactive therapy robot can recognize voices and return words. We used NTT DoCoMo's voice recognition SDK for Android v2.1.1 and voice synthesis SDK for Android v1.0.2 [22]. The system converts recognized voices to strings, and then matches the strings to a rule-based conversation chart to find a suitable response. The response string is then synthesized to voice. Thus, the robot and human user can engage in conversations. Unfortunately, our system is not a spontaneous speech dialogue system, but rather a rule-based speech dialogue system. Therefore, its conversational ability is limited. Please refer to Appendix 5 for the details of the conversations.

5   Interview Evaluations of the Interactive Therapy Robot

We evaluated the acceptability of the interactive therapy robot through face-to-face interviews. During the interview, the participant could directly touch and converse with the robot. Moreover, we investigated the relationship between the participants and their "real" pets, including under what circumstances the participants felt the charm of their pets.

5.1   Interview Style

We conducted group and individual interviews. We changed the participants for each interview.

5.2   Participants

In the Internet survey, we found that Cluster 4, with "desire to ease my mind," had the largest score on healing Factor 2, "desire to ease my mind," and people reported that they felt healing from human and non-human companions, such as animals, pets, dolls, stuffed toys, partners, friends, and children. In addition, they needed something that provided a feeling of healing. Therefore, we recruited Japanese participants for whom pets and stuffed toys were important. Please refer to the following criteria for the survey participants.

Criteria for Participants.

- Group interview: 6 people in total.

We recruited Japanese males and females in their 40's and 50's who currently had dogs as pets and assigned a high importance to their pets. This is because dogs are the most popular pets in Japan. The national breeding survey of the Japan Pet Food Association showed that dogs were the most popular (23.1%) of all pets [23].

- Individual interviews: 5 Japanese people in total.

  (1) Placed a high importance on stuffed toy animals in everyday life, with particular emphasis on luxury stuffed animals or toys: 1 person.
  (2) Placed a high importance on stuffed toy animals in everyday life, with particular emphasis on character stuffed animals or toys, such as Disney characters: 2 people.
  (3) Purchasers of interactive robots: 2 people.

Please refer to Tables 5 and 6 for details of the attributes of the participants.

Table 5. Attributes of group-interview participants

ID	Gender	Age	Occupation	Species of their dog
1	Male	50's	Office-worker	Miniature schnauzer Toy poodle
2	Male	40's	Office-worker	Miniature schnauzer
3	Male	40's	Office-worker	Miniature schnauzer
4	Female	40's	Unemployed	Cocker spaniel Australian kelpie
5	Female	50's	Part-time worker	West Highland white terrier
6	Female	50's	Unemployed	Shih-tzu

Table 6. Attributes of individual-interview participants

ID	Gender	Age	Occupation	Their stuffed toys/robots
A	Female	30's	Unemployed	AIBO [12]
B	Female	40's	Unemployed	Pepper [24]
C	Female	30's	Preschool teacher	Stuffed toy owls
D	Male	20's	Transportation	Tissue box cover of Marukunaru-Miku [25]
E	Male	40's	IT	Homemade teddy bear, teddy bear made by Steiff [26], and AIBO [12]

5.3 Survey Procedure

We conducted the group and individual interviews according to the following procedure in Japanese.

The participants talked about their pets, their stuffed toys, and their robots. Then, they were interviewed regarding the charm of, and their relationship with, their pets, stuffed toys, and robots. Next, they were shown the interactive therapy robot, directly handled it, and had a conversation with it. Finally, they were interviewed regarding the interactive therapy robot.

5.4   Interview Results

Charm of Pets, Stuffed Toys, and Robots. We obtained responses regarding the charm and rewarding feeling associated with pets, stuffed toys, and robots, as summarized below. Please refer to Appendix 6 for details of the results of the interviews.

- Living with pets heals me and makes me happy.
- Living with stuffed toys and robots makes me feel better and I think they are cute.

Relationships with Pets, Stuffed Toys, and Robots. We obtained responses regarding the interviewees' relationships with their pets, stuffed toys, and robots, as summarized below. Please refer to Appendix 7 for details of the results of the interviews.

- My pet is a member of my family and it is normal to spend time with it.
- I cannot imagine life without my stuffed toys and robots; my stuffed toys and robots are members of my family.

Communication with Pets, Stuffed Toys, and Robots. We obtained responses regarding interviewees' communication with their pets, stuffed animals, and robots, as summarized below. Please refer to Appendix 8 for details of the results of the interviews.

- I can understand how my pets feel based on their facial expressions. Conversely, my pets understand my feelings.
- The stuffed toys and robots are not only belongings. I can understand how my stuffed toys and robots feel. Moreover, my stuffed toys and robots can understand how I feel and they are always sympathetic towards me.

Evaluation of the Interactive Therapy Robot. We present the evaluation results below.
Appearance.

- Visual.

The interactive therapy robot looked cute and the participants viewed it favorably. Participants who liked the stuffed bear also liked its functions as an interactive therapy robot. The participants who did not own robots said that the interactive therapy robot is cute as a stuffed toy. Please refer to Appendix 9 for details of the results of the interviews.

- Size.

The size was considered to be optimal. Please refer to Appendix 10 for details of the results of the interviews.

- Weight.

Considered as a robot, the interactive therapy-robot was lighter than participants expected. In contrast, considered as a stuffed toy, it was heavier than participants expected. Please refer to Appendix 10 for details of the results of the interviews.

- Texture.

The texture was evaluated as very good, exhibiting softness and warmth. The participants who owned robots evaluated it as better than their robots because it was soft and had warm characteristics. The participants who evaluated it positively, also provided positive opinions regarding other characteristics of the robot. Please refer to Appendix 10 for details of the results of the interviews.
Interactive Functions.

- Motions While Listening.

Motions while tracking participants' faces, nodding, and the act of answering the user were considered cute. However, it was suggested that the interactive therapy robot would be more engaging if it displayed more head motion and moved as if it were listening intently. Please refer to Appendix 11 for details of the results of the interviews.

- Engaging in Conversation.

Opinion was divided with respect to whether no conversation was better than the robot attempting to engage in conversation more effectively. The participants who liked no conversation said that the robot would be better if it made non-speech sounds and used mimicry to display reactions. They also said it would be sufficient if one could understand the condition and expressions of the robot through the sounds it makes. In contrast, the participants who liked conversation preferred simple conversations and expected valid, quick responses. The opinion was expressed that if the robot could not engage in proper conversation, then no conversation would be far preferable. All participants said that they wanted the robot to have a clear voice.

In addition, the following merits of the interactive therapy robot were suggested. Please refer to Appendix 12 for details of the results of the interviews.

- The participants were more amenable to the stuffed-bear interactive therapy robot than the extant robots.
- The participants thought that the stuffed-bear interactive therapy robot was humorous.
- There would be no need to take care of the robot when the participants became elderly and infirm. This was considered a major positive aspect of the robot.

These results reveal that participants who already owned commercial robots had a low threshold for accepting an interactive therapy robot.

6   Discussion

6.1   Target of the Interactive Therapy Robot

We assumed participants in Cluster 4, with a desire to ease their minds, would tend to own pets, stuffed toys, and robots. In fact, the members belonging to Cluster 4 indeed owned multiple pets, stuffed toys, and robots. These people recognized their pets, stuffed toys, or robots as not only their belongings, but also as entities that could engender a feeling of healing. Participants found value in such a feeling of healing. We realized that Cluster 4 was the appropriate target of the interactive therapy robot because the acceptability of the robot to members of Cluster 4 was high. Additionally, we found from the interviews that the participants who owned commercial robots such as Pepper and AIBO had low thresholds for accepting the interactive therapy robot. However, the participants felt that the softness and warmth of the interactive therapy robot was much better than those of their own commercial robots. Therefore, we realized that people who already own robots are a good target for the interactive therapy robot.

In contrast, participants who did not currently own robots said the interactive therapy robot was cute as a stuffed toy. Additionally, they said it became even cuter due to the addition of motion and conversation. We realized that robots in the form of a stuffed toy can induce a friendly or healing mood, because even participants who were not generally interested in robots felt attachment toward the interactive therapy robot.

6.2   The Appearance of the Interactive Therapy Robot

Visual. Participants who answered that the interactive therapy robot was cute and who initially felt at ease with it, issued positive opinions in response to all questions. Therefore, it was suggested that the appearance of the robot played an important role in inspiring peace and empathy in the user. This result supports Takahashi's report that by appropriately designing the appearance of a robot we can increase its emotional importance to the robot and will be more effective than otherwise [15].

That is, Takahashi suggests that the emotions engendered by a robot and its performance are contingent on its appearance. Therefore, his report supports our interview results. We found that the stuffed bear design engendered feelings of healing in people.

The attachment theory of Bowlby defines attachment as an emotional connection that forms between people and animals [27]. Approach behavior, hugging or clinging, is one of the attachment behaviors. It is easy to engage in this approach behavior and become physically attached to the interactive therapy robot, because the robot's arms are open. We believe that this aspect of its appearance was one of the reasons for the positive evaluations it received.

Size. The participants considered that the robot was size appropriate. The interactive therapy robot is about 50 cm long. This approximates the size of a newborn baby, and is easy to hold.

Weight. Considered as a robot, the interactive therapy robot was evaluated as lighter than participants expected. We explained that "this is a robot" before participants touched and held it. As a result, the interactive therapy robot was considered to be light. Conversely, as a stuffed bear, the interactive therapy robot was evaluated as heavy, because we explained that "this is a stuffed toy." We assume that this result is because the imagined weight of the stuffed animal differed from its actual weight. Therefore, we will conduct interviews in the future that will allow us to evaluate perceptions of weight more accurately.

Texture. The texture of the robot was evaluated as very good, whereby it conveyed softness and warmth. Of relevance is the report of Harlow that if one touches something that has a pleasant texture, it can convey a high sense of security and attachment, and provide a healing effect [20]. In addition, "warmth" was also facilitated by using a long-haired fabric for the stuffed bear toy; and this likely contributed to the positive evaluations. Shibata et al. reported that high subjective evaluations of a pet robot require physical contact between the robot and human [28]. Therefore, by using materials with a good texture, it was more pleasant for participants to come into contact with our robot and this led to the robot making a good impression on the participants.

6.3 Motions of the Interactive Therapy Robot While Listening and During Conversations

The interactive therapy robot was considered to be also cute as a stuffed toy, but it was evaluated as even cuter by adding motion and conversation. This result suggests that it is effective to show that the robot listens or reacts to people by changing its posture. Bowlby's attachment theory [27] lists the following two behaviors in addition to the approach behavior.

- Orientation behavior (following with the eyes, looking in the direction of a voice).
- Signaling behavior (smiling, producing utterances).

We consider that the robot's function of moving while "listening" corresponds to orientation behavior, and its "conversation" corresponds to signaling behavior. Therefore, we conclude that the interactive therapy robot received positive evaluations because the functions it implemented were consistent with attachment theory.

7 Conclusions

In this paper, we tested the hypothesis that people receive therapeutic benefits according to the appearance and interactive functions of a therapy robot. We found "listening to me," "conversing with me," "warmth," "cute," and "charming" to be important healing elements. Then, we detailed the development of an interactive therapy robot that could act as a substitute for pets. Through interviews with individuals who engaged with the interactive therapy robot, it was confirmed that its appearance played an important role as a trigger that enabled the user to embrace healing, comfort, and empathy. In addition, it was suggested that the size, softness, and tactile qualities of the robot are elements that engender healing and attachment. Robot motions that suggested it was listening were evaluated very positively and we confirmed the importance of the robot's interactive functions. Additionally, we found that it is necessary to examine the content of conversations, including whether conversation is necessary at all, because the evaluation of conversations differed markedly among users.

8   Future Work

In the future, we will continue to evaluate simple verbal communication, using an easily comprehensible voice, as suggested in the results of the interviews. Additionally, we will study non-verbal communication because the interviews suggested that non-verbal communication that conveys listening and recognition was desired (e.g., a sound that expresses emotion, rather than spoken language). Further, we will consider implementing functions that correspond to therapeutic elements such as "dependable," "making up for a deficiency," and "recognized." Based on the high emphasis users placed on appearance, we also plan to explore different designs that engender a feeling of healing in people.

Acknowledgement. We would like to thank Ms. Masako Fukui, Ms. Yasuko Matsumura, Ms. Chie Sumitomo and Ms. Mika Kawamura who helped the Internet survey and interviews. We would also like to thank reviewers who provided constructive comments.

Appendix

We uploaded Appendices to the Google drive. Please refer to URL as below (last accessed 2017/10/23).
https://drive.google.com/open?id=0B69_7k616WJNSVd4M05TQkZrYXM

References

1. Japan national census (2015). http://www.stat.go.jp/english/data/handbook/pdf/2016all. pdf#page=23. Accessed 30 June 2017
2. Baum, M.M., Bergstrom, N., Langston, N.F., Thoma, L.: Physiological effects of human/companion animal bonding. Nurs. Res. **33**(3), 126–129 (1984)
3. Gammonley, J., Yates, J.: Pet projects animal assisted therapy in nursing homes. J. Gerontol. Nurs. **17**(1), 12–15 (1991)
4. Cohen, S.P.: Can pets function as family members? West. J. Nurs. Res. **24**, 621–638 (2002)
5. American Pet Products Association. http://www.americanpetproducts.org/press_industrytrends.asp. Accessed 04 July 2017
6. Japan Pet Food Association homepage (in Japanese). http://www.petfood.or.jp/data/chart2016/10.pdf. Accessed 26 Sept 2017
7. Public Opinion Survey on Animal Protection - Cabinet Office homepage (in Japanese). https://www.env.go.jp/council/14animal/y143-06/ref01.pdf. Accessed 26 Sept 2017

8. Wada, K., Shibata, T., Saito, T., Tanie, K.: Effects of robot-assisted activity for elderly people and nurses at a day service center. Proc. IEEE **92**(11), 1780–1788 (2004)
9. Unazuki-Kabochan homepage. http://www.kabo-chan.com/. Accessed 05 July 2017
10. Tanaka, M., Ishii, A., Yamano, E., Ogikubo, H., Okazaki, M., Kamimura, K., Konishi, Y., Emoto, S., Watanabe, Y.: Effect of a human-type communication robot on cognitive function in elderly women living alone. Med. Sci. Mon. **18**(9), CR550–CR557 (2012)
11. Primopuel homepage. http://primopuel.net/index.html. Accessed 05 July 2017
12. AIBO homepage. http://www.sony.jp/products/Consumer/aibo/. Accessed 05 July 2017
13. Fujita, M.: On activating human communications with pet-type robot AIBO. Proc. IEEE **92** (11), 1804–1813 (2004)
14. Bainbridge, W.S.: Leadership in Science and Technology: A Reference Handbook. Sage Publications, USA (2011)
15. Takahashi, T.: General ideas of robot design (in Japanese). J. Robot. Soc. Jpn. **22**(8), 966–969 (2004)
16. Mori, Y., Saito, Y., Kamide, H.: Evaluation of impressions for hug dolls (in Japanese). Int. J. Affect. Eng. **11**(1), 9–15 (2012)
17. Kawaguchi, M.: Megatrend 2014–2023 (in Japanese), pp. 122–126. Nikkei Business Publications, Japan (2003)
18. Tanno, H., Matsui, Y.: The functions of friendship in undergraduates (in Japanese). Tsukuba Psychol. Res. **31**, 21–30 (2003)
19. Asakawa, K., Sano, T., Kogawa, M., Azuma, Y., Keiko, M.: The healing effects of pet animals on college students: A health psychological study (in Japanese). Bull. Hyogo Univ. Teach. Educ. Engl. **1**(20), 115–119 (2000)
20. Harlow, H.F.: Nature of love. Am. Psychol. **13**, 673–685 (1958)
21. Yano Research Institute Ltd.: Character Business's 2014 Year-Book (in Japanese), p. 415. Yano Research Institute (2014)
22. Docomo developer support homepage (in Japnese). https://dev.smt.docomo.ne.jp/?p=index. Accessed 06 Mar 2016
23. Japan Pet Food Association homepage (in Japnese). http://www.petfood.or.jp/data/chart2014/02.html. Accessed 10 July 2017
24. Pepper homepage (in Japanese). https://www.softbank.jp/robot/. Accessed 19 June 2017
25. Derived character of VOCALOID™ HATSUNE MIKU homepage (in Japanese). http://miku.sega.jp/. Accessed 10 July 2017
26. Steiff homepage (in Japanese). http://www.steiff.co.jp/. Accessed 12 July 2017
27. Bowlby, J.: Attachment and Loss. Attachment, vol. 1. Basic Books, New York (1969)
28. Hamada, T., Yokoyama, A., Shibata, T.: Development of robot therapy (in Japanese). J. Soc. Instrum. Control Eng. **42**(9), 756–762 (2004)

Lost Puppy: Towards a Playful Intervention for Wandering Dementia Patients

Yacintha Aakster[1], Robby van Delden[2](✉) ⓘ, and Stefan Lentelink[3]

[1] Creative Technology, University of Twente, Enschede, The Netherlands
yacintha.aakster@gmail.com
[2] Human Media Interaction, University of Twente, Enschede, The Netherlands
r.w.vandelden@utwente.nl
[3] Roessingh Research and Development, Enschede, The Netherlands
s.lentelink@rrd.nl

Abstract. Many nursing homes for dementia patients struggle with residents that wander towards the exit with the intention of leaving. Several types of interventions have been used to deal with this issue. Unfortunately, many of them are quite forceful, or are unsuitable for the specific context of certain nursing homes. In this paper, we investigate the possibility to using a more playful persuasive intervention. The design itself is in the form of a lost puppy, equipped with several actuators and sensors, that has to be brought 'home', in order to steer residents unknowingly away from the exit. Our first pilot indicated that residents noticed the puppy and showed interest in the device, and might be distracted from the exit. However, the puppy in its current form did not yet lead the residents away from the exit. Based on our contextual analyses, related work, and received feedback, we share our design insights which could be helpful for creating playful interventions for people with dementia.

Keywords: Dementia · Wandering · Playful intervention · Play
Design · Exit · Care home

1 Introduction

Around 47 million people worldwide have dementia [42]. Dementia is an umbrella term for the deterioration of cognitive functions caused by damaging of the cells in the brain and the connections between the cells [2]. The most common type of dementia is Alzheimer's disease [2,42]. The symptoms and characteristics of dementia affect people's everyday functioning and can involve (but are not limited to) memory loss, affected judgement, aggression, loss of willpower, and disorientation of time and place [14,42]. In general, in the early stages of dementia, people are able to remain at home with the help of family caregivers [23,43]. When the workload of caregivers becomes too high, the people with dementia

© Springer International Publishing AG, part of Springer Nature 2018
A. D. Cheok et al. (Eds.): ACE 2017, LNCS 10714, pp. 84–102, 2018.
https://doi.org/10.1007/978-3-319-76270-8_7

often move into a nursing home. Wandering behaviour of people with dementia, especially prevalent for those with Alzheimer's disease, represents a major
challenge regarding this group [20]. Kleine et al. and Burns et al. indicated that
respectively 17.4% and 18.5% of their subjects showed wandering behaviour,
with subjects with more severe dementia showing higher rates of wandering
behaviour [9,20].

Given this high prevalence rate of people with dementia in our society, it is
not surprising to see a serious interest of Human-Computer Interaction (HCI)
researchers in people with dementia [24]. Joddrell and Astell indicated they found
three directions regarding HCI for people with dementia: screening and assessment, addressing activity of daily living (ADL), and providing leisure activities
[19]. In this paper we focus on a playful interactive intervention for people with
dementia who wander towards the exit with the intention of leaving. The intervention we envision is not aiming for therapeutic goals or cognitive stimulation.
Instead, we want to use playful aspects to unknowingly steer people with dementia away from the exit in a more pleasurable way than current alternatives. The
case study we present here is for one specific nursing home, where many residents
stroll freely through the building. Several of them are in a far developed stage
of dementia, and therefore not allowed to leave without supervision. A chip in
their shoe prevents the exit door from opening when they stand in front of it[1],
which can lead to confrontation and confusion. Residents can get upset, cause a
scene in the entrance hall, and even become aggressive towards caregivers. This
requires the receptionist and caregivers to step in by calming them down and
taking them somewhere else.

To address this issue we propose our *Lost Puppy* concept: a stuffed puppy
located near the exit, that is equipped with a motion sensor and several actuators
(sound and light) to attract the attention of wandering residents who might go
towards the exit. The puppy entices the person to return the puppy to the
lost puppy's parent, a non-interactive stuffed dog placed a little further away,
intended to lead the resident away from the exit.

In the remainder of this paper we will explain how we came to the design
of the *Lost Puppy* prototype, and share our insights. In Sect. 2, we start with
related work, including other interventions for wandering residents. In Sect. 3,
we summarise previously identified aspects for addressing the senses that are relevant when designing interactive technology for people with dementia. Section 4
reports on the context of the exit, by conducting a small observational study
of the entrance, and several sets of semi-structured interviews with the activity
manager, receptionist, and psychologist. In Sect. 5, we give an overview of the
design and concept of the proposed puppy prototype, with which we did a first
preliminary evaluation that is reported in Sect. 6. In Sect. 7, we discuss some
of the weaknesses of our concept, future improvements, and share important
design insights. These insights are an important part of the paper, as they point
to important aspects and useful directions for the design of interactive technology

---

[1] A system that is used by more nursing homes, for instance the commercial system
'Door Guardian' [32].

for people with dementia. And finally, we conclude our work in Sect. 8 with a short conclusion.

The main contributions of this paper are: (1) to inspire others with our concept to consider a more subtle entertainment perspective than the common forceful devices and interventions to address wandering behaviour (and perhaps related issues); and (2) to provide interesting and useful insights into research and design aspects when working on interactive technology for people with dementia.

2   Related Work

For our project we looked at several existing interventions in the literature and those that are commercially available. There are several interventions that help to prevent people with dementia from leaving a nursing home, including preventing doors from opening, delayed opening of doors, hidden doors or controls, signalling an alarm, and surveillance [44]. Alternative ideas we found include a 'phantom bus stop' that makes residents patiently wait for a bus that will never arrive, but might calm down residents and allow caregivers to pick them up at a known location, see [34]. Another method is to use visual deterrents, for instance stickers disguising the door as a book closet, or even less subtle by using yellow signs saying 'STOP', see [36]. Both the signage and door covering stickers were rejected as valid options by the nursing home. A door-sticker with bricks was tried once, but was recognised as covering an exit and subsequently peeled off by a resident.

Interactive technology was seen by the nursing home, and our project team, as a powerful tool that might help to address the wandering problem in different ways. Morrissey et al. indicate that in HCI for people with dementia, technology is often seen as a solution to behavioural decline [24]. For instance, a prompting device using artificial intelligence to help in a routine like washing hands [22], and other forms of assistive technology, including agendas, video calls, or location tracking [19]. Besides technology for activities of daily living (ADL), one can make a distinction between digital leisure activities for pure entertainment and those for cognitive stimulation or therapeutic interventions [19]. Included in the former are creative digital activities such as painting a vase or music making, activities that are (more) difficult to perform without technology [5, 19, 30]. Included in the latter, mainly therapy-related, is research intended to aid current interventions and therapies by introducing additional technology. For example, providing audio and video material using a touch screen interface for reminiscence therapy [11]. An activity for the elderly that can be used for therapy purposes and entertainment is the PARO robot, a robotic baby seal [40]. Similarly in-between is the provision of leisure activities stimulating physical, cognitive, and social aspects in a playful way such as an interactive table projection [3]. This shows that technology is not always 'fixing' behaviour seen in people with dementia, but can also be an entertaining tool to enhance their existing activities.

Similar to the more comprehensive 'nighttime wandering system' of Radziszewski et al., that encouraged people with dementia to go back to bed in a soothing way with lighting and the use of media at night, we are interested in an interactive system that can be used during the day to gently steer people in an entertaining and playful way [28]. Nudging interventions (i.e. transparent ways to change behaviour without economic incentives [35]) like these, have been used as a successful way of 'ambient influence' to steer the behaviour of the general public, for instance to get people to use the stairs instead of the elevator [31].

3   Addressing the Senses of People with Dementia

When designing for people with dementia, several aspects of (multi-modal) sense-making should be considered. Several studies suggest this goes beyond only the age-related aspects (see [6] for a more extensive overview). We target several design oriented aspects and address four senses: visual, auditory, olfactory and tactile. We had omitted the sense of taste beforehand as it is beyond the scope of our project.

According to Jakob and Collier [16,17], the use of visuals can be effective, but is often too much emphasized as a sensory stimulus for people with dementia. Both Habell and Jakob and Collier mention that people with dementia can have a false visual perception, for instance mistaking a staircase for a waterfall, or a high glare floor surface for a river [12,17]. The confusion and decline in visual function is why Jakob and Collier discourage using shiny objects, moving lights (e.g. a disco ball), and suggest facilitation of slower light intensity changes [17]. The use of visual cues, including signs/icons and objects, can nonetheless be a suitable way to prompt certain behaviour [5,12]. Building on his experience as an architect for dementia care centres, Habell suggests that colour coding might be effective, for example giving accessible doors a bold colour [12].

People with dementia might not be able to detect auditory stimuli as well as other people. Hearing loss is a common occurrence in the ageing process. Also, Uhlmann et al. and Lin et al. have found a correlation between hearing loss and the severity of cognitive dysfunction [21,39]. Hearing impairment should therefore be taken into account when using auditory stimuli to attract the attention of people with severe dementia. In terms of auditory stimuli, music has proven to be a useful tool in stimulating people with dementia [6,30]. It can be used as a way to comfort people but also allows them to reminisce about earlier times. Spiro indicates that memory for music is special for people with dementia, as it is a complex skill that has been demonstrated to be more persistent than other information abilities [33]. Nair et al. conclude, based on a literature review and their baroque music intervention study (with negative effects), that especially preferred music genres help, rather than music of a general genre [26].

Olfactory deficits are more prominent in people with Alzheimer's disease; deteriorating olfactory discrimination, odour identification, and the olfactory detection threshold [10]. Nevertheless, the use of smells can be beneficial for people with Alzheimer's disease. For example, a small scale aromatherapy study indicated towards improvement of cognitive functioning and some improvement in conceptual understanding [18]. More directly related to HCI research, Gowans et al.

speculated that smell will have strong connections with memory functions and therefore also suggested the inclusion of smell in their set of (touchscreen operated) reminiscence devices for residents [11].

The sense of touch can be used in a passive and an active way. Passively, to comfort people with dementia and make them feel safe, by providing soft or fluffy materials. And actively, by providing them with objects with which they can interact in engaging ways. For example, sensory cushions are objects that contain different materials for a tactile and multi-faceted experience (vision, smell, hearing, and even taste) [17]. Another distinction can be made whether touch is used instrumentally, as part of a task, or as an expressive form, which is more emotional [6]. We refer the reader to [15] for an overview and several studies on technology addressing social touch and emotional aspects. Touch can be an effective stimulus, but in order to attract people with dementia, and in order to establish interaction, the objects should look inviting and meaningful [17].

4   Context of the Exit

The first author did four observations at the location, each lasting about 3 hours and performed during different time frames: 1x morning, 2x midday, and 1x midday/afternoon. Weather conditions may have been of influence. Due to sunny and warm weather, many people (e.g. employees and supervised residents) went outside for a walk or to sit in the sun. On average, about 55 people walked in and out every hour during the observed hours. The entrance hall shows several remarkable points, such as the large contrast in light intensity, see Fig. 1. Compared to the bright incoming sunlight, the entrance hall is quite dark. Providing sunlight to the residents is important [12] but residents are also drawn by this. Where the building is well designed for its visitors, who naturally feel where the exit is and where to find information, the design seems less favourable for its wandering residents. The receptionist also plays a role, and can be seen as a multi-sensory stimulus for the residents. The receptionist talks, moves and attracts people, creating an auditory, visual, and social stimulus. In front of the exit, there is a small gift shop. Some residents were observed to be drawn to this shop to look at, and touch, stalled and displayed items (e.g. shiny jewellery and things wrapped in squeaky plastic foil). And lastly, the decor of the entrance hall creates a funnel-like path towards the exit, feeling natural to follow.

4.1   Interviews

To get a more personal insight into the behaviour of the residents, beyond a general description of people with dementia, the first author interviewed an activity manager, a receptionist, and a psychologist. A semi-structured interview was used starting with 11–14 questions depending on the expertise of the interviewee. Responses were audio recorded and consent was given for this. We will briefly share the most important findings.

Fig. 1. A shadow/highlight corrected photo of the entrance hall of the nursing home. Notice the funnel effect with attractive light of the exit, the position of the receptionist (blurred for privacy), and the shiny items near the gift shop on the right.

Activity Manager. The activity manager has been working for the nursing home for more than ten years. He organizes and manages activities for the residents with the focus on physical activity and engagement. His goal is to keep residents active and for that reason most activities are related to sports in a playful way.

For giving instructions to the residents, he stated it is important to maintain the order of: (1) having some 'small talk'; (2) showing an explanatory photo or picture; and (3) performing the activity. In other words, explain, demonstrate, and then let them try it out themselves. *'Only words are not enough.'* He also mentioned that the best way to reach residents, for him personally, is to use humour. Making residents laugh makes them comfortable and relaxed, and makes them more willing to participate. The activity manager tried incorporating the Kinect into activities about 3 years ago, but the relation between physical actions and the screen were not understood by the residents. However, considering new kinds of technologies, he continued that *'the people coming into the nursing home nowadays are a bit more familiar with it'.*

Receptionist. The interviewed receptionist has been working at the nursing home for eight years. Her primary task is to be a receptionist, but an important part of her job is also to interact with the residents that come to her desk, or the exit.

She indicated that residents who go to the exit most often come just after the lunch, when the sun is shining right on the glass around the exit, and when the employees change shift. She mentioned that the latter is an important stimulus for residents, because employees gather at the desk. Residents sometimes end up at the exit by accident as a result of their wandering, and sometimes because they planned to. It is the hardest to distract or change the mind of the latter group of residents. It is also more common that this group of residents get upset or aggressive. To lead residents away from the exit, the receptionist uses a personal approach (including the use of names) which she feels is the most effective.

Psychologist. The interviewed psychologist has been working in the field of elderly care for over eight years. She does neurological research on dementia and is involved with the residents. She decides, based on a person's stage of dementia, symptoms, and behaviour, what the best care for this person would be.

When asked about the utility and applicability of sensory stimuli in guiding residents away from the exit, the psychologist stated she could imagine it being useful. People with dementia often have difficulties with focussing and are easily distracted and attracted by stimuli. She strongly believes that providing a counter stimulus that is more attractive than the exit could help in solving this problem. The psychologist explained that the time it takes to process sensory stimuli is different for people with dementia as opposed to healthy people. A person with dementia needs more time to process sensory stimuli, and therefore it is important to provide these stimuli a little bit longer than normal. She experiences dementia as a progressive disease that slowly takes away memories, starting with the last learned things and making its way back through time. People with dementia have a different perception of the world because they have lost memory of the things learned recently. Mentally they could be back 40 years, making it harder to incorporate newer technologies, as was indicated by the activity manager as well. The psychologist feels that a combination of both an autonomous distraction from a technological intervention and a personal, human, approach is preferable and probably most effective.

5   Design of the Proposed Puppy Prototype

5.1   A Stuffed Animal

Taking into account the insights from the literature, observations, and interviews mentioned above, the first author created 50 ideas for concepts through individual brainstorming. All ideas were then evaluated mainly by the first author, in four successive phases. Input from two occupational therapists was used as input for phases three and four. In the first phase, 24 seemingly unrealistic or infeasible ideas were filtered out. In the second phase, the remaining ideas were scored on the following principles: feasibility; innovativeness; comfortability; distractability/attractiveness; fit with the environment; and safety. The principles were scored between one to five points for each concept. The ideas that scored 20 points or higher, with a maximum of 30 points, were then elaborated upon giving concept descriptions. In the third phase the resulting top 12 of concepts were subsequently pitched to the two collaborating occupational therapists. During this third phase, the therapists indicated the general expected effectiveness of the concepts, they did this based on their expertise in the field of dementia and experience with residents of the nursing home. The gathered feedback was used to come to a top three of concepts. In the fourth phase these three concepts were assessed by weighing of pros and cons by the first author. The *Lost Puppy* concept was selected because of its expected effectiveness (as indicated in phase three by the therapists) in combination with its soft and playful character.

The *Lost Puppy* concept consists of a stuffed animal in the shape of a puppy, paw prints on the floor that indicate the direction of the goal, and a larger stuffed animal in the shape of a dog to represent the puppy's parent. The concept is supported by a storyline about the puppy being lost and needing to be brought back home, barking for attention. This home is located elsewhere in the residence where the parent dog is laying in a dog basket. The route from the puppy in the entrance hall to its parent dog is indicated by small paw prints on the floor. By giving residents the task to bring back the puppy, an interaction can be established that will engage them for a longer time. By performing this task, residents are unknowingly distracted from their own goal (i.e. going to the exit) and being led away from the stimuli that could re-attract them towards the exit. See Fig. 2, for an overview of the intervention.

The choice of animal in this concept was a dog, based on people's familiarity with dogs and the importance of recognition in design for people with dementia, see [1,5,17,26]. Also, a dog was a good fit for the storyline. There is however, a possibility that people have a fear of dogs. For that reason, a puppy was used instead of a mature dog because they are considered to be more approachable. Puppies also possess certain physical properties (infantile) that can stimulate caregiving in people [7]. Giving care to a vulnerable puppy can raise a feeling of responsibility in residents, and therewith stimulate them mentally. In another study, such a nurturing aspect with tangible properties in playful activities has also been indicated by proxies of residents as bringing pleasure [37]. Succeeding in reuniting the puppy with its parent can provide a feeling of complaisance and adds a clear goal.

5.2   Location

The location of the puppy was decided based on a small set of tests. For the tests, a stuffed animal in the shape of a small dog was placed at different locations in the entrance hall of the nursing home. For the course of an hour for each location, the first author observed whether the dog would be spotted or not by

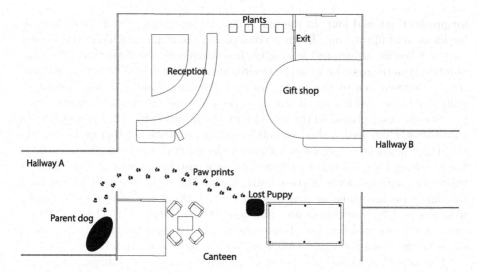

Fig. 2. A schematic overview of the exit location of the nursing home with the *Lost Puppy* concept.

the resident. The most reactions were witnessed when the dog was put on top of a pool table that had a black cover on it. At this location there was a large contrast between the black canvas and the light coloured fluffy animal. Therefore, we decided to use this location. However, to allow the pool table to be used, we used a moveable cart in front of the table on which the puppy could sit.

5.3   Technical Implementation

The implemented system consisted of a commercially available stuffed puppy of around 35 cm long, 15 cm wide, and 15 cm in height, see Fig. 3. To keep the dog light enough and better resistant to being accidentally dropped, the speakers were not embedded in the puppy. Instead, they were included in a moveable pedestal on which the puppy was placed. The pedestal also included a semi-transparent window with a Philips Hue colour changing LED lamp behind it to strengthen the visual attractiveness. Also a note was added around the puppy's neck prompting to bring it back home. A passive infrared motion sensor was connected to an Arduino to trigger a randomly selected barking sound when motion was detected. Five different barking sounds were included, ranging from more whiny to excited barking. Paw prints were placed on the floor to prompt the direction to walk to, the location of the non-interactive 'parent dog' positioned around the corner, as indicated in Fig. 2.

Fig. 3. Two photos of the implementation of the *Lost Puppy* concept. On the left, the puppy and motion sensor are placed on a pedestal with inside the Philips Hue with control interface, speaker, and laptop running the software. On the right, the installation can be viewed as a resident would see it when walking through the entrance hall.

6   Pilot Evaluation

The goal of the pilot evaluation was to gain insight into how effective the intervention is and to indicate whether it is indeed possible to divert the attention of residents away from the exit with such an intervention. In order to gain insights into the effectiveness of the elements of the intervention (i.e. puppy, paws and parent dog, note, and active involvement of the receptionist), starting with the puppy we added one element every 90 min (while including the previously added elements). In total, the observations were performed over the course of seven hours. The exact numbers of interactions observed were not kept because observations were performed from several points of view and the exit was not always within sight (e.g. when observing interactions with the parent dog). People with dementia are a rather vulnerable user group, and therefore we worked in close cooperation with the nursing home to perform the user test. We started with a test of one hour to discover any major flaws and to be sure that no dangerous situations could occur during testing.

Puppy. Residents in the entrance hall did notice the puppy and some approached it. One resident walked by the puppy, and said to the puppy when it started barking *'It's going to be fine'*. Later that same resident walked by again and responded to the puppy's barking by saying *'Calm, calm'*. The resident stood next to the puppy for a couple of minutes but did not pet or pick up the puppy. There was one resident, usually quite active around the exit and regularly attempting to leave, who asked how the system actually worked, even being interested in the technical details. She did not think the puppy was real, but did pet the puppy and seemed to be amused by the whole system for quite a while.

In the facility there were several groups of residents with visitors. In one group, a visitor suggested to approach the puppy. The group seemed to be very amused and delighted by the puppy and its barking, and one of the residents left a little flower with the puppy. Usually the visitors reacted with the most enthusiasm to the puppy and encouraged the residents to approach and pet the puppy. This created a social situation in which the puppy was central. They would stand around the puppy, listen to its barking, and some also petted the puppy.

There was one resident later that day who came to the exit with the intention of leaving. When the receptionist suggested to go to the puppy, the resident responded saying the puppy on top of the box was fake but that there was a dog inside of that box, because it could be recognised that the barking came from there. However, the resident did not care to seek this out. She did continue to have a conversation with the receptionist and then decided to sit down. There were also residents that passed by the puppy without noticing it, or its barking. It slowly became busier in the entrance hall because lunch hour was approaching, which sometimes made it difficult to hear the barking. The receptionist therefore suggested to turn up the volume.

Paws and Parent Dog. The paw prints seemed to help to gain attention from residents. Residents stopped to look at them and made comments such as *'how funny'*. One resident in the entrance hall had already noticed the puppy, and also noticed the paw prints. He even followed the paw prints for a little while, but not far enough to spot the 'parent dog'. There were also residents coming from the location of the parent dog, walking towards the entrance hall. These residents walked past the parent dog but almost all residents did seem to notice it. Most of these residents responded by smiling, and some reacted verbally both in a group setting and when alone. It did not result in any physical interaction with the dog.

Note. The prompting note 'Lost: bring me to Hallway A', was not noticed by many residents. There was one resident who noticed the note by herself, but she did not engage in further interaction. The visitors that accompanied the residents did notice the note, but they also seemed to lack the confidence to pick up or take the puppy. Therefore, they did not encourage the residents to do so either.

Active Involvement of the Receptionist. The receptionist was instructed to point residents towards the puppy when they came to the exit, and explain that the puppy was lost and had to be brought back to the 'parent dog'. With the receptionist's assistance, residents seemed to approach the puppy more often than without her encouragement. Some residents walked up to the puppy upon her instructions, but on arrival they would look at it and walk away again. Some residents did not immediately follow up on the receptionist's instructions, but when she physically guided them they would follow her. The residents did not show interest in bringing the dog to Hallway A, and said things such as *'I have to pee first'* or *'No, it is dead'*, without being really bothered by that latter possibly shocking interpretation. The receptionist did state that the puppy provided a natural topic to talk about with residents and that she did not feel uncomfortable to do so. She did not see a change in the behaviour of the residents during the tests, as she believes that most of the residents are too 'faded' to be able to grasp the idea of a lost puppy. She noticed that residents refused to step on the paw prints and therefore (ironically) even suggested to place them directly in front of the exit.

7   Discussion

In this work, we created a playful interactive intervention to address the issue of wandering in people with dementia in a nursing home. Our pilot evaluation was very exploratory and tested for only one day. Therefore, long term testing is needed to gain more insight into the interaction and effectiveness of its elements. Such evaluations could also use more quantitative measures with a fairer comparative research methodology (e.g. comparing identical time slots).

Nonetheless, the current study showed that the *Lost Puppy* concept can attract residents walking through the entrance hall. When noticed, the *Lost Puppy* system also seems to have a general positive effect on the residents and the atmosphere in the entrance hall. However, the intervention does not succeed in drawing the attention of residents for a long time. Residents did not complete the suggested task of bringing the puppy to its parent. The intervention did not prevent residents who purposefully wanted to leave from going to the exit either. For the residents who did not end up at the exit during testing, we can only speculate if they were steered away by the intervention or by something else. In this discussion we suggest improvements for the current prototype in order to make the *Lost Puppy* a more suitable intervention. Furthermore, in the subsequent paragraphs we will share more general insights for designing such a playful intervention for people with dementia.

7.1   Improve the Setting, Sensors, Sounds, and Stimuli of the Puppy

Similar to the importance of the physical layout of the entrance, the location and setting of the *Lost Puppy* are also essential. Currently the puppy was placed on top a large pedestal in the entrance hall. To some people this made the puppy less approachable, as if the puppy was exhibited and they were not allowed to touch it. Therefore, it is recommended to place the puppy in a location that is perceived more accessible. Another point regarding the setting is that if the puppy is actually brought to the parent, the puppy in the entrance hall needs to be replaced. We recommend that the receptionist keeps a small storage of puppies nearby, to refill the *Lost Puppy* spot, and occasionally collects the puppies from the parent somewhere nearby. The receptionist present during the evaluation was more than willing to do this.

The receptionists and caregivers at work during the testing indicated that the sounds were sometimes too soft when there was noise in the entrance hall. Therefore, it is recommended to provide the receptionist with the possibility to change settings of the installation, including changing the volume of the barking sounds and to mute it when there is for example a performance (e.g. a children's choir) in the hall.

Currently, the stimuli of the puppy were not sufficing to go beyond attracting the residents. Therefore, we recommend as a first attempt to include more stimuli. For example, the puppy should, similar to the PARO robot, move its head and tail [40]. This could make it appear more natural and, combined with other improvements (e.g. adaptive (barking) sounds), persuade the residents to initiate more action, hold their attention during execution, and finally succeed to bring the puppy to the parent steering the residents away from the exit.

7.2   Design for Dementia Insights: Towards Guidelines

The current study does not yet allow us to establish strong guidelines, but sharing our first insights might help others. We based our insights on related work, interviews, and feedback from residents. And we welcome future research to test, strengthen, and add more of these insights. Several of the insights extend the work of Jakob and Collier regarding design principles and recommendations for multisensory environments (MSEs)[2].

Getting Informed. Regarding the design process we first reiterate that it is important to **include people with dementia (and people close to them) in the process**, and to educate oneself regarding dementia [19,38]. This can also include education about more specific elements, in this case wandering behaviour and analysis of the exit situation. In this particular study, we leaned in the beginning and concept generation more on the proxies of the residents (i.e. the activity manager, psychologist, receptionist, and occupational therapists), than on direct interactions with the residents. It might have been beneficial to also include more family members. In our opinion the goal of the intervention, unknowingly prevent the residents from leaving, could have been a too confronting topic to incorporate residents as full design partners. For the informal location test and pilot study we did use both the verbal and non-verbal feedback of the residents as much as possible. For insights into proper participatory design and co-design for people with dementia we refer to [13] and [38].

---

[2] The principles consisted of: feeling comfortable and safe; meaningful and familiar; multisensory experience; stimulation and relaxation; control and interaction; and age appropriate and usable. These were accompanied with 3 design recommendations: using textiles and soft materials (encouraging playful engagement), lighting and lights (gradual changes), and low-tech vs high-tech (multi-modal but preventing a technical appearance by using familiar elements). We refer the interested reader to [17] or their more informal and extensive guidebook [16] for a complete description.

Over-Stimulation. It is important to **prevent over-stimulation** for this target group. Too much sensory stimuli can be easily overwhelming. As described by Reisberg et al.'s *Stage 3 - mild cognitive decline scale*, affected concentration can become apparent for people with dementia [29]. This supports the advice for multi-sensory rooms for residents with dementia by Jakob and Collier, to de-clutter spaces and **create visual focus** points [16]. For example, guiding visual focus with lights that gradually change colour (e.g. with a Philips Hue or light path of LEDs [28]), with moving parts (e.g. moving limbs of a seal [40]), or by increasing contrast (e.g. as seen in the informal location test by choosing the proper background)[3].

Goals and Prompts. Another aspect is to **include clear goals** during the entire interaction [1] with the **use of appropriate prompts** during the interaction. Clear goals can also be intuitive goals. For example, showing, in a virtual environment, dots of paint in combination with a blank vase can be enough to trigger residents to start painting [5]. In our intervention we included a clear goal, but it might not have been clear during the entire interaction. Emphasizing for instance the paws with additional gradually changing lights might have helped to make the goal clearer, and could have prompted the users. The written prompt *'to return the puppy'* to its parent's location was not successful. Even auditory prompts (not given by a person) might be ignored when they are hard to understand. Another consideration is that it can also be speculated that prompts using synthetic speech might be harder to understand than naturally spoken text, especially for people with dementia [1]. In the prompts given by a system, it is also important that it is clear what to do, but in the meanwhile preventing that residents become insecure about whether they are capable to perform the task [30]. More extensive, simple and short but very specific, preferably multi-modal prompts seem to be needed.

Personal Approach. In general it helps to **use tailoring and personalization** to persuade people [27]. For our target group this could for instance be done by using the residents name for prompting (as was mentioned in an interview with the receptionist), adapting content to personal preferences (e.g. changing to preferred music although this might be logistically problematic [26]), or triggering remaining memories with certain topics [12,41]. However, considering privacy-security reasons, and considering that 'a significant number of subjects' got upset when personal pictures were included (they could not remember the depicted moments or persons), Gowans et al. argue against the use of such personalization [11]. Therefore, it is important to consider what type of personalisation is used and if the benefits outweigh its consequences.

---

[3] Shiny objects were observed to attract attention at the gift shop near the exit, and reflective surfaces can be fascinating for some individuals [38]. However, shiny object/glare/reflections could be misinterpreted by residents and be detrimental and confusing [6,17].

Recall. In the design clearly **link to recognisable and/or familiar elements** [1,5,17,26]. As people with dementia in general have severe trouble learning new skills or memorising new procedures, the interaction should build on recognisable and intuitive elements. Furthermore, according to Jakob and Collier, using familiar elements can help to make users feel safe [17]. One way to address this familiarity is using technology to mimic animals, like the PARO robotic seal [40]. It seems that this could trigger the caregiving tendencies indicated for real human-animal interaction, especially when using infantile characteristics which is known as the baby schema [7].

Incorporating Sounds. When applicable, make sounds originate actually from the object itself, or at least **incorporate the origin of sounds** into the design. It might be hard for residents to make the cognitive link between the object and sounds playing from a distance. This link was previously also suggested by Gowans et al. [11]. Even though the speaker was really close, the difference in location was noticed for our puppy by one resident, leading her to conclude the puppy was fake. Furthermore, considering the high occurrence of hearing problems of people with Alzheimer's disease [39], it could be useful to have adjustable audio. The audio should be audible but not too loud, preventing discomfort and over-stimulation of others.

Humour, Fun, and Laughter. If possible in a suitable manner, **try to incorporate humour** into the system. Several sources mention stimulation of humour or laughter for residents [4,12,23]. Our current design already triggered some smiling, laughs and giggles, as well as remarks as *'how funny'* and *'look at that'*. The interviewed activity manager also mentioned humour as an important feature to reach residents.

Social Interaction. Embrace the attractive value, the effect that 'people attract people', and incorporate facilitation of the social interactions it can trigger. In other words: **use the interactive piece as a 'honey pot'** [8]. This 'enticing honey-pot' effect [8] has been proven to exist for embodied play experiences in public spaces [25]. As was indicated in the interview, it also seemed that residents were attracted when employees gathered. Furthermore, a demonstration effect was seen where people (mostly family visitors) would talk about the puppy to the residents and even pet it. Related to this we also advise to consider the **use of the system as 'conversation piece'** as this might support and stimulate social interaction. This was seen here, as well as suggested for other systems for people with dementia [38,41], and in a general population interacting in public spaces [25].

Age Appropriate Design. Together with staff and residents we identified that there could be a thin line between offering a too childish toy and providing an effective steering interactive intervention. A too childish looking system might make residents less willing to use it, as was also demonstrated in another study by one participant leaving a music activity because it looked too childish [30]. This perfectly fits with Jakob and Collien's principle to **make it age appropriate and usable** [17]. We follow them and others in the advice to address people with dementia with respect, taking them for full, addressing what they can while taking into account the things they have trouble with, their peculiarities, and the individual differences [17,23,24,41]. Perhaps targeting/picking the proper play experiences according to the stage of dementia could be a small help herein [4].

To emphasize the importance of providing pleasurable interactions for people with dementia using an appropriate multi-modal interaction, fitting the person's preferences, we end this discussion with this inspiring quote:

> *'The emphasis in descriptions of the course of the syndrome tends to be on long-term degeneration. Nevertheless, in a favourable environment and with care based on respect and love, people with dementia can, in spite of their limitations, laugh, dance, sing and cry, mean something special to someone else, care for a fellow resident, and enjoy good food, beautiful music and pleasant smells.'* [23, p. 4]

8   Conclusion

This study focused on developing an interactive playful intervention to steer people with dementia living in a nursing home unknowingly away from the exit. Our proposed *Lost Puppy* concept has not yet succeeded in achieving its goal. However, our study, building on the research of others, resulted in several insights into the design for people with dementia regarding this subject. We believe that these insights can inspire and support future initiatives towards subtle playful interactive interventions for people with dementia.

Acknowledgements. This study was part of a bachelor assignment and is the result of a cooperation between the University of Twente (Human Media Interaction research group), Roessingh Research and Development (Telemedicine Group), and Liberein (location Bruggerbosch). We would like to thank all staff members from Bruggerbosch who provide 24/7 residential care for people with dementia, and in particular Nienke de Haan and Manon Scheffer for the time they invested and their valuable insights. And finally, we would like to thank Dennis Reidsma, Lynn Packwood, and Monique Tabak, and our other colleagues involved in this project for their valuable input. This project was indirectly sponsored as part of a collaborative effort between Roessingh Research and Development and Liberein (location Bruggerbosch).

References

1. Alm, N., Astell, A., Gowans, G., Dye, R., Ellis, M., Vaughan, P., Newell, A.F.: An interactive entertainment system usable by elderly people with dementia. In: Stephanidis, C. (ed.) UAHCI 2007. LNCS, vol. 4555, pp. 617–623. Springer, Heidelberg (2007). https://doi.org/10.1007/978-3-540-73281-5_65
2. Alzheimer's Association: What is dementia? http://www.alz.org/what-is-dementia.asp. Accessed 29 July 2017
3. Anderiesen, H.: Playful design for activation: co-designing serious games for people with moderate to severe dementia to reduce apathy. Ph.D. thesis, TU Delft, Delft, The Netherlands (2017). Chapter: Intermezzo: Active Cues Tovertafel - a product description
4. Anderiesen, H., Scherder, E., Goossens, R., Visch, V., Eggermont, L.: Play experiences for people with alzheimer's disease. Int. J. Des. **9**(2), 1–11 (2015)
5. Astell, A., Alm, N., Dye, R., Gowans, G., Vaughan, P., Ellis, M.: Digital video games for older adults with cognitive impairment. In: Miesenberger, K., Fels, D., Archambault, D., Peňáz, P., Zagler, W. (eds.) ICCHP 2014. LNCS, vol. 8547, pp. 264–271. Springer, Cham (2014). https://doi.org/10.1007/978-3-319-08596-8_42
6. Behrman, S., Chouliaras, L., Ebmeier, K.: Considering the senses in the diagnosis and management of dementia. Maturitas **77**(4), 305–310 (2014)
7. Borgi, M., Cirulli, F.: Pet face: mechanisms underlying human-animal relationships. Front. Psychol. **7**, 2981–29811 (2016)
8. Brignull, H., Rogers, Y.: Enticing people to interact with large public displays in public spaces. In: Rauterberg, G.W.M., Menozzi, M., Wesson, J. (eds.) Proceedings of the IFIP International Conference on Human-Computer Interaction, INTERACT 2003, pp. 17–24. IOS Press (2003)
9. Burns, A., Jacoby, R., Levy, R.: Psychiatric phenomena in alzheimer's disease. iv: disorders of behaviour. Br. J. Psychiatry **157**, 86–94 (1990)
10. Djordjevic, J., Jones-Gotman, M., Sousa, K.D., Chertkow, H.: Olfaction in patients with mild cognitive impairment and alzheimer's disease. Neurobiol. Aging **29**(5), 693–706 (2008)
11. Gowans, G., Campbell, J., Alm, N., Dye, R., Astell, A., Ellis, M.: Designing a multimedia conversation aid for reminiscence therapy in dementia care environments. In: Extended Abstracts on Human Factors in Computing Systems, CHI 2004, pp. 825–836. ACM, New York (2004)
12. Habell, M.: Specialised design for dementia. Perspect. Pub. Health **133**(3), 151–157 (2013)
13. Hendriks, N., Truyen, F., Duval, E.: Designing with dementia: guidelines for participatory design together with persons with dementia. In: Kotzé, P., Marsden, G., Lindgaard, G., Wesson, J., Winckler, M. (eds.) INTERACT 2013. LNCS, vol. 8117, pp. 649–666. Springer, Heidelberg (2013). https://doi.org/10.1007/978-3-642-40483-2_46
14. Holzer, C., Warshaw, G.: Clues to early alzheimer dementia in the outpatient setting. Arch. Fam. Med. **9**(10), 1066–1070 (2000)
15. Huisman, G.: Social touch technology: extending the reach of social touch through haptic technology. Ph.D. thesis, Universiteit Twente, Enschede, The Netherlands (2017)

16. Jakob, A., Collier, L.: A guide book: how to make a Sensory Room for people living with dementia. Kingston University, London, England (2014). http://fada. kingston.ac.uk/de/MSE_design_in_dementia_care/doc/How%20to%20make%20a %20Sensory%20Room%20for%20people%20with%20dementia.pdf. Unpublished manuscript
17. Jakob, A., Collier, L.: Sensory enrichment for people living with dementia: increasing the benefits of multisensory environments in dementia care through design. Des. Health **1**(1), 115–133 (2017)
18. Jimbo, D., Kimura, Y., Taniguchi, M., Inoue, M., Urakami, K.: Effect of aromatherapy on patients with alzheimer's disease. Psychogeriatrics **9**(4), 173–179 (2009)
19. Joddrell, P., Astell, J.A.: Studies involving people with dementia and touchscreen technology: a literature review. JMIR Rehabil. Assist. Technol. **3**(2), e10 (2016)
20. Klein, D.A., Steinberg, M., Galik, E., Steele, C., Sheppard, J.M., Warren, A., Rosenblatt, A., Lyketsos, C.G.: Wandering behaviour in community-residing persons with dementia. Int. J. Geriatr. Psychiatry **14**(4), 272–279 (1999)
21. Lin, F.R., Yaffe, K., Xia, J., Xue, Q.L., Harris, T.B., Purchase-Helzner, E., Simonsick, E.M.: Hearing loss and cognitive decline in older adults. JAMA Intern. Med. **173**(4), 293–299 (2013)
22. Mihailidis, A., Boger, J., Canido, M., Hoey, J.: The use of an intelligent prompting system for people with dementia. Interactions **14**(4), 34–37 (2007)
23. Ministry of Health, Welfare and Sport, Zorgverzekeraars Nederland [Health insurance Companies Netherlands], Alzheimer Nederland, ActiZ: Guideline for integrated dementia care [excerpt] (2009). http://ec.europa.eu/social/BlobServlet? docId=8275. Accessed 8 Oct 2017
24. Morrissey, K., Lazar, A., Boger, J., Toombs, A.: HCIxDementia workshop: the role of technology and design in dementia. In: Proceedings of the 2016 CHI Conference Extended Abstracts on Human Factors in Computing Systems, pp. 484–491. ACM, New York (2017)
25. Müller, C., Wan, L., Wulf, V.: Dealing with wandering in institutional care: exploring the field. In: Proceedings of the 7th International Conference on Pervasive Computing Technologies for Healthcare, PervasiveHealth 2013, pp. 101–104. ICST (Institute for Computer Sciences, Social-Informatics and Telecommunications Engineering), Brussels (2013)
26. Nair, B.R., Browne, W., Marley, J., Heim, C.: Music and dementia. Degenerative Neurol. Neuromuscul. Dis. **3**, 47–51 (2013)
27. Oinas-Kukkonen, H., Harjumaa, M.: Persuasive systems design: key issues, process model, and system features. Commun. Assoc. Inf. Syst. **24**(28), 485–500 (2009)
28. Radziszewski, R., Ngankam, H., Pigot, H., Grégoire, V., Lorrain, D., Giroux, S.: An ambient assisted living nighttime wandering system for elderly. In: Proceedings of the 18th International Conference on Information Integration and Web-Based Applications and Services, iiWAS 2016, pp. 368–374. ACM, New York (2016)
29. Reisberg, B., Ferris, S.H., de Leon, M.J., Crook, T.: The global deterioration scale for assessment of primary degenerative dementia. Am. J. Psychiatry **9**(3), 1136–1139 (1982)
30. Riley, P., Alm, N., Newell, A.: An interactive tool to promote musical creativity in people with dementia. Comput. Hum. Behav. **25**(3), 599–608 (2009). Including the Special Issue: Enabling elderly users to create and share self authored multimedia content

31. Rogers, Y., Hazlewood, W.R., Marshall, P., Dalton, N., Hertrich, S.: Ambient influence: can twinkly lights lure and abstract representations trigger behavioral change? In: Proceedings of the 12th ACM International Conference on Ubiquitous Computing, pp. 261–270. ACM, New York (2010)

32. Secure Care: Wander management solutions. http://www.securecare.com/hubfs/Brochures/DG_Brochure.pdf?t=1495550876843. Accessed 18 Oct 2017

33. Spiro, N.: Music and dementia: observing effects and searching for underlying theories. Aging Ment. Health **14**(8), 891–899 (2010)

34. Taylor, K.: The phantom bus stop. Hektoen Int. J. Med. Humanit. (free online journal) **6**(4) (2014). http://hekint.org/the-phantom-bus-stop/. Accessed 18 Oct 2017

35. Thaler, R., Sunstein, C.: Nudge: Improving Decisions about Health, Wealth, and Happiness. Yale University Press, New Haven (2008)

36. The Alzheimer's store: Wandering. http://www.alzstore.com/alzheimers-dementia-wandering-s/1828.htm. Accessed 18 Oct 2017

37. Treadaway, C., Fennell, J., Kenning, G., Prytherch, D., Walters, A.: Designing for wellbeing in late stage dementia. In: Proceedings of the Third International Conference Exploring the Multi-dimensions of Well-Being; Co-creating Pathways to Well-Being, pp. 126–129 (2016)

38. Treadaway, C., Kenning, G.: Sensor e-textiles: person centered co-design for people with late stage dementia. Working Older People **20**(2), 76–85 (2016)

39. Uhlmann, R.F., Larson, E.B., Rees, T.S., Koepsell, T.D., Duckert, L.G.: Relationship of hearing impairment to dementia and cognitive dysfunction in older adults. JAMA **261**(13), 1916–1919 (1989)

40. Wada, K., Shibata, T., Saito, T., Tanie, K.: Effects of robot-assisted activity for elderly people and nurses at a day service center. Proc. IEEE **92**(11), 1780–1788 (2004)

41. Wallace, J., Thieme, A., Wood, G., Schofield, G., Olivier, P.: Enabling self, intimacy and a sense of home in dementia: an enquiry into design in a hospital setting. In: Proceedings of the SIGCHI Conference on Human Factors in Computing Systems, CHI 2012, pp. 2629–2638. ACM, New York (2012)

42. World Health Organization: Fact sheet dementia (2017). http://www.who.int/mediacentre/factsheets/fs362/en/. Accessed 18 Oct 2017

43. Yaffe, K., Fox, P., Newcomer, R., Sands, L., Lindquists, K., Dane, K., Covinsky, K.E.: Patient and caregiver characteristics and nursing home placement in patients with dementia. JAMA **287**(16), 2090–2097 (2002)

44. Zeisel, J., Hyde, J., Levkoff, S.: Best practices: an environment behavior (e-b) model for alzheimer special care units. Am. J. Alzheimer's Care Relat. Disord. Res. **9**(2), 4–21 (1994)

A Dynamic Scenario by Remote Supervision: A Serious Game in the Museum with a Nao Robot

Damien Mondou$^{(\boxtimes)}$, Armelle Prigent, and Arnaud Revel

L3i - University of La Rochelle, La Rochelle, France
damien.mondou@univ-lr.fr
http://l3i.univ-larochelle.fr

Abstract. This paper presents a new approach to designing and supervising an interactive experience. The approach is implemented by creating a serious game with a Nao robot. This game allows youth to discover the ethnographic artifacts of La Rochelle's natural history museum in a playful manner. The design phase of the game is divided into two steps. The first step defined the atomic behaviors grouped within the pattern. In the second step, the agents implementing these patterns were created; they specified the contents and behaviors to be executed on the controlled process, in our case the Nao robot. The first objective is to externalize the contents of the game (e.g. robot speech) and the real behaviors of the process (e.g. the different postures and gestures of the Nao) in a database. The second objective is to be able to define a serious game without constraints on the process piloted.

Keywords: Robot · Serious game · Supervision · Game design

1 Introduction

Museums continually search for new ways to both increase their visitor count and allow visitors to discover the museum artifacts while gaining new knowledge. For several years, the serious game has demonstrated that it can playfully help users increase their understanding of a subject. The benefits of learning through play have been demonstrated [9,24]. Thus, many cultural sites have been equipped with fun features that allow visitors to find out about the collections or works of art in another manner.

For it, museum's curators may use on-screen games [7], augmented reality [17], transmedia and virtual immersion solutions [5] to allow visitors to navigate the artifacts and to learn about the cultural and artistic items at the cultural center. A possible continuation of these serious games is playing with a robot, which has been proposed for several years.

© Springer International Publishing AG, part of Springer Nature 2018
A. D. Cheok et al. (Eds.): ACE 2017, LNCS 10714, pp. 103–116, 2018.
https://doi.org/10.1007/978-3-319-76270-8_8

There are many advantages to interactive games with a robot. Robot-based computer vision systems can be integrated into the museum space and challenge a visitor to participate. Thus, a simple visitor can become a player for part of their visit. In addition, people can visit the museum and play without having to be equipped with a tablet, phone or others equipments which might interfere with their visit.

In collaboration with the Museum of Natural History of La Rochelle in France, we have developed an interactive experience for young visitors. This serious game allows the youth to discover, in ainteresting manner, the ethnography section of the museum. This serious game is embedded in the Nao robot, that was initially developed by the French company Aldebaran (now Softbank Robotics). Nao encompasses a set of sensors (e.g. a camera, sonar, and tactile sensors) that allow it to perceive the environment. This robot is also able to interact with a person through its microphones and speakers. Thanks to a serious game, Nao is in charge of the playful discovery of the museum's artifacts.

In parallel with this experience and in the framework of a transdisciplinary study conducted with a laboratory specialized in marketing research, we studied the reactions of visitors to the presence of a robot in a cultural place. We found that, depending on the age of the visitor, the reactions differ. Children responded quicker to the robot and could be impatient waiting for the robot's response; adults were more hesitant. Thus, it is important to plan for different visitor scenarios (e.g. accounting for the individual's age).

It is important to note that scripting a game through a robot creates new challenges in design, especially when several scenarios are desired. For instance, the user can interact with the robot in various manners, which means these different interactions must be precisely orchestrated. Thus, the robot can move and gesture; see, recognize, and talk to the visitor; and wait for the visitor's responses. Another issue is that the current programming interfaces do not allow for content outsourcing, which is a challenge for the replicability of the interactive experience (e.g. in another museum).

In this paper, we offer an approach for the supervision of interactions with the robot through a high-level model to represent the different execution contexts.

We propose a formal model for the scenario, a generic supervision tool and the connection from Nao to the supervision tool (wrapper). After describing the interactive experience with Nao, developed for the museum, we will present the method for the game's modeling and dynamic supervision.

2   Robots in Everyday Life

Robots become more and more present in our everyday lives and allow us to simplify our daily activities. For instance, at King's College London, the receptionist is a robot named Inkha (Fig. 1(b)). Robots can also be found in supermarkets to help shoppers find different products and provide nutritional advice, such as LoweBot [19], Aiko Chihira [23], and Pepper [3]. Robots can also be major actors in artistic works, such as Nao [2] and Poppy [13]. Artists and scientists

(a)   (b)   (c)   (d)

Fig. 1. Experiences with robots in museums

have proposed a human-robot dance performance at the School of Moon in 2016 in order to question perceptions and representations of the body.

In this article, we are particularly interested in the presence of robots in cultural places. We have found several projects that introduce robots in museums for the reception and orientation of the visitors. Since 2014 at the National Museum of Emerging Science and Innovation in Tokyo, two robots have been in charge of welcoming visitors and can also read the news to them. At the Eppur Si Muove exhibition at the Museum of Modern Art in Luxembourg, a Nao robot with the base of a mobile robot (Fig. 1(a)) is itself an interactive work and is responsible for guiding and presenting the works to the public [10]. In France, as part of a project on the artificial esthetism of machines, the robot Berenson (Fig. 1(c)) was deployed at the Quai Branly Museum. This robot behaves like an art critic, as he expresses an emotion when he sees a work. His opinion will evolve thanks to the reactions of the people around him [4]. Furthermore, some museums, because of their architecture, are not accessible to people with a motor handicap. The Oiron castle museum in France observed this issue and, on the first floor of the museum, introduced a robot that is able to be remotely controlled by a joystick from the ground floor, which allows individuals with a handicap to visit the works that were previously inaccessible to them. This robot is called Norio (Fig. 1(d)) and has been used in the museum since November 2014 [11].

3   Playing with Nao in the Museum

The scenario proposed in our experiment aims to allow the visitor (or player) to interact with the Nao robot to discover the Museum's Kanak masks collections. The robot asks the player a number of questions. This first experiment of dynamic supervision is based on an interactive quiz. With each new question, the player is required to move around the museum to find the answer and give it to the robot. Players can start a session with Nao at any time since a visual recognition algorithm allows the robot to continue the question sequence with the visitor (Fig. 2).

Fig. 2. Nao in the La Rochelle museum, France

The experiment, shown in Fig. 3, proceeds as follows. At the beginning of the session, Nao is in a waiting position, the robot remains so until it detects the presence of a human in its field of vision. Then, Nao attracts the visitor's attention by calling and inviting the individual. Once the visitor is close enough to Nao, the robot asks the individual to place themselves in front of Nao in order to trigger the visual recognition algorithm, which will allow the robot to identify the player during the different phases of the session. If the face is recognized, Nao resumes the question sequence with this identified visitor. If the robot does not recognize the face, Nao asks the visitor if they want to play; if the visitor refuses, Nao goes back into the waiting situation. If the user accepts, then Nao records the visitor's face with an identifier and starts the quiz.

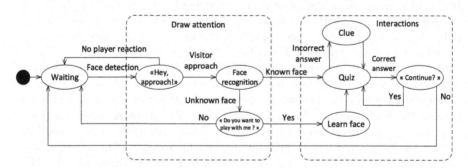

Fig. 3. The interactive experience scenario

3.1   First Approach: The Linear Programming of Nao

The first game session was completed by a purely linear development through the graphical programming tool called Choregraphe, which was delivered with Nao - and supported by Softbank Robotics - in order to pilot Nao. Choregraphe is a simple tool for combining predefined behaviors and descriptions of new behaviors, with Python language support. The pre-existing behaviors provided to Nao can be modified, since the Python code is accessible from Choregraphe. This tool offers some visual abstraction, which is then interpreted by the robot's NAOqi, the software that runs on the robot and controls it. The visual language of Choregraphe is translated through behaviors. Each behavior is defined by a name, input(s), output(s), parameter(s), and typically a Python script that contain the commands to be executed. When a signal arrives at the input, the behavior is loaded and performed. Once the output is stimulated, the box is onloaded (Fig. 4).

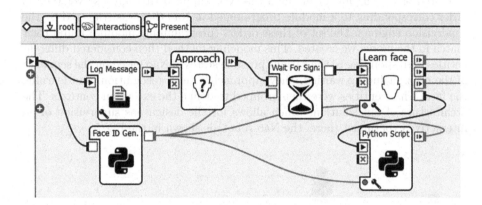

Fig. 4. Choregraphe programming for the game

The entire interactive experiment in the museum was modeled and implemented through Choregraphe. The model obtained can be compared to a Petri net [20] where the places are behaviors (modeled by boxes) and the transitions are the links between these behaviors. While this tool has proven to be effective, it does not meet all of the researchers' expectations. For instance, Choregraphe does not make it possible to define a scenario, accounting for the **space** for which it was designed. The goal is to be able to deploy this type of experience in different museums with minimal processing effort. In order for this experience to be adaptable to various museums, the **contents** of the experiment must also be modified. Though the **interactions** are relatively simple and the sequence with a player contains only three questions, the possible modifications of the dialogues and, the content or the re-scheduling of the interactions proved to be laborious and hazardous when they intervened shortly before a session with the public. The final limitation concerns the **temporality** of the experience. We wish to be able to apply a duration period to a particular event in the scenario, such as a time limit on how long the visitor has to answer the question posed by the robot.

3.2   Modeling and Dynamic Supervision of the Game

These different limitations led the researchers to propose a new architecture allowing to take into account the activity's temporality, to manage external contents and to facilitate the deployment of the same scenario in another museum. Softbank Robotics proposed a software development kit (SDK) in C++ and Python to control Nao. Thus, we used the Python SDK in our approach. The first step consisted of developing a wrapper which would allow dialogue to occur between the robot and the supervision engine. Therefore, the robot's sequence consisted of waiting for a command that was supplied through a server (i.e. an order corresponding to a module programmed in Nao that was triggered by the supervision engine). The set of these orders (programming module) found their match in the model we created. This modeling method then considered different entities corresponding to the various possible states of Nao based on the sequence of the quiz, including waiting, "hey, approach", facial recognition, and learning the face. These entities were then grouped to define the execution contexts. The architecture of our solution, which allows for the design ans supervision of an interactive experiment (here, the Nao robot) is shown in the Fig. 5.

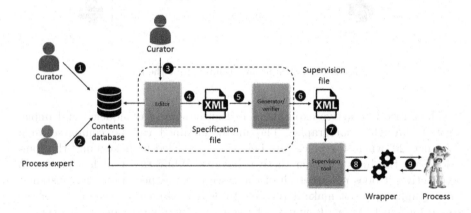

Fig. 5. Architecture of the design and supervision of an interactive experience

As shown in Fig. 5, in the first step, the museum's curator and process' expert define the contents (e.g. the text of presentation of the works and quiz) and the executable behaviors (e.g. postures and gestures) respectively and then insert them into the database. The museum's curator can then design the interactive experience through the model's editor. The curator uses the contents present in the database to construct its scenario, associating the robot's behavior and speech and obtaining a specification file in XML format (Fig. 7). This file is then used to generate the supervision file which contains the scenario modeled by timed automata as the input of the supervision tool. This tool, described in the following section, will then pilot the robot thanks to the scenario designed by the curator.

4   A Dynamic Supervision Approach

The final objective of our work is proposing a platform that allows for dynamic adaptation to the user and that permits the supervision of the activity, taking into account the content, interactivity, time, and space. Indeed, designing an interactive experience that fully corresponds to a user is tricky. A way of managing the quality of the experience is adjusting the content to the user's context. In this case, the management of the activity is based on an *a priori* modeling approach called *top-down*, as management have been used in web adaptation [8,26] and in a video game adaptation framework [14–16].

We propose a formal model of the game's execution based on two layers of modeling. The behaviors of the entities are modeled by input/output finite state machines, and the objective is to leave a significant possibility of choice to the user while guaranteeing the quality of the narrative framework. A first approach of dynamic supervision has been proposed in [21,22], and having given rise to a supervision framework called #Telling. We propose an extension of this work that facilitate the control allows content outsourcing and time constraints representation. Thus, #Telling, whose modeling is divided into three layers, can supervise the activity based on the execution scenes. Although this framework's effectiveness has been proven, it does not allow for the temporal dimension to be taken into account, in either the definition of the behavior or in the transition from one situation to another. Finally, content management is not supported. We propose a new model that is able to address these issues and simplify the modeling phase of the experiment using the two-layer model, which is described in the next section.

4.1   Two-Layers Model

Formal models have been proven to be effective for controlling interactive experiments. Petri nets are often used to model and verify asynchronous activities, particularly serious games [1,18]. Linear logic approaches have been used to represent ressources consumption [6]. In our approach, we use timed I/O finite state machines networks, which are more suited to represent synchronous systems with time constraints. Modeling an interactive experience is divided into two parts:

– We first describe the experience in an abstract manner, by defining the reusable entities (e.g. behaviors and patterns), modeled by timed automata. This step creates the *declarative layer*;

– By instantiating patterns into agents, which are grouped into scheduled execution contexts, we define the *implementation layer*.

The process of creating an interactive system is illustrated in Fig. 6.

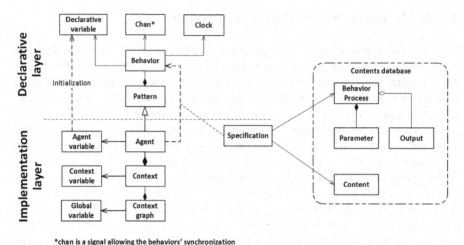

*chan is a signal allowing the behaviors' synchronization

Fig. 6. Two-layer approach for interactive modeling with content management

Declarative Layer. The declarative layer is the layer in which we define the generic entities of the modeled system, namely the atomic behaviors that can be executed. These behaviors are associated with declarative variables (e.g. integers, strings or Boolean) and channels, which are signals that allow several behaviors to be synchronized. The behaviors are then grouped into patterns that represent a set of entity specific behaviors that can be reused by the multiple inheritance principle.

Implementation Layer. The implementation layer is the layer where the designer defines the agents, that can instantiate the behaviors of several patterns and aggregate atomic behaviors not present in the instantiated patterns. This principle of multiple inheritance allows the designer to reuse the patterns defined in the declarative layer as many times as necessary without needing to redefine the patterns. When the designer is defining the agents, for each behavior they specify the content or action to be performed on the process. These agents are then linked in **execution contexts** representing the specific context in which agents interact with each other.

4.2 Example of the Model for the Robot in Museums

We used our two-layer model to pilot the Nao robot in the natural history museum. We now present examples of behaviors for the implementation of the

```
<specification id="Nao">
    <declarative_layer>
        <chan id="confirmGame"/>
        <clock id="X"/>
        <behavior id="say" .../>
        <behavior id="animate"  .../>
        <behavior id="detectPerson"  .../>
        <behavior id="speechReco"  .../>
        <pattern id="animatedSay">
            <behavior id="say" priority="1"/>
            <behavior id="animate" priority="2"/>
        </pattern>
    </declarative_layer>
    <implementation_layer>
        <agent id="speechAwait">
            <pattern id="animatedSay"/>
            <behavior id="say" class="Module" value="673" success="" fail="">
                <parameter id="language" value="french"/>
                <parameter id="speedSpeech" value="90"/>
                <content value="9"/>
            </behavior>
            <behavior id="animate" class="Gesture" value="247" success="" fail=""/>
        </agent>
        <agent id="speechExplain">
            <pattern id="animatedSay"/>
            <behavior id="say" class="Module" value="673" success="" fail="">
                <parameter id="language" value="french"/>
                <parameter id="speedSpeech" value="90"/>
                <content value="6"/>
            </behavior>
            <behavior id="animate" class="Gesture" value="247" success="" fail=""/>
            <behavior id="speechReco" class="Module" value="675" success="" fail="">
                <parameter id="language" value="french"/>
                <parameter id="dictionnary" value="oui;non"/>
                <parameter id="confidence" value="45"/>
                <output id="wordRecognized">
                    <value="oui" launch="confirmGame!"/>
                    <value="non" launch="noGame!"/>
                    <default launch="noGame!"/>
                </output>
            </behavior>
        </agent>
        .
        .
        <context id="await">
            <agent id="speechAwait"/>
            <agent id="peopleDetection"/>
        </context>
        .
        .
        <contextGraph>
            <clock id="Y"/>
            <global_variable id="nbPlayer" type="integer" value="0"/>
            <context id="await" init="true">
                <successor id="await" synchronization="errorDetection?" timeMin="" timeMax="" update=""/>
                <successor id="explain" synchronization="detectUser?" timeMin="" timeMax="" update=""/>
            </context>
            .
            .
        </contextGraph>
    </implementation_layer>
</specification>
```

The module 673 corresponding to the speech module is associated with the behavior «say» . The content number 9 will be uttered by the Nao robot in French at a speed of 90%.

Association of the gesture with the id 247 in database with the behavior «animate»

Output of the speech recognition module. Two answers are expected "oui" or "non". A specific signal is then sent for each case.

Fig. 7. Scenario specification in XML format

serious game embedded in the robot. In the declarative layer, we defined two behaviors, including "say" and "animate". Our scenario contains several phases in which the robot had to make a speech while being animated. We combined these two behaviors in an "animatedSay" pattern. This pattern can be reused as many times as necessary in the implementation layer.

For example, we wanted to define a "speechAwait" agent who would be responsible for attracting visitors. This agent would implement the previously defined "animatedSay" pattern. When defining the agent, the designer would perform a specification of the "say" and "animate" behaviors.

Thus, according to Fig. 7, the module with ID number 673 in the database is associated with the "say" behavior and corresponds to the speech module programmed in Nao. With this behavior, we associated the content with ID number 9, which represents the speech uttered by the robot. Speed speech and language parameters had to be entered.

The interactive experience thus scripted was modeled by timed automata. We then obtained a supervisory file, as the input of our supervision tool.

4.3   Dynamic Supervision

This section introduces the dynamic supervision of the interactive experience. Since the interactive experience has been modeled, our supervision tool was responsible for running the experience and invoking it remotely in the Nao robot. The aim of our platform was to dissociate the modeling and the supervision of the activity. It was then possible to use the same model to control different processes, provided one develops a specific client for each process. A sequence diagram of the supervision is detailled in Fig. 8.

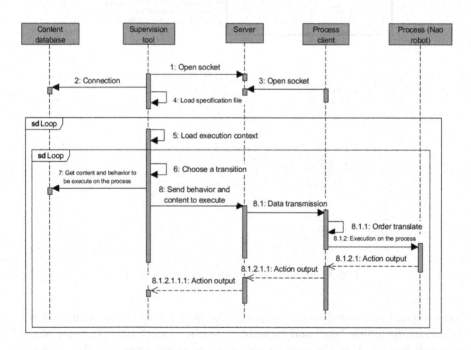

Fig. 8. Supervision sequence diagram

This supervision tool uses the specification file previously generated as an input and loads the defined context graph (Fig. 9). The transition from one

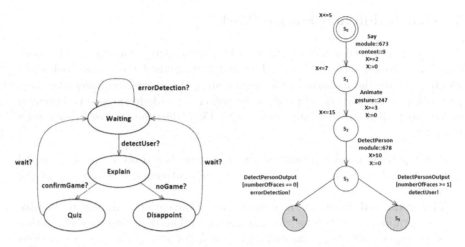

Fig. 9. Context graph of the serious game

Fig. 10. Context "Waiting" modeled by time automaton

context to another is completed by receiving signals (e.g. errorDetection, wait, detectUser, noGame and confirmGame) from a source context. The transition can also be done via global variables to which we can apply guards and updates, like an automaton. Thus, we define four contexts:

- **Waiting:** The robot goes into the rest position and waits until it detects the presence of a visitor. If a detection problem occurs, the context re-executes with the signal *errorDetection*. Otherwise, the supervision tool changes to the *Explain* context;
- **Explain:** At this step, the serious game is presented and the robot asks the visitor if they want to play;
- **Disappoint:** The visitor left or does not want to play. Nao expresses disappointment;
- **Quiz:** Here, the robot utilizes a facial recognition to determine if it knows the player. If Nao knows the individual, the robot waits for the answer to the question previously asked; otherwise, Nao learns the player's face and ask them a question.

Each context is defined as a timed automaton, and each transition resembles a command to be executed on the process. An example of the context "Waiting" is shown in Fig. 10.

This serious game is executed on the Nao robot. We use the Python SDK provided by Softbank Robotics to control the robot through a client developed for this purpose. Each controlled process must possess its own client in order to interpret the data received from the server. The client links the supervision tool and the controlled process. Nao receives orders from the supervision tool and translates them into a language that is understandable by the robot.

5   Conclusion and Future Work

This paper presented a supervision model for interactive experiences. The modeling was divided into two steps. The first step defined the atomic behaviors grouped within the pattern. In the second step, the agents implementing these patterns were created; they specified the contents and behaviors to be executed on the controlled process (the Nao robot). Our contribution lies in two main points:

- **A simplified construction of the scenario** based on a two-layer model that helped with the modularity, reuse and automatic construction of the entities;
- **The external content management.** Conventional design tools (like Choregraphe) do not allow this management. The modeling and adaptation of an experiment from one museum to another would have been laborious tasks. Thanks to our approach, the contents were managed externally. Our supervision tool was then in charge of recovering the contents in the database to control the process.

With the exception of the editor for designing the supervision's input file (which was thus designed manually), which is under development, all of these features were implemented. To test this approach, we modeled a simple serious game with the Nao robot. The validation of our model allows us today to consider the design of a more complex game. In the long run, we aim to combine this top-down approach with a bottom up approach [12,25] in order to integrate a relevance loop. Thus, due to the observations made during the execution of the activity and the machine learning process, we aim to be able to modify the *a priori* model by adding or removing behaviors. The machine learning process will allow the experience to be adaptated to the actual behavior of the end user, which is nearly impossible to predict during the design. Finally, we want to extend our model to the management of the locations where the different contexts of the scenario are executed; this outreach will allow us to take advantage of the visitors' real-time geolocation thanks to the e-beacon technology. It will also be possible to choose the dialogues and behaviors of the robot according to the observed displacements of the visitor.

References

1. Araújo, M., Roque, L.: Modeling Games with Petri Nets. Digital Games Research Association (DiGRA) (2009)
2. Aspord, E., Becker, J., Grangier, E.: Link human/robot. Van Dieren (eds.) (2014)
3. Boom, D.V.: Pepper the humanoid robot debuts in France (2015). https://www.cnet.com/news/pepper-the-popular-humanoid-robot-debuts-in-france/
4. Boucenna, S., Gaussier, P., Andry, P., Hafemeister, L.: A robot learns the facial expressions recognition and face/non-face discrimination through an imitation game. Int. J. Soc. Robot. **6**(4), 633–652 (2014)

5. Carrozzino, M., Bergamasco, M.: Beyond virtual museums: experiencing immersive virtual reality in real museums. J. Cult. Heritage **11**(4), 452–458 (2010)
6. Champagnat, R., Estraillier, P., Prigent, A.: Adaptative execution of game: unfolding a correct story. In: Proceedings of the 2006 ACM SIGCHI International Conference on Advances in Computer Entertainment Technology, ACE 2006. ACM, New York (2006). https://doi.org/10.1145/1178823.1178941
7. Coenen, T., Mostmans, L., Naessens, K.: Museus: case study of a pervasive cultural heritage serious game. J. Comput. Cult. Herit. **6**(2), 8:1–8:19 (2013)
8. De Virgilio, R.: AML: a modeling language for designing adaptive web applications. Pers. Ubiquitous Comput. **16**(5), 527–541 (2012)
9. Dietze, D.: Playing and Learning in Early Childhood Education. Wadsworth Publishing Company, Belmont (2011)
10. Henaff, P.: Entre art et science: Guido, un robot guide espiègle au musée d'art moderne de luxembourg. session vidéo, Journées Nationales de la Recherche en Robotique (JNRR) (2015)
11. Khlat, M.: Norio, the robot guide of the oiron castle (2014). http://www.tourmag.com/Norio-the-robot-guide-of-the-Oiron-Castle_a71190.html
12. Kop, R., Toubman, A., Hoogendoorn, M., Roessingh, J.J.: Evolutionary dynamic scripting: adaptation of expert rule bases for serious games. In: Ali, M., Kwon, Y.S., Lee, C.-H., Kim, J., Kim, Y. (eds.) IEA/AIE 2015. LNCS (LNAI), vol. 9101, pp. 53–62. Springer, Cham (2015). https://doi.org/10.1007/978-3-319-19066-2_6
13. Lapeyre, M., Rouanet, P., Oudeyer, P.Y.: Poppy: a new bio-inspired humanoid robot platform for biped locomotion and physical human-robot interaction. In: Proceedings of the 6th International Symposium on Adaptive Motion in Animals and Machines (AMAM), Darmstadt, Germany, March 2013
14. Liapis, A., Martínez, H.P., Togelius, J., Yannakakis, G.N.: Adaptive game level creation through rank-based interactive evolution, pp. 1–8, August 2013
15. Louchart, Y., Aylett, R.: Emergent narrative, requirements and high-level architecture, p. 308 (2004)
16. Magerko, B.: Building an interactive drama architecture (2003)
17. Miyashita, T., Meier, P., Tachikawa, T., Orlic, S., Eble, T., Scholz, V., Gapel, A., Gerl, O., Arnaudov, S., Lieberknecht, S.: An augmented reality museum guide. In: Proceedings of the 7th IEEE/ACM International Symposium on Mixed and Augmented Reality, pp. 103–106. ISMAR 2008. IEEE Computer Society, Washington (2008)
18. Natkin, S., Vega, L.: A Petri Net model for the analysis of the ordering of actions in computer games. In: GAME ON 2003, France, January 2003, London, October 2003
19. Prnewswire: Lowe's introduces lowebot - the next generation robot to enhance the home improvement shopping experience in the bay area (2016). www.prnewswire.com/news-releases/lowes-introduces-lowebot--the-next-generation-robot-to-enhance-the-home-improvement-shopping-experience-in-the-bay-area-300319497.html
20. Reisig, W.: A Primer in Petri Net Design. Springer Compass International. Springer, Heidelberg (2011)
21. Rempulski, N.: Synthèse dynamique de superviseur pour l'exécution adaptative d'applications interactives. Ph.D. thesis, Université de La Rochelle (2013)
22. Rempulski, N., Prigent, A., Courboulay, V., Perreira Da Silva, M., Estraillier, P.: Adaptive storytelling based on model-checking approaches. Int. J. Intel. Game. Simul. (IJIGS) **5**(2), 33–42 (2009)

23. Reuters: Humanoid robot starts work at Japanese department store. http://www.reuters.com/article/us-japan-robot-store-idUSKBN0NB1OZ20150420
24. Samuelsson, I.P., Fleer, M.: Play and Learning in Early Childhood Settings: International Perspectives. Springer, Dordrecht, London (2008)
25. Spronck, P., Ponsen, M., Postma, I.S.k.E.: Adaptive game AI with dynamic scripting, pp. 217–248 (2006)
26. Wang, C., Wang, D.Z., Lin, J.L.: ADAM: an adaptive multimedia content description mechanism and its application in web-based learning. Exp. Syst. Appl. **37**(12), 8639–8649 (2010)

Hugvie as a Therapeutic Agent in the Improvement of Interaction Skills in Children with Developmental Disabilities: An Exploratory Study

Diana Leonor Garcês Costa[1], Yoram Chisik[2(✉)], and Ana Lucia dos Santos Faria[2]

[1] Achada Fisioclinic, Funchal, Portugal
[2] Madeira Interactive Technologies Institute (M-ITI), Funchal, Portugal
ychisik@gmail.com

Abstract. In this exploratory study we examined the use of a Hugvie, a "huggable" pillow with an expressionless vague human form as a means of engaging and maintaining the attention of 8 children between the ages of 2 to 8 years old with a history of communication and language developmental delay and difficulties with social interaction as part of ongoing communication and speech therapy treatment in a speech pathology clinic. Results from 40 individual sessions indicate Hugvie to be an effective means of drawing and engaging the attention of the children and in facilitating the goals and objectives of the treatment plan when compared with conventional therapy aids such as toys and digital applications. The study validates previous observations related to robotic interfaces with minimalistic facial expression and sets a path for further inquiry into tangible speech therapy aids.

Keywords: Assistive technologies · Children · Complex communication needs
Multisensory interaction

1 Introduction

The ability to effectively communicate with others is an essential need for the well-being of an individual and a core element of human social interaction. Most children naturally acquire the communication and language skills common within their cultural and linguistic context in a seemingly effortless manner [19]. However, children clinically diagnosed with a developmental disorder such as autism spectrum disorder (ASD), attention deficit disorder or hyperactivity disorder experience difficulties in communication, language acquisition and in effectively expressing themselves and interacting with others [2].

In order to address the complex communication needs of children with developmental disorders, a speech and language pathologist (SLP) or speech therapist (as they are more commonly known), performs an evaluation of the communication abilities of the child. This generally involves an assessment of the child's language and communication skills (understanding language and expression, social interaction, attention and

© Springer International Publishing AG, part of Springer Nature 2018
A. D. Cheok et al. (Eds.): ACE 2017, LNCS 10714, pp. 117–127, 2018.
https://doi.org/10.1007/978-3-319-76270-8_9

listening). For younger children, these are typically carried out informally through play-based activities and formally through standardized tests. The assessment in combination with a report from the child parents is used to establish a functional diagnosis on the basis of which, health professionals and teachers responsible for the care and treatment of the child, define a treatment plan based on a selection and/or combination of evidence based approaches for developing communication competences.

Engaging and maintaining the attention of the child is a critical challenge in pediatric speech therapy due to the competing demands on children in therapy settings, namely, being in an unfamiliar setting with an unfamiliar adult, the language and cognitive demands of the activities, alongside the child's attention span difficulties associated with their developmental disorder. To address this challenge, play-based therapy approaches, such as the Developmental Individualized Relationship (DIR) model/Floortime, have been developed and have been shown to be effective, in improving functional developmental levels and communication skills in children with autism and other developmental disorders in a number of recent studies [4, 5, 15, 17]. The approach essentially seeks to engage the child at his own level, following the lead of the child in finding an object and/or an activity that captivates the child's attention and then, building an interaction around that object/activity. For instance, if the child is playing with a car, the therapist will join in the activity and add a functional meaning to it, such as a language construct, to engage the child in an activity that furthers the goals of the treatment.

The capacity of robots to excite and draw the curiosity of children and their ability to embody certain aspects of human communication (speech, expression, body language) in a highly predictable way, as opposed to the often unpredictable behaviour exhibited by humans [3, 10, 16, 20], has led to a growing interest, within pediatric therapy, in the use of robots as therapeutic agents, not only to engage children and to improve imitation and repetition of movements [6], but also to engage and improve social skills [7, 8].

However, the role and use of robot-based intervention has divided opinions in the therapeutic community for a number of reasons:

- The majority of studies in the field are conducted in robotics labs where the emphasis is largely on the engineering aspects of the robot thus studies tend to focus only on specific parts of the therapy as opposed to a therapy session or a treatment plan.
- Most studies employ robots with a variety of facial, body and motion features but with a fixed position, which limits the interaction of the child with the robot to the interaction under study, limiting the ability of the child to lead the process.
- The capacity of robots to embody a range of facial expressions and body motions can be overwhelming to children with ASD although studies with robots with minimalistic facial expressions, such as KASPAR [12], or vague animalistic form, such as Auti [1], have begun to address this issue.

Overall, there is a lack of substantive clinical evidence based research to validate the efficacy of child-robot interaction within pediatric therapy, in general and speech therapy in particular, as opposed to specific therapy segments [7, 11]. The complex communication needs of children with developmental disorders require an individual treatment plan that is specifically devised based on a functional evaluation of his/her communication and fine-tuned by the therapist during the therapy sessions, based on the condition and mood of the child in each session.

In this exploratory study we aim to address these three issues by exploring the use of a Hugvie [13], a "huggable" pillow with an expressionless vague human form within the context of long term therapy, as opposed to individual lab experiments of children with developmental disorders and complex communication needs.

As suggested by previous studies [1, 12], we hypothesize that Hugvie's lack of a face and its vague, yet suggestive and highly tactile humanoid form would be an attractive medium to children with developmental disorders. Its simple form and tactile nature might reduce the complexity of the interaction and provide a low barrier entry point for the children, allowing them to explore Hugvie on their own terms and, in turn, guide the therapist through their interactions with Hugvie, thereby increasing the potential for complex interactions and, consequently, progress and success in the treatment program. This study aims to validate previous findings and build a foundation for a more comprehensive and long-term clinical study of the efficacy of Hugvie and similar agents in speech therapy.

2   The Study

Hugvie [13], developed by ATR Hiroshi Ishiguro Laboratory, is a pillow with a vague human form designed as a huggable presence agent. Hugvie, measures 75 cm in length and weighs 600 grams. It is filled with microbeads and thus is highly pliable but capable of returning to its original shape once it is released from a hug (or any form of squeezing). In addition, Hugvie contains pockets into which a cell phone and/or other electronics can be inserted, allowing people to interact with and experience the presence of others while hugging it. Studies conducted with Hugvie showed reduced stress levels in people talking with loved ones via a phone embedded in a Hugvie [18, 21] and showed potential in engaging children in storytelling activities involving a large group of children [14].

Hugvie thus provide a platform we can utilize in play-based therapy sessions, both as a physical artefact and as an electronic device, in order to test our hypothesis, explore the ways in which children react to and interact with a low complexity agent such as a Hugvie and gauge the nature of the interaction plus its potential as a therapeutic agent in speech language therapy.

3   Participants

For this study 8 children between the ages of 2 to 8 years old were drawn from the clinical practice of the first author in <removed for blind review> after approval by the parents and the board of the clinic. The children were selected to participate in this study on the basis of their age and interaction skills. All the participants have a history of communication and language developmental delay, have difficulties with social interaction and have been undergoing treatment at the clinic for at least 1 month and thus are familiar with the facility and the therapist, as noted below:

C1: Male, 2 years old, diagnosed with developmental delay. Non-verbal with low interaction skills, communicates by pointing and eye gaze. Been in therapy for 6 months.

C2: Male, 3 years old, diagnosed with Autism. Non-verbal, low interaction with others and activities, mainly communicates via tantrums. Been in therapy for 6 months.

C3: Male, 3 years old, diagnosed with Autism. Non-verbal, communicates by gestures, low interaction and low joint attention. Been in therapy for 1 month.

C4: Female, 4 years old, diagnosed with a specific language impairment. Verbal, low collaboration, low attention in activities. Been in therapy for 1 year.

C5: Male, 5 years old, diagnosed with a specific language impairment. Verbal, low collaboration, low attention in activities. Been in therapy for 1 year.

C6: Male, 5 years old, diagnosed with a specific language impairment. Verbal, low collaboration, low attention in activities. Been in therapy for 1 year.

C7: Female, 8 years old, diagnosed with a specific language impairment and attention deficit disorder. Verbal, low collaboration in activities. Been in therapy for 9 months.

C8: Male, 8 years old, with a specific language impairment and attention deficit disorder. Verbal, low collaboration in activities. Been in therapy for 9 months.

4 Methodology

The children engaged with Hugvie in particular play scenarios that were incorporated into five 45-min therapy sessions, developed according to the specific therapeutic goals for each child and conducted in a familiar therapy room in the clinic. All 40 therapy sessions were conducted over a 16-week period between September and December 2016, in accordance with the planned therapy schedule of each child.

Hugvie was incorporated into the therapy sessions in one of three forms aimed at exploring three initial research questions:

4.1 RQ1: How Would the Children Respond to Hugvie?

In each therapy session, a wide range of toys is available to the children with the child leading the way in choosing a toy and/or activity to engage in. In the first two sessions Hugvie was introduced as a play partner to gauge the children initial reaction to it (Fig. 1).

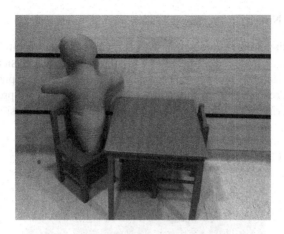

Fig. 1. Hugvie set in the play-therapy area

4.2   How Would Children Respond to Technology Embedded in Hugvie?

Listening and responding is a critical element of speech and communication processes and thus we wanted to see if the children would respond and interact with Hugvie if it spoke. For this we inserted an iPhone equipped with the *Grid Player* application [9] into Hugvie. When presented with Hugvie the children were asked whether they would like to engage in a meal time role-play, blowing bubbles or spinning a wheel, as illustrated in Fig. 2. During play the therapist remotely triggered the voice output option of *Grid Player* to utter the Portuguese expressions "Mais" (more) or "Outra vez" (do it again), using a synthesized female voice, to see if the child would respond to the request by repeating the action. Hugvie was presented this way during the third and fourth sessions.

Fig. 2. Hugvie with an embedded iPhone during a blowing bubbles activity

4.3   Is It just a Novelty Effect?

To see whether the children interaction with Hugvie is just the result of its novelty in the 5th session we introduced a frog pillow of similar size and physical properties to Hugvie but with a slightly more complex appearance as an additional play partner to see whether the children opt to go with the novelty of the frog or would prefer to continue to play with Hugvie with whom they have played over the past 4 sessions (Fig. 3).

Fig. 3. The frog

Due to privacy concerns the sessions were not videotaped. However, detailed observational notes were taken by the conducting therapist following the end of each session.

5   Observational Notes

Due to the lack of video footage, detailed coding of the children interaction with Hugvie was not possible. Therefore, only a qualitative description of the children behaviour during the therapy sessions is provided at this point.

C1: During the first session, the child was curious but hesitant, he looked at Hugvie and then at the therapist at first gesturing at Hugvie but not making any sounds and later exploring Hugvie by touching and moving him around. In the second session Hugvie was directly used by the therapist as part of cause and effect exercises with the child maintaining attention and engagement throughout the session through his interaction with Hugvie. During the 3rd and 4th sessions the child was surprised by the fact Hugvie was able to talk, at first searching for the source of the sound and later engaging with Hugvie in the bubble making activity, effectively taking turns and waiting for Hugvie to ask for more bubbles. When introduced to the frog, the child appeared confused by the choice and turned around to play by himself leaving both Hugvie and the frog behind.

C2: During the first session the child regarded Hugvie with suspicion but after encouragement by the therapist he started exploring Hugvie through touch and later engaged in role play with Hugvie. C2 is prone to tanturms during the sessions but Hugvie had a calming effect for the child as he physically sought Hugvie and calmed down after hugging him. During the 3rd and 4th sessions the child was surprised by the fact Hugvie was able to talk and not only sought the source of the sound but wanted to physically remove the iPhone from Hugvie as he perceived it as a foreign object. During the bubble making activity he responded quickly to the words uttered by Hugvie but looked at the therapist for feedback as though he knew the sounds were not uttered by Hugvie himself but as a result of action by the therapist however he was able to maintain his attention throughout the activity in all sessions. When he was asked, at the 5th session, to choose between Hugvie and the frog, C2 looked at Hugvie, smiled and jumped to it.

C3: During the first session C3 was very curious about Hugvie exploring him by touch and smell and then proceeding to give him a very strong hug. During the second session, the curiosity was gone but he engaged in role playing with Hugvie while speaking to him. During the 3rd and 4th sessions the child was surprised by the fact Hugvie was able to talk, at first searching for the source of the sound and later engaging with Hugvie in the bubble making activity. During the 5th session C3 explored both the frog and Hugvie and then chose Hugvie as a playmate.

C4: During the first session C4 was very happy to see Hugvie, she smiled, touched Hugvie and asked if she could play with it. In both the first and second sessions she interacted with Hugvie through role play and persisted in the activity far longer than she does with other activities. At the end of both sessions she addressed Hugvie as a person and said goodbye to him. During the 3rd and 4th sessions C4 was somewhat shocked by the fact that Hugvie spoke had difficulty in understanding the synthesized voice used by the *Grid Player* application and repeatedly asked Hugvie "What are you saying?" and then started to respond with the action request by Hugvie, she continued to pay attention and completed the entire activity. In session 5 when presented with the frog C4 looked at the frog then at Hugvie and decided to hug Hugvie and then proceeded to play with him instead of the frog.

C5: During the first session C5 was unenthusiastic when he saw Hugvie for the first time. He cried and had a tantrum but after a while looked at Hugvie and asked what was it. When told it's a playmate he started to explore Hugvie by touching it and after encouragement from the therapist started to play with it. There were no issues during the second session and C5 interacted with Hugvie using role play. During the 3rd and 4th sessions C5 was surprise by the sound emanating from Hugvie he proceeded to find the Iphone inserted into Hugvie and refused to interact with Hugvie in anyway during both sessions. However, when presented with the frog during the 5th session, C5 not only chose Hugvie over the frog, she looked at the frog with a very displeased expression.

C6: During both the first sessions C6 was very enthusiastic when he saw Hugvie, he asked many questions about hugvie, expressed a high level of interest both through speech and physical interaction than he usually does for other activities and maintained a higher level of attention than usual. During the 3rd and 4th sessions C6 asked why Hugvie was talking. Encouraged by the therapist, he listened to Hugvie and was able to complete the tasks and maintain attention in the activities. When presented with the frog during the 5th session, C6 asked what it was and when asked to choose between Hugvie and the frog, he chose Hugvie and saying specifically that he was going to choose his friend "abraços" (hugs).

C7: When C7 saw Hugvie for the first time she was uninterested and specifically asked whether she had to play with him. After encouragement from the therapist she started to play with Hugvie and described him has a very nice partner, easy to hug. She later said she was sad because he had no legs. In both of the initial sessions she paid higher attention to the activities and was more communicative than normal. During the 3rd and 4th sessions C7 found the ability of Hugvie to make sounds both curious and distracting as she had difficulty in understanding the synthesized voice used by the *Grid Player* application and therefore asked "what did he say?" after each time Hugvie spoke. Despite that during the role play activities she waited quietly for Hugvie command and then performed the task that Hugvie was asking. She was very collaborative in the two sessions. When presented with the frog C7 looked at him and said he was ugly then looked at Hugvie told the therapist she wanted to play with him and gave him a hug

C8: During the first session C8 was very curious about Hugvie and asked many questions about what Hugvie can do and what he was going to do with it. In both of the first sessions his level of collaboration and attention were much higher than usual. Although C8 is usually very cooperative he also has great difficulty in maintaining attention on a specific task, however during all of the sessions he was able to maintain his attention till the end of the activity listening and responding to the requests made by Hugvie. When he felt tired during some of the sessions he asked the therapist if he could lie on the floor and rest with Hugvie. When presented with the frog C8 observed both, looked at one and then the other, then looked at the therapist and chose Hugvie, smiling.

6   Discussion

The primary aim of this initial study was to explore whether Hugvie could be effective in attracting and engaging the attention of the children in related therapy activities, and whether its lack of expression and tangible vaguely human form would be an advantage or a hindrance in the therapy process.

The observational results of the study confirm that Hugvie was a highly effective agent in facilitating the session, not only in its ability to draw and engage attention but also in its ability to help the children calm down and maintain their own sense of direction and control when they were overwhelmed or tired. The children extensively explored and interacted with Hugvie using all their senses, they touched, moved around, hugged and smelled Hugvie in addition to talking and listening to him. C2 specifically sought out Hugvie during a tantrum in one of the sessions and calmed down after hugging Hugvie and C8 asked whether he could sleep with Hugvie after feeling tired following a session. The children with verbal communication abilities referred to Hugvie using terms of affection such as "abraços" (hugs) and "amiguinho" (little friend), which they came up with by themselves. C4 made sure she said good-bye to Hugvie when she left a session, suggesting they treated him with a degree of affection and attachment.

Compared with the traditional aids used in standard therapy sessions in the clinic, which range from physical toys to computer games and programs, Hugvie demonstrated to be particularly effective in, not only gaining the attention of the children and promoting interaction, but also for maintaining their engagement with specific therapeutic tasks, such as joint attention and turn taking, throughout the sessions. Although we did not take precise time measurements during this exploratory study, there was a distinct and noticeable improvement in the level of attention, interaction and perseverance with an activity with all the children during their interaction with Hugvie.

Therapists working in clinical practice need to address a wide gamut of communication and social interaction conditions in relation to the specific diagnosis of each child. In addition, each therapy session tends to be quite intense, both for the child and the therapist, as the difficulty experienced by the therapist in trying to engage the child in an activity may be just as great as the difficulty experienced by the child in maintaining that engagement. Hugvie seems to be an effective mediator between the child and the therapist both in its physical form and with the addition of electronics providing an effective conduit for the therapy and related activities. This is particularly evident with C5 and C6 two children of the same age and similar diagnosis but with different manifestations in therapy and in their initial reaction to Hugvie.

As speech therapy interventions for young children tend to be play-based, the fact that children were beginning to incorporate Hugvie into different kinds of play activities, e.g. exploratory play: touching, smelling, squeezing (C1, C2, C3, C4, C5); functional play whereby children requested bubbles or cuddles (C1, C2, C3, C8); and make-believe play sequences (C3, C4, C5, C6, C7) is promising and shows potential for providing opportunities for imaginative play and extending role play so that children can experience different social interactions as they work on their communication and language goals.

7   Future Work

This study shows that Hugvie holds great promise as a therapeutic agent in speech therapy as it provides an Opportunity for multisensory learning that capitalises on its touch, vibration and sound properties which in turn allow for increased levels of engagement and concentration by the children. In future work, we intend to further explore Hugvie's potential as a therapeutic tool by:

- Exploring the dynamics that exist between the child and the therapist, the ways in which Hugvie alters this dynamic and they ways in which we can use Hugvie as a scaffolding mechanism during therapy sessions and beyond.
- Extending play contexts whilst mapping out the skills that are being worked on, e.g. turning taking, attention and listening, initiating communication, receptive language skills etc.
- Exploring the ways in which we can increase the motivation of the child through personalization, e.g. incorporating favourite songs, familiar stories/voices so that rewards are embedded in the therapeutic activity.
- Exploring the potential for embedding a wider range of electronics to further potentials for interaction, mediation and play.
- Exploring the potential for long-term interaction between a child and a Hugvie. As the overall treatment plan encompasses activities at the clinic and activities at home and/or other care environments, Hugvie can act as both a companion to the child

providing a source of relief and encouragement and as a therapeutic or communication agent to the therapist or care giver.

- Building on the long-term interaction point by exploring the ways in which the activities involving Hugvie can be stepped up/stepped down in complexity throughout the course of the intervention. E.g. gradually increasing language complexity 'spoken' by Hugvie in make-believe play sequences.
- Exploring generalisability, will the children use the skills acquired during their interaction with Hugvie in every day communication?
- Explore the ethical considerations of giving robots human-like qualities, e.g. the use of familiar voices and the implications of blurring the boundaries between the real and the virtual and of using partial humanoid forms for children with learning difficulties.

Acknowledgments. The authors would like to thank Hiroshi Ishiguro and Hidenobu Sumioka of ATR Hiroshi Ishiguro Laboratories for providing the Hugvie and for their support and encouragement. In addition the authors would like to extend their thanks to Seray Ibrahim of the UCL Institute of Education and to the anonymous reviewers for their helpful comments and suggestions during the writing of this paper.

References

1. Andreae, H.E., Andreae, P.M., Low, J., Brown, D.: A study of auti: a socially assistive robotic toy. In: Proceedings of the 2014 Conference on Interaction Design and Children (IDC 2014), NY, USA, pp. 245–248. ACM, New York (2014)
2. Beukelman, D., Mirenda, P.: Augmentative and Alternative Communication: Supporting Children and Adults with Complex Communication Needs, 4th edn. Paul H. Brookes, Baltimore (2013)
3. Cabibihan, J.-J., Javed, H., Ang, M., Aljunied, S.M.: Why robots? a survey on the roles and benefits of social robots in the therapy of children with autism. Int. J. Soc. Robot. 5(4), 593–618 (2013)
4. Casenhiser, D.M., Binns, A., McGill, F., Morderer, O., Shanker, S.G.: Measuring and supporting language function for children with autism: evidence from a randomized control trial of a social-interaction-based therapy. J. Autism Dev. Disord. 45(3), 846–857 (2015)
5. Casenhiser, D.M., Shanker, S., Stieben, J.: Learning through interaction in children with autism: preliminary data from a social-communication-based intervention. Autism 17(2), 220–241 (2011)
6. Colton, M.B., Ricks, D.J., Goodrich, M.A., Dariush, B., Fujimura, K., Fujiki, M.: Toward therapist-in-the-loop assistive robotics for children with autism and specific language impairment. In: 2009 AISB New Frontiers in Human-Robot Interaction Symposium, vol. 24, p. 25 (2009)
7. Diehl, J.J., Schmitt, L.M., Villano, M., Crowell, C.R.: The clinical use of robots for individuals with autism spectrum disorders: a critical review. Res. Autism Spectr. Disord. 6(1), 249–262 (2012)
8. Giullian, N., Ricks, D., Atherton, A., Colton, M., Goodrich, M., Brinton, B.: Detailed requirements for robots in autism therapy. In: 2010 IEEE International Conference on Systems Man and Cybernetics (SMC 2010), pp. 2595–2602 (2010)

9. Grid Player. produced by Smartbox Assistive Technology Ltd. https://thinksmartbox.com/product/grid-player/
10. Howard, A.: Robots learn to play: robots emerging role in pediatric therapy. In: Proceedings of the Twenty-Sixth International Florida Artificial Intelligence Research Society Conference, pp. 3–8 (2013)
11. Huijnen, C.A.G.J., Lexis, M.A.S., Jansens, R., de Witte, L.P.: Mapping robots to therapy and educational objectives for children with autism spectrum disorder. J. Autism Dev. Disord. **46**, 2100–2114 (2016)
12. KASPAR. http://www.herts.ac.uk/kaspar/the-social-robot. Accessed 1 Feb 2017
13. Kuwamura, K., Sakai, K., Minato, T., Nishio, S., Ishiguro, H.: Hugvie: communication device for encouraging good relationship through the act of hugging. Lovotics **1**(1), 10000104 (2014)
14. Nakanishi, J., Sumioka, H., Ishiguro, H.: Impact of Mediated Intimate Interaction on Education: A Huggable Communication Medium that Encourages Listening. Front. Psychol. **7**(510), 1–10 (2016)
15. Pajareya, K., Nopmaneejumruslers, K.: A pilot randomized controlled trial of DIR/Floortime™ parent training intervention for pre-school children with autistic spectrum disorders. Autism **15**(5), 563–577 (2011)
16. Ricks, D.J., Colton, M.B.: Trends and considerations in robot-assisted autism therapy. In Proceedings of the 2010 IEEE International Conference on Robotics and Automation (ICRA 2010), pp. 4354–4359. IEEE (2010)
17. Solomon, R., Van Egeren, L., Mahoney, G., Quon Huber, M., Zimmerman, P.: PLAY project home consultation intervention program for young children with autism spectrum disorders: a randomized controlled trial. J. Dev. Behav. Pediatr. **35**(8), 475–485 (2014)
18. Sumioka, H., Nakae, A., Kanai, R., Ishiguro, H.: Huggable communication medium decreases cortisol levels. Sci. Rep. **3**, 3034 (2013)
19. Tomasello, M.: Origins of Human Communication. MIT press, Cambridge (2010)
20. Valadão, C.T., Goulart, C., Rivera, H., Caldeira, E.: Bastos Filho, T.F., Frizera-Neto, A., Carelli, R.: Analysis of the use of a robot to improve social skills in children with autism spectrum disorder. Res. Biomed. Eng. **32**(2), 161–175 (2016)
21. Yamazaki, R., Christensen, L., Skov, K., Chang, C.-C., Damholdt, M.F., Sumioka, H., Nishio, S., Ishiguro, H.: Intimacy in phone conversations: anxiety reduction for danish seniors with hugvie. Front. Psychol. **7**, 537 (2016)

A Week Without Plastic Bags: Creating Games and Interactive Products for Environmental Awareness

Anna Gardeli, Spyros Vosinakis, Konstantinos Englezos, Dimitra Mavroudi, Manolis Stratis, and Modestos Stavrakis

Department of Product and Systems Design Engineering,
University of the Aegean, Syros, Greece
{agardeli,spyrosv,modestos}@aegean.gr

Abstract. Interactive technologies and digital games can be valuable tools in raising awareness and persuading people to adopt more environmental friendly behaviour. Appropriate methods and paradigms for designing such systems and successfully blending the 'fun' element with the messages to be communicated are still under research. In this paper, we investigate the benefits and drawbacks of using games and playful interactive technologies for influencing people's behaviour towards the environment, through a series projects developed and publicly presented during a campaign for reducing the use of plastic bags. We present the design process and methodology adopted, the resulting projects, and a number of observations and preliminary results based on their public use.

Keywords: Persuasive technologies · Games · User motivation
User engagement · Environmental sustainability · Pro-environmental behavior

1 Introduction

Interactive technologies and gamification are rapidly growing research topics that have the potential to inform, educate and change people's behavior about environmental problems related to ecological sustainability [1, 2]. Interacting through persuasive technologies and ecologically-focused gamification transposes game mechanics and game design techniques to involve and motivate people to act, while at the same time disseminate essential information about human intervention to nature. The value and effectiveness of interactive technologies and games in education and sensitization about environmental/ecological problems has been shown through numerous scientific studies [3, 4].

An important aspect of this research area is the incorporation of appropriate motivational and playful elements in the design of interactive systems to attract and retain users' interest, whilst achieving their educational or persuasive goals. Despite the recent emergence of generic methodologies and guidelines for designing persuasive systems [5, 6], the successful selection and combination of design elements and technologies that lead to the expected awareness or behavior change, is still an open issue. There is

© Springer International Publishing AG, part of Springer Nature 2018
A. D. Cheok et al. (Eds.): ACE 2017, LNCS 10714, pp. 128–138, 2018.
https://doi.org/10.1007/978-3-319-76270-8_10

a growing need for further paradigms and use cases in a variety of areas that will eventually provide rich feedback on various design choices with respect to the target group and the desired outcomes.

Our research is along this line. We focus on design approaches for pre-environmental behavior through physical play and motivation within a social context and by using interactive technologies and computer games. In this paper, we present the development and an initial evaluation of a number of games and interactive systems that were publicly displayed in an information and awareness campaign for the reduction of plastic bags in the marine environment (LIFE14GIE/GR/001127). Selected student groups from two courses, in collaboration with their tutors, developed and tested eight different games and interactive installations that aimed to promote the campaign's goals in informing and educating people about the environmental problem through play and interaction. To achieve these primary goals, the games/interactive installations focused to attract people's attention, instill interest, engage them in understanding the problem with plastic bags and the environment and motivate them to participate in activities that promote ecological sustainability. In addition, the interactive installations motivated users to actual recycling through play.

2   Related Work

Over the last years, numerous studies and projects have applied persuasive technologies, motivational elements and playfulness in a wide variety of domains such as health and fitness, safety, environmental sustainability and more [7]. As being described by Fogg [8], persuasion is "an attempt to shape, reinforce, or change behaviors, feelings, or thoughts about an issue, object, or action". Persuasive technologies and gamification are motivational systems that rely on the assumption that technology can influence human behavior and habits. Designing for persuasion - or change - must be on purpose of "guiding the user towards an attitude or behavior change" [9] while at the same time keeps him/her motivated and engaged with the task/activity at hand.

Digital or hybrid games have grown to be a strong educational and persuasive tool, given their entertaining and motivating nature. Games intended for social and behavioral change are called games for change, and they mainly aim "to promote reflection and positive behavior changes in players in the physical world, through characteristics that persuade players to consider the social or political issue presented in the game" [10]. Instead of words, images or moving picture, games use their rule-based approach and interactions to persuade players. That rhetoric technique, called procedural rhetoric, is based on the abstraction of physical world systems in the game and it is directly linked to the game elements, mechanics and gameplay [6].

Numerous studies (e.g. [11, 12]) also suggest that interactive installations combining a digital interface with physical activity present strong indicators of producing positive behavior change results, especially when combined with entertaining elements. A typical example is the "playful toothbrush" system [13], an interactive game with motivational and educational purposes. With a vision-based motion tracker the system makes a game out of the activity of brushing one's teeth, where the user brushes the teeth of a 'virtual self' through physical interaction. Another example which focuses on pro-environmental behavior is "Gaia", a multiplayer mobile augmented reality game combined with a public installation that helps users learn about waste management and recycling in a fun way. Users walk in the city to collect virtual objects through their mobile interface and bring them to the recycle bins, whilst learning facts and tips about recycling.

Some approaches additionally provide a form of feedback to users concerning the effects of their actions to help them reflect and improve their future behavior. For example, UBIGreen investigates a mobile tool for tracking and supporting green transportation habits [14]. A mobile phone-based application provides personal awareness about green transportation behaviors through iconic feedback. Small graphical rewards are earned by selecting pro-environmental means of transportation, and the user performance is also reflected in the phone's wallpaper. Another example is BinCam [12], a smart recycle bin that informs the users' social network about her recycling behavior by posting images of thrown-away items whenever the lid opens and closes. As such, it helps users reflect on their own and other people's waste-related habits.

Finally, several influential projects and approaches in developing interactive installations and games also emerged from 'The Fun Theory' campaign, an initiative that aimed in exploring people's environmental behavior and persuade them to change by allowing them to experience the fun side of acting responsibly [15]. It focused in exploring three aspects of human behaviour: environmental psychology, fun theory, operant conditioning. Among others, projects included a piano staircase for motivating people exercising by using traditional stairs instead of escalator, 'The World's Deepest Bin' for motivating the collection of garbage and placement in an interactive bin, and the 'Bottle Bank Arcade Machine' about recycling glass bottles and cans.

3   Design Process

'Week without plastic bags' was a campaign organized in the island of Syros as part of the LIFE DEBAG project, which included many different actions with informative and educative purposes, such as training seminar for primary and secondary education teachers, beach litter cleanup actions, etc. Its main objective is to inform about environmental issues related to the use of plastic bags and to persuade consumers to replace them with more environmental friendly solutions. The Department of Product & Systems Design Engineering of the University of the Aegean supported the project by implementing interactive technologies and games that promoted the campaign's messages as co-ordinated student projects in two different courses: computer games/edutainment and interaction design. The methodological framework used for developing the projects was based on the following phases: (1) preliminaries and introduction, (2) briefing, (3) research, (4) design, and (5) evaluation.

The first phase was initiated by a presentation and analysis of the main goals of the LIFE DEBAG project. Course tutors and the collaborating scientists from the project explained the main objectives and provided guidelines regarding the methods and techniques that should be used in the following phases. Preliminary activities also included project planning which involved team assembly, role assignments (coding, physical computing, visual & industrial design, interaction design, communication design and research) and the documentation of a project plan.

Following educational material that has already been taught during the lectures and tutorials of the two courses, students formed groups (3–4 students) and started briefing (phase 2) by defining goals, constraints and future design directions of the project. The main methodological tools that assisted in this phase was the eight-step design process for creating persuasive technologies [5] and the P.A.C.T. scoping technique [16] followed by a preliminary use of exploratory scenarios and early sketches [17, 18].

The methodological core for researching, designing and evaluating (phases 3–5) interactive installations and games was mainly based on design approaches in HCI and Interaction Design for games, digital product and service design [16, 19]. It encompassed a number of design goals focusing in dealing with product's behavior, visual and physical form, interaction, playability and digital interactive content. The research, design and evaluation processes that the students followed involved a multilayered set of techniques for (a) conducting research, (b) collecting data and (c) modeling raw information, (d) defining requirements, (e) laying out a basic design framework, (f) defining interactive content and mechanics (especially in the case of digital games), (g) designing prototypes (low & high fidelity) and (f) testing and evaluation.

The research perspective in this work was human-centered and followed a user-driven design research. The methodological tool for conducting research was based on the scoping technique of P.A.C.T. [16] and the first four steps from Fogg's design process [5], which provided the grounds for analyzing: People (receptive audience), Activities in terms of Actual and Target Behavior, and Inhibitors of Target Behavior, Context and the Technologies involved.

Students conducted interviews with stakeholders and other close collaborators from the LIFE DEBAG project campaign. They mainly focused in analyzing users, their behavior and everyday activities. Understanding pro-environmental behavior of people and their engagement with the ecological problem of plastic bags led to the analysis of the actual contexts where people mainly come in close contact with getting, using or disposing a plastic bag (e.g. supermarkets, shops, beaches and other coastal environments, and household). Moreover, contexts where people gather, have time to spend in learning and getting informed about environmental issues have also been identified. Analysis of potential technologies and experimentation on physical computing and games design techniques were the final stages of the research agenda. The main outcomes of the research can be summarized in Table 1.

Analyzing and modeling raw data by the use of personas was the core of developing models that explained what was observed. The last step in modeling information and towards the definition of requirements was done through the use of scenarios or stories about personas interacting with an anticipatory version of the future product.

The next phase involved the definition of the design framework where students focused on interaction and games design, physical computing, and visual and industrial design for the interactive installations. In the case of digital games, the students further focused on selecting and applying appropriate game world aesthetics, story and mechanics that balance well with the intended purpose and the messages to be communicated, using the popular Mechanics-Dynamics-Aesthetics (MDA) approach [20].

Table 1. People, activities, target behavior and inhibitors in four different contexts.

People	Activities	Target behavior	Inhibitor(s)	Context
Market customers	Use free plastic bags for carrying goods	Avoid plastic bags Use reusable cloth bags	Forget to carry cloth bags Prefer plastic bags for reuse Lack of motivation to avoid plastic bags	Super markets Shops Kiosks
Tourists Working personnel at beach or coastal areas, kids	Carry items in plastic packaging/bags Playing with plastic toys Relax Listen to music	Collect and recycle plastic waste Avoid carrying plastic bags and packaging Avoid leaving waste	Lose things at the beach Not motivated to collect and recycle plastics Not informed about environmental issues	Beaches Coastal areas
Adults relaxing and socializing Kids Tourists	Socializing Playing games Relaxing	Learn about environmental threats Collect plastic packaging and bags	Lack of time, no visible information spot	Public places, meeting points Cultural sights
Family	Doing household activities, playing games, relaxing	Avoid using plastic bags for packaging	Not informed about threats, not informed about alternatives, formed a strong habit	House

Finally, the design process concluded by designing low fidelity prototypes followed by more detailed designs of highly interactive games and installations. A series of (play)testing and refinement led to the final prototypes, which were publicly presented and tested during the LIFE DEBAG campaign.

4   Description of the Projects

In total, eight projects have been implemented, six interactive installations and two platform computer games. Five projects focused on informing and educating about collecting and recycling plastic waste of the coastal and marine environment while also promoted actual recycling through play. Two projects focused on the replacement of plastic bags by cloth bags principally in urban environments. One project focused on informing and providing awareness about the consequences of plastic bag use. Concerning the interaction techniques, the two computer games are presented through a visual/graphical interface, one of the installations uses a hybrid GUI and physical interaction, while the rest use physical and tangible interaction alone. Table 2 presents a summarized description of the projects and Fig. 1 shows selected screenshots and concept designs.

Table 2. The eight implemented projects with their aims and content, motivational factors and technology – user interface employed.

Name	Aim/content	Motivational factors	Technology/UI
Bag to the future	Replacement of plastic bags in everyday life	Rewards, points, progress, visual or audio feedback	Unity game engine
Finding bags	Consequences of the use of plastic bags	Rewards, points, progress, visual or audio feedback	Unity game engine
Arbino	Rewards for good behavior	Rewards, points	Arduino, NFC technology
Bagar	Rewards for good behavior, consequences of the use of plastic bags	Rewards, points, visual or audio feedback	Arduino, NFC technology, motion sensors, mobile app
DE - BAG	Replacement of plastic bags in everyday life	Rewards	Arduino, NFC technology
SEArch	Consequences of the use of plastic bags	Visual or audio feedback	Arduino, NFC technology
The JunkBox	Rewards for good behavior	Visual or audio feedback	Arduino, motion sensors

Fig. 1. Concept designs and screenshots from a selection of the implemented projects.

The two platform games have been developed on the Unity game development platform and both provided a desktop and a tablet version. The interactive installations have been developed using the physical computing platform Arduino, sensors, actuators, NFC/RFID technology, and other peripherals.

Bag to the future (digital game). The first game was built on two main content objectives: the replacement of plastic bags in everyday life and the awareness of the consequences of their use. Based on the fact that the negative effect on the environment of the use of plastic bags is not immediately visible, the future self of the young character appears to inform him about the situation in the future where the problem is most visible and unavoidable. As a mission, he/she has to collect all the plastic bags, with a device called "bag-exterminator", and replace them with fabric bags, baskets or different temporary storage means, friendlier to the environment. His/her purpose is to save the future by changing the behavior and habits of the grown-ups, who use plastic bags recklessly every day. His/her mission is secret, so the user is playing against time and noise.

Finding bags (digital game). The second game informs about the factors that contribute to the destruction of the underwater environment and the dangers that marine life is facing, that can either be trapped by a plastic bag or consume it. The main goal of the game is to clean the ocean by collecting plastic bags in an underwater environment and transfer them with safety to the vessel, where they will be recycled. A secondary goal is to save fishes and turtles if they are trapped by a plastic bag. There is not a winning situation you can collect as many bags and save as many fishes and turtles as you can. The game uses microsimulations to show the level of pollution. The game overs when your time is up or the pollution level is too high.

Bagar (interactive installation and game). Bagar is a hybrid installation and interactive ecosystem includes: an application that run on portable devices (tablet or smartphone), an interactive installation with physical prototype and infrastructure based on web technologies. The main functionality is based on the speed/judgment/reflex game logic where users try to place the waste at the correct position in the bin/system. The system personalizes users, records users' performance and rewards users with a LIFE DEBAG cloth bag considering their score. Users can see their ranking, the total number of plastic bags they have loaded into the bin and participate in a knowledge questionnaire, that addresses the topics that the project deals with.

Arbino (interactive installation and game). Based on the game genre of treasure hunting, the main goal of this project was the collection and placement of plastic bags in an interactive bin. The system identifies the number of the collected bags using proximity and presence sensors, and stores the actual score. Users, who collect a large number of bags, get rewarded by the system with a LIFE DEBAG cloth bag, automatically delivered by the corresponding mechanical output of the system.

JunkBox (interactive installation). JunkBox is an interactive recycle bin and music jukebox, that can be used in coastal environments where users (swimmers, beach visitors, tourists, kids etc.) have time to relax and entertain while can collectively participate in recycling. Users are prompted to collect plastic waste and place it in the interactive installation. In turn, the system identifies the number of items collected by its sensors, sums and stores the actual score for each user and provide reward by allowing to select and play songs from a database, like a real jukebox.

Grow and Throw (interactive installation). Throw & Grow is an interactive installation for watering plants and a recycle bin. The design of the system is based on volunteer action for preserving the environment. Through a personalized engagement with the process, users will be interested in adopting "their own plant" and gain personal emotional satisfaction through helping the environment. The bin identifies object delivery through its sensors and provides its user with the ability to water a plant locally or remotely to another installation, depending on user preference.

SEArch (interactive installation and game). SEArch is an interactive, physical game, based on a combination of a treasure hunt and Q&A type of games that has an informative purpose. The gaming process includes using a map to locate three hidden objects that are placed in a specified area. Users are then prompted to answer a number of questions, concerning the effect of plastic waste at sea, in order to win the game. The interactive installation consists of a physical box that houses the electronic parts and affords interaction, a map and a physical board that presents the story and information.

DE – BAG (interactive installation). DE - BAG is an interactive installation and product designed to prevent consumers from purchasing plastic bags at sale points in supermarkets and shops. The idea of the project is that cloth bags can support NFC technology for affording intact transactions: collect or redeem rewards or collected points, gamify point collection among users/customers at the cashier's desk.

5   Public Presentation and Preliminary Evaluation

During the 'Week without plastic bags' campaign, visitors had the chance to interact with the systems that have been implemented by our student groups, which were presented in public exterior and interior spaces (Fig. 2). Users were mainly children about 7 to 12 years old, usually formed in groups, accompanied either by parents or teachers while many university students and other adult passersby (tourists, town residents) visited the event. We used a combination of in situ observation, video recording, questionnaires and interviews in order to evaluate user enjoyment and motivation and gain some initial understanding about possible benefits and pitfalls of our design choices.

Regarding user experience, we reached some findings implying that users were *attracted*, *engaged* and *motivated*. Initially, the presentation (physical and interactive elements) of the projects managed to draw the attention of multiple users. Most of them (mainly children) returned to play/interact multiple times with the prototypes, in the same or different days, which is a strong indicator of engagement.

As expected, we noticed that gamification and playfulness had an important role in users' enjoyment and motivation. Installations and games that strongly incorporated these aspects had a higher return rate compared to static installations that just communicated a message. Gamification mechanisms, such as, providing instant feedback on performance to create competition and giving rewards, played a major role in keeping the users engaged and motivated. In addition, we observed that this repeated use of the persuasive systems was of high importance in developing targeted user behavior in the long run. In short term, it allowed monitoring user performance over time and observing their progress. We further noticed that the social aspect in the public installations was strong. Users exhibited social behavior and intentionally collaborated with each other. In some cases, users learnt how to play/interact by watching others. Children had a tension to collaborate with each other, although our games/systems have been designed to be single-user. There were groups of two or more people in front of the screen or installation, discussing and helping each other to fulfil the purpose of each game/task. After their interaction, a lot of users communicated their knowledge and experience to other passersby, motivating them to participate as well. Users exhibited online social behavior by disseminating their score and achievements on social networks even on the games/installations that did not support the features (they used manual methods). This way, the message, and some knowledge, were disseminated to more individuals. Based on these findings, we suggest that persuasive systems, especially public ones, should incorporate social and collaborative features in their design.

In most cases, users needed different levels of support depending on interaction complexity, and gameplay. Younger users needed more assistance with complex tasks, and a few of them failed to complete more than one task. Furthermore, a limited number of users diverged from the actual scenarios and tried to explore different features of the systems. In addition, most users preferred the tablet device to the laptop for the two digital games, despite the fact that laptops also had touch screens.

We also made a number of observations regarding technical issues. Given the ambient noise of the environment, especially during the outdoor presentations, the sound in most projects was low; alternative techniques (visual or haptic) should be used as feedback. Environmental lighting conditions affected the calibration of the sensors and thus auto-calibration mechanisms needed to be implemented. Finally, physical prototypes were prone to failure when users acted beyond the specified limits of the experiments.

Fig. 2. Visitors interacting with the projects in the central square of Hermoupolis, Syros

6 Conclusions

This work outlined the methodological steps and decisions towards the development of a set of prototypes that aimed at informing and educating users in a playful and engaging way about the problem of plastic bags. The findings of our preliminary evaluation concerning user interaction indicate positive results, though interactive installations that where detached from their actual context of use (e.g. DE-BAG, JunkBox) had lower impact and should be evaluated again. Our observations suggest that interactive technologies and computer games can improve the dissemination of information about environmental problems and contribute towards the advance of awareness and user engagement. After a week in participating the campaign and based on performance measurements (between sessions) and questionnaire feedback (pre and post intervention), users, passersby and audience exhibited a significantly higher degree of awareness for the project's goals. Finally, project stakeholders of the environmental problem that participated to the gathering and workshops identified interest towards further development and extension of the current work in different areas/disciplines.

References

1. Gardner, G.T., Stern, P.C.: Environmental Problems and Human Behavior, 2nd edn. Allyn & Bacon, Boston (2002)
2. Vlek, C., Steg, L.: Human behavior and environmental sustainability: problems, driving forces, and research topics. J. Soc. Issues **63**(1), 1–19 (2007)
3. Froehlich, J.: Gamifying green: gamification and environmental sustainability. In: The Gameful World: Approaches, Issues, Applications, pp. 563–596 (2015)
4. Reidsma, D., Katayose, H., Nijholt, A. (eds.): ACE 2013. LNCS, vol. 8253. Springer, Cham (2013). https://doi.org/10.1007/978-3-319-03161-3
5. Fogg, B.J.: Creating persuasive technologies: an eight-step design process. In: Proceedings of the 4th International Conference on Persuasive Technology, p. 44 (2009)
6. Oinas-Kukkonen, H., Harjumaa, M.: Persuasive systems design: key issues, process model, and system features. Commun. Assoc. Inf. Syst. **24**(1), 28 (2009)
7. de Vries, P.W., Oinas-Kukkonen, H., Siemons, L., Beerlage-de Jong, N., van Gemert-Pijnen, L. (eds.): PERSUASIVE 2017. LNCS, vol. 10171. Springer, Cham (2017). https://doi.org/10.1007/978-3-319-55134-0
8. Fogg, B.J.: Persuasive Technology: Using Computers to Change What We Think and Do. Morgan Kaufmann, Amsterdam (2002)
9. Hamari, J., Koivisto, J., Sarsa, H.: Does gamification work? – A literature review of empirical studies on gamification. In: 47th Hawaii International Conference on System Sciences, pp. 3025–3034 (2014)
10. Hosse, I.R., Zuanon, R.: Games for change: the strategic design of interactive persuasive systems. In: Antona, M., Stephanidis, C. (eds.) UAHCI 2015. LNCS, vol. 9177, pp. 442–453. Springer, Cham (2015). https://doi.org/10.1007/978-3-319-20684-4_43
11. Chiu, M.C., et al.: Playful bottle: a mobile social persuasion system to motivate healthy water intake. In: Proceedings of the 11th International Conference on Ubiquitous Computing, NY, pp. 185–194 (2009)

12. Thieme, A., et al.: We've bin watching you: designing for reflection and social persuasion to promote sustainable lifestyles. In: Proceedings of the SIGCHI Conference on Human Factors in Computing Systems, NY, pp. 2337–2346 (2012)
13. Chang, Y.-C., et al.: Playful toothbrush: Ubicomp technology for teaching tooth brushing to kindergarten children. In: Proceedings of the SIGCHI Conference on Human Factors in Computing Systems, NY, pp. 363–372 (2008)
14. Froehlich, J., et al.: UbiGreen: investigating a mobile tool for tracking and supporting green transportation habits. In: Proceedings of the SIGCHI Conference on Human Factors in Computing Systems, pp. 1043–1052. ACM (2009)
15. The Fun Theory (2009). http://www.thefuntheory.com/. Accessed 28 July 2017
16. Benyon, D.: Designing Interactive Systems: A Comprehensive Guide to HCI and Interaction Design. Pearson, Harlow (2010)
17. Carroll, J.M.: Making Use: Scenario-Based Design of Human-Computer Interactions. MIT Press, Cambridge (2000)
18. Preece, J., Sharp, H., Rogers, Y.: Interaction Design: Beyond Human-Computer Interaction, 4th edn. Wiley, New York (2015)
19. Goodwin, K.: Designing for the Digital Age: How to Create Human-Centered Products and Services. Wiley, New York (2009)
20. Hunicke, R., LeBlanc, M., Zubek, R.: MDA: a formal approach to game design and game research. In: Proceedings of the AAAI Workshop on Challenges in Game AI (2004)

A Tentative Assumption of Electroacoustic Music as an Enjoyable Music for Diverse People

Takuro Shibayama[1,4(✉)], Hidefumi Ohmura[2], Tatsuji Takahashi[1], and Kiyoshi Furukawa[3]

[1] Tokyo Denki University, Ishizaka, Hatoyama-machi, Saitama 350-0394, Japan
takuro@mail.dendai.ac.jp
[2] Tokyo University of Science, 2641 Yamazaki, Noda-shi, Chiba 2780-022, Japan
[3] Tokyo University of the Arts, 12-8 Ueno-Park, Taito-ku, Tokyo 110-8714, Japan
[4] ZKM | Institute for Music and Acoustics, Lorenzstr. 19, 76135 Karlsruhe, Germany

Abstract. Music went through a huge transformation between the end of the 19th century and the beginning of the 20th. Part of this transformation involved the separation of music intended for entertainment, which everyone can enjoy, and music that is primarily artistic and philosophical. The latter became more esoteric: today this type of 'artistic' music is often called 'contemporary music', and it has yet to win many supporters. The reason for this is believed to be that the artistic expression of music is 'difficult' for many people to interpret. However, we disprove this theory, developing a workshop aimed at creating electroacoustic, or contemporary, music with a diverse group of people. From these workshops, we determine that electroacoustic music is actually experienced as 'enjoyable' by many people. This paper describes our tentative assumption that both our artistic and research activities support this idea, and its implications to integrating aesthetic and philosophical points of view.

Keywords: Aesthetics · Funology · Avant-Garde music expression
Electroacoustic music

1   Introduction

'Contemporary' music developed between the end of the 19th century and beginning of the 20th. While *contemporary music* literally refers to any current music, today the term has come to mean music of a style that greatly deviates from 'conventional' music, which has a clear tonality and rhythm. This type of music has long seemed esoteric, and there are many who feel listening to this music is painful. Indeed, several musicians have supported this popular views, including Adorno, who refused to appreciate commercial popular music, insisting instead on creating purely artistic music [1], and Boulez, who understood contemporary musicology as the fusion between science and mathematics [2]. These and similar ideologies may be part of why contemporary music does not have as many listeners as other musical entertainment. However it remains unclear whether contemporary music is truly esoteric or unpleasant to listen to in and of itself.

© Springer International Publishing AG, part of Springer Nature 2018
A. D. Cheok et al. (Eds.): ACE 2017, LNCS 10714, pp. 139–152, 2018.
https://doi.org/10.1007/978-3-319-76270-8_11

Over the course of this study, we separately implemented artistic workshops and research into the emotions music evokes. Each activity supports the same answer to the above question: people can enjoy listening to contemporary music. In this paper, we try to integrate both individual initiatives to show how they support our findings.

1.1 Workshop

Over the past 10 years, one of the authors have carried out numerous workshops focused on creating concrete music (*musique concréte*), which is a music composed of various recorded sounds rather than musical tones, with participants who have little to no expertise in musical composition [3, 4]. Most participants are people who have never even listened to this type of music. Pierre Schaeffer, a French sound engineer and composer, developed concrete music in 1948. Along with electronic music, which started in Germany at about the same time, concrete music is one of the major foundations of experimental computer music, or electroacoustic music.

These workshops asked participants to compose their own concrete music using a computer. Most participants were able to compose a piece while enjoying their final product. Therefore, we determined that concrete music, although considered to be difficult to understand, is actually enjoyable for most people.

Therefore, these workshops allowed us to reconsider common assumptions about modern music and ask the following questions:

(A) Is concrete music truly 'esoteric'?
(B) Why have so many people assumed this type of music to be difficult to understand and enjoy?
(C) It is easier for people to create 'esoteric' music than appreciate the modern music made by others?

To answer these questions, we had to understand the meanings and significance of 'esoteric', or electroacoustic, music in these workshops.

1.2 Research on Emotions Evoked by Music

We also attempt to design music generation systems that can adjust the complexity of a piece's musical structure by controlling the cognitive bias adaptive reasoning model [5] and the occurrence of sounds using the amount of information entropy [6]. These systems are based on Meyer's work, who defined music as a human emotion, or a series of anticipations about what comes next [7]. Narmour [8] and Huron [9] inherited his viewpoint, but there is as of yet no musical generation system that quantitatively addresses human expectation. Our two models, therefore, were designed to generate traditional music based on quantitative data of human expectation. However, these models show a tendency for some people to feel 'interested' secondary to a situation's extremely high complexity. Our original research question did not allow us to generate an un-supervised model. However, our finding that people found this music 'interesting' allowed us to link this research with the workshop described in Sect. 1.1.

1.3 Moving Toward Integration

Through workshop and music emotion research, we were convinced that people can enjoy music with high complexity. In this paper, we suggest that concrete music is more complicated than conventional music, but that contemporary music, which is generally regarded as esoteric, can actually be enjoyed by anyone. These results are corroborated by our music generation system, despite this not being its primary purpose. We propose the possibility of integrating concrete music into the field of computer-generated music (i.e. Funology [10]), with the academic validities and viewpoints contained within this field to expand the idea of human 'fun'.

2 Workshop Methods

In 2011, one of the authors started carrying out concrete music workshops in art museums throughout Japan. The workshops are based on the syllabus for a concrete music composition class taught through the correspondence education department of Osaka University of the Arts, where one of the writers has been a lecturer since 2005. The students there have little prior knowledge of contemporary music and information technology, meaning that the class discussion went beyond computer-generated music to include the wider experience of concrete music. Through these, we found that although concrete music is often lumped with contemporary music and is also said to be too esoteric for the general public, people enjoy the experience of listening to and creating concrete music. This finding inspired us to introduce new educational approaches encouraging more people to experience the production of concrete music. The goal of our workshops, therefore, is to position the creation of a "work space" as relational and project art, in line with the perspective developed within the field of fine art in recent years [11]. Through this approach, we believe that we can develop activities to expand the field of concrete music, which was founded in 1948. The process of carrying out our workshops convinced us that 'concrete music is joyful music.'

These workshops were generally held from 1–5 p.m. on a weekend. People of all ages, from elementary school students to adults, participated and produced music together using computers. Most workshops were structured as follows:

(A) Participants listen to sample audio materials (Schaeffere, Russolo, Merzbow, Henry, etc.).
(B) Participants record the sound of items they brought from home.
(C) Recorded sounds are transferred to one laptop computer.
(D) Participants make a montage using editing software (i.e. Audacity).
(E) While composing their compilation, participants were urged to describe their composition using words. For example, high/low, hard/soft, movement/no movement, and light/dull, etc.
(F) Participants create a 10–20 s monophonic soundtrack.
(G) Facilitators collect tracks from each participant and play separately, making comments as they go.
(H) Finally, all participants' tracks are played at the same time.

When recording sounds, participants are encouraged to listen to the sounds origi-
nating from each item they brought, rather than trying to put on a musical performance
with said item. When creating the montages, participants are instructed to think of some
metaphor of imaginative vision that is evoked by the sound, as described in Step (E).

3 Scientifically and Academically Relevant Workshops

During the musical workshops, one of the authors was struck by how many participants
laughed together while creating music from everyone's individual work. We suggest,
therefore, that the creation of artistic music creates an affinity that is not felt when merely
appreciating such music. In light of this hypothesis, we offer a reanalysis of some of our
previous studies.

3.1 Activity 1: Measuring the Effects of the Workshop

It was interesting to note that participants uniformly enjoy the final Step (H), when all
tracks are played together, despite the fact that individual participants do not necessarily
recognize that their work is being played with that of the other participants. In other
words, the participants enjoyed listening to the music, even though the final piece has a
much greater complexity than when listening to each person's individual recording.

In our 2011 workshop, we conducted a questionnaire survey to evaluate people's
impressions of the following music: 'Risveglio di una città', by futurist composer Luigi
Russolo; 'Etude aux chemins de fer', by Pierre Schaeffer, the founder of concrete music;
and computer-generated noise music by Merzbow (Masami Akita). This questionnaire
asked participants to listen to the same audio clips and answer the same questions before
and after the workshop. We observed that participants' impressions improved after
completing the workshop. This shows that the creation of concrete music enables people
to enjoy music that deviated from 'traditional' definitions of music. However, this survey
has some limitations: our use of the same listening material for both the before and after
questionnaires cannot eliminate the possibility that evaluations improved simply
because people became accustomed to the sound. Therefore, there is room for improvement in this survey.

3.2 Activity 2: Electroacoustic Listening Experiment

In 2011, we conducted an experiment to determine whether functions like the elapsed
syntax of concrete music existed. This was intended to verify our hypothesis that the
progressive continuity of acoustic materials is a consequence, even though the listener
is creating inevitability. To accomplish this, we divided a historically distinguished
concrete music piece into 33 parts and produced three sound tracks that arranged these
sound fragments randomly. We asked 100 different subjects to compare these tracks,
including the original piece, however, subjects were not informed which was the original. Nor were most subjects knowledgeable of concrete music.

The results showed that most subjects could not differentiate between the tracks, even though the sounds were in a different order. Even if the chronological sequential order of the electroacoustic music is replaced by a random order, there is no change in listeners' impressions.

In order to make this experiment more precise, we incorporated Schaeffer's understanding of the categorization of acoustic sound materials [12] and the perception of multimodal sound with more modern cognitive science ideas. For instance, Gaver points out that listening to sounds based on affordance theory will complementarily affect both perception and interpretation, rather than physical analysis, which is based on acoustics [13]. This process of clarifying the image of sounds in concrete music, based on an ecological listening experience, is highly compatible with the metaphorical exterior cognitive model proposed by Lakoff [14, 15]. These ideas are a useful strategy for updating Schaeffer's theory about Helmholtz-based acoustics and the relationship between Saussure-based linguistics and the structure of concrete music. However, while we assumed in our analysis that the listener sees no clear causal relationship in the chronological order of the acoustic materials, it is possible that these listeners are somewhat musical themselves, as in our proposed hypothesis. These findings are important clues to the design of the generation model of electroacoustic music. It is important to consider that when people listen to electroacoustic music, they may be 'watching' the photographic scene of each acoustic material being played rather than listening to the sequence of acoustic sounds. Regardless, our findings in this experiment provide major insight into the generative model of electroacoustic music. If we interpret the results of this experiment as if the arrangement of acoustic material in electroacoustic music is coincidental and inevitably undifferentiated, the affinity with our concept oriented in the middle region between consciousness and unconsciousness, shown in Sect. 4, increases.

3.3   Activity 3: Music and Emotion (Symmetric Cognitive Bias)

In 2010, we started designing a music generation model based on human expectation. This research is based on Meyer's theory that music is the continued anticipation for the next musical event [7]. His proposal was subsequently utilized by Narmour in his IR (implication-realization) theory [8] and Huron in his ITPRA (imagination, tension, prediction, reaction, and appraisal) theory [9]. However, neither of these theories develop a music generation model based on quantitative data.

For the purposes of creating such a model, we focus on cognitive bias, an illogical inference model peculiar to humans. Cognitive bias is human-specific non-logical reasoning about the causal relationship of an event. This non-logical reasoning is regarded as the foundation of human intuition. There are several types of cognitive bias, including representative heuristics, but we applied a mathematical model that treats human reasoning based on a symmetric cognitive bias as the probability of an event occurring.

For cognitive bias in causal relationships, $p \Rightarrow q$, where only human beings have inverse reasoning such as $q \Rightarrow p$, the inference behind $\neg p \Rightarrow \neg q$, etc. The former is symmetric bias, the latter is called mutually exclusive bias. We treat the concatenation of existing music from the preceding sound to the following sound as the minimum unit of expectation of music, based on the transition probability, 'loosely symmetric model' (LS), already used in fields to which machine learning has been applied [16]. This system can generate new pitch elements by applying the condition probability, the LS model, and the 'rigidly symmetric model' (RS) to the transition probability of the preceding sound of the existing music and the transition probability of the following sound. As a result of comparing the generated pitch elements, we found that a loosely symmetric model close to the human thought model generates the pitch element most in line with the human sense.

However, there are problems with this system. It can only cope with machine learning by its supervisor and it was difficult to properly incorporate rhythm. In other words, this system can only generate a tonal pitch set that composes a melody based on Western classical music theory as a variant of the original.

We are now paying attention to experience while trying to create an impression evaluation experiment using this system. This experience includes a composer and cooperative researcher, who both laughed when a pitch structure randomly generated by the RS model has a strong symmetry of reasoning. This implies that elements of the music were 'funny' or 'interesting'. However, we cannot determine the exact meaning of the laughter. The RS model has far more states that can be derived as a result than the LS model; it also is better at inference and divergent reasoning.

3.4 Activity 4: Music and Its Complexity

Based on the above music generation system using symmetry cognitive bias, we considered how to realize generation in the unsupervised model. Therefore, we designed a new model treating the accuracy of an event's occurrence by controlling the information entropy mentioned above [6, 17]. In this model, it was possible to variably adjust both the rhythm and pitch between the normal distribution and the uniform distribution from the centre value to the periphery.

First, one period is divided into 32, and each of these are divided into six levels (Fig. 1). By variably controlling the occurrence probability of sound at each timing from the normal distribution to the uniform distribution range, it is possible to control the complexity of the rhythm (Fig. 2). Pitch element is also generated by this method: pitch element can generate the perfect fifth zone in the key circle by 12 tones on the left and right from the central axis as one set. When this distribution approaches a uniform distribution, the probability that the musical intervals of the 12 sounds appear in the octave becomes equivalent, and when approaching the normal distribution, the probability that only the central sound appears in a certain adjustment becomes high.

What is important about this model is the inverted U-shaped function of the Berlyne [18]. This shows the correlation between music complexity and listener satisfaction (Fig. 3). It suggests that a certain complexity is necessary for listeners to appreciate music; listeners feel pleasure when the complexity of a piece is very high or low.

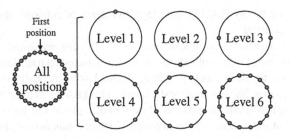

Fig. 1. Six levels of timings of sounds.

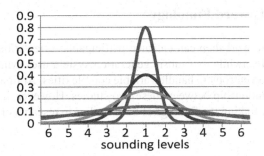

Fig. 2. Probability distributions for sounding points.

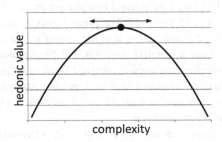

Fig. 3. Inverted U function, originally proposed by Berlyne in 1971

The features of the system we designed include the following three points: (a) it can generate music without a supervisor, (b) the vertex of the inverted U-function of the bar line can be shifted left and right, and (c) since music can be generated at various complexities, this system can also introduce the generation of electroacoustic music composed of more complex sound materials than musical tones. Currently, based on (c), we are attempting to generate concrete music from pieces of recorded sound material. This system can generate not only the timing of sound, but also the sequence of sound materials based on their complexity and control of their contrast.

Although the degree of complexity is a computational concept, we map this concept to an acoustic image we can understand, as mentioned in Sect. 2. The image in which the acoustic material is being forged serves as the label of the image using Lakoff's language metaphor theory [14, 15] and the 'movement' of concrete music is drawn as the shade of the contrast.

It is believed useful to design sequence order with the argument as a label. This system has a wide range of complications, from music based on traditional music theory with clear pitches to electroacoustic music formed from acoustic material without distinct pitch elements, like electroacoustic music. This enables us to create a complexity oriented music structure. In this process of system design, we our focused attention on the possibility that the vertices of the inverted U-shaped function of this bar line have widths on the left and right depending on the era and individual tastes.

4   Strategies Toward Funology

Our concrete music workshop can enhance participants' orientation towards highly complex music. Meanwhile, our music generation system uses symmetric cognitive bias and information entropy to handle variable complexities. At first glance, it seems as if there is no relationship between these two studies. However, in this section, we clarify connection, linking the findings of both studies to research on complexity and consciousness.

4.1   Activity Example 4 – Music and Its Complexity

One of the authors of this study first listened to a piano piece by Schönberg using early 12-tone theory when he was 15 years old. The piece seems to be a collection of sounds that cannot be experienced in any order, and the author's first reaction was, 'This is really music?' This was not a negative reaction, but playful and with laughter. It is necessary to examine whether this laughter derived from awkwardness or, as Bergson suggests, due to 'inserting an irrational idea into an idiomatic phrase' [19]. From this perspective, human kind may have acquired through evolution a type of creativity that utilizes deviations regarded as irrational.

On the other hand, however, as mentioned in Sect. 2, many participants in our workshops felt 'uncomfortable' when listening to the materials presented (i.e. pieces by Russolo, Schaeffer, Merzbow, and Henri). While discomfort does not immediately seem like a situation in which laughter is appropriate, participants gradually found joy in the process of recording sounds from the non-musical items they brought and in the composition of concrete music from these acoustic materials. At this point, participants started to laugh at the abstract musical 'movement' born from their individual compositions. The participants of this workshop, those who were able to enjoy the final composition and appreciate the esoteric music, clearly believe that this vertex shifted to the right. In addition, it may be conceivable that the vertex of Berlyne's inverted U-function shifts based on individual and cultural differences.

It is reasonable to think that the vertex of pleasure (hedonics) shifts throughout history as well. For example, any historical music was, at one point, the 'newest' music of its era. For example, J. S. Bach's complex musical piece dedicated to Friedrich the Great; J. G. Müthel's compositions, in which all the undulations of human emotions are notated in the scores; and Beethoven's work, including the appearance of a full chorus in the final movement of the Ninth Symphony. While there is no way to ascertain whether the music was popular when it was first composed or merely gained popularity as time went on, by the beginning of the 20th century, it was certainly true that any music labelled 'contemporary' would face the utmost rejection from listeners.

Has the complexity of music changed over time? It is true that Western music became more complicated in the shift from the Romantic to Modern period. There was a transition from using three chords (C or Dm) to four (CM7 or Dm7), an increased frequency of key changes, and a trend towards collapsing tonality (and the appearance of atonality). All these suggest that complexity has increased as a combination of frequency ratios. Nattiez positions the rise of noise music and electroacoustic music as the extension of these trends [20].

On the other hand, if we observe the contrast between the end of polyphonic music and the rise of monophonic music, or the appearance of minimal music against the total serialism technique, we cannot assume that music today has continued to become more complex over time. From a relative point of view, we can see that popular musicality tends to go back-and-forth between two poles of complication and simplification. Today we human beings are in a period that values complexity. Since the beginning of the modern era, Western music, including amusement music, philosophical and esoteric music, and world music has been recorded and circulated. In no time, until now, has traditional music of the past been replayed so often. The diversification of musical expression after modernization expanded the left and right width at the vertex of the inverse U-shaped function and accelerated its fluidity. This process can be regarded as an extension of the object people associate with the word *music* (Fig. 4).

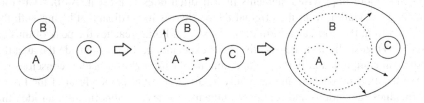

Fig. 4. *kansei*'s process of expansion. The left end refers to a state where only A can be regarded as 'music'. The centre refers to a state in which both A and B are regarded as 'music' as a result of people's mind-sets expanding. As creative attitudes increase, they progress toward the right end of the figure, where A, B, and C, universal realms of the human mind, are all considered 'music'.

We believe that understanding the complexity of musical structures and human pleasure as complementary results in additional possibilities for music generation and increased potential for musical expression and education. In the next section, we describe in detail the possibilities this has for academic and scientific development, and how these developments can be positioned against the growth of artistic expression, what we refer to as Funology.

4.2 Extension of Awareness and Recognition

This next sections examines the two experiments described above based on both their complexity and creativity. We hypothesize that lovers of complicated music have increased choices of probability. According to Meyer's theory, an experienced listener can predict more future possibilities for where a piece of music will go. The listener feels joyful when results betray that expectation. It involves more reasoning skills when there are diverse states of being.

Marvin Minsky, a leading expert in artificial intelligence research, explains human reasoning, defining the ability to detect certain kinds of differences at a conscious/ unconscious level as a 'difference-engine' [21]. He defines this 'difference-engine' as reasoning at the conscious/unconscious level. He also points out that the function of the 'difference-engine' decreases as humans use that function throughout the day. Minsky assumes that music plays a role in returning human reasoning to its original conditions: he writes that listening to music is one way to restore this function. The word *music* here, of course, refers to music with a melody or harmonic structure. However, humans have transformed music into something more complicated and with complex acoustic representation. Music that has undergone such transformation disappoints the majority of listeners when they first listen to it, as the structure itself is complicated. For example, 'Risveglio di una città', composed by Russolo, and 'Le sacre du printemps', composed by Stravinsky, are typical examples. This music greatly deviates from previous music of its time, it the pieces' complexity disrupted listeners' reasoning.

Music during the Baroque Period was often styled on variations on 'La Folia', a musical piece composed of sequential variations on a theme with a fixed form of the melody positioned at the beginning. 'La Folia' implies that musical performance used to include more improvised elements than it often does at present. As this variation progresses, deviation from the original theme 'leaves the ordinary'. Playing with this deviation from the norm as a form of madness, 'La Folia' reaches the peak of musical ecstasy. When such music betrays listener's expectation, it exists outside the area that he/she can comprehend: there is a large amount of information his/her consciousness cannot handle, and he/she can grasp only a part. 'La Folia' is the plural of the French *foli* (madness/deviation) and references human madness or abnormality, an idea that began with Michel Foucault's concepts of psychological/pathological analysis [22]. Foucault presents theories of who defines 'abnormal', and how the criterion for abnormality is set [23]. He points out the involvement of society and culture on the creation of abnormalities. This abnormality can be interpreted as a thing made from the difference of both poles of 'deviation' on the spectrum of what is 'normal' in society. The boundary also corresponds to each individual area of consciousness/unconscious.

Human beings have been trying to orient consciousness to the outside of itself since ancient times. In 1954, Aldous Huxley published his book *The Door of Perception* [24], in which he consumes a substance extracted from cacti roots, often consumed by Native Americans in sacred rituals. Huxley describes his experience in detail and writes his conclusions. The substances he takes are similar to mescaline and lysergic acid; consuming them gives rise to a state of conscious arousal and a sense that consciousness connects with information outside the self. Native Americans thought that it possible to engage with the universal world by taking this substance. Huxley's view is unique, however, in that he concludes that artists can reach this heightened state of consciousness without taking such any substances.

Tor Norreteranders studies the role of consciousness in his book, *User Illusion,* understanding it as a function to eliminate unnecessary information within a subject's environment [25]. Norreteranders insists that human consciousness can be recovered by looking at a tree's green leaves or the mountain ridgelines at sunset. Yet, despite their benefits, these landscapes have a high degree of complexity when contrasted with cities, which are artificially and geometrically constructed. In other words, eliminating unnecessary information also eliminates some of the richest sensory information. Norreteranders concludes his work with the belief that 'subliminal' parts of our mind (other than consciousness) make up the "sublime."

In recent years, scholars have hypothesized that a symptomatic schizophrenic thinking pattern is formed when symmetry is transiently strengthened at the symmetry of cognitive bias in human inference. When symmetry becomes stronger, the situation assumed by reasoning increases. In other words, assuming the possibility of every situation is also an assumption of an impossible situation. It can be regarded as synonymous with increased complexity in reasoning. Logical reasoning without symmetric bias is scattered, rule-based reasoning. When the 'loosely symmetric model' (LS) is added to that, the inference approaches human intuition. And when a 'rigidly symmetric model' (RS) is used, it becomes excessive inference and approaches delusion. What is 'proper' and what is 'excess'? Who decides the standard? How do individuals become conscious of it?

The observation of the boundary between human consciousness/unconsciousness is based on the theories exemplified in this section. Expanding the area of conscious to the unconscious may have played a major role in the formation of human culture. What supported the movement is an illogical inference unique to humans, because illogical human reasoning has a higher degree of complexity than other animals, which perform only logical reasoning. It is reasonable that irrational behaviors became a source of artistic ideas, which may have been triggered by illogical reasoning in human history. From such a viewpoint, the increase in complexity in the music structure and the increase in complexity in human reasoning may have occurred in the course of the transformation of human culture. This implies that to be 'artistic' is to have rich ideas or make connections between human intuition and delusion.

4.3 Deconstruction of Belief

Imaging having a conversation with someone that goes something like this: 'Do you like music?' 'Yes, I like music'. What kinds of things are you associating with the word *music*? For example, if someone listens to Indian music every day, the words 'I like music' are insufficient, and an additional explanation is necessary to make clear that 'music' refers to 'Indian Music'. Likewise, if someone listens to concrete music, misunderstandings will arise if they merely use the word 'music' to communicate this.

In other words, *music* is often used in an implicit and limited way. In many cases, the word *music* refers to the most frequently played, best-selling, and most famous music that is liked by the majority of people. Most of this music is quite different from the concrete music we study here, and in most cases is composed based on Western traditional music theory.

Needless to say, this music plays an important role in connecting people's minds. Because music can invite consensus, it can arouse overall united group brain activity [26, 27]. Some even suggest that music may have been learned prior to language [28]. However, our workshops show that other kinds of music can have these benefits too, even music that many people may question as such on first listen. J. P. Guildford, the founder of personality psychology, defines the necessary attitudes for creativity [29]. His definition, specifically the following three traits, has a great influence on our study in this paper. These traits include directing diversity, tolerance to rules, and diffusion type with creativity rather than convergent type. Because electroacoustic music, which we use in our study, is based on creating non-rule-based music, our workshop encourages participants to assume more complexity than they would normally expect in regular music.

Using these assumptions, it is possible to clearly show that (i) people can learn to make highly complex concrete music, (ii) the creation of art is more diverse than many people assume, and (iii) a software system based on Berlyne's proposed inverse U function can be used to vary the hedonics point and further the field of Funology. Points (i) and (ii) attempt to extend the scope of the word *music* and enable us to be conscious of the circumstances compelling us to 'buy existing music and listen'. It enables us to transition from thinking of music as something given by society to something we create. Point (iii) demonstrates how computers can be applied to entertainment in order to further expand the framework of 'entertainment'.

In order to further examine the possibilities of the above three conclusions, we are preparing to integrate our past studies and put together a large-scale study that combines the creative field with empirical research. This will allow us to explore the possible connections between art and science, or the field of Funology, through a new acoustic expression applied computer. Moreover, the development of such a tool can be synchronized with the development of Funology in the anthropological field.

5   Conclusion

In Japan, contemporary music, including electroacoustic music, is still fairly marginal. However, we are convinced that this kind of music, generally regarded as esoteric, has the possibility of being enjoyed by many people. We offer a new way for people to appreciate this music—not just the general listening of music, but the actual creation of music. This topic is not novel: the popularity of amateur bands, global expansion of karaoke, and movement of 'handmade' 'zines' demonstrate that many people are now expressing their own creativity rather than merely appreciating the work of 'professional' artists.

However, our approach is fundamentally different from that amateurs expressing their artistic side, such as works like *The Portsmouth Sinfonia* or other outsider art. As computers become less expensive and more easily obtainable, we believe that increased creativity make everyone creators of their own art. Therefore, our research is directed at the transition from 'appreciators' to 'creators', a recent proposal within the art field that expands people's enjoyment of works of art. We do not deny that the idea of 'things that can be enjoyed' already exists. However, we think that to extend this premise is useful for developing computer technology related to human entertainment. The effects and evaluation methods for such participatory workshops have not yet been established, and it is necessary to complete much further research in order to verify how these workshops can contribute to society. For that purpose, we are currently working on the following studies: (a) design of an electroacoustic music generation system that can control complexity, (b) development of a concrete music composition workshop and evaluation methods for the workshop, and (c) quantification methods for improving creativity and *kansei*, or 'human sensation, expansion'. Putting together (a), (b), and (c), we call our future research the 'Denshi Onkyo People Project'. The words *denshi onkyo* are Japanese and refer to electroacoustic music. This enables environmental design that can address both the creation and activation of creative fields and the formation of a place within the academic canon.

In the future, we hope to expand the field of our studies to Germany, the Netherlands, France, and other countries. We are preparing to acquire scientific data from each nation and compare the results. By doing so, we can verify whether our findings are particular to Japan's social and cultural background or whether this is a global phenomenon.

Increasing the number of people who can enjoy esoteric music may help boost social innovation. Enjoying esoteric music, that has high complexity increases the number of assumable inferences, and by increasing such individuals, we also expand the areas that society can assume. Finally, many people can share their ideas in the enlarged hypothetical area. Of course, in order for such fluid creation of artwork to become the established social order, it is necessary to form a certain equilibrium between the intention to increase complexity and to suppress it. However, if we inductively grasp the possibility that as many as people as possible will be subjective and creative, it is reasonable to think that the proposals in this paper have the possibility of helping arouse social innovation.

Acknowledgments. This work was partly supported by JSPS KAKENHI grant numbers 17K12808.

References

1. Adorno, T.: Philosophy of Modern Music. Continuum, New York (1971). (Trans.) Mitchell, A.G., Bloomster, W.
2. Boulez, P., Nattiez, J.-J.: Jalons (pour une decennia). Bourgois, Paris (1993)
3. Saitama Muse Forum (SMF). www.artplatform.jp
4. Denshi Onkyo People Project. www.d-o-people.net
5. Ohmura, H., Shibayama, T., Takahashi, T., Shibuya, S., Okanoya, K., Furukawa, K.: Melody generation system based on generalization by human causal intuition. In: Proceedings of Internal Conference of Society of Instrument and Control Engineers, Akita, pp. 2005–2010 (2012)

6. Ohmura, H., Shibayama, T., Takahashi, T., Shibuya, S., Okanoya, K., Furukawa, K.: Modeling of melodic rhythm based on entropy toward creating expectation and emotion. In: Proceedings of International Conference of Sound and Music Computing, Stockholm, pp. 61–66 (2013)
7. Meyer, L.B.: Emotion and Meaning in Music. University of Chicago Press, Chicago (1956)
8. Narmour, E.: The Analysis and Cognition of Basic Melodic Structures. University of Chicago Press, Chicago (1990)
9. Huron, D.: Sweet Anticipation: Music and the Psychology of Expectation. MIT Press, Cambridge (2007)
10. Blyth, M.A. (ed.): Funology, From Usability to Enjoyment. Kluwer Academic Publishers, Dordrecht (2004)
11. Bourriaud, N.: L'esthétique Relationalle. Les Presse Du Reel, Dijon (1998)
12. Schaeffer, P.: Traité des Objets Musicaux: Essai Interdisciplines. Seul, Paris (1966)
13. Gaver, W.: What in the world do we hear? An ecological approach to auditory event perception. Ecol. Psychol. 5(1), 1–29 (1993)
14. Lakoff, G., Johnson, M.: Metaphors We Live by. University of Chicago Press, Chicago (1980)
15. Lakoff, G.: Women, Fire and Dangerous Things: What Categories Reveal About the Mind. University of Chicago Press, Chicago (1987)
16. Takahashi, T., Nakano, M., Shinohara, S.: Cognitive symmetry: illogical but rational biases. Symmetry Cult. Sci. 21(1), 1–3 (2010)
17. Ohmura, H., Shibayama, T., Hamano, T.: Music system with quantitative controllers based on expectations for pitch and rhythm structure. In: Proceedings of Knowledge and System Engineering (KSE) 2016, Hanoi (2016)
18. Berlyne, D.E.: Aesthetics and Psychobiology. Appleton Century Crofts, New York (1971)
19. Bergson, H.: Le Rire. Essai sur la Signification du Cozmique, Paris (1900)
20. Nattiez, J.-J.: Musicologie Générale et Sémiologie. Bourgois, Paris (1987)
21. Minsky, M.: Emotion Machine: Commonsense Thinking, Artificial Intelligence, and the Future of the Human Mind. Simon and Schuster, New York (2006)
22. Foucault, M.: Maadie mentale et Personnalité. Presses Universitaires France, Paris (1954)
23. Foucault, M.: L'Histoire de la folie àl'âge classique. Edition Gallimard, Paris (1961)
24. Huxley, A.: The Doors of Perception. Chatto and Windus, London (1954)
25. Norretranders, T.: The User Illusion: Cutting Consciousness Down to Size. Penguin Books, London (1999)
26. Benzon, W.: Beethoven's Anvils: Music in Mind and Culture. Basic Books, New York (2002)
27. Small, C.: Musicking: The Meanings of Performing and Listening. Wesleyan University Press, Washington D.C. (1998)
28. Mithen, S.: The Singing Neanderthals: The Origins of Music, Language, Mind, and Body. Harvard University Press, Cambridge (2007)
29. Guilford, J.P.: Nature of Human Intelligence. McGraw-Hill Inc., New York (1967)

Voice Animator: Automatic Lip-Synching in Limited Animation by Audio

Shoichi Furukawa[1]([✉]), Tsukasa Fukusato[3], Shugo Yamaguchi[1],
and Shigeo Morishima[2]

[1] Waseda University, Tokyo, Japan
furukawa7246@ruri.waseda.jp, wasedayshugo@suou.waseda.jp
[2] Waseda Research Institute for Science and Engineering, Tokyo, Japan
shigeo@waseda.jp
[3] The University of Tokyo, Tokyo, Japan
tsukasafukusato@is.s.u-tokyo.ac.jp

Abstract. Limited animation is one of the traditional techniques for producing cartoon animations. Owing to its expressive style, it has been enjoyed around the world. However, producing high quality animations using this limited style is time-consuming and costly for animators. Furthermore, proper synchronization between the voice-actor's voice and the character's mouth and lip motion requires well-experienced animators. This is essential because viewers are very sensitive to audio-lip discrepancies. In this paper, we propose a method that automatically creates high-quality limited-style lip-synched animations using audio tracks. Our system can be applied for creating not only the original animations but also dubbed ones independently of languages. Because our approach follows the standard workflow employed in cartoon animation production, our system can successfully assist animators. In addition, users can implement our system as a plug-in of a standard tool for creating animations (Adobe After Effects) and can easily arrange character lip motion to suit their own style. We visually evaluate our results both absolutely and relatively by comparing them with those of previous works. From the user evaluations, we confirm that our algorithms is able to successfully generate more natural audio-mouth synchronizations in limited-style lip-synched animations than previous algorithms.

Keywords: Lip-synching · Limited animations · Animation filtering

1 Introduction

Limited animation (LA) is a traditional hand-drawing technique used to create cartoon animations that reuses some frames instead of redrawing entire frames. The LA technique has the advantage of animators being able to create much more expressive and stylized animations as compared to those generated from 3DCG. This is the reason LA is still popular globally despite the growth of 3D animation. However, it is both time-consuming and costly to produce high quality LA-style cartoons. This is especially true because drawing animated frames

© Springer International Publishing AG, part of Springer Nature 2018
A. D. Cheok et al. (Eds.): ACE 2017, LNCS 10714, pp. 153–171, 2018.
https://doi.org/10.1007/978-3-319-76270-8_12

Closed Lip   Partly Open Lip   Open Lip

Fig. 1. Examples of key images.

while maintaining lip-audio synchronization is very laborious and requires well-experienced animators.

In general, character lip motion in LA is created by replacing a few lip images (referred to as "key images") that usually represent the closed, partly open and open lip positions (Fig. 1). This approach is similar to that used in flipbooks. Two approaches have been employed to produce speech animations: the "after-recording" and the "pre-scoring" approaches.

The after-recording process basically requires (1) placing key images that follow character script, (2) recording the voice of a voice-actor performing while watching the animated frames, and (3) putting the recorded audio track over the animated frames. However, step (1) is tedious for animators and requires well-trained animators since animators have to imagine suitable lip motions based only on the script. Furthermore, because the speed of voice-actors varies among one another, the created lip motion does not synchronize perfectly with the audio in step (3). As a result, animators are required to repeatedly revise the frames for better lip-audio synchronization. In animation, refining components to address not only lip-audio mismatching but also drawing errors, among others, is called a "retake". According to our interview of the staff of an animation studio, a 30-min animated film generally includes about 200 retakes with 30% of the retakes being related to lip-synching. Furthermore, because audiences are very sensitive to lip-audio de-synchronization, lip-synch retakes are essential for the airing of the film.

On the other hand, pre-scoring is a technique in which animators produce the lip motion based on a pre-recorded voice-acting audio track. In this process, lip-sync retakes could actually be reduced, but the fact remains that animators are still required to repeatedly and laboriously place key images. Furthermore, for dubbing of different languages, the original audio track is just replaced by new translated version resulting in even greater lip-audio de-synchronization.

In this paper, to address these problems, we propose a method that automatically produces lip-synched LA-style animations. Our system does not require any other additional items outside of typical workflows employed in cartoon animation. Our system uses only the voice-actor's voice and a few key images as the input. First, we estimate the motion of the voice-actor's lip from the audio track. We employ a state-of-the-art formant-based method that works in real-time. Since it is language independent, we can create not only the original animations but also dubbed films. After obtaining the lip motion, we convert it to character lip motion represented by the key images. For this last part, there are two challenging obstacles to producing natural character lip transitions. The first obstacle is how to take correspondences between continuous lip motion and a few discrete key images (we refer to this as the "spatial alignment problem (SAP)"). The second obstacle is in the determination of a suitable timing for the replacement of the key images so that the animation maintains a natural lip movement appearance (we refer to this as the "temporal alignment problem (TAP)"). In this paper, we propose novel methods based on adaptive thresholding and afterimage effects to solve SAP and TAP. In order to faithfully adhere to typical workflows in animation production, we demonstrate our system in Adobe After Effects, which is a standard tool for animators to create animations. In After Effects, animators can easily tune the generated lip transition to suit their personal expressive style. Furthermore, based on the lip transition generated by our system, animators can learn how to draw a natural transition. In summary, our contributions are

- An efficient language-independent system for creating high quality LA-style lip-synch animations using only voice audio and a few key images. This means our system can work for creating both the original animations and dubbed films.
- Algorithms for solving SAP and TAP based on adaptive thresholding and afterimage effects that achieve a natural lip transitions using only a few lip images.
- The possibility of various application both in entertainment production, such as cartoon animations and games, and in the training of animators based on a natural lip motions automatically generated from audio.

In this paper, we evaluate our results both absolutely and relatively by visually comparing them with those of previous works that generate LA-style motion. These previous algorithms can include motionless or flickering mouth motions. From user evaluations, we confirm that animations generated using our proposed techniques results in more natural audio-mouth synchronization.

2   Related Work

2.1   Lip-Sync Animation

Various 3D facial models for cartoon characters have been used in the field of computer graphics. The blendshape technique, which is a common method employed to animate the facial expression of 3D characters, is based on the linear combination of base poses (referred to as "key shapes") such as happiness, sadness, laughter, anger, and more. In this technique, manually controlling the linear parameters is very laborious for creators. To address this, Weise et al. [16] proposed a system that transfers the facial expressions of the actor to various characters using RGB-D data obtained from professional equipment. Weise et al. [15] demonstrated a real-time system that captures facial expressions by utilizing a commodity depth sensor, and achieved more interactive control of character facial expressions. Moreover, Cao et al. [3] captured facial expressions with high accuracy by combining facial depth data with sparse facial landmarks. These methods work successfully when character key shapes are ready to be used, but the problem remains that key shapes are created for each character in a time-consuming process, which greatly hinders its practical adoption in, for example, film and gaming applications. In addition, although these methods can success-fully produce realistic and lip-synched full animations, they are difficult to apply directly in LA-style animation production.

In general, LA-style films are recorded at 24 frames per second, and each drawn image is displayed three times (referred to "on threes") resulting in eight drawings per second. Kawamoto et al. [9] mainly focused on the laborious task in creating character key shapes and proposed lip-synched-animation system, which included a function that converts original animations to LA-style shot on threes. While this converting function can produce LA-like animations, their method cannot be directly applied to produce traditional LA-style lip-synched animations, which consist of a few key images, such as those shown in Fig. 1. This is due to the fact that it is difficult to take correspondences between various visemes, which are the visual units to distinguish sounds, and only a few key images to represent natural character's lip motion.

Other audio-based approaches have also been proposed. Bregler et al. [2] segmented new audio into three sequent phonemes (referred to "triphones") and created realistic speech animations by selecting video frames that correspond to the triphones and stitching them together. Ezzat et al. [7] and Chang et al. [4] demonstrated an alternative approach that constructs a generative model to produce mouth images corresponding to input phonemes. These methods succeeded in creating realistic speech animation, but it remains problematic to create LA-style animations because of the small number of key images to take the correspondences to various phonemes.

2.2 Stylized Cartoon Animation

Approaches to stylize 2D/3D animations have been discussed for a long time. For instance, procedural rules defined by a physical simulation (e.g. squash-and-stretch and temporal effect) have been used for stylization. Kazi et al. [10] developed a 2D sketching system that simplifies the creation of dynamic illus-tration with motion principals. By using these amplifiers, the user can control the movements and deformations of an underlying background grid. In addition, Dvorovzvnak et al. [6] generated stylized 2D animations by transferring exem-plars drawn by artists. These approaches allow the animators to reflect their personal styles by user interaction. On the other hand, some approaches focus on converting any motion, such as 3D skeletal motion, to LA-like style by using a temporal filter [11,12,14]. For example, using motion capture data (MoCap), Kitamura et al. [11] demonstrated a LA-like converter by omitting frames that

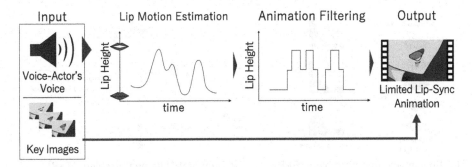

Fig. 2. System overview.

included relatively fast or slow motion. Although these methods can allow for expressive appearance, it is difficult to maintain global timing of the character motion. Therefore, it is hard to achieve suitable audio-mouth synchronization when applying these techniques.

2.3   Lip Motion Capture and Estimation

There are a lot of approaches to obtaining the lip motion of the voice actor. For example, image-processing-based approaches (e.g. facial landmarks detection) is a basic way to capture lip movements. However, it is difficult to produce robust results in environments with unstable or irregular lighting. Moreover, additional efforts are required on the part of the production staff in order to prepare for additional equipments (e.g. video cameras) for capturing in a recording studio. In addition, visual recording risks disturbing the usual performance style of the voice-actor. Phoneme-based methods such as HMM are also common approaches to computing lip motion. However, to use them successfully for a variety of languages, users are required to switch between language-specific phoneme-models. In addition, the reduction in work speed results in increased stress on the animators and therefore working rapidly is essential for software to assist animators. Therefore, in this paper, we employ a state-of-the-art formants-based method that works in real-time to obtain lip motions.

3   System Overview

Our proposed system utilizes only pre-recorded a voice-actor's voice track and three key images ("closed," "partly open," and "open" lip) as inputs, and automatically creates a LA-style lip-synched animation. Our system mainly consists of two steps (refer to Fig. 2): "Lip Motion Estimation" (refer to Sect. 3.1) and "Animation Filtering" (refer to Sect. 3.2). Firstly, in "Lip Motion Estimation", we compute the lip motion of the voice-actor from the input audio track. By using a formant-based method, various languages (e.g. English, Chinese or Japanese)

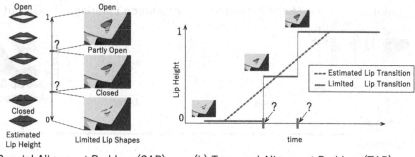

(a) Spacial Alignment Problem (SAP)   (b) Temporal Alignment Problem (TAP)

Fig. 3. Overview of SAP and TAP.

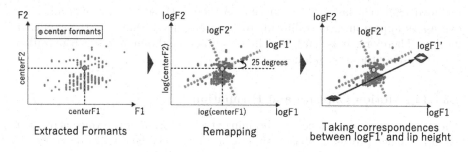

Extracted Formants   Remapping   Taking correspondences between logF1' and lip height

Fig. 4. Overview of lip motion estimation.

can be used here. In "Animation Filtering", our system converts the lip transitions to the LA style. Here, we tackle two challenging problems (Fig. 3). Firstly, for SAP, the difficulty lies in how to take correspondences between continuous distance from upper to lower lip (referred to as "lip height") and a few discrete key images. Secondly, for TAP, a timing has to be determined in which the replacement of the key images results in natural lip motions. Our key idea to solve the SAP is to take correspondences between one peak of the continuous lip transition and one movement of the character's lip by adaptive thresholds. By doing so, the converted lip transition can simulate the voice-actor's lip motion well. To address the TAP, the key idea is to sample lip transitions and perform interpolation while taking into account afterimage effects. By employing these methods, our proposed system can automatically create high quality of lip-synched animations that are comfortable for viewers to watch.

3.1 Lip Motion Estimation

First, we estimate the lip motion from the input voice track. In regard to lip motion capturing, we employ the state-of-the-art formant-based method proposed by Ishi et al. [8]. The original paper aimed at real-time control of the lips of a humanoid-robot. For this paper, however, we modify some parameters of the method for generating character lip motion at the later steps. Here, we briefly explain its principle concept (refer to Fig. 4) and highlight the modifications that we make.

First, input audio data is pre-emphasized by $1 - 0.97z^{-1}$ to enhance its high frequency and framed by using 32[ms] of hamming window while shifting it by 10[ms]. Then, based on linear predictive coding (LPC), the first and the second formant (denoted as F1 and F2) are extracted. In phonetics, a vowel space, which is the set of (F1, F2) obtained from speaker's voice, differs from speaker to speaker. In order to normalize the difference, the set of (F1, F2) computed from the input voice track is remapped into a log space (logF1 vs. logF2). The origin is moved to speaker-specific center formants, which are the center coordinates of the speaker's vowel space (denoted as (centerF1, centerF2)) resulting in a new origin at (log centerF1, log centerF2). Next, the axes are rotated around the new origin counterclockwise by 25 degrees and the new axes are noted as logF1' and logF2'. As a result, logF1' corresponds to lip height one-to-one. Note that some restrictions are prescribed in the original paper to distinguish between vowels and consonants. Moreover a particular lip height value is used during consonant periods. Furthermore, when a period greater than or equal to 0.2[s] exhibits low power of the input audio signal, the lip height during the period is decayed by multiplying it by 0.9.

In our proposed system, we use a monophonic audio track that is captured at more than 44.1[kHz] and 16[bit]. We set the LPC order as 64. Since the average outline of the vowel spaces is dramatically different depending on the gender, we define the average center formants as specific values in terms of gender: (centerF1, centerF2) = (500 Hz, 1450 Hz) for male and (centerF1, centerF2) = (500 Hz, 1600 Hz) for female. This achieves simplified normalization of individual utterance while preserving fine accuracy by only selecting the gender of the input voice track. This approach is very practical for animators as compared to the original GUI-based normalization techniques. Next we calculate lip height using Eq. (1) with a height scale of 0.5.

$$\text{lip\_height} = 0.5 + \text{height\_scale} * \text{logF1}' \qquad (1)$$

We distinguish vowels, consonants, and voiceless periods by simply using the power of the signal (the mean square of signal amplitude) as Table 1. Note that the threshold can vary depending on the recording environment. Next, during periods of uttering consonants, we determine the lip height by taking the product of the previous lip height of a vowel period with a weight parameter α. In this paper, we use $\alpha = 0.5$. Additionally, while human lips would be gradually close after utterance, characters in LA open and close theirs quickly. Considering this, we therefore set the decaying parameter as 0.5 instead of 0.9. Then we normalize the lip height so that it ranges from 0 to 1 and apply a 9-frame sized smoothing filter.

Because the analysis window for LPC is shifted by 10[ms] resulting in the sampling frequency of 100[Hz], we are required to downsample the lip height to 24[fps] for LA-style. Then, we take the $floor(100 * \frac{1}{24} * i)$-th value of the calculated lip height as the i-th value of downsampled one and denote it as an "estimated lip transition (ELT)."

Table 1. Distinction of vowels, consonants and soundless periods.

Periods where power of signal $\geq$ a threshold	$\Rightarrow$ vowels
Periods where power of signal $<$ a threshold for less than 0.2[s]	$\Rightarrow$ Consonants
Periods where power of signal $<$ a threshold for not less than 0.2[s]	$\Rightarrow$ Voiceless

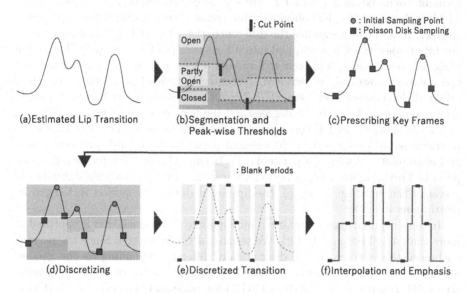

Fig. 5. Processes of animation filtering.

3.2   Animation Filtering

Figure 5 shows the outline of the animation filtering process. In this part, our system converts the ELT obtained in Sect. 3.1 into a natural LA-style lip transition suitable for characters.

Peak Segmentation and Peak-Wise Thresholds. While ELT includes continuous lip shapes, the input key images only represent discrete shapes. Therefore, we need to take correspondences between these continuous and discrete values. One simple solution is to set constant thresholds for entire frames. For example, the quantized lip height at the t-th frame ($L(t)$) is defined as follows.

$$L(t) = \begin{cases} 0 & (0 \leq \text{ELT}[t] < \frac{1}{3}) \\ 1 & (\frac{1}{3} \leq \text{ELT}[t] < \frac{2}{3}) \\ 2 & (\frac{2}{3} \leq \text{ELT}[t] \leq 1) \end{cases} \quad (2)$$

where $L(t)$ corresponds to the key image number (0: closed, 1: partly open and 2: open), and $ELT[t]$ is the estimated lip height at the t-th frame. However, these thresholds can cause a motionless or flickering appearance resulting in the audience easily identifies the lip-audio de-synchronization. The reason is that the audiences are very sensitive not to the discrepancy between local instant lip shapes and audio, but to that between the lip motion and the audio. Therefore, to approximate the motion represented by ELT, we propose an adaptive method. Inspired by adaptive thresholding for binary images, our key idea is to take correspondences between a local peak of ELT and one movement of character's lip from open to close using locally adaptive thresholds. We first detect abrupt transitions of ELT by placing cut points at i-th frame where $(ELT[i + 1] - ELT[i]) > 0$ and $ELT[i] - ELT[i - 1] \leq 0$). Here, the first frame is regarded as an initial cut point and the last frame is considered to indicate the end of the final segment. Then, we set peak-wise thresholds based on the maximum and the minimum values in each segment as below.

$$\text{threshold1}[n] = \min[n] + \tau_1 \tag{3}$$

$$\text{threshold2}[n] = \frac{(\max[n] - \min[n])}{2} + \min[n] + \tau_2 \tag{4}$$

where $\text{threshold1}[n]$ and $\text{threshold2}[n]$ means lower and upper thresholds from the n-th to the $(n + 1)$-th cut points respectively. Note that the last terms τ_1 and τ_2 are the factors to avoid the overlap of threshold1 and threshold2 that results when the maximum and the minimum are equivalent (in this paper, we set $\tau_1 = 0.01$ and $\tau_2 = 0.02$). Lastly, using Eq. (5), ELT is quantized to the number of key images (as shown in Fig. 5(b)).

$$L(t) = \begin{cases} 0 & (0 \leq ELT[t] \leq \text{threshold1}[n]) \\ 1 & (\text{threshold1}[n] < ELT[t] \leq \text{threshold2}[n]) \\ 2 & (\text{threshold2}[n] < ELT[t] \leq 1) \end{cases} \tag{5}$$

when the n-th cut point $\leq t <$ the $(n + 1)$-th cut point.

Key Framing and Discretization. We determine key frames, where the ELT's values are discretized based on the peak-wise thresholds defined at the previous step. We consider frames with local maxima as the crucial frames to achieve lip-audio synchronization. These frames are initially taken as key frames (as shown in Fig. 5(c): "Initial Sampling"). Next, as inspired by Dunbar et al. [5], we apply Poisson Disk Sampling [5] to ELT in order to pick up other key frames (as shown in Fig. 5(c): "Poisson Disk Sampling"). From our experience, a disk size of five frames can provide the resolution that is similar to LA-style animation. Finally, at the prescribed key frames, our system quantizes ELT by taking the thresholds as reference (Fig. 5(d) and (e)).

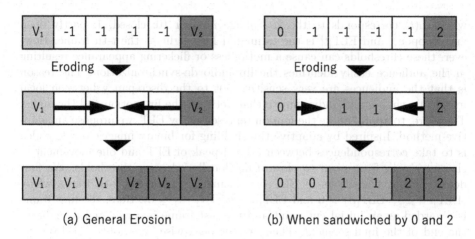

Fig. 6. Example of interpolation.

Interpolation and Motion Emphasis. In limited animations, it is because of the afterimage effect that results by replacing frames (as is done for a flipbook) that viewers have the impression that the character's lip are moving. In addition, the afterimage effect causes a viewer perception delay. That is to say, when image "A" switches to image "B" at time t, viewers generally feel the change a little later, at time $t + \delta$. Considering this effect, we interpolate the frames between key frames. These interpolated frames are referred to as "blank frames".

We first dilate the values at key frames like "image dilation". Here, the values of the blank frames are represented as -1, and the size of the dilation window is 2 frames, which means the dilated value at the i-th frame is the maximum value from the i-th to the $(i+1)$-th frame. Furthermore, each of remaining blank periods is interpolated by eroding it using its head and tail values (denoted as V_1 and V_2 in Fig. 6). Note that when the blanks are sandwiched by the values 0 and 2, the center frame(s) is(are) interpolated by a value of 1 for smooth transitions. As a result of these processes, the interpolated transition precedes ELT a little resulting in a natural LA-style lip motion.

In the discretized transition, a value except 0 sometimes lasts for a long periods over several frames due to the interpolation. This is especially true because the dilation can erode the smaller value. Our solution for this has the common idea with a limited-style-converting algorithm proposed by Kawamoto et al. [9], in which, in each constant period, one key frame whose mouth shape is different from that of the previous period is selected. We emphasize the transition by inserting different values in periods where the same value of the quantized lip height lasts (we denote the length of such a period as l), as shown in Table 2. Here, the reason for processing $9 \leq l$ and $6 \leq l < 9$ separately, and for the number of inserted frames is to generate a similar resolution to that of the on-threes method. After this emphasizing process, the final animation is produced by placing key images following the obtained transition (Fig. 5(f)).

Table 2. Emphasis of Lip Transition.

if the value is 2		
when $9 \leq l$	$\Rightarrow$ inserting three frames of "1" centering the middle frame.	(Fig. 7(a))
when $6 \leq l < 9$	$\Rightarrow$ inserting "1" at the half of the period.	(Fig. 7(b))
if the value is 1		
when $9 \leq l$ and the post value is 0		
	$\Rightarrow$ inserting three frames of "2" centering the middle frame.	(Fig. 7(c))
when $9 \leq l$ and the post value is 2		
	$\Rightarrow$ inserting three frames of "0" centering the middle frame.	(Fig. 7(d))
when $6 \leq l < 9$	$\Rightarrow$ inserting "0" at the half of the period.	(Fig. 7(e))

4 Results and Discussion

We created 36 limited animation films using our method. In these animations, male voice-actors spoke 18 audio tracks (three scripts in English, Chinese, and Japanese, each). Female voice actors provided 18 as well. Each of the sentences was selected from the 1st to 4th set of "Harvard Sentences [13]" at random and used without change for English or being translated for Chinese or Japanese. The sampling frequency of each audio track was 48[kHz]. The threshold mentioned in Sect. 3.2 was 10^4 and the other used parameters were the same as those referred in Sects. 3.1 and 3.2. Figure 9 describes one of our results. In Fig. 9, the first row shows the input audio track and the script. The second row shows the voice-actor's lip transition estimated by the method described in Sect. 3.1 and the third is the obtained limited transition. Comparing the second and the third, although our result is discretized, it simulates the similar motion to the original transition well.

From related works, we select three algorithms that can be expanded in order to produce traditional LA-style lip-synched animations composed by key images. We compare our result with the transitions created by these algorithms. In Fig. 9, the forth row shows the result generated by using an algorithm for converting to LA-style that was proposed by Kawamoto et al. [9]. Here, we treat the frames in vowel periods as key frames and our adaptive thresholding is used for the quantization. After applying the converting algorithm and linearly interpolating between key frames, the result transition is then obtained by simply thresholding the interpolated values ($0 \leq$ the value $v \leq 0.5$ to 0, $0.5 < v \leq 1.75$ to 1 and $1.75 < v$ to 2). Furthermore, the forth and the bottom row in Fig. 9 show the results generated by using the methods of Kitamura et al. [11] and Morishima et al. [12] respectively. Note that each result also employs our adaptive thresholds for the quantization. In addition, for the method proposed by Kitamura et al. [11], as described in the original paper, we set 4 as the number of frame-omitting process and 1/3 of the total number of frames for frame-holding process. In Fig. 9, a still period can be observed in both Kawamoto et al. and Kitamura et al. results. This results in a motionless appearance. In addition, spiky motion exists in Kitamura et al. and Morishima et al. results, which results in a flickering

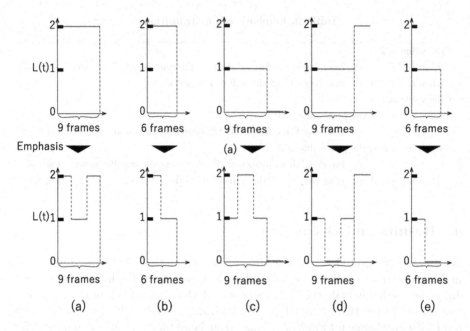

Fig. 7. Emphasis of transition.

appearance. Furthermore, the lip-moving period of the result in Morishima et al. does not match with the original audio track.

In the following parts, we discuss additional experiments that were conducted to visually evaluate our results both absolutely and relatively as compared to previous works.

4.1   User Study A: Naturalness

To assess the naturalness of our results, we performed a crowdsourced experiment. We invited 100 participants and paid a fixed sum for the experiment regardless of the quality, i.e., 0.10 U.S. dollars. The evaluation period lasted approximately 10 min. for each participant. First, we showed the 18 male animations generated by our proposed method. Then, the participants completed a survey regarding the lip-audio sync quality. The answers were scored on a seven-point Likert scale wherein a score of 1 was noted as "highly unnatural" and a score of 7 as "highly natural". We also conducted a scoring experiment for the 18 female animations in the similar manner.

Figures 10 and 11 show the results of the survey. The obtained scores were positive. In fact, all of the average scores except Q8 in Fig. 11 were larger than 4, which was noted as "neither natural nor unnatural". From these quantitative absolute evaluations, we confirmed that the participants were satisfied with the quality of our results. In regard to the female Q8, the animation included a periodic lip motion resulting in the relatively motionless appearance. This can be because the sampling interval mentioned in Sect. 3.2 was a little longer to maintain the original motion. In this situation, our method can be improved by interactive control of the sampling intervals.

4.2   User Study B: Our Method Vs. Previous Methods

We randomly selected (2 English + 2 Chinese + 2 Japanese) × 2 gender = 12 films from the 36 results mentioned at the beginning of this section. Then, we invited 15 participants to compare them with animations generated using the (1) Kawamoto's method, (2) Kitamura's method, and (3) Morishima's methods described above. Each question required the participants to watch a video wherein four animations generated by the four different methods were placed in random order. The participants were asked to decide how "natural" they looked. Note that this study was conducted independently of "User Study A" and a seven-point Likert scale was used for each task where a score of 1 is noted as "highly unnatural" and a score of 7 as "highly natural".

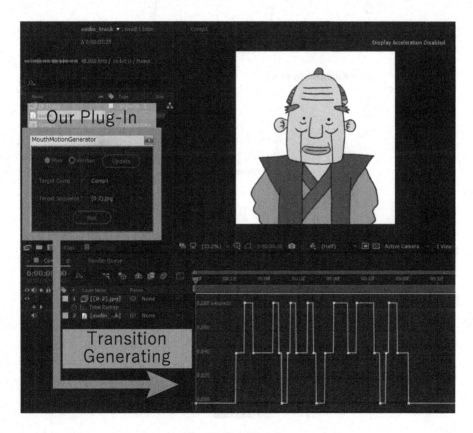

Fig. 8. Our Plug-In.

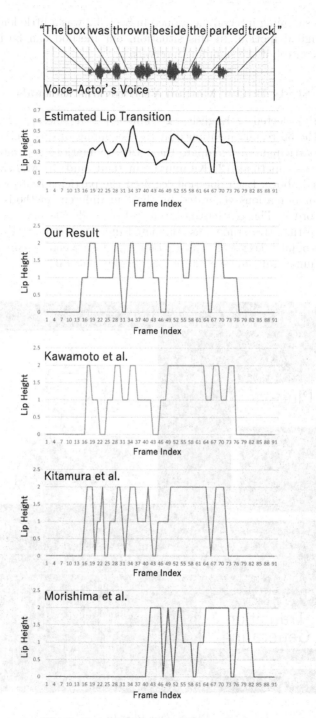

Fig. 9. Our result and previous methods.

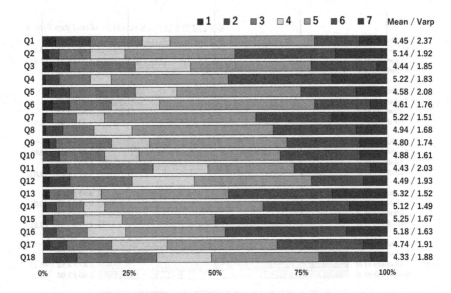

Fig. 10. Scores of user study a: male.

Figure 12 shows the results of an analysis of the answers. It is confirmed that our results have higher average scores as compared to the previous methods. Furthermore, we calculated p-values by running a Wilcoxon signed-rank test. For this, we used a function implemented in the "coin" package of R language [1].

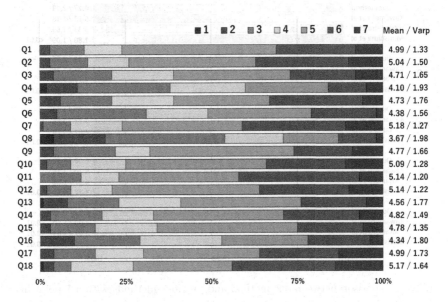

Fig. 11. Scores of user study a: female.

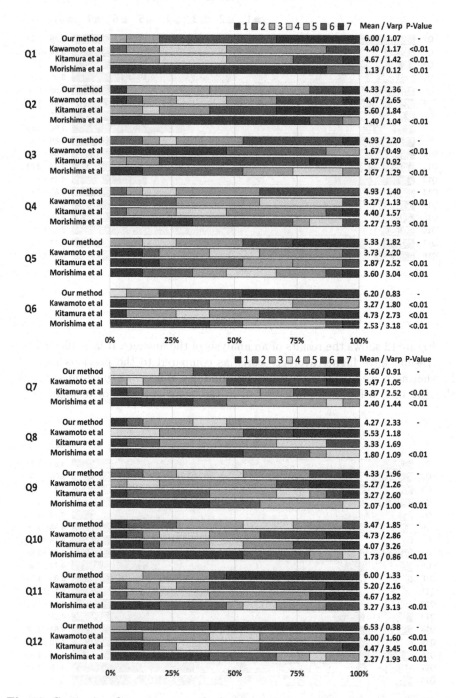

Fig. 12. Comparison between our method and previous methods with a 7-point likert scale.

As the result, 62.5% of questions wherein our results have higher average scores as compared to Kawamoto et al., 55.6% of those to Kitamura et al., and 100% of those to Morishima et al. have p-values that are less than 0.01. We conclude that in these questions, the scores were significantly different. In a few questions, although from the statistical test significant difference was not detected, our results received relatively lower scores than Kawamoto et al. or Kitamura et al. results. This can be because the quantized lip values at some consecutive key frames were the same resulting in the motionless or periodic appearance. To address this situation, our system requires to iteratively apply the motion emphasis process or implement interactive controls of the interval of sampling. As mentioned above, however, in these questions, the statistical test did not show the significant difference. Therefore, we plan to conduct additional evaluations with more samples to verify the dependencies on scripts.

5   Implementation

In addition, we implemented our method as a plug-in for Adobe After Effects, which is a standard tool following the workflow of creating cartoon animations (shown in Fig. 8). In regards to user interaction, the user first loads the key images and a recorded voice track and simply selects the gender through a button click. The changing of the gender just switches center formants, as described in Sect. 3.1. Then, by clicking the "run" button, our system automatically calculates the natural lip transition of the character, and the key images are placed following the transition. Modifications of the generated transition is intuitive and is performed interactively. Because our method is quick and because it fits into existing workflows, animators can find use of the proposed system without much disturbance. In fact, we received positive feedback from users of the system prototype. For example, an amateur animator thought that the rapid performance contributes to its usability and that it is especially convenient when generating long speech animations.

6   Conclusions and Future Work

In this paper, we proposed a new method to automatically generate limited animation (LA) style lip-synched animations using only a voice-actor's audio track and a few images that represent closed, partly open, and open lip. Our key ideas to generate natural lip transition are based on (1) taking correspondences between the continuously changing lip height of the voice-actor and the discretized key images using adaptive thresholds and on (2) sampling and interpolating lip transitions while taking into account afterimage effects. Our method (1) solves the spatial alignment problem and (2) solves the temporal alignment problem. We obtained highly positive scores about the appearance of our results. Additionally, highly positive scores were obtained when our results were compared to those using previous methods. These scores mean that our results can achieve high-quality audio-lip synchronization in LA-style animations. In addition, the results, which took into account various languages (English, Chinese, and Japanese), strongly suggest that our system can work for expanded multi-language productions. This means that animators can produce animations with less concern for the target language since the proposed method automatically addresses this aspect. We also demonstrated that our method can be successfully implemented as a plug-in in Adobe After Effects, which is a widely used tool in the field of animators. As a result, we propose that our system faithfully adheres to existing workflows in animation.

One of the limitations of our method is that it is difficult to directly apply the method for generating speech animations that include head rotations since lip shapes differ from frame to frame. However, as our method mainly focuses on generating a natural character lip transitions, animators can use the generated transition as a drawing guide. In practical scenes, the number of speech frames in which the character's head rotates is much less than that without head rotation because drawing frame by frame is time-consuming and costly. In addition, such frames require well-trained animators and they allow for personal influences. Practically, our method would be used as follows. For scenes without character head rotation, animators can efficiently produce high-quality lip motions using our method. For scenes with character head rotation, the system can serve as a guide for animators. As a part of future work, and with the aim of improving our system, image interpolation methods can be implemented to automatically generate speech animations with head rotations.

In addition, LA-style animations sometimes have speech scenes using multiple (more than three) key images to exaggerate character lip motions. In order to be able to apply our method to these types of scenes, we plan to (1) distinguish vowels and consonants more accurately by taking into account formant bandwidth, to (2) separate consonants into sub-categories (e.g. fricatives, laterals, or plosives) and to (3) take fine correspondences between the mouth shapes of the voice-actor and the key images.

There is demand for online lip-synching of LA characters. For example, in the testing of character lip motion for animation directors, in the development of remote avatars for communication entertainment and more. In this paper, we proposed a quick method for LA-style lip-synched animations. The system can be expanded for the use in real-time applications. In future works, we aim to optimize our algorithm for online applications.

Acknowlededments. This work was supported in part by the Japanese Information-Technology Promotion Agency (IPA), JST ACCEL Grant No. JPMJAC 1602, and JSPS Grant No. 17H06101, Japan.

References

1. coin: conditional inference procedures in a permutation test framework. https://cran.r-project.org/web/packages/coin/index.html. Accessed 22 Oct 2017
2. Bregler, C., Covell, M., Slaney, M.: Video rewrite: driving visual speech with audio. In: Proceedings of the 24th Annual Conference on Computer Graphics and Interactive Techniques, pp. 353–360. ACM Press/Addison-Wesley Publishing Co. (1997)
3. Cao, C., Hou, Q., Zhou, K.: Displaced dynamic expression regression for real-time facial tracking and animation. ACM Trans. Graph. (TOG) 33(4), 43 (2014)
4. Chang, Y.J., Ezzat, T.: Transferable videorealistic speech animation. In: Proceedings of the 2005 ACM SIGGRAPH/Eurographics Symposium on Computer Animation, pp. 143–151. ACM (2005)
5. Dunbar, D., Humphreys, G.: A spatial data structure for fast poisson-disk sample generation. ACM Trans. Graph. (TOG) 25(3), 503–508 (2006)
6. Dvorožňák, M., Bénard, P., Barla, P., Wang, O., Sýkora, D.: Example-based expressive animation of 2D rigid bodies. ACM Trans. Graph 36(4), 10 (2017)
7. Ezzat, T., Geiger, G., Poggio, T.: Trainable videorealistic speech animation. ACM Trans. Graph. (TOG) 21(3), 388–398 (2002)
8. Ishi, C.T., Liu, C., Ishiguro, H., Hagita, N.: Speech-driven lip motion generation for tele-operated humanoid robots. In: Auditory-Visual Speech Processing 2011 (2011)
9. Kawamoto, S.I., Yotsukura, T., Anjyo, K., Nakamura, S.: Efficient lip-synch tool for 3D cartoon animation. Comput. Anim. Virtual Worlds 19(34), 247–257 (2008)
10. Kazi, R.H., Grossman, T., Umetani, N., Fitzmaurice, G.: Motion amplifiers: sketching dynamic illustrations using the principles of 2D animation. In: Proceedings of the 2016 CHI Conference on Human Factors in Computing Systems (2016)
11. Kitamura, M., Kanamori, Y., Mitani, J., Fukui, Y., Tsuruno, R.: Motion frame omission for cartoon-like effects. In: Proceedings of International Workshop on Advanced Image Technology (IWAIT), pp. 148–152. KSBE (2014)
12. Morishima, S., Kuriyama, S., Kawamoto, S., Suzuki, T., Taira, M., Yotsukura, T., Nakamura, S.: Data-driven efficient production of cartoon character animation. In: ACM SIGGRAPH 2007 Sketches, p. 76. ACM (2007)
13. Rothauser, E.: IEEE recommended practice for speech quality measurements. IEEE Trans. Audio Electroacoust. 17, 225–246 (1969)
14. Wang, J., Drucker, S.M., Agrawala, M., Cohen, M.F.: The cartoon animation filter. ACM Trans. Graph. (TOG) 25, 1169–1173 (2006)
15. Weise, T., Bouaziz, S., Li, H., Pauly, M.: Realtime performance-based facial animation (TOG). ACM Trans. Graph. 30, 77 (2011)
16. Weise, T., Li, H., Van Gool, L., Pauly, M.: Face/off: live facial puppetry. In: Proceedings of the 2009 ACM SIGGRAPH/Eurographics Symposium on Computer Animation, pp. 7–16. ACM (2009)

Polymorphic Cataloguing and Interactive 3D Visualization for Multiple Context of Digital Content: MoSaIC

Hiroyo Ishikawa[1(✉)] and Kunitake Kaneko[1,2]

[1] Research Institute for Digital Media and Content, Keio University, Yokohama, Japan
hiroyo@hvrl.ics.keio.ac.jp
[2] Faculty of Science and Technology, Keio University, Yokohama, Japan

Abstract. In this paper, we propose two methods of interactive visualization of the MoSaIC catalogue.

We proposed a conceptual modeling for manifold relationships among digital content files as polymorphic catalogues and its visualization system (MoSaIC-II) before. In the modeling, two structures are provided to express the relationships. One is "grouping objects". The other is "associating between two objects". The relationship is constructed by using the combination of two structures, and it is described by using directed graph called a MoSaIC catalogue. Multiple catalogues can be connected by shared objects polymorphically.

To visualize the catalogue, we propose two methods which are polymorphic topology view and layer view in MoSaIC system using 3D computer graphics. In the previous method, some objects might be overlapped depending on object connections. Then a lot of objects and complex connection of edges can users feel complicated. Using the new methods, object overlap and the complexity of catalogue and object connections can be improved.

In the polymorphic topology view, users can see topology of connected objects avoiding object overlaps. Furthermore, we propose the layer view to show objects aligned by a catalogue creator. In the layer view, users can see connected objects which are aligned and exhibited on each catalogue layer. In this method, a complex connection of edges is improved and comparatively a lot of objects can be handled.

Keywords: Digital curation · Graph visualization · Multiple-context

1 Introduction

Recently, more and more digital content is used on the Internet. Many museums and libraries open their archives of digitized analogue work. Because the content adds keywords and descriptions, we can search digital content by keywords. However, when we don't know appropriate keywords, it is difficult to find a target content by searching. In many cases, users don't access archives without purpose. However, related content may be provided in some archives or search engines as recommendations, for example, the Google knowledge graph [1], Google doodle [2] illustrating a topic related to this

© Springer International Publishing AG, part of Springer Nature 2018
A. D. Cheok et al. (Eds.): ACE 2017, LNCS 10714, pp. 172–186, 2018.
https://doi.org/10.1007/978-3-319-76270-8_13

day, and Wikipedia main page [3]. It is very useful way for users to access and enjoy content easily.

Another way to find content is to use a digital curation site and a content curation site [4, 5]. On the curation sites, links listing digital content with curator's writing provided. The users can easily access digital content from the links without searching. It is very useful to provide links of related digital content for users. The content, however, is limited to a certain theme. The users have to browse other sites or search something repeatedly on the web to find digital content of a related theme. That is, for watching useful content, it is important to find digital content related to each other.

On the other hand, museums have devised various methods to be open their archives to the public. Rijksmuseum Amsterdam has introduced a system to show personal collections of Rijks item images. In this system, users can collect a part of an image. Additionally, related collections which created by other users can be shown when collections include common images [6]. The Metropolitan Museum of Art has published item lists curated by museum staff from each theme. Some keywords are added to characteristic parts of images, users can search them by keywords [7]. Such systems are useful to find new content.

If multiple digital curation site and collection site are associated by common content, we can implement efficient browsing by follow the links. Such link information allows users to find digital content, like an association game, from networks. Then users can understand various relations and contexts. Additionally, to understanding the content it also encourages the way users find for new related content and gain new information or knowledge. However, it is difficult to achieve that kind of multi curation on ordinary web technique. Therefore, we thought about connecting content of archives, digital curations and collections by related content and proposed polymorphic cataloguing [8]. In this method, one catalogue is created for one theme by abstracting relationships among the content as a directed graph. The catalogues can be connected by shared objects. So we can access content included in the catalogues while labeling each catalogue. To access archives through polymorphic catalogues, the catalogues have to be visualized.

There are many visualization methods of a directed graph [9]. As a way to express and visualize relationships of many content and various themes, some applications are to express the connection between web pages, songs or words, user information by using 2D graphs to visualize them [10, 11]. These can express and visualize the connections between content evenly, however it is difficult to express the polymorphic catalogues we proposed.

To visualize polymorphic catalogue, we proposed a visualization method where catalogues are layered and objects are connected by arrows [8, 12]. Then we developed a content browsing system using the visualization result as a graphical interface. The system was effective, however, there were some problems of overlapped objects and complex connections by a lot of objects and edges.

Therefore, in this paper, new methods are proposed to avoid these problems. To solve the problem of overlapped objects, we propose a method which is like a radial tree. Additionally, we propose a method which layered each catalogue completely for a lot of objects and graph edges.

2   Polymorphic Cataloguing

2.1 Modeling of Relationships

Various relationships among objects are determined, by a combination of order, corre-spondence, reference, connection, equivalence relation and so on. However, it is very difficult to strictly define every kind of relationships. Therefore, in this research, we avoid describing for the semantics of each relationship. We propose a modeling to abstract various relationships among objects. In this modeling, two structures are provided as an abstract of conceptual model.

(1) Grouping objects
(2) Associating between two objects

(1) is to create a group of objects gathered by a specific purpose, for example, cate-gorization, and clustering. (2) is to associate two objects, it means various semantics as mentioned in above.

The relationships are expressed by the combination of the two structures. One cluster of relationships is dealt with as one catalogue described by a directed graph. Examples of the modeling are shown in Fig. 1.

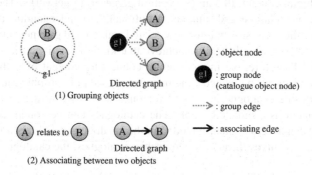

Fig. 1.   Two structures for modeling of relationships. (1) The group g1 includes the object A, B and C. In the directed graph, the node g1 connects the node A, B and C by group edges. (2) The object A relates to the object B. In the directed graph, the node A connects to the node B by an associating edge

In the graph data, an object is shown by a node. In the case of grouping, a group node is added for each group, but one group is possible in one catalogue, group elements are connected by group edges. It is not possible to group a catalogue to itself. In the case of associating, two nodes are connected by an associating edge. It is not possible to asso-ciate a node to itself.

When the catalogue is an element of another catalogue, the catalogue needs to include a group. The group may be empty. That is, the group node means a catalogue object node.

In this paper, the catalogue is a connected graph. The node and the edge have are added metadata. The file object node has file ID and owner ID. The catalogue object node and the edge have catalogue ID and owner ID. All connected node of a node are ordered. The system deal with catalogue ID and file ID as object ID, but can distinguish between a catalogue and a file. Nodes don't have catalogue information, but the catalogue elements can be known by gathering nodes connected by the same catalogue edges.

2.2 Cataloguing Objects with Properties

Property information can be set to each object. The properties used in this paper are title, description, thumbnail (for files) and object map (for catalogues). Title description and object map are text files.

Thumbnail is an image file. Titles or thumbnails in visualized results can be helped to distinguish the objects. Object map is used only in layer view (see in Sect. 3.2) to position objects.

Each property can be set one by each catalogue. The properties are set to each object node by directed graph in each catalogue, because properties are regarded as digital content files.

Example of cataloguing with properties is shown in Fig. 2. Catalogue properties are set to a group node by property edges. The catalogue which has no group is added an invisible catalogue node and the properties are set to the node. The property edge has catalogue information, so system can distinguish properties by each catalogue. The property edge, invisible catalogue node and property node are not visualized as a graph.

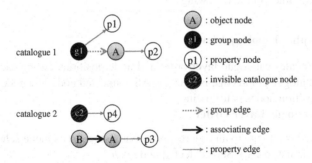

Fig. 2. Example of catalogue with properties. A property of catalogue 1 is set to the group node g1. A property of catalogue 2 which has no group is set to the invisible catalogue node c2. To the shared node A, the property p2 is set in catalogue 1, and the property p3 is set in catalogue 2. Property p2 and p3 may be the same.

The shared objects can be set different properties by each included catalogue. However, the thumbnail of a file is one prepared by an original file owner. Title, description, and map file of a catalogue set by another catalogue are not available except the title. The title is available for the catalogue object node in another catalogue.

3 Visualization of Catalogue

We propose two methods to visualize catalogues described by directed graphs. One is polymorphic topology view, the other is layer view.

The flow of visualization part is the following.

1. Select an object node and a catalogue by a user.
2. Gather objects connected to the select object from a database.
3. Decide new object positions by polymorphic topology view or layer view.
4. Draw and move objects from current position to new position.

In the polymorphic topology view, the selected node is set at the center and the graph is expands outwards, radially. Arbitrary node is located at the center of nodes which are connected to itself. Basically each catalogue area is layered. Each node is shown on the layer of an applicable catalogue. In the case of a shared node, it is shown on higher priority catalogue layer.

In the layer view, start catalogue is set to the main catalogue. The main catalogue is set to the lowest layer. Each node is shown on the layer of the applicable catalogue. The position of nodes can be set with an object map by a catalogue creator. The nodes shared in multiple catalogues are shown each layer of the applicable catalogue, however the horizontal position of the same object node is the same. The order of catalogue except the main catalogue is decided by the selected catalogue and catalogue connection. These methods are explained in the following.

3.1 Polymorphic Topology View

This method decides catalogue layer order and node positions on the each layer. The direction of catalogue graph edge is ignored. All connected node of a node are ordered. The flow to position nodes is following.

Decide Catalogue Layer Order

a. Add selected catalogue to an ordered catalogue list (c-list). Queue selected node to a check node list (n-list). Set a selected node to n_i.

b. Acquire catalogues $\{c_j : j = 0 \dots m - 1\}$ in which n_i is included.

   For $\{c_j : j = 0 \dots m - 1\}$,
   - add c_j to the c-list.
   - add ordered nodes included in c_j to the n-list. The ordered nodes are acquired by the flowing.
     • Create the spanning tree (tree- c_j - n_i) in which the root is n_i from c_j. A spanning tree is obtained by breadth first search from the root node.
     • Extract nodes from the tree- c_j - n_i by breadth-first search.

c. Dequeue from the n-list to n_i.
   Add n_i to an ordered object list (o-list).

d. (iv) Repeat from (ii) to (iii) until the n-list is empty.

A spanning tree is obtained by breadth first search from a root node. In adding catalogues or queuing nodes to the each list, a repetition is avoided. The c-list is catalogue layer order.

Position Nodes on Each Catalogue Layer. Process the following for each catalogue c_i of the c-list.

a.   Create spanning tree.

Create the spanning tree from ci, in which the root node n_r is the highest priority node of the o-list.

b.   Calculate weight of connected nodes.

Weights of all connected nodes are calculated. Two weights are on one connected nodes shown in Fig. 3 (1). A weight of node i from node j is calculated by formula (1). Here, $\{c_k | k = 0 \dots m - 1\}$ is connected node of node i expect node j, w_{cki} is a weight of node c_k from node i. If node i has no child node, $w_{ij} = 1$.

$$w_{ij} = 1 + \sum_{k=0}^{m-1} w_{c_k i} \tag{1}$$

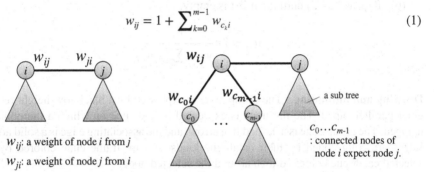

(1) Weights of connected nodes.   (2) Calculate a weight of node i from j.

Fig. 3. Weights of connected nodes.

c.   Decide node positions
   (1)   Decide n_r position. When ci is the selected catalogue, n_r is fixed at current position. When ci is not the selected catalogue, the position is decided already.
   (2)   Set n_r to node i.
   (3)   Acquire nodes connected to node i in ci. Queue not positioned nodes to a check-node-list (n-list).
   (4)   Decide position connected nodes as shown in Fig. 4. Each center angle of circular sectors of connected node is calculated by formula (2).

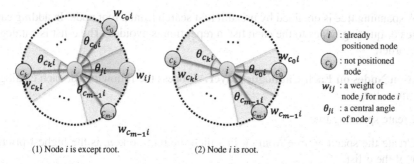

(1) Node i is except root.   (2) Node i is root.

Fig. 4. Weights and central angles of circular sectors of connected nodes. Connected nodes of node i are concentrically located in which node i is the center. When node i is not the root, the node i is located previously, and already positioned node (node j) is existed in connected nodes of the node i. The nodes $\{c_0 \ldots c_{m-1}\}$ are located as shown in (1). When node i is the root as shown in (2), node j doesn't exist and c_0 is located on the node j position of (1). (Color figure online)

(5) Dequeue from the n-list to node i.

(6) Repeat (3)–(5) until the n-list is empty.

$$\theta_{c_k i} = 2\pi \frac{w_{ic_k}}{w_{ij} + \sum_{l=0}^{m-1} w_{c_l i}} \tag{2}$$

Drawing and animating. The group node is expressed by a black low-height rectangular parallelepiped. The file node is expressed by the cube on which a thumbnail is mapped. The group edge is a dashed line arrow, and the associating edge is a solid arrow. Edges are color-coded by their catalogue kinds. A wire frame cube colored by the selected catalogue color is drawn around the selected node.

Selected catalogue is set on the lowest layer. Other layers are set in the order in the paragraph (1). Shared nodes are shown on higher priority catalogue layer, from each catalogue, however edges are drawn from other layers. If useless space exists, for example less objects, an upper layer moves down to the same height of a lower layer.

An example of visualization result is shown in Fig. 8 (1). Visualization result is used as a visual interface. Users can change viewpoint and scale freely by using touch device. Selecting node on the visualized graph will changes the center of graphs and each node position. Nodes are animating from the current position to a new position, so we can watch the moving of nodes.

3.2 Layer View

This method decides catalogue layer order. Node positions on the each layer are set by the object map of the property. If the object map is not set, the positions are set from result of the polymorphic topology view. Catalogues are layered from the main catalogue in order from the bottom. The main catalogue is selected by a user in advance. The order of layers is decided in the following.

Decide Catalogue Layer Order. In this method, catalogue connection information is needed. When two catalogues have a shared object, these catalogues are connected. Each catalogue keeps the last selected object. Flow chart is shown in Fig. 5. Some variables and a sub process are shown in Fig. 6.

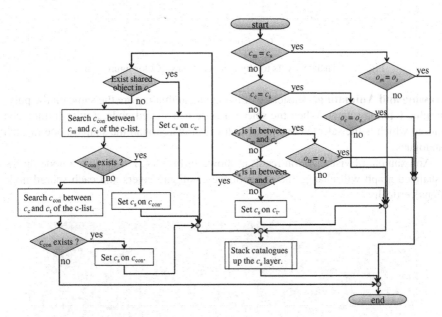

Fig. 5. Flow chart of deciding catalogue layer order. c_{con} is a catalogue connected to c_s.

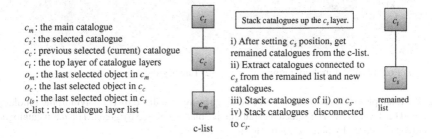

c_m : the main catalogue
c_s : the selected catalogue
c_c : previous selected (current) catalogue
c_t : the top layer of catalogue layers
o_m : the last selected object in c_m
o_c : the last selected object in c_c
o_{ls} : the last selected object in c_s
c-list : the catalogue layer list

Stack catalogues up the c_s layer.

i) After setting c_s position, get remained catalogues from the c-list.
ii) Extract catalogues connected to c_s from the remained list and new catalogues.
iii) Stack catalogues of ii) on c_s.
iv) Stack catalogues disconnected to c_s.

Fig. 6. Catalogue layers and variables used in Fig. 5.

Translate Layers to Align Shared Nodes. Upper layers are translated to align shared node vertically shown in Fig. 7. When there are multiple shared nodes in one catalogue, the selected node takes priority and all objects are translated. If the selected node is not included, the lowest layer position takes priority. Then other shared nodes are moved to align respectively.

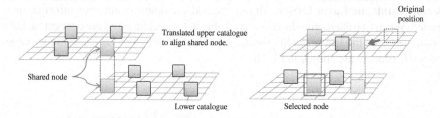

Fig. 7. Translate layers to align shared nodes. (Color figure online)

Drawing and Animating. Basically drawing and animating are the same on the polymorphic topology view. When the selected node is a shared node, a wire frame cube colored which is the selected catalogue color is drawn around the shared node in each catalogues.

An example of visualization result is shown in Fig. 8 (2). Selecting a node on the visualized graph will change the order of the catalogue layers and each shared node aligns vertically.

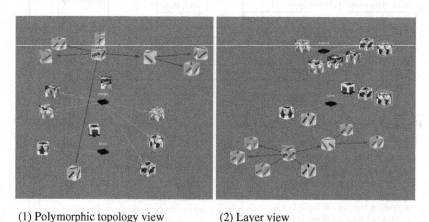

(1) Polymorphic topology view   (2) Layer view

Fig. 8. Examples of visualization. Three catalogues are visualized by (1) polymorphic topology view and (2) layer view. The selected catalogue is "black" colored by green. The main catalogue is "crayons" colored by blue in (2). (Color figure online)

4   Experiments

4.1   Experiment System: MoSaIC

Experiment system consists by a computer and two 4K touch displays (32 in.). An example of displays is shown in Fig. 9. The layer view is shown at the right side display, and content files shown at the left side. In this system, available media as digital content file are image, movies, audio (supported format by DirectShow(R)), pdf and text.

Fig. 9. MoSaIC system.

4.2 Experiments

Comparison between the previous method and the proposed method. Examples of
the same catalogues are visualized by the previous method and the proposed method
(the polymorphic topology view) are show in Fig. 10. Two objects are located on the
same position in the previous method (1). It can be seen that overlapping is avoided in
the polymorphic topology view (2). In the case of (3), because many edges are crossed
and complicated, it is difficult to understand connections of objects. In the polymorphic
topology view shown in (4), the crossed and complicated edges are improved, and it can
be seen that it is easy to understand the object connections.

An example of many catalogues and objects are shown in Fig. 11. The results of the
previous method and polymorphic method show few differences in appearance. The
edges are crowded so it is difficult to select an object. In the layer view, there are no
vertical obstructive edges. Even though the catalogue structure is very high, user can
select an object by changing viewpoint and view size with rotation, translation and scale
of the catalogue structure.

Comparison between the polymorphic topology view and the layer view. An
example of fewer objects in catalogues is shown in Fig. 12. In the polymorphic topology
view, because there are not so many edges, user can see the relationships among the
objects, even though the objects are connected directly. In the layer view, to see catalogue connections users have to select an object and observe marked objects.

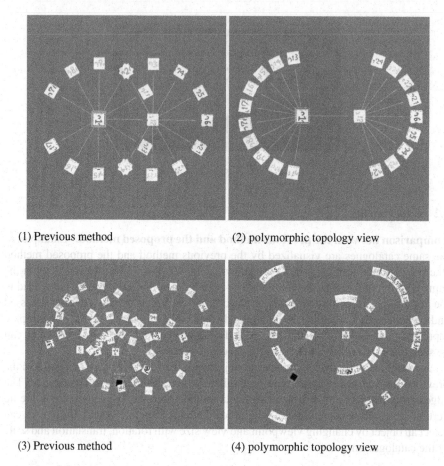

(1) Previous method   (2) polymorphic topology view

(3) Previous method   (4) polymorphic topology view

Fig. 10. Examples of the comparison between the previous method and the proposed method (the polymorphic topology view). Overlapped objects occurred shown in (1). In the polymorphic topology view, overlapped objects are avoided shown in (2). In the case of (3), edges are crossed and complicated. The crossed edges are avoided and complicated connections are improved in the polymorphic topology view shown in (4).

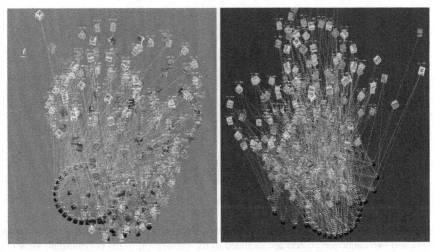

(1) Previous method   (2) polymorphic topology view

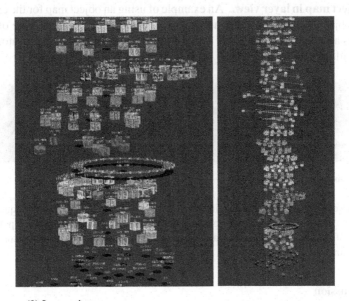

(3) Layer view

Fig. 11. An example of seventy three catalogues, one hundred and ninety file objects and seventy three catalogue objects visualized by three methods. Many edges are crowded in the previous method (1) and polymorphic topology view (2). In the layer view (3), there is no vertical direction edge, however, the height of catalogue structure is about three times as tall as (1) and (2). Enlarged image of a part of the left side image is shown in the right side. The same objects with the selected object are marked by red wire frame cubes. (Color figure online)

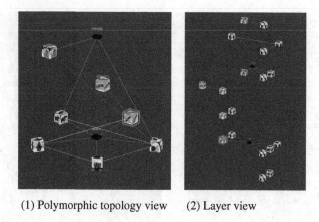

(1) Polymorphic topology view   (2) Layer view

Fig. 12. An example of the catalogues which have fewer objects. Seven catalogues, seven file objects and two catalogue objects are included in the catalogues. In the polymorphic view (1), there are three layers. In the layer view (2), there are seven layers.

Using object map in layer view. An example of using an object map for the catalogues in which objects are connected sequentially is shown in Fig. 13. In the case of no map, the objects are located on a straight line. In the case of using map, the creator can edit object positions.

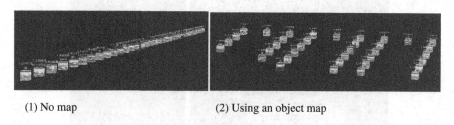

(1) No map   (2) Using an object map

Fig. 13. An example of the catalogue in which thirty six objects are connected sequentially. In the case of no map (1), the object positions are set from the result in polymorphic topology view. In the case of (2), the object positions are set from the object map which the creator edited the object positions.

4.3 Discussion

It can be seen that object overlap which occurred in the previous method is avoided shown in Fig. 10. However, when the weights of nodes are imbalance, the light weighted objects are too near each other in the polymorphic topology view. Thus, there is room for improvement on this weighting.

In the case of the catalogues which have many objects shown in Fig. 11, it is difficult to follow edges between objects on the polymorphic topology view. In the layer view, however, it is easier to select an object than the polymorphic topology view, because of edges are removed between different catalogues. In this case, catalogue connections can be seen by searching the same object with the selected object.

In the case of the catalogues which have fewer objects shown in Fig. 12, because there are many layers on which a few objects are shown in the layer view, it is not easy to understand the relationships at a glance. On the other hand, the polymorphic topology view connecting objects directly even between different catalogues is still easier understand than the layer view.

The effectiveness of the object map is shown in Fig. 13. Creators can edit object positions in the maps and provide a virtual space like an exhibition room designed freely in the layer view.

From these experiments, it can be seen that it is effective to select an appropriate view and use object maps according to the number of objects or depending on the complexity of the catalogue.

5 Conclusion

In this research, we proposed two methods (the polymorphic topology view and the layer view). An interactive visualization of the MoSaIC catalogues is improved the problems occurred in the previous method.

We developed the new system MoSaIC using the proposed methods as a visual interface, and examined the effectiveness of them. In the polymorphic topology view, overlapped objects were avoided by changing the center angle of graph connection by connected object weights. In the layer view, the complexity of the catalogue and the object connections were improved by layered catalogues.

In this paper, the system deals with connected graphs and catalogues which are connected. We have to improve the MoSaIC system to deal with disconnected graphs and disconnected catalogues.

Additionally, evaluation of the polymorphic cataloguing is needed. For example, we have to investigate similarity or difference between Human recognition and conceptual modeling by polymorphic cataloguing.

The current system is a stand-alone system and accesses content files stored in internal HDD by a simple Database. In the future, we aim that museums and libraries will be connected by the Internet and will share the archives and the catalogues. Researches about an autonomous distributed global Catalogues sharing mechanism is a work in progress [13].

Acknowledgments. This work has been supported in part by MEXT (Ministry of Education, Culture, Sports, Science and Technology) - Supported Program for the Strategic Research Foundation at Private Universities 2012-2017.

References

1. Google official blog. http://googleblog.blogspot.jp/2012/05/introducing-knowledge-graph-things-not.html
2. Google doodles. https://www.google.com/doodles
3. Wikipedia main page. https://en.wikipedia.org/wiki/Main_Page
4. Digital Curation Resource Guide. http://digital-scholarship.org/dcrg/dcrg.htm
5. Beagrie, N.: Digital curation for science, digital libraries, and individuals. Int. J. Digit. Curation **1**(1), 3–16 (2006)
6. Rijks studio. https://www.rijksmuseum.nl/en/explore-the-collection
7. One met. Many worlds. http://onemetmanyworlds-eng.tumblr.com/
8. Ishikawa, H., Saito, H., Miyashita, Y., Kaneko, K.: Polymorphic cataloguing and viewing system for using digital archives: MoSaIC. In: International Conference on Virtual Systems and Multimedia, VSMM 2014, Hong Kong, pp. 176–179. IEEE (2014)
9. Herman, I., Melançon, G., Marshall, M.S.: Graph visualization and navigation in information visualization: a survey. IEEE Trans. Vis. Comput. Graph. **6**(1), 24–43 (2000)
10. Songrium. http://songrium.jp/
11. Flickr Graph. http://www.visualcomplexity.com/vc/project.cfm?id=91
12. Nodem repository. http://repo.nodem.org/?objectId=276
13. Miyashita, Y., Ishikawa, H., Teraoka, F., Kaneko, K.: Catalogue: graph representation of file relations for a globally distributed environment. In: Proceedings of the 30th Annual ACM Symposium on Applied Computing (SAC 2015), Salamanca, pp. 806–809. ACM (2015)

Leveraging Icebreaking Tasks to Facilitate Uptake of Voice Communication in Multiplayer Games

Kieran Hicks[1]([✉]), Kathrin Gerling[2], Patrick Dickinson[1],
Conor Linehan[3], and Carl Gowen[1]

[1] University of Lincoln, Lincoln, UK
khicks@lincoln.ac.uk
[2] KU Leuven, Leuven, Belgium
[3] University College Cork, Cork, Ireland

Abstract. Voice Communication (VC) is widely employed by developers as an essential component of online games. Typically, it is assumed that communications through this mechanism will be helpful and enjoyable, but existing literature suggests that the entry into VC can be problematic. In this paper, we present a study that attempts to mitigate player discomfort when first engaging with VC with strangers, through the use of traditional icebreaking tasks. We integrate these into the game *RET,* an online cooperative first person shooter which requires effective communication for players to succeed. An online user study with 18 participants suggests that icebreaking tasks can contribute to a positive VC experience, but their inclusion also creates further issues to be considered for successful integration.

Keywords: Voice communication · Player experience · Game design

1 Introduction

Voice communication (VC) is increasingly seen as a standard feature in online multiplayer gaming, e.g. *Overwatch* [4], The *Division* [37] and, *Destiny* [7]. A small body of research on the topic suggests that, on the one hand, VC may promote a feeling of connection between players, and facilitates coordinated play [42]; on the other hand, VC can make players feel more vulnerable and open to new types of antisocial behaviour [40, 41]. Given the increased popularity of online multiplayer modes, the integration of VC as the default method for player coordination in contemporary games, but many of the initially reported issues still remain [42], suggesting a need for game designers and researchers to develop ways of facilitating positive VC experiences.

In our paper, we address this issue by leveraging traditional icebreaking tasks which are small group based tasks designed to introduce people to each other and encourage conversation. We use these to support the on-boarding phase of games, as this is a key element in retaining players [32]. We present *RET*, a three-player online game in which the successful completion of team challenges requires effective communication between players. In a study with 18 participants, we explore the impact of in-game icebreaking tasks on player experience, and perceptions of VC. This was achieved through a study

© Springer International Publishing AG, part of Springer Nature 2018
A. D. Cheok et al. (Eds.): ACE 2017, LNCS 10714, pp. 187–201, 2018.
https://doi.org/10.1007/978-3-319-76270-8_14

using post-hoc surveys and interviews. Our results show that icebreaking tasks are generally effective in bringing players together, but that adaptations are necessary to seamlessly integrate them into games and ensure adequate re-playability. Building on these findings, we discuss strategies for the development of in-game icebreaking tasks to facilitate entry into VC, and discuss the wider implications that VC has for player experience.

This paper makes the two main contributions: (1) We present one approach to reducing player discomfort when first engaging with VC, through the design and evaluation of in-game icebreaking tasks. (2) We discuss issues surrounding the wider integration of icebreakers into online multiplayer games.

2   Background

We provide an overview of previous work on the use of VC in games along with insights into icebreaking tasks to facilitate social interaction in gaming settings and beyond.

2.1   Voice Communication in Games

Since the late 1990s, VC has been used as an alternative to text chat in online games. It was first used for back channel communication through third-party voiceover-IP software, such as TeamSpeak [31]. More recently, VC has been built directly into games; for example, in the Xbox LIVE online multiplayer platform [40]. In early online games, voice chat was sought frequently in competitive team-based first-person shooter (FPS) games to support fast-paced combat [40]. Likewise, in the massively multiplayer online (MMO) genre, strategic advantage was a primary factor that increased the uptake of VC [40, 44]. Recently some games, such as DayZ [8] have made use of the voice communication as a game mechanic, through an in-game proximity system that only allows nearby players in the game world to communicate [10]. Voice has also been used as a method for control in single player games [9].

Previous work has broadly explored player motives to engage in VC. Beyond using it to gain competitive advantage, some players use online gaming not just to connect with their teammates and opponents, but also as a way of staying in touch with friends [44], and research suggests that gaming communities may form for both social and cooperative reasons [45]. Within these communities, players may receive social and emotional support [33] and there is evidence that voice communication in games has positive social effects; for example, a reduction of loneliness among players [44]. In this context, research suggests that VC conveys more information about the communicator than text [40], and may therefore establish increased trust between conversation partners [6].

Wadley et al. [40] found that players considered voice to have greater emotional impact than text, with profound implications for player experience. For example, one rude player can demoralise the rest of the team [40]. Previous research also identified concerns regarding anxiety and harassment that were detrimental to players' experiences of VC [39–41]. Other problematic aspects include player behaviour that adds unnecessary noise to the voice channel e.g. television programs being picked up by the microphone [17], and technical difficulties especially when using third-party tools [39].

2.2 Icebreakers to Facilitate Social Interaction

Icebreakers have been long used as a method of familiarising strangers in small groups to increase collaboration and encourage positive communication. For example, they are applied to introduce groups of adult learners [12], or as a means to initiate conversation in public spaces [26]. Icebreakers have also been found to be a method of supporting increased collaboration and aiding in the development of online communities [14], e.g., in an emerging online learning community users were asked to name a film character that they identified with, revealing a piece of personal information whilst encouraging discussion [14]. Different types of icebreaking tasks can be employed depending on the nature of the existing relationship between participants, situations in which the participants will be strangers, tasks that facilitate introductions and getting to know each other are successful [43] e.g. asking a group to sort into alphabetical order encourages introductions [42, 43].

Interestingly, games are often applied as icebreaking tasks [26], rather than being viewed as a setting that could benefit from icebreaking activities. For example, Jarusriboonchai et al. [21] leveraged a co-located game that involved players asking simple questions as an introductory icebreaking task. Generally, research suggests that games can be more effective than traditional icebreaking tasks, highlighting the benefits of a playful setting [11].

3   RET: A System to Study Icebreaking Tasks in Games

In order to study the impact of icebreaking tasks to facilitate VC in online gaming, we created *RET*, a co-operative online game. The goal of *RET* is to progress through a series of challenges that vary in activity such as jumping on platforms and navigating mazes (See Fig. 1). The game is played with three players; each is given either the *Healer, Tank* or *Damage* role at random upon starting the game. These three roles each have a different ability requiring players to work together. *RET* was implemented using the Unity3D engine [38] and was distributed via the game marketplace itch.io.

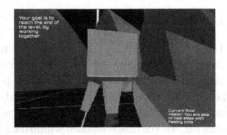

Fig. 1. Gameplay view of RET.   **Fig. 2.** Observing the health of a teammate.

3.1 Gameplay

RET is a first person shooter to be played with three persons that features a total of nine puzzles (see Fig. 3) that must be solved co-operatively and require players to both discuss tactics and swap between roles (e.g., the role of *Healer* must be swapped between players to heal each other). The *Tank* role allows the player to raise a large shield that can be used to defend both themselves and fellow players, The *Damage* role is able to shoot and destroy enemies that exist through the level whilst also having a higher jump to reach certain platforms, and the *Healer* role is granted the ability to shoot orbs that heal fellow players. There are some instances in which the game uses distributed information across players, e.g., a player cannot see their own health value and instead must rely on other players to keep them informed (See Fig. 2).

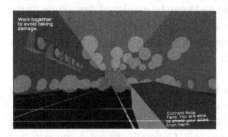

Fig. 3. Puzzle solving.   **Fig. 4.** Engaging with the icebreaking task.

Controls. Players can navigate the environment using the WASD keys to move, space to jump, and the mouse to orientate and look around. Unique abilities associated with roles can be accessed through the left mouse click. The players' avatar is able to interact with certain objects in the environment by pressing the F key, and each player can request to change roles with other players.

Voice Communication. As RET implements information sharing as a core mechanic, it lends itself to voice communication to facilitate this process. The game features an in-game voice communication solution implemented via an open channel with an always on microphone (i.e., continuous transmission). A text-based chat channel is also included.

3.2 Integration of Icebreaking Tasks

Traditional icebreaking tasks prominently feature information exchange, e.g., users are tasked with arranging the group into alphabetical order which prompts participants to ask each other's names or participants are posed with a statement such as "*what x items could you not live without*" [43]. RET builds on these previously successful icebreaking tasks [15] and uses simple questions to encourage players to interact with each other (See Fig. 4). The task is situated within the game world and takes about 90 s to complete. When first joining the game, players are prompted to answer several questions e.g., *What is your favourite hobby?*, *What is your favourite movie?*, *Where are you from?*, *Current favourite game?*. Once all players have completed this part, a prompt appears that introduces the team and encourages players to greet each other by speaking their nickname displayed on each player's avatar. After 30 s, answers are shared with the group by displaying them above each avatar. The game then encourages players to discuss; however, to see answers, players need to be in close proximity in the virtual space. Therefore, they do not just have to engage in verbal communication but also interact through physical location of their avatars. This process is repeated three times, then the main game begins by teleporting all players into the starting area of the first level.

4   Study: Exploring the Effects of Icebreaking Tasks in Multiplayer Games

Here, we report results of a study we carried out to gain insights into both player perceptions of the game *RET* and the integration of icebreaking tasks to facilitate engagement with VC.

4.1   Research Questions

We aim to answer two main questions related to the integration of in-game icebreaking tasks in *RET*, (1) what effect does the inclusion of these icebreaking tasks have on the player experience of *RET* and (2) if the icebreaking tasks had any effect on reducing player perceived discomfort in using VC with strangers.

4.2   Measures

In our study, we use post-game questionnaires and interviews to gain insights into player experience, combining quantitative and qualitative data.

Questionnaires. We made use of several standard questionnaires and a custom post-game questionnaire. This was done through an in-game survey approach as Frommel et al. found that integrated questionnaires can help minimise gameplay interruptions [16]. The first few questions focused on demographic information. Following this, participants were asked to rate several statements on a seven-point Likert scale, for example, *"I enjoyed the communication method"* and *"I felt comfortable using the communication method"*. This part of our study focused on participant enjoyment and feelings toward VC. Finally, participants were asked to fill in the Player Experience and Needs Satisfaction (PENS) Questionnaire [27] as this has previously been applied in games research [3]. Through using the PENS questionnaire after each condition, we gained insight into how the icebreaking task affected the player experience. When participants had played through all three conditions, they were asked to rate each condition on a Likert scale between 1–7 where 1 is "Dislike" and 7 is "Like".

Interviews. After the play session was complete, participants were invited to take part in a short one-on-one open interview. This interview was semi-structured with several questions that all participants were asked surrounding feelings of discomfort and shyness and what effects they felt the icebreaker had on the game. At the end of the interview, participants were given an opportunity to ask questions relating to the research.

4.3 Participants and Procedure

We recruited 18 participants through social media including Facebook, Twitter, and an online learning support system at <Removed for Review> (1 female, average age 22, SD = 3.42). Participants took part in groups of three, each session lasted around 1.5 h. Participants were compensated with a £10 Amazon voucher. The research was approved by the ethics board at <removed for blind review> and all participants gave informed consent.

All participants took part remotely to accurately simulate the context of online multiplayer gaming. At the start of the session, participants were then given a brief overview of the game *RET* and the general procedure. We followed a within-subjects design (counterbalanced using Latin square) with all participants experiencing three conditions: *VC but no icebreaking task, VC and icebreaking task, Icebreaking task but no VC.* After playing through each condition, participants were asked to complete the integrated post-play survey. At the end of the study, participants were asked to rate the three conditions, and participate in a closing interview.

4.4 Quantitative Results

Data were analyzed using Friedman's ANOVA, and we followed up with Wilcoxon signed-rank tests for pairwise comparisons. Results for the initial post-game statements reveal that of the three communication methods, participants prefer the inclusion of $(X^2(2) = 19.097, p < .05)$. Participants enjoyed VC over text (text M = 2.88, SD = 1.91, VC M = 6.00, SD = 1.15; Z = −3.224, p = 0.001). There was no significant difference in enjoyment between voice with and without icebreakers. Though slightly higher feelings of comfort were reported (without icebreaker M = 5.66, SD = 1.63, with icebreaker M = 5.83, SD = 1.60) the difference was not significant.

Results for the PENS questionnaire show that *RET* provided players with a generally positive player experience (see Fig. 5). In terms of perceived competence, we found significant differences between all conditions $(X^2(2) = 7.969, p < .05)$. Pairwise comparisons revealed no significant difference in perceived competence in the voice communication conditions. There was a significant difference for relatedness $(X^2(2) = 8.853, p < .05)$, pairwise comparisons showed a significant difference between conditions with voice and without $(Z = −2.180, p = 0.029)$, but not between voice with icebreaker and voice without icebreaker.

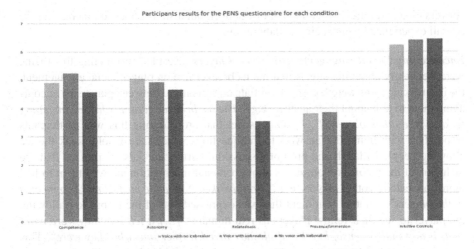

Fig. 5. PENS [27] results for *RET (7 = strongly agree, 1 = strongly disagree).*

4.5 Data Analysis

Interview data were analysed using a Thematic Analysis approach according to Braun and Clarke [2]. Responses were coded, and descriptive category codes were applied to 486 data points with a total of 31 categories emerging (See Fig. 6).

Fig. 6. Breakdown of themes emerging from interviews.

4.6 Qualitative Results

Our results reveal four key themes, *Benefits of Icebreaking Tasks* (89 occurrences), *Negative Effects of Icebreaking Tasks* (77 occurrences), *Effects of Cooperative Mechanics* (176 occurrences), and *Players' Ambivalent Perspectives on VC* (131 occurrences) which is comprised of two subthemes *Positives of VC* (70 occurrences) and *Negatives of VC* (61 occurrences).

Theme 1: Benefits of Icebreaking Tasks

This theme emerged around the perceived benefits that the icebreaking task provided, focusing on two aspects; its effects on social engagement through the encouragement of conversation and relieving feelings of discomfort, but also its effects on increasing the overall experience by enhancing collaboration.

Encouraging Social Engagement Between Players. Results surrounding this theme were frequently about the effects that the icebreaker had on player social engagement, the icebreaking tasks were reported to initiate conversations between players by encouraging them to talk about their answers e.g. *"The ice breaker certainly helped in getting to know the other players [...]"*. One aspect that arose during this was participants responding with humorous answers to the questions which then would break the ice allowing people to laugh and prompt discussion. Participants also expressed that the inclusion of the icebreaker questions about personal information allowed them to feel more connected to other players, e.g., *"I really liked it, it made me feel more connected to the players"*. Another sentiment that was expressed was of the icebreaker allowing the player to see their fellow players as real humans *"[...] it felt like they were more real, if that makes sense, like I had already dived further into who they were"*. This sentiment occurred frequently e.g. *"I have to admit it did kinda humanise everyone if that makes sense as it was a bit comforting."* These results reveal that by learning and sharing a piece of personal information it facilitated players to feel more connected and to humanise each other.

Effect of Icebreakers on Player Experience. Responses in this theme focus on the ways in which the icebreaker had an effect on player experience beyond social engagement. Participants stated that they were more inclined to communicate openly with other players after participating in the icebreaking tasks. Additionally, they suggested icebreakers enabled them to communicate more efficiently. Participants also reported how they would like to see the icebreaking task in other games, discussing what potential benefits it could enable. Additionally, participants reflected again on the humanising nature of icebreakers discussed in the previous theme e.g., *"team based games like MOBA's may benefit from this as there is a lot of anger and hate thrown around in a match and having this information may be a way to make people think that there is another person behind the screen"*. Lastly, participants felt the benefits of the icebreaking tasks were more pronounced when using VC over text-based communication.

Theme 2: Negative Effects of Icebreaking Tasks

This theme addresses concerns that participants voiced regarding the inclusion of icebreaking tasks. It explores issues relating to repeated and continued use, along with perspectives on personal information sharing.

Players' Concerns. Results show that participants had ambivalent thoughts on the inclusion of icebreaking tasks. While clearly acknowledging the benefits that the tasks provided, players also highlighted the risk that participation in icebreakers might become burdensome over time. Participants suggested that it would be important that players were given an opt-out. Some participants further suggested that icebreakers could interfere with players' immersion, breaking the context of the game if icebreakers were not directly embedded into play, for example stating that *"they were somewhat detrimental to the experience as it took the attention away from the game that the players were* *wanting to play.*". Participants also found the inclusion of the icebreaking task confusing as it was not something they were used to in games. Lastly, participants considered the implementation of the icebreaker problematic as it required them to share personal information with strangers, introducing the risk of vulnerability if they for example revealed their gender.

Suggestions for Improvement. Throughout the analysis, participants frequently expressed ideas, opinions, and suggestions on how the icebreakers could be modified depending on the game, genre or group of players participating. The suggestions in this theme ranged from large changes such as all players having a small biography shared with other players, and small scale suggestions such as lengthening or shortening the amount of time between each round of icebreaking tasks. Participants also expressed the desire to increase integration of icebreaking tasks, directly linking information exchange with play (e.g., implementing *"a large door with the word "UP" can only be opened by the player who gave this as one of his answers"*). In contrast, other participants suggested playing icebreaking tasks during natural breaks of play, for example, to cover waiting times when the game was loading.

Theme 3: Effects of Cooperative Mechanics

This theme details participants' reflections of the effects of cooperative mechanics on player experience. In particular, codes that emerged in this theme address effects on communication, reflections on teamwork and aspects of the design that participants either enjoyed or disliked.

Mechanics Encouraging Communication. Participants expressed the effect that the forced cooperation elements and the role-based nature of the game had on communication between players. Many participants felt that the inclusion of such mechanics facilitated and encouraged communication. Additionally, participants reported that role swapping and hidden information also encouraged communication, for example stating that *"Instead of simply accepting who is whom, we had to find out ourself with the voice/ text and help each other out as much as possible."* While they realised that game mechanics increased communication, participants were also quick to point out possible positives and negatives that could emerge from them. For example, one participant expressed dismay having died several times, not having judged their (invisible) remaining health correctly, and finding it too difficult to communicate with other players to receive accurate information within good time.

Player Reflections on Teamwork and Collaboration. Participants shared reflections on the gameplay experience surrounding teamwork and the sense of perceived fellowship which emerged from the inclusion of the communication mechanics in addition to the differing communication methods of VC and text. The results that fall into this category generally comprise participants' recollections of specific moments where they were required to use communication, for example, one player outlined that *"after going through the barriers as medic I had to ask my team what my health was and whether I need to heal"*. Participants also reported that the game mechanics acted as a natural icebreaker by facilitating a common means for communication among fellow players, as the game provides a reason to communicate. Participants expressed feeling less anxious initially speaking, as conversations already were ongoing.

Theme 4: Players' Ambivalent Perspectives on Voice Communication

Player perspectives on the general inclusion of VC in video games were ambivalent. This theme is split into two sub-themes; the player perceived positives and negatives.

Positives of Voice Communication. The most frequently occurring node in this sub-theme was on the effects of VC on social engagement; participants expressed that they felt the communication was much more natural and likely to occur when using VC due to the more efficient and personal nature. Participants also expressed their opinions on the specific implementation of VC that we chose for RET (open mic, always on). Some participants considered the open mic a great feature that reduced discomfort as it made communication more easily accessible, with one participant commenting that *"I prefer to just be able to talk, every time I have to push a button to talk it distracts me from the game and ruins my immersion"*.

Negatives of Voice Communication. Participants also reflected on the negative side of VC. For example, participants frequently stated that they would avoid using VC due to fears of harassment regarding gender, or that they may speak English as a second language. Tying into this, participants also revealed that they would try to avoid using VC entirely with strangers and instead just use it with friends or a mixture between the two, for example, one participant stating that *"[..] I would never go in blind so to speak and just start talking to strangers"*. Participants also stated that inexperience using VC as a cause for lack of engagement. Lastly, participants noted that VC was sometimes hard to understand due to low volume or internet quality, creating awkward situations (e.g., asking someone to repeat themselves several times).

5   Discussion

In this paper, we outline challenges and opportunities associated with the use of VC, and present RET, a game that leverages traditional icebreaking tasks to facilitate VC. Our results demonstrate that icebreaking tasks can contribute to a positive VC experience, but also show that additional considerations are necessary to optimally integrate icebreaking tasks into playful environments. Here, we discuss strategies for in-game icebreaker design, and we reflect on the wider implications of the increasing use of VC in games.

5.1   The Effects of Icebreaking Tasks on Player Experience

Players experience awkwardness when speaking to strangers that icebreaking tasks can help reduce, creating a more positive experience by providing increased opportunity for communication. However, that does not mean that icebreakers are without risk; based on the results of our thematic analysis, there are issues which may negatively impact the player experience, if not confronted. The impact that in-game icebreaking tasks have is dependent on the design and implementation of the task. If integrated with care, as outlined in the following section, there is opportunity for player experience to be improved. Poor implementation such as repetitive or overly personal tasks will have a negative effect on not just the icebreaker experience but the game as a whole. Additionally, it is important to keep in mind that quantitative results regarding player experience suggest that icebreaking tasks had no effect on how the game was generally perceived, suggesting that although players may experience discomfort in the onboarding phase, this does not translate into a generally negative player experience.

5.2   Adapting Icebreaking Tasks to Games

Our results show that traditional icebreaking tasks need to be further developed to be fully suitable for gaming environments. Here we will discuss the most important aspects for improvement and adaption to player feedback.

Appropriate Content for In-Game Icebreaking Tasks: Personal Preferences Rather Than Personal Information

Traditionally, icebreaking questions encourage individuals to share personal information. For example, in RET we included a question that prompted players to state where they are from. Our results suggest that the revealing nature of voice communication already requires players to share more personal information than they may be comfortable with. Hence, when directly involving players in communication, designers should avoid asking players to reveal information that could expose them to harassment directly targeting aspects of their personality (see Study 1). There is a balancing act in the design of these questions, as they also serve as the foundation for players getting to know each other. Instead of asking player to reveal personal *information*, we therefore suggest designers focus on perhaps less vulnerable personal *preferences*. For example, a question such as '*What is your favourite movie?*' allows a player to express an aspect of their person without revealing substantial personal information. This raises the issue of how to deal with the repetitive nature of in-game icebreaking tasks. When wishing to follow a question-answer format, it is therefore important to consider other sources of information relevant to play, for example leveraging performance data (e.g., weapon usage, most helpful player etc.) to inform the generation of questions tying the icebreaker further into the overall experience.

Exemplary Game Mechanic: Sharing preferences could be implemented in a fighting game before the round countdown. For example, a statement such as "I like character X the most" could appear and prompt players to rate it between 1 to 5 with 5 being "Love it" and 1 being "Don't agree". Values could be assigned to controller buttons, and when both players have rated the statement their answers would appear on the screen for discussion. This avoids requiring the player to reveal personal information but still allows personality to show through character preferences.

Implementation of In-Game Icebreaking Tasks: Integrating Solutions Into the Main Game

Icebreaking tasks in traditional environments are often presented as standalone activities facilitated by a moderator. The implementation we chose in RET was similar. However, while this approach was generally effective, there were concerns around the extra activity breaking immersion and flow of the game. To address this issue, we suggest to further explore the direct integration of icebreaking activity through game mechanics. For example, players could be engaged in puzzles that require information exchange for successful completion. Additionally, designers should consider rewarding active icebreaker participation with vanity items that can be used outside of the task, adding value to the icebreaking tasks for players beyond social engagement.

Exemplary Game Mechanic: Apossible implementation in an Online RPG game could be reward mechanisms that are associated with the icebreaking task, e.g., players obtaining collectable tokens through participation. Because RPGs tend to focus on long-term progression, tokens could be collected and then used to purchase vanity items such as costumes or changing spells visual effects. Thereby, the icebreaking task would form part of the game, contribute to progression, and therefore be more likely to be meaningful to players.

6   Limitations and Future Directions

There are some limitations that need to be considered when interpreting our work. Most importantly, our game *RET* was designed as a small-scale research tool and therefore only connects three players at a time. Additionally, only a small number of female participants were enrolled in our study, suggesting limited generalizability to women playing games, and raising questions around self-selection. Future work should explore ways of scaling up and connecting larger groups of players to investigate whether and how dynamics change with an increase of player numbers. Likewise, it would be interesting to study the impact of icebreaking tasks in games in an in-the-wild setting to explore how players interact in a non-research context. Moving beyond challenges that the integration of VC in games poses, exploring opportunities and strengths that are provided by voice communication seems like another valuable avenue: our work suggests that VC does have large potential to bring players together; if designers are looking to build communities, leveraging the effects that VC has on ties between players could be a valuable design opportunity, for example, by creating games that play with social relationships and directly draw from closeness between players as a game mechanic.

7   Conclusion

Voice communication has become an important feature in multiplayer games that is increasingly integrated as a mandatory feature that players are asked to engage with. Our work shows that there are distinct challenges that relate to the revealing nature of VC, suggesting that it may not only contribute to player experience by creating social bonds between players, but may also discourage players from further engagement as a result of player discomfort regarding voluntary and accidental sharing of personal information and characteristics (e.g., gender). While our work outlines some opportunities to address player discomfort when first engaging with VC, we need to consider a comprehensive approach to VC in games that implements mechanisms to reduce discomfort and player harassment. This is particularly important as problems with VC often affect the on-boarding phase of games when players are new to the game, a stage during which player relationships with a game are arguably most fragile and players are most likely to withdraw from a game altogether.

References

1. Augar, N., Raitman, R., Zhou, W.: Wikis: collaborative virtual learning environments. In: Weiss, J., Nolan, J., Hunsinger, J., Trifonas, P. (eds.) The International Handbook of Virtual Learning Environments, pp. 1251–1269. Springer, Dordrecht (2006). https://doi.org/10.1007/978-1-4020-3803-7_52
2. Barrick, M.R., Mount, M.K.: The big five personality dimensions and job performance: a meta-analysis. Pers. Psychol. **44**(1), 1–26 (1991)
3. Birk, M., Mandryk, R.L.: Control your game-self: effects of controller type on enjoyment, motivation, and personality in game. In: Proceedings of the SIGCHI Conference on Human Factors in Computing Systems, pp. 685–694 (2013)
4. Blizzard Entertainment. Video Game. Overwatch (2016)
5. Braun, V., Clarke, V.: Using thematic analysis in psychology. Qual. Res. Psychol. **3**(2), 77–101 (2006)
6. Burgoon, J., Bonito, J., Ramirez, A., Dunbar, N., Kam, K., Fischer, J.: Testing the interactivity principle: effects of mediation, propinquity, and verbal and nonverbal modalities in interpersonal interaction. J. Commun. **52**(3), 657–677 (2002)
7. Bungie. Destiny (2014). www.destinythegame.com. Accessed 04 Mar 2016
8. Bohemina Interactive. DayZ (2013). www.dayzmod.com. Accessed 04 Mar 2016
9. Carter, M., Allison, F., Downs, J., Gibbs, M.: Player identity dissonance and voice interaction in games. In: Proceedings of the 2015 Annual Symposium on Computer-Human Interaction in Play, pp. 265–269 (2015)
10. Carter, M., Gibbs, M., Wadley, G.: Death and dying in DayZ. In: Proceedings of The 9th Australasian Conference on Interactive Entertainment: Matters of Life and Death, vol. 9, p. 22 (2013)
11. Depping, A.E., Mandryk, R.L., Johanson, C., Bowey, J.T., Thomson, S.C.: Trust me: social games are better than social icebreakers at building trust. In: Proceedings of the 2016 Annual Symposium on Computer-Human Interaction in Play (2016)
12. Chlup, D.T., Collins, T.E.: Breaking the ice: using ice-breakers and re-energizers with adult learners. Adult Learn. **21**, 34–39 (2010)
13. Clear, T.: Global virtual teams and 3D collaborative virtual environments. In: Software Innovation and Engineering New Zealand Workshop 2007, SIENZ 2007, Auckland, New Zealand (2007)
14. Dixon, J., Crooks, H., Henry, K.: Breaking the ice: supporting collaboration and the development of community online. Can. J. Learn. Technol./La revue canadienne de l'apprentissage et de la technologie **32**, 99–117 (2006)
15. France, E.F., Anderson, A.H., Gardner, M.: The impact of status and audio conferencing technology on business meetings. Int. J. Hum. Comput. Stud. **54**(6), 857–876 (2001)
16. Frommel, J., Rogers, K., Brich, J., Besserer, D., Bradatsch, L., Ortinau, I., Schabenberger, R., Riemer, V., Schrader, C., Weber, M.: Integrated questionnaires: maintaining presence in game environments for self-reported data acquisition. In: Proceedings of the 2015 Annual Symposium on Computer-Human Interaction in Play, pp. 359–368 (2015)

17. Gibbs, M.R., Hew, K., Wadley, G.: Social translucence of the *Xbox Live* voice channel. In: Rauterberg, M. (ed.) ICEC 2004. LNCS, vol. 3166, pp. 377–385. Springer, Heidelberg (2004). https://doi.org/10.1007/978-3-540-28643-1_48

18. Gibbs, M.R., Wadley, G., Benda, P.: Proximity-based chat in a first person shooter: using a novel voice communication system for online play. In: Proceedings of the 3rd Australasian Conference on Interactive Entertainment, vol. 3, pp. 96–102 (2004)

19. Gosling, S.D., Rentfrow, P.J., Swann, W.B.: A very brief measure of the Big-Five personality domains. J. Res. Pers. **37**(6), 504–528 (2003)

20. Hew, K., Gibbs, M.R., Wadley, G.: Usability and sociability of the Xbox Live voice channel. In: Pisan, Y. (ed.) Proceedings Australian Workshop on Interactive Entertainment (IE2004), pp. 51–58. Creative and Cognitive Studios Press, Sydney (2004)

21. Jarusriboonchai, P., Malapaschas, A., Olsson, T.: Design and evaluation of a multi-player mobile game for icebreaking activity. In: Proceedings of the 2016 CHI Conference on Human Factors in Computing Systems, pp. 4366–4377 (2016)

22. Knapp, B.: Ventrilo (2002). www.ventrilo.com

23. Nacke, L.E., Bateman, C., Mandryk, R.L.: BrainHex: preliminary results from a neurobiological gamer typology survey. In: Anacleto, J.C., Fels, S., Graham, N., Kapralos, B., Saif El-Nasr, M., Stanley, K. (eds.) ICEC 2011. LNCS, vol. 6972, pp. 288–293. Springer, Heidelberg (2011). https://doi.org/10.1007/978-3-642-24500-8_31

24. Nacke, L.E., Bateman, C., Mandryk, R.L.: BrainHex: a neurobiological gamer typology survey. Entertainment Comput. **5**(1), 55–62 (2014)

25. Löber, A., Schwabe, G., Grimm, S.: Audio vs. chat: the effects of group size on media choice. In: 40th Annual Hawaii International Conference on System Sciences, HICSS 2007, vol. 40, p. 41 (2007)

26. Nasir, M., Lyons, K., Leung, R., Moradian, A.: Cooperative games and their effect on group collaboration. In: vom Brocke, J., Hekkala, R., Ram, S., Rossi, M. (eds.) DESRIST 2013. LNCS, vol. 7939, pp. 502–510. Springer, Heidelberg (2013). https://doi.org/10.1007/978-3-642-38827-9_43

27. Przybylski, A.K., Rigby, C.S., Ryan, R.M.: A motivational model of video game engagement. Rev. Gen. Psychol. **14**, 154–166 (2010)

28. Rogers, Y., Brignull, H.: Subtle ice-breaking: encouraging socializing and interaction around a large public display. In: Workshop on Public, Community, and Situated Displays (2002)

29. Salinäs, E.L.: Collaboration in multi-modal virtual worlds: comparing touch, text, voice and video. In: Schroeder, R. (ed.) The Social Life of Avatars. Computer Supported Cooperative Work, pp. 172–187. Springer, London (2002). https://doi.org/10.1007/978-1-4471-0277-9_10

30. Sallnäs, E.-L.: Effects of communication mode on social presence, virtual presence, and performance in collaborative virtual environments. Presence: Teleoper. Virtual Environ. **14**(4), 434–449 (2005)

31. TeamSpeak. TeamSpeak Communication System (1999). https://www.teamspeak.com/. Accessed 04 Mar 2016

32. Thomsen, L.E., Petersen, F.W., Drachen, A., Mirza-Babaei, P.: Identifying onboarding heuristics for free-to-play mobile games: a mixed methods approach. In: Wallner, G., Kriglstein, S., Hlavacs, H., Malaka, R., Lugmayr, A., Yang, H.-S. (eds.) ICEC 2016. LNCS, vol. 9926, pp. 241–246. Springer, Cham (2016). https://doi.org/10.1007/978-3-319-46100-7_24

33. Taylor, T.L.: Play Between Worlds: Exploring Online Game Culture. MIT Press, Cambridge (2009)

34. Triebel, T., Guthier, B., Plotkowiak, T., Effelberg, W.: Peer-to-peer voice communication for massively multiplayer online games. In: 6th IEEE Consumer Communications and Networking Conference, CCNC 2009, vol. 6, pp. 1–5 (2009)
35. Toups, Z.O., Kerne, A., Hamilton, W.A., Shahzad, N.: Zero-fidelity simulation of fire emergency response: improving team coordination learning. In: Proceedings of the SIGCHI Conference on Human Factors in Computing Systems, pp. 1959–1968 (2011)
36. Turkle, S.: Life on the screen: identity in the age of the internet, vol. 3, pp. 99–100. Simon and Schuster, New York (1995)
37. Ubisoft. The Division (2016). http://tomclancythedivision.ubi.com/game/en-gb/home/. Accessed Mar 04 2016
38. Unity Technologies. Unity (2016). https://unity3d.com/company
39. Wadley, G., Gibbs, M.R., Benda, P.: Towards a framework for designing speech-based player interaction in multiplayer online games. In: Proceedings of the Second Australasian Conference on Interactive Entertainment, vol. 2, pp. 223–226 (2005)
40. Wadley, G., Gibbs, M., Benda, P.: Speaking in character: using voice-over-IP to communicate within MMORPGs. In: Proceedings of the 4th Australasian Conference on Interactive Entertainment, vol. 4, p. 24 (2007)
41. Wadley, G., Gibbs, M.R., Ducheneaut, N.: You can be too rich: mediated communication in a virtual world. In: Proceedings of the 21st Annual Conference of the Australian Computer-Human Interaction Special Interest Group: Design: Open 24/7 (2009)
42. Wadley, G., Carter, M., Gibbs, M.: Voice in virtual worlds: the design, use, and influence of voice chat in online play. Hum. Comput. Interact. **30**, 336–365 (2015)
43. West, E.: The big book of icebreakers: quick, fun activities for energizing meetings and workshops. McGraw Hill Professional, New York (1999)
44. Williams, D., Caplan, S., Xiong, L.: Can you hear me now? The impact of voice in an online gaming community. Hum. Commun. Res. **33**(4), 427–449 (2007)
45. Williams, D., Ducheneaut, N., Xiong, L., Zhang, Y., Yee, N., Nickell, E.: From tree house to barracks the social life of guilds in world of warcraft. Games Cult. **1**(4), 338–361 (2006)
46. Wilson, M.L., Reeves, S., Coyle, D., Chi, E.H.: RepliCHI workshop II. In: Workshop Proceedings of the SIGHCHI Conference on Human Factors in Computing Systems (2014)

Including Non-gamers: A Case Study Comparing Touch and Motion Input in a 3D Game for Research

Isabelle Kniestedt[✉], Elizabeth Camilleri, and Marcello A. Gómez Maureira

University of Malta, Msida, Malta
ikniestedt@gmail.com, bethcamilleri94@gmail.com,
ma.gomezmaureira@gmail.com

Abstract. While digital games are becoming increasingly popular as a choice for research stimuli, their complex nature brings about challenges. The design of the games and designers' reliance on established conventions may hinder their use in research, particularly with 'non-gaming' test subjects. In this study, we explored how players performed using a 1-to-1 motion control scheme using a tablet's gyroscope to control the camera as compared to a traditional touch-based joystick in a 3D first-person game. Results showed that players – particularly those less experienced with games – found the game more enjoyable and exciting with motion controls than with joystick controls. Additionally, while experienced players performed better than inexperienced ones when using the joystick, this difference was not present when using the motion controls. We therefore believe motion-based control schemes can be beneficial in making research using games more accessible to a wider range of participants, and to limit influence of prior gaming experience on gathered data.

Keywords: Digital games · Input controls · Research stimulus

1 Introduction

Digital games, both commercial and custom made, have a long-standing history of being used as research tools in a variety of fields and studies [5,20]. Some advantages of using games as research stimuli are their ability to make abstract experiment tasks more approachable and understandable [12]. Due to their design they can also provide ideal tools to elicit certain emotions [32], and they provide a safe, virtual environment to explore research topics through experiments that might otherwise be dangerous, deemed unethical [11], or physically impossible for participants to take part in. Using games in this context comes with certain challenges. Commercial, off-the-shelf games have the potential to introduce uncontrolled or unknown variables into the experiment setup that can influence test results. Games developed specifically for research can limit the amount of variables in play, but budget restrictions do not always allow

© Springer International Publishing AG, part of Springer Nature 2018
A. D. Cheok et al. (Eds.): ACE 2017, LNCS 10714, pp. 202–218, 2018.
https://doi.org/10.1007/978-3-319-76270-8_15

for dedicated designers and developers, leading to the use of very straightforward gaming tasks that often do not offer the same affordances as professionally developed games [11], therefore not taking full advantage of the medium.

Another concern is accessibility to test participants, an often varied and undefined 'target audience'. Games are more ubiquitous than ever before, with the mobile industry projected to take up almost a quarter of the entire games market in 2017 [3]. Casual games are characterized by being especially easy to pick-up-and-play by those who would not usually consider themselves 'gamers' [2]. When using more complex game systems, a certain level of gaming experience is generally required (e.g. being able to use an analog game controller, or knowledge of using the 'WASD' keys on a keyboard to move around in a game environment). In order to use games to effectively test human behavior, however, participants cannot be limited to 'gamers'. Ideally, games that are to be used for such test experiments should therefore be easily accessible to a general population and prior gaming experience should not influence the data gathered in such experiments.

The case study presented here was motivated by this design concern of accessibility while developing a tablet game for research purposes. A requirement of this project was that the player explores a 3-dimensional environment, for which we developed a motion-based control scheme utilizing the strength of natural mapped interactions [19]. These controls use the tablet's gyroscope to directly control the first-person in-game camera, resulting in the player looking around the virtual environment as if they were taking a picture with the tablet in the real world. This was then compared to 'traditional' controls using an on-screen joystick operated by touch input, as is often seen in commercial mobile games [9].

With this comparison we tried to answer two questions. The first was whether it would be less challenging for inexperienced players to navigate a virtual 3D environment using the motion controls, as compared to the touch-based equivalent of an analog game controller. The second question was whether the motion controls would introduce any variables in the experiment setup that researchers should be aware of if they utilize this input method in their own studies. This paper describes the testing of the game using a mixed-method approach to data gathering in an attempt to capture various possible effects of the control scheme on player experience. The resulting discussion is informed by our experience in iteratively developing and testing the game. Our aim is to contribute to the growing body of work related to the use of video games as research stimuli by suggesting that careful design of input methods can aid in issues regarding participant selection and the quality of data, an approach that so far, to our knowledge, has been overlooked.

2   Background

Using games as research tools is not a new notion; experiment tasks assigned to participants in which their performance is scored can often be labeled or perceived as a game [5]. Games, however, have become increasingly varied, complex, and sophisticated over time, as has the technology that mediates them. This can make them suitable for new types of research [29], but also makes them less predictable and harder to utilize in a controlled experiment setting. With many studies across disciplines using game-like stimuli in some capacity [1,13,29], the body of work specifically concerned with using games in this capacity has also grown. So far, efforts are widespread and varied, ranging from specific contributions focused on a particular experiment task or field [7,8,23] to more general guidelines concerning stimulus design and experiment setup [5,6,11,12,20,26]. Notable recurring topics are the advantages and disadvantages of using commercial and custom-made games, how to select appropriate games for a specific study, approaches to data logging, and how to work towards being able to generalize results across studies.

Participant selection is mentioned as part of these studies, but solutions are lacking, with the consensus seemingly being that extensive logging and strategic participant selection are the best way to approach the issue of varying player ability. McMahan et al. [20] describe the importance of considering player background when using commercial games as a research stimulus, stating that prior game experience can affect enjoyment and anxiety, as well as a participant's attitude and motivation, when participating in a research study using digital games. They suggest to either include or exclude participants based on their experience, or to passively gather data on participant background to take prior experience into account during data analysis. This coincides with suggestions from other authors, stating the importance of detailed logging to explain differences in data between participants or participant groups [5]. Similarly, Järvelä et al. [11] suggest being "selective" with participants and to pay special attention to prior gaming experience. They state that basic skills in playing digital games are preferred, as time spent on learning takes time away from the experiment tasks, and a lack of basic skills is likely to negatively influence quality of the data.

This conclusion is far from ideal, as it means excluding possible participants based on a non-essential skill not necessarily related to the topic of a given study. It also raises a secondary concern, namely that a certain amount of practice time with the game is needed to gain consistent results across participants, or for the research task to 'stabilize' [13]. Even when limiting participants based on prior experience, not all games are the same, and different participants will require different times to become accustomed to the game they need to play. Any effort to ease this process, and include participants of different backgrounds, should be worth exploring. With gaming becoming increasingly common as a pastime, it would seem solutions could be found within the game industry.

Researchers have paid specific attention to the usability of mobile games and the effects of input methods on performance, for instance by comparing virtual and physical controls [4]. In these comparisons, virtual controls often perform worse than their physical counterparts, likely due to a lack of tactile feedback. As Teather and MacKenzie [26] state, there is relatively little research comparing gyroscope-based controls (or 'tilt' controls) to touch controls (using an on-screen equivalent of a traditional game controller or direct touch input through gestures). In their research they found that previous studies yielded conflicting results in terms of player performance when being subjected to the different controls. Their own results show little difference in performance between the two styles (tilt-based motion and touch control), although touch control still slightly outperformed tilt in the highest game levels. It is important to note that their study, as well as others exploring similar topics, all used 2-dimensional games as their experiment stimulus, with none exploring the types of controls in a 3D environment. One exception is a comparison of three first-person shooter games on *iPod Touch* [9], where one of the games offered a tilt-based input method to control the camera combined with touch input using virtual joysticks for movement. Hynninen [9] concludes that tilt input performed worse than pure touch-based controls using virtual joysticks and swiping gestures. None of the input methods performed well, however, when compared to traditional mouse and keyboard controls in similar games, suggesting it was not just the tilt controls that impacted performance, but rather a poor adaptation of controls familiar to first-person shooter players to a new platform. It is also important to note that while testing 3-dimensional games, the game used in their study does not directly map the position and rotation of the device to that of the game camera, but rather uses a tilting motion to gradually turn the camera, which likely lacks the speed and precision necessary for the fast game-play associated with first-person shooters.

Popularized by Nintendo when they released the Nintendo *Wii*, the game industry has shown a trend for producing different types of controls in an effort to broaden their audience to include casual gamers and those who would not consider themselves 'gamers' at all. Referred to as 'natural interaction techniques' [19], these types of controls mimic realistic movements, e.g. swinging the *Wii Mote* like a racket while playing virtual tennis. Since players already know how to perform the intended action, the learning curve is lower than when learning an abstract control system. Based on earlier research showing that natural interactions can provide greater usability than non-natural interactions for some tasks, MacMahan et al. [19] explored the effects of natural interactions in *Mario Kart* [22] on the Nintendo *Wii*. Their findings show players performing worse when using the motion controls than when using the physical game controller, with suggested reasons for the bad performance being the game's poor use of the Wii remote's sensors, latency issues, and the use of large muscle groups over smaller muscles which contribute to a lack in precision. This is indicative of a similar issues found when comparing touch-based controls with tilt input, as described above. Combating this issue of precision, as well as making the controls as intuitive as possible, was one of our main concerns while developing the game, which we will describe in detail next.

3   The Game

The game used in this study is a single-player tablet game that was originally created for cognitive science research into human foraging behavior [27]. We were asked to create a game based on a 2-dimensional visual searching task, which would be used to test the same behavior in a 3D environment. A central design concern was making the game accessible to non-gamers, as the underlying cognitive task is not exclusive to those who play games frequently. In our experience of performing research with games we found that 3D navigation can be a significant obstacle for novice gamers. Additionally, participants that do not consider themselves gamers tend to be concerned with performing well during an experiment using a game, which could impact data gathered (especially related to performance and emotional state) [20].

In the game, the player takes on the role of a squirrel gathering food for its family. The player controls the squirrel from a first-person perspective and explores a park where 'target' (positive) and 'distractor' (negative) objects are spread across the environment. The default mode for the game has the player on a two-minute timer in which they try to gather as many of the target objects as possible. Objects are collected upon collision, meaning players simply run into the objects to collect them. Collecting target objects grants points, while distractor objects temporarily restrain the player and negatively impact their score by resetting it to zero (Fig. 1).

Fig. 1. Game with joystick controls (left) and early play-tester using motion controls (right)

We relied on fairly simple game mechanics, using points and a timer reminiscent of older 'arcade' style video games. In order to emphasize the exploratory aspects of the game, we attempted to create an interesting game-play experience by putting players in an unfamiliar perspective: that of a small animal exploring a large environment. This was done through the scale and design of the digital environment, the positioning of the camera and its field of view, movement speed and sound effects.

The controls developed for this game, in this paper referred to as the **motion** control scheme, use the tablet's gyroscope to orient the first-person camera to where the player points the device. In this sense it works as if one would take a picture using the tablet's camera, but instead of looking at real-life surroundings it looks into the virtual environment. In practice, this has the player physically turning their body to turn around in the game, as well as point the tablet up and down to look above or below them in the game environment. This control scheme's limitation is that it requires the player to either stand up or be seated on a swivel chair in order to play the game comfortably, as being seated on a static chair hinders movement. The only other control in the game is the 'move' button, which is located at the bottom left of the screen. By holding the button pressed the player will move forward in the direction they are looking. Releasing the button will make the player stop moving.

In addition to the motion controls, we developed a second input method more akin to controls commonly used in commercial mobile 3D games. We refer to this scheme as **joystick** controls. The joystick controls have the same movement button in the bottom left of the screen. However, instead of positioning and turning the tablet to look around, players use a virtual joystick on the bottom right of the screen, mimicking a standard video game controller and control schemes found in commercial games.

3.1   Iterations and User Testing

Development and refining of the game took place over a 13 month period, in which both the game and the controls went through multiple iterations. The controls were subject to user testing from several weeks into the project and continued to be tested and developed throughout the time leading up to the experiment described in this study. We conducted a pilot study to the work presented here with 12 participants after the completion of the first fully functional prototype. Both control schemes were tested and compared, and the results informed both the design of this experiment and adjustments to the game's parameters (e.g. movement speed, camera field of view, and joystick responsiveness). Overall responses to the game were positive, leading us to assume that the majority of participants would find the game engaging and therefore ensuring that the results of the study would not be impacted by unsatisfactory game-play. Further testing was done in the context of cognitive science research, which led to additional adjustments to the design and helped fine-tune both control schemes. Through this iterative process, we feel confident that both control methods are comparable to those of commercial games, and should not negatively impact our findings.

4   Experiment Design

We tested two experiment conditions: **playing the game using the motion controls,** and **playing the game using the joystick controls.** Participants played both conditions in succession, playing two 'rounds' of the game, each with a fixed length of two minutes, under each condition. Starting conditions were alternated between participants to control for potential influences due to experimentation order—players with even participant numbers started with motion controls, while players with odd participant numbers started with joystick.

For the experiment, the target and distractor objects in the environment were walnuts and acorns of two different sizes; players were asked to collect the small nuts (0.8 scale from the default size), while the large nuts (1.2 scale from default) acted as distractors. The environment, as well as the position and type of objects found within, was consistent between tests. This made the control scheme the only difference in the game between conditions.

After having played both conditions (for a total of four game rounds) the participants answered a questionnaire in which they ranked the two conditions with respect to several emotion states. During play we also recorded psychophysiological measurements using a wristband sensor as an additional, unbiased indicator of player experience [15], and logged game metrics to analyze player behavior and performance.

4.1 Measurements

The survey consisted of two parts: questions related to demographic information, and preference ranking of the two conditions. Demographic data gathered included age and gender. We also documented gaming frequency, differentiating between frequency in playing 'mobile' and 'other' games (i.e. PC or console) as a general separation of 'casual' and 'hardcore' gamers [14]. Players could choose from 5 options: 'Less than a few times a year', 'A few times a year', 'A few times a month', 'A few times a week', and 'Multiple times a week'.

Players were then asked to state their preference between the two conditions with respect to several emotion states: *enjoyment, challenge, distraction, frustration,* and *excitement.* Each question followed the same structure (e.g. 'Which of the two control schemes do you feel was more enjoyable?'). We based our decision to ask players to annotate their experience in the form of pairwise preferences rather than rely solely on ratings (e.g. Likert scale) on research which shows that people rate emotions better in relative terms than in absolutes, and thus yield more reliable annotations of player experience [21,31]. Through a 4-alternative forced-choice (4-AFC) protocol, players could choose the first or second condition that they played, as well as indicate no preference by selecting either 'Both' or 'Neither'. We used this 4-AFC protocol so as to not force a preference where there potentially was none, with the intent of making player choices clearly motivated and more meaningful [30]. Below each question was a comment box where participants could freely elaborate on their choice. In addition to these questions, players were asked to rate their general enjoyment of the game (irrespective of the control scheme) on a scale from 1 to 10.

To measure player behavior and performance we logged game metrics, including amount and type of items collected (positive and negative), player position (recorded at 10 Hz), and camera rotation (10 Hz). Each of these were logged with a time code so that player route and collection events could be checked against sensor data. One of the advantages of using a digital stimulus for research is the ability to record player behavior and analyze it afterwards [5]. In this case we were particularly interested in the way and amount that participants moved in the virtual environment between test conditions, as well as their performance in regards to item collection.

Psycho-physiological data (also referred to as biometric data) was collected using the *Empatica E4* wristband sensor [18,24], which tracked *heart-rate* (reported at 1 Hz, based on blood volume pulse captured via a PPG sensor) and *electro dermal activity* (EDA) (4 Hz). Over the last decade, metrics and biometrics have become a part of the quality assurance practice of several notable game development studios. Similarly, game research has adopted the use of biometrics to study a variety of topics, e.g. game features, events, and emotional effects [15]. While different studies have shown conflicting results and the connection between psycho-physiological data and emotional states does not yet show itself to be completely reliable, we included biometric measurements in our study to gain an additional indicator of how the different controls might affect the players' experience and to provide an additional data point on a subject that is still much debated [10,15]. Additionally, we deemed it important to add measurements that provided unbiased data to counter possible designer-bias.

4.2 Procedure

Tests were carried out over the duration of a week at the University of Malta. Participants were gathered through a combination of convenience and purposive sampling. As sampling from the university campus showed a pattern of less gaming experience, we purposely included participants from the university's digital games course.

The game was played on an *iPad 4th Gen*. The laptop used to gather data from the iPad and biometric sensor after each session was set up on a central table, with chairs for the researchers on one end and the swivel-chair for the participant on the other. Participants were asked to read through a general information sheet and sign the consent form, while the researchers assigned them an ID and prepared the game and sensor. Next, they asked the participants to put on the sensor, or helped them to put it on if requested.

Two baseline readings of the biometric data were gathered against which the measurements taken during the game were compared: 30 s with the participant sitting still (used as a baseline to the data collected while playing with the traditional controls), and 30 s while moving the arm with the sensor in circles (used as a baseline to the data collected while playing with motion controls). During the baseline readings, participants were asked to count along with a metronome ticking at 80 beats per minute with the goal of still engaging the participants in a task (as they would be in the game). Based on previous tests we found that while using the joystick, players were largely motionless. While playing with the motion controls, players move their arms up and down and turn around in the chair. It should be noted that in none of our tests this led to participants moving very fast or suddenly; their movements were generally controlled and steady. The baseline readings should therefore be comparable to the play sessions, and the motion of the game should not have negatively influenced the sensor data.

Participants played two rounds (of two minutes each) with the first control scheme (alternating which one they started with between participants). Scores from collected objects aggregated between rounds, and players were encouraged to aim for a high-score at the beginning of the experiment session. Once the timer ran out, players saw their score and were able to progress independently to the next round. After finishing the second round they were returned to the game's main menu. One of the researchers then changed the control scheme, before handing them the iPad a second time. They then played another two rounds with the other control scheme, before being asked to take off the sensor. The session concluded with the participant filling in the survey.

For both game metrics and biometric data, we only looked at the second round that participants played in each condition. This was so that players had one round to get used to each of the controls, and limit the effects of players getting used to a control scheme on the data.

4.3   Data Processing

Data from the metrics logged in-game and the psycho-physiological sensor was processed before evaluation. First, game logs were parsed for positions and rotation of the player camera for each participant, in order to analyze the in-game behavior of participants. Similarly, data was parsed for positive and negative pickup events as well, which were used as a measure of player performance. We aggregated the spatial distance between subsequent player positions and the difference between subsequent camera rotations to explore differences in overall player movement.

Five different sub-measures were derived from the sensor data: *Median*, *Median Absolute Deviation (MAD)*, *Slope*, *Travel*, and *Onsets* (for EDA only). Additionally, each sub-measure was calculated for each of the baseline readings (i.e. motionless and in motion) taken at the start of the experiment. We then divided the sub-measures of an experiment session by the sub-measures of the respective baseline to derive a value that expresses the relative change of a participant's sub-measure as compared to their baseline. An exception was the sub-measure of Slope, which is expressed in measure per minute. Outliers in the data (values larger than $3 * MAD$ [16]) were removed and the sensor data was pre-processed with a Gaussian filter (window width $= 4 *$ measure frequency).

After calculating the sub-measures across all participants we performed a Shapiro-Wilk test of normality under an alpha level of 0.05, and again removed outliers (values larger than $3 * MAD$, this time across participants rather than across sensor measures over time for each individual participant) that resulted in $p < 0.05$. Sub-measures that still showed a deviation from normality after this were omitted from further analysis and are not reported in this study. All of the data processing was facilitated by custom-made scripts, while statistical analysis of measures across all participants was conducted with the statistical software JASP [17].

5   Results

We concluded the research experiment after having tested $N = 31$ participants, 48.4% of which were female. The median age was 20.50 ($M = 23.57, SD = 8.25$). The median for the frequency of playing mobile video games was 3 out of 5 ($M = 2.94, SD = 1.44$), and 3 out of 5 for non-mobile video games ($M = 3.03, SD = 1.35$). To recall, this measure was taken through a nominal scale going from 'Less than a few times a year' (converted to 1), 'A few times a year' (2), 'A few times a month' (3), 'A few times a week' (4), to 'Multiple times a week' (converted to 5).

In order to determine whether individual measures differed between the two test conditions, we performed Bayesian Paired Samples T-Tests, opting for a Cauchy prior width of 0.707, in accordance with research by Wagenmakers et al. [28]. The value of the Bayes Factor BF (BF_{10}) indicates the likeliness that a given hypothesis is not equal to its null-hypothesis, i.e. the assumption that there is no significant difference between the tested conditions. A BF_{10} value of 1 indicates that there is an equal chance of the hypothesis being different from the null-hypothesis as there is of them being similar. A value lower than 1 indicates that the null-hypothesis is more likely. Unlike classical hypothesis testing, the Bayesian T-Test can therefore be used to confirm the null-hypothesis, rather than only reject it [25], making it particularly helpful for this study. The results for each individual measure, as well as their corresponding mean and standard deviation, are shown in Table 1. Mean values for game metrics correspond directly to player actions (distance corresponding to meters, rotations corresponding to degrees), while mean values for sensor measures are percentages with regards to their respective baselines (a mean of -33 indicating a decrease of 33% over

Table 1. Bayesian Paired Samples T-Test of game metrics and sensor measures. Measures with (†) indicate *anecdotal evidence for* a significant difference between conditions ($BF_{10} > 1$, but $BF_{10} < 3$). Measures in **bold** indicate at least *moderate evidence against* a significant difference between conditions ($BF_{10} < 0.333$).

Measure	Mean$_{Motion}$	SD$_{Motion}$	Mean$_{Joystick}$	SD$_{Joystick}$	BF$_{10}$	Error%
Distance traveled	115.274	23.698	106.554	24.852	0.752	9.89e-5
Camera rotations	4557.140	1387.413	3842.211	1074.532	†1.655	2.92e-8
Total pickups	18.000	8.896	17.774	8.578	**0.193**	3.36e-4
Positive pickups	17.226	9.694	17.290	9.093	**0.192**	3.42e-4
Negative pickups	0.774	1.117	0.484	0.851	0.533	5.04e-5
Heart-rate median	1.173	11.414	−6.303	19.137	†1.284	7.19e-8
Heart-rate slope	−0.613	3.799	−0.651	6.287	**0.207**	1.36e-4
Heart-rate travel	−28.120	55.118	−33.883	51.636	**0.276**	2.31e-4
EDA median	33.263	33.133	58.145	67.534	†1.059	2.02e-7
EDA MAD	119.205	204.899	116.577	196.896	**0.201**	4.04e-5
EDA travel	−17.911	64.016	−0.649	75.966	**0.269**	1.35e-4

baseline). The majority of measures indicate evidence *for* the null-hypothesis. In Table 1 this is indicated by values in **bold** for $BF_{10} < 0.333$, which means that for a given measure it is at least 3 times more likely that empirical (small) differences are *not* significant. Three measures suggest anecdotal evidence *for* significant differences (indicated by (†) for $BF_{10} > 1$, but $BF_{10} < 3$). For these measures we further conducted the more widely used Student T-Test, which showed significant differences ($p < 0.05$) for two results: 'Camera Rotations' – $t(30) = 2.237$, $p = 0.033$, and 'Heart-rate Median' – $t(29) = 2.224$, $p = 0.034$.

After playing the game in both test conditions, participants were asked to rate their enjoyment between 1 ('did not enjoy at all') and 10 ('enjoyed it a lot'), which resulted in a median rating of 7 out of 10 ($M = 7.19$, $SD = 1.2$), with 87.1% stating they would play again. Participants were further asked to rank which of the two conditions was more *enjoyable, challenging, distracting, frustrating,* and *exciting.* The distribution of the responses is shown in Fig. 2. Clear preference was given to motion controls in both enjoyment (77.4%) and excitement (80.6%). Joystick controls were more frequently deemed challenging (48.4%—Bayesian Binomial Test, against > 0.25: $BF_{10} = 44.531$) and frustrating (51.6%—$BF_{10} = 44.531$).

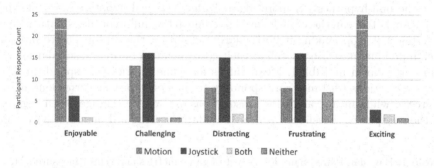

Fig. 2. Frequency distribution of self-reported preferences regarding which condition was more 'Enjoyable', 'Challenging', etc. Participants could forgo ranking by choosing 'Both' or 'Neither'.

Participants were asked to elaborate on their survey choices through written comments. Out of 31 participants, 10 did not comment on their choices, while the rest of the participants filled out all or some of the comment fields. For the states of *enjoyment* and *excitement*, half of participants made comments related to moving around being more fun than remaining stationary. Positive aspects mentioned were turning speed, ease of motion, and a higher level of "immersion". Four people specifically commented on preferring the joystick controls, finding movement easier without physically turning around and one participant reporting slight motion sickness. Among the reasons for the joystick being considered more *challenging* was having to divide attention between two actions (i.e. turning and moving). Similar arguments were given for *distracting* and *frustrating*, with divided attention (e.g. through keeping track of thumb position) being listed as a reason for the joystick to distract from the game.

Finally, we looked at potential influences that could impact the comparison between the two experiment conditions. Chi-Squared Tests between 'Play Frequency' (mobile and non-mobile) and self-reported preferences did not show evidence for preferences being influenced by how frequent participants play video games (all tests $p > 0.05$). Looking at correlations (Pearson's r, $p < 0.05$), we found that 'Play Frequency (non-mobile)' correlated with 'Distance Traveled (Joystick)' ($r = 0.404$, $p = 0.024$). A Bayesian Independent Samples T-Test (Cauchy Prior 0.707) between start conditions showed that the majority of measures had a $BF_{10} < 0.333$ and none had a value above $BF_{10} > 1$, indicating that no significant differences were due to starting condition.

6 Discussion

During this study we were interested in effects on player experience and performance, as well as the ease of use of the motion as compared to joystick controls, between participants with varying levels of game playing experience. Regarding player performance, measured by the amount of items collected, we did not see a significant difference between conditions. This suggests that regardless of prior gaming experience, participants performed equally well in both test conditions. This is in contrast with other studies, where motion-based controls negatively impacted performance [9,19]. We consider this a positive result for our study, as it suggests that the motion controls do not cause players to under-perform like other tilt-based input methods or when compared to joystick controls used in commercial games. We believe the direct mapping of the camera to the position and rotation of the tablet to be the main reason for this difference, as it provides a higher level of accuracy and control than other tilt-based input methods.

Other measures of particular interest were distance traveled and degrees of camera rotation. With the goal of the game being the exploration of an environment and the collection of items dispersed throughout said environment, we consider the amount that participants traveled indicative of how easy it was to move around. Frequency of playing non-mobile games (i.e. PC or console games) showed a positive correlation to distance traveled in the joystick condition. It stands to reason that those who are more likely to be familiar with analog controllers would need less time to master the joystick input scheme. This suggests a learning curve for those who did not have this prior experience. The fact that we did not find significant evidence of a difference in the motion control scheme suggests that the learning curve was equal regardless of prior experience. With the survey results suggesting that participants in general enjoyed using the motion controls more, we consider this the strongest indication that the motion controls were able to bridge the gap between participants of varying gaming backgrounds and experience.

A student t-test showed a significant difference in camera rotations between conditions, with an increased amount of rotations when using motion controls. This is not completely surprising, as every movement of the tablet is recorded by the game, while the use of the joystick requires purposeful action to turn the camera. However, the difference is large enough that we do not think accidental movement is the sole explanation. The physical movement of the motion controls requires more effort from the player to turn and look around. A possible explanation for this difference could be, as participants stated in their written and verbal comments, that the act of moving physically was more fun than using the joystick and caused them to feel more 'in the game', comparing it to a virtual reality experience. Alternatively, it is also a possibility that the joystick controls were generally perceived as less interesting to use, which led to participants being more efficient in how they used them. Overall, it would suggest that the motion controls contributed to the sense of exploration and 'looking around' we attempted to stimulate in our original design.

Overall, there are not many indications of the motion controls causing subconscious responses in players' biometric measures, suggesting the control scheme can be used in research without introducing hidden variables that could influence data collection of this kind. We did find evidence in the heart rate median, which was higher compared to the relative baseline when using motion controls. Although we did not find significant correlations between game ranking and heart rate data, we speculate that this difference can be explained for similar reasons as the increase in camera rotation. Since the motion controls were deemed more exciting by the majority of players, the increase in the heart rate can be another expression of the participants' excitement while playing. Here we want to reiterate the importance of recording a baseline reading that takes the motion of the controls into account in order to accurately compare the biometric data. As described earlier, we attempted to take a baseline measure that reflected the amount of motion the players would experience while playing the game for each condition. We therefore believe the difference can be explained by the participants' emotional state, rather than through the act of being in motion. However, we make room for the possibility that, despite our efforts, the movement of the controls still had some effect on the data, which could be remedied by changes in the baseline procedure.

We recognize that our sample size is relatively small, but the data so far seems to indicate that the motion controls can indeed make research games more accessible to inexperienced participants. Tests throughout the game's development have shown that the motion controls are easier to get used to and require less explanation for non-gamers. This does not mean, however, that these particular controls will work for every study. First, there is the requirement for participants to move. While not a concern for our purposes, space and other limitations (e.g. using more sensitive sensor equipment) could prevent motion controls from being used in a particular study. Second, this game was developed as a visual searching task. Moving the tablet to search for items is closer to the physical action of foraging than the use of a game controller, making the controls an appropriate choice. While research participants were encouraged to get a high score, (turning) speed was not an essential part of the game experience (as it would be in, for example, a first-person shooter game). Accuracy was a necessity as target and distractor items could be positioned close together, requiring careful navigation to only collect the correct one. As it stands, we consider the current control scheme to be useful for games that require the navigation and exploration of 3D environments where either no or only simple actions are required. A single button, or similar input, at minimum is required to move the player forward, and an additional button could be implemented for simple interactions (e.g. talk, jump, open a door, read a message, pick up an object). Careful interface design would be necessary to make the use of an additional button intuitive (e.g. 'move' and 'action' buttons should not be placed too close to one another on the screen, as we experienced in earlier versions of the game).

At this time, we do not exclude any particular game from using this type of control, as appropriate interface and input design can mediate a lot of potential issues with games that require more complex controls. We do, however, foresee potential issues with certain types of games, for instance first-person shooters and other games that require quick reflexes. The current control scheme does provide the accuracy needed for such a game, but a person's physical turning speed could be an issue if the game requires a certain level of speed. Additionally, rapidly turning around could cause physical issues (e.g. dizziness or nausea) in some participants. By designing the game in such a way that it does not require players to turn around in too large increments too fast, these issues could be mediated. However, this type of controls is likely to be less fast and accurate in general than those using a mouse and keyboard, where players often can move in multiple directions (e.g. backwards and by strafing) using only the small motions of button presses. Comparing the motion controls to a setup such as this was out of the scope for this study, but would be valuable to explore in future work. While limiting movement can ease the learning curve for inexperienced players, it would be interesting to see the two compared directly. Another type of game for which it would be harder to utilize this type of control is a racing game, or any other game that through its metaphor (e.g. sitting in a car) restricts a player's movement. Follow-up studies using the control scheme in different games could illuminate which other types of research experiments could benefit from using this type of control specifically.

7   Conclusion

This study explored the effects of two input methods on player experience and performance when interacting with a 3D game in a research setting. The concern regarding prior gaming experience among participants and its influence on data quality has led to the suggestion of excluding participants inexperienced with games from research experiments. It was our goal to bridge the gap between experienced and inexperienced participants, allowing inexperienced players to be a part of research studies without impacting data. We tested two controls: a motion-based control scheme mimicking the use of a tablet's camera, and 'traditional' video game controls in the form of a virtual joystick. Our results show that the motion controls were generally preferred by players, deemed more enjoyable and exciting, and can limit differences in player behavior among participants with varying game playing experience. Players' performances were not negatively impacted by the motion controls, and much of the biometric data points to evidence against significant differences between the two conditions. We therefore suggest that the use of carefully designed, non-conventional controls, such as the motion-based interaction explored in this study, can limit impacts due to prior gaming experience without introducing hidden variables in the experiment setup. We hope this study motivates further exploration into this topic.

Acknowledgments. We would like to thank all test participants that took part in both the pre-tests and the final experiment for their time and feedback. We also want to thank Francesca Borg Taylor-East for her contribution to the initial development of the game. Last, but not least, we are very grateful to Prof. Ian Thornton for his continued enthusiasm and support as we developed this game for his research and continued to improve it into a universal tool to be released to the academic community.

References

1. Calvillo-Gámez, E., Gow, J., Cairns, P.: Introduction to special issue: video games as research instruments. Entertain. Comput. **2**(1), 1–2 (2011)
2. Casual Games Association: Casual games market report 2007 (2007). http://www.casualgamesassociation.org/pdf/2007_CasualGamesMarketReport.pdf
3. Casual Games Association: Towards the global games market in 2017: a broad look at market growth by screen and region (2014). http://cdn2.hubspot.net/hubfs/700740/Newzoo_Games_Industry_Growth_Towards_2017.pdf?t=1455182596586
4. Chu, K., Wong, C.Y.: Mobile input devices for gaming experience. In: 2011 International Conference on User Science and Engineering (i-USEr), pp. 83–88. IEEE (2011)
5. Donchin, E.: Video games as research tools: the space fortress game. Behav. Res. Methods **27**(2), 217–223 (1995)
6. Elson, M., Quandt, T.: Digital games in laboratory experiments: controlling a complex stimulus through modding. Psychol. Popul. Media Cult. **5**(1), 52 (2016)
7. Harteveld, C., Sutherland, S.C.: Personalized gaming for motivating social and behavioral science participation. In: Proceedings of the 2017 ACM Workshop on Theory-Informed User Modeling for Tailoring and Personalizing Interfaces, pp. 31–38. ACM (2017)
8. Holmgård, C., Togelius, J., Henriksen, L.: Computational intelligence and cognitive performance assessment games. In: 2016 IEEE Conference on Computational Intelligence and Games (CIG), pp. 1–8. IEEE (2016)
9. Hynninen, T.: First-person shooter controls on touchscreen devices: a heuristic evaluation of three games on the iPod touch. Master thesis (2012)
10. Järvelä, S.: Measuring digital game experience: response coherence of psychophysiology and self-reports. Master thesis (2017)
11. Järvelä, S., Ekman, I., Kivikangas, J.M., Ravaja, N.: Digital games as experiment stimulus. In: Proceedings of DiGRA Nordic 2012, pp. 6–8 (2012)
12. Järvelä, S., Ekman, I., Kivikangas, J.M., Ravaja, N.: A practical guide to using digital games as an experiment stimulus. Trans. Digit. Games Res. Assoc. **1**(2), 85–115 (2014)
13. Jones, M.B., Kennedy, R.S., Bittner Jr., A.C.: A video game for performance testing. Am. J. Psychol. **94**, 143–152 (1981)
14. Juul, J.: A Casual Revolution: Reinventing Video Games and Their Players. MIT Press, Cambridge (2010)

15. Kivikangas, J.M., Chanel, G., Cowley, B., Ekman, I., Salminen, M., Järvelä, S., Ravaja, N.: A review of the use of psychophysiological methods in game research. J. Gaming Virtual Worlds **3**(3), 181–199 (2011)

16. Leys, C., Ley, C., Klein, O., Bernard, P., Licata, L.: Detecting outliers: do not use standard deviation around the mean, use absolute deviation around the median. J. Exp. Soc. Psychol. **49**(4), 764–766 (2013)

17. Love, J., Selker, R., Marsman, M., Jamil, T., Dropmann, D., et al.: JASP (v.0.7) (2015). Computer software

18. McCarthy, C., Pradhan, N., Redpath, C., Adler, A.: Validation of the Empatica E4 wristband. In: 2016 IEEE EMBS International Student Conference (ISC), pp. 1–4. IEEE (2016)

19. McMahan, R.P., Alon, A.J.D., Lazem, S., Beaton, R.J., Machaj, D., Schaefer, M., Silva, M.G., Leal, A., Hagan, R., Bowman, D.A.: Evaluating natural interaction techniques in video games. In: 2010 IEEE Symposium on 3D User Interfaces (3DUI), pp. 11–14. IEEE (2010)

20. McMahan, R.P., Ragan, E.D., Leal, A., Beaton, R.J., Bowman, D.A.: Considerations for the use of commercial video games in controlled experiments. Entertain. Comput. **2**(1), 3–9 (2011)

21. Metallinou, A., Narayanan, S.: Annotation and processing of continuous emotional attributes: challenges and opportunities. In: 2013 10th IEEE International Conference and Workshops on Automatic Face and Gesture Recognition (FG), pp. 1–8, April 2013

22. Nintendo: Mario Kart Wii. Published by Nintendo (2008)

23. Raffert, A., Zaharia, M., Griffiths, T.: Optimally designing games for cognitive science research. In: Proceedings of the Cognitive Science Society, vol. 34 (2012)

24. Ragot, M., Martin, N., Em, S., Pallamin, N., Diverrez, J.-M.: Emotion recognition using physiological signals: laboratory vs. wearable sensors. In: Ahram, T., Falcão, C. (eds.) AHFE 2017. AISC, vol. 608, pp. 15–22. Springer, Cham (2018). https://doi.org/10.1007/978-3-319-60639-2_2

25. Rouder, J.N., Speckman, P.L., Sun, D., Morey, R.D., Iverson, G.: Bayesian t tests for accepting and rejecting the null hypothesis. Psychon. Bull. Rev. **16**(2), 225–237 (2009)

26. Teather, R.J., MacKenzie, I.S.: Comparing order of control for tilt and touch games. In: Proceedings of the 2014 Conference on Interactive Entertainment, pp. 1–10. ACM (2014)

27. Thornton, I.M., Kniestedt, I., Camilleri, E., Gòmez Maureira, M., Kristjánsson, Á., Prpic, V.: Simulating foraging in the wild using an ipad. Presented at ECVP 2017 (2017)

28. Wagenmakers, E.J., Love, J., Marsman, M., Jamil, T., Ly, A., Verhagen, J., Selker, R., Gronau, Q.F., Dropmann, D., Boutin, B., et al.: Bayesian inference for psychology. Part II: example applications with JASP. Psychon. Bull. Rev. **24**, 1–19 (2017)

29. Washburn, D.A.: The games psychologists play (and the data they provide). Behav. Res. Methods **35**(2), 185–193 (2003)

30. Yannakakis, G.N.: Preference learning for affective modeling. In: 2009 3rd International Conference on Affective Computing and Intelligent Interaction and Workshops, pp. 1–6, September 2009

31. Yannakakis, G.N., Martínez, H.P.: Ratings are overrated!. Front. ICT **2**, 13 (2015). http://journal.frontiersin.org/article/10.3389/fict.2015.00013
32. Yannakakis, G.N., Paiva, A.: Emotion in games. In: Calvo, R.A., D'Mello, S., Gratch, J., Kappas, A. (eds.) Handbook on Affective Computing, pp. 459–471. Oxford University Press, Oxford (2014)

Player Adaptivity and Safety in Location-Based Games

João Jacob[1(✉)] ⓘ, Ana Lopes[1] ⓘ, Rui Nóbrega[1,2] ⓘ,
Rui Rodrigues[1,2] ⓘ, and António Coelho[1,2] ⓘ

[1] FEUP, Faculdade de Engenharia da Universidade do Porto, Porto, Portugal
{joao.jacob,ruinobrega,rui.rodrigues,acoelho}@fe.up.pt,
ana.isabel.crist.lopes@gmail.com
[2] INESC TEC, Instituto de Engenharia de Sistemas e
Computadores – Tecnologia e Ciência, Porto, Portugal

Abstract. Location-based games require, among other things, obtaining or computing information regarding the players' physical activity and real-world context. Additionally, ensuring that the players are assigned challenges that are adequate and safe for the current context (both physical and spatial) is also important, as it can improve both the gaming experience and the outcomes of the exercise. However, the impact adaptivity has in the specific case of location-based exergames still has not been researched in depth. In this paper, we present a location-based exergame and compare different play-through sessions when playing both the context sensitive and the regular versions of the game. Results show that the adaptive version provided a significantly safer gameplay experience. These results showcase the impact in player health and safety that player adaptivity achieves in location-based exergames.

Keywords: Exergames · Location-based games · Player adaptivity
Game design · Mobile computing

1 Introduction

Location-based games (games that use the player's physical location and incorporate it into the game in some way [19]) require obtaining or computing information regarding the players' physical activity, current location and context. Additionally, ensuring that the players are assigned challenges that are adequate to their physical ability, safe and adapted for the current context (both physical and spatial) is also important, as it can improve both the gaming experience and the outcomes of the game. So, the relevant information gathering of both player and context proves to be useful in determining the performance of the former in the latter. There are some models that combine the challenge's difficulty and the player's skill, for both regular games and, more recently, exergames, the Game Flow Model [20] or the Dual Flow Model [17] respectively.

What differentiates these games from others is their pervasiveness and the use of this information to improve the player's experience and safety. This is an open challenge in the field of adaptivity.

Our work, in this paper, presents techniques for using sources of geographical information to provide location-based games with context-aware content. Additionally, we

© Springer International Publishing AG, part of Springer Nature 2018
A. D. Cheok et al. (Eds.): ACE 2017, LNCS 10714, pp. 219–238, 2018.
https://doi.org/10.1007/978-3-319-76270-8_16

test how some of this information may be used by a location-based game, GhostChase, in order to improve the player's experience and safety.

1.1 Location-Based Games

Even though recent, location-based games have already become popular [12]. Location-based games, are games that use the player's physical location as input, or that access or generate information associated to a location. The first commercial game (2002) was Botfighters [19], a pay-per-locate game. Each player had to destroy enemy robots (other players) earning credits for each kill. These games have since then gained a considerable amount of popularity. For instance, Geocaching [14] is one such popular location-based game, with over one million of users. The dynamics behind that game is treasure hunting: a player stashes a cache somewhere in the real world and creates a puzzle that other players must solve to get to the physical location of that cache. This location-based game does not require a mobile device to play. Some of these location-based games can also be considered exergames, games that require the user to perform physical activity as a means of interacting with the game. Games such as "Zombies, Run!" [3], a jogging-while-escaping-from-zombies exergame, or "Geo Wars" [9] a location-based strategy exergame, which promotes and rewards the player for performing physical activity in his/her surrounding environments.

The importance of game adaptivity in location-based games and exergames was also explained by Jacob and Coelho, as a means to overcome the issues these types of games commonly present [10]. These games can benefit from analyzing player performance and adaptivity of the proposed challenges. This way, levels and quests can be generated or adapted to better suit that particular player or the current context (both physical and spatial).

1.2 Adaptivity

An adaptive game has been defined by D. Charles and B. Magerko as games that recognize player input and are able to adequately change their behavior (be it gameplay mechanics or game elements [1, 11]) so as to ensure a better experience. As such, this methodology can be applied to different games, such as exergames [16] or health games [5, 18], mobile games [2] and others, entertainment or otherwise [11].

Adaptivity plays an important role in this work as it will cover the part of the solution where the game will dynamically change itself in order to better accommodate the current player's status.

1.3 Pervasive Exergames

Pervasive exergames are defined as being exergames that have some awareness, via sensors or remote services, of data or information that is relevant to their goals and challenges [8], being similar to a context-aware application or service in that regard [15].

Unlike many exergames, these context-aware games monitor services and sensors to ensure the player is being challenged in a way that blends with the current context.

Usually through GPS, heart rate and accelerometer sensors, the game can be aware of the player's physical condition. Mobile phone's camera and location services' APIs can provide the application with some information regarding the surroundings of the player [2, 7].

This context awareness can be used to not only improve the gaming experience itself [16], but the quality of measurements, such as more accurately calculating the expended energy in a gaming session [13].

The players of these games could potentially benefit from adaptivity. However, these games are currently very limited as to how aware they are of the player's surroundings and how they can take into account the geo-information and adapt the game's challenges and goals with it.

2   Gathering Geo-Information

The issue of gathering geo-referenced data and preparing it for usage in the context of location-based games is one of the main problems faced in the creation of location-based games that is inexistent in regular, non-context aware, games [10]. As such, there is a need for accessing multiple sources of geo-referenced data and providing developers with means of using that data in location-based games. Taking this in consideration we have developed *GeoStream*.

GeoStream aims to become a solution for gathering remote geo-temporal data from 3rd party services, allowing an extensible means for developers to compute information from distinct sources.

2.1   GeoStream

The *GeoStream* API allows for developers to specify a geographical area for which geo-referenced data will be accessed, gathered and made accessible to the developers.

As Fig. 1 shows, a map is comprised by the center position (in a Location-Based Game it will often be the player's real physical position) and vertical and horizontal offset values that, depending on the context, can be pixels, meters (for UTM coordinates) or degrees (for Latitude and Longitude coordinates), determining the bounding box where the game will take place. Additionally, the map is divided in "chunks" that allow for the dynamically loading the close surroundings of the desired location, as the player moves.

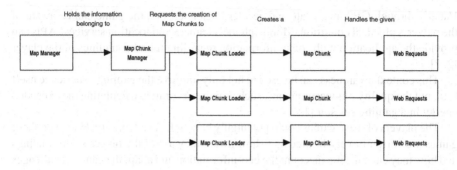

Fig. 1. Hierarchy and information flow of a Map Manager entity and its components.

Figure 2 summarizes how the GeoStream API is structured. A Map Manager will choose what Map Chunks to load and unload depending on the position of the game entity it tracks. As that entity, usually the player, moves towards a border of the map, whenever the limits of a chunk are traversed, new chunks are requested and older chunks may be discarded. Chunks that are marked to be discarded will be removed from the game, including all the georeferenced entities and information that were created with it. These entities, named Features, comprise any type of geo-referenced structure, and are what populates these chunks. As such, features can be rivers, trees, bridges, buildings, bus stops, roads, sidewalks and other man-made or natural structures.

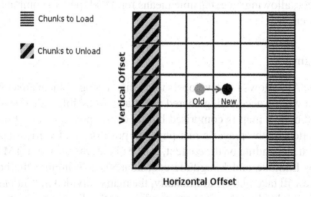

Fig. 2. Depiction of the dynamic loading and unloading of map chunks as the player moves East.

This architecture is further refined by the existence of a hierarchy between the Map, its Chunks and different web services that require either a pair of coordinates to function (such as a Weather Service) or a bounding box to be defined (such as getting a Satellite Image of a portion of the earth, or querying data from a GIS). Callbacks for these services are responsible for returning geographical information in an asynchronous model, in the form of Features, to the respective Chunk.

Depending on its usage, GeoStream may be used to generate graphical representations of the information it retrieved (see Fig. 3). However, defining what information to retrieve and how it is displayed or used is left to the developer [6].

Fig. 3. Island of Manhattan (Generated using GeoStream).

3   Grappher – A Node-Based Editor for Pervasive Games

A traditional issue with the creation of adaptive, mobile exergames is the constant need of tweaking, reparametrizing, deploying and testing the game with different players in order to collect data and restart this cycle. The possibility of applying a RAD (Rapid Application Development) philosophy is of interest to the area of adaptive game development as it could allow designers to focus on testing and readjusting the game as quickly as possible, avoiding the need of redeploying and restarting the game.

Grappher is a Unity3D editor plugin that allows for a game designer to quickly parametrize a game's setting via a node-based editor. The user can choose different sources of data (sensors, web-services, game parameters or functions, Grappher parameters, etc.) or program his/her own (see Fig. 4). Any graph created in Grappher is stored in a remote server, and can be reused in other graphs.

Any saved graph can be loaded via the Grappher Loader component (see Fig. 5). Additionally, this component allows the developer to specify when the graph should be executed (if continuously, only once, or on a certain event), as well as how frequently should the application check for a new version of this graph. This allows for a deployed game, using these graphs, to be reparametrized remotely, as it will automatically update to the latest version of every graph (if possible) during runtime. This can, ultimately, remove the need to redeploy or repackage the application, and incentives developers to tweak and test the game with minimal effort.

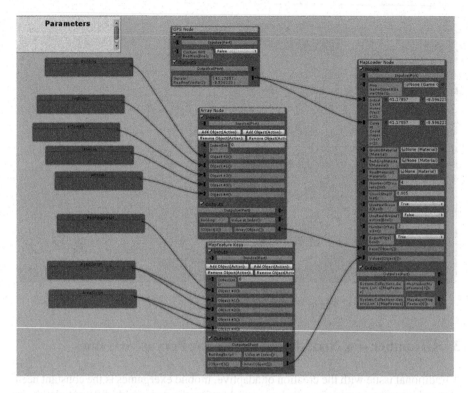

Fig. 4. Depiction of a graph parametrizing the GeoStream framework in Grappher. Most notably, defining what features to be post-processed in GhostChase (Buildings, Roads and Areas).

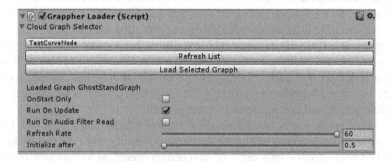

Fig. 5. Grappher loader component in Unity3D

4   GhostChase – A Case Study

GhostChase, is a mobile location-based exergame that showcases the combination of the *GeoStream* platform with the game adaptivity framework *Grappher*. In it, a set of ghosts is chasing the player as if they were in the surroundings of the real-world location of the player. The player must therefore flee from the pursuing ghosts by physically moving in the real world, reaching a game-suggested haven (a real physical location) before they catch him/her (see Fig. 6). The game is played on an Android smartphone with both headphones and Android wear enabled smartwatch being optional.

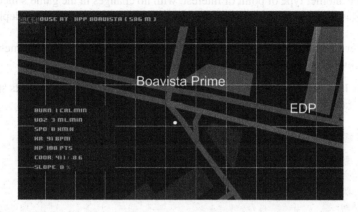

Fig. 6. GhostChase appearance.

The Relative Gross Volume of Oxygen consumed and the player's Burn Rate are computed using the following formulae, already studied [4]:

$$RGVO2\left(\frac{\frac{mL}{Kg}}{\min}\right) = 0.2 * Speed + 0.9 * Speed * Slope + 3.5 \tag{1}$$

$$Burn\,Rate\left(\frac{Cal}{\min}\right) = \frac{RGVO2}{1000} * Weight * 5 \tag{2}$$

Although the above equations over-estimate oxygen consumption and burn rate, they serve as an acceptable indicator for the intensity of the current activity and its benefits.

Since the game requires the player to run around, it encourages only glancing the phone when absolutely needed, as it guides the player with audio-based turn-by-turn navigation to the safehouse. Whenever ghosts are getting closer to the player, a continuous beeping sound is played. The pitch, tempo and volume of that sound increase whenever the ghost gets closer to the player. Conversely, they fade into silence when the player evades the ghost(s). If a ghost touches the player, it will make the player lose health at the rate of one health point per second. If the player's health reaches zero, it is game over. If the player safely reaches the safehouse, the game is won.

GhostChase makes use of *GeoStream* to generate the buildings' footprints, calculate the safehouse position (a hospital in the area, if none exists, the game will only spawn ghosts and effectively start when the player's surroundings contain one) and determine the shortest known path to it. It also makes use of several local sensors to determine the player's real-world position, speed and heart rate via *Grappher*. It is noteworthy that other sources of information were available and could be used to foster adaptivity and safety, such as time of day, weather conditions, type of road, real time traffic information among others. *Grappher* is used to bridge the parametrization of game mechanics and geographical information, via two distinct graphs. For instance, the safehouse could just as easily be another type of point of interest, with no changes in the game's mechanics, with the developer needing only to make the change in the graph, no redeployment needed.

In order to test how adaptivity and player safety in location-based games can be achieved, two profiles for the game were created:

- **GhostChaseB (see** Fig. 7) – A non-adaptive version of the game. Ghosts spawn at a fixed rate, every 30 s, approximately 50 m behind the player.

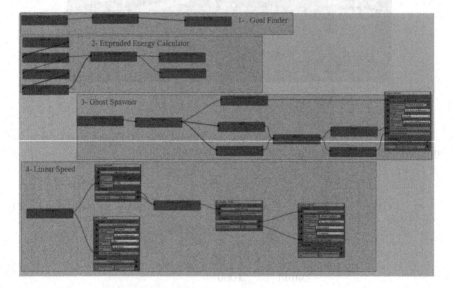

Fig. 7. GhostChaseB profile in Grappher. Features 4 sub-graphs responsible for: finding the goal, calculating VO2 consumption and burn rate, spawning ghosts and defining their speed.

- **GhostChaseA (see** Fig. 8) – An adaptive version of the game. Using *GeoStream*, the game has access to context sensitive geographical information. This version of the game stops ghosts from spawning when the player is within 50 m of a crosswalk for safety reasons.

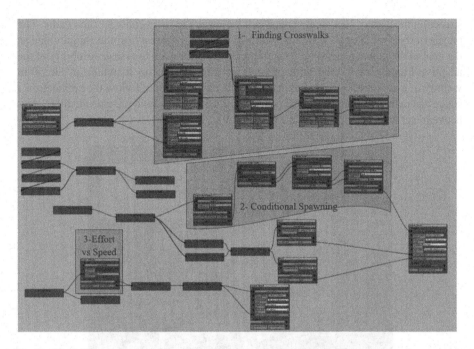

Fig. 8. GhostChaseA profile in Grappher. Based on the GhostChaseB file, it features 3 new parts: finding the crosswalks, using them to decide if it safe to spawn ghosts, and variable ghost speed.

5   Adaptivity in GhostChase

In order to determine if player safety can be improved through game adaptivity, potentiated by making use of context-relevant geographical information (via GeoStream), three scenarios were devised. They would differ only in location. Each scenario requires the game to be tested twice, once using the adaptive profile (GhostChaseA) and another with the non-adaptive (GhostChaseB), in an arbitrary order. As GhostChaseA version of the game doesn't spawn ghosts when the player is near a crosswalk, it should demonstrate a clear difference between both versions of the game when the player is near a crossroad. However, as these scenarios are meant to place the player in potentially dangerous real-life situations (playing the game near a crossroad), all data were obtained by simulating the player's movement, by first creating several pre-defined paths in a GPS mocking application with slightly differing in speed and position as they would if ran by the same person. All simulated player stops at a crosswalk respected the minimum waiting time of one minute, unless specified in the scenarios.

These scenarios are as follows:

GhostChase Scenario #1 (GC1)
In this scenario, we intend to showcase the potential of adaptivity in improving the player's safety in a simple real-life situation. As such, we test the differences in ghost

spawning mechanics in a single crosswalk, between the two versions of the game. The player starts at a college's campus, and must run to the nearest hospital (highlighted as the goal in the game, as per Fig. 9), going first to a crosswalk to assess the ability of the adaptive framework to deal with pre-defined safety rules (no spawning in the 50-m vicinity of a crosswalk). In this experience, the player is not to follow the application's suggested path, as it contained no crosswalks and, as such, would provide no differences between versions (compare Fig. 10 with Fig. 9).

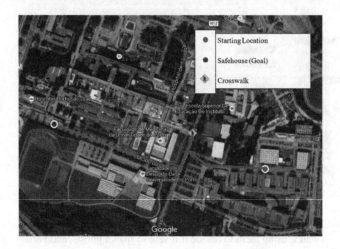

Fig. 9. GC1 experimental design map overview.

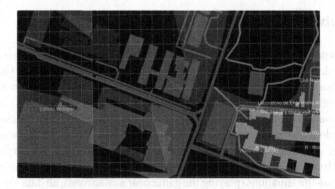

Fig. 10. A suggested path for the GC1 experiment.

The protocol for this experiment is as follows:

- The player starts in the college's campus.
- Once the game starts, the player moves (running or walking) to that specific pedestrian crossing.

- As the player arrives at that crosswalk, he/she spends at least one minute in that location, ensuring that ghost spawning differences between both versions of the game are evident.
- After said minute has passed, the player resumes the game, going to the safehouse.
- The game ends when the player arriving at the safehouse.

The protocol is repeated for the second version of the game.

GhostChase Experiment #2 (GC2)
In this instance, the player starts near the *Casa da Música* in Porto and has to go to the nearest hospital (see Fig. 11). In this situation, the path contains several crosswalks that should make clear the context awareness capabilities of the adaptive version of the game and its potential benefits in improving the player's safety.

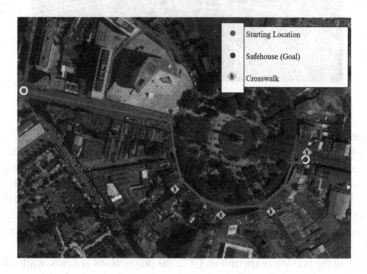

Fig. 11. GC2 experimental design map overview.

Note that both the adaptive and non-adaptive versions of the game, had the player starting from a position with no nearby crosswalks and through a path with multiple crosswalks. It was designed as follows:

- The player starts in area with no crosswalks nearby.
- Once the game starts, the player moves (running or walking) according to the game's suggested path.
- As the player arrives at that crosswalk, he/she spends at least one minute in that location.
- After said minute has passed, the player resumes the game, going to the safehouse, following the suggested path.
- The game ends when the player arrives at the safehouse.

Repeat the protocol for the second version of the game.

The suggested path will have the player cross at or near multiple crosswalks that are recognized by the *GeoStream* API as such (Fig. 12).

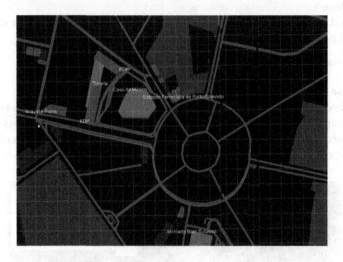

Fig. 12. A suggested path for the GC2 experiment.

GhostChase Experiment #3 (GC3)

In the third experiment, the player starts in the west side of the Île-de-la Cité in Paris and must go to the hospital near the Nôtre Dame. This is to showcase that the access to geographical information and adapting the game to it is only restrained by what data is accessible for the current location. The path contains some crosswalks, close to the initial position of the player. This experiment is also meant to highlight how the proposed context awareness would function in different locations if context-relevant information is available.

Contrary to the previous experiment, GC2, the player starts at a crosswalk and passes by a few crosswalks (see Fig. 13). It was designed as follows:

- The player starts at a crosswalk.
- Once the game starts, the player moves (running or walking) according to the game's suggested path.
- As the player arrives at that crosswalk, he/she is not meant to spend any time at the crosswalk.
- The game ends when the player arrives at the safehouse.

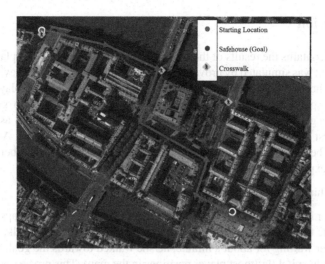

Fig. 13. GC3 experimental design map overview.

Repeat the protocol for the second version of the game.

Similar to the GC2 experiment the player is supposed to follow the path the application delineated, meeting multiple crosswalks (Figs. 13 and 14). However, in this experiment (GC3), the player starts at a crosswalk and is not expected to spend any time near the crosswalks that are along the way. The idea is to test different starting conditions (near a crosswalk) and if a fast-paced player will notice differences in the game (spending no time waiting to cross the road).

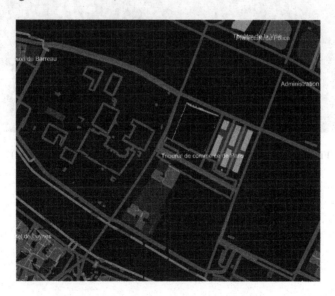

Fig. 14. Suggested path for the GC3 experiment.

6   Discussion

This section contains the results of the three simulated experiments. The players' physical movement was simulated by providing mock locations to the mobile device, through a mobile application with pre-defined paths. Game events, such as the player's movement, ghost spawn positions and directions were logged and used to generate the following images. Tests were simulated and not done in the real world, as one of the goals is to test user safety in playing the different versions of the game. As the user's safety could be compromised in one or both versions, using realistic albeit simulated data for our experiments was considered important.

(a) **GhostChase Experiment #1 (GC1)**

The player initially started in the rightmost position seen in the heatmaps of Figs. 15 and 16, inside the college campus. Then he/she proceeds to the crosswalk, signaled in the map. After waiting for about a minute, he/she walked towards the goal, an entrance of the closest hospital (leftmost player positions in the map). This process was repeated for both versions of the game.

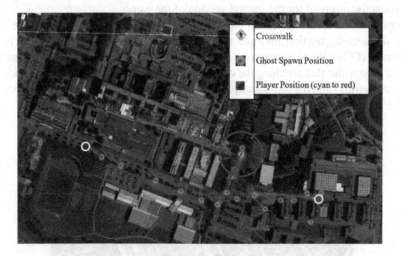

Fig. 15. GC1 GhostChaseB gameplay session. (Color figure online)

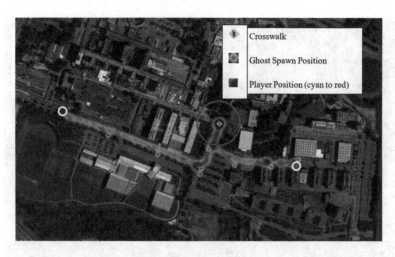

Fig. 16. GC1 GhostChaseA gameplay session. (Color figure online)

As previously explained in the section *GhostChase – A Case Study*, the adaptive version of the GhostChase game- GhostChaseA is aware of crosswalks. If it any are present and are less than 50 m from the player's current position, no new ghosts will spawn. For them to spawn, the player will have to go to a new position where no "crossings" are within 50 m.

The red arrows represent the approximate direction the ghost was moving towards to when it spawned.

The red circle in both those images has a radius of approximately 50 m. In the GhostChaseB version of the game, it is possible to see that ghosts did spawn when the player was within 50 m of the pedestrian crossing. In the other image, of the GhostChaseA version, no ghosts spawned within 50 m of the crosswalk.

(b) GhostChase Experiment #2 (GC2)

The player initially started in the leftmost position seen in the heatmaps of Figs. 17 and 18 and proceeded to the goal following the path given by the application. The player stopped for approximately one minute in each of the first three crosswalks encountered, in both variations of the GC2 experiment.

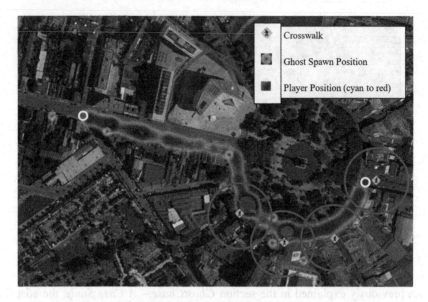

Fig. 17. GC2 GhostChaseB gameplay session. (Color figure online)

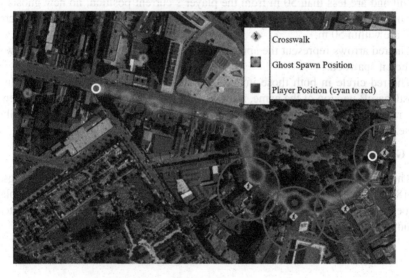

Fig. 18. GC2 GhostChaseA gameplay session. (Color figure online)

The differences between the adaptive and non-adaptive versions of GC2 are even more evident than in the GC1 experiment.

Similar to what occurred with the GC1 experiment, it is visible how the adaptive version of the game differs from the non-adaptive version of the game. In the GC2 non-adaptive version, ghosts would continue to spawn well within 50 m of crosswalks when the player was standing near them (as it is visible from their movement vectors, in red).

However, in the adaptive one, ghosts only spawned in the street the player started at, as the application found no crosswalk nearby. When the player entered the roundabout, as it contains several crosswalks nearby, and since their safety areas (circles in red in both images) overlap each other, the player saw no ghosts spawning until the end of the game session. This further proves that the system is well aware of the surroundings of the player and can be used by a game to provide challenges that are both adequate to the player's fitness level and surroundings.

(c) **GhostChase Experiment #3 (GC3)**

The player initially started in the leftmost position seen in both heatmaps maps of Figs. 19 and 20 and proceeded to the goal following the path given by the application. In this case, the player did not stop when near any crosswalk and continued following the given path as if no time was spent waiting to cross a road.

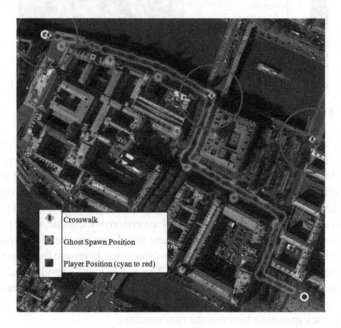

Fig. 19. GC3 GhostChaseB gameplay session. (Color figure online)

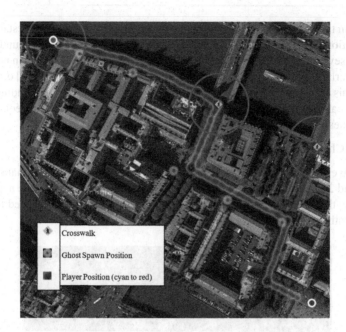

Fig. 20. GC3 GhostChaseA gameplay session. (Color figure online)

As expected, in this scenario the differences between the adaptive and non-adaptive versions are less evident. As the player spends less time inside the safety area of a crosswalk, the number of ghosts that spawn in the non-adaptive version of the game is not much higher than those that spawn in the adaptive counterpart. However, it is still visible, particularly at the starting point, that ghosts do spawn well within the vicinity of the crosswalks, in the case of the non-adaptive version of the game, while none appear in the adaptive counterpart. Even in cases where the player may have no problems with crossing quickly, the system will prevent ghost spawning to ensure the player is not too focused in the game while crossing the road. This experiment's results final part of the path is very similar between adaptive and non-adaptive versions, as the player movement speeds are equivalent and no crosswalk is near the player, resulting in a comparable number of ghosts spawning between the two versions.

Considering all three experiments, in distinct locations, with different surroundings, one can determine that the adaptive version of the GhostChase game is more aware of the player's real-life surroundings and is capable of changing the game's behavior whenever the player is close to some locations (in the experimental cases, crosswalks). As such, it is possible to reinforce a player's safety regarding real world surroundings through location-based game adaptivity. Additionally, as *GeoStream* is able to provide access to more geographical, contextually relevant information, both adaptivity and player safety could be improved through parametrization via *Grappher*. For instance, having the player follow a less traffic intensive route, or a safer route that has pedestrian roads. Accessing weather information could also be used to parametrize the game's difficulty as the players' mobility is impacted by it.

7   Conclusions and Future Work

We have presented GhostChase, a location-based game that is able to access varied geo-information sources and incorporate that information in-game thanks to *GeoStream*, an API for aggregating and accessing geo-referenced data from several third-party sources.

Our current results with GhostChase and *GeoStream/Grappher* show a potential benefit for the player's experience and safety by making location-based games aware of potentially dangerous real-world situations and adapting their mechanics accordingly. It is our intention to provide a generic methodology through which already existing location-based games may adapt their own challenges and mechanics in accordance with context-sensitive information.

These results, albeit based in simulated gameplay sessions to avoid exposing real users to dangerous situations in this testing phase, use real data and realistic gameplay behavior. This provides good evidence of the GIS-based adaptivity capabilities of the proposed solution. Nevertheless, it is our goal to expand the tests to experiments in controlled and uncontrolled physical spaces in the future, as well as integrating other adaptivity and safety elements.

Acknowledgements. This work is part of João Jacob's PhD and the submission of this paper has been partially supported by FourEyes, FourEyes is a Research Line within project "TEC4Growth – Pervasive Intelligence, Enhancers and Proofs of Concept with Industrial Impact/ NORTE-01-0145-FEDER-000020" financed by the North Portugal Regional Operational Programme (NORTE 2020), under the PORTUGAL 2020 Partnership Agreement, and through the European Regional Development Fund (ERDF).

References

1. Berger, F.: Evaluating an implementation of an adaptive game-based learning architecture. In: Masthoff, J., Mobasher, B., Desmarais, M.C., Nkambou, R. (eds.) UMAP 2012. LNCS, vol. 7379, pp. 351–355. Springer, Heidelberg (2012). https://doi.org/10.1007/978-3-642-31454-4_34

2. Campbell, A.G., Grady, M.J.O., Connor, N.E.O.: FreeGaming: mobile, collaborative, adaptive and augmented exergaming categories and subject descriptors. In: Proceedings of the 8th International Conference on Advances in Mobile Computing and Multimedia, pp. 173–179 (2010)

3. Erenli, K.: The impact of gamification: a recommendation of scenarios for education. In: 2012 15th International Conference on Interactive Collaborative Learning (ICL), pp. 1–8 (2012). https://doi.org/10.1109/ICL.2012.6402106

4. Filardo, R.D., Rosendo da Silva, R.C., Petroski, E.L.: Validação das equações metabólicas para caminhada e corrida propostas pelo American College of Sports Medicine em homens entre 20 e 30 anos de idade. Rev. Bras. Med. Esporte **14**(6), 523–527 (2008). https://doi.org/ 10.1590/S1517-86922008000600010

5. Göbel, S., Hardy, S., Wendel, V.: Serious games for health: personalized exergames. In: Proceedings of the 18th ACM International Conference on Multimedia, pp. 1663–1666 (2010). http://dl.acm.org/citation.cfm?id=1874316. Accessed 9 Dec 2013

6. Goncalves, J.S.V., Rossetti, R., Jacob, J., Goncalves, J., Olaverri-Monreal, C., Coelho, A., Rodrigues, R.: Testing advanced driver assistance systems with a seriousgame-based human factors analysis suite. In: IEEE Intelligent Vehicles Symposium Proceedings, pp. 13–18 (2014)
7. Görgü, L., Campbell, A.G., McCusker, K., Dragone, M., O'Grady, M.J., O'Connor, N.E., O'Hare, G.M.P.: Freegaming: mobile, collaborative, adaptive and augmented exergaming. Mob. Inf. Syst. 8(4), 287–301 (2012). https://doi.org/10.3233/MIS-2012-00147
8. Hardy, S., El Saddik, A., Gobel, S., Steinmetz, R.: Context aware serious games framework for sport and health. In: Proceedings of the 2011 IEEE International Symposium on Medical Measurements and Applications, MeMeA 2011, pp. 1–5 (2011). https://doi.org/10.1109/MeMeA.2011.5966775
9. Jacob, J.T.P.N., Coelho, A.F.: Geo wars–the development of a location-based game. Rev. Prisma. Com. 14, 1–13 (2011). http://revistas.ua.pt/index.php/prismacom/article/view/972. Accessed 11 July 2011
10. Jacob, J., Coelho, A.: Issues in the development of location-based games. Int. J. Comput. Games Technol. 2011, 1–7 (2011). https://doi.org/10.1155/2011/495437
11. Lopes, R., Bidarra, R.: Adaptivity challenges in games and simulations: a survey. IEEE Trans. Comput. Intell. AI Games 3(2), 85–99 (2011). https://doi.org/10.1109/TCIAIG.2011.2152841
12. Matyas, S.: Playful geospatial data acquisition by location-based gaming communities. Int. J. Virtual Real. 6(3), 1–10 (2007)
13. Mortazavi, B., Pourhomayoun, M., Ghasemzadeh, H., Jafari, R., Roberts, C.K., Sarrafzadeh, M.: Context-aware data processing to enhance quality of measurements in wireless health systems: an application to MET calculation of exergaming actions. IEEE IoT J. 2(1), 84–93 (2015). https://doi.org/10.1109/JIOT.2014.2364407
14. O'Hara, K.: Understanding geocaching practices and motivations. In: Proceedings of the SIGCHI Conference on Human Factors in Computing Systems, pp. 1177–1186 (2008). https://doi.org/10.1145/1357054.1357239
15. Salber, D., Dey, A.K., Abowd, G.D.: The context toolkit: aiding the development of context-enabled. In: CHI 1999 Proceedings of the SIGCHI Conference on Human Factors in Computing Systems, pp. 434–441 (1999). https://doi.org/10.1145/302979.303126
16. Silva, J.M., El Saddik, A.: An adaptive game-based exercising framework. In: 2011 IEEE International Conference on Virtual Environments, Human-Computer Interfaces and Measurement Systems Proceedings, pp. 1–6 (2011). https://doi.org/10.1109/VECIMS.2011.6053847
17. Sinclair, J., Hingston, P., Masek, M.: Exergame development using the dual flow model. In: The 5th International Conference on Intelligent Environments – IE 2009, pp. 1–7 (2009). https://doi.org/10.1145/1746050.1746061
18. Smeddinck, J., Siegel, S., Herrlich. M.: Adaptive difficulty in exergames for Parkinson's disease patients. In: Proceedings of Graphics Interface 2013, pp. 141–148 (2013). http://dl.acm.org/citation.cfm?id=2532154. Accessed 9 Dec 2013
19. Sotamaa, O.: All the world's a botfighter stage: notes on location-based multi-user gaming. In: Cultures, pp. 35–44 (2002)
20. Sweetser, P., Wyeth, P.: GameFlow: a model for evaluating player enjoyment in games. Comput. Entertain. (CIE) 3(3), 3 (2005). https://doi.org/10.1145/1077246.1077253

Dreadful Virtualities: A Comparative Case Study of Player Responses to a Horror Game in Virtual Reality and Flat Screen

Marta Clavero Jiménez[1](✉), Amanda M. S. James[1],
Marcello A. Gómez Maureira[2], and Isabelle Kniestedt[2]

[1] Independent Researcher, Copenhagen, Denmark
derkonai@gmail.com, mastokja@gmail.com
[2] University of Malta, Msida, Malta
ma.gomezmaureira@gmail.com, ikniestedt@gmail.com

Abstract. As Virtual Reality (VR) technology has become consumer ready, questions concerning its effects are becoming more urgent, specifically in regards to content that involve strong emotions such as horror games. This study compares player responses while playing the same game in two conditions: room-scale VR and a conventional monitor. We developed a test game, based on a commercial title, and combined semi-structured interviews, questionnaires and psycho-physiological measures to analyze differences between setups. Participants' self-reports of fright were similar in both conditions on their first playthrough. However, results across different measures indicated an elevated experience of fear in VR upon playing the game a second time. The sensation of spatial presence afforded by VR emerged as the main argument for making the experience more intense and enhancing the immediacy of virtual threats. Our results show that while VR does not necessarily provide a more intense horror experience than conventional setups, it is less impacted by pre-existing knowledge of game content, providing a longer-lasting intensity to the experience.

Keywords: Virtual reality · Horror games · Game user research

1 Introduction

The art of scaring ourselves in the form of horror fiction has enticed people throughout time and across cultures. Horror is a popular theme in videogames, and one that is in itself enriched by the interactive nature of games. Game designer and writer Richard Rouse argues that it is only logical that videogames and horror are a perfect match since many of the classic horror elements lend themselves well to this interactive medium [47].

© Springer International Publishing AG, part of Springer Nature 2018
A. D. Cheok et al. (Eds.): ACE 2017, LNCS 10714, pp. 239–260, 2018.
https://doi.org/10.1007/978-3-319-76270-8_17

Games create an experience for the players, intensifying horror through gameplay [40], a feature that has attracted a lot of research into the emotional effects, and the impact of horror-gaming on videogame audiences.

Taking into consideration the popularity and appeal of horror in videogames, it is no wonder that, with the advent of consumer-ready Virtual Reality (VR) in 2016, a myriad of horror experiences are being developed for this medium [6,17,52]. Alongside disempowered protagonists, sinister atmosphere, and claustrophobic environments, the 'jump-scare' – a sudden effect meant to startle players – has been a common ingredient in the development of horror games [42]. The excessive use of this technique in many current VR horror titles has, however, sparked concerns among developers and researchers alike [8,50]. "When the headset is on there is seemingly no escape. Do developers take into account the psychological differences between previous gaming horror experiences and that of VR?" [32].

The general intuition among game developers is that playing in VR is more impactful and effective at eliciting certain emotions than an experience on a conventional screen. Particularly, horror experiences could be too intense when wearing a head mounted display. Taking the headset off to break the spell of the virtual space takes more effort than with traditional gaming interfaces; the illusion of being physically in the virtual space makes any fictional threat feel quite real [16]. VR offers a fascinating format for exploring the horror genre, which is why it is important to understand the medium and its effects.

While the literature suggests that VR has the potential to elicit strong emotions in players, there is a lack of comparative studies offering empirical evidence. Additionally, previous research on the topic of fear and videogames has mostly focused on the emotional effects of a single medium. This paper presents the adapted design and implementation of a horror game as a research tool, and the subsequent study in which it was used to identify and compare players' experiences. We examined the differences in emotional responses elicited by playing the same horror game in room-scale Virtual Reality (indicated as VRc, or VR condition) and on a conventional flat screen monitor (indicated as SCc, or screen condition). Being aware of the existence and impact of these differences between mediums can provide insight for future empirical studies, and be used by VR horror game developers to make informed decisions for the implementation of their ideas. Furthermore, there is an interest in using psycho-physiological measures in game studies, as well as game development, to gain unbiased data on emotional experiences. Inspired by similar previous studies [3,29] and related literature [39], this study was performed with the following research question and hypotheses in mind:

What are the self-reported and measurable psycho-physiological differences in fright responses when comparing the same game experience played in two different mediums?

H1: Participants will report experiencing higher levels of fear in VRc than in SCc. Psycho-physiological measures will indicate increased emotional arousal (corresponding with fright responses) in VRc.

H2: Participants will report experiencing less or no fear on re-play, regardless of the medium. Psycho-physiological measures will follow the same pattern, showing lower levels of arousal on re-play, regardless of the medium.

2 Theoretical Foundation

The development of the game used in this study was based on an understanding of the characteristics of horror fiction, and within the medium of videogames in particular. Inspired by Perron's concept of survival horror as an 'extended body genre' [40], we made the connection with Gregersen and Grodal theories about the embodied experience of videogames [14]. This link lead us to review the literature regarding the processes of embodied emotions, particularly concerning fear and the sensation of spatial presence, which informed the design of the research experiment.

2.1 Horror

Supernatural horror opens up a lot of possibilities when it comes to game design, especially when having to develop a consistent and believable world. Horror's long roots in folklore give ample opportunity to build on existing antagonists, such as werewolves or similar monsters, that our basic instinct associates with dangerous predators. Its implicit association with darkness, or obstructed scenery brings forth an instinctual fear in most people, inspiring a sense of vulnerability and uncertainty. Moreover, the fact that supernatural elements are common in horror allows for interesting and different game mechanics without them being inconsistent with the game-world [47]. We can say that 'habituation' and 'knowing' largely decrease the potential for horror to elicit strong emotions of fear, and that the unpredictability of a fright-inducing experience is part of the thrill that makes us seek the experience in the first place [23,41,54].

Horror, a genre that is primarily defined by its intention of transferring the physical reactions associated with the emotion of fear, is considered a 'body genre' [58]. Perron [40] expanded on this notion with the concept of 'extended body genre' when referring to videogames. In the same line, Gregersen and Grodal [14] argue that "interacting with videogames may lead to a sense of extended embodiment, ... where one experiences both agency and ownership of virtual entities" due to an interactive feedback loop where multi-sensory and proprioceptive systems are being activated. Gerrig and Rapp indicate that Coleridge might have been wrong when he coined the popular term "suspension of disbelief". When taking into consideration the psycho-physiological processes involved in our emotional experiences with media, the case is more akin to a "willing construction of disbelief". Audiences must engage their conscious cognitive processes in order to reject and contextualize, while their automatic processes are being activated by the stimuli provided by media [13].

2.2   Embodied Emotions

Fear belongs to what cognitive theorists call 'basic emotions'. Neurocognitive studies, such as those conducted by LeDoux [26], indicate that basic emotions are processed by a fast pathway through the limbic system, while cognitively evaluated secondary emotions (e.g. thrill and excitement) emerge by means of consciousness mechanisms processed by the slow pathway through the frontal lobes. Fear is a multifaceted emotion with associated action tendencies and physiological responses, automatically activated by specific perceptual triggers (real or otherwise). Once the fear module is activated, it requires conscious effort to cognitively evaluate the emotional experience in order to influence and regulate behaviors [37,38].

Consciousness mechanisms are an important notion to take in consideration when studying the emotional effect of horror-inducing media. Grodal [15] makes the case that the field of cognitive psychology provides a useful vantage point to study and describe videogames. Our brains did not exactly evolve to experience emotionally-charged fictional horror in film or game form, and thus, the automatic fast pathway reacts to mediated stimuli very similarly to real stimuli. One of the proposed reasons about why our response to mediated horror is less intense than to real-life situations, is that we are able to evaluate emotions cognitively and to correctly attribute bodily changes to more or less controllable external sources [37]. This processing allows us to be able to ride a roller-coaster, watch a horror film in the cinema, or play a scary game in VR. The frequency, persistence, and level of emotional charge of these mediated stimuli, influence how much of a strain it is for the consciousness mechanism to assess and regulate responses [15].

Previous studies about fear in the context of videogames have combined different methods in order to establish a connection between emotions, physiological data, and player behavior [36,53]. The physical component, these bodily responses associated with horror-gaming, can be measured using sensors capable of recording fear-related physiological arousal [19,20]. Although opinions are divided on the use of 'biometrics' to measure fear in games, with some researchers suggesting that only jump-scares can be adequately measured, this study is an attempt to capture another kind of fear, namely ongoing suspense.

A review of 134 publications assessing biophysical patterns found that it is possible to differentiate between basic emotions based on autonomic nervous system activity [22]. Increases in EDA and decrease in temperature are some of the most useful indicators of fear-related responses [4,5,9,10,25,28]. Despite the plethora of studies, there is no golden standard when it comes to accurately mapping physiological responses with discrete emotions [31]. For this reason, to elucidate the specificity of the emotional valence, it is necessary to take into consideration the context (i.e. a horror-gaming situation in an experimental setting), the self-reported measures, and the qualitative data gathered from interviews. When used in combination with self-reporting qualitative methods, physiological measures can provide a more rigorous portrayal of the player's emotional experience [30]. This is even more important when we take into consideration that some people might repress their emotional reactions to fright-inducing media in their self-reports [53].

Prinz's theory on embodied emotions proposes that "emotions are perceptions, and they are used to perceive our relationship to the world" [43]. It also states that emotions are "perception of affordances", allowing us to perceive what a situation affords regarding behavioral responses. Neuroscientific discoveries supplement this theory with the addition of cognitive appraisals as part of the emotional process, explaining complex emotions [26]. These premises connect with the concepts of spatial presence and immersive technologies, as well as their emotional impact.

2.3   Spatial Presence and Immersion

The term immersion and spatial presence are frequently brought up as a central component regarding emotional response in videogame players, especially in regards to VR. Lynch and Martins [29] argue that the interactive elements, characteristic of videogames, are the possible cause of an enhanced state of presence and immersion, and that this seems to be a key component when participants reported feeling more frightened. The definitions of the terms are not without contention in the academic world, including some cases where the two terms are being used interchangeably. Ermi and Mäyrä [12] argue that immersion is a term describing the experience felt when becoming involved in, and giving attention to a mediated experience, and its ability to stimulate imagination, challenge us or stimulate our senses.

Willans [57] builds on Prinz's theory of embodied emotions in his argument for spatial presence as a perceptual emotion. This perception is affected by our interpretation of environmental stimuli such as sight, hearing, touch, proprioception, balance/motion, smell and taste [18]. Spatial presence in VR is evoked when stimuli from the virtual environment overpower the stimuli of the real world environment enough to trigger the emotion of 'being there' [57].

Virtual reality is a powerful affective medium that affords a high sense of presence [45]. With the introduction of room-scale VR, which allows natural locomotion in a dedicated room-sized space, the virtual environment feels even closer to reality [59]. This heightened sensory immersion, particularly when experiencing room-scale VR, can amplify the effects of horror elements [32] and enhance the sensation of spatial presence [57].

3   The Game

In order to have a high level of experimental control, we created the research stimulus based on the design of an existing commercial game: *P. T.* — the standalone playable teaser of *Silent Hills* [21]. The virtual space in *P. T.* features a series of perceptual triggers that effectively activate the human fear module [38], moreover, this title has been recognized by game critics as one of the most compelling horror game experiences in recent years [1,51]. Adapting an existing commercial game made our research tool closer, experience-wise, to real-life gaming

Fig. 1. Game layout as seen from above (left) and in-game screenshots (right). A non-euclidean solution creates the illusion of the virtual space being bigger on the inside. This allows for areas (e.g. bathroom) to occupy the same space as the other rooms.

situations, contributing to higher levels of ecological validity [34]. Additionally, this approach allowed us to minimize the impact of confounding variables, and to log in-game events.

3.1 Design and Implementation

Using the game engine Unity, we developed an adaptation of the game that could be played in room-scale VR, as well as non-VR. Since designing for room-scale VR is a more complex challenge due to its unique set of constraints and considerations (e.g. natural gestures and locomotion, playing within a room with a fixed size, etc.) [49], we designed the VR version first. The other version was developed afterwards by introducing changes in the design that made it possible to play the game with a gamepad controller in front of a PC monitor. We acknowledge that this introduces a certain amount of bias in our study towards VR, since the level layout and the interactions were designed with the constraints of room-scale VR in mind. Nevertheless, we deem the resulting PC version close enough in terms of experience, pacing and mechanics to other similar horror games, including the source material.

To avoid introducing confounding variables beyond the different types of control schemes and output methods for each condition, the two game versions were essentially the same, differing only in terms of control and field of view. The levels of the game world were designed in such a way that the player moves through the physical play area and the game world at a 1:1 ratio, meaning that the size of the playable VR area correlates exactly with the size of the

Table 1. Overview of the individual game loops. All letter indications are based on Fig. 1. Note that the player transitions into the next loop by walking through the loop door and traversing the corridor in the order $A \rightarrow B \rightarrow C$. Walking in the other direction does not trigger the next loop.

Loop 0	Dimly lit concrete room. After a short monologue, a door opens into section A of the corridor.
Loop 1	Lights are on in all sections. A radio report describing a familicide is heard.
Loop 2	Light in A is off; B and C on. The bathroom door rattles and knocking is heard when the player passes B.
Loop 3	Lights in A and C are on; B is off. The loop door slams shut on approach, then the bathroom door opens slightly and a baby's cry is heard. The bathroom door closes on approach and the loop door opens.
Loop 4	Lights in A and B are off; C is on. Cries of a woman can be heard. A tall and mangled female figure is standing in C. As the player approaches, all lights go off. The figure disappears; her cries increase in volume. Approaching the loop door causes all lights to turn on and the cries to stop.
Loop 5	Lights in A and C are off; B is on. On approach to B, the bathroom door opens. On entering the bathroom, the door closes behind, and one of the controllers becomes a flashlight. The sound of a door opening can be heard, followed by footsteps. The door rattles and opens after a short pause.
Loop 6	All lights are on. The radio is playing the same report as before. On approach, the loop door slams shut, the radio stops playing, and all lights turn off. Footsteps and heavy breathing can be heard from the upper floor. The female figure approaches the banister of an interior balcony and looks down at the player. After a while the figure retreats and the loop door opens.
Loop 7	All lights are on. As the player walks, footsteps and heavy breathing can be heard from behind. The figure's shadow is projected on the walls in front of the player. A distorted version of the radio report plays on the radio.
Loop 8	All lights are off and the flashlight is the only source of light. The player can hear the figure's steps and heavy breathing behind them.
Loop 9	All lights are off. The loop door is locked and loud ringing of a phone can be heard as soon as the player enters A. When the players approaches the telephone in C, a voice tells them: "You have been chosen". The virtual space fades to black and the game ends

game world. The simplicity of the level design and architecture in the source material lent itself well for this room-scale VR adaptation, where the game world is confined to the play area space. The level geometry and size of the game world were modified accordingly to fit the virtual space in a 3.15 by 3.3 m VR playable area.

Besides adjusting the level design of *P.T.*, the game used in this study has a modified sequence of events and content. The game levels are referred to as *loops* (see Table 1 for descriptions). Although a virtual body representation seems to increase the reports of spatial presence when compared to having no actual body representation in the virtual world, it can also be disturbing for players if the movements of the virtual body are not aligned with theirs [48]. Considering that tracking a full body in VR is currently not technologically feasible, we avoided implementing a virtual body representation instead of having something that would disturb the players [49].

Due to practical constraints in VR development, as well as the goals for the experimental design, we did not implement content that (1) was intended to startle players with sudden scare effects (jump-scares), (2) had progression puzzles that would cause the duration of the test to be unpredictably long, and (3) would likely induce simulator sickness.

4   Pilot Test

A pilot test was conducted to refine the data gathering tools and the test procedure, and to identify possible issues that could hamper the quality of the research experiment [24,56]. A prototype of the VR version of the game was used to test the procedure and gameplay. This version of the game only included loops 1, 2, 4, 7 and 9. A total of 26 participants were part of the pilot test, 2 females (8%) and 24 males (92%). One of the objectives of the pilot test was to assess the ecological validity of the stimulus material, since 'jump-scares' and gating mechanisms were removed in the process of adaptation. Overall, participants reported being entertained and as scared as in similar experiences. As a result of the pilot-test the function to turn off the flashlight was removed, as it confused players. The behavior of the ghost character in loops 4, 7, and 8, was adjusted, and an audio intro was added to serve as mood-setting. Additionally, bugs were identified and dealt with. We handed participants an early version of the questionnaire and conducted an interview after the play-session. As a result, we shortened both the questionnaire and interview, and modified the phrasing of some items.

5   Experiment Design

The experiment ran for six days with a total of 29 participants. Two versions of the same horror game were used as stimulus material. Participants engaged with the stimulus material twice, once in each medium. The order of the test conditions alternated between participants; half of participants experienced the game first in VRc followed by SCc, and vice versa. The research process was based on a mixed-methods approach, combining game metrics, psycho-physiological measurements, observation, interviews and questionnaires. This approach was chosen to explore various angles and to gain as complete a picture of differences in player experience between both conditions as was possible within the scope of the study.

5.1   Equipment

The same laptop, with specifications that are considered sufficient by the developers of the VR equipment, was used for both conditions, as well as ear-enclosing headphones with sonic isolation. An *Empatica E4* wristband sensor was used to record psycho-physiological responses. The sensor was chosen as a compromise between level of invasiveness, the need to measure participants in motion (specifically in the VRc), and budgetary constraints. A recent study [44] compared the E4 sensor to a laboratory sensor and found it to be as accurate for the purposes of emotion recognition. Another study [33] compared the sensor to a portable electrocardiogram (ECG) and found that the ECG performed better 5% of the time. While this suggests an improvement over the E4 sensor, we argue that even with a difference in data quality, the Empatica sensor can provide valid results, especially given that fear-related physiological responses are relatively strong compared to other emotional responses.

VR condition (VRc): The HTC Vive is comprised of a headset, two wireless controllers, and two base stations enabling 360 o room-scale tracking. The tracking area in this test was 3.15 by 3.3 meter. The Vive includes sensors in the headset and wireless controllers that pick up infrared signals from the base stations to track the position and movement of the player inside the VRc area (see Fig. 2). For the VRc, participants were instructed to mind the cable connecting the display device to the machine running the game; basic instructions regarding wearing the headset and holding the controllers was also provided. Participants used natural locomotion to navigate the virtual space of the game, completing a total of nine clockwise loops around the play area.

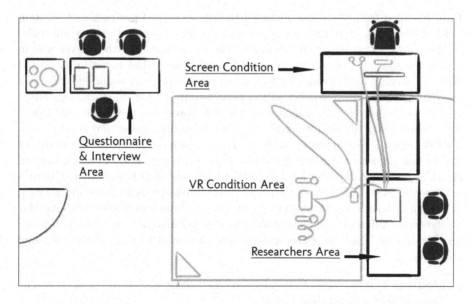

Fig. 2. Schematic showing the testing environment and setup.

SC condition (SCc): The participants were seated at a desk where they played the game using a 17 in. monitor connected to the laptop and an Xbox 360 controller. Instructions were provided regarding the controller and its button functionality, and a printed guide was available for reference.

5.2   Questionnaire and Interview Data

The questionnaire used in the experiment consisted of three parts: *pre-experiment*, *post-session*, and *post-experiment*, each of which was administered at a different time during the experiment. The pre-experiment section was administered as a structured interview, and consisted mainly of items that sought to profile participants' familiarity with, and disposition toward horror games. Participants were also asked about their experience with different types of VR headsets with the purpose of addressing the influence of novelty-excitement during the VR version of the experiment. The post-session part consisted of nine closed questions where participants were asked to rate different aspects of their experience on a unipolar 10 point Likert scale. It was administered twice, right after the participant finished each of the test conditions. The post-experiment section followed the second post-session questionnaire, and was mainly aimed at gathering demographic information. The experiment ended with a semi-structured interview, the goal of which was to gain insight into the participant's subjective game experience, as well as provide context to the participant's measured responses.

5.3   Game Metrics and Psycho-Physiological Measures

Data recorded from the game included the player's head position and rotation (with a frequency of 10 Hz), and gameplay events. Position and rotation information was contextualized by recording the room and loop the player was in at a given time. Game events were single occurrences that typically consisted of doors opening and closing, lights turning off and on, and sound effects. Each entry into the log was recorded with a time stamp and logged chronologically.

For psycho-physiological measures, the E4 sensor was used to record *heart-rate* (reported by the device based on the blood volume pulse and captured via a PPG sensor), *electrodermal activity* (EDA), peripheral *skin temperature*, as well as time stamps for synchronization of data through an event mark button. Heart rate (HR) is reported at 1 Hz, while EDA and skin temperature (Temp.) are reported at 4 Hz. For these measures we established baseline readings for each participant (described further in the next section), which were used to control for idiosyncratic differences in participants, as well as differences in activity between test conditions. The raw sensor values were processed to express the following measures:

1. **Median:** The *median* of the measure, indicating the 'typical' value of the measure over a given time frame.

2. **Median Absolute Deviation (MAD):** The MAD of the measure, indicating deviations over a given time frame from the data's *median*. This measure is meant to capture consistent fluctuations, as MAD should be less influenced by few temporary outliers.
3. **Slope:** The linear polynomial of the measure over a given time frame, indicating a general trend and steepness of a measure.
4. **Travel:** Aggregate of absolute differences between individual measures over a given time frame. This measure is meant to capture both continuous and temporary fluctuations. The measure is divided by the amount of measures to make it comparable.
5. **Onsets (EDA only):** Indicates the amount of peaks (phasic skin conductance measurements) with a threshold of $0.01\mu S$ (processed through Ledalab using Continuous Decomposition Analysis [2]). Peaks are divided by the amount of measures to make them comparable.

Data from the game and the sensors was processed before subsequent evaluation by removing outliers (values larger than $3 * MAD$ [27]). Sensor data was further pre-processed with a Gaussian filter (window width $= 4 *$ measure frequency), and brought into context to a participant's baseline measure. Each of the sensor measures therefore directly expresses an in- or decrease of the baseline in percent, with the exception of 'Slope', which is reported as change of a measure per minute.

6   Procedure

Participants were recruited by use of convenience sampling through social media, physical flyers, and word of mouth. People with phobias that could be triggered by the contents of the game, health issues that might get triggered by flashing lights or sudden emotional distress, as well as those lacking basic game-playing experience were excluded. The test area for the experiment was equipped with AC units, keeping the temperature at $21\,^\circ$C, to minimize the impact on skin temperature measures. All conditions in the room (i.e. light conditions, closed windows, doors, noise levels, etc.) were kept the same throughout the experiment sessions. The experiment procedure was divided into four stages, as shown in Fig. 3: Briefing, first play (VRc or SCc), second play (using the remaining condition), and interview/debriefing. Experiments alternated between VRc and SCs as the starting condition for each participant. The briefing stage started with introductions, followed by participants reading and signing the consent form, and the opportunity to ask questions regarding the form and the test. After this, a pre-experiment questionnaire was administered to establish prior experience with horror games and VR, and the participant was fitted with the E4 sensor.

A baseline recording for the psycho-physiological measures was taken before playing each condition, which functioned as a base value against which the measurements taken during each test were compared. In VRc this meant that participants walked, at a leisurely pace, within the VRc area, counting out loud

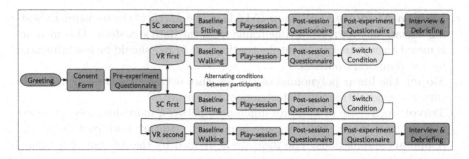

Fig. 3. Flowchart illustrating the sequence of the experiment with alternating starting conditions.

until 80. For SCc, the procedure for baseline recording was done with the participant counting until 80 while seated. This approach was chosen to establish a baseline under physical conditions similar to those required in the play-session minus the stimulus material. A test conductor then explained the controls of the respective version of the game, and helped the participant with the necessary equipment. Participants were also reminded that the test could be terminated at their will at any time, and informed that the test conductors would not talk to them during the play-session (an exception to this rule was made whenever tracking problems occurred). Once the participant was ready, the test conductor initialized the game. Once each of the play-sessions concluded, the post-session questionnaire was administered.

After the participant had finished both testing conditions and post-session questionnaires, they were asked to fill in the post-experiment section of the questionnaire as well and participate in a semi-structured interview. Both test conductors were part of the debriefing and interview process. Audio recordings of the interviews were made for later analysis. To conclude the experiment, participants were given the option to ask questions, and were handed a formal debriefing information sheet.

7   Data Analysis and Results

The experiment was conducted with $N = 29$ participants[1], 31% of which were female. 89.6% of participants were age 18–34. While all participants played both conditions, 6 participants did not fully complete playing the VRc. All participants completed the SCc and completed the VRc at least up to the 5th loop. The majority of participants had played or had watched others play horror games, and 43% had played (or had watched others play) *P.T.*. Two thirds of participants (61%) had some experience in game development, and 75% had tried some form of VR before.

---

[1] Due to a loss of data, questionnaire results were based on $N = 28$.

Q1 How scary did you find the experience?			
	Mean	Std. Dev	Median	N
VRst	6.07	1.98	6.50	N=14
SCst	5.43	2.47	5.00	N=14
VRnd	6.43	2,17	7.00	N=14
SCnd	3.64	1.95	4.00	N=14

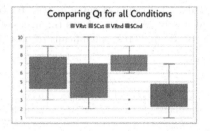

Fig. 4. Questionnaire results for Q1

7.1 Questionnaire

When asked whether participants expected sudden scare effects ('jump scares'), 75.9% answered 'Yes'. When directly comparing both test conditions at the end of the experiment, 79.3% ranked VRc as scarier than SCc (BF_{10} = 4301.85, against 0.5). A closer analysis of this question, reveals that if the VRc was first, participants unanimously chose VRc as scarier than SCc. However, when the SCc was first, only 64.2% chose VRc as scarier, while 14.3% reported both condition as equally scary, and 21.4% expressed that the SCc was scarier. Additionally, 27 participants (93.1%) indicated VR as their preferred condition. After playing each condition, we asked participants to rate how scary they found the experience (Q1) on a scale from 1 to 10 (see Fig. 4). When directly comparing conditions for scariness ratings, there was no significant difference between conditions as the first experience. Looking at differences between conditions on the second play, however, SCc was rated significantly lower (Mann-Whitney $U = 33$, $N1 = N2 = 14$, SCnd vs. VRnd, $p = 0.002753$ two tailed; alpha level 0.05).

7.2 Interview

Interviews were transcribed and coded through a mixed approach. The coding scheme was produced by deriving codes from the literature and from data-centric themes [7].

Participants' reports centered around the influence of 'expectations' and 'knowing', as well as the experience of spatial presence, movement, interactions, and embodiment. Participants generally expected the game to contain (more) 'jump-scares', due to the genre. Some also expected more traditional horror-game gameplay and interaction. These expectations were built on participants' previous experience with the genre and had a influence on their first condition play-session.

Participants reported that 'knowing' had a big influence on how scared they felt, with participants that experienced VR as the first condition citing 'knowing' as the reason they felt little or no fear during the SCc play-session. This was not the case for participants who experienced SC as first condition. Although 'knowing' still was cited as reducing the experience of fear in their VR play-session, most participants still found VR to be the scarier condition regardless.

Table 2. Results of game metrics for both conditions combined, and for 1st and 2nd play only. $M_{condition}$ shows the mean of a measure per condition; BF_{10} is the result of a Bayesian T-Test. Significant results are bold.

	Overall			1st Play Only			2nd Play Only		
	M_{SCc}	M_{VRc}	BF_{10}	M_{SCc}	M_{VRc}	BF_{10}	M_{SCc}	M_{VRc}	BF_{10}
Play duration	450.1 s	516.5 s	0.713	540.5 s	538.2 s	0.385	411.4 s	475.5 s	0.707
Horizontal rotations	20.44 °/s	28.82 °/s	**5.1e+5**	21.60 °/s	30.49 °/s	**4614**	20.06 °/s	25.82 °/s	**5.582**
Vertical rotations	6.48 °/s	10.56 °/s	**12413**	6.20 °/s	10.99 °/s	**27.52**	6.75 °/s	10.10 °/s	1.894

They stated that feeling spatially present in the game influenced these feelings greatly (e.g. *"I knew what was going to happen, but some things that had already happened still had a bigger effect on me in the VR than with the monitor. That door effect – Bathroom door loop 5 – was the one that affected me the most."*)

Spatial presence was a big factor when participants reported on why they felt scared in VR. Some expressed that in VR they could not look away from the game, and therefore felt more a part of the game itself rather than an onlooker. The visual isolation in VR added to the feeling of spatial presence as well as to their experience of fear (e.g. *"I completely forgot for a few seconds where I was, and what I was doing, and I thought that I was actually in that situation, and obviously that is something that for me will throw me off completely and scare me."*). This greater sense of embodiment within the game was also reflected in the way they reported movement, interactions, and visceral reactions to the game in VR.

7.3   Sensor Measures and Game Metrics

Game metrics (shown in Table 2) and sensor data (shown in Table 3) were analyzed for statistically significant differences between test conditions. Bayesian T-Tests were conducted (Cauchy prior width 0.707 [55]) for all sensor and game metrics, using paired samples for first and second play sessions combined, and independent samples for analyzing differences in the individual play sessions. The Bayesian T-Test returns a Bayes Factor BF, with the notation BF_{10}, indicating the assumption that a given hypothesis is not equal to its null-hypothesis. A BF_{10} of 1 indicates an equal chance of tested conditions being different as opposed to them being similar. A value lower than 1 indicates that the null-hypothesis is more likely; meaning that the Bayesian T-Test can be used to *confirm the null-hypothesis* rather than only reject it [46]. Note that we consider results with a $BF_{10} > 3$ or $BF_{10} < 0.333$ significant, that is, instances in which the likelihood of difference (or similarity) is at least 3 times higher than its inverse possibility.

The analysis of sensor and game metrics is based on varying sub-samples due to some participants not completing all game loops, as well as due to the removal of outliers for a given measure. It should be noted that outliers were removed both from the raw data of a participant, as well as from the processed

Table 3. Results of the sensor metrics for HR, EDA, and skin temperature. $\Delta M_{condition}$ shows the mean of a measure per condition in % based on the corresponding baseline measure (e.g. -5.0 is 5% lower than baseline); BF_{10} is the result of a Bayesian T-Test. 'Slope' is shown directly in measure change per minute, and does not use a baseline. Horizontal rows separate measures of both conditions combined, 1st play only, and 2nd play only. Significant results are bold.

	Median			MAD			Slope			Travel		
	ΔM_{SCc}	ΔM_{VRc}	BF_{10}	ΔM_{SCc}	ΔM_{VRc}	BF_{10}	x/min_{SCc}	x/min_{VRc}	BF_{10}	ΔM_{SCc}	ΔM_{VRc}	BF_{10}
$HR_{Overall}$	0.833	3.125	**0.240**	58.92	120.7	0.409	0.003	–0.136	**0.244**	–45.26	–10.06	**8.183**
$EDA_{Overall}$	31.17	233.0	**38.72**	128.5	861.4	**5.557**	0.010	0.084	**4.473**	–28.51	205.2	**1054**
$Temp._{Overall}$	0.468	–0.887	0.607	21.65	152.7	2.129	≈ 0	–0.055	**4.490**	–56.79	–23.17	**5.749**
$HR_{1stPlay}$	–3.546	3.828	0.463	60.59	154.2	1.006	0.504	0.335	0.372	–45.314	–1.491	**3.129**
$EDA_{1stPlay}$	78.80	221.3	2.352	410.9	711.3	0.586	0.023	0.066	0.859	32.76	169.02	2.566
$Temp._{1stPlay}$	–0.913	–2.641	1.302	103.1	185.4	0.474	–0.025	–0.050	0.489	–49.93	–29.01	0.902
$HR_{2ndPlay}$	5.211	2.472	0.368	57.12	48.10	0.366	–0.499	–0.607	0.368	–31.02	–31.20	0.359
$EDA_{2ndPlay}$	16.74	128.07	**12.26**	79.50	649.79	**5.879**	–0.003	0.072	**4.462**	–39.50	236.13	**46.84**
$Temp._{2ndPlay}$	1.849	0.742	0.644	29.41	68.63	0.441	0.013	–0.071	**20.12**	–58.35	–35.89	0.802

measures across participants. In general, the sub-sample size for SCc was $n \approx 28$, and $n \approx 27$ for VRc in combined session results (with the exception of 'play duration' where VRc was $n \approx 22$). For the analysis of first and second play sessions, the sub-sample size was $n \approx 14$ for SCc and $n \approx 13$ for VRc (≈ 11 for 'play duration').

Apart of the sensor measures shown in Table 3, onsets were evaluated for EDA measures, with the result $\Delta M_{SCc} = -0.023$, $\Delta M_{VRc} = 0.087$, $BF_{10} = 14.44$ for both play sessions combined. For first play: $\Delta M_{SCc} = -0.007$, $\Delta M_{VRc} = 0.097$, $BF_{10} = 3.32$. And for second play: $\Delta M_{SCc} = -0.03$, $\Delta M_{VRc} = 0.053$, $BF_{10} = 7.19$. This means that the conditions differ significantly in regards to the amount of measured EDA onsets.

In addition to the analysis of play sessions as a whole, results from the individual loops were explored to discover which game loops had the most impact. In terms of game metrics, loop 8 lasted significantly longer in VRc than in SCc ($BF_{10} = 31.59$). Differences in camera rotation are mostly impacted by the loops 0, 2, 5 and 6, all of which are higher in VRc. For HR, loop 8 shows a significant difference for MAD ($BF_{10} = 118.9$) and travel ($BF_{10} = 39.04$), both of which had a lower mean in SCc than in VRc. EDA is generally most influenced by the loops 3–8, with the most significant differences in loops 5 and 7. For temperature, loop 5 had the most pronounced impact (slope $BF_{10} = 317.4$, lower in VRc) on the overall measure.

8   Discussion

The intent of this study was to examine the differences in player experience, especially regarding fright responses, when comparing the same horror game in two different setups. We expected to find participants reporting higher levels of fear in

VRc than in SCc, and for these reports to be backed up by psycho-physiological measures (H1). When asked to compare the two experiences directly in the post-experiment questionnaire, participants reported that the game was scarier when playing VR, regardless of it being the first or second test condition. Previous experience with VR headsets, or lack thereof, had no significant influence on these outcomes. The results of the questionnaire are in line with comments made during the interviews, with most of the participants reporting that they found the experience scarier in VR. Reasons for this related to feeling a strong sense of 'being there' in VRc, and that this made the overall VR experience more intense. This notion of spatial presence was also mentioned by those that found SCc to be scarier, with them stating that although they did not find the VRc to be scarier, they did 'feel it more' physically. However, when asked to rate the experience individually after each session, only a marginal difference between first conditions was found.

Regarding psycho-physiological data, significant differences were found in EDA and skin temperature when considering the second session, corroborating the results from the questionnaire. No significant difference was found between conditions when participants played the first condition (experiencing the game as new). During the second play, however, participants showed significant measures between conditions, suggesting VRc continued to cause intense emotional responses despite players being familiar with the game at this point. This result contradicts our second assumption that participants would experience less or no fear responses on re-playing the same game, regardless of medium (H2). Additionally, questionnaire responses showed that the order in which the conditions were played had a significant impact on how scary participants rated the game. No significant differences were found in the ratings for VRc as the first or second condition. In contrast to this, we did see significant differences between SCc as first and second condition. Participants elaborated on this in the interviews, stating the game was significantly less scary when playing SCc after VRc, while VRc was still considered to be scary even after playing SCc first. A common reason cited for this difference was that knowing the sequence of events and being familiar with the game influenced how intensely fear was felt during second play-sessions. Participants playing VRc first reported experiencing less fear in the second condition as they 'knew what was going to happen'. This knowledge had less impact on participants playing VRc second, with participants reporting that although they knew what was going to happen, the experience in VR was still scary. Spatial presence and the physicality inherent of VR was cited as the main reason for the VRc being more impactful and intense despite knowing what would happen.

Knowing the full extent of 'any danger', consequences and all, will reduce anxiety and fear [35]. We expected that participants would become habituated to the game during their experience with the first condition, and that the intensity of their emotional response would therefore diminish. The results show that habituation had an effect on the intensity of fear measured and reported, but that the effect is only noticeable when switching from VRc to SCc, but not vice versa. A possible reason for the decline in fear response from VRc to SCc could be that the game has no randomized events, minimal interaction options, and no death scenario. The knowledge that there are no consequences for the participant's actions seems to increase the habituation effect when playing the game on SC as second condition. This habituation, however, does not seem to have any significant influence when looking at the responses from the participants who had SC as first condition and VR as second condition.

In addition to analyzing differences over the duration of a play session, we also considered observed differences within particular loops. Differences were observed in EDA values (median, travel, and onsets) for loops 3 through 8, with values being significantly higher in VRc. Abrupt increases in EDA (onsets) are typically associated with short-term events and occur in the presence of distinct environmental stimuli [11]. We therefore consider it likely that these differences were caused by the events in those loops (e.g. the sudden closing of a door, changes in lighting conditions, and audio cues). This suggests that changes in audio and light conditions might have a greater effect in VR. It can also indicate that the sensation of spatial presence afforded by VR enhanced the immediacy of a perceived threat. This corresponds to self-reports of players getting startled by the encounter with the ghost in loop 4, specifically mentioning that the confrontation had more of a 'physical' impact in VR, as well as other events, e.g. to the bathroom door opening in loop 5.

Game metrics indicated that people looked around more in VR, which correlates with statements from the interviews. Evidence for this difference stops being significant around Loop 6, which suggests that players got used to the repeating environment, or that the novelty of being in VR wears out over time. A larger difference was found when comparing the first session, suggesting that players felt less of an urge to look around when already familiar with the environment. In regards to play duration, no significant differences were found between conditions. Loop 8 is an exception to this, and shows players taking significantly longer to complete the loop in VRc than SCc. With the lights being off in this loop, this finding suggests that the darkness required more effort to navigate in VR. Other sensor readings (increases in EDA measures and a decreasing slope in temperature) suggest a more intense emotional response consistent with fear. A possible explanation for the findings in this loop could be that the events in previous loops, combined with knowledge of horror fiction tropes, created suspense, a precursor to fear [23].

One notable finding in this study was the absence of consistent significant differences in heart rate values. This challenges our expectations of finding elevated heart rate in relation to emotional arousal. Given the nature of the stimulus material — a suggestive horror game that relies mostly on suspense and atmosphere instead of sudden startle effects — we suggest that the stimulus used might not lend itself well to measurements of heart rate. Another possible explanation is that, since heart rate values were always computed against their respective baseline reading, participants could have had an already elevated heart rate due to stress caused by being part of an experiment or as a result of anticipatory fear, which is a common occurrence before playing a horror game. Future studies could remedy this by establishing a longer baseline procedure, and taking baseline measurements at a separate time from the experiment (e.g. some days apart).

Any study is limited by the technology of the time, especially when investigating the effects of new technologies on users. Participants stated that the VR headset's cable was a distraction and, for some, a source of anxiety as they were concerned with tripping. Although many current commercial VR sets rely on cables, and our setup is therefore comparable to one that a player might have at home, we cannot exclude the effect this may have had on the gathering of data. For future research we would suggest the use of a wireless VR set when possible to limit this influence. It is also possible that data was influenced by the relative 'newness' of VR as a technology, and participants seemed to favor VR during interviews and in questionnaire answers. This influence is likely to decrease as more people become accustomed to VR. While this study provides an important data point regarding the differences in game experience between VR and monitors, future studies will be needed to see whether the findings remain the same as VR continues to become more generally used as a medium.

9 Conclusion

With this study we aimed to provide empirical data regarding a general intuition among game developers, namely that horror games in VR provide more intense emotional experiences than when played on a traditional monitor. To this end we developed a horror game and tested it in both conditions, using a mixed-method approach to data gathering to gain a full picture of player experience in both setups.

The data shows that when directly compared after having experienced both conditions, VR is subjectively considered to provide a more intense, frightening experience than playing on a screen. However, most of the data (both in psycho-physiological measures and questionnaire answers) points towards VR being more intense *only* when playing the game for a second time. This largely contradicts the literature regarding the role of uncertainty in the horror fiction experience, and suggests that VR is less impacted by 'knowing what is to come', with players still experiencing notable fear responses. Although our data does not necessarily support the assumption that playing an atmospheric horror game in VR is always more frightening than when played on a screen, it shows that subjectively players do consider it as such. More interestingly, it shows that horror games enjoy a longer lasting appeal when played in VR than they do on a monitor, suggesting the physical responses and sensation of spatial presence induced by the technology contribute to the continued intensity of the experience. Additionally, this study serves as a first data point for psycho-physiological measures for player experience of horror games in VR, which, we hope, will be a foundation for more empirical research on the topic.

Acknowledgments. First and foremost we would like to thank Mikkel Svendsen, for pouring hours upon hours of his spare time into developing the game that was used for this research. He offered his technical advice, enthusiasm, and support throughout the whole process. We are most thankful to Yasmin Marie Cachia, for her generous assistance and her advice during the experimental phase of this project. Huge thanks to the lecturers and staff members at the Institute of Digital Games at the University of Malta, for allowing us to use their equipment and their space, and for wholeheartedly participating in our research. Many thanks to Marco Scirea and Daniel Cermak for the many conversations and guidance. Thank you as well to all test participants and playtesters, this project would have been impossible without your enthusiastic participation.

References

1. Bakalar, J.: P.T. is pure video-game marketing genius. https://www.cnet.com/news/p-t-is-pure-video-game-marketing-genius/ (2014). Accessed 14 Apr 2017
2. Benedek, M., Kaernbach, C.: A continuous measure of phasic electrodermal activity. J. Neurosci. Methods **190**(1), 80–91 (2010). https://doi.org/10.1016/j.jneumeth.2010.04.028
3. Blackmore, K.L., Coppins, W., Nesbitt, K.V.: Using startle reflex to compare playing and watching in a horror game. In: Proceedings of the Australasian Computer Science Week Multiconference, ACSW 2016, pp. 72:1–72:7. ACM, New York(2016). https://doi.org/10.1145/2843043.2843482
4. Cacioppo, J.T., Berntson, G.G., Larsen, J.T., Poehlmann, K.M., Ito, T.A.: The psychophysiology of emotion. In: Lewis, R., Haviland-Jones, J. (eds.) Handbook of Emotions, vol. 2, 2nd edn, pp. 173–191. Guilford Press, New York (2000). Chap. 11
5. Collet, C., Vernet-Maury, E., Delhomme, G., Dittmar, A.: Autonomic nervous system response patterns specificity to basic emotions. J. Auton. Nerv. Syst. **62**(1–2), 45–57 (1997). https://doi.org/10.1016/s0165-1838(96)00108-7
6. Cooper, D.: 6 upcoming VR horror games with the most potential, 23 August 2016. https://gamerant.com/6-best-upcoming-vr-horror-games-666/. Accessed 13 Apr 2017
7. Cote, A., Raz, J.G.: Game research methods. In: In-depth Interviews for Games Research, pp. 93–116. ETC Press, Pittsburgh (2015). http://dl.acm.org/citation.cfm?id=2812774.2812784
8. Crecente, B.: Experts set to meet with fed government about need for VR ethics, more research. http://www.polygon.com/2017/3/24/15055542/vr-government-regulation, Mar 2017. Accessed 13 Apr 2017
9. Dawson, M.E., Schell, A.M., Filion, D.L.: The electrodermal system. In: Cacioppo, J.T., Tassinary, L.G., Berntson, G.G. (eds.) Handbook of Psychophysiology, 2n edn, pp. 200–223. Cambridge University Press, New York (2007). Chap. 8
10. Ekman, P., Levenson, R., Friesen, W.: Autonomic nervous system activity distinguishes among emotions. Science **221**(4616), 1208–1210 (1983). https://doi.org/10.1126/science.6612338
11. Empatica Support: What should I know to use EDA data in my experiment? Empatica Support, May 2016
12. Ermi, L., Mäyrä, F.: Fundamental components of the gameplay experience: analysing immersion. In: De Castell, S., Jenson, J. (eds.) Worlds in Play: International Perspectives on Digital Games Research, vol. 21, pp. 37–54. Peter Lang, New York (2005). Chap. 3

13. Gerrig, R.J., Rapp, D.N.: Psychological processes underlying literary impact. Poetics Today **25**(2), 265–281 (2004)
14. Gregersen, A.L., Grodal, T.K.: Embodiment and interface. In: Perron, B., Wolf, M.J. (eds.) Video Game Theory Reader 2, pp. 65–83. Routledge, New York and London (2008). Chap. 4
15. Grodal, T.: Stories for eyes, ears, and muscles - story as embodied simulation. In: Embodied Visions: Evolution, Emotion, Culture, and Film, Chap. 6, pp. 129–155. Oxford University Press, Oxford (2009)
16. Hackett, P., Hickman, C., Hurd, T., Schwartz, A., Stephan, S.: A year in roomscale: design lessons from the HTC VIVE & beyond, March 2016. http://www.gdcvault.com/play/1023661/A-Year-in-Roomscale-Design. From VRDC - GDC 2016, San Francisco
17. Hunt, C.: The 10 best horror games for VR, 21 July 2017. https://www.vrheads.com/best-horror-games-vr, Accessed 24 July 2017
18. Jerald, J.: The VR Book: Human-Centered Design for Virtual Reality. Morgan & Claypool, New York (2016)
19. Karamnejad, M., Choo, A., Gromala, D., Shaw, C., Mamisao, J.: Immersive virtual reality and affective computing for gaming, fear and anxiety management. In: ACM SIGGRAPH 2013 Posters, SIGGRAPH 2013, pp. 74:1–74:1. ACM, New York (2013). https://doi.org/10.1145/2503385.2503466
20. Keir, Z.M., Kroll, B.M., Ludwig, K.D., Schuler, E.J., Vigen, L.M.: The somatic and autonomic nervous system's response to a fear stimulus. J. Hum. Physiol. **1**, 1–8 (2011)
21. Kojima Productions: P.T. (2014)
22. Kreibig, S.D.: Autonomic nervous system activity in emotion: a review. Biol. Psychol. **84**(3), 394–421 (2010). https://doi.org/10.1016/j.biopsycho.2010.03.010
23. Krzywinska, T.: Reanimating lovecraft: the ludic paradox of Call of Cthulhu: dark corners of the earth. In: Perron, B. (ed.) Horror Video Games: Essays on the Fusion of Fear and Play, pp. 267–287. McFarland & Company Inc., Jefferson (2009)
24. Lankoski, P., Björk, S.: Game Research Methods. ETC Press, Pittsburgh (2015). http://dl.acm.org/citation.cfm?id=2812774.2812776
25. Lanzetta, J.T., Orr, S.P.: Excitatory strength of expressive faces: effects of happy and fear expressions and context on the extinction of a conditioned fear response. J. Pers. Soc. Psychol. **50**(1), 190–194 (1986). https://doi.org/10.1037/0022-3514.50.1.190
26. LeDoux, J.E.: Emotion circuits in the brain. Annu. Rev. Neurosci. **23**(1), 155–184 (2000). https://doi.org/10.1146/annurev.neuro.23.1.155
27. Leys, C., Ley, C., Klein, O., Bernard, P., Licata, L.: Detecting outliers: do not use standard deviation around the mean, use absolute deviation around the median. J. Exp. Soc. Psychol. **49**(4), 764–766 (2013). https://doi.org/10.1016/j.jesp.2013.03.013
28. Lichtenstein, A., Oehme, A., Kupschick, S., Jürgensohn, T.: Comparing two emotion models for deriving affective states from physiological data. In: Peter, C., Beale, R. (eds.) Affect and Emotion in Human-Computer Interaction. LNCS, vol. 4868, pp. 35–50. Springer, Heidelberg (2008). https://doi.org/10.1007/978-3-540-85099-1_4
29. Lynch, T., Martins, N.: Nothing to fear? An analysis of college students fear experiences with video games. J. Broadcast. Electron. Media **59**(2), 298–317 (2015). https://doi.org/10.1080/08838151.2015.1029128

30. Mandryk, R.L., Inkpen, K.M., Calvert, T.W.: Using psychophysiological techniques to measure user experience with entertainment technologies. Behav. Inf. Technol. **25**(2), 141–158 (2006). https://doi.org/10.1080/01449290500331156

31. Mauss, I.B., Robinson, M.D.: Measures of emotion: a review. Cogn. Emot. **23**(2), 209–237 (2009). https://doi.org/10.1080/02699930802204677

32. May, G.: Could VR horror be too... horrifying? 3 November 2016. https://www.wareable.com/vr/virtual-reality-horror-experiences-too-real-ethics-555

33. McCarthy, C., Pradhan, N., Redpath, C., Adler, A.: Validation of the empatica e4 wristband. In: 2016 IEEE EMBS International Student Conference (ISC), pp. 1–4. IEEE (2016)

34. McMahan, R.P., Ragan, E.D., Leal, A., Beaton, R.J., Bowman, D.A.: Considerations for the use of commercial video games in controlled experiments. Entertainment Comput. **2**(1), 3–9 (2011). http://www.sciencedirect.com/science/article/pii/S1875952111000127. Video Games as Research Instruments

35. Niedenthal, S.: Patterns of obscurity: gothic setting and light in resident evil 4 and silent hill 2. In: Perron, B. (ed.) Horror Video Games: Essays on the Fusion of Fear and Play, pp. 168–180. McFarland & Company Inc., London (2009)

36. Nogueira, P.A., Torres, V., Rodrigues, R., Oliveira, E., Nacke, L.E.: Vanishing scares: biofeedback modulation of affective player experiences in a procedural horror game. J. Multimodal User Interf. **10**(1), 31–62 (2016)

37. Öhman, A.: Fear and anxiety: Evolutionary, cognitive, and clinical perspectives. In: Lewis, M., Haviland-Jones, J.M. (eds.) Handbook of Emotions, 2nd edn, pp. 573–593. The Guilford Press, New York (2000)

38. Öhman, A., Mineka, S.: Fears, phobias, and preparedness: toward an evolved module of fear and fear learning. Psychol. Rev. **108**(3), 483–522 (2001). https://doi.org/10.1037/0033-295x.108.3.483

39. Perron, B.: Horror Video Games: Essays on the Fusion of Fear and Play. McFarland & Company Inc., Jefferson (2009)

40. Perron, B.: The survival horror: the extended body genre. In: Perron, B. (ed.) Horror Video Games Essays on the Fusion of Fear and Play, pp. 121–143. McFarland & Company Inc., Jefferson (2009)

41. Perron, B.: Silent Hill: The Terror Engine. University of Michigan Press, Ann Arbor (2012)

42. Picard, M.: Haunting backgrounds: transnationality and intermediality in Japanese survival horror video games. In: Perron, B. (ed.) Horror Video Games: Essays on the Fusion of Fear and Play, pp. 95–120. McFarland & Company Inc., New York (2009)

43. Prinz, J.J.: Gut Reactions: A Perceptual Theory of Emotion. Philosophy of Mind Series. Oxford University Press, Oxford (2004)

44. Ragot, M., Martin, N., Em, S., Pallamin, N., Diverrez, J.M.: Emotion recognition using physiological signals: laboratory vs. wearable sensors. In: Ahram, T., Falcão, C. (eds.) International Conference on Applied Human Factors and Ergonomics, pp. 15–22. Springer, Cham (2017)

45. Riva, G., Mantovani, F., Capideville, C.S., Preziosa, A., Morganti, F., Villani, D., Gaggioli, A., Botella, C., Alcañiz, M.: Affective interactions using virtual reality: the link between presence and emotions. CyberPsychol. Behav. **10**(1), 45–56 (2007). https://doi.org/10.1089/cpb.2006.9993

46. Rouder, J.N., Speckman, P.L., Sun, D., Morey, R.D., Iverson, G.: Bayesian t tests for accepting and rejecting the null hypothesis. Psychon. Bull. Rev. **16**(2), 225–237 (2009). https://doi.org/10.3758/PBR.16.2.225

47. Rouse, R.: Match made in hell: the inevitable success of the horror genre in video games. In: Perron, B. (ed.) Horror Video Games: Essays on the Fusion of Fear and Play, pp. 15–25. McFarland & Company Inc., Jefferson (2009)

48. Sanchez-Vives, M.V., Slater, M.: Opinion: from presence to consciousness through virtual reality. Nat. Rev. Neurosci. **6**(4), 332–339 (2005). https://doi.org/10.1038/nrn1651

49. Schell, J.: Making great VR: six lessons learned from I expect you to die, 26 June 2015. http://www.gamasutra.com/blogs/JesseSchell/20150626/247113/Making_Great_VR_Six_Lessons_Learned_From_I_Expect_You_To_Die.php. Accessed 18 Mar 2017

50. Schwartz, A., Reimer, D., Leiby, A., Moss, P., Under, D., Brackenridge, R., Hollander, A.: The Reality of Authoring in the Virtual Frontier, August 2014. http://www.youtube.com/watch?v=YEm6copWtYU. From Unite 2014; Developer Conference, Seattle

51. Smith, D.: What it's like to play the best game of 2014, which is about to disappear forever in 2 days, April 2015. http://www.businessinsider.com/silent-hills-pt-review-2015-4?r=US&IR=T&IR=T. Accessed 14 Apr 2017

52. Source VR: The best VR horror games December 2016. http://vrsource.com/best-vr-horror-games-current-upcoming-4092/ (15 Dec 2016). Accessed 13 Apr 2017

53. Sparks, G.G., Pellechia, M., Irvine, C.: The repressive coping style and fright reactions to mass media. Commun. Res. **26**(2), 176–192 (1999). https://doi.org/10.1177/009365099026002004

54. Therrien, C.: Games of fear: a multi-faceted historical account of the horror genre in video games. In: Perron, B. (ed.) Horror Video Games: Essays on the Fusion of Fear and Play, pp. 26–45. McFarland & Company Inc., Jefferson (2009)

55. Wagenmakers, E.J., Love, J., Marsman, M., Jamil, T., Ly, A., Verhagen, J., Selker, R., Gronau, Q.F., Dropmann, D., Boutin, B., et al.: Bayesian inference for psychology, part ii: example applications with JASP. Psychon. Bull. Rev. **24**, 1–19 (2017)

56. Weedon, B.: Game metrics through questionnaires. In: El-Nasr, M.S., Drachen, A., Canossa, A. (eds.) Game Analytics: Maximizing the Value of Player Data, Chap. 23, pp. 515–537. Springer, London (2013). https://doi.org/10.1007/978-1-4471-4769-5_23

57. Willans, T.: Spatial presence in virtual worlds as a perceptual emotion: an expansion on cognitive feeling? In: 2012 Sixth International Conference on Complex, Intelligent, and Software Intensive Systems, pp. 899–904. IEEE, July 2012. https://doi.org/10.1109/cisis.2012.209

58. Williams, L.: Film bodies: gender, genre, and excess. Film Q. **44**(4), 2–13 (1991). https://doi.org/10.2307/1212758

59. Wilson, P.T., Kalescky, W., MacLaughlin, A., Williams, B.: VR locomotion: walking>walking in place>arm swinging. In: Proceedings of the 15th ACM SIGGRAPH Conference on Virtual-Reality Continuum and Its Applications in Industry - Volume 1, VRCAI 2016. ACM, New York (2016). https://doi.org/10.1145/3013971.3014010

HapPull: Enhancement of Self-motion
by Pulling Clothes

Erika Oishi[✉], Masahiro Koge, Takuto Nakamura, and Hiroyuki Kajimoto

The University of Electro-Communications, 1-5-1 Chofu-ga-oka, Chofu, Tokyo, Japan
{oishi,koge,n.takuto,kajimoto}@kaji-lab.jp

Abstract. The realism of audiovisual media with self-motion, such as racing games and movies, is enhanced by the sensation of bodily motion. In various studies, this sensation is presented by actually moving the user's body in accordance with the audiovisual motion. However, such devices tend to be bulky, and compact devices can only simulate one sensation. In our previous study, we proposed a simple and effective system for simulating self-motion. The compact system uses DC motors and string to pull the user's clothes and thus elicit both skin sensation and deep sensation. However, the system only pulls the clothes backward. Here, we present our improved system named HapPull, which pulls the user's clothes both forward and backward and presents torque by pulling the clothes diagonally. We investigated whether users perceived the presented sensation as acceleration or velocity, and found that the physical sensation that is related to the traction force created by our system depends on the nature of the visual stimulus.

Keywords: Haptic · Pulling clothes · Self-motion

1 Introduction

In audiovisual media with self-motion, such as racing games and movies, the sense of motion is considered to be the key to realism. The sense of motion is a multisensory event that includes the vestibular sensation caused by the acceleration, deceleration and inclination of the body, the deep sensation caused by the inertia of the body, and the skin sensation caused by the wind blowing over the whole body. In various studies, these sensations are created by actually moving the user's body in accordance with the motion. However, such devices tend to be bulky, and compact devices can only present a single sensation to a limited body area.

To address this issue, we previously proposed a simple and effective system for creating self-motion by pulling the user's clothes, which elicits both skin sensation and deep sensation [1]. In a racing game, acceleration and wind are presented by pulling the body backward and fluttering the clothes. SPIDAR [2] is a representative method of

---

T. Nakamura—JSPS Research Fellow

© Springer International Publishing AG, part of Springer Nature 2018
A. D. Cheok et al. (Eds.): ACE 2017, LNCS 10714, pp. 261–271, 2018.
https://doi.org/10.1007/978-3-319-76270-8_18

moving the user's body by pulling with string, whereas we used the user's clothes as a medium for presenting force and skin sensation to a wide area of the body.

In our previous study, we developed a prototype (Fig. 1) that pulls clothes backward from the shoulders and investigated whether users perceived the sensation as acceleration or another physical quality, and found that they experienced the sensation as velocity. However, when applied to create self-motion in a car racing game, many users claimed that the traction force was not in natural accordance with velocity. There might be several reasons for these incompatible results, but we presume that a main reason is that the system cannot present deceleration because it only pulls the clothes backward. Therefore, in this study, we developed HapPull that pulls clothes both forward and backward by adding two motors in front of the body, and investigated in detail whether users perceived the presented sensation as acceleration or velocity.

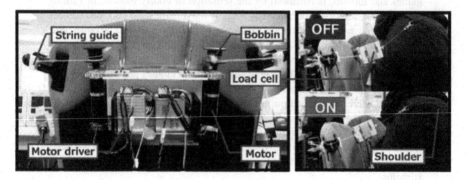

Fig. 1. Previous system [1]

2   Related Work

Vection is often used to improve the sense of self-motion with visual or auditory stimuli [3–6]. Vection refers to the illusion of self-motion created by seeing moving stimuli. However, the inconsistency between visual and bodily sensations often causes motion sickness.

While the sense of self-motion is occasionally presented using a motion platform [7–9], such systems tend to be bulky. Cheng [10] proposed a motion platform that does not require a large-scale device by carrying the user's body with another person. However, there is a risk of dropping the user or performing the wrong operation.

To cope with these issues, several studies have proposed compact systems to present part of the sensation of motion. Several studies attempted to improve self-motion by presenting tactile flow to the body using chair that vibrated in accordance with the visual contents [11, 12]. However, this method only presents skin sensation, and interpretation is necessary to relate the tactile sensation to bodily motion. A type of suit has also been developed to create whole-body vibration [13, 14], but although it is quite effective in creating a sense of immersion, it is still hard to express bodily motion.

Some studies have used compact systems that deliver electrical stimulation. Aoyama [15] simulated virtual head motion by stimulating the vestibular organs electrically. While the sensation is quite strong, the total stimulation time is limited because of safety issues. The Teslasuit [16] presents whole body tactile sensation through electrical stimulation, but again, the electrical stimulation is not safe enough for general use.

The sense of motion can also be expressed by presenting wind [17, 18]. However, creating the sensation of wind over a large area of the body typically requires a huge blower.

Our method is inspired partly by a low-cost motion platform by pulling the user's body with bandages and air cushions [19]. The acceleration force is presented by a haptic device that is used to shake parts of the user's body while seated [20–22]. In contrast to previous methods, we used string to pull user's clothes, which causes both force sensation and skin sensation to a wide area of the body.

3   System

3.1   System Configuration

HapPull (Fig. 2) is composed of a chair with a backrest, motors each with a gear head (Maxon, 25 RE φ25 mm, 10 W, 26 GP B φ26 mm, gear ratio 19:1), bobbins, Kevlar string, clips, a frame, and a microcontroller (NXP, mbed LPC1768).

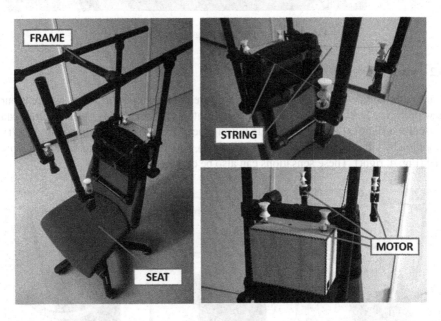

Fig. 2. System

A box containing the microcontroller is attached to the backrest of the chair. The system has four motors with bobbins for winding string, two of which are placed about

0.3 m in front of the user's body and the other two about 0.2 m from the back of the body. As shown in Fig. 3, the clips with string are attached to the shoulders of the user's clothing. The system can effectively pull the upper body by using the motors to reel in the string and pull the clothes. The microcontroller controls the motor current. Each motor can provide a force of up to about 10 kg.

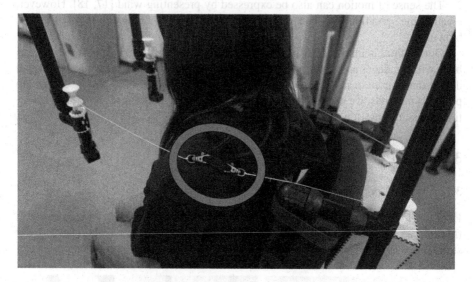

Fig. 3. Method of attaching clips to the user

3.2 Sensation

Our first prototype only used two motors to present the backward traction, whereas our new prototype has two additional motors in front of the user's body. As a result, it can present translational force by strongly pulling the clothes in one direction (Fig. 4, left), vibration by vibrating the motors (Fig. 4, center), and torque by pulling on the diagonal line (Fig. 4, right). These sensations can also be combined.

Fig. 4. Sensation induced by HapPull (left: pressure; center: vibration; right: torque)

4   Experiment

The purpose of this study was to simulate the sensation of motion by presenting a traction force to the body to create a feeling of inertia that matches the audiovisual content. We assumed that the sense of self-motion should improve by presenting the traction force in accordance with acceleration in the audiovisual content because the inertia force is physically related to acceleration. However, as mentioned in the introduction, in our previous study the users experienced the traction force as velocity, not acceleration. We presume that the main reason for this incompatibility was that our previous system only pulled the clothes backward. Another possible reason is that the experiment used a sinusoidal forward-backward motion as the visual stimulus, which we experience rarely in our daily lives. In our follow-up experiment using a car driving stimulus, many participants felt that the traction force was not in accordance with the velocity.

Therefore, in this experiment, we investigated whether users perceived the sensation presented by our new system, which can exert forward and backward force, as acceleration or velocity. We also used two types of visual stimuli to investigate whether the type of stimuli affects the results.

4.1   Methods

Because the most suitable method of presenting a traction force might differ depending on the context of the user's motion, we prepared two different visual stimuli. In the first, the visual stimulus moves forward and backward in a sinusoidal manner, as described in Eq. (1) (VA condition). In this condition, velocity is as shown in Eq. (2) and acceleration is as shown in Eq. (3). This condition can be interpreted as a reciprocating movement similar to playing on a swing. The second visual stimulus presents a repetitive forward and stopping movement, as in Eq. (4) (VB condition). This can be interpreted as a car moving forward then stopping. In this condition, velocity is a sine wave with an offset, as shown in Eq. (5). Note that velocity does not have a negative value in this case. Acceleration is a sine wave, as shown in Eq. (6). In both conditions, the frequency is set to 0.1 Hz. The optical flow of the stimulus, shown in Fig. 5, was rendered using Unity (Unity Technologies, Inc.) and presented using a head-mounted display (Oculus VR Inc., Oculus Rift Development Kit 2, resolution 1920×1080 (one eye 960×1080), horizontal angle of $90°$, diagonal angle of $110°$). A fixation point was positioned at the center of the visual stimulus.

$$x = A \sin\left(2\pi ft - 1/2\pi\right) \tag{1}$$

$$v = 2\pi fA \sin\left(2\pi ft\right) \tag{2}$$

$$a = 4\pi^2 f^2 A \sin\left(2\pi ft + 1/2\pi\right) \tag{3}$$

$$x = A(t + \sin\left(2\pi ft - \pi\right)) \tag{4}$$

$$v = A(1 + 2\pi f \sin(2\pi ft - 1/2\pi)) \tag{5}$$

$$a = 4\pi^2 f^2 A \sin(2\pi ft) \tag{6}$$

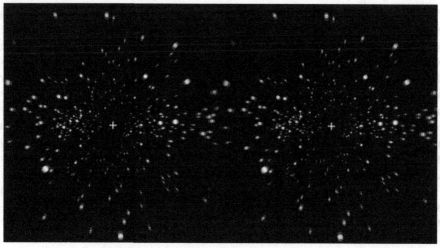

Fig. 5. Visual stimulus (left: view of left eye, right: view of right eye)

Traction force was presented under four conditions: in accordance with the acceleration (HA+ condition), in the opposite direction to the HA+ condition (HA− condition), in accordance with the velocity (HV+ condition), and in the opposite direction to the HV+ condition (HV− condition). The traction force in the VA condition is shown in Fig. 6 and that in the VB condition is shown in Fig. 7. A positive value in the graph means the two front motors are moving and pulling the body forward, whereas a negative

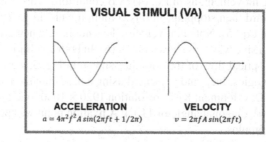

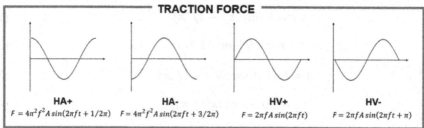

Fig. 6. Traction force in the VA condition

value means the two rear motors are moving and pulling the body backward. The maximum force was normalized and set to about 10 kg. The sinusoidal frequency was 0.1 Hz.

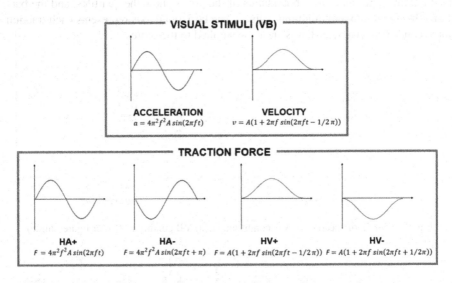

Fig. 7. Traction force in the VB condition

To control the clothing type and to facilitate the attachment of the clips, we provided the participants with a hooded sweatshirt to wear. They were instructed to sit on the chair that housed our system, and to wear the head-mounted display and noise canceling headphones (BOSE, QuietComfort15). First, the visual stimulus for the VA or VB condition was presented without traction force as a reference stimulus. Second, the visual stimulus was presented with the four traction force conditions. Each condition was evaluated on a 7-point Likert scale where the reference stimulus was scored as 4. The participants were asked to rate their subjective feeling of speed (1: very weak, 4: neutral, 7: very strong), acceleration (1: very weak, 4: neutral, 7: very strong), immersion (1: very weak, 4: neutral, 7: very strong) and incompatibility (1: very strong, 4: neutral, 7: very weak) for each condition. "Incompatibility" here means the subjective mismatch between the visual and haptic sensation. The same procedure was then repeated for the other conditions, and the order of the conditions was counterbalanced. Sixteen participants aged 20–33 participated in the experiment and each participant completed eight trials, one for each condition.

When riding in a vehicle, the body usually experiences an inertial force in the opposite direction to the acceleration. Therefore, we hypothesized that the HA− condition would be the best condition for simulating traction force.

4.2   Results and Discussion

The user feedback scores are shown in Figs. 8, 9, 10 and 11. The red lines show the median, the upper and lower boundaries of the boxes show the quartiles, and the bars show the maximum and minimum values. The horizontal axis represents each traction force condition. The Steel-Dwass test was applied to the scores.

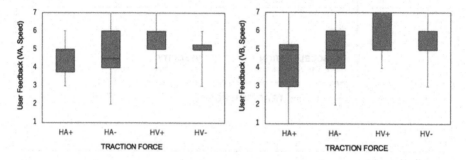

Fig. 8. Feeling of speed (left: VA condition, right: VB condition) (Color figure online)

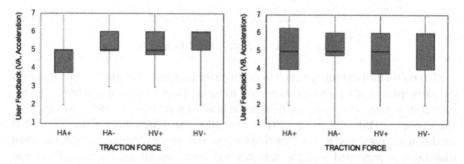

Fig. 9. Feeling of acceleration (left: VA condition, right: VB condition) (Color figure online)

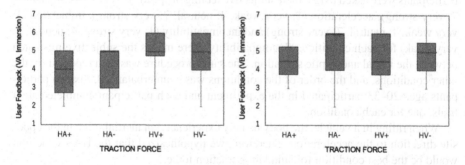

Fig. 10. Feeling of immersion (left: VA condition, right: VB condition) (Color figure online)

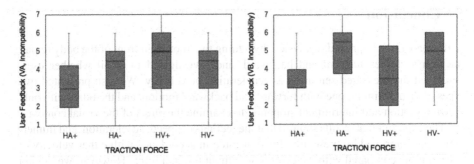

Fig. 11. Feeling of incompatibility (left: VA condition, right: VB condition) (Color figure online)

Feeling of Speed. Figure 8 shows the scores for the feeling of speed. We did not find a significant difference between conditions. However, all of the median values exceeded 4, which means that the feeling of speed was improved by our system, regardless of the presentation method.

Feeling of Acceleration. Figure 9 shows the scores for the feeling of acceleration. We did not find a significant difference between conditions. Similar to the feeling of speed, all of the median values exceeded 4, indicating that the feeling of acceleration was improved by our system.

Feeling of Immersion. Figure 10 shows the scores for the feeling of immersion. Again, we did not find a significant difference between conditions, but all of the scores were equal to or larger than 4.

Feeling of Incompatibility. Figure 11 shows the scores for the feeling of incompatibility. We did not find a significant difference between conditions for either visual stimulus. However, the scores showed a large deviation, which may have been caused by differences in the interpretation of the visual stimuli. The users' comments suggested that the traction force was interpreted either as the body's inertia itself, or as the driving force by another person. These two interpretations represent different scenarios with opposite directions of force, indicating that more realistic visual stimuli, such as a car driving scene, should be presented to prevent different interpretations. In addition, some participants provided low scores in almost all conditions, due to the discordance in the strength of the visual stimuli and the strength of the traction force created by pulling the clothes. Hence, we should adjust the strength of the traction force in accordance with the visual stimuli.

Overall, users tended to favor the VA with HV− condition. In the VB condition, they tended to favor the HA− and HV− conditions. This result was similar to our previous experiments. That is, the traction force for visual stimuli with forward and backward motion was interpreted as velocity. The traction force for visual stimuli with only forward motion was interpreted as acceleration. Therefore, the physical sensation that is related to the traction force created by our system depends on the nature of the visual stimulus.

5 Conclusion

In this paper, we improved our system by adding two motors in front of the body to pull the user's clothes forward and backward, and investigated in detail whether users perceived the presented sensation as acceleration or velocity. We also presented two types of visual stimuli, one with forward and backward motion, and the other with only forward motion and intermittent stopping, to examine the effect of the visual context.

The experimental results showed that the feelings of speed, acceleration, and immersion were improved by presenting traction force in accordance with either velocity or acceleration, compared with the condition without traction force. However, we did not find a significant difference between conditions for either type of visual stimuli. The feelings of speed, acceleration, and immersion were improved if the user felt that the haptic sensation synchronized with the visual stimuli, no matter what type of physical quality they expressed. In other words, these results may suggest the robustness of our method, although we need to conduct further studies.

We provide two examples of how our system can be applied to enrich the virtual-reality experience. One is a swing ride, which moves forward and backward like a pendulum. The user gets on the swing in the virtual space and experiences the thrill of the ride. Because our experimental results showed that the participants tended to prefer the HV+ with the VA condition, the traction force is exerted in the direction of travel in accordance with the velocity of the ride. The other example is a racing game, which moves forward then stops, as in the VB condition. The user drives the vehicle using a handle and an accelerator pedal in virtual space. Because the experimental results showed that the participants tended to prefer the VB condition with the HA− and HV− conditions, the traction force is exerted in accordance with both velocity and acceleration. Specifically, our system pulls the user's body to the rear when the vehicle starts to accelerate, presents a constant force while the vehicle moves at a constant velocity, and pulls the user's body sharply forward when the vehicle stops suddenly. The system also presents torque when the vehicle turns a curve.

As our next step, we will investigate the usefulness of vibratory sensation and torque sensation, and will apply our system to actual games.

Acknowledgements. This research was supported by the JST-ACCEL Embodied Media Project (JPMJAC1404).

References

1. Oishi, E., Koge, M., Sugarragchaa, K., Kajimoto, H.: Enhancement of motion sensation by pulling clothes. In: Proceedings of ACM Symposium on Spatial User Interaction 2016, pp. 47–50 (2016)
2. Buoguila, L., Cai, Y., Sato, M.: New haptic device for human scale virtual environment scaleable – SPIDAR. In: Proceedings of ICAT 1997, pp. 93–98 (1997)

3. Sugiura, A., Tanaka, K., Takada, H., Kojima, T., Yamakawa, T., Miyao, M.: A temporal analysis of body sway caused by self-motion during stereoscopic viewing. In: Antona, M., Stephanidis, C. (eds.) UAHCI 2015. LNCS, vol. 9176, pp. 246–254. Springer, Cham (2015). https://doi.org/10.1007/978-3-319-20681-3_23

4. Nojima, T., Saiga, Y., Okano, Y., Hashimoto, Y., Kajimoto, H.: The peripheral display for augmented reality of self-motion. In: Proceedings of International Conference on Artificial Reality and Telexistence, pp. 308–309 (2007)

5. Ito, H., Takano, H.: Controlling visually induced self-motion perception: effect of overlapping dynamic visual noise. J. Physiol. Anthropol. Appl. Hum. Sci. 23(6), 307–311 (2004)

6. Väljamäe, A., Larsson, P., Västfjäll, D., Kleiner, M.: Travelling without moving: auditory scene cues for translational self-motion. In: Proceedings of International Conference on Auditory Display, pp. 9–16 (2005)

7. MediaMation: MX4D. http://www.mediamation.com/products_x4d.html

8. CableRobot simulater, Fraunhofer IPA. http://www.cablerobotsimulator.org/

9. Simworx: 360° rotating flying theatre. http://www.simworx.co.uk/360-flying-theatre/

10. Cheng, L., Lühne, P., Lopes, P., Sterz, C., Baudisch, P.: Haptic Turk: a motion platform based on people. In: Proceedings of the SIGCHI Conference on Human Factors in Computing Systems, pp. 3463–3472 (2014)

11. Israr, A., Poupyrev, I.: Tactile brush: drawing on skin with a tactile grid display. In: Proceedings of the SIGCHI Conference on Human Factors in Computing Systems (2011)

12. Amemiya, T., Hirota, K., Ikei, Y.: Concave-convex surface perception by visuo-vestibular stimuli for FiveSenses theater. In: Proceedings of Virtual and Mixed Reality - New Trends, pp. 225–233 (2011)

13. Lemmens, P., Crompvoets, F., Brokken, D., Eerenbeemd, J., Vries, G.: A body–conforming tactile jacket to enrich movie viewing. In: Proceedings of the World Haptics, pp. 7–12 (2009)

14. Konishi, Y., Hanamitsu, N., Outram, B., Kamiyama, Y., Minamizawa, K., Sato, A., Mizuguchi, T.: Synesthesia Suit. In: Hasegawa, S., Konyo, M., Kyung, K.-U., Nojima, T., Kajimoto, H. (eds.) AsiaHaptics 2016. LNEE, vol. 432, pp. 499–503. Springer, Singapore (2018). https://doi.org/10.1007/978-981-10-4157-0_84

15. Aoyama, K., Iizuka, H., Ando, H., Maeda, T.: Four-pole galvanic vestibular stimulation causes body sway about three axes. Sci. Rep. 5, 10168 (2015)

16. Teslasuit. https://teslasuit.io/

17. Kulkarni, S., Fisher, C., Pardyjak, E., Minor, M., Hollerbach, J.: Wind display device for locomotion interface in a virtual environment. In: Proceedings of EuroHaptics Conference 2009 and Symposium on Haptic Interfaces for Virtual Environment and Teleoperator Systems, pp. 184–189 (2009)

18. Seno, T., Ogawa, M., Ito, H., Sunaga, S.: Consistent air flow to the face facilitates vection. Perception 40(10), 1237–1240 (2011)

19. Steinemann, A., Tschudi, S., Kunz, A.: Full body haptic display for low-cost racing car driving simulators. In: Proceedings of IEEE Virtual Reality (2011)

20. Danieau, F., Fleureau, J., Guillotel, P., Mollet, N., Lécuyer, A., Christie, M.: HapSeat: producing motion sensation with multiple force-feedback devices embedded in a seat. In: Proceedings of the 18th ACM Symposium on Virtual Reality Software and Technology, pp. 69–76 (2012)

21. Ouarti, N., Lécuyer, A., Berthoz, A.: Haptic motion: improving sensation of self-motion in virtual worlds with force feedback. In: Proceedings of IEEE Haptics Symposium (2014)

22. Bouyer, G., Chellali, A., Lécuyer, A.: Inducing self-motion sensations in driving simulators using force-feedback and haptic motion. In: Proceedings of IEEE Virtual Reality (2017)

Promoting Short-Term Gains in Physical Exercise Through Digital Media Creation

Oral Kaplan[1]([⊠]), Goshiro Yamamoto[2], Takafumi Taketomi[1],
Yasuhide Yoshitake[3], Alexander Plopski[1], Christian Sandor[1],
and Hirokazu Kato[1]

[1] Nara Institute of Science and Technology, Nara 630-0192, Japan
{oral.kaplan.nv4,takafumi-t,plopski,sandor,kato}@is.naist.jp
[2] Kyoto University Hospital, Kyoto 606-8507, Japan
goshiro@kuhp.kyoto-u.ac.jp
[3] National Institute of Sports and Science in Kanoya, Kagoshima 891-2311, Japan
y-yoshi@nifs-k.ac.jp

Abstract. Although regular physical exercise is associated with various health benefits, low rates of adherence remain as an intricate problem. In this paper, we discuss a new emotional facilitator named productivity for increasing adherence to regular physical exercise by promoting short-term gains. We introduce how it can be utilized in digital exertion games to encourage physical activity and maintain high intrinsic motivation. We define how it can be used to encourage regular practice of physical exercise and support users in maintaining high levels of intrinsic motivation. We believe inclusion of design ideas disclosed in this paper will lead to more engaging experiences with higher adherence to physical exercise.

Keywords: Physical exercise adherence · Digital exergames
Exercise motivation · Emotional facilitators

1 Introduction

Physically active lifestyle has been consistently associated with various health benefits such as lower incidence of cardiovascular diseases or improved mental health [1,2]. Most of these beneficial effects only manifest and persist as a result of regular physical exercise [3]. Despite all this, poor adherence rates to training programs remain as a frequently reported problem [4,11].

Previous research in psychology consistently demonstrated the positive effects of emotional facilitators on regular practice of physical exercise [5]. These are grouped into four categories:

1. Perceived competence,
2. Perceived social interaction,
3. Novelty experience,
4. Perceived physical exertion.

© Springer International Publishing AG, part of Springer Nature 2018
A. D. Cheok et al. (Eds.): ACE 2017, LNCS 10714, pp. 272–277, 2018.
https://doi.org/10.1007/978-3-319-76270-8_19

These facilitators have been frequently employed by information scientists to design systems that would increase adherence rates to physical exercise [6–8]. Among these facilitators, *achievement*; a subcategory of perceived competence, has been commonly utilized in exercise applications due to its strong connection with long-term goal oriented structure of physical exercise. For example, fitness trackers typically employ gamification metaphors such as filling empty bars to represent current progress; followed by rewards upon reaching predefined goals. Yet, it is widely accepted that this concept does not produce satisfactory results in terms of inducing long-lasting improvements in user behaviour [9]. Usually a significant decline in exercise motivation is observed when rewards are removed from the equation. Additionally, since short-term gains are difficult to observe or quantify, high drop-out rates in up to 50% of administered programs are observed within the first six months [4].

In this paper, we discuss a new emotional facilitator named productivity for increasing adherence to regular physical exercise through promotion of short-term gains in digital exertion games. We define how it can be used to encourage regular practice of physical exercise and support users in maintaining high levels of intrinsic motivation. We believe inclusion of ideas disclosed in this paper will result in engaging digital exertion game designs with higher adherence rates to physical exercise.

2   Productivity in Digital Exertion Games

Derived from to produce, productivity refers to state of generation, creation or enhancement. We aim to assist users' with developing and retaining high intrinsic motivation levels in exertion games through embedding productivity. Our current approach is to utilize digital content creation as a catalyst to bolster motivation during preliminary phases of physical exercise. Surely preferred content must meet specific qualifications; for instance being comparable and repeatedly accessible.

3   Music Composition Through Physical Exercise

Short musical compositions are one of the potential candidates that we currently consider for digital content creation. Primarily, positive influence of music on physical exercise has been confirmed in numerous studies from physiological and psychological standpoints [16,17]. Additionally, perceived choice of music has been shown to have a correlation with exercise intrinsic motivation [15]. Due to frequent observation of *"Exercise is boring."* as an internal barrier, we anticipate middle-aged and elderly to be the most suitable target group for this particular content type [12]. Yet, this age group requires additional circumstances to be considered while designing physical exercise applications. These might include age-related decline of cognitive functions; such as attention, information processing speed, and memory retention, or physiological health and fine motor skills [10].

4   Design

Our current design concepts revolve around a simple card game widely known as concentration to address previously mentioned elements of elderly exercise. We have developed a simple prototype which consists of four cards; one target and three possible matches. We hope to address issues related to diminished memory retention through utilizing this game. We propose squats to address physical exercise needs due to its proven benefits and applicability [13]. Music is included in gameplay as a feedback mechanism to specifically represent correct execution of this movement. We also employ lateral arm raises to add more variation to possible input combinations.

Typical scenario starts with all four cards facing down. A default sound loop starts playing with game initialization. Target card is displayed to users for a certain amount of time after initialization and flipped back. Following this step, the deck of three possible choices is revealed and flipped back; similar to target card. Finally, users are expected to execute a physical gesture; squat or arm raise, for making a selection (Fig. 1).

Fig. 1. Physical gestures are employed for card selection.

Utilization of productivity comes into action after selection process in the form of music. When correct card is selected, an additional sound loop of a different instrument starts to play. Selecting the correct card consecutively leads to introduction of more loops; which leads to a complete song when combined. The number of loops included; aka the song itself, corresponds to adequate or poor exercise performance. Song length is usually fixed between a couple seconds to a minute; allowing effortless comparison between multiple sets of exercise.

4.1   Drawing Through Physical Exercise

An another design concept that we currently consider replaces the art medium with paintings. Similar to music, simple full body gesture can be used to administer physical exercise routines. Just like building a puzzle, proper execution of physical gestures can reveal pieces from a drawing. Resulting content can effortlessly be shared on social network platforms; leading to possible increase in motivation through social acceptance and support.

5 Discussion

Short-Term Gains

In this paper, we mainly address intrinsic motivation regulation in physical exercise through short-term gain promotion. In most cases, commercially available products such as smart watches place their main focus on end goals to ensure physically active users. Such approach fails to support users in building a sufficient level of intrinsic motivation; which results in commitment issues and high drop out rates among participants [4].

Although our idea of short-term gain promotion revolves around digital content creation, other forms of media, material or concepts would also be suitable for application. Ultimately, we believe if participants of physical exercise can realize their short-term progress, intrinsic motivation can be built in to promote regular physical exercise.

Long-Term Goals

Even though our focus is on short-term gains, the importance of long-term goals is also undeniable. We believe gains and goals can be simultaneously promoted in both short and long-term conditions. As an example, creating short musical compositions on a day-by-day basis can be uninspiring and tedious. On the other hand, combining each composition for formation of a complete song might lead to an increase in long-term performance and motivation of users.

Additionally, a band or orchestra setting similar to Guitar Hero can be employed to boost intrinsic motivation development through perceived social interaction. Promoting the act of collective creation can result in a higher sense of belongingness and lead to improved adherence rates in physical exercise classrooms.

Reaching Users

It is obvious to us that distinct user groups differ in physical exercise preferences. The approach we introduce in this paper must be tailored to selected user group according to their specific needs. Although we only introduced middle-aged and elderly, designs can be tailored to professional athletes, participants of recreational sports, or children. These groups can further be divided into sub-groups depending on age, profession, or social background.

A Variety of Sports

Sports repetitive in nature such as cycling can also be considered as a target of our approach. In professional cycling, athletes might pedal five to six thousand times in an hour. Recorded pedalling data can be simplified into a shorter digital content and used to perform brief assessment of their performance; such as left-right balance or efficiency. As an example, data from one hour long sessions can be sonified into a few seconds long files where undesired results can be represented in the form of sudden increase in pitch values.

6 Future Work

In this paper, we do not strictly relate our idea with a specific user group. Since we believe different users might have different needs, it is apparent that our idea requires formal testing with different users. As our first and most important future work, we are planning to have long-term experiments; preferably with elderly participants.

Considering our approach depends on content creation, providing necessary tools and materials is utmost importance. It is obvious to us that the creatable content would have a great impact on both intrinsic motivation development and adherence rate. We aim to investigate this branch of our approach in the near future too.

We are hoping to verify and modify multiple points in our approach with a series of pilot tests in the near future. We are aiming to confirm effects of social interaction; especially in elderly settings. Supporting multiplayer modes is also included in our design concepts for the future. Currently we are working on a scenario which builds on top of our music based approach to bring multiple individuals together in a band or orchestra context. Through one participant one instrument concept, we are aiming to allow groups of people to create digital content in a collective manner.

7 Conclusion

In this paper, we describe an emotional facilitator named productivity for increasing adherence to physical exercise through digital exertion games. We demonstrate how it can be utilized in digital exertion game contexts. Future directions that we are interested in include qualitative and quantitative user studies, introduction of additional design concepts, multiple game modes, and applications to various user groups. We believe our efforts will contribute to advances in building intrinsic motivation and higher adherence rates to regular physical exercise.

Acknowledgements. This work was supported by the MIC/SCOPE #162107006.

References

1. Paffenbarger, J., Ralph, S., Robert, T.H., Alvin, L.W., Lee, I.M., Jung, D.L., Kampert, J.B.: The association of changes in physical-activity level and other lifestyle characteristics with mortality among men. New England J. Med. **328**(8), 538–545 (1993)
2. Reiner, M., Niermann, C., Jekauc, D., Woll, A.: Long-term health benefits of physical activity-a systematic review of longitudinal studies. BMC Public Health **13**(1), 813–821 (2013)
3. Mujika, I., Padilla, S.: Detraining: loss of training-induced physiological and performance adaptations. Part I. Sports Med. **30**(2), 79–87 (2000)

4. Annesi, J.: Effects of a cognitive behavioral treatment package on exercise attendance and drop out in fitness centers. Eur. J. Sport Sci. **3**(2), 1–16 (2003)
5. Wienke, B., Jekauc, D.: A qualitative analysis of emotional facilitators in exercise. Front. Psychol. **7**, 1296 (2016)
6. Gerling, K.M., Schulte, F.P., Masuch, M.: Designing and evaluating digital games for frail elderly persons. In: Proceedings of the International Conference on Advances in Computer Entertainment Technology, pp. 62–69 (2011)
7. Wouters, P., Van Nimwegen, C., Van Oostendorp, H., Van Der Spek, E.D.: A meta-analysis of the cognitive and motivational effects of serious games. J. Educ. Psychol. **105**, 249–265 (2013)
8. Trout, J., Christie, B.: Interactive video games in physical education. J. Phys. Educ. Recreation Dance **78**(5), 29–45 (2007)
9. Nicholson, S.: A RECIPE for meaningful gamification. In: Reiners, T., Wood, L.C. (eds.) Gamification in Education and Business, pp. 1–20. Springer, Cham (2015). https://doi.org/10.1007/978-3-319-10208-5_1
10. Levy, R.: Aging-associated cognitive decline. Int. Psychogeriatr. **6**(1), 63–68 (1994)
11. Shimada, T., Kuramoto, I., Shibuya, Y., Tsujino, Y.: Keep healthy with fun: an entertainment system for keeping the motivation of daily, dull, and monotone exercise. In: Proceedings of the International Conference on Advances in Computer Entertainment Technology, pp. 280–281 (2007)
12. Manaf, H.: Barriers to participation in physical activity and exercise among middle-aged and elderly individuals. Singap. Med. J. **54**(10), 581–586 (2013)
13. Campbell, A.J., Robertson, M.C., Gardner, M.M., Norton, R.N., Tilyard, M.W., Buchner, D.M.: Randomised controlled trial of a general practice programme of home based exercise to prevent falls in elderly women. BMJ **315**(7115), 1065–1069 (1997)
14. Fiatarone, M.A., O'Neill, E.F., Ryan, N.D., Clements, K.M., Solares, G.R., Nelson, M.E., Roberts, S.B., Kehayias, J.J., Lipsitz, L.A., Evans, W.J.: Exercise training and nutritional supplementation for physical frailty in very elderly people. New England J. Med. **330**(25), 1769–1775 (1994)
15. Markland, D.: Self-determination moderates the effects of perceived competence on intrinsic motivation in an exercise setting. J. Sports Exerc. Psychol. **21**(4), 351–361 (1999)
16. Karageorghis, C.I., Terry, P.C., Lane, A.M.: Development and initial validation of an instrument to assess the motivational qualities of music in exercise and sport: the Brunel music rating inventory. J. Sports Sci. **17**(9), 713–724 (1999)
17. Edworthy, J., Waring, H.: The effects of music tempo and loudness level on treadmill exercise. Ergonomics **49**(15), 1597–1610 (2006)

Towards Player Adaptivity in Mobile Exergames

João Jacob[1]([✉]) ⓘ, Ana Lopes[1] ⓘ, Rui Nóbrega[1,2] ⓘ,
Rui Rodrigues[1,2] ⓘ, and António Coelho[1,2] ⓘ

[1] FEUP, Faculdade de Engenharia da Universidade do Porto, Porto, Portugal
{joao.jacob,ruinobrega,rui.rodrigues,acoelho}@fe.up.pt,
ana.isabel.crist.lopes@gmail.com
[2] INESC TEC, Instituto de Engenharia de Sistemas e Computadores – Tecnologia e Ciência,
Porto, Portugal

Abstract. Exergames require obtaining or computing information regarding the players' physical activity and context. Additionally, ensuring that the players are assigned challenges that are adequate to their physical ability, safe and adapted for the current context (both physical and spatial) is also important, as it can improve both the gaming experience and the outcomes of the exercise. However, the impact adaptivity has in the specific case of virtual reality exergames still has not been researched in depth. In this paper, we present a virtual reality exergame and an experimental design aiming to compare the players' experience when playing both adaptive and regular versions of the game.

Keywords: Exergames · Adaptivity · Virtual reality · Mobile
Game development · Pervasive games

1 Introduction

Exergames (games that promote some form of physical exercise in the gameplay) require obtaining or computing information regarding the players' physical activity and, often, current location and context. Additionally, ensuring that the players are assigned challenges that are adequate to their physical ability, safe and adapted for the current context (both physical and spatial) is also important, as it can improve both the gaming experience and the outcomes of the exercise. So, the relevant information gathering of both player and context proves to be useful in determining the performance of the former in the latter. There are some models that combine the challenge's difficulty and the player's skill, for both regular games and, more recently, exergames, the Game Flow Model [32] or the Dual Flow Model [27] respectively.

However, determining the actual impact and player perception of adaptivity in virtual reality exergames is different as the level of immersion of the experience is distinct from that of traditional games.

Our work, presented in this paper, aims to provide insights into how to develop a workflow towards adaptivity for mobile virtual reality exergames. We present two versions of the same game, both authored via a custom tool, one with fixed difficulty and another adaptive and propose a comparison between them in regards of player

© Springer International Publishing AG, part of Springer Nature 2018
A. D. Cheok et al. (Eds.): ACE 2017, LNCS 10714, pp. 278–292, 2018.
https://doi.org/10.1007/978-3-319-76270-8_20

performance, physical exertion levels as well as immersion and tiredness perception. Our proposed methodology allows for a comparison between non-adaptive and adaptive gameplay sessions, helping game designers in understanding the impacts and adequacy of the difficulty and strain their exergames and their player profiles may cause.

2   Player Adaptivity

An adaptive game [10, 21] has been defined, as a type of games that recognize player input and are able to adequately change their behavior (be it gameplay mechanics or game elements [4, 20]) so as to ensure a better experience.

As such, this methodology can be applied to different games, such as exergames [26] or health games [12, 28], mobile games [8] and others, entertainment or otherwise [20].

The importance of game adaptivity in location-based games and exergames was also explained in [17], as a means to overcome the issues these types of games commonly present.

Adaptivity plays an important role in this work as it will cover the part of the solution where the game will dynamically change itself in order to better accommodate the current player's status.

3   User Profiling

The creation of player profiles to drive the adaptation of a game's behavior is not recent. There is a patent dated from as early as 1997 that claims "A method of adaptive computer game play based on profiling" [3]. Furthermore, the relation between player personality types and game behavior has also been explored with positive results, identifying personality types with actions in games [31] and vice versa, presenting a relationship between demographics, game preferences and in-game behavior [19].

Player-centered game-design also benefits by the ability of correctly profiling users and their interests [10], be it to dynamically adapt the game to the player's preferences or to create a game that appeases to the tastes of a generic user profile. User profiling can be used as a basis for adaptivity, by matching a player's behavior to the closest profile that fits, and treating the player as having that profile and game preferences.

User profiling can contribute towards player adaptivity, as it helps identifying the type of player and adequate challenges to them. Since location-based exergames have several dynamic game conditions, such as the player's physical state or the location the game is being played at, these variables, that may better define the context for adaptivity purposes, are not considered when adapting a game solely through user profiling techniques.

4   Exergames and Serious Games

Exergames have been popularized by the Nintendo Wii and PlayStation Eye. However, exergaming can be traced back to the 1980's, through the Nintendo accessory, the

PowerPad, and was also present in the 1990's via Konami's Dance Dance Revolution [33]. Studies have shown how these games are more physically intensive than regular videogames and positively impact the user's health [29, 34]. Although many of these games focus on being fun, mainly those sold by the entertainment industry, there are many with other goals, such as rehabilitation and health maintenance. These are called serious games, as they are games whose main focus is not entertainment.

Serious exergames are used, primarily as training, maintenance or rehabilitation tools [33].

A large number of rehabilitation games appeared as rehabilitation tools, thanks to the availability of the Nintendo Wii and Wii Fit. These studies have shown, from an early start, that these games could be useful in therapeutic scenarios [30], and even how they could be useful in the areas of prognosis and treatment of physical disabilities [22] such as Cerebral Palsy [15] and Parkinson [2, 28]. Even in scenarios where the goal is to treat psychological ailments, exergames show their potential [24].

Training exergame-based tools, such as the Online-Gym show the feasibility [9] of creating a virtual environment where physically remote people may interact and perform exercises virtually side by side. Balance and fall-prevention exergames have also shown positive results. A study of static balance assessment in patients suffering from chronic stroke showed that participants that used the Wii-Fit performed better than those training only with conventional methods, even after three months [16]. Other studies with an elderly population showed how these games can potentially improve balance, particularly as they allow the patients to practice safely in their homes [1, 5].

The potential benefits of serious exergames is widely recognized in many areas of application. These exergames could also benefit from adaptation and player-specific profiles to potentially tailor and adequate their mechanics and goals to the player's physical condition and whereabouts.

5   Context-Aware Exergames

Context-aware exergames are defined by being exergames that have some awareness, via sensors or remote services, of data or information that is relevant to their goals and challenges [14], being similar to a context-aware application or service in that regard [25].

Unlike many exergames, these context-aware games monitor services and sensors to ensure the player is being challenged in a way that blends with the current context. Usually through GPS, heart rate and accelerometer sensors, the game can be aware of the player's physical condition. Mobile phone's camera and location services' APIs can provide the application with some information regarding the surroundings of the player [8, 13].

This context awareness can be used to not only improve the gaming experience itself [26], but the quality of measurements, such as more accurately calculating the expended energy in a gaming session [23].

The players of these games could potentially benefit from adaptivity. However, these games are currently very limited as to how aware they are of the player's surroundings and how they can take into account the geo-information and adapt the game's challenges and goals with it.

6 Estimating Player Effort

There are several methods for calculating and estimating a person's gait, expended energy and effort. In the context of this work, we focused on Eqs. 1 to 3, used for calculating the players' effort. The reasoning behind this is two-fold: not only are these equations well known, they also rely on the parameters of Age (A), Resting Heart Rate (RHR) and Current Heart Rate (CHR), which are easily acquirable.

So, by using the Haskell equation for calculating the Maximum Heart Rate [11]

$$MHR(A) = 220 - A \tag{1}$$

and Karnoven's Heart Rate Reserve formula [18]

$$HRR(MHR, RHR) = MHR - RHR \tag{2}$$

it is possible to determine the current intensity of the physical exercise using the Karvonen method [18]

$$E(CHR, RHR, HRR) = \frac{CHR - RHR}{HRR}. \tag{3}$$

An effort value of 0, when the current heart rate is the same as that of the resting heart rate, means that the person can be considered to be rested. Conversely, an effort of 1 is attained when the person's heart is performing at the theoretical maximum. As the above formula shows, effort values vary linearly with the CurrentHR (as the RestingHR and HRReserve are considered constants, even though they can vary from person to person).

7 Grappher – A Node-Based Editor for Pervasive Games

A traditional issue with the creation of adaptive, mobile exergames is the constant need of tweaking, reparametrizing, deploying and testing the game with different players in order to collect data and restart this cycle. The possibility of applying a RAD (Rapid Application Development) philosophy is of interest to the area of adaptive game development as it could allow designers to focus on testing and readjusting the game as quickly as possible, avoiding the need of redeploying and restarting the game.

Grappher is a Unity3D editor plugin that allows for a game designer to quickly parametrize a game's setting via a node-based editor. The user can choose different sources of data (sensors, web-services, game parameters or functions, Grappher parameters, etc.) or program his/her own (see Fig. 1.). Any graph created in Grappher is stored in a remote server, and can be reused in other graphs.

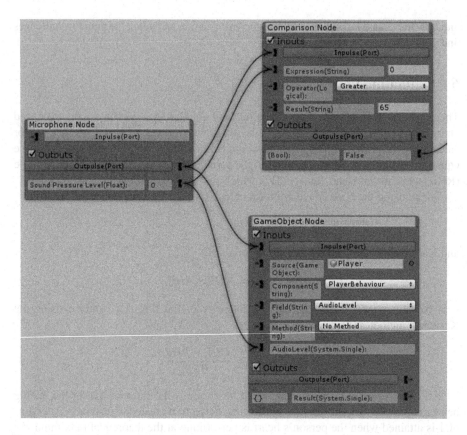

Fig. 1. Depiction of a graph with three nodes (a sensor, a component and a comparison node) in Grappher.

Any saved graph can be loaded via the Grappher Loader component (see Fig. 2). Additionally, this component allows the developer to specify when the graph should be

Fig. 2. Grappher Loader Component in Unity3D.

executed (if continuously, only once, or on a certain event), as well as how frequently should the application check for a new version of this graph. This allows for a deployed game, using these graphs, to be reparametrized remotely, as it will automatically update to the latest version of every graph (if possible) during runtime. This can, ultimately, remove the need to redeploy or repackage the application, and incentives developers to tweak and test the game with minimal effort.

8   User Study

In order to assess the impacts that the use of Grappher may have regarding player adaptivity it would be necessary to compare the players' experience of playing a game that can be both adaptive and non-adaptive. As such, it was necessary to develop such a game and to expose its mechanics so as to parametrize them to either be adaptive (depending on several factors) or not. In this paper, we present GhostStand, a mobile virtual reality exergame that allows us to test the impact that player adaptivity may have in the experience of playing this type of games.

8.1   GhostStand – A Mobile Virtual Reality Exergame

The GhostStand game is a VR (Virtual Reality) First Person Exergame where the player must fend off enemy ghosts from his/her position, using a sword.

In the real world, the user is equipped with a mobile head mounted display (HMD), headphones, a smartwatch and a mock sword as per Fig. 3. The game requires the player to be alert as the ghosts can come from different directions. Interactions are limited to looking around (3 degrees of freedom) and swinging the sword (3 degrees of freedom) at the incoming enemies.

Fig. 3. User playing GhostStand with a Mobile HMD, Headphones, Smartwatch and Sword.

As Fig. 4 shows, a dark and gloomy atmosphere characterizes the game from an early start. This was to help minimize possible problems with immersion or discomfort, as with current mobile VR technology it is not uncommon for the space between pixels to be visible to the naked eye. So, a darker image helps in masking this effect.

Fig. 4. Concept art for the GhostStand game.

The game has the following characters and items:

- **Ghosts**: the enemies in the game. They are attracted to the player and will attempt to kill him.
- **Pillars of Light**: four of these structures are present in the scene. They serve two purposes. To serve as beacons, making the orientation of the player relative to them an easier task, and as a spawn location for the Ghosts.
- **Restless Samurai Spirit**: the player embodies this character, a spirit continuously tormented by the Ghosts.
- **Spirit Sword**: the player's character wields a sword capable of defeating the incoming Ghosts. It can be used defensively, by blocking the Ghosts' attempts to harm the player or by shoving them away, or offensively, by violently hitting the Ghosts, banishing them definitely.
- **Gloomy Moon**: A big, dark moon rests low and centered between the four Pillars of Light. It serves no purpose, other than providing ambiance and as a very specific point of reference to the player, as it is used for the calibration process of the sword.

These game elements behave in accordance to the following mechanics:
Pillars of Light:

- Spawn Ghosts at certain intervals
- Spawned Ghosts share the same characteristics, within parametrized limits (speed, hit speed resistance and time to live)

Ghosts:

- Have varied maximum speeds, resistance (the minimum sword swinging speed they must be hit at in order to die) and a time-to-live of 40 s.
- Will attempt to converge at the Player's position. They will gravitate towards the player, from their own spawn points. However, they are susceptible to bumping

against the ground, each other, the Player, and the sword, meaning that their initial straight trajectory can become curved or elliptical.

- Cast a red shadow on the platform the Player's avatar is at, making it easier to guess their distance and position.
- When bumping against the player, will remove one point from the player's life points pool.
- When hit, will either flash in a red color and move away from the player, if the speed it was hit was less than their resistance, or, if said speed is greater than their threshold, they will instantly die.

Player:

- Can freely look around.
- Can move the sword around by moving his/her right hand around the three axes (the player cannot, however, thrust the sword forward).
- Can block Ghosts from attacking, by placing the sword between the ghosts and himself/herself.
- Can push away Ghosts by swinging or flicking the sword gently.
- Can kill Ghosts by hitting them with great arm speed.
- Is awarded points based on the speed at which each Ghost was killed.
- Can die when player life points pool reaches zero points, from an initial 100 points.
- Can re-align his/her field of view with the sword by looking at the Gloomy Moon, placing his/her right hand on the chest and, with the left hand, touching the Smartwatches display. A small vibration is felt on the wrist, indicating that the calibration process was concluded.

The Fig. 5 shows a perspective view of the game, in design time. The player is standing between the four pillars of light. Since the player does not know from where the next enemy spawned will be coming from, he/she must periodically look around at the pillars of light.

Fig. 5. Third person view of the game in design time.

The player's avatar body is translucent, so as to give the player the ability to see his/her avatar's body, in first person, but without intruding too much on the game itself. Also noticeable (Fig. 5) is that the avatar's arms and wrists follow the swords orientation. This is thanks to the avatar being fully rigged as a humanoid, allowing for the game engine's (Unity3D) inverse kinematic features to be used, fully. As such, as the player moves the wrist around, so do the avatar's hands, arms and shoulders, further enhancing the player's experience. The size of the platform the player is standing at is roughly the same length of that of the sword. This means that whenever the ghosts cast their red shadow on the platform, they will most likely be in range of the player's sword.

The Fig. 6 is representative of what the players see when experiencing the Ghost-Stand game. In this particular screenshot, in Fig. 6, the player did not have the sword within view. The game's UI present in this screenshot is meant for debugging only and was changed for the experimental setup, by removing "Effort", "Maximum Swing Speed" and "Time Left" from it, and leaving only "Health" and "Score" for the player to see.

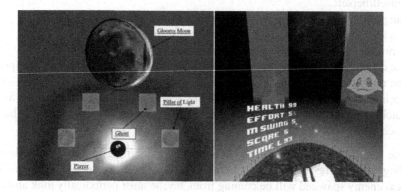

Fig. 6. Layout of a level in ghostStand (Left). In-game screenshot (Right).

A slight vignette effect and monochromatic noise were added to each individual camera image, better hiding the current limitations of the smartphone-based head-mounted displays used, as they usually have very big, visible pixels and the dark space between them is often also noticeable. Sound effects for ghost spawning, dying, and hitting the player were added, as well as for the sword swinging and hitting the ghosts. An eerie music with random sound effects (such as heavy breathing, maniacal laughter and storm brewing) was added in order to muffle external sounds and enhance the experience and immersion levels.

9   Experimental Setup

To ascertain the impact of player adaptivity in GhostStand, two game versions were designed using Grappher: a non-adaptive and an adaptive one. Both feature the same game elements, albeit with different parametrizations.

– **Non-adaptive version** (Fig. 7): This version defines a constant spawn interval (15 s) between each ghost. One of the four possible spawning locations is chosen randomly.

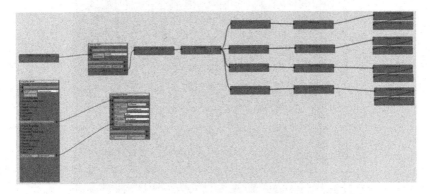

Fig. 7. Graph of the non-adaptive version. The split between four possible spawn locations is visible. The lower part (a distinct sub-graph) is responsible for computing the player's effort.

– **Adaptive version** (Fig. 8): The adaptive version of the game considers the player's Effort (presented in the section Estimating Player Effort of this paper) and uses a custom function to calculate a spawn interval, depicted in Fig. 9.

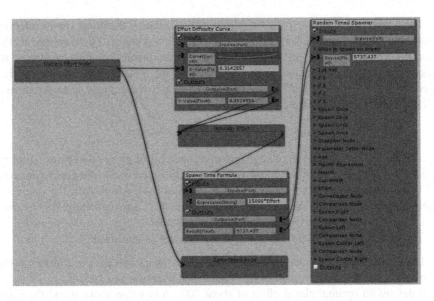

Fig. 8. Graph of the adaptive version. The non-adaptive configuration (rightmost node) is reused and reparametrized to become adaptive.

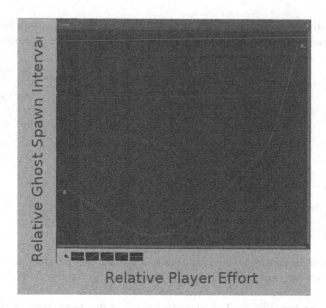

Fig. 9. Function defining the relation between player effort and spawning interval (relative values).

The adaptivity function, $f(Effort)$, allows for calculating the ghost spawn interval, depending on the current effort reading. The function's domain (0 to 1) represents the effort percentage from 0% (at rest) to 100% (maximum theoretical physical strain). Its range represents the coefficient to be multiplied by the non-adaptive ghost spawning interval of 15 s. So, the actual ghost spawning interval in the game is, at each moment, calculated by the following expression.

$$GhostSpawnInterval(s) = 15 \times f(Effort). \tag{4}$$

The Fig. 9 shows that the relative spawning interval of ghosts decreases (from an initial value of 0.7) as the player starts performing more exercise, up until approximately 0.3 (30%) of effort (at which point, it has a value of 0.4). Afterwards, the spawning interval increases steadily up until 70% effort (value of 1, approximately) accelerating past a value of 1.8 of relative spawning interval past that.

The idea behind the exemplified adaptivity function is multifold:

- The game has an initial warming-up phase, where the game's pace accelerates as the player's effort increases, well beyond that of the non-adaptive version.
- It defines an optimal player effort of about 30%. Any value above it and the game will decrease its pace.
- If the player pushes beyond this, progressively being more strained, the game will reduce the ghost's spawn rate concomitantly. This is meant to serve as a means of both ensuring the player's safety (as the game will not require the user to maintain the current degree of physical effort).

The experiment itself was designed for indoors, limiting the amount of possible external factors. As such, a sound lab available at the facilities was used, as it had sound insulation and controlled lighting.

The following list details the equipment required for the user to play the game, visible in Fig. 10:

- A BoboVR Z3 mobile HMD case for the mobile phone to be placed in it
- A OnePlus One smartphone, running Android 6.0.1
- A LG Watch R smartwatch, running Android 6.0.1
- A wired stereo headset
- A lightweight plastic "sword", designed to add heft to the players' arm movement

Fig. 10. Equipment used in the GhostStand experiment.

Both a questionnaire and informed consent form were created. The questionnaire is meant to provide insight about player perception of the game and how it may correlate with data from the player's gameplay session. The Informed Consent Form was needed to inform the players of potential health hazards (motion sickness, malaise, fatigue or injuries).

The questionnaire was based on the Game Engagement Questionnaire [6] and on an adaptive exergame master thesis questionnaire [7]. The GEQ questions provide insight into the psychological state and general gaming experience of the players, useful for determining if the players did enter a state of flow, boredom or stress, while the other questions are specifically tailored for exergames, useful in evaluating the physical state the player was in during gameplay.

10   Conclusion

This paper presented a study into the importance and impact player adaptivity may have in virtual reality exergames, a relatively novel type of games. We have presented Ghost-Stand, a VR mobile exergame with adaptive game challenges that asks its players to strike down ghosts by moving their arms in the real world. Our methodology for determining the potential benefits of adaptivity in this genre of games was to create two versions of GhostStand, using our tool Grappher, one with no adaptivity and another where the player's age and heart rate play an important role in deciding the pace of the game. We do not claim that the adaptivity profile used in the GhostStand adaptive version is ideal, as other variables could also be added to it (swing speed, hit rate, life remaining, etc.). However, in order to determine if there are differences between an adaptive and non-adaptive version of the same game, these would be unnecessary. The preliminary results suggest that, much like their classic brethren, VR exergames do benefit from adaptivity, ensuring that the player is motivated to be physically pushed all the while ensuring that the player is not risking harm. Additionally, in the particular case of virtual reality games, ensuring that these mechanisms do not break the immersion of the virtual reality experience is also of interest. Further testing GhostStand with improved and varied adaptivity profiles, as well as testing other games, the addition of new variables and frameworks for supporting the easier creation of adaptivity profiles for these types of games are also part of our future line of research.

Acknowledgements. This work is part of João Jacob's PhD and the submission of this paper has been partially supported by FourEyes, FourEyes is a Research Line within project "TEC4Growth – Pervasive Intelligence, Enhancers and Proofs of Concept with Industrial Impact/NORTE-01-0145-FEDER-000020" financed by the North Portugal Regional Operational Programme (NORTE 2020), under the PORTUGAL 2020 Partnership Agreement, and through the European Regional Development Fund (ERDF).

References

1. Agmon, M., Perry, C.K., Phelan, E., Demiris, G., Nguyen, H.Q.: A pilot study of Wii Fit exergames to improve balance in older adults. J. Geriatr. Phys. Ther. **34**(4), 161–167 (2011). https://doi.org/10.1519/JPT.0b013e3182191d98
2. Barry, G., Galna, B., Rochester, L.: The role of exergaming in Parkinson's disease rehabilitation: a systematic review of the evidence. J. Neuroeng. Rehabil. **11**(1), 33 (2014). https://doi.org/10.1186/1743-0003-11-33
3. Begis, G.: Adaptive gaming behavior based on player profiling, pp. 1–5 (2000). US Patent: US6106395 A
4. Berger, F.: Evaluating an implementation of an adaptive game-based learning architecture. In: Masthoff, J., Mobasher, B., Desmarais, M.C., Nkambou, R. (eds.) UMAP 2012. LNCS, vol. 7379, pp. 351–355. Springer, Heidelberg (2012). https://doi.org/10.1007/978-3-642-31454-4_34
5. de Brito, C., Jacob, J., Nóbrega, R., Santos, A.: Balance assessment in fall-prevention exergames. In: Proceedings of the 17th International ACM SIGACCESS Conference on Computers & Accessibility, pp. 439–440 (2015). https://doi.org/10.1145/2700648.2811342
6. Brockmyer, J.H., Fox, C.M., Curtiss, K.A., Mcbroom, E., Burkhart, K.M., Pidruzny, J.N.: Journal of experimental social psychology the development of the game engagement questionnaire: a measure of engagement in video game-playing. J. Exp. Soc. Psychol. **45**(4), 624–634 (2009). https://doi.org/10.1016/j.jesp.2009.02.016
7. Burt, C.: Having Fun, Working Out: Adaptive and Engaging Video Games for Exercise (2014)

8. Campbell, A.G., Grady, M.J.O., Connor, N.E.O.: FreeGaming: mobile, collaborative, adaptive and augmented ExerGaming categories and subject descriptors. In: Proceedings of the 8th International Conference on Advances in Mobile Computing and Multimedia, pp. 173–179 (2010)

9. Cassola, F., Morgado, L., de Carvalho, F., Paredes, H., Fonseca, B.: Online-gym: a 3D virtual gymnasium using kinect interaction. Procedia Technol. **13**, 130–138 (2014). https://doi.org/10.1016/j.protcy.2014.02.017

10. Charles, D., Kerr, A., McNeill, M.: Player-centred game design: player modelling and adaptive digital games. In: Proceedings of the Digital Games, vol. 285, pp. 285–298 (2005)

11. Fox, S.M., Haskell, W.L.: The exercise stress test: needs for standardization. In: Cardiology: Current Topics and Progress, pp. 149–154 (1970)

12. Göbel, S., Hardy, S., Wendel, V.: Serious games for health: personalized exergames. In: Proceedings of the 18th ACM International Conference on Multimedia, pp. 1663–1666 (2010). http://dl.acm.org/citation.cfm?id=1874316. Accessed 9 Dec 2013

13. Görgü, L., Campbell, A.G., McCusker, K., Dragone, M., O'Grady, M.J., O'Connor, N.E., O'Hare, G.M.P.: Freegaming: mobile, collaborative, adaptive and augmented exergaming. Mob. Inf. Syst. **8**(4), 287–301 (2012). https://doi.org/10.3233/MIS-2012-00147

14. Hardy, S., El Saddik, A., Gobel, S., Steinmetz, R.: Context aware serious games framework for sport and health. In: Proceedings of MeMeA 2011 - 2011 IEEE International Symposium on Medical Measurements and Applications, pp. 1–5 (2011). https://doi.org/10.1109/MeMeA.2011.5966775

15. Hernandez, H.A., Ye, Z., Nicholas Graham, T.C., Fehlings, D., Switzer, L.: Designing action-based exergames for children with cerebral palsy. In: Human Factors in Computing Systems: Proceedings of the SIGCHI Conference, (CHI 2013), pp. 1261–1270 (2013). https://doi.org/10.1145/2470654.2466164

16. Hung, J.W., Chou, C.X., Hsieh, Y.W., Wu, W.C., Yu, M.Y., Chen, P.C., Chang, H.F., Ding, S.E.: Randomized comparison trial of balance training by using exergaming and conventional weight-shift therapy in patients with chronic stroke. Arch. Phys. Med. Rehabil. **95**(9), 1629–1637 (2014). https://doi.org/10.1016/j.apmr.2014.04.029

17. Jacob, J., Coelho, A.: Issues in the development of location-based games. Int. J. Comput. Games Technol. 1–7 (2011). https://doi.org/10.1155/2011/495437

18. Karvonen, M.J., Kentala, E., Mustala, O.: The effects of training on heart rate; a longitudinal study. Ann. Med. Exp. Biol. Fenn. **35**, 307–315 (1957)

19. Van Lankveld, G., Spronck, P., Van den Herik, J., Arntz, A.: Games as personality profiling tools. In: 2011 IEEE Conference on Computational Intelligence and Games, CIG 2011, pp. 197–202, September 2011. https://doi.org/10.1109/CIG.2011.6032007

20. Lopes, R., Bidarra, R.: Adaptivity challenges in games and simulations: a survey. IEEE Trans. Comput. Intell. AI Games **3**(2), 85–99 (2011). https://doi.org/10.1109/TCIAIG.2011.2152841

21. Magerko, B.: Adaptation in digital games. Computer **41**(6), 87–89 (2008). https://doi.org/10.1109/MC.2008.172

22. Meleiro, P., Rodrigues, R., Jacob, J., Marques, T.: Natural user interfaces in the motor development of disabled children. Procedia Technol. **13**, 66–75 (2014). https://doi.org/10.1016/j.protcy.2014.02.010

23. Mortazavi, B., Pourhomayoun, M., Ghasemzadeh, H., Jafari, R., Roberts, C.K., Sarrafzadeh, M.: Context-aware data processing to enhance quality of measurements in wireless health systems: an application to MET calculation of exergaming actions. IEEE Int. Things J. **2**(1), 84–93 (2015). https://doi.org/10.1109/JIOT.2014.2364407

24. Paulo, S.: Exergames: Jogos digitais para longeviver melhor (2015)

25. Salber, D., Dey, A.K., Abowd, G.D.: The context toolkit: aiding the development of context-enabled. In: CHI 1999 Proceedings of the SIGCHI Conference on Human Factors in Computing Systems, pp. 434–441 (1999). https://doi.org/10.1145/302979.303126

26. Silva, J.M., El Saddik, A.: An adaptive game-based exercising framework. In: 2011 IEEE International Conference on Virtual Environments, Human-Computer Interfaces and Measurement Systems Proceedings, pp. 1–6 (2011). https://doi.org/10.1109/VECIMS.2011.6053847

27. Sinclair, J., Hingston, P., Masek, M.: Exergame development using the dual flow model. In: The 5th International Conference on Intelligent Environments – IE 2009, pp. 1–7 (2009). https://doi.org/10.1145/1746050.1746061

28. Smeddinck, J., Siegel, S., Herrlich, M.: Adaptive difficulty in exergames for Parkinson's disease patients. In: Proceedings of the 2013 Graphics, pp. 141–148 (2013). http://dl.acm.org/citation.cfm?id=2532154. Accessed 9 Dec 2013

29. Song, H., Peng, W., Lee, K.M.: Promoting exercise self-efficacy with an exergame. J. Health Commun. 16(2), 148–162 (2011). https://doi.org/10.1080/10810730.2010.535107

30. Sousa, F.H.: Uma revisão bibliográfica sobre a utilização do Nintendo® Wii como instrumento terapêutico e seus fatores de risco. Revista Espaço Acadêmico 8(123), 155–160 (2011)

31. Spronck, P., Balemans, I., Van Lankveld, G.: Player profiling with fallout 3. In: Proceedings of the Eighth AAAI Conference on Artificial Intelligence and Interactive Digital Entertainment, pp. 179–184 (2009)

32. Sweetser, P., Wyeth, P.: GameFlow: a model for evaluating player enjoyment in games. Comput. Entertain. (CIE) 3(3), 3 (2005). https://doi.org/10.1145/1077246.1077253

33. Tanaka, K., Parker, J., Baradoy, G., Sheehan, D., Holash, J.R., Katz, L.: A comparison of exergaming interfaces for use in rehabilitation programs and research. Loading 6(9), 69–81 (2012)

34. Whitehead, A., Johnston, H., Nixon, N., Welch, J.: Exergame effectiveness: what the numbers can tell us. In: Proceedings of the 5th ACM SIGGRAPH Symposium on Video Games - Sandbox 2010, pp. 55–62, October 2010. https://doi.org/10.1145/1836135.1836144

A Hybrid Virtual-Augmented Serious Game to Improve Driving Safety Awareness

Lucía Vera[1] , Jesús Gimeno[2] , Sergio Casas[2](✉) , Inma García-Pereira[2],
and Cristina Portalés[1]

[1] Institute of Robotics and Information and Communication Technologies (IRTIC),
University of Valencia, Valencia, Spain
[2] Computer Science Department, University of Valencia, Valencia, Spain
Sergio.Casas@uv.es

Abstract. The use of 3D virtual content and Augmented Reality (AR) in certain applications allows designing tools and serious games that are more attractive to the potential users. Focusing on the area of learning and education, these technologies can be adapted to the requirements of the application that needs to be developed, to the available devices on which they are expected to run and also to the learning content. However, in most applications only a single interaction paradigm and a single visualization mode is used, restricting the potential benefits of the system. In this paper, we propose a software application designed to improve driving safety awareness and learning for both adults and children, in which we combine different interaction and visualization modes. The application is shaped as a hybrid virtual-augmented "Game of the Goose" in which AR, tactile interaction and 3D virtual content are brought to the user in a combined but meaningful way. The combination of these different interaction paradigms creates an educational tool which is much more intuitive and engaging. In this serious game, multiple players/users can participate simultaneously and players obtain, on the one hand, an intuitive interaction, simple and realistic based on AR and, on the other hand, an increase in the sense of immersion by means of virtual content, for a given set of driving-related situations. This provides a much more tailored learning system, making the users focus in the given driving situations. The paper describes the objectives set in the development of the application, the design and implementation decisions taken and a comprehensive but preliminary assessment performed with 285 users which provides satisfactory and promising results.

Keywords: Serious game · Augmented Reality · Virtual content
Driving safety · Awareness

1 Introduction and Related Work

Driving is a complex task. It involves a variety of visual, physical and cognitive skills such as quick reactions to environment changes and decision making upon unpredictable risky situations. Driving simulators, serious games, and computer-based driving applications in general, allow training some of these skills in a safe manner and also increasing

© Springer International Publishing AG, part of Springer Nature 2018
A. D. Cheok et al. (Eds.): ACE 2017, LNCS 10714, pp. 293–310, 2018.
https://doi.org/10.1007/978-3-319-76270-8_21

social awareness on driving safety – including special driving groups that require particular attention such as racing drivers, children or drivers with previous criminal records.

Vehicle simulators and computer-based vehicle-related applications are very convenient for a variety of reasons since they have a number of advantages with respect to performing experiments in real conditions with real vehicles [1]: they can improve safety and reduce risks; they provide an economical cost reduction; the number of tests could be increased; potential human damage is almost inexistent; instructors and trainees are more available; the conditions of the tests/lessons could be varied (climate, environment, distractions); there is always the possibility of repeating the same tests with the same conditions; tests could be objectively analysed; trainees could benefit from a debriefing of their actions, etc.

Many computer-based driving applications make use of virtual content and Virtual Reality (VR) technology. Although some of them are intended to evaluate or promote driving safety, the different case studies and the conditions in which they work are very diverse. For instance, in [2] a study on fatigue among eldest drivers was performed. In this case, a big screen and a fixed-base simulator (with no motion cues) was used. Another example is [3] where the drivers are people with autism disorders. In [4] a study on the prediction of vehicle collisions in young adults was performed. In [5] a motion-based simulator is used to study patterns in the way drivers perform curve driving. These are just a few examples of the hundreds of references about driving simulation that can be found in the literature. Most of these works make use of realistic graphics, 3D sound and sometimes motion platforms to provide motion cues. However, the majority of them are focused on teaching physical skills and not in driving safety awareness. In addition, the interaction paradigm is restricted to VR. The authors believe that the combination of multiple types of stimuli and different interaction paradigms could provide a significant benefit for increasing awareness. Although driving simulators and VR could play an important role, other interaction paradigms could also be helpful. An example of a successful combined/hybrid interaction for driving safety awareness is ROMOT [6], which uses VR and Augmented Reality (AR) technologies (among others) to provide awareness-raising on several aspects of driving rules and road traffic safety. However, in this work the AR part is almost anecdotic and the interaction is limited to certain moments.

In this regard, AR is a technology that can also provide a successful learning environment. As defined by Azuma, this technology requires computer-based systems that can simultaneously: (i) combine virtual and real objects; (ii) are interactive in real-time; (iii) provide a 3D registration system so that virtual and real objects can be properly combined [7]. Examples of AR applications that are helpful for learning or awareness-raising are [8–11]. The number of works dealing with AR learning applications is quite high since it is a technology that is both affordable and practical. It is important to note that millions of people around the planet own mobile devices capable of providing AR features. A review of AR applications for learning can be found in [12]. This technology has also been used for driving, although the number of works is smaller. Examples of the use of AR to driving are [13–15].

On the other hand, although simulators play an important role in training skills (driving simulators are especially relevant for learning particular driving skills) they may not be the perfect choice to provide awareness and learning capabilities different than physical skills. There are other choices to provide learning that can be as effective and are usually less expensive. One of these solutions are the serious games.

Sometimes the differences between serious games and simulators are very subtle and some simulators could also be considered as serious games. However, it is generally accepted that a simulator is a computer application that tries to recreate or replicate some situation, experience or natural phenomenon. Although many simulators are designed as games, they do not have to be games. Serious games, on the contrary are computer-based games with a particular learning purpose. In this regard, they do not need to perfectly recreate a particular phenomenon or situation and can use several interaction paradigms such as VR and AR, or even others.

Serious games have shown to be an effective tool for learning [16]. For this reason, hundreds of serious games with various purposes have been proposed. Driving has also been the subject of some serious games. In [17] an evaluation of the behaviour of people with respect to driving is performed. Driving manufacturers, such as Renault, have been also interested in developing serious games for driving. "The Good Drive" [18] is probably the perfect example. This tool is a video-game environment designed to support people that want to obtain a driving license, reducing the number of hours (and hence the financial cost) they need to get the license. Serious games can also be applied to assess driver information systems, ergonomics [19] and Advanced Driver Assistance Systems (ADAS) [20]. The problem of awareness-raising, related or not with driving, has also been dealt by means of serious games [21–23]. Research suggests that these applications are hugely successful in generating public interest and an increase of awareness [24].

Despite the great number of works dealing with driving and road safety, the combination of several of the aforementioned technologies to provide benefits for driving safety has not been explored, to the best of our knowledge. In this regard, this paper describes a hybrid virtual-augmented serious game designed to improve driving safety awareness. The game is targeted to all the actors involved in road accidents (drivers, passengers and pedestrians) since it would be a mistake to consider drivers as the sole group responsible for accidents. The novelty of the application with respect to other systems dedicated to similar objectives consists in considering simultaneously several interaction paradigms with different levels of presence. The pedagogical content of the game has been designed by a group of psychologists specialized in driving safety. Consequently, the interaction paradigms and the visualization features are chosen to match the expected level of immersion, entertainment and engagement needed to fulfil the transfer of knowledge and the awareness-raising. The system is designed to be specially appealing for young people. This is the reason why it is conceived as a serious game. The game, however, is not designed just to entertain youngsters and it can also be used by adults, since it can be adapted to different profiles and ages.

The paper is organized as follows. This section has introduced the tool and has reviewed related works on the topic. The application is described in Sect. 2. Section 3 deals with the system's architecture. Section 4 shows some experiments performed with real users in a driving safety exhibition where this application was used. Finally, Sect. 5 is dedicated to draw conclusions and outline future work.

2 Description of the System

The application presented in this paper is part of a broader set of training and educational actions that have been designed to perform a driving safety exhibition to promote safe driving and awareness-raising on this important issue. One implementation of this exhibition is deployed (see Fig. 1) and underway in the Kingdom of Saudi Arabia (KSA). Sadly, this country is one of the leaders in mortality rates due to road traffic accidents. The situation is so critical that national authorities are developing massive plans to increase driving safety awareness, especially for children, since cultural aspects have a great deal of importance in driving safety and teaching children on how to properly behave behind the wheel guarantees a brighter future. As children and teenagers are eager to learn by playing and are more sensitive to technological applications, a serious game seems the perfect choice to engage them in these topics. Our serious game is designed to coexist with other driving safety applications and complementary training elements in a massive driving safety interactive exhibition, using augmented reality, mixed reality and virtual reality applications, such as ROMOT [6]. In any case, the proposed application works independently with respect to the rest of elements in the exhibition.

Fig. 1. Driving safety awareness exhibition in the city of Dammam, KSA. The hybrid serious game is in the foreground. ROMOT is in the background.

The application is setup as an educational serious game which combines the AR paradigm and 3D virtual content, in order to raise awareness on the hazards related to road safety. The dynamics of the game is based on the popular "Game of the Goose", with a board consisting of a track with consecutive spaces that players use to move a virtual token towards the end of the track by means of virtual dice (Fig. 2).

Fig. 2. Interaction space of the application

However, in this case, not only is the advance around the board related with the value obtained by casting the dice, but it also comes with the need to properly response to questions that are raised when the token falls in each of the spaces of the board. Players need to answer these questions in order to advance through the game and successfully complete it. These questions are, of course, about driving safety and are formulated and designed by a group of psychologists experts in driving safety.

The use of AR provides several advantages: (i) an easy customization and modification of the game with respect to a traditional board game; (ii) the possibility that different users play simultaneous but independent games; (iii) it makes people more involved and participate actively in the game, contrary to a regular video-game.

The game set-up consists of a table with a flat image on top and a cylindrical image in the middle acting as AR marker, so that the user can enable the AR features of the game (Fig. 3). The element of play is a mobile device (preferably a tablet due to its larger screen, although a mobile phone can be used too). Players need to identify themselves first by logging in through the mobile device. Once they have been granted access through the registration platform, players can use their device's camera to point to the game table in order to start the game. The cylindrical marker makes possible to use the AR capabilities from any near location, which allows, in turn, to offer the possibility to provide multiplayer capabilities: several players can use the system simultaneously although they do not directly compete with each other; the result of the game depends only on the actions of the person playing the game, although the final score will be eventually compared with the results of previous players.

Fig. 3. Some users playing the game

The board resembles an uphill road (Fig. 3) and a car is used as the game token. Although an actual printed image is used as a reference frame to mark the limits of the board (see Figs. 2 and 3), both the token and the board are virtual. Players need to move this virtual token towards the final space to complete the game. The token moves through the road as the users cast the dice and answer questions related with driving safety. All the visualization and interaction is performed through the mobile device (dice, token displacement, board, questions, answers, etc.).

Once the player falls into a space of the board, the AR scene is hidden, and the game changes the interaction and visualization modes to show only virtual content to the players. This virtual content comes in various forms and it is designed to challenge the driving safety knowledge of the people playing the game by means of driving safety-related questions. If players successfully answer a question, they are rewarded with a good score. Otherwise, they are penalized with a bad score. In either case, they are informed of the correct answer and its rationale, receiving an immediate feedback. Due to the theme of the game, which is focused on road safety, two types of questions have been included in the application:

- 2D questions, which are used to focus the attention of players on a particular subject (Fig. 4).

Fig. 4. 2D question within the interactive game

- 3D questions with virtual content, which are designed to portrait a particular driving situation in which some kind of risk is present and the player needs to respond to a specific question. These 3D questions recreate driving situations with virtual cars and virtual pedestrians (avatars). There is some degree of interaction, since players can move the "look-at" direction of the virtual camera (although not the point of view) by actually tilting the tablet, but the user does not control the driving situation. They are privileged observers of the virtual content and the amount of virtual presence is not meant to reach full immersion. Therefore, this virtual content cannot be considered as a 100% pure VR application nor as a driving simulator, although it shares many of the features and advantages of these applications.

In the case of the 3D scenes, where a specific situation is analysed, players either join a scene in third-person view (Fig. 5) or get involved as if they were in control of the situation by means of a first-person view (Fig. 6). These two visualization modes are chosen according to the particular situation being recreated, trying, thus, to use the proper amount of immersion in the virtual environment to achieve the goals the system is designed for.

In all cases, the application provides a virtual presenter that narrates the situation, formulates the question and enumerates the possible answers. The system uses a pedagogical methodology based on immediate feedback, so that for every question of the game (Fig. 7) the player gets not only an immediate result but also an explanation/ justification about the proper answer (Fig. 8). Thus, players can learn from their mistakes and can get also motivated with their successful answers.

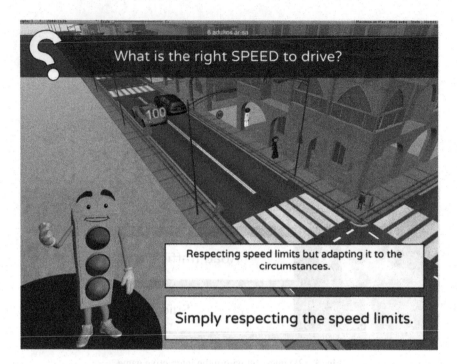

Fig. 5. 3D question with a third-person situation

In the case of scenes/questions with virtual 3D content, the feedback is accompanied by a recreation - in the simulated environment - of the consequences of the answer being selected (both wrong and correct). This way, players can visualize the consequences of their choices. The potentiation of the sensation of immersion is aimed at increasing their awareness on driving safety by actually "experiencing" the consequences of wrong behaviour behind the wheel. For all questions, a final explanation is given. In case the answer is correct, the positive situation is visualized. On the contrary, in case a wrong answer is given, the consequences of the negative situation are recreated first and later the correct situation is shown alongside the explanation.

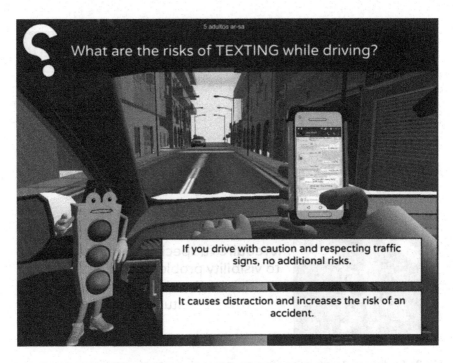

Fig. 6. 3D question with a first-person situation

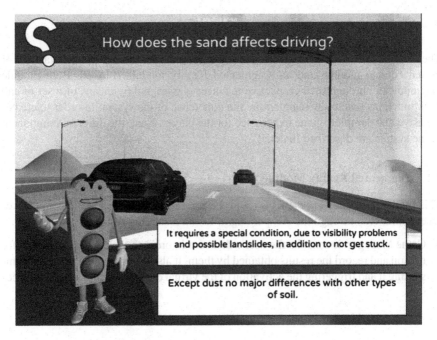

Fig. 7. Virtual presenter asking a question with two possible answers

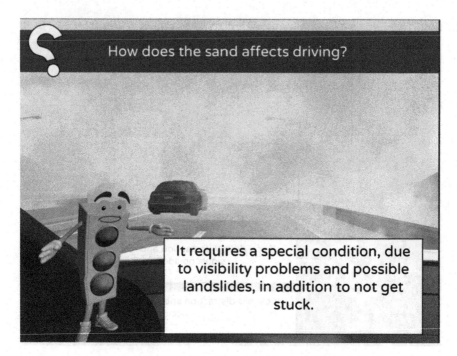

Fig. 8. Feedback and explanation of the answer to enhance learning and increase awareness

3   Architecture

The system is structured in two different modules that perform independent tasks: a 3D virtual content module and an Augmented Reality module (Fig. 9). Both modules communicate through their respective manager classes and by means of a set of callback functions that allow maintaining the coherence of the system in order to create a cohesive and complete game experience for the player. Next, the different components of the system are described in detail.

3.1   Augmented Reality Module

This module manages the gameplay and the recreation of the game elements (token, dice, board, etc.) through the AR paradigm. Its main submodules are:

- Game Manager: it consults the user's database in order to lookup the players' information and record the results obtained by them. It also controls the flow of the game, starting it and triggering the activation of the virtual content module when it is necessary.

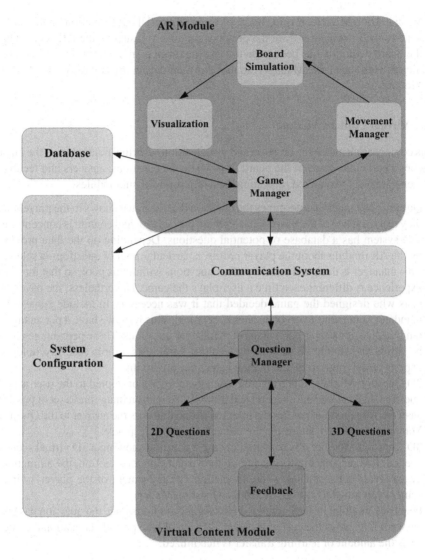

Fig. 9. System's architecture

- Movement Manager: it deals with the random generation of numbers to simulate the dice. It also determines the movement of the token and the target space of the board. Then it yields control of the application to the Board Simulation Module, so that the simulated environment is actually simulated and displayed.
- Board Simulation Module: it is in charge of deciding which elements need to be visualized depending on the location the user is placed with respect to the AR mark. It handles the coherence of the board with the virtual dice cast and simulates the motion of the vehicle-token towards the target space of the board, according to the point of view of the user.

- Visualization Module: it is in charge of visualizing all the information on the screen. It takes the information from the previous module to visualize the AR scene. Once the board evolution has been depicted and the token is in the right place, it communicates with the Game Manager, so that this module can invoke the Virtual Content Module.

3.2 Virtual Content Module

This component handles the creation and visualization of virtual content once the player reaches a particular space of the board. It is where the questions, answers and feedback are generated and visualized. It is composed of a series of submodules:

- Question Manager: it determines the question that the game shows to the player once they reach a space of the board. This is where the pedagogical content is concentrated. The system has a database of potential questions. Depending on the data provided by the AR module about the player profile, a particular pool of questions is selected. This manager is designed to ask random questions within this pool, so that the game experience is different each time a user plays the game. Nevertheless, the psychologists who designed the game decided that it was necessary to include some set of mandatory questions everybody should be asked. This way, we have a percentage of random questions and a percentage of mandatory questions. These percentages could be varied and should be decided by teaching specialists, in this case psychologists experts on driving safety and human behaviour on driving.
- 2D Question Module: it is triggered when the question prompted to the user is a 2D question. In this case, the question text is presented with an image and a set of possible answers. The module handles the interaction and transfers the answer to the Question Manager in order to determine the correctness of the response.
- 3D Question Module: it is triggered in case a question showing a 3D virtual scene is needed. It is responsible for managing the virtual camera's motion, the animations, avatars, etc. It also manages the interaction, the movement of the player's virtual camera and transfers the answer to the Question Manager.
- Feedback module: it is triggered to give feedback to users once the question has been answered. It shows the correct answer, as the goal is to provide educational content so as the amount of learning transfer is maximized.

The application is supported by an external database that provides vital information. On the one hand, it provides a big question repository with their corresponding 3D scenes depicting dynamic virtual content. On the other hand, as the users need to sign up before using the application, we can gather some data about the players and personalize both the entertainment experience and the teaching procedure. In this regard, the game uses two different age groups to select the questions: under 18 years old and over 18. The game also stores the scores users obtain when they complete the game and some other useful data such as the time spent to complete it.

Finally, there is a communication module that acts as a bridge between the two main modules of the system. It is based on call-back functions that are called from either module (AR or virtual content) in order to maintain the coherence of the system.

4   Experiments and Results

As the goal of the application is to increase awareness on driving safety, it is important to assess the system, since the entertainment envelope is just an "excuse" to obtain more important goals: get people engaged with driving safety issues.

To assess the application, the results of 285 players were analysed in a preliminary evaluation of the game. These people used the system in a national driving safety awareness exhibition in Dammam, KSA on December 2016. The population sample consists of 181 men (64%) and 104 women (36%), and covers a wide spectrum of ages (Fig. 10). Users were provided with the same tablet models so that there were no differences in the game performance, no need to use their own mobile devices to install the application and the registration process was easier. All age groups present more men than women due to cultural reasons of the country where the experiment was carried out, but this does not mean that the application or the questions are designed only for men, as it can be used by both genders. Since one of the goals of the application is to engage youngsters, it is good to see that the size of each age group decreases as their age increases. This suggests that the game is appealing for children, since the exhibition did not have any age restriction and no group was expected to be significantly more numerous. There were 98 persons under the age of 16, 81 persons between 16 and 24 years, 52 between 25 and 34, and 54 persons older than 34 years. The size of the experiment is large enough to draw some conclusions about the use of the tool.

The application is designed to store several indicators regarding the use of the system. Of course, one of them is the final score, but the game also stores some other data such as the amount of time the application was used, the language the player selected, the number of rounds etc. Figure 11 shows a box plot of the use times for each group (by gender and age). As it can be seen, mean use time varies from 7 to 9 min. Although there are some differences (men between 25–34 seem to be the fastest group), these differences are small between age groups and also between men and women. Variability is also quite similar and not very high. Therefore, we imply that the difficulty in the use of the application has been relatively similar and small.

If we take a look at the scores, grouping the results per age and gender, they are fairly similar, with some remarkable exceptions. As Fig. 12 shows, mean scores (with a maximum of 100 points) ranges from 57 to 73. Although no group has scored mean values below 50, which could be considered as a failure, it is also true that no particular group got results that could be deemed as outstanding. This may be caused by the context in which the results were taken, since the experiments were performed in a driving safety exhibition created precisely because the lack of driving safety awareness in the country. Therefore, some driving safety concepts are suspected not to be previously rooted in many of the participants of the experiments.

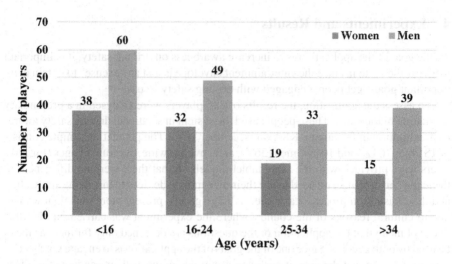

Fig. 10. Number of people in the experiment, per age and gender

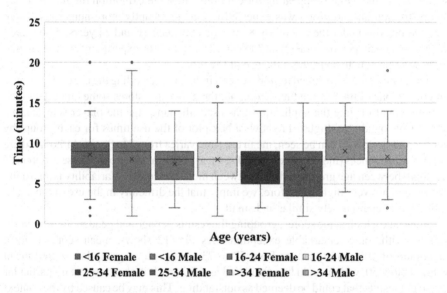

Fig. 11. Box plot of the use time, per age and gender

Mean score results show that males between 25 and 34 seem to be the group less aware on driving safety, whereas younger people (under the age of 16) seem to perform better. These results could be caused by the recent efforts of national authorities in targeting younger audiences to make them much more aware about the dangers of driving and decrease mortality rates. The rest of the groups performed rather similarly, although the dispersion varies from group to group and it is quite higher in males than in female groups, especially in middle age groups. This could indicate that the groups

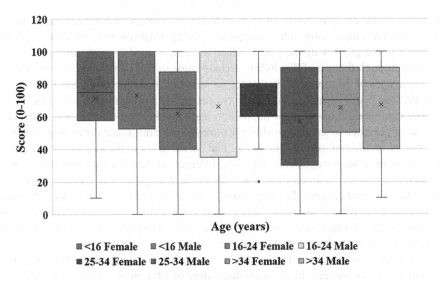

Fig. 12. Mean score, per age and gender

between 16 and 34 years old include both sensible people and also some quite dangerous drivers.

However, is important to realize that the transfer of knowledge caused by a particular question of the application occurs after the participants were scored for that particular question: first a driving situation is presented to the user, then they are asked about the situation (they answer with the knowledge they had before using the application plus the knowledge they have gathered from previous questions of the game), then they get graded, and finally the right answer is given to them. For this reason, it is difficult to know how much of the score is caused by the application. Thus, neither scores, nor use times provide a clear picture of the advantages of using this application. It is necessary to study how these two indicators correlate as this information would be much more valuable.

Thus, the next step is to study the correlation between the time spent by players using the application and the score they obtained. For the 104 women in the experiment, the correlation between use time and score is 0.5. For the 181 males, the correlation coefficient raises to 0.61. The differences may be caused by social and cultural factors that are not the focus of our study. Luckily, the group of children (under 16 years old) stands out again showing a correlation coefficient of 0.67 for women and 0.65 for men. Therefore, the more time the application is used, the higher score people get. Although correlation does not always imply causation, this suggests that the use of the application is indeed effective.

5   Conclusions and Further Work

This paper describes a serious game designed to raise awareness on driving safety. The application implements a virtual-augmented "Game of the Goose". The novelty of the application is the combination of augmented reality, user interaction through tactile input and 3D virtual content to reproduce dangerous driving situations and provide immediate feedback to the players of the game, which are encouraged to apply the knowledge obtained through the use of this hybrid serious game to real driving situations. One of the advantages of this approach is that the game is both fun and useful and follows the principle that learning through fun is always easier than through tedious lessons.

The combination of different interaction and visualization modes causes that the amount of presence in the real world vary through the game as the different paradigms are utilized in different parts of the game. The choice of these paradigms is not casual, since each one allows us guiding players to different teaching aspects, which is in turn the key aspect and the main reason for designing the game with these features, as suggested by psychologists. In this regard, as there are not technical aspects that are specific to the driving awareness problem, this application structure could be used to raise awareness on other topics, provided that a group of experts in that particular issue is included in the development of the system.

The reception of the game has been very favourable. The fact that nearly 300 people wanted to use the system during a driving safety exhibition is a great success itself. Moreover, we reported no cases in which the game was started but not finished and a few reports of people playing more than one round. Even though the game does not take a great deal of time to complete, this suggest that people really liked it. Moreover, we have been able to objectively measure the performance of a sizeable group of people playing the game, finding that young people are more likely to correctly answer the questions prompted by the game. The relatively high correlation between use times and final scores also suggests that this serious game is an effective tool for increasing driving safety awareness, especially for younger people, which is very good news for the future, although the assessment is still preliminary.

Of course, there is a substantial amount of future work that can be done to continue and enhance this application. On the pedagogical side, we would like to perform a complete assessment comparing the exact amount of knowledge transfer the game may provide, although all evidences already suggest that the tool is indeed effective. To do so, it is necessary to perform a double assessment of the people who use this tool. One before they use it, and another one after they have played the game, which is complex and has to be properly designed by learning specialists.

On the technological side, there are a number of modifications that could be applied to the system. For instance, VR glasses could be used to recreate the 3D virtual content. In addition, as the virtual content already features realistic graphics, this 3D content could also be enhanced by adding other perceptual cues such as motion cues or olfactory cues. Another option is to turn the non-AR content into a VR vehicle simulator. Nevertheless, it would be necessary to analyse if the different modifications/additions increase the ability of the system to provide benefits for driving safety and awareness-raising. In this regard, some simulators and other fully immersive VR applications cause simulator sickness to some people. Therefore, the effectiveness of the system may be reduced and it is possible that other interaction paradigms with less immersion capabilities are more effective albeit less flamboyant. Since learning and awareness-raising are the ultimate goals of the system, the addition of more technology is not always a synonym of greater success.

References

1. Casas, S., Fernández, M., Riera, J.V.: Four different multimodal setups for non-aerial vehicle simulations—a case study with a speedboat simulator. Multimodal Technol. Interact. **1**(2), 10 (2017)
2. Vallières, É.F., et al.: Perceived fatigue among aging drivers: an examination of the impact of age and duration of driving time on a simulator (2015)
3. Cox, S.M., et al.: Driving simulator performance in novice drivers with autism spectrum disorder: the role of executive functions and basic motor skills. J. Autism Dev. Disord. **46**(4), 1379–1391 (2016)
4. McManus, B., et al.: Predicting motor vehicle collisions in a driving simulator in young adults using the useful field of view assessment. Traffic Inj. Prev. **16**(8), 818–823 (2015)
5. Reymond, G., et al.: Role of lateral acceleration in curve driving: driver model and experiments on a real vehicle and a driving simulator. Hum. Factors **43**(3), 483–495 (2001)
6. Casas, S., et al.: On a first evaluation of ROMOT—a RObotic 3D MOvie theatre—for driving safety awareness. Multimodal Technol. Interact. **1**(2), 6 (2017)
7. Azuma, R.T.: A survey of augmented reality. Presence Teleoperators Virtual Environ. **6**(4), 355–385 (1997)
8. Haugstvedt, A.-C., Krogstie, J.: Mobile augmented reality for cultural heritage: a technology acceptance study. In: 2012 IEEE International Symposium on Mixed and Augmented Reality (ISMAR). IEEE (2012)
9. Vlahakis, V., et al.: Archeoguide: an augmented reality guide for archaeological sites. IEEE Comput. Graph. Appl. **22**(5), 52–60 (2002)
10. Dickey, R.M., et al.: Augmented reality assisted surgery: a urologic training tool. Asian J. Androl. **18**(5), 732 (2016)
11. Portalés, C., Perales, C.D., Cheok, A.D.: Exploring social, cultural and pedagogical issues in AR-gaming through the live lego house. In: Proceedings of the International Conference on Advances in Computer Entertainment Technology. ACM (2007)
12. Dunleavy, M., Dede, C.: Augmented reality teaching and learning. In: Spector, J., Merrill, M., Elen, J., Bishop, M. (eds.) Handbook of Research on Educational Communications and Technology, pp. 735–745. Springer, New York (2014). https://doi.org/10.1007/978-1-4614-3185-5_59
13. Jose, R., Lee, G.A., Billinghurst, M.: A comparative study of simulated augmented reality displays for vehicle navigation. In: Proceedings of the 28th Australian Conference on Computer-Human Interaction. ACM (2016)
14. Kim, H., et al.: Look at Me: augmented reality pedestrian warning system using an in-vehicle volumetric head up display. In: Proceedings of the 21st International Conference on Intelligent User Interfaces. ACM (2016)
15. Kane, V., et al.: Depth perception in mirrors: the effects of video-based augmented reality in driver's side view mirrors. In: 2016 IEEE Virtual Reality (VR). IEEE (2016)
16. Connolly, T.M., et al.: A systematic literature review of empirical evidence on computer games and serious games. Comput. Educ. **59**(2), 661–686 (2012)
17. Genious: Genious Serious Games - Driving (2017). http://www.genious-seriousgames.com/portfolio-item/driving/. Accessed 19 July 2017
18. Renault: The Good Drive (2017). https://group.renault.com/en/news/blog-renault/the-good-drive-a-serious-game-for-learning-to-drive/. Accessed 19 July 2017
19. Gonçalves, V.J.M.: Applying serious games to assess driver: information system ergonomics (2014)

20. Goncalves, J.S., et al.: Testing advanced driver assistance systems with a serious-game-based human factors analysis suite. In: 2014 IEEE Intelligent Vehicles Symposium Proceedings. IEEE (2014)
21. Cetto, A., et al.: Friend inspector: a serious game to enhance privacy awareness in social networks (2014). arXiv preprint: arXiv:1402.5878
22. Madeira, R.N., et al.: LEY!: persuasive pervasive gaming on domestic energy consumption-awareness. In: Proceedings of the 8th International Conference on Advances in Computer Entertainment Technology. ACM (2011)
23. Lehtonen, E., et al.: Learning game for training child bicyclists' situation awareness. Accid. Anal. Prev. **105**, 72–83 (2017)
24. Rebolledo-Mendez, G., et al.: Societal impact of a serious game on raising public awareness: the case of FloodSim. In: Proceedings of the 2009 ACM SIGGRAPH Symposium on Video Games. ACM (2009)

Cheer Me!: A Video Game System Using Live Streaming Text Messages

Yu Matsuura[✉] and Sachiko Kodama

The University of Electro-Communications, 1-5-1 Chofugaoka, Chofu, Tokyo 182-8585, Japan
{yu.matsuura,sachiko.kodama}@uec.ac.jp

Abstract. Nowadays, video game live streaming has gained popularity. To make communication between the streamers and the viewers more direct, we developed a game system in which the viewer can participate and reflect their own emotion by posting chat messages on a live streaming service. The system evaluates and classifies the emotion of the viewers' messages into nine levels through a text analysis API. The smaller the level, the more negative emotions the sentence has, and the higher the level, the more positive they are. When the system evaluates the emotion of the message, the message sentence appears on the game screen in real time. The sentences have different effects, which help or bother the streamer's play depending on classification. In a user test, five subjects were interviewed. All of them answered that they felt a strong awareness of participation and that they thought that the system activated communication between the streamer and the viewers. A "big hole" trick, which was designed so that player could pass the scene only when he could receive the viewers' messages, gave them excitement.

Keywords: Live streaming · Viewer participation · Video games
Chat message

1 Introduction

Live streaming of video games gained popularity during the 2010s. Nowadays, many professional streamers are generating sustainable revenue from viewer subscriptions and donations. Watching such live streams tends more and more towards becoming a new kind of entertainment on its own [1]. Viewers can communicate with streamers using chats on live-streaming platforms. However, streamers can only reply to the chat messages in many cases. There is still room where the chat messages can be further utilized.

Aiming at a more direct communication between streamers and viewers, we developed a game system that reflects the viewers' emotions by evaluating chat messages. When a message is posted, the text graphically appears on the game screen. The text plays some role, which helps or bothers players (Fig. 1).

© Springer International Publishing AG, part of Springer Nature 2018
A. D. Cheok et al. (Eds.): ACE 2017, LNCS 10714, pp. 311–317, 2018.
https://doi.org/10.1007/978-3-319-76270-8_22

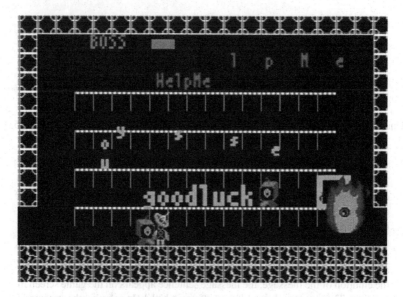

Fig. 1. Proposed Cheer Me! system. A text posted by viewers graphically appears on the game screen. The text helps or bothers player. This figure shows that the text "bless you" is attacking the enemy.

The contributions in this paper are as follows:

1. The game system reflects viewers' emotion. Viewers can participate without inputting the specific message designated for the game.
2. By designing effects not limited to the game situations, viewers can participate regardless of the delay of message reflection.

2   Related Work

Live-streaming platforms have been investigated recently. Lessel [2] developed a viewer participation system for video card game. However, since the system requires a dedicated platform, it places a burden on viewers to use.

"TwitchPlaysPokemon" [3] is a live streaming program in which viewers can operate a video game "Pokémon Red Version" by posting commands of the controller buttons on chat. One hundred and twenty two million commands were posted to the program. "Nico-Reversi" [4] is an online Reversi game in which viewers can vote position on chat. The streamer can play with the viewers. These viewer participation systems have the same point that viewers become players. However, viewers of live-streamed video games access the streaming to watch the streamers' gameplay. Therefore, the viewer participation system should be able to keep the viewers as a viewer.

"Live from PlayStation" [5] is a live streaming service in which users can watch video games of PlayStation 4 being played. The service has an "Interact" button. When viewers use this button, some changes occur in the streamed game. For example, viewers can give recovery items to the streamer, or decide whether the game can be continued when the streamer fails. However, they can use the Interact button in only one way. Hence, the system cannot fully reflect the viewers' intentions.

"Choice Chamber" [6] is a game for viewer participation. Viewers can participate in real time by answering choices of questions displayed on the screen using chat. However, there are two issues in the game. One is that the questions are limited to the game situations. Hence, the streamer must wait reflection of the choices. As a result, the immediacy of the game is lost. Furthermore, this participation method cannot apply to other games, because it needs dedicated game design. The other is that the method reduces the value of usual messages not answering to the question. Smith [7] argued that viewers are heightening their enjoyment using chat messages telling the streamers to do certain things or asking them questions. Therefore, it is necessary to consider viewer participation methods that can solve these issues.

In contrast to these previous systems, the Cheer Me! system can keep viewers as a viewer and reflect their intentions regardless of the delay of message reflection. The system reflects the intentions using the viewers' emotions evaluated from usual chat messages not answering to the specific questions. The proposed system suggests a path for applying viewer participation method to existing or future games, especially action game.

3   Cheer Me!

We developed a game system "Cheer Me!", which reflects the viewers' emotions by evaluating chat messages on a live streaming platform. Streamers play the game while streaming the game screen alone. Figure 2 provides an overview of the game system. The system consists of two parts—an evaluation program and a game program.

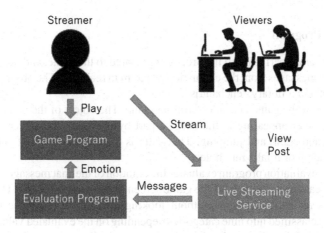

Fig. 2. System overview

3.1 Evaluation Program

The evaluation program has two roles—receiving chat messages from a live streaming service's server, and evaluating the viewers' emotions from the chat messages.

The program is written in PHP, and accesses a live-streaming service server in which chat messages are saved. When chat messages are posted in a stream, the program receives the messages and evaluates them in real time.

An emotion evaluation is done through communication with the Text Analytics API [8]. Text Analytics API is a web service provided by Microsoft. When the Text Analytics API inputs a sentence, it evaluates the emotion contained in the sentence with a value from 0 to 100. The smaller the value, the more negative emotions the sentence has, and the higher the value, the more positive they are.

However, the API can evaluate only English and Spanish. To use other languages, the evaluation program communicates with the Translator Text API [9] before evaluation to translate if the sentence is not in English (Fig. 3).

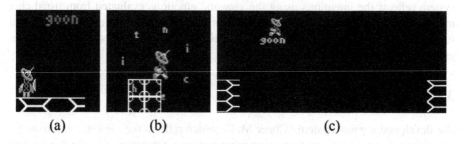

| (a) | (b) | (c) |

Fig. 3. (a) The sentence of the viewer's message appears on the game screen, (b) Skill effect of Positive level 3, (c) The player character is passing through a "big hole" trick by using the skill effect of Positive level 1.

3.2 Game Program

The game program performs all the processing related to the game, and the reception of the value and messages from the evaluation program in real time. The program is written in JavaScript and a library "enchant.js".

The genre of the game is a side-scrolling game. The object of the game is to defeat the boss character appearing in the deepest part by operating the player character by moving left and right, and jumping. The game is over when hit points of the player character reach 0 or it falls into holes.

When the evaluation program evaluates the emotion of the chat message, the message sentence appears from the right of the game screen and moves to the left. Therefore, the streamer can read the messages without looking away from the game screen. The sentences are classified into nine categories depending on the evaluated values, and have different effects depending on the classification.

The sentence has two effects—collision effect and skill effect. These help or bother the streamer's play. The collision effect is the effect when the player character collides with the sentence. If the emotion of the sentence is positive, the hit points increase by

1, and if negative, they decrease by 1. Since all posted chat messages are reflected, the sentences can fill up the screen. Therefore, to reduce the risk of a "game over" without the manipulation of the streamer, we designed the increase/decrease value of a hit point to be 1. The skill effect is the effect when colliding with a sentence while pressing the space key, and has a greater influence on the game situation than the collision effect. Thus, the streamer can choose either the collision effect or the skill effect when the player character collides with the sentence. Table 1 shows the correspondence between the emotion evaluation values and skill effects. Owing to the specifications of the system, a delay of approximately 5~15 s occurs from the time a viewer posts a message until the live streaming service delivers the game screen reflecting the message to the viewer. Therefore, skill effects are designed to help or bother streamers regardless of the situations and viewers can participate the game regardless of the delay time. In addition, if the evaluation value of the sentence is from 20 to 79, the player character can ride on the sentence; otherwise the sentence moves while chasing the player character in the vertical direction.

Table 1. Correspondence between evaluated values and skill effects.

Classification	Evaluated value	Skill effect
Negative level 4	0–9	Five enemies homing in on the player character appear
Negative level 3	10–19	The number of characters enemies appear
Negative level 2	20–29	Three enemies appear
Negative level 1	30–39	An enemy flying in the sky appears
Neutral	40–59	Attack to throw the sentence ahead
Positive level 1	60–69	Fly in the sky
Positive level 2	70–79	Attack (homing enemy)
Positive level 3	80–89	Make a barrier with sentences
Positive level 4	90–99	Attack five times (homing enemy)

In the middle of the stage, we prepared a "big hole" trick that cannot be jumped over with a normal jump. There are two ways to pass through the trick. One is to ride on top of the sentence, and another is to use the skill effect of positive level 1. Thus, the streamer can pass only by using the viewer's message.

4   Evaluation

A user test was performed to examine whether the game system activates communication between the streamer and the viewers.

4.1   Method of a User Test

The subjects of the test comprised four males aged 22–23 and one female aged 22 in the laboratory of the University of Electro-Communications. Subjects played this game system five minutes per person and streamed the game screen and their voices.

Meanwhile, the other four people not streaming watched the stream and posted a chat message freely in Japanese. The test was performed using website "niconico" [10] most popular live-streaming platform in Japan. After the streams of all five subjects finished, a questionnaire on this game system was conducted. In addition, we recorded the streamed video and observed it later. All subjects used Google Chrome as a browser on a Windows desktop PC for the broadcasting and viewing. The questionnaire comprised four items to be answered with "yes · no", and a field for free comments.

4.2   Results

Table 2 shows the results of the questionnaire. The results show that the subjects feel the viewers' participation and think that the game system activates communication between a streamer and viewers. In the comments field, one subject wrote, "I felt that cheering helps the streamer directly", and another subject wrote, "The feeling that I want to cheer is strengthened." These comments indicate that the system of reflecting positive messages may have made viewers post cheering messages. Furthermore, a certain subject commented, "I got a strong impression when the streamer passed through the big hole trick using messages I posted.", so the experience of changing the game situation has the possibility of giving the viewer excitement.

Table 2.   Results of the questionnaire

Question	Yes	No
Q1. When you broadcast, did you feel that viewers were participating?	4	1
Q2. When you viewed, did you feel that you were participating?	5	0
Q3. Were you enjoying viewing compared to ordinary live streaming?	5	0
Q4. Do you think that the game system activates communication between a streamer and viewers?	4	1

On the other hand, there was a comment, "If the message posted was judged as negative contrary to intention, it bothers the streamer and I feel sorry". In the recorded video, there are some messages that are posted as cheering, but are judged as negative. These messages often contained abbreviated words, grammatically incorrect words, and slang not in the dictionary. Since the emotion evaluation program communicates with the translation API, we presumed that an erroneous evaluation of emotions occurred from the mistranslation of these words.

On the scene of the big hole trick, a message like ASCII art expressing a bridge by a symbol such as "~" "+" was posted. However, the game system cannot reflect the viewer's intention to bridge the big hole because Text Analytics API cannot evaluate such symbols. Contemplating on how to use such messages may broaden the range of the way to communicate.

In the recorded video, all subjects were able to answer questions or directions about playing from viewers by their voice without stopping playing. Therefore, we believed that the proposed system didn't prevent usual communication between the viewers and the streamer.

5   Conclusion

In this paper, we presented and tested a new game system that reflects the viewers' emotions included in their chat messages.

The results of the user test indicate that subjects feel the viewers' participation and think the game system activates communication between a streamer and viewers. Furthermore, all subjects were able to answer chat messages without stopping playing. Thus, we believed that the system didn't prevent usual communication between the viewers and the streamer.

As future work, we would like to consider the game genre fitted to the viewers' interactions. There was a user comment that "the feeling that I want to cheer is strengthened." We believe that reflecting the viewers' messages may be suitable in fighting games such as those used in eSports, because the audiences' cheering has a strong relationship with both eSports and real sports.

References

1. Kaytoue, M., Silva, A., Cerf, L., Meira Jr., W., Raïssi, C.: Watch me playing, i am a professional: a first study on video game live streaming. In: Proceedings of the 21st International Conference on World Wide Web, pp. 1181–1188 (2012)
2. Lessel, P., Vielhauer, A., Krüger, A.: Expanding video game live-streams with enhanced communication channels: a case study. In: Proceedings of the 2017 CHI Conference on Human Factors in Computing Systems, pp. 1571–1576 (2017)
3. TwitchPlaysPokemon. https://www.twitch.tv/twitchplayspokemon. Last accessed 28 July 2017
4. Iyoda, A., Sano, S., Watanabe, K.: Prototyping of interactive live streaming contents with audience comments. SIG Technical reports, 2009-HCI-135(14), pp. 1–5 (2009). (in Japanese)
5. Live from PlayStation. http://manuals.playstation.net/document/en/ps4/share/viewer.html. Last accessed 28 July 2017
6. Choice Chamber. http://www.choicechamber.com. Last accessed 23 Oct 2017
7. Smith, T., Obrist, M., Wright, P.: Live-streaming changes the (video) game. In: Proceedings of the 11th European Conference on Interactive TV and Video, pp. 131–138 (2013)
8. Text analytics API. https://azure.microsoft.com/en-us/services/cognitive-services/text-analytics/. Last accessed 28 July 2017
9. Translator Text API. https://azure.microsoft.com/en-us/services/cognitive-services/translator-text-api/. Last accessed 28 July 2017
10. niconico. http://www.nicovideo.jp/. 23 Oct 2017

Exploring the Use of Second Screen Devices During Live Sports Broadcasts to Promote Social Interaction

Marco Cruz[1] , Teresa Romão[1(✉)] , Pedro Centieiro[1,2] , and A. Eduardo Dias[1,2]

[1] NOVA Lincs, Faculdade de Ciências e Tecnologia, Universidade NOVA de Lisboa,
2829-516 Caparica, Portugal
mas.cruz@campus.fct.unl.pt, tir@fct.unl.pt, pcentieiro@gmail.com
[2] Viva Superstars Digital Media Lda, Madan Parque, Rua dos Inventores,
2825-182 Caparica, Portugal
eduardo@vivasuperstars.com

Abstract. The rise of mobile technology has transformed the once passive activity of watching a live sports broadcast into an active experience. Nowadays, it is common practice for sports fans to communicate, interact and share information with others through social mobile applications not only after, but also during the broadcast of a live sport event. However, sometimes the discussion between fans is not contextualised and the social applications used by them lack tools to register moments that can promote social discussions. Furthermore, not all sports fans can watch an event TV broadcast, making it impossible to express a concrete opinion about it. To address this issue, we developed ReactIt, a system developed for smartphones and smartwatches, that allows users to share automatically generated videos containing specific moments of a football match along with their emotional reaction, to engage fans and promote social interaction between them. Results from user tests were very positive regarding the interaction with both devices, and users manifested great interest in using ReactIt in a real life environment.

Keywords: Smartphone · Smartwatch · Second screen · Emotional reactions
Video sharing · Social interaction · Social network · Sports events

1 Introduction

Sports have the ability to bring people together. The competitiveness and the uncertainty of the end result are two factors that lead people to watch a sport activity. Since the Neolithic age of 7000 BC, there are indications of sports assisted by crowds, where there are evidences showing a wrestling match surrounded by people watching it [1]. This proves that competition is something that is in our blood, as well as the enjoyment of seeing others compete, which has made the world of sports evolve so much, from ancient times to the present. These days, sports continue in constant evolution, thanks to the use of new technologies and rules that allow a fairer and more balanced competition.

Sports in general have the ability to make fans emotionally engage with the event. Since sports are competitive physical activities, it is natural that our emotional state

© Springer International Publishing AG, part of Springer Nature 2018
A. D. Cheok et al. (Eds.): ACE 2017, LNCS 10714, pp. 318–338, 2018.
https://doi.org/10.1007/978-3-319-76270-8_23

changes during a sports event, where the emotions and the level of satisfaction of the spectators are directly related with the performance of the team they support. Watching a sport event confers a more social and global sense of experience, due to the existing social platforms. Increasingly, fans turn to social online platforms to communicate, interact and share information with other viewers during the broadcast of an event, providing a less lonely experience, and giving the feeling of watching the event together with the other fans. Even after an event, the discussion continues on these social platforms, where users share news associated with the event, support and indignation messages, as well as photos and videos containing moments of the event. As long as the content shared arouses a positive or a negative reaction, it will promote social interactions. Videos are one of the best types of content to engage users on social platforms, especially in the context of sports. The fact that different fans may have different opinions regarding specific moments of an event, means that videos have the ability to promote social discussion, and that is something we took advantage of, in this work.

Nowadays people have the habit of having their mobile phone, tablet or laptop nearby while watching television [2]. With the impetus these devices had in recent years, several concepts for second screen applications have been explored in the sports field [3, 4]. At this time, the most used devices for the use of second screen applications are smartphones and tablets [5], due to their mobility. Although smartwatches are not yet so popular and have not been exploited in this context, due to their recent market introduction, they have enormous potential for the development of social applications. These devices can be best suited for applications that require short and fast interactions than other mobile devices. In addition, they have the constant ability to monitor the user's contextual and physiological data.

Given the emotional impact of sports events and people's interest in expressing their opinions and emotions on social platforms during an event, we developed ReactIt, a new concept that emotionally engages sports fans, allowing a more social and entertaining experience. It allows the sharing of automatically generated videos by the system that contains specific moments of a football match, promoting social interactions between fans, through their reactions (opinions and emotions). The system was developed for smartphone and for smartwatch, which is a device that has not yet been much explored in the world of second screen applications, and has features that a smartphone does not have. User tests were conducted to evaluate the concept provided by ReactIt, the users' reactions, the system's usability, and to extract insights for future work.

2   Related Research

People are inseparable from their mobile devices, even at home, where they keep their devices near while watching TV. To take advantage of this behaviour, new second screen applications are appearing on the market. Due to the huge variety of existing second screen applications, and to the different forms of interaction provided by them, a large number of applications were studied [6], where the authors classified their functionalities according to the type of interaction they allow, being these, social sharing, gamification and extras, and expanded experience. The work described in this paper focuses on social sharing, which allows a Human-to-Human interaction where people share and interact with others, such as exchanging opinions on what they are watching or even sharing content related to the broadcasted show. Several studies have been conducted in this area, such as [7], where it is concluded that viewers are more motivated to share messages in real time, when they are watching television alone, in order to feel more connected within a community of users, even knowing that the message may not be seen by anyone. Other studies [8, 9] concluded that during the broadcast of a television show, viewers are more likely to share personal opinions and messages not addressed to anyone, just wanting to be part of a larger group.

Sports in general are undoubtedly one of the most talked about themes on social network, generating millions of live reactions. They have the ability to emotionally engage fans because of its nature. For this reason, second screen applications are the perfect combination when viewing sports events live broadcasts. Fans are not so socially involved when watching a sports event at home, compared to the fans that are on the venue. In order to solve or at least soften this problem, new concepts were developed and tested, allowing the fans to establish a greater emotional connection during a game. Among them is WeFeel [3], a system that allows users to share their emotions and opinions in real time through a mobile device during a sports event TV broadcast. Users can express their emotional state in the different moments of the match, through a set of emotions available on the application, and complement it with a comment. The system presents users' emotions and comments on the television screen rather than on the mobile device, thus creating a different experience where the users are not forced to turn the attention away from the television to visualize the reactions of their friends.

Another concept that also allows fans to share their opinions is WorldCupinion [4]. This system aimed to understand whether mobile devices could serve as a communication channel to share non-verbal information that represents emotional reactions during the transmission of sport event on television. To see if real-time sharing of emotions was an appealing concept, WorldCupinion was tested during the FIFA World Cup in 2010, as it is an event of enormous interest to the public around the world, and where spectators are extremely emotionally involved with the event. In WorldCupinion, users could choose the team they wanted to support, and express their thoughts during a match, through a set of opinions available on the application, and also observe the opinions of the other users.

The developed system (ReactIt), goes beyond simply sharing opinions and emotions with the other fans. When a user shares an emotion or opinion which is associated with a match moment, the system automatically generates a video that contains the shared match moment and makes it available to all his friends. This way, friends may watch the match moment before reacting to it, even when they are not watching the match on TV, promoting social interaction no matter where or when.

3 ReactIt

Like any other second screen application, the goal of ReactIt is to improve the user experience during a television broadcast, in this case during the broadcast of sports events, in particular football. ReactIt explores not only the use of smartphones, but also smartwatches in order to allow fans to express themselves. The system allows the sharing of reactions (opinions and emotions) along with the videos containing the corresponding moments of a sports event, engaging and promoting social interactions between the fans. The idea of ReactIt is to enable a quick and simple way to share our emotional state regarding a match moment, with our friends and other users that also use ReactIt, as well as to see how they react to the same match moment. Just as fans express their opinions and emotions with their friends at the venue or in public places, such as a cafe or a bar, we want to encourage the fans that are at home, to do the same. When a user shares a match moment, a small video is automatically generated by the server. This video has a 10 s length and contains the specific moment that the user registered through ReactIt.

When reacting to a match moment shared by a friend, the user downloads the associated video and reacts to it (expresses an opinion and emotion). Since users are used to share information on social networks (including videos), ReactIt allows an easy way to share videos during a match, generating social interactions between fans. And because of this functionality, the use of ReactIt can also be extended to users who cannot watch the match live on television. The idea of generating a video is simple: the user is not required to immediately react to a match moment shared by a friend at the time the share is made. Since there is a video associated with that moment, the user can choose to react during an eventless period of the match, for example when the ball goes out of the field, or when the match is over. Thus, when the user wants to react to the moment shared by his friend, he knows exactly what he is reacting to, since he can watch the video first. All the match moments that were shared throughout the match and the reactions expressed by the users, are stored in the system. Thus, at the end of the match, it is possible to make an analysis of the users reactions regarding the different moments shared during the match.

ReactIt can be used by any kind of sports fan who would like to be aware of the important moments of a match in real time, whether he is watching the match live on television or not (as illustrated by Fig. 1). Thus, a possible use of this system can be seen as follows:

1. The user has a mobile device (a smartphone or a smartwatch) with ReactIt installed, and he is in the comfort on his sofa watching a sports event on the television. At some point in the match, the referee awards a penalty that leaves the fans divided over his decision. The user registers the moment of the foul with a simple touch in the centre of the screen of the mobile device (Fig. 2a) and then reacts through a set of available opinions and emotions (Fig. 2b and c). The user wants to know the reaction of his friends and shares the moment he registered associated with his own reaction, with simply 3 touches (more details in the next sub-section).
2. His friends, who may or may not be watching the match, and who also have the application on their devices, receive a push notification (alert).
3. When they touch on the notification, they watch a video that contains the last 10 s prior to the time when the moment was registered. After watching the video, they may react by choosing an opinion and an emotional state.

4. The user who registered the moment is notified as soon as his friends react, and can make an analysis of the data, consulting the different shared moments of the match and the results obtained regarding the opinions and emotions expressed by their friends.

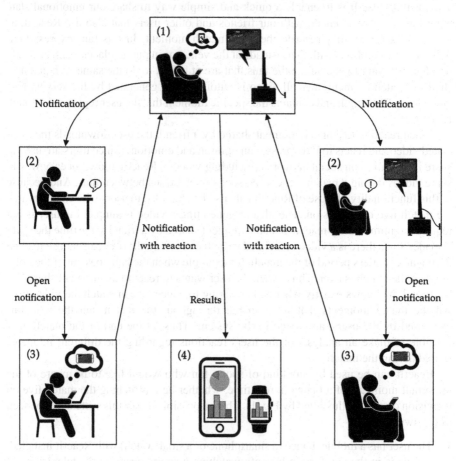

Fig. 1.   ReactIt – system usage example.

3.1   Smartphone Application

The application is composed by 3 sections: registration of a match moment, visualization of match moments and users' reactions, and user profile (Fig. 2). These sections are accessed through a menu at the bottom of the screen (tab bar). The menu is always visible, in order to allow the user to quickly access any of the sections.

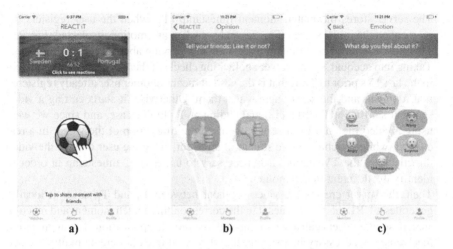

Fig. 2. Sharing a video of a match moment through ReactIt using the smartphone. (a) Initial screen where a moment can be registered. (b) Opinion selection screen. (c) Emotion selection screen.

The application was designed in a clear and intuitive way, allowing users to perform any task, in a simple and fast way, through a minimal number of interactions. The goal is not to divert the focus too much from first screen, the television displaying the match. So, in order to react to a match moment, users have to classify the moment with a "thumbs up" or "thumbs down", which is a type of classification that users are already familiar with, from other social networks like YouTube. This classification allows the users to have a better perception of the positive and negative opinions of the fans regarding the different actions in the match. In addition to the opinion a user may have regarding a match moment, we find that emotions are an essential aspect in applications developed for communication between viewers during a live broadcast, since it allows a more detailed reaction. Take for instance the introduction of emotions by Facebook in 2016. This was one of the biggest changes to Facebook in recent years, as it moved away from the simplistic and iconic "thumbs up" interaction to a set of six different emotions (like, love, haha, sad, wow, and angry), in order to allow users to better express themselves (and ultimately, to further analyse users' interaction with content). In our case, we used an emotions assessment interface inspired in the one used by WeFeel [3]. This is based on the CAAT's model [11], proposed by Cardoso et al., which was built upon Plutchik's Circumplex Model of emotions [12]. The final model (used in a sport context) contains 6 emotions [13] (anger, connectedness, unhappiness, elation, surprise and worry) associated with a colour.

Figure 2 illustrates the process of a user sharing a video of a match moment with his own associated reaction. The user starts by registering the moment by touching on the ball which is centred on the screen (Fig. 2a). Then he gives his opinion (Fig. 2b) and next, he selects an emotion through our emotions assessment interface (Fig. 2c).

Once a user selects the emotion, this information is sent to the server application, which starts generating the corresponding match moment as follows:

1. The server stores the match moment timestamp (T_1) when the user registers the moment on the initial screen (Fig. 2a) and not when an emotion is selected (Fig. 2c). This way, users can take time to react without worrying about losing the moment.
2. Taking into account T_1, the server application checks if there is a registered moment in the last 15 s prior to T_1. If that is the case, it means another user already registered that moment, and the server aggregates them. Otherwise, it starts cutting a video segment starting at $T_1 - 10$ s (T_0) and ending at T_1. In our case, and since we were using a video file on a local server, we used the timestamp of the video. In a real context, while watching a live stream of an event, since the user obtains the video directly from the TV station, it is necessary to use a UTC timestamp in order to identify the different match moments.
3. Then, the server creates the video segment between T_0 and T_1, saves it locally, generates a URL, and associates it to the corresponding match moment and reaction shared, so other users can access it through the mobile application. The aggregation mechanism is necessary in a system like this, so it does not create multiple video segments for the same match moment that was registered by the users with just a few seconds difference.
4. A push notification is sent to all user's friends so they can react to that moment.

When a friend touches on the notification the application downloads the 10-s video, and as soon as he finishes watching the video, he may react giving his opinion and selecting an emotional state.

There are two types of notifications in ReactIt. When a user shares a moment, all his friends receive a yellow notification (Fig. 3a), in order to inform them that someone is asking his opinion. As soon as his friends react to the match moment he shared, the user receives a green notification (Fig. 3b). This is a response notification that specifies the opinion, the emotion, and the corresponding time of the moment (expressed in "minutes:seconds").

Fig. 3. Different notifications used on the smartphone application. (a) User receiving a yellow notification. (b) User receiving a green notification. (Color figure online)

The system stores every moment shared during the match, so no one is required to immediately react after receiving a notification. Since each moment has a video associated with it, users can choose to react when they want, either during eventless periods of the match, in the half time or when the match is over.

By selecting "Matches" in the lower menu of the screen, users can select the match where there are still moments to react to (Fig. 4a). On this screen the idea is to prioritize the matches that are being broadcasted live, and whose teams belong to the list of favourite teams of the user (defined in the user profile). When selecting a match, the user has access to a list with all the moments shared during that match (Fig. 4b). Each moment has an associated avatar of the user who shared the match moment. It is possible for multiple users to share one match moment at or near the same time. In this situation, the system aggregates the two (or more) shares into one, only generating the video of the first share, and displaying an image with an aggregation of the users' avatars. Below the match time, it is possible to know how many friends reacted to that moment, and on the right side how many users (worldwide) in the system reacted to the same moment. When a certain moment becomes popular, that is, when at least 50% of the users reacted to that moment, a red trending icon is shown.

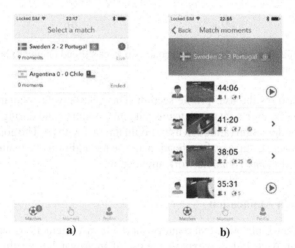

Fig. 4. (a) List of matches ordered by the user favourite teams (finished matches are at the end of the list). (b) List with all the moments shared during a match.

In this list there may be match moments that the user has not yet reacted, such as the ones at minutes 35:31 and 44:06 which have a "play" icon on the right side. When the user selects them, the video corresponding to that moment is played and once it is finished, the system asks for the user's reaction. The system only allows the user to see the other users' reactions to a match moment, when he already reacted to it. The idea is that the user must not be influenced by the opinions of the other users. The remaining moments that the user has already reacted to, such as the ones at minutes 38:05 and 41:20 (in Fig. 4b), have an arrow on the right side, which upon selection allows the user to access the match moment details screen (Fig. 5). In these screens, users can see the distribution of the users' opinions through a pie chart (Fig. 5a), and the distribution of the emotions through a bar chart (Fig. 5b). Above the charts, users can switch between reactions from friends and reactions from all users of the system (worldwide). By scrolling down, it is still possible to see the friends' opinions and emotions individually.

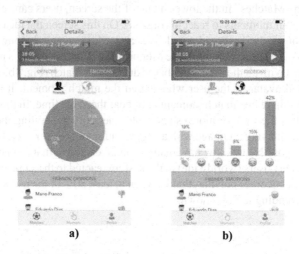

a)   b)

Fig. 5. Details of a match moment (smartphone): (a) User's friend opinions pie chart. (b) Users worldwide emotions bar chart.

The last section is the user profile section. This section was populated with place-holder data (e.g. the user's favourite teams, city and country) and during our tests it did not require user interaction (although users could interact with it). The goal was for users to feel that they were using a real application, hence the addition of a feature of this kind, which is included in any social network application.

3.2 Smartwatch Application

Since ReactIt is an application that requires short and fast interactions when registering a match moment, we decided to explore the use of smartwatches for this type of quick interactions. It is quicker to share a match moment through a smartwatch, unless the user is constantly with the smartphone in hand waiting to register a moment when something interesting happens in the match. The system was developed for Apple Watch, which has a feature that keeps the device on standby when it is not being used, saving energy. When the user turns the wrist in order to use the smartwatch, it auto-matically activates and opens the last application, allowing users to quickly interact with it.

Due to the small screen space, we do not include access and management of the user profile on the smartwatch, being only possible to access it through the smartphone. In addition, some changes had to be made to the interface. In the smartwatch application, users react to a moment through an opinion and an emotional state, like they do in the smartphone application. However, the emotions assessment interface had to be adapted to fit the screen, without deviating much from the WeFeel' model [3]. Figure 6 shows the different screens that allow a user to share a match moment on the smartwatch, and react through an opinion and an emotion.

a)   b)   c)

Fig. 6. Sharing a video of a match moment through ReactIt using the smartwatch. (a) Initial screen where a moment can be registered. (b) Opinion selection screen. (c) Emotion selection screen.

Notifications are an important feature in smartwatches since they allow to perceive important information with gentle alerts on the wrist (like small vibrations and alert sounds). That is why ReactIt also has a notification control system in the smartwatch. As already mentioned, a user can receive two types of notifications (Fig. 7): when a friend shared a moment and he wants to know the user's reaction, and another to inform the user about a friend's reaction to a moment he shared.

a)   b)

Fig. 7. Different types of notifications used on the smartwatch application. (a) User receiving a push notification when a friend shared a moment. (b) User receiving a push notification when a friend reacted to a moment.

Just like the smartphone application, when a user receives a notification to react to a match moment, he can choose to see it later, through the "Dismiss" button or touch on the notification, and watch the video containing the moment (which is something possible with an Apple Watch). Therefore, we included the possibility of watching the video through the smartwatch with a zoom effect (Fig. 8). This zoom cuts the sides of the video, but since in football the camera is always focused on the ball, the relevant video content are usually in the centre, so it is unlikely to miss a moment due to the lateral cuts of the video.

Fig. 8. Video with a modified resolution on the smartwatch.

The screens that contain the list of the different matches (Fig. 9a) and all the moments shared during a match (Fig. 9b) were adjusted taking into account the characteristics of the smartwatch. Because of the small screen space, the teams are identified by their abbreviation, since the full name would take up too much space or simply would not fit. Also for space reasons, the video thumbnail was removed and placed in the match moment details screen.

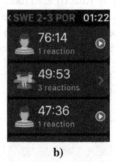

Fig. 9. (a) List of matches on the smartwatch. (b) List of moments shared during a match on the smartwatch.

The details of a match moment in the smartwatch application are presented differently than in the smartphone application. There are no tabs because they are inconsistent with the interface design for smartwatches, so a page-based navigation was used, where the user simply swipes left or right to see the details of a moment (Fig. 10).

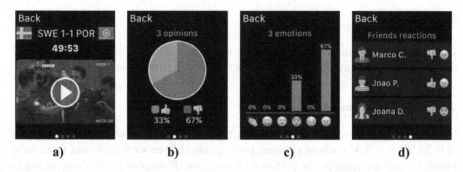

a)   b)   c)   d)

Fig. 10. Details of a match moment on the smartwatch application. (a) Accessing the video. (b) User' friends opinions pie chart. (c) Users worldwide emotions bar chart. (d) Friends' individual opinions and emotions.

Wearables typically have the capability to monitor user physiological data. At this stage, ReactIt was developed for Apple Watch, which contains a heart rate sensor. Since watching a sports event can be very emotional for the fans, ReactIt continuously captures the user's heart rate when watching a live broadcast. At the end of the match, the smartwatch application synchronizes the user's heart rate data with the smartphone, where the user can see a chart with the heart rate values throughout the match (Fig. 11), by accessing the user profile. This data shows in which moments of the match the user was more emotional. For now, this information is only for the curiosity of the users, but in the future we intend to relate it with the shared match moments and the corresponding emotions, and study those relations.

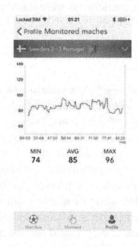

Fig. 11. User's heart rate throughout a match displayed on the smartphone application.

4   Evaluation

User tests were conducted to evaluate the concept provided by ReactIt, the users' reactions and the system usability, and to extract insights for future work.

4.1   Participants and Methodology

User tests were conducted with a total of thirty-one participants, with ages 17–45 years ($\bar{x} = 26.06$, $\sigma = 6.32$), where eighteen participants (fifteen were male and three were female) tested the smartphone prototype running on iPhones and thirteen participants (eleven were male and two were female) tested the smartwatch prototype running on an Apple Watch Series 0. Some of the test sessions were carried out with three participants using the system simultaneously, and some with two participants. Before starting the tests, we explained the ReactIt's concept to the participants, and during the tests, we observed the behaviour of the participants, took notes, and provided assistance if anyone had a problem.

ReactIt was tested in a room with a Smart TV in the centre where a football match was displayed. A summary of a match between the Portuguese national team and the Swedish national team from the qualifier for the FIFA World Cup 2014 was used during the tests. Some important moments of the game were selected and compiled in a 12-min video which contained fouls, dangerous plays and goals from both teams. All reactions during the tests were stored in the system, so in each test users could see the reactions of all the participants from the previous tests, that on a real environment would be all the users of the system.

After the match was finished, participants were asked to answer a questionnaire with which we evaluated the ReactIt's usability and entertainment value.

4.2   Questionnaire

Two questionnaires were created, one for the smartphone test and another for the smartwatch test, as there were some specific features of each device that we wanted to test. The questionnaires were divided into 3 sections. The first section included participants' personal data, such as age, sex, and some habits they had while watching sports events broadcasts on television. This section contained the same statements in both questionnaires. The second section focused on usability and entertainment aspects, where we intended to evaluate the entertainment concept provided by ReactIt, as well as usability and user experience aspects. This section had a few different statements in both questionnaires. And finally, the general aspects, where we wanted to know if the participants found the concept interesting and if they would use the application in a real life environment. The last two sections (2 and 3) comprised statements to be rated using a Likert-type scale, which ranged from 1 ("strongly disagree") to 5 ("strongly agree"). Table 1 presents section 2 statements for the smartphone questionnaire, Table 2 presents section 2 statements for the smartwatch questionnaire, and Table 3 presents section 3 statements, which are the same for the smartphone and the smartwatch questionnaires.

Table 1. Usability and entertainment section for the smartphone questionnaire.

Statements
2. Usability and entertainment
2.1. I immediately understood how to share a moment with my friends
2.2. I can quickly share a moment with my friends without losing focus on the match
2.3. I did not miss any important moment while sharing a match moment with my friends
2.4. It is easy to access my friends' reactions
2.5. It is easy to understand my friends' reactions
2.6. The notification colour helps distinguish between a friend asking for my reaction and a friend that reacted to a match moment I shared
2.7. I am likely to react to game moments shared by my friends during the match
2.8. I am likely to react to game moments shared by my friends during the half time or when the match ends
2.9. ReactIt makes me feel like I am watching the match with friends
2.10. Even if I was not watching the game on TV, I think I could be aware of the most important moments of the match through ReactIt

Table 2. Usability and entertainment section for the smartwatch questionnaire.

Statements
2. Usability and entertainment
2.1. I immediately understood how to share a moment with my friends
2.2. I can quickly share a moment with my friends without losing focus on the match
2.3. I didn't miss any important moment while sharing a match moment with my friends
2.4. It is easy to access my friends' reactions
2.5. It is easy to understand my friends' reactions
2.6. I was able to understand the content of the videos
2.7. I like the idea of being able to check my heart rate throughout the match
2.8. I'm likely to react to game moments shared by my friends during the match
2.9. I'm likely to react to game moments shared by my friends during the half time or when the match ends
2.10. ReactIt makes me feel like I am watching the match with friends
2.11. Even if I was not watching the game on TV, I think I could be aware of the most important moments of the match through ReactIt

Table 3. General aspects section for the smartphone and smartwatch questionnaires.

Statements
3. General aspects
3.1. I liked to use ReactIt
3.2. It is easy to learn how to use ReactIt
3.3. I find ReactIt an interesting concept

4.3   Results and Discussion

During the test sessions, users were free to share and react to any moments of the match. In total, 174 moments of the match were registered by the participants, and there was a total of 334 reactions to those registered moments. Figure 12 presents the relation between the most important moments of the match video and the number of reactions expressed by the participants.

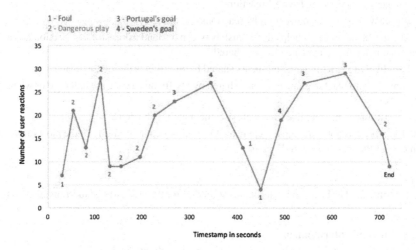

Fig. 12.   Relation between the most important moments on the video and the users' reactions.

In an analysis of the first section of both questionnaires (personal data and sports habits), we observed that the majority of the participants (51.6%) watch sports events on television on a weekly basis, 22.6% on a monthly basis, 16.1% watches it fortnightly, and only 9.7% rarely watches sports events on TV.

The most used devices by the participants during the broadcast of a sport event are the smartphone (71%), the computer (42%), and the tablet (29%). 16% of the participants stated they did not use any device. From the participants who use a device, 55% access social networks to perform activities related to the event, 48% browse the web, 39% participate in chat conversations, 23% exchange SMS with their friends, and only 3% make voice calls. These results show that users are used to interact with other viewers or their friends during live broadcasts on television.

Lastly, we have found out that 32% of the participants have the habit of discussing event situations frequently, through technological means, 32% only discuss sometimes, 20% rarely discuss, and 16% discuss very often.

Smartphone results.   Regarding the results of the usability and entertainment section of the smartphone questionnaire (Fig. 13), the results show that the vast majority of participants (77.7%) strongly agree that it is easy to understand how to share a moment of the match with friends (statement 2.1 in Table 1). The results of statements 2.2 and 2.3 were positive, but not as positive as we expected. Although most have agreed that

ReactIt allows one to quickly share a moment without losing focus on the match (statement 2.2), some have had a neutral response (22.2%) and others have disagreed (11,1%). Regarding the statement 2.3, 33.3% of the participants strongly agreed that they did not lose any important situation while sharing a moment of the match, 27.8% agreed, and 38.9% were neutral. Since the presented video was a compilation with some important moments of a match (not a complete match), it contained a greater frequency of important moments than a complete match. In this case, there was little time (only about 30–40 s) between two important moments, so participants did not have much time to share, react or explore the application without losing any important situation in the video. Instead, during a complete match, there are many more eventless periods in which users can take advantage of to react and explore the application.

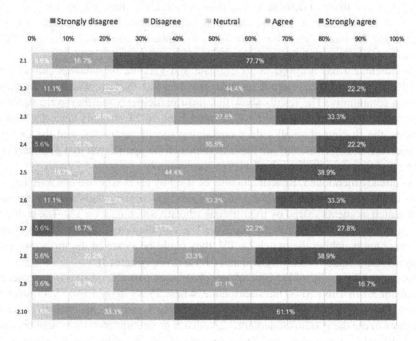

Fig. 13. Results from the usability and entertainment section of the smartphone questionnaire.

Most participants agreed (55.5%) that it was easy to access their friends' reactions (statement 2.4), and 22.2% strongly agreed. But there were also those who remained neutral (16.7%) and those who disagreed (5.6%). After the tests, in an informal conversation with the participants, we noticed that some of them did not realize that they could also access their friends' reactions by touching on the notifications they received. Despite this, participants were able to understand the different charts with the distribution of their friends' opinions and emotions (statement 2.5), where 38.9% strongly agreed and 44.4% agreed. Since notifications are an essential part of the application, it is important that they be as intuitive as possible. We also tried to understand, through statement 2.6, whether the different colours of the notifications helped the participants to identify the different types of notifications 33.3% of participants strongly agreed and another

33.3% agreed. There were participants with a neutral response (22.2%) and some disagreed (11.1%). In conversation with the participants, we understood that several participants immediately understood the different notification' types as soon as they received one of each type, others only realized after they have received several notifications.

With statements 2.7 and 2.8, we wanted to understand the participants' habits when using ReactIt. More precisely, when they are most likely to react to match moments shared by their friends. We found that 50% of the participants (27.8% strongly agree and 22.2% agree) stated that they were likely to react to match moments shared by their friends during the match, and 72.2% (38.9% strongly agree and 33,3% agree) stated that they were likely to react during the half time break, or after the match is over. We believe the answers to these statements were also negatively influenced by the video we presented. In a real match, it is expected that the users would use the application more often during the match, since there are a lot of eventless periods where users can take advantage to interact with the application.

Statement 2.9 has allowed us to evaluate and validate the concept provided by ReactIt. The idea of the system is to make fans feel like they are watching the match within a community. The results show that most participants felt they were watching the match with their friends, where 61.1% agreed and 16.7% strongly agreed. The notifications, the sharing of small videos containing specific moments, and the fact that reactions are shown in a chart are characteristics of the application that give users the feeling that they are watching the match in a community.

As already mentioned, ReactIt can also be used by users who are not watching the sports event. Since each moment has an associated video, they can visualize and react to the match moments shared by their friends who are watching it on TV. The results of the last statement (2.10) were very positive. The vast majority considered that even if they were not watching the match on TV, they could be aware of the most important moments of the match (33.3% agreed and 61.1% strongly agreed).

Regarding the results of the general aspects section, participants liked to use ReactIt (statement 3.1 in Table 3) on the smartphone, where 55.5% agreed and 38.9% strongly agreed. The vast majority of the participants strongly agreed (77.8%) that it is easy to learn how to use the system (statement 3.2). Also, a great enthusiasm was demonstrated during the tests. Almost everyone (44.4% agreed and 50% strongly agreed) found ReactIt an interesting concept (statement 3.3).

Smartwatch results. The results of the usability and entertainment section of the smartwatch questionnaire (Fig. 14) were also positive. The results show that all the participants immediately understood how to share a moment (statement 2.1 in Table 2), where 53.8% strongly agreed and 46.2% agreed. Since sharing a moment is an important feature in ReactIt, it is important to be as intuitive as possible.

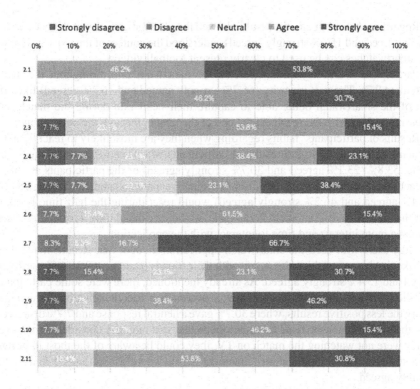

Fig. 14. Results from the usability and entertainment section of the smartwatch questionnaire.

As with the smartphone application, most participants were able to share moments of the match with friends without losing focus on the game (statement 2.2), where 30.7% strongly agreed and 46.2% agreed. Most of the participants also considered that they did not miss any important moment of the match while they were sharing moments (statement 2.3). The results to these statements were a little more positive for the smartwatch, which may indicate that this device is more suitable for this type of interaction (a possibility we need to further explore).

The results of the smartwatch regarding statements 2.4 and 2.5 were mostly positive. 61.5% (38.4% agreed and 23.1% strongly agreed) of the participants considered it easy to access friends' reactions (statement 2.4), as well as 61.5% (23.1% agreed and 38.4% totally agreed) of the participants were able to understand their friends' reactions (statement 2.5). But there were also participants who had a less positive feedback. During the course of the tests, we noticed that most users, upon receiving a notification with a reaction from a friend, did not touch on it to view the different charts with the distribution of the reactions, unlike participants who used a smartphone did. We believe that the fact that the participants were not familiar with the device (as acknowledged from the first section of the questionnaire regarding the personal data and sports habits) contributed to the less positive results regarding statement 2.4 and consequently of statement 2.5.

Regarding statement 2.6, the results showed that the vast majority of the participants (61.5% agreed and 15.4% strongly agreed) understood the content of the videos, showing that smartwatches can be used to clearly present football videos.

Participants were very enthusiastic to see their heart rate throughout the match (statement 2.7). The vast majority (66.7% strongly agreed and 16.7% agreed) liked the idea of the smartwatch being able to capture their heart rate during the match, and accessing a chart with the results at the end of the match, through the smartphone.

Results of participants' habits regarding when they are most likely to react to match moments, were similar to the results of participants who tested ReactIt on the smartphone. 53.8% (23.1% agreed and 30.7% strongly agreed) of the participants are likely to react to moments shared by their friends during the match (statement 2.8), and 84.6% (38.4% agreed and 46.2% strongly agreed) would react during the half time break or after the match is over (statement 2.9). Again, we believe that during a real match, users will have more interest and time to interact with the application.

Most users who used the smartwatch application thought that ReactIt made them feel like they were watching the match with their friends (statement 2.10), where 46.2% agreed and 15.4% strongly agreed. As already mentioned, there were some participants who did not immediately understood how to access their friends' reactions, which may justify the less positive results, where 30.7% gave a neutral response and 7.7% disagreed. Like the participants who used the smartphone, the vast majority considered that, even if they were not watching the match on TV, they could be aware of the most important moments through the application (statement 2.11), where 53.8% agreed and 30.8% strongly agreed.

Regarding the results of the general aspects section, participants also liked to use ReactIt (statement 3.1 in Table 3) on the smartwatch (61.5% agreed and 30.8% strongly agreed). Although the majority found that the system is easy to learn by using the smartwatch application (30.8% agreed and 46.2% strongly agreed), there were some participants who had a less positive opinion (15.4% were neutral and 7.6% disagreed). The results of the statement 3.3 were similar to the ones obtained for the smartphone application. Participants found ReactIt an interesting concept, with the results divided by approximately 50% between strongly agree and agree.

Finally, when informally asked, users promptly considered the video feature (the possibility of watching a video of an important moment of the match) as the most distinctive feature that would make them use ReactIt over other social applications they use to exchange comments and opinions while watching a TV show.

5 Conclusions and Future Work

This paper presents a system that enables sports fans to have a more social and enjoyable experience while watching sports events on television. It allows users to share automatic generated videos, that contains a specific moment of a football match, with their friends in a simple and non-intrusive way, in order to create social interactions between the fans. This feature not only allows users that are watching the match to later analyse all the match moments, but it also allows users that cannot watch the match (and would like to), to follow the match and to be aware of its important moments.

The feedback received during the tests was very positive. The vast majority of the users considered that ReactIt was easy to learn and they liked to use both devices. They also found it an interesting concept and were very enthusiastic about using it in a real life environment, such as watching a football match on TV in the comfort of their sofa. This satisfaction was evident not only on the users who tested ReactIt on the smartphone, but also on those who used the smartwatch application. This is very encouraging since so far this device has not been so much explored in the development of second screen applications. Furthermore, with the feedback we received, we could validate the idea that these devices can also have a place in the second screen applications world. Although the results of the user tests were very encouraging, further tests should be performed in the future to overcome the limitations of the accomplished ones, such as testing the application during a real life football match TV broadcast (90 min) with different users interacting with the applications at the same time in different locations, to evaluate their experience in a real environment.

The tests were performed in a controlled environment, and therefore we did not take into account the fact that users may be watching the match on different TV providers, and the broadcast delays of the match, since at this stage, the focus was to test the concept with the different devices and see how users interact with them. In the future we intend to explore a possible synchronization mechanism to fix the problem regarding the broadcast delays, and at the same time adapt the aggregation algorithm used when different users register the same moment, so it can work on a real environment with thousands of simultaneous users.

We explored this concept in the context of football, as it is one of the most watched sports in the world, but this concept can be applied to any sport, or other TV broadcast genre, that users would like to exchange opinions and emotions about.

Acknowledgements. This work is funded by FCT/MEC NOVA LINCS PEst UID/CEC/ 04516/2013.

References

1. Debate. Is technology good for our society? http://bit.ly/29qhgcJ. Last accessed 31 July 2017
2. Businessinsider. What People Are Really Doing When They Pretend to Watch TV (2014). http://read.bi/1mc88Lw. Last accessed 31 July 2017
3. Centieiro, P., Cardoso, B., Romão, T., Dias, A.E.: If you can feel it, you can share it!: a system for sharing emotions during live sports broadcasts. In: Proceedings of the 11th Conference on Advances in Computer Entertainment Technology (ACE 2014), Article No. 15 (2014)
4. Shirazi, A.S., Rohs, M., Schleicher, R., Kratz, S., Schmidt, A.: Real-time nonverbal opinion sharing through mobile phones during sports events. In: Proceedings of the SIGCHI Conference on Human Factors in Computing Systems (CHI 2011), pp. 307–310. ACM Press (2011)
5. Statista. Statistics and facts on second screen usage. http://bit.ly/29lu3kF. Last accessed 31 July 2017

6. Morales, G.D.F., Shekhawat, A.: The future of second screen experience. In: Workshop on Exploring and Enhancing the User Experience for Television (CHI 2013) (2013)
7. Schirra, S., Sun, H., Bentley, F.: Together alone: motivations for live tweeting a television series. In: Proceedings of the SIGCHI Conference on Human Factors in Computing Systems (CHI 2014), pp. 2441–2451 (2014)
8. Murkherjee, P., Wong, J., Jansen, B.: Patterns of social media conversations using second screens. In: Proceedings of the International Conference on BigData/SocialCom/CyberSecurity (ASE 2014) (2014)
9. Wohn, D.Y., Na, E.: Tweeting about TV: sharing television viewing experiences via social media message streams. First Monday **16**, 3–7 (2011)
10. Nielsen. Super Bowl 50: Nielsen Twitter TV Ratings Post-Game Report (2016). http://bit.ly/1O3ttyb. Last accessed 31 July 2017
11. Cardoso, B., Romão, T., Correia, N.: CAAT: a discrete approach to emotion assessment. In: Proceedings of the SIGCHI Conference on Human Factors in Computing Systems Extended Abstracts (CHI EA 2013), pp. 1047–1052. ACM Press (2013)
12. Plutchik, R.: The nature of emotions. In: Emotion: Theory, Research, and Experience. Theories of Emotion, vol. 1, pp. 35–56. Academic Press, New York (1980)
13. Lee, S., Heere, B., Chalip, L.: Identifying emotions associated with professional sport team brands. In: Proceedings of the Conference of the North American Society for Sport Management (NASSM 2013), Hackney, pp. 390–391 (2013)

Picognizer: A JavaScript Library for Detecting and Recognizing Synthesized Sounds

Kazutaka Kurihara[1(✉)], Akari Itaya[1], Aiko Uemura[2], Tetsuro Kitahara[2],
and Katashi Nagao[3]

[1] Department of Computer Science, Tsuda University, 2-1-1, Tsuda-machi, Kodaira-shi,
Tokyo 187-8577, Japan
kurihara@tsuda.ac.jp, m17aitay@gm.tsuda.ac.jp
[2] Department of Information Science, Nihon University, 3-25-40 Sakurajosui, Setagaya-ku,
Tokyo 156-8550, Japan
{uemura,kitahara}@chs.nihon-u.ac.jp
[3] Department of Media Science, Graduate School of Information Science, Nagoya University,
Furo-cho, Chikusa-ku, Nagoya 464-8601, Japan
nagao@nuie.nagoya-u.ac.jp

Abstract. In this paper, we describe and evaluate Picognizer, a JavaScript library that detects and recognizes user-specified synthesized sounds using a template-matching approach. In their daily lives, people are surrounded by various synthesized sounds, so it is valuable to establish a way to recognize such sounds as triggers for invoking information systems. However, it is not easy to enable end-user programmers to create custom-built recognizers for each usage scenario through supervised learning. Thus, by focusing on a feature of synthesized sounds whose auditory deviation is small for each replay, we implemented a JavaScript library that detects and recognizes sounds using traditional pattern-matching algorithms. We evaluated its performance quantitatively and show its effectiveness by proposing various usage scenarios such as an autoplay system of digital games, and the augmentation of digital games including a gamification.

Keywords: Audio event detection and recognition · Template matching
Digital games · Gamification

1 Introduction

In their daily lives, people are surrounded by various synthesized sounds, such as sound effects in digital games, traffic instructions, advertisements, and state notifications of home electrical appliances and information devices. We define synthesized sounds as sounds replayed by machines, such as computers, whose auditory deviation is small for each replay. An electronic voice that records and replays speech is also categorized as a synthesized sound.

When a detector or a recognizer is provided to reuse these synthesized sounds not only as signals to people but as inputs to a computer system, standalone electrical appliances in today's living environment can be linked with various internet services and the

© Springer International Publishing AG, part of Springer Nature 2018
A. D. Cheok et al. (Eds.): ACE 2017, LNCS 10714, pp. 339–359, 2018.
https://doi.org/10.1007/978-3-319-76270-8_24

Internet of Things (IoT) network. This will greatly enrich people's daily lives. This is a contribution to the entertainment computing community and the development of the maker movement, which has gained momentum in recent years.

In this paper, we focus on detecting and recognizing sound effects in digital games as a kind of synthesized sound. Augmenting digital games using sound effect detection and recognition can add new entertainment value to existing digital games or achieve nongame purposes, such as social welfare. The latter has been called the toolification of games, a peripheral concept of gamification that Kurihara [1] proposed. It has been difficult to realize the development of augmented systems reusing existing digital games because of matters of intellectual property rights and because of the difficulty gaining source code. With our proposed technology, however, it becomes possible to gain the inner state of a game from an external attachment instead of from gaining and editing the original source code and to process the information based on what is gained.

Recently, considerable progress has been made in the field of pattern recognition as a key technology for detecting and recognizing sounds. In this, supervised machine learning using deep learning has made particularly impressive progress [2], although it requires the collection of a massive data set, a labeling effort, and a large amount of computational resources. Thus, end-user programmers who want to introduce such recognition technology currently use recognizers or APIs developed and released by the companies or research institutions with such resources. These recognizers are usually designed not for recognizing user-specified sounds but for recognizing versatile sounds, such as spontaneous speech.

However, these state-of-the-art technologies are not necessarily required for detecting and recognizing synthesized sounds, such as the sound effects in digital games. This is because satisfactory accuracy can be achieved using traditional template-matching approaches because of the small auditory deviation of each replay. Unfortunately, an easy-to-use library that can detect and recognize synthesized sounds using a traditional template-matching approach on a web browser has not yet been developed or reported in the literature.

In this paper, we propose Picognizer, an easy-to-use JavaScript library that detects and recognizes synthesized sounds[1]. With this library, a user-specified target sound and sound collected through a microphone are analyzed to extract common audio features, such as the power spectrum, and compared using a matching algorithm, such as dynamic time warping, to calculate a cost. When the cost is below a threshold, we consider the target sound to be detected.

We can also build a recognizer, i.e., an identifier that says which target is detected from multiple candidates, by calculating costs for the multiple targets and comparing them with one another. Hereafter, we use "detect" instead of "detect and recognize" to simplify the description when mentioning Picognizer's functionality, although it has the potential to create recognizers.

---

[1] A demo video of Picognizer is available from the following link: https://youtu.be/CoYJmNdxPNY.

After detection, various information systems can be triggered through internet services, such as myThings [3], which is an IFTTT-like service from Yahoo Japan, to control IoT devices, such as Sony MESH [4] (Fig. 1).

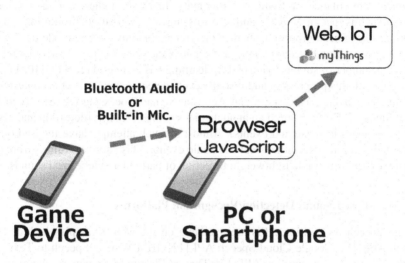

Fig. 1. Overview of Picognizer.

The library is written only in the client-site JavaScript, so users can use the library in their web browser without installing anything. In addition, the library is written in Node.js, which is currently under development, and will run on small computers, such as the Raspberry Pi, so gadgets can be developed for the detection of synthesized sound.

In this paper, we report the implementation of the prototype and its evaluation with so-called 8-bit sound sources, such as the Nintendo Entertainment System. We focus on 8-bit sound sources because it is relatively easy to design an application for gamification despite its acoustic simplicity.

The rest of this paper is composed as follows. In the next section, we look at related work. Then we describe details of the implementation of our proposed system and the evaluation of its fundamental performance. Then we show various use case scenarios. Finally, we discuss some points for improvement and future work.

2 Related Work

2.1 Audio Event Detection/Sound Event Detection

Although the recognition of sounds not limited to speech and music has attracted relatively little attention until recently, the number of attempts to recognize nonspeech/nonmusical sounds is increasing. In particular, the detection of certain sounds from an auditory scene (called audio event detection/sound event detection) has garnered great attention. Cai et al. [5] detected some highlighted sound effects (specifically, laughter, applause, and cheers) using a hidden Markov model toward movie summarization.

Pikrakis et al. [6] studied gunshot detection in the context of violence detection in movies. They used Bayesian networks to classify eight sound classes, such as gunshot, music, speech, and screams. Harma et al. [7] investigated the use of acoustics to achieve automatic surveillance of living environments. In these studies, common acoustic features, such as spectra, MFCCs, and zero crossing rates, were used. In addition, various techniques have been proposed, such as hierarchical auditory scene modeling [8] and sparse representation based on nonnegative matrix factorization [9]. As in other related fields, the number of studies that use deep learning has increased recently [10, 11].

Along with this progress in audio/sound event detection studies, some contest-style attempts have begun. The Audio and Acoustic Signal Processing (AASP) Technical Committee of IEEE has started an annual contest called DCASE (detection and classification of acoustic scene and events). Almost all such attempts have focused on the robust and accurate detection of real-life audio events. This approach differs from ours in that we focus on simple lightweight detection of particular synthesized sounds.

2.2 Web-Based Sound Detection/Recognition Platforms

Various speech recognition APIs are available on the web. Examples include Bing Speech API [12], Google Cloud Speech API [13], IBM Watson Speech to Text [14], and docomo speech recognition API [15]. These APIs aim to recognize general speech using a large-scale training data set and advanced machine learning techniques; they do not aim to detect particular user-specified sounds.

When users input musical audio signals using the built-in microphone on their smartphone, they can determine the name of the song being played using a web service such as Shazam [16]. The recent popularization of electronic music distribution has increased the need for such services. Shazam's web API is not open to the public at the moment; the API may become open and be used for developing various services in the near future.

2.3 Implementation of Sound Recognition/Detection in IoT Devices

Amazon Echo [17] and Listnr [18] are IoT devices for audio recognition. Their mechanism is as follows. The IoT microphone constantly picks up surrounding sounds. These sounds are processed through cloud-based audio recognition; as a result, various internet services start to work cooperatively. The main idea behind this application is to pick up speech, but it is an open system to which users can add their own audio recognition system, so various applications are possible. Our proposed system can also introduce and use this device as an additional audio recognition terminal, so both can coexist.

MagicKnock [19] has the same hardware composition as an IoT microphone device but collects and detects vibration patterns of users' knocks against the side that is set and uses these data as inputs for some information systems.

2.4 Programming Environment

Sikuli [20] is a Python programming environment that enables GUI automation, such as clicking a specific icon with a mouse. By taking a screenshot of an icon and putting that screenshot directly into the programming code, users can command that this image be targeted. When the programming works, it conducts image detection using template matching. The difference between this system and our proposed system is that the former is targeted to images whereas the latter is targeted to sounds; however, both augment existing ready-made systems as external attachments. The image- and audio-based augmentations of existing systems are possible using Sikuli together with our proposed system.

IFTTT [21] and myThings are simplified programming services that enable description of control of IoT devices or various web services using IF-THEN rules, i.e., the combination of a trigger condition and an invoked action. These services are designed for end-user programmers to use in their daily lives. Using the meshblu server, an MQTT message broker server, users can connect our proposed system with myThings.

Srt.js [22] is a framework that enables users to readily augment video content by embedding JavaScript with its execution time schedule as a form of subtitle information in YouTube videos. Srt.js is relevant to this study because both systems are client-side JavaScript frameworks that augment existing content as external attachments.

3 Picognizer

3.1 Implementation

Picognizer is a library that detects synthesized sounds written only in JavaScript. It works in web browsers that can manage microphone inputs with *getUserMedia*. Operation checks have been done in Firefox and Chrome for Windows and Mac PCs and in Firefox for Android. In addition, implementation of a Node.js version is currently under development so that it will be able to be used on small computers, such as the Raspberry Pi.

The system workflow of Picognizer is shown in Fig. 2. When the target sound source is inputted in the form of a wav or mp3 file, with the common processing steps, such as normalization and a low-pass filter, the JavaScript library Meyda [23] extracts 17 kinds of auditory features as a vector, including the power spectrum and MFCC. The same extraction of the feature vector for the microphone input is processed when detection starts.

The target feature vector and the input feature vector are compared using dynamic time warping or direct comparison, and their distance, the so-called cost, is calculated. To implement dynamic time warping, we extended dtw [24], an npm (a common package manager for Node.js) package of one-dimensional dynamic time warping, to multiple dimensions. The direct comparison method does not consider expansion and contraction of the input sound data and the target sound data as dynamic time warping does; instead, it compares those sound data naïvely per frame and calculates their cost. If the cost is below a threshold, we consider the target sound to be detected.

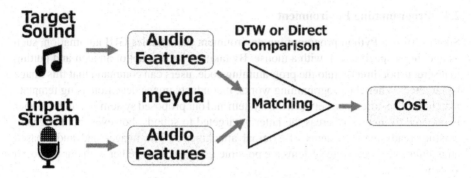

Fig. 2. Workflow of Picognizer.

In both dynamic time warping and direct comparison, it is necessary to define the distance function between the feature vectors to calculate the cost in each frame. For the situation in which the target sound is included but other sound is also mixed, we define and use the following asymmetric distance function, *Asym_Dist*.

$$Asym\_Dist(\textbf{target}, \textbf{input}) = Dist(\textbf{target}, Mask(\textbf{target}, \textbf{input})) \tag{1}$$

In this function, **target** is the target feature vector, **input** is the input sound's feature vector, and *Dist(A,B)* is the Euclidian distance between vector **A** and vector **B**. *Mask(A,B)* is a vector made by masking vector **B** with vector **A**. $Mask_i$ (**A,B**), the ith element of *Mask(A,B)*, is defined as follows:

$$Mask_i(\mathbf{A}, \mathbf{B}) = min(\mathbf{A}_i, \mathbf{B}_i) \tag{2}$$

Figure 3 is a graphical explanation of this function.

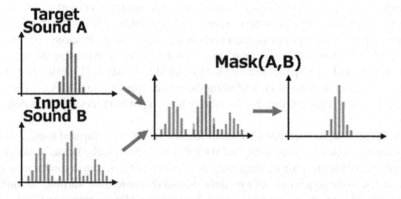

Fig. 3. Graphical explanation of *Mask(A,B)*. Naïvely comparing target *A* with input *B* results in low performance when *B* contains noise derived from sources such as background music. To exclude the noise, *Asym_Dist* calculates the Euclidean distance between *A* and *Mask(A,B)*.

3.2   How to Use

Use in Web Browsers. This section explains how to use Picognizer in web browsers. It is not necessary to install anything to use Picognizer. Simply by accessing the following URL one can use Picognizer.

https://qurihara.github.io/picognizer/script.html?cri=10&surl=http://xxx.net/bg_red.js&src=http://zzz.com/target.mp3

Table 1 shows all configuration parameters that the user can specify as the query string.

Table 1. Detection parameters for browser-based Picognizer.

Parameter	Description
src	Target sound file URL (.wav or .mp3)
st, et	Start time and end time for slicing the target audio file to apply
surl	JavaScript file URL executed on detection
cri	Threshold value for cost
mode	Cost calculation algorithm ("dtw" or "direct" for direct comparison)
wfunc	Window function [default; "hamming" for Hamming window)
ft	Meyda audio feature (default: powerSpectrum)
frame	Interval for each feature extraction (default: 0.02)
dur	Interval for each cost calculation (default: 1.0)

In this example, the target sound file is designated by the *src* parameter, the threshold of the cost is designated by the *cri* parameter, and the JavaScript file that is executed when the cost is below the threshold is designated by the *surl* parameter. Figure 4 shows the screenshot when a user accesses the URL. When the user clicks or taps the "Picognize" button and allows the browser to use its microphone, detection is activated. On the screen, the time series history and threshold of the cost are shown graphically, and the user can adjust the threshold to an appropriate level using the slide bar. The following script is an example that turns the color of the background screen red when a sound is detected.

```
setup = function(){
  console.log("Initialized.");
}
onfire = function(){
  document.bgColor = 'red';
}
```

Here the *setup* function is executed when the website is loaded, and the *onfire* function is executed when the cost gets below the threshold. In this way, Picognizer can embed all of the necessary information for detecting synthesized sounds as a URL text. Thus, it is easy to save and share the information with others.

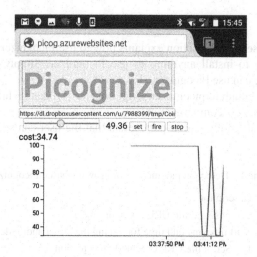

Fig. 4. Screenshot of browser-based Picognizer.

Enabling execution of arbitrary JavaScript is possible but may generate security concerns. To alleviate these worries, we have developed a way to add a security measure by limiting its use. The main function of Picognizer is to connect with various IoT devices and internet services using the detection of a synthesized sound as its starting point. The following URL realizes this by limiting the approved action after detection to sending a trigger to Meshblu server, an MQTT message broker.

https://qurihara.github.io/picognizer/trigger.html?cri=33&src=http://zzz.com/target.mp3&myuuid=XXXXXX&mytoken=YYYYYY&server=192.168.0.1

Here server, myuuid, and mytoken are the account information needed to connect to Meshblu. When this information is inserted, Picognizer can be linked with various IoT devices connected to the same Meshblu server and can be connected with myThings, enabling easy collaboration with various internet services.

Fig. 5. Screenshot of browser-based Picognizer with the recording UI.

We have also developed usage targeting the scenario to begin from the recording of the target sound in the real world using a microphone. As the following example shows, when the user accesses the following URL, the UI for recording on the browser appears (Fig. 5).

https://qurihara.github.io/picognizer/reco.html?myuuid=XXXXXX&mytoken=YYYYYY&server=192.168.0.1

Direct JavaScript Coding. Instead of using the ready-made website shown in the previous section, users can code JavaScript directly. In this way, users have more detailed control over actions, such as the setting of the low-level detection parameters or the simultaneous cost calculation of the several target sound sources. These can be described as follows.

```
var Pico = require('./Pico');
var P = new Pico;
var option = {
    windowFunc:"hamming",
    mode:mod,"direct",
    feature:["mfcc"],
    framesec:0.1,
    duration:1.0
};
P.init(option);
P.recognized(['audio1.mp3','audio2.mp3'],
    function(cost){
        //do something with an array of cost
});
```

Ways to Input Sounds. The inputting of sounds to Picognizer depends on how the targeted synthesized sound is replayed. When the targeted synthesized sound is replayed on a PC, preparing the virtual microphone device (sometimes called the stereo mixer device), which deals with the sound as input data through the microphone, makes it possible for Picognizer to detect the sound on the web browser working on the same PC without any disturbance by noise (Fig. 6). When the sound is generated by devices equipped with an audio output terminal socket, the influence of noise can be reduced by inputting the sound to the device that Picognizer is working on using appropriate audio cables. Figure 7 shows an example of a wired connection from the headphone terminal socket of a TV or monitor to the microphone input of a smartphone, and Fig. 8 shows an example of a wireless connection using a Bluetooth audio receiver. When the sound is replayed in other circumstances, the sounds generated in the real space are collected through the physical microphone connected with the device that Picognizer is working on. In this case, the influence of noise, such as from environmental sounds, is great, so careful preprocessing of the collected sound such as noise reduction and fine adjustment of the threshold may be necessary (Fig. 9).

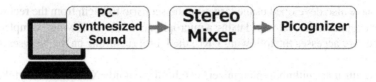

Fig. 6. Connection using a virtual microphone device on a PC.

Fig. 7. Connection with an audio cable.

Fig. 8. Connection with wireless Bluetooth audio.

Fig. 9. Connection with a physical speaker and a microphone through aerial sound transmission.

4   Basic Performance Evaluation

We evaluated Picognizer using the Nintendo Entertainment System game Super Mario Brothers. We chose this 8-bit sound source because it is relatively easy to design an application for gamification despite its acoustic simplicity. Namely, such 8-bit old games are useful and practical because they tend to be simple and therefore have rich "redundant spaces [1]," i.e., spatiotemporal opportunities for the coexistence of the player's behavior and another game/nongame element that differs from the optimized way to achieve the primary purpose of the game.

4.1 Test Data Set

We conducted four experiments. Detailed configurations of each experiment can be described as follows:

1. Detection of a target sound effect without BGM
2. Detection of a target sound effect mixed in a BGM
3. Detection of a target sound effect without BGM, allowing overlapping of another artifact sound effect
4. Detection of a target sound effect mixed in a BGM, allowing overlapping of another artifact sound effect.

The test data set for each experiment was constructed in the following manner. We chose three sound effects as our detection targets: getting a coin, a small jump, and getting a 1-up mushroom. Monaural 35 s length input sources with a sampling frequency of 22050 Hz were created to contain one of the three target sound effects at least five times, spread randomly. Nine sound effects in Super Mario Brothers, excluding the target sound effects, were chosen randomly as artifacts and repeatedly mixed into the input source. For experiments 1 and 2, no overlapping of multiple sound effects was allowed, although overlapping was allowed in experiments 3 and 4.

We chose three BGMs: outdoor stage BGM, underground stage BGM, and star BGM when Mario becomes invincible. After experiments 1 and 3, one of the three BGMs was mixed into the input sound source with the signal-to-noise (SN) rate set as 0 dB and 5 dB for experiments 2 and 4, respectively.

Finally, we manually labeled all onset times for the mixed sound effects, including the targets, and the artifacts for each input source so that the evaluation tool could determine them.

4.2 Methods

Our informal pilot evaluation showed that among various audio features, the power spectrum generally achieved the best performance for sound effect detection in Super Mario Brothers. Thus, we fixed the audio feature only to the power spectrum.

In each experiment, we compared the detection performance among various parameter combinations regarding the distance function and the cost calculation algorithm. We chose the Euclidean distance function and *Asym_Dist* as the distance function parameters and DTW and direct comparison as the cost calculation algorithm parameters.

We used a 64bit Windows7 machine (Intel Core i7-470K 3.5 GHz CPU, 16 GB RAM). All the computation was done in real time. The input sounds are captured by "stereo mixer," a Windows' virtual microphone device to prevent environmental noise. For each experiment, the power spectrum was extracted as the audio feature vector every 40 ms, and then we calculated the cost between the target sound effect and the input sound. We used a Python evaluation tool, mir_eval [25], to the test data set to compute recall, precision, and F-measure, with acceptable deviation in terms of the detected onset time of each sound effect of ± 50 ms from the actual time. We manually determined the threshold value to obtain the best recall in each condition. We did this because we believe that it is possible to reduce false positives in the future by integrating Picognizer with other technologies, such as Sikuli, which deals with visual detection.

4.3 Results

Tables 2, 3, 4 and 5 show the result of experiments 1 and 2. In the S/N [dB] column, clean corresponds to the results of experiment 1. Similarly, 5 dB and 0 dB correspond to the results of experiment 2. We compared the impacts of distance functions (Euclidean distance and *Asym_Dist*) and cost calculation algorithms (DTW and direct comparison), respectively.

Table 2. Results of Euclidean distance and DTW conditions in experiments 1 and 2.

Sound effect	BGM	S/N [dB]	F-measure	Precision	Recall
coin	outdoor	clean	0.750	0.750	0.750
		5	0.667	0.714	0.625
		0	0.545	1.000	0.375
jump	underground	clean	0.545	1.000	0.375
		5	0.462	0.600	0.375
		0	0.462	0.600	0.375
1up	star	clean	0.500	0.667	0.400
		5	0.500	0.667	0.400
		0	0.500	0.667	0.400

Table 3. Results of Euclidean distance and direct comparison conditions in experiments 1 and 2.

Sound effect	BGM	S/N [dB]	F-measure	Precision	Recall
coin	outdoor	clean	1.000	1.000	1.000
		5	0.875	0.875	0.875
		0	0.667	0.714	0.625
jump	underground	clean	0.889	0.800	1.000
		5	0.842	0.727	1.000
		0	0.842	0.727	1.000
1 up	star	clean	1.000	1.000	1.000
		5	1.000	1.000	1.000
		0	1.000	1.000	1.000

From these results, we can see that the combination of *Asym_Dist* and direct comparison achieved the best detection performance.

Next, Tables 6, 7, 8 and 9 show the results of experiments 3 and 4. Again, clean corresponds to the results of experiment 3. Similarly, 5 dB and 0 dB correspond to the results of experiment 4. We again compared the impacts of distance functions (Euclidean distance and *Asym_Dist*) and cost calculation algorithms (DTW and direct comparison), respectively.

Table 4. Results of *Asym_Dist* and DTW conditions in experiments 1 and 2.

Sound effect	BGM	S/N [dB]	F-measure	Precision	Recall
coin	outdoor	clean	0.750	0.750	0.750
		5	0.625	0.625	0.625
		0	0.400	0.429	0.375
jump	underground	clean	0.545	1.000	0.375
		5	0.400	1.000	0.250
		0	0.222	1.000	0.125
1 up	star	clean	0.444	0.500	0.400
		5	0.444	0.500	0.400
		0	0.100	0.067	0.200

Table 5. Results of *Asym_Dist* and direct comparison conditions in experiments 1 and 2.

Sound effect	BGM	S/N [dB]	F-measure	Precision	Recall
coin	outdoor	clean	1.000	1.000	1.000
		5	1.000	1.000	1.000
		0	0.933	1.000	0.875
jump	underground	clean	0.941	0.889	1.000
		5	0.889	0.800	1.000
		0	0.889	0.800	1.000
1 up	star	clean	1.000	1.000	1.000
		5	1.000	1.000	1.000
		0	1.000	1.000	1.000

Table 6. Results of Euclidean distance and DTW conditions in experiments 3 and 4.

Sound effect	BGM	S/N [dB]	F-measure	Precision	Recall
coin	outdoor	clean	0.600	0.857	0.462
		5	0.455	0.556	0.385
		0	0.421	0.667	0.308
jump	underground	clean	0.194	0.167	0.231
		5	0.200	0.176	0.231
		0	0.333	0.600	0.231
1 up	star	clean	0.444	0.667	0.333
		5	0.500	1.000	0.333
		0	0.235	0.182	0.333

Table 7. Results of Euclidean distance and direct comparison conditions in experiments 3 and 4.

Sound effect	BGM	S/N [dB]	F-measure	Precision	Recall
coin	outdoor	clean	0.870	1.000	0.769
		5	0.636	0.778	0.538
		0	0.636	0.778	0.538
jump	underground	clean	0.553	0.382	1.000
		5	0.867	0.765	1.000
		0	0.867	0.765	1.000
1 up	star	clean	1.000	1.000	1.000
		5	1.000	1.000	1.000
		0	1.000	1.000	1.000

Table 8. Results of *Asym_Dist* and DTW conditions in experiments 3 and 4.

Sound effect	BGM	S/N [dB]	F-measure	Precision	Recall
coin	outdoor	clean	0.636	0.778	0.538
		5	0.571	0.750	0.462
		0	0.333	0.600	0.231
jump	underground	clean	0.261	0.300	0.231
		5	0.267	1.000	0.154
		0	0.143	1.000	0.077
1 up	star	clean	0.400	0.500	0.333
		5	0.400	0.500	0.333
		0	0.400	0.500	0.333

Table 9. Results of *Asym_Dist* and direct comparison conditions in experiments 3 and 4.

Sound effect	BGM	S/N [dB]	F-measure	Precision	Recall
coin	outdoor	clean	0.870	1.000	0.769
		5	0.818	1.000	0.692
		0	0.762	1.000	0.615
jump	underground	clean	0.963	0.929	1.000
		5	0.963	0.929	1.000
		0	0.929	0.867	1.000
1 up	star	clean	1.000	1.000	1.000
		5	1.000	1.000	1.000
		0	1.000	1.000	1.000

From these results, we can again see that the combination of *Asym_Dist* and direct comparison achieved the best detection performance.

4.4   Discussion

Throughout the experiments, the combination of *Asym_Dist* and direct comparison achieved perfect 1.0 F-measure scores in many conditions and was never less than 0.762, which is considered a practical detection performance.

Regarding the distance functions, we can infer that the masking operation of *Asym_Dist* worked well to prevent lower performance due to the mixing of BGM and the artifacts. *Asym_Dist* is theoretically effective when the overlap between the spectrum of the target sound and the spectrum of nontarget sounds is small. We believe that the good characteristics of the sounds in Super Mario Brothers led to the success of this evaluation. Further studies are needed with other digital games with different audio characteristics.

Regarding the cost calculation algorithms, we can conclude that the direct comparison algorithm can use characteristics of synthesized sounds that do not stretch or shrink too much for each replay. However, this algorithm does not recover when the start time of the calculation is delayed or some frames are missing. Thus, to maximize the benefit, faster machines, such as modern notebook PCs, are required to minimize the *frame* and *dur* parameters in Table 1, which means frequent feature extractions and cost calculations to minimize the harmful effects of calculation delays and missing discriminative frames. However, although DTW requires more calculation overhead per cost computation than does direct comparison, it has a certain robustness against calculation delays and missing frames. Thus, the user may reduce the average calculation overhead using DTW with coarsened *frame* and *dur* parameters, which means a low-frequency cost calculation, to make the most of a low-speed machine, such as a smartphone, that cannot afford excessive calculations with direct comparison. Quantitative evaluations of this parameter optimization based on machine power will be addressed in future work.

5   Example Usage Scenarios

In this section, we describe some example usage scenarios for Picognizer, in particular those that have to do with the detection of sound effects in existing digital games.

5.1   Augmentation of Digital Games

Toolification of Games. Figure 10 shows an example of a real-world augmentation of the popular Nintendo Entertainment System game Super Mario Brothers. In this system, a real-world coin is ejected when the player obtains a coin in the game. Ejection of coins is realized by a servo motor controlled by a Sony MESH GPIO tag invoked by Picognizer, which detects the sound effect associated with obtaining a coin in the game. We can assume the ejection of coins to be a reward for the player when the system provides the real coins or a penalty, or an expense for the player when he or she must provide his or her own real coins. This system is a real-world implementation of Coins for Two, which allows a player to raise money for charity by playing Super Mario Brothers [1]. The system is typically used at charity events: A money collection box is placed below the coin ejector, and players can place their real coins in the ejector.

Fig. 10. An example of the toolification of games using Super Mario Brothers. Picognizer detects the sound effect associated with gaining a coin to eject a real coin.

The player can raise a sum of money based on coins obtained in the game. Thus, the player must survive to acquire more coins to donate more money. This transforms the value in raising money for charity, which may expose economic discrepancies, as the result of effort within the rules of a game that is fair for everyone. Specifically, players can raise money according to the results of their play, regardless of their economic status. This may encourage people to raise money because it may decrease hesitation among anyone, rich or poor, who may be sensitive to disclosing his or her economic status.

Kurihara [1] defined the toolification of games, a peripheral concept of gamification, as when augmentation of an existing game achieves nongame values, such as social welfare, as this example shows. Picognizer can help developers to implement the toolification of games readily without the burden of obtaining and modifying the source code of existing host games.

Integration with Philips Hue. Figure 11 shows an example of augmentation of a digital game. In this scenario, the popular smartphone game Monster Strike [26] was augmented with Philips Hue [27], an IoT lighting solution. Monster Strike alerts the player by generating a siren sound and changing the screen to red when a boss enemy appears. This augmentation system listens to the audio stream of the game and detects the alert sound to change the real-world lighting to red to enhance the entertainment value. In this case, a wired connection is not necessary because a Bluetooth audio connection is used between the smartphone and the PC on which Picognizer is working. This wireless functionality releases the player from any physical constraints of using Picognizer. This scenario can be applied to larger scale game events or parties in which a large number of participants play or watch digital games in a facility where the lighting and sound delivery systems are synchronized with the game play.

Fig. 11. An example of augmentation of the smartphone game Monster Strike. The real-world lighting, delivered by an IoT lighting solution, Philips Hue, turns red when the game alerts the player of the boss enemy's arrival.

5.2 Autoplay System for Digital Games

Figure 12 shows an autoplay system for QuickDraw, a game for Nintendo Switch 1-2-Switch [28]. In QuickDraw, a player wins when he or she pushes a button faster than the opponent after moving a pistol-like game controller to the horizontal direction. The game system synthesizes a "Fire!" sound as the starting signal while displaying "Fire!" text on the screen. The autoplay system listens to the audio stream of the game and detects this "Fire!" sound using Picognizer to rotate a game controller attached to an IoT motor, Webmo. The Webmo is fixed to a box built with Lego-like toy bricks that has a structure to push the button of the game controller when it rotates to the horizontal direction.

Fig. 12. An example of an autoplay system for QuickDraw, a game for Nintendo Switch. The game controller is manipulated physically by an IoT motor Webmo.

In this scenario, we applied Picognizer to a digital game to estimate the state of the game using only audio clues. With Picognizer and Sikuli, which can deal with visual clues, end-user developers can build autoplay systems for more complex games.

6 Discussion and Future Work

6.1 Support for Setting Parameters

In Picognizer, which uses traditional pattern matching, the cost (distance) between the target audio data and the input data is calculated automatically, whereas the threshold value of the cost (which determines whether the target sound has been detected) is set manually by users once when they configure a new detector. In the current implementation, the UI offers a slide bar to set the threshold and a graphical display of the cost, but there could be more detailed support. For example, the system could estimate a threshold value by observing both negative examples that do not contain the target sound and positive examples that do contain the target sound.

In addition, for users unfamiliar with audio detection, it would be helpful to implement a wizard that recommends features or detection parameters based on the properties of the targeted audio data, the performance of the user's machine, and the user's needs. More specifically, through dialogue, we could collect information on users' needs, such as whether they want to focus on replayed speech or the sound effects in digital games, or whether they want to increase recall at the cost of calculating overhead, or whether they want to manage the data using a low-power computer. These are matters for future work.

6.2 Extension to Sounds with More Complex Audio Properties

In this work, we targeted 8-bit sound sources, such as the Nintendo Entertainment System, to evaluate our prototype with no environmental noise. Synthesized sounds vary, and it is not easy to create high-quality detectors for every kind of target. Although the current prototype can also be applied to digital games that have more complex audio properties, as shown in Sect. 5, future work will focus on introducing the recent techniques proposed in the Music Information Retrieval research field and tuning to those sound sources and evaluating their performance.

6.3 Application to Synthesized Sounds in Nongame Contexts

In this work, we conducted a performance evaluation with a focus on sound effects in digital games. However, users may want to detect many other kinds of synthesized sounds. Although evaluations with a focus on such nongame synthesized sounds have not yet been conducted, the current prototype can be applied to such situations.

Figure 13 demonstrates one such application, which delivers push notifications to a smartphone when Picognizer detects a well-known alert sound synthesized by the McDonald's Japan's French fry potato fryer to tell the best time to finish cooking. It is an important research direction to evaluate the performance and interface design compared to other techniques for detecting synthesized sound, such as those summarized in the related work section above.

Fig. 13. An example of the detection of synthesized sounds in a nongame context. An alert sound from McDonald's French fry potato fryer is detected and a push notification is delivered to the user.

6.4 Toward Supervised Machine Learning

In this paper, we focus on a traditional template-matching approach that allows users to create custom-made synthesized sound detectors. When it becomes widely used, we will accumulate usage data for the browser-based Picognizer on the server. A promising future research direction is to create a versatile recognizer that is specially trained for synthesized sounds based on the usage data and state-of-the-art supervised machine learning techniques.

7   Conclusion

In this study, we developed Picognizer, a JavaScript library that enables end-user programmers to readily develop information systems by detecting synthesized sounds as the starting point. Here we evaluated its basic performance, suggested various applications for use, and discussed its effectiveness and future visions. We will extend the target to more complex and varied synthesized sounds and work on improving accuracy for sounds collected through a microphone along with environmental noise. We also aim to extend its use with the implementation of Node.js, which makes it possible to work with embedded devices. After we release Picognizer to the public, we will be committed to popularizing it and collecting examples of its use by holding workshops.

Acknowledgements. This work was supported by JSPS KAKENHI Grant Numbers JP15H02735, JP16H02867, JP17H00749.

References

1. Kurihara, K.: Toolification of games: achieving non-game purposes in the redundant spaces of existing games. In: Proceedings of ACE 2015, pp. 31:1–31:5 (2015)
2. Hinton, G., Deng, L., Yu, D., Dahl, G.E., Mohamed, A.R., Jaitly, N., Senior, A., Vanhoucke, V., Nguyen, P., Sainath, T.N., Kingsbury, B.: Deep neural networks for acoustic modeling in speech recognition: the shared views of four research groups. IEEE Signal Process. Mag. **29**(6), 82–97 (2012)
3. myThings. https://mythings.yahoo.co.jp/. Accessed 28 July 2017
4. Sony MESH. http://meshprj.com/. Accessed 28 July 2017
5. Cai, R., Lu, L., Zhang, H.-J., Cai, L.-H.: Highlight sound effects detection in audio stream. In: Proceedings of IEEE International Conference on Multimedia and Expo (ICME), vol. III, pp. 37–40 (2003)
6. Pikrakis, A., Giannakopoulos, T., Theodoridis, S.: Gunshot detection in audio streams from movies by means of dynamic programming and Bayesian networks. In: Proceedings of IEEE International Conference on Acoustics, Speech, and Signal Processing (ICASSP), pp. 21–24 (2008)
7. Harma, A., McKinney, M.F., Skowronek, J.: Automatic surveillance of the acoustic activity in our living environment. In: Proceedings of IEEE International Conference on Multimedia and Expo (ICME) (2005)
8. Imoto, K., Shimauchi, S.: Acoustic event analysis based on hierarchical generative model of acoustic event sequence. IEICE Trans. Inf. Syst. **E990D**(10), 2539–2549 (2016)
9. Lu, X., Yu, T., Matsuda, S., Hori, C.: Sparse representation based on a bag of spectral exemplars for acoustic event detection. Proceedings of IEEE International Conference on Acoustics, Speech, and Signal Processing (ICASSP), pp. 6255–6259 (2014)
10. Wang, Y., Neves, L., Metze, F.: Audio-based multimedia event detection using deep recurrent neural networks. In: Proceedings of International Conference on Acoustics, Speech, and Signal Processing (ICASSP) (2016)
11. Cakir, E., Parascandolo, G., Heittola, T., Huttunen, H., Virtanen, T.: Convolutional recurrent neural networks for polyphonic sound event detection. IEEE/ACM Trans. Audio Speech Lang. Process. **25**(6), 1291–1303 (2017)
12. Bing Speech API. https://azure.microsoft.com/ja-jp/services/cognitive-services/speech/. Accessed 28 July 2017
13. Google Cloud Speech API. https://cloud.google.com/speech/. Accessed 28 July 2017
14. IBM Watson Speech to Text. https://www.ibm.com/watson/developercloud/speech-to-text.html. Accessed 28 July 2017
15. Docomo Speech Recognition API. https://dev.smt.docomo.ne.jp/?p=docs.api.page&api_name=speech_recognition&p_name=api_usage_scenario. Accessed 28 July 2017
16. Shazam. https://www.shazam.com/. Accessed 28 July 2017
17. Amazon Echo. https://www.amazon.com/dp/B00X4WHP5E. Accessed 28 July 2017
18. Listnr. https://listnr.cerevo.com/ja/. Accessed 28 July 2017
19. MagicKnock. http://magicknock.com/. Accessed 28 July 2017
20. Yeh, T., Chang, T.-H., Miller, R.C.: Sikuli: using GUI screenshots for search and automation. In: Proceedings of UIST 2009, pp. 183–192 (2009)
21. IFTTT. https://ifttt.com/. Accessed 28 July 2017
22. Srt.js. http://www.unryu.org/top-english/srtjs. Accessed 28 July 2017
23. Rawlinson, H., Segal, N., Fiala, J.: Meyda: an audio feature extraction library for the web audio API. In: The 1st Web Audio Conference (WAC), Paris, France (2015)

24. Sakoe, H., Chiba, S.: Dynamic programming algorithm optimization for spoken word recognition. IEEE Trans. Acoust. Speech Signal Process. **26**, 43–49 (1978)
25. Raffel, C., McFee, B., Humphrey, E.J., Salamon, J., Nieto, O., Liang, D., Ellis, D.P.W.: mir_eval: a transparent implementation of common MIR metrics. In: Proceedings of the 15th International Conference on Music Information Retrieval (2014)
26. Monster Strike. http://us.monster-strike.com/. Accessed 28 July 2017
27. Philips Hue. https://www2.meethue.com. Accessed 28 July 2017
28. 1-2-switch. https://www.nintendo.co.jp/switch/aacca/. Accessed 28 July 2017

Towards an Emotion-Driven Adaptive System for Video Game Music

Manuel López Ibáñez[1](✉), Nahum Álvarez[2], and Federico Peinado[1]

[1] Department of Software Engineering and Artificial Intelligence,
Complutense University of Madrid, c/Profesor José García Santesmases 9,
28040 Madrid, Spain
manuel.lopez.ibanez@ucm.es, email@federicopeinado.com
[2] Artificial Intelligence Research Center, National Institute of Advanced Industrial
Science and Technology, 2-3-26 Aomi, Koto-ku, Tokyo 135-0064, Japan
nahum.alvarez@aist.go.jp

Abstract. Perfectly adaptive music is a long dreamed goal for game audio designers. Although numerous systems have been developed in both academic and industrial contexts, currently there is no unified method for producing this type of content – not even an agreement on input variables, output variations or assessment criteria. Our research aims to create an audio system for video games that improves the experience by adapting environmental music to emotions associated with the ongoing narrative. This system combines short audio tracks of pre-designed music in real time, using player behavior and emerging feelings as main cues. In this paper, we identify some of the issues that dynamic music faces through the study of current adaptive and procedural techniques, and describe how our sound system architecture attempts to solve them. In the end, we claim that a sonification method like the proposed one could improve player engagement by adapting music to each game situation, driven by a solid focus on emotional storytelling.

Keywords: Interactive digital storytelling · Affective computing
Player experience · Sound design · Procedural content generation

1 Introduction

Designing sound and music for video games has always been a task with an intrinsic difficulty. As in many other interactive experiences, sound designers and musicians cannot predict all possible outcomes, so video game music should be *dynamic*, that is, not designed with a fixed timeline in mind but aimed towards a large set of possible player actions, reactions and in-game situations.

Thus, it makes sense to create music that is not strictly responsive (as in a rhythm game) but "automatically adaptive" in some form, looking for an improved experience for the player, where ambient sound around him would fit his circumstances. Such capability moves audio production tasks closer to software system design, not being an isolated task for the musician anymore, but having a much tighter relationship with the overall game architecture.

So as to consider most issues and difficulties that current audio systems need to tackle, in the next section we review scientific literature on adaptive and procedural sound design, as well as on the role of emotions in player experience.

In Sect. 3 we identify the main issues of dynamic and procedural music composition and the solutions proposed until now. Section 4 contains a description of our system architecture, which aims to improve and unify current methods for adapting music in narrative video games, taking into account basic emotional changes of the story as a reference. This is illustrated with a dialogue between an in-game character and the player.

The last section outlines preliminary conclusions about improvements on player engagement that could be achieved with this emotion-driven adaptive system for dynamic music.

2   Adaptive Music and Basic Emotions

Recently, an increased interest in developing new models for the understanding of auditory perception has been developed. For example, Asutay et al. [1] provide an evaluation system which considers the emotional meaning attached to a sound as an important factor when identifying audio, along with signal characteristics.

Ekman [2] also states that designing sound for video games has to take into account the non-linear nature of the media, so as to improve the emotional response achieved during a gaming session. This author considers there is a "readiness to act" at the core of every emotion, and consequently, emotions prepare a player for certain types of actions. Thus, sound in video games should be centered on guiding these possible actions and adapting to them, instead of following a linearity of any kind. This "readiness to act" can also add coherence to emotions felt during gameplay.

One of our claims is that dynamic music design for games has to consider the emotional nature of audio, so a need arises: to have a simple taxonomy which allows to classify basic emotions felt by players during a standard gaming session. Paul Ekman designed a taxonomy including 5 basic emotions [3], widely used today. "Surprise", though not considered a basic emotion, is added as the sixth element of this list, as Ekman considers it perfectly describes a sudden change in feelings:

- Anger: Wrath, ire. Generates displeasure and inclination to belligerence.
- Disgust: Repugnance, aversion. Implies distaste for something.
- Fear: Urgency to avoid a certain situation which can inflict pain, damage, anxiety or simple aversion.
- Joy: Being delighted, glad, fortunate or pleased by something or someone.
- Sadness: Sorrow, unhappiness and grief. The feeling associated to dark, negative or bad things.

- Surprise: A sudden and unexpected feeling. Associated to discovery or learning without warning, whether the discovered piece of information is negative or positive.

Although Paul Ekman himself and other authors have identified many more subtle and complex emotions, the simplicity and universality of this list makes it suitable for our needs, as it would make the process of sorting sounds according to emotions and desirable player reactions a task achievable in most game scenarios.

Yanagisawa and Murakami [4] even propose a system to quantify emotional quality ("*kansei* quality") of a sound, by using certain parameters like "strong", "silent", "dull" or "hard" in a survey taken by neutral subjects. Though being applied to physical product design in the mentioned article, this method could be of use in video games if utilised properly. For example, we can increase the level of fear induced by an atonal melody by raising its intensity.

Besides, Jørgensen [5] points out that game audio has a dual role: on one hand, it serves the purpose of supporting the general feeling of an environment ("ambient music"); on the other, it gives players pieces of information about the game. A *layered* audio design system may then be appropriate, because it would make easy to select a set of sound tracks that fulfill both the requirements of the environment and the characters.

As will be explained in the next section, numerous music design systems have tried to adjust to events happening in-game and to player emotions. However, most initiatives are merely environmental – they depend on a change of scenery or a cinematic sequence to work properly. This usually happens due to two main reasons: lack of human resources or insufficient computational capacity. Our proposal aims to slightly decrease human intervention while greatly decreasing computational needs when composing layered, fully adaptive music for video games.

3   Problems of Current Dynamic Music Systems

The interactive entertainment industry offers many cases of *ad hoc* systems for generating dynamic music. Modern examples include the vertical re-orchestration of Red Dead Redemption, which uses a large pool of "music stems", all recorded in A minor at 130 beats per minute in order to be easily combined. Tomb Raider Legend developed the concept of micro-scoring for adapting its more than 180 min of music to different game characters and environments; Halo[1] series combines vertical and horizontal techniques with some randomization in its proprietary audio engine, etc.

Though dynamic audio design is a valued asset in this industry, as all previous examples show, most of the time it is achieved in a traditional, non-adaptive manner. Dynamic audio design techniques are more expensive, and have a practical limitation: because it is not possible to predict every potential in-game situation, an undetermined amount of "sound holes" or inconsistencies may

---

[1] https://www.halowaypoint.com.

appear during the experience unless a completely adaptive approach is taken. Classic dynamic music is usually associated with seamlessly changing between different audio environments or scripted situations [6]. What we propose, however, is to fully adapt to player actions, even when there is not a way to predict what could happen during gameplay.

On the other hand, Collins [7] states that the major handicap of procedural music in current video games is available technology. As most of these methods produce a lower quality result in terms of audio fidelity, producers are worried about reducing the level of player immersion. Besides, system performance lowers considerably when using procedurally generated sound and music, which becomes a problem when playing on low-end equipment, like game consoles or mobile devices. Even popular game engines like Unreal Engine[2] understand procedural audio as an experimental, uncommon feature, which offers low quality results.

Jewell, Nixon and Prügel-Bennett [8] try to improve the complexity and general quality of procedurally-generated music by adding semantic information to genetic algorithms, achieving better results. Nevertheless, this technique cannot be applied to real-time gaming, due to their processing cost and the level of adjustment needed to achieve a sufficiently good piece of music.

Luhtala et al. [9] find another interesting solution to the problem of audio quality in procedural music by adding a variety of synth modules to their system, in a way that makes it possible to process "raw" generated data by using Virtual Studio Technology (VST) instruments, among other techniques. Again, the same problem emerges from this approach: the processing power required for utilising high quality VSTs in multiple tracks while generating dynamic music is such that a commercial game with state-of-the-art graphics could not run, even on a current high-end system.

Another interesting issue was noted by Böttcher et al. [10], who found a clear lack of attention from most users to sound quality and music composition when they are playing. We also observed this effect in a previous experiment with users of a Virtual Reality demo [11]. Emotions arise as a side effect of music and, as stated by Eladhari [12], sound does not have a protagonist role in a video game unless it conveys important, gameplay-related information.

Lastly, Livingstone and Brown [13] stand up for the need of a sound system that allows to dynamically adjust music in a video game depending on player emotions. This would bring a "cinematic" feel to video game soundtracks, thus improving the perception of music in video game production. We followed this suggestion when proposing our adaptive system for dynamic music.

4 Proposal of an Emotion-Driven Adaptive System

Our take on the problems mentioned above is materialized on a system that allows to create audio atmospheres which adapt to the emotions arisen during

---

[2] https://www.unrealengine.com/what-is-unreal-engine-4.

a gaming session. This system does not generate music from scratch, due to limitations found in procedural techniques; instead, it combines pre-designed fragments of music (in the form of short sound tracks) to achieve the desired effect, avoiding the problem of low-fidelity sound. In its current version, the system is meant to work with in-game dialogues that allow the player to confront different characters and emotional situations, choosing from a variety of possible responses.

The proposed architecture (see Fig. 1) works as follows:

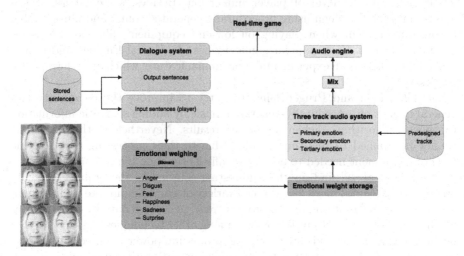

Fig. 1. Architecture of our emotion-driven adaptive music system. Photos from Bennett and Šabanović [14].

- The game engine includes a dialogue system which the user can interact with in two ways: receiving messages from a non-player character (NPC) (*text output*) and choosing answers to those messages (*input choice*) from a series of options.
- The dialogue system takes information from a database of tree-form short dialogues. These dialogues are designed by a human, and try to induce a variety of emotional responses in the player. In our initial configuration, the player can choose from 3 different answers each time a text output is shown on screen, representing the expression of a feeling.
- Every possible answer has an "emotional weighing", containing a real value in a range from 0 to 1 for one of the 6 basic emotions of Ekman [3]. For example, receiving a declaration of war will have an anger value of 1, and watching a butcher work will have a disgust value of 0.5.
- The "emotional weights" of characters' messages and player choices are stored, so that the system can remember the emotional context of a playing session. With each addition, the stored basic emotion variables with a higher value in the last seconds of gameplay are selected. Our intention is to select

a maximum of 3 concurrent emotions (that correspond to 3 different music tracks) depending on their accumulated weight.

- We establish a maximum of 3 tracks for two reasons: Sometimes, emotions can overlap (e.g. anger and disgust generate loathing), which means at least 2 simultaneous tracks are needed to create such a complex atmosphere. Besides, we add a third track so as to be able to include remembrance in the experience. If, for example, our chosen tracks are prioritized in the following order: anger, disgust and happiness, we can produce a sense of loathing (anger and disgust) while hinting at a lost happiness.
- Due to this decision, currently we work with a 3-track audio system managing fragments of music each delta second. Once in that period of time, the emotion variables are read and a new piece of music related to those feelings starts playing if necessary. The resulting music should represent the selected basic emotions. If no emotional answers are given, the previous loop will keep playing indefinitely.
- All tracks are chosen from a database of predesigned fragments of music, created by a human composer, sharing a tempo of 110 beats per minute. All of them will be loops, with lengths that range from 5 s to 15. The system is not designed to allow a sequence of quick changes in ambient music (less than 5 s each), due to the minimum duration of the loops used.
- Every time a new track is selected and played, it adjusts to a fixed tempo *grid*, skipping up to a beat if necessary. Once a combination of two or more tracks is playing, they are mixed in the audio engine. Intensity (volume) is established depending on the values of emotional weight, for a normalized intensity of 1. Primary emotions have a normalized (non-logarithmic) intensity of 0.5, followed by secondary (0.3) and tertiary (0.2) emotions.
- The resulting ambient music plays through the game engine's audio system. This makes it possible to spatialise the mix or to add an extra layer of effects.

5   Conclusions

Considering the disparity of approaches given to dynamic music generation in commercial video games, the proposed system architecture aims to constitute a versatile option for having emotion-driven ambient music without the low quality sound and high processing cost of a more complex, procedural system. Due to its architecture, it can work in every commercial game engine in the market, and can potentially adapt to every type of game, as long as there are emotional interactions in it.

Besides, the proposed audio managing technique acts as an "assistant" instead of as a "proxy" for musicians. This means the final result can be shaped by both human creativity and computational adaptability, resulting in sound tracks which are natural to compose and flexible to recombine at the same time. Although this means our system requires expert knowledge, it gives musicians the capacity to create realistic audio tracks for video games, while maintaining instantaneous adaptability.

For further research and testing of the system, we are currently building a prototype and a testbed game in Unity[3]. This prototype will be played by real users while taking both quantitative and qualitative measures, such as: live recording of play sessions and Self-Assessment Manikin Test (SAM) for measuring emotions [15].

Once the system works as intended, and after adjusting it according to the results achieved in the experimental phase, a plugin for popular game engines as Unity or Unreal can be developed, so as to allow musicians and sound designers to use it with ease.

Acknowledgements. This article was funded by the Complutense University of Madrid (grant CT27/16-CT28/16 for predoctoral research), in collaboration with Santander Bank and NIL research group.

References

1. Asutay, E., Västfjäll, D., Tajadura-Jiménez, A., Genell, A., Bergman, P., Kleiner, M.: Emoacoustics: a study of the psychoacoustical and psychological dimensions of emotional sound design. AES J. Audio Eng. Soc. **60**(1–2), 21–28 (2012)
2. Ekman, I.: Psychologically motivated techniques for emotional sound in computer games. In: AudioMostly 2008, pp. 20–26 (2008)
3. Ekman, P.: An argument for basic emotions. Cogn. Emotion **6**(3), 169–200 (1992)
4. Yanagisawa, H., Murakami, T., Noguchi, S., Ohtomi, K., Hosaka, R.: Quantification method of diverse kansei quality for emotional design: application of product sound design. In: ASME 2007 International Design Engineering Technical Conferences and Computers and Information in Engineering Conference, pp. 461–470 (2007)
5. Jørgensen, K.: What are these grunts and growls over there? Computer game audio and player action. Ph.D. thesis (2007)
6. Strank, W.: The legacy of iMuse: interactive video game music in the 1990s. In: Moormann, P. (ed.) Music and Game: Perspectives on a Popular Alliance, pp. 81–91. Springer Fachmedien Wiesbaden, Wiesbaden (2013). https://doi.org/10.1007/978-3-531-18913-0_4
7. Collins, K.: An introduction to procedural music in video games. Contemp. Music Rev. **28**, 5–15 (2009)
8. Jewell, M.O., Nixon, M.S., Prugel-Bennett, A.: CBS: a concept-based sequencer for soundtrack composition. In: Proceedings - 3rd International Conference on WEB Delivering of Music, WEDELMUSIC 2003, pp. 105–108 (2003)
9. Luhtala, M., Turunen, M., Hakulinen, J., Keskinen, T.: 'AIE-studio' - a pragmatist aesthetic approach for procedural sound design. In: Proceedings of the 8th Audio Mostly Conference, AM 2013, pp. 1–6 (2013)
10. Böttcher, N., Martínez, H.P., Serafin, S.: Procedural audio in computer games using motion controllers: an evaluation on the effect and perception. Int. J. Comput. Games Technol. **2013**, article no. 6 (2013)
11. López Ibáñez, M., Álvarez, N., Peinado, F.: A study on an efficient spatialisation technique for near-field sound in video games. In: Proceedings of the 4th Congreso de la Sociedad Española para las Ciencias del Videojuego, Barcelona (2017)

---

[3] https://unity3d.com/es.

12. Eladhari, M., Nieuwdorp, R., Fridenfalk, R.: The soundtrack of your mind: mind music - adaptive audio for game characters. In: Proceedings of the 2006 ACM SIGCHI International Conference on Advances in Computer Entertainment Technology, New York, p. 54 (2006)
13. Livingstone, S., Brown, A.: Dynamic response: real-time adaptation for music emotion. In: Second Australasian Conference on Interactive Entertainment, Sydney, pp. 105–111. Creativity & Cognition Studios Press (2005)
14. Bennett, C.C., Šabanović, S.: Deriving minimal features for human-like facial expressions in robotic faces. Int. J. Social Robot. **6**, 367–381 (2014)
15. Bradley, M.M., Lang, P.J.: Measuring emotion: the Self-Assessment Manikin and the Semantic Differential. J. Behav. Ther. Exp. Psychiatry **25**(1), 49–59 (1994)

Koto Learning Support Method Considering Articulations

Mayuka Doi and Homei Miyashita

Meiji University, Nakano-ku, Tokyo 1648525, Japan
cs172030@meiji.ac.jp, homei@homei.com

Abstract. Playing the Koto requires various skills such as reading Koto scores and understanding string positions instantly. In addition, there are many articulations, and some of them have no information about the timing for switching fingers or pushing a string down in Koto scores. Therefore, learning to play the Koto is difficult. In this paper, we propose a method to support beginners in practicing the Koto considering articulations. The method directly presents information for effective Koto performance, such as the string positions color-coded by fingering, timing of picking, picking directions, and articulations to the strings and soundboard. An experimental system presents this information by using projection mapping. We evaluated its effectiveness for beginners and an experienced person by comparative experiments through three user studies. As a result of these studies, we found that beginners were able to learn the Koto more effectively than by the traditional method, but our system is not useful for experienced people.

Keywords: Koto · Music · Instrument learning · Projection mapping

1 Introduction

A Koto [1–3] is a traditional Japanese 13-stringed[1] musical instrument. Koto players need to master play techniques such as hand shapes, how to pick strings, and how to apply power; to read Koto scores; and to understand string positions instantly. Koto scores are written in string names and unique articulation symbols (see Fig. 1). Therefore, it is difficult to read Koto scores and imagine the melodies. Moreover, there are over 20 articulations of the Koto [1, 2]. Mastering some of them is difficult because there is no information about the timing for switching fingers or pushing a string down in Koto scores. In addition, the Koto has 13 strings, but there is no sign that specifies string positions; thus, beginners are not able to play the Koto smoothly, and their motivation easily decrease.

---

[1] Strings are named "一," "二," "三," "四," "五," "六," "七," "八," "九," "十," "斗," "為," and "巾" from the back.

© Springer International Publishing AG, part of Springer Nature 2018
A. D. Cheok et al. (Eds.): ACE 2017, LNCS 10714, pp. 368–383, 2018.
https://doi.org/10.1007/978-3-319-76270-8_26

Fig. 1. Example of a Koto score (Soukyoku Gakufu "Sawai Tadao Koto Kyousokubon Daiichisyuu" © 2004 Sawai Tadao)

In this paper, we present a method to support learning to play the Koto including 20 articulations for beginners. The method directly presents useful information for Koto performances, such as the string positions color-coded by fingering, timing of picking, directions to move fingers, and articulations to the strings and soundboard called Ryukou. An experimental system indicates this information by using projection mapping (see Fig. 2). Therefore, beginners who are not able to read Koto scores and do not understand string positions are able to learn to play the Koto including articulations.

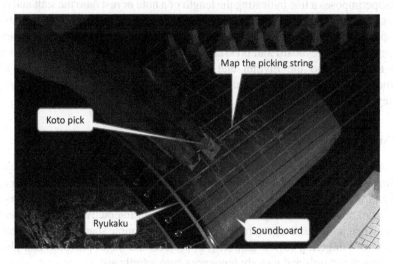

Fig. 2. Koto learning with the system

We conducted two user studies with beginners to evaluate their motivation perform-ance in their learning process. In addition, we conducted a user study with an experienced person to evaluate the learning efficiency when learning with the proposed method compared to that without it. The results of a week-long between-participants study show that the proposed method facilitates playing with fewer errors. However, it is not effective for experienced people.

The main contributions of this work are as follows:

1. We proposed a method to support the learning of the Koto considering articulations.
2. We conducted two user studies with beginners. One investigated the effectiveness of the proposed method while using it for a week and then not using it, and the other investigated the improvement in reading Koto scores.
3. We carried out a user study with an experienced person and provided an index for removing assistance.

2   Related Work

2.1   Augmented Pianos

P.I.A.N.O. [4] projects a note-information-based piano roll onto the piano to facilitate the mapping of notes onto piano keys for beginners who do not have sight-reading knowledge. It supports correct fingering by showing different colors and some articulations. Takegawa et al. [5] constructed a system to support learning the correct keying and fingering for playing a piano using a fingering recognition technique in real-time for beginners. It projects information about the keys, fingers, and score onto the keyboard and a display. Moreover, they developed a system to support the understanding of the different durations of each note and rest and the reading of a music staff for beginners [6]. It superimposes a line indicating the length of a note or rest onto the staff and checks the length. MirrorFugue [7] presents the recoded hand gestures of a remote collaborator to support remote lessons for beginners. Andante [8] projects animated characters walking along the keyboard and pressing the physical keys with each step onto a fallboard to understand the rhythm and musical expression. Raymaekers et al. [9] constructed a system that presents the time until keying on keys and a shooting game with keys used as a game controller.

2.2   Augmented String Instruments

Sano and Go [10] proposed a system to support the playing of the Koto by projecting the string position and Koto score corresponding the current performance position onto the Koto for beginners. However, articulations were not considered, and players were not able to know the flow of piece. ChinAR [11] is an interactive system for learning the Guqin that indicates the gesture and position using simple shapes such as circles and triangles with fingering colors. guitAR [12] projects the finger positions and phrasing instructions for chords and melody sequences onto a fretboard.

2.3   Music Games

Rocksmith [13], Yousician [14], and Synthesia [15] are music games using real instruments. Guitar Hero [16] is a guitar game using a controller shaped in the form of a guitar. These games show note information on virtual instruments displayed on the screen, so players do not need to have score-reading skills. However, players need to map note information to instruments or controllers.

3   System

3.1   System Configuration

Figure 3 shows experimental system configuration. A projector is mounted above the Koto to show information along the entire lengths of the strings. Moreover, gray paper is placed on the soundboard near Ryukaku (see Fig. 2) in order to make it easy to see. In addition, the system is supposed to be used in a dark room. Therefore, lighting equipment is set near the music stand to read a Koto score, and the rings of the Koto picks for each finger are coated with different fluorescent paints.

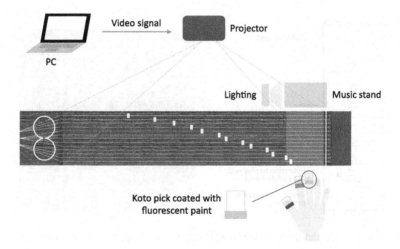

Fig. 3. System structure

3.2   Presented Information

The composition of the information is as follows:

- Lines indicating the landmarks of the string positions color-coded by fingering
- Arrows showing the timing of picking and directions in which the fingers should be moved
- Simple symbols of the articulations

- Separation lines indicating the separation of the beat
- A line indicating the landmarks of the correct picking position

The system directly projects this information onto the strings and soundboard for a span of one measure flowing from the left to the right with the metronome. The tempo is able to be changed. In order to make it easy to understand the correspondence between the Koto score and the performance support information, the length of the line of the landmark is adjusted to the size of the string name on the Koto score, except for five articulations: Nagashizume, Hireken, Uraren, tremolo, and arpeggio. The line of these exceptions is adjusted to the sound length. In addition, Koto players pick strings 2–4 cm to the left of Ryukaku with Koto picks. Therefore, the marker line is projected 3 cm to the left of Ryukaku to pick strings at the correct position. At the time at which an arrow overlaps the line showing the correct picking position, learners pick the specified string with the specified fingering finger and articulation. Thus, they are able to play the Koto correctly with the correct timing.[2] Figure 4 shows an example of the correspondence between a Koto score and the performance support information. Figure 5 shows the details of some of the articulations and the corresponding presented information targeted by the method. The colors of the fingers in Figs. 4 and 5 correspond to those of the rings of Koto picks in Fig. 3.

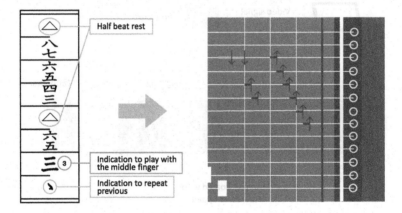

Fig. 4. A Koto score and an example of the presentation of the performance support information corresponding to it

---

[2] You can watch a demonstration video at (https://www.youtube.com/watch?v=xoVm-ZoQdvlk.)

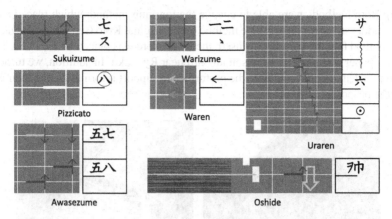

Fig. 5. Details of the articulations

3.3 Mapping

Although the strings of the Koto are thin and not horizontal, the system exactly maps information onto every string. In addition, it is able to save and read string positions.

3.4 Implementation

We used an NEC PC-LZ650NSS personal computer (PC), whose platform was Windows 10; a 6-foot-wide Koto; and a QUMI VIVITEK QUMI Q5-RD projector. In addition, we implemented the system using Processing and Pure Data.

4 Evaluation

We conducted two experimental studies to investigate the effectiveness of the proposed method in the elements of Koto performance when a Koto beginner is practicing the picking, fingering, and rhythm of a new score. In addition, we conducted an additional user study in order to assess whether the method for beginners is also useful for experienced people. In all user studies, tuning and alignment were carried out by the first author.

4.1 User Study 1: One-Week Performance

In this user study, we examined the learning effect of the proposed method compared that of the traditional method using the test performance, a subjective evaluation, a motivation score, and the performance delay time. Moreover, we investigated the transition from each method to other methods.

Method. In this evaluation, we compared the traditional method, which uses the string names written on paper. The paper was placed on the soundboard near Ryukaku (see

Fig. 6). Both methods were able to change the marking method, which placed a mark on the middle string, or the baseline method of the original Koto (see Fig. 6). Regardless of the method that the participants used, the Koto score was placed on the music stand, and gray paper was placed on the soundboard near Ryukaku. In addition, we turned off the light so that learners could see the performance support information and their hands using the proposed method.

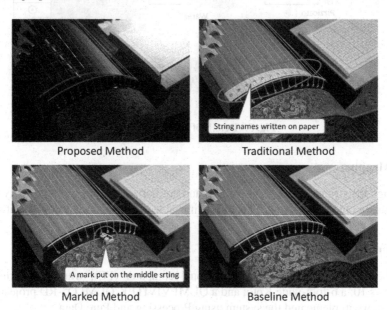

Fig. 6. Photographs showing the various methods

Participants. A total of six beginners for playing the Koto participated in the study, and three participants used each method considering their musical experiences. All participants were students recruited from a local university, 1 female and 5 male.

Trial Piece. We choose part 1 of "Huyunohi (Tadao Sawai)" from the beginning to bar 46, except for bars 29–42 as the trial piece. The total numbers of bars and notes are 32 and 331, respectively. It includes three articulations, Sukuizume, pizzicato, and Awase-zume. A Koto teacher confirmed that the degree of difficulty of the selection is appropriate. In the experiment, we used the Koto score, which extracted only this part.

Flow of the User Study. The user study was conducted for five consecutive days, and its schedule is summarized in Table 1. It was designed in imitation of the related work [4]. This user study consisted of two phases, practice and test phases. Participants practiced the trial piece for 15 min and were able to change methods at any time freely during the practice phase (P1–P5). In the test phase (T1–T5), they played the Koto using the proposed or traditional method. All phases (P1–P6, T1–T7) were accompanied by the sound of a metronome, and its speed was set to 60 bpm. After the final test on each day, participants evaluated their motivation (P1–P6) with a seven-point Likert scale and a subjective performance evaluation (T1–T7) out of 10 with reasons. Finally, they freely articulated their opinions and impressions about the experiment.

Judgment. Figure 7 shows the method used to judge the performance mistakes and examples. There are seven types of articulation errors: change Sukuizume to basic (see Fig. 7(e)), change basic to Sukuizume (see Fig. 7(f)), change pizzicato to basic (see Fig. 7(g)), change basic to pizzicato (see Fig. 7(h)), change Sukuizume to pizzicato (see Fig. 7(i)), change multiple sounds to a single sound (see Fig. 7(j)), and a gap in picking multiple strings of 0.5 s or more (see Fig. 7(k)). The performance delay time was determined as the time caused by a tempo shift, repeat, and suspension. We judged mistakes on the basis of recorded videos and sound waveforms of the test performances.

Table 1. User study schedule

Day	Details
1st	First introduction (taught how to put Koto picks on fingers, assume a posture, read a Koto score, and play the Koto including articulations)
	Confirmation of the trial piece (listen to a model performance, one time)
	Practice (P1)
	Test performance (T1)
2nd	Confirmation of the trial piece
	Practice (P2)
	Test performance (T2)
3rd	Confirmation of how to pick and the trial piece
	Practice (P3)
	Test performance (T3)
4th	Similar to the second day (P4, T4)
5th	Confirmation of the trial piece
	Practice (P5)
	Test performance (T5)
	Practice with marked method (P6)
	Test performance with marked method (T6)
	Test performance with baseline method (T7)

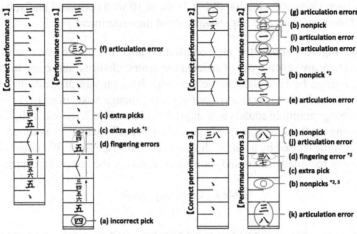

*1 We do not judge fingering error.   *2 We do not judge articulation error.   *3 We judge two nonpicks.

Fig. 7. Judgement of errors

Results and Considerations

Learning Performance. Figure 8 shows the averages of the numbers of missed picks (incorrect picks, nonpicks, and extra picks), fingering errors, and articulation errors for each test performance by the participants for each method. Since the proposed method directly presents the string positions color-coded one-by-one, there were many nonpicks because the participants fell behind the presented information. Nevertheless, the numbers of incorrect picks, fingering mistakes, and extra picks caused by rephrasing were few. We were concerned about inducing mistakes because the marker lines projected onto the strings were also projected onto the soundboard. However, it was concluded that the participants became used to it on the second day, and there was not a significant effect. With the traditional method, the correspondence between the

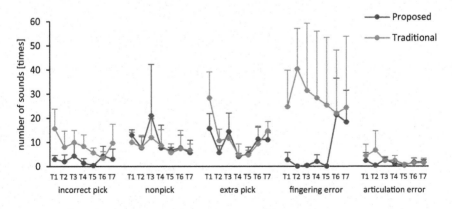

Fig. 8. Numbers of picking, fingering, and articulations errors in T1–T7

position at which the string name is written and string may be different from different viewpoints. Therefore, there were many incorrect picks and extra errors caused by repetition. In addition, one participant did not notice mistakes and finished T1–T5.

We used a t-test for the analysis, and a significant difference exists for incorrect picking in P5 at a significance level of 5%. We instructed the participants to play pizzicato with the middle finger or ring finger of the left hand. However, there was a participant who played with the left index finger. We regarded it as acceptable and did not count it as a fingering error. We are not able to confirm that a significant difference exists for fingering. However, participants using the proposed method played with fewer fingering errors, and there were trials in which they were able to play without mistakes. Moreover, the differences in the fingering errors were rather pronounced because the consciousness about the fingering was becoming weak when using the traditional method. In addition, all participants using the traditional method mistook the same part in all trials. A significant difference does not exist for articulation errors because articulations are not difficult. The number of mistakes in T3 increased because the participants were retaught how to play, and the number of nonpicks increased for the proposed method in T3 because a Koto pick fell off the finger.

In the trials with the marked method, there were more mistakes in the group using the proposed method than in that using the traditional method in T6. However, the number of mistakes in T7 with the baseline method decreased and was less than the group using the traditional method because participants in the group using the proposed method noticed their mistakes in T6 and corrected them.

Performance Delay Time. Figure 9 shows the times used for each method in the practice phases (P1–P6) for each participant, and Table 2 summarizes the performance delay time of each test for each person. We allowed participants to change methods during practice, but no one changed. The group with the proposed method, two in T6 and one in T7, repeated. The group with the traditional method—all in T1, T3, and T7, one in T2, and two in T5 and T6—repeated.

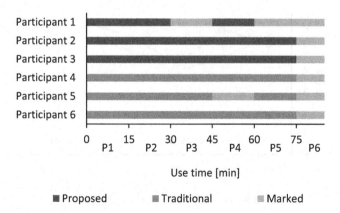

Fig. 9. Times used for each method for each participant in P1–P6

Table 2. Performance delay times of each participant in T1–T7 [beat]

Participant	T1	T2	T3	T4	T5	T6	T7
1	0	0	0	0	0	0	0
2	0	0	0	0	0	10	4
3	0	0	0	0	0	27	27
4	31	3	7	4	1	1	6
5	40	1	3	0	1	6	4
6	87	34	9	4	0	2	6

Subjective Evaluation. Figure 10 shows the average scores of the subjective performance evaluations of each participant for each method. The evaluations of the proposed method were higher than those of the traditional method. Significant differences were confirmed at a significance level of 5% in T1, T2, and T4. The evaluation of T3 decreased because participants were retaught how to play.

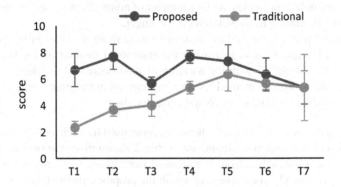

Fig. 10. Subjective performance evaluations in T1–T7

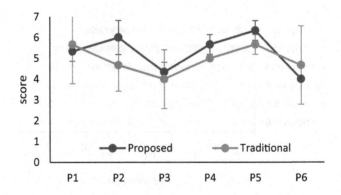

Fig. 11. Motivation scores in P1–P6

Motivation Score. Figure 11 shows the average motivation scores of each participant for each method. Although there are no significant differences, two participants using the traditional method said "I did not feel like I made progress, except on the first day," and there was a person that played phrases unrelated to the trial piece during practice.

From the reasoning provided from participants' descriptions, the group using the proposed method was conscious of the tempo on the second day and was practicing with their attention focused on the part that was not played well on the second day at the earliest or the fourth day at the latest. On the other hand, the group using the traditional method practiced while conscious of the tempo on the third or fourth day. By using the proposed method, they were able to practice at a higher level.

4.2 User Study 2: Verification of an Improvement in Reading Ability

We examined the improvement in reading Koto scores, where a Koto score was considered to be read after it became possible to play roughly using the proposed method, and the Koto score was read at the beginning using the traditional method. Participants using the proposed method watched the presented information rather than a Koto score. Therefore, our hypothesis was that the ability to read Koto scores would be higher for the traditional method than the proposed method.

Experimental Design. The participants were same as those in user study 1. We choose part 1 of "Akinohi (Tadao Sawai)" from bar 45 to bar 64 as the trial piece. The total numbers of bars and notes are 20 and 133, respectively. It includes two articulations, Kakizume and pizzicato. A Koto teacher confirmed that the degree of difficulty in the selection is appropriate. In this user study, we used the Koto score, which extracted only this part and added the fingering number to the part played with the middle finger. All of the participants practiced with the marked method for 5 min. Afterwards, they played with the marked method as the test performance and clapped their hands at the timing of picking strings with a metronome (45 bpm) as a rhythm check.

The metronome was not used in the practice and test phases in order to neglect consciousness except rhythm and confirm participants' understanding of the rhythm. Therefore, we instructed the participants to play with a natural tempo without rephrasing during the test performance. The judgement of errors was the same as that for user study 1.

Results and Considerations. The results are shown in Fig. 12. A significant tendency was observed for incorrect picking by a t-test at a significance level of 5%. There were no fingering errors, except for one participant, because there was no misleading fingering in the trial piece. Two people in the group using the traditional method were not able to read the places where the pizzicato and repetition symbols were written together. However, all participants using the proposed method were able to read and play correctly. In other words, the visualization of the articulations using the proposed method promoted the understanding of the symbols in the Koto score. In both groups, one person skipped part of the phrase that repeats a quarter of a beat twice and half of a beat once, and they were not able to clap their hands accurately in the rhythm check. We confirmed that the others were able to understand the rhythm.

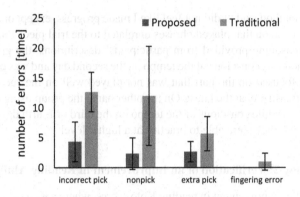

Fig. 12. Numbers of picking and fingering errors

4.3 User Study 3: Verification of the Usefulness for Experienced People

In this study, we investigated the effectiveness of the proposed method for experienced people.

Experimental Design. The first author of this paper, who has played the Koto for about 9 years, participated in this experiment, and we compared the proposed method with the baseline method. The trial piece of the proposed method was part 1 of "Otokirara (Tadao Sawai)" from bar 56 to bar 75 (20 bars, 252 notes), and that of the baseline method was part 1 of "OKOTO (Hikaru Sawai)" from bar 115 to bar 134 (20 bars, 148 notes). A Koto teacher confirmed that the degrees of difficulty of the selections are the same. Experiments were first conducted with the baseline method and then carried out with the proposed method. Using both methods, the participant played a prepractice test after looking over each trial piece score once. After that, the participant practiced for 7 min and then played after the practice test. The proposed method was used only in the practice phase, and all tests were carried out using the baseline method. Regardless of the method used by the participant, the Koto score was placed on a music stand, and we turned off the light so that the performance support information and participant's hands were able to seen when using the proposed method. The judgement of mistakes was the same that used for user study 1.

Results and Considerations. Figure 13 shows the results. For those who are familiar with Koto scores, the baseline method is more effective than the proposed method. When using the proposed method, the participant found that it was best to follow the presented information with her eyes. Therefore, it is impossible to memorize the performance during the practice phase. As a result, the number of errors increased. On the other hand, it was possible to memorize the Koto score with the string names to practice watching the Koto score with the baseline method. Thus, there were few errors. If experienced people use the proposed method, we find that it is only effective for basic practice sessions such as practicing articulations, practicing fast finger movements, and confirming picking or fingering mistakes after playing to some degree with the baseline method.

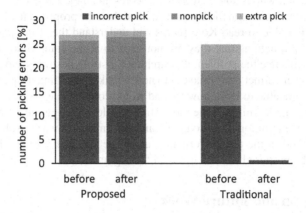

Fig. 13. The number of picking errors of before and after practice by experienced people

5 Discussion

5.1 Limitations

There were no rhythm mistakes in user study 1 when listening to the model performance. However, there were mistakes in user study 2 because there was no model performance. Participants using the proposed method said that it is effective for understanding the flow of the song, but we are not able to conclude that it was due to the effect of the proposed method completely because they were listening to pitches that were not able to be understood from the Koto scores. In general practice, learners play the Koto while being taught how to play by Koto teachers or by listening to sound sources. Therefore, the proposed method is expected to be useful for actual learning.

5.2 Comparison of the Proposed and Traditional Methods

When using the proposed method, none of the participants were lazy and avoided practicing. Practices were semicompulsive, the pieces of performance support information moved left-to-right one-by-one. On the other hand, when using the traditional method, a participant did not concentrate on practicing because he was tired. Hence, he was not able to practice reading the Koto score and finding the corresponding string positions passively.

5.3 Usefulness of the Proposed Method

Even if learners play the Koto by using the proposed method, they are not able to remember the string names in the Koto score. In addition, the sounds assigned to the strings change depending on tuning. Therefore, by only memorizing sounds, they must memorize the tuning and change that into the strings on that basis. In other words, an experienced person who is able to read Koto scores and understand the string positions learned more effectively with the baseline method than the proposed method. However, beginners are not able to read Koto scores and understand the string positions. Thus, they must perform actions that they are not used to at the same time. The proposed method is able to solve the problem of searching for string positions and to prevent the memorization of incorrect performances to notice picking and fingering errors. In addition, beginners are able to learn how to read Koto scores efficiently after playing with the proposed method. Although the motivation was lower using the proposed method than that using the traditional method, the number of mistakes was less than that for the traditional method in the test performance using the baseline method. Therefore, we consider that the proposed method is useful for beginners.

6   Conclusion and Future Work

In this paper, we introduced a method to support beginners who are not able to read Koto scores and understand string positions instantly in learning the Koto. Our method presents performance support information on the strings and soundboard directly by using projection mapping. This information is composed of the string positions color-coded by fingering, timing of picking, directions to pick, articulations, and the one beat separation lines of one measure. Moreover, the performance support information moves from left to right for one measure. We conducted two user studies with beginners to compare the learning performance, motivation, self-evaluation, and improvement in reading a Koto score when using the proposed method and traditional method, which uses string names written on paper. Further, a user study with an experienced person was also conducted to compare the learning performance of the proposed method to that with the baseline method.

The results showed that beginners were able to play the Koto including articulations and learn more efficiently by using the proposed method. Particularly, the presentation of the performance strings colored for fingering and the direction to pick was useful for understanding the string positions and flow of the song and maintaining motivation. Therefore, the numbers of incorrect picking and fingering errors were less than those of the traditional method. Moreover, by visualizing the performance support information, the experimental participants noticed mistakes by themselves, even though there was no judgment function. In addition, the skill in reading a Koto score and performing improved compared to that of the traditional method. However, the proposed method had the opposite effect for experienced people. We expect that the timing of the effect of the proposed method is reversed when players are able to understand Koto scores and find the string positions written on the Koto score. This finding is useful as an index for removing the assistance provided by the proposed method.

In the future, we will improve the proposed method to reduce the performance support information gradually and introduce a mechanism to increase the time for reading Koto scores at a stage at which a performance is stable. Moreover, we will construct an experimental system and conduct experiments to evaluate the hypothesis of the useful stage of the proposed method.

Acknowledgments. We are grateful to Koto teacher Mayuko Kobayashi and all of the participants in this study.

References

1. Hukunaga, C.: Yasashiku manaberu Koto kyouhon (in Japanese). Choubunsya, Tokyo (2003)
2. Yamaguchi, O., Tanaka, K.: Hougaku Koto hajime (in Japanese). Edition KAWAI, Tokyo (2002)
3. Wikipedia. https://en.wikipedia.org/wiki/Koto_(instrument)
4. Rogers, K., Röhlig, A., Weing, M., Gugenheimer, J., Könings, B., Klepsch, M., Schaub, F., Rukzio, E., Seufert, T., Weber, M.: P.I.A.N.O.: faster piano learning with interactive projection. In: Ninth ACM International Conference on Interactive Tabletops and Surfaces, pp. 149–158. ACM, New York (2014). https://doi.org/10.1145/2669485.2669514
5. Takegawa, T., Terada, T., Tsukamoto, M.: Design and implementation of a piano practice support system using a real-time fingering recognition technique. In: 37th International Computer Music Conference, pp. 387–394 (2011)
6. Takegawa, T., Terada, T., Tsukamoto, M.: A piano learning support system considering rhythm. In: 38th International Computer Music Conference, pp. 325–332 (2012)
7. Xiao, X., Ishii, H.: MirrorFugue: communicating hand gesture in remote piano collaboration. In: Fifth International Conference on Tangible, Embedded, and Embodied Interaction, pp. 13–20. ACM, New York (2011). https://doi.org/10.1145/1935701.1935705
8. Xiao, X., Tome, B., Ishii, H.: Andante: walking figures on the piano keyboard to visualize musical motion. In: International Conference on New Interfaces for Musical Expression 2014, pp. 629–632 (2014)
9. Raymaekers, L., Vermeulen, J., Luyten, K., Coninx, K.: Game of tones: learning to play songs on a piano using projected instructions and games. In: The ACM CHI Conference on Human Factors in Computing Systems, pp. 411–414. ACM, New York (2014). https://doi.org/10.1145/2559206.2574799
10. Sano, K., Go, K.: Koto performance support system for beginners (in Japanese). Forum Inf. Technol. **11**(3), 491–492 (2012)
11. Zhang, Y., Liu, S., Tao, L., Yu, C., Shi, Y., Xu, Y.: ChinAR: facilitating Chinese Guqin learning through interactive projected augmentation. In: Third International Symposium of Chinese CHI, pp. 23–31. ACM, New York (2015). https://doi.org/10.1145/2739999.2740003
12. Löchtefeld, M., Gehring, S., Jung, R., Krüger, A.: guitAR: supporting guitar learning through mobile projection. In: The ACM CHI Conference on Human Factors in Computing Systems, pp. 1447–1452. ACM, New York (2011). https://doi.org/10.1145/1979742.1979789
13. Rocksmith. https://rocksmith.ubisoft.com/rocksmith/en-us/home/
14. Yousician. http://www.yousician.com/
15. Synthesia. http://www.synthesiagame.com/
16. Guitar Hero. https://www.guitarhero.com/

Evaluation of the Game Exermon – A Strength Exergame Inspired by Pokémon Go

Alf Inge Wang$^{(\boxtimes)}$ ⓘ, Kristoffer Hagen ⓘ, Torbjørn Høivik ⓘ,
and Gaute Meek Olsen ⓘ

Norwegian University of Science and Technology, Trondheim, Norway
alfw@idi.ntnu.no, kristoffer.hagen@ntnu.no, torhoe@gmail.com,
gaute.meek@gmail.com

Abstract. Sedentary lifestyle has become a major concern across the world as a result of an increasing number of desk jobs, and a steady increase in digital media consumption. This type of lifestyle can cause major health issues. The immensely popular game Pokémon Go has proven that it is possible to develop games that will motivate people of all ages to be physical active. Our exergame, Exermon, got its inspiration from Pokémon games as well as the Tamagotchi games, where our goal was to motivate the player to do strength exercises to evolve a fantasy character. This paper describes the Exermon game concept, and presents the results from an evaluation of the game where the focus was on the physical, motivational, enjoyment, and engagement effects of playing the game, as well as evaluating the game control, progression and social interaction.

Keywords: Exergame · Exertion game · Computer game · Physical activity
Strength training · Pokémon Go

1 Introduction

Physical activity has many positive effects on quality of life, and thus an increasing sedentary lifestyle has become a major concern across the world. Physical activity promoted through exergames has many benefits such as lower risk of early death, coronary heart disease, stroke, high blood pressure, type-2 diabetes, metabolic syndrome, colon cancer, breast cancer and reduced symptoms of depression. Most existing exergames can classified into the two categories of games to stimulate to general physical movement of the player [1–9] and games for elderly or patients to improve physical strength and balance [10–13]. Further there are exergames that explores the borders of the physical and virtual world [14–22]. Exergames focusing on muscle strengthening in general, which are not used for physical treatment are underrepresented in the literature on exergames, although there are some examples [23–26].

According to the U.S. Department of Health and Human Services, muscle-strengthening physical activity should be included at least 3 days of the week as part of 60 or more minutes of daily physical activity [27]. Adults should also do muscle-strengthening activities that are moderate or high intensity and involve all major muscle groups two or more days a week, as these activities provide additional health benefits. The challenge

© Springer International Publishing AG, part of Springer Nature 2018
A. D. Cheok et al. (Eds.): ACE 2017, LNCS 10714, pp. 384–405, 2018.
https://doi.org/10.1007/978-3-319-76270-8_27

both for children and adults is to have the motivation to do muscle strengthening activities. Our proposed solution to address this problem is to create a motivating, enjoyable and engaging game that can provide health benefits from strength training.

In terms of numbers, Pokémon Go can be considered to be the most successful commercial exergame to promote physical activity with more than 650 million downloads worldwide [28]. To be able to succeed in the game, the player must move around in the physical world to capture pokémons appearing on specific locations, and walk to PokéStops and Pokémon gyms that can be found at predefined physical locations. Although similar games have been developed before, Pokémon Go is the first to become a major success in terms of number of users and income. The Pokémon Go phenomena that surprised media and researchers the most was the fact that this game was able to get typical gamers who previously stayed in-door and were not physically active, to walk long distances for many hours [29, 30]. The Pokémon Go game has demonstrated the power of motivation an exergame can have on physical activity, and that a game can potentially change behavior related to physical activity.

Our Exermon game with the goal to promote physical strength training was inspired by games like Pokémon and Tamagotchi. The target audience for this game is young adults unlike many games for physical strength which focus on rehabilitation of elderly [11–13, 31, 32]. Another difference with our approach is that our Exermon game was designed as a real game containing real gameplay, unlike many research prototypes that only uses game technology such as Wii Fit, Wii balance board, Kinect, PlayStation Move or Wii mote to support tracking of body movements [33]. Similarly, many research prototypes focus on motor skill learning [34] and not actual building muscles. We believe that an exergame like Exermon has a great potential both in terms of engagement, gameplay and motivation for strength training. This paper presents the concept of the Exermon game as well as an evaluation of the game.

2   Background

This section presents related work, some basic principles for strength training, and the theoretical framework used for the game design of the Exermon game.

2.1   Related Work

There are several examples of exergames on the mobile platform similar to our Exermon game, but most of these games focus on motivating the player to walk or just physically move. In [33], Wylie and Coulton describe the heart rate and movement controlled mobile exergame Health Defender inspired by the arcade classic Space Invaders. The objective of this game is to encourage players to exercise during gameplay through triggered bonuses, and to improve both gaming experience and personal health. To trigger a bonus, the player must actively work out during gameplay to raise the heart rate to match the target exertion rate. Player experiences show that such games have the potential for both improving health as well as wellbeing [35]. Other similar approaches are Fish'n'Steps that links a player's daily foot step count to the growth and activity of an animated virtual character (a fish in a fish tank) [8], LocoSnake that is a location-based version of the classic Snake mobile game in which users can control the snake by walking [36], SmartRabbit that is a mobile running game where players compete against other players using a smartphone with GPS [35], Lutfen that is a multi-player game designed to be played at the campus of University College Dublin (UCD) where the players are encouraged to move between different zones [37], and iFitQuest that is a location-aware mobile exergame designed to target adolescent children consisting of a number of mini-games including interacting with Non Player Characters (NPCs), visit landmarks and collect items [9]. There are also several similar games that combine learning and physical movement [38–40], where the exertiation is just a side-effect of the game being location-aware. A common characteristic of the games above is that they all have a simple game mechanism to stimulate the player to physically move to achieve an award or complete a task in the game.

In addition to mobile exergames, other platforms are used including the Nintendo Wii, the PlayStation Move, special-purpose controllers, and a combination of exercise equipment and games [41]. One example of a combination of the use of exercise equip-ment and gaming is the PedalTanks game, where an exercise bike is used to control a multiplayer tank game [42]. A user study where the PedalTanks game was played 132 times over three days by 8 participants showed that the game scored better on both subjective enjoyment and degree of physical activity compared to moderately paced walk [7]. There are also other similar exercise bike games made such as PaperDude [43] and a game combining an exercise bike, VR and Kinect [44]. An alternative approach is to use interactive ski-poles, a mini stepper in combination with a heart-beat monitor to control a biathlon game (combination of skiing and shooting) [45].

Some researchers limit the definition of exergames to only involve aerobic-type activities. Oh and Yang proposed to redefine exergames as a combination of exertion and video games including strength training, balance, and flexibility activities [46]. Most research on exergames has so far focused on aerobic-type activities, but there are some exceptions. In [23], a project where the purpose was to describe the acute exercise responses, heart rate, and rate of perceived exertion to exergaming using full-body isometric muscle resistance and to determine whether these responses are different during single- versus opponent-based play. In [24], Marshall et al. describes the design and study of two multi-player games that encourage players to use brute force directly against other players. The first game is Balance of Power, which is a tug-of-war style game implemented with the Kinect, while Bundle is a playground-inspired chasing game implemented with smartphones. Brains & Brawn is strategy card game for muscle-strengthening inspired of games like Heartstone and Pokémon [26]. Playtesting the game demonstrated that players were incented to exercise with correct form and showed favorable attitude toward the game. Another example is the Remote Impact game where two remote players are facing a sensitive playing area, on which the shadow of the remote person is projected [19]. The players can talk to and hear each other through voice connection between the two locations. Once the game starts, both players try to execute and impact on each other's shadow through punches, kicks and throws. The system recognizes when there has been a hit or a miss. Players can dodge hits by ducking or moving out of the way, just as in traditional contact sports. More points are scored by hitting the opponent harder. The player with the most points wins the game. The aim with this project was like our Exermon project: To encourage designers to make exergames that include extreme forceful behaviors, which can contribute to general fitness and weight loss while at the same time being social and entertaining.

One example of a game which is very close to our Exermon game is World of Workout, which is a mobile role-playing game where the character evolves based on the exercises the user performs in reality [25]. In this game, the accelerometer on a smartphone was used to measure activities such as jumping jacks and sit-ups without having to specify specifically the exercise being performed. The evaluation of the game showed that there was a direct connection between exercise, in-game progress and motivation, that the sensors worked for the most part recognizing the physical activities, and the ability to automatically differentiate particular activities proved difficult.

Although the goal of the game Pokémon Go is not strength training, there are several similarities with our Exermon game as well as differences [28]. The core goal with both games is the same: training a monster that can be used to fight other monsters. The main difference is that in Pokémon Go, much of the gameplay evolves around walking around and catching pokémons, not performing strength exercises. Another noticeable difference is that Pokémon Go is a location-aware and augmented reality game. A possible extension to our Exermon game could be to also include location-aware gameplay to encourage the player to both walk and do strength exercises. Another difference is that the exercise is explicit in Exermon (you are directly encouraged to do strength exercises), while the physical movement in Pokémon Go is more a side effect of playing the game (implicit). The main positive physical effect with Pokémon Go reported is how the game has increased the players' physical activity level and socialization [29]. Some have also been worried about children safety in playing the Pokémon Go game, focusing on protecting against injuries, predators, and inappropriate situations [47].

2.2 Strength Training

Our motivation to make an exergame based on strength training was based on the fact that there are very few exergames with such focus, and there are many benefits from strength training, including reduced risk of injuries, reduced pain in muscles and joints, better body posture, increased muscular endurance, and increased muscular power [48, 49]. A strength exercise is doing a controlled movement to the degree such that micro tears are made in the muscle tissue. These tears are then continuously repaired by the muscle fibers, which expands to cover the gap. This in turn makes the muscle larger and able to exert more power. The American College of Sports Medicine recommends exercising strength training at least two times per week, doing ten to twelve repetitions of eight to ten different exercises, which covers all major muscle groups[1]. Feigen-baum found that between four and ten repetitions will progress a person's strength, and between twelve and twenty will work on the muscles endurance [50].

---

[1] ACSM Information on Resistance Training for Health and Fitness: http://www.acsm.org/docs/brochures/resistance-training.pdf.

There are mainly two main approaches for strength training: Free weight training and body weight training. In *free weight training*, the person exercising uses weight such as dumbbells, barbells and kettlebells as resistance. It is essential to find weights that fit your own fitness level. The main challenge with free weight training is that the steep learning curve for inexperienced persons and the need for some expertise and training to perform the exercises correctly. In *body weight training*, a person uses his or her own body as resistance by countering the force that gravity exerts on it. The learning curve of body weight training is minimal, and most people learn these exercises during physical education in school. Also since your own weight is used, the risk for injuries is less than for free weight training.

2.3   The Theoretical Framework for the Game Design

The game design of the Exermon game is based on the focus areas to make a game fun to play: Challenge, fantasy and curiosity [51]. It is crucial for an immersive game to provide the appropriate level of *challenge*. If the game is too easy, the player will get bored and if it is too hard the player will get frustrated. To provide a challenge, a game must present the player with goals to be achieved, it must provide feedback to notify the player if she or he is getting closer or farther away from reaching the goal, and it must provide some kind of randomness to give the game some unpredictability. The goal of the challenge is to boost the player's self-esteem when overcoming a challenge. *Fantasy* is used in a game to make it more appealing and interesting. Malone distinguishes between extrinsic and intrinsic fantasy, where the former means that the fantasy objects or situations are influenced by the skill of the player but not the other way around. For the latter, the player's skill affects the fantasy, and the skill also depends on the fantasy. The use of fantasy is important to create player emotions, which will improve the player's attachment to the game. *Curiosity* can mainly be divided into two sub-categories: Sensory curiosity - which involves the use of graphics and audio to enhance the player experience, and cognitive curiosity – which mean that the player does not get the complete picture of the game in the beginning, but the game will open as the player progresses.

The *gameflow framework* is based on the concept of flow, which is defined as a state is reached where a person will have an intense and focused concentration on what he/she is doing, merged action and awareness, loss of self-consciousness, in control of their actions, reduced sense of time, and experiences the activity as rewarding [52]. Specifically, in the gameflow framework, Sweetser and Wyeth specify eight elements to increase the flow in games. These eight elements are that the game must require *concentration* to play, it must provide an appropriate *challenge* and match the player's skill level, it must support development and mastery of *player skills*, it must provide the player with a sense of *control* over their actions in the game, it should have *clear goals* on what to do and when to do them, it should provide the player with appropriate and timely *feedback*, it must yield *immersion* where the player experience deep but effortless involvement in the game, and it should support and create opportunities for *social interaction*.

Dual flow is a concept used in relation to exergames [53]. When the dual flow state is reached, the player gets an effect from the exercising, and finds the game attractive at the same time. The main difference between dual flow and gameflow is that the effect of exercise is also measured. It is crucial that the intensity of the workout matches the player's fitness level. When the player gets in better shape, it is important that the intensity also increases [54].

There is an overlap of three theoretical frameworks presented above, they individually have nuances that improve game design. The game design of the Exermon game was founded on the theory on intrinsic motivation, gameflow and dual flow. We wanted to design a highly enjoyable, engaging and immersive exergame, which would directly affect the player's motivation to do strength exercises. The next section will describe the game design more in detail.

3   Exermon – Exergame for Strength Training

This section describes the game concept and gameplay.

3.1   Introduction to the Exermon Game

The name of our exergame is Exermon, a combination of the words <u>exer</u>cise and <u>mon</u>ster. The player chooses a personal monster to train called an "exermon". The appearance of the exermon depends on the player doing body weight exercises to grow and keep it being alive. When the player is exercising, the exermon will gain stats based on the exercise and repetitions. The player will see the monster get stronger by raising the stats, but can also risk death of the monster if the player is not exercising over a period of time. The caring and growth of the exermon was inspired by the Tamagotchi game where a player needs to take care of their digital alien pet. The more the player will exercise, the more the monster will evolve as shown in Fig. 1.

Fig. 1. Evolution of an exermon avatar

The exermons live on an island where they can fight other monsters or fight bosses in an arena. The player can connect with friends to compare their monsters and fight them. To get a monster that fights well, the player needs to keep exercising to boost the monster's health points, power, and speed.

3.2 Gameplay

Strength training demands great concentration and a focus on the exercise being performed. This means that the person exercising will not be able to interact with the game during the workout. The game consists of three main parts: Training, Planning, and Fighting. The physical activity will take place in the *training part*, where the game tracks the player's exercises using a smart phone's proximity and accelerometer sensors. The proximity sensor is used to count push-ups and handstand push-ups by monitoring the change of distance between the phone laying on the floor and the chest or the head of the player. For sit-ups, squats, hang-ups, dips, table-ups, Bulgarian squats, glute bridge, hanging leg-raises and pistol squats, the player's motion is captured by the accelerometer. The accelerometer captures acceleration on all three axes (x, y, and z). If the sensor output value exceeds the threshold value in one direction, the game knows the player is halfway through a repetition, and waits for a movement in the other direction to detect a completion of a repetition. In the training phase, the game will also stimulate the player through sound and graphics. After completing an exercise, the player will be able to see that the stats of her or his exermon have increased. The visual appearance of the exermon will also evolve over time as the player carry out more strength exercises.

The *planning part* of the game is where the player gets an overview, the progress, and the status of the game. The player is presented with the actions available, an overview of accomplishments, and an overview of the player's social network. The planning part is the hub of the game. Figure 2. shows screenshots from training and planning modes.

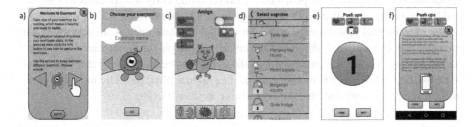

Fig. 2. Screenshots from (a) the welcome screen, (b) initial choosing an exermon, (c) the planning and status screen, (d) choose exercise screen, (e) execute exercise screen, and (f) exercise information screen

The *fighting part* of the game is where the player directly will interact with the game and reap the fruits of her or his physical training. The fighting is carried out in a first-person boxing style where you are boxing a computer-generated opponent. The player fights by swiping on the screen trying to hit the opponent's avatar that is constantly moving. Fighting against computer-generated opponents can be done in three different modes: Arena, Boss fight, and Friend fight. In the *Arena mode*, the player is given a rank and moved up and down in rank according to how well the player fights. The player will face harder and harder opponents as she or he climbs the ranking. The goal of this mode is to be ranked as number one. In the *Boss fight mode*, the player faces an extremely hard opponent with a lot of health points, power and speed. The player is awarded greater rewards from beating a boss than winning a battle in the Arena mode. At the beginning of a week, a boss is generated according to the player's stats to motivate the player to exercise an appropriate amount through the week to conquer the boss. In the *Friend fight mode*, the player can fight a friend's exermon. The exermon is controlled by the computer, but has the characteristics of your friend's exermon. The more a friend has exercised and evolved her or his exermon, the harder it is to defeat it in a fight because of the higher stats. It is also possible to earn badges in the Exermon game to promote side goals. Whenever a player earns a badge, the game presents this achievement through a cool visual effect triggering sensory curiosity. Figure 3. shows screenshots from the fighting mode.

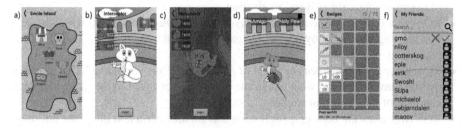

Fig. 3. Screenshots from (a) the Exermon island, (b) an opponent in arena mode, (c) boss fight, (d) fighting an opponent, (e) the badges screen, and (f) search for friends' screen

In addition to the elements described above, the Exermon game includes a store where the player can buy exercise boost that gives double number of stats gained from exercising. The player can also buy boosters that will increase health points, power or speed stats. The gold coins used in the store can be won from battling opponents. Finally, the Exermon game offers the player to choose from a total of nine exermons, which varies in terms of color and race as shown in Fig. 4.

Fig. 4. Available exermons

4   Research Questions and Research Approach

The research goal of the evaluation presented in this article was to investigate the effect of an exergame for strength training. The research approach used for in this evaluation was the Goal/Question/Metrics (GQM) paradigm [55], where first the research goal is defined at the conceptual level. The next step is to define a set of research questions at the operational level, and finally describe a set of metrics to answer the research questions (quantitative level). Our research goal was defined according to the GQM template to be:

The purpose of this study was to *evaluate the effect of using a game as a motivation for strength training* from the point of view of *an adult* in the context of *everyday life*.

The following research questions (RQs) were defined by decomposing the research goal:

- RQ1 *What is the physical effect from playing the Exermon game?* This research question investigates if the player increase the amount of exercise from playing the game, whether the player get physically stronger, and if the game can match the individual player's fitness level.
- RQ2 *What is the motivation effect of playing the Exermon game?* This research question investigates if the game can motivate the player and how the various aspects of the game affect the players' motivation.
- RQ3 *What is the enjoyment effect of playing the Exermon game?* This research question investigates the enjoyment of the game and what aspects of the game produce enjoyment.
- RQ4 *What is the engagement effect of playing the Exermon game?* This research question investigates to what extent the player gets engaged in the game and what elements of the game that engages.
- RQ5 *How does the control, progression and social interaction affect the Exermon game experience?* This research question investigates the users control of the game, the progression of the game, and how social interaction is stimulated in the game.

To answer the five research questions above, data from four data sources (both qualitative and quantitative) are analyzed:

- A *questionnaire* (quantitative) consisting of 19 statements that reflects theory on intrinsically motivating instruction [56], the gameflow framework [57], and the dual flow model, as well as questions related to demographics. The statements are answered with a non-standard 4-level Likert Scale from strongly disagree to strongly agree to avoid neutral responses.
- *Observation* (qualitative) of a limited set of the test-subjects with focus on the research questions above.
- *Interviews* (qualitative) of a limited set of the test-subjects with focus on the research questions above.
- *Logs* of the player data from the game (quantitative) including exercise events, fight events, and friend (social) events.

5   Results

The Exermon game was tested on 24 subjects, and the demographics of the subjects are shown in Fig. 5. The gender distribution was 71% male vs. 29% female. The majority of subjects were between 21–30 years old. Before the evaluation started, half of the subjects exercised 3–4 times per week, 33% 1–2 times per week, and 13% did not exercise at all. One of the subjects exercised 7 or more times per week before testing the Exermon game.

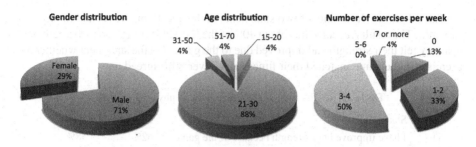

Fig. 5. Demographics of test-subjects

All 24 subjects tested the Exermon game over a two-week period, and answered a questionnaire after the test period was over. For observation and interviews, we used stratified sampling where you define your samples (strata) based on population characteristics such as age and gender. The strata defined were young adults between 18 and 25 years old of both genders. From the 24 test-subjects, four female and four males in the age 18 to 25 years old were picked for observation and interview.

The results reported in this section are based on results from the questionnaire, the observations, the interviews, and logs from the game server.

5.1 Physical Results (RQ1)

An important part of this experiment was to investigate whether a game like Exermon could increase motivation for doing strength exercises. In our survey, the subjects were asked to report how often they worked out before testing the game, and how often they worked out during the test period. Figure 6 shows that around 60% of the test-subjects exercised the same amount in the test period, while around 40% increased the amount of physical exercise. Out of the ten test-subjects who increased the amount of exercise, eight did 1–2 extra exercises per week, while two did 3–4 extra exercises a week during the test period. Also among those who increased their exercise per week while playing, 30% of them did not exercise at all before playing the game, 50% exercised 1–2 times per week, and the remaining 20% exercised 3–4 times per week.

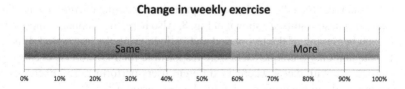

Fig. 6. Change of amount of exercise after playing the game

Table 1 shows the results of two statements in the questionnaire related to physical strength[2]. The results revealed that about 40% of the test-subjects agreed to the statement that they felt their strength had improved due to the game. On the statement whether the exercises in the game matched their fitness level over 80% agreed.

Table 1. Results from statements related to physical strength

ID	Statement	Disagree	Agree
S1	I have improved my strength because of the game	62%	38%
S2	The exercises matched my fitness level	17%	83%

Our evaluation lasted 14 days, and we recorded every time someone had finished an exercise in the game. Figure 7 shows the day-to-day records of exercise events in the game over the two weeks the test lasted. The figure shows that most exercise events occurred the first four days where the peak was day two with 150 events. At day five, the event count stabilized around 25–50 events per day, with another peak at the end of the period (day 12). The average exercise event count for the period was 65.2 per day, which computes to 2.7 exercise events per subject per day.

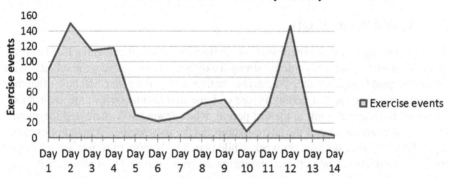

Fig. 7. Exercise events registered during the test period

Our data also recorded the number of unique users executing exercise events during the test period. These results are shown in Fig. 8. Also here, the number of unique users peaked at the beginning of the test period and varied during the test period. It is interesting to note that only 8 unique users were responsible for 147 exercise events on day 12. This contrasts with day 2 where 17 different users performed 150 exercises. The average number of unique users per day for the test period was 8.1.

---

[2] In the presentation of the data, the results from the questionnaire grouped in to the two responses disagree and agree. This means that strongly disagree and disagree are put into one group, and strongly agree and agree are put into another group.

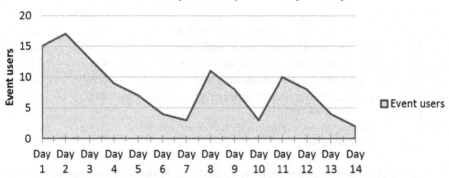

Fig. 8. The number of unique users exercising day by day during the test period

An observation of eight test-subjects showed that they all did the exercises correctly. By correctly, we mean that they performed the exercises to the best of their abilities, not cheating or doing it halfway. The majority pushed themselves to do as many repetitions as possible. The observations exposed the exercises to be physically demanding shown by heavy breathing and verbal confirmation about getting tired. The exercises the participants chose were pistol squats, push-ups, squats, sit-ups, dips, and glute bridge.

From the interviews, we found that 50% of the subjects had increased the amount of exercising because of the Exermon game. One of the interviewees elaborated: "I have exercised more because of the game, I like this kind of training". In the interview, three subjects said that they had gotten stronger by being able to do more repetition from the game. Three other subjects said that they were already exercising a lot and did not feel that the Exermon game had contributed to improved strength, even though one of them had increased the number of workouts during the test period.

5.2   Results on Motivation (RQ2)

Table 2 shows the results from the statements related to various aspects of motivation. On the first statement over 90% of the subjects agreed that they were motivated to play the game before each session. This shows that the game itself was a motivation for the subjects. The response was rather varied on how various aspects of the game motivated the subjects. Close to 40% agreed that the character's appearance in the game motivated the subject to work out more. Similarly, about 40% that knowing that the player's character could die made them work out harder. However, one aspect of the game that clearly motivated the subjects was the feature to unlock all the exercises in the game (70% of the subjects agreed to this statements). Similarly, over 80% of the subjects agreed that being able to beat an opponent who previously appeared unbeatable motivated to work out. Finally, over 60% of the subjects agreed that the feature that made it possible to compare the user's exermon with other players' exermons motivated to improve.

Table 2. Results from statements related to motivation

ID	Statement	Disagree	Agree
S3	I was motivated to play the game before each session	8%	92%
S4	My character's appearance inspired me to work out more	58%	42%
S5	Knowing that my character could die made me work out harder	62%	38%
S6	I wanted to play more to unlock all the exercises	30%	70%
S7	Beating an opponent who previously appeared unbeatable gave me great motivation to work out	17%	83%
S8	Being able to compare my exermon with my friends' exermons motivated me to improve	37%	63%

Our observations revealed some more details related to how the game design affected the motivation of the subjects. It was obvious also from the observations that beating friends was a motivation to improve the exermon's stats to be able to fight better. This again meant that the player had to exercise more to boost the exermon's stats. One of the test-subjects lost motivation when his friend did not manage to follow his progress in exermon stats, as it became too easy to defeat his friend's exermon. After the participants had exercised, some hurried back to look at the image of their exermon to see if it had improved his visual appearance. Being able to obtain badges clearly motivated two of the female test-subjects to exercise more to get a new badge. One of the test participants had bought an exercise boost item before the observation. Because if this, she really tried to maximize the amount of repetitions she could do to boost the stats as much as possible.

In the interview, the interviewees focused on different elements of the game that made it motivating. Six out of eight were clearly motivated, while two were less. Some told us that the rivalry against friends was the major motivation factor, while others focused on appearance and development of their exermon, and keeping it alive.

5.3 Results on Enjoyment (RQ3)

Table 3 describes the results on statements related to enjoyment in the questionnaire. 100% over the subjects enjoyed playing the game, while over 90% felt better at the game the more they played. Also, close to 80% found the fantasy world in the game to be appealing.

Table 3. Results from statements related to enjoyment

ID	Statement	Disagree	Agree
S9	I enjoyed playing the game	0%	100%
S10	I felt better at the game the more I played	8%	92%
S11	I found the fantasy world in the game appealing	21%	79%

The observations and interview also clearly showed that the subjects enjoyed the game. While playing in the arena, one of the test-subjects shouted, "it is fun to fight!". When we told the test-subjects to play the game, the group was divided into two. Some knew right away what they wanted to do and went in the arena or found friends to battle without any explanation. Others felt a little insecure about what to do and needed more instruction on what their next step was going to be. However, for both groups we observed that the test-subjects smiled and enjoyed different parts of the game. The observations of subjects also revealed different attitudes towards the audio in the game. Some players muted the music during gameplay, while others moved according to the music and enjoyed it. One of the test-subjects celebrated his victories, and after defeating a friend shouted out to his friend who were nearby: "Hah, I beat you!".

In the interview, all participants said they enjoyed playing the game, and especially the fighting part of the game. One of the participants exclaimed: "I was excited" about the fighting in the game. Two participants said that the exercising got more exciting because the game gave feedback when you completed a repetition in terms of increase in stats and a sound that was played. Although all subjects enjoyed the game, three players pointed out that the game gets a little boring in the long term because the lack of features and monotonous fighting.

5.4 Results on Engagement (RQ4)

Table 4 shows the results from statements on engagement. In general, it was obvious that the test-subjects got engaged by the game as over 90% felt engaged, close to 80% were completely focused on the task they were doing, and over 80% were curious on how their exermon would evolve. However, only 25% of the subjects agreed that they were so engaged in the game that they became less aware of their surroundings. We believe there are two reasons for the latter. First, games on mobile devices such as smart phones are generally less immersive than games played on larger screens, as it is easier to focus on the surroundings on a small screen. Second, the Exermon game takes the player in and out of the gameplay on purpose, as the player must carry out strength exercises.

Table 4. Results from statements related to engagement

ID	Statement	Disagree	Agree
S12	I felt engaged in the game	8%	92%
S13	I was completely focused on the task I was doing	21%	79%
S14	I was so engaged in the game that I became less aware of my surroundings	75%	25%
S15	I was curious on how my exermon would evolve	17%	83%

Our observations revealed that the majority of test-subjects concentrated hard to do their best while playing the game. The interview documented variation in the mount of engagement in the game. Some subjects were really engaged in the beginning, but lost the engagement after a while. Others were really engaged throughout the game, relating to their exermon and trying to achieve the best result possible. "I was really focused while fighting, because I really wanted to win" was the response from one participant. Two players said they were lacking engagement in the game.

5.5 Results on Control, Progression and Social Interaction (RQ5)

Table 5 shows the results from statements related to controlling the game and the progression of the game. The majority of the test-subjects felt they were in control of what they were doing in the game (close to 80%), as well as it was clear what they had to do to progress in the game (over 80%). Fewer, but the majority, said that the game presented clearly the tasks to accomplish (67%), and that the game had an appropriate difficulty level (71%).

Table 5. Results from statements related to control and progression

ID	Statement	Disagree	Agree
S16	I felt in control of what I was doing in the game	21%	79%
S17	It was clear that I was making progress in the game	17%	83%
S18	I was presented with clear tasks to accomplish	33%	67%
S19	The game had an appropriate difficulty level	29%	71%

Our observations showed that the subjects understood that they made progress in the game by viewing their rank and stats. Initially, some subjects had some problems understanding what to do in the game. We also noticed that everyone had challenges that matched their skill level. This was because they started by working out to improve their stats, and progressed up to the opponent's level.

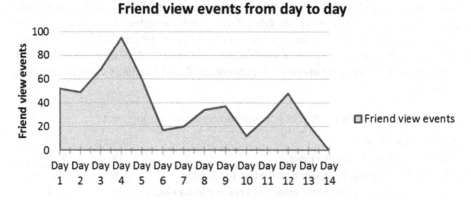

Fig. 9. Records of friend view events

During the test period, we also logged data on fighting activities in the game, what kinds of fights were fought, and friend events. Our data revealed that most fighting activity was around the first days of the test period, but there were also frequent fights around day 8-9 and day 12. The average number of fights per day in total was 129.3, which computes to 5.4 fights per test-subject per day. Further, our data showed that 83% of the fights were arena fights, 11% were fights with friends, and 6% were boss fights. Figure 9 shows number of times a player looked at a friend's game stats per day over the test period. As we can see the number of friend view events varied over time with a peak on day four with over 90 friend view events. The average amount of friend views per day was 38.7 (1.6 per player per day).

6 Discussion

This section presents and discusses some technical challenges in the Exermon game, the problem of cheating, and threats to validity of the result.

6.1 Technical Issues

From tests during the development of the Exermon game, it was found that the tracking of the various exercises using the proximity and accelerometer sensors varied among different Android smartphones. It was therefore decided to include a question about how the phone tracked the exercises in the questionnaire. The results from the survey showed that for 37.5% of the test-subject, the game counted about the correct number of repetitions. For 25% of the test-subjects, the game counted fewer repetitions than they actually did, and for 37.5% the game counted more repetitions than they actually did. This means that for 62.5% of the test-subjects, the smart phone did not count the correct repetition when exercising all the time. Our observations of the eight test-subjects showed that the majority got exactly the correct number of exercise repetitions, except for two participants who had problems with the dips exercise where it counted several repetitions while getting into position and none when actually doing the repetitions. One of the two said "I lost focus on doing the exercise physically correct, because I was more focused on getting the phone to count the number of repetitions correctly." In addition, one person did not get any repetitions counted while doing the glute bridge exercise. One person had a lower tier smartphone without a proximity sensor, which meant that no repetitions for push-ups were counted. Further, one of the persons we observed decided to do the exercise without the phone, and afterwards simulated the repetitions by shaking the phone. The main problem with exercise counting is the great variation sensor responses in various Android smartphones. A possible solution to this problem is to add a calibration or learning mechanism to the game, to teach the game what should be recognized as an exercise repetition. This problem is not unique to tracking exercises on smart phones, but are also a problem when playing commercial exergames using dedicated exercise sensors in games like EA Active, or the Kinect sensor on games like XBOX Fitness and Shape Up. Another solution to this problem suggested by one of the observed test-subjects was to add a possibility to adjust the count after an exercise, which brings us to the other challenge of the Exermon game – cheating.

6.2 Cheating

By using sensors in a smart phone to count exercise repetitions, it will be easy to cheat the game by simply moving the phone according to the pattern required to recognize a strength exercise. This is a challenge for almost all exergames. If the players want to cheat the physical movements, there are always ways of doing this. We were of course aware of this problem and thus included a question in the questionnaire about cheating. The results showed that 42% of the test-subjects said they had not cheated at all. Further, 29% said they cheated a few times in the game, 25% said they had cheated many times, and one person said he had cheated all the time. The subjects that cheated a few times explained their cheating that they wanted to test which movements were picked up by the phone and counted as repetitions, to avoid the death of his or her exermon, or correct the number of repetition the game did not recognize. Those who cheated many or all the times, wanted to gain stats to beat opponents in the arena, the boss and friends' exermons, or did not want to do a lot of exercising. We acknowledge that cheating is a major concern for all exergames including Exermon, and currently there are no easy solutions to prevent it. However, if the player is interested in getting stronger physically in the first place and play together with friends who agree on a code of honor about not cheating, this issue should not be a major concern. Experiences from other exergames we have worked with shows that players interested in playing exergames have an initial motivation for improving their physical health, although they might lack motivation to do the physical exercises. Their motivation for improving their physical shape is our best weapon to avoid cheating in exergames. It is always a way to trick the sensors.

6.3   Threats to Validity

The evaluation of the Exermon game cannot be classified as a controlled experiment, but rather a quasi-experiment. To counter the lack of a controlled environment and a detailed experimental design, we used four sources of data, both qualitative and quantitative. We believe that the combination of data sources provides a realistic evaluation of the game.

The Hawthorne effect states that the behavior of individuals will change as they become aware that they or their actions are under observations [58]. We did overt observations, which mean that the test-subjects were aware of our observations and that the Hawthorne effect might have influenced our results, giving us a more positive feedback and data that we otherwise might have gotten.

Generalization of the results of this quasi-experiment is limited, as the results are related to this particular game and to the length of the study. However, we believe the results are useful for other researchers working on games to motivate physical strength. Due to the limited length of the study, it is hard to say anything about the potential lasting effects of similar exergames. However, the initial results are very positive, and we believe an improved and extended version of the Exermon game with more depth in gameplay should motivate players over a longer period of time.

7   Conclusion

In this paper, we have presented the Exermon game, which is a new type of exergame combining role-playing game elements, first-person boxing, caring for a monster, and strength exercises. The goal of developing Exermon was to motivate players to do strength exercises to get their monster, their exermon, to grow and evolve. Further, our paper describes the results from the evaluation of the game where 24 subjects tested the game over two weeks, and where five research questions were answered through a survey, observations, interviews and logs from the game server.

The *first research question* investigated whether there were any physical effects from playing the Exermon game (RQ1). The survey showed that above 40% the test-subjects exercised more than they did before when playing the game, where most did 1–2 extra exercises per week, and a few 3-4 extra exercises per week. The survey also showed that 40% of the test-subjects felt their strength had improved due to the game. Our logs from the game showed that most test-subjects exercised mostly in the beginning of the test period and at the end. To conclude, we found that the game gave a positive physical effect but not on all test-subjects.

The *second research question* focused on the motivational effect of playing the Exermon game (RQ2). The survey showed that over 90% of the test-subjects were motivated to exercise by the game itself, but it was found a great variation in what parts of the game that motivated the test-subjects to perform strength exercises. About 40% were motivated by the exermon's appearance, 40% were motivated by the fact that their exermon could die in the game, 70% were motivated by feature to unlock all exercises in the game, over 80% were motivated from the goal of defeating a previously unbeatable opponent, and 60% were motivated by the feature of playing against other players' exermons. To conclude, the game has a motivational effect on the players, but there is room for improvement for making the game even more motivational.

The *third research question* investigated the enjoyment effect of playing the Exermon game (RQ3). The survey showed that all test-subjects enjoyed playing the game, that 90% felt better the more they played the game, and about 80% found the fantasy world in the game appealing. The observations of the test-subjects clearly confirmed that the test-subjects enjoyed the game, and especially the fighting part. The only challenge found was that a few subjects got less enthusiastic over time as the game was running out of content. To conclude, the game was found to be enjoyable, but more content should be provided to keep the game enjoyable over time.

The *fourth research question* focused on whether the players were engaged by the Exermon game (RQ4). In general, the game was found to be engaging of almost all test-subjects (90%), and about 80% were completely focused the task they were doing. However, we found that only 25% of the test-subjects were so engaged that they became less aware of their surroundings. One part of the game that made it engaging was the players' curiosity of their exermons evolution.

The *fifth research question* investigated the control, progression and social interaction in the game (RQ5). The survey showed that the majority of players felt control over their actions in the game, the progress was easy to follow and easy to understand what to do, and the difficulty level was appropriate. The players also found social component of the game motivational, although there is a potential to improve it through direct fights between friends.

The main challenges revealed in our evaluation of the game were found to be the possibility of cheating the strength exercises, and issues related to the game recognizing repetitions of exercises using smartphone sensors. The evaluation of the Exermon game shows that there is absolutely a great potential for exergames for strength training. The main challenges are technical as well as cheating, and the game design and inclusion of social features are essential for the success of such games.

Another challenge with exergames like Exermon, is that such games require the players to be interested in doing strength exercises in the first place. The effect of the game is to boost the motivation for doing physical training, and not to motivate those who are not interested in doing strength exercises in the first place. A weakness with the approach is that the strength exercises themselves are not directly related to the fantasy of the game, but rather have an indirect effect on the fantasy through evolving the monsters. Future research includes investigating exergame concepts where the exercises and the fantasy is tightly integrated, as well as examining the long-term effects of such exergames.

Acknowledgements. Our sincerest thanks go out to all the participants of the testing process. Without you, we would not have been able to conduct this study, and write this paper. You know who you are.

References

1. Unnithan, V.B., Houser, W., Fernhall, B.: Evaluation of the energy cost of playing a dance simulation video game in overweight and non-overweight children and adolescents. Int. J. Sports Med. **27**, 804–809 (2006)
2. Göbel, S., Hardy, S., Wendel, V., Mehm, F., Steinmetz, R.: Serious games for health: personalized exergames. In: Proceedings of the 18th ACM International Conference on Multimedia, pp. 1663–1666. ACM (2010)
3. Gao, Y., Mandryk, R.: The acute cognitive benefits of casual exergame play. In: Proceedings of the SIGCHI Conference on Human Factors in Computing Systems, pp. 1863–1872. ACM (2012)
4. Ketcheson, M., Ye, Z., Graham, T.: Designing for exertion: how heart-rate power-ups increase physical activity in exergames. In: Proceedings of the 2015 Annual Symposium on Computer-Human Interaction in Play, pp. 79–89. ACM (2015)
5. Chatta, A., Hurst, T., Samaraweera, G., Guo, R., Quarles, J.: Get off the couch: an approach to utilize sedentary commercial games as exergames. In: Proceedings of the 2015 Annual Symposium on Computer-Human Interaction in Play, pp. 47–56. ACM (2015)
6. de Souza, L.M., Yildirim, I.G., Kolesnichenko, A., Park, T.: World of riders: exercising is fun. In: Proceedings of the 2016 Annual Symposium on Computer-Human Interaction in Play Companion Extended Abstracts, pp. 55–60. ACM (2016)
7. Hagen, K., Chorianopoulos, K., Wang, A.I., Jaccheri, L., Weie, S.: Gameplay as exercise. In: Proceedings of the 2016 CHI Conference Extended Abstracts on Human Factors in Computing Systems, pp. 1872–1878. ACM (2016)
8. Lin, J.J., Mamykina, L., Lindtner, S., Delajoux, G., Strub, H.B.: Fish'n'Steps: encouraging physical activity with an interactive computer game. In: Dourish, P., Friday, A. (eds.) UbiComp 2006. LNCS, vol. 4206, pp. 261–278. Springer, Heidelberg (2006). https://doi.org/10.1007/11853565_16
9. Macvean, A., Robertson, J.: iFitQuest: a school based study of a mobile location-aware exergame for adolescents. In: Proceedings of the 14th International Conference on Human-Computer Interaction with Mobile Devices and Services, pp. 359–368. ACM (2012)

10. Gerling, K.M., Miller, M., Mandryk, R.L., Birk, M.V., Smeddinck, J.D.: Effects of balancing for physical abilities on player performance, experience and self-esteem in exergames. In: Proceedings of the 32nd Annual ACM Conference on Human Factors in Computing Systems, pp. 2201–2210. ACM (2014)

11. Gerling, K.M., Schild, J., Masuch, M.: Exergame design for elderly users: the case study of SilverBalance. In: Proceedings of the 7th International Conference on Advances in Computer Entertainment Technology, pp. 66–69. ACM (2010)

12. Barry, G., Galna, B., Rochester, L.: The role of exergaming in Parkinson's disease rehabilitation: a systematic review of the evidence. J. Neuroeng. Rehabil. **11**, 1 (2014)

13. Tsai, T.-H., Chang, H.-T., Huang, G.-S., Chang, C.-C.: WaterBall: the exergaming design for rehabilitation of the elderly. Comput. Aided Des. Appl. **9**, 481–489 (2012)

14. Alavesa, P., Schmidt, J., Fedosov, A., Byrne, R., Mueller, F.F.: Air tandem: a collaborative bodily game exploring interpersonal synchronization. In: Proceedings of the 2015 Annual Symposium on Computer-Human Interaction in Play, pp. 433–438. ACM (2015)

15. Hämäläinen, P., Marshall, J., Kajastila, R., Byrne, R., Mueller, F.F.: Utilizing gravity in movement-based games and play. In: Proceedings of the 2015 Annual Symposium on Computer-Human Interaction in Play, pp. 67–77. ACM (2015)

16. Rebane, K., Kai, T., Endo, N., Imai, T., Nojima, T., Yanase, Y.: Insights of the augmented dodgeball game design and play test. In: Proceedings of the 8th Augmented Human International Conference, p. 12. ACM (2017)

17. Choi, W., Oh, J., Edge, D., Kim, J., Lee, U.: SwimTrain: exploring exergame design for group fitness swimming. In: Proceedings of the 2016 CHI Conference on Human Factors in Computing Systems, pp. 1692–1704. ACM (2016)

18. Raffe, W.L., Tamassia, M., Zambetta, F., Li, X., Pell, S.J., Mueller, F.F.: Player-computer interaction features for designing digital play experiences across six degrees of water contact. In: Proceedings of the 2015 Annual Symposium on Computer-Human Interaction in Play, pp. 295–305. ACM (2015)

19. Mueller, F.F., Agamanolis, S., Gibbs, M.R., Vetere, F.: Remote impact: shadowboxing over a distance. In: CHI 2008 Extended Abstracts on Human Factors in Computing Systems, pp. 2291–2296. ACM (2008)

20. Sato, K., Kuroki, K., Saiki, S., Nagatomi, R.: Improving walking, muscle strength, and balance in the elderly with an exergame using Kinect: a randomized controlled trial. Games for Health J. **4**, 161–167 (2015)

21. Chao, Y.-Y., Scherer, Y.K., Wu, Y.-W., Lucke, K.T., Montgomery, C.A.: The feasibility of an intervention combining self-efficacy theory and Wii Fit exergames in assisted living residents: a pilot study. Geriatr. Nurs. **34**, 377–382 (2013)

22. Chang, Y.-J., Chen, S.-F., Huang, J.-D.: A kinect-based system for physical rehabilitation: a pilot study for young adults with motor disabilities. Res. Dev. Disabil. **32**, 2566–2570 (2011)

23. Bonetti, A.J., Drury, D.G., Danoff, J.V., Miller, T.A.: Comparison of acute exercise responses between conventional video gaming and isometric resistance exergaming. J. Strength Cond. Res. **24**, 1799–1803 (2010)

24. Marshall, J., Linehan, C., Hazzard, A.: Designing brutal multiplayer video games. In: Proceedings of the 2016 CHI Conference on Human Factors in Computing Systems, pp. 2669–2680. ACM (2016)

25. Bartley, J., Forsyth, J., Pendse, P., Xin, D., Brown, G., Hagseth, P., Agrawal, A., Goldberg, D.W., Hammond, T.: World of workout: a contextual mobile RPG to encourage long term fitness. In: Proceedings of the Second ACM SIGSPATIAL International Workshop on the Use of GIS in Public Health, pp. 60–67. ACM (2013)

26. Richards, C., Graham, T.: Developing compelling repetitive-motion exergames by balancing player agency with the constraints of exercise. In: Proceedings of the 2016 ACM Conference on Designing Interactive Systems, pp. 911–923. ACM (2016)

27. Buchner, D.M., Bishop, J., Brown, D.R., Fulton, J.E., Galuska, D.A., Gilchrist, J., Guralnik, J.M., Hootman, J.M., Johnson, M.A., Kohl III, H.W., Lee, S.M., Loughrey, K.A., McDivitt, J.A., Simons-Morton, D.G., Smith, A.W., Tilson, W.M., Troiano, R.P., Wargo, J.D., Willis, G.B., Rodgers, A.B.: 2008 Physical Activity Guidelines for Americans. U.S. Department of Health and Human Services (2008)

28. Wikipedia: Pokémon Go. Wikipedia (2017)

29. Clark, A.M., Clark, M.T.: Pokémon go and research - qualitative, mixed methods research, and the supercomplexity of interventions. Int. J. Qual. Methods 15(1) (2016). SAGE Publications, London

30. McCartney, M.: Margaret McCartney: game on for Pokémon Go. BMJ: Br. Med. J. 354, i4306 (2016)

31. Wüest, S., Langenberg, R., Bruin, E.D.: Design considerations for a theory-driven exergame-based rehabilitation program to improve walking of persons with stroke. Eur. Rev. Aging Phys. Act. 11, 119 (2013)

32. Smith, S.T., Schoene, D.: The use of exercise-based videogames for training and rehabilitation of physical function in older adults: current practice and guidelines for future research. Aging Health 8, 243–252 (2012)

33. Wylie, C.G., Coulton, P.: Mobile exergaming. In: Proceedings of the 2008 International Conference on Advances in Computer Entertainment Technology, pp. 338–341. ACM (2008)

34. Di Tore, P.A., Raiola, G.: Exergames in motor skill learning. J. Phys. Educ. Sport 12, 358 (2012)

35. Wylie, C.G., Coulton, P.: Mobile persuasive exergaming. In: 2009 International IEEE Consumer Electronics Society's Games Innovations Conference, pp. 126–130. IEEE (2009)

36. Chittaro, L., Sioni, R.: Turning the classic snake mobile game into a location–based exergame that encourages walking. In: Bang, M., Ragnemalm, E.L. (eds.) PERSUASIVE 2012. LNCS, vol. 7284, pp. 43–54. Springer, Heidelberg (2012). https://doi.org/10.1007/978-3-642-31037-9_4

37. Gorgu, L., O'Hare, G.M., O'Grady, M.J.: Towards mobile collaborative exergaming. In: Second International Conference on Advances in Human-Oriented and Personalized Mechanisms, Technologies, and Services, CENTRIC 2009, pp. 61–64. IEEE (2009)

38. Wang, A.I., Forberg, S., Øye, J.K.: Knowledge war - a pervasive multiplayer role-playing learning game. In: European Conference on Game Based Learning (ECGBL 2016). ACPI, Glasgow (2016)

39. Wang, A.I., Ibánez, J.D.J.L.G.: Learning recycling from playing a kinect game. Int. J. Game-Based Learn. (IJGBL) 5, 25–44 (2015)

40. Wu, B., Wang, A.I.: A pervasive game to know your city better. In: Proceedings of the 2011 IEEE International Games Innovation Conference (IGIC 2011), pp. 117–120 (2011)

41. Yim, J., Graham, T.: Using games to increase exercise motivation. In: Proceedings of the 2007 Conference on Future Play, pp. 166–173. ACM (2007)

42. Hagen, K., Weie, S., Chorianopoulos, K., Wang, A.I., Jaccheri, L.: Pedal tanks. In: Chorianopoulos, K., Divitini, M., Hauge, J.B., Jaccheri, L., Malaka, R. (eds.) ICEC 2015. LNCS, vol. 9353, pp. 539–544. Springer, Cham (2015). https://doi.org/10.1007/978-3-319-24589-8_53

43. Bolton, J., Lambert, M., Lirette, D., Unsworth, B.: PaperDude: a virtual reality cycling exergame. In: CHI 2014 Extended Abstracts on Human Factors in Computing Systems, pp. 475–478. ACM (2014)

44. Shaw, L.A.: Development and evaluation of an exercycle game using immersive technologies. The University of Auckland, New Zealand (2014)

45. Nenonen, V., Lindblad, A., Häkkinen, V., Laitinen, T., Jouhtio, M., Hämäläinen, P.: Using heart rate to control an interactive game. In: Proceedings of the SIGCHI Conference on Human Factors in Computing Systems, pp. 853–856. ACM (2007)
46. Oh, Y., Yang, S.: Defining exergames & exergaming. In: Proceedings of Meaningful Play, pp. 1–17 (2010)
47. Serino, M., Cordrey, K., McLaughlin, L., Milanaik, R.L.: Pokémon Go and augmented virtual reality games: a cautionary commentary for parents and pediatricians. Curr. Opin. Pediatr. **28**, 673–677 (2016)
48. Winett, R.A., Carpinelli, R.N.: Potential health-related benefits of resistance training. Prev. Med. **33**, 503–513 (2001)
49. Hunter, G.R., McCarthy, J.P., Bamman, M.M.: Effects of resistance training on older adults. Sports Med. **34**, 329–348 (2004)
50. Feigenbaum, M.S., Pollock, M.L.: Prescription of resistance training for health and disease. Med. Sci. Sports Exerc. **31**, 38–45 (1999)
51. Malone, T.W.: What makes things fun to learn? heuristics for designing instructional computer games. In: The 3rd ACM SIGSMALL Symposium and the First SIGPC Symposium on Small Systems. ACM Press, Palo Alto (1980)
52. Nakamura, J., Csikszentmihalyi, M.: The concept of flow. Flow and the Foundations of Positive Psychology, pp. 239–263. Springer, Dordrecht (2014). https://doi.org/10.1007/978-94-017-9088-8_16
53. Sinclair, J., Hingston, P., Masek, M.: Exergame development using the dual flow model. In: Proceedings of the Sixth Australasian Conference on Interactive Entertainment, p. 11. ACM (2009)
54. Sinclair, J., Hingston, P., Masek, M., Nosaka, K.: Testing an exergame for effectiveness and attractiveness. In: 2010 2nd International IEEE Consumer Electronics Society's Games Innovations Conference, pp. 1–8. IEEE (2010)
55. Basili, V.R.: Software modeling and measurement: the Goal/Question/Metric paradigm. University of Maryland for Advanced Computer Studies (1992)
56. Malone, T.W.: Toward a theory of intrinsically motivating instruction. Cognit. Sci. **5**, 333–369 (1981)
57. Sweetser, P., Wyeth, P.: GameFlow: a model for evaluating player enjoyment in games. ACM Comput. Entertain. **3**, 3 (2005)
58. Gale, E.A.: The Hawthorne studies—a fable for our times? QJM **97**, 439–449 (2004)

Photo Curation Practices on Smartphones

Xenia Zürn[1]([✉]) [iD], Koen Damen[1] [iD], Fabienne van Leiden[1] [iD],
Mendel Broekhuijsen[1,2] [iD], and Panos Markopoulos[1,2] [iD]

[1] Eindhoven University of Technology, Eindhoven, The Netherlands
{x.k.zurn,k.h.b.damen}@student.tue.nl,
f.z.v.leiden@alumnus.tue.nl,
{m.j.broekhuijsen,p.markopoulos}@tue.nl
[2] University of Technology Sydney, Sydney, NSW, Australia

Abstract. With camera-enabled phones always at hand, people tend to build large photo collections on these devices, which in turn creates the need of curating such collections. This paper describes a study of curation activities performed on smartphones aiming to identify design opportunities for applications that will help users manage and organize their photo collections. Semi-structured interviews with young adults show that curation on smartphones does not happen without external triggers and is an activity that they postpone and avoid as much as possible. The most usual trigger for curation activities is running out of storage space. Rather than specialized applications participants are content with camera roll applications that are built into their phones. They do not like how photographs are mixed in the camera roll, but value the overview, chronological order and serendipity it allows in viewing. Furthermore, they appreciate automated backup of their photo collections.

Keywords: Photo curation · Smartphone · PhotoUse · Interaction design
Design research

1 Introduction

The introduction of digital cameras 25 years ago [17] made the cost of taking and storing photos negligible, resulting in a sharp increase in the number of photos captured and stored [5]. For the broader public, the primary role of digital photography has shifted from capturing special events and family life, to a means of communicating with friends, shaping identity, and supporting social bonds [4, 11]. Smartphones have become a key enabler in this evolving role of digital photography as they offer convenient and quick photo capturing and sharing. As a result, there is an increasing number of photos stored on mobile phones. Moreover, people use cloud storage where they keep various personal photo collections from different sources and captured through various devices. People often navigate and manage these photo collections using their smartphones which makes the development of applications supporting curation on the smartphone increasingly relevant. The goal of this paper is to understand this particular use of the smartphones and to identify design opportunities that can support and improve current and future photo curation practices on smartphones.

© Springer International Publishing AG, part of Springer Nature 2018
A. D. Cheok et al. (Eds.): ACE 2017, LNCS 10714, pp. 406–414, 2018.
https://doi.org/10.1007/978-3-319-76270-8_28

2   Related Work

The advances in media capture and media sharing technologies have changed digital photography practice (e.g. [6, 9, 12, 14]). Rodden and Wood investigated how people organize and browse through their digital photo collections using PC software called Shoebox [14]. They found that the browsing features of digital files made it easier to organize them, but their study was limited to users with relatively small collections. However, several studies acknowledge that the sheer amount of data makes it increasingly difficult to properly manage and retrieve the photos (e.g. [1, 12, 19]). Frohlich et al. [6] identified a number of requirements for tools that can support digital photography, which they called PhotoWare. To understand how to support emerging photo practices, Kirk et al. introduced the PhotoWork model in which they describe the activities that people perform after capturing and prior to sharing a photo [12]. Their work aims to give designers a better understanding of the workflow. Building on that work, Broekhuijsen et al. proposed the PhotoUse model [3], which provides a holistic perspective to designing solutions encompassing less attractive photo tasks, such as curation. Van House and Churchill [10] described that curation in the context of digital media involves deciding on what to keep, in what format and structure to preserve it, and deciding on the methods of (re)presentation. According to the PhotoUse model, photo curation consists of four photo activity categories:

- Organizing: tagging, moving, categorizing, naming, captioning, archiving and deleting pictures.
- Triaging: assessing and selecting for a specific purpose (e.g. sharing, decorating, presenting).
- Managing: filing, backup, downloading and uploading.
- Editing: retouching, cropping, combining, correcting and changing.

While Broekhuijsen et al. [3] focused on the use of homebound devices, we are interested to see how these practices apply to mobile-only practices. In our study, we use the PhotoUse model to analyze current photo curation activities that people perform on their smartphone and identify design opportunities for mobile curation applications.

When looking at commercial mobile curation applications, we see that almost all smartphones that are currently on the market have at least one default application for organizing and viewing photos. Even though native photo applications differ in User Interface, features and specific use [18], they all feature a main camera roll that provides access to all photos stored in the phone as a continuous list. These applications also have the option to view the photos organized in folders, which are often automatically created by the application. The smartphone user is able to manually create folders and to move, name and categorize the photos. Many of these built-in applications also offer some tools for editing. Moreover, most smartphones support cloud-based applications that allow for managing photo collections that are stored in the cloud.

3   Curating Photo-Collections on Smartphones

In this study, we set out to understand curation activities on the smartphone and to identify design considerations for smartphone applications to support curation. We gathered information about these curation activities through semi-structured interviews with smartphone users in which we asked about their photo collections, their curation activities on their smartphones and the applications they use for curation. We applied the laddering method [8] to encourage participants to explain their motives and to make suggestions.

3.1   Participants

We applied homogeneous purposive sampling [13] targeting participants who store a large number of photos on their phones; at least about a thousand photos. The participants (N = 11, 5 male, 6 female) were Industrial Design students from the authors' personal and professional network. Students belong to the group of young adults and are therefore a group of active smartphone users, who use their smartphone for both social and professional purposes. The selected participants owned different smartphones. The participants therefore had one of the following default applications on their smartphone: Gallery (Android), Photos (iOS) or Windows Photo Gallery (Windows).

3.2   Procedure

At the start of the interview sessions the participants were fully briefed about the aims of the study and the meaning of curation in the context of digital media (consisting of triaging, organizing, managing and editing). Informed consent was obtained, where we committed to confidentiality and anonymity of the data. The sessions started with semi-structured interviews about the different applications they use on their smartphones for curating photos, lasting about 15 min. Participants then showed their photo collection to explain their curation activities. The total session lasted about 30 min.

3.3   Data Analysis

One of the two researchers who were present at the interview sessions took notes. Also, interviews were audio-recorded. The responses were transcribed and translated from Dutch to English. Interviews were transcribed in full, and the transcriptions were coded following the iterative steps of thematic analysis as described in the work of Braun and Clarke [2]. The themes were refined until there was consensus between the first three authors of this work.

4   Findings

The findings represent the information contributed by the participants in the sessions. We present the photo activities on smartphones following the activity categories of the

PhotoUse model [3] that relate to curation. Participants are referred to with their participant number (P1 to P11).

The participants' smartphone photo collections ranged from 900 to >14,000 photos. In some cases, the photos were stored on a cloud-based application (e.g. Google Photos, Google Drive and iCloud), but they were still accessible on the smartphone.

4.1 Applications

Almost all participants used the default application available as part of the operating system of the phone for organizing and retrieving photos. Two participants referred to this as the chronological 'camera roll'. Participants use what is pre-installed on their phones and rarely consider other applications for curation purposes.

"The album application was already on the phone and that is enough for what I need." – P6.

Next to the pre-installed applications, these participants used in total three applications, *Dropbox*[1], *Google Drive*[2], and *iCloud Drive*[3], for managing photos and six applications for editing photos, *Instagram*[4], *Lumibee*[5], *Photo Editor*[6], *Pixlr*[7], *Schets*[8], and *Snapseed*[9].

4.2 Curating Activities

Organizing. Almost all participants indicated that they never look at their photo collections deliberately without an external trigger. It can be daunting to start curating a large photo collection. Going through a photo collection and curating the photos is seen as too much work, too time consuming and therefore is considered a last resort activity. As P8 explains: *"I have many photos where there are three similar photos and only one is good, yet I still keep the other two. But I have reached a point where I am not going to start with it anymore; I have 9,000 pictures. I would only do that if I would be at a place without internet for a long time and I was extremely bored." – P8*

The most important trigger for the majority of the participants to curate their photos is the limited amount of storage on their smartphones. *"I often receive a notification that my phone has no storage space anymore, so then I have to delete pictures. I then select around 300 and I delete them all at once." – P1*

In many cases the phone is seen as a place to 'dump' photos. This is related to the value of the photos taken with a smartphone *"I do organize photos on my laptop in folders, but I see my phone more like a dump place for photos. About once or twice a*

---

[1] https://www.dropbox.com/.
[2] https://drive.google.com/.
[3] https://www.iclouds.com/.
[4] https://www.instagram.com/.
[5] http://www.lumibee.photo/.
[6] https://www.adobe.com/products/aviary.html.
[7] https://pixlr.com/.
[8] https://www.sonymobile.com/nl/apps-services/sketch/.
[9] https://play.google.com/store/apps/details?id=com.niksoftware.snapseed&hl=nl.

year I transfer the photos from my phone on my computer, but because there are so many photos, I don't feel like organizing them. [...] Overall, you can conclude that I do not organize [my photos] on my phone, because quality is worse [than my camera] and photos are quickly taken, and not well thought-through." – P3

Photos that enter the smartphone's collection via WhatsApp or other social media are also of diverse quality and value: *"WhatsApp group photos are the biggest problem; I want the photos of [design related] projects and my [design project] client and girlfriend but not all the photos of a crazy party on Saturday."* – P5

Triaging. An important trigger to curate the photos is the role of smartphones in social gatherings. If photos are selected for sharing, some participants pay a lot of attention to curating these photos. *"After a holiday I want to make a nice album. Place the photos in a good order and add some text, so I can show this as a slideshow presentation [to my family or friends]. This [photo-album] is nice to share with people who were with me on holiday so they can add photos as well."* – P7

Another reason for participants to browse through photos and curate their collection is when they need a photo for educational or work-related purposes: *"When I have to write a report, I will search for a specific photo."* – P5

Even when a structure or browsing method is provided by the smartphone software (e.g. event-based, people-based, or grouped by theme such as food), most participants prefer using the camera roll to retrieve photos. The camera roll is mainly valued for its overview and chronological order: *"I will check the approximate date, for example if I need a picture from carnival [popular celebration that takes place in the late winter] I will look into February and then I can find the photo."* – P1

If participants browse through the camera roll, they enjoy stumbling upon photos in a serendipitous manner: *"I actually never look at my photos. If by accident I come across a photo it may be interesting."* – P6

Managing. To upload and make a backup of the photo collection, most participants use cloud services to store photos. Almost half of all participants mention that this happens automatically; a quality that is being valued: *"I value Dropbox because it uploads to the cloud. And also the possibility to access [files] via other devices. Especially that this happens automatically."* – P6

Editing. Editing activities are particularly important prior to sharing photos on social media. *"Sharing is my trigger to edit photos. I wouldn't do that for myself."* – P10

Summary of Findings. In summary, the findings from our study were that

1. Participants install applications for editing and managing, but not for organizing and triaging.
2. Curation does not happen without external triggers and is seen as a last resort activity.
3. Lack of storage space is the most important trigger to curate photos, which makes deleting the most frequent curation activity.
4. Participants do not like that photos of different values are presented together in the applications they use.

5. Social gatherings are important triggers for editing and triaging photos.
6. Participants enjoy the camera roll for its chronological order, overview and serendipity it stimulates.
7. Participants appreciate automatic backup.

5   Design Considerations

Based on our findings we can identify three design opportunities that can be considered
in developing novel curating applications for smartphones. These design opportunities
are based on suggestions made by the participants, which we then developed further.

5.1   Make Curating More Fun

Noting that participants generally do not engage in curation activities without external
triggers, we believe that there is an opportunity to improve the curation experience by
making curating on the smartphone more fun.

One way how this could be achieved is with gamification elements for curating
activities. By repeatedly confronting players with a similar type of problem *"until
players achieve a routinized, taken-for-granted mastery of certain skill"* [7], a feeling
of competence can be created. Competence in games is associated with enjoyment [16].
Gamifying curating activities could make users feel competent which might result in
enjoying the activity more and thus increasing intrinsic motivation to perform curation
activities. For example, the gamification elements achievement could be implemented
by giving rewards for assessing, sorting and tagging photos. Rewards for weekly objectives could challenge users to perform a certain amount of actions each week. A weekly
objective could be, say, to put ten percent of the photo collection in folders and earning
a new editing filter as a reward.

Another approach pertains to making curation more social. From our findings we
see that participants curate for social purposes or in social settings. Curation could be
turned into a social activity that is performed with others. After having been together on
a trip, a shared album could be created in which the photos of all partakers are gathered
and curated together. The partakers could rate the photos and in this way decide together
which photos are the best photos of the trip. This could be represented by a ranking list
with the top photos.

5.2   Support Deleting

Improving ease of use and the user experience relating to deleting unwanted photos
could be given higher priority, as it is the most executed curating activity, albeit force-
fully: *"The biggest irritation is the size of the files and the need to delete files to make
room; this has almost become a weekly activity. Maybe the phone can automatically
create suggestions of what to remove."* - P5

To support deleting, the smartphone could proactively make suggestions on what to
delete [12]. Since valued photos are mixed with less valued ones, the smartphone could

make inferences based on source (e.g. incoming photos from instant messaging applications like WhatsApp[10]) to make it easier to delete or manage them as a group. A way to do this by sending daily notifications with suggestions to delete certain photos. Another option would be to delete photos semi-automatically, by placing these in a temporary trash folder. Users would be notified to review photos in the temporary trash folder at suitable moments, e.g. during lunchtime or before going to bed. This also relates to the theory of disposition of possessions by C. Roster, which mentions that people have several stages of throwing something away [15]. *"It would be nice to rate photos with stars and all other photos would become junk. If you want to remove photos it takes a lot of time. You cannot select them all together because then you would be scared that you throw important photos away."* – P5.

When automating curation processes on the smartphone, it should be taken into account that although participants value suggestions, they want to be in control of the final curation decisions. People do not trust the smartphone to be "smart enough" to understand which photos belong together [19]: *"It should be easy to separate the photos in albums. But I still want to do this myself."* – P7

5.3 Provide Overview and Support Reminiscing

From our findings, we also gained insights into the use of photos for reminiscing, even though the focus of our study was on curation: the camera roll function is the most used and most valued feature of photo applications for retrieving, because of the overview it provides. It is therefore worth supporting this overview function in new applications for smartphones. However, the camera roll is not be the most suitable tool for retrieval and could benefit from some improvements: *"A better presentation of the photos would be nice, so I don't need to search too long for a specific photo."* – P7

Therefore, we recommend changing the way people view their photo collections, e.g. by making the chronological overview more appealing with an option to make photos bigger and to group similar photos. Important and most viewed photos could be marked as favorites, allowing easier access instead of the current situation, which requires a lot of scrolling of the whole collection of pictures.

Further development in the overview function or other applications could focus more on supporting reminiscing with the smartphone's photo collections. Two important experiences we found for this are *serendipitous photo retrieval* and being able to *see the context of the photos* in the camera roll (e.g. automated sorting based on social connections): *"When I look at my photos, I have to scroll back from bottom to top. It is quite fast, however maybe having a random button would be fun such that you become inspired, since you already know the order of your photos and you know what's coming next. That's why I barely look at old photos."* – P10. We have already discussed how a reward system could be supported system based on achieving curation objectives. A possible reward in that context could be to earn 'random button presses'. For example, if the daily objective is reached, five random button presses are earned. Lastly, regarding

---

[10] https://www.whatsapp.com/.

context one participant states: *"It would be nice if the WhatsApp photos were sorted based on the source [group/person] they came from." – P5*

6 Conclusion

This study has focused on different kinds of curation activities on smartphones. Through semi-structured interviews we acquired insights in smartphone use regarding photos, curation activities and its triggers, and retrieval activities. Based on suggestions by the participants we propose three design directions that can be considered in developing novel curating applications for smartphones; (1) make curation more fun, (2) support deleting, (3) provide overview and support reminiscing. These design directions are directly applicable on current smartphone photo-applications. However, we are not aware of current curation applications that successfully address all these design considerations. The reported insights in smartphone curation activities and the suggested design considerations can guide the design of future applications that support curation activities on smartphones.

Clearly, given the magnitude of the study the results presented would need to be validated with a larger and more representative sample in order to generalize to a broader population. On the other hand, the participants interviewed are early adopters and savvy with interactive media which helps understand evolving trends in this field. Further, as we are more interested in the implications for designing interactive applications, applying these findings to the design of novel applications and field testing is recommended in order to reliability of the recommendations derived.

Acknowledgements. This research was supported by STW VIDI grant number 016.128.303 of The Netherlands Organisation for Scientific Research (NWO), awarded to Elise van den Hoven. We would like to thank all participants for their input and we would like to thank the reviewers for taking the time to review our work.

References

1. Bergman, O., Tucker, S., Beyth-Marom, R., Cutrell, E., Whittaker, S.: It's not that important: demoting personal information of low subjective importance using GrayArea. In: Proceedings of the SIGCHI Conference on Human Factors in Computing System, pp. 269–278. ACM, New York (2009). https://doi.org/10.1145/1518701.1518745
2. Braun, V., Clarke, V.: Using thematic analysis in psychology. Qual. Res. Psychol. 3(2), 77–101 (2006). https://doi.org/10.1191/1478088706qp063oa
3. Broekhuijsen, M., van den Hoven, E., Markopoulos, P.: From photowork to photouse: exploring personal digital photo activities. Behav. Inf. Technol. 36(7), 754–767 (2017). https://doi.org/10.1080/0144929X.2017.1288266
4. Van Dijck, J.: Digital photography: communication, identity, memory. Vis. Commun. 7(1), 57–76 (2008). https://doi.org/10.1177/1470357207084865
5. Frohlich, D., Fennell, J.: Sound, paper and memorabilia: resources for a simpler digital photography. Pers. Ubiquit. Comput. 11(2), 107–116 (2006). https://doi.org/10.1007/s00779-006-0069-4

6. Frohlich, D., Kuchinsky, A., Pering, C., Don, A., Ariss, S.: Requirements for photoware. In: Proceedings of the 2002 ACM Conference on Computer Supported Cooperative Work, pp. 166–175, New Orleans, Louisiana, USA (2002). https://doi.org/10.1145/587078.587102

7. Gee, J.P.: What video games have to teach us about learning and literacy. Comput. Entertain. 1(1), 20 (2003). https://doi.org/10.1145/950566.950595

8. Gutman, J.: Exploring the nature of linkages between consequences and values. J. Bus. Res. 22(2), 143–148 (1991). https://doi.org/10.1016/0148-2963(91)90048-3

9. Van House, N.: Collocated photo sharing, story-telling, and the performance of self. Int. J. Hum.-Comput. Stud. 67(12), 1073–1086 (2009). https://doi.org/10.1016/j.ijhcs.2009.09.003

10. Van House, N., Churchill, E.: Technologies of memory: Key issues and critical perspectives. Mem. Stud. 1(3), 295–310 (2008). https://doi.org/10.1177/1750698008093795

11. Kindberg, T., Spasojevic, M., Fleck, E., Sellen, A.J.: The ubiquitous camera: an in-depth study of camera phone use. IEEE Pervasive Comput. 4(2), 42–50 (2005). https://doi.org/10.1109/mprv.2005.42

12. Kirk, D., Sellen, A., Rother, C., Wood, K.: Understanding photowork. In: Proceedings of the SIGCHI Conference on Human Factors in Computing Systems, ACM Press, NY (2006). https://doi.org/10.1145/1124772.1124885

13. Miles, M., Huberman, A., Saldana, J.: Qualitative Data Analysis: A Sourcebook. Sage Publications, Beverly Hills (1984)

14. Rodden, K., Wood, K.: How do people manage their digital photographs? In: Proceedings of the SIGCHI Conference on Human Factors in Computing Systems, pp. 409–416. ACM Press, NY (2003). https://doi.org/10.1145/642611.642682

15. Roster, C.: Letting go: the process and meaning of dispossession in the lives of consumers. Adv. Consum. Res. 28(1), 425–430 (2001)

16. Ryan, R.M., Rigby, S., Przybylski, A.: The motivational pull of video games: a self-determination theory approach. Motiv. Emot. 30(4), 344–360 (2006). https://doi.org/10.1007/s11031-006-9051-8

17. Said, C.: Dycam model 1: The first portable digital still camera. MacWeek oct (1990)

18. Wagoner, A.: Gallery or Photos for Android, which should you use? Android Central (2015). http://www.androidcentral.com/gallery-or-photos-android-which-should-you-use. Accessed 20 June 2016

19. Whittaker, S., Bergman, O., Clough, P.: Easy on that trigger dad: a study of long term family photo retrieval. Pers. Ubiquit. Comput. 14(1), 31–43 (2009). https://doi.org/10.1007/s00779-009-0218-7

The Handling of Personal Information
in Mobile Games

Stefan Brückner[✉] ⒾⒹ, Yukiko Sato, Shuichi Kurabayashi ⒾⒹ, and Ikumi Waragai

Graduate School of Media and Governance, Keio University, 5322 Endoh,
Fujisawa, Kanagawa 252-0882, Japan
{bruckner,yukisato,kurabaya,ikumi}@sfc.keio.ac.jp

Abstract. The management of personal consumer information by corporate entities is a politically and socially sensitive subject. This paper examines how personal information is handled by mobile game developers and displayed inside mobile games. 38 mobile games from 29 developers were examined, chosen based on their popularity as expressed by the rankings in the Google Play store. An investigation was made into the type of information that is required during the registration process, what information is optional, and what information is finally displayed in the game and to whom. In a second step, the privacy policies of the 29 mobile game developers were compared, examining them for differences in content. Lastly, the reaction of game developers to written requests for information disclosure and deletion was investigated. Results suggest that how personal information is displayed in-game is largely dependent on the game genre. Privacy policies, while following the same template, differ in how detailed they are held. Lastly, replies to inquiries about information and requests for deletion varied greatly and sometimes were at odds with a company's privacy policy. This investigation indicates the necessity of accumulating and sharing know-how and best practices for the design of privacy policies and the proper handling of personal information.

Keywords: Mobile games · Personal information · Information privacy
Privacy policy

1 Introduction

Current economic, societal and technological trends facilitate the increasing collection, storage and utilization of (private) user information by corporations providing digital services. Surveys point to growing consumer concern as to how such data is handled by those entities that gather it [1]. While empirical evidence shows that stated consumer attitudes towards the disclosure of personal information often run contrary to actual consumer behavior [2–4], economic (and image) losses of companies after publicly known data breaches show that consumers do react to a perceived mishandling of their personal information. The fear of such a mishandling can even cause consumers to abstain from fully embracing digital services, leading to losses of potential customers for businesses [2, 5–7].

© Springer International Publishing AG, part of Springer Nature 2018
A. D. Cheok et al. (Eds.): ACE 2017, LNCS 10714, pp. 415–429, 2018.
https://doi.org/10.1007/978-3-319-76270-8_29

While data security [8], consumer and legislator attitudes towards gathering personal data [2–4], or the legal and economic ramifications of data breaches [5–7] have been the object of scientific debate, there has been no research to-date, investigating how personal information is actually handled in the context of digital, especially mobile, games. Mobile games have become an integral part of global entertainment culture and are a central element in the expansion of the global digital games market. According to Newzoo [9], the global digital games market will exceed 1 billion USD in revenue in 2017, 42% of which is generated by mobile games, topping all other forms of digital play. By 2020, mobile games are predicted to generate half of all revenue in the global games market [9] with 213 million players in the US alone [10]. As of April 2016, mobile gamers in the US, on average, play 1.3 mobile games a day [11]. The global spread of mobile gaming also contributes to an increasing accumulation of user data by game developers and publishers, making privacy information management in gaming apps an important issue. Gaming apps may explicitly or implicitly acquire many pieces of personal information in the long term, because they can record user behavior, such as usage of in-app purchases and geolocations, while users are playing.

This article aims to clarify what kind of personal information is displayed in digital mobile games, how mobile game developers handle personal information gathered by them, and how they react to requests for disclosure or deletion of personal information. It is hoped that this work will encourage further research into the topic of how personal (user) information is gathered, shared, displayed and treated by game developers and publishers. While this paper is not able to provide a satisfactorily comprehensive analysis of all questions pertaining to the relationship between personal information and games, it strives to provide an overview of how such information is treated in mobile games, thereby establishing a basis for further scholarly inquiry.

To this end, a three-step approach was employed. First, 38 popular mobile game applications were examined as to how and what kind of personal user information is gathered and displayed in-game. Second, the privacy policies of the respective developers were analyzed and third, the reaction of game developers to written requests for information disclosure and deletion was investigated. The remainder of this paper is structured as follows: In Sect. 2, after presenting a working definition of "personal information", based on a brief discussion of existing legal concepts, the methodological framework of this study is introduced. Section 3 provides a detailed picture of this paper's results, which are further discussed in Sect. 4, which concludes this paper.

2   Method

The American National Institute of Standards and Technology (NIST) defines "Personally Identifiable Information" (PII) as [12]:

> any information about an individual maintained by an agency, including (1) any information that can be used to distinguish or trace an individual's identity, such as name, social security number, date and place of birth, mother's maiden name, or biometric records; and (2) any other information that is linked or linkable to an individual, such as medical, educational, financial, and employment information.

While PII is a term predominantly used in the US context, the European Union uses a slightly different definition for "Personal Data", with Article 2 of the EU directive 95/46/EC stating that:

> personal data' shall mean any information relating to an identified or identifiable natural person ('data subject'); an identifiable person is one who can be identified, directly or indirectly, in particular by reference to an identification number or to one or more factors specific to his physical, physiological, mental, economic, cultural, or social identity;

The fast-paced changes in the digital landscape and the increasing shift to a data-based economy, or as Zuboff [13] puts it: to "surveillance capitalism", constantly pose new challenges to legislators and judges in defining what constitutes personal information. Based on the above-mentioned definitions, in the context of digital games, personal information in the context of this article will encompass data such as login information (login name/email address and password), persistent identification numbers generated by the system, nicknames/usernames, location data and any data pertaining to an individual user.

To determine, how personal information is displayed, 38 mobile games from 29 developers were downloaded and examined (Table 1). The samples were chosen according to the German Google Play Store's top free and top grossing game rankings from July 3, 2017. The 16 "top free" and 25 "top grossing" game applications were analyzed, leading to a sample size of n = 38 because of overlap between the rankings.

First, the handling of personal information *in-game* was investigated. What kind of information is required or asked for when playing the game for the first time? What kind of personal information is displayed in the game and who can see it? The display of personal information was divided into two categories, information that can be seen only by the user themselves (and the respective developer), and information which other players can access. Also, it was differentiated between optional and required information input.

In the next step, the content of the privacy policies of the chosen game developers was compared. This was done through a qualitative analysis, categorizing privacy policy content related to personal information. The aim in this comparison was to examine how the content of privacy policies is related to the display and handling of personal information by mobile game developers. In all cases, the (often legally binding) English version of each privacy policy was used. In cases where two separate versions for Europe and the US exist, the European version was referenced. All privacy policies were accessed via the corresponding link in the Google Play Store, on July 15, 2017.

Lastly, the reaction of corporations to user requests for information disclosure and deletion was tested by contacting the developers. Contact took place in two stages: First was a request for the disclosure of what kind of personal information is gathered and stored by the company. If applicable, this included a reference to the relevant parts of the respective privacy policy. After this request was fulfilled, the next step was to send a request for deletion of the user's personal information. Communication with developers was carried out in German as far as possible, switching to English only when communication in German was not accommodated. Developers that are represented with more than one game in this analysis were only contacted for the game with the highest place in the rankings.

Table 1. Overview of analyzed games

Game title	Developer	Release
Bubble Witch 3 Saga	King	2016
Candy Crush Saga	King	2012
Candy Crush Saga Soda	King	2014
Castle Clash: Königsduell	IGG	2015
Castle Crush	Fun Games For Free	2017
Clash of Clans	Supercell	2013
Clash of Kings	Elex Wireless	2014
Clash Royale	Supercell	2016
Cooking Craze - Ein lustiges Restaurant Spiel!	Big Fish Games	2017
Farm Heroes Saga	King	2013
Final Fantasy Brave Exvius	Square Enix Co, Ltd.	2016
Final Fantasy XV: A New Empire	Epic Action LLC	2017
Fishdom	Playrix Games	2016
Forge of Empires	InnoGames GmbH	2015
Futurama: Worlds of Tomorrow	TinyCo	2017
Game of War - Fire Age	Machine Zone, Inc.	2014
Gardenscapes - New Acres	Playrix Games	2016
Goodgame Empire: Four Kingdoms	Goodgame Studios	2013
Hay Day	Supercell	2013
Herumzappeln - Fidget Spinner	Words Mobile	2017
Huuuge Casino	Huuuge	2015
Ich Einfach unverbesserlich	Gameloft	2013
King of Avalon: Dragon Warfare	Diandian Interactive Holding	2016
Lords Mobile	IGG.COM	2016
Marvel Sturm der Superhelden	Kabam	2014
Mobile Strike	Epic War	2015
Pokémon Go	Niantic, Inc.	2016
Roll the Ball: Schieberätsel	BitMango	2015
Stadt Land Fluss - Wörterspiel	Fanatee Games	2014
Star Wars Galaxy of Heroes	Electronic Arts	2015
Subway Surfers	Kiloo	2012
Summoners War: Sky Arena	Com2uS	2014
Super Mario Run	Nintendo Co., Ltd.	2017
The Floor is Lava	Ketchapp	2017
The Last Day on Earth: Survival	Kefir!	2017
Township	Playrix Games	2013
Wort Guru	Word Puzzle Games	2017
Wort Meister	Word Mania Studio	2017

3   Results

3.1   Requirement and Display of User Information

On a basic level, many mobile games do not only handle information that the player provides via direct input in the game interface. Linking mobile games to out-of-game user accounts is common practice. Figure 1 details what kind of personal information is shown by how many of the sampled mobile games. Of the 38 games analyzed here, only four did not require any information input and had no option to link the game with an out-of-game account: "Fidget Spinner", "Wort Guru", "Wort Meister" and "The Floor is Lava". These games also did not display or require the input of any personal information from the user. Interaction with other players during the games is not possible, as they are single-player games, that do not require an active internet connection.

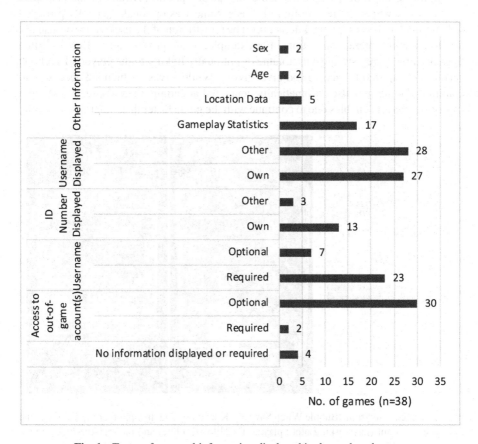

Fig. 1. Types of personal information displayed in the analyzed games

Of the remaining 34 games, 30 offered the option to link the game with an outside account like Facebook, Google+, or a specific account by the developer, such as an "IGG account" by IGG. Linking the game to such an account often enables functions such as the ability to play on more than one device or to save the game state, so that the game can be continued from where it was left off, even after the application is deleted from a device. In "Hay Day" and "Gardenscapes" linking your game to a Facebook account is necessary to enable interaction with other players. "Marvel: Sturm der Superhelden" and "The Last Day on Earth: Survival" require a link to an outside account like Google Play.

The question of the necessity of account linkage also directly relates to how players are identified in-game. In the examined games, two ways of distinguishing between players can be seen. First, through the use of (player-chosen) user names, second by numerical or alphanumerical system generated IDs. Out of 38 games, 23 required the selection of a user name, while this was optional in 7 games. In games with the option of linking to an out-of-game account like Facebook, it was often also possible for players to use, for instance, their Facebook name (and profile photo) instead of a nickname.

Games in which the registration of a user name was optional, generally provided only limited options for player interaction. The registration of the user name was usually tied to enabling interaction options. For example, in the puzzle game "Bubble Witch Saga 3" (Fig. 2), registering a user name or optionally linking to the player's Facebook account, is required to receive and give "lives". While "lives", which are necessary to continue playing, are also automatically generated at certain intervals, receiving them from other players enables one to continue with the game faster than otherwise possible.

Fig. 2. Screenshots from "Bubble Witch Saga 3" (King) showing the option of linking the game to another account (left), asking other players for "life" (middle) and the registration of a user name

In-game, displaying user names seems to be the preferred method of identifying users. Out of 38 games, a system generated ID was displayed in only 13. Out of those, viewing another player's ID was only possible in 3. In contrast, 28 games displayed user names[1]. User names can be chosen by the player themselves Generally, the use of a unique name is required. While games like "Clash Royal" (Fig. 3) require the player to choose a user name after the tutorial phase and players can only interact with other players after this, games like "Final Fantasy XV: A New Empire" allow players to play the game without changing the default user name, consisting of a series of numbers. The latter only requires a unique user-chosen name to enable the game's chat function.

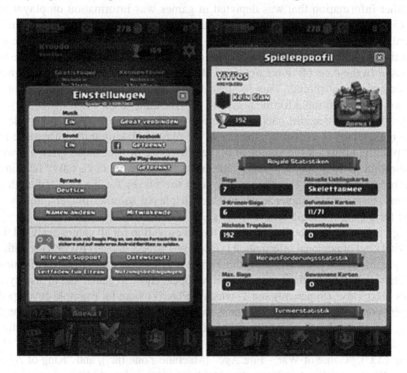

Fig. 3. Screenshots from "Clash Royale" (Supercell)

Figure 3 shows screenshots from the game "Clash Royale", depicting the unusual display of both user ID and user names. Both can be seen by the player himself, as well as by other players. However, the user ID displayed to the player in the settings screen (Fig. 3 left side, below the word "Einstellungen") differs from the user ID displayed in the profile screen showing information about other players (Fig. 3 right side, below the user name). Among the analyzed games, this system is unique to "Clash Royale" and "Clash of Clans" (both by Supercell). "Final Fantasy Brave Exvius" displays the same

---

[1] The games "Hay Day" and "Gardenscapes" are counted as "requiring the registration of a username", as a name for your "farm" or "garden" is needed. However, the user name is thereafter not shown in-game. Interaction with other players is only possible via linking your game to a Facebook account.

user ID to the user and other players, while most other analyzed games only display the user name.

Aside from user names and IDs, other player information that was commonly shown in-game was statistical information about a user's state of play. 17 games showed such information to other players. In competitive match-based games, this included for example data on how many matches a player participated in, how many he won or lost, and data on his favorite playing strategy (for example Fig. 3 right side).

Other information that was depicted in games was information on player location (5 games), the player's age (2), and the player's sex (2). Location information typically only consisted of the country the player resided in or the language he uses. Only the games "Pokémon Go" and "Huuuge Casino" displayed more precise location data. In the case of "Pokémon Go", this included precise GPS data on where a "Pokémon" was captured. This is however not visible to other players. "Huuuge Casino" made it optional for the player to provide data on the town where they live. If the player does record such information, it is accessible by all other players. "Huuuge Casino" also displays the sex of the player, making it the only game to do so explicitly, although the choice of player character or user name often allows for assumptions as to a player's sex. Aside from "Huuuge Casino", only "Ich einfach unverbesserlich" (Eng. Despicable Me) asks the player for his sex, although it is optional. Data on the player's age was not displayed to other players, and is only asked for during the registration process.

Figure 4 shows the detailed results of the investigation for all games analyzed. How and what kind of personal information is displayed largely appears to coincide with two factors, game developer and game genre. Especially the latter seems to be very influential in determining what kind of information developers chose to gather and to display. The games "Hay Day" (Supercell) and Township (Playrix) were for example developed by different companies. However, the game design is exceedingly similar. As can be seen in Fig. 4, they display the same characteristics in relation to the display and handling of personal information. Similarly, the games "Final Fantasy XV: A New Empire" (Epic Action LLC), "Game of War – Fire Age" (Machine Zone Inc.), and "King of Avalon: Dragon Warfare" (Diandian Interactive Holding) exhibit almost identical game design, also evident in the way personal information is displayed.

	Access to out-of-game account(s)		Username		ID Number Displayed		Username Displayed		Other Information			
	Required	Optional	Required	Optional	Own	Other	Own	Other	Gameplay Data	Location Data	Age	Sex
Wort Guru												
Final Fantasy XV: A new Empire		■	■				■					
Castle Crush		■					■					
Wort Meister												
The Floor is Lava												
Gardenscapes - New Acres		■					■					
Futurama: Worlds of Tomorrow		■			■							
Clash Royale							■					
Roll the Ball: Schieberätsel		■		■								
Cooking Craze - Ein lustiges Restaurant Spiel!		■										
The Last Day on Earth: Survival	■											
Ich Einfach unverbesserlich					■						■	
Subway Surfers		■						■				
Herumzappeln - Fidget Spinner												
Stdt Land Fluss - Wörterspiel		■										
Super Mario Run		■			■							
Summoers War: Sky Arena		■					■					
Clash of Clans							■					
Pokemon Go							■				■	
Clash of Kings		■					■					
Hay Day							■					
Candy Crush Saga		■	■				■					
Candy Crush Saga Soda		■	■				■					
Lords Mobile		■		■			■					
Mobile Strike		■					■					
Castle Clash: Königsduell		■					■					
Game of War - Fire Age		■					■					
Huuuge Casino - Slots Spiele Kostenlos		■					■					■
King of Avalon: Dragon Warfare		■					■					
Marvel Sturm der Superhelden	■						■					
Forge of Empires							■					
Township		■					■					
Bubble Witch 3 Saga		■	■				■					
Farm Heroes Saga		■	■				■					
Star Wars Galaxy of Heroes		■					■					
Final Fantasy Brave Exvius		■					■					
Fishdom		■					■					
Goodgame Empire: Four Kingdoms		■					■					

Fig. 4. Analysis results

3.2 Privacy Policies

A detailed examination of each developers' privacy policy is outside the scope of this preliminary study. Instead the focus lies in a brief comparison of what is covered in the privacy policies and wherein they differ. First, on a formalistic point, the privacy policies of the 29 companies analyzed vary greatly in their length (Fig. 5). Discounting the privacy policy of Ketchapp, which could not be found, the word count ranges from 413 words (Word Mania Studio) to 7,729 words (Kebam) with an arithmetic average of around 2400.

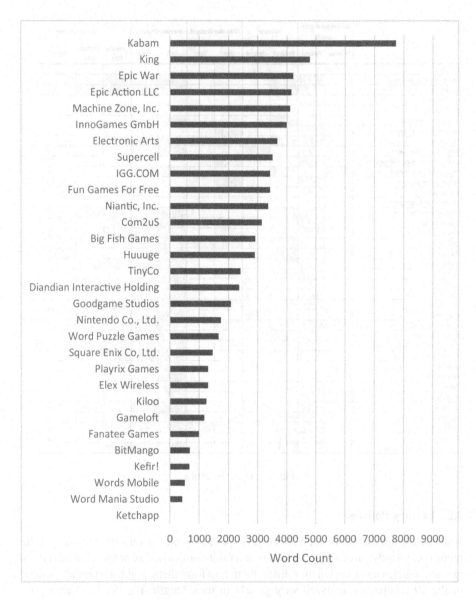

Fig. 5. Privacy policy word count

Content wise, there are five discernible topics that most companies cover to varying extents (Fig. 6). The method and extent of their data (1) *collection*, how they (2) *use* this data, with whom they (3) *share* the data gathered, how the data is (4) *secured*, and lastly, how and to what extent the (5) *users have access* to the data gathered from them Among the privacy policies examined, 16 also explicitly mentioned legal provisions regarding the use of their services by children under the age of 13.

Company Name	Word Count	Collection	Use	Sharing	Security	User Access	Children
Word Puzzle Games	1.652						
Epic Action LLC	4.149						
Fun Games For Free	3.413						
Word Mania Studio	413						
Ketchapp	N/A						
Playrix Games	1.303						
TinyCo	2.397						
Supercell	3.497						
BitMango	678						
Big Fish Games	2.911						
Kefir!	659						
Gameloft	1.175						
Kiloo	1.241						
Words Mobile	498						
Fanatee Games	988						
Nintendo Co., Ltd.	1.730						
Com2uS	3.133						
Niantic, Inc.	3.349						
Elex Wireless	1.301						
King	4.787						
IGG.COM	3.414						
Epic War	4.210						
Machine Zone, Inc.	4.104						
Huuuge	2.894						
Diandian Interactive Holding	2.358						
Kabam	7.729						
InnoGames GmbH	3.981						
Electronic Arts	3.661						
Square Enix Co, Ltd.	1.456						
Goodgame Studios	2.071						

Fig. 6. Content Comparison of privacy policies

Generally, the content of the privacy policies, especially with concern to the categories collection, use, and sharing is largely identical, most likely adapted from existing templates conforming to current legal standards. There are, however, some exceptions. For example, "Words Mobile" provides only a minimalistic policy [14], stating vaguely:

WordsMobile may collect personal and non-personal information from you when you use the Service. Personal information is information that specifically identifies an individual, including, but not limited to, an individual's name, phone number, credit card or other billing information, email address and home address.

Electronic Arts presents a more detailed picture of which kind of information they gather. According to their privacy policy, this includes, among other things: email addresses, user names, dates of birth, telephone numbers, passwords, security questions and answers, demographic details, names, billing information, IP address, browser information and device identifiers [15]. How detailed privacy policies are held does not directly seem to correlate with the size of a company. The privacy policy of Square Enix is, for example, comparatively less detailed than the one of Epic Action LLC.

Of the examined polices, 24 provide details on how one's personal information, gathered by the company, can be accessed, deleted or altered. In most cases, an email address is mentioned where inquiries can be made. However, some companies place a charge on such inquiries. Square Enix for examples mentions that "[The] Company will charge a separately specified fee for requests for notification of the disclosure and purpose of use of Personal Information." [16].

3.3 Information Disclosure and Deletion

While privacy policies have explicitly stated the possibility of accessing one's personal information or having it deleted. In practice, this has proven rather difficult. For a preliminary examination of developer reaction to requests for information disclosure and deletion 13 companies were contacted. Three in April, the remaining 10 between July 10 and July 13, 2017 (Table 2).

Table 2. Overview of replies to disclosure and deletion requests

Company	Contact date	Reply disclosure	Reply deletion
Big Fish Games	07.10.2017	Privacy policy	Delete app Change email address
Com2uS	04.25.2017	Details	Possible per mail
Epic Action LLC	07.10.2017	Privacy policy	Delete app
Fanatee Games	07.10.2017	Details	No data
Fun Games For Free	07.10.2017	Privacy policy	Delete app
Gameloft	07.10.2017	Details	Possible per mail
IGG	07.13.2017	None	
Niantic	07.10.2017	None	
Nintendo	04.25.2017	Privacy policy	Possible in app
Playrix Games	07.10.2017	None	
Square Enix	07.10.2017	Details	Delete app
Supercell	04.25.2017	Details	Possible per mail
Word Puzzle Games	07.10.2017	None	

In the first mail, developers were asked to disclose all data gathered from the user, the purpose for gathering that data and whom the data is shared with. The time until the first reply to our contact varies greatly between companies. For example, Com2uS generally answered queries within two working days, while Word Puzzle Games did not answer at all as of July 30, 2017. Many companies utilize automated replies, either to ensure users that their query was received (e.g. Gameloft) or to send them a series of frequently asked questions, asking users to contact them again, if their questions were not answered (e.g. Niantic). After receiving a reply from the request for information disclosure, a second request, asking for the deletion of all personal information, was sent.

Table 2 shows the reactions to the requests for information disclosure and deletion. "None" signifies that a satisfactory reply as to what user information was gathered, was not received by July 30, 2017. This does not mean that there was no reply at all. For example, as mentioned above, Niantic employs a system of automatic replies, while the mail exchange with IGG was hindered by linguistic barriers, and was therefore not concluded in time.

Out of the nine companies where a mail exchange was successfully completed, four answered a request for information disclosure by referencing their privacy policy, while the remaining five provided details in their reply as to what information was collected, how it was used, and whom it was shared with. Among the latter, answers were in general consistent with the relevant privacy policy, although they remained rather general and vague. One of the clearest answers was provided by Supercell, first listing what kind of information they gather (device ID, MAC, IMEI, OS version, email address, location etc.) and summarizing it as "Wir sehen also: Mit was für einem Gerät, du dich wann und von wo aus einloggst" (we can see what device you use, and where and when you log-in).

Replies to requests for deleting user information were mixed. Nintendo offers an option to delete user data by a button in the settings screen of its game "Super Mario Run", which was pointed out in their reply. Fanatee claimed that they do not save any user data ("Wir haben keinerlei Daten über dich gespeichert"). Four companies implied that deletion of the application would be sufficient in order to delete any user information, which Big Fish Games supplemented by advising to change the registered email address, before deleting the app. Only Supercell and Gameloft offered to delete all personal information, for which they required user authentication, either by official documents (like passports) or by providing clear information about when an account was created, how often and from where it was accessed, etc.

4 Discussion and Conclusion

This preliminary study aimed at providing an overview of how personal user information is displayed in mobile games, how developers of mobile game claim to handle such information, and how they react to user requests for disclosure or deletion of personal information. Findings show, that while there is some variety in what kind of personal data is required and/or displayed, the genre seems to play a great role in determining how user information is handled in a mobile game.

The samples in this study were chosen by their popularity, based on the Google Play Store ranking from a single day. Therefore, it is possible (and likely) that the games examined in this study are not representative of the majority of mobile games. There is a noticeable bias for puzzle games (Bubble Witch Saga 3, Candy Crush Saga, Candy Crush Saga Soda, Farm Heroes), building and strategy/building games (Final Fantasy XV: A New Empire, Hay Day, Township, Game of War – Fire Age etc.). Other genres, e.g. RPGs, are not included. To provide more comprehensive and representative results, a random sample big enough to allow for statistic examination would be needed.

Privacy policies of game developers generally follow the same standard patterns, of covering the topics data collection, use, sharing, security and user access, although there exists a great discrepancy in how detailed these topics are covered, depending on the company. While the sample does not show any clear link between company size and how detailed a privacy policy is held, this could also be attributed to the limited sample size of n = 29. A more detailed survey, with a greater sample size and accounting for different variables is necessary to examine what influences the detailedness of privacy policies.

Company reactions to requests for information disclosure or deletion showed a mixed picture. While two companies accommodated a request for information deletion, the others did not. This can also be seen to stand in contrast to their privacy policies, where it is generally stated that requests to delete information can be directed at the them by mail. This hints at a gap between the actual handling of personal user information by game developers and what is stated in their privacy policies. However, to ascertain the existence of such a gap, a more thorough investigation, informed by legal expertise, is required. The scope of this study allowed only a limited examination of developer reactions. To validate the results, the sample size needs to be increased. As, depending on the company, mail exchanges can continue for more than two weeks, more time needs to be allotted as well. Lastly, contacting the same company more than once, using different accounts and wording for the requests could also possibly contribute to more precise results.

This study focused mainly on how game developers treat personal user information. It has been established that the kind of information required to register for a game and the kind of personal information displayed in-game, varies. The next logical step is the examination of user reception and preferences. While it entails certain methodological difficulties, investigating actual user attitudes concerning the use of personal information in games appears to be a promising field of further inquiry.

As mentioned in Sect. 1, mobile gaming has become an integral part of global entertainment culture, with a steadily increasing market share and number of players. However, similar to developments in other fields affected by digitization, such as social network services, online stores, etc., this also enables game developers and publishers to gather vast amounts of personal information about game users, thereby creating legal and ethical challenges as to how this data is managed.

Based on the results of this investigation, disparities between a company's privacy policy and the way it actually manages private user information are evident. Accordingly, there is a need for, in the case of mobile games, which are often from small-scale game developers and publishers, to accumulate know-how and establish best practices for privacy policy design and the handling of personal information, e.g. creating in-game possibilities for users to view, alter, and delete their information. There are currently several ways under discussion, as to how users of mobile devices can retain ownership and keep watch over the information they provide [17, 18]. Adopting such approaches for mobile game applications could possibly mitigate user concerns. Finally, privacy policies could potentially also benefit from considering the genre/type of game they are valid for. As different game genres tend to require different forms of information, comprehensibility and conciseness of privacy policies could profit from being more closely tailored to a specific game. Current efforts towards creating a system for the automatic generation of privacy policies (AutoPPG) [19] could help to establish non-generic privacy policies that are easy-to-understand, comprehensive, and precise.

References

1. European Commission: Special Eurobarometer 359: Attitudes on Data Protection and Electronic Identity in the European Union, Brussels (2011)
2. Acquisti, A., Grossklags, J.: Losses, gains, and hyperbolic discounting: an experimental approach to information security attitudes and behavior. In: 2nd Annual Workshop on "Economics and Information Security", UC Berkeley (2003)
3. Acquisti, A., Grossklags, J.: Privacy and rationality in individual decision making. IEEE Secur. Priv. **3**(1), 26–33 (2005)
4. Norberg, P.A., Horne, D.R., Horne, D.A.: The privacy paradox: personal information disclosure intentions versus behaviors. J. Consum. Aff. **14**(1), 100–126 (2007)
5. Jenkins, A., Anandarajan, M., D'Ovidio, R.: 'All that Glitters is not Gold': the role of impression management in data breach notification. Western J. Commun. **78**(3), 337–357 (2014)
6. Gatzlaff, K.M., McCullough, K.A.: The effect of data breaches on shareholder wealth. Risk Manage. Insur. Review **13**(1), 61–83 (2010)
7. Manworren, N., Letwat, J., Daily, O.: Why You Should Care About the Target Data Breach. Bus. Horiz. **59**(3), 257–266 (2016)
8. Föck, M., Fröschle, H.: Schutz der Unternehmensdaten: Data Leakage Protection (DLP). HMD Praxis der Wirtschaftsinformatik **48**(5), 28–34 (2011)
9. Newzoo: The Global Games Market Will Reach $108.9 Billion in 2017 With Mobile Taking 42%, https://newzoo.com/insights/articles/the-global-games-market-will-reach-108-9-billion-in-2017-with-mobile-taking-42/, last accessed 2017/07/28
10. Statista: Number of Mobile Phone Gamers in the United States From 2011 to 2020 (In Millions). https://www.statista.com/statistics/234635/number-of-mobile-gamers-forecast/. Accessed 29 July 2017
11. Statista: Average number of mobile games played daily and monthly in the United States as of April 2016. https://www.statista.com/statistics/596593/number-mobile-games-played/. Accessed 12 Oct 2017
12. National Institute of Standards and Technology: Guide to Protecting the Confidentiality of Personally Identifiable Information (PII), Gaithersburg (2010)
13. Zuboff, S.: Big other: surveillance capitalism and the prospects of an information civilization. J. Inform. Technol. **30**(1), 75–89 (2015)
14. WordsMobile Stuido: Privacy Policy, http://www.words-mobile.com/policy.htm. Accessed 15 July 2017
15. Electronic Arts Inc.: Privacy Policy. http://tos.ea.com/legalapp/WEBPRIVACY/US/en/PC/. Accessed 15 July 2017
16. Square Enix: Privacy Policy. http://www.jp.square-enix.com/privacy/index2_en.html. Accessed 15 July 2017
17. Saroiu, S., Wolman, A., Agarwal, S.: Policy-carrying data: a privacy abstraction for attaching terms of service to mobile data. In: HotMobile 2015 Proceedings of the 16th International Workshop on Mobile Computing Systems and Applications, pp. 129–134. ACM Press, New York (2015)
18. Mun, M., Hao, S., Mishra, N., Shilton, K., Burke, J., Estrin, D., Hansen, M., Govindan, R.: Personal data vaults: a locus of control for personal data streams. In: Co-NEXT 2010 Proceedings of the 6th International Conference, Article no. 17, pp. 1–12. ACM Press, New York (2010)
19. Yu, L., Zhang, T., Luo, X., Xue, L.: AutoPPG: towards automatic generation of privacy policy for android applications. In: SPSM 2015 Proceedings of the 5th Annual ACM CCS Workshop on Security and Privacy in Smartphones and Mobile Devices, pp. 39–50. ACM Press, New York (2015)

A Serious Mobile Game with Visual Feedback for Training Sibilant Consonants

Ivo Anjos[1]([envelope]) [ORCID], Margarida Grilo[2], Mariana Ascensão[2], Isabel Guimarães[2],
João Magalhães[1], and Sofia Cavaco[1]

[1] NOVA LINCS, Department of Computer Science,
Faculdade de Ciências e Tecnologia, Universidade NOVA de Lisboa,
2829-516 Caparica, Portugal
i.anjos@campus.fct.unl.pt, {jm.magalhaes,scavaco}@fct.unl.pt
[2] Escola Superior de Saúde do Alcoitão,
Rua Conde Barão, Alcoitão, 2649-506 Alcabideche, Portugal
{margarida.grilo,mascensao,iguimaraes}@essa.pt

Abstract. The distortion of sibilant sounds is a common type of speech sound disorder (SSD) in Portuguese speaking children. Speech and language pathologists (SLP) frequently use the isolated sibilants exercise to assess and treat this type of speech errors.

While technological solutions like serious games can help SLPs to motivate the children on doing the exercises repeatedly, there is a lack of such games for this specific exercise. Another important aspect is that given the usual small number of therapy sessions per week, children are not improving at their maximum rate, which is only achieved by more intensive therapy.

We propose a serious game for mobile platforms that allows children to practice their isolated sibilants exercises at home to correct sibilant distortions. This will allow children to practice their exercises more frequently, which can lead to faster improvements. The game, which uses an automatic speech recognition (ASR) system to classify the child sibilant productions, is controlled by the child's voice in real time and gives immediate visual feedback to the child about her sibilant productions.

In order to keep the computation on the mobile platform as simple as possible, the game has a client-server architecture, in which the external server runs the ASR system. We trained it using raw Mel frequency cepstral coefficients, and we achieved very good results with an accuracy test score of above 91% using support vector machines.

1 Introduction

Speech is one of the most important aspects of our life. While regular mistakes are made by children when they are still learning how to speak and learning the language, these mistakes tend to disappear gradually as children grow up. However there are cases in which the mistakes continue even when the child grows older. In these cases the child may have a speech and/or language disorder.

© Springer International Publishing AG, part of Springer Nature 2018
A. D. Cheok et al. (Eds.): ACE 2017, LNCS 10714, pp. 430–450, 2018.
https://doi.org/10.1007/978-3-319-76270-8_30

While there are many types of speech and language disorders, here we focus on speech sound disorders (SSD). A SSD occurs when a child produces speech sounds incorrectly, after an age at which these mistakes were not supposed to happen [1, 25].

When a child has a SSD, she should be observed by an SLP, who can assess the type and severity of the disorder, and then she should be clinically followed by the SLP to treat the disorder. As part of the treatment to correct the speech errors, SLPs use specific types of speech production exercises that must be performed multiple times in each speech therapy session.

The SLP has to find ways to make the repetition of the exercises enjoyable, in order to keep the child motivated. Most times this is accomplished by transforming the exercises in some sort of game that the child can play. This would be relatively simple with a few repetitions, but given the extensive number of repetitions required to achieve speech improvements, keeping the child motivated may be a hard task. To further motivate the child, many SLPs also use some kind of reward system. For instance, the child may be rewarded with a game for the last five minutes of the session if he performs well during the session. Most times this last game includes also some sort of therapy exercise.

Whereas traditionally children attend speech therapy sessions once a week, more intensive therapy has been proven to lead to faster improvements [4, 5, 14]. In particular, when the intensive training is done at home (home training) it can increase the overall exercise practicing time substantially. This is particularly useful when children attend speech therapy sessions only once a week, and as a consequence they do not repeat the speech exercises as often as desirable. With home training children can practice the exercises recommended by their SLP whenever they have free time.

These two concepts of intensive training (with more frequent sessions per week) and home training are becoming more popular in recent years, and some studies have already proven that this type of training is very beneficial [5, 7, 12]. These studies show considerable improvements when children have more than the regular weekly session. In the cases where children cannot attend more than one session per week, home training has been proved as a good alternative for those extra sessions. The major benefit from intensive training and home training is a faster improvement rate, which can also lead to more motivation. When children are motivated they tend to overcome their problems more easily, so this kind of cycle is beneficial.

In spite of all the benefits of home training, this may not be straightforward to implement when the right tools are not available. The problem is how can children practice the speech exercises at home? Who is going to verify if they are doing the exercises correctly? Well, the first obvious choice would be the parents, but, for multiple reasons including lack of time, this is not always possible. This leaves room for a combined clinical and technological solution to emerge.

Some software systems to assist children to train their exercises have already been proposed for several disorders. Nonetheless, some systems like Articulation Station, and Falar a Brincar do not have any type of ASR system [2, 8], which leads to the problems that we described above: children are always depending

Fig. 1. Child playing the proposed game comfortably at home.

on another person other than themselves to train their exercises. This can lead to lower weekly training times, which will lead to slower improvements.

There are other systems that have an ASR system or use some sort of sound analysis, like sPeAK-MAN, Star, and ARTUR - the ARticulation TUtoR, that have the goal of helping children with articulation problems [3,10,27], Talker [26], Speech Adventure, that was developed for children with cleft palate or lip [23], and Flappy Voice and the Remote Therapy Tool for Childhood Apraxia, which focus on apraxia [15,21]. All of these systems rely on game like exercises to keep children motivated and engaged while training, and are developed for the English language. While its main focus is not on speech therapy training, the *Interactive Game for the Training of Portuguese Vowels* uses an ASR system to distinguish the EP vowels [6]. Vithea is another system developed for EP [30]. It aims to help people with aphasia. This system has a virtual therapist that guides the patient through their exercises and uses an ASR system to validate the exercises.

While many native Portuguese children need to attend speech therapy to correct SSDs related to the production of distorted sibilant sounds, there is a lack of software systems to assist with the training of these sounds. As a contribution to fill this gap, we propose a serious mobile game that focus on the EP sibilant consonants, the *serious mobile game for the sibilant consonants*. While our game can also be used during the speech therapy sessions, our main goal is to provide a game that can be used for home training and does not require the supervision of parents (Fig. 1). Thus, our game uses an ASR system to identify if the child is performing the exercise correctly and therefore decrease the need of an adult to monitor the child.

The game incorporates the isolated sibilants exercise, which is an exercise used by SLPs to teach children to correctly produce the sibilant consonants. It runs on mobile platforms like tablets, iPads and smartphones, which children usually are keen on using. As thus, we are not only providing means for home training the sibilants, but also to motivate children on doing the exercises often. The game's main character is controlled in real time by the child's voice and its behaviour gives visual feedback to the child on his speech productions. The game is implemented with a client-server architecture, where the client is the mobile game application and the server has an ASR system that classifies the child speech productions.

The *Serious Game for the Sustained Vowel Exercise* (SVG) [16], previously proposed by some of our team members, and which, like the present work is also part of the BioVisualSpeech project, uses sound analysis to control the movement of the main character. While at first glance, the SVG may look similar to the present work, there are some fundamental differences. The SVG is developed for the sustained vowel exercise, which consists of saying a vowel for a few seconds with approximately constant intensity. In its current version, that game does not use an ASR system and it does not distinguish the vowel that is being produced. It uses sound analysis to determine the intensity of the speech production and the phonation time, independently of the produced phoneme. The proposed game, on the other hand is developed for the isolated sibilants exercise. It distinguishes the produced sibilant with the help of an ASR system. On the other hand, the intensity variation of the production is not important for the proposed game. Finally, the SVG is a game to be used during the speech therapy sessions, whereas our game can be used both during the speech therapy sessions but also at home.

In the remaining sections we explain the sibilants exercise (Sect. 2), we discuss the main characteristics of the proposed game (Sect. 3), and its ASR system (Sect. 5), and the feedback we received from both SLPs and children (Sect. 6).

2   Sibilant Consonants and the Isolated Sibilants Exercise

Sibilant sounds are a specific group of consonants, and happen when the air flows through a very narrow channel in the direction of the teeth [11]. This channel can be created in different places and this creates different types of sibilant sounds. There are two types of sibilant sounds in EP: alveolar, and palato-alveolar, these regions can be seen in Fig. 2. In each of these sibilant types, the vocal folds can be used or not, resulting in a voiced or a voiceless sibilant, respectively. An example of this is the sound [z] (e.g. *z* in "zip"), which is voiced because it uses the vocal folds, and the sound [s] (e.g. *s* in "sip"), that does not use the vocal folds and as a result it is a voiceless sibilant. These two sounds are alveolar fricatives, so they are produced by creating a narrow channel in the same location, and the only difference between them is the use of the vocal folds.

There are four different sibilant consonant sounds in EP: [z] as in zebra, [s] as in snake, [ʃ] as the *sh* sound in sheep, and [ʒ] as the *s* sound in Asia. [z], and [s] are both alveolar sibilants, while [ʃ], and [ʒ] are palato-alveolar sibilants. Both [z] and [ʒ] are voiced sibilants, and [s] and [ʃ] are voiceless sibilants.

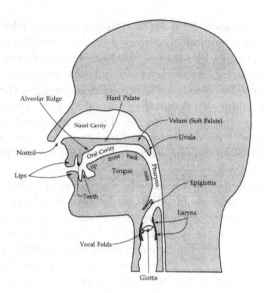

Fig. 2. Diagram with the names of the main places of articulation [13].

In the words given above as an example, "zip" and "sip", there is also one interesting characteristic, that is between these two words only a single sound varies: [z] and [s]. This creates what is called a minimal pair, which is a pair of words where only a single sound varies. Given their similarities, the words in a minimal pair are very easy to confuse and it is common to use one instead of the other. This is a very common SSD, especially in children. It is even more problematic when the minimal pair consists of two sibilants like in our example (the sounds [z] and [s] from "zip" and "sip"), because here the only difference between the two different sounds is the use of the vocal folds. Another reason for the choice of the four sibilant sounds named above is that they also appear in many minimal pair words (e.g. "sink" and "zinc"). Even thought the sounds [ʒ] and [ʃ] do not appear in any usual minimal pair words in English, there are some in EP (e.g. *"jacto"*, *"chato"*).

The most usual sibilant mistakes committed by children are distortion errors. These can consist of (1) exchanging the voiced and voiceless sounds, for example exchanging a [s] that is voiceless, for a [z] that is produced in the same location of the vocal tract but is voiced, or (2) exchanging the vocal tract local of production which results in producing another sibilant [22].

When a child has a SSD that influences his production of the sibilant consonants, the SLP usually starts by observing how the child reacts to the hearing and production of the isolated sibilants. The process starts by trying to understand if the child can distinguish the different sibilants when hearing them as isolated sounds. If he can, the next step is to practice the *isolated sibilants exercise*, which consists of producing a specific sibilant sound for some duration of time. The main goal of this exercise is to teach the child how to distinguish between the different sibilant sounds, and also how to produce each one of them.

Once the child is able to say the sibilant consonants correctly, the SLP then starts asking for multiple productions of the different sibilants always alternating both the vocal tract local of production and the use of the vocal folds, in order to try to understand if the child can always produce the correct sibilant or if sometimes the child exchanges from one sibilant to another. This process is done with the isolated sibilants exercise and is the base to detect what the child problem is. Only after the problem is correctly identified and the child can say the isolated sibilants correctly, they can move on to more complex exercises like using the sibilant sounds inside words and in multiple positions within a word.

As it will be discussed in detail in subsequent sections, our solution is to incorporate the isolated sibilants exercise in a computer game that motivates the child on exercising often. An important characteristic of the game is that children do not control the main character with a keyboard or other usual input method, but instead the character is controlled only by the child's voice; the child has to do the isolated sibilants exercise correctly in order to make the character move towards a target.

3   Game and Architecture

We propose a serious game for mobile platforms for intensive training of the sibilant consonants for correction of distortion errors. The aimed age group of this game are children from five to nine years old, because usually at these ages the regular phonological development exchange errors have already disappeared.

The game incorporates the isolated sibilants exercise, which is an exercise frequently used by SLPs during the therapy sessions. While the game can be used at the therapy session, our main purpose is to offer a solution that can be used at home to give children the opportunity of having more intensive training even when it may be difficult for them to attend more than one therapy session per week.

3.1   System Platform and Game Engine

Our proposal, as already mentioned, is to create a game that children can use to practice the therapy exercises for the sibilant consonants either in the session or at home. Thus, the first decision that had to be made was if the game was going to be developed for a mobile format, like a tablet or a smartphone, or for laptops and desktop computers. After some research we concluded that the tablet market in Portugal is still expanding (Fig. 3). In 2014 the share of monthly active tablet users was 42.38% and by 2021 this value is projected to reach 52.07% of the total population [29]. The slower predicted expansion for future years is mainly because almost half of the population already has a tablet and does not need a new one. So this is a good indicative that if the game is developed for tablets, it can reach a very large audience. Moreover, being developed for a mobile platform, the game allows the child to play comfortably anywhere in the house, and even outside provided there is an internet connection (as it will be explained in Sect. 3.2, the game will need access to the internet).

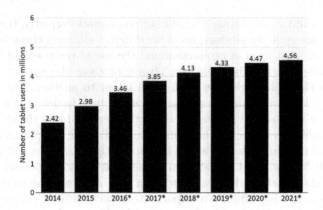

Fig. 3. Forecast of number of tablet users in Portugal from 2014 to 2021 (in million users) [28].

The next challenge was to choose the platform, that is, to decide if the game was going to be developed for Android, iOS or both. Even though Android has a larger market share [18], iOS still has a significant amount of users. Thus our decision was to develop the game for both platforms. Instead of developing the game twice, one for each operating system, we decided to use Unity because this allows for it to be developed only once, while creating executable files for each platform.

3.2 System Architecture

Since this game is designed to be used at home, it can not depend on the SLP to decide if the exercise is being correctly executed, nor the parents since many times they are not available. So the best option is to use automatic speech recognition to provide feedback on whether the exercise is executed correctly.

The game will run in mobile platforms, but using an ASR system that executes the speech recognition in the mobile platform can be very demanding which could cause delays in the regular execution of the game. So the best alternative is to use a client-server architecture, where the game sends the sound samples to the server, and the server sends back information on whether the productions were correctly produced (Fig. 4). This kind of architecture also gives us more flexibility when choosing what to use for the ASR engine, and also allows changing the algorithm at anytime without having to change the mobile application.

Client

The client application has to send the sound that the child is producing to the server. In order to do this, the application captures segments of sound of a determined length. When a segment reaches its desired length the client sends it to the server. The client then awaits for the server to respond whether the sound production in the segment is correct or not. When the client receives the answer

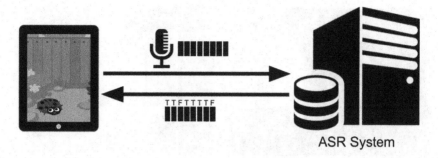

Fig. 4. Client-server architecture. The client is the mobile application, that captures segments of sound, and then sends them to the server. The server has to extract the sound features from each segment and uses an ASR system to classify them. Afterwards the server sends the response back to the client, which can now provide the feedback to the child.

it provides visual feedback to the child through the character's movement. In case of positive feedback this cycle continues until the character reaches its goal. Given this type of connectivity with the server, the client always needs to have a stable internet connection.

Server

When the server receives a new segment of sound it first has to extract its features, and then uses them in the previously trained ASR system in order to get a response on whether the speech segment is correct or not (Sect. 5 discusses the features and algorithms used to classify the child productions). The server then sends this answer back to the client and waits for the next speech segment. To train this ASR system, we used child speech productions of the sibilant sounds (more details in Sect. 4).

3.3   Mobile Game

As briefly explained above, the proposed game uses the isolated sibilants exercise. In order to play the game the child has to say one of the four sibilant consonants addressed by the game: [z], [s], [ʃ], or [ʒ].

The game includes four scenarios, one for each of the addressed sibilant sounds (Fig. 5). These scenarios were created with the help of a visual artist and with images from *Freepik* [9]. To create the scenarios we took into account the aimed age group of five to nine years old children. Each of the scenarios has a different character, and the game goal is to move it to a specific location. The characters or game goal are related to the addressed sibilant sound, which is very helpful to provide visual cues to the child.

(a)   (b)

(c)   (d)

Fig. 5. The four game scenarios. (a) The scenario for the [z] consonant. (b) The scenario for the [s] consonant. (c) The scenario for the [ʃ] consonant. (d) The scenario for the [ʒ] consonant.

Visual feedback and visual cues

In order to control the character, children do not use a keyboard or any other regular input method, but instead they use only their voice. Each character responds to a different sibilant sound. To make the character move, the child has to say that specific sibilant correctly. The character's movements give visual feedback to the child about his sound productions. The feedback is positive when the production is correct, in which case the character moves towards the goal. The character keeps moving while the child is producing the sibilant consonant correctly. If the production is not correct, the character stops moving to give negative feedback to the child. In the case of negative feedback, there are two available modes: one in which the exercise has to be repeated from the beginning and another in which the character waits for a correct production to continue moving towards the target. This type of visual feedback is very intuitive for children and also a good way to motivate them on trying to say the sibilant consonants correctly.

The scenario in Fig. 5a is used to train the [z] sibilant. The main character, a bumblebee, moves towards the beehive, which is the game target, while the child is saying the [z] sibilant correctly. The characters or goal of each scenario are always related to a word in EP that starts with the specific sibilant used in the scenario. For instance, a bumblebee was chosen for the [z] sibilant scenario because the EP word for bumblebee starts with a [z] sibilant (*zangão*). The scenario used to train the [s] sibilant has a snake that moves towards the log while the child is saying the [s] sibilant correctly (Fig. 5b), and the scenario used for the [ʒ] sound has a ladybug that flies towards a flower while the child is saying the [ʒ] sibilant correctly (Fig. 5d). The EP word for snake starts with the [s] sibilant (*serpente*) and the EP word for ladybug starts with the [ʒ] sibilant (*joaninha*). Finally, there is a scenario for the [ʃ] sibilant (Fig. 5c). In this case the main character, a boy, has to run away from the rain until the end of the street, which is the game target. The rain comes from a gray rainy cloud that follows the boy while he moves. The boy is able to run away from the rain while the child says the [ʃ] sound correctly. The EP word for rain starts with the [ʃ] sibilant (*chuva*).

Instead of relying only on the SLP explanations, it is important that the game provides visual cues to help the children remember the exercise and sound that they should produce. An interesting idea was to relate the type of movement of the character with the use of the vocal folds. This idea came from the flying movement of the bumblebee, and that the [z] sibilant is a voiced one. We did not want a very complex motion in order not to distract the child, so the movement was simplified to a sinusoidal wave, that can be modified by changing its amplitude and frequency. We applied the same concept to the movement of the ladybug, since the [ʒ] sound is also voiced. We decided to use a simple straight line movement for the remaining sounds, [s] and [ʃ], for the snake and the boy running away from the rain respectively, because these are voiceless sibilants. This is achieved by using the same code, but with a zero amplitude parameter.

Parameterization of the game

The distance separating the initial position of the main character (starting point) from the target (end point) is related to the speech duration needed to make the character move until it reaches the target. The isolated sibilants exercise can be done with shorter or longer reproduction of the sibilants by varying the distance between the starting point and end point. This possibility is very useful for SLPs because every child is different and the exercise needs to be adapted to his current state or problem. While developing games for speech therapy, we must be very careful to not restrict the options of the SLPs. For instance in this case, if the time that a child has to reproduce the sibilant sound was always the same, this would not suit every child in the same way. So, the best alternative is to give SLPs the most options and adjustable parameters, so that they can have all the needed flexibility to better adjust the exercise to the problems of each child. As a response to these observations, there are many parameters that can be adjusted in all four scenarios:

- the starting and end points,
- the time the character takes to move from the starting to the end point,
- the amplitude and frequency of the movement for the voiced consonants.

Implementation details - modularity and extensibility

Another very important characteristic of these scenarios is that given the client-server system architecture, each one can be individually built and animated, since they are all completely independent from each other. To accomplish this, they all share three main classes, that are responsible for recording the microphone input, the connection to the server, and create the movement of the character. The main game cycle of each of the scenarios, is processed as follow, the microphone class is always recording the input sound, when this recording reaches a certain length it is sent to the server by using the helper class, that manages the connections to the server, and then the response from the server is used to compute the current state of the game: proceed (if the child is producing the correct sound) or stop (if the child is not producing the sibilant sound correctly). If the child is producing the correct sound, the movement class is used to produce the animation that moves the character towards the target, and the main cycle continues until the character reaches the target. If the child does not produce the correct sound, the game finishes and the main cycle stops its execution.

With this base main cycle and with the help of the three main classes, it is very simple to add other scenarios for these sounds, and even to new sounds. In the latter case, in order to have the game characters moving as a response to the added type of sounds, the game's ASR system would need to be trained, in order to recognize the new class of sounds. The re-trained ASR system would be updated in the server, but the base code would not need any changes. More complex scenarios can also be built using this base, as proven by our scenario for the [ʃ] sound, that has two moving characters (the boy and the rain) and uses the same logic for the base main game cycle and also relies on our three main helper classes, with some additional code to control the movement of the rain.

4   Sound Data

In order to train the ASR system, we collected data in three schools in the Lisbon area. There were 90 children participating in the recordings with ages between 4 and 11 (Table 1a). The recordings were made using a dedicated microphone and a DAT equipment (the setup used can be seen in Fig. 6). While we tried to make the recordings in a quiet room, there was noise coming from the outside, especially during recess.

We collected eight different samples from each child which correspond to short and long repetitions of the sibilant sounds [ʃ], [ʒ], [s], and [z]. Table 1b shows the number of samples from each sound. There was always an SLP participating in the recordings, who gave all the necessary indications to the children.

The sound productions from each child were recorded in a single file. This means that every file includes the sibilant sounds and also every indication from the SLP. In order to be able to use this data, every file had to be split in separated samples, one for each of the eight child productions that it contains. To automatize this process, we created an algorithm that measures the energy

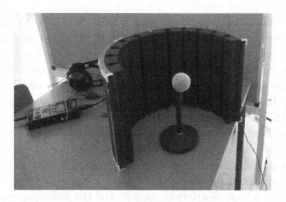

Fig. 6. The setup used for the recordings. On the left there is one of the DAT equipment's used, and on the right the microphone, with an acoustic foam around it.

Table 1. Recorded data. (a) Number of children who performed the recordings. (b) Number of samples from each sound.

Age	Boy	Girl	Both
4	1	0	1
5	3	8	11
6	0	4	4
7	3	8	11
8	16	14	30
9	11	13	24
10	4	4	8
11	0	1	1
Total	38	52	90

(a)

Sound	Number of Samples
[ʃ]	203
[ʒ]	215
[s]	214
[z]	210
Total	842

(b)

in the beginning of the file (to measure the sound level of the *no speech* signal) and then identifies the peaks of energy, which have high probability of being regions containing speech. In this way the files are automatically split into smaller files that contain single productions of sound. Afterwards we still needed to listen to each of these samples, to identify which files contain the child sibilant productions, and delete the remaining files (SLP speech, or noises). When all the files were split we obtained a total of around 2600 smaller files, from which 842 were the child sibilant productions we are interested in.

5   Automatic Recognition of Isolated Sibilant Consonants

An important characteristic of our game is the visual feedback given to the child through the movement of the main character. In order to provide useful visual feedback to the child, the game must react almost instantly to the child's voice. Given the inherent communication delay from the client-server architecture, we have to consider carefully the classification algorithm in order to reduce the time that it takes to classify a group of samples as much as possible. This leads to the exclusion of some sort of algorithms, like for instance lazy ones, as those usually take more time to classify samples since they do not have a previous training phase to learn the model, but instead they delay the learning until any request is made to the system, and since these results are always based on a local feature space, this process happens at every request. The game's time restrictions also require that some algorithms that are more complex and take more time to compute an answer must be avoided.

Given the game's time restriction, we selected the following classifiers for this study: support vector machines (SVM) with radial basis function (RBF) kernel, linear discriminant analysis (LDA), and quadratic discriminant analysis (QDA). An important characteristic of these classifiers is that all three of them support multiclass classification. Given that we are trying to distinguish between the four different sibilant sounds, this is a simple and effective way to do it. Since all three classifiers share this characteristic, this was also useful because it provided us with an easy way of comparing the algorithms and features that were being tested.

5.1 Feature Vectors

We use the raw Mel frequency cepstral coefficients (MFCC) as features for all three classifiers. As an illustration, Fig. 7 shows the MFCCs (matrix) obtained for a [z] sound. Our feature vectors consist of columns of the MFCCs matrix. MFCCs are commonly used in ASR systems and, as it will be seen below, we obtained very good results with the combination of these features and classifiers.

While historically the number of MFCCs used is thirteen, there are also studies that use different numbers of coefficients. In particular Carvalho *et al.* had good results using different numbers of coefficients to classify isolated phonemes (the EP vowels) [6].

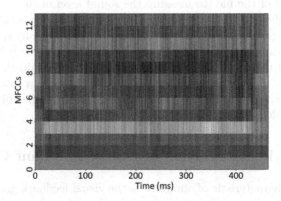

Fig. 7. The MFCCs matrix with 13 coefficients, obtained for a [z] sound.

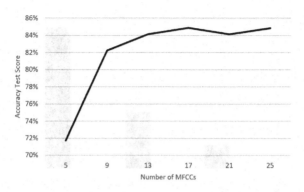

Fig. 8. Accuracy test scores of the multiclass SVM classifier with RBF kernel, using different numbers of MFCCs.

We trained the multiclass SVM classifier with different numbers of MFCCs, ranging from 5 to 25 coefficients, as seen in Fig. 8. The accuracy of the test score is really low when using only 5 MFCCs, but it rapidly increases with the use of more coefficients. This basically means that by using a small number of coefficients, our machine learning algorithm does not have enough distinct data to correctly separate the four different sibilant sounds, but when using more data (more coefficients), the four sounds can be more easily separated. The increase in score starts to slow down at around 13 MFCCs, and above that the differences between scores can be easily attributed to the margin of error of the training of each classifier. So we decided to use 13 coefficients since our results did not show any particular improvements when using more than 13 coefficients. This result is also confirmed by most literature, that usually uses around 12 to 13 MFCCs [17, 19, 20, 24].

5.2   Classification Results

We trained the LDA, QDA and multiclass SVM with the MFCCs feature vectors and the data described in Sect. 4. As stated previously, these are all multiclass classifiers which means that we can easily train them with the same data set, and get comparable results.

The three classifiers were trained in the following way:

- Once we computed the MFCCs matrices from all sounds, we built the feature vectors by selecting columns from these matrices. Given the limitations of the SVM training complexity, we did not use the whole matrices. Instead, we selected around 20000 columns by choosing 66 random samples of each sound for each child. These vectors were labeled with the corresponding sibilant. We use one class for each sibilant, so we have 4 different classes.
- We then used stratified sampling on this set of data to get the training and test set, using a test set size of 30%.
- We also used a stratified 5 fold cross validation within our training set.

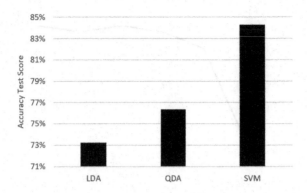

Fig. 9. Accuracy test scores of the three multiclass classifiers.

Figure 9 shows the accuracy of the test scores for these three multiclass classifiers. As can be observed in the figure, QDA performs better than LDA, which is expected since QDA is not limited to a linear space to try separate all four classes, in contrast with LDA that can only learn linear boundaries. Even thought QDA give us considerably better scores than LDA, our multiclass SVM classifier has a test score almost 8% higher than QDA, meaning it is around 8% more accurate, giving us less errors in the classification of the four different sounds.

Since the multiclass SVM with the RBF kernel gave the best results with a considerable margin, we focused on this classifier to try to achieve even better results. The multiclass SVM can loose accuracy in some sounds, due to having to adjust to all four classes at the same time. So we replaced the multiclass SVM with four SVMs, one for each class. The idea was to create one SVM classifier, also with the RBF kernel, to classify each of the four different sibilant classes. This way we could fine tune each one of the four classifiers, which here we call *single-sibilant* SVM, in order to improve our classification scores.

Each single-sibilant SVM was trained with the same method that was described above, the only change was that for each classifier, the labels of the data were changed to true or false depending on the sound that was being trained. For instance, when we trained the classifier for class [s], all samples from sibilant [s] were labeled *true*, and the remaining samples were labeled *false*. Doing this for each sound, let us achieve our goal of one classifier for each sound. The parameters for each classifier were then fine tuned to try to achieve the best accuracy scores for each of the four classes.

Figure 10 shows the results obtained with this approach. The multiclass SVM has the same score for all sounds, since it is always the same classifier, and the score is an average of all the correct labels for all classes. The four single-sibilant SVMs approach brought us better results in the classification of all four sounds, by a margin of around 8%. In addition, it can be observed that these are quite high accuracy test scores (above 91%).

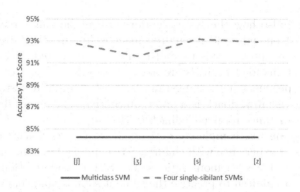

Fig. 10. Accuracy test scores of the multiclass SVM, and four single-sibilant SVMs (both with the RBF kernel) for all four classes.

6   Feedback from Potential Users

As future work we will validate our game solution and our ASR system with real users. In a first phase we are planning on validating it during speech therapy sessions, since this will allow having SLPs confirming that our ASR system is performing as expected. After this test is complete, another interesting way to validate our solution is to give our solution as homework to some children, selected by the SLPs according to their needs, and see if using the game at home contributes towards faster improvements.

In the meantime we were able to collect feedback from both SLPs and children. While this was not a formal validation, their feedback, which is discussed below, was important to assess the potential of the game.

6.1   Feedback from SLPs

We were always in contact with multiple SLPs to have impartial feedback about our work. In an initial phase, we created a simple prototype of the game that was used to demonstrate our proposed scenarios to some SLPs and explain the mechanism of the game. We collected feedback from four SLPs that work with children, one with four years of experience, two with eight, and one with thirteen years of experience. All four SLPs agreed that the scenarios were adequate for the aimed age group, and that the game would provide a good way of training the sibilant sounds. Another interesting aspect, is that all of them already use some sort of homework, but not in a mobile platform given the lack of this type of systems for EP. Also, all of them noticed a faster improvement when children used homework, this can probably be attributed to the extra weekly training time.

When asked if they would rather use our system in their sessions or at home, the results were a bit mixed. There was one SLP who only wanted to use the system during the sessions. The remaining were interested in trying it a few times during their sessions first, in order to understand how children react to the system, and also how the system performs. But they all agreed that if the system is robust enough, and if children react well to it, they would use it as homework. In our opinion, this type of feedback is expected, given the lack of this type of systems for EP, SLPs are not completely confident on them. They first need to experiment it to understand that using an ASR system combined with the game visual feedback is a good alternative that allows decreasing the need of adult assistance to give feedback to the child.

After our game was completely developed, we got feedback from one SLP with four years of experience with children. We explained her the game concept, and also performed some demonstrations. The SLP considered that our system, is a good way for children to practice the sibilant sounds, and that the scenarios are very interesting for children within the aimed age group. Like some of the SLPs we talked to previously, she would first use our system during the sessions to make sure that everything is working as expected, in order not to mislead the children. But she added that once she verified that the game works correctly, she would use it as home training. She already uses other types of homework with her patients, with very good results. Home training with the proposed game would have the advantage of increasing the motivation of the child and reducing the need of adult supervision. The idea of using the movement of the character as a visual cue for the use of the vocal folds was something that she considered very important, since she already tries to incorporate those types of cues when performing the exercises with children. As an additional visual cue, she gave the advice of trying to incorporate the same idea to the background of the scenarios. Basically using more straight lines in the scenarios where the vocal folds are not used, and the opposite when the vocal folds are used.

6.2   Feedback from Children

This work was presented at the European Researchers Night (ERN) 2017, at the National Museum of Natural History and Science in Lisbon. This is an event open to the general public and that runs simultaneously in several cities in Europe. The goal of ERN is to show citizens the importance and the impact of science in their everyday life and in the development of the society, and also demystify the image of researchers as someone distant and inaccessible. During the event researchers demonstrate and explain their work to the public through activities.

At the ERN 2017 we had the opportunity to show our work to both children and parents. We had the game set up to allow children to try it, and at the same time explain to parents the importance of these types of games for children that are attending speech therapy (Fig. 11). We used a laptop, a screen and an external microphone.

Around fifty children tried the game. We were able collect some opinions and to see the children's reactions to the characters and the way of controlling the game. Not all children who tried the game were attending speech therapy, but our goal here was not to understand if the game was classifying the speech production correctly or if it contributes to faster speech improvements. We only aimed to assess if the graphics, characters and type of interaction with the game

Fig. 11. Child playing the proposed game during the European Researchers Night 2017.

appealed to the children. We had children from all ages trying the game, from some very young children to some twelve year old children. While the game was designed for children from five to nine years old, all children trying the game at ERN liked the scenarios and characters regardless of their age. They also reacted very well to the type of interaction with the game, that is, controlling the characters only with their voice.

7   Conclusion and Future Work

Here we proposed the *serious mobile game for the sibilant consonants*, a serious game for mobile platforms for correction of sibilant sounds distortion in EP. The game is designed for home training and uses the isolated sibilants exercise. As identified by our team, there is a lack of systems that focus on EP, and even those that do, do not have exercises to practice the isolated sibilants exercise. Another very important aspect is that children should not be restricted to only practice their exercises during their therapy sessions or when their parents have time to supervise them. Instead children should be able to do these exercises at home, even when their parents do not have time, since this would allow them to perform the exercises more frequently, which can lead to faster improvements, thus motivating them even further.

Our solution solves both these problems by offering a mobile game with which children can practice their EP sibilant sounds. The game is implemented with a client-server architecture in which all the complex computation is done in the server. In this way the game can be played even on low end devices, with the only restriction of having an internet connection. This allows more children to benefit from our solution and perform their exercises nearly anywhere.

With the help of an ASR system that classifies the child speech productions, the game is controlled only by the child's voice. In order to achieve the game goal, the child has to perform the isolated sibilants exercise correctly. In addition, the game gives immediate visual feedback to the child about his speech. Our ASR system got very good results, with accuracy test scores of above 91% when using SVMs and MFCCs. As future work we will explore more machine learning algorithms to improve these scores, such as hidden Markov models and artificial neural networks. However, we must keep in mind that we can not develop a computationally expensive system because of our response time restrictions. Thus the next goal is to balance more complex algorithms in order to try improve our ASR system performance, but at the same time maintaining the very low response time that we currently have.

While a formal validation has been planned as future work, we were able to gather feedback from both SLPs and children. The feedback from children confirmed that children of the aimed age group liked the characters, scenarios and that they also reacted well to the way of controlling the character with their voices. The SLPs that we contacted showed interest in our solution, and consider it a good way for children to train the sibilant sounds at home. They all consider that this type of visual feedback is a good way to let children know if they are producing the sounds correctly or not, and that it will probably be more motivating than the regular exercises they do in their speech therapy sessions. Nonetheless, almost all of them would first like to try the game in their sessions, to check if our ASR system is accurate and if children react well to the game.

Acknowledgments. This work was supported by the Portuguese Foundation for Science and Technology under projects BioVisualSpeech (CMUP-ERI/TIC/0033/2014) and NOVA-LINCS (PEest/UID/CEC/04516/2013).

We thank the SLPs Diana Lança and Catarina Duarte for their availability and feedback. We also thank all the 3rd and 4th year SLP students from Escola Superior de Saúde do Alcoitão who collaborated in the data collection task. Many thanks also to Inês Jorge for the graphic design of the game scenarios. Finnally, we would like to thank the schools from Agrupamento de Escolas de Almeida Garrett, and all the children who participated in the recordings.

References

1. American Speech-Language-Hearing Association (ASHA) - Speech Sound Disorders: Articulation and Phonological Processes. http://www.asha.org/public/speech/disorders/SpeechSoundDisorders/. Accessed 28 July 2017
2. Articulation Station. http://littlebeespeech.com/articulation_station.php. Accessed 5 Jan 2016
3. ARTUR - the ARticulation TUtoR. http://www.speech.kth.se/multimodal/ARTUR/. Accessed 16 Jan 2016
4. Barratt, J., Littlejohns, P., Thompson, J.: Trial of intensive compared with weekly speech therapy in preschool children. Arch. Dis. Child. **67**(1), 106–108 (1992)
5. Sanjit, K., Bhogal, R.T., Speechley, M.: Intensity of aphasia therapy, impact on recovery. Stroke **34**(4), 987–993 (2003)
6. Carvalho, M.I.P., et al.: Interactive game for the training of Portuguese vowels (2012)

7. Denes, G., et al.: Intensive versus regular speech therapy in global aphasia: a controlled study. Aphasiology **10**(4), 385–394 (1996)
8. Falar a Brincar. https://falarabrincar.wordpress.com/. Accessed 16 Jan 2016
9. Freepik. http://www.freepik.com/. Accessed 28 July 2017
10. Ganapathy, S., Thomas, S., Hermansky, H.: Comparison of modulation features for phoneme recognition. In: 2010 IEEE International Conference on Acoustics Speech and Signal Processing (ICASSP), pp. 5038–5041. IEEE (2010)
11. Guimarães, I.: Ciência e Arte da Voz Humana. Escola Superior de Saúde de Alcoitão (2007)
12. Hall, P.K., Jordan, L.S., Robin, D.A.: Developmental apraxia of speech: theory and clinical practice, p. 200. Pro Ed (1993)
13. Image Quiz: Vocal Tract. http://www.imagequiz.co.uk/img?img_id=ag5zfmltYWdlbGVhcm5lbnIQCxIHUXVpenplcxifotErDA. Accessed 30 July 2017
14. Kreimer, S.: Intensive speech and language therapy found to benefit patients with chronic aphasia after stroke. Neurol. Today **17**(12), 12–13 (2017)
15. Lan, T., et al.: Flappy voice: an interactive game for childhood apraxia of speech therapy. In: Proceedings of the First ACM SIGCHI Annual Symposium on Computer-Human Interaction in Play, pp. 429–430. ACM (2014)
16. Lopes, M., Magalhães, J., Cavaco, S.: A voice-controlled serious game for the sustained vowel exercise. In: Proceedings of the 13th International Conference on Advances in Computer Entertainment Technology, p. 32. ACM (2016)
17. Matejka, P., Schwarz, P., et al.: Analysis of feature extraction and channel compensation in a GMM speaker recognition system. IEEE Trans. Audio Speech Lang. Process. **15**(7), 1979–1986 (2007)
18. Mobile Operating System Market Share in Portugal, 2016 to 2017. http://gs.statcounter.com/os-market-share/mobile/portugal/#yearly-2016-2017-bar. Accessed 25 July 2017
19. Nefian, A.V., et al.: A coupled HMM for audio-visual speech recognition. In: 2002 IEEE International Conference on Acoustics, Speech, and Signal Processing (ICASSP), vol. 2, pp. II–2013. IEEE (2002)
20. Nwe, T.L., Foo, S.W., De Silva, L.C.: Speech emotion recognition using hidden Markov models. Speech Commun. **41**(4), 603–623 (2003)
21. Parnandi, A., et al.: Development of a remote therapy tool for childhood apraxia of speech. ACM Trans. Access. Comput. (TACCESS) **7**(3), 10 (2015)
22. Preston, J., Edwards, M.L.: Phonological awareness and types of sound errors in preschoolers with speech sound disorders. J. Speech Lang. Hear. Res. **53**(1), 44–60 (2010)
23. Rubin, Z., Kurniawan, S.: Speech adventure: using speech recognition for cleft speech therapy. In: Proceedings of the 6th International Conference on Pervasive Technologies Related to Assistive Environments, p. 35. ACM (2013)
24. Sharma, S., et al.: Feature extraction using non-linear transformation for robust speech recognition on the Aurora database. In: Proceedings of the 2000 IEEE International Conference on Acoustics, Speech, and Signal Processing, ICASSP 2000, vol. 2, pp. II1117–II1120. IEEE (2000)
25. Shriberg, L.D., Paul, R., Flipsen, P.: Childhood speech sound disorders: from post-behaviorism to the postgenomic era. In: Speech Sound Disorders in Children, pp. 1–33 (2009)
26. Talker. http://speech-trainer.com/children-speech-therapy. Accessed 15 Jan 2016

27. Tan, C.T., et al.: sPeAK-MAN: towards popular gameplay for speech therapy. In: Proceedings of the 9th Australasian Conference on Interactive Entertainment: Matters of Life and Death, p. 28. ACM (2013)
28. The Statistics Portal - Forecast of tablet user numbers in Portugal from 2014 to 2021 (in million users). https://www.statista.com/statistics/566416/predicted-number-of-tablet-users-portugal/. Accessed 02 Feb 2016
29. The Statistics Portal - Forecast of the tablet user penetration rate in Portugal from 2014 to 2021. https://www.statista.com/statistics/568594/predicted-tablet-user-penetration-rate-in-portugal/. Accessed 02 Feb 2016
30. VITHEA - Virtual Therapist for Aphasia treatment. https://vithea.l2f.inesc-id.pt/wiki/index.php/Main_Page. Accessed 16 Jan 2016

Optimized HMD System for Underwater VR Experience

Hiroyuki Osone[1(✉)], Takatoshi Yoshida[2], and Yoichi Ochiai[1]

[1] University of Tsukuba, Tsukuba, Japan
soneo.tsukuba@gmail.com
[2] The University of Tokyo, Tokyo, Japan

Abstract. We designed a head mounted display (HMD) that is suited for underwater use. To reduce the buoyancy, we developed an internal optical design in which the viewing angle of the HMD remains wide even when the device is filled with water. Two types of HMD were prepared and tried in subject experiments. The first is an off-the-shelf HMD that was water-tightened with adhesive and vinyl tape. The second is a rectangular parallelepiped type HMD with a structure that can be filled with water. Subjects evaluated these HMDs in terms of clearness, wideness of view, ease of swimming, and feeling of immersion while watching 360° video in underwater. Until now, there had been no discussions regarding the optics of HMDs used in water. This research has established a method for the optical design of an HMD that can be used underwater and was first evaluated by subjects.

Keywords: Head-mounted display (HMD) · Virtual reality
Wearable devices

1 Introduction

Many people exercise in water. However, when swimming in a pool, they may get bored. Therefore, studies on virtual reality (VR) and augmented reality (AR) in water have been made. Yamashita et al. [10] made the AquqCAVE, which allows you to experience VR in an aquarium. Its associated payload is low but the cost of setting up the environment is high. Users cannot swim, over a wide area, and so this system cannot be used by many people simultaneously. Zhang, Tan, and Chen have created a head-mounted display (HMD) [1] that can be used underwater. However, air enters the device's structure, which greatly increases buoyancy and makes swimming uncomfortable. In another study carrid out by Quarles [7], water was present in the internal structure of the HMD. However, he does not address its properties from an optical point of view, and thus, the viewing angle is unknown. Therefore, we designed an optimal HMD for swimming. Because there is no air layer in the proposed HMD, we expected that buoyancy would not be an issue and that the HMD could be easily worn while swimming. Though swimming in a pool has low entertainment value, by

© Springer International Publishing AG, part of Springer Nature 2018
A. D. Cheok et al. (Eds.): ACE 2017, LNCS 10714, pp. 451–461, 2018.
https://doi.org/10.1007/978-3-319-76270-8_31

wearing this HMD, one can enjoy VR while swimming comfortably. Our study is the first to evaluate underwater VR by subject experiments.

1.1 Contributions

- We designed the HMD with a sufficiently wide viewing angle even if water fills its internal structure. This ingenuity makes it comfortable to swim while wearing the HMD because buoyancy is greatly reduced.
- There was no discussion regarding optics in studies regarding conventional underwater HMDs. Our HMD, which can be used underwater, was designed optically properly and was evaluated by subjects for the first time by in this research.
- Subject experiments were conducted to evaluate VR experienced in water. The first evaluation of underwater VR was carried out in this study (Fig. 1).

Fig. 1. We have designed, taking optics into account, an HMD that ensures a sufficient field of view even when its internal structure is filled with water. This reduces the buoyancy, so that the user can swim comfortably while enjoying VR

2 Related Works

2.1 Head-Mounted Displays

In this study, we propose an HMD best suited for use while swimming underwater. However, our main objective is to promote the use of head-mounted immersive VR. A historical investigation of HMDs has been presented by Rolland and Hua [13]. Recently, inventions regarding low-cost HMDs such as Google Glass and Oculus Rift[1] have gained attention. The former, proposed by Mann et al. [5], was developed commercially. The use of low-cost HMDs that uses a smartphone

---

[1] https://www3.oculus.com/en-us/rift/.

as a display, proposed by Olson et al. [6], is spreading. Among them, HMDs that anyone can easily use to experience VR with cardboard and a smartphone, such as like Google Cardboard, are widely used.

We are not the first to propose a HMD that is usable in water. Zhang et al. [1], designed an waterproofed HMD, and Quarles et al. [7] developed an HMD that was designed with a structure that allowed it to be filled with water. However, buoyancy was a significant issue in the former study, which made it difficult to swim comfortably in water. The optics involved in the latter study were not discussed. Thus, we created an HMD that maintains the field view suitable for swimming underwater by using an optical design that allows water to fill in its internal structure, thereby reducing buoyancy.

2.2   Underwater VR/AR

Frohlich et al. [4] and Takala et al. [8] used a simulation system similat to a cave on which underwater environments are drawn. They surrounded the users in the room and projected 3D images of the ocean world onto the walls to create an enclosing simulation. Such environments are more comprehensive than PC games to completely enclose users in a virtual world. Thus, they can be used to target more human senses and make the simulation more extensive. However, the cost of setting up such an environment is high. Several systems immerse users in a pool or aquarium to simulate the experience of being in the ocean. For example, Blum et al. [9] visually enhanced a normal swimming pool with virtual marine objects displayed on mobile PC devices mounted in front of a submarine mask using augmented reality and a waterproof HMD. Bellarbi et al. [2] put tablets and sensors in a waterproof casing to display fish and submarines with AR markers that enabled underwater interactions. However, because the case has to be held in the hand, the user cannot swim. Likewise, Yamashita et al. [10] developed a computer-expanded aquarium with a rear projection on an acrylic wall surrounding swimmers and providing a stereoscopic environment with an immersive feel, like a cave. These systems are realistic because users are actually immersed in water, which is difficult to simulate on land. On the other hand, it is also costly to install these environments, and thus, it is difficult to spread the use of these systems to many people.

2.3   Position of This Study

By capitalizing on the portability of VR goggles as mentioned in the section titled "Head-Mounted Displays", we designed HMD that are comfortable for swimming in pools, an activity that could otherwise be boring. In order to prevent a significant increase in buoyancy, its internal optical design was developed so that the interior can be filled with water. Because the payload is low and environment settings are unnecessary, it is possible to play on the way home from work or to play with lots multiple people (Fig. 2).

	Environmental cost	
	Low	High
User-friendly	This study Zahang[1] Quarles[7]	Yamashita[10] Torsten[4]
Not user-friendly	Abdelkader[2]	

Fig. 2. A chart of related works on (underwater VR/AR).

3   Designing the Underwater Head Mounted Display

In this section, we explain the configuration of our HMD, which uses smart-phones, plano-convex lenses and underwater goggles designed in this research.

3.1   Optical Design

First, as a prototype, we attached the lens of a Google Cardboard to underwater goggles and watched a video of Google Cardboard VR video underwater. However, the image fell to the center of the field of view and appeared triple. Then, we developed an optical design, using Zemax OpticStudio[2], that meant that the screen could be seen underwater with almost the same viewing field as that provided by Google Cardboard out of the water.

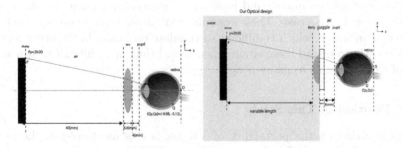

Fig. 3. Optical system of Google Cardboard (left) and Optical system of our HMD (right). The variable length is used to optimize focusing of the image.

---

[2] http://www.zemax.com/opticstudio.

Table 1. Parameters of the eye model

Part	Curvature radius [mm]	Thickness [mm]	Refractive index	Clear Semi-Diameter [mm]
Cournea	7.8	0.5	1.38	6.0
Aqueous	6.7	1.5	1.34	6.0
Aqueous	11.0	1.6	1.34	11.0
Iris	-	0.1	1.34	1.4
Lens	10.0	3.7	1.42	5.0
Vitreous	−6.0	16.6	1.34	5.0
Retina	−11.0	-	-	11.0

Optimization by Numerical Simulation. The optical design system of the proposed system is the same as the one proposed by Osone et al. [11]. Since the focus and the image are symmetrical, we only needed to consider the optical design for one eye. First, the optical system of Google Cardboard when used in the air was reproduced in OpticStudio, as shown in Fig. 3 (left). We used an iPhone 7 as display. Its height was 58.00 mm when laid sideways, so we set the ray from the top to 29.0 mm and the ray from the center to 0 mm. The wavelength of the ray was set to $0.59\,\mu m$, which is a general wavelength that defines the focal length of the lens. The eye model downloaded and used on the official site of Zemax was downloaded and used[3].

The center of the retina of the eyeball model was set as the origin of the coordinate system. When reproducing the optical system using Google Cardboard in the air, a ray coming from a height of y = 29.0 mm reached the retina at the coordinates shown in Fig. 3. This figure also shows the effects of the optical system for a ray coming from a height of y = 0 mm. Our HMD, shown in Fig. 3 (right), was designed so that the coordinates of the image formed by the retina are almost the same as those obtained when a Google Cardboard is used in the air. We tried each of the plano-convex lenses sold by Edmund Optics one by one, and repeated the optimization calculations for the image on the retina with the distance between the display and the lens as a variable. For each lens, the coordinates for a ray with y = 29 mm reaching the retina were examined, as shown in Table 1. We chose to use a lens with a diameter of 25 mm and a focal length of 25 mm, with which the coordinates obtained were the closest to the coordinates obtained when using a Google Cardboard.

We only needed to consider the optical design for one eye. First, as shown in the Fig. 3 (left), the optical system of Google Cardboard when used in the air was reproduced. The display had a height of 58.00 mm when laid sideways, so our calculations used a ray coming from a height of 29.0 mm and a ray coming from the center at a height of 0 mm. The wavelength of the light beam was set

---

[3] http://customers.zemax.com/os/resources/learn/knowledgebase/zemax-models-of-the-human-eye.

to 0.59 μm. The eye model used on the official site of Zemax was downloaded and used. The optical system was set as shown in Fig. 3 (right). It was designed so that the coordinates of the image formed on the retina are almost the same as those obtained when a Google Cardboard is used in the air. We tried each of the plano-convex lenses sold by Edmund Optics one by one, and repeated the optimization calculations for the image on the retina with the distance between the display and the lens as a variable. For each lens, the coordinates on the retina obtained for a ray coming from a height of y = 29 mm reaching the retina were examined as shown in the Table 1. We chose to use a lens with a diameter of 25 mm and a focal length of 25 mm, with which the coordinates obtained were closest to the coordinates obtained when using a Google Cardboard (Table 2).

Table 2. Lens data.

Diameter [mm]	Focal length [mm]	Variable length [mm]	Qy [mm]	Qz [mm]
Google cardboard	-	-	−9.08	−5.11
20	20	45.8	−10.13	−8.00
22.5	22.5	51.7	−9.77	−6.42
25	25	65.8	−8.38	−4.13
30	30	69.9	−8.02	−3.73

Gaussian Optics. In this section, we described the optimal optical design for our HMD, which is to be used in an underwater environment. The ray tracing diagram of the proposed system in an underwater environment is shown in Fig. 3 (right). Because there is water between the display and the lens, there is a difference in the distance between the object lens and the eye lens from what it would be without the water. When the focal length of the lens and the distance between the lens and the pupil are given, the goal is to find the distance between display and lens connecting the image without causing blurring on the retina.

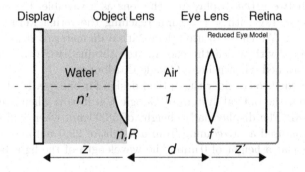

Fig. 4. Optical system of our HMD.

Table 3. Parameters in Fig. 4 and their meaning

Parameter	Letter	Number
Display-lens	z	68.9
Image distance of the reduced eye model	z'	17.0
Focal length of the reduced eye model	f	16.7
Distance between eye and lens	d	11.5
Curvature radius of lens	R	16.8
Refractive index of lens material	n	1.673
Refractive index of water	n'	1.33

First, we rewrote the system presented in Fig. 3 into an equivalent optical system using a reduced eye model, as shown in Fig. 4. Let z be the distance between the display and the lens. See Table 3 for the meanings of the other parameters shown in Fig. 4. By doing ray tracing based on Gaussian optics, the following equation is obtained for ray matrix M to derive the convex lens of the reduced eye model from the plano-convex lens.

$$M = \begin{pmatrix} A & B \\ C & D \end{pmatrix} \tag{1}$$

$$= \begin{pmatrix} 1 & 0 \\ -\frac{1}{f} & 1 \end{pmatrix} \begin{pmatrix} 1 & d \\ 0 & 1 \end{pmatrix} \begin{pmatrix} 1 & 0 \\ 0 & n \end{pmatrix} \begin{pmatrix} 1 & 0 \\ \frac{n-n'}{nR} & \frac{n'}{n} \end{pmatrix} \tag{2}$$

$$= \begin{pmatrix} 1.235 & 15.30 \\ -0.0535 & 0.420 \end{pmatrix} \tag{3}$$

The image conditions at this time satisfy the following expression.

$$z = \frac{B + Dz'}{A + Cz'}$$

Thus, the optimum distance between the display and the lens was calculated to be $z = 68.9$ mm. This value is close to the value of the variable length calculated in the previous chapter when using our lens.

3.2 Buoyancy and Center of Gravity Evaluation

We designed the 3D model of the enclosure using Rhinoceros. For the sake of simplicity, the head was a ball with a diameter of 20 cm and a weight of 5 kg, and its center was set as the origin of the coordinates. For the other objects, their weight was measured and the volume was calculated from the model. The additional volume of tape and adhesives was ignored. The relationships between the center of gravity, weight, volume, and so on are shown in the Fig. 5. Considering these values, when a person puts on a watertight HMD, their head tends to float in the water, but, when the a person puts on our designed HMD, their head tends to sink in the water.

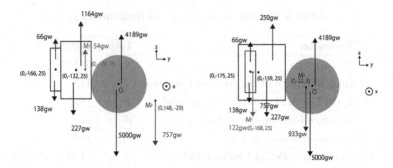

Fig. 5. Watertight HMD (left) and our proposed HMD (right). In each subfigure, M1 is the center of gravity of the corresponding HMD and M2 is the center of gravity of all objects.

3.3 External Design

The HMD was built by laser cutting on acrylic material. Because each person's vision is different, a mechanism was provided that allows focus adjustment by varying the distance between the display and the lens. More specifically, a vertical hole was made in the upper part of the HMD and a screw was passed through. In this way, after adjusting the position of the smartphone, the screw was tightened with a screwdriver so that its position would remain fixed.

4 Evaluation

In this section, the HMD experience was evaluated through subject experiments in terms of wide-view clearness, swimming comfort, and feeling of immersion.

4.1 Method

Participants. Six male volunteers (ages 18–22) were recruited through social media. The participants average height and weight were 173.7 cm (SD = 3.5, range 169–180) and 63.0 kg (SD = 8.4, range 51–79), respectively. All participants had normal or corrected vision. Each participant was briefly informed of the purpose of the study and told that they could abort the experiment and take a break at any time. Furthermore, they were provided with a consent form to complete and sign. No participant reported feeling any motion sickness.

System Setup and Performance. Two types of HMD were prepared for the experiments. The first was an off-the-shelf HMD water-tightened with adhesive and vinyl tape. The second was the proposed HMD, which has a structure that allowed water to fill its inside.

Subjects swam freely while looking at a 360° video delivered as content for Google Cardboard from YouTube using an iPhone 7. The movie's display was automatically adjusted according to the subject's position by detecting movement using the accelerometer and the gyro sensor of the iPhone 7. When the subjects swam, they wore a snorkel, nose plugs, and earplugs according when desired.

4.2   Imagery Assessment

Whether it was clearly visible in a wide field of view was evaluated by the subjects. Their average scores on a seven-point Likert scale (0 = negative, 6 = positive) were calculated. For the watertight HMD, the average was 3.2 out of 6 (SD = 1.0). For the HMD we made, the average was 4.2 out of 6 (SD = 0.7). This result proves that there was sufficiently large field of vision.

4.3   Feeling While Swimming

We asked each subject to assess the ease of moving their head underwater on a seven-point Likert scale (0 = negative, 6 = positive), both for the watertight HMD with a higher buoyancy and for the proposed HMD with a lower buoyancy. For the watertight HMD, the average was 2.8 out of 6 (SD = 2.1). For the HMD we made, the average was 3.2 out of 6 (SD = 2.2). This result doesn't prove that users can swim comfortably by wearing an HMD subject to less buoyant force. However, all subjects could swim without push proposed HMD to water, and watertight HMD is needed to push in the water. It shows the HMD is useful.

4.4   Immersion into Virtual Reality

The factor analysis of an iGroup presence questionnaire (iPQ)[4] describes three factors that collectively affect presence on a seven-point Likert scale (0 = negative, 6 = positive). Spatial presence is related to the sense of operating in virtual space instead of operating something from outside. Involvement describes attention to the real and virtual environments during simulation, and realness is a comparison of the experience of the real world and the virtual world. The overall assessment of the presence is derived from the average of the ratings of these three factors and from the evaluation of another question about general existence. For the watertight HMD, the average overall presence of all reported participants was 2.78 out of 6 (SD = 1.72). Average spatial presence was M = 2.92 out of 6, (SD = 1.83), average involvement was M = 2.70 out of 6 (SD = 1.22), and average realness was M = 2.70 out of 6 (SD = 1.55). For our proposed HMD, the average overall presence of all reported participants was 3.31 out of 6 (SD = 1.72). Average spatial presence, average involvement and average realness were M = 3.15 out of 6 (SD = 0.96), M = 3.52 out of 6, (SD = 1.70) and for M = 3.40 out of 6 (SD = 0.47), respectively. Through this result, we can infer that even though the participants were engaged and present in a virtual underwater world, they behaved as if they were scuba diving in real life. In other words, our HMD made it possible to experience the virtual world more naturally.

---

[4] http://www.igroup.org/pq/ipq/construction.php (last accessed October 21, 2017).

5　Discussion

Since players do not notice the surrounding walls or people, there is a need to implement a system to avoid obstacles. For example, Slawson et al. [12] showed that visible light tracking using an LED is possible even underwater. By expanding this system and using it three-dimensionally, it would be possible to specify the position of the players.

In addition, focus will be lost if a player uses this HMD in the air. By adding a mechanism that changes the position of the display so that the focal length is appropriate both in water and in air, swimmers would be able to see without interruption when taking their heads out of the water.

6　Conclusion

In this research, we have designed an HMD, taking optics into account, which ensures a sufficient field of view even when its internal structure is filled with water. This reduced buoyancy, and the evaluations by subjects proved that the proposed device is actually useful. Therefore, in this paper, we have described a device that allows users to enjoy VR comfortably in the water.

Acknowledgments. We would like to thank all contributors who supported our laboratory via the crowdfunding project.

References

1. Zhang, W., Tan, C.T., Chen, T.: A safe low-cost HMD for underwater VR experiences. In: SIGGRAPH ASIA 2016 Mobile Graphics and Interactive Applications, p. 12. ACM (2016)
2. Abdelkader, B., Christophe, D., Samir, O., Samir, B., Alain, D.: Augmented reality for underwater activities with the use of the dolphyn. In: 2013 10th IEEE International Conference on Networking, Sensing and Control (ICNSC), pp. 409–412. IEEE (2013)
3. Jain, D., Sra, M., Guo, J., Marques, R., Wu, R., Chiu, J., Schmandt, C.: Immersive scuba diving simulator using virtual reality. In: Proceedings of the 29th Annual Symposium on User Interface Software and Technology, pp. 729–739 (2016)
4. Torsten, F.: The virtual oceanarium. Commun. ACM **43**(7), 94–101 (2000)
5. Steve, M.: Through the glass, lightly [viewpoint]. IEEE Technol. Soc. Mag. **31**(3), 10–14 (2012)
6. Olson, J.L., Krum, D.M., Suma, E.A., Bolas, M.: A design for a smartphone-based head mounted display. In: 2011 IEEE Virtual Reality Conference, pp. 233–234. IEEE (2011)
7. Quarles, J.: Shark punch: a virtual reality game for aquatic rehabilitation. In: 2015 IEEE Virtual Reality (VR), p. 375. IEEE (2015)
8. Takala, T., Savioja, L., Lokki, T.: Swimming in a virtual aquarium (2005)
9. Lisa, B., Wolfgang, B., Stefan, M.: Augmented reality under water. In: SIGGRAPH 2009: Posters. ACM, Article No. 97 (2009)

10. Yamashita, S., Zhang, X., Rekimoto, J.: AquaCAVE: augmented swimming environment with immersive surround-screen virtual reality. In: Proceedings of the 29th Annual Symposium on User Interface Software and Technology, pp. 183–184. ACM (2016)
11. Osone, H., Yoshida, T., Ochiai, Y.: Optimized HMD system for underwater VR experience. In: ACM SIGGRAPH 2017 Posters. ACM (2017)
12. Slawson, S., Conway, P., Justham, L., West, A.: The development of an inexpensive passive marker system for the analysis of starts and turns in swimming. Procedia Eng. **2**(2), 2727–2733 (2010)
13. Rolland, J., Hua, H.: Head-mounted display systems. In: Johnson, R.B., Driggers, R.G. (eds.) Encyclopedia of Optical Engineering, pp. 1–13. Marcel Dekker, New York (2005)

Magnetic Table for Levitating Food for Entertainment

Kevin Stanley Bielawski[1,2]([✉]), Nur Ellyza Abd Rahman[1,2], Azhri Azhar[1,2],
Kasun Karunanayaka[1,2], Mohammed Rabea Taleb Banalzwaa[1,2],
Ibrahim Gamal Mahmoud Moteir[1,2], and Adrian David Cheok[1,2]

[1] Imagineering Institute, Iskandar Puteri, Malaysia
{kevin,ellyza,azhri,kasun,rabea,ibrahim,adrian}@imagineeringinstitute.org
[2] City, University of London, London, UK
http://imagineeringinstitute.org/

Abstract. In this paper, we discuss our work towards a new dining platform that uses magnetic levitating food and magnetic utensils in an initial prototype device. The ultimate goal of the project is a complete table with dynamic levitating food, but the current implementation is a set of levitating magnets that can be encased in food hovering over static locations. We investigated different weights and shapes of 3-D printed objects to mimic food and found that the levitating magnets are strong enough to support lightweight food. This magnetic levitating table can produce a playful and entertaining dining experience by moving and rotating to stay in place. The key novelties of this paper are the integration of food with a magnetic levitating table for playful interactions and novel dining experiences.

Keywords: Magnetic levitation · Magnetic food · Levitating food

1 Introduction

Food is a basic human need, and the experience of eating food has been explored for maximum enjoyment. The variety of restaurants and methods for experiencing food are vast, yet new technology allows for novel and interactive ways to enjoy the basic activity of eating [7,11,19,21]. Furthermore, new technology and studies have sought to create enhanced multisensory virtual environments for dining experiences [8,13,22].

One aspect of the dining experience that has recently received attention is the haptic experience of holding utensils, and how it may affect taste and overall experience. In one study, virtual chopsticks were used to enhance a virtual reality dining experience by providing force feedback when a user picked up food with chopsticks [13]. In another study, the effect of the texture of plateware was investigated, and the researchers found that food tasted rougher when eaten off of rougher plates [5]. Another study found that the freshness of pretzels differed between holding a crisp pretzel end or a soft pretzel end, regardless of

© Springer International Publishing AG, part of Springer Nature 2018
A. D. Cheok et al. (Eds.): ACE 2017, LNCS 10714, pp. 462–469, 2018.
https://doi.org/10.1007/978-3-319-76270-8_32

the crispness of the tasted pretzel [2]. In another study, the weight of cutlery was suggested as a factor in perception of the taste of food, with heavier utensils resulting in a better experiences [18].

One concept that was previously proposed for novel dining experiences is the use of magnetic levitation [1,20]. Magnetic fields can be used to levitate food, move food, modify the weight of utensils, add dynamic textures, and create novel dining experiences. Magnetic levitation is commonly used in high-speed trains [14] and bearing-less motors [6,9], but it has also been applied to other fields [12,16]. Magnetic levitation has also been investigated as a novel haptic experience with researchers investigating methods to apply force to users on a magnetic inverted pendulum [4] and moving a levitating magnet using a haptic actuator [3].

In this paper, we describe our approach for magnetically levitating food to enhance dining experiences. We use a combination of permanent magnets and electromagnets to levitate a permanent magnet that can be encased within food. We investigate the feasibility of different shapes of food that can be levitated with this system, and find that shapes with larger moments of inertia and lower masses are suitable for levitation.

2   Prototype

Our approach uses permanent magnets to provide the levitation force and electromagnets to provide a centering force for the system, Fig. 1. This approach builds on previously described work for levitating a magnet [15]. The basics of the operation of our device use the unstable equilibrium at the center of a ring magnet to provide the force of levitation to a floating magnet. When moved off of the center of the ring magnet, the levitating magnet will be attracted to the ring magnet, so electromagnets are used to push the levitating magnet back to the center of the ring.

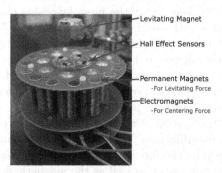

Fig. 1. Our system is composed of a ring of permanent magnets to provide levitating forces, a set of electromagnets to provide centering forces, Hall effect sensors for position sensing, and a levitating magnet.

Our system consists of a set of 16 cylindrical magnets with a diameter of 1 cm each in a ring with a total diameter of 9 cm at the centerline of the magnets. The cylindrical magnets produce a levitating force, and a set of 8 electromagnets provide a restoring force along the x- and y- axes, with two electromagnets on either side of the center of the structure in the x- and y- directions. The position of the magnet is sensed using a set of four Hall-effect sensors (Honeywell SS494B) located near the center of the structure. The Hall-effect sensors indicate the position of the levitating magnet and are used in a proportional-derivative (PD) control system implemented with an Arduino Pro-Mini, Fig. 2.

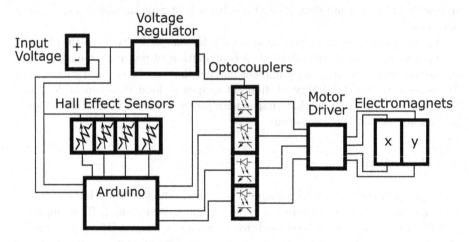

Fig. 2. Our system consists of Hall effect sensors for sensing the levitating magnet position, a PD controller implemented with an Arduino Pro-Mini, optocouplers, motor drivers, and electromagnets.

In our system, we used several different strengths and sizes of levitating magnets, but ultimately found that the most favorable magnet was a stack of two grade N52 magnets with one having a diameter of 2.5 cm and a height of 1 cm, and the additional magnet having a diameter of 2 cm with a height of 0.5 cm. Based on our modeling and experiments, the proper levitating magnet was determined based on the balance of the attractive force of the magnets forming the ring and the potential restoring forces of the electromagnets used to restore the magnet to the original position.

The dynamics of the system were determined using a combination of modeling and experimental verification. Modeling was done using FEMM 4.2 [17] in planar mode to determine the forces on the levitating magnet due to position and current in the electromagnet as well as the magnetic field ($|B|$), Fig. 3. The materials used in the model corresponded to the materials in the system, but the exact dimensions were determined using experimental verification. Verification was performed by determining the height at which a magnet levitated at the center of the ring with no electromagnetic input while is was constricted to motion in the vertical direction. In the model, a levitating magnet would require a total vertical force equal to its weight at that location. The size of the ring magnets were tuned to obtain a proper result. Similarly, the magnetic field could be used to tune the model electromagnets, with measured magnetic field corresponding to the simulated magnetic field at a particular current. The current to the electromagnets was changed from no current to maximum current while the magnetic field was read at the Hall-effect sensors. As the electromagnetic field from a solenoid is given by $\mathbf{H} = ni$ [10], where n is the turn density and i is the current, our results showed a linear correlation between the measured magnetic field and the current in the electromagnets. This was tuned in the model based on the number of turns simulated coils. Ultimately, after tuning the model system, it was used to determine a relationship between current in the coils, position of the levitating magnet, and the force on the levitating magnet. For sufficiently small motion of less than 5 mm, we found the equation of motion in a single axis to be $F = m\ddot{x} = 7.6x\,(t) + 0.012i\,(t)$ N, where $x\,(t)$ is the position in m, and $i\,(t)$ is the current represented by the pulse-width modulated (PWM) signal. Our model system was used to develop a control system using PD control. The PD controller had a relatively high derivative component with a lower proportional component. This model system was then used to understand how to make the levitating magnet more stable.

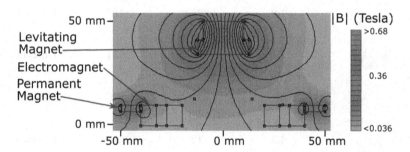

Fig. 3. The magnetic flux density, $|B|$, due to the levitating magnet, permanent magnets, and electromagnetic coils that have a current of half of the maximum current. The magnetic fields and forces of the permanent and electromagnets were modeled using FEMM 4.2. The current in the electromagnetic coils was varied per an experimentally-derived relationship between the supplied PWM control signal and the resulting magnetic field.

After successfully testing the system to levitate magnets, different shapes of magnetic foods were tested on the system. In order to determine the effects of added masses to the magnetic foods, we used 3-D-printed shapes. The 3-D-printed shapes had changes in the total mass, size, and distribution of mass. Furthermore, the shapes were intended to mimic shapes of common foods, including pears, pumpkins, onions, and pizzas.

3   Effects of Objects on Levitation

We tested multiple different 3-D printed objects with changes to the size, mass, and mass distributions. We found that the center of mass needs to be at the same center of mass of the levitating magnet, otherwise the object would not levitate. Furthermore, we found that, except for lightweight and heavy objects, high moments of inertia were favorable to low moments of inertia for stable levitation (see Table 1). The table is best suited for levitating lightweight, disk-shaped objects with a height approximately equal to the height of the levitating magnets, which is about 25 mm.

Table 1. Success of levitating different shapes

Shape	Maximum Diameter (cm)	Mass (g)	Moment of Inertia (g·cm^2)	Stability
	10.5	40	233	Stable
	5.0	23	55	Unstable
	7.0	25	102	Unstable
	10	75	511	Unstable
	12	34	226	Stable
	4.5	12	22	Unstable
	3.5	5	6.8	Stable

This work showed that in the current system, several common shapes of food could be stably levitated for interactive displays and even to be removed from the magnet and eaten. This could provide an attractive display to entice customers to order food or be used as a unique dining experience where floating food is directly consumed and brought out on a levitating plate.

4   Applications to Levitating Food

Our results show that stable levitation of food is possible and can provide a novel dining experience. It can also be used to entice customers to enter a store as an attractive display. People interacting with the levitating magnets often take photos and play with the levitating table. When used as an element in dining, it can provide a unique and playful dining experience.

Our system currently consists of three of these tables arranged to levitate three magnets holding food, Fig. 4. This system is interactive, but users must remove the magnet from the food before eating. This can be done either by disposing of the magnet, or carefully removing the food from the levitating magnet without disturbing the magnet away from the controllable region of the table. The system is likely best used as a display in its current form, but it can also be an interactive way to dine or present a dish to a customer.

Fig. 4. Our current system consists of three tables positioned to levitate magnets holding food. (a) Food is represented with different 3-D printed objects, and (b) real food is tested and can levitate. The real food in (b) is (from left to right) a dried kiwi, a white fungus, and a prune.

5 Future Work

Our current device has some limitations that will be overcome in future work. Currently, the height of the levitating magnet is determined by the ring of permanent magnets in the system. This cannot be changed dynamically, except by adding weight to make the height lower. Furthermore, the system is confined to a single levitating location. We did some investigation into if we could move the magnet, but found that the system works best if the levitating magnet remains at the center of the ring magnet, and becomes less stable when moved away from center. We plan to extend our work in the future to use only electromagnets so that the levitating magnet can be fully manipulated for six-dimensional control, including the height, planar motion, and angle of the magnet. This work will enable a fully novel dining experience with food moving around the table automatically without being manipulated by hand.

In addition to extending the magnetic table for full motion of levitating magnets, we will also investigate novel methods of interacting with the magnetic dining table. These methods will include levitating food, moving food, modifying the weight of the utensils, and adding dynamic textures to a meal. We expect that these novel interactions will enhance dining experiences to create new methods for interacting during meals.

6   Conclusions

In this paper, we have discussed our simulation, development, and technical results on a novel platform for a magnetic dining table. The current system consists of a set of permanent magnet rings that provide levitation force combined with electromagnets that provide a centering force. We investigated the use of different shapes of food that can be levitated with the current system and found that shapes with larger moments of inertia were more likely to be stable. The system can be currently implemented for unique dining experiences with lightweight food that has been shaped with an opening for the levitating magnet. The key novelties of this paper are the integration of food with a magnetic levitating table for playful interactions and novel dining experiences.

References

1. Abd Rahman, N.E., Azhar, A., Johar, M.A.M., Karunanayaka, K., Cheok, A.D., Gross, J., Luis, A.: Magnetic dining table and magnetic foods. In: Proceedings of the 13th International Conference on Advances in Computer Entertainment Technology, p. 33. ACM (2016)
2. Barnett-Cowan, M.: An illusion you can sink your teeth into: haptic cues modulate the perceived freshness and crispness of pretzels. Perception **39**(12), 1684–1686 (2010)
3. Berkelman, P., Dzadovsky, M.: Magnet levitation and trajectory following motion control using a planar array of cylindrical coils. In: ASME Dynamic Systems and Control Conference, pp. 767–774 (2008)
4. Berkelman, P.J., Hollis, R.L., Salcudean, S.E.: Interacting with virtual environments using a magnetic levitation haptic interface. In: Proceedings, 1995 IEEE/RSJ International Conference on Intelligent Robots and Systems 1995 'Human Robot Interaction and Cooperative Robots', vol. 1, pp. 117–122. IEEE (1995)
5. Biggs, L., Juravle, G., Spence, C.: Haptic exploration of plateware alters the perceived texture and taste of food. Food Qual. Prefer. **50**, 129–134 (2016)
6. Bleuler, H.: A survey of magnetic levitation and magnetic bearing types. JSME Int. J. Ser. 3, Vibr. Control Eng. Eng. Ind. **35**(3), 335–342 (1992)
7. Ganesh, S., Marshall, P., Rogers, Y., O'Hara, K.: Foodworks: tackling fussy eating by digitally augmenting children's meals. In: Proceedings of the 8th Nordic Conference on Human-Computer Interaction: Fun, Fast, Foundational, pp. 147–156. ACM (2014)
8. Iwata, H., Yano, H., Uemura, T., Moriya, T.: Food simulator: a haptic interface for biting. In: Proceedings, Virtual Reality, pp. 51–57. IEEE (2004)
9. Jayawant, B.: Review lecture-electromagnetic suspension and levitation techniques. In: Proceedings of the Royal Society of London A: Mathematical, Physical and Engineering Sciences, vol. 416, pp. 245–320. The Royal Society (1988)
10. Jiles, D.: Introduction to Magnetism and Magnetic Materials. CRC Press, New York (2015)

11. Khot, R.A., Aggarwal, D., Pennings, R., Hjorth, L., Mueller, F.: Edipulse: investigating a playful approach to self-monitoring through 3D printed chocolate treats. In: Proceedings of the 2017 CHI Conference on Human Factors in Computing Systems, pp. 6593–6607. ACM (2017)
12. Kim, W.J., Trumper, D.L.: High-precision magnetic levitation stage for photolithography. Precis. Eng. **22**(2), 66–77 (1998)
13. Kitamura, Y., Douko, K., Kitayama, M., Kishino, F.: Object deformation and force feedback for virtual chopsticks. In: Proceedings of the ACM Symposium on Virtual Reality Software and Technology, pp. 211–219. ACM (2005)
14. Lee, H.W., Kim, K.C., Lee, J.: Review of Maglev train technologies. IEEE Trans. Magn. **42**(7), 1917–1925 (2006)
15. Li, C., Li, L.: The stable magnetic levitation of a cylindrical ferromagnetic object. J. Supercond. Novel Magn. **27**(12), 2773–2778 (2014)
16. Liu, Y., Zhu, D.M., Strayer, D.M., Israelsson, U.E.: Magnetic levitation of large water droplets and mice. Adv. Space Res. **45**(1), 208–213 (2010)
17. Meeker, D.: Femm 4.2. User's Manual, Virginia (2009)
18. Michel, C., Velasco, C., Spence, C.: Cutlery matters: heavy cutlery enhances diners' enjoyment of the food served in a realistic dining environment. Flavour **4**(1), 26 (2015)
19. Narumi, T., Kajinami, T., Tanikawa, T., Hirose, M.: Meta cookie. In: ACM SIGGRAPH 2010 Posters, p. 143. ACM (2010)
20. Rahman, N.E.A., Azhar, A., Karunanayaka, K., Cheok, A.D., Johar, M.A.M., Gross, J., Aduriz, A.L.: Implementing new food interactions using magnetic dining table platform and magnetic foods. In: Proceedings of the 2016 Workshop on Multimodal Virtual and Augmented Reality, p. 5. ACM (2016)
21. Wei, J., Cheok, A.D., Nakatsu, R.: Let's have dinner together: evaluate the mediated co-dining experience. In: Proceedings of the 14th ACM International Conference on Multimodal Interaction, pp. 225–228. ACM (2012)
22. Wei, J., Peiris, R.L., Koh, J.T.K.V., Wang, X., Choi, Y., Martinez, X.R., Tache, R., Halupka, V., Cheok, A.D.: Food media: exploring interactive entertainment over telepresent dinner. In: Proceedings of the 8th International Conference on Advances in Computer Entertainment Technology, p. 26. ACM (2011)

FunCushion: Fabricating Functional Cushion Interfaces with Fluorescent-Pattern Displays

Kohei Ikeda[1]([✉]) [iD], Naoya Koizumi[2] [iD], and Takeshi Naemura[1] [iD]

[1] The University of Tokyo, Hongo 7-3-1, Bunkyo-ku, Tokyo, Japan
{ikeda,naemura}@nae-lab.org
[2] The University of Electro-Communications,
Chofugaoka 1-5-1, Chofu-shi, Tokyo, Japan
koizumi.naoya@uec.ac.jp

Abstract. We introduce FunCushion, a digital fabrication method for customized fluorescent-pattern displays on cloths of cushion interfaces with push detections. The displayed patterns are printed out onto cloths by an inkjet printer with transparent fluorescent ink, and the patterns can interactively be made to glow with an ultraviolet light source embedded inside the cushion. Furthermore, push detection using infrared light can be easily integrated with the display for interaction. The displays are adaptable to 3D shapes, illuminate with multi-color and gradation, and can be integrated with static visual print and embroidery. This method enables end-users and designers to create soft, everyday products with fluorescent-pattern displays in a lab. Technical evaluations revealed effective materials for the display. Application examples demonstrate FunCushion's applicability.

Keywords: Fluorescence · Ultraviolet light · Printing display
Cushion · Cloth · Deformable User Interfaces (DUI)
Digital fabrication

1 Introduction

Cloth is a fundamental material for soft toys, furnitures and everyday commodities such as cushion blocks, sofa and clothing. It beautifully decorates the appearance of these products and provide comfort due to the softness. If visual contents can be dynamically displayed on cloths without compromising the softness, they can enhance the aesthetics of furniture (Fig. 1b). Furthermore, they can add interactivity and new ways of playing to conventional soft toys (Fig. 1c)

Electronic supplementary material The online version of this chapter (https://doi.org/10.1007/978-3-319-76270-8_33) contains supplementary material, which is available to authorized users.

by integrating the displays with input sensing. Whereas sensing methods for cloths and soft objects have been well studied, display methods on cloths have room for improvement. The display methods can be categorized into projection-based methods and visible light-emitting diode (LED) integration. The former projects images onto the surface of cloths from the outside of soft objects, but it often suffers from occlusion and calibration and cannot be applied to portable devices. On the other hand, the latter method uses LEDs or optical fibers on the surface of cloth to emit display light. However, this method has difficulty displaying fine patterns and large images. When a light source is embedded inside soft objects to achieve a smoother touch, then diffusion of lights by the covering materials disturbs the display quality.

Fig. 1. FunCushion is a digital fabrication method enabling end-users and designers to create fluorescent-patttern displays on cloths of cushion interfaces with push detection: (a) printed fluorescent-pattern (b) lampshade (c) interactive cushion block (d) interactive plush toy (e) wristrest with e-mail notification.

This paper introduces FunCushion, a novel method that can display light-emitting fine patterns on cloth while retaining the softness, and a fabrication method to make the display as shown in Fig. 1a. This is achieved by combining fluorescent ink and ultraviolet (UV) light; specifically, we inkjet-print the patterns on cloths with transparent fluorescent ink and embed a UV light source inside the soft object, in which the soft materials also work as a diffuser to improve the display. The display method can be easily combined with push detection using infrared (IR) lights; thus, we implemented a UV/IR module to simplify the fabrication process. This paper presents four contributions:

1. A novel display method for cloth that displays light-emitting fine patterns while retaining the softness by using UV light and transparent fluorescent inks.
2. Integration of two invisible lights to display fine patterns and detect user motion simultaneously.
3. A digital fabrication process by using fluorescent inkjet printing and a UV/IR module.
4. Technical evaluations to reveal the effective materials (cloth and soft diffuser) to improve the quality of the display.

FunCushion enables end-users and designers to create interactive everyday objects made of cloths. We demonstrate the wide applicability of FunCushion through application examples.

2   Related Work

2.1   Deformable User Interfaces (DUI)

The flexible devices called Deformable User Interfaces (hereinafter, DUI) which can deform into various shapes by physical input have been developed to give users higher degrees of freedom of input in Human Computer Interaction [1–3]. They provide physical flexibilities, allow various input movements such as pushing, bending and stretching. They can also be applied to 3D shapes. Furthermore, everyday soft products made of cloths have been augmented to DUI for sensing human behavior by integrating electronics into them [4]. Sugiura et al. provide a pressure sensing method that can be easily embedded into a ready-made pillow cushion and maintain its softness by using IR light sources and receivers [5]. FunCushion introduces customized cloth displays for DUI that can be embedded into daily soft products and integrated with Sugiura et al.'s pressure sensing method using IR light without compromising the tactile feels and the softness.

2.2   Interactive Fabric Applications and Fabrications

Cloths are essential materials for creating many wearable or carried objects such as clothes, bags, and cushions. Novel fibers, yarns, and weaving technologies have been developed to increase functionality and aesthetic quality. In particular, interactive cloths that include e-textiles are powerful technologies for creating smart wearable and mobile products. They intelligently support daily life by sensing input gestures and displaying visual contents at the positions close to users and enhance the aesthetic qualities of cloths [6,7]. However, these techniques have not yet been established in the fabrication process. The major methods to build interactive cloths are stitching conductive yarns or optical fibers, embroidery, printing conductive inks, and connecting electronic components and microcontrollers [8–14]. Furthermore, digital fabrication methods of interactive soft products have also been developed to enable end-users and designers to create interactive fabric applications [15–17]. Whereas sensing methods for cloths and soft objects have been well studied, display methods on cloths have room for improvement. We thus introduce a novel displaying method called FunCushion and its digital fabrication method.

2.3   Cloth Displays

A cloth display is a cloth that contains embedded display technology and can present information by computer. To take advantage of the properties of cloth, four requirements must be satisfied.

1. *Tactile feel and softness*: The tactile feel and the softness of soft objects are essential for soft user interfaces. Impairment of the original tactile feels and softness of soft objects must be avoided.
2. *Displaying Fine Pattern*: Cloth displays are required to achieve fine patterns to clearly display small icon buttons and aesthetic decorative fine patterns.

3. *Applicability to portable objects*: Cloth displays should be applicable to daily portable and wearable products such as clothes, bags, and plush toys.
4. *Visibility control*: The visibilities of the displays are required to be controlled. The display systems should be invisible and not affect the original look of the fabric when the displays are not working.

No previous method meets all these requirements at the same time. The major display methods can be categorized into two types.

Projection-based method: A projection-based method using a camera and a projector [18,19] can display fine visual contents without compromising the tactile feel of cloths. Although the method provides flexibility of cloths, it often suffers from occlusion and calibration and cannot be applied to portable and wearable objects. Thus, display equipment should be embedded in soft objects for ubiquitous and wearable computing.

Visible LED integration: The other type of method is integrating visible LEDs with objects. In previous work, researchers stitched the visible LEDs to the surface [20] or wove optical fibers into cloths [21–23]. However, these methods impair the original tactile feel and softness of cloths, and the quality of displays is limited by their size. In other works, the visible LEDs were embedded into soft objects [24], but when light sources are embedded inside soft objects to achieve a smoother tactile feel, diffusion of lights by the covering materials disturbs the quality of the display.

The previous methods have difficulty providing both the necessary softness and fine pattern at the same time. Therefore, we chose a method for directly printing patterns onto cloths with functional inks.

2.4   Printed Displays with Functional Inks

Printed displays with functional inks are powerful technologies in ubiquitous and wearable computing. They achieve fine patterns and are adaptable to various sizes and shapes. Functional inks change their colors or emit light in response to physical stimulations such as heat [25] and UV light [26,27] by energy projection. However, these methods need a laser system, so they are not suitable for outside use because they present safety issues. On the other hand, there are other energy providing methods that use printed circuits. Researchers developed thin flexible printed displays by printing the display patterns with thermochromic [28] or electroluminescence [29] onto paper. Printscreen [29] introduced thin-film customized displays that can be printed onto thin substrates with the electroluminescence and the conductive ink. However, they cannot be printed onto cloths. Furthermore, functional inks are also used for fabric displays. Many fabric displays use non-emissive color-changing inks such as thermochromic inks [30–33] and photochromic inks [34]. They have long switching intervals of color-changing. AmbiKraf [30] and TempTouch [33] achieve rapid color-changing by using Peltier elements, but these elements impair the softness.

We choose to use light-emitting inks because they have short switching intervals and their light-emitting patterns are also visible in dark environments. This paper introduces an emissive printed cloth display with fluorescent inkjet-printing.

3   FunCushion

We propose FunCushion, a fluorescent-pattern display on cloth of a cushion interface with push detection. It can display a glow pattern on cloth in response to the user's pushing action. The display system consists of a UV-LED, a soft diffuser, a UV-pass visible-cut filter, transparent fluorescence, and cloth, as shown in Fig. 2. A light-emitting pattern is printed on the surface of cloth by an inkjet printer with transparent fluorescent ink. UV light is emitted to the printed area from the UV-LED. The soft diffuser also works as a diffuser of UV light, without which the LED is so directional that the patterns do not glow homogeneously. A UV-pass visible-cut filter is inserted since otherwise the visible light slightly provided by the UV-LED leaks out around the printed pattern, decreasing the contrast of the display.

The sensing system for push detection consists of an IR-LED, an IR-receiver, and a soft diffuser (Fig. 2). We detect a user's push by receiving reflected IR light and measuring the density of the soft diffuser [5]. The amount of the reflected IR light changes as the density of the diffuser changes when pressure is applied to the diffuser. The display and sensing system can be integrated in the same position without interfering with each other since the wavelengths of two invisible light sources are sufficiently different.

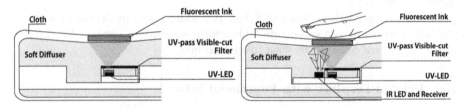

Fig. 2. System configuration of FunCushion. Display only (left half) and integration with push detection (right half).

The diffuser, cloth, and combination of a UV-LED and filter need to increase the contrast and uniformity of the display. Moreover, the diffuser should be soft and stably change the amount of the reflected IR as the diffuser's density changes. The cloth should be for inkjet printing and not fluorescent itself. We evaluated the luminance and contrast of the display using several materials.

4   Fabrication Process

This paper proposes a digital fabrication approach to create customized cloth displays. The fabrication process consists of two steps: (1) digital designing and printing a light-emitting pattern and (2) embedding a UV/IR module for displaying and sensing inside a soft object. We introduce two printing approaches: direct printing onto cloth and heat transfer.

4.1   Printing

Direct Printing onto Cloth. Light-emitting patterns can be easily designed by using a standard graphics editor such as Adobe Illustrator or Photoshop. The patterns can be printed by using a household inkjet printer (Epson PX-105), three color fluorescent inks (Soken SKI-TRC-R69, G69, B69), and A4-sized cloths for the printer (240 μm thick, Plus IT-325CO, Fig. 3a). The direct printing method enables designers to print the patterns onto cloths rapidly without ink bleed. The printed fluorescent patterns are transparent without UV light and visible only when UV light within 350 nm to 400 nm illuminates; thus, the system can control visibility of the patterns (Fig. 3b).

Heat Transfer onto Cloth. The heat transfer method enables patterns to be fixed onto cloths of various sizes, thicknesses, and textures. The user designs a light-emitting pattern reflected in the horizontal direction and prints it onto a semi-transparent transfer sheet (less than 160 μm thick, Elecom EJP-WPN, Fig. 3d). The sheet is fixed on the cloths by using a heating iron (Fig. 3c).

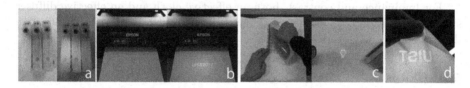

Fig. 3. Three color fluorescent inks (a) and two printing methods: direct printing onto cloth (b) and heat transfer (c) using thin transfer sheet (d). Printed patterns can interactively glow due to UV light (b, c).

4.2   Controller: UV/IR Module

We implemented a UV/IR module to embed light sources easily and a light receiver for displaying and sensing in a soft object. To display high contrast images, a UV LED should be powerful and emit only UV light. We selected a 365 nm UV-LED with a powerful center wavelength (690 mW at 500 mA forward current, irradiation angle is 110°, Nitride NS365L-6SVG) and a UV-pass visible-cut filter (Sigmakoki UTVAF330U) for energy sources. To detect user action, the photoreflector must include an IR pass filter. We thus selected Genixtek TPR-105F, which is the same photoreflector as in previous research [5]. To make customization easy, we choose Arduino for the controller. End-users can display fine patterns and detect a user's push on the cloth of soft objects easily with the above two steps.

5   Materials

In our proposed method, the cloth and soft diffuser are the essential materials. When end-users and designers fabricate daily soft products, they need to be able to choose various cloths and diffusers with different textures, softness, etc. in accordance with their preferences and the products' uses. FunCushion supports various cloths and diffusers. On the other hand, the quality of the display and the input sensitivity differ depending on the type of cloth and soft diffuser. It is thus important to investigate optically effective materials for output and input of the system. FunCushion needs to satisfy three requirements.

1. *Sufficient luminance of the display*: The display has to emit light with sufficient luminance. In the specifications of standard RGB (sRGB), the screen luminance level is defined as $80 \, cd/m^2$, which is the sufficient value of luminance in a dark environment.
2. *Sufficient contrast of the display*: To display a pattern clearly, sufficient contrast is required. Contrast means the luminance ratio between a fluorescent area and a non-fluorescent area.
3. *Change of IR-reflectivity for push sensing*: To stably detect a user's push, the amount of reflected IR light needs to greatly change when pressure is applied to the cushion.

For luminance and contrast, both an effective cloth and an effective diffuser should be considered. On the other hand, for IR-reflectivity, only an effective diffuser should be considered.

5.1   Cloths

We printed fluorescent patterns onto three types of cloths by using the direct printing and heat transfer methods. The direct printing method supports the cloths dedicated to inkjet printing. We could print fluorescent patterns on 100% white cotton cloth (240 μm thick, A4 size, Plus IT-325CO) and linen cloth (50% hemp and 50% cotton, 350 μm thick, A4 size, Kawaguchi 11-287) by using the inkjet printer. This method has difficulty printing onto heavy, large, and coarse cloths. The heat transfer method, in contrast, allows for printing onto cloths of various sizes, thicknesses, and textures. We used a semi-transparent transfer sheet (less than 160 μm thick, Elecom EJP-WPN) that supports white and light color cloths. We could adhere the sheets to the white cotton canvas (graded number: No. 11).

To achieve sufficient luminance and contrast (Requirements 1 and 2), the texture of cloth must be fine, and a large amount of fluorescent ink must be able to be coated on cloth. We compared luminance and contrast of the three cloths in a technical evaluation.

5.2   Soft Diffusers

We used 100% polyester cotton, natural cottons, and BREATHAIR® (Toyobo) as soft diffusers. Polyester cotton and organic cotton are commonly used for handicrafts and consumer products. BREATHAIR® (Toyobo) is a cushion material developed by Toyobo [35] that has high resilience, water permeability, air permeability, and pressure durability.

To realize sufficient luminance and contrast (Requirements 1 and 2), a soft diffuser must transmit a lot of UV light. To greatly change IR-reflectivity (Requirement 3), a soft diffuser must reflect IR light and its density must greatly change in accordance with the pressure. In this paper, we compared luminance and contrast of the three soft diffusers in a technical evaluation.

6 Display Primitives

This section provides a systematic overview of display primitives of FunCushion. We developed new display primitives on the basis of a combination of fluorescent inks and UV-LEDs. They are divided into spatial control and luminescent color.

6.1 Spatial Control and Luminescent Color

Spatial Control. There are two types of spatial control of segments: unified control with one UV-LED and separate control of multi-segments with multiple UV-LEDs. For the unified control, light emission of multi-segments can be controlled all together at the same time with one UV-LED (Fig. 4a). This is suitable for illuminating a large area at one time.

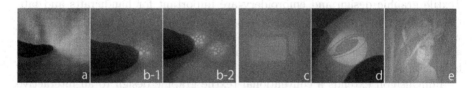

Fig. 4. Display Primitives of FunCushion. Spatial control is classified into two types: (a) unified control and (b) separate control. FunCushion enables images to be displayed with single color (c), multiple colors (d), and gradation (e).

On the other hand, multiple segments can be separately controlled with multiple UV-LEDs. Separate control of segments enables designers to create matrix displays that dynamically change the visual contents (Fig. 4b-1, b-2). We propose a new system configuration for separate control of multi-segments (the top half in Fig. 5). The optical path from UV-LEDs can be controlled by placing a soft frame with small holes on UV-LEDs. We implemented the matrix display by creating the soft frame (the bottom half in Fig. 5). The small holes can be made by laser-cutting on the NR rubber that does not transmit the UV light. Soft diffusers used in Fig. 2 were put in the holes to diffuse UV light.

The minimum segment size of the matrix display is 13 mm square, and the minimum distance between each segment is 15 mm. The rubber construction affects the softness of the object. The paper provides two directions for end-users, one is the matrix example that can present dynamic contents with more rigid

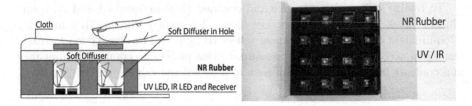

Fig. 5. System configuration and implementation of matrix display. Small holes are made by laser-cutting on NR rubber and filled with soft diffusers.

interface, and the other is highly comfortable display but with static contents. The former is suitable for products that users do not push input to the surface of objects.

Luminescent Color. Images of displays can be printed with not only a luminescent single color but also multiple colors and gradation (Fig. 4.c, d, e) by using three fluorescent inks (R, B, G). An image can be printed in 255 levels of gradations for each color.

6.2   Integration with Static Visual Print and Embroidery

Textile graphic design and embroidery are important for handicrafts and fabricating daily soft products. People choose textile graphic design in accordance with their preferences when they make a bag, clothing, or a cushion cover. They also customize them by embroidering and sticking on a patch. FunCushion can be combined with textile graphic design and embroidery

FunCushion extends a conventional textile graphic design to an interactive one by combining a fluorescent print with a static visual print in two ways: overlaying the same image on the static visual print (Fig. 6a), and printing a different image beside the static visual print (Fig. 6b). The former simply highlights the pattern by illuminating it (Fig. 6a). The latter adds interactive visual content related to the static visual print (Fig. 6b). While static visual images can be printed with an inkjet printer or laser printer, a fluorescent pattern can also be combined with a textile design of a commercially available cloth by using a heat transfer sheet (Fig. 6c).

Fig. 6. Integration with static visual print (a, b, c) and embroidery (d, e).

FunCushion also extends conventional embroideries and makes them interactive. An embroidery patch can be combined with a fluorescent pattern onto cloths after it is printed (Fig. 6d). When the linen cloth (Kawaguchi 11–287) is used, the designer can directly embroider on it with a needle.

7   Push Sensing

To design interactions, the relationship of positions between push sensing and the display must be considered. In this section, we provide an overview for determining the position of push sensing in accordance with it use. The relationships of positions are classified into two types: integration at the same position and at different positions.

Same Position. When push sensing is placed at the same position as a display, a light-emitting pattern is expected to work as buttons for a user to push. For instance, patterns work as icon buttons on a cushion for remotely controlling equipment in a room (Fig. 7a) or as pixels of a touch matrix display (Fig. 4b-1, b-2).

Different Positions. Push sensing is placed at a different position from a display when two positions are not required to match. We provide example situations.

1. *Input without looking at the area*: When an input sensor is integrated into a position that cannot be seen while a user is inputting, it may be separated from a display. For instance, visual contents are displayed on the backrest of a sofa in accordance with the users' sitting positions in Fig. 7b.
2. *Different area sizes*: When the input and output areas are different sizes, their positions do not necessarily have to match. For instance, the light-emitting area is larger than the input area in Fig. 4a and c.
3. *Remote uses and multiple users*: When multiple users use systems together to communicate remotely, input and output positions may be separated. In response to an input to one device, the other device displays visual contents such as message illustrations at the remote location.

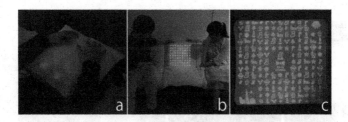

Fig. 7. Application examples of positional relationship between input and output: (a) cushion with remote control buttons, (b) sofa with display on its backrest, and (c) decorative Christmas cushion for children.

8   Shapes and Durability

8.1   3D Shapes

A display must be adaptable to complex 3D shapes and shape deformations to be embedded into soft products made of cloths such as plush toys and cushions. FunCushion supports flat surfaces, simple curved surfaces, and complex 3D shapes composed of doubly curved surfaces. After printing a pattern onto a cloth, a designer can make a 3D shape by cutting, folding, and sewing. We demonstrate the applicability of FunCushion to 3D shapes through four application examples. We also describe the possibilities of the products from the viewpoint of user's experience.

- *Lampshade*: FunCushion is applicable to a ruled surface product (Fig. 8left). We implemented the lampshade as an example of products that do not have IR input. This application shows applicability of products with UV output only. This lamp shade works as a standard room light with the white LED at night. After turning off the light, the UV-LED lights up and works as an ambient illumination with fluorescent patterns in bedroom. Applications without IR input such as the lampshade does not provide interactivity, but they can be used to simply decorate furnitures and clothing in living space.
- *Wristrest*: We introduce the another ruled surface product for office. In this application, a notification display of an e-mail is integrated into a conventional wrist rest (Fig. 1e). This ambient display gently glows as necessary without impairing the appearance of the conventional wrist rest.
- *Cushion Blocks*: We implemented the kids' cushion blocks(Fig. 8 right) as an example of products that have IR input. Each block dynamically displays pictures on the surface in response to user's push or grip input.
- *Plush Toy*: FunCushion is also adaptable to a 3D soft product with a doubly curved surface such as a plush toy. It extends a conventional plush toy to an interactive and decorative one. The turtle plush toy (Fig. 1d) changes its body's appearance interactively in response to a user's push. This was implemented with the heat transfer method.

Fig. 8. Applications of FunCushion: lampshade (left half) and cushion blocks (right half).

– *Sofa*: FunCushion can be embedded into large soft furniture such as a sofa. We implemented an interactive sofa with a matrix display (Fig. 7b) that supports communication of users in a living space. The matrix display has the 9×9 pixels in the backrest and five pressure sensors are embedded in each of two sheets. The purpose of it is to make a conversation trigger by displaying some pictures such as heart shape on the backrest in living space when two users sit on the both sides.

8.2   Durability

The surface cloths of FunCushion are durable for shape-deformations with pushing, bending, stretching, crumpling, and sewing (Fig. 9). It can be embedding into various soft products for ubiquitous and wearable computing. The electronics in the objects limit the flexibility of the cloths depending on their size. Since the electronics are not elastic, only the surface cloths can be pinched and stretched. To make the entire interfaces bendable, we fix the electronics in urethane foams and cover them by diffusers. This makes the positions of the electronics reasonably durable to bending, while the durability depends on the relative size of the entire interfaces compared to the electronics. The interfaces can be bent if flexible circuits are used, and this can be addressed as future work.

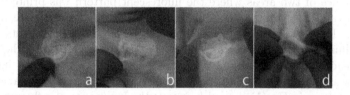

Fig. 9. Durability to shape-deformations: (a) pushing, (b) bending, (c) stretching, and (d) crumpling.

9   Technical Evaluation

We evaluated the quality of the display and investigated effective cloths and diffusers for our system. The quality was evaluated from the viewpoint of luminance and contrast.

9.1   Cloths

We evaluated the luminance and the contrast of the display with several cloths. Three types of 90 mm x 90 mm cloths were compared: 100% cotton cloth (Plus IT-325CO), linen cloth (50% hemp and 50% cotton, Kawaguchi 11-287), and cotton canvas (graded number: No. 11) with a heat transfer sheet (Elecom EJP-WPN3). The cotton (IT-325CO) and linen (11-287) cloths were printed on by

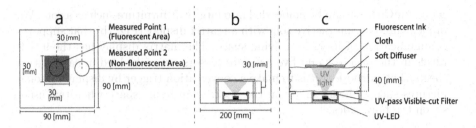

Fig. 10. Experimental setup for measuring luminance. (a) Measured points on cloth. (b) Setup to compare cloths. (c) Setup to compare soft diffusers.

using an inkjet printer. The transfer sheet was adhered to the cotton canvas with a heating iron.

The experimental setups are shown in Fig. 10b and c. A 30 mm × 30 mm square pattern was printed on a 90 mm x 90 mm cloth twice by using an inkjet printer with a fluorescent ink (Soken SKI-TRC-B69), (Fig. 10a). A 365 nm UV-LED (Nitride NS365L-6SVG) and a UV-pass visible-cut filter (Sigmakoki UTVAF-50S-33U) were set on the bottom of a 200 mm × 200 mm × 200 mm acrylic box, and a cloth with the fluorescent pattern was set 3 mm above the filter (Fig. 10b). A forward current of 0.1 A was applied to the UV-LED, and the luminance of two areas where the fluorescent pattern was printed (fluorescent area) and not printed (non-fluorescent area) on the cloth are measured (Fig. 10a). The forward current was gradually increased in increments of 0.1 A, and the luminance was measured. This trial was repeated until the forward current reached 0.5 A. The luminance was 0.01 cd/m^2 without UV light. The contrast was calculated as the luminance ratio (R) of two luminance values (l_f, l_n) as shown in Eq. (1). l_f and l_n means the luminance of a fluorescent area and a non-fluorescent area, respectively.

$$R = l_f/l_n \tag{1}$$

The results are shown in Fig. 11. The graphs show the relationship between a forward current of a UV-LED and the luminance of fluorescent (Fig. 11a) and non-fluorescent (Fig. 11b) areas. The luminance values should be high for the fluorescent areas (Fig. 11a) and low for the non-fluorescent areas (Fig. 11b). In Fig. 11a, the cotton cloth (IT-325 CO) always had the highest luminance values of all three cloths. From the two graphs (Fig. 13a and b), the cotton cloth also always had the highest contrast.

Figure 12 shows the differences in the enlarged views of fluorescent contours depending on the compared cloths. The cotton cloth has a fine weave, and the area where the fluorescent ink applied to the cloths is larger than that of linen cloths (Fig. 12a, b). These enlarged views show that the cotton cloth has the highest sharpness (Fig. 12a) of the three cloths. From the results, the cotton cloth (IT-325 CO) is the most effective of the compared cloths.

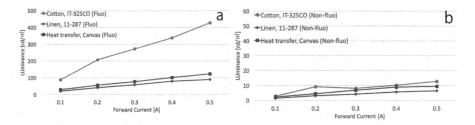

Fig. 11. Luminance of fluorescent area (a) and non-fluorescent area (b) with three types of cloths.

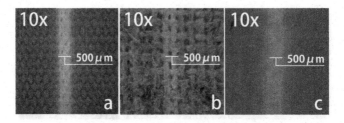

Fig. 12. Enlarged views of fluorescent contours printed on three cloths: (a) cotton cloth (Plus IT-325CO), (b) linen cloth (Kawaguchi 11-287), and (c) cotton canvas (graded number: No. 11) with the heat transfer sheet (Elecom EJP-WPN3).

9.2 Diffusers

We evaluated the luminance and the contrast of the display using multiple diffusers. Three types of soft diffusers 40 mm thick were compared: 100% polyester cotton, organic cotton, and BREATHAIR® (Toyobo). The experimental setup is shown in Fig. 10c. This experiment was also conducted by using a 365 nm UV-LED, UV-pass visible-cut filter, and cotton cloth (IT-325 CO) with the fluorescent pattern The forward current was gradually increased in increments of 0.1 A, and the luminance was measured at two areas on the cloth (Fig. 10a). This trial was repeated until the forward current reached 0.5 A. The contrast was calculated in the same way as in the previous experiment (1).

The results are shown in Fig. 13. BREATHAIR® has the highest luminance values at the fluorescent area when a forward current between 0.2 A to 0.5 A was applied (Fig. 13a). Its luminance could reach the required luminance 80 cd/m² [36] at a 0.5 A forward current. The polyester cotton had the second highest luminance values and could reach luminance 60 cd/m² at a 0.5 A forward current. The luminance of non-fluorescent areas did not reach 10 cd/m² for any diffuser (Fig. 13b). From the two graphs (Fig. 13a and b), BREATHAIR® always had the highest contrast.

Figure 14 shows the difference in the enlarged view of the compared soft diffusers. This enlarged view shows that BREATHAIR® has the largest gap between the fibers and has a structure that allows more UV light to pass through

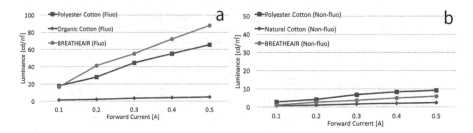

Fig. 13. Luminance of fluorescent area (a) and non-fluorescent area (b) with three types of diffusers.

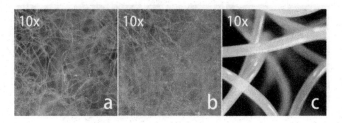

Fig. 14. Enlarged view of three diffusers: (a) 100% polyester cotton, (b) organic cotton, and (c) BREATHAIR® (Toyobo).

(Fig. 14c). From the results, BREATHAIR® is the most effective of the compared soft diffusers.

10   Discussion

10.1   System Thickness and Effect on Display and Sensing

The thickness of the entire system ranges from 20 mm (the soft diffuser is 15 mm thick and the visible-cut filter is removed to reduce the size) to 50 mm (the diffuser is 40 mm thick). If it is thin, the UV light does not sufficiently diffuse, and if it is thick, the luminance does not reach $80\,cd/m^2$. The illuminated area with one UV-LED ranges from 15 mm square to 45 mm square. In the point of view of sensing, the system can detect only light push at the minimum, while it can detect deep push at the maximum.

10.2   Discussion of Illuminations and Other Materials

In the paper, we targeted the sufficient luminance at $80\,cd/m^2$ and only BREATHAIR and IT-325CO cloth reached the value at the 40 mm diffuser thickness. However, $80\,cd/m^2$ is a target that has sufficient visibility in a bright room (we will correct the sentence), and other materials tested should also achieve it by reducing the thickness. End-users can select the materials and its thickness in his/her preference. It is hard for some fabrics such as jeans, dark-colored fabrics, wool to apply our method since they do not transmit lights. On the other hand, it is also hard for sparsely woven textiles because fluorescent ink is only sparsely adhered.

10.3   Heat and Power Supply

The effect of heat by a UV-LED needs to be considered. Strong heat dissipation is not needed when about 0.04 A forward current is applied to a UV-LED from an output pin of a microcontroller but is needed when about 0.4 A forward current is applied. If designing a bright display, we recommend using a heat sink.

The limitation of this system is power supply. When a power source is required to supply energy to only a microcontroller, a lithium-ion-polymer battery can be used. However, battery capacity is insufficient for long-time use. In the future, a wireless power supply will solve this problem.

11   Conclusion

This paper introduced FunCushion, a digital fabrication method of customized fluorescent-pattern displays on cloths of cushion interfaces while retaining the softness. The display can be integrated with the previous push detecting method [5] by using two invisible lights. The display is adaptable to 3D shapes and illuminates with multiple colors and gradation. Furthermore, it can be integrated with static visual print and embroidery. This method enables end-users and designers to create soft everyday products with soft displays in lab. The experiments revealed that cotton cloth and BREATHAIR® (Toyobo) are effective materials for the display.

References

1. Schwesig, C., Poupyrev, I., Mori, E.: Gummi: a bendable computer. In: Proceedings of the SIGCHI Conference on Human Factors in Computing Systems (CHI 2004), pp. 263–270. ACM (2004)
2. Vlack, K., Mizota, T., Kawakami, N., Kamiyama, K., Kajimoto, H., Tachi, S.: GelForce: a vision-based traction field computer interface. In: CHI 2005 Extended Abstracts on Human Factors in Computing Systems (CHI EA 2005), pp. 1154–1155. ACM (2005)
3. Wessely, M., Tsandilas, T., Mackay, W.E.: Stretchis: fabricating highly stretchable user interfaces. In: Proceedings of the 29th Annual Symposium on User Interface Software and Technology (UIST 2016), pp. 697–704. ACM (2016)
4. Sugiura, Y., Igarashi, T., Inami, M.: Cuddly user interface. IEEE Comput. **49**(7), 14–19 (2016). Special Issue on 21st User Interfaces
5. Sugiura, Y., Kakehi, G., Withana, A., Lee, C., Sakamoto, D., Sugimoto, M., Inami, M., Igarashi, T.: Detecting shape deformation of soft objects using directional photoreflectivity measurement. In: Proceedings of the 24th annual ACM symposium on User interface software and technology (UIST 2011), pp. 509–516. ACM (2011)

6. Kan, V., Fujii, K., Amores, J., Zhu Jin, C.L., Maes, P., Ishii, H.: Social textiles: social affordances and icebreaking interactions through wearable social messaging. In: Proceedings of the 9th International Conference on Tangible, Embedded, and Embodied Interaction (TEI 2015), pp. 619–624. ACM (2015)

7. Jacobs, M., Worbin, L.: Reach: dynamic textile patterns for communication and social expression. In: CHI 2005 Extended Abstracts on Human Factors in Computing Systems (CHI EA 2005), pp. 1493–1496. ACM (2005)

8. Poupyrev, I., Gong, N.W., Fukuhara, S., Karagozler, M.E., Schwesig, C., Robinson, K.E.: Project Jacquard: interactive digital textiles at scale. In: Proceedings of the 2016 CHI Conference on Human Factors in Computing Systems (CHI 2016), pp. 4216–4227. ACM (2016)

9. Buechley, L., Eisenberg, M., Catchen, J., Crockett, A.: The LilyPad Arduino: using computational textiles to investigate engagement, aesthetics, and diversity in computer science education. In: Proceedings of the 2008 CHI Conference on Human Factors in Computing Systems (CHI 2008), pp. 423–432. ACM (2008)

10. Castano, L.M., Flatau, A.B.: Smart fabric sensors and e-textile technologies: a review. Smart Mater. Struct. 23(5), 053001 (2014)

11. Post, E.R., Orth, M., Russo, P.R., Gershenfeld, N.: Electronic textiles: a platform for pervasive computing. IBM Syst. J. 39, 3 (2000)

12. Marculescu, D., Marculescu, R., Zamora, N.H.: E-broidery: design and fabrication of textile-based computing. Proc. IEEE 91(12), 1995–2018 (2003)

13. Holleis, P., Paasovaara, S., Häkkilä, J.: Evaluating capacitive touch input on clothes. In: Proceedings of the 10th international conference on Human computer interaction with mobile devices and services (MobileHCI 2008), pp. 81–90. ACM (2008)

14. Lee, S., Kim, B., Yoo, H.-J.: Planar fashionable circuit board technology and its applications. J. Semicond. Technol. Sci. 9(3), 174–180 (2009)

15. Ngai, G., Chan, S.C., Cheung, J.C., Lau, W.W.: The TeeBoard: an education-friendly construction platform for e-textiles and wearable computing. In: Proceedings of the 2009 CHI Conference on Human Factors in Computing Systems (CHI 2009), pp. 249–258. ACM (2009)

16. Peng, H., Mankoff, J., Hudson, S.E., McCann, J.: A layered fabric 3D printer for soft interactive objects. In: Proceedings of the 33rd Annual ACM Conference on Human Factors in Computing (CHI 2015), pp. 1789–1798. ACM (2015)

17. Hudson, S.E.: Printing teddy bears: a technique for 3D printing of soft interactive objects. In: Proceedings of the 2014 CHI Conference on Human Factors in Computing Systems (CHI 2014), pp. 459–468. ACM (2014)

18. Lepinski, J., Vertegaal, R.: Cloth displays: interacting with drapable textile screens. In Proceedings of the Fifth International Conference on Tangible, Embedded, and Embodied Interaction (TEI 2011), pp. 285–288. ACM (2011)

19. Seaakes, D., Yeo, H.-S., Noh, S.-T., Han, G., Woo, W.: Mirror mirror: an on-body t-shirt design system. In: Proceedings of the 2016 CHI Conference on Human Factors in Computing Systems (CHI 2016), pp. 6058–6063. ACM (2016)

20. Fujimoto, M., Naotaka, F., Terada, T., Tsukamoto, M.: Lighting choreographer: an LED control system for dance performances. In: Proceedings of the 13th international conference on Ubiquitous computing (UbiComp 2011), pp. 613–614. ACM (2011)

21. Berzowska, J., Skorobogatiy, M.: Karma Chameleon: Bragg Fiber Jacquard-Woven photonic textiles. In: Proceedings of the Fourth International Conference on Tangible, Embedded, and Embodied Interaction (TEI 2010), pp. 297–298. ACM (2010)

22. Hashimoto, S., Suzuki, R., Kamiyama, Y., Inami, M., Igarashi, T.: LightCloth: senseable illuminating optical fiber cloth for creating interactive surfaces. In: Proceedings of the 2013 CHI Conference on Human Factors in Computing Systems Pages (CHI 2013), pp. 603–606. ACM (2013)

23. Gauvreau, B., Guo, N., Schicker, K., Stoeffler, K., Boismenu, F., Ajji, A., Wingfield, R., Dubois, C., Skorobogatiy, M.: Color-changing and color-tunable photonic bandgap fiber textiles. Opt. Express 16(20), 15677–15693 (2008)

24. Goldstein, H.: Not Ready to Wear. IEEE Spectrum 44(1), 38–39 (2007)

25. Saakes, D., Inami, M., Igarashi, T., Koizumi, N., Raskar, R.: Shader printer. In: SIGGRAPH 2012 Emerging Technologies (SIGGRAPH 2012). ACM (2012)

26. Saakes, D., Chiu, K., Hutchison, T., Buczyk, B.M., Koizumi, N., Inami, M., Raskar, R.: Slow display. In SIGGRAPH 2010 Emerging Technologies (SIGGRAPH 2010). ACM (2010)

27. Hashida, T., NIshimura, K., Naemura, T.: Hand-rewriting: automatic rewriting similar to natural handwriting. In: Proceedings of the 2012 ACM International Conference on Interactive Tabletops and Surfaces (ITS 2012), pp. 153–162. ACM (2012)

28. Tsujii, T., Koizumi, N., Naemura, T.: Inkantatory paper: dynamically color-changing prints with multiple functional inks. In: Proceedings of the Adjunct Publication of the 27th Annual ACM Symposium on User Interface Software and Technology (UIST 2014), pp. 39–40. ACM (2014)

29. Olberding, S., Wessely, M., Steimle, J.: PrintScreen: fabricating highly customizable thin-film touch-displays. In: Proceedings of the 27th Annual ACM Symposium on User Interface Software and Technology (UIST 2014), pp. 281–290. ACM (2014)

30. Peiris, R.L., Tharakan, M.J., Cheok, A.D., Newton, O.N.: AmbiKraf: a ubiquitous non-emissive color changing fabric display. In: Proceedings of the 15th International Academic MindTrek Conference: Envisioning Future Media Environments (MindTrek 2011), pp. 320–322. ACM (2011)

31. Wakita, A., Shibutani, M.: Mosaic textile: wearable ambient display with non-emissive color-changing modules. In: Proceedings of the 2006 SIGCHI International Conference on Advances in Computer Entertainment Technology (ACE 2006). ACM (2006)

32. Berzowska, J.: Very slowly animating textiles: shimmering flower. In: SIGGRAPH 2004 Sketches (SIGGRAPH 2004), p. 34. ACM (2004)

33. Peiris, R.L., Nakatsu, R.: TempTouch: a novel touch sensor using temperature controllers for surface based textile displays. In: Proceedings of the 2013 ACM International Conference on Interactive Tabletops and Surfaces (ITS 2013), pp. 105–114. ACM (2013)

34. Melin, L.: The information curtain: creating digital patterns with dynamic textiles. In: CHI 2001 Extended Abstracts on Human Factors in Computing (CHI EA 2001), pp. 457–458. ACM (2001)

35. Toyobo, CO. LTD: TOYOBO BREATHAIR — Cushion Materials (2017). http://www.toyobo-global.com/seihin/breathair/

36. International Electrotechnical Commission: Colour Measurement and Management in Multimedia Systems and Equipment - Part 2-1: Default RGB Colour Space - sRGB (1998)

Immersion and Togetherness: How Live Visualization of Audience Engagement Can Enhance Music Events

Najereh Shirzadian[1], Judith A. Redi[2], Thomas Röggla[1(✉)], Alice Panza[1],
Frank Nack[3], and Pablo Cesar[1,2]

[1] Centrum Wiskunde & Informatica, Science Park 123, Amsterdam, Netherlands
t.roggla@cwi.nl
[2] Delft University of Technology, Mekelweg 2, Delft, Netherlands
[3] University of Amsterdam, Science Park 904, Amsterdam, Netherlands

Abstract. This paper evaluates the influence of an additional visual aesthetic layer on the experience of concert goers during a live event. The additional visual layer incorporates musical features as well as bio-sensing data collected during the concert, which is coordinated by our audience engagement monitoring technology. This technology was used during a real Jazz concert. The collected measurements were used in an experiment with 32 participants, where two different forms of visualization were compared: one factoring in music amplitude, audience engagement collected by the sensors and the dynamic atmosphere of the event, the other one purely relying on the beat of the music. The findings indicate that the visual layer could add value to the experience if used during a live concert, providing a higher level of immersion and feeling of togetherness among the audience.

1 Introduction

This paper evaluates if and how a real-time live visualization adds value to the experience of concert goers. We have developed an additional visual aesthetic layer on top of the music, coordinated by our audience engagement monitoring technology using GSR (Galvanic Skin Response) sensors. Our wearable bio-sensing technology provides a reliable, fine-grained, and continuous mechanism to quantify the experience of people. This measurement technology was used during a real concert organized by a well known (international) institution that periodically hosts a series of Jazz events. The measurements were used during a lab experiment where we tested two visualizations on 32 participants. One of which factoring in the level of audience engagement collected by the sensors, the other one purely relying on the beat and amplitude of the music. The results indicate that the visual layer could add value to the concert experience, providing a higher level of immersion and feeling of togetherness among people. Thus, the final visualization combines the music amplitude, the level of audience engagement collected using the GSR sensors and the dynamic atmosphere of the event.

© Springer International Publishing AG, part of Springer Nature 2018
A. D. Cheok et al. (Eds.): ACE 2017, LNCS 10714, pp. 488–507, 2018.
https://doi.org/10.1007/978-3-319-76270-8_34

Enriching a music event with visual content is an art field in itself which began in the late 1980s and has since been further developed worldwide by video artists, the so-called 'VJs' [12,29]. As technology progresses, opportunities for making musical events even richer are blooming. Experiments have shown how combining music with visuals, but also light and even smell, can provide the audience with an enhanced experience. Dekker refers to these performances as *synaesthetic performances*, synthesizing various media and therefore creating a physical and psychological connection with the public [6]. User generated content has also played an important role in this development [10]. For example, Engström et al. [8] have proposed to bring the trend of collaborating on media content into the nightclub scene. An app was designed that allows users to directly upload videos to the VJ following requirements gathered with artists and audience.

Traditionally, performances are visually enriched by coordinating and visualizing the active participation of the audience, involving them in the creation process [4,15,30]. Our work instead explores a more transparent and less intrusive approach: real-time monitoring of audience engagement based on wearable sensors. Wearable sensors have recently become a reliable source of information about the affective state of people, and are commercially used for several distinctive applications such as well-being and gaming [22,23]. Among wearable sensors, the most relevant for monitoring audience engagement are those capable of tracking physiological signals such as Heart Rate or Galvanic Skin Response (GSR). Especially the latter has been shown in a number of studies to correlate with user arousal [18,19,31], i.e. the level of activation of a person [25]. As a consequence, GSR signals have been used in literature as a proxy measure for engagement, which we use as the basis of our proposed visualization enriching the experience for concert goers.

We leverage the power of sensing the state of crowds attending a concert through physiological sensors. Such a real-time source of data is then used for creating a visualization that enriches the actual concert, triggering higher immersion and feeling of togetherness within the audience. Based on interviews with professionals and audience members, we gathered a number of requirements for developing the visualization.

At the aesthetic level, the artistic goals were to create a 'collective artwork', which dynamically transforms based on the level of engagement of the crowd. Still, the visualization was kept abstract enough, so no direct conclusion regarding the quality of the music could be drawn, which could in turn negatively affect the musicians or the crowd. Finally, audience members can identify themselves if they would feel like it, providing extra awareness about his/her state and his/her relationship with others at the event.

From a more scientific point of view, we hypothesize that by augmenting a live event with a visualization of the audience engagement, we deliver a richer experience. In particular, we propose a new visualization approach that extends existing models based only on music, taking into consideration the atmosphere of the event. The overlap of these two sources of information makes the audience experience a multi-layered event, which combines music and higher awareness of the audience engagement. As a result, we define our research question as: *Does the integration of user engagement information add value to the user experience of a live musical event in terms of increased immersion and togetherness?*

In the remainder of this paper we further report our efforts, using mixed-method methodologies: interviews with professionals and audience members, an experiment in which GSR data was collected from a relatively large crowd at a live Jazz concert, and a second experiment in which 32 audience members evaluated the visualization based on immersion and togetherness in a lab setting. Section 2 examines previous research in the fields of visual enrichment of music events, measurement approaches of audience engagement, immersion and togetherness. Section 3 describes the mixed-methodology approach used, and the rich data set collected during the various experiences. Section 4 describes the developed visualization and Sect. 5 reports the results. Finally, Sect. 6 provides an analysis of the results and a discussion of these.

2   Related Work

2.1   Visual Enrichment of a Concert

Music visualization has a big role in the artistic scene, dating back to the late 1980s. So called 'video jockeys' or 'VJs' are video artists usually working in live performances, complementing music with visuals [6]. While the working field for VJs expands also towards museums, art galleries, live shows and concerts, the main field still remains the nightclub scene [9]. Still, the development of user centered media reveals new opportunities in visual enrichment of music events. Engström et al. state that the importance of user generated content is increasing when it comes to the production of hybrid media [10]. In a 2008 study, they investigated new ways for the audience to contribute to live visuals, using a mobile app to upload videos directly to the VJ. The experiment showed that this increased participation to the visuals triggered a new collective experience [8]. In addition, it is known that, as social beings, we are strongly affected by the opinion (or affective state) of others around us, them being virtually or spatially collocated [13].

This leads us to hypothesize that enriching visualization with data reflecting the audience affective state may further increase the user's feeling of participation and immersion in the event.

2.2   Sensing User Engagement

Engagement has been defined by Attfield as 'a quality of the user experience that emphasizes the positive aspects of interaction – in particular the fact of being captivated by a resource' [2], p.9, and similarly described as a state of high affective involvement of a user with an experience [28].

Previous work has identified a number of ways for monitoring the level of engagement of people with experiences, but those are mostly based on self-report [21]. Gathering data during a live concert puts practical constraints on the measurement, since it should not affect the users' experience of the event. In this regard, wearable sensors offer a valuable alternative to self-reported data [20]: being attached to the user skin in a relatively unobtrusive way, they can gather measurements of the affective state of the users without harming the user experience. Lang found a linear correlation between GSR and human arousal [18]. Building on these results, a number of studies have leveraged the power of GSR sensors to better understand user experiences during live performances.

Wang et al. measured the GSR response of a group of test users during a live performance which was also recorded on video. Later, the video recording was compared with the data gathered from the sensors and results from questionnaires and interviews: the researchers validated that GSR sensors are an accurate proxy for measuring audience engagement [31]. Latulipe also supports the approach of interpreting GSR signals as audience engagement after running an empirical study with 49 participants. A video of a dance performance was presented to the participants, who were equipped with GSR sensors and scales that allowed them to self-report their current state of emotional reaction [19]. The two measurements were found to be correlated.

At this stage, it is important to mention that arousal itself may not be sufficient to characterize engagement: an indication of the positivity of the state (valence) would be missing. Since the GSR sensors can only measure arousal, and not valence, it is not possible to state if the experienced emotion is positive or negative. In this regard, Latulipe ran an exploratory study, where she showed audience engagement data of performances to performance arts experts. These experts stated that without a causal explanation, the valence factor would not be interesting anyway, since valence is a very subjective variable [19]. Based on this result, we propose in this paper to use GSR as a proxy measurement for arousal, being well aware of the need of furthering this research in the future to include valence measurements in the visualizations.

2.3   Enriched Performances: Immersion and Togetherness

Previous works have considered a number of approaches to provide feedback to musicians, actors, and producers. Some examples include off-line visualization tools [24], real-time mechanisms such as mobile phone usage [30] and messages [4], and audience movement [15]. We nevertheless explore audience engagement as the basic element for creating the visualizations. In particular, we explore the effect of the visualization on the level of immersion and togetherness of the crowd.

Immersion is an aspect which occurs in gaming, as well as virtual environments, but also in visiting art exhibitions or watching movies. Jennett et al. state that immersion consists of three features [16]: (1) Lack of awareness of time; (2) Loss of awareness of the real world and (3) Involvement and sense of being in the task environment. Several measurement questionnaires have been developed and tested. Witmer et al. define immersion and involvement as two important aspects for experiencing presence. They introduced a 'presence questionnaire' to measure presence in virtual environments [32]. Jennett et al. developed a questionnaire to measure immersion in games [16]. They base their definition of immersion on two descriptive studies of Brown and Cairns and Haywood and Cairns. In the first study, 'gamers' were interviewed about their experience in playing computer games [3], the second study dealt with children in an interactive exhibition [14].

Along with immersion, we are also interested in increasing the sense of togetherness in the audience. In our research, the aspect of 'togetherness' is equated to the degree of 'feeling part of a group'. In a music show, the audience member can feel as part of the audience, but also - when included with GSR data in the visualization - part of the concert/show. Previous works describe different approaches to measure the feeling of being part of a group. The 'group attitude scale' (GAS) is a measurement tool with 20 items, which was developed to measure attraction to a group. The selected items were tested in several studies and provide a valid measure of attraction to groups [11]. Besides text-based measurement tools, there are also graphical measurement options to get an insight in to what degree a person feels part of a group. Schubert et al. developed a pictorial scale of 'Ingroup-Outgroup Overlap' and 'Self-Group Overlap' (OSIO) [27], building up on the 'inclusion of others in self' (IOS) scale of Aron et al. [1]. The tested and proven OSIO measurement scales are easy to use and well understood.

3   Methodology and Data Collection

This research followed a mixed-methodology approach: both requirement gathering and evaluation were done using qualitative and quantitative mechanisms. First, requirements were gathered through interviews with musicians and concert organizers. Then, GSR data was gathered from the audience of a live concert. Requirements from the audience perspective were also gathered through questionnaires. According to these requirements, visualizations were created, which were evaluated quantitatively in a second experiment with potential audience members. Additionally, a qualitative evaluation was conducted with the musicians and the concert organizer, as described in Sect. 5. The real concert, which we based our requirements on, was organized by a cultural institute in a major European capital.

3.1   Requirement Gathering with Performers and Event Organizers

Initial interviews provided first insights and information about the requirements and expectations of the visualization. A concert organizer and the musicians were interviewed in a semi-structured way in order to gain more knowledge about what the persons in different roles would expect from a visualization that shows the audience's engagement. The interviews with the concert organizer and the musicians were held in person or on the phone, recorded and transcribed.

Insights gained from the interviews showed that sensing and feeling the audience is very important for the musicians interviewed.

"Otherwise I would only record CDs. If you enter the stage, you already feel the atmosphere, so you know what the vibe is a little bit." - Musician 1.

Both musicians pointed out that a live visualization during the concert would not be valuable for them. In part, that was because their eyes are closed during playing; partly it was because - should the visualization show low audience engagement - they would feel insecure about their play and get influenced by the visualization. Still, both musicians mentioned, if the visualization would show a very highly engaged audience, the visualization would influence them in a positive way and strengthen them in their play. In general, the musicians saw the potential of a live visualization more for the audience than for themselves:

"Maybe for the audience it would be better. Maybe it should be projected behind you and then the audience can see. Because I think this is really interesting. Maybe it even creates a feeling of collectiveness." - Musician 1.

The perspective of the concert organizer followed this direction. A live visualization of the audience engagement would not be used for evaluations of the event.

"You cannot evaluate art, put it into numbers" - Concert Organizer.

Rather, the concert organizer saw this concept as a new way to form a collective artwork, giving the concert an added artistic visual value. Understanding the concerns of the artists that the visualization might make them feel insecure, the concert organizer pointed out clearly that it was crucial for the event that the musicians would feel at ease and had their space to perform their art, without being disturbed. In addition, a live visualization of the audience engagement would have to be coordinated very closely to the choreography of the performing artist, to create harmony in the performance.

3.2   Requirement Gathering with Concert Audience

To gather audience requirements, 40 concert attendees were given questionnaires after the concert. The concert attendees were a mixed crowd of students and culturally interested people between 19 and 70 years, mixed in gender (15 male, 25 female) and mainly based in the city where the experiment was held. Attendees' expectations for future audience engagement visualizations were investigated through a set of 12 questions investigating (1) their experience with the GSR sensors during the concert (see Sect. 3.4); (2) their interest in seeing live data visualized during the concert and which added value they would find in it and (3) privacy concerns. All questions were formulated as statements and attendees were asked to indicate their level of agreement with them on Likert scales from 1 to 5, (1 = 'I fully disagree', 5 = 'I fully agree'). A yes/no question also investigated whether they believed that a live visualization could influence their concert experience.

Results from the questionnaires showed that the users were very interested in the gathered data (mean rating of 4.55) and also very interested in a live visualization during a concert (mean of 4.075). The users were interested in the general mood of the audience (mean of 3.8), but still wanted to be able to identify themselves in the visualization (mean of 3.7). Privacy concerns were voted as not very high (mean rating of 2.1). 77 percent of the attendees stated that a live visualization would influence their concert experience. In comparison, whether the visualization would enrich the experience or distract them from the music, the users were quite indecisive. Both mean values are found in the middle of the scale, while the users tend to say that the visualization would rather distract from the music (mean: 3.2), than enrich the experience (mean: 2.85).

When asked whether visualizations would influence their concert experience, audience members were consistent with the impression of the musicians (see Sect. 3.1):

"If everyone seemed to be enjoying themselves it might make me feel better. If everyone seemed bored, however, it may make me feel bored too"

"I might get carried away with the general vibe even if it's not my own personal experience"

"Probably I would be influenced by the opinion/feeling of the other people so I would be distracted"

Finally, an unexpected feature appeared while scanning the questionnaire results: Some audience members saw the potential of 'gamification' in the visualized data, wanting to try to influence their engagement values:

"It would be a great sideshow for those not engaged by the main show. Also a lot of people would probably try to see if they could influence the visualization/ compete for who could set the highest GSR"

3.3   Summary of the Requirements

The requirements were gathered through semi-structured interviews and questionnaires with both professionals and concert goers. The most important findings that drove the development work, were that the visualization should be intended for the audience and not necessarily for the musicians and that the audience rated the privacy concerns low, while being very interested in the physiological data and its visualization.

3.4   GSR Data Collection

The quantitative requirement gathering was set up with the audience of the concert. The concert was acoustically and visually recorded and the recordings were temporally aligned. During the concert, the engagement of 40 users was gathered with GSR sensors and stored (see Fig. 1). This was achieved by setting up two *Raspberry Pis* running specialized software, which acted as receivers for the wireless sensors. Each one of them was responsible for capturing the data sent out by one of the groups of sensors. This data was then forwarded to a laptop which acted as a central hub, processing and storing the data (see Fig. 2).

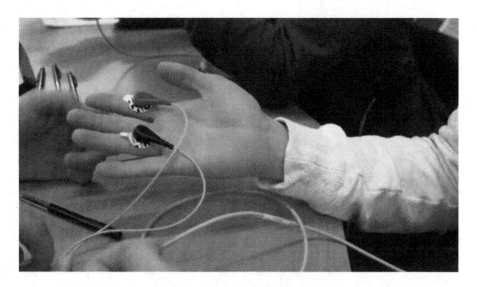

Fig. 1. Audience member with GSR sensor

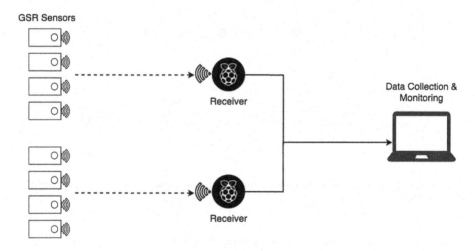

Fig. 2. Network architecture for collecting GSR data streams during the Jazz concert

In order to collect the data, we deployed an optimized network infrastructure and a monitoring system at the venue (see Fig. 3) which could handled large volumes of real-time data from the wearable sensors. Hence, it was possible to collect data from several users at the same time. The entire recording process was synchronized and controlled and the GSR measurements were sent to the receivers through wireless transmission.

After the concert, the collected data was run through an algorithm to rid it of artifacts introduced, for instance, by the electrodes temporarily losing contact to

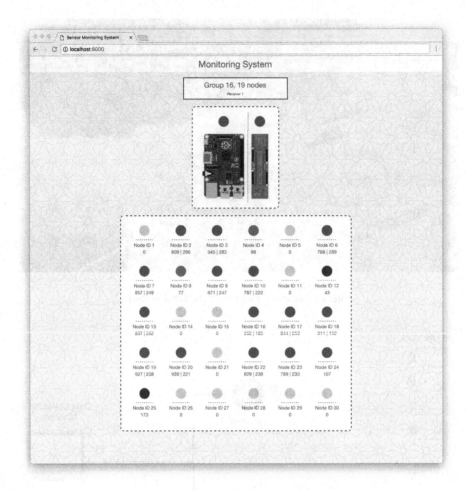

Fig. 3. Network monitoring software, controlling the state of the sensors during the Jazz concert

a participant's skin, or data packets getting lost in transit to the receivers. As a first step, the data for each sensor were then aligned to the general timeline with a granularity of 1 s. As a consequence, if the receiver had received more than one GSR sample for a specific sensor within one second, it would take the average value of those samples. On the other hand, if the receiver did not receive any data from a sensor during a specific second, the value was interpolated from the two adjacent values in the timeline. Finally, the resulting file was analyzed for artifacts. These artifacts manifest themselves through sudden vertical jumps in a sensor's GSR value from one second to the next. This was fixed by differentiating the data for each sensor and zeroing all entries for which the derivative was larger than a certain value. The data was then integrated numerically using a cumulative sum to restore the original signal without the artifacts. Empirically, we found that zeroing values which were more than four standard deviations away from the mean for a given sensor provided a robust way of removing the artifacts without impacting the original signal. A similar process to remove these kind of artifacts was followed by Kocielnik et al. [17] in their experiments.

4   Creation of the Visualizations

Based on the requirements gathered from the concert organizer, the musicians and the audience, and on the collected GSR data, two visualizations were created for comparison purposes using Processing[1], a programming language that allows for the creation of visualizations based on different input types. While one visualization just takes the music as an input, the second visualization takes two parameters as input: the music and the data gathered from the sensors.

The main objective was to create a 'collective artwork', based on the changes of the GSR data in order to show that the audience is triggering and influencing the visualization. We opted for a dynamic visualization, from which conclusions regarding the quality of the music could not be drawn, as directly requested by the musicians and the event organizer. In addition, we wanted to meet the requirements of the audience members to identify themselves in the visualization. Thus, each sensor (audience member) was shown individually as a circle, that moved along the y-axis of the screen according to the value of engagement (as gathered by the GSR sensor). The radius of the circle responded to the

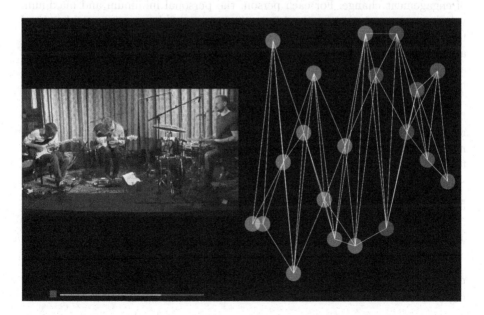

Fig. 4. left side: video recording; right side: visualization with absolute values

[1] https://processing.org.

amplitude of the music. Additionally, the circles were plotted in different colors, to make the identification more evident. In this example, five colors were used, so each four circles were plotted in the same color. The audience member with the sensor 'blue2' could identify herself/himself as the second blue circle on the screen.

Even though the requirement collection phase showed that the audience was interested in getting information about its 'average mood' in a live visualization, the decision was made not to show the relative/absolute average value of the GSR signals explicitly. Given that the circles represented individual audience members, having a reference 'average mood' indicator, such as a line crossing the visualization horizontally, would have made it possible for the audience to detect how many and which people were currently less engaged than the average. Therefore, the final visualization only showed the audience members as circles, floating over the screen, driven by their GSR data, changing size with the amplitude of the music. Still, the connection of the audience was important for the concept of the visualization. Therefore, the audience members were connected to each other with lines. The movement of the audience member pulled the lines with them.

By analyzing the GSR data manually, it was also discovered that the values of the GSR changed gradually, but very slowly. During a concert lasting for one hour, there was movement visible, but it was hardly recognizable for the viewer. To intensify the movement of the visualization, we decided to represent relative changes in engagement with respect to each individual's range of engagement change. For each person, the personal minimum and maximum values were stored, then mapped from the bottom of the screen to the height of the screen (see Fig. 4). Every person's circle floated in its own range of minimum and maximum values, representing each person's individual/relative experience and reaction to the music. In addition, to increase the visual focus on movement, the new position of the circle was updated every 5 s.

Eventually, an abstract, constantly changing, collective artwork was created, triggered by the feelings of the audience and the music. Even though the 'general mood' of the audience was not explicitly shown with a line anymore, the constant movement and re-formation of the abstract visualization could be understood as the 'general mood' of the room.

5   Evaluation of the Visualizations

To eventually answer our research question:

whether enriching visualizations with audience engagement data during a concert would increase the audience immersion and feeling of togetherness in the event

we performed a controlled experiment. The visualizations described in Sect. 4 were implemented for excerpts of the concert during which GSR data were collected. They were then displayed alongside the video of the corresponding concert excerpt in a split-screen fashion (see Fig. 4, showing the concert recordings on the left side and the visualization on the right side). A time-line in the bottom left corner of the screen allowed to jump to different parts of the show.

Music excerpts were played along with their corresponding visualizations (with and without sensor data) to 32 of participants in a laboratory setting. Although we recognize that this approach has limited ecological validity (as the visualizations were not shown live during an event), we opted for the controlled setting to be able to collect reliable quantitative data. In addition, following our original mixed methodology, a qualitative evaluation was also performed through semi-structured interviews with the concert organizer in person and one of the musicians on the phone. The interview with the concert organizer was recorded and transcribed. Due to technical issues, the recording of the musician failed, therefore the key concepts extracted from the interview, were summed up and confirmed with the musician via e-mail.

5.1   Experimental Design

We conducted a full-factorial quantitative evaluation with 32 potential concert visitors. Participants were mainly students, researchers and young professionals, assembled in opportunist sampling fashion. The main factor under investigation was the presence of engagement data (through GSR) within the visualization. We created two visualizations: one as described in Sect. 4, and the other very similar, but not reacting to sensor data. A second issue was whether the effect of including GSR data in the visualization would depend on the level of 'energy' of the music piece that was being performed. A calmer music piece may have generated limited changes in audience arousal, in turn creating minimum added value in the visualization. Thus, to be able to generalize our results, we created visualizations for two different concert excerpts: a calmer one, and a more energetic one. Finally, because of the complexity of the task (i.e., evaluating music visualizations), we were forced to provide our participants with context about the research, and mention that they would see music visualizations that do or do not react on sensor data. One possible issue there may have been that the sole knowledge of the presence of sensor data in the visualization may have biased the participants. To control for this, for each video and visualization (with and without sensor data) we performed two repetitions, one in which the participant was told that sensor data were visualized, and one in which the participant was told that only music was being visualized. We combined the effects of the three factors (visualization of sensor data, energy of the music piece played, and communication of the presence of sensor data in the visualization) in a full-factorial design, for a total of $2 \times 2 \times 2 = 8$ conditions (see Fig. 5).

Measurements. We developed a short questionnaire to evaluate the feeling of Immersion and Togetherness of participants in presence of the visualizations. The questionnaire included four items to measure immersion adapted from Zhu et al. [33], and Schubert et al. [26], and three items to measure togetherness, adapted from previous research of the 'group attitude scale' [11] and 'assessment of Self-Group Overlap' [27] (see Table 1). In addition, participants were asked to report

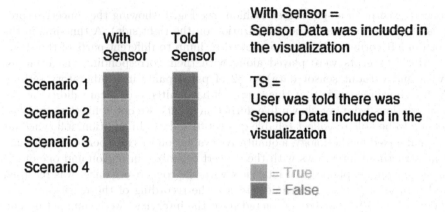

Fig. 5. Full-Factor experiment setup

the extent to which they appreciated the music piece played in the video, on a 5-point Likert scale.

Protocol. Participants were seated in front of a screen. The experiment was held with either three or 4 participants at the same time. Prior steps of the research were explained beforehand. Participants were asked to imagine themselves in the audience of the Jazz concert, wearing the GSR sensors, while seeing the visualizations projected behind the band. Participants were shown two excerpts (1:15 min) of the recorded concert, enriched with the two visualizations. Each excerpt was tested in a full-factor procedure. One excerpt was chosen from a calm play, the other one from a rhythmic, energetic part of the concert. In total, each participant watched eight video clips (the reader can find them here: http://goo.gl/2BL0rL), each lasting 75 s. The order of the clips was randomized to prevent an influence of fatigue and memory on the results. After each video clip, participants were asked to fill in the questionnaire to self-report their level of immersion and togetherness.

Table 1. Questionnaire for the evaluation of the visualization

Aspect	Nr. items	Based on	Measure scale
Immersion	4	[33], [26], [11]	5-point Likert
Togetherness	1	[11]	5-point Likert
Togetherness	2	[27]	OSIO
Liked Music	1	-	5-point Likert

5.2   Results: Quantitative Analysis

We first analyzed the internal consistency of the questionnaire for the Immersion and the Togetherness items separately. For the four Immersion items, we obtained a Chronbach's alpha of 0.879 (excellent internal consistency). We could then conclude that the four items were measuring the same underlying construct, and thus they could be combined (summed) into a single dependent variable hereafter referred to as 'Immersion'. Similarly, for the three togetherness items we found a value of alpha of 0.75 (very good). The three items were then combined into a single variable hereafter referred to as 'Togetherness'.

To verify whether our three fixed factors (visualization of sensor data, energy level of the video and communication of whether sensor data were visualized or not) had an effect on Immersion and Togetherness, we resorted to Linear Mixed Effect (LME) models. LMEs extend classic linear models to properly model data obtained from repeated measures designs (such as ours, where all subjects evaluated all experimental conditions). LMEs allow modelling the repeated measures factors (in our case, the participants) as random effects in the model, thereby accounting for individual differences in the visualization preferences. In effect, a different intercept is estimated per participant, consequently modelling individual participant biases in the Immersion and Togetherness evaluations.

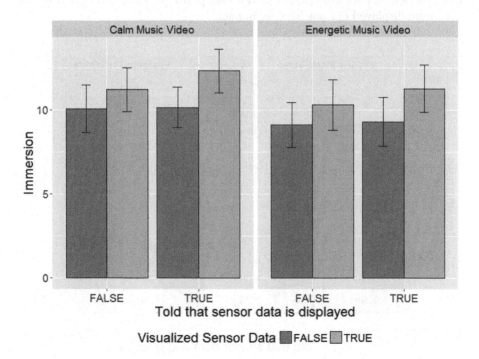

Fig. 6. Immersion levels as affected by the visualization of sensor data, the energy level in the video, and whether participants were informed or not of the presence of sensor data in the visualization

We investigate the impact of the three fixed factors on Immersion and Togetherness through the likelihood ratio testing [5]. We fit first a minimal (null) model including only the random effect (participants) as a predictor. We then iteratively add a term to it for each of the three fixed factors (extended models). Whenever an extended model is found to fit the data significantly better (as evaluated through an ANOVA) than the null model or than a model accounting for a lower number of fixed factors, the newly added factor is considered to have a significant effect on the dependent variable.

With respect to Immersion, we found both the energy level of the concert excerpt ($p = 0.005$) and the visualization of sensor data ($p < 0.001$) to have a significant effect. A model including both factors also performed better than models including only either of them. The fact that participants were told or not that sensor data were included in the visualization did not have a significant effect ($p = 0.69$). These findings can be visually inspected in Fig. 6). Clearly, the visualization of sensor data has the biggest effect on immersion, while the impact of the level of energy of the video is smaller.

Regarding togetherness, we find similar results. In this case, however, the level of energy of the video does not significantly improve the goodness of fit of the model. As visualized in Fig. 7, the presence of sensor data in the visualization is the best predictor of Togetherness (significant with $p < 0.001$), which is higher when the sensor data are visualized. Whether participants were told that sensor data were displayed did not have an impact.

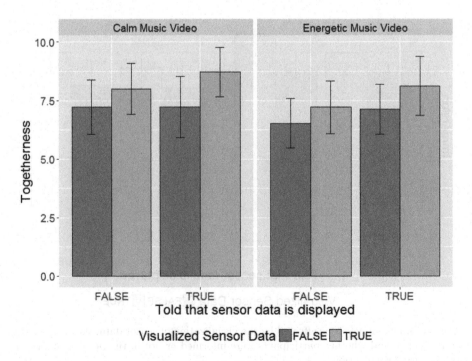

Fig. 7. Level of togetherness

It should be noted that the togetherness values are fairly low (the maximum achievable value, having summed three items, would be 19, while on average, the togetherness feeling gets at most close to 9). This may be due to the fact that participants were shown recordings of the event, thus it was difficult for them to fully identify themselves with the audience as if they were actually attending the live event.

Finally, we found a moderate correlation between the extent to which participants liked the music excerpt played in the video and both Immersion and Togetherness (Spearman correlation coefficient of 0.41 and 0.48, respectively). This indicates that there is a tendency of participants to feel more immersed in the event and involved with the audience when they like the music better. In fact, by adding this variable as covariate in the models, we found it to have a significant effect in improving the model fit to the data, for both Immersion and Togetherness ($p < 0.001$ in both cases).

5.3   Results: Qualitative Analysis

The qualitative evaluation confirmed that the created visualization was perceived as a 'collective artwork', which enriches the concert. The concert organizer remarked its potential added value:

"It would increase the live-experience when the audience is included in the uniqueness. Emotions are always unique - what you feel in this moment, you will never feel in this way again. This is why people go to concerts - to feel this uniqueness of the moment. And seeing this uniqueness of the moment visualized for the audience, this is an incredible added value"

Furthermore, she stated, *"It is not about only the listening. When you go nowadays to a cultural event, you want to feel and experience."*

As the design process was discussed, she agreed with the decision not to show the 'average mood' in the visualization, since a concert experience is *"highly individual."*

"The average is not relevant, we don't need the average. [...] We live in a society where we become more and more individualized and in a 'narcissist' kind of way we want to be mirrored [in the visualization]. We all want to know more about us... And it also looks nicer!"

Finally, she highlights the collaborative aspect of a concert, which is represented in the visualization by the connecting lines between the circles (audience members).

"The atmosphere of the evening is created by the cooperation of all involved participants, also the audience, of course."

6 Discussion and Future Research

The main goal of the study was to determine whether a live visualization would add value to the experience of a concert. This question can be confirmed. Still, the study revealed that there are various further research areas which occur in this field of human arousal during live events. For the cultural scene, the outcomes are valuable and serve as inspiration for which purposes such visualizations could be useful and how they could be integrated into events in order to create multi-layered shared experiences.

We are aware that the lab experiment set-up is not ideal as we simulated a live concert experience but are certain that it should not really affect the initial results we obtained, as we mad use of real measurements. However, as the experiments were not conducted in live concerts, the real-time algorithms to process the data are not needed for now but we used them as in the future they are necessary. Thus, we do understand that we just explored the potential experience space and got very confident results that our approach is a very good idea. It is important to mention that to be further validated, our method needs to be tested in a live scenario. Although we found well-defined, statistically significant effects of sensor data visualization on Immersion and Togetherness, the average absolute values of these two dependent variables were relatively low (around the middle of the scale, in fact). This indicates that for participants it was still difficult to fully imagine themselves in the live concert situation. Furthermore, user testing with different kinds of identifications within the visualization are needed, in order to make it easy and understandable for the concert attendee to identify herself/himself in the visualization.

The quantitative evaluation showed clearly that adding sensor data to the visualization of live music contributes to create a greater feeling of Immersion and Togetherness with the audience. Immersion was found to be influenced also by the energy level of the music played in the video excerpt: people felt more involved with the calm music video (and corresponding visualization) than with the energetic one. This result goes against our initial hypothesis that more energetic music would generate higher arousal in the audience, thereby making the visualization of sensor data more conspicuous. Also contrary to our initial hypothesis, we found that informing participants that sensor data was visualized or not did not have a significant impact on Immersion and Togetherness: the visualization of sensor data, rather than the knowledge of it, was most compelling for participants. Finally, we found a 'halo effect' [7] of music likability on Togetherness and Immersion. The more participants liked the music in the excerpt, the higher was their feeling of immersion and togetherness. This effect is not dissimilar from other results found e.g. in literature on visual experiences, where users more interested and engaged with the video content rated their QoE higher and were also more tolerant to impairments due to, e.g. video compression [33].

Both criteria of the collective artwork and the requirement of no evaluating the music quality were confirmed. The 'general mood' was only shown implicitly through the re-formation of the visualization; the decision to not show the average mood through a plotted line was welcomed by the concert organizer, addressing the previous concern that the visualization could be used for concert evaluation.

The visualization was developed based on requirements from the three different stakeholders in live music events: the organizer, the musician, and the audience. In order to bring the visualization closer together with the music act, it would be advisable to define and adjust the visual elements beforehand with the musicians and concert organizer into an integral and complete audio-visual concept for a deeper experience. This was also supported by the evaluation conducted with the concert organizer.

With respect to data collection, it should be noted that human arousal is a very sensitive variable, which can be triggered by various elements. Further research should be conducted to learn more about the confounding variables. In a live setting at a concert or a nightclub, the emotions of the audience are not only triggered by the music, but also by social interaction, conversations, personal thoughts; in addition, stimulants such as alcohol could influence human arousal. Further research should examine how different factors influence the GSR data and thus the visualization.

Finally, from a more practical perspective, the data was gathered, stored and pre-processed before it was used as an input for the visualization. Further work is needed to streamline these steps and make the data processing and visualization possible in real time, during a concert or at a nightclub.

7   Conclusion

The study presented in this paper showed that an additional visual aesthetic layer, provided by a visualization combining physiological parameters in the from of audience engagement levels and the beat and amplitude of the music, on top of the music performance during a live concert could provide a higher level of immersion of togetherness among the audience. The experiment also demonstrated that there is a tendency of participants to feel more immersed in the event and involved with the audience when they like the music better. Thus, the visualization of unique moments during the concert deepens and enriches the experience of the audience. For musicians and concert organizers, the presented approach of visualization is not (yet) seen as a feature in the daily concert business but rather as an experimental way towards new collaborative artworks and concert experiences. The aspect of evaluation of the event through sensor data is not welcomed neither by the musicians nor the concert organizer. Rather, it is the emotional, artistic, collaborative aspect, that appeals to the interviewed experts.

References

1. Aron, A., Aron, E.N., Smollan, D.: Inclusion of other in the self scale and the structure of interpersonal closeness. J. Pers. Soc. Psychol. **63**(4), 596 (1992)
2. Attfield, S., Kazai, G., Lalmas, M., Piwowarski, B.: Towards a science of user engagement (position paper). In: WSDM Workshop on User Modelling for Web Applications, pp. 9–12 (2011)
3. Brown, E., Cairns, P.: A grounded investigation of game immersion. In: CHI 2004 Extended Abstracts on Human Factors in Computing Systems, pp. 1297–1300. ACM (2004)
4. Cerratto-Pargman, T., Rossitto, C., Barkhuus, L.: Understanding audience participation in an interactive theater performance. In: Proceedings of the 8th Nordic Conference on Human-Computer Interaction: Fun, Fast, Foundational, NordiCHI 2014, pp. 608–617. ACM, New York (2014)
5. Davison, A.C.: Statistical models, vol. 11. Cambridge University Press, Cambridge (2003)
6. Dekker, A.: Synaesthetic performance in the club scene. In: 3rd Conference on Computational Semiotics for Games and New Media, p. 24 (2003)
7. Dion, K., Berscheid, E., Walster, E.: What is beautiful is good. J. Pers. Soc. Psychol. **24**(3), 285 (1972)
8. Engström, A., Esbjörnsson, M., Juhlin, O.: Mobile collaborative live video mixing. In: Proceedings of the 10th International Conference on Human Computer Interaction with Mobile Devices and Services, pp. 157–166. ACM (2008)
9. Engström, A., Esbjörnsson, M., Juhlin, O.: Nighttime visual media production in club environments. In: Night and Darkness: Interaction after Dark-workshop, at CHI (2008)
10. Engström, A., Esbjörnsson, M., Juhlin, O., Norlin, C.: More tv!-support for local and collaborative production and consumption of mobile tv. In: Adjunct Proceedings of EuroITV, pp. 173–177 (2007)
11. Evans, N.J., Jarvis, P.A.: The group attitude scale a measure of attraction to group. Small Group Res. **17**(2), 203–216 (1986)
12. Faulkner, M.: VJ: Audio-Visual Art and VJ Culture. Laurence King Publishing Ltd, London (2006)
13. Hall, E.T., et al.: The Silent Language, vol. 3. Doubleday, New York (1959)
14. Haywood, N., Cairns, P.: Engagement with an interactive museum exhibit. In: McEwan, T., Gulliksen, J., Benyon, D. (eds.) People and Computers XIX–The Bigger Picture. Springer, London (2006). https://doi.org/10.1007/1-84628-249-7_8
15. Jacquemin, C., Gagneré, G., Lahoz, B.: Shedding light on shadow: real-time interactive artworks based on cast shadows or silhouettes. In: Proceedings of the 19th ACM International Conference on Multimedia, MM 2011, pp. 173–182. ACM, New York (2011)
16. Jennett, C., Cox, A.L., Cairns, P., Dhoparee, S., Epps, A., Tijs, T., Walton, A.: Measuring and defining the experience of immersion in games. Int. J. Hum. Comput. Stud. **66**(9), 641–661 (2008)
17. Kocielnik, R., Sidorova, N., Maggi, F.M., Ouwerkerk, M., Westerink, J.H.: Smart technologies for long-term stress monitoring at work. In: 2013 IEEE 26th International Symposium on Computer-Based Medical Systems (CBMS), pp. 53–58. IEEE (2013)
18. Lang, P.J.: The emotion probe: studies of motivation and attention. Am. Psychol. **50**(5), 372 (1995)

19. Latulipe, C., Carroll, E.A., Lottridge, D.: Love, hate, arousal and engagement: exploring audience responses to performing arts. In: Proceedings of the SIGCHI Conference on Human Factors in Computing Systems, pp. 1845–1854. ACM (2011)

20. Martella, C., Gedik, E., Cabrera-Quiros, L., Englebienne, G., Hung, H.: How was it? exploiting smartphone sensing to measure implicit audience responses to live performances. In: Proceedings of the 23rd ACM International Conference on Multimedia, MM 2015, pp. 201–210. ACM, New York (2015)

21. O'Brien, H.L., Toms, E.G.: What is user engagement? a conceptual framework for defining user engagement with technology. J. Am. Soc. Inf. Sci. Technol. 59(6), 938–955 (2008)

22. Picard, R.: Affective media and wearables: surprising findings. In: Proceedings of the 22nd ACM International Conference on Multimedia, MM 2014, pp. 3–4. ACM, New York (2014)

23. Picard, R.W.: Automating the recognition of stress and emotion: from lab to real-world impact. IEEE MultiMedia 23(3), 3–7 (2016)

24. Röggla, T., Wang, C., César, P.S.: Analysing audience response to performing events: a web platform for interactive exploration of physiological sensor data. In: Proceedings of the 23rd ACM International Conference on Multimedia, MM 2015, pp. 749–750. ACM, New York (2015)

25. Russell, J.A.: Evidence of convergent validity on the dimensions of affect. J. Pers. Soc. Psychol. 36(10), 1152 (1978)

26. Schubert, T., Friedmann, F., Regenbrecht, H.: The experience of presence: factor analytic insights. Presence 10(3), 266–281 (2001)

27. Schubert, T.W., Otten, S.: Overlap of self, ingroup, and outgroup: pictorial measures of self-categorization. Self Identity 1(4), 353–376 (2002)

28. See-To, E.W., Papagiannidis, S., Cho, V.: User experience on mobile video appreciation: How to engross users and to enhance their enjoyment in watching mobile video clips. Technol. Forecast. Soc. Chang. 79(8), 1484–1494 (2012)

29. Shanken, E.A.: Art and Electronic Media. Phaidon Press Limited, London (2009)

30. Tseng, Y.-C., Huang, Y.-C., Wu, K.-Y., Chin, C.-P.: Dinner of luciérnaga: an interactive play with iphone app in theater. In: Proceedings of the 20th ACM International Conference on Multimedia, MM 2012, pp. 559–568. ACM, New York (2012)

31. Wang, C., Geelhoed, E.N., Stenton, P.P., Cesar, P.: Sensing a live audience. In: Proceedings of the 32nd Annual ACM Conference on Human Factors in Computing Systems, pp. 1909–1912. ACM (2014)

32. Witmer, B.G., Singer, M.F.: Measuring presence in virtual environments. Technical report, DTIC Document (1994)

33. Zhu, Y., Heynderickx, I., Redi, J.A.: Understanding the role of social context and user factors in video quality of experience. Comput. Hum. Behav. 49, 412–426 (2015)

Accuracy Evaluation of Remote Photoplethysmography Estimations of Heart Rate in Gaming Sessions with Natural Behavior

Fernando Bevilacqua[1,2](✉) ⓘ, Henrik Engström[1] ⓘ, and Per Backlund[1] ⓘ

[1] University of Skövde, Skövde, Sweden
{fernando.bevilacqua,henrik.engstrom,per.backlund}@his.se
[2] Federal University of Fronteira Sul, Chapecó, Brazil
fernando.bevilacqua@uffs.edu.br

Abstract. Remote photoplethysmography (rPPG) can be used to remotely estimate heart rate (HR) of users to infer their emotional state. However natural body movement and facial actions of users significantly impact such techniques, so their reliability within contexts involving natural behavior must be checked. We present an experiment focused on the accuracy evaluation of an established rPPG technique in a gaming context. The technique was applied to estimate the HR of subjects behaving naturally in gaming sessions whose games were carefully designed to be casual-themed, similar to off-the-shelf games and have a difficulty level that linearly progresses from a boring to a stressful state. Estimations presented mean error of 2.99 bpm and Pearson correlation $r = 0.43$, $p < 0.001$, however with significant variations among subjects. Our experiment is the first to measure the accuracy of an rPPG technique using boredom/stress-inducing casual games with subjects behaving naturally.

Keywords: Games · Emotion assessment
Remote photoplethysmography · Computer vision
Affective computing

1 Introduction

In human-computer interaction (HCI) research, the study of the relation between users and systems is of interest. Within the context of games research in particular, the relation between the player and the game is an important topic. Such relation comprehends concepts as engagement and immersion [7] and the investigation of the elements that influence such concepts. To perform such investigations, researchers need to rely on methods that are able to capture the user's state within the proposed context. Questionnaires about the user's emotional state are common tools used in the process, e.g. to obtain information about

© Springer International Publishing AG, part of Springer Nature 2018
A. D. Cheok et al. (Eds.): ACE 2017, LNCS 10714, pp. 508–530, 2018.
https://doi.org/10.1007/978-3-319-76270-8_35

stress and boredom levels. As a side effect, however, questionnaires require a shift in attention, hence breaking or affecting the level of engagement/immersion of the user. As an addition to (or replacement of) questionnaires, physiological signals have been used to obtain information from users without causing interruptions [6,32,40,50]. Heart rate (HR), for instance, is a source of information to measure emotional states [21], which can be used to detect emotions such as stress [9] or boredom [49].

Computer games were proved to provoke alteration in the mean HR of players at stressful periods of gameplay [35,38]. A common approach to obtaining HR measurements is the use of physical sensors attached to a player. They allow a continuous measurement of the signal, however they are intrusive and might restrict player's motion abilities, e.g. a sensor attached to a finger prevents the use of that finger. The intrusive approach also increases user's awareness of being monitored [17,48,49], which disturbs the results of any game research investigation being performed. As an alternative, investigations [27] have shown that it is possible to remotely measure HR by analyzing a video of a subject using remote photoplethysmography (rPPG) [1]. The remote detection of HR proved a promising approach to infer boredom/stress levels [22] or cognitive stress [25] of a person. Experiments regarding such approaches, however, were performed under extremely controlled situations with few game-related stimuli. A significant limitation of such approaches was that subjects were asked to remain still during the experiment. Another problem is that subjects had limited interaction with the content being presented: they performed tasks mentally (e.g. counting), watched videos/images or performed gamified cognitive tests for a short period of time. Those are artificial situations that are unlikely to happen in real-life situations, especially in a gaming session with a challenging game lasting for several minutes. In that situation, the subject will probably move and present variations of facial actions during the gaming session [4].

rPPG-based methods for HR measurement are tools that can be used by the HCI community, particularly in games research, however its reliability within a context involving natural behavior must be checked. The methods are sensitive to noise caused by movement, facial expressions or changes in illumination (e.g. screen activity reflected on user's face), which are all likely to happen in such sessions with natural behavior. Those interferences may cause the rPPG technique to produce unreliable remote estimations of the HR signal, resulting in misleading investigations. It is important to establish the reliability of remote HR measurements under situations with natural behavior, where users are not instructed to behave differently than what they usually do. In that light this paper presents an analysis of the remotely estimated HR signal of users within such natural context. We developed a set of casual-themed, similar to off-the-shelf games that were carefully designed to present stressful and boring moments, which should induce players to present variations of HR. During the gaming sessions, the player's HR signal was remotely estimated using the work by Poh et al. [31], an established rPPG technique for HR estimation. A physical sensor was used as ground truth. A comparison and analysis of the accuracy of remote HR estimations are presented and discussed. The main contribution of this paper is the accuracy evaluation of an established rPPG technique within the context of gaming sessions where users behave naturally instead of following movement constraint rules, e.g. remain still. The use of rPPG allows a continuous and unobtrusive measurement of player's HR, which might be used as a replacement for questionnaires and physical sensors in the investigations of the emotional state of users. In the games industry, game designers might use rPPG to create self-balancing games that adjust the current difficulty level based on the estimated stress/boredom state of players.

2   Related Work

The use of physiological signals to infer information about users is a recurrent research topic [20–22]. To provide an introduction for readers unfamiliar with rPPG, we introduce its general structure and the core techniques in the field. Additionally we present works involving physiological signals, in particular HR, and game-related materials commonly used for detection of emotional states of users.

2.1   Principles of rPPG

The principle of rPPG is the contact-less monitoring of human cardiac activities by detecting variations in the absorption of light on human skin using an RGB camera [43]. There exist initiatives to classify [27,36] and formally model the algorithmic principles [45] of rPPG techniques. Rouast et al. [36] propose a general algorithm framework composed of three phases that are common to all rPPG techniques: signal extraction, signal estimation and heart rate estimation. The use of different techniques in each of such steps results in a wide range of variations in rPPG approaches.

Early initiatives regarding rPPG analyzed the acquired video with a manually detected/defined region of interest (ROI) as a source of data, few (or no use of) signal filtering and signal extraction based on the average of image brightness [39] or colors [43]. The use of automatic detection of the ROI for each video frame improved estimations, however the process was still affected by noise caused by facial activity and movement, for instance. The work of Poh et al. [30] was the first in the field to rely on Blind Source Separation (BSS) to improve the signal-to-noise ratio (SNR). The authors extracted the signal using automatic definition/tracking of the ROI (based on 60% width of a Viola and Jones [44] bounding box) and the average of the color channels. The three raw signals (derived from R, G and B) were filtered, detrended and decomposed using Independent Component Analysis (ICA). The second component generated by ICA was interpolated and a custom algorithm detected peaks to identify the HR. The authors further improved the technique by selecting the ICA component whose power spectrum contained the highest peak [31] and by incorporating alternate frequency bands (i.e. orange and cyan) into the extraction phase [26].

Datcu et al. [10] present a similar approach, however using Active Appearance Models (AMM) [12] to segment the face of the subject into ROIs. Li et al. [24] also use a different ROI, based on facial landmarks, and a combination of additional steps to mitigate noise caused by illumination, motion and facial expressions by removing signal outliers. Bousefsaf et al. [5] propose a variation of the previously described approaches, using a skin detection procedure to select pixels in the signal extraction phase.

Different approaches that are not based on the average of colors of the face can also be found in the literature. Those techniques use knowledge of the color vector of the different components to perform the signal extraction. Wang et al. [46] focus on the definition of a plane orthogonal to the skin-tone, ignoring pixels outside the subspace of skin pixels in the signal estimation phase. Similarly de Haan and Jeanne [11] also use a skin model to generate a chrominance-based PPG signal, which is calculated as a combination of the intensities of the color channels in the video instead of their average. Those techniques aim to be more resilient than BSS-based techniques regarding motion noise. Balakrishnan et al. [3] are the first to completely move away from color-based initiatives and perform the signal extraction based on head movements. Irani et al. [19] further improved the technique by using a moving average filter applied to the trajectory of the feature points being tracked to remove the noise produced by other sources of motion, e.g. respiratory activity.

The different settings in each phase of an rPPG technique result in a trade-off between advantages and disadvantages. Estimation based on head movement, e.g. Balakrishnan et al. [3], does not rely on previous knowledge about colors nor requires visible skin area to work. However it is outperformed by other methods when subjects are not completely still [24] since it is significantly affected by subject motion. Techniques based on pre-defined skin-tone models, e.g. de Haan and Jeanne [11], Wang et al. [46] better adapt to changes in illumination (including non-white light sources), however they suffer performance degradation when the skin mask is not properly defined (or is noisy) or the pre-defined skin model is inaccurate [45]. Finally BSS-based methods, e.g. Poh et al. [31], rely on BSS techniques (e.g. ICA) which are ideal to de-mix the estimated PPG signal from noise. However such techniques are unable to deal with periodic motion (i.e. exercise situation) and its statistical nature requires a long signal to enable an accurate measurement [45]. Despite such limitations, the ICA-based rPPG technique by Poh et al. [31] presents the best SNR for HR estimation under stationary situations (i.e. non-exercising) with different illumination conditions when compared to other techniques [46]. The work is also extensively cited in the literature and often used as a benchmark for new techniques, which makes it a consolidated and robust solution.

2.2   HR Measurement for Emotion Detection

The foundation of HR-based approaches for emotional estimation draws on the theory that physiological signals are linked to emotion regulation [2,13,37]. Physiological signals, such as HR, are hard to fake because of their link with the autonomic nervous system, differently from facial expressions [23], for instance. As a consequence, HR and its derivatives, such as heart rate variability (HRV), have been used as reliable sources of information in different emotion estimation methods [22]. Additionally it has been used as an indication of perceived interest and confusion in mobile applications [47] and as a possible measurement of engagement by quantitative approaches [33].

The significant variation of physiological signals, however, is an obstacle to its use in emotional estimation. Signals increase during emotional arousal, but decrease in response to attention engagement, which makes the measurement of engagement, for instance, a non-trivial process [33]. Despite such challenges, the use of HR and HRV has been demonstrated in a continuous arousal monitor [16] as well as a detection mechanism for mental and physical stress based on physical and mental tasks [14,42]. Results indicate higher HRV during the mentally demanding task when compared to the rest period. The HR mean alone also has been shown to be a measurement of frustration in a game [35]. As previously mentioned, however, the use of sensors that require physical contact might disturb the user experience or be sensitive to noise. Even when users state they forgot about the use of physical sensors during a gaming session, researchers still face noisy data due to subject motion affecting the sensors [8].

2.3 Natural Behavior and Accuracy of rPPG Techniques

The use of remote measurement of physiological signals, such as rPPG, has already been applied to emotion detection. Signals as HR and HRV were used to remotely detect stress [6,26,28], for instance. Since the estimations of rPPG techniques are significantly affected by external noise, e.g. subject's movement, experimental results are usually accompanied by accuracy evaluations regarding the estimations of the employed rPPG technique. In the majority of the cases, subjects are typically instructed to stay still [36], which improves the accuracy of the rPPG technique. In some other cases, however, authors evaluate the accuracy of the HR estimation under scenarios where subjects are instructed to act naturally. Despite the fact that such works present experiments where subjects are told to behave naturally, their accuracy evaluation is based on artificial or simple human-computer interactions. Subjects are idly staring at the camera [18,51], faking an interaction with a computer [30], working on a task, i.e. making a website [29] or mentally subtracting numbers [25], or performing arbitrary movements [41], e.g. head rotation in different degrees.

Another important factor is the material the subjects are interacting with, such as images [15] or gamified cognitive tests [28]. With such materials, users take a passive role with limited possibilities of interaction, more likely resulting in less emotional and corporal manifestations. If games are used instead, users can take an active role in the interaction and are more likely to behave in a natural way, e.g. featuring facial expressions and moving the body [4]. That natural behavior directly affects the remote measurements of physiological signals.

The previously mentioned experiments lack further analysis of the accuracy of rPPG when applied to a situation involving games as elicitation materials and users behaving naturally. In that context, we designed and carried out an experiment focused on further exploring the accuracy evaluation of an rPPG technique applied to gaming sessions involving natural behavior. Our experiment is based on the previously mentioned findings that HR varies according to stress/frustration and that facial expressions can convey contextual information about emotional state [15]. As opposed to previously mentioned works and their accuracy evaluation, in our experiment each subject spends an average of 25 min in the session, playing three different games that were custom-made to provoke emotional reactions similar to off-the-shelf games. Subjects were also not instructed regarding how they should move, so body and facial reactions are likely to be the ones the subject would normally present under a gaming context. The novelty of our approach consists of using carefully designed game material as emotion elicitation sources, using induced boring-to-stressful game mechanics to produce variations in the emotional state and HR of participants, based on the previously mentioned findings that HR varies according to stress/frustrations. We aim to explore the accuracy of rPPG-estimated HR readings of subjects during such interaction. To the best of our knowledge, this is the first experiment to measure the accuracy of an rPPG technique with the use of boredom/stress-inducing games with subjects behaving naturally.

3   Experiment

Twenty adult participants of both genders (10 female) with different ages (22 to 59, mean 35.4, SD 10.79) and different gaming experience gave their written consent to participate in the experiment. The study population consisted of staff members and students of the University of Skövde, as well as citizens of the community/city. Subjects were seated in front of a computer, alone in the room, while being recorded by a camera and measured by a heart rate sensor. The camera was attached to a tripod placed in front of the subjects, approximately 0.6 m of distance; the camera was slightly tilted up. A spotlight, tilted 45° up, placed at a distance of 1.6 m from the subject and 45 cm higher than the camera level, was used for illumination; no other light source was active during the experiment.

The participants were each recorded for about 25 min, during which they played three games (detailed in Sect. 3.1). Each game was followed by a questionnaire which subjects answered to provide self-reported stress/boredom measurements about the game. The questionnaire featured, for instance, questions with a 5-point Likert scale related to how the player felt related to stress/boredom at the beginning/end of the game (1: not stressed/bored at all, 5: extremely stressed/bored), e.g. *"On a scale from 1 to 5, how bored did you feel at the beginning of the game?"*. The questionnaire was used to check if subjects perceived the games as being boring at the beginning and stressful at the end, which was the intended design of the games to provoke variations in physiological signals during the gaming session. The first two games were followed by a 138 s rest period, where the subjects listened to calm classic music. The last game was followed by an additional questionnaire about age and gaming experience/profile. The order which the games were played was randomized among subjects. Participants received instructions from a researcher that they should play three games, answer a questionnaire after each game and rest; they were told that their gaming performance was not being analyzed, that they should not give up in the middle of the games and that they should remain seated during the whole process.

3.1   Games and Stimuli Elicitation

The three games used in the experiment were 2D and casual-themed, played with mouse or keyboard in a web browser. When keyboard was used as input, the keys to control the game were deliberately chosen to be distant from each other, requiring subjects to use both hands to play. It prevents any facial occlusion during the game play, e.g. hand interacting with the face. The games were carefully designed to provoke boredom at the beginning and stress at the end, with a linear progression between the two states (adjustments of such progression are performed every 1 min). The game mechanics were chosen based on the capacity to fulfill such linear progression, along with the quality of not allowing the player to kill the main character instantly (by mistake or not), e.g. by falling into a hole. The mechanics were also designed/selected in a way to ensure that all subjects would have the same game pace, e.g. a player must not be able to deliberately control the game speed based on his/her will or skill level, for instance. Figure 1 shows each one of the games.

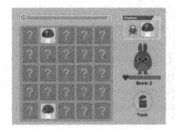

Fig. 1. Games used in the experiment. From left to right: Mushroom, where the player must sort bad from good mushrooms by analysing color patterns; Platformer, where the player must jump over or slide below obstacles while collecting hearts; Tetris, which is a clone of the original version of the game, however without hints about the next piece to enter the screen.

The **Mushroom** game is a puzzle where the player must feed a monster by dragging and dropping mushrooms in rounds. In a given round, mushrooms are displayed in a grid and the player has a limited time in seconds to collect good and discard bad (poisonous) mushrooms. Boredom is induced at the beginning of the game with fewer mushrooms to deal with and plenty of time for the task. Stress is induced by increasing the number of mushrooms and reducing the time available to drag them. The stress progression continues to happen until the player is unable to deal with the number of mushrooms within the available time. This leads to mistakes that will eventually decrease the health bar to zero, terminating the game. The **Platformer** is a side-scrolling game where the player must control the main character while collecting hearts and avoiding obstacles (skulls with spikes). The character can jump or slash, however the player is not able to move the main character left or right. The character's health bar decreases when an obstacle is hit and it increases when a heart is collected. At the beginning, boredom is induced with a slow pace and almost no hearts or obstacles appearing on the screen. Stress is induced by a faster game pace with several obstacles on the screen and almost no hearts to collect. The stress progression continues until the player is unable to deal with the obstacles, causing consecutive hits (mistakes) which decrease the health bar until zero, when the game ends. Finally the game **Tetris** is a modification of the original Tetris game. In our version of the game, the next block to be added to the screen is not displayed, so the player is unable to predict future moves. Additionally the down key, usually used to speed up the descendant trajectory of the current piece, is disabled. As a consequence, the player is not able to adjust the pace of the game according to his/her skills. In the beginning, boredom is induced with a low speed for the falling pieces. Stress is induced by making the pieces fall faster.

The games used the same seed for random calculations, which ensured that all subjects received the same sequence of game elements, e.g. pieces in the Tetris. According to previous analysis [4], results with statistical significance show the subjects perceived the games as being boring at the beginning and stressful at the end.

3.2   Data Collection

During the whole experiment, subjects were recorded using a Canon Legria HF R606 video camera. All videos were recorded in color (24-bit RGB with three channels × 8bits/channel) at 50p frames per second (fps) with pixel resolution of 1920 × 1080 and saved in AVCHD-HD format, MPEG-4 AVC as the codec. At the same time, subject's HR was measured by a TomTom Runner Cardio watch (TomTom International BV, Amsterdam, Netherlands), which was used as ground truth. The watch was placed on the left arm, approximately 7 cm away from the wrist, like a regular wrist watch, and its use was unobtrusive, so it did not affect the movements of the subjects, who could still use both hands to play the games. The watch recorded the HR at 1 Hz.

4   Methodology

The following subsections present the methodology we used to analyze the HR data obtained from the ground truth, as well as how we applied an rPPG technique to extract and analyze the HR from the video recordings. Subject 9 had problems to play the Platformer game, so data from this subject, in this particular game, was not used in any analysis nor results.

4.1 Data Analysis

Firstly we divided the videos of each game session into several video segments of 60 seconds each, denoted as V_i, where $i \in [1, 2, ..., n]$ represents the interval (1 comprehends the time from 0:00 until 1:00, 2 comprehends the time from 1:00 until 2:00, and so on). The use of 60 seconds as the duration of each video segment is based on the work by Poh et al. [31]. Since the games have a constantly increasing difficulty level, different subjects might have played the same game for longer or shorter periods of time. As a consequence, the interval n represents the last available interval for each subject and it is likely to be different among subjects. Any remaining video segment of less than 60 seconds was discarded, i.e. if the duration of a game session was not multiple of 60. We then calculated $HR_{gt}(V_i)$, which is the mean HR of a subject while playing during the video segment V_i, calculated from ground truth. We excluded from the calculation any HR values equal to zero assuming they were miss-readings.

As previously mentioned in Sect. 2, the rPPG technique proposed by Poh et al. [31] is consolidated, extensively mentioned in the literature and presents the best SNR for HR estimation under non-exercising situations. For those reasons, we selected such technique (refereed as the rPPG technique from now on) to perform the extraction of HR from the video segments. We calculated $HR_{video}(V_i)$, which is the estimated HR from video segment V_i obtained with the rPPG technique. The evaluation of the accuracy of HR_{video} when compared to HR_{gt} was based on statistical methods used by previous works [24,31,36]. The measurement error is calculated as:

$$HR_{error} = HR_{video} - HR_{gt} \qquad (1)$$

where HR_{video} is the set of HR estimations by the rPPG technique from the video segments and HR_{gr} is the set of HR means calculated from the ground truth obtained from the watch, as previously described. HR_{error} was calculated with video segments of a given game (for the analysis of that game) or with all available segments (for the analysis of all games combined). We also calculated the following measurements: mean of HR_{error} denoted as M_e; standard deviation of HR_{error} denoted as SD_e; root mean squared error (RMSE) of HR_{error}; mean of error-rate percentage, calculated as:

$$M_{eRate} = \frac{1}{N} \sum_{i=1}^{N} \frac{|HR_{error}(V_i)|}{HR_{gt}(V_i)} \qquad (2)$$

where V_i is a video segment and N is the total of video segments for a given game (or for all games); finally the linear correlation between HR_{video} and HR_{gt} accessed using Pearson's correlation coefficient r.

4.2 Implementation of the rPPG Technique

The selected rPPG technique was implemented in Matlab R2016a according to the original paper by Poh et al. [31]. Since we had no access to the custom algorithm to detect peaks mentioned in the article, such step was replaced by the identification of the highest peak in the frequency domain after an FFT operation. This operation is commonly used in the HR estimation phase of rPPG techniques, as explained in Sect. 2.1. The implementation of the rPPG technique was validated with a procedure similar to the one described by Li et al. [24]. Firstly we manually inspected all video recordings from the experiment and exerted a segment V_i' of 30 s (1500 frames) from each video where the subject presented the least amount of body motion and facial activity. We obtained a testing set of 20 video segments of 30 seconds each, totalizing 30000 frames of data. The mean HR calculated from ground truth for the testing set was 76.8 bpm (SD 13.4 bpm, min. 55 bpm, max. 110 bpm). We then applied the rPPG technique to each of those V_i' segments to estimate the HR, evaluating the estimated values using ground truth and the statistical methods previously described. Results are present in Table 1. The numbers indicate the implemented rPGG technique produces accurate and statistically significant results for the estimations, which are aligned with those reported in the original paper. Therefore we assume the rPPG technique is correctly implemented and further accuracy measurements obtained during our analysis are due to subject activity, not implementation errors.

Table 1. Performance of the rPPG technique applied to the testing set

M_e (bpm)	SD_e (bpm)	RMSE (bpm)	M_{eRate} (%)	r
−0.25	1.41	1.40	1.52	0.99*

* p < 0.001

5 Experimental Results

The performance of the rPPG technique regarding the extraction of the HR is presented on Table 2. The first three rows of the table present the performance evaluation calculated with data from each game, while the last row presents the same performance evaluation calculated with data from all games combined. Regarding the analysis of all games combined, the mean estimation error M_e was 2.99 bpm (SD_e 18.83 bpm), RMSE was 19.03 bpm and M_{eRate} was 10.31%. The low value for M_e describes the overall accuracy of the technique, however the high values for SD_e and M_{eRate} suggest significant variation among the estimations. As demonstrated by M_{eRate}, which is the mean of error-rate percentage, the estimation error of the rPPG technique was equivalent to 10.31% of the expected HR value calculated from ground truth, on average. On a game level, the mean estimation error M_e was 2.96 bpm (SD_e 19.45 bpm) in the Mushroom game, 0.31 bpm (13.51 bpm) in the Platformer game and 5.18 bpm (21.45 bpm) in the Tetris game. RMSE and M_{eRate} were 19.59 bpm and 10.88% in the Mushroom game, 13.43 bpm and 7.82% in the Platformer game, and 21.97 bpm and 11.64% in the Tetris game, respectively. All three games presented significantly higher values for SD_e and M_{eRate}, which also suggests considerable variations in the estimation error during the analysis of subjects for each game. In particular, the estimations performed during the Platformer game presented the lowest values for M_e, RMSE and M_{eRate}, which indicates the rPPG technique performed with lower errors and fewer variations among subjects in the Platformer game than it did in the other two games.

Table 2. Accuracy measurements of the rPPG technique when applied to the video segments of a given game and of all games

Game	M_e (bpm)	SD_e (bpm)	RMSE (bpm)	M_{eRate} (%)	r
Mushroom	2.96	19.45	19.59	10.88	0.45*
Platformer	0.31	13.51	13.43	7.82	0.55*
Tetris	5.18	21.45	21.97	11.64	0.37*
All	2.99	18.83	19.03	10.31	0.43*

* p < 0.001

The Pearson's correlation coefficient r regarding HR_{gt} (mean HR calculated from the ground truth) and HR_{video} (mean HR estimated via rPPG) is 0.45, 0.55 and 0.37 for the Mushroom, Platformer and Tetris game, respectively. All correlations have statistical significance, $p < 0.001$. The correlation is illustrated in Fig. 2. For all three games, there is a positive and medium strength correlation between HR_{gt} and HR_{video}, which indicates the estimations performed by the rPPG technique are aligned with ground truth data. The correlation is stronger in the Platformer game, followed by the Mushroom game and finally by the Tetris game.

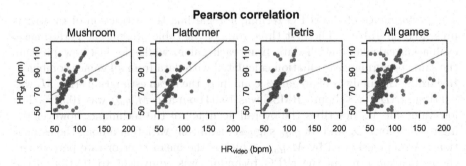

Fig. 2. Statistical correlation of HR_{gt} and HR_{video} when applied to the video segments of each game, as well as to the video segments of all games.

To better analyze the variations regarding estimation errors among subjects, Figs. 3 and 4 show a distribution of values of M_e, RMSE and M_{eRate} for all games combined and individually. The x-axis represents intervals of values of M_e, RMSE or M_{eRate} while the y-axis represents the percentage of subjects that presented an estimation error within the interval informed in the x-axis. Regarding the distribution of values of M_e, shown in Fig. 3, overall 66.1% of the subjects presented estimations with M_e within the interval [−5 bpm, 5 bpm]. For the remaining 33.9% of the subjects, M_e was spread within the interval [−20 bpm, 35 bpm]. On a game level, M_e was within the interval [−5 bpm, 5 bpm] for 65%, 68.4% and 65% of the subjects of the Mushroom, Platformer and Tetris game, respectively. The values for M_e are more equally distributed for the Platformer game, which explains the lower values of SD_e for that game when compared to the Mushroom and the Tetris game, which present less equally distributed values of M_e. The distribution of values of RMSE, shown in Fig. 4 in the first row, indicate that overall values were lower than 10 bpm for 59.4% of the subjects, while the remaining of the subjects had RMSE varying from 10 bpm to 50 bpm. On a game level, RMSE was lower than 10 bpm for 50%, 68.5% and 60% of the subjects of the Mushroom, Platformer and Tetris game, respectively. Regarding M_{eRate}, shown in Fig. 4 in the second row, overall 69.5% of subjects had HR estimations that were up to 10% different than the expected HR from ground truth. On a game level, in total 73.7% and 70% of the estimations performed by the rPPG technique during the Platformer and the Tetris game, respectively, presented M_{eRate} interior or equal to 10%. Those values are slightly better than the 65% of the subjects with M_{eRate} up to 10% in the Mushroom game. Despite the fact that M_{eRate} was similar for both the Platformer and Tetris games, the former presented no subjects whose M_{eRate} was greater than 30%, while the later presented 10% of the subjects with M_{eRate} greater than 30%.

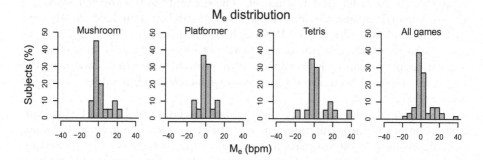

Fig. 3. Distribution of values of M_e for all games. The x-axis represents intervals of values of M_e while the y-axis represents the percentage of subjects that presented an estimation error within the interval informed in the x-axis.

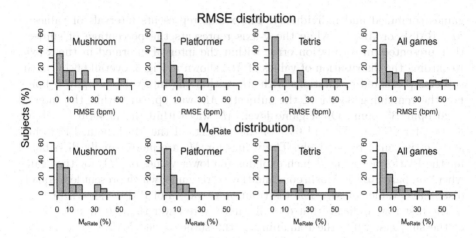

Fig. 4. Distribution of values of RMSE and M_{eRate} for all games. The x-axis represents intervals of values of RMSE or M_{eRate} while the y-axis represents the percentage of subjects that presented an estimation error within the interval informed in the x-axis.

6   Discussion

The results obtained indicate that the use of the selected rPPG technique to estimate HR from videos of gaming sessions is possible in certain circumstances. When the technique was applied to a testing set of 20 manually selected 30 s long video segments, whose subject's facial activity and body movement were minimal, the estimations were significantly accurate. As demonstrated by Table 1, the mean of error-rate M_{eRate} was 1.52% and the Pearson's correlation coefficient was $r = 0.99$ for that testing set. Those results were expected since the videos featured an unrealistic condition where subjects remained mostly still with a neutral face. When the rPPG technique was applied to all gaming sessions, however, body movement and facial activity significantly impacted the estimation performance. It is aligned with previously described works in the literature, which indicate the estimation error increases when subject activities increase [46].

The elevated values for SD_e, the standard deviation of M_e, suggest significant variations in the estimations among subjects in each video segment. As per our understanding, the estimation discrepancies do not seem to be caused by errors equally spread among all gaming sessions, but due to a subset of problematic ones instead. The discrepancies and skewness of the estimations are visible in the scatter plot of the estimated and expected HR values in Fig. 2. It shows a cluster of points for each game, however it is surrounded by significantly wrong estimation points. In the Mushroom game, for instance, 5 estimations (bottom right of the chart) were in the interval [120 bpm, 181 bpm] bpm, which is significantly outside the expected ground truth interval of [80 bpm, 110 bpm]. Similar significantly wrong estimations can also be seen in the Platformer and the Tetris game. The skewed distribution of values of M_e, M_{eRate} and RMSE illustrated in Figs. 3 and 4 also support that indication. Considering the estimations for all games, in total 69.5% of them presented M_{eRate} related to an estimation value that was less than 10% different than the expected HR from ground truth. Additionally 59.4% of all estimations presented RMSE lower than 10 bpm. That result is slightly worse when compared to similar works that used rPPG techniques and subjects featuring natural movements, whose reported RMSE was between 0.11 and 7.28 bpm. A direct comparison of our results to the ones of such similar works is unfair however. Despite the fact that the aforementioned works present experiments where subjects are told to behave naturally, their accuracy evaluation is based on artificial human-computer interactions, as previously described in Sect. 2.3. Our accuracy results account for body and facial movement caused by games whose focus is entertainment, not artificial interactions. As a consequence, our results are more connected to a scenario involving real and spontaneous reactions to games, showing that the rPPG technique can be used, however estimations are skewed by factors such as natural facial activity and subject movement.

The differences in estimation also seem to be connected to the particularities of each game and subject. Considering the distribution of values of RMSE and M_{eRate}, both the Platformer and the Tetris games presented more estimations with lower error than the Mushroom game. The Mushroom game presented 15% of its estimations with RMSE greater than 30 bpm and M_{eRate} greater than 30%, which are significantly wrong estimations. In order to further explore such differences in estimations, we analyzed the variations of movement and size of the ROI used to track the subject's face along the videos. A stable ROI (both in shape and movement) is required for a precise extraction of the plethysmographic signal, so significant variations in the ROI lead to estimation errors. We calculated the mean position of the center point of the ROI for each subject in each gaming session. For each subject in each game session, we calculated the Euclidean distance between the center point of the ROI of each frame and the mean center point of the ROI previously calculated (for that subject in that session). Similarly we calculated the mean length of the ROI diagonal for each subject in each game session, subtracting it from the length of the ROI diagonal of each frame in that gaming session. Since game sessions differ in time duration, we normalized the subject's progress in the game using the interval [0, 1], where 0 is the start point of the gaming session and 1 its end. Measurements were also subtracted from the sessions mean to facilitate analysis and comparison among different games/subjects.

Figure 5 illustrates some of the patterns we observed in the investigation of the distance of the ROI central position. Each row in the figure contains three charts showing the variations of the ROI central position along the gaming sessions of a given subject. The first row contains the investigation of subject 17, who presented, for all his/her gaming sessions combined, −0.33 for M_e (SD_e 1.4) and 1.39 for RMSE (low estimation errors). The second row shows subject 3, who presented 11.47 for M_e (SD_e 16.47) and 19.62 for RMSE (moderate to high estimation errors). Finally the third row shows subject 1, who presented 15.94 for

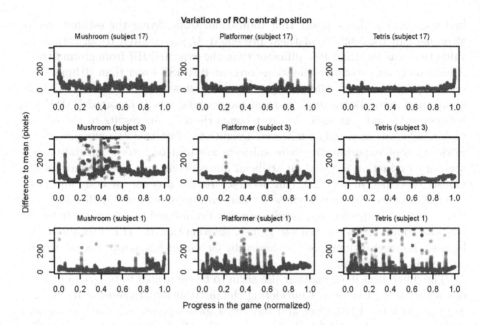

Fig. 5. Variations of distance of the ROI central position for subjects 17 (low estimation errors), 3 (moderate to high estimation errors) and 1 (high estimation errors) during their gaming sessions. Values were subtracted from session mean to facilitate analysis and comparison among different games/subjects.

M_e (SD_e 28.5) and 31.96 for RMSE (high estimation errors). The estimations performed on subject 17 were significantly accurate and the charts regarding the variation of the ROI central position show a stable progression along all gaming sessions. The distance variation remains mostly concentrated within the interval of [0, 100] pixels for all games, which suggests the subject presented few or short movements during gaming sessions. Subject 3 also presented low variation in the Platformer and the Tetris game, however there is a significant variation in the ROI central position in the Mushroom gaming session. The chart indicates significant distance variations of the ROI that is above 200 pixels in a certain period of the game. Finally subject 1 presents high variations in the ROI distance in all gaming sessions, as demonstrated by points above the 200 pixels mark regarding the difference to mean. The Tetris game, in special, present distance variations above 200 pixels during almost the whole session.

Figure 6 illustrates the same subjects regarding the investigation of the variations of the ROI diagonal length. Similarly to the variations of the ROI central position, the variation of the ROI diagonal length is lower for subject 17 (first row of charts in the figure), since the majority of the values are close to zero. Subject 3 also presents low variations in the ROI diagonal length during the Platformer and the Tetris game, however there are significant changes in the ROI size during a period in the Mushroom game. In such period, the length of the ROI

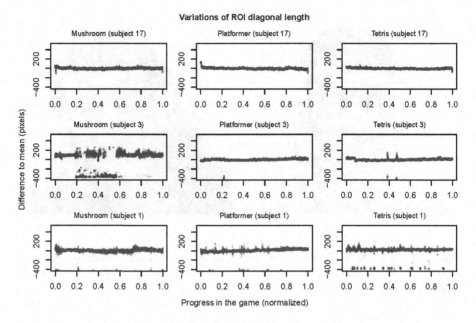

Fig. 6. Variations of ROI diagonal length for subjects 17 (low estimation errors), 3 (moderate to high estimation errors) and 1 (high estimation errors) during their gaming sessions. Values were subtracted from session mean to facilitate analysis and comparison among different games/subjects.

diagonal is negative, i.e. -400 pixels, which indicates the size of the detected ROIs for those frames was smaller than the mean ROI diagonal length. It could be caused by a wrongly detected face (false-negative), for instance. Finally subject 1 presents, to some extent, variations of the ROI diagonal length during the majority of his/her gaming sessions. Those constant variations could be caused by the inability of the face tracking algorithm to stably and continuously detect the subjects face along the frames of the video. The chart shows a distribution of values along the zero mark regarding difference to mean, however they are more spread than those of subject 17, for instance, which indicates higher instability of the ROI size/detection for subject 1. In the Tetris session of subject 1, for instance, there is extreme variation in the ROI diagonal length with values close to -400 pixels, similarly to the ones of subject 3 in the Mushroom game. Such extreme variation could also be explained by a wrongly detected face area during those frames.

An inspection of the videos of subjects with patterns similar to the ones of subjects 3 and 1 revealed sensitive amount of movement and facial activity, including occlusion of the face by the subject's hand, as illustrated by Fig. 7. Any facial occlusion influences the face tracking algorithm used (Viola and Jones), since it might wrongly detect the face position or do not detect it at all. A flawed face detection step affects the extraction of the plethysmographic signal, because

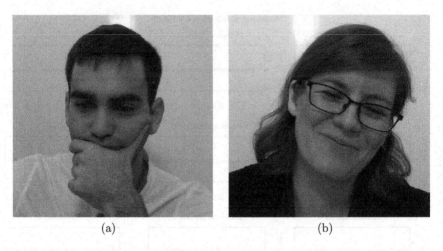

(a)   (b)

Fig. 7. Examples of body movement and facial activity during gaming sessions. (a) Partial face occlusion by subject's hand; (b) Head tilt and movement during laugh action.

noise is extracted along with the raw signal, making the rPPG technique unable to separate it properly. Despite our efforts to create games that prevented face occlusion by the subject's hand, such behavior seems to be natural in boring situations. Both Mushroom and Tetris games were more likely to allow players to place a hand in the face to express boredom, since the games could still be played with a single hand when the gameplay speed was not elevated. The Platformer game, on the other hand, is less likely to allow players to use only a single hand to play, which reduced chances of face occlusion interfering with the face tracking algorithm. This could also explain why estimations made during the Platformer game were more accurate than those performed during the other two games. Those extreme cases with facial occlusion are probably affecting the error rates in our analysis, producing less accurate estimations. We could have removed such extreme and flawed cases from our analysis, however our aim is to test how the selected rPPG technique performs in natural gaming situations. A dataset with untreated videos of gaming sessions with natural interactions might produce sub-optimal HR estimations, however it is our understanding that stressing the rPPG technique with less artificial videos provides researchers with insights about possible problems and accuracy limits of such tool.

We speculate that the variations regarding movement and size of the ROI, which directly influence estimation accuracy of the rPPG technique, seem to be connected to the unique behavior of each user as well. As illustrated by Figs. 5 and 6, subjects present different movement patterns. Previous analysis of the videos indicates significant differences regarding facial activities among subjects [4]. It strengthens the idea of a user-tailored model able to deal with such peculiarities, which is more likely to produce better estimations. A method that operates its estimations based on the average user behavior is prone to be significantly affected by specific user behavior outside the expected mean pattern, causing a skewed distribution of estimation errors such as the ones presented on Fig. 4 regarding M_{eRate} and RMSE. Finally, as previously mentioned, a stable ROI is required for an accurate HR estimation, which is corroborated by the lower estimation errors achieved when subjects were mostly still (Table 1). As a consequence, it is possible to speculate that a more robust algorithm for face detection, which is better prepared to deal with the natural movements of subjects, is likely to produce a more stable ROI and consequently more accurate HR estimations. The accuracy of the estimation is also likely to improve by integrating a method to identify noise in the signal, e.g. ROI is wrongly detected or subject is moving too much, and discard problematic frames (or the whole window) accordingly.

6.1 Limitations

Some limitations of the experimental procedure and analysis should be noted. The 1-minute long duration of each video segment used for the estimation of HR may affect the results. The ideal length of the video segment used for estimation (called window size) is not agreed upon in the literature [36]. In general, it depends on the characteristics of the rPPG technique being applied as well as the hardware configuration, such as camera framerate [34]. We selected a 1 min analysis window based on the information of the original work by Poh et al. [31]. Additionally our experimental procedure consists of games whose difficulty level changes every 1 min, so that value is aligned with the window size used for HR estimation. As previously described, the statistical nature of ICA, part of the selected rPPG employed in the experiment, demands longer video samples to produce accurate results. The longer the video, however, the higher the chances of subject motion, which increases noise. A trade-off between the duration of the video segments and the estimation accuracy could be better investigated. Our experimental setup used an external light source to minimize noise caused by changes in illumination, which should narrow the estimation error to causes as subject movement and/or facial activity. It is likely, however, that other factors might impact the estimation accuracy, such as facial hair, e.g. beard and hair over the forehead area, use of glasses, and skin color.

7   Conclusion and Future Work

This paper presented the description and results of an experiment focused on the accuracy evaluation of a remote photoplethysmography (rPPG) technique in a gaming context. The technique was applied to estimate the HR of subjects behaving naturally in gaming sessions with induced boredom and stress. In total twenty adults of different ages and gaming experiences participated in the experiment, where they played three different games while being recorded by a video camera and monitored by a HR sensor. The games used in the experiment were carefully designed and implemented to have a difficulty level that linearly increases over time, from a boring to a stressful point.

Previous work with experiments involving emotions and rPPG were performed under extremely controlled situations with few game-related stimuli. Subjects were not interacting with a complete digital game in any of the experiments, which hindered the accuracy evaluation of rPPG techniques within the context of games research, for instance. Authors commonly used images, videos or text as content to produce the emotional stimuli, in experimental sessions lasting from 20 s to 10 min. The aforementioned non-game stimuli content is less likely to produce the reactions of a real gaming session, e.g. spontaneous body movement and facial actions. As opposed to such works, in our experiment each subject spent an average of 25 min in the session, playing three different games that were custom-made to provoke the emotional reactions similar to a natural play session. Subjects were also not instructed regarding how they should move, so body and facial reactions are likely to be the ones the subject would normally perform under a gaming context.

The recordings of game sessions of each subject were divided into video segments of 1 min each. The rPPG technique by Poh et al. [31] was applied to each of those video segments to estimate the HR of subjects. We performed an accuracy evaluation of the estimated HR obtained from the video segments in relation to the HR calculated from ground truth. Overall the estimations of the rPPG technique presented mean estimation error of 2.99 bpm (SD 18.83 bpm), RMSE of 19.03 bpm and a positive and medium strength Pearson correlation of $r = 0.43$, $p < 0.001$. On average, the estimation error of the rPPG technique was up to 10.31% of the expected value calculated from ground truth. Additionally we performed an exploratory investigation regarding factors that impacted the accuracy of the rPPG technique, such as variations in the region of interest (ROI) used to remotely extract the HR signal. Further analysis is still required, however our numbers suggest factors connected to the type of the game being played and the unique behavior of each subject influenced the estimations. Among the causes of such influence we identified body movement, e.g. head tilt and rotation, and facial occlusion by subjects hand.

Our results provide researchers with information related to the reliability of a remote HR measurement technique when applied to the context of games research. We believe our experimental setup is a novel approach in the exploration of the accuracy of rPPG-estimated HR readings of subjects in a gaming context. To the best of our knowledge, our experiment is the first to measure the accuracy of an rPPG technique with the use of three boredom/stress-inducing games with subjects behaving naturally. Future work involves investigation of facial activity as well as body movement as a complementary source of information to be used along with remote HR estimation in a multimodal analysis for the identification of stress and boredom in games. As demonstrated, subject movement affects rPPG estimations, however it is an inherent characteristic of a gaming session with natural behavior. We will analyze the use of such signals in a user-tailored approach, focusing on the particular behavior of each user instead of the average pattern.

Acknowledgment. The authors would like to thank the participants and all involved personnel for their valuable contributions. This work has been performed with support from: CNPq, Conselho Nacional de Desenvolvimento Científico e Tecnológico - Brasil; University of Skövde; EU Interreg ÖKS project Game Hub Scandinavia; UFFS, Federal University of Fronteira Sul.

References

1. Allen, J.: Photoplethysmography and its application in clinical physiological measurement. Physiol. Meas. **28**(3), R1–R39 (2007). https://doi.org/10.1088/0967-3334/28/3/r01

2. Appelhans, B.M., Luecken, L.J.: Heart rate variability as an index of regulated emotional responding. Rev. Gen. Psychol. **10**(3), 229 (2006)

3. Balakrishnan, G., Durand, F., Guttag, J.: Detecting pulse from head motions in video. In: 2013 IEEE Conference on Computer Vision and Pattern Recognition, pp. 3430–3437. Institute of Electrical and Electronics Engineers (IEEE), June 2013. https://doi.org/10.1109/cvpr.2013.440

4. Bevilacqua, F., Backlund, P., Engstrom, H.: Variations of facial actions while playing games with inducing boredom and stress. In: 2016 8th International Conference on Games and Virtual Worlds for Serious Applications (VS-GAMES), pp. 1–8. Institute of Electrical and Electronics Engineers (IEEE), IEEE, September 2016. https://doi.org/10.1109/vs-games.2016.7590374

5. Bousefsaf, F., Maaoui, C., Pruski, A.: Continuous wavelet filtering on webcam photoplethysmographic signals to remotely assess the instantaneous heart rate. Biomed. Signal Process. Control **8**(6), 568–574 (2013). https://doi.org/10.1016/j.bspc.2013.05.010

6. Bousefsaf, F., Maaoui, C., Pruski, A.: Remote assessment of the heart rate variability to detect mental stress. In: Proceedings of the ICTs for Improving Patients Rehabilitation Research Techniques, pp. 348–351. Institute for Computer Sciences, Social Informatics and Telecommunications Engineering (ICST), IEEE (2013). https://doi.org/10.4108/icst.pervasivehealth.2013.252181

7. Boyle, E.A., Connolly, T.M., Hainey, T., Boyle, J.M.: Engagement in digital entertainment games: A systematic review. Comput. Hum. Behav. **28**(3), 771–780 (2012)

8. Brogni, A., Vinayagamoorthy, V., Steed, A., Slater, M.: Variations in physiological responses of participants during different stages of an immersive virtual environment experiment. In: Proceedings of the ACM Symposium on Virtual Reality Software and Technology - VRST 2006, pp. 376–382. ACM, Association for Computing Machinery (ACM) (2006). https://doi.org/10.1145/1180495.1180572

9. Choi, J., Gutierrez-Osuna, R.: Using heart rate monitors to detect mental stress. In: 2009 Sixth International Workshop on Wearable and Implantable Body Sensor Networks, pp. 219–223. IEEE, Institute of Electrical and Electronics Engineers (IEEE), June 2009. https://doi.org/10.1109/bsn.2009.13

10. Datcu, D., Cidota, M., Lukosch, S., Rothkrantz, L.: Noncontact automatic heart rate analysis in visible spectrum by specific face regions. In: Proceedings of the 14th International Conference on Computer Systems and Technologies, CompSysTech 2013, pp. 120–127 (2013). ACM, New York. ISBN 978-1-4503-2021-4. https://doi.org/10.1145/2516775.2516805, http://doi.acm.org/10.1145/2516775.2516805

11. de Haan, G., Jeanne, V.: Robust pulse rate from chrominance-based rPPG. IEEE Trans. Biomed. Eng. **60**(10), 2878–2886 (2013). https://doi.org/10.1109/tbme. 2013.2266196
12. Edwards, G.J., Taylor, C.J., Cootes, T.F.: Interpreting face images using active appearance models. In: Proceedings of the 3rd International Conference on Face & Gesture Recognition, FG 1998, p. 300, Washington, DC, USA (1998). IEEE Computer Society. ISBN 0-8186-8344-9. http://dl.acm.org/citation.cfm?id=520809. 796067
13. Fenton-O'Creevy, M., Lins, J.T., Vohra, S., Richards, D.W., Davies, G., Schaaff, K.: Emotion regulation and trader expertise: Heart rate variability on the trading floor. J. Neurosci. Psychol. Econ. **5**(4), 227 (2012)
14. Garde, A., Laursen, B., Jørgensen, A., Jensen, B.: Effects of mental and physical demands on heart rate variability during computer work. Eur. J. Appl. Physiol. **87**(4–5), 456–461 (2002)
15. Giannakakis, G., Pediaditis, M., Manousos, D., Kazantzaki, E., Chiarugi, F., Simos, P.G., Marias, K., Tsiknakis, M.: Stress and anxiety detection using facial cues from videos. Biomed. Signal Process. Control **31**, 89–101 (2017). https://doi.org/ 10.1016/j.bspc.2016.06.020
16. Grundlehner, B., Brown, L., Penders, J., Gyselinckx, B.: The design and analysis of a real-time, continuous arousal monitor. In: 2009 Sixth International Workshop on Wearable and Implantable Body Sensor Networks, pp. 156–161. Institute of Electrical and Electronics Engineers, IEEE, June 2009. https://doi.org/10.1109/ bsn.2009.21
17. Healey, J.A., Picard, R.W.: Detecting stress during real-world driving tasks using physiological sensors. IEEE Trans. Intell. Transp. Syst. **6**(2), 156–166 (2005)
18. Hsu, Y.C., Lin, Y.-L., Hsu, W.: Learning-based heart rate detection from remote photoplethysmography features. In: 2014 IEEE International Conference on Acoustics, Speech and Signal Processing (ICASSP), pp. 4433–4437. Institute of Electrical and Electronics Engineers (IEEE), IEEE, May 2014. https://doi.org/10.1109/ icassp.2014.6854440
19. Irani, R., Nasrollahi, K., Moeslund, T.B.: Improved pulse detection from head motions using DCT. Institute for Systems and Technologies of Information, Control and Communication (2014)
20. Jerritta, S., Murugappan, M., Nagarajan, R., Wan, K.: Physiological signals based human emotion recognition: a review. In: 2011 IEEE 7th International Colloquium on Signal Processing and its Applications, pp. 410–415. IEEE, Institute of Electrical and Electronics Engineers (IEEE), March 2011. https://doi.org/10.1109/cspa. 2011.5759912
21. Kivikangas, J.M., Chanel, G., Cowley, B., Ekman, I., Salminen, M., Järvelä, S., Ravaja, N.: A review of the use of psychophysiological methods in game research. J. Gaming Virtual Worlds **3**(3), 181–199 (2011). https://doi.org/10.1386/jgvw.3. 3.181_1
22. Kukolja, D., Popović, S., Horvat, M., Kovač, B., Ćosić, K.: Comparative analysis of emotion estimation methods based on physiological measurements for real-time applications. Int. J. Hum. Comput. Stud. **72**(10–11), 717–727 (2014). https://doi. org/10.1016/j.ijhcs.2014.05.006
23. Landowska, A.: Emotion monitoring verification of physiological characteristics measurement procedures. Metrol. Meas. Syst. **21**(4), 719–732 (2014). ISSN 2300-1941. https://doi.org/10.2478/mms-2014-0049

24. Li, X., Chen, J., Zhao, G., Pietikainen, M.: Remote heart rate measurement from face videos under realistic situations. In: 2014 IEEE Conference on Computer Vision and Pattern Recognition, pp. 4264–4271. Institute of Electrical & Electronics Engineers (IEEE), June 2014. https://doi.org/10.1109/cvpr.2014.543

25. McDuff, D., Gontarek, S., Picard, R.: Remote measurement of cognitive stress via heart rate variability. In: 2014 36th Annual International Conference of the IEEE Engineering in Medicine and Biology Society, pp. 2957–2960. Institute of Electrical and Electronics Engineers (IEEE), August 2014. https://doi.org/10.1109/embc.2014.6944243

26. McDuff, D., Gontarek, S., Picard, R.W.: Improvements in remote cardiopulmonary measurement using a five band digital camera. IEEE Trans. Biomed. Eng. **61**(10), 2593–2601 (2014). https://doi.org/10.1109/tbme.2014.2323695

27. McDuff, D.J., Estepp, J.R., Piasecki, A.M., Blackford, E.B.: A survey of remote optical photoplethysmographic imaging methods. In: 2015 37th Annual International Conference of the IEEE Engineering in Medicine and Biology Society (EMBC), pp. 6398–6404. IEEE, Institute of Electrical and Electronics Engineers (IEEE), August 2015. https://doi.org/10.1109/embc.2015.7319857

28. McDuff, D.J., Hernandez, J., Gontarek, S., Picard, R.W.: COGCAM: Contact-free measurement of cognitive stress during computer tasks with a digital camera. In: Proceedings of the 2016 CHI Conference on Human Factors in Computing Systems - CHI 2016. Association for Computing Machinery (ACM) (2016). https://doi.org/10.1145/2858036.2858247

29. Monkaresi, H., Calvo, R.A., Yan, H.: A machine learning approach to improve contactless heart rate monitoring using a webcam. IEEE J. Biomed. Health Inform. **18**(4), 1153–1160 (2014). https://doi.org/10.1109/jbhi.2013.2291900

30. Poh, M.-Z., McDuff, D.J., Picard, R.W.: Non-contact, automated cardiac pulse measurements using video imaging and blind source separation. Opt. Express **18**(10), 10762 (2010). https://doi.org/10.1364/oe.18.010762

31. Poh, M.-Z., McDuff, D.J., Picard, R.W.: Advancements in noncontact, multiparameter physiological measurements using a webcam. IEEE Trans. Biomed. Eng. **58**(1), 7–11 (2011)

32. Rani, P., Liu, C., Sarkar, N., Vanman, E.: An empirical study of machine learning techniques for affect recognition in human-robot interaction. Pattern Anal. Appl. **9**(1), 58–69 (2006)

33. Ravaja, N., Saari, T., Laarni, J., Kallinen, K., Salminen, M., Holopainen, J., Järvinen, A.: The psychophysiology of video gaming: Phasic emotional responses to game events. In: International DiGRA Conference (2005)

34. Roald, N.G.: Estimation of vital signs from ambient-light non-contact photoplethysmography (2013)

35. Rodriguez, A., Rey, B., Vara, M.D., Wrzesien, M., Alcaniz, M., Banos, R.M., Perez-Lopez, D.: A VR-based serious game for studying emotional regulation in adolescents. IEEE Comput. Grap. Appl. **35**(1), 65–73 (2015). https://doi.org/10.1109/mcg.2015.8

36. Rouast, P.V., Adam, M.T.P., Chiong, R., Cornforth, D., Lux, E.: Remote heart rate measurement using low-cost RGB face video: A technical literature review. Front. Comput. Sci. 1–15 (2016). https://doi.org/10.1007/s11704-016-6243-6

37. Schubert, C., Lambertz, M., Nelesen, R.A., Bardwell, W., Choi, J.-B., Dimsdale, J.E.: Effects of stress on heart rate complexitya comparison between short-term and chronic stress. Biol. Psychol. **80**(3), 325–332 (2009)

38. Sharma, R., Khera, S., Mohan, A., Gupta, N., Ray, R.B.: Assessment of computer game as a psychological stressor. Indian J. Physiol. Pharmacol. **50**(4), 367 (2006)

39. Takano, C., Ohta, Y.: Heart rate measurement based on a time-lapse image. Med. Eng. Phys. **29**(8), 853–857 (2007). https://doi.org/10.1016/j.medengphy.2006.09. 006

40. Tijs, T.J.W., Brokken, D., IJsselsteijn, W.A.: Dynamic game balancing by recognizing affect. In: Markopoulos, P., de Ruyter, B., IJsselsteijn, W., Rowland, D. (eds.) Fun and Games. LNCS, vol. 5294, pp. 88–93. Springer, Heidelberg (2008). https://doi.org/10.1007/978-3-540-88322-7_9

41. Tran, D.N., Lee, H., Kim, C.: A robust real time system for remote heart rate measurement via camera. In: 2015 IEEE International Conference on Multimedia and Expo (ICME), pp. 1–6. IEEE, Institute of Electrical and Electronics Engineers (IEEE), June 2015. https://doi.org/10.1109/icme.2015.7177484

42. Vandeput, S., Taelman, J., Spaepen, A., Van Huffel, S.: Heart rate variability as a tool to distinguish periods of physical and mental stress in a laboratory environment. In: Proceedings of the 6th International Workshop on Biosignal Interpretation (BSI), New Haven, CT, pp. 187–190 (2009)

43. Verkruysse, W., Svaasand, L.O., Nelson, J.S.: Remote plethysmographic imaging using ambient light. Opt. Express **16**(26), 21434 (2008). https://doi.org/10.1364/ oe.16.021434

44. Viola, P., Jones, M.J.: Robust real-time face detection. Int. J. Comput. Vis. **57**(2), 137–154 (2004)

45. Wang, W., den Brinker, A., Stuijk, S., de Haan, G.: Algorithmic principles of remote-PPG. IEEE Trans. Biomed. Eng. 1 (2016). https://doi.org/10.1109/tbme. 2016.2609282

46. Wang, W., Stuijk, S., de Haan, G.: A novel algorithm for remote photoplethysmography: Spatial subspace rotation. IEEE Trans. Biomed. Eng. **63**(9), 1974–1984 (2016). https://doi.org/10.1109/TBME.2015.2508602. ISSN 0018–9294

47. Xiao, X., Wang, J.: Towards attentive, bi-directional MOOC learning on mobile devices. In: Proceedings of the 2015 ACM on International Conference on Multimodal Interaction - ICMI 2015, pp. 163–170. ACM, Association for Computing Machinery (ACM) (2015). https://doi.org/10.1145/2818346.2820754

48. Yamaguchi, M., Wakasugi, J., Sakakima, J.: Evaluation of driver stress using biomarker in motor-vehicle driving simulator. In: 2006 International Conference of the IEEE Engineering in Medicine and Biology Society, pp. 1834–1837. IEEE, Institute of Electrical and Electronics Engineers (IEEE), August 2006. https:// doi.org/10.1109/iembs.2006.260001

49. Yamakoshi, T., Yamakoshi, K., Tanaka, S., Nogawa, M., Shibata, M., Sawada, Y., Rolfe, P., Hirose, Y.: A preliminary study on driver's stress index using a new method based on differential skin temperature measurement. In: 2007 29th Annual International Conference of the IEEE Engineering in Medicine and Biology Society, pp. 722–725. IEEE, Institute of Electrical and Electronics Engineers (IEEE), August 2007. https://doi.org/10.1109/iembs.2007.4352392

50. Yun, C., Shastri, D., Pavlidis, I., Deng. Z.: O' game, can you feel my frustration? In: Proceedings of the 27th International Conference on Human Factors in Computing Systems - CHI 2009, pp. 2195–2204. ACM, Association for Computing Machinery (ACM) (2009). https://doi.org/10.1145/1518701.1519036

51. Zhao, F., Li, M., Qian, Y., Tsien, J.Z.: Remote measurements of heart and respiration rates for telemedicine. PLoS ONE **8**(10), e71384 (2013). https://doi.org/10. 1371/journal.pone.0071384

eSport vs irlSport

Christopher McCutcheon[1]([✉]) ⓘ, Michael Hitchens[2] ⓘ, and Anders Drachen[3] ⓘ

[1] Torrens University Australia, Leura, Australia
christopher.mccutcheon@laureate.edu.au
[2] Macquarie University, Macquarie Park, Australia
michael.hitchens@mq.edu.au
[3] Digital Creativity Labs, University of York, York, UK
anders.drachen@york.ac.uk

Abstract. This paper examines in-real-life (irl) sport and eSports in an attempt to clarify the definition of eSport. The notion of physicality and embodiment are central to the need for clarity in understanding of what eSports are and whether they are sport or some other activity. By examining existing definitions of eSport and irlSport we can identify the similarities and differences between these activities. Methodologically the paper uses the philosophical process of critical thinking and analysis to examine the various approaches taken to defining both eSport and irlSports. Our aim is to highlight the inherent problem of the definition of eSports and irlSports (and the privileging of the term sport as it currently applies only to irlSports). We find that eSports are sports and that the definition of sport should be expanded to include sub-categories of irlSports and eSports.

Keywords: eSport · irlSports · Competitive video games · Embodiment
Virtual play spaces

There are few words in the English language which have such a multiplicity of meanings as the word sport [1].

eSport has similar multiplicity, for example:

eSports commonly refer to competitive (pro and amateur) video gaming that is often coordinated by different leagues, ladders and tournaments, and where players customarily belong to teams or other "sporting" organizations which are sponsored by various business organizations [2].

and

"Esports is computer games played in a competitive environment" [3].

A. Drachen—Part of this work was conducted in the Digital Creativity Labs (www.digitalcreativity.ac.uk), jointly funded by EPSRC/AHRC/InnovateUK under grant no EP/M023265/1.

A. D. Cheok et al. (Eds.): ACE 2017, LNCS 10714, pp. 531–542, 2018.
https://doi.org/10.1007/978-3-319-76270-8_36

1   Introduction

Throughout the history of humanity's attempts to understand sport from a theoretical or philosophical perspective, the theorists and philosophers have in general taken to view sport in terms of physicality. As eSports emerge from the niche 'gamer-nerd' segment to be embraced by a wider, mainstream audience and culture there is an increasing need to clarify our understanding of what eSports are and how they relate to traditional embodied sports or 'in-real-life' or irlSports[1].

Clarity is required as the current definition of sport does not take into consideration the discipline of eSports. Decisions are being made, laws enacted, resources invested without a functioning definition or anything but a lay understanding of what eSports actually are. The notion that physicality is central to the concept of irlSport has never really been questioned. The current focus upon physicality creates some interesting challenges when we attempt to understand how eSports match up or compare to traditional in-real-life (irl) sports. In this paper we will attempt to rectify part of the problem by investigating the various definitions that we have of eSports and irlSports[2]. We argue that the definition of sport must change to accommodate the rapid growth of eSports. Ultimately however, it is open for debate whether eSports are indeed sports, or some other category of sports-like or sportive competitive behaviour.

eSports are considered to be, in general, a competitive approach to computer games. For example, Hamilton et al. [4] defined eSports to be "the high-level play and spectating of digital games". Several other authors and theses agree in general terms with the simple definition of eSports as competitive computer games [5, 6]. There are several issues with the current definition of irlSports which we believe are problematic. Any of these issues are sufficient to demand a new look at how irlSports and eSport are defined, and the relationship (if any) between them.

Some of the identified issues with the current (philosophical) definition of irlSport which have a bearing or impact upon the subsequent definition or understanding of eSport:

It is impossible to define an open system without reverting to arbitrary stipulation[3]. All sport activities are social systems, social systems are open to change and thus constitute open systems. Therefore sports are open systems and impossible to define without arbitrary stipulation. We contend that the notion of physicality is such an arbitrary stipulation.

The philosophical definition of sport was essentially set in its current form in 1985. There has been little to no new investigation of our understanding of what sport really

---

[1] irl = in real life. A term used by gamers and other online populations to mean anything that happens in real life, or outside of the game/MMO/internet environment.

[2] Hemphill started the inquiry in 2005 with his work, Cybersports. In that paper he questioned the privileging of the 'real' over the virtual. Part of the underlying thesis of this paper harks back to that investigation of Hemphill's – to question the othering of the virtual as not real, and to challenge the notion that sport must be likewise grounded in the physical or the 'real'.

[3] Stipulation; the practice of defining any object or thing by declaring it so. Stipulation is not a desired method of philosophical inquiry or a preferred definitional approach as it can lead to arbitrariness, and the fuzzy edge of a set becomes a problematic case for any stipulation.

is (ontology) since. Therefore, the emergent sportive practice of eSport, which came after the development of the current prevailing definition, does not fit comfortably within the current definition of sport, and as such leaves that current definition outside of the necessary and sufficient conditions to ontologically describe sport in all of its forms.

Physicality is a core element of the currently accepted definition of sport. Physicality itself is problematic in terms of monist embodiment (no mind/body split) and distributed communication/embodiment systems.

Online, distributed personality (leaky body concept [7]), genetic modification technology, body modification, prosthetics, anthropomorphism and nanotechnology (not an exhaustive list by any measure) all muddy the concept of physicality, humanity and embodiment. Again leaving the current definition of sport on shaky grounds – eSports adds further to the problematic definition that sports are at their core games with the skillful exercise of physicality as their distinguishing feature from the aforementioned said core class of games.

This paper will examine eSports by, in part, examining the (philosophical) literature on irlSport and hopes to determine a forward pathway for determining a method of definition or class-object analysis for the irlSports-eSport juncture.

Methodologically, the paper uses the philosophical method of critical thought and analysis. It examines the underlying definitional approaches to eSport and irlSport and concludes that there are fundamental problems with the current approaches to defining both. By considering the role of physicality and outcomes in understanding eSport the paper suggests a potential avenue of approach to dealing with the problem, and identifying pathways for future work.

2   eSport: Impact and Popularity

eSports commonly refer to competitive (pro and amateur) video gaming that is often coordinated by different leagues, ladders and tournaments, and where players customarily belong to teams or other "sporting" organizations which are sponsored by various business organizations [2].

Hamari and Sjöblom [2] stated that eSports are becoming one of the most rapidly growing media in the world; that growth being driven by the increasing number of online games and broadcasting channels such as pod and vod casting, youtube and twitch streaming just to name the more obvious and accessible. This is supported by Heaven [8] who indicated that better video-streaming and internet speeds are enabling greater engagement with eSports.

Meanwhile Sjöblom et al. [9] indicated that eSports streaming is at the centre of a major shift in the broadcast media landscape. An example of this is provided by the July 2017, Sydney leg of the Overwatch World Cup qualifiers; which we believe were the first eSports matches broadcast on Australian free to air television[4].

eSport has made its way into popular culture and is being recognized by mainstream society. According to Hamilton, Kerne and Robbins [4] "The Global StarCraft League (GSL) finals at Blizzcon 2011…engaged 25,000 co-located and 300,000 online

---

[4] No supporting data available at the time of writing. Broadcast on 7Mate.

viewers." Snider [10] claimed that in 2013 League of Legends (a popular eSport) had 32 million players each month.

Similarly, Wingfield [11] indicated that (as at 2014) an estimated 70 million people watch eSports online[5] and the 2013 League of Legends championship achieved an online viewership of 8.5 million; compared to the 7.2 million viewers of the ITV broadcast of the FA Cup Finals (Wigan vs Manchester City) in the same year [12].

eSports leagues are a central feature of the eSports communities and growth of the phenomena. Multiple eSports leagues and competitions have emerged all over the world – ESL Gaming, Major League Gaming, World Cyber Games (defunct), and more recently, the League of Legends and Overwatch World Cups [13–18].

Coats and Parshakov [19] analyzed the prize pools in eSports tournaments, finding that eSports players are risk averse and advising that there should be a larger spread of the prize pool to incentivize players. Whilst Hollist [20] argued that there is a need for regulation of labor relations in eSports as current laws are inadequate to properly regulate eSports in regards to employer-employee relations and employment conditions and employee (player) health. There is a considerable amount of interest in eSports from various sectors of the academy – commercial gaming [21], grassroots eSports communities [22], eSports and streaming content [9, 23], nationality [24], training and physicality [25] and so on.

To sum up, in the words of Hamari and Sjöblom [2], "During recent years, eSports (electronic sports) have become one of the most rapidly growing forms of new media driven by the growing provenance of (online) games and online broadcasting technologies".

It is clear that eSports have become significant in both business and societal terms, and therefore it is important to develop a clear definition or understanding of what eSports actually are.

3   eSports: Current Definitions and Approaches

e-sports, a catchall term for games that resemble conventional sports insofar as they have superstars, playoffs, fans, uniforms, comebacks and upsets. But all the action in e-sports occurs online, and the contestants hardly move [26].

There are an astounding number of eSports definitions in both the academic and non-academic literature. Unfortunately all of them are stipulative and have not been tested; and as such cannot function as definitions from a philosophical point of view. However, they generally suffice for a 'working definition' point of view.

Hemphill's definition, as a sport philosopher, is arguably the closest there is to an acceptable eSport definition [27]: "electronically extended athletes in digitally represented sporting worlds." (p. 199). Hemphill updated and extended this in 2015 '… contrary to the claim about them being virtual or merely games, sport-themed computer games that involve human immersion and skillful, physical interactivity can be considered sport, at least in the classic formulation of sport as the demonstration of physical prowess in a game' [28].

---

[5] Wingfield did not provide information on the timeframe over which this number was accrued.

Wagner [6] defined eSports as "an area of sport activities in which people develop and train mental or physical abilities in the use of information and communication technologies." The fundamental problems associated with this definition are due to the overly broad nature of the foundation upon which Wagner laid it.[6]

Hamari and Sjöblom [2]: "a form of sports where the primary aspects of the sport are facilitated by electronic systems; the input of players and teams as well as the output of the eSports system are mediated by human-computer interfaces" [2]. A clear development upon Wagner. Martončik [29] follows a similar train of thought.

Alternatively Hutchins [30] suggests that the eSport model is nothing more than a template overlaid upon the traditions, mores and performative culture of mainstream sports broadcasting. The intention of such being to tap into the continuity of broadcast sports, and in doing so be accepted as a sport by virtue of being called a sport and appearing like a sport. Or to put it another way if it walks like a duck, talks like a duck and looks like a duck, it must be a duck; Essentially Wittgenstein's family resemblance model.

Karhulahti [21] neatly summed up the working definitions as:

> With nuance, they all perceive esport through two criteria: technological specificity (computers, cyberspace, electronics) and advanced competition (athleticism, professionalism, sport). These criteria are directly connected to the videogame culture so that esport is recognized as an "extension of gaming."

Therefore the working definition can be distilled down to two generic views of eSport; eSport is computer mediated competitive sportive or sport-like behavior. To clarify:

- Sportive – has the features of a sport according to the Suits-Meier formulation of sport in the philosophy of sport literature, but does not necessarily 'look' like a traditional sport. E.g. League of Legends [31] or Overwatch [32]
- Sport-like – a digital representation of an irlSports which on the surface appears to be a sport but may not be categorized as a sport according to the Suits-Meier formulation. For example, FIFA 17 [33].

The fundamental problem however, is that there has not been an examination of the metaphysical or ontological foundations underlying pronouncements on what eSports are. There have been stipulated, but relatively sensible working definitions made (see all of the above literature). Those definitions, for the most part have functioned well enough for researchers looking at issues surrounding eSports (regulation, player management, prize money, gambling, game design and mechanics and so on and so forth) but to date, no single clear investigation into the nature of eSports, or their relationship to irlSports, or to the foundational disciplines of games, play and ludology (which will have to be left to further study due to space restrictions here). Therefore, it is difficult, and somewhat irresponsible, to rely on lay, or untested definitions of the concept of eSports, and/or their relationship to irlSports.

---

[6] Wagner bases his definition of eSports on that of the work of Tiedemann [53], which seems overly broad; so broad as to essentially include all human activity as sport. Further, Tiedemann does not take into consideration the generally accepted Suits-Meier definition of sport.

4   Defining eSports or Re-defining irlSport? Why not Both!

It may not be possible to come to a unified and acceptable (analytic/essentialistic phil-osophical) definition of sport that will have the necessary and sufficient conditions to encompass both eSport and irlSports. Therefore the next two viewpoints may have long term merit in the evolution of an acceptable understanding of eSports.

Karhulahti [21] considered eSport not from the competitive and technology lever-aged point of view that many authors have taken, but from the economic 'pay-for-play' point of view, and introduced the idea of "Executive Ownership" (p. 46), where the owner of the intellectual property – i.e. the game company that develops and maintains the game, servers and 'playing fields', has ultimate power and ownership over when and even how the game/sport is played. Karhulahti further suggests that eSport be described as economic Sport, rather than electronic. Karhulahti points out that her view of economic eSport should encompass any commercial game (with attached Executive Ownership structure – holder of absolute power in regards to property rights over the game) that has a competitive, social and instructional structure surrounding it.

Interestingly, Karhulahti's definition does have a remarkable similarity to Bernard Suits' [34, 35] original definition of sport, sans the physicality component (more on this later).

A second alternative viewpoint is that of Wittgenstein's [36] notion of family and community that can easily be applied to a definitional approach to eSports.

Wittgenstein claimed there cannot be an essentialistic[7] definition of irlSports because there are no necessary and sufficient conditions which are broad enough to cover all aspects but specific enough to limit out non-sport elements.

If we accept Wittgenstein's thesis then it is basically impossible to essentially define the product of any social (human defined) system. Therefore, sport, and presumably eSport, as the product of social systems, are both open sets and therefore cannot be defined[8]. Thus any attempt to close the set is arbitrary and therefore stipulative; which ultimately defeats the purpose of defining the fundamental essence of eSport and irlSports.

Wittgenstein offered a different way in which we can view of eSport/irlSport; that sport may be characterised upon the idea of family resemblance or commonality. Under this approach, eSports are sports because of the broad family resemblance between them and irlSports. The family name (eSports are in fact named eSports) automatically making them a sub-set of the class sport. It is all in the name, similar things share a similar name.

In addition there is the socially accepted role that eSports plays in the eSports community. eSports fulfil the same social role as irlSports within the gamer community. As such eSports can be considered to be equivalent to irlSports for the social niches that accept eSports as sports. This is known as the equivalency clause:

---

[7] Essentialistic is taken to mean any underlying essential or fundamental truth or knowing of a thing.

[8] However, a method (class membership) may be substituted instead of definition. To be honest we are delving into the semantics/deconstruction of the definition of 'definition'; which is somewhat out of the scope of this paper.

For example, overheard at the Sydney leg of the 2017 Overwatch World Cup Cosplayer 1, whilst enthusiastically cheering after the Australian team win over Japan, turned towards Cosplayer 2 and yelled joyously, "Now I get sport!" [37].

Evidence of an eSports community is provided by Kozachuk, Foroughi and Freeman [38] who described the eSport as being in a state of "drastic growth", with increasing numbers of player and competitions and "millions of spectators" globally. Likewise Freeman [39] added that, "esports players extremely emphasize the sense of community, belongingness, cohesion, and comradeship among them."

The final word here goes to Gunatilaka, [40] commenting on the Sydney leg of the 2017 Overwatch World Championship:

> *To anyone in doubt of whether esports should be considered a sport, take it from me - it is sport and it deserves to be. These tournaments feel exactly the same as packed out footy games. Forget the fact that compared to traditional sports, esports has little physical exertion. The amount of teamwork, training, skill and dedication required to compete at this level is legitimate.*

5   What is irlSport?

The current presiding definitions of games, play and sport fail to take into consideration the changing nature of the online or virtual world and the technology and culture that drives, sustains and surrounds these worlds. The terrain has significantly changed since Klaus Meier [41, 42] suggested some changes to Bernard Suit's [35, 43–47] definition of games and sport in 1989. It has become important to re-examine the definition of sport and performance and, indeed, the western cultural understanding of what a sport is in light of the development and impact of eSports.

Any such "definition" offered must, of course, be founded in an academic discourse, discipline or assumption; and as previously evidenced, there are many relevant and acceptable discourses within the sport, recreation and physical education sphere [48, 49][9]. Each discourse presents a different viewpoint and aims to achieve a different agenda. In the case of sport philosophy, the discipline inherited its foundational discourse and understanding of physicality, humanity and activity primarily from physical education, and has never really challenged those inherited basic embodiment assumptions; arguably remaining basically essentialist throughout its existence as a distinct discipline.

We contend that the generally accepted definition of sport provided by Suits and Meier does not adequately cover eSports or virtual/online and distributed playing fields. By relying upon the concept of *physicality*, the current generally accepted understanding of irlSport excludes many eSport instantiations and practices, and provides important gatekeeper and policy development organizations (such as government funding agencies) with an incorrect philosophical and in-practice foundation on which they base their activities.

---

[9] Blumenfeld noted these different points of view in terms of play. He indicated the difficulty in determining exactly what play is stems from "…the different points of view which must be, but have not always been, clearly distinguished…" [48].

Osterhoudt [50] and Paddick [51] as prime examples of the state of the discipline, emphasize physicality as "a necessary component (and intrinsic good) of sport" [52].

5.1 The Suits/Meier Formulation for Sport

"Games are the voluntary attempt to overcome unnecessary or gratuitous obstacles" [27].

The Suits/Meier formulation is generally accepted within the discipline of the philosophy of sport as the standard account for a definition of sport. This definitional approach has two distinct phases. The definition of games, which form the basis for the definition of sports.
The Suits [35, 47] formulation of games can be summarized as follows, games are:

- Goal oriented
- Rules based
- Where the rules prohibit the use of more efficient means over less efficient means, and,
- The rules are accepted just because they make the activity possible

Suits [34, 35] continued to define sport in such a manner:
A game is also a sport if:

- It is a game of skill,
- The core skill is physical,
- The game has a wide following, and
- The following has achieved a certain level of stability

This is the currently accepted "definition" of sport (Meier's modification of Suits):

*...all sports are indeed games. That is, a game may also correctly be termed a sport if it possesses the additional characteristics of requiring **physical skill or prowess** [our emphasis] to be demonstrated by the participants in the pursuit of its goal* [42].

We claim that eSports meets all the aspects currently required of the definition of sport. A simple 'in your own head' analysis will confirm that eSports are games.

Further; eSports fit into the above definition of sport if we consider that physicality is inherent in any human embodied activity. That is to say we are all meat; thinking requires the physical brain to occur, therefore eSports are physical. Also, of course, using a controller or mouse and keyboard is also physical.

As previously evidenced, eSports demonstrate skillful participation and enjoy a wide following; adhering to Suits [35, 43–47] original definition of sport.

This permits an examination of eSports alongside irlSports. Are eSports 'just' sports? To answer, as sports are not 'just' games then no, eSports are not just sports. There is a difference between the two similar but related concepts.

What sets eSports apart from sports? When we remove the notion of physicality that traditionally defined the difference between sport and games, and nominally defines the difference between sport and eSport, we are left in the undesirable position that games, sport and eSport are all the same thing; which clearly they are not.

Hamari and Sjoblom [2] question the 'location' of irlSports vs eSports and declare that irlSports exist within the 'real' world whilst eSports exist outside of the 'real' world inhabiting virtual computer mediated environments. However, phenomenology principles could easily argue that this is a false premise since, the computer mediated delivery systems themselves are both in the world and of the world and therefore, any virtual environment is automatically in the 'real' world by virtue of inheriting its realness from its very existence.

irlSports are practiced in an arguably different form of embodiment and reality to that of eSports. Inasmuch that if we accept, for conveniences sake, the notion that the irlSports play-space is both in and of the world, whilst the eSport play-space could be argued that it is primarily only of the world[10].

We can also refer to the concept of the leaky body [7], if we can accept that an irlAthlete can have their body boundaries and identity extended beyond the physical instantiation and biological limitation. Then clearly it should also be acceptable to apply the leaky body concept to the practice of sport (not just the practitioner) and thus also extend sport beyond the 'physical' limitations to include unbound examples; eSport.

A further approach would be to simply extend the prevailing definition of sport to encompass eSport as a sub-set, much like the definition of games was extended to include sport. Therefore, conceivably, we can conclude that eSports are sports (they really are) but they're a particular type/category/subset of sport, with, as yet to be clearly determined or defined parameters.

6   Where to Next?

Ideally, sport as a whole should remove references to physicality, as it is arbitrary, limiting and ambiguous. Additionally, physicality seems less important to eSports practice, however, there are similarities between irlSports and eSport on this front, in that eSport does contain physicality (reaction time, fine motor skills etc.) as a central feature of success. Or to put is very plainly and simply; physicality matters to eSport but is not all important. Additionally there needs to be clarity around accepting or rejecting eSports as a category of sports.

Finally, we suggest that there is potential for conceptualizing all sport not just in terms of physicality but more importantly goal directed skillful embodiment, whilst still embracing Suits notion of unnecessary obstacles and the play-space. We would suggest that characterizing sport in terms of outcomes within the world or impact upon an environment rather than privileging physicality would be a place to start this investigation. Where:

- Skillful can mean intentional, with skill and practice, and predominately non-random.
- Embodiment can mean any form of authentic cognitive lived embodiment regardless of physical form.
- Goal directed can mean any form of intentional action seeking a (prescribed/preferred) outcome; regardless of achieving the outcome.

---

[10] Although eSport must be in the world for it to exist.

- Playspace can mean any place in which play, games and sports are instantiated. The play space may be real, virtual, conceptual or imagined, or any variant as yet unidentified.

Therefore, we may consider an overall category of sport containing the sub-categories of eSport and irlSports. Further, the sub-categories of eSport and irlSports can be differentiated from each other by the embodiment typically expressed during their execution or performance (physical and virtual) and the environments/play spaces that they typically inhabit. Additionally, a third category of sportive behavior may be identified in those sports that exhibit crossover features of both irlSports and eSport. Specifically those activities that use virtual reality and motion capture devices (and future devices of this ilk) to translate full-embodied physical actions into a virtual eSports play space.

Sport is more than just irlSports. irlSports does not encapsulate all sport and eSport is more than just competitive computer gaming.

References

1. Graves, H.: A philosophy of sport. Contemp. Rev. **78**, 877–893 (1900)
2. Hamari, J., Sjöblom, M.: What is eSports and why do people watch it? Internet Res. **27**, 211–232 (2017)
3. Schubert, M., Drachen, A., Mahlmann, T.: Esports analytics through encounter detection. In: MIT SLOAN Sports Analytics Conference, pp. 1–18 (2016)
4. Hamilton, W., Kerne, A., Robbins, T.: High-performance pen + touch modality interactions: a real-time strategy game eSports context. In: Proceedings of the 25th Annual ACM Symposium on User Interface Software and Technology (UIST 2012), pp. 309–318 (2012)
5. van Ditmarsch, J.: Video Games as a Spectator Sport: How Electronic Sports Transforms Spectatorship (2013)
6. Wagner, M.G.: On the scientific relevance of eSports. In: International Conference on Internet Computing, pp. 437–442 (2006)
7. Shildrick, M.: Leaky Bodies and Boundaries: Feminism, Postmodernism and (Bio) Ethics. Routledge, London (1997)
8. Heaven, D.: Esports: Pro video gaming explodes with big prize pots. https://www.newscientist.com/article/mg22329823.900-esports-pro-video-gaming-explodes-with-big-prize-pots/#.VR9OzeEyRxI
9. Sjöblom, M., Törhönen, M., Hamari, J., Macey, J.: Content structure is king: an empirical study on gratifications, game genres and content type on Twitch. Comput. Hum. Behav. **73**, 161–171 (2017)
10. Jenny, S.E., Manning, R.D., Keiper, M.C., Olrich, T.W.: Virtual(ly) athletes: where eSports fit within the definition of "sport". Quest **69**, 1–18 (2016)
11. Wingfield, N.: In E-Sports, Video Gamers Draw Real Crowds and Big money. https://www.nytimes.com/2014/08/31/technology/esports-explosion-brings-opportunity-riches-for-video-gamers.html
12. Plunkett, J.: BBC's FA Cup final coverage nets peak of nearly 9 million (2015). https://www.theguardian.com/media/2015/jun/01/bbc-fa-cup-final-coverage-nets-peak-of-nearly-9-million
13. Blizzard Entertainment: Overwatch World Cup 2017. https://worldcup.playoverwatch.com/en-gb/#group-stage

14. Riot Games: World Championships. http://www.lolesports.com/en_US/worlds/world_championship_2016/schedule/elim/Quarterfinals
15. Major League Gaming: Call of Duty World League. http://www.majorleaguegaming.com/
16. World Cyber Games: About the World Cyber Games of the Past. http://worldcybergames.com/
17. Australian eSports League: Welcome to eSports. http://ael.org.au/
18. Turtle Entertainment: ESL Gaming. https://www.eslgaming.com/
19. Coates, D., Parshakov, P.: Team vs. Individual Tournaments: Evidence From Prize Structure in eSports Basic Research Program (2016)
20. Hollist, K.E.: Time to be grown-ups about video gaming: the rising esports industry and the need for regulation. Ariz. Law Rev. **57**, 823–847 (2015)
21. Karhulahti, V.-M.: Reconsidering esport: economics and executive ownership. Phys. Cult. Sport. Stud. Res. **74**, 43–53 (2017)
22. Curley, A.J., Nausha, M.: Challenges and Best Practices in Supporting Grassroots eSports Communities, pp. 1–5 (2016)
23. Karhulahti, V.-M.: Prank, troll, gross and gore: performance issues in esport live-streaming. In: 1st International Joint Conference on DiGRA FDG, pp. 1–13 (2016)
24. Parshakov, P., Zavertiaeva, M.: Success in eSports: Does Country Matter? (2016)
25. Kari, T., Karhulahti, V.-M.: Do e-athletes move? A study on training and physical exercise in elite e-sports. Int. J. Gaming Comput. Simul. **8**, 53–66 (2016)
26. Segal, D.: Behind league of legends, e-sport's main attraction. https://www.nytimes.com/2014/10/12/technology/riot-games-league-of-legends-main-attraction-esports.html
27. Hemphill, D.: Cybersport. J. Philos. Sport. **32**, 195 (2005)
28. Hemphill, D.: Cybersport. In: Torres, C.R. (ed.) The Bloomsbury Companion to the Philosophy of Sport, pp. 346–348. Bloomsbury Publishing, London (2015)
29. Martončik, M.: E-Sports: playing just for fun or playing to satisfy life goals? Comput. Hum. Behav. **48**, 208–211 (2015)
30. Hutchins, B.: Computer gaming, media and e-sport. In: TASA Conference 2006, Perth, Western Australia, pp. 1–9 (2006)
31. Riot Games: League of Legends (2009)
32. Blizzard Entertainment: Overwatch (2016)
33. Electronic Arts: FIFA 17 (2016)
34. Suits, B.: The trick of the disappearing goal. J. Philos. Sport. **16**, 1–12 (1989)
35. Suits, B.: Tricky triad: games, play, and sport. J. Philos. Sport. **15**, 1–9 (1988)
36. Wittgenstein, L.: Philosophical Investigations. Wiley-Blackwell, Chichester (West Sussex) (2009)
37. McCutcheon, C.: Personal recollection (2017)
38. Kozachuk, J., Foroughi, C.K., Freeman, G.: Introduction. In: Exploring Electronic Sports: An Interdisciplinary Approach, Proceedings of the Human Factors and Ergonomics Society Annual Meeting, pp. 2118–2122 (2016)
39. Freeman, G.: How, if at all, does eSports shape players' online and offline social/interpersonal relationships? In: Exploring Electronic Sports: An Interdisciplinary Approach, Proceedings of the Human Factors and Ergonomics Society 2016 Annual Meeting, p. 2119 (2016)
40. Gunatilaka, L.: Falling for eSports. https://www.facebook.com/notes/screenplay/falling-for-esports-blog/2093700917323067/
41. Meier, K.V.: Performance prestidigitation. J. Philos. Sport. **16**, 13–33 (1989)
42. Meier, K.V.: Triad trickery: playing with sport and games. In: Morgan, W.J., Meier, K.V. (eds.) Philosophic Inquiry in Sport, pp. 23–35. Human Kinetics, Champaign (1995)
43. Suits, B.: What is a game? Philos. Sci. **34**, 11–17 (1967)

44. Suits, B.: The elements of sport. In: Osterhoudt, R. (ed.) Philosophic Inquiry in Sport, pp. 48–64. Human Kinetics, Springfield (1973)
45. Suits, B.: The Grasshopper: Games, Life and Utopia. NonPareil, Boston (2005)
46. Suits, B.: Words on play. J. Philos. Sport. **4**, 117–131 (1977)
47. Suits, B.: The elements of sport. In: Morgan, W.J., Meier, K.V. (eds.) Philosophic Inquiry in Sport, pp. 8–15. Human Kinetics, Champaign (1995)
48. Blumenfeld, W.: Observations concerning the phenomenon and origin of play. Philos. Phenomenol. Res. **1**, 470–478 (1941)
49. Champlin, N.L.: Are sports methodic? J. Philos. Sport. **4**, 104–116 (1977)
50. Osterhoudt, R.: "Physicality": one among the internal goods of sport. J. Philos. Sport. **XXIII**, 91–103 (1996)
51. Paddick, R.J.: What makes physical activity physical? J. Philos. Sport. **2**, 12–22 (1975)
52. Hsu, L.: Revisiting the concept of sport. J. Humanit. Soc. Sci. **1**, 45–54 (2005)
53. Tiedemann, C.: Sport (and culture of physical motion) for historians, an approach to precise the central term(s). In: Teja, A., Krüger, A., Riordan, J. (eds.) Sport and Cultures, Proceedings of the 9th International Congress of the European Committee for Sport History (CESH), Crotone, Italy, pp. 410–416 (2004)

Heritage Hunt: Developing a Role-Playing Game for Heritage Museums

Suzanne de Kock and Marcello A. Gómez Maureira[✉]

University of Malta, Msida MSD 2080, Malta
suusdekock@gmail.com, ma.gomezmaureira@gmail.com
http://www.um.edu.mt/

Abstract. Artefacts in museums are fundamentally de-contextualized in the way that they are displayed. This papers describes the development of *Heritage Hunt*, a mobile game prototype developed for the National Museum of Archaeology in Malta, that looks at roleplaying and the portrayal of history at a small-scale level to promote a better understanding of the every-day cultural context of displayed artefacts. We conducted a small, explorative study across different development stages to assess this approach. The final prototype was tested in the museum space, with results indicating that roleplaying can be beneficial to direct the attention of visitors towards less prominent artefacts, as well as encourage visitors to consider different perspectives in history.

Keywords: Museum games · Role-playing · Game design
User experience testing

1 Introduction

Archaeology, history, and natural history museums provide visitors with the opportunity to learn about the past through the immediacy of physical artefacts. They provide a space for curiosity and dialogue, frequently augmented by textual information or interactive interfaces. Yet, the preserved artefacts remain fundamentally de-contextualized; a piece of history, often displayed mere steps away from another artefact that may have been created hundreds of years later. After all, the original context of each artefact lies centuries in the past, if not longer, and is connected to a space that rarely corresponds to its modern whereabouts.

In this paper we discuss the design and creation of *Heritage Hunt*, a video game for tablets and smart-phones that attempts to bridge this gap. The game aims to inform its players of the everyday cultural context of the artefacts on display, how they were used at the time, and how different people of the time might have looked at them in different ways. In order to achieve this goal, the game uses elements of role-playing in order to give the player a sense of personal involvement in the narrative of the game. It contextualizes artefacts through small fictional narrative elements in a historical setting; supplementing already

© Springer International Publishing AG, part of Springer Nature 2018
A. D. Cheok et al. (Eds.): ACE 2017, LNCS 10714, pp. 543–556, 2018.
https://doi.org/10.1007/978-3-319-76270-8_37

displayed information that focuses on the larger scope. As a research effort, *Heritage Hunt* is an indicative case study that aims to explore the benefits and challenges of developing a narratively-driven, multi-user mobile game for museums focusing on history. As part of this effort we present the results of user tests at different stages of the development, and the modifications that were informed by them. Due to the small scale nature of the research, we see its use primarily in informing museums with limited resources. Our message therefore is less that playful interactivity is a completely novel concept, but rather that their use is not common place and should be considered even in smaller venues. Here, the particular way in which *Heritage Hunt* presents history can provide an example to build upon.

2   Related Work

Before we describe the development of *Heritage Hunt*, we want to highlight prior work that informed the development of this project; starting from considerations regarding the museum environment, and the impact of role-playing on social interactions.

2.1   Learning in Museum Spaces

In general, a wide range of demographics visit museums to learn in an informal manner [12]. Museum visitors have varying levels of motivation, prior knowledge and interest, and learn in highly idiosyncratic ways. This diversity in learning and engagement means that the museum has to be versatile and prepared to accommodate the needs of various kinds of visitors. Falk and Dierking [6] have proposed a model of learning in museums that recognizes a personal, sociocultural, and physical context.

The personal context focuses on the individual motivations and the prior knowledge that visitors bring to the museum space. Whether a person learns or not depends on whether they have the motivation and attention span to do so. What Falk and Dierking propose is that the museum has to make the effort to motivate the visitors and give them many opportunities to engage with the exhibits.

The sociocultural context of museum learning focuses on how people learn in groups. Much of the time visitors to museums come in small groups; they are rarely visited alone [12]. Furthermore, a study conducted on the learning experience of students in a museum showed that the students were more likely to remember parts of their visits that included social interaction [8].

The physical context is considered to be the architectural structure of the museum as well as any physical media within. The displays, in terms of artefacts, written signage, and interactive displays, all count towards the physical context of museum learning. This includes the layout and the order in which a visitor experiences the exhibit [2,6]. Even the language used on informational plaques affects the relationship between the museum and the visitor [11].

2.2   Interactivity and Museums

While interactivity in general does not require technical components, we base our project on technically afforded interactivity. Frequently, these interactive experiences tend to be one-way streets of information accessed by menial tasks, such as the press of a button or the manipulation of a screen. Witcomb [14] questions the nature of this sort of interaction, and how beneficial it is for the visitor considering the linearity of the information flow. An audio guide would be an example of this, where the information presented is completely linear with no significant input from the user. In contrast to such linear interactivity, spatial interaction [9] does not 'feed' information to the visitors. Instead it lets the visitors draw their own conclusions, using the imaginative aspects of interactivity. It invites the visitors to become co-authors of the content presented to them. The visitor is presented with small standalone narratives that are spread over a large space. There is a loose organisation in the design, but the visitors are free to move around the museum's exhibits to pick and choose what they want to experience. Dialogic interactivity [14] revolves around creating a dialogue between the visitor and the content. In this form of interactivity, content is presented with a central theme under the recognition that artefacts have a context that is often not fully known, and is thus open for discussion. Witcomb [14] encourages museums to become a space in which discussion is promoted by posing questions and showing different points of view, and acknowledging that there is no single truth when it comes to interpreting artefacts that are taken out of their original context.

2.3   Roleplaying Games

When looking at games that combine a social context with storytelling, roleplaying games (RPGs) are arguably the most well-known implementation of these aspects. Roleplaying, whether mediated through digital devices or not, is defined by putting oneself into the shoes of someone else; a character who a player of the game makes decisions as. Bowman suggests that "[a roleplaying game] should establish some sense of community through a ritualized, shared story-telling experience amongst multiple players. RPGs also should involve some form of game system, which provides the framework for the enactment of specific scenarios and the solving of problems within them." [4, pp. 11–12]. A large part of what motivates a player to empathize with a character is through decision making on behalf of that character. Players face obstacles by the game system and have to figure out how to overcome them with the tools at their disposal [5]. Often they must agree on a course of action together with other players, thus introducing additional opportunities for social interaction.

Heritage museums use historical reconstructions as a way to provide something akin to live-action roleplaying to involve the visitor in history [10]. These reconstructions use actors and roleplaying to make history come to life for the visitor, and the visitor's participation is crucial to the experience. Other ways that museums and sites have been engaging the visitor are virtual reconstructions.

They allow the player to traverse a digital space to see the way scholars think history could have looked. An example of this is *Pterosaurs: Flight in the Age of Dinosaurs*, installed at the American Museum of Natural History, which lets its players traverse a digital space as a pterosaur [7].

Aside from reconstructional roleplaying, museums have also been using interactivity in museums to put their visitors in the shoes of the researchers and get them to understand the process of archaeologists, anthropologists, or curators. An example of this is *MicroRangers*, and application-based game that teaches the players about microbiology and ecosystems, sending them on missions given to them by virtual scientists [1].

3   Research Approach

The primary focus of this study is to explore the potential of using roleplaying elements in combination with an every-day historical narrative within a mobile video game. This exploration is guided by principles of user experience research, which "focuses on a person's perception and the responses resulting from the use or anticipated use of a product, system, or service" [3, p. 4]. When considering the approach of user experience research for game development, Takatalo et al. say that "although the designer may have a clear idea of the user experience that the game system should provide, this experience will not necessarily be the gamers' experience" [13, p. 24].

In practice this meant that the development of *Heritage Hunt* alternated between phases of conceptual and technical work on the game, and phases of testing prototypes of the game (at various stages of completion) with participants. Apart of evaluating aspects of usability, we were further interested in whether the design goal of the game–promoting an understanding of the everyday cultural context of artefacts–was achieved. At this point we need to point out that the scope of this research is necessarily limited to that of an exploratory study due to budgetary constraints. As such the project should be understood as an early investigation that should be followed by further research and practical development.

The user experience testing that was conducted for this project took place in the form of focus groups carried out before the conceptualization of the application, preliminary tests with a paper and a digital prototype, and an on-site testing session at the National Museum of Archaeology in Malta with the final iteration of the digital prototype.

4   The Game

Heritage Hunt was developed specifically for the Phoenician exhibit of the National Museum of Archaeology in Malta. In the game, two or three players are tasked to solve a mystery surrounding the fictional robbery of a grave that takes place during the time of the Phoenician empire. All events and interactions of the game are mediated by a mobile application that acts as digital 'game master'.

Fig. 1. Tomb artefact acting as initial starting point (left); visitor scanning the QR code of an artefact to reveal a clue (middle); screenshot of the game showing the main hub (right).

Players discover details of the story as they investigate specific artefacts in the exhibit with the purpose of gathering clues to solve the crime. The application is responsible for revealing these story details only when players interact with corresponding artefacts, which is done by scanning a QR code identifier.

Players choose one of three characters at the start of the game, each of which receives details of the story that are unique to the perspective of that character. In order to discover all clues (and thus, complete the entire narrative), players must share the information they have gathered through their game characters with each other. In the end, players are asked to decide which of the suspects they have come across has committed the crime, resulting in either a wrongful, or rightful conviction, each of which is described within the narrative of the game.

By describing the same artefact in different ways according to a character's viewpoint, the game encourages players to understand an artefact in its day to day context, as well as its context in relation to different people at that time in history. The game focuses on a small, localized narrative of an event that could have taken place in a small community as a way to create an experiential understanding of the time period, and the role that artefacts played in society at that time.

4.1   The Characters

The players are asked to choose one of three characters: the aristocrat, the servant, or the merchant. These characters were chosen for their archetypal roles in society, giving the players a choice of viewpoint through which to view the world. The use of three characters was chosen in order to account for groups of visitors to museums as well as to have a manageable distribution of clues. The game can also be played by two characters, which increases the amount of information and clues that is given to each individual character.

4.2 Playing the Game

The game starts at a particular artefact: the physical re-creation of a Phoenician tomb (see Fig. 1). By having a set starting point, a place could be chosen for players to stand idle and read the game content without blocking the flow of visitors in the exhibit. In order to start the game, each player scans the QR code at the tomb. They are then asked to choose the character they want to play as. At this point, players are given information about the character, the way that they relate to the grave and to each other, and the suspects of the crime. Following this point in the game, players can investigate at their own pace, and in any order by finding other artefacts that have a QR code attached to them. Scanning these codes gives each character a different narrative, which may or may not include a clue to solve the mystery. Some clues are only given to specific characters. At any point during the game, players can re-read their own clues in the 'Found Clues' menu, or find a summary of what they have found and a description of the suspects in the 'Suspect' menu. The 'Codex' menu provides additional information about the Phoenicians for curious players. Whenever players think they have enough information, they can accuse one of the suspects. They are then given a brief description of what happens to the suspect, indicating whether their accusation was correct or not. The game then ends automatically.

The length of a play session is largely dependent on how fast players gather clues, and whether they decide to look at other exhibitions in-between investigating game-related artefacts. In general, the game has been designed to take about 15 to 20 min when played at a slow pace, and with other museum-related activities taking place in the meantime.

5 Development Process

In this section, we describe two of the earlier tests (using incomplete versions of the game) that took place during development. Each test informed the development of the game in its own way, and served as an intermediary check to see whether design expectations were being met. The first version of the game was informed by two focus groups, with a total of 10 participants. These helped to identify issues with existing interactivity in museums and informed basic design decisions in early concept development. One such a decision was to develop for mobile devices, as they allow for a high degree of independence in when and how to interact with the game and cause minimal disturbance to the existing exhibit. Based on the comments and opinions gathered in these sessions, a first prototype (centred around a narrative-based game) was created specifically for the National Museum of Archaeology in Malta.

5.1 Paper Prototype Testing

The first prototype of the game consisted of an early version of the game narrative, printed on paper and conveyed to players with vocal instructions.

The goal of this testing session was to find out how users might want to interact with the game, and whether the narrative of the game was considered engaging. Three participants, game design students that had not been part of the focus group sessions before, were invited to play the game as a group in a large lecture room. Printed photographs of artefacts were distributed across the room to roughly simulate the museum environment for which the game was developed. Participants were given a short explanation of the game and how to play it, while a moderator simulated the functionality of the digital application by revealing different parts of the game narrative depending on the characters that each participant had chosen. When all clues had been given, the participants were encouraged to discuss their findings and who they thought committed the crime. Afterwards the participants were interviewed together about their experience.

The test revealed that visual representations of involved characters and artefacts, while planned to be part of the game eventually, were considered crucial by the participants. Throughout the session, participants were engaged in the question of which of the suspects was responsible for the crime; something that remained a topic for discussion in the post-game interview. Discussion on the game's length and complexity remained short, with participants stating that both seemed appropriate. Apart of this, participants stressed the need for a concluding narrative after accusing a suspect, which could in itself be used to reveal whether or not a group had made the right choice. Finally, participants commented on the fact that the game had provided them with a more 'personal connection' with artefacts that they would have considered uninteresting in a regular museum visit.

5.2   Digital Prototype Testing

After the testing of the paper prototype, a first digital prototype was developed. This prototype had the basic functionality of the game, such as scanning of a QR code to indicate gathering of a clue, as well as visual references in the form of photos of the artefacts. The digital prototype still lacked the functionality to complete the game, however, and the interface had not yet been designed in regards to visual aesthetics. Similar to the paper prototype test session, the digital prototype was tested in a simulated museum environment with photos indicating the positions of the artefacts. Three different students of a game studies course at the local university were once again invited to test the game. At this point we were primarily interested in observing how participants handled the application, and whether it was able to guide the play session without additional explanations. In general, participants behaved similar to those who had played the paper prototype: remaining mostly together as a group, discussing their take on the story whenever a new clue came in, and finally deliberating who to accuse.

In the concluding interview, participants highlighted the uneven text distribution amongst player characters and the slow response of the QR scanner as problems. While participants mentioned that the game gave them a human perspective on the artefacts, they also made clear that testing outside the museum setting was a limiting factor. Participants felt unconnected to the artefact itself and would have enjoyed to explore it up close, especially after having played through a narrative that involved them so prominently. Overall, the digital prototype managed to fulfil its purpose, as players remained engaged throughout, and were able to progress through the parts of the game that had been implemented by this point.

After the test session, we focused our development efforts on implementing the suspect accusation mechanic, improving the speed and handling of the QR scanner (e.g. by indicating a target distance through lining up the code with visual markers), and added visual elements to the application to make it more appealing.

6   On-Site User Testing

The final test within the scope of this study used a feature complete version of the game, and took place at the National Museum of Archaeology in Malta. We received permission to test the game in the Phoenician exhibit for one afternoon, and were further given the opportunity to test the game with members of the staff to get feedback from their perspective, which we evaluated separately from the responses of museum visitors. One caveat for this test session was the request by the museum to approach visitors only on their way out of the exhibition in order to not disturb their regular experience. This meant that all test participants played the game with at least some prior knowledge of the featured artefacts. Data for this test was collected in two steps: a researcher observed the way participants played, and afterwards conducted short exit interviews with the participants. The following questions were asked, all of which were followed up with the request to elaborate (Fig. 2):

1. *What did you like/dislike about the game?*
2. *How did going through the exhibit with the game compare to going through without?*
3. *Would you play a game like this again?*
4. *Did playing the game change the way you understand the Phoenicians?*

When interviewing staff members, we replaced the last two questions with: *(3) Do you think that an application like this would be a useful addition to a museum exhibit?* and *(4) Is there anything you would like to see added or changed to make the game more museum friendly?*

Participants were each given a small tablet with the application running, as well as instructions of the goal of the game, and how to operate the QR scanner (i.e. where the camera on the device is located). After participants had finished the game and accused a suspect, a researcher would take them aside and ask them about their experience.

6.1   Testing Results

Tests were conducted with 13 people, 3 of which were museum staff. Test sessions involved two 2-player sessions with senior couples, a 2-player session with a

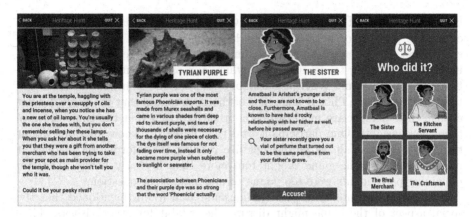

Fig. 2. Screenshots of the final prototype, from left to right: (1) clue found when scanning the oil lamp artefact, (2) codex entry relevant to the narrative, (3) suspect screen with clues found so far, (4) accusation screen.

middle-aged couple, a 2-player session with students, a 2-player session with children (under the age of 10), and a 3-player session with the museum staff. In general, testing sessions lasted between 10 and 15 min. In contrast to prior test sessions, all player groups spread out in order to find clues, only convening once they had found all the clues. Four of the participants went through every piece of information offered by the application (including the 'Codex' screen with supplementary information), while the other nine only used the 'Codex' and 'Suspects' screen when they were stuck. In most of the sessions, participants asked for assistance by the researcher to inform them whether they had found every clue available. Apart of this, older participants tended to require assistance with scanning QR codes, suggesting that our efforts to make this aspect more user friendly were not fully successful.

In the post-game interviews, both staff and visitors expressed enjoyment of the game, highlighting that the game provided additional background regarding the every-day context of exhibited artefacts. All groups suggested they would play a game like this again if given the chance. The test session conducted with two children suggested that the narrative was difficult to grasp in its entirety for younger participants, but at the same time did not seem to hinder engagement with the mystery, or the involved artefacts. One couple mentioned that they liked how the game presented them with a different experience than they normally would have found in a heritage museum. Another couple enjoyed that they had to think about the clues critically, and required thought from the players to solve. In general, most participants expressed interest in the narrative and its characters, as well as having the narrative revolve around the exhibited artefacts. On the other hand, one participant thought that the artefacts were not involved enough, and found that too much time was spent looking at the game screen. Apart of the game content, three of the tested groups mentioned trouble with using the QR scanner, though they also mentioned that handling became easier once they got used to it. One participant mentioned that a more expressive positive or negative feedback would have been appreciated at the completion of the game. Another comment was made in regards to the social impact of gathering to discuss clues, which one participant mentioned as the best part of the game. When asked about whether the game changed the way they understood the Phoenicians, four of the visitors said that the game did not change their perspective much, while another four said that the game did give them new insights. One participant said that he hardly knew anything about the Phoenicians at all, as he did not like reading the information plaques at museums, and so the game taught him more than he knew before. The two remaining participants were too young to understand the question.

Finally, in our interview with the museum staff it was mentioned that the social aspect of the game might disrupt the exhibit for other visitors. They suggested a designated spot outside of the exhibit (but still inside the museum) where the players might be able to discuss their findings. The museum staff was particularly enthusiastic about the game's ability to raise interest for exhibition artefacts that could be considered less 'eye-catching' than others.

7   Discussion

Out of all test sessions, the final on-side test session was, predictably, the most revealing. While this does not devalue the impact of the prior evaluations, it is also clear that simulated evaluation sessions can only serve as a rough indication. Where before players had stuck together and discussed their thoughts after each new clue, in the museum setting all of the participant groups split up and only discussed their findings at the end. The participants were observed to be quieter, likely due to the fundamentally hushed atmosphere of the exhibit. They engaged in fewer discussions throughout, instead reading both artefact signage and game narrative on their own, before coming together to complete the game. Something that did not show in our previous tests (in a simulated museum environment) was that many people go through an exhibit at their own pace, even when visiting in a group. Several of the participants had gone around on their own during their initial visit of the exhibit as well, and then continued this behaviour when they started playing the game. The lack of social interaction did not seem to impact whether participants enjoyed the experience, however. From our perspective, there is no 'wrong' way to play the game, and especially given concern by the museum staff that discussion could distract other visitors, it is encouraging that different forms of play can be accommodated. The suggestion of the museum staff to provide designated areas at which a suspect can be accused could easily be implemented and would allow the museum to strike a balance between not disturbing non-playing visitors, while offering visitors the possibility to engage with artefacts through a mobile game.

The test provided valuable insight into how different museum visitors interact with the game, especially when comparing very young players with seniors. Although seniors experienced some trouble in using the tablet, they were still interested in the game itself and were observed to be very engaged with the content. They, also, answered that they would play a game like this again if they had the chance, suggesting that the game does not have an upper age limit. Although an increasing amount of seniors will likely be familiar with smartphones and tablets as these devices continue to become more ubiquitous, developers should consider further ways of mediating issues in using the game's technology (e.g. through interface design or exploring alternative hardware).

One of the user tests included two children of the ages seven and nine. The text-heavy nature of the game, for which a minimum level of reading comprehension is required, proved to be too complex to follow for the seven-year-old. The nine-year-old was engaged in the experience, despite not being fully capable of drawing conclusions from the text independently. Towards the end of the test she noted that the game had been fun. This was an unexpected finding, as the game does not feature many things that children are used to in modern games (e.g. many visual cues, sounds, or animations). It suggests that this kind of gaming experience could potentially work for children, but in its current state would not work without direct supervision and participation from an adult as well.

Those looking to develop games for museum spaces need to deal with a wide ranging target audience. A possible solution for varying ages could be to implement the selection of an age-range or difficulty at the start of the game. Our results indicate that age is not a factor in whether participants enjoyed the game, but content will need to be tailored to different age groups. In addition to age, differences in nationality are also a frequent occurrence. Museums generally provide their information material in different languages, and this needs to be considered for any game in a museum space as well; even in our small user test the use of only English text caused a problem. Any story-based game developed for general museum visitors (i.e. not only children) will therefore need a minimum amount of content that is adapted and translated to accommodate these differences.

In regards to the original aim of this project – to develop a game that promotes a better understanding of the everyday cultural context of the artefacts on display – the test brought mixed results, with the same amount of people reporting that the game gave them new insights as there were people reporting it did not. A reason given by one of the more sceptical participants was that the game did not relate to the artefacts enough to think more about their use. Although the game draws clear connections to the artefacts on display, the point could be made that the information about them is not integral to the clues (i.e. the information important to a player focused on solving the mystery) being collected. While the aim is to give an impression of the daily use of such an item, it is possible some players are more focused on getting the relevant information for their goal of finishing the game, therefore not spending more time thinking about the larger context. Future games could remedy this by putting the relevant artefacts themselves more at the centre of the story. The game may have worked as intended on those players that felt like they had gotten a better understanding of the Phoenicians from playing the game, however. Further testing and more in-depth interviews would be needed to explore how the game works for different players.

Factors that likely influenced how participants interacted with the game, were some of the testing limitations. Participants played the game after having finished their visit of the exhibit, rather than as a simultaneous activity. We consider it likely that this contributed to some participants being more focused on finishing the game rather than spending time thinking about the artefacts and the historical context of the mystery. In terms of data gathering, it is possible that participants were influenced by the presence of the game's developer and were less forthcoming in their answers than had the test been conducted by an external party. Although we considered direct observation of player behaviour by the game designer to be valuable at this stage in the project, it is possible participants were less critical of their experience or forthcoming in their answers. Further testing of such a game should ideally happen in closer collaboration with the museum in question and be performed by the museum staff or an external party.

Overall, the user tests confirmed that there is a demand for games in museum spaces, and show the potential universal appeal of roleplaying, narrative-based games in such spaces. Moving forward, we would consider alternatives to QR codes in any future iterations or projects. Although they functioned as intended, the use of Bluetooth beacons or similar technology would be less obtrusive in a museum space, and potentially be less difficult to interact with for older participants. It would allow for players to be notified of a clue automatically once they are in close proximity, rather than having to scan a code. This could help in keeping the player's focus on the exhibit and the larger context of the story, rather than finishing the game.

Additionally we foresee potential in the creation of authoring tools for museum staff. This type of game can easily be adapted to different exhibits by replacing the text and images. It would therefore be an inexpensive way of continuously delivering new content relevant to what is on display at a given time.

8 Conclusion

The aim of this study was to explore the possibility of narrative-based games to enhance visitors' museum experiences. Through narrative and role-playing elements, we attempted to provide visitors with a more complete picture of the people living in the past than out-of-context artefacts tend to provide. This was done by connecting objects on display to a story, in which the players take on the roles of historical figures as they try to solve a mystery.

The process of developing this game brought to light some of the challenges in designing games for museum spaces, for instance the importance of tailoring content to visitors of different ages and backgrounds. It also showed how simulated testing, while essential to the development process, does not always provide the same results as testing within the actual museum space. It is therefore essential that games developed for museums are done so in close collaboration with the museum involved and are extensively tested in the intended environment. Targeted research in how museum spaces affect player behaviour could prove very beneficial in these efforts.

The results of our tests suggest that there is a demand for interactive and game-like experiences within museum spaces. While such experiences can be found in museums all over the world, their implementation is far from being ubiquitous and participants in our study were still surprised about the concept of playing in a museum. Our user tests further suggest specific potential for narrative and roleplaying elements to contextualize heritage exhibits, and to engage a range of visitors, with half of the participants indicating that playing the game deepened their understanding of the Phoenician people.

The further back in time one goes, the less is often known about a culture. With only physical artefacts remaining and little representations of people (e.g. through statues or paintings), a game like *Heritage Hunt* can help visitors relate to the people of ancient civilizations and gain an understanding that is difficult to conceive from artefacts alone. This paper takes the first steps towards introducing roleplaying mechanics to museum spaces in the hope that others will follow in the footsteps towards combining innovation and games in heritage museums.

Acknowledgements. We would like to thank the participants in this study for their time, as well as the staff of the National Museum of Archaeology of Malta for their support.

References

1. American Museum of Natural History: MicroRangers (2015). http://www.amnh.org/learn-teach/families/microrangers/. Accessed 16 Mar 2017
2. Bennett, T.: The Birth of the Museum: History, Theory, Politics. Routledge, London (1995)
3. Bernhaupt, R.: User experience evaluation in entertainment. In: Bernhaupt, R. (ed.) Evaluating User Experience in Games, pp. 3–7. Springer, London (2010). https://doi.org/10.1007/978-1-84882-963-3_1
4. Bowman, S.L.: The Functions of Role-Playing Games: How Participants Create Community, Solve Problems and Explore Identity. McFarland, Jefferson (2010)
5. Daniau, S.: The transformative potential of role-playing games: from play skills to human skills. Simul. Gaming **47**(4), 423–444 (2016)
6. Falk, J.H., Dierking, L.D.: Learning From Museums: Visitor Experiences and the Making of Meaning. Altamira Press, Walnut Creek (2000)
7. Ferreira, B.: How games are changing the museum experience (2016). http://motherboard.vice.com/en_us/article/yp3wwj/how-games-are-changing-the-museum-experience. Accessed 16 Mar 2017
8. Kelly, L., Groundwater-Smith, S.: Revisioning the physical and on-line museum: a partnership with the coalition of knowledge building schools. J. Mus. Educ. **34**(1), 55–68 (2009)

9. Marty, P.F., Jones, K.B.: Museum Informatics: People, Information, and Technology in Museums. Routledge, London (2012)
10. Mortara, M., Catalano, C.E., Bellotti, F., Fiucci, G., Houry-Panchetti, M., Petridis, P.: Learning cultural heritage by serious games. J. Cult. Herit. **15**(3), 318–325 (2014)
11. Ravelli, L.: Museum Texts: Communication Frameworks. Routledge, London (2006)
12. Smithsonian Institution: Results of the 2004 Smithsonian-wide Survey of Museum Visitors (2004). http://www.si.edu/content/opanda/docs/rpts2004/04. 10.visitors2004.final.pdf. Accessed 15 Mar 2017
13. Takatalo, J., Häkkinen, J., Kaistinen, J., Nyman, G.: Presence, involvement, and flow in digital games. In: Bernhaupt, R. (ed.) Evaluating User Experience in Games, pp. 23–46. Springer, London (2010). https://doi.org/10.1007/978-1-84882-963-3_3
14. Witcomb, A.: Re-imagining the Museum: Beyond the Mausoleum. Psychology Press, London (2003)

Words in Freedom: A Manifesto Machine as Critical Design

Simone Ashby[✉] ⓘ, Julian Hanna ⓘ, Sónia Matos, and Ricardo Rodrigues ⓘ

Madeira Interactive Technologies Institute (M-ITI), Funchal, Portugal
{simone.ashby,julian.hanna,sonia.matos,ricardo.rod}@m-iti.org

Abstract. Words in Freedom is a design project aimed at artists, activists, and others that draws from research on the manifesto to create a studio environment or 'Manifesto Machine'. Drawing primarily on the sub-disciplines of Design for Good and Critical Design, this project seeks to enhance conscious self-expression and empowerment while questioning design's inbuilt optimism and the effects of automation on human agency. When we automate for improved performance, what do we lose in the process? Do the benefits outweigh the loss of agency? How can technology aid expression without over determining it? Ultimately, Words in Freedom seeks to create a collaborative writing environment that strikes the right balance between freedom and constraint, agency and inspiration. We trace the manifesto's return to prominence in digital form, arguing for its usefulness as a potent discursive artifact. We then describe the Manifesto Machine as a set of tools to help write and disseminate persuasive manifestos, introducing our initial prototype (or probe, as in Reflective Design) as a means of conducting our primary research, engaging with groups and understanding social practices around declaring principles and beliefs.

Keywords: Manifestos · Activism · Critical Design · Reflective Design
Collaborative virtual environments

1 Background

'Manifestos exist to challenge and provoke' [8].

How to write a manifesto? The manifesto may be defined as 'a declaration of artistic aims and principles loosely based on the revolutionary political form of the 19th century, for example *The Communist Manifesto*. It is usually a pamphlet-length, polemical, public declaration' [9]. According to F.T. Marinetti, the leader of Italian Futurism and the most prolific manifesto writer of the 20th century, the key elements of any manifesto are 'violence and precision' [19]. Manifestos must be bold and direct like the advertisements they imitate.

The manifesto is currently one of most vital and adaptable online genres. The sudden acceleration in mobile computing a decade ago, including the rapid rise of social media and image-and-slogan-dependent 'meme culture', combined with the mainstreaming of political activism, have contributed to the manifesto's timeliness. Today the manifesto is more relevant than ever: no grassroots political movement, startup, online zine or

© Springer International Publishing AG, part of Springer Nature 2018
A. D. Cheok et al. (Eds.): ACE 2017, LNCS 10714, pp. 557–566, 2018.
https://doi.org/10.1007/978-3-319-76270-8_38

hacker collective is complete without a declaration of principles. From Postcapitalism [21] to Xenofeminism [11], Occupy [18] to Black Lives Matter [2], movements are using manifestos to announce themselves to the world.

Building on the 'manifesto moment' heralded by the current era of online activism, we present the preliminary results of a new project, Words in Freedom, which analyses innovations in form, content, and dissemination signaled by the digital manifesto (and its analogue predecessor), maps what has been done in recent years, and grows the capacity for future interventions in the form of a 'Manifesto Machine'. While we are designing a tool or 'machine' for making manifestos, our purpose extends beyond simple technical facilitation and what Dunne and Raby call 'design's inbuilt optimism' [6]. We want to encourage users to reflect – through collaboration, conscious expression, and public dissemination – on what they stand for and why, and how their beliefs might intersect with the beliefs of others. In so doing, we hope to invite reflection on the productive and potentially undervalued role of criticality in HCI, in effect fusing two sub-disciplines: Design for Good [1] and Critical Design [6]. As Tonkinwise has argued: 'Designing that does not … Criticize, Provoke, Discourse, Interrogate, Probe, Play, is inadequate designing' [22].

One area where Critical Design and HCI diverge is in their approach to problem solving. Generally speaking Critical (or Speculative) Design seeks not to solve a problem *per se* but to stage it dramatically, to encourage engagement, invite reflection, and embody critique. Frequently cited aims of Critical Design and Design Fiction include provoking action and debate [7, 13], opening up discursive spaces [12], forcing conversations [3], and 'inspir[ing] and encourag[ing] people's imaginations to flow freely' [6]. These aims correspond closely with the aims of the manifesto itself – which exists 'to challenge and provoke' [8] – making the Manifesto Machine an ideal Critical Design object.

Combining Critical Design with the digital manifesto also opens the way towards greater attention to activism, engagement and critical self-reflection within the field of HCI. Our work shares affinities with Reflective Design, which 'supports scepticism' about its own design and draws on critical approaches to HCI in 'folding critical reflection into the practice of technology design' [20], and Participatory Design, in which users play an active role in the design process [5]. In particular, we position our initial prototype as a technological probe [10] as framed by [20] for understanding users and social practices, and as a means of inviting critical reflection as the basis for inspiring further design.

2   Introduction

As social media in the age of political crisis demonstrates, people want to say something and want to be heard. The difficulty is that it is sometimes hard to know what to say, which is why so many opinions are just reposts of the opinions of others [16]. It is hard to know what you believe until you say it out loud, or how to say it confidently and clearly.

In a recent interview [4], the filmmaker Adam Curtis argued that the weakness of early social media-led manifestations such as Occupy and Tahrir Square was that participants had no unified or articulated vision, only processes, networks, channels of dissemination. There was a powerful desire for change, but no vision yet of that better world. What these movements failed to do, according to Curtis, was to harness people's desires with a clear dramatic vision, to excite imaginations with narratives of power that have always been at the heart of politics and history. One answer to this shortcoming is the manifesto, which creates dramatic narratives of power (e.g. 'A spectre is haunting Europe' [14]) and performative visions of possible futures to seize the imagination and win converts. One key question that emerges is thus how can we facilitate the creation of compelling narratives in our Manifesto Machine?

Given this backdrop, we sought to build a creative and collaborative environment that gives like-minded individuals the tools and inspiration to draft, design, and disseminate coherent and persuasive manifestos. As Laboria Cuboniks, the artist collective that wrote 'The Xenofeminist Manifesto' (2015), states: 'The whole point of writing something like [a manifesto] is to try to reshape the discursive chessboard' [11]. That is what we are challenging users to do with the Manifesto Machine: to empower artists and activists to overcome barriers to participation (shyness, lack of knowledge, sense of authority) and discover the freedom-within-constraints that manifesto writing offers, with the ultimate goal of supporting activism and changing society as a whole.

3 Designing for Bold Expression

Our approach to the Manifesto Machine began with the definition of a set of constraints, which we determined were necessary to encourage wider participation and engagement, and to steer the interaction. The main constraints govern: idea generation and text input, canvas, typeface and control panel aesthetics, and publishing. Manifestos usually follow strict templates handed down from well known historical examples: *The Communist Manifesto*, the US *Declaration of Independence*, avant-garde manifestos of Futurism, Dada, Surrealism, etc. Common features of the manifesto might include: a preamble, providing an account of events leading up to the present; a numbered list of tenets, usually complaints or demands; a call (or series of calls) to action; and so on. Drawing on some of these templates for our initial probe, we assembled a stock of keywords and phrases to assist idea generation and guide the writing process. While we do not intend to emphasize the use of stock phrases in successive iterations of the Manifesto Machine, our immediate objective was to sidestep the barrier less experienced authors face in undertaking a new writing project: the blinking cursor in a sea of white.

Initially, we conceived of these elements as fitting inside old-fashioned typesetter drawers (Fig. 1). In the current iteration (Figs. 2, 3 and 4), phrases (e.g. 'We affirm', 'We declare') appear in searchable drop-down lists, arranged by rhetorical category (e.g. 'Intentions') on the left of the canvas. The user can drag and drop text elements onto the canvas and position them as desired. Inputting new text elements dims the background and places focus on the text box. Users can also free-type in the canvas and add their own words and phrases to the 'My Words' drawer and enable them to be shared with other users.

Fig. 1. Paper prototype fashioned after a 19th century typesetter cabinet, with pull-out drawers for selecting boilerplate phrases.

Fig. 2. The Manifesto Machine desktop and mobile visualizations.

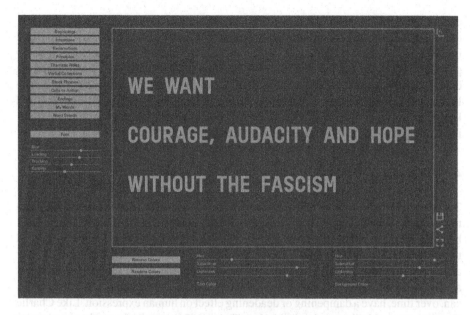

Fig. 3. Initial Manifesto Machine probe, which enables the user to play with text and background color. Color transformations that are applied to the canvas are also applied to the entire interface.

Fig. 4. Close-up of drop-down lists.

For the canvas, typeface, and control panel aesthetics, we aimed for a balance between freedom, usability, consistency, and minimum standards for a well designed end product. Sliders allow the user to choose from a curated selection of avant-garde, open-source fonts, and control size, leading, tracking, and kerning. Color is manipulated in the same way, governing the hue, saturation, and lightness for both text and background. There are additional options to reverse or select a random color scheme (opposite complementary colors, based on color theory), and to save, share or adjust screen size. Font manipulations happen in real time with browsing. For the canvas, both portrait and landscape views are possible, with aesthetic choices extending to the entire interface, including control panels, to minimize distraction.

4 Discussion

The automation of uncomfortably human actions, actions with heart, risks taking us into the territory of the uncanny – the same phenomenon that creates an empathetic 'valley' between people and humanoid robots [15]. The user might ask: Am I being encouraged to automate my political views? My self-expression? My values and principles? My anger and outrage? Allowing technology to facilitate too much thinking, feeling, or acting on our behalf – for example, re-tweeting a meme to express political dissent – can, over time, have a dampening or deadening effect on human expression. Like Charlie Chaplin's assembly line worker in *Modern Times* (1936), we risk becoming less human and more machine-like (Fig. 5).

Fig. 5. Charlie Chaplin in assembly line scene from *Modern Times* (1936).

Increasingly, we permit corporate entities such as Facebook and Twitter to do our protesting for us, rather than engaging directly through collective action and mobilization. At risk are our rhetorical skills and our ability to argue and act outside our bubble. Confronting our own passivity and willingness to allow our deepest selves – our values, principles, political beliefs, etc. – to be automated and controlled by corporations, sold for entertainment, is the first step towards ensuring that the Manifesto Machine can truly function as an effective tool for enabling bold expression.

Our project questions technologies that enhance and automate self-expression, thus functioning on two levels: as both tool and critique. Much of the work still lies ahead of us in deploying the aforementioned medium-fidelity probe within a co-design setting with activist and artist groups for an initial exploration of user experiences with collaborative manifesto writing. With respect to collaboration, we acknowledge that functionalities around group discussion, weighing solutions, and reaching compromise remain to be understood and built into the design. These are insights that can only be gained through interventions with the current and subsequent probes.

In terms of critique, we expect that these interventions will offer early insights into the satisfaction and comfort level felt by new authors tasked with putting beliefs into words (and images) in a technology mediated context. For example, does the end product adequately reflect users' true beliefs? How can technology aid expression without over-determining it? How can a manifesto writing environment play a supporting role without diminishing authorial agency? Is the language of historical manifestos useful for self-expression in the digital age? What other affordances do people require to enable an effective collaborative writing experience that yields meaningful expression aided by clear communication design? Is the manifesto inherently static, or should it be allowed to evolve over time? Does the Manifesto Machine merely lead users in the direction of shallow sloganeering and inauthentic expression? How do we define meaningful expression in the digital age?

Drawing on the constructive provocation, self-awareness, healthy scepticism, and co-design feedback of Critical Design, Reflective Design, Participatory Design, and similar critical approaches, Words in Freedom aims at facilitating meaningful self-expression without replicating the co-optation for commercial or entertainment value propagated by corporate entities such as Facebook and Twitter. We want to help users rationalize their feelings in such a way as to be able to externalize problems, discuss with groups of collaborators, and propose and share ideas in a participatory process.

5   Conclusions and Future Work

In this paper we have presented a Manifesto Machine that explores design affordances to enable ordinary users to create eye-catching and persuasive statements of principle. We showcased our earliest efforts – creating a collaborative online environment, importing and combining bold exclamations and calls to action from historical manifestos, and playing with vivid complementary colors – with an emphasis on making manifesto writing easier. And yet, this is only the first step in the process of designing an effective and engaging manifesto studio environment that helps users create and collaborate actively on meaningful expression.

As indicated above, the next step will be a participatory design study, involving a selection of artist and activist groups, which uses the current iteration of the Manifesto Machine as a technological probe for exploring the balance between agency and passivity with regard to technology and sociopolitical expression.

Fig. 6. Early example of a critical take on meme activism from Jenny Holzer's *Truisms* series [23].

Fig. 7. An old Solari airport arrivals board becomes a public display for a manifesto.

Manifestos are bold proclamations, but they are also ephemeral by nature: they are written for the moment, to be hurled across barricades or pushed into the hands of strangers. Preserving this ephemerality and temporality will be important. Using interaction design to create new possibilities in activist practices, rather than aiming primarily to solve problems, is another essential element to the Manifesto Machine. Thus, additional future work will involve user studies *in situ*, testing how collaborative writing might best be supported (e.g. borrowing from the book sprint methodology), how different forms of dissemination could work, and what kind of media could be used to encourage participation. We also aim to move beyond the internet, where 'memefestos' are viewed and quickly forgotten, to more public, tangible, analogue forms of output. Following the example of artists such as Jenny Holzer [e.g. 23] (Fig. 6), we have already experimented with a Solari display [17] that has been hacked to receive text (Fig. 7).

Acknowledgments. We gratefully acknowledge the financial support of the Associated Robotic Laboratories LARSyS (PEstLA9-UID/EEA/50009/2013) that made this research possible.

References

1. AIGA (American Institute of Graphic Arts), Design for Good. http://www.aiga.org/design-for-good. Accessed 29 July 2017
2. Black Lives Matter, Guiding Principles. http://blacklivesmatter.com/guiding-principles/. Accessed 28 July 2017
3. Bleecker, J.: Design Fiction: A Short Essay on Design, Science, Fact and Fiction, March 2009. http://drbfw5wfjlxon.cloudfront.net/writing/DesignFiction_WebEdition.pdf. Accessed 23 May 2017
4. Chapo Trap House Podcast Interview With Adam Curtis, 12 December 2016. https://soundcloud.com/chapo-trap-house/episode-65-no-future-feat-adam-curtis-121216. Accessed 04 Feb 2017
5. DiSalvo, C., Clement, A., Pipek, V.: Participatory design for, with, and by communities. In: Simonsen, J., Robertson, T. (eds.) International Handbook of Participatory Design, pp. 182–209. Routledge, Oxford (2012)
6. Dunne, A., Raby, F.: Speculative Everything: Design, Fiction, and Social Dreaming. MIT Press, Cambridge (2013)
7. Dunne, A., Raby, F.: Critical Design FAQ (2011). http://www.dunneandraby.co.uk/content/bydandr/13/0. Accessed 28 July 2017
8. Hanna, J.: Manifestos: a manifesto. In: The Atlantic, 24 June 2014. https://www.theatlantic.com/entertainment/archive/2014/06/manifestos-a-manifesto-the-10-things-all-manifestos-need/372135/. Accessed 03 Mar 2017
9. Hanna, J.: Key Concepts in Modernist Literature. Palgrave Macmillan, London (2008)
10. Hutchinson, H., Mackay, W., Westerlund, B., et al.: Technology probes: inspiring design for and with families. In: Proceedings of the SIGCHI Conference on Human Factors in Computing Systems, pp. 17–24. ACM (2003)
11. Laboria Cuboniks: The Xenofeminist Manifesto. http://www.laboriacuboniks.net. Accessed 11 Mar 2017
12. Lindley, J., Coulton, P.: Back to the future: 10 years of design fiction. In: Proceedings of the 2015 British HCI Conference, pp. 210–211. ACM (2015)
13. Malpass, M.: Between wit and reason: defining associative, speculative, and critical design in practice. Des. Culture **5**(3), 333–356 (2013)
14. Marx, K., Engels, F.: The communist manifesto. In: Tucker, C. (ed.) The Marx-Engels Reader, pp. 335–362. Norton, New York (1972)
15. Mori, M.: Bukimi No Tani (The Uncanny Valley). Energy **7**, 33–35 (1970)
16. Morozov, E.: The brave new world of Slacktivism. In: Foreign Policy, 19 May 2009. http://neteffect.foreignpolicy.com/posts/2009/05/19/the_brave_new_world_of_slacktivism. Accessed 29 July 2017

17. Nisi, V., Jorge, C., Nunes, N., Hanna, J.: Madeira story generator: prospecting serendipitous storytelling in public spaces. In: The Proceedings of Entertainment Computing, pp. 15–27 (2016)
18. Occupy Movement, The 'GlobalMay Manifesto' of the International Occupy Assembly, 11 May 2012. https://www.theguardian.com/commentisfree/2012/may/11/occupy-globalmay-manifesto. Accessed 28 July 2017
19. Perloff, M.: The Futurist Moment: Avant-Garde, Avant-Guerre, and the Language of Rupture. University of Chicago Press, Chicago (2004)
20. Sengers, P., Boehner, K., David, S., Kaye, J.: Reflective design. In: Proceedings of the 4th Decennial Conference on Critical Computing, pp. 49–58. ACM (2005)
21. Srnicek, N., Williams, A.: Inventing the Future: Postcapitalism and a World Without Work. Verso, London (2016)
22. Tonkinwise, C.: Just Design: Being Dogmatic About Defining Speculative Critical Design Future Fiction. https://medium.com/@camerontw/just-design-b1f97cb3996f. Accessed 28 May 2017
23. Waldman, D.: Jenny Holzer. Guggenheim, New York (1989)

Omnidirectional Video in Museums – Authentic, Immersive and Entertaining

Jaakko Hakulinen[✉] ⓘ, Tuuli Keskinen ⓘ, Ville Mäkelä ⓘ, Santeri Saarinen ⓘ,
and Markku Turunen ⓘ

University of Tampere, Tampere, Finland
{jaakko.hakulinen,tuuli.keskinen,ville.mi.makela,
santeri.saarinen,markku.turunen}@uta.fi

Abstract. Omnidirectional video (ODV) provides possibilities for capture and presentation of cultural content for museums and other exhibitions. 360° video capture can record authentic environments and activities, and enables immersive viewing of such material. We present the potential of ODV by reporting the learnings from long-term user experience data collection with two ODV-based museum installations; a head mounted display (HMD) based rally simulator, and a road grader simulator utilizing three projectors and haptic feedback. The results show the value of immersion, provide insights into the possibilities and challenges of interactivity, and show, how haptic feedback can improve the overall experience. The results also provide support to the use of physical elements in museum installations. In addition, we managed to avoid cyber sickness, a common problem with immersive VR content, in the installations. Overall, the respondents strongly support the conception that these kinds of installations would make museums more desirable places to visit.

Keywords: Omnidirectional video · 360° video · Museum installation
User experience · Immersion · Haptic feedback · Head mounted display

1 Introduction

360° video, aka omnidirectional video (ODV) provides possibilities for the capture and presentation of cultural content for museums and other exhibitions. Video can be used to capture authentic places, environments and activities, and full spherical 360° capture enables immersive viewing of such material. The limitation is that ODV is still static video in spherical form, and therefore ways to interact with it are restricted. Still, within the restrictions, many kinds of interactions are possible. Compared to modeling 3D graphics, ODV capture is cost efficient and it ensures authenticity of the resulting material and thus can also have significant cultural-historical value. To produce 360° video, the captured place or activity needs to be physically accessed. However, video can often be captured in locations and during activities, where most museum goers would not be able to go to or join in real life. It is also possible to capture historic events which cannot be experienced any other time.

© Springer International Publishing AG, part of Springer Nature 2018
A. D. Cheok et al. (Eds.): ACE 2017, LNCS 10714, pp. 567–587, 2018.
https://doi.org/10.1007/978-3-319-76270-8_39

In many cases, ODV is viewed with what can be considered immersive setups. Head-mounted displays (HMD) are the most common and most immersive. Still, CAVE type solutions utilizing multiple projectors or displays can also reach significant levels of immersion [11]. Both share the fundamental interaction where content can be observed naturally by turning one's head towards a point of interest - whether it be accessed through the viewport of a HMD, or observed in a CAVE via the surrounding displays. The resulting immersion can lead to interesting and engaging experiences and is therefore often desirable.

In the context of museums, 360° video can be valuable for several reasons. For visitors, it can provide engaging experiences, which can attract more people. The engagement can also have pedagogical value as engaged visitors may absorb more information. When visitors are allowed to choose what part of the omnidirectional video they are looking at, different visitors may also focus on details that are particularly interesting to them. ODV can also provide means to record culturally significant environments and experiences in an efficient and comprehensive manner.

To study the possibilities of ODV in the context of museums we created two installations to automobile and road museum Mobilia (Kangasala, Finland); a simulator of a vintage road grader, followed by a rally simulator. These utilize ODV in different ways. The HMD-based rally simulator provides a more common approach with minimal interaction but the viewing takes place inside an actual rally car. In contrast, the road grader simulator features a rough physical replica of a grader interior, utilizes three projectors, and provides more interactivity (compared to the rally simulator) as the system reacts to pedals and a steering wheel. Both installations utilize audio (vehicle sounds, speech), and the grader simulator also features haptic feedback in the simulator's seat.

In this paper, we look at the subjective feedback collected with several iterations of the installations. This work provides understanding on the effects of additional modalities, different levels of immersion, and different levels of interactivity on user experience. The work considers also the target user group in the museum which includes children in great proportion. Feedback for the four versions of the road grader was gathered during a period of two years starting from June 2015, and feedback for the rally simulator was gathered for one year starting from June 2016. The results illustrate the value of immersive viewing and show how haptic feedback can improve the overall experience. We also present effects of different interaction metaphors. Finally, we discuss how cyber sickness can be avoided, as demonstrated by our HMD-based rally simulator installation.

Next, we will provide background on the utilization of ODV in interactive installations. Sections 3 and 4 describe our installations and the feedback we have collected during their deployment in the museum environment. Section 5 summarizes and discusses our experiences and findings, focusing on immersion, interactivity and the potential of additional modalities. We believe these concepts are critical in understanding the potential of ODV. The paper is closed with conclusions in Sect. 6.

2   Related Work

ODVs have been used in many domains and contexts. Remote operations and telepresence applications were the first serious applications [5, 7, 21, 35], therapeutic [9, 24, 28] and education [10] solutions have also been studied and consumer products have followed recently. Many of these applications offer interactive content and have UI elements which are often crucial features for pleasant user experience [4, 28]. Different interaction techniques in interactive omnidirectional video (iODV) [11] applications have also been studied. Desktop based interfaces [19] exists and most recent work has focused on HMD-based interaction, where head orientation and dwell-time based interaction is common [11]. Gesture-based interaction [2, 22, 25, 29, 37] and second-screen interfaces [36] have been studied as well. ODV has also been used to simulate AR interactions [3]. Some applications have utilized also additional modalities [26]. Argyriou et al. [1] as well as Saarinen et al. [30] have presented guidelines for omnidirectional videos in their research.

Simulators and other interactive installations in museums form one potential application of ODV. It has been utilized in various settings with historical and cultural content. Cultural heritage has been recorded and displayed [15, 16, 20], and various performances and events have been captured [e.g., 6, 17] and even used as part of theatrical experiences [8].

The application of ODVs usually relies on immersive approach. Immersion and (the feeling of) presence have been given various definitions by different authors. Slater [31] separates the two so that immersion is purely objective measure defined by rendering software and display technology. Related parameters include display field of view (FOV), field of regard (FOR), resolution, update frequency, and support for stereoscopy. In contrast, presence is "an individual and context-dependent user response" to using a system, an individual's experience of 'being there'. In this paper, we focus mostly on the objective immersion per Slater's definition, but also inquire about users' subjective views on feeling involved. A significant challenge with immersive virtual content consumption, including ODV content is that some users experience cyber sickness [27] as the result. This can be battled with well-designed content and interaction.

In immersive virtual reality, ODV can be contrasted to 3D content created either by modeling, utilizing existing CAD models or by capturing objects and environments, for example, with photogrammetry or laser scanning. Creating 3D content is in most cases a time-consuming process which requires high expertise. In contrast, capturing ODVs is possible with little training, in particular with the latest consumer grade cameras. The ODV captures a lot of detail, and where the virtual content should carefully match some real environment, ODVs can be particularly valuable.

ODV can be viewed in different ways. The recent advances in VR technology have made head mounted displays (HMD) the most discussed way but options range from viewing with regular computers (e.g., YouTube, Vimeo and Facebook support 360° video) to hand-held devices with magic lens style interaction and CAVE like environments consisting of multiple projectors or multiple large displays. From the interaction point of view, most ODV viewing setups allow users to control the viewing direction, be it by head orientation in HMD, device orientation with a hand-held mobile phone, or with mouse on desktop use. The weakness of ODVs is that it limits the user's movement in the virtual world. The user can only move between separate videos, unlike with full 3D content, where free exploration can be enabled. However, there are other forms of interaction possible with ODV content, which can be combined in novel ways. In addition to the traditional video controls (playback rate and position) [19], ODV allows different viewing projections which can create interesting effects. For example, so called small-planet projection (stereographic projection) creates an interesting view into videos, particularly to videos captured while the camera is moving.

While the array of ODVs applications found in literature provides many ideas and illustrations of the possibilities, the evaluations have been small-scale and mostly done in laboratories. As technology now allows real-life application of ODV-based solutions, there is need to validate the value of these solutions with real users and in real context. In the following, we present the long-term evaluations of two ODV-based museum installations and an analysis of feedback collected over several iterations. The results provide insights into aspects of such installations valued by museum visitors.

3   Road Grader Simulator

We looked at the possibilities of creating an interactive ODV based installation by building a road grader installation. The system is a simulator of a vintage road grader based on ODV, audio, and haptic feedback. It is targeted especially for families with children, including grandparents with their grandchildren. This target user group was specified by the museum personnel. An approach with a physical steering wheel and pedals was chosen since the target user group, according to the museum staff, values activities which resemble physical driving. The simulator is installed in a dedicated, darkened room and is part of the main exhibition of the museum. The simulator has been available for visitors since June 2015 and over the two years we have updated the system three times, resulting in four different iterations. Subjective feedback has been collected with a questionnaire the whole time and the collected feedback has both guided our development steps and provided data on the effects of these updates. These results are presented per iteration and discussed in the following. We start by describing the technical setups, and the system's evaluation procedure along with the findings.

3.1   System Description

The content of the road grader installation is based on 4K resolution (3840 * 1920 pixels, 25 fps) ODV. Although using videos makes it impossible to allow users to drive around freely, ODV was chosen because it is more cost-efficient to produce than 3D models, ensures the authenticity of the content and a real historical grader was available for capturing realistic material. A camera setup capable of capturing full spherical video was attached on the roof of the grader and a microphone was placed inside the cabin while the grader was driven around on small roads.

The current system setup of the simulator can be seen in Fig. 1. It consists of a large display (three full-HD projectors with picture area of about 6 * 1.5 m), a seat with haptic feedback, a steering wheel and brake and accelerator pedals, a computer, an audio speaker, and a set of sensors. The sensors are a 3D accelerometer and gyroscope for the steering wheel (Yocto3D by YoctoPuce[1]), linear potentiometers for the pedals (connected via a YoctoKnob), and a light sensor looking through a hole in the seat (YoctoLight) to detect whether someone is sitting on it. The setup is mechanically robust since the visitors cannot apply force directly to the sensors. The seat has a device called Buttkicker[2] to provide strong vibration feedback.

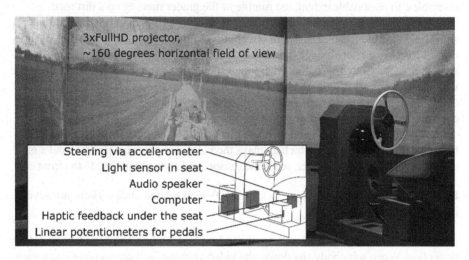

Fig. 1. The road grader simulator setup.

The display setup originally consisted of a single full-HD projector covering ~53° of the driver's field of view. This was later upgraded to three projectors whose image covers about 160° of the driver's horizontal field of view with the total horizontal resolution of 5760 pixels, which is higher than the resolution of the utilized video material. The display surfaces are flat and there are clearly visible edges between the three projection surfaces. The distance from driver's seat to the projection screens is roughly 2.5 m. The room is dimmed so that very little outside light comes in to ensure good contrast in the projected picture. The driver's seat is lit with a spotlight hanging from ceiling.

The steering wheel movement is limited to roughly 65° per direction so a single accelerometer can tell the steering angle. This is a mechanically simple solution with minimal moving parts. In the first version, the steering wheel rotation was unlimited and used a pulse counter rotated via a set of gears. The update was made because user feedback indicated that the initial solution did not provide good experience, and the implementation was prone to fail. For the third version we also updated the software so that a more distinct visual response to accelerating and braking is provided.

---

[1] http://www.yoctopuce.com/.

[2] http://www.thebuttkicker.com/.

The pedals and their mounting are from an old utility vehicle and therefore very sturdy. The linear potentiometers sensing the pedal movements are attached to the mounting and hidden inside the encasing of the system.

The haptic feedback on the seat utilizes a low frequency audio transducer which physically rumbles the seat in vertical direction based on audio signal. The audio is the same the users hear, consisting of engine sounds and various other noises the grader makes. The seat is mounted on rubber feet to allow movement. The resulting effect resembles, to reasonable extent, the rumble of the grader running on a dirt road.

The light sensor in the seat detects if somebody is sitting, and it is placed under a small hole near the front edge. There is a spotlight illuminating the seat, which ensures that the light sensor gets enough light in the darkened room when nobody is sitting down, and communicates to the visitors where they should go in the room. The only problem with the light sensor solution was that initially it was located too far back so that small children did not cover the sensor when sitting down. This was problematic since small children are in the target user group of the installation.

The computing hardware and software consists of PC computer running an HTML-based front end application, which displays the video and plays back audio, and a back end which acts as an http-server, reads the sensors and serves their data to the front end.

Interactivity. The system plays back the ODV and related audio. There are several interactive elements.

Sitting Down. When nobody is sitting, the video plays back in a so-called small planet projection. When somebody sits down, the video animates in three seconds into a view close to first person perspective (the camera was placed on the roof of the grader so the viewpoint is somewhat higher than in real life and vehicle interior is not visible).

The Break and Acceleration. The pedals control a simple simulation of driving speed and the related engine rpm. No gear changes were included in the simulation and the grader is simulated so that it never comes to complete halt, even if break is fully depressed. The speed is communicated in three different ways.

First, video playback rate is varied. There are two rates, 0.5 when the user is braking and 1.0 times original rate otherwise. The rate is not mapped directly to the virtual vehicle speed as playback of the high resolution (4K) video at random rates is unreliable. As people are not very good at detecting minor changes in video playback rate, this solution has not resulted in any negative feedback.

Second, audio matches the simulated engine RPM. From the recordings, sound clips with different constant RPM values and samples with increasing and decreasing RPM were selected. Based on the simulated engine RPM, appropriate samples are selected and played back with varying playback rate (rate adjustment changing the pitch of the sound to match the exact RPM). The software selects the sample, which matches the current situation with minimal change from the original sampling rate to create realistic vehicle sounds. The audio is both played back via the audio speaker and fed to the Buttkicker to create haptic feedback.

Third, video projection changes somewhat based on the speed. With the ODV both viewing direction and the field of view can be adjusted. The field of view of the central projector varies so that high speed has narrower field of view than slow speed (the average FOV is 60° and it can change ±15°). This effect emphasizes the appearance of motion even when the video playback speed does not change. In addition, the camera view tilts so that in fast speed the camera looks slightly downwards, displaying more road near the vehicle while slow speed shows more sky, further affecting the experienced speed.

Steering. Turning the steering wheel adjusts a set of visual parameters to provide some feeling of steering. Camera heading adjusts so that steering left turns the camera left and vice versa (i.e., like in a real vehicle). User comments indicated that some people would assume the camera to turn the other way and we experimented with both mappings. The maximum view rotation is about ±30°. We also tried rolling the camera sideways but this effect was considered potentially nauseating and was never included in the production versions. The virtual camera can also move sideways inside the video sphere creating some distortion somewhat similar to sideways movement. This effect is used to small extent, the maximum offset being 0.06 * video sphere radius.

The Iterations. The four main versions and the changes between them can be seen in Table 1.

Table 1. Summary of the different versions of the road grader simulator

Version	Main features	Main changes compared to the earlier version
1: "baseline"	1 projector (~53° FOV) unlimited steering wheel rotation	–
2: "haptic"	1 projector, haptic feedback	Haptic feedback (Buttkicker) installed
3: "3 screens"	3 projectors (~160° FOV), haptic feedback, steering limited to ±65°	Added projectors, steering wheel rotation limited
4: "inverted steering"	3 projectors, haptic feedback, limited steering with inverted visual effect	Camera turning logic changed to turn to the opposite direction as the steering wheel

3.2 Evaluation

We wanted to understand the user experience the installation provides and monitor, how the upgrades change it. Therefore, we collected subjective feedback from users with a questionnaire. With the data over the four iterations, we can also look at the roles of different elements in the experience. The long-term evaluation presented here covers data from altogether 215 respondents received between mid-June 2015 and early-June 2017.

Subjective Data Collection. User experiences were collected with a paper-form questionnaire. Because a suitable questionnaire was not readily available, one was created to correspond with the context, and the objectives of the system. The custom questionnaire was required partly due to the target user group. We needed a question-naire, which children, possibly with the help of their parents can fill in without guidance. This required simple phrasing and limited length, making most existing questionnaires, especially those focused on immersion and presence, unsuitable. We also wanted to cover aspects specific to the content. Thus, in addition to more general user experience aspects the questionnaire inquired about immersion and the appeal of the system in the context of a (automobile) museum. The questionnaire design was based on our earlier user experience evaluations and questionnaire development [e.g., 14, 33], including our earlier museum installation evaluations [32].

The questionnaire includes ten statements with a five-step rating scale on the range of *Totally disagree – Neither agree or disagree – Totally agree*. The statements can be seen in Fig. 2. In addition, the overall liking of the system was inquired with a five-step smiley face scale ranging between extremely unhappy (1) – extremely happy (5). To support and explain the quantitative results, the questionnaire includes open-ended sentences inquiring the best and worst features of driving the road grader, as well as other comments considering the driving or the simulator. The questionnaire ends with a background information section asking the respondent's age, gender (Boy/male, Girl/female, Other), personal interest towards technology (e.g., cars), gaming and history as statements rated on a similar disagree–agree scale as the user experience statements.

A table for filling in the questionnaire, and a return box, are situated in the vicinity of the simulator in the same room. Although an electronic questionnaire would have reduced the required work, a paper-form was selected to avoid equipment maintenance and to ensure approachable feedback mechanism for non-technical museum visitors such as older people with their grandchildren. In order to motivate people to provide feedback small product prizes have been raffled amongst the respondents who have provided their contact information.

Respondents. Between mid-June 2015 and early-June 2017, i.e., concerning all four versions of the road grader simulator, we received feedback from altogether 215 respondents (103 boy/male, 66 girl/female, 4 other, 42 did not answer). The ages of the respondents varied between 1.5–68 years (mean = 22.9, SD = 17.9), the age group of 0–10-year-olds covering about 38%, 11–20-year-olds about 19%, 21–35-year-olds about 15%, 36–50-year-olds about 18%, 51–64-year-olds about 9%, and 65-year-olds or older only about 2% of the responses. The respondents were very interested in technology (median 5/5), and somewhat interested in gaming and history (median 4/5).

3.3   Results

A summary of the user experience statement responses for the different versions is presented in Fig. 2. As can be seen from the statement results, already the first version received good ratings from the users. They totally agreed that the first impression of the simulator was interesting and that these kinds of simulators would increase their interest in museum visits. Along with the experience in general, respondents mentioned, e.g., the possibility to turn the steering wheel and to push the pedals as the most positive things about the simulator. This indicates that people, especially children, liked the

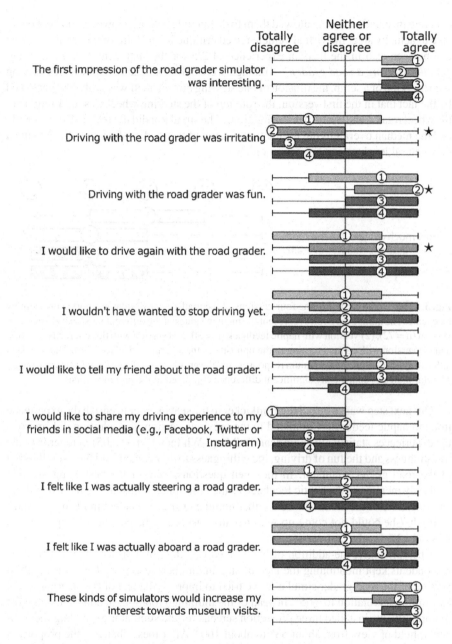

Fig. 2. Reported user experiences about the road grader simulator. The numbered circles represent the median experience values of the different versions: (1) baseline version (n = 63–72), (2) version with haptic feedback (n = 29–32), (3) version with three screens (n = 57–62), and (4) version with camera turning to the opposite as the steering wheel (n = 32–37). The whiskers indicate the minimum and maximum responses, and the gray boxes indicate the interquartile range. The stars indicate statistically significant differences compared to the previous version.

concrete installation which allowed them to do tangible actions. However, one not being able to actually steer the virtual vehicle raised critique in one third of the feedback. This can be seen also in the median experience of 2/5 for the statement "*I felt like I was actually steering a road grader*". Although we would not be able to allow free driving with this kind of a setup, the illusion of one steering him-/herself was probably weakened by the fact that in the first version, the rotation of the steering wheel was not limited but the wheel rotated endlessly to both directions. The simulator did not feel realistic enough, and the median overall liking for the first version of the road grader simulator remained on a neutral level, as can be seen in Fig. 3.

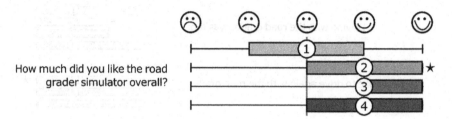

Fig. 3. The overall likings of the four versions of the road grader simulator reported on a smiley face scale. The numbered circles represent the median values of the different versions: (1) baseline version (n = 72), (2) version with haptic feedback (n = 30), (3) version with three screens (n = 62), and (4) version with camera turning to the opposite as the steering wheel (n = 36). The whiskers indicate the minimum and maximum responses, and the gray boxes indicate the interquartile range. The star indicates statistically significant difference compared to the previous version.

Our next step was to install the Buttkicker to the seat in order to enrich the experience through haptic feedback. Compared to the previous version, this addition did improve the experiences statistically significantly (Mann-Whitney U, p < 0.05) in regards to the irritatingness and the fun of driving, the willingness to drive again, and the overall liking of the road grader simulator. In the open questions, 18% of the best thing answers explicitly mentioned the haptic feedback as the best things. Considering the worst thing answers, 29% of the mentions were either nothing or the respondent marked a "-" indicating he/she could not come up with negative aspects, whereas the same proportion was only 2% for the first version.

Unsurprisingly, the addition of haptic feedback did not help with the fact that the respondents kept mentioning the lack of steering in their feedback. Thus, for the third version of the road grader simulator, we tried to improve the feel of the steering wheel by limiting its rotation to ±65°, instead of the unlimited rotation. In addition, and most importantly, we installed three projection screens for the simulator expanding the horizontal field of view from about 53° to about 160°. After these changes, the proportion of positive mentions about the scenery and pictures increased, and the respondents felt slightly stronger as if they would have been actually aboard a grader. However, there were no statistically significant (Mann-Whitney U) differences in the experiences compared to the previous version with haptic feedback addition. This was a rather unexpected result. It may be that the screens are too far away from the user, and as the installation space is still rather large, expanding the horizontal field of view was not enough to enable the feeling of immersion: the ceiling, the floor and the walls on extreme left and right of the user were still visible.

People have different expectations on how a virtual environment should react to turning the steering wheel. First, our simulator functioned so that turning the steering wheel to the left turned also the view to the left, i.e., one would see further to the left, like in the real driving situation. In the fourth version, we changed this to the opposite to see whether it would affect the user experiences. Rather surprisingly, changing the camera to turn to the opposite direction as the steering wheel showed no statistically significant changes (Mann-Whitney U) in the experiences. However, regarding the worst things answers, the proportion of lack of steering mentions doubled from about 30–33% for the previous three versions to about 61% for this fourth version. Also, the medians for the statements of people feeling like steering a road grader or being aboard one dropped a step after changing the camera turning logic, although the change was not statistically significant.

Our findings from the iterative development of the road grader simulator show that haptic feedback is important for such a setup combining omnidirectional video and concrete, physical elements – a grader cabin with a seat, steering wheel and pedals in this case. It is impossible to allow free steering for this kind of a simulator. Instead, turning the steering wheel turns the virtual camera, not the vehicle itself. This resulted in critique throughout the feedback by the respondents. In order to provide a richer experience, we are developing a new solutions for more realistically mimicking steering by visual effects. The respondents were also rather neutral considering the statement *"I felt like I was actually aboard a road grader"*. One obvious reason for this might be that the camera was situated on top of the roof instead of the cabin when shooting the ODV with the actual road grader. However, the limited field of view of the display and lack of actual grader interior and windows which allowed the users to see the room around them most likely were even more significant factors.

4   360° Rally Simulator

After experimenting with a projector based system, we wanted to investigate the experiences created by an immersive head mounted display ODV installation in the same place (Rally Museum in Mobilia). The system uses ODV recorded inside a rally car during real-world rally driving. The target user group still includes children but the installation is directed more towards adult visitors. The video is shot from the car of a well-known rally driver, and thus, visitors can find value in both the immersive experience and the factual content. The installation, set up inside a real rally car, has been in the Rally Museum since its opening in June 2016, and subjective feedback from one year of use is reported in this article.

4.1   System Description

The 360° rally simulator is a system built for the Samsung Gear VR headset and Samsung mobile phones. It utilizes Oculus Mobile VR SDK for displaying the visual material on

Gear VR. The content is 4K (3840 * 1920 pixels, 25 fps) ODV. The simulator is set up inside an actual rally car which is part of the Mobilia Rally Museum collection. Inside the car, the users are able to sit either on the driver's or the co-driver's seat, and while sitting on the driver's seat, also keep their hands on the steering wheel (although the steering wheel does not control the simulator). The car used in the installation is different and older than the car the videos were recorded in. The simulator application is used by putting on the Gear VR headset and separate headphones. See Fig. 4 for the physical setup in the museum.

Fig. 4. In the 360° rally simulator installation, the user is able to sit in a real car and experience a rally stage through VR glasses and headphones.

The application consists of several ODVs and audio recorded inside a rally car during two practice stages by many times national rally champion Juha Salo and his co-drivers Marko Salminen and Henri Arpiainen. First, winter-time material with snowy scenery was available for the museum visitors, and for the last four months, it was replaced with material recorded during a summer time practice session. The video materials consist of runs through test tracks and commentary discussion between the driver and co-driver afterwards. The audio consisting of engine sounds and car intercom speech enhances the experience since it allows the users to listen to the pace notes read by the co-driver and hear engine and other sounds. In addition, there is an initial short video from the starting position where the user can activate the driving video by looking at an arrow in the front of them. The videos were recorded with the camera placed between the heads of the driver and co-driver so that viewing most of the interior, including pace notes, steering wheel and pedals, is possible. Information about the video (driver, co-driver, car and location) is overlaid on the ceiling of the car with a 3D text element, which is visible when the user looks up with the HMD. This combination of video, audio and actual physical car environment was designed to provide a novel and exciting experience for the visitors.

4.2   Evaluation

In order to study museum visitors' experiences with the rally simulator, subjective feedback from the users has been collected with a questionnaire. One of our main goals was to study the effects of a different presentation medium (HMD) on the experience, as opposed to the three-projector setup of the previous simulator. We also wanted to understand how interesting the visitors find the video material without interactivity and how they experience the physical installation. We were also inquiring about cyber sickness as it is a well-known challenge with immersive VR content.

Subjective Data Collection.   Similar to the road grader simulator, user experiences of the rally simulator were collected with a paper-form questionnaire. For consistency and comparability reasons, the questionnaire created for the road grader simulator was taken as the basis even though the target user group was somewhat different. In addition to changing the wording to refer to the rally experience, an item inquiring the respondent's physical seat within the car (driver's seat or co-driver's seat) and a statement inquiring whether the simulator caused the respondent nausea were added. Also, the inquiry about the respondent's personal interest in history was replaced with interest in rally racing. The final 11 statements rated on a disagree–agree scale for the rally simulator can be seen in Fig. 5.

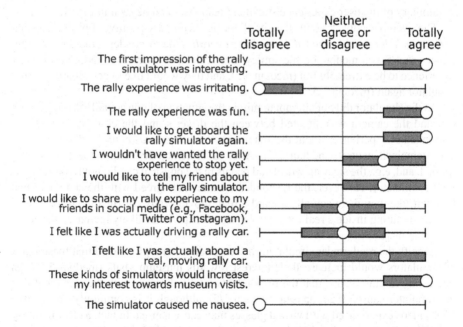

Fig. 5. Reported user experiences with the rally simulator. The whiskers indicate the minimum and maximum responses, the gray boxes indicate the interquartile range, and the white circles represent the median values (n = 273–286).

The questionnaire has been available for rally museum visitors since the simulator's first deployment in June 2016. A table for filling in the questionnaire, and a return box, are situated in the vicinity of the simulator. To motivate people to provide feedback, product prizes have been raffled amongst the respondents of the rally simulator questionnaire as well.

Respondents. Between mid-June 2016 and early-June 2017, we received feedback from altogether 304 respondents (159 boy/male, 103 girl/female, 2 other, 40 did not answer). 256 of these respondents experienced the winter-scenery rally, and for the remaining 48 respondents (~16%), the summer-scenery material was presented. The ages of the respondents varied between 4–70 years (mean = 32.0, SD = 17.9), the age group of 0–10-year-olds covering about 16%, 11–20-year-olds about 17%, 21–35-year-olds about 19%, 36–50-year-olds about 32%, 51–64-year-olds about 13%, and 65-year-olds or older only about 3% of the responses. A clear majority, 94%, of those who reported their physical seat, sat on the driver's seat. The respondents were very interested in technology (median 5/5), and somewhat interested in gaming as well as rally racing (median 4/5).

4.3   Results

A summary of the user experience statement responses can be seen in Fig. 5.

The overall feedback about the simulator has been very positive. For the question *"How much did you like the rally simulator overall"*, the respondents rated their experiences as 4/5 as a median on the smiley face scale. The users have reported the rally experience to be extremely fun (median 5/5), and they would like to get aboard the rally simulator again (median 5/5).

As the simulator did not attempt to mimic the situation of one actually driving a rally car, and the camera was situated between the driver's and the co-driver's seat, the respondents' experiences about the statement *"I felt like I was actually driving a rally car"* remained neutral (median 3/5). After all, interactivity within the system was limited, and, e.g., the steering wheel and pedals in the physical car did not have on effect on the simulator. However, the respondents somewhat agreed with the statement that they felt like they were actually aboard a real, moving rally car (median 4/5). This is logical, as sitting inside a real rally car during the experience likely increased the sense of "being there".

As with the road grader simulator, the respondents strongly agreed that these kinds of simulators would increase their interest towards museum visits (median 5/5). An interesting finding is also that the respondents totally disagree with the statement that the simulator caused them nausea (median 1/5), although it is commonly known that 360° videos experienced with virtual glasses may cause nausea. In fact, a clear majority of 79% totally disagreed and 10% somewhat disagreed with the simulator causing them nausea. Only 11 individuals out of the 280 respondents (4%) totally agreed with the statement.

Considering the open-ended questions, the respondents admired the experience in general, the authenticity, i.e., as if they would have been aboard a real car, and the possibility to sit in a real car. Also, the feeling of speed, the possibilities provided by the ODV, i.e., the ability to look around, and the audio including the pace notes, were mentioned as positive aspects. The negative comments about the rally experience concentrated on the issues related to contrast and lighting of the video material throughout the responses (about 24% of negative mentions). The videos displayed the car interior properly but the environment outside the car was often overexposed, and the road and its surroundings were hardly visible. In the winter recordings this was mostly due to snowy environment while in the summer recordings (available to the museum visitors since mid-January 2017), direct sunlight created strong contrasts. The material change (from the winter to the summer material) actually decreased some user experience measures (Mann-Whitney U, $p < 0.05$): statements related to first impression, irritatingness and willingness for future use were rated worse.

Overall, the museum visitors obviously have enjoyed our 360° rally simulator a lot, despite some justified critique: When asking for the worst thing about the rally experience, about 16% of the mentions explicitly stated there was nothing negative and about 13% of the mentions were a "-" indicating that those respondents could not come up with negative aspects. Also, when asking free-form comments, about 43% of the mentions were positive such as *"a nice idea"*, *"more of these things"*, or *"a nice addition to a museum"*.

5   Discussion and Future Work

Constructing and iteratively refining the two ODV based museum installations has given us understanding of the possibilities and challenges of utilizing 360° video in such applications. The long-term collection of feedback has provided us overall understanding of museum goers' attitudes and experiences and also provided us some data on the effects of various upgrades we have introduced to the installations.

The overall feedback to the road grader was positive. The driving was considered fun and the installation was considered something that increases willingness to visit museums. However, the visitors reported that they did not feel like they were actually steering the road grader. Over the revisions, we were able to improve the experience, especially with haptic feedback, but also got some mixed results, particularly with steering mapping adjustment. The rally simulator received overall favorable feedback, it was considered fun and the visitors reported that they would have liked to continue using it. While people did not feel like driving the rally car, they reported that they felt like being inside one. The possibility to focus on the different details of a real-life rally car was valued and the pace notes were also considered interesting.

Looking at the user experiences and comments received, we raise *immersion, interactivity* and *additional modalities* as the key elements relevant to ODV based museum installations.

5.1 Immersion

The immersive nature of the ODV provided genuine value. As earlier work suggests, the HMD based installation seemed to have more beneficial immersion. While the novelty value of a VR headset may play some role in the positive user experience, the objective immersion of the headset is significantly better than the immersion our projector based system could provide. While the horizontal coverage of the projection was close to human field of view, the vertical coverage was much smaller and room floor and ceiling were clearly visible to drivers. This, together with the fact that the simple cabin did not include windows or ceiling limited the immersion. We assume that this is the cause to the rather minimal improvement to the user experience when we added two more projectors to the installation.

In museums, social interaction is often an important part of the experience. From this point of view, HMD based material presentation is not optimal, since it isolates people. It can be argued that, e.g., projection based viewing solutions, which support multiple simultaneous users would be better. In museum settings also issues related to public displays like honey-pot effect can be relevant, overly complex and ambiguous installations may be avoided by visitors.

The downside of the immersion is that immersive solutions are prone to cause simulator sickness, aka, cyber sickness [27]. Especially when VR content, e.g., an ODV is viewed with a HMD, unpredictable camera movements can cause cyber sickness [13]. It is possible to stabilize the video, in particular camera rotations in post-processing [12]. However, shooting videos with a moving camera should always be considered very carefully. Having at least a part of the view stable can reduce unpleasant effects. Our respondents reported minimal ill effects, and while people who know they are prone to cyber sickness likely did not try the installation, the reported numbers are still surprisingly low indicating that the rally simulator was very successful in avoiding cyber sickness. This is probably mostly due to the fact that the rally videos consisted mostly of the fixed car interior, and moving scenery was visible only through car windows. This provided plenty of fixed, clear focus points for the viewers. In addition, the installation contained a couple of minutes of material and the resulting short usage sessions most likely helped as well. Finally, watching the video in the firm cup seats of the rally car provided a stable and comfortable environment.

5.2 Interactivity

In the road grader simulator, we experimented with creating an interactive application with ODV as the primary content. The simulator reacted to accelerator and brake pedals with realistic engine sounds and subtle visual effects. This part of interaction seemed effective. However, the feedback on steering wheel rotation never resulted in adequate feeling of control, as seen in the user experience data. The free form feedback also supports this conclusion. While the users liked that they could "drive" the road grader, they also complained that they could not actually steer it. The fact that inverting the visual steering feedback caused only slight change in the user experience tells that the users did not really feel they were driving a vehicle. Instead, the metaphor for some of the users was steering the world as opposed to steering the camera [34]. At the moment, the installation may appear more interactive than it really is, which can hurt the user experience. We are currently building a solution where more realistic driving simulation controls virtual camera position and heading inside the 3D video sphere with realistic steering model. This solution requires a video, where the vehicle is not visible, a 3D model will be used instead. With these updates we wish to increase the feeling of actually steering the grader, but we acknowledge that we will lose some of the benefits of ODV, namely some of the authenticity and low production costs.

To provide any benefit, a museum installation must first capture the attention of the visitors and intrigue them to interact. The most common use case is that a visitor will use each installation once. Therefore, immediate usability of the installations is critical. Issues studied with public displays, such as the barrier of first use and levels of engagement and related models like audience funnel [18] and honey-pot effect [23] can be valuable tools but at the same time, the interaction must be easy to understand and not intimidate visitors. Utilizing physical elements and genuine items as part of the installations is recommendable in museum settings. These elements can both guide and attract the users and add value to the experience. Both of our installations have received a good number of users and museum personnel consider them worthwhile additions to the exhibits, event when they cause additional maintenance burden. The added value of the physical elements separate the installations from what the visitors could experience already at home and immersion and interactivity separate them from the other exhibits.

5.3 Additional Modalities

Audio-visual material can benefit from other modalities as well. Haptic sense, both tactile and kinesthetic, were involved in our installations. The real rally car, while interesting to the visitors by itself, as the environment to view the videos added tactility to the experience. Similarly, the grader was interesting, particularly to small children since it allowed them to steer and operate the pedals. The haptic feedback added to the seat in the grader created a statistically significant and noteworthy improvement to the user experience and illustrates how active haptic feedback solutions can provide value. Many of the measures improved with the introduction of this feedback showing that good haptic feedback can improve the overall experience, instead of being just a gimmicky addition. With the use of, potentially authentic, physical props and additional feedback modalities museum installations can provide experiences which cannot be found elsewhere.

6 Conclusions

Omnidirectional video, aka 360° video, can be used to efficiently create authentic and immersive experiences and thus has great potential to be utilized in museum installations. Where it is possible to record material related to the exhibit, ODV can provide engaging and entertaining experiences which can also provide valuable information and understanding to the visitors. In this paper, we presented two systems based on ODV material, one viewed with a head-mounted display and the other utilizing a three-projector setup. The installations also utilized physical props and additional modalities. The reported experiences and the analysis of the roles of immersion, interactivity and additional modalities can help others interested in building similar installations. We consider immersion and interactivity to be important factors to help understand the possibilities of ODV based solutions. In museum settings physical elements of the installations can also have an important role.

Authenticity of the presented material is key in museum context and when video capture is an option, ODV can be valuable. In comparison to traditional video, the installations can be more interactive. Even the baseline possibility to control the viewing direction can be appreciated as it allows the visitors to focus on details most interesting to them. Furthermore, the engagement, created via the interactivity and immersion can lead to both user satisfaction and potentially efficient communication of information. Overall, ODV based technology can create entertaining and effective museum installations. The production costs of such installations can also be reasonable; ODV camera solutions are now available at almost all price categories, and programming interactive ODV applications is reasonably easy with tools like Unity3D.

ODV can be especially useful in cases where the immersive nature of ODV is inherently valuable. In our two cases, this value was in (virtually) being inside a special type of vehicle not generally accessible to the public. Similarly, this value may be in a building or a location that is hard to access, or an activity that is rare or dangerous in real life. The user experience data we collected shows that immersive ODV viewing experience can create good and valued experiences. In museum environments, it is often possible to enrich the viewing experience further by adding physical props and some interactivity. In our case, the real rally car, even when it did not match the specific vehicle in videos, nor did the camera position the user's location, enriched the viewing experience. We were also able to minimize cyber sickness in the HMD based installation. In the case of the grader simulator, the realistic seat, especially after the addition of haptic feedback, and the realistic steering wheel and pedals added to the experience.

The limitation of ODV compared to 3D modelled content are the fewer interaction possibilities. ODV based solutions can still provide reasonable level of interactivity and when the installations are properly designed, the authenticity of video content and the reasonable productions costs make them viable options. The museum context best supports short usage sessions and the possibilities of ODV based solutions can efficiently fulfill the required level of interactivity. The immersive nature of these solutions can create memorable experiences enhancing the overall museum experience. Respondents to our user experience questionnaires strongly support the idea that these installations can make museums more desirable places to visit.

Acknowledgements. This work was done as a part of MIRACLE project, financed by Tekes – the Finnish Funding Agency for Innovation. We appreciate the involvement and input of Mobilia personnel who participated in the design process, data collection and maintenance of the installations. We thank also Juha Salo and his co-drivers for the possibility to record the materials.

References

1. Argyriou, L., Economou, D., Bouki, V., Doumanis, I.: Engaging immersive video consumers: challenges regarding 360-degree gamified video applications. In: 15th IEEE International Conference on Ubiquitous Computing and Communications and 2016 International Symposium on Cyberspace and Security (IUCC-CSS 2016), pp. 145–152. IEEE (2016). https://doi.org/10.1109/iucc-css.2016.028
2. Benko, H., Wilson, A.D.: Multi-point interactions with immersive omnidirectional visualizations in a dome. In: ACM International Conference on Interactive Tabletops and Surfaces (ITS 2010), pp. 19–28. ACM, New York (2010). https://doi.org/10.1145/1936652.1936657
3. Berning, M., Yonezawa, T., Riedel, T., Nakazawa, J., Beigl, M., Tokuda, H.: pARnorama. 360 degree interactive video for augmented reality prototyping. In: The 2013 ACM Conference on Pervasive and Ubiquitous Computing (UbiComp 2013), pp. 1471–1474. ACM, New York (2013). https://doi.org/10.1145/2494091.2499570
4. Bleumers, L., Van den Broeck, W., Lievens, B., Pierson, J.: Seeing the bigger picture: a user perspective on 360° TV. In: 10th European Conference on Interactive TV and Video (EuroiTV 2012), pp. 115–124. ACM, New York (2012). https://doi.org/10.1145/2325616.2325640
5. Boult, T.E.: Remote reality via omnidirectional imaging. In: ACM SIGGRAPH 98 Conference Abstracts and applications (SIGGRAPH 1998), p. 253. ACM, New York (1998). https://doi.org/10.1145/280953.282215
6. Concert - 360-degree Video from ZuZuVideo. https://www.youtube.com/watch?v=1Kp1_icG328
7. De la Torre, F., Vallespi, C., Rybski, P.E., Veloso, M., Kanade, T.: Omnidirectional video capturing, multiple people tracking and identification for meeting monitoring. Technical report (2005). http://repository.cmu.edu/robotics/128/
8. Decock, J., Van Looy, J., Bleumers, L., Bekaert, P.: The pleasure of being (there?): an explorative study into the effects of presence and identification on the enjoyment of an interactive theatrical performance using omnidirectional video. AI Soc. **29**(4), 449–459 (2014). https://doi.org/10.1007/s00146-013-0487-6
9. Fassbender, E., Heiden, W.: Atmosphaeres – 360° video environments for stress and pain management. In: Ma, M., Oliveira, M.F., Baalsrud Hauge, J. (eds.) SGDA 2014. LNCS, vol. 8778, pp. 48–58. Springer, Cham (2014). https://doi.org/10.1007/978-3-319-11623-5_5
10. Ekola, L., Järvinen, A.: KÄÄNNEKOHTA: 360-videon soveltuminen viittomakielen tulkkausharjoitteluun. Bachelor's thesis. Diaconia University of Applied Sciences, Degree Programme in Sign Language Interpretation (2014). https://publications.theseus.fi/bitstream/handle/10024/73100/Ekola_Jarvinen.pdf?sequence=1
11. Kallioniemi, P., Mäkelä, V., Saarinen, S., Turunen, M., Winter, Y., Istudor, A.: User experience and immersion of interactive omnidirectional videos in CAVE systems and head-mounted displays. In: Bernhaupt, R., Dalvi, G., Joshi, A., K. Balkrishan, D., O'Neill, J., Winckler, M. (eds.) INTERACT 2017. LNCS, vol. 10516, pp. 299–318. Springer, Cham (2017). https://doi.org/10.1007/978-3-319-68059-0_20
12. Kasahara, S., Nagai, S., Rekimoto, J.: First person omnidirectional video: system design and implications for immersive experience. In: ACM International Conference on Interactive Experiences for TV and Online Video (TVX 2015), pp. 33–42. ACM, New York (2015). https://doi.org/10.1145/2745197.2745202
13. Kasahara, S., Rekimoto, J.: JackIn head: immersive visual telepresence system with omnidirectional wearable camera for remote collaboration. In: 21st ACM Symposium on Virtual Reality Software and Technology (VRST 2015), pp. 217–225. ACM, New York (2015). https://doi.org/10.1145/2821592.2821608

14. Keskinen, T.: Evaluating the user experience of interactive systems in challenging circumstances. Ph.D. thesis. Dissertations in interactive technology 22, University of Tampere (2015). http://urn.fi/URN:ISBN:978-951-44-9972-2

15. Kwiatek, K.: How to preserve inspirational environments that once surrounded a poet? Immersive 360° video and the cultural memory of Charles Causley's poetry. In: 18th International Conference on Virtual Systems and Multimedia (VSMM 2012), pp. 243–250. IEEE (2012). https://doi.org/10.1109/vsmm.2012.6365931

16. Kwiatek, K., Woolner, M.: Transporting the viewer into a 360° heritage story: panoramic interactive narrative presented on a wrap-around screen. In: 16th International Conference on Virtual Systems and Multimedia (VSMM 2010), pp. 234–241. IEEE (2010). https://doi.org/10.1109/vsmm.2010.5665980

17. Mammut   #project360.   https://play.google.com/store/apps/details?id=ch.mammut.project360&hl=en

18. Michelis, D., Müller, J.: The audience funnel: observations of gesture based interaction with multiple large displays in a city center. Int. J. Hum. Comput. Interact. 27(6), 562–579 (2011). https://doi.org/10.1080/10447318.2011.555299

19. Neng, L.A.R., Chambel, T.: Get around 360° hypervideo. In: 14th International Academic MindTrek Conference: Envisioning Future Media Environments (MindTrek 2010), pp. 119–122. ACM, New York (2010). https://doi.org/10.1145/1930488.1930512

20. Okura, F., Kanbara, M., Yokoya, N.: Fly-through Heijo palace site: augmented telepresence using aerial omnidirectional videos. In: ACM SIGGRAPH 2011 Posters (SIGGRAPH 2011), Article 78. ACM, New York (2011). https://doi.org/10.1145/2037715.2037803

21. Onoe, Y., Yamazawa, K., Takemura, H., Yokoya, N.: Telepresence by real-time view-dependent image generation from omnidirectional video streams. Comput. Vis. Image Underst. 71(2), 154–165 (1998). https://doi.org/10.1006/cviu.1998.0705

22. Pakkanen, T., Hakulinen, J., Jokela, T., Rakkolainen, I., Kangas, J., Piippo, P., Raisamo, T., Salmimaa, M.: Interaction with WebVR 360° video player: comparing three interaction paradigms. In: 2017 IEEE Virtual Reality (VR), pp. 279–280. IEEE (2017). https://doi.org/10.1109/vr.2017.7892285

23. Parra, G., De Croon, R., Klerkx, J., Duval, E.: Quantifying the interaction stages of a public display campaign in the wild. In: 8th Nordic Conference on Human-Computer Interaction: Fun, Fast, Foundational (NordiCHI 2014), pp. 757–760. ACM, New York (2014). https://doi.org/10.1145/2639189.2639216

24. Peñate, W., Pitti, C.T., Bethencourt, J.M., de la Fuente, J., Gracia, R.: The effects of a treatment based on the use of virtual reality exposure and cognitive-behavioral therapy applied to patients with agoraphobia. Int. J. Clin. Health Psychol. 8(1), 5–22 (2008)

25. Petry, B., Huber, J.: Towards effective interaction with omnidirectional videos using immersive virtual reality headsets. In: 6th Augmented Human International Conference (AH 2015), pp. 217–218. ACM, New York (2015). https://doi.org/10.1145/2735711.2735785

26. Ramalho, J., Chambel, T.: Windy sight surfers: sensing and awareness of 360° immersive videos on the move. In: 11th European Conference on Interactive TV and Video (EuroITV 2013), pp. 107–116. ACM, New York (2013). https://doi.org/10.1145/2465958.2465969

27. Rebenitsch, L., Owen, C.: Review on cybersickness in applications and visual displays. Virtual Reality 20(2), 101–125 (2016). https://doi.org/10.1007/s10055-016-0285-9

28. Rizzo, A.A., Ghahremani, K., Pryor, L., Gardner, S.: Immersive 360-degree panoramic video environments: research on creating useful and usable applications. In: Jacko, J.A., Stephanidis, C. (eds.) Human-Computer Interaction: Theory and Practice, Part 1, pp. 1233–1237. Lawrence Erlbaum Associates, Mahwah (2003)

29. Rovelo Ruiz, G.A., Vanacken, D., Luyten, K., Abad, F., Camahort, E.: Multi-viewer gesture-based interaction for omnidirectional video. In: 32nd ACM Conference on Human Factors in Computing Systems (CHI 2014), pp. 4077–4086. ACM, New York (2014). https://doi.org/10.1145/2556288.2557113

30. Saarinen, S., Mäkelä, V., Kallioniemi, P., Hakulinen, J., Turunen, M.: Guidelines for designing interactive omnidirectional video applications. In: Bernhaupt, R., Dalvi, G., Joshi, A., K. Balkrishan, D., O'Neill, J., Winckler, M. (eds.) INTERACT 2017. LNCS, vol. 10516, pp. 263–272. Springer, Cham (2017). https://doi.org/10.1007/978-3-319-68059-0_17

31. Slater, M.: A note on presence terminology. Presence Connect **3**(3), 1–5 (2003)

32. Turunen, M., et al.: Multimodal media center interface based on speech, gestures and haptic feedback. In: Gross, T., Gulliksen, J., Kotzé, P., Oestreicher, L., Palanque, P., Prates, R.O., Winckler, M. (eds.) INTERACT 2009. LNCS, vol. 5727, pp. 54–57. Springer, Heidelberg (2009). https://doi.org/10.1007/978-3-642-03658-3_9

33. Turunen, M., Hakulinen, J., Melto, A., Heimonen, T., Laivo, T., Hella, J.: SUXES - user experience evaluation method for spoken and multimodal interaction. In: 10th Annual Conference of the International Speech Communication Association, ISCA, pp. 2567–2570 (2009)

34. Ware, C., Osborne, S.: Exploration and virtual camera control in virtual three dimensional environments. In: The 1990 Symposium on Interactive 3D Graphics (I3D 1990), pp. 175–183. ACM, New York (1990). https://doi.org/10.1145/91385.91442

35. Yagi, Y.: Omnidirectional sensing and its applications. IEICE Trans. Inf. Syst. **E82-D**(3), 568–579 (1999)

36. Zoric, G., Barkhuus, L., Engström, A., Önnevall, E.: Panoramic video: design challenges and implications for content interaction. In: 11th European Conference on Interactive TV and Video, pp. 153–162. ACM, New York (2013). https://doi.org/10.1145/2465958.2465959

37. Zoric, G., Engström, A., Barkhuus, L., Ruiz-Hidalgo, J., Kochale, A.: Gesture interaction with rich TV content in the social setting. In: Exploring and Enhancing the User Experience for Television, Workshop of ACM SIGCHI Conference on Human Factors in Computing Systems (CHI 2013) (2013)

Photographing System Employing a Shoulder-Mounted PTZ Camera for Capturing the Composition Designated by the User's Hand Gesture

Shunsuke Sugasawara[✉] and Yasuyuki Kono

Graduate School of Science and Technology, Kwansei Gakuin University,
2-1 Gakuen, Sanda 669-1137, Japan
{enm85486,kono}@kwansei.ac.jp

Abstract. We have developed the wearable system for photographing of the scenery/composition designated by the user's hand frame with a shoulder-mounted camera. The hand frame is the gesture of making a rectangular enclosure with both hands when the user considers the composition of a picture. The system detects the hand region of the user from an image of a head-mounted camera, and gets a "picking region image" by recognizing the hand gesture. The picking region is the region in the hand frame indicated by the user through the image of the head-mounted camera. It photographs high resolution image of the similar composition as the picking region image, called "target region image" by controlling PTZ (pan/tilt/zoom) of the shoulder-mounted camera. It performs robust control on noise such as the user's body sway.

Keywords: Shoulder-mounted camera · PTZ
Feature point tracking · Wearable system

1   Introduction

We have developed the wearable system for photographing of the scenery/ composition designated by the user's hand frame with a shoulder-mounted camera. An example of a hand frame is shown in Fig. 1. The hand frame is the action of making a rectangular enclosure with both hands when the people decides the composition of a picture. The hand frame is easy and intuitive method of decides composition. The photographing of the determined composition with the camera has two problems. One is that the scenery designated by the naked eye is different from the scenery through the camera lens. Another is that it takes some actions before transition from a hand frame to an attitude of photographing. In this research, we aim to create the wearable system that take the similar composition as the designated region by the user's hand frame with the shoulder-mounted PTZ (pan/tilt/zoom) camera.

A. D. Cheok et al. (Eds.): ACE 2017, LNCS 10714, pp. 588–600, 2018.
https://doi.org/10.1007/978-3-319-76270-8_40

Fig. 1. A hand frame

2   Related Work

Fuchi et al. [1] proposed a system that photographs the range designated by the user's hand gesture with three cameras installed on the ceiling. It's usable environment is limited, because their system requires to install cameras preliminarily. Furthermore, the taken pictures are not from user's view. Chu and Tanaka [2] proposed an interaction technique enabling users to control digital camera's functions such as pan, tilt, and shutter using hand gestures when taking self-portrait pictures. Our proposed wearable system saves an arbitrary area in the user's viewpoint as a still image. Sakata et al. [3] proposed a system that supports remote collaborative work with shoulder-mounted camera and laser pointer. It always photographs and projects the remote collaborator's instruction as a laser on fixed point by estimating the operator's motion and controlling the panning and tilting of the camera. Their research doesn't control the zoom function of the camera. In this research, the system controls pan/tilt robustly against the user's body sway to hold a specific region even after zooming the camera.

3   System Configuration

The system configuration is shown in Fig. 2. The user wears an HMD (Head-Mounted Display) with a camera for checking the composition of the picture and the PTZ camera on the right shoulder for taking high resolution picture of the similar composition as the picking region image. (1) The picking region is the region in the hand frame indicated by the user through the image of the head-mounted camera. (2) The system searches for the region equivalent to the picking region image from the image of the shoulder-mounted camera, and determines the discovered region as the target region. (3) The system controls the PTZ of the shoulder-mounted camera and saves the camera image as a still image.

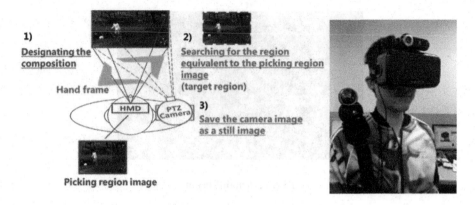

Fig. 2. System configuration

4   Getting a Picking Region Image

In this research, the system gets a picking region image designated by the user to perform gesture determination process on user's hand region detected from the image of the head-mounted camera. The rough flow of user operations is shown in Fig. 3. (II) To detect skin color region from an image of a head-mounted camera, we apply the expression proposed by Song et al. [4] to each pixel and the image is binarized in skin color region. (III) Since the hand region and the background region with similar RGB values may overlap, the edges obtained by applying the Sobel filter to the image of the head-mounted camera are set as boundary lines and these are separated. (IV) It detects two regions from the largest region after separation. It decides that the one located on the lower left is the left-hand and the one located on the upper right is the right-hand region.

The system recognizes hand gestures from hand region detection image obtained above. (V) This system recognizes three hand gestures: designation (of a picking region), waiting (for photographing), performing (for photographing). User performs these hand gestures successively on this system.

The "designation" hand gesture determines the composition shown by user's hand frame as the picking region. User's view in the HMD while recognizing the hand gesture is shown in Fig. 4, where the red rectangle is designated region and has the base of the fingers of the right hand and the left hand as the diagonal. User can freely modify the size and the position of the picking region by moving the position of hands. In order to recognize this hand gesture, the system detects the hand frame. We define the hand frame as a state where the left and right hands are in proper positional relationship and the thumb and forefinger are open at right angles. First, it detects thumb tip and forefinger tip. Next, it searches a pixel of hand region so as if drawing a circle toward the forefinger with the thumb tip as the center (a round search), and assumes the found point is the base of fingers. It calculates the closing angle of each line connecting the thumb tip and the forefinger tip, the forefinger tip and the base. A similar search is performed

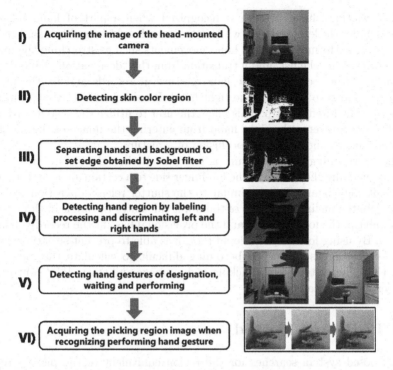

I) Acquiring the image of the head-mounted camera

II) Detecting skin color region

III) Separating hands and background to set edge obtained by Sobel filter

IV) Detecting hand region by labeling processing and discriminating left and right hands

V) Detecting hand gestures of designation, waiting and performing

VI) Acquiring the picking region image when recognizing performing hand gesture

Fig. 3. User operations for getting a picking region image

Fig. 4. Recognition of designation hand gesture

centered on the found point, and the crossing angle is determined again using for new found point. These processes are continued until the crossing angle begins to increase. If the minimum crossing angle until the end is approximate to a right angle, the system decides the point that creates the crossing as the base and the hand region forms a hand frame.

The "waiting" hand gesture is recognized when a part of hand region is detected under the left forefinger while detecting a hand frame. This hand gesture is able to be performed with less hand movements such as stretching the middle finger or loosening the fist, and a transition from the "designation" hand gesture is smooth. After recognizing the hand gesture, it records and fix the picking region size and stop detecting the right hand. It records the relative position of the base to the forefinger tip. This allow the user to utilize the system with only the left hand, prevents the right hand from entering the image of the shoulder-mounted camera and becoming occlusion of a picture.

The "performing" hand gesture is recognized when the system detects the action of inclining the thumb to the forefinger side to a certain angle and standing it at right angle again. This is similar to the shutter release operation. In order to calculate the inclination angle of thumb, it calculates the angle of three points the thumb tip, the forefinger tip and the provisional base at the recorded relative position. By using for the provisional root, it is able to prevent situations where the base position is shifted or becoming difficult to calculate the inclination angle. (VI) The system gets a picking region image and starts PTZ control of a shoulder-mounted camera.

5   PTZ Control Method

The proposed system searches for the region equivalent to the picking region image designated by the user from the image of the shoulder-mounted camera, and controls the PTZ of the shoulder-mounted camera so that the discovered region is shown on the its whole screen. The region in the camera image may be moved due to the influence of such as the user's body sway. In order to track this, we implement robust control focusing on the positional difference of feature points. The rough flow is shown in Fig. 5. (A) The system searches for the region equivalent to the picking region image from the image of the shoulder-mounted camera, and determines the discovered region as the target region. (B) It pans and tilts the camera so that the target region moves to the center of the camera image. It estimates the positional difference of feature points in the camera image per pan/tilt degree. (C) If the target region is in the center, the system performs to zoom so that the target region is shown on the entire screen of the camera image. (D) It detects the positional gap between the camera image and the target region. (E) It pans/tilts so that the positional gap is eliminated. If the positional gap is equal to or less than the threshold value, the camera image is saved as a still image.

5.1   Estimation of the Positional Difference of Feature Points

The system requires to figure out the positional difference in the x direction and the y direction of feature points in the camera image to eliminate the positional gap between the target region and the camera image. It calculates the positional difference of feature points to track feature points by comparing the frames

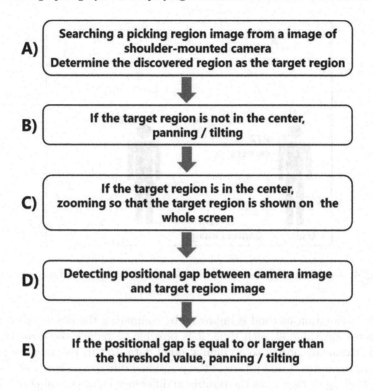

A) Searching a picking region image from a image of shoulder-mounted camera
Determine the discovered region as the target region

B) If the target region is not in the center, panning / tilting

C) If the target region is in the center, zooming so that the target region is shown on the whole screen

D) Detecting positional gap between camera image and target region image

E) If the positional gap is equal to or larger than the threshold value, panning / tilting

Fig. 5. Flow of PTZ control

just before and after panning/tilting. An example of observation is shown in Fig. 6. While capturing an object A in which the position/shape is invariant, if the camera is panned to the right, A appearing in the camera image moves to the left. It can calculate positional difference by panning from the difference in coordinates of A. However, the positional difference of feature points is affected by the positional relationship between the user and the object in real space. The system doesn't limit the usable environment, therefore, it observes the actual positional difference on the environment to acquire images and control pan/tilt continuously. It uses AGAST [5] for feature points detection and Lucas-Kanade method [6] for feature points tracking.

The observed positional difference contains errors due to the noise such as the user's body sway or changing in the feature points group detected. We implement a method to estimate the positional difference without errors by observation applying Kalman filter [6]. Kalman filter is a process for estimating and controlling an appropriate state of a certain linear dynamic system from observation values including errors. In this filter, two phases are executed for each one step of time. One is the prediction phase that estimates next state of the system using for the information learned in the past and another is the correction phase that acquires the current observation value and adjusts the estimation method model.

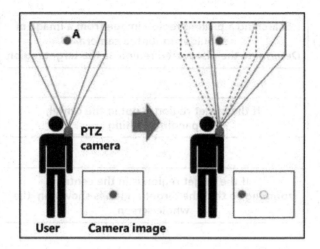

Fig. 6. An example of observation for positional difference of feature points

Since the estimation method is improved by comparing the predicted value and the observation value at each time, it is possible to reduce the error from the prediction value according to accumulation of data. In this research, we prepare for two Kalman filters and estimate the positional difference separately for panning and tilting. It estimates the positional difference before panning or tilting is executed, and after execution, acquires the actual the positional difference and adjusts the estimation method model.

5.2   Tracking the Target Region

The target region in the camera image may move due to the user's body sway. The system controls PTZ to track the target region. After zooming, when the entire target region is contained in the camera image, the camera image is saved as a still image. PTZ control in the system is divided into two phases. The former phase (phase 1), PTZ control for "approaching" the target region, is a process from the initial state of shoulder-mounted camera operation until the target region is centered by panning/tilting and adjusted the zoom magnification. It performs template matching to track the target region from the camera image. The latter phase (phase 2), PTZ control for "staying" in the target region, is a process of controlling the panning/tilting in order to eliminate the positional gap between the camera image and the target region after zooming. It performs feature points tracking to track the target region from the camera images.

When the "performing" hand gesture is detected from the images of the head-mounted camera, the target region image is acquired and the phase 1 is launched. It searches the target region from the image of the shoulder-mounted camera. It utilizes for template matching of a picking region image as a template image for the search method. It obtains the coordinates of discovered target region, and if the target region isn't in the center, controls the panning/tilting of the camera so that the image to move to the center. It performs observes and estimates the positional difference of feature points described in Sect. 5.1. When the target region is detected at the center of the camera image, the system controls zooming so that the target region is equal to the size of the camera image.

After Zooming, the phase 2 is launched. It detects feature points from the camera image and the target region image, and performs feature point tracking between these images. The system calculates the positional gap between the camera image and the target region image from feature points that can be tracked. It pans and tilts the camera to the direction for decreasing the positional gap. By estimating the positional difference of feature points per panning/tilting from the estimation method described in Sect. 5.1, the rotation angle necessary for eliminating the positional gap is obtained. However, position and posture of the shoulder-mounted camera are always fluctuating due to the user's body sway, so it is difficult to obtain the image as expected. The system again calculates the positional gap after the panning/tilting and continues control. If the positional gap is equal to or less than the threshold value, it determines that the photographing is successful and saves the camera image as a still image. We set the threshold to be half of the positional difference of the feature points in the x direction 1-degree panning and in the y direction 1-degree tilting. This is to prevent situations where the positional gap increases after panning/tilting.

6 Experiment

6.1 Experimental Method

We conducted an experiment to evaluate the effectiveness of the PTZ control method in this system. A subject wears the cameras on the head and the right shoulder. The camera mounted on the right shoulder is a PTZ camera. A subject look see the image of the head-mounted camera in an upright state and designates five regions as picking regions. The five regions are, in order, upper left, upper right, lower left, lower right, and center of the camera image. It is shown in Fig. 7. In the eight different environments, we determine the similarity between the image of the picking region specified from the head-mounted camera image and the image saved as a still image from the shoulder-mounted PTZ camera. The eight environments are defined as Environment 1 to Environment 8, and shown in Fig. 8. The similarity calculation obtains the value of zero mean normalized cross correlation [6] of between the saved image and the picking region image expanded to the same size. The value when two images are perfectly matched is 1, and the value when the two images are not correlated at all is 0. The higher the similarity between two images, the more positive the value. In this experiment, the head-mounted camera and the shoulder-mounted camera acquire the image of 640 pixels horizontal and 480 pixels vertical. Regarding the picking region, the horizontal size was fixed at 400 pixels and the vertical size

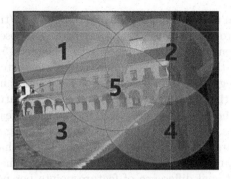

Fig. 7. Designated five regions

Fig. 8. Environment 1 to Environment 8

was fixed at 300 pixels. At the time of executing the PTZ control, experimenter is always in a state in which the right arm is being lowered, and it is assumed that the experimenter doesn't intentionally move the body.

6.2   Result

Results of experiments in eight environments are shown in Tables 1, 2, 3, 4, 5, 6, 7 and 8. The rows 1, 2, 3, 4, 5 of the table are regions in the image of the head-mounted camera shown in Fig. 7. The table shows the success or failure of photographing and the similarity when the region is designated as the picking region. The success or failure of photographing is judged to be failed in the case where the target region is missed for some reason. Furthermore, if a shoulder-mounted camera image is saved as a still image however an erroneous region is, it is judged as a failure. In the case where the correct region is saved it is judged to be successful.

Table 1. Result of experiment in Environment 1

	1	2	3	4	5
Success or failure of photographing	Success	Success	Success	Success	Success
Similarity	0.528	0.420	0.584	0.446	0.393

Table 2. Result of experiment in Environment 2

	1	2	3	4	5
Success or failure of photographing	Failure	Success	Success	Success	Failure
Similarity	-	0.733	0.822	0.712	-

Table 3. Result of experiment in Environment 3

	1	2	3	4	5
Success or failure of photographing	Success	Success	Success	Failure	Success
Similarity	0.496	0.681	0.809	-	0.762

Table 4. Result of experiment in Environment 4

	1	2	3	4	5
Success or failure of photographing	Success	Success	Success	Failure	Success
Similarity	0.496	0.681	0.809	-	0.762

Table 5. Result of experiment in Environment 5

	1	2	3	4	5
Success or failure of photographing	Failure	Success	Success	Failure	Success
Similarity	-	0.850	0.709	0.662	0.831

Table 6. Result of experiment in Environment 6

	1	2	3	4	5
Success or failure of photographing	Success	Success	Success	Failure	Success
Similarity	0.662	0.681	0.535	-	0.586

Table 7. Result of experiment in Environment 7

	1	2	3	4	5
Success or failure of photographing	Success	Failure	Success	Success	Success
Similarity	0.642	-	0.735	0.368	0.574

Table 8. Result of experiment in Environment 8

	1	2	3	4	5
Success or failure of photographing	Success	Failure	Success	Failure	Success
Similarity	0.621	-	0.474	-	0.563

7 Discussion

7.1 Limitation

We obtained the experimental result photographing was successful 30 out of 40 regions. The system has some limitations.

In Environment 4, the system failed on the lower right region. The causes include halation of an image. Halation is a phenomenon in which an especially highlighted part of the image blurs white. We think that the system executed to pan/tilt with an erroneous rotation angle and the positional gap increased, because of erroneous feature point tracking in strong light hit parts. The rotation angle and the execution time of the next panning/tilting increase in proportion to the length of the positional gap. Thus, the system erroneously obtains a frame in the middle of panning/tilting. The system loses track of the target region and judges as a failure, because feature points are hardly detected from the frame in the middle. We think that it improves the PTZ control accuracy by removing points having outliers from feature point groups. It is required to set a standby time for frame acquisition after execution in proportion to the rotation angle of panning/tilting.

In the photographing of the lower right region of the environment 5, still images were saved for the wrong region. The designated picking region image and the saved image is shown in Fig. 9. The reason is that the distribution of pixel values is similar between the picking region and the wrong region, and it is thought that the template matching was erroneous. We think that it is possible to reduce errors by limiting the search range using for the positional relationship between the two cameras.

Fig. 9. The picking region image (left) and saved image (right) of the Region 4 of Environment 5

Although the photographing was successful, the similarity decreased in several cases due to the roll of the saved image being shifted to left compared with the picking region image, because the shoulder-mounted camera fell off the top of the shoulder. As an example, the picking region image and saved image of the upper left region of the Environment 4 are shown in Fig. 10. Implementing adjustment of the zoom magnification and two-dimensional affine transformation enables the system to save the image in which the gap of the rolling direction is corrected with less decreasing the image quality so much. Feature point matching of ORB features is robust to rotation and varying illumination. The system performs ORB feature point matching after zooming, and calculates the rolling gap using for the positional relationship of the matching points between the picking region image and PTZ camera image. Since the error in the initial setting matching is large, it reduces erroneous matching to restrict the positional relationship.

Fig. 10. The picking region image (left) and saved image (right) of the Region 5 of Environment 4

7.2   Usability

We mainly implemented two interactive technics, hand detection and shoulder-mounted PTZ camera control. These technics have the potential to be applicable to various applications.

The hand detection method can be implemented employing only a monocular camera regardless of indoor or outdoor environment. The interface based on this method is intuitive, since the user can operate a system just by holding their hand in front of the camera. Besides activating each function of a system, it can be applied for indicating a specific region on computer vision.

We implemented PTZ camera control robust to the user's body sway as a wearable system. This camera control matches compositions from two different viewpoints and maintains them by removing the influence of external factors. We think that this method can be applied in the field of personal robot or remote annotation. Sharing objects to be gazed with others will promote mutual understanding.

8   Concluding Remarks and Future Work

In this research, we have developed the system for photographing of the same composition designated by the user's hand frame with a shoulder-mounted PTZ camera. The system gets the picking region image to detect a particular hand gesture from the image of the head-mounted camera. It searches for a region equivalent to the picking region image from the image of the shoulder-mounted camera, and decides the discovered region as the target region. It controls panning/tilting/zooming so that the target region is shown on the whole screen of the shoulder-mounted camera. When the shoulder-mounted camera puts the entire target region in the camera image, the camera image is saved as a still image.

As a result of the experiments, we successfully photographed 30 PTZ camera images out of 40 regions, and showed the effectiveness of this system. However, the system has some limitations. I would like to respond to these, and revalidate by taking into account the size change of the picking region and the user's body sway.

In the future, we have plan to develop the photographing system employing a small Unmanned Aerial Vehicle (UAV), a drone. This system requires a smartphone instead of HMD, and a drone instead of a shoulder-mounted PTZ Camera. It is difficult to track a target region with a shoulder-mounted PTZ Camera when trying to take a very small far region. We think that this problem can be solved by flying a drone equipped with a camera to the position where it can photograph. Furthermore, it is inconvenient for the user to wear video see-through HMD on a daily basis. We think that setting the pinch-out operation on the touch panel of the smartphone to the designated operation of the picking region enables a burden on the user to be reduced. We want to develop an interface to automatically generate the flight plan of the drone based on computer vision and implement it in a wearable system.

References

1. Fuchi, K., Takahashi, S., Tanaka, Z.: A system for taking a picture by hand gesture. In: Proceedings of the 70th National Convention of IPSJ, Japan (2008)
2. Chu, S., Tanaka, J.: Hand gesture for taking self portrait. In: Jacko, J.A. (ed.) HCI 2011. LNCS, vol. 6762, pp. 238–247. Springer, Heidelberg (2011). https://doi.org/10.1007/978-3-642-21605-3_27
3. Sakata, N., Kurata, T., Kourogi, M., Kuzuoka, H., Billinghurst, M.: Remote collaboration using a shoulder-worn active Camera/Laser. In: Multimedia, Distributed, Cooperative, and Mobile Symposium (Dicomo 2004), Japan, pp. 377–380 (2004)
4. Song, J., Sörös, G., Pece, F., Fanello, S.R., Izadi, S., Keskin, C., Hilliges, O.: In-air gestures around unmodified mobile devices. In: ACM User Interface Software and Technology Symposium (UIST 2014), USA, pp. 319–329 (2014)
5. Mair, E., Hager, G.D., Burschka, D., Suppa, M., Hirzinger, G.: Adaptive and generic corner detection based on the accelerated segment test. In: Daniilidis, K., Maragos, P., Paragios, N. (eds.) ECCV 2010. LNCS, vol. 6312, pp. 183–196. Springer, Heidelberg (2010). https://doi.org/10.1007/978-3-642-15552-9_14
6. Bradski, G., Kaehler, A.: Learning OpenCV - Computer Vision with the OpenCV Library. O'Reilly Media, USA (2008)

Roulette++: Integrating Physical Lottery Process with Digital Effects

Misturu Minakuchi$^{(\boxtimes)}$

Kyoto Sangyo University, Kyoto 6038555, Japan
mmina@acm.org

Abstract. Roulette is a popular lottery device. After a ball is placed into a disk of roulette, it decides the result based on the hole of the disk in which the ball enters. Because the ball keeps rotating for a while, it is possible to raise the anticipation of the players from the time the ball is inserted until the result is determined. We propose a "Roulette++" system, which further enhances the excitement by using a flat dish shape with several holes so that the ball makes complex movements such as bouncing off a hole. It also tracks the movement of the ball with a camera and provides visual and auditory effects based on the movement. In this way, the physical device can arouse the players' excitement while ensuring randomness.

Keywords: Chance · Randomness · Lottery · Roulette · Digital effects

1 Introduction

Roger Caillois stated that the *Area*, or chance, is one of the key elements of a play [1]. We can regard chance as the antithesis of *Agon*, or competition. Chance sometimes supersedes the player's efforts, abilities, and skills, which can, for instance, lead to beginners beating experts. Thus, the element of chance can introduce tension into play.

Although chance is an essential and important element of play, it is not a certainty in play involving a computer. The AR dice tower [2] is an attempt to solve this problem by using the combination of physical randomness and computing. Visual and auditory effects excite the players while randomness is ensured by using a physical dice.

We propose another device that integrates physical randomness and computing. It is a roulette-like device that is enhanced with visual and auditory effects, which are based on the movement of the ball.

2 Approach

We can easily observe players and identify those who feel happy or unhappy about the results of a game based on chance. Some players enjoy the process of

© Springer International Publishing AG, part of Springer Nature 2018
A. D. Cheok et al. (Eds.): ACE 2017, LNCS 10714, pp. 601–607, 2018.
https://doi.org/10.1007/978-3-319-76270-8_41

determining the results in gambling. For example, some craps players may enjoy rolling the dice and some slot machine players may enjoy the actions of the reels. In this way, the lottery process until results are known to the players is important to enhance the entertainment value of any game based on chance.

Roulette is a lottery device takes a moderate amount of time to generate the results and the steps and rules of the game are very easy to follow. Some arcade medal game machines adopt variations of roulette, such as one with a flat dish with several holes (Fig. 1). Such variations of roulette extend the period for which the ball rotates and makes complex movements by bouncing off a hole during rotation.

Fig. 1. Example of a roulette used in an arcade medal game machine.

Utilizing these characteristics, some game machines use roulette-like devices for significant lotteries such as jackpots. Figure 1 shows a lottery device of the medal game machine, Galileo Factory™, a product of the Sega Corporation. When a player gets a challenge for the jackpot, a ball is placed into this device. If the ball falls into the hole in the center, the player hits the jackpot and gets a large number of medals. The player thus watches the movement of the ball with anticipation and anxiety.

No sound and visual effects such as lights or video accompany the roulette games in casinos. Arcade medal game machines play sound and flashlights when the ball is rolling. These machines also play loud music with fanfare to celebrate jackpots. However, these visual and auditory effects are unrelated to the process of the lottery, i.e., the movement of the ball.

Hence, we use a camera to track the ball and to play effects based on the movement of the ball.

3   Implementation

Figure 2 shows the overview of Roulette++. The disk is placed at the bottom, the USB camera is set on the top, and the projector is placed on the side of the frame to project the video over the disk.

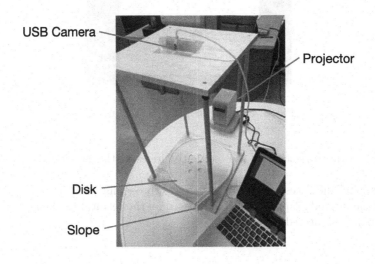

Fig. 2. Overview of the Roulette++.

The disk is about 260 mm in diameter and the central part is slightly dented. It has nine holes with a diameter of 17 mm each. The disk consists of four slices that are created by a 3D printer. We also created a slope to throw the ball into the disk at an appropriate angle and speed.

We used a rubber ball with a diameter of 18–20 mm. The rubber ball sometimes makes irregular moves when it is repelled from a hole unlike harder balls made of glass and steel. This irregular behavior is preferable as it enhances the unpredictability and consequently the entertainment involved in the lottery process. Bigger balls roll powerfully and smoothly, but they throw a larger shadow on the projected image.

The USB camera on the top of the frame captures the entire disk with a resolution of 640 × 480 pixels at 30 fps. The OpenCV for Processing is used to threshold and process the image to locate a cluster of a pre-defined size range. Figure 3 shows an example of thresholded images. The black circle depicts the detected ball, the red circles show the positions of the holes, and the green line shows the trajectory of the ball for verification of the process. The ball that is of a high contrast color such as red and blue against the white disk can be stably detected in an ordinary environment of a room with average brightness.

The program considers the center of the bounding box of the located cluster as the ball position. The current implementation performs the following three kinds of visual and auditory effects based on the ball position:

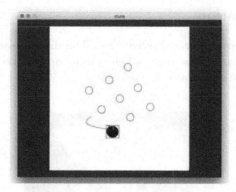

Fig. 3. Example of a thresholded image.

- Displays the trajectory of the ball with circles at the previous ball positions (Fig. 4).
- Highlights the holes to which the ball is approaching (Fig. 5).
- Plays animated graphics and sound based on the result, i.e., the hole in which the ball has entered (Fig. 6).

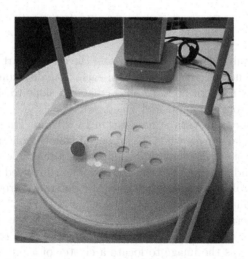

Fig. 4. Trajectory of the ball.

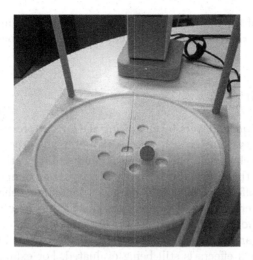

Fig. 5. Highlights of the holes.

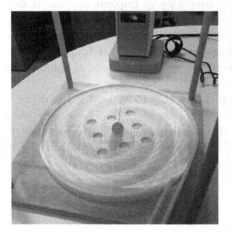 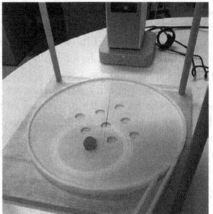

Fig. 6. Effects of the results. Left: jackpot. Right: fail.

4   Observation

We demonstrated Roulette++ at our open campus event held for three days in August 2017. Dozens of people experienced the device with and without visual and auditory effects. Everyone replied that the setting with effects was more exciting. In the setting without effects, many people did not react much when the ball entered a hole. In contrast, many people apparently regretted or delighted when they saw the result in the setting with effects. Because the effect of the losing was disappointing to ring the bell, there were some people who laughed when seeing the result. Many people agreed that the movement of the ball itself was tricky and interesting, but they also told that the trajectory display and the highlighting of the approaching hole were effective for emphasizing the fun. Some commented that it would be better to predict the movement of the ball and display it.

5   Discussion

Roulette++ entertains players by enhancing the lottery process with visual and auditory effects based on the situation. Although many studies have been conducted on the psychological effects of visual and auditory stimuli, it is difficult to find studies on their effects in actual game play. For example, Spenwyn et al. investigated the effects of light and music on gambling behavior [3], but the light and music were unrelated to the situations of the game play. It is obvious that visual and auditory effects arouse the anticipation and excitement of players. Many video games and gambling machines adopt such effects, although the effectiveness of such effects is still being evaluated. For example, Bramley and Gainsburg investigated how to use sounds at slot machines [4].

Another benefit of Roulette++ is its simplicity of implementation. It uses only one USB camera while the arcade medal game machines uses several sensors to detect the hole in which the ball drops. The alignment of the camera and the projector is completed in one minute using a setup utility. This simplicity of the configuration is suitable for utilizing the device for a wide range of applications including board games.

One of the pending issues that we are still trying to address is the delay in detecting the ball position. Display of the trajectory is delayed, especially when the speed of the ball is high. To solve this problem, we intend to use of high-performance PCs and cameras, to predict the next position of the ball and to optimize the disk shape to slow down the ball.

6   Conclusion

We proposed Roulette++, which performs visual and auditory effects based on the process of the physical lottery to arouse the players' anticipation and excitement. It can track the ball and detect the result of the lottery with a simple mechanism. In future studies, we aim to solve the problem of delay and to improve effect patterns.

Acknowledgment. We would like to thank Mr. Yudai Fujii who contributed in building the prototype of the system. This work was supported by JSPS KAKENHI Grant Number JP15K00510.

References

1. Caillois, R.: Les jeux et les hommes. Gallimard (1958)
2. Sasaki, N., Hirata, K., Morino, K., Minakuchi, M.: AR Dice Tower: integrating physical randomness with digital effects. In: Proceedings of the 13th International Conference on Advances in Computer Entertainment Technology (ACE 2016), Article 43, 6 pages (2016)
3. Spenwyn, J., Barrett, D.J.K., Griffiths, M.D.: The role of light and music in gambling behaviour: an empirical pilot study. Int. J. Ment. Health Addict. 8(1), 107–118 (2010)
4. Bramley, S., Gainsbury, S.M.: The role of auditory features within slot-themed social casino games and online slot machine games. J. Gambl. Stud. 31(4), 1735–1751 (2015)

Online Communication of eSports Viewers: Topic Modeling Approach

Ksenia Konstantinova[1], Denis Bulygin[1], Paul Okopny[2], and Ilya Musabirov[1(✉)]

[1] National Research University Higher School of Economics, St. Petersburg, Russia
ilya@musabirov.info
[2] Uppsala University, Uppsala, Sweden

Abstract. This paper represents a brief overview of the communication of eSports viewers during the broadcasts of Dota 2 tournaments on the streaming platform Twitch.tv. We employed a topic modelling algorithm Twitter-LDA to analyse the contents of chat messages. We found that different stages of the stream can trigger different ways of behaviour depending on the type of the content. Game sessions more often had short emotional expressions, while breaks and moments of game inactivity included more analytical discussions and sociability.

1 Introduction

This work is dedicated to the understanding of how viewers react to video action on Twitch.tv during different stages of eSports tournament broadcast.

We applied the probabilistic topic modelling algorithm Twitter-LDA to extract topics of chat messages. This algorithm helps capture viewers' collective reactions to game events. We analysed chats of two Dota 2 majors' live streams during games and in breaks between games.

During the game, the conversation is mostly reactive to the game events: fans express their feelings, talk about broadcast problems and features and cheer for favourite teams. During breaks between games, viewers are more diverse in topics, and these topics go beyond only reflecting stream events, including more analytical discussions and sociability.

2 Dota 2, Streaming, eSports

Twitch.tv is a live-streaming service, a platform for interactive game spectatorship. Viewers (people who watch the game broadcast) can communicate with a streamer (a person who is broadcasting) or each other using built-in chat. Besides text, viewers actively use emojis in their communication. Emojis can be referred to as a universal language, which supplements text with emotions or additional meanings, which are hard to express with just text [1].

In this work, we analyse live streams of tournaments in Dota 2, a free-to-play online game, which is also an eSports discipline. Dota 2 tournaments' broadcasts attract millions of viewers on online streaming platforms.

© Springer International Publishing AG, part of Springer Nature 2018
A. D. Cheok et al. (Eds.): ACE 2017, LNCS 10714, pp. 608–613, 2018.
https://doi.org/10.1007/978-3-319-76270-8_42

3   Related Work

The academic inquiry of chat communication in streaming platforms probably started with [2] by Hamilton et al. The authors investigated Twitch.tv to attempt to describe how a combination of video streaming and chat communication affects players' experience. They treated a live stream as a hybrid form of media, which provides people with experience of social spectatorship as they are "[...] sharing rich experiences of play" [2].

Hamilton et al. pointed out that chat communication plays a crucial role in participation culture formation. Being disrupted by an overwhelming flow of messages ("waterfall of text" [2, p. 7]), chat communication becomes less meaningful for viewers, thus reducing the satisfaction of both streamer and viewers.

Recktenwald in [3] developed the idea of emotional response and interaction between video stream and viewers. He stated that bursts of messages are closely related to actions of the streamer and particular events in the stream.

A burst of messages can be provoked not only by a game event but also by other viewers' or moderators' behaviour. These "waterfalls of text" cause clutter in the chat which makes it difficult for a viewer to communicate with others in the chat. Thus, this type of emotional response sometimes is considered antisocial [4].

Viewers often employ emojis to enhance their text communication. As the pace of a stream is fast, an emoji, which requires only a few keystrokes, is a fast and simple way to communicate an emotional response to whatever is going on in the stream. In addition, emojis are often employed to convey emotions, which otherwise could not be expressed briefly and accurately in text [1].

4   Data and Methods

In this paper, we focus on the analysis of chat messages that are connected with broadcast- and game-related events. Employing the Chatty[1] application, we collected 1.3 million messages from two Dota 2 tournaments: Epicenter: Moscow (May 2016) and Boston Major (December 2016).

We gathered additional information on game- and broadcast-related events (e.g., the death of a character or the end of a game) from Dotabuff website and Open Dota 2 API.

To detect spectators' anticipation and reaction we marked time slots covering 30 s before and 90 s after as related to a particular event. We also marked chat messages during the breaks between games to analyse the shift in chat contents.

To extract frames of viewers discussions, we applied the probabilistic topic modelling algorithm Latent Dirichlet Allocation (LDA) [5]. Provided with a collection of text documents, LDA derives a pre-determined number of topics. Each topic is represented by a set of words which often co-occur in the same documents.

---

[1] chatty.github.io/.

Specifically, we employed a modification of the LDA algorithm called Twitter-LDA [6], which gets a set of messages with a common attribute as one text document, and each message is assigned to one topic only. Thus, it allowed us to analyse shot messages from the chat.

Because the only important LDA parameter defined by a researcher is the number of topics, we fitted models in the range between 30 and 70 topics. We chose a 50-topic model because the messages were quite heterogeneous in terms of topics and the topics were interpretable enough to be labelled.

To highlight associations between topics and game activity, we used the $G\hat{2}$ log-likelihood ratio [7]. We separated text messages into two categories due to the timestamps of game events. The $G\hat{2}$ log-likelihood ratio showed the prevalence of each topic in periods of game (in)activity based on frequencies of messages on each topic. We then applied the same logic to compare topics' frequencies during games and breaks.

5   Analysis and Results

Based on the LDA output, we labelled and categorised topics. For each topic, we looked at the top 20 tokens with the highest probability to name given topics (see Table 1).

Table 1. Topic examples

Group	Spam	Emojis	Emojis
Category	Spam	Sarcasm	Confusion
Topic	#0	#16	# 38
Top-20 of topic words	**jebaited nam fishmoley taxibro yetiz** na dota **superlongmessage** laugh eu players damn feels beautiful **spam** emotes 17 tv twitch large	9k **lul** mmr **4head pogchamp** miracle **kappa** 2k kreygasm chat 3k 1k aui **elegiggle** 8k 4k 5k player brokeback tinker	**wutface residentsleeper** navi game pogchamp kappa **ttours** start **scamaz** wtf kappawealth smorc dallove **boring** naga orospu purge Sikeyim aliens hype

After applying the $G\hat{2}$ log-likelihood ratio to topics, we obtained probabilities for each one to occur during active or inactive periods of the game, and during games or in breaks between games. Each topic was assigned to the specific category and characterised by prevalence in different broadcast modes (see Fig. 1) or in different stream modes (see Fig. 2).

Inactive periods of the broadcast mainly include voting for teams and players, communication on chat with other viewers, the discussion of the audio quality of the stream and analytics, and mocking other viewers or players.

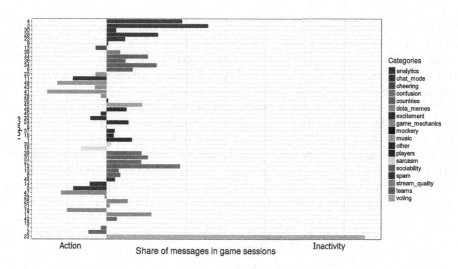

Fig. 1. Topic prevalence in two stages of game session (log-likelihood ratio)

During inactive game periods, fans get more emotional and show a decreased variety of discussion topics. Mostly, spectators cheer for their favourite teams, discuss the game session itself or show their excitement and spam messages, connected to Dota or local jokes.

During breaks between games, players focus on discussions of game analysis, players, and teams. The topical distribution is similar to the one during inactive periods of games with some minor distinctions. For example, viewers discuss chat limitations and moderation policies (category *chat mode*) during inactive periods of a game, but not in breaks.

We extracted the number of topics reflecting the emotional response of viewers, which can be seen by short expressions and emojis (see Fig. 1). For example, such emojis as *Kreygasm, SwiftRage*, or word "awoo" in topic #11 (*excitement*) express positive reaction to the game.

In addition, viewers can mock players' or casters' actions by writing "fired" or "322" (an expression of the low level of casters' performance). This reaction is reflected in topic #35 (*mockery*) and includes "gg" (good game), which is a sarcastic evaluation of players' decisions and actions.

Sarcasm is another category of emotional topics (#16, #33). It consists of such words as "9k", "LUL", "mmr", "Kappa". The phrase "9k mmr" reflects the high personal ranking of particular players. That is why viewers add an emoji *LUL* in the case that a player does something that contradicts his high ranking. *Kappa* is the most popular emoji on the Twitch.tv, which usually denotes sarcasm per se.

During the game, viewers also chant (topic #13) for teams. Usually, it presents copy-paste messages for supporting the favourite team in trouble. These types of messages are closely connected to names of concrete players and teams (#15, #2). Players and teams are also mentioned with "voting" category, which is a feature of the streaming platform that provides viewers with the possibility to foretell the winner (!vote) and choose the most valuable player (!mvp).

Regarding less emotional topics, spectators can also comment on the video itself, which is reflected in the categories "stream quality", "game mechanics", "analytics", "music". While categories of analytics and music are specific for breaks between games, the stream quality and game mechanics are more relevant for analysing chat communication during the game.

Inactive periods of game sessions and breaks between games also can be represented by topics related to social interaction in the chat. Thus, viewers can talk to each other (*sociability*), write copy-paste messages (*spam*, *dota memes*) and even get muted by moderators or a chatbot (*chat mode*); viewers can also reflect on teams' or tournaments' origin as well (*countries*). *Sociability* shows viewers talking to each other in a chat room; for example, viewers can send an emoji *HeyGuys* to greet other spectators.

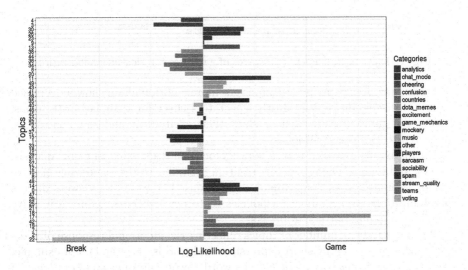

Fig. 2. Topic prevalence during games and breaks (log-likelihood ratio)

6   Conclusion

A live-streaming community can both spectate and discuss the main aspects of the broadcast. During an active period of game sessions, viewers are more emotional: drama on screen leads to the burst of text messages in chat rooms. Action, which usually can be pointed as a new turn in the actual game, is more appealing and lets people get involved in the game they watch. Pasting emojis and short expressions is common here; thus, it can be explained by the importance of being immediate and reacting as fast as possible, as Zhou et al. claimed [6].

Unlike event-intense periods, inactive periods are less thematically driven. During breaks and inactive periods of the game, viewers interact with each other, socialise, and discuss in-game events. The flow of messages is less intense than during the active game periods. However, we can still witness cascades of messages here. They are more specific and refer to the stream itself: bugs of the game and troubles with sound cause a tremendous response, which consists of specific emojis or phrases.

Communication between stream viewers is connected to the contents of a stream and in-game events. This connection and the event-driven nature of stream chats still require more detailed investigation, which will be the focus of our future work.

Acknowledgements. The article was prepared within the framework of the Academic Fund Program at the National Research University Higher School of Economics (HSE) in 2017–2018 (grant No. 17-05-0024) and by the Russian Academic Excellence Project 5–100.

References

1. Zhou, R., Hentschel, J., Kumar, N.: Goodbye text, hello emoji: mobile communication on wechat in China. In: Proceedings of the 2017 CHI Conference on Human Factors in Computing Systems, pp. 748–759. ACM (2017)
2. Hamilton, W.A., Garretson, O., Kerne, A.: Streaming on twitch: fostering participatory communities of play within live mixed media. In: Proceedings of the 32nd Annual ACM Conference on Human Factors in Computing Systems, pp. 1315–1324. ACM (2014)
3. Recktenwald, D.: Toward a transcription and analysis of live streaming on twitch. J. Pragmat. **115**, 68–81 (2017)
4. Seering, J., Kraut, R., Dabbish, L.: Shaping pro and anti-social behavior on twitch through moderation and example-setting. In: Proceedings of the 2017 ACM Conference on Computer Supported Cooperative Work and Social Computing, pp. 111–125. ACM (2017)
5. Blei, D.M.: Probabilistic topic models. Commun. ACM **55**(4), 77–84 (2012)
6. Zhao, W.X., Jiang, J., Weng, J., He, J., Lim, E.-P., Yan, H., Li, X.: Comparing twitter and traditional media using topic models. In: Clough, P., Foley, C., Gurrin, C., Jones, G.J.F., Kraaij, W., Lee, H., Mudoch, V. (eds.) ECIR 2011. LNCS, vol. 6611, pp. 338–349. Springer, Heidelberg (2011). https://doi.org/10.1007/978-3-642-20161-5_34
7. Agresti, A.: An Introduction to Categorical Data Analysis, 2nd edn. Wiley, Hoboken (2007)

The Development of an Augmented Virtuality for Interactive Face Makeup System

Bantita Treepong[✉] ⓘ, Panut Wibulpolprasert ⓘ, Hironori Mitake,
and Shoichi Hasegawa ⓘ

Department of Information and Communication Engineering,
Tokyo Institute of Technology, Tokyo, Japan
{treepong.b,panut,mitake,hase}@haselab.net

Abstract. In this paper, we focus on developing an interactive face makeup system that allows the user to practice applying makeup on their face without using real makeup materials. In our system, feature points on the human face were tracked by Kinect and mapped to a 3D face model. Face textures were generated and mapped on the model by using UV mapping technique. The makeup tools were developed for providing tangible interactions to users. Users can perceive a realistic makeup feeling by using our makeup tools. When the user applies the makeup, the program will paint the color on a face model, which synchronized with the users' movement in real-time. The system is evaluated by a subjective evaluation method. The result shows that our system can provide a new and attractive makeup experience to the users compared to other makeup applications.

Keywords: Face makeup · Augmented virtuality · Tracking system

1 Introduction

In our modern society, makeup is one of the main contributors of human beauty. There are more than 88 billion views of beauty contents consist of makeup tutorials and review of cosmetic products videos on YouTube [1]. This indicates that considerable amount of women pay attention to cosmetic. One in three women usually wears makeup every time before leaving the house and more than 50% of women feel that wearing good makeup helps them become more self-confident [2]. However, one basic issue is that they do not know which makeup material is suitable for their skin tone. They have to spend a fair amount of money to buy several makeup materials in order to find a suitable material. Moreover, sometimes they need to spend a lot of time with makeup before they step outside. In addition, women who have no makeup experience also feel that doing makeup is very troublesome.

© Springer International Publishing AG, part of Springer Nature 2018
A. D. Cheok et al. (Eds.): ACE 2017, LNCS 10714, pp. 614–625, 2018.
https://doi.org/10.1007/978-3-319-76270-8_43

Nowadays, many interactive makeup applications have been developed, such as [3–5]. The simplest type of application is a 2D makeup application, for examples [6]. In this case, a camera is used for capturing the user's face. The user can select the makeup color and style through its 2D user interface(UI). However, this kind of applications is unattractive and inflexible because it just overlay your selected makeup on the captured image which can limit the user's viewpoint. Furthermore, the makeup styles, e.g. eyebrow shape, the thickness of eyeliner and the shape of cheek brush, are limited, so the user can not generate their own makeup style.

Another type of makeup application is smart mirror application, such as [7,8]. Here, the video camera is usually used for capturing the user's face and the makeup result will be overlaid on the captured video in real-time. Therefore, it will allow the user to see the makeup result in a different viewpoint. Furthermore, this kind of application uses the smart mirror as a display system instead of using the normal monitor. The smart mirror can fill the gab between virtual and real environment for providing the realistic feeling to the user. The common weak point of these applications is that the user can not improve their makeup skill. The applications provide only static makeup function that allows the user to select the makeup style through its UI. It does not provide the function for applying the makeup by themselves. Rahman et al. [9] also developed a smart mirror system for supporting the user in cosmetic products selection. They attached the IR emitter on their mock-up cosmetic tool for tracking the tool movements. A RFID tag also attached on the tool for indicating it's the texture and material. Before the users apply the makeup, they have to scan the tool to the RFID reader, then the system will generate a makeup texture on a 3D model based on the scanned product. They also provide a recommendation scheme that shows the information of the similar products of different brands. Though this system can help the users to make a decision support in cosmetic selection easier, the variety of makeup tools and color still limited depend on their developed cosmetic tools.

Besides, some researchers also developed a makeup application based on an augmented reality system [10,11]. For example, Almeida et al. [10] combine an AR technology in their makeup application on a mobile phone. This application uses AR for assisting a user to apply a makeup following the given tutorial. The user's face was captured and tracked by using a camera on a mobile phone. Then, a semi-transparent image of makeup is superimposed on the captured image in step-by-step for guiding a user to apply a makeup in a specific area. However, the application still needs a skin tone detection function which can help a user to be able to find a suitable cosmetic color with user's skin tone.

In this paper, we present the interactive face makeup system that allows users to practice the makeup on their face without the use of real makeup materials. The aim of this system is for supporting the makeup training when users have an extra time. By using this system, the users can try to apply makeup as many times as they want on the virtual face without the need to actually clean their face. Moreover, they can choose the makeup color which is suitable for their skin tone and try to find their makeup style by practicing with our system.

2 Makeup Survey

The makeup survey was conducted from 49 people with 94% of female and 6% of male. The age group of respondents is between 22–40 years old. The propose of this survey is to analyze the general makeup behaviors of people. The data of this survey is used for making a decision within a specified area of makeup. The survey is separated into 2 parts: the makeup in daily life and the difficulty of makeup.

In the first part, we ask about a simple makeup that respondents wear every day. The face powder, lipstick, and brush-on are the top three makeup materials that people usually wear in their daily life. In the second part, most of the respondents think that applying the shading and highlighting is the most difficult process of the makeup while applying the eyeshadow, eyeliner and shape the eyebrow are respectively the second, third, and forth. Table 1 shows the result of both first and second part of the makeup survey.

Table 1. The makeup survey result

Makeup process	Percentage	
	Everyday makeup	Makeup difficulty
Apply face primer	53	27
Apply face powder	84	10
Apply eyeliner	31	43
Apply eyeshadow	27	45
Shape eyebrows	47	39
Face brushing	57	12
Apply lipstick	71	10
Shading and highlighting	NA	47
Other	6	NA

3 Proposed Method

This section gives the overview of our proposed method. The system requirement is consists of a real-time face tracking and touch detection function of the makeup tools. For the real-time face tracking, most people usually deform their face for applying makeup in the exact area. Therefore, the face expression tracking process is essential for the makeup system. Also, the touch detection function is important because it can provide a realistic makeup feeling to the

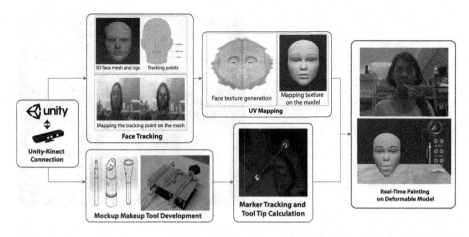

Fig. 1. The figure displays process overview of our method. They are separated into 3 parts: (1) Face tracking and UV mapping, (2) The development of the makeup tools, and (3) Real-time painting system

user. This function can help the user to feel and know which part of their face has makeup.

The system consists of a Kinect camera for capturing the movement of the human face in real-time, the mock-up makeup tools for providing the tangible interaction to the user when they apply the makeup, the Arduino Uno board, and the computer monitor. The process overview of our system is illustrated in Fig. 1. The propose of this research is to develop an augmented virtuality system to practice applying makeup. The user can experience a makeup feeling without the use of real makeup materials. By using this system, the user can improve their makeup skill and help them to be self-reliant with their own makeup style.

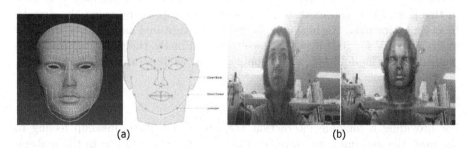

Fig. 2. (a) The 3D face mesh and the 33 feature points of the human face, and (b) The tracking points were mapped on the 3D face model.

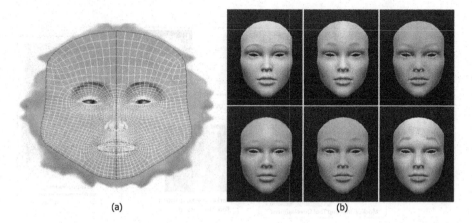

(a)   (b)

Fig. 3. (a) The captured image was mapped on the unwrapped uv texture, and (b) The mapping result of images that are captured form six subjects.

3.1 Face Tracking and UV Mapping

At the beginning, a 3D model of the human face is created in an Autodesk 3ds Max software. A hierarchical set of a facial skeleton of the model is generated by using rig system on a BonyFace plug-in for 3ds Max. The model is imported to the Unity software. The Kinect 2.0 is used for capturing and tracking the human face in this step. The 33 feature points of the human face including eye, eyebrow, mouth, nose, cheek, jaw, and chin, are tracked by using Kinect high detail face points function [12]. Those points are mapped to the facial skeleton of the model. Then, the face model will be able to move corresponding to the user's facial expression in real-time, as shown in Fig. 2.

To overlay the face texture on the 3D model, UV mapping technique, which is the process for projecting a 2D image to a surface of a 3D model, is used in this step. First, the mesh of 3D model is unwrapped by using the unwrap function in 3ds max. An image of the subject is captured and mapped onto the unwrapped UV for generating the face texture. Finally, the generated texture is applied on the model to see the mapping result, as illustrated in Fig. 3.

3.2 Development of Makeup Tools

For providing a tangible interaction and giving a realistic makeup feeling to the user, the makeup tools have been developed. As mentioned in the makeup survey section, we found that the lipstick, face powder, and brush-on are the top 3 makeup materials that people usually apply in their daily life. While shaping the eyebrow is also one of the difficult parts for makeup. As a result, in the preliminary step, we pick up lipstick, cheek brush, and eyebrow pencil as the focused makeup tools in our system.

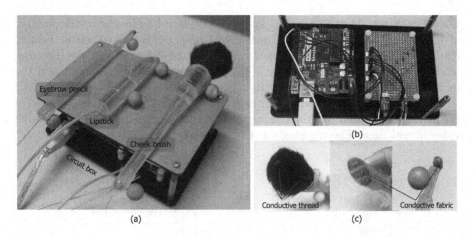

Fig. 4. (a) The hardware prototype includes of eyebrow pencil, lipstick, cheek brush, and circuit box, (b) Inside the circuit box consists of Arduino Uno, and low-pass filter circuit board, and (c) The conductive materials are attached on the tip of makeup tools.

Hardware Design. The prototype of the lipstick, eyebrow pencil, and cheek brush are developed, as shown in Fig. 4(a). The main part of the prototypes are the conductive materials which are used to detect touches between the prototype and the user's face, as can be seen in Fig. 4(c). The conductive fabric is put on the tip of lipstick and eyebrow pencil while the conductive thread is assembled inside the brush. When users brush their cheek or apply the lipstick by using our tools, the conductive materials will receive the touching data and send the data to the circuit board, as shown in Fig. 4(b), for filtering out the high frequency. The filtered data will be sent to the Arduino for processing and then the final data will be sent to the computer via serial port. For the lipstick, the conductive fabric was separated into 3 layers for detecting a different touch area and providing a different brush size in our face painting program according to the touch area.

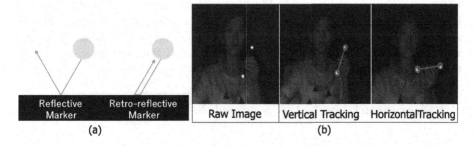

Fig. 5. (a) Property of retro-reflective marker (b) Raw image captured from Kinect IR camera (left), and tracking result (middle and right)

Tool Tracking. The tool tracking system is developed for localizing the position of our makeup tools. The system consists of a Kinect camera and retro-reflective markers. The retro-reflective marker can reflect the light back in the direction where it comes, as depicted in Fig. 5(a). With this property, the position of the marker can be found by capturing its reflected light.

The Kinect IR camera is used for capturing the markers. The reflected area of the markers is tracked by determining the area of the white pixel in the captured video in real-time. The tracking results are shown in Fig. 5(b).

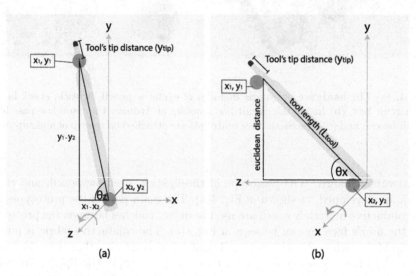

(a)   (b)

Fig. 6. The coordinate system and the relationship of marker and tool shows in front view (a) and side view (b)

Tooltip Calculation. Since the markers are not exactly attached to the makeup tool's tip, the tooltip calculation method is applied for calculating the relationship between the marker and the makeup tool's tip. First, the rotation angle of z-axis (θ_z) is calculated by using the slope data between the top and the bottom markers, as illustrated in Fig. 6(a), and the rotation angle of x-axis (θ_x) is calculated by using Euclidean distance and the length between two markers, as illustrated in Fig. 6(b). The angle can be described by (1). After the angles were calculated, the rotation matrix of z and x and the position vector of the tool's tip can be calculated by using (2), and (3) respectively.

$$\theta_z = \arctan\left(\frac{y1 - y2}{x1 - x2}\right), \theta_x = \arccos\left(\frac{\sqrt{(x1 - x2)^2 + (y1 - y2)^2}}{L_{tool}}\right) \quad (1)$$

$$R_{zx} = \begin{bmatrix} cos\theta_z & -sin\theta_z & 0 \\ sin\theta_z & cos\theta_z & 0 \\ 0 & 0 & 1 \end{bmatrix} \begin{bmatrix} 1 & 0 & 0 \\ 0 & cos\theta_x & -sin\theta_x \\ 0 & sin\theta_x & cos\theta_x \end{bmatrix} \quad (2)$$

$$P_{tooltip} = R_{zx} \begin{bmatrix} 0 \\ ytip \\ 0 \end{bmatrix} + \begin{bmatrix} x1 \\ y1 \\ z1 \end{bmatrix} \qquad (3)$$

3.3   Face Painting

The final step is the development of face painting system for real-time painting on a deformable model. The system is developed using a Unity3D framework. The workflow of the system is shown in Fig. 7. First, when a user applies the makeup by using our makeup tools, the conductive materials which are used as the touch sensor will detect if the tool has touched on the user's face or not. When the tool is touching, the software will project a ray-cast according to the tracking position of the tool's tip. Once the ray-cast hit a mesh collider of the face model, it will paint preselected color on the face model in the same position as the user did in the real world.

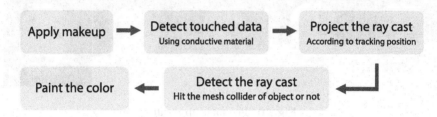

Fig. 7. The workflow of face painting process

4   Evaluation

A subjective evaluation was conducted to evaluate the user satisfaction and the performance of the system. Five subjects were asked to apply makeup by using our system. The subjects have to use our makeup tools, which include lipstick, eyebrow pencil, and cheek brush. The subjects can choose their own makeup color and try to apply the makeup in their own style. While the subjects apply the makeup on their face, the monitor will display corresponding makeup result on the face model in real-time as depicted in Fig. 9. Finally, the interval scale questionnaires, as shown in Fig. 8, were given to the subjects to ask about their satisfaction after they have used our makeup system.

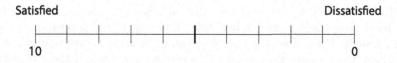

Fig. 8. The example of interval scale questionnaire

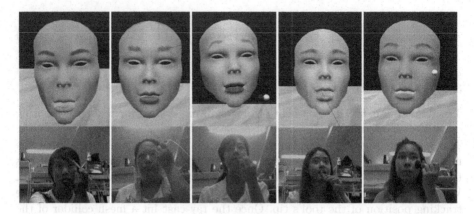

Fig. 9. The subjects applied a virtual makeup by using our system

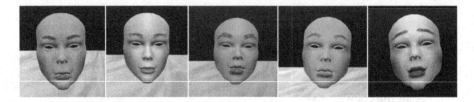

Fig. 10. The makeup result

5   Result and Discussion

Figure 10 shows the makeup results. The evaluation results were separated into 2 parts; tools evaluation, and overall system evaluation. Figure 11(a) shows the evaluation result of each makeup tools. The graph shows user satisfaction level of the brush shape and the color tones of each makeup tools. The comfortable level of a tactile sensation when subjects used our mock-up tools compare with real cosmetic tools also shows in this graph. As can be seen, most subjects are satisfied with the shape, the color tone, and the tactile sensation of the cheek brush. They think that it provides a realistic makeup on their face model. Also, it can make them feel comfortable and give them a realistic makeup feeling when they apply the makeup because our brush tool made from the real brush material.

However, the satisfaction level of the brush shape of the eyebrow pencil is less than 50% because they feel that the thickness of a line is too thick when they are shaping the eyebrow, so it is difficult to control and paint their eyebrows in the desired shape. The comfortable level of the tactile sensation of eyebrow pencil and lipstick also less than cheek brush because both of them made from resin which is a hard material, so it provides a less realistic tactile sensation to the subjects compare with the real makeup tools.

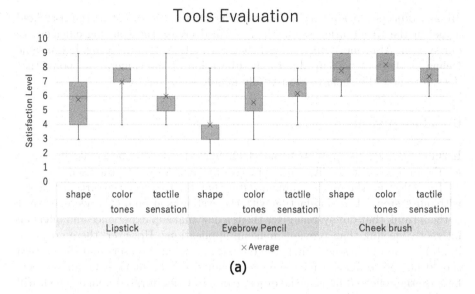

(a)

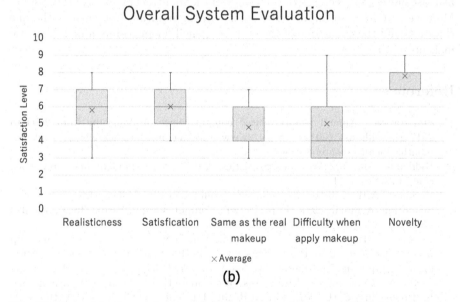

(b)

Fig. 11. The subjective evaluation result (a) Tool evaluation, and (b) Overall system evaluation

Figure 11(b) shows the evaluation result of the overall system. It is apparent that most subjects think our system is creative and provide them a new feeling with virtual makeup. The evaluation result demonstrates that our system provides a realistic feeling to the subjects and they are satisfied with our system at 60% average. Nevertheless, the system is quite difficult to use because if there are any objects blocking the tools from the camera viewpoint or the user hold a tool in the wrong orientation, then it will decrease the tracking efficiency of our system. Also, most subjects feel that our system does not provide the same feeling as the real makeup due to the limitation of the camera viewpoint that does not allow the them to realistically handle the tools.

6   Conclusions

In summary, we have presented a novel augmented virtuality face makeup system for the propose of providing an interactive makeup feeling to the users.

By collecting the user's comment after they try to apply the virtual makeup with our system, their satisfaction with the system is around 60% average. Most of them think that our system gives them a new makeup experience and offers an interactive feeling than previous makeup applications. However, there are some limitations in our system. First, the distance between the users and the camera should not be too close and the camera should not be blocked by any objects because the reflected light of the object can affect the infrared image, which will increase noises and decrease the efficiency of the tool tracking part of the system. Moreover, we have to improve the quality in the painting step such as the line thickness and the color tone of the eyebrow pencil for providing a more realistic makeup result.

References

1. Statista Inc.: Annual beauty-related content views on YouTube from 2009 to 2017 (in billions) (2017). https://www.statista.com/statistics/294655/youtube-monthly-beauty-content-views/
2. Hidden in Makeup: Woman's Statistics (2017). http://hiddeninmakeup.weebly.com/statistics.html
3. Bermano, A.H., Billeter, M., Iwai, D., Grundhöfer, A.: Makeup lamps: live augmentation of human faces via projection. Comput. Graph. Forum **36**(2), 311–323 (2017)
4. Nakagawa, M., Tsukada, K., Siio, I.: Smart makeup system: supporting makeup using lifelog sharing. In: Proceedings of the 13th International Conference on Ubiquitous Computing, UbiComp 2011, New York, NY, USA, pp. 483–484. ACM (2011)
5. Hieda, N., Cooperstock, J.R.: sharedFace: interactive facial projection mapping. In: Proceedings of the 2015 Virtual Reality International Conference, VRIC 2015, New York, NY, USA, pp. 18:1–18:4. ACM (2015)
6. Impala, Inc. Beauty: IMAN Cosmetics, Virtual beauty application for cosmetic products recommendation (2015–2017). http://www.imancosmetics.com/beauty-app
7. Iwabuchi, E., Nakagawa, M., Siio, I.: Smart makeup mirror: computer-augmented mirror to aid makeup application. In: Jacko, J.A. (ed.) HCI 2009. LNCS, vol. 5613, pp. 495–503. Springer, Heidelberg (2009). https://doi.org/10.1007/978-3-642-02583-9_54
8. Modiface Inc.: Modiface In-store AR mirrors (2017). http://modiface.com/

9. Rahman, A.S.M.M., Tran, T.T., Hossain, S.A., Saddik, A.E.: Augmented rendering of makeup features in a smart interactive mirror system for decision support in cosmetic products selection. In: 2010 IEEE/ACM 14th International Symposium on Distributed Simulation and Real Time Applications, pp. 203–206, October 2010

10. de Almeida, D.R.O., Guedes, P.A., da Silva, M.M.O., Vieira e Silva, A.L.B., do Monte Lima, J.P.S., Teichrieb, V.: Interactive makeup tutorial using face tracking and augmented reality on mobile devices. In: Proceedings of the 2015 XVII Symposium on Virtual and Augmented Reality, SVR 2015, Washington, DC, USA, pp. 220–226. IEEE Computer Society (2015)

11. Nishimura, A., Siio, I.: iMake: computer-aided eye makeup. In: Proceedings of the 5th Augmented Human International Conference, AH 2014, New York, NY, USA, pp. 56:1–56:2. ACM (2014)

12. Microsoft: High definition face tracking (2017). https://msdn.microsoft.com/en-us/library/dn785525.aspx

UPP (Unreal Prank Painter): Graffiti System Focusing on Entertainment of Mischievous Play

Shunnosuke Ando[✉][ID] and Haruhiro Katayose

School of Science and Technology, Kwansei Gakuin University,
2-1 Gakuen, Sanda, Hyogo 669-1337, Japan
{ehl82387,katayose}@kwansei.ac.jp
http://ist.ksc.kwansei.ac.jp/~katayose/

Abstract. Mischief is a behavior that is socially inappropriate, though is not clearly hostile towards other people and things. Mischief is said to have the unique potential to provide pleasant sensations and challenging experiences for mischief makers or players. From this, mischief can be the subject of entertainment as long as it has no critical negative influence on society. In this research, we focused on "graffiti" among the various forms of mischief. We describe the design and implementation of the *Unreal Prank Painter*, which is an entertainment system beyond mere "drawing," powered with augmented reality (AR).

Keywords: Graffiti · Mischief · AR

1 Introduction

Humans are always asked to act "appropriately" in society [1]. Indeed, the ability of environmental adaptability to select behavior and the existence of psychological desire to reinforce it are known [2]. However, research shows a psychology in which human beings desire to choose theirown willful actions. From this psychology, we experience stress due to the necessity of taking socially appropriate actions, and the energy that repels the causes of stress increases. This psychology is called "psychological reactance" (aka Taboo psychology, the Caligula effect), and it refers to the psychology where interest and attention are further raised by things being prohibited [3].

Mischief is one of the typical behaviors caused by "psychological reactance." Mischief is a socially inappropriate act, though the purpose is not the act itself, but rather to enjoy the nearby reactions to their deliverables and influences. Mischievous people enjoy providing surprising and interesting experiences to other people in their surroundings and for themselves, using behaviors that deviate from social rules and appropriate actions [4]. Because mischief depends heavily on rules and environments in specific places, it has good compatibility with games that also use them, such as location information games and mixed reality

A. D. Cheok et al. (Eds.): ACE 2017, LNCS 10714, pp. 626–636, 2018.
https://doi.org/10.1007/978-3-319-76270-8_44

(MR) games, etc. [5]. *Shhh!* by Linehan et al. (2013) [6] is a game focused on mischievous subjects. The mischief makers or players reportedly enjoy playing the game and show remarkable creativity in accomplishing mischievous tasks.

Players reportedly gain unique experiences in games with mischievous themes, which indicate that mischief can be one form of entertainment, as long as they have no critical negative influence on society. However, the absolute number of games is small, and many undeveloped parts exist such as place and kids of mischief. Therefore, in this research, we focused on "graffiti" and extended it from the viewpoint of augmented reality (AR) to construct a content creation platform that enables "graffiti," not merely "drawing," including entertainment as a form of mischief.

In Sect. 2, we discuss related work on mischief and graffiti. We then describe the approaches and implementation of the Unreal Prank Painter in Sects. 3 and 4. Section 5 presents an evaluation on how well the Unreal Prank Painter meets the approach mentioned in Sect. 3. Subsequently, in Sect. 6, we outline the research results described in this paper and the future prospects.

2   Related Work

Mischief is a socially inappropriate act, but the purpose is not the act itself, but to enjoy the nearby reactions to their deliverables and influences. The pleasure of mischief is to provide a surprising experience to those nearby and to the players themselves by creating unique situations in the environment by these actions [4]. One type of play that uses this to motivate players to take actions that create heterogeneous circumstances in the surrounding environment and that provide enjoyment to the players and the people in the surrounding environment [6]. "Bollocks," which is played by elementary and junior high school students in the UK is an example. *Bollocks* is a school game in which players sequentially make utterances in a louder voice than the previous players until multiple players (mainly students) anger the teacher. The conflicting act forced by the game (making a sound) creates a situation deviating from the everyday against the rule of society in the school environment (to be quiet), providing an exhilarating experience for the players.

Games and plays are similar to the rules of society, especially in buildings, in that rules exist individually and depend on the environment (type of game) [5]. Linehan et al. were inspired by this point and created *Shhh!*, which electronically expanded "Bollocks" as a game that leads players to take socially inappropriate actions as part of the gameplay. *Shhh!* is a game where you intentionally make sounds in the library, measure their volume with a designated application, and compete on the basis of score. *Shhh!* pays attention to the rule of the library (the need to be quiet) and forces players to act socially inappropriately by setting the act of "intentionally making noise" as a necessary requirement of the game. As a result, the player is conscious of social rules more than usual and has embarrassing emotions, but the player reportedly actively participates in the game and gets a uniquely entertaining experience. Linehan et al. suggested that a game with electronically expanded mischief can provide exhilaration and satisfaction to players. However, relatively few applications electronically expand mischief, and many points have not been considered enough, such as places and kinds of mischief. Also, in *Shhh!* by Linehan et al., the location is limited to libraries, and because players are not free to choose places the entertainment of mischievous acts that are done through free will in nature may be reduced.

Graffiti is an act of "drawing in the city," and it has aspects as socially inappropriate behavior and as artwork, so how the graffiti get recognized depends on places, scenes, the content to be drawn, etc. [7]. The socially inappropriate behavior of graffiti is composed of inappropriateness as a form of vandalism to the city and inappropriateness of the content depicted. On the basis of the aforementioned, the authors consider that for an application to satisfy both mischievous and artistic elements of graffiti, (1) users need to have the ability to decide the content and location arbitrarily, (2) graffiti practitioners need to have the ability to imagine the possibility of their act being "browsed" by an unspecific number of other people, (3) a possibility needs to exist to encounter graffiti, and (4) the intention and message of graffiti practitioners need to be correctly transmitted to those who browsed the graffiti. Doing graffiti electronically enables preventing vandalism to the city while keeping the freedom of the content drawn by the player. Many applications are said to use graffiti, such as *Graffiti Simulator* [8] by Kingspray. Graffiti Simulator is an application using virtual reality (VR), and it performs coloring on a virtual object prepared in virtual space. However, the graffiti behavior in Graffiti Simulator is reflected only in virtual space, so graffiti can only be done in virtually prepared situations. This ends up providing a space for which graffiti is permitted for players, and the premise of mischief (a socially improper act) is not considered.

HoloDoodle [9] by Capitola VR is an example of a graffiti application related to MR and AR. HoloDoodle uses HoloLens, which allows users to draw graffiti in the airspace of an MR-Environment. HoloDoodle enables arbitrary digital graffiti in real space. However, because 3D space needs to be tracked, preparation and the right settings are required for synchronization to share items. Therefore, this application has problems with satisfying the graffiti's element of browsing an unspecific number of others and with satisfying the possibility of encountering graffiti.

3   Approaches

Applications and systems that electrically perform "graffiti" provide entertainment as airspace drawing using VR/AR. However, in terms of entertainment as mischief, they are insufficient. Satisfying self-empathy and thrill (based on the feeling of morality) of graffiti practitioners is necessary to guarantee the entertainment value of graffiti. These are guaranteed by "browsing" the graffiti from third parties.

The great benefit of implementing digital graffiti is that it can prevent damaging the object on which graffiti has been performed. However, users find it difficult to feel the reality of "graffiti" in a system where everything is completed in the Cyber World (or Virtual Environment).

In this research, we focused on the graffiti's aspect as a type of mischief and implemented a graffiti system, the *Unreal Prank Painter (UPP)*, which utilizes a form that (1) draws graffiti in AR applications cooperating with real space and (2) is browsed by going to "the place." Accomplishing these should secure the entertainment value of original graffiti. Specifically, for graffiti practitioners, we have a real experience of (1) doing graffiti at "the place of interest" in real space and (2) that they can imagine the possibility of being "browsed" by a third party. For third parties, the possibility of encountering "graffiti" written by someone on "the place of interest" is guaranteed. Also, from a legal point of view, the crime of property destruction can be avoided.

To satisfy the aforementioned concept, GPS, plane estimation technology, and servers are used. GPS is used for roughly linking the graffiti and "the place" where it is drawn. Plane estimation is used to set the canvas of graffiti and also to link graffiti to more detailed positions. The linked information is saved to the server, and other users can browse the graffiti performed on the object at "the place." We gave the choice of anonymous/signed as an option of this application to satisfy both aspects of entertainment as mischief and as art for the users who draw graffiti. Also, by implementing the system of "adding to existing graffiti," we aim to provide the entertainment of secondary/n^{th} creation.

4   Application Design

The outline of the UPP is shown in Fig. 1. The UPP is composed of *Graffiti Mode* and *Gallery Mode*, which are modes to perform graffiti and to browse graffiti, respectively. In this chapter, we will describe the design of the UPP.

In *Graffiti Mode*, players can spray electronic graffiti on the plane of a real landscape using GPS and plane estimation. Moreover, the drawn graffiti can be saved together with a feature point map and GPS data to the cloud server.

In *Gallery Mode*, two pieces of data, a feature point map, and a graffiti image can be obtained according to the current position of the player, and they are stored in the server. Based on this information, graffiti drawn at the place is reproduced. At this time, this graffiti can be edited and re-uploaded. In that case, existing graffiti are erased.

4.1   Design of Graffiti Mode

A screen image of the graffiti mode and an explanation are shown in Fig. 2. To provide a graffiti experience with no sense of incongruity to the player, we need to arrange graffiti on a real landscape appropriately. In this application, we assume that "graffiti" is performed on an arbitrary plane and set a graffiti canvas using plane estimation.

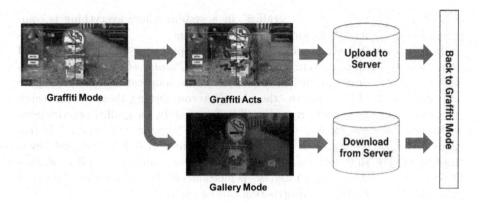

Fig. 1. Outline of UPP

Figures 3 and 4 show produced graffiti. In these figures, the estimated plane can be viewed from different angles, and the graffiti on the plane are deformed according to the angle. This aims to make graffiti appear as if it were done on the actual target. SmartAR [10] developed by SONY were used for plane estimation.

The graffiti were painted using the ray casting method. Colors, brush thickness, etc. can be freely changed by the user with the interface on the screen to ensure the freedom of expression of graffiti.

In addition, the graffiti can be released to the public by uploading it to the server. At this time, four kinds of data, (1) the image data in which graffiti is shown together with the landscape, (2) the image data of the graffiti itself, (3) the GPS data of the point where the graffiti was made, and (4) the feature point group data used for plane estimation, are stored on the server. These data are used when presenting graffiti to third parties in order to place them in the same place where the graffiti were drawn so that they can be viewed together with the surroundings.

4.2 Design of Gallery Mode

A screen image of the gallery mode is shown in Fig. 5. In this mode, the player can view images of graffiti stored on the server based on their position in real space. If graffiti does not exist at that position, the image is not displayed. By selecting the presented image, the corresponding feature point group data and graffiti image data are downloaded from the server. This feature point group is used as an AR marker, and a graffiti image is presented when the viewer sees it in the camera. As a result, the viewer can browse the graffiti not only as an image but together with the surrounding situation in the same way as the nature graffiti. The Fig. 6 shows the situation of viewing the same graffiti from multiple machines. We can see that the graffiti are presented at different angles for each machine.

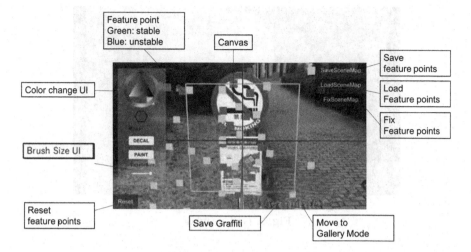

Fig. 2. Rakugaki mode

Fig. 3. Graffiti: front

Fig. 4. Graffiti: side

Fig. 5. Gallery mode

Fig. 6. Gallery mode

5   Evaluation and Discussion

5.1   Setting of Evaluation Items and Evaluation by Evaluation Table

On the basis of the approach described in Sect. 3, we set evaluation items from
the requirements that are considered necessary for actually using the UPP. After
that, we determined whether or not this application satisfies each item. Evaluation criteria are shown in Table 1.

Performing Graffiti

As mentioned in Sect. 3, we aimed to construct an application that enables
entertainment as a form of mischief in graffiti acts. Therefore, players need

to be able to perform mischief in arbitrary places without any mechanical discomfort. Also, graffiti need to be set in public because the mischief should not be self-contained. We set the evaluation items of this condition as "implementation of graffiti mode". In this item, we evaluated "graffiti without mechanical discomfort," "movability in real space," and "sharing graffiti," which are considered important when graffiti is done in a graffiti application.

Blowsing Graffiti

We need to convey the intention of the graffiti actor by sharing the graffiti itself and the information on the surrounding environment to other people. We set the evaluation item for this as an "implementation of the gallery mode." For this item, whether or not "the display of graffiti" are displayed with surrounding information was determined. Also, the graffiti needs to be viewed relatively easily to show this kind of passive mischief. We evaluated this as "ease of viewing."

Usability

Because this application has multiple players and involves their operations, whether or not players can easily and accurately perform these operations is important. The evaluation was performed as "the usability of graffiti mode" and "the usability of gallery mode."

5.2 Discussion

In this research, we developed and implemented the "UPP" as a platform for graffiti content creation based on the premise that mischief can be a subject of entertainment as long as it has no critical negative influence on society. We have developed applications, particularly concentrating on function building. By designing a strict position based on "graffiti" and "browsing," we aimed to satisfy both the mischievous and artistic aspects of graffiti. As a result, we successfully implemented "UPP" with the function of drawing virtual "graffiti," which goes beyond mere "drawing" in real space. We also implemented the function of real-space-based graffiti presentation to a third party. This application successfully provides the possibility of mischievous and artistic graffiti by giving the user a choice of being anonymous or signing the work. Also, this application allows adding some drawings to existing graffiti, so this function has great possibilities. Examples of application include providing entertainment of secondary/n^{th} creation and/or usage as a communication tool. However, tasks also exist. One significant issue is that, because it takes a form of AR application, it still has some lack of reality in the graffiti experience. We aimed to add realities by using third parties, but further evaluations are still needed to know the actual effect. A significant problem exists in the current UI pertaining to the functions when paying attention to the player's experience. The current UI has many operation items, and it is complicated; thus it may impair the players' experience. Furthermore, because of the problem of frame rate, graffiti lines may be interrupted during high-speed input. Measures such as complementation of the intervals

Table 1. Evaluation table

Evaluation item	Evaluation	Notes
Implementation of graffiti mode		
Graffiti without mechanical discomfort	Good	Succeeded in setting the proper position of a real landscape using the SmartAR plane estimation.
Movability in real space	Excellent	Using a smartphone enabled easily moving around while maintaining sufficient functions.
Sharing graffiti	Average	Succeeded in sharing graffiti using a cloud server. However, problems occurred such as not being able to set graffiti at the position assumed by the player on the real space due to the accuracy of the GPS.
Implementation of gallery mode		
Display of graffiti	Good	Based on the downloaded feature point map, graffiti is displayed successfully at the same point it was drawn.
Ease of viewing	Average	The player needs to adjust the position of the camera because the canvas is not displayed unless the downloaded feature point group is included in the camera. Presenting the landscape image gives information on the place where the feature point group exists, but it is not enough.
Usability		
Usability of graffiti mode	Bad	Many steps are required to save graffiti, so the degree of difficulty is relatively high.
Usability of gallery mode	Bad	The user interface (UI) is difficult to understand, and players are not properly guided

according to the input speed of the lines are necessary because not being able to draw the image intended by the player can severely damage the user experience.

Problems remain with the performance of the equipment but not the application itself. Although GPS is used to specify the position on the real space of graffiti, it has an error of about 10 m on average. Errors are reduced in a Wi-Fi environment, yet large errors are generated in the GPS in indoor use without a Wi-Fi environment. As a result, a situation arises wherein the graffiti cannot be put at the place intended by the player. Also, due to the performance of the machine, a relatively long time is needed to save graffiti in some cases. These are areas to improve but we consider the importance to be low, considering the expected future improvements in the performance of equipment.

What is considered to contribute most to the future development of the UPP is the use of electronic advantages of graffiti. In the application we have created, we faithfully simulate real graffiti, but the electronic advantages are not necessarily consistent with the reduction in the entertainment quality of graffiti. For example, in the present version of the UPP, only a single graffiti can be created at a single place, just like with real graffiti, but a plurality of graffiti can be arranged electronically. Furthermore, the viewable range can also be electronically expanded. These factors need to be experimentally set because how they affect the fun and user experience is unknown.

6   Conclusions

In this research, we focused on the aspects of graffiti as antisocial acts, and by fulfilling this we aimed to add entertainment as a form of mischief to graffiti. We proposed and developed an AR application for smartphones, the "Unreal Prank Painter," which (1) gives players their own freedom to select graffiti placement and (2) enables cooperation in real space. In this research, we focused on the construction of the system and implemented graffiti that is free and fits real space. In addition, we constructed a sharing method that conveys the graffiti without excess or deficiency. A prototype has been completed for implementation. Evaluations of an application on the experience of the players, including a field survey, are in short supply, so we plan to conduct a large-scale evaluation experiment in the future.

References

1. Byrne, D.R., Baron, R.A.: Social Psychology, 9th edn. Pearson, London (1999)
2. Bandura, A.: Social Learning Theory. Prentice Hall, Englewood Cliffs (1977)
3. Fukada, H.: Psychological Reactance (Shinri-teki Reactance Riron) (JP), Bulletin of Faculty of Education, Hiroshima University (1997)
4. Kirman, B., Linehan, C., Lawson, S.: Exploring mischief and mayhem in social computing or: how we learned to stop worrying and love the trolls. In: CHI 2012 Extended Abstracts on Human Factors in Computing System (2012)

5. Kirman, B., Linehan, C., Lawson, S.: Blowtooth: a provocative pervasive game for smuggling virtual drugs through real airport security. Pers. Ubiquit. Comput. **16**, 767–775 (2012)

6. Linehan, C., Bull, N., Kirman, B.: BOLLOCKS!! designing pervasive games that play with the social rules of built environments. In: Reidsma, D., Katayose, H., Nijholt, A. (eds.) ACE 2013. LNCS, vol. 8253, pp. 123–137. Springer, Cham (2013). https://doi.org/10.1007/978-3-319-03161-3_9

7. Hirayama, Y., Morosawa, K.: 7246 Graffiti and paintings in the context of urban space Summaries of technical papers of Annual Meeting Architectural Institute of Japan. F-1, Urban planning, building economics and housing problems (2007)

8. Kingspray Graffiti: Graffiti simulator. http://infectiousape.com/. Accessed 11 Feb 2017

9. Capitola VRi: HoloDoodle. http://capitola-vr.com/. Accessed 9 Oct 2017

10. SONY: SmartAR. http://www.sonydna.com/sdna/solution/SmartAR_SDK.html. Accessed 11 Feb 2017

Interactive Dance Choreography Assistance

Victor de Boer[1]([✉]), Josien Jansen[1], Ana-Liza Tjon-A-Pauw[1], and Frank Nack[2]

[1] Department of Computer Science, Vrije Universiteit Amsterdam, Amsterdam, The Netherlands
v.de.boer@vu.nl, josienjansen1@gmail.com, analizatjon7@gmail.com
[2] Informatics Institute, Universiteit van Amsterdam, Amsterdam, The Netherlands
f.m.nack@uva.nl

Abstract. Creative support for the performing arts is prevalent in many fields, however, for the art of dance, automated tools supporting creativity have been scarce. In this research, we describe ongoing research into (semi)automatic automated creative choreography support. Based on state-of-the-art and a survey among 54 choreographers we establish functionalities and requirements for a choreography assistance tool, including the semantic levels at which it should operate and communicate with the end-users. We describe a user study with a prototype tool which presents choreography alternatives using various simple strategies in three dance styles. The results show that the needs for such a tool vary based on the dance discipline. In a second user study, we investigate various methods of presenting choreography variations. Here, we evaluate four presentation methods: textual descriptions, 2D animations, 3D animations and auditory instructions in two different dance styles. The outcome of the expert survey shows that the tool is effective in communicating the variations to the experts and that they express a preference for 3D animations. Based on these results, we propose a design for an interactive dance choreography assistant tool.

Keywords: Dance choreographies · Dance representation · Performing arts
Creativity support

1 Introduction

The arrival of digital media and computational tools have opened up new possibilities for digital creativity [1]. In the field of dance, digital technologies have been used for instructing, and assessing dance as well as opportunities to expand dance resources and redefine the learning process [2, 3]. However, tools supporting automatic dance creativity are scarce.

According to [4], making choreographies in the traditional way is very costly and time-consuming. The use of accurate computer software can be really helpful to make it less costly and time-consuming. Another difficulty dancers can come across, is lack of inspiration for making a new choreography [5]. Smart technology can provide suggestions for choreography elements or for more variety in steps, addressing this challenge.

When making choreographies, a choreographer typically starts from a particular stimulus such as a specific physical movement, a musical phrase, a visual image, or a

© Springer International Publishing AG, part of Springer Nature 2018
A. D. Cheok et al. (Eds.): ACE 2017, LNCS 10714, pp. 637–652, 2018.
https://doi.org/10.1007/978-3-319-76270-8_45

state of mind [6]. It requires choreographers to engage with inner motivations to express feelings as well as to dialogue with the external environment, whether that be visual, aural, tactile or kinesthetic environmental stimulus [7]. Furthermore, the goal of a dance production, as with any other art, is the creative exploration of an idea. Within dance, this exploration takes place through the choices made regarding choreographic expression, musical accompaniment, costuming, lighting, scenic elements, and props [8]. Choreographers can build a piece on their own or with other dancers, either way, this is an iterative and interactive process where technology can play an assistive role. We include the external stimulus to discover what inspires a choreographer in a creative process.

In this paper we investigate to what extent choreographers can be supported by semi-automatic dance analysis and the generation of new creative elements. In Sect. 3, we outline specific needs and requirements for a new tool based on the state-of-the-art and through a survey. This includes the selection of appropriate semantic level at which should operate and communicate with the end-users. Based on the results we developed a simple prototype choreography assistant which uses various strategies for creative support. We evaluate this in three dance styles. In Sect. 4, we then focus on the presentation methods of these choreography variations. In a second user study, we investigate which methods of presenting choreography variations.

2 Related Work

2.1 Automatic Creativity and Dance

As technology continues to develop, the possibilities of integrating it in the process of creating dance increases as well. Stoppiello and Coniglio believed that linking the actions of a performer to the sound and imagery that accompanied them would lead to new modes of creation and performance [9]. Merce Cunningham's "Biped" choreography integrated computer-captured dance movements and interpreted it with hand-drawn graphics, so that animated and abstract dance characters projected on a screen moved along with and among the real dancers [10]. In the media video "Ghostcatching" Bill T. Jones's recorded actions, a portrait of Jones as performer, was used to animate abstract dancers in an 8,5 min virtual dance [11]. What these dance productions all have in common is that they aim to discover new ways of creating dance and this study has the same goal, however, we are focused on the choreographers' needs in this process and not on the end product that the audience observes.

Burton et al. [12] researched how Laban Movement Analysis (LMA) could be useful for more expressive human-machine interaction. Jadhav et al. describe similar research in the field of automated choreography, focusing on Indian Bharatanatyam Dance [13]. Their goal was a computer program that generate new experimental steps for them. Here they faced two main challenges: (1) to avoid impracticable (not doable) and impractical (not practiced) dance steps, and (2) to generate steps that had surprise value or novelty. In order to model the dance steps, a classification was needed whereby there is a clear representation of human movements, at a higher level than LMA notation. Following this, we use dance terms because of their usability.

Other studies have created systems where interactive environments are used to create, practice and perform choreographies including a virtual reality-based tele-immersive environment [14] or interactive augmented reality for live performances [15]. Sheppard et al. developed an application where multiple participants interact independent of physical distance, which resulted in tele-immersive dance (TED), a highly interactive collaborative environment [16]. Such tele-immersive environments have a similar framework as the choreography assistant tool. Except this tool would give suggested variations and generate it in real-time, that part is missing in the previous mentioned systems.

2.2 Dance Sensing

Several kinds of systems exist to capture movements of the human body. These include motion sensing systems such as markerless 3D camera clusters [17], cameras with reflective markers [18], wireless sensor modules worn at wrists and ankles [19], wearable wireless sensor nodes [20], pressure sensing floors [21] and a kinect-based human skeleton tracking system [22]. These studies demonstrate how well movements can be tracked and how motion detection can be used in various forms. This sensing –although non-trivial- is out of scope of this research.

2.3 Dance Representation

Most choreographies are never stored in retrievable forms. They either are retained in memory of the choreographer or are stored in video registrations. However, retrieving information from (large libraries of) is not easy as video is a "blind medium", which is meaningless until one watches it [23].

Several representation languages for human movement have been developed. One study discusses the Labanotation system that is used for analyzing and recording movement. It comprises a symbolic notation, related to music notation, where symbols for body movements are written on a body parts [24]. One study developed a method to generate coded description from motion-captured data with the Labanotation Editor [25]. As a follow up, the researchers developed XML for Labanotation to represent text and interchange data via the Internet. With LabanXML specific motion patterns can be searched, dance movements analyzed and body motion archived [26]. Wilke et al. used Labanotation to develop a LabanDancer system and translate Labanotation scores into 3D human figure animations, because most dancers and choreographers cannot read or write the notation [27].

The Benesh Movement Notation is another well-known dance notation. Benesh is written like a music score: on a five line stave that is read from left to right and from the top of the page to the bottom. According to Bianchini et al., Labanotation and Benesh notation are not capable to be integrated into a software environment [28]. It is also hard to analyze dance movements within the existing dance notations. Both notations are quite comprehensive and therefore difficult to learn [29].

A more common way of communication among dancers are style-specific *dance terms*. For example in classical ballet, common terms like the third position, pas-de-deux and plié are terms most western-educated dancers understand. Recent work by El Raheb et al. has led to the development of a hierarchical vocabulary based on classical ballet syllabus terminology (Ballet.owl) implemented as an OWL-2 ontology [30]. Their BalOnSe tool provides a web interface for ballet that allows the user to annotate classical ballet videos with terms from this ontology. The ontology consists of steps in dance terms and indicates the corresponding type of step. We build on this ontology for our dance-terms based prototype. In Sect. 3 we investigate the appropriate representation level for communicating dance variations to users.

2.4 Dance Presentation

Most digital tools for dance contain UI presentation elements, mostly divided into visual and auditory presentations. Dancers are stimulated by visual presentations such as visual effects [15], lighting [31], and 3D virtual rooms [32]. Visual effects could be presented as 2D animations where abstract figures, circles and lines are used or written text is shown to an audience [33–35]. The effects can be presented as 3D animations as well. One example is texture-mapped drawings around a 3D character [10]. Another example is the study where 3D images are based on a motion-captured human body with kinematic models, hand-drawn lines modelled as mathematical curves and sampled charcoal strokes [11]. There are also studies that use animated human figures with models based on hierarchical skeletons [21, 25, 36].

In addition to the visual presentations, there is the notion of aural stimuli that may be used in the choreography process. These stimuli usually come from music, but from auditory pitches or noises that movements produce as well [37–39]. The previously mentioned presentations are used as a basis for the development of our presentation methods.

One of the most influential and significant works that used animated figures for choreography is the work of Merce Cunningham. He used a computer system called Life Forms, which is an interface that supports choreography and where the tool becomes a "visual idea generator" [2, 6]. Another paper presents the evolution of Life Forms, DanceForms, which lets choreographers try out ideas and animations before ever meeting with live dancers [4]. These studies show how people interact with computer systems in their creative process. However, this is a static way where people sit behind a computer and create pieces with clicks of a mouse. In Sect. 4, we discuss how to presents the interaction in a more dynamic way in the dance studio.

3   Dance Representation

In this section, we describe an investigation into how choreographers make choreographies and what their general attitude towards technological help in this area is. This gives us the opportunity to identify requirements for an assistant in dance analysis to generate new creative elements in choreographies. To this extent we first describe the setup and results of a survey, followed by a design of a prototype and a user study.

3.1 Survey Setup

To get insight in the attitude of dancers towards the use of technology within the process of creating choreographies, we conducted an online survey. This survey included questions on how choreographers develop choreographies. We included questions about awareness and use of various dance notations and to what extent users are willing to use digital technologies to support them in their creative process. The survey and its results is described in detail in [40]. Here we reproduce the most important findings. The questionnaire was distributed among Dutch choreographers through within Dutch dance communities through social media. 54 choreographers (9 male, 45 female) responded. Almost 75% of the participants followed a certified dance education.

3.2 Survey Results

With respect to dance notations, the survey results confirmed earlier findings from [23] that most choreographers store choreographies through written notation, in memory, or video registration. 61% of the respondents use the aforementioned dance terms for making and remembering their choreographies. Almost 80% of the respondents report not being able to work with dance notations as Laban and Benesh.

To determine the acceptance of digital tools for creative support, participants were asked about willingness to adopt a tool that, for example, gives new variations based on an existing choreography. A significant sub-group (55%) of the respondents does have a positive attitude towards such tools. However, the dancers with a negative attitude are often very negative, where they give arguments such as loss of human aspects of dance, loss of ownership of a choreography or possible difficulty to work with such tools. We also asked participants to rate the importance of various features of choreographies on a 1 (very important) to 5 (not important) Likert scale. As the results in Table 1 show, musicality, creativity and emotion turned out to be the most important aspects in choreographies.

Table 1. Avg. importance ratings of choreography aspects on a Likert scale 1 (high) to 5 (low)

Aspect	Avg. rating
Originality	2.15
Musicality	1.57
Creativity	1.78
Technique	2.30
Symmetry	2.41

To end the questionnaire, an open question was asked about potential features for a potential choreography assistant tool. Using a MoSCoW method, a list of requirements for a choreography assistant tool was developed. Participants indicate that:

- The tool must work with different dance styles
- A dancer must be able to add their existing choreography to the tool
- The tool is able to give new suggestions for choreography variations
- The suggestions must be based on different, rule-based strategies
- The dancer must be able to see the choreography at any moment (written)
- The dance notation used is dance terms
- The tool must be "easy to use", and have fast variation generation time (seconds) The tool is able to explain complex movements in have simplified body movements (legs, arms, belly, knees, hips and head)

3.3   Prototype

Based on the requirements from the previous section, we developed a prototype choreography assistant tool. This prototype is a mobile application (to facilitate use at any time and any place) for dancers where users can enter a choreography consisting of different subsequent steps and the prototype generates variations based on different strategies. When opening the application, the user chooses a dance style. The prototype supports classical ballet, modern dance and street dance. The user continues in a new screen where they can enter their choreography in ten steps, using dance terms (see Fig. 1)[1].

Fig. 1.   Screenshot of the mobile choreography assistant prototype

Dance ontologies.   For classical ballet, these dance terms are based on the BalOnSe ontology from [30], as introduced in Sect. 2.3. In the prototype, 78 ballet steps from BalOnSe were implemented. For modern dance, an ontology from Phyllis Eckler was

---

[1] The prototype is developed as a simple Android application which can be used with a minimum SDK version of 17. The application and source code are available at https://github.com/biktorrr/Dancepiration.

used to implement steps for this dance style. This ontology exists of 57 modern dance steps[2]. For street dance, this was more difficult. There were no existing ontologies for street dance steps found, so a partial ontology for this dance style consisting of 31 steps was made based on experience of one of the authors of this paper.

Generating variations. To generate new variations based on the entered choreographies, we implemented two main strategies. The first strategy replaces one random step by another random new step from the same dance style. The second strategy takes the ontology hierarchy into account and replaces a random step in the choreography by one that shares a 'parent' step in the ontology hierarchy. For example, a specific type of jump is replaced by a different type of jump. The expectation is that the variations based on the ontologies will be more appreciated by the dancers than the completely random option. A third strategy randomly selects either one of the other two strategies or changes more than one step. We however did not evaluate this third variation. The variations are triggered by the user pressing one of three buttons. In the screenshot shown in Fig. 1, these are the buttons labeled 1–3.

3.4   User Study

Setup. We evaluated the prototype in a user study done with six Dutch students from the dance academy Codarts. The participants were asked to (1) choose at least one dance style and make a simple choreography and enter it in the prototype. They were asked to rate this choreography on a 10-point scale. Next, the participant was asked to generate variations using both the random and the ontology-based strategy, each three times. The strategies were not explained to the participants and the buttons were numbered not named.

For each variant, participants were asked to rate the new choreography on a 10-point scale again. Participants were also asked to indicate the executability of the variation and to indicate how correct, creative, helpful and meaningful the variation was on a Likert scale from 1 (very bad) to 5 (very good). Finally, participants were asked what their opinion about the application in general was and what variant they prefer the most.

Results. The random-based variations are compared to ontology-based ones in Table 2 based on different aspects. This shows that in every single aspect the ontology-based variant is outperforming the random variations. For the average choreography score and correctness this difference is statistically significant.

In Table 3, the four aspects per dance style are shown including the differences between the two variants. When looking at the results from dance style perspective, it seems that ballet is the worst performing dance style. The correctness of ballet is the lowest in comparison to the other dance styles. It is also the only dance style whereby the random variant performs better than the ontology-based variant. Interesting is the rating of creativity, whereby ballet is the best performing. One participant indicated in

---

[2] These steps were retrieved from the web document at http://faculty.lacitycollege.edu/ecklerp/modern_dance_terminology.htm.

the user study for ballet variations: "These variations are not logic and fitting, however they are very creative."

Table 2. Average ratings of two variants (grade on a 1–10 scale) and differences in assessment of different elements (on 1–5 scale). *, ** indicates statistical significance at $\alpha = 0.10$ and $\alpha = 0.05$ respectively (t-test/anova).

Score	Original	Random	Ontology-Based	Difference	
Average grade	*6.17*	*5.50*	*6.35*	**+0.85**	**
Correctness		2.89	3.37	**+0.48**	*
Creativity		3.19	3.37	+0.18	
Helpfulness		2.59	3.00	+0.41	
Meaningfulness		2.70	2.96	+0.26	

Table 3. Average ratings per aspect based on dance styles *, ** indicates statistical significance at $\alpha = 0.10$ and $\alpha = 0.05$ respectively (t-test/anova).

Element	Style	Random	Ontology-Based	Difference	
Correctness	Ballet	2.89	2.56	−0.33	
	Streetdance	2.78	3.56	**+0.78**	*
	Modern	3.00	4.00	**+1.00**	**
Creativity	Ballet	3.44	3.56	+0.12	
	Streetdance	2.78	3.11	+0.33	
Helpfulness	Ballet	2.67	2.67	0.00	
	Streetdance	2.44	2.89	+0.45	
	Modern	2.89	3.44	+0.55	
Meaningfulness	Ballet	2.89	2.78	−0.11	
	Streetdance	2.33	2.67	+0.34	
	Modern	2.89	3.44	+0.55	

For the question which variants they preferred, 90% expressed preference for the ontology-based variation instead of the random option.

Discussion. In general, the variations based on the ontologies are considered better than the original choreography. The participants indicated they would like to work with a complete application for preparing dance choreographies and lessons.

The ontology-based variation results in the highest-rated choreographies for most aspects and styles. For classical ballet, the tool performed the worst in general among while classical ballet is the most researched dance style with the most extended ontology. A possible reason for this is that classical ballet is the most strict dance style in terms of existing dance terms. The other dance styles are very flexible in their steps and there are a lot more possibilities for follow-up steps. The aspect correctness can be seen as one of the most important aspects of this application. When a suggestion is not execut-able, the whole choreography will be considered to be bad. This confirms findings from [13], which also concludes that this is especially difficult to achieve.

4 Dance Presentation

In the previous section, we have shown the potential of a choreography assistance tool based on dance term representation. We did not discuss the influence of presentation method of choreography variations. The prototype described in Sect. 3 has a very basic text-based User Interface. In this section, we investigate which presentation methods are considered most effective by end-users for an interactive dance choreography assistant tool. To this end, we developed a second prototype, where choreography variations can be presented in four different methods. In this experiment, we focus on two new dance styles: Hip-hop and Dancehall[3].

4.1 Four Presentation Methods

We here first describe the four presentation methods, which include both visual and auditory modalities. The visual methods (shown in Fig. 2) consisted of textual descriptions, 2D animations and 3D animations and the auditory method consisted of voice-overs. The reason for choosing these four presentation methods is that they differ from each other in the sense that they each present a different approach but propose the same variation.

- **Textual descriptions.** The textual descriptions were based on Laban and Benesh movements. However, as Sect. 3 shows, most dancers are not familiar with these notations, we used (Dutch) written descriptions of individual poses and movements. Rather than using dance terms, here we use detailed descriptions of these poses ("start with legs apart at a shoulders' length, bend knees slightly"). This was done to ensure that the presentation methods could be used for a range of dance styles, including less formal ones for which appropriate training is needed.
- **2D animations.** The 2D animations were created with Stykz (https://www.stykz.net/) which is a multi-platform animation program to develop stick figures. The software is frame-based, so every frame can be customised individually. Therefore, every movement can be animated and modified as desired. The body parts were created with added lines and adjusted by clicking on the points and dragging them in the wanted direction. The timeline and speed could be adjusted with the controller panel and the play button generated the end product in another window without the dots.
- **3D animations.** The 3D animations were created with the choreography software DanceForms 2 (http://charactermotion.com/products/danceforms/), which is designed to visualize dance steps or entire routines in an easy-to-use 3D environment. The 3D animations for this study consisted of one character and were made from scratch, however, large groups of characters or existing sequences from the Dance-Forms database could be used as well.

---

[3] More information about the dance styles can be found at https://en.wikipedia.org/wiki/Hip-hop_dance and http://www.gangalee.net/dancehall_info.php respectively.

- **Auditory descriptions.** The textual instructions were converted to audio versions using Google Translate text-to-speech. This resulted in audio versions of the same instructions.

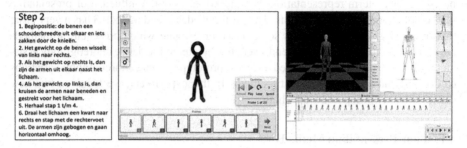

Fig. 2. Three of the four presentation methods (auditory is omitted). From left to right: textual, 2D animation (Styx tool) and 3D animation (DanceForms)

4.2 Setup

Seven experts participated in the experiment. These participants were gathered from Beatz dance studio in the Netherlands. All participants were trained in two dance styles for this experiment. Before the user study started the participants were asked to sign an informed consent letter and fill out a pre-experiment survey on background information of the participant.

Next, the participants were taught a simple choreography. As the variations were generated before the experiment and to ensure that each participant started with the same choreography, they were shown choreographies for each of the two styles, consisting of 16 counts of steps. After this, three pre-programmed variations were shown using one of the four presentation methods. To increase immersion, the visual methods were presented using a large projection screen. Each participant was asked to execute the movements to demonstrate that they understood the presented variations before moving to the next variation. After three variations for one method, the next method was presented. This resulted in 12 variations per dance style per participant. Figure 3 shows participants for each of the four styles.

Fig. 3. Four participants during the 2nd user experiment. From left to right this shows variations presented through textual, 2D animation, 3D animation, and auditory instructions.

The participants were then asked to give their assessment on the presentation methods in a post-experiment survey. Here participants were asked to for each of the presentation methods (1) give an overall assessment; (2) indicate how creatively stimulating these are; (3) how understandable the method is; and (4) whether the method disrupts the creative process. Scores were given on a 1–10 scale. The entire survey can be found in [41].

4.3   Results

Figure 4 shows the results for the overall assessment for the four presentation methods for the two dance styles in two boxplots. These show mean values, variance and range of values. Even though variance is quite substantial (especially for the Textual method), the patterns are very similar between the two styles. This indicates that there is little difference between the styles in how the methods are perceived. Both plots show that the 3D animation is consistently rated highest (with one notable negative outlier in the hip-hop), followed by textual descriptions.

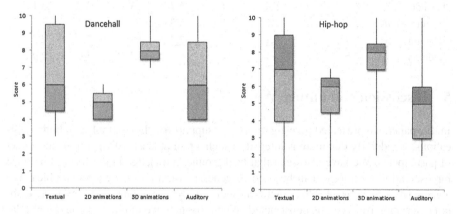

Fig. 4. Boxplot showing medians, variation and extremes of overall assessment of four presentation methods for Dancehall (left) and Hip-hop (right)

Table 4 shows the mean scores for the four criteria (including overall assessment) aggregated over the two dance styles. This shows that for each of scores, the 3D-animations outperform the other presentation methods. When asked directly which method they preferred, five out of seven participants indicated a preference for the 3D-animations.

Discussion. The overall assessment of the presentation methods of the two dance styles shows that both datasets are balanced around the same scores. The medians in all cases differ at most with 1. Overall, the results show that the participants have a neutral or positive attitude towards the four presentation methods. However, the scores of the 3D animations were significantly higher than the other presentation methods. Thus, the participants prefer the 3D animations as a method to stimulate their creativity, because it is clear to understand and does not interrupt the creative process. This presentation method is considered to be the most effective and accepted for the interactive dance choreography assistant tool.

The participants were neutral towards the 2D animations and the auditory instructions. Regarding the 2D animations they were less positive about the clear understanding of the variations and more positive about the level of interruption in the creative process. This suggests that the animations were not clear enough to understand and requires further development. Moreover, this means that the animations were not interrupting the process. Regarding the auditory descriptions the participants were less positive about the stimulation of creativity and more positive about the clear understanding of the variations.

Table 4. Mean scores and variance for the four assessment criteria for the two dance styles combined. The highest means are underlined.

	Overall assessment		Stimulation of creativity		Understandability		(Un-) disruptiveness	
	μ	σ	μ	σ	μ	σ	μ	σ
Textual	6.5	3.1	5.4	2.6	6.7	3.3	6.1	3.1
2D animations	5.4	1.9	5.8	2.3	5.5	2.2	6	3
3D animations	_7.7_	2	_7.1_	2.2	_7.7_	2.1	_7.7_	2.5
Auditory	5.6	2.8	4.7	2.6	6.3	2.6	5.6	2.9

5   Discussion and Future Work

In this paper, we presented investigations into support for choreography. In both applications, we identify that there is interest in such a tool at least with a significant subset of participants. We have also seen that background knowledge in the form of a dance representation (ontology) can be used to generate variations on choreographies. We acknowledge that our rules for generating such variations are quite basic and more elaborate variation rules can be constructed. Where for now we only use hierarchical relations, other relations between steps can be exploited. For example, the steps could be annotated with information about difficulty, 'level of energy', emotional valence or other features, which can be incorporated in the rules. Eventually, we could use Machine Learning to identify 'good' choreography fragments and base variations on such learned material.

Another limitation of the studies is that we investigated short choreographies. With more elaborate choreographies, successful variation strategies are likely to differ from shorter ones. This would require further investigation. Similarly, the user studies described here are performed with limited numbers of participants. To more robustly affirm the findings, larger and more longitudinal studies will be insightful.

Here, we also looked at dance as a standalone art form, whereas in practice music plays a big role in developing and performing choreographies. Combining dance representations and rules with representations for music can result in new possibilities for generating choreography variations [42].

Finally, the results of these investigations provide input for the representation, variation generation and presentation parts of a choreography assistance tool. The method of user input is out of scope for this research, but should be investigated in detail. Such an input method can consist of an extended version of the input method described in Sect. 3, can consist of speech recognition, or ideally be interpreted from motion-captured dance movements [16, 17].

6 Conclusion

In this paper, we presented an investigation into the requirements and possibilities of automated choreography assistant tool. Results show that indeed choreographers can be assisted by semi-automatic analysis of choreographies and the creative generation of new choreography elements. However, from the questionnaire we identify two sub groups of choreographers, one of which has a very positive and one a negative view on such a tool. The survey corroborates existing research in the conclusion that such a tool should be based around dance terms as a representation language. Dance ontologies can be developed or reused to represent choreographies and to base variations on. For some dance styles, this approach is more successful than for others but that hierarchies in these ontologies can be exploited to design executable variations.

We furthermore explored which presentation methods of choreography variations are considered to be effective in the UI of an interactive dance choreography assistant tool. A user study with manually created variations showed that 3D animations received the most positive assessment and are therefore preferred by the experts.

The research presented in this paper shows the potential value of semi-automatic analysis of dance and creative generation of new elements in the choreography as well as as presentation during the choreography process.

Acknowledgements. The authors would like to thank express our gratitude towards all participants in the user studies and surveys as well as to the students of Codarts and Beatz Dance Studio. We also want to thank Kelsey Ketting and Marije Koning for their support.

References

1. Plucker, J.A., Beghetto, R.A., Dow, G.T.: Why isn't creativity more important to educational psychologists? potentials, pitfalls, and future directions in creativity research. Educ. Psychol. **39**(2), 83–96 (2004)
2. Parrish, M.: Technology in dance education. In: Bresler, L. (ed.) International Handbook of Research in Arts Education. Springer International Handbook of Research in Arts Education, vol. 16, pp. 1381–1397. Springer, Dordrecht (2007). https://doi.org/10.1007/978-1-4020-3052-9_94
3. Risner, D., Anderson, J.: Digital dance literacy: an integrated dance technology curriculum pilot project 1. Res. Dance Educ. **9**(2), 113–128 (2008)
4. Calvert, T., Wilke, W., Ryman, R., Fox, I.: Applications of computers to dance. IEEE Comput. Graph. Appl. **25**(2), 6–12 (2005)

5. Van Dyke, J.: Intention: questions regarding its role in choreography. J. Dance Educ. **1**(3), 96–101 (2001)
6. Calvert, T.W., Bruderlin, A., Mah, S., Schiphorst, T., Welman, C.: The evolution of an interface for choreographers. In: Proceedings of the INTERACT 1993 and CHI 1993 Conference on Human Factors in Computing Systems, pp. 115–122. ACM, May 1993
7. Nahrstedt, K., Bajcsy, R., Wymore, L., Sheppard, R., Mezur, K.: Computational model of human creativity in dance choreography. Urbana **51**, 61801 (2007)
8. Latulipe, C., Wilson, D., Huskey, S., Gonzalez, B., Word, M.: Temporal integration of interactive technology in dance: creative process impacts. In: Proceedings of the 8th ACM Conference on Creativity and Cognition, pp. 107–116. ACM, November 2011
9. Coniglio, M.: The importance of being interactive. In: New Visions in Performance, pp. 5–12 (2005)
10. Abouaf, J.: "Biped": a dance with virtual and company dancers. IEEE Multimedia **6**(3), 4–7 (1999)
11. Dils, A.: The ghost in the machine: merce cunningham and Bill T. Jones. PAJ: A J. Perform. Art **24**(1), 94–104 (2002)
12. Burton, S.J., Samadani, A.-A., Gorbet, R., Kulić, D.: Laban movement analysis and affective movement generation for robots and other near-living creatures. In: Laumond, J.-P., Abe, N. (eds.) Dance Notations and Robot Motion. STAR, vol. 111, pp. 25–48. Springer, Cham (2016). https://doi.org/10.1007/978-3-319-25739-6_2
13. Jadhav, S., Joshi, M., Pawar, J.: Art to SMart: an automated BharataNatyam dance choreography. Appl. Artif. Intell. **29**(2), 148–163 (2015)
14. Chan, J.C., Leung, H., Tang, J.K., Komura, T.: A virtual reality dance training system using motion capture technology. IEEE Trans. Learn. Technol. **4**(2), 187–195 (2011)
15. Brockhoeft, T., Petuch, J., Bach, J., Djerekarov, E., Ackerman, M., Tyson, G.: Interactive augmented reality for dance. In: Proceedings of the Seventh International Conference on Computational Creativity, June 2016
16. Sheppard, R.M., Kamali, M., Rivas, R., Tamai, M., Yang, Z., Wu, W., Nahrstedt, K.: Advancing interactive collaborative mediums through tele-immersive dance (TED): a symbiotic creativity and design environment for art and computer science, October 2008
17. Yang, Z., Yu, B., Wu, W., Diankov, R., Bajscy, R.: Collaborative dancing in tele-immersive environment. In: Proceedings of the 14th ACM International Conference on Multimedia, pp. 723–726. ACM, October 2006
18. Wechsler, R., Weiß, F., Dowling, P.: EyeCon: a motion sensing tool for creating interactive Dance, Music, and Video Projections. In: Proceedings of the AISB 2004 COST287-ConGAS Symposium on Gesture Interfaces for Multimedia Systems, pp. 74–79 (2004)
19. Aylward, R., Paradiso, J.A.: Sensemble: a wireless, compact, multi-user sensor system for interactive dance. In: Proceedings of the 2006 Conference on New Interfaces for Musical Expression, pp. 134–139. IRCAM—Centre Pompidou, June 2006
20. Park, C., Chou, P.H., Sun, Y.: A wearable wireless sensor platform for interactive dance performances. In: 2006 Fourth Annual IEEE International Conference on Pervasive Computing and Communications, PerCom 2006, pp. 52–59. IEEE, March 2006
21. Srinivasan, P., Birchfield, D., Qian, G., Kidané, A.: A pressure sensing floor for interactive media applications. In: Proceedings of the 2005 ACM SIGCHI International Conference on Advances in Computer Entertainment Technology, pp. 278–281, June 2005
22. Alexiadis, D.S., Kelly, P., Daras, P., O'Connor, N.E., Boubekeur, T., Moussa, M.B.: Evaluating a dancer's performance using kinect-based skeleton tracking. In: Proceedings of the 19th ACM International Conference on Multimedia, pp. 659–662, November 2011

23. Ramadoss, B., Rajkumar, K.: Semi-automated annotation and retrieval of dance media objects. Cybern. Syst. Int. J. **38**(4), 349–379 (2007)
24. Loke, L., Larssen, A.T., Robertson, T.: Labanotation for design of movement-based interaction. In: Proceedings of the Second Australasian Conference on Interactive Entertainment, pp. 113–120. Creativity & Cognition Studios Press, November 2005
25. Nakamura, M., Hachimura, K.: Development of multimedia teaching material for Labanotation. In: ICKL (International Council of Kinetography Laban) Proceedings of the Twenty-Second Biennial Conference, pp. 150–160 (2002)
26. Nakamura, M., Hachimura, K.: An XML representation of labanotation, labanXML, and its implementation on the notation editor labaneditor2. Rev. Nat. Cent. Digitization (Online Journal) **9**, 47–51 (2006)
27. Wilke, L., Calvert, T., Ryman, R., Fox, I., Bureau, D.N.: From Dance Notation to Human Animation: The LabanDancer Project. New York Times (1932)
28. Bianchini, S., Levillain, F., Menicacci, A., Quinz, E., Zibetti, E.: Towards behavioral objects: a twofold approach for a system of notation to design and implement behaviors in non-anthropomorphic robotic artifacts. In: Laumond, J.-P., Abe, N. (eds.) Dance Notations and Robot Motion. STAR, vol. 111, pp. 1–24. Springer, Cham (2016). https://doi.org/10.1007/978-3-319-25739-6_1
29. Herbison-Evans, D.: A human movement language for computer animation. In: Tobias, J.M. (ed.) Language Design and Programming Methodology. LNCS, vol. 79, pp. 117–128. Springer, Heidelberg (1980). https://doi.org/10.1007/3-540-09745-7_9
30. El Raheb, K., Papapetrou, N., Katifori, V., Ioannidis, Y.: BalOnSe: ballet ontology for annotating and searching video performances. In: Proceedings of the 3rd International Symposium on Movement and Computing, p. 5. ACM (2016)
31. El-Nasr, M.S., Vasilakos, A.V.: DigitalBeing–using the environment as an expressive medium for dance. Inf. Sci. **178**(3), 663–678 (2008)
32. Jung, S.H., Bajcsy, R.: A framework for constructing real-time immersive environments for training physical activities. J. Multimedia **1**(7), 9–17 (2006)
33. Bailey, H.: Ersatz dancing: negotiating the live and mediated in digital performance practice. Int. J. Perform. Arts Digit. Media **3**(2–3), 151–165 (2007)
34. Gonzalez, B., Carroll, E., Latulipe, C.: Dance-inspired technology, technology-inspired dance. In: Proceedings of the 7th Nordic Conference on Human-Computer Interaction: Making Sense Through Design, pp. 398–407. ACM, October 2012
35. Latulipe, C., Huskey, S.: Dance. Draw: exquisite interaction. In: Proceedings of the 22nd British HCI Group Annual Conference on People and Computers: Culture, Creativity, Interaction, vol. 2, pp. 47–51. British Computer Society, September 2008
36. Neagle, R.J., Ng, K., Ruddle, R.A.: Developing a virtual ballet dancer to visualise choreography. In: Proceedings of the AISB, pp. 86–97, March 2004
37. Hagendoorn, I.: Some speculative hypotheses about the nature and perception of dance and choreography. J. Conscious. Stud. **11**(3–4), 79–110 (2004)
38. Sevdalis, V., Keller, P.E.: Captured by motion: Dance, action understanding, and social cognition. Brain Cogn. **77**(2), 231–236 (2011)
39. Qian, G., Guo, F., Ingalls, T., Olson, L., James, J., Rikakis, T.: A gesture-driven multimodal interactive dance system. In: 2004 IEEE International Conference on Multimedia and Expo, ICME 2004, vol. 3, pp. 1579–1582. IEEE, June 2004
40. Jansen, J.: Support for choreographers by semi-automatic dance analysis and the generation of new creative elements. M.Sc. thesis. Vrije Universiteit Amsterdam 2017 (2017)

41. Tjon-a-Pauw, A.: A comparison of UI presentation methods for an interactive dance choreography assistant tool M.Sc. thesis. Vrije Universiteit Amsterdam 2017 (2017)
42. Meroño-Peñuela, A., et al.: The MIDI linked data cloud. In: d'Amato, C., et al. (eds.) ISWC 2017. LNCS, vol. 10588, pp. 156–164. Springer, Cham (2017). https://doi.org/10.1007/978-3-319-68204-4_16

DanceDJ: A 3D Dance Animation Authoring System for Live Performance

Naoya Iwamoto[1], Takuya Kato[1], Hubert P. H. Shum[2(✉)], Ryo Kakitsuka[1],
Kenta Hara[3], and Shigeo Morishima[4]

[1] Waseda University, Tokyo, Japan
iwamoto@toki.waseda.jp, {takuya_lbj,kakitsuka.99821}@ruri.waseda.jp
[2] Northumbria University, Newcastle upon Tyne, UK
hubert.shum@northumbria.ac.uk
[3] Meiji University, Tokyo, Japan
mactkg@gmail.com
[4] Waseda Research Institute for Science and Engineering, Tokyo, Japan
shigeo@waseda.jp

Abstract. Dance is an important component of live performance for expressing emotion and presenting visual context. Human dance performances typically require expert knowledge of dance choreography and professional rehearsal, which are too costly for casual entertainment venues and clubs. Recent advancements in character animation and motion synthesis have made it possible to synthesize virtual 3D dance characters in real-time. The major problem in existing systems is a lack of an intuitive interfaces to control the animation for real-time dance controls. We propose a new system called the *DanceDJ* to solve this problem. Our system consists of two parts. The first part is an underlying motion analysis system that evaluates motion features including dance features such as the postures and movement tempo, as well as audio features such as the music tempo and structure. As a pre-process, given a dancing motion database, our system evaluates the quality of possible timings to connect and switch different dancing motions. During runtime, we propose a control interface that provides visual guidance. We observe that disk jockeys (DJs) effectively control the mixing of music using the DJ controller, and therefore propose a DJ controller for controlling dancing characters. This allows DJs to transfer their skills from music control to dance control using a similar hardware setup. We map different motion control functions onto the DJ controller, and visualize the timing of natural connection points, such that the DJ can effectively govern the synthesized dance motion. We conducted two user experiments to evaluate the user experience and the quality of the dance character. Quantitative analysis shows that our system performs well in both motion control and simulation quality.

N. Iwamoto and T. Kato contributed equally to this work.

Electronic supplementary material The online version of this chapter (https://doi.org/10.1007/978-3-319-76270-8_46) contains supplementary material, which is available to authorized users.

Keywords: Human-computer interaction · Character animation
DJ controllers · Dance

1   Introduction

Dancing is one of the most popular physical activities across every age group, race and region around the world. It can be regarded as a form of self-expression and a means of communication. The use of dance to enhance musical expression has been popular for centuries in musicals, opera and ballet. Video of well designed dance motion can be played along a musical score to achieve a similar effects.

In recent years, dance animation using digitally generated characters has become more and more popular in musical animation mega hits such as the animation "Frozen". Apart from such a kind of *pre-rendered* dance animation, real-time dance authoring has also been introduced. Using novel sensors such as the Microsoft Kinect and motion capture systems, the real-time control of characters had become more accessible. These interfaces allow the user to create computer generated dance motions with intuitive actions. While we can enjoy various live performances acted by computer generated character in the world, most of these live performances only show the 2D video created in advance as an offline process. The difficulty of live scene authoring lies not only on the skills of the performers but also the technical complexity to achieve a high quality performance. Therefore, we propose a character control system that requires a relatively low skill level to control the character, as well as adapts well in existing live stage performance frameworks.

A challenge for real-time dance authoring is that while many dance movements are based on normal motion, dance differs in that its motion normally requires a beat. In music and dance, the beat is an audible or visual cue demarcating the division of a certain sequence. Dancers continually change their poses while maintaining the beat. The rhythm of musical content is normally characterized by a repeating sequence of beats. Dance and music have evolved together over centuries to match one another by sharing the beat. Many existing interfaces have not been able to achieve high quality dance as these principles are not taken into account.

To address this problem, we came up with a hypothesis that the creation of real-time dance can be improved by allowing the users to understand the beat of both motion and music. This hypothesis came up when observing the interaction of the disk jockey in music. A disk jockey, known as a DJ, is a person who introduces and plays music especially on the radio or at a club or live performance. Their performance often involves intricate and seamless mixing to connect one piece of music with another, which is recognized as a way of performing music without playing musical instruments. Their interaction with the music normally takes the beat of the music into account. Since both dance and music share the same principles, we anticipate that by providing a means for the user to maintain the beat when creating dance motion would result in a highly usable system.

We present a novel dance authoring interface called *DanceDJ* based on such a hypothesis. By mimicking the interaction of the musical DJ, the system allows users to control dance motion more intuitively and create high-quality dance motion in real-time. By implementing the synchronize button that synchronizes the dance motion with the music played by the other electronic instruments, the user can match the beat of the dance motion to that of the music. In contrast to the music DJ, the connectivity and beat of the dance motion tend to be more abstract than that of the music, which affects the usability when connecting the dance motion. To support the users, we have implemented a novel feature to estimate the connectivity of the dance motions. The system automatically calculates the beat of the dance by using the motion intensity to estimate the probability of the frame wise dance connectivity, which represents how well the beat of dance and music matches together. This feature helps the users to achieve a DJ-like experience when interactively creating dance motion and allows users to create, as well as realizing our hypothesis of the beat and correlation with music.

We have produced a fully usable system for real-time dance authoring. Experimental results show that high-quality dance motion can be synthesized in real-time using the proposed DJ interface. We have preformed quantitative user studies to support the usability of the system. For the user, we have evaluated how well users have been able to create high-quality dance motion intuitively. For the audience, we have evaluated how plausible the created dance motions are by looking at the dance motion results our system has created in real-time. We have also conducted tests of using our system in real-world live performances.

There are two major contributions in this paper:

- To design a novel DJ interface for real-time dance authoring based on dance and music beat correlations.
- To introduce a novel dance and music beat evaluation function that evaluates how well a pose in a dance synchronizes to that of another dance using the estimated beat information of motion and music.

The rest of the paper is organized as follow. Section 2 describes the related research of this project. Section 3 describes the DJ interface we have implemented for real-time dance authoring. Section 4 explains the design of the transition function that estimate the quality of switching from one motion to another based on the beat pattern. Section 5 explains how we visualize the results of the transition function for effective dance controls. Section 6 details the user study we have preformed to support the usability of the system. Finally, Sect. 8 concludes and discusses the system.

2   Related Work

In this section, we introduce works related to our system. There are numerous related works for creating character motion interactively. Mainly, this work can be divided into user interaction when creating character motion and DJ-like interactions.

2.1   User Interfaces for Character Control

Numerous interfaces have been introduced to control character motion. One of the favorite ways is the performance-based approach. The interface, which uses motion capture and video of human motion has been popular in creating 3DCG animation creations [4,5,11,15,20]. Depth camera based motion sensing opens another pathway for real-time character controls [16,17,23,28]. While they fulfill the demands of recreating accurate human motion, this interface relies upon the user's ability to perform the demanded motion. Additionally, editing the character motion requires other interactions, such as sketch-based interaction [2,3,8,9,13]. While these interfaces are easy to use, they do not match our demand for real-time motion creation. Interfaces that control the bones of the characters [10,12,26,27], such as ones introduced by [6], allows users to create dance motion intuitively. These character-shaped interfaces that interactively deform the characters' bones allow users to create arbitrary poses. Despite its intuitiveness in creating bone shapes for a specific frame, these interfaces are not suitable for creating character motion in real-time using only two hands to control the whole body. One of the ways to create character motions is to set motion coordination keys to individual buttons like the character controls in video games [25]. This way, the user can press various buttons to control the character. While the usability of such character control would be familiar to those who play video games, the user is required to memorize the dance motions allocated to each particular button. This forces the users to either memorize a large number of button allocated motions or the designer to limit variety of the motions allowed to the user.

2.2   DJ-Like Interaction in Research

Due to the creative nature of mixing, many types of research have focused upon the interaction of DJ's. The interaction of DJ's has been analyzed in various ways to realize similar applications or improve their actions. While many of these applications introduce a novel interface alternative to the traditional DJ interface, the form of DJ interfaces has not changed drastically. Accordingly, recent researchers have applied the DJ interaction to other applications to take advantage of its high usability [7,18,19]. Target applications which apply a DJ-like interface vary from data visualization, 3DCG visualization to Robot motion control. In these researches, sliders and turntables have been installed in various applications. They have proved that DJ-like interactions can increase usability and provide the user with a novel experience of interaction with the target application, especially when this interaction is in real-time.

Our proposed user interface is inspired by the interface called "Robot-Jockey", which was introduced by [22]. This interface introduced a novel interaction for creating dance motion of a robot using the DJ-like interaction of controlling tempo and motion in real-time. Since the primary objective of this interface is to provide the means of creating the robot's motions in real-time with intuitive interaction, their interface only needs to select very limited motions such as kicking or punching from the database. The limited selection of motions can be sufficient for a robot which only has a few actuators to control the body, while 3DCG characters have several more joints, bones and skin to consider. Accordingly, we follow the idea of controlling dance motions in real-time using a DJ-like interface while we improve the system to be sufficient to control 3DCG characters.

2.3 Implementation Requirements

Taking the shortcomings of related applications towards our potential users into account, we set our implementation requirements as follows:

Intuitive motion control:
We select and control the parameters of the character motion that are necessary for the live-action remixing of dance motions.

Intuitive interface:
Our interface is based on the MIDI interface. The MIDI interface is a well-designed, intuitive, and very popular interface for many fields and requires real-time interactions.

Works in real-time:
Our interface can create dance motions in real-time, which allows usage in live performances such as concerts.

In developing our interface, we have tried to achieve all of the goals which the works cited above have not yet completely satisfied. As related works and products have not been able to fulfill the requirements set out above, we believe that this makes our interface advantageous for application in numerous settings.

3   DanceDJ Interface

To verify our hypothesis described in Sect. 1, we developed the prototype of DanceDJ to author character's dance motion with a DJ interface. A simple live performance work flow is shown in Fig. 1. Firstly, the DJ plays music and shares the beat with the DanceDJ system using a local network in real-time. While we evaluated our system playing only along DJ, the use of electronic instruments and existing online beat estimation systems would allow the proposed system to be applicable for wide variety of music genre. Next, the DanceDJ operator controls an input dance motion to synchronize with the received beat. Finally the character which is assigned the dance motion is projected on a screen or stage in front of audiences. From the audience's perspective, it looks like the character is dancing while synchronized with the music played by the DJ. In our experiment, the DJ used a DJ software package called *Traktor*, and sent music information to other device with a software called *Ableton Link*. The DJ interface sends a MIDI signal distributed at each button or slider into the DanceDJ system.

A typical DJ interface for music controls is shown in Fig. 2. This interface has many buttons and sliders to control music. The left and right part that have

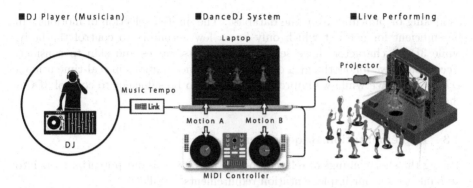

Fig. 1. System overview of DanceDJ with live performance setup. (a) DJ plays music sending the tempo into DanceDJ using local network. (b) Dance DJ receives the tempo and allows the user to synchronize. (c) Audiences can enjoy watching the virtual avatar's dance synchronized with the music on the stage/screen as a visual expression of the music.

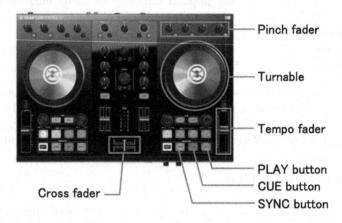

Fig. 2. Common DJ interface; buttons, fader and turntables are equipped for mixing two music.

similar buttons and sliders are for controlling two pieces of music respectively. The play button is for playing/pausing the music. The tempo faders adjust the speed of the music tempo. The turntables adjust playback speed to match tempos or beats. In the middle, the cross fader blends the two pieces of music assigned to the left and right parts. The sync buttons are used for automatic music tempo tuning based on the other assigned music.

To author the character's dance motion, we map the different dance motion control functions onto the DJ controller as shown in Table 1. The principle of such a mapping design is to conserve the meaning of the buttons such that DJs can transfer their skills from music controls to dance controls. The tempo faders are

Table 1. Mapping function between DJ and dance parameters

DJ-interface	Dance control parameters
Tempo fader	Motion speed
Cross fader	Mixing dance motion
Pinch fader	Sound effect
Turntable	Moving in few sequence
PLAY	Start/Stop dance animation
SYNC	Synchronization between music and dance
CUE	Visualization of the transition point

assigned with a motion speed control function. The play buttons start and pause a dance motion. The turntables are used to playback sequences of dance motion. The cross fader interpolates two different dance motions. The sync buttons are used for automatic tempo tuning of the selected dance motion based on the received music tempo. We use the cue button for the visualization function as described in Sect. 4 to find a smooth transition point between different dance motions.

Fig. 3. DanceDJ's system screen in a prototype stage. (a) For audience, the center's character displayed for a user is only projected to the projection screen. (b) For a user, the system displays three characters, which left and right are assigned different motions respectively, and center is a result interpolated dance motions between left and right by using cross fader.

In Fig. 3, we show a simple DanceDJ's system screen. From the user's perspective, the screen has three columns displaying the same character; the left and right columns display two different dance motions, and the center column displays the result that is interpolated from the left and right dance motions dependent on the cross fader's value. The audience can only see the resultant character in the center column.

Our system employs a data-driven approach to synthesize a new dance motion. We constructed a dance database that consisted of 16 dance motions from a Japanese video website *niconico*. In our study, this number of dance motions were sufficient for our experiments and a live performance for about half an hour. The dance motions were created by various amateur users, and the duration was about 3 min each. All dance motions are retargetted to the same structure with the same number of joints, which facilitates efficient motion interpolation. In our experiment, we used motion data with 70 joints included finger joints. Joints are represented using quaternions and we use *Spherical Linear Interpolation (SLERP)* for interpolating the joints between two dance motions.

It is a challenge to mix motions seamlessly and avoid sudden jumps of postures. While a DJ is able to mix different music by ad-lib as they have memorized the music, requiring the DJ to memorize all the dance choreography for dance mixing would be difficult. We address the problem by proposing a technical solution and by providing visual guidance. For the technical solution, we propose a novel transition function to evaluate a connectivity between two different dance motions based on the motion tempo, postures and the original music tempo assigned to each dance motion, which is detailed in Sect. 4. As the visual guidance, we visualize a result of the transition function to users on the system screen in real-time, which is described in Sect. 5.

4   A Transition Function for Dance Motions

We describe a transition function to evaluate how well a frame in a dance can seamlessly transition to a frame in another dance. This function supports a user to narrow down the transition frame candidates of a selected dance motion. It consists of two terms including (1) the beats of both music and motion $E_{beat}(i,j)$, and (2) the similarity of human poses $E_{pose}(i,j)$:

$$E_{trans}(i,j) = w_1 E_{beat}(i,j) + w_2 E_{pose}(i,j), \tag{1}$$

where i and j are the beat indexes of two different dance motions, w_1 and w_2 are weights from 0.0 to 1.0 for the evaluation functions $E_{beat}(i,j)$ and $E_{pose}(i,j)$ respectively. These weight parameters are controlled by the user using the pinch fader of the DJ interface. $E_{beat}(i,j)$ and $E_{pose}(i,j)$ are described in the next two subsections.

4.1   Beat Matching Between Music and Motion

Considering that dance motion represents music beats as physical expression, the dance motion beat is related to joint angular velocity or angular moment. Therefore, we first compute the *Weight Effort* using a sum of angular velocity for each dance motion database. We then define motion beat from the minimum value in each a window range [21]. Since each dance motion comes with a corresponding piece of music, we obtain the window range from the beat of the music.

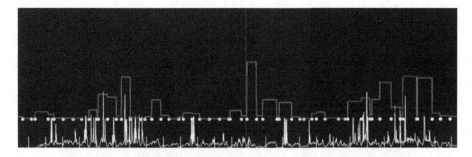

Fig. 4. An analyzed result for arbitrary dance motion. The wave information is *Weight Effort (WE)* considered the sum of angular velocity for the all joints at each frame. Dot circles represents dance motion beats calculated from the *WE* value

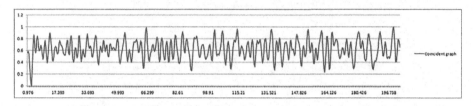

Fig. 5. The beat evaluation result (E_{beat}) of transition function applied for arbitrary music and the dance motion created by artists. When the music beat and the motion beat are completely matching, the result becomes a constant sine curve.

We use the *Songle* API to analyze the beat of the corresponding music. The beat information has a set of both time position and beat count, and we compute the beat per minutes (BPM) by calculating the average beat over time.

From the results as shown in Fig. 4, we found that the dance motion beat does not always match the music beat because the dance motion beat is not at a constant interval. We expect that a smooth dance transition should happen at the frame when the beat of both music and motion matches. Therefore we design the beat evaluation function $E_{beat}(i, j)$ to evaluate a beat matching rate between the motion and the music. To evaluate a beat's coincidence factor of motion tempo with music tempo, we approximate the discretized motion tempo into a continuous function using a Gaussian distribution. The range of those values are from 0.0 to 1.0. We set 0.1 as the *sigma* value used in Gaussian distribution. The result is shown in Fig. 5.

4.2 Posture Similarity

To seamlessly connect the different dance motions, we compute the similarity of the posture based on the sum of root mean square distance in joint positions for all joints [14]. Considering two dance motions, the frame-wise pose similarity can be calculated and represented using a similarity matrix as shown in Fig. 6. The X-axis represents the frame number of a dance motion, and the Y-axis

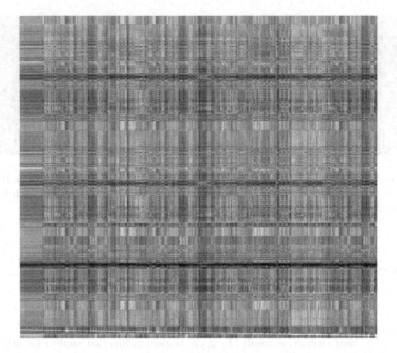

Fig. 6. A result of *Motion Graph* applied for two different dance motions; The width and height of the image corresponds to the number of frames for each two dance motions. The corresponded frame colored with white represents high similarity of two postures.

represents that of another dance. A darker pixel indicates a high similarity at the corresponding frame pair.

We conduct the similarity calculation for all dance motion combinations as an pre-process to reduce on-line computation time. During run-time, given two poses from two dance motions, the calculated value is retrieved as the result of the posture similarity function $E_{pose}(i, j)$.

5   Visual Guidance for Motion Transition

In this section, we describe how to visualize the dance motion's information on the system screen to assist a user in transitioning smoothly between two different dance motions.

An example of the graphical interface is shown in Fig. 7. Our system has three partitions on the system screen; the left and right columns are for editing, and the center is for visualizing the mixing result. If a user sets the cross fader to the right side, the user can select the next dance motion and edit it on the left side.

In particular, tn the top left and right hand corners of Fig. 7, we display basic information including the input dance motion, the music title, duration,

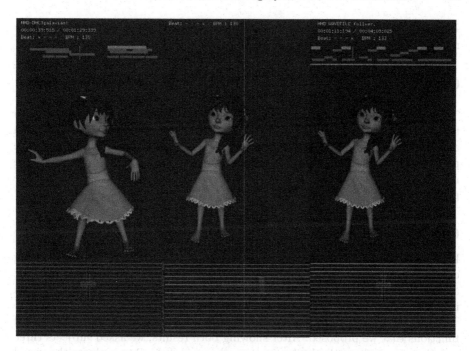

Fig. 7. Final system screen; we show the beat information below. In the upper right hand corner visual guidance based on the transition function for seamless transition in shown. (Color figure online)

beat, BPM and structure. The lines at the bottom left and right hand sides show the music beat of the dance motion, which scrolls upwards during the playback of a dance motion. The corresponding color indicates the quality of transitions calculated from Eq. 1. At the bottom of the center column, the colored lines represent music beat of four counts received from the DJ through *Ableton Link*. When the user pushes the Sync button on the DJ interface, the interval width of the music beat bars are fitted to the width of the beat received from the DJ.

5.1   Visualization of Transition Frames

Here, we describe a visual process for assisting the user in transitioning between different dance sequences.

When the user searches for the next transition point by pushing the cue button, the system uses Eq. 1 to evaluate a smooth connection. A time-line that visualize the results of the transition function is shown below both the music structure. It indicate time-line information that takes the global similarity (based on music and motion features such as tempo and pose) with the other candidate dance motion into account. We use red to represent large values and blue to represent small values. Similarly, the color of the time-lines below the dancing character is updated using the same color scheme. It represents on the local similarity between the current selected dance frame and the other candidate's motion in the neighbor frame range.

6   User Study

To evaluate the effectiveness of our system, we conducted user studies from the perspectives of both audiences and users. There were 17 people (15 men and 2 women) and 12 people (11 men and 1 woman) for the user and audience perspective studies respectively. Their ages ranged from 21 to 30 years old. While no one had DJ experience, 25% of the subjects had dance experience and stage performance.

6.1   Audience Perspective

In the study of audience perspective, we first showed two dance animations using our system synchronized with music played by a DJ for a few minutes. The first animation was controlled by an experienced user without the transition function nor automatic beat synchronization. We call such a system the prototype system. The second animation was controlled by the same user using the full range of functions that we proposed. After showing both results, we asked subjects three questions for each synthesized animation shown in Table 2 to evaluate the visual effectiveness of the dance motion synthesized using the *transition function*. The results in Fig. 8 show that our system consistently out-performs the prototype system in all three questions. It demonstrates that our system helps to improve

Table 2. Questions for audiences; (7-points Likert scale, 7: most agree; 1: least agree)

No.	Question
Q1	Were you satisfied with the animation result?
Q2	Is the connection between different dance sequences natural?
Q3	Did you feel that the animation result matched both the dance and music?

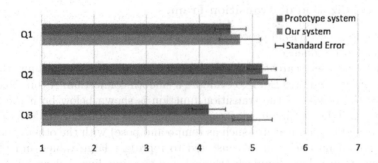

Fig. 8. Result of the user evaluation from audience perspective. (Color figure online)

the quality of dance mixing. We used a two-tailed Wilcoxon signed-rank test and found no significant differences in the results between the two systems (p-values were more than 0.05).

6.2   User Perspective

In the study of the user's perspective, we first explain the usage of the prototype system to the subject for 5 min. The subject then used the system while listening to a DJ playing music for 10 min. Next, we explained our full system consisting the visualized transition function and automatic beat synchronized function for 5 min. The subject then used it for 10 min.

We finally asked each subject to evaluate the systems with five questions shown in Table 3. Figure 9 shows the averaged results of the user study. In Q1, Q2 and Q3, our system scores significantly higher than the prototype system. A two-tailed Wilcoxon signed-rank test was conducted to demonstrate that the difference between the average score was statistically significant. In Q4, most subjects suggested that our system was more adaptable in mapping transition between dance motion than the prototype system, as shown in Fig. 10. In Q5, the transition function with the visual guidance allows subjects to intuitively control without taking much time, as shown in Fig. 11.

Table 3. Questions for users; Q1–Q4 (7-points Likert scale, 7: most agree; 1: least agree), Q5 (open ended)

No	Question
Q1	Could you naturally connect dance motion sequences?
Q2	Could you match both dance and music?
Q3	Were you satisfied with the dance animation you controlled.
Q4	Did you feel that the mapping relationship between each button and motion function was adaptable?
Q5	How long did it take you to control the dance motion satisfactorily?

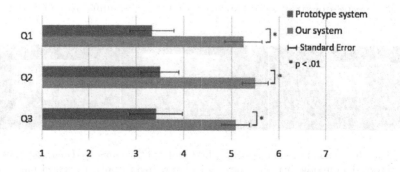

Fig. 9. Result of the user evaluation from user perspective.

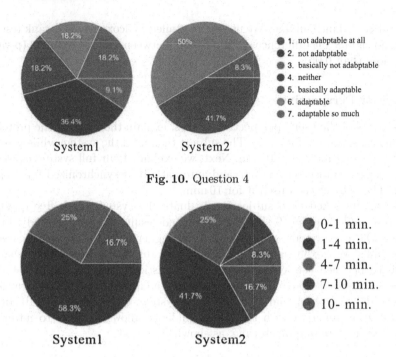

Fig. 10. Question 4

Fig. 11. Question 5

The results of user evaluation show that our method was more effective in transitioning seamlessly from both the audience and user's perspective.

6.3 Other Feedback

As a separate user study, we also conducted a live performance with a DJ in a music club. The synthesized character's dance motion was projected to a large 2D screen using a projector. There were about 20–30 audience. There were positive reaction from the audience when the character was synchronized with the DJ's music. During our live performance we met a opportunity to collaborate with

Fig. 12. The scene of live performance. Left and right persons are DanceDJ player and DJ player. The middle person is next VJ player. Incidentally, DanceDJ player and a VJ player started a novel collaboration.

VJ). We mixed two video channel half and half, and the VJ made the visual effects such as the dance floor for our dancing character by ad-lib. This is shown in Fig. 12.

7   Discussions

Experimental Feedback: As an evaluation, we conducted two experiments to evaluate both audience and user perspective. Since all the subjects were asked to evaluate the prototype prior to evaluating our Dance DJ, comparison might not be fairly evaluated. To counterbalance the evaluation more, we conducted an additional experiment in reverse order to evaluate detailed advantages of our system. From our experiments, we found that DanceDJ has some rooms of improvement for audiences and users. For example, because our system can assist user to seamlessly connect different dance motion naturally, sometimes many audiences do not notice the transition's timing. This raises the problem that the system may not encourage dramatic effects at the transition like what DJs do between drastically different songs. As our future work, we will design diverse connecting function, such as for a mash-up affection, which provide user intuitive control to create different varieties of dance motion simply by changing the function. Some future directions are listed below:

Emotional Enrichment: We wish to visualize the emotional features of music in real-time. A character's facial and body motion are synchronized with music emotional features perceived by the audiences. We then integrate existing techniques such as automatic facial motion synthesis [1] and motion filter [24] using the pinch fader to enrich quality of the animation.

Database Limitation: For all the experiments, we used a motion database created by armature artists. Hence, the quality and the number of the motion database are limited. In the future, we will collect more dance motions and corresponded music data-set from the video shared in different video hosting services.

Helping Users with Disabilities: Since it only requires a few simple control to create the dance motion, we believe that the system could help those who cannot dance due to physical disabilities for enjoying dancing. We plan to evaluate how to better serve such a user group by providing a system to generate virtual dance characters.

Artists Collaboration: We believe that the users of our system, DanceDJs, have a possibility to be a type of major artists in the field, such as DJs or VJs. Since the collaboration with DJs has proven to be successful, the collaborations with VJs will be a very interesting direction to move forward for exploring future possibilities.

8 Conclusion

We have presented DanceDJ, a novel DJ-like controller for creating dance animation in real-time. We have presented the transition function and visual guidance for user control. The transition function considered both synchronization between the music and human motion beats, and posture similarity with next dance's posture. By visualizing the transition function's results, this system allows the user to intuitively and effectively transition into the next dance motion. We evaluated the effectiveness from audience and user perspectives by conducting user evaluation.

In our future work, we will add a motion effect function for changing the dynamics of dance motions with the pinch fader. By collaborating with Video Jockeys (VJs), we will represent the dancing character and the background environment more attractively. Furthermore, our system will adopt a motion exploring function to find arbitrary dance motions from dance motion database as soon as possible as an on-line process. We believe DanceDJ has a good potential to conduct a new style of live performance in collaboration with DJ, VJ and real dancers on a stage.

Acknowledgement. This work was supported in part by JST ACCEL Grant Number JPMJAC1602, Japan. It was also supported by the Engineering and Physical Sciences Research Council (EPSRC) (Ref: EP/M002632/1) and the Royal Society (Ref: IE160609).

References

1. Asahina, W., Okada, N., Iwamoto, N., Masuda, T., Fukusato, T., Morishima, S.: Automatic facial animation generation system of dancing characters considering emotion in dance and music. In: SIGGRAPH Asia 2015 Posters (SA 2015), pp. 11:1–11:1. ACM, New York (2015). http://doi.acm.org/10.1145/2820926.2820935
2. Choi, B., i Ribera, R.B., Lewis, J.P., Seol, Y., Hong, S., Eom, H., Jung, S., Noh, J.: SketchiMo: sketch-based motion editing for articulated characters. ACM Trans. Graph. **35**(4), 146:1–146:12 (2016). http://doi.acm.org/10.1145/2897824.2925970
3. Choi, M.G., Yang, K., Igarashi, T., Mitani, J., Lee, J.: Retrieval and visualization of human motion data via stick figures. Comput. Graph. Forum **31**(7pt1), 2057–2065 (2012)
4. Dontcheva, M., Yngve, G., Popović, Z.: Layered acting for character animation. In: ACM SIGGRAPH 2003 Papers (SIGGRAPH 2003), pp. 409–416. ACM, New York (2003). http://doi.acm.org/10.1145/1201775.882285
5. Fender, A., Müller, J., Lindlbauer, D.: Creature teacher: a performance-based animation system for creating cyclic movements. In: Proceedings of the 3rd ACM Symposium on Spatial User Interaction (SUI 2015), pp. 113–122. ACM, New York (2015). http://doi.acm.org/10.1145/2788940.2788944
6. Glauser, O., Ma, W.C., Panozzo, D., Jacobson, A., Hilliges, O., Sorkine-Hornung, O.: Rig animation with a tangible and modular input device. ACM Trans. Graph. **35**(4), 144:1–144:11 (2016). http://doi.acm.org/10.1145/2897824.2925909

7. Groth, P., Shamma, D.A.: Spinning data: remixing live data like a music dj. In: CHI 2013 Extended Abstracts on Human Factors in Computing Systems (CHI EA 2013), pp. 3063–3066. ACM, New York (2013). http://doi.acm.org/10.1145/2468356.2479611

8. Guay, M., Cani, M.P., Ronfard, R.: The line of action: an intuitive interface for expressive character posing. ACM Trans. Graph. 32(6), 205:1–205:8 (2013). http://doi.acm.org/10.1145/2508363.2508397

9. Hahn, F., Mutzel, F., Coros, S., Thomaszewski, B., Nitti, M., Gross, M., Sumner, R.W.: Sketch abstractions for character posing. In: Proceedings of the 14th ACM SIGGRAPH/Eurographics Symposium on Computer Animation (SCA 2015), pp. 185–191. ACM, New York (2015). http://doi.acm.org/10.1145/2786784.2786785

10. Held, R., Gupta, A., Curless, B., Agrawala, M.: 3D puppetry: a kinect-based interface for 3D animation. In: Proceedings of the 25th Annual ACM Symposium on User Interface Software and Technology (UIST 2012), pp. 423–434. ACM, New York (2012). http://doi.acm.org/10.1145/2380116.2380170

11. Ishigaki, S., White, T., Zordan, V.B., Liu, C.K.: Performance-based control interface for character animation. ACM Trans. Graph. (SIGGRAPH) 28(3), 61 (2009)

12. Jacobson, A., Panozzo, D., Glauser, O., Pradalier, C., Hilliges, O., Sorkine-Hornung, O.: Tangible and modular input device for character articulation. ACM Trans. Graph. 33(4), 82:1–82:12 (2014). http://doi.acm.org/10.1145/2601097.2601112

13. Jin, M., Gopstein, D., Gingold, Y., Nealen, A.: Animesh: interleaved animation, modeling, and editing. ACM Trans. Graph. 34(6), 207:1–207:8 (2015). http://doi.acm.org/10.1145/2816795.2818114

14. Kovar, L., Gleicher, M., Pighin, F.: Motion graphs. ACM Trans. Graph. 21(3), 473–482 (2002). http://doi.acm.org/10.1145/566654.566605

15. Lee, J., Chai, J., Reitsma, P.S.A., Hodgins, J.K., Pollard, N.S.: Interactive control of avatars animated with human motion data. ACM Trans. Graph. 21(3), 491–500 (2002). http://doi.acm.org/10.1145/566654.566607

16. Liu, Z., Huang, J., Bu, S., Han, J., Tang, X., Li, X.: Template deformation-based 3-D reconstruction of full human body scans from low-cost depth cameras. IEEE Trans. Cybern. 47(3), 695–708 (2017)

17. Liu, Z., Zhou, L., Leung, H., Shum, H.P.H.: Kinect posture reconstruction based on a local mixture of Gaussian process models. IEEE Trans. Vis. Comput. Graph. 22(11), 2437–2450 (2016)

18. Norman, A., Amatriain, X.: Data jockey, a tool for meta-data enhanced digital DJing and active listening. In: ICMC. Michigan Publishing (2007)

19. Ragnhild, M.M., Mckelvin, M., Nest, R., Valdez, L., ping Yee, K., Back, M., Harrison, S.: SeismoSpin: a physical instrument for digital data. In: CHI 2003 Extended Abstracts on Human Factors in Computing Systems, pp. 832–833. ACM Press (2003)

20. Shiratori, T., Hodgins, J.K.: Accelerometer-based user interfaces for the control of a physically simulated character. ACM Trans. Graph. 27(5), 123:1–123:9 (2008). http://doi.acm.org/10.1145/1409060.1409076

21. Shiratori, T., Nakazawa, A., Ikeuchi, K.: Dancing-to-music character animation. Comput. Graph. Forum 25(3), 449–458 (2006). http://dx.doi.org/10.1111/j.1467-8659.2006.00964.x

22. Shirokura, T., Sakamoto, D., Sugiura, Y., Ono, T., Inami, M., Igarashi, T.: Robo-Jockey: real-time, simultaneous, and continuous creation of robot actions for everyone. In: Proceedings of the 7th International Conference on Advances in Computer Entertainment Technology (ACE 2010), pp. 53–56. ACM, New York (2010). http://doi.acm.org/10.1145/1971630.1971646

23. Shum, H.P.H., Ho, E.S.L., Jiang, Y., Takagi, S.: Real-time posture reconstruction for Microsoft kinect. IEEE Trans. Cybern. **43**(5), 1357–1369 (2013)

24. Wang, J., Drucker, S.M., Agrawala, M., Cohen, M.F.: The cartoon animation filter. ACM Trans. Graph. **25**(3), 1169–1173 (2006). http://doi.acm.org/10.1145/1141911.1142010

25. Yazaki, Y., Soga, A., Umino, B., Hirayama, M.: Automatic composition by body-part motion synthesis for supporting dance creation. In: 2015 International Conference on Cyberworlds (CW), pp. 200–203, October 2015

26. Yoshizaki, W., Sugiura, Y., Chiou, A.C., Hashimoto, S., Inami, M., Igarashi, T., Akazawa, Y., Kawachi, K., Kagami, S., Mochimaru, M.: An actuated physical puppet as an input device for controlling a digital manikin. In: Proceedings of the SIGCHI Conference on Human Factors in Computing Systems (CHI 2011), pp. 637–646. ACM, New York (2011). http://doi.acm.org/10.1145/1978942.1979034

27. Zhai, S., Milgram, P.: Quantifying coordination in multiple DOF movement and its application to evaluating 6 DOF input devices. In: Proceedings of the SIGCHI Conference on Human Factors in Computing Systems (CHI 1998), pp. 320–327. ACM Press/Addison-Wesley Publishing Co., New York (1998). http://dx.doi.org/10.1145/274644.274689

28. Zhang, P., Siu, K., Zhang, J., Liu, C.K., Chai, J.: Leveraging depth cameras and wearable pressure sensors for full-body kinematics and dynamics capture. ACM Trans. Graph. **33**(6), 1–14 (2014). http://doi.acm.org/10.1145/2661229.2661286

Automatic System for Editing Dance Videos Recorded Using Multiple Cameras

Shuhei Tsuchida$^{(\boxtimes)}$ ⓘ, Satoru Fukayama ⓘ, and Masataka Goto ⓘ

National Institute of Advanced Industrial Science and Technology (AIST),
Central 2, 1-1-1 Umezono, Tsukuba, Ibaraki, Japan
{s-tsuchida,s.fukayama,m.goto}@aist.go.jp

Abstract. As social media has matured, uploading video content has increased. Multiple videos of physical performances, such as dance, are difficult to integrate into high-quality videos without knowledge of video-editing principles. In this study, we present a system that automatically edits dance-performance videos taken from multiple viewpoints into a more attractive and sophisticated dance video. Our system can crop the frame of each camera appropriately by using the performer's behavior and skeleton information. The system determines the camera switches and cut lengths following a probabilistic model of general cinematography guidelines and of knowledge extracted from expert experience. In this study, our system automatically edited a dance video of four performers taken from multiple viewpoints, and ten video-production experts evaluated the generated video. As a result of a comparison of another automatic editing system, our system tended to be performed better.

Keywords: Video editing · Dance · Computational cinematography
Automation

1 Introduction

As social media has progressed, many videos have been uploaded to the Internet for private or public purposes. High-quality videos are likely to be shared by many people, leading to increased opportunities for dance performers. Therefore, video content is an important tool for a performer to become well known. Sponsored professional dance videos are regularly uploaded on social media, attracting fans and increasing the recognition of performers. However, these attractive and sophisticated videos are usually achieved with professional techniques used in movies and TV. Thus, it is difficult to create a high-quality dance video for amateur performers. One reason is the lack of knowledge of video photography and editing. However, the principles of home video editing is not ideal for videos that include intense movement such as dance performance. In this paper, we focus on video editing, and propose a system that automatically generates more attractive and sophisticated dance videos, which can be used by non-specialists. The system creates a single dance video by automatically editing performance

A. D. Cheok et al. (Eds.): ACE 2017, LNCS 10714, pp. 671–688, 2018.
https://doi.org/10.1007/978-3-319-76270-8_47

videos taken from multiple camera angles according to a probabilistic model created based on the principles of video editing and principles obtained from preliminary interviews.

The remainder of this paper is organized as follows. In Sect. 2, we introduce related work. In Sect. 3, we explain our system: we describe the principles of video editing, explain the system outline, and explain the probabilistic model based on these principles. In Sect. 4, we discuss the evaluation experiments we conducted and the results and considerations. In Sect. 5, we discuss the limitations of our system and summarize this paper in Sect. 6.

2   Related Works

Several automatic video-editing systems have been proposed, such as that developed by Heck et al. [1]. However, few are focused on dance-video editing. Our automatic editing system was designed to enable better editing of dance and show performances. We therefore surveyed studies on other automatic video-editing and support systems.

Arev et al. [2] used insight to share the focus of peoples attention and determine where important actions in the scene are being done. The system selects the camera by combining its function and cinematography guidelines and determines the timing of cutting. Ranjan et al. [3] proposed an automatic editing system for meetings that applies television production principles. Zsombori et al. [4] proposed a system that automatically generates video of events based on media annotations and highlights specific people during events. Lu and Grauman [5] presented a video-summarization technique to discover the story of egocentric videos. Given a long input video, their technique selects a short video that shows an essential event. Jain et al. [6] re-edited widescreen video by using pan, cut, and zoom based on gaze data. Shin et al. [7] proposed a system for converting the content of a blackboard-style lecture video into a readable interactive lecture note with graphics in the corresponding text. Kumar et al. [8] presented a system that focuses on each performer in stage-performance video to crop the video and presents a divided-screen video. For panoramic video, Sun et al. [9] proposed a system to automatically extract the region of interest and control a virtual camera. Roininen et al. [10] described how to model the shot cut timing of professionally edited concert videos. Mate and Curcio [11] presented an automatic video-remixing system that intelligently processes user-generated content in combination with sensor information. Truong et al. [12] proposed QuickCut, which can quickly create narration videos. The system treats narrated videos of appropriate sizes as clips, taking into account the length of narration and length of motion. Leake et al. [13] proposed a system for efficiently editing video of dialogue-driven scenes. Jeong and Suk [14] proposed a method to enhance dance video by selecting seven emotion categories to be communicated to viewers.

It is also worth noting research on movement and emotion. Nam et al. [15] stated that the speed of motion of an object is the most influential factor on emotions. Montepare et al. [16] clarified that walking characteristics, such as the swing amount, step length, weight and walking speed of the arm, differentiate the emotions expressed by pedestrians.

From the aforementioned studies, we can see that action and emotion are closely related. Our system focuses on the behavior of performers and makes dance video more attractive and sophisticated through editing.

3   Automatic Dance-Video-Editing System

We look at the process of editing videos taken from multiple viewpoints into a single video. An editor selects a video clip, determines how long the clip will be, and selects the next video clip. This is equivalent to selecting one camera at a time and transitioning. This means that if there are two successive shots that take into account the camera before the transition and the appropriate camera work according to the movement of the performer, it can be regarded as an estimation problem. This problem can be solved by estimating the appropriate camera work depending on the movement of the performer while selecting the camera at each moment. In this paper, we define the minimum time unit as one beat (synonymous with a quarter-note) and treat the selection of an effective camera for each beat as an optimization problem. We aim to generate more attractive and sophisticated dance videos by using the constraints and evaluation functions based on preliminary interviews and the principles of video editing.

3.1   Principles of Video Editing

There are principles of professional video editing, and editors take into account these principles and make edits based on their own experience. Similarly, to generate a more attractive and sophisticated dance video through editing, it is necessary to edit according to the dance performance based on these principles. Therefore, we enumerate the principles of general video editing that can be adapted to dance videos from the guidelines of cinematography and the empirical principles that can be adapted to dance videos determined from interviews of video production experts. We define a shot far from the subject as a long shot and a shot near the subject as an up shot. We define a video of a length of one beat as one shot and a series of consecutive shots from the same camera as one cut.

Principle 1. Switch camera according to beat. *Video Production: Disciplines and Techniques* [17] contains the following description. *"edits should be made at appropriate points at the end of a sentence on the narration track in a documentary, for example, or on the beats of the music."* Dancing to music is common, and most of the time it is adapted to the beat of the music. Therefore, Therefore, the timing of switching cameras must be adjusted to the beat.

Principle 2. The maximum length and minimum length of a cut are changed according to user preferences. *Grammar of the Edit* [18] contains the following description. *"a shot lasting more than three seconds is viewed by* *some producers and directors as 'boringly long.'"* As for the length of a cut, it cannot be stated unconditionally that the shorter the cut length, the more attractive and sophisticated it is. Therefore, setting the maximum and minimum cut lengths will be entrusted to the editor. This paper specifies that the difference between maximum and minimum lengths increases so that the cut length is selected within a wide range.

Principle 3. Switch to a camera with different composition to prevent 'jump cut'. *Grammar of the Edit* [18] states that *"Editing together two shots of similar camera angles will cause a jump at the cut point. Differing camera angles and framing will help prevent the 'jump cut' in the mind of the viewer."* The jump cut is an edit that combines two shots of the same subject from slightly changed camera positions. This type of editing provides an effect of skipping time. Switching to a camera with different composition can prevent jump cuts.

Principle 4. The closer the shot, the shorter the cut length. The more distant the shot, the longer the cut length. *Grammar of the Edit* [18] states that *"In deciding the length of a shot, it is essential to give the eyes enough time to read and absorb the visual information. If you are questioning the 'proper' duration for a shot, then you could describe, in your mind, what you are seeing in the shot."* The appropriate time for cutting is equal to the time that the situation can be explained. In a closer shot, the information is clear enough to tell a viewer in a short time, so the cut length is short. A more distant shot has more information, so the cut length needs to be longer.

Next, we interviewed four experts: three people who were involved in video production work and one who graduated from a body expression and cinematic arts department. We had them watch the dance video prepared in advance and interviewed them about editing techniques and what they care about when shooting dance. We defined the following two items based on the comments obtained.

Principle 5. Make the main camera recognizable. From the previous interview received the following comments. *"It is good to be able to recognize that this is the main cut the creators want to show.", "It is important for creators to think that this cut is main.", "Put a side dish inside a long shot."* A 'side dish' refers to a shot that emphasizes movements, in contrast to a long shot from which is easy to obtain overall information. From these comments, it is important that the main camera is designated so that the viewer can recognize the main camera.

Principle 6. Decide what to emphasize and when to vary the pace. From the previous interviews, we received the following comments. *"I will emphasize the best part by up shot and make sure that this cut does not continue to some extent", "If you cut video that focuses on performer's feet every time he kicks his feet, positive impression will fade. Choosing a better shot with priority is ideal.", "I think it is important to consider how much the balance is the best to repeat between up shot and long shot.", "Slow and high speed. A viewer is tired of switching the cut at a constant speed. We sometimes make an extreme change in the number of cuts according to the tune."*

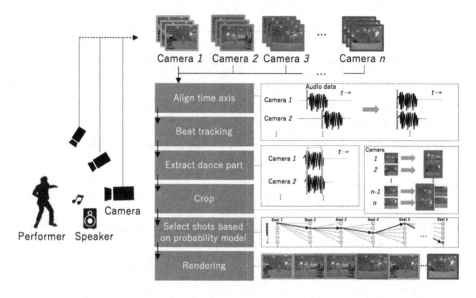

Fig. 1. System overview

We developed our system based on these six principles. We interpreted these principles, as described in Sect. 3.2, to construct the system.

In Principle 3, the composition was assumed to be the size of the motion vector on the video. By increasing the difference in the size of the motion vector between the cameras that are transited, the video switches to different compositions. In Principle 5, we predict that the camera will be recognized as the main camera by increasing the percentage of only one video. In Principle 6, what is considered an attractive shot depends on the case. Therefore, we assume that the attractive part of this time has intense movement (the reverse situation is technically compatible). Our system balances the relatively intense movement and non-intense movement areas throughout the whole video.

3.2 System Overview

The system overview is shown in Fig. 1. The system flow is as follows.

1. An editor puts dance videos taken from multiple places into our system. All videos must be recorded with the same song playing during shooting. However, it is not necessary to shoot at the same time.
2. The system extracts the audio data of each video and takes the correlation function of the music data used in the dance and the extracted audio data. The system cuts the movie according to where the correlation is maximized. As a result, the time axis can be aligned since the start of all videos is at the start of the song.
3. It calculates the beat positions in the song using the beat-tracking method proposed by Böck et al. [19].

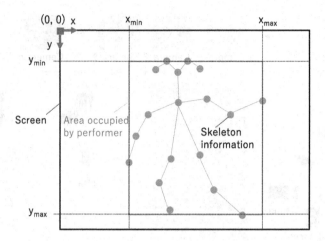

Fig. 2. Area occupied by performer on screen

4. It extracts the dance-performance part. Currently, the system does not perform automatic detection of choreographed parts of performers. Therefore, it must determine in advance how many beats there are from the beginning of the song to when the performer starts to dance and how many more beats until the performer stops dancing.

5. It acquires the performer's skeleton information using the OpenPose library by Cao et al. [20]. The difference between the maximum (x_{max}) and minimum (x_{min}) values in the x-axis direction of the obtained skeleton information is defined as the area occupied by the performer by multiplying the difference between the maximum (y_{max}) and minimum (y_{min}) values in the y-axis direction (Fig. 2). The system calculates R, the percentage of the screen area S_a occupied by the performer.

$$R = \frac{y_{max} - y_{min}}{x_{max} - x_{min}} / S_a \tag{1}$$

6. The image is cropped so that all calculated R fall between 0 and 1.0 and the average value is 0.55 to 0.65. The center of the crop is the center position of the area occupied by the performer. Moreover, in the upper 40% camera, which is up shot of all cameras, the system produces the cropped videos centered on the nose and the cropped videos centered on the average position of the heel position of both feet. The system calculates the average optical flow per camera and treats a video with a large average as one of the shots (Fig. 3).

7. A video of one beat is defined as one shot. The system selects shots based on the probabilistic model for each shot and saves the order in which the evaluation-function value for the selected shot is maximized.

8. The system generates a single video based on the saved order.

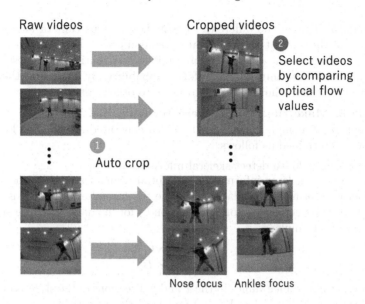

Fig. 3. Auto crop function flow

3.3 Probabilistic Model

The following probability distributions are generated based on principles 2 to 6.

Principle 2. The maximum and minimum lengths of a cut are changed according to user preferences. In this paper, the minimum and maximum cut lengths are 2 and 12 beats, respectively. If the duration of the camera before the transition being used is shorter than the minimum length we set, the probability of transition to the same camera is $1 - (N - 1) \cdot 1^{-20}$, and the other is 1^{-20}. If the duration of the camera before the transition being used is longer than the maximum length we set, the probability of transition to the same camera is 1^{-20}, and others are uniformly distributed. Where N is the total number of the cameras.

Principle 3. Switch to a camera with different composition to prevent 'jump cut'. We defined x_t as the camera to capture the image used at time t and n as the camera index. The optical flow is calculated with the Gunnar Farneback method [21]. We compute W_t^n, the average value of optical flow for all $0 < t < t_{max}$ for camera n. We normalize W_t^n so that $\sum_n W_t^n = 1$.

$$p(x_t) = \frac{W_t^n}{\sum_n W_t^n} \tag{2}$$

Principle 4. The closer the shot, the shorter the cut length. The more distant the shot, the longer the cut length. The system squares the average optical flow of each camera calculated by Principle 3, and the normalized one is expressed by probability distribution. The square of the average is experimentally determined to increase the difference. From the previous camera location, the probability of the current camera location is assumed to be moved to another camera according to the calculated probability distribution. The destination-camera number is determined by a uniform probability. By doing this, the higher the degree of up shot, the easier it is to move to other cameras.

Principle 5. Make the main camera recognizable. The system increases the percentage of a single camera in the video generated at the end. The main camera was determined as follows:

1. Use OpenPose [20] to detect skeletal information.
2. The amount of skeleton information not obtained in a frame is b_f; the amount of skeleton information available is B; the total number of frames is F; and the rate of undetected skeleton information (γ for 'no data') is expressed with the following formula:

$$\gamma = \frac{1}{F} \sum_{f=1}^{F} \frac{b_f}{B} \tag{3}$$

Moreover, the variance values in the x and y directions of the skeleton number in all frames are denoted as $V(x_{all})$ and $V(y_{all})$, respectively.
3. The main camera is the camera that maximizes the following formula:

$$m = \frac{V(x_{all}) + V(y_{all})}{\gamma} \tag{4}$$

The system selects the main camera at a probability of 60% and others in the uniform probability distribution. We use the normalized value of m as the probabilistic model to determine a shot at the first beat of the video.

Principle 6. Decide what to emphasize and when to vary the pace. The system uses a shot with an intense movement when a relatively intense movement is carried out throughout all the videos. The average optical flow per beat of every camera is calculated, and the median value is used as a threshold value. If the average is higher than the threshold, it is a shot that includes an intense movement. If the average is lower than the threshold, it is a shot that does not include an intense movement. The average optical flow per beat is normalized and expressed as a probability distribution. If it does not include an intense movement, the system normalizes the maximum optical flow minus the average and uses it as a probability distribution. If it includes an intense movement, the system normalizes the average optical flow and uses it as a probability distribution.

Probabilities corresponding to Principles 2 to 6 are P_2, P_3, P_4, P_5, and P_6. The system generates a video in which the following evaluation function $O(x_{1:T})$ is maximized ($x_{1:T} = x_1, x_2, ..., x_T$, $T = t_{max}$). However, the coefficient follows the following equation, $a_2 + a_3 + a_4 + a_5 + a_6 = 1$.

$$O(x_{1:T}) = \sum_{t=1}^{T} \log P(x_t) \tag{5}$$

$$P(x_t) = a_2 P_2(x_t) + a_3 P_3(x_t) + a_4 P_4(x_t) + a_5 P_5(x_t) + a_6 P_6(x_t) \tag{6}$$

4 Experiment

4.1 Procedure

We conducted an expert evaluation experiment to investigate whether the principles are reflected in the system and whether it is capable of generating more attractive and sophisticated video. We shot a dance performance of four performers, two males and two females, as editing material. The performers genres were all different: BREAK, HIPHOP, WACK and POP, in order of movement intensity. Performers created choreography that combined the basic movements for each genre. The beats per minute for the songs used were 109, 129, 93, and 92, respectively, and the choreography ranged from the start of the song to 16–64 beats. We used ten cameras (HERO5 Session, by GoPro) and a speaker (Computer MusicMonitor, by Bose). The layout of the cameras are shown in Fig. 4. The height of each camera is indicated by its color in the diagram. We adjusted each camera so that the subject was at the center of the screen. The layout of the cameras in BREAK and HIPHOP are on the left in Fig. 4, the layout in POP and WACK on the right. To prevent other cameras from entering between the subject and camera, shooting was done using two separate cameras.

We prepared seven different videos from each dance video. We decided to vary the coefficients used in the system one at a time to prevent the number of combinations from exploding. For the first video, we set the following ratios: $a_2 : a_3 : a_4 : a_5 : a_6 = 3 : 2 : 5 : 3 : 3$. For videos 2~6, we changed the coefficients one at a time to zero. For the seventh video, we created a simple automatic editing system that generates a single video as the baseline system (Baseline). It operates with the following algorithm:

1. The system calculates the average optical flow of every frame. It calculates the average of them of each beat.
2. It normalizes the average optical flow for each camera.
3. For each beat, the system selects a camera with the maximum normalized optical flow.

By doing this, a shot that includes relatively intense movement becomes easier to select.

We prepared a total of 28 videos from four performer's dance videos based on the seven ways described above.

The experts were ten experts (8 males and 2 females) who work in video production or who were educated in video production. They had experience of between 1 and 20 years (average of 8.6 years). They watched 14 videos of 2 performers and evaluated them based on a 7-point Likert scale; from 1 not agree to 7 totally agree. They watched the videos in random order.

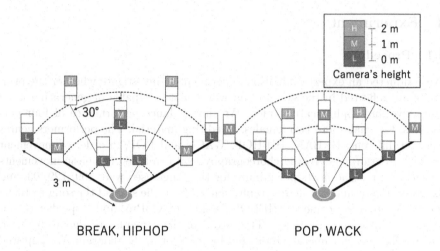

BREAK, HIHOP   POP, WACK

Fig. 4. Camera layouts

In addition to four questions on editing principles (items #1–4), there were two evaluation items that are considered important in editing (#5–6), and one item that measures the skillfulness of editing (#7). We give the evaluation items below.

Q1: The video switches were between shots with different compositions.
Q2: The closer the shot, the shorter the cut length. The more distant the shot, the longer the cut length.
Q3: I can recognize the main camera.
Q4: The video has a varied pace to emphasize certain cuts.
Q5: I feel dynamic.
Q6: I can grasp the overall situation.
Q7: This editing is attractive.

We conducted the questionnaire using Google Forms. The questionnaire was expected to take about 30 min. The experts could take a break even while answering the questionnaire. In addition, they could review the video multiple times and re-evaluate it compared to the previous video. While the experts watched the videos, the browser screen was maximized. While watching videos, the experts wore earphones or headphones, and we asked them to listen to the audio. After they finished all answers, we received their oral feedback about the system.

4.2 Results and Consideration

The results of Q1~Q4 based on editing principles are shown in Fig. 5. The vertical axis indicates the average scores of Q1~Q4 given by all experts. The vertical bars indicate standard deviation, and the horizontal axis represents valid and invalid coefficients. The coefficient of constant is expressed as 1 if it is more than 0, and 0 if it is 0.

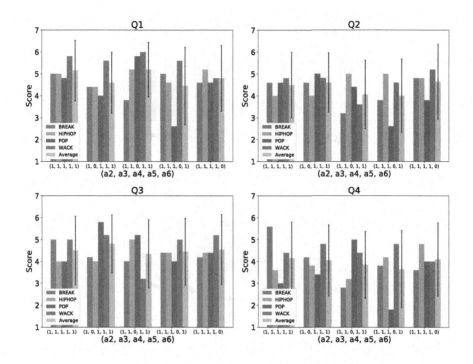

Fig. 5. Questionnaire results regarding Q1~Q4

We assessed the difference between the average scores for each constraint regarding Q1 by using analysis of variance (ANOVA). There was no significant difference; however, all the coefficients (1, 1, 1, 1, 1) in Q1 were enabled, the coefficients (1, 0, 1, 1, 1) corresponding to Q1 were disabled, and the score of (1, 0, 1, 1, 1) was lower than that of (1, 1, 1, 1, 1) for all performers. This indicates that constraints function based on principle due to an invalid constraint.

We assessed the scores of Q2 by using ANOVA. There was no significant difference; however, all the coefficients (1, 1, 1, 1, 1) in Q2 were enabled, the coefficients (1, 1, 0, 1, 1) corresponding to Q2 were disabled, and the score of (1, 1, 0, 1, 1) was lower than that of (1, 1, 1, 1, 1) for three of the four performers. Constraints did not function depending on performance.

We assessed the scores of Q3 by using ANOVA. There was no significant difference. All the coefficients (1, 1, 1, 1, 1) in Q3 were enabled, the coefficients (1, 1, 1, 0, 1) corresponding to Q3 were disabled, and there was no trend of change. At this time, the main camera was chosen with a probability of 60% as a constraint to recognize the main camera. However, this was not sufficient.

We assessed the scores for Q4 by using ANOVA. There was no significant difference. All the coefficients (1, 1, 1, 1, 1) in Q4 are enabled, the coefficients (1, 1, 1, 1, 0) corresponding this item were disabled, and there was no trend of change. We assumed that the attractive part of this time had intense movement.

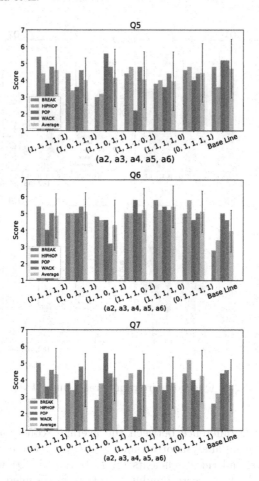

Fig. 6. Questionnaire results regarding Q5∼Q7

However, the parts that should be emphasized differed between experts. Therefore, it seems that a trend could not be determined.

The results of Q5–Q7 are shown in Fig. 6. Recall that Baseline was the system of using only optical flow.

Next, we look at the results of two items that are considered important in editing, extracted from preliminary interviews.

We assessed the difference between the average scores of Q5 by using ANOVA. There was no significant difference. The coefficients (1, 1, 1, 1, 1) in Q5 with our system had high scores. When all coefficients (1, 1, 1, 1, 1) were valid, the score tended to be high because the overall balance was good by selecting up shot when the performer moved intensely. With Baseline, however, the experts felt dynamics because the cut was switched at short intervals.

We assessed the difference between the average scores of Q6 by using ANOVA. There was a significant difference ($F_{(6,139)} = 5.54, p < .05$). We also assessed the difference by using an Fishers Least Significant Difference (LSD) test. There was also significant differences between the scores of Baseline and all except constraint $(1, 1, 0, 1, 1)$ $(p < .05)$. With Baseline, the cut was switched at short intervals because the length of the cut was not considered. As a result, the overall situation was difficult to grasp and received a low score. Additionally, there were significant differences between the scores of constraints $(1, 1, 1, 0, 1)$, $(1, 1, 1, 1, 1)$ and constraint $(1, 1, 0, 1, 1)$ $(p < .05)$. This shows that using Principle 4 is effective in recognizing the main camera because the difference between the short cut length and a long one becomes clearer.

Finally, we look at the results of an item that measures goodness throughout editing. We assessed the difference between the average scores of Q7 by using ANOVA. There was no significant difference. However, compared with our system, Baseline scores tended to be low; therefore, our system is likely to be effective. Specifically, our system's scores were higher for BREAK and HIPHOP. It was not very effective for WACK, and Baseline tended to be higher for POP. We examined the average optical flow for each performer (Fig. 7). The vertical axis indicates the average optical flow for each beat, and the horizontal axis indicates beats. POP is a dance with a many movements, such as robotic dance. The average optical flow rapidly decreased intermittently, as shown in Fig. 7. In our system, the intense movement was taken as a part that should be emphasized, and the system divided the cases by the median of optical flows. However, this is likely to cause the system to emphasize parts intermittently and affect other constraints. As mentioned above POP has many fine movements; therefore, if there are few up shots, the video will be difficult to understand. Regarding Q6, Baseline enabled relatively understandable editing for only POP. In this regard, we must consider it necessary to confirm the total amount of movement throughout a dance and adjust the parameters.

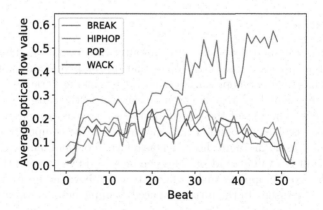

Fig. 7. Average optical flow value per beat

5   Discussion

5.1   Limitations

This section explains the limitations of our system. This system is based on a performers movements. Therefore, the performer must be captured within the frame of the camera. Moreover, it is expected that this system will not work well for multiple performers because it was designed for one performer. This system is vulnerable to beat-tracking errors. If the beat-tracking results are wrong, the timing of camera switches will not be on beat. Performances must be taken with fixed cameras. In a moving camera, the motion of the camera is captured as an optical flow. It is necessary to develop a system that takes into account moving cameras. The same song needs to be used when shooting videos. If there is video content with a different song, the system cannot align the time axis of both video content. Moreover, just like the previous reason, the video should not contain a large amount of noise. Our system involved only ten cameras; if there are too few or too many cameras, it may not work well. This can be handled by increasing the content by cropping and limiting the number of videos selected. Currently, it is necessary to determine the choreography part of the dance in advance. It is possible to think of a method of automatically recognizing dance choreography, but there is various noise during shooting. For example, some performers felt out the mood beforehand, and half were dancing before the start of the choreography. It is considered that cooperation of the performer is necessary, such as limiting activity before the performance and preparing gestures at the beginning of the choreography. As we described in the previous section, our system may not work well depending on the genre of dance.

Although our system has some limitations, as described above, it can be sufficiently improved in the future.

5.2   Interview

We conducted oral interviews via video call after the evaluation. Through interviews with ten experts, we selected topics that overlapped among multiple evaluators. The most common opinion was that the original material was not attractive and there was little change in composition. One of the causes of this was the size of the shot. The size of the person on the screen was cropped to a ratio of 0.1 to 1.0. We received an opinion that the change in the composition was small because there was no more up shot, such as a face, foot, and hand, and that this made it difficult to evaluate videos. This can be solved by changing the crop size. However, the fixed cropped frame is likely to not follow the performer because he/she moves intensely. In the future, we need to implement a crop function that follows movement automatically.

We also found that camera arrangement is also important. In this study, 10 cameras were placed within 120° in front of the dancer, 1~3 m deep and 0~2 m high. However, some experts pointed out that it was difficult to create a video that can produce a clearer difference than other videos, even when editing videos from cameras placed in this range. One expert said that they set a shot that is taken out largely from theory, such as a shot from the top of the performer and one from the viewpoint of the performer, for example, as an accent. We received an opinion from experts that if we can improve the above two points in terms of material, we could make a video with more easily and distinctly differences.

We received an opinion from experts that if we can improve the above two points regarding material, we could make a clear video that was easier to evaluate. In the future, it is considered worth working as a new research question on systems for collecting these attractive materials.

Experts often gave their opinions about the first and last cuts. In fact, our system does not take into account these cuts. For example, although the pose taken at the end of the performers choreography was stopped, many cuts with a short interval were observed. It turned out that this was not ideal for editing. In the future, we will incorporate the concept of pose into our system, where the performer is considered to be in a pose if he/she has stopped for more than a certain period of time. We will then consider a method of selecting the camera with the best viewing position. Regarding pose, there was an opinion that when the performer's movement was slow, the experts had a negative impression when the cut was switched. We need to investigate the relationship between movement intensity and length of cut.

We have also received many opinions stating that the link with music is very important. We received an opinion that it was attractive when the viewer felt that the movement and music matched. In the future, we need to examine the balance between the movement of a shot and information obtained from music.

5.3 Principles and Constraints

We compared the scores of when all constraints were satisfied and those of when one constraint was omitted and could not confirm a significant difference. However, as there were some constraints that showed trends, it is likely that those constraints were functioning. In addition, even if the constraint is omitted, the combined effects of other constraints might follow a principle. In the future, we need to conduct a wider ranging investigation, such as comparing a constraint that enables only one coefficient with others. Furthermore, we could not confirm the relationship between the constraints and the overall evaluation. Therefore, we need to examine the video materials so that there is a clear difference.

5.4 Interactivity

The numerical values on the system were determined experimentally in advance because it was difficult to verify all parameters. The editor can also control these parameters interactively. The minimum and maximum lengths based on Principle 2 should be set to shorten the length of the cut if an editor prefers to shorten the cut length. If the editor prefers a long cut, he/she can set the minimum and maximum lengths to increase the length of the overall cut. Regarding

Principle 5, we developed a system to automatically determine the main camera. However, there is also a method with which the editor can select this main camera and he/she can adjust the percentage of the main camera in the video. Regarding Principle 6, the parts to emphasize are currently determined while looking at the optical flow. However, there is a method with which the editor can also select a range of the parts to emphasize. Our system selects a video that maximizes the evaluation function. However, the editor can choose a video that matches his/her preferences from several candidates that the system provides. In addition, it is possible to add a function that can easily modify the generated video, such as by switching the cut and adjusting the length.

5.5 Expandability

In the future, we can cite various methods of expandability in developing video-editing systems. Currently, it is assumed with our system that the camera is fixed: i.e., not capable of moving. If the system is capable of moving the camera, it can be used to shoot a dance performance at an optimum angle while moving the camera with a drone. However, the system is difficult to implement in real-time because of slow computation speed. If the processing speed is improved, it can be adapted to live-performance streaming. For example, the system can acquire videos from a number of smartphones of several audience members watching the performance on a street. The system can conduct a streaming distribution that automatically adjusts the cut of the videos and selects the most attractive video.

Various methods can be considered, such as generating visual effects according to a performers movement, or applying effects that are more emphasized on the important parts of the video. In the interviews, there were experts who said that there is knowledge about the arrangement of cameras and video-editing, but knowledge about visual effects is poor. If we can propose an accurate visual effect to enhance the attractiveness of a video, there is a need for such a feature. Moreover, the camera work with the proposed system can also be applied to virtual reality (VR) space. A system should be considered to automatically transition the camera in VR space to show the virtual dancing character better. It should also be specialized for dance performances. However, it can be applied to other events such as sports. For example, in weight training, we can see online a number of videos to learn how to train. If there is a system that makes weight training more attractive and sophisticated, it can be adapted to such videos.

6 Conclusion

We focused on video-editing, and proposed a system that automatically generates more attractive and sophisticated dance videos even when used by non-specialists. The system creates a single dance video by automatically editing performance videos taken from multiple locations according to the probabilistic model created based on the principles of video editing and those determined from preliminary interviews. We conducted an evaluation experiment in which our system automatically edited a dance video of four performers taken from multiple viewpoints. Ten video-production experts evaluated the generated videos. The system tended to perform better than a baseline automatic editing system. In addition, we developed discussions based on interviews and showed the system expandability. We will further extend this system and launch a web service based on it.

Acknowledgments. This work was supported in part by JST ACCEL Grant Number JPMJAC1602, Japan.

References

1. Heck, R., Wallick, M., Gleicher, M.: Virtual videography. ACM Trans. Multimed. Comput. Commun. Appl. (TOMM) **3**(1) (2007). https://doi.org/10.1145/1198302. 1198306. Article No. 4
2. Arev, I., Park, H.S., Sheikh, Y., Hodgins, J., Shamir, A.: Automatic editing of footage from multiple social cameras. ACM Trans. Graph. (TOG) **33**(4) (2014). https://doi.org/10.1145/2601097.2601198. Article No. 81
3. Ranjan, A., Birnholtz, J., Balakrishnan, R.: Improving meeting capture by applying television production principles with audio and motion detection. In: Proceedings of CHI 2008, pp. 227–236. ACM, New York (2008). https://doi.org/10.1145/1357054.1357095
4. Zsombori, V., Frantzis, M., Guimaraes, R.L., Ursu, M.F., Cesar, P., Kegel, I., Craigie, R., Bulterman, D.C.: Automatic generation of video narratives from shared UGC. In: Proceedings of Hypertext 2011, pp. 325–334. ACM, New York (2011). https://doi.org/10.1145/1995966.1996009
5. Lu, Z., Grauman, K.: Story-driven summarization for egocentric video. In: Proceedings of CVPR 2013, pp. 2714–2721. IEEE, New York (2013). https://doi.org/10.1109/CVPR.2013.350
6. Jain, E., Sheikh, Y., Shamir, A., Hodgins, J.: Gaze-driven video re-editing. ACM Trans. Graph. (TOG) **34**(2) (2015). https://doi.org/10.1145/2699644. Article No. 21
7. Shin, H.V., Berthouzoz, F., Li, W., Durand, F.: Visual transcripts: lecture notes from blackboard-style lecture videos. ACM Trans. Graph. (TOG) **34**(6) (2015). https://doi.org/10.1145/2816795.2818123. Article No. 240
8. Kumar, M., Gandhi, V., Ronfard, R., Gleicher, M.: Zooming on all actors: automatic focus + context split screen video generation. Comput. Graph. Forum **36**, 455–465 (2017). https://doi.org/10.2312/wiced.20171070. Article No. 2
9. Sun, X., Foote, J., Kimber, D., Manjunath, B.S.: Region of interest extraction and virtual camera control based on panoramic video capturing. IEEE Trans. Multimed. **7**(5), 981–990 (2005). https://doi.org/10.1109/TMM.2005.854388
10. Roininen, M.J., Leppnen, J., Eronen, A.J., Curcio, I.D., Gabbouj, M.: Modeling the timing of cuts in automatic editing of concert videos. Multimed. Tools Appl. **76**(5), 6683–6707 (2017). https://doi.org/10.1007/s11042-016-3304-7
11. Mate, S., Curcio, I.D.: Automatic video remixing systems. IEEE Commun. Mag. **55**(1), 180–187 (2017). https://doi.org/10.1109/MCOM.2017.1500493CM

12. Truong, A., Berthouzoz, F., Li, W., Agrawala, M.: QuickCut: an interactive tool for editing narrated video. In: Proceedings of UIST 2016, pp. 497–507. ACM, New York (2016). https://doi.org/10.1145/2984511.2984569

13. Leake, M., Davis, A., Truong, A., Agrawala, M.: Computational video editing for dialogue-driven scenes. ACM Trans. Graph. (TOG) **36**(4) (2017). https://doi.org/10.1145/3072959.3073653. Article No. 130

14. Jeong, K.A., Suk, H.J.: Jockey time: making video playback to enhance emotional effect. In: Proceedings of the 2016 ACM on Multimedia Conference, pp. 62–66. ACM, New York (2016). https://doi.org/10.1145/2964284.2967183

15. Nam, T.J., Lee, J.H., Park, S., Suk, H.J.: Understanding the relation between emotion and physical movements. Int. J. Affect. Eng. **13**, 217–226 (2014). https://doi.org/10.5057/ijae.13.217. Article No. 3

16. Montepare, J.M., Goldstein, S.B., Clausen, A.: The identification of emotions from gait information. J. Nonverbal Behav. **11**(1), 33–42 (1987). https://doi.org/10.1007/BF00999605

17. Foust, J.C., Fink, E.J., Gross, L.S.: Video Production: Disciplines and Techniques. Taylor and Francis, Abingdon (2012)

18. Bowen, C.J.: Grammar of the Edit. Taylor and Francis, Abingdon (2013)

19. Böck, S., Krebs, F., Widmer, G.: Joint beat and downbeat tracking with recurrent neural networks. In: ISMIR, pp. 255–261 (2016)

20. Cao, Z., Simon, T., Wei, S.E., Sheikh, Y.: Realtime multi-person 2D pose estimation using part affinity fields. In: CVPR (2017)

21. Farneback, G.: Two-frame motion estimation based on polynomial expansion. In: Bigun, J., Gustavsson, T. (eds.) SCIA 2003. LNCS, vol. 2749, pp. 363–370. Springer, Heidelberg (2003). https://doi.org/10.1007/3-540-45103-X_50

Structured Reciprocity for Musical Performance with Swarm Agents as a Generative Mechanism

Insook Choi[✉]

University of Salford, Manchester, M5 4WT, UK
insook@insookchoi.com

Abstract. A creative inquiry introduces a swarm simulation as a generative mechanism, providing a third agency in music creation alongside agency of composition and performance. When applying an evolutionary model such as swarms to music the challenge is to develop a performance interaction model beyond improvised explorations so that the model can facilitate the integrities for, and emerging dynamics in, all agencies. To minimize a performer's cognitive overload another challenge is management of dataflow in interactive architecture for generating music. An interaction model for structured reciprocity is investigated as a design solution that applies model-based indirection. In the scope of musical composition, reciprocity is exhibited as a time dependent relationship between a performer's actions and evolutionary swarm tendencies applied to generate musical outcomes. Reciprocity is structured using levels of indirection as a construct of mapping data from a swarm simulation to an interactive music performance application. The paper presents an approach to encoding, activating, generating and measuring reciprocity. A comparative case study demonstrates the implementation of these concepts in two musical works. The paper concludes (1) reciprocity in interactive applications helps optimize actions to leverage emergent tendencies, including their intuitive qualities, towards realizing desired outcomes; and (2) data analysis from the case study indicates temporal signatures of reciprocity are related to indirection in interaction scenarios for generative musical performance.

Keywords: Reciprocity · Swarm simulation · Musical performance
Cognitive cycle · Sound design pattern · Gesture · Emergent behavior
Interaction design · Evolutionary model · Assistive interface

1 Introduction

Complexity in generative factors in musical performance steers a research agenda for designing interactive experiences. This study aims at gaining insights towards a generalizable principle of structured reciprocity. The principle here is applied to designing efficient and intuitive musical interactions and performance scenarios. Reciprocity in an interactive scenario characterizes a relationship of time-coupled decisions exchanged between a human participant and computation. Cases of creative process focus on where and when decision-making takes place and the transparency of it. A simple interactive system is chosen to emphasize facile real-time selections. The hypothesis is that

© Springer International Publishing AG, part of Springer Nature 2018
A. D. Cheok et al. (Eds.): ACE 2017, LNCS 10714, pp. 689–712, 2018.
https://doi.org/10.1007/978-3-319-76270-8_48

reciprocity may provide a signature of dynamic selection flow: a process of deferring and taking decisions to render shared creative output.

To investigate reciprocity this work identifies musical composition and performance applications that use generative properties of simulated swarm agents. While musical performance is highly specialized, the use of dynamic simulation in musical creation incorporates multiple constructs also applied widely in interactive media and digital games. To ascertain suitable assumptions concerning musical creation, this case study applies autoethnographic methods to consult the composer and to articulate her criteria for composing musical performance experiences.

The relationship between generative arts and generative mechanisms is commonly understood with the definitions anchored on computational autonomy and causality [1, 2]. Implied in [3] a generative formalism yields how a mechanism can be materialized in arts. Romero and Machado [4] preface two different criteria between an artistic perspective and a scientific standpoint. For the former, the challenge has to do with accepting an evolutionary approach through well-established artistic practices and venues. For the latter, the challenge is to innovate and develop autonomous systems that would bring evolvable aesthetics and new models of human-machine interaction.

This paper examines reciprocity as a structured relationship between a performer and a dynamic simulation, where the simulation is applied as a generative mechanism for the interactive production of musical outputs. In musical creation to engage a complex system such as a swarm simulation presents an overarching question: What is the model of engagement? Musical creation draws upon a literature of musical practice, and evolutionary simulation draws upon a literature of computational practice. If the motive for using a simulation is to automate music generation, the automata can be designed with layers of rules and algorithms that influence musical outputs. However when situating a human performer in an engagement model, the design problem space becomes much larger to draw one clean model to work with. For musical performance using generative agents the composer devises ways for performers to engage literatures of both music and computation. Reciprocity is a signature of this dynamic engagement and may be structured to optimize sound production and performance to leverage the integrity of the evolutionary system in terms of inherent qualities and emergent patterns.

1.1 In and Out of a Musical Paradigm

To study in context a creative technology application such as game design for gameplay experience, assumptions posited will consult criteria and literature of game practice. For computational music creation and performance this paper adopts the same approach. Composition and performance are original sources that bring about interactive sound production and inform listening experience. The fundamental tools of interactive music generation applied in this work are consistent with digital music technology standards. However the works reported here are experimental compositions, meaning they do not reproduce established musical genres but rather develop new classes of references and computational applications. The paper discusses two musical works that present a human performer controlling a "super agent" to interact with autonomous agents in a dynamic visualization of a swarm simulation. In these compositions, swarm agents are given sounds to play with and the performer plays with the swarms to influence the sounds. Agents' collective data controls digital transformations of sounds. Swarms' emergent properties greatly influence the sounds, while the performer can influence but cannot completely control the agents' behaviors. This configuration introduces indirection as a condition for reciprocity between a performer and simulated agents.

In terms of the social simulation, through a super agent the swarm agents perceive the performer's movement as movements of their own kind. In the world of swarms the perceivable environment is inherently contradictory because a super agent is not constrained by agents' binding social rules. What it can evoke, on the surface, is a meta-phor of a conductor and an orchestra. However a conductor and orchestra share a common goal towards shaping musical events from the beginning to end given musical literature to follow. Towards progressing a coherent common goal, music performance rules are enforced a priori, cultured with shared repertoires, and manifest through unspoken collaborative agreements. Yet why should we entrain swarms to simulate human musicians when swarms already exhibit emergent patterns? Study of reciprocity aspires towards visions of future use cases, and can also function to guide us what not to do.

Prior Work in ALife-Informed Music Computation. The purpose and assessment value of the works in the field of experimental composition depart from what some people may think of as music. Therefore an experimental musical approach may depart from some research agendas in the AI community that aim to learn by modeling well-known musical styles or recognized behaviors [5–10]. Originality is also emphasized historically, for composers encouraged to learn but not to imitate previous genres. Evolutionary computing has been applied through an iterative training process to generate musical outputs including scores and recordings of synthesized sounds [11–15]. Bilotta and Pantano proposed a mathematical mediation to translate CA to musical language in order to transfer the semantics of complexity to a range of musical expres-sions [16]. The process methodology in their work comes close to structuring reciprocity between a generative mechanism and music, employing "musification codes" as a struc-ture that evokes aspects of reciprocity, a mathematical formalization to decode CA and re-encode them as music. The codes providing options to read a matrix frame (a grid), population growth patterns given input entropy, or local behaviors read through color or binary code. For social models, Miranda et al. applied a multi-agent listening model in composition with a genetic algorithm, given initial musical materials, feature detec-tion and evaluation rules, and each agent adjusts its own deviation with respect to the collective outputs [17].

The above examples apply IEC – Interactive Evolutionary Computation, a process requiring extensive training and assessment to apply creative choices. Tod and Werner [18, p. 319] describe this process as creating a "fitness bottleneck" and respond by applying autonomous musical agents to perform creative selections. While the process is efficient, the agents' aesthetic preferences drift without human supervision until they generate "unlistenable" music. A goal is to design a system that balances human over-sight with agents' decision efficiency, which can provide exploration of emergent prop-erties without iteration over a predetermined fitness function. Autonomous agents in flocking and swarm systems meet this requirement and methods have been implemented for efficient real-time interaction. Unemi [19] developed evolutionary efficiencies for breeding agents using a form of NIEC (Narrowly-defined IEC) [20] and Sayama [21] further optimized breeding with real-time interaction using HIEC (Hyperinteractive Evolutionary Computation).

Generative music methods extract data from simulated swarm agents to control audio signal generators. Interaction methods may be classified according to the rate and regularity of scheduled data flow between a swarm system, human users, and sound generators. Murray-Rust et al. [22] and Huepe et al. [23] adopt methods that apply human control during initialization only, with autonomous run-time operation dedicated to agent-agent interaction. Blackwell [24], Grace [25], and Davis and Karamanlis [26] adopt methods to provide real-time re-initialization of swarm behavioral parameters and run-time modification of the mapping from agents' data to sound control. In these approaches the control changes are infrequent and irregular with respect to the simulation time step, and the user does not interact directly with individual agents. Other work using agents in real-time performance includes EvoMove [22–27], which applies a commensal computing scheme to provide a movement-based musical companion for dancers, with sounds conceived as ambient feedback rather than presenting a musical structure.

The above research exhibits a collective concern for management and application of emergent behaviors and methods for designing relationships between agents' tendencies and musical content. Schacher et al. [28] implement architecture for real-time performance interaction with agents, with further focus on symmetry of swarm simulation and musical structure, summarizing relationships in five classes: formal, ontogenetic, conceptual, interaction, and ecological. These are defined in terms of mapping mechanisms, classified by the extent and kind of separation between agent data and musical signal output. The concept of *designing indirection* introduced in Sect. 2 below encompasses these functions. Social interaction between agents and human players is introduced by Choi and Bargar [29] and reflected by Schacher et al. as "…a shared space within which the perceptual and behavioural properties of simulated entities and humans overlap and interrelate [op cit p. 53]." Bisig and Kocher describe performance interactions where "…human behaviour interferes with the emergent swarm behaviour and begins to form a meta-system, that might exhibit different states than the purely closed world of simulation [30, p. 105]." The engineering of reciprocity addresses structure and design of these formations. Collectively swarm music research establishes practice of social agent simulation applied to generative music with recent examples of interactive performance. Introducing a concept of reciprocity encompasses and reframes prior research perspectives, with relevance for broader examination of reciprocity in the design and assessment of human performance with interactive social agents.

1.2   Basis for Reciprocity

The concept of reciprocity in composition relates to eliciting structure of emergent behaviors in sound rather than reproducing legacy structures or known musical styles. A mutual challenge arises to encompass the domains of performance, compositional works with evolutionary models, and the definition of composition. Ringer and Crossley-Holland [31] define composition as, "the act of conceiving a piece of music, the art of creating music, or the finished product. These meanings are interdependent and presume a tradition in which musical works exist as repeatable entities. In this sense, composition is necessarily distinct from improvisation." Here the distinction between composition and improvisation lies on the existential manifestation of the work as repeatable entity. Emergent properties contribute to interactive creation and challenge traditional boundaries that define repeatability.

The implementation of reciprocity introduces how composition is conceived for situating a performer in this work. Production of musical tones and events is inherently circular with an intimate feedback through auditory perception [32]. Kinaesthetic interaction between performer and instrument encodes a musical signal, for which the performer's movement determines the features of the signal. The choice of how to govern further movement is directed by listening to the previous states generated by previous motions. The circuit of internalization of a current state of movement, externalization of previous states to guide current state, and projection of future states to build desired hysteresis, is so highly integrated at a performer's sensorimotor level that it is difficult to separate. However the quality of performances is shaped through these fleeting moments of dual sensory-motor and cognitive processing: internalization and externalization along with consulting the musical score toward higher-level projection of future states. At the core, the chain of kinaesthetic interaction produces music, and listening shapes the chaining. These observations are experientially based supported by encouraging discoveries in neural mechanisms' temporal percepts. Recent studies suggest the brain does not process time in a serial mechanism but in distribution: interval timing is processed by feedback loops, and through these loops the output of an internal clock serves to dynamically modify its own input [33, 34]. Reciprocity is enacted by listening in this context: a performer listens and mediates the simulation with an action, utilizing auditory feedback (sensory) to guide movements (motor), where the kinaesthetic dynamic that feeds the performer's auditory perception is extended by simulated agents' dynamics.

Reciprocity is illustrated here for two compositions with musical elements synthesized by eliciting structure of emergent swarm behaviors. Each composition constitutes two components, a score and a system of interaction. The two works, Mutandrum and Human Voice, are encoded in a computer system for programming interactive digital sound and for routing sound control data from the swarm simulation. The composer's selection and design of agents' tendencies is encoded alongside the sound synthesis design. The software encoding requires a performer's interaction to realize the compositions. For performers the compositions are represented as musical scores that indicate musical sequences but do not adopt traditional western music notation. Both scores provide blueprints for performers to work with: (1) navigation plans to move within constraints from one local free form to the next while agents play by rules at all times; (2) plans to initialize diverse types of swarms that were curated during the composition process using NIEC and HIEC. The plans are expressed in the form of scores to function as time-based musical roadmaps. The scores by no means convey all audible details or musical depth that is programmed in the composition software. The scores provide a layout of basic elements including notated instructions and a high-level rule: Move from one section to the next until all sections are exhausted. In the form of scores, at least, they structure activity so that the activity is repeatable and rehearsable. Performance here is twofold: for agents, rule-based behavioral movements; for human players, locally free form play along with agents, guided by the score. A performer does not improvise but responds to the score and to agents with situational awareness and makes decisions in a context for playing both, the composition and the swarm.

2   Rationale and Research Methods

Case studies of two compositions of this author will be presented with a comparative analysis. From experience working with nonlinear dynamical systems such as the chaotic Chua's circuit [35, 36], this author recognized that nonlinearity and self-organizational principles are often implied in a creative process itself, at subconscious level while encountering material suggestions and imageries, and at conscious level while translating them into tangible ideation. The agency of composition can be articulated by the traces of its processes and the agency of performance is articulated through realizing the composition. However other agency is challenging to articulate, such as the source of inspiration, whether it sparked as spontaneous brain chemistry or intuition. Another challenge is the management of dataflow in performance architecture to minimize a performer's cognitive overload during the complex audiovisual and sensorimotor interaction with a swarm's dynamics. To assess this complex scenario most psychoacoustics-related findings are not readily applicable, because they largely rely on isolated stimulus tests in simple settings. However, the recent discussions in neural basis of music perception [37] and the ERP processing time window [38] indicate more promising directions. Works presented here was motivated three ways: (1) to articulate examples and implications of the hidden agency of creative choice, by introducing swarms as visibly working through an artistic inquiry; (2) to explore how swarm dynamics may yield new pathways in music creation, and further how this inquiry may contribute to the artificial life research agenda; (3) to gain quantitative insights for designing indirection for a complex evolutionary interaction, by constructing data through the case study.

2.1   Analytic Autoethnographic Method

The workflow for this research begins with a music composition process, continues to a music performance process, and culminates in an assessment process that reflects on previous stages to develop an analytical position. This workflow exhibits parallels with interaction design, then implementation, then testing. The case studies here draw upon musical work by this author as composer and performer. With awareness there may be many shortcomings in autoethnographic methodology in general [39], the methodology adapted here can be best described as an analytic autoethnography [40], including numerical data, towards establishing a new theoretical framework bridging art and science. Each step of the way keeps in sight the requisite variety [41] between the two domains with an attempt to avoid blind spots. This method recalls cybernetics of observing systems as introduced by von Foerster's analysis of self-organizing systems and their dependence upon energy and structure in their environments [42]. Self-reflexive research is performed by truly searching again one's creative results, with a reflective investigation that is objectively driven. The aim is to formalize and reframe methodologies, techniques, and aesthetic criteria, along the way noting right or wrong design intuitions, and other factors constituted for finishing the two works.

Framing Research Questions. When designing a system to compose in and compose with, the creative and technical problem space hinges on non-typical conditions that juxtapose two domains: a music composition that uses a fixed notated score, and an evolutionary system that exhibits emergent behaviors. By explicating this problem the working question is framed: How do you work with a collective body that follows simple rules and self organizes, and displays unexpected patterns of behaviors, to produce and perform music that can be reproducible and rehearsed? This questions motivates a series of investigations that were undertaken roughly in the following order:

1. How swarms work:
   a. How swarms work when engaged by a player
   b. How swarms work to control sound synthesis
   c. How indirection can be designed, using knowledge gained from (a) and (b), leading to how to work with swarms
2. How to work with swarms
   a. How to work with swarms when the compositional plan is exogenous to the swarms' world – applying compositional agility for planning with adaptability
   b. How to work with swarms within an overall plan – applying compositional strategies for performance
   c. How to work with swarms in multiple levels of indirection and time scale

Through these research questions, three types of agencies are articulated: swarm, composition, and performance. The undercurrents of discussion are based on results obtained from investigations with this framework. Sections 3 and 4 apply the two framing topics, how swarms work and how to work with swarms, drawing upon comparisons of the two compositions. Section 3 introduces two techniques: emergent feature analysis and procedural sound design patterns. Section 4 surveys musical structure, discusses model-based indirection, and introduces PGAU as a tool for quantifiable analysis of performance engagement with agents. Section 5 focuses on reciprocity, and Sect. 6 reviews the investigation of indirection and time scale, using the LIDA framework [43, 44] for comparison with temporal studies of cognitive cycles.

3 How Swarms Work in Performance

The model applied in this work is the heterogeneous swarm model developed by Sayama [21]. Unlike Reynolds' canonical flocking algorithm [45] the agents are decentralized with no leader. To initialize, typically 100 to 300 agents are set in motion with constrained random positions and initial velocities. From this initial condition, each agent's motion is dynamically influenced as it behaves with respect to other agents it detects within its perceptual range, simulating social engagement, otherwise straying in random motion. Sayama provides an efficient matrix method called a recipe, in which the number of agents and rules of behaviors can be initialized as a set of parameterized values, creating an agent behavioral type. Initializing more than one recipe for separate sets of agents forms heterogeneous swarms. Any agent that perceives another is affected in movement regardless of behavioral type.

Data is extracted from performances with swarms using touch sensitive surfaces. Agents are visualized, a performer can touch the visual display and agents respond. Data from swarms is interpreted to generate sound control data transmitted to real-time sound synthesis engines. Data mapping includes pattern recognition and feature extraction from swarm behaviors, applying a model based design of indirection that prolongs temporal dynamics, discussed is Sect. 4.2. Details of system configuration are reported in [46].

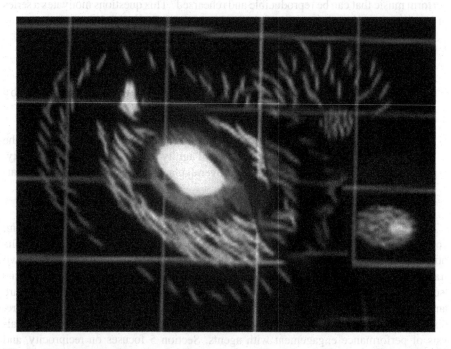

Fig. 1. Color visualization of agents by type, from *Mutandrum*. The area within each grid measures approximately three inches by four inches. Resolution constraints are discussed in Sect. 4.1. The performers' hand is distorting the image projection to the right of center. (Color figure online)

Visualization of Swarms. Agents are visualized by colored pixels. A mixture of colored agents represents the simulation's current state. This simplicity, that agents represent nothing more than visualized state, provides an important baseline to investigate sound with swarm dynamics in tandem with its visual presentation. The whimsical behaviors of agents spontaneously bond with others then stray, creating a constant redistribution of the visual mix, a dynamic field for emergent patterns. The evolutionary trajectory of a given type of agent can be anticipated as to its patterns over time, however the detailed trajectories and patterns of heterogeneous swarms are not predictable beyond a local limit. Often clusters of agents forming patterns are a dominant visual feature; cluster formation is adopted for sound design to reflect this feature, focusing on tracking clusters at the cost of not tracking behavior by agent type.

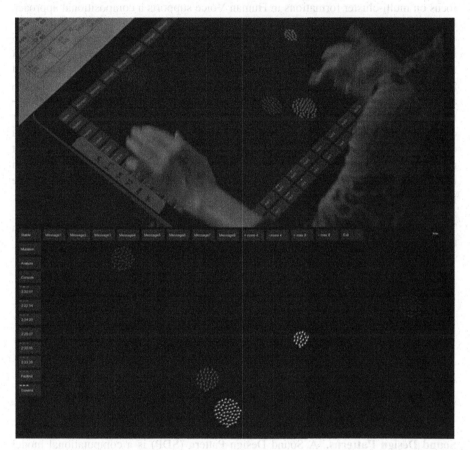

Fig. 2. Color visualization of cluster formation on a touch sensitive screen, from Human Voice, showing performance configuration. (Color figure online)

Color is used differently in the two compositions to support differences in performance requirements. In Mutandrum color visualizes individual agent type and this relates to tone quality transformations (see Fig. 1). In Human Voice color visualizes collective agent behavior and this relates to the number of active sound sources (see Fig. 2). Visualization conveys structural differences of the two musical works, in terms of different types of sounds and different methods for agent data to transform sounds. In Mutandrum, agents' color by type highlights heterogeneous clusters and illustrates distributions of agent types. Visualizing clusters' internal structure draws attention to clusters' internal dynamics, and this data is applied to control timbre transformations (tone quality) of sounds. In Human Voice, agents' color is determined by cluster sequencing and aids the performer's control of sound by illustrating and tracking the progressive number of clusters. The number of clusters determines the number of active sound sources, a requirement specified in the performance score. To summarize: the focus on inter-agent dynamics in Mutandrum supports a timbre-dominant compositional approach, and the focus on multi-cluster formations in Human Voice supports a compositional approach based on polyphony and counterpoint.

Emergent Feature Analysis. Cluster formation is a prominent emergent feature of swarm behavior and is important for control of musical events and structures. Emergent features are not formally modeled in the swarm simulation, so to extract data of clusters and other features for sound control the performance system implements feature recognition. Table 1 presents types of swarm data grouped by duration range required for extracting the data. In Table 1 agent data AD1, AD2, and AD3 depend upon AD4 – data of cluster recognition. AD4 requires automated feature detection, as the clusters are not represented in the simulation. Emergence of these features is uncertain and influenced by a performer, therefore AD4 durations required to induce phase transitions may be prolonged beyond the values indicated in Table 1.

Table 1. Agent data grouped by duration range required for feature formation, data extraction and feature recognition of swarm state

Agent data type	Agent data source	Duration range needed to extract feature data
AD1	Number of Agents in each Cluster	15–20 ms
AD2	Energy of Agents	25–35 ms
AD3	Area of each cluster	50–70 ms
AD4	Position of each Cluster in performance space	75–100 ms
AD5	Velocity of each Cluster	80–120 ms
AD6	Cluster Deformation	250 ms to 2 s
AD7	Cluster Divide	1 s to 3 s
AD8	Cluster Merge	500 ms to 2 s

Sound Design Patterns. A Sound Design Pattern (SDP) is a computational model designed to generate coherent combinations of audible attributes [46, 47]. Attributes and their transformations can be organized by duration range, combining the duration required to generate a pattern and the duration required to recognize the pattern, such as a performer responding to influence a pattern. Table 2 presents SDP types based on duration ranges of audible attributes used in SDPs. Multiple time scales of sound transformation are concurrent in a sound, and attributes of shorter duration contribute to attributes of longer duration. SDP types group sound control parameters to coordinate control data across multiple duration ranges. SDPs are not equivalent to sound sources; several SDP can combine to control a single sound source, or one SDP can contribute to the transformation of several sound sources. Combining SDPs provides a method to control features and transformations of complex sounds, and enables the use of swarm data to control transformations of attributes concurrently at multiple time scales. The lower half of Fig. 6 compares the duration ranges of agents' emergent behavior and SDP audible attributes. The durations of swarm features suggests a "best fit" model by applying swarm data to SPD types of similar duration.

Table 2. Audible attributes of Sound Design Patterns grouped by Duration Range.

SDP type	Audible attributes of sounds	Duration range of SDP
SDP1	Pitch change, loudness change	50 ms–200 ms
SDP2	Timbre, Resonance, Filtering	200 ms–500 ms
SDP3	Sound Source Location cues; Spatial and Directional cues	450 ms–2.0 s
SDP4	Sound Event (from onset to evolution to termination)	500 ms up to many seconds
SDP5	Patterns of Rhythm, Tempo, Spoken Words, Melody	1 s up to many seconds

4   How to Work with Swarms in Experimental Performance

Traditional music composition dimensions include (1) form and tonal relationship, (2) temporal arrangement of elements including structure of repetition, (3) thematic development, (4) harmonic progression, and (5) instrumentation. Working with swarms does not deviate from these dimensions, but shifts paradigms in the ideation of the elements in them.

4.1   Experimental Compositional Dimensions

(1) FORM: In both compositions, the musical form organizes types of agents' collective behavior and associates these to sounds. Behavioral types are used to organize musical structure.

(2) TEMPO: In both compositions, the agents' behaviors were systemically studied for temporal signature then categorized by tempo and temporal agility: the degree of slow to fast, and the range of fluctuation in tempo caused by the degree of stability in swarm dynamics. The temporal signatures are investigated through alternating sound synthesis methods then curated as musical elements using coupled sets of parameters mapping swarm domain to sound range. To produce exact repetition a coupled set is initialized with the same initial condition.

(3) THEME: Thematic development in music often relies on recognizable units of tones and rhythms. In Mutandrum repeated patterns output by tone generators were modulated by swarm dynamics, applying progressive fragmentation. In Human Voice, phrases with spoken texts functioned as semantic themes with musical meanings, which are not solely dependent on the meaning of individual texts but emerge from combinatorial bindings according to swarm dynamics.

(4) PROGRESSION: Harmonic progression is a dominant technique in Western common practice tonal music. In these works the function of progression is carried by timbre (Mutandrum) and texture (Human Voice). Instead of melody and

harmony, Mutandrum applies techniques for progressive derivation of spectral evolution (tone quality) in sounds, using swarms' evolutionary dynamics. Human Voice exploits additional progression in poetic form and linguistic content by generating multiple voices that present spoken texts in layers.

(5) ORCHESTRATION: Instrumentation is orchestrated by sound source selection and by Sound Design Patterns (SDP), and these associations are controlled by selected behavioral tendencies of swarms; see Tables 1 and 2 and the discussion below regarding sound source selection and manipulation.

Mutandrum: Musical Goals and Features. Mutandrum explores the plasticity of sound in relationship to the plasticity of swarms, described as "sound tangibility" in [47]. This describes the kinesthetic relationship of motion dynamics between a human agent and simulated agents, and how auditory feedback confirms that relationship. The ability to engage a visualization of agents through a touch interface evokes an interactive "electro-visual-acoustic" experience, with attributes determined by relative visual and audible responsiveness. To explore audiovisual plasticity, swarm clusters' symmetry and shape deformation are identified as top priority for feature recognition. Cluster deformation data is applied to synchronize transformations of sounds with changing cluster shapes, ensuring an obvious local correspondence between performer's action, swarm response and sound response. To further establish local correspondence the cluster's position in x-axis in the performance space drives the stereo position of the sound source associated with the cluster. Additionally the temporal dynamics of the micro-movements, or "jitters" of the agents are emphasized by sounds. When swarm jitter values are highest the sounds return strong rhythmic features and a notable pulse. When swarm jitter values are attenuated the sounds return sustained tones focusing on timbre transformations.

Compositional choices in Mutandrum reflect the physical limitations of the capacitive surface used for the original performance, supporting only two simultaneous touch points on a 36 by 48-in. table top. The reliable resolution of position sensing for touch interaction was an area of roughly 0.3 in. square with fuzzy boundaries, approximating a differentiable resolution of 160×120 units. Agents visualized at 1024×768 pixels scaled to 48×36 in. producing a unit of about 0.05 in./pixel. The ratio of this resolution to the rate of change of agents' movements and the lower-resolution capacitive sensing determines the rate of change of sound control data. Given these constraints, manipulation of large clusters is most accurate and reliable; in response compositional design focuses on spectral explorations therefore strategizes with a limited number of sound sources. During the flow of the performance, a maximum of four complex sources are made available, and the concurrent number of sound sources varies from section to section. The quality of sounds is determined by a dominant frequency and spectral (tone quality) portrait. Cluster size determines the frequency: the larger the cluster the lower the fundamental frequency. The shape of clusters influences the spectral resonance. To avoid the feature recognition task of disambiguating complex cluster shapes, data extraction is only applied to detect relative deviation from the symmetry of the native cluster state, which is usually circular. The deformation data is applied to vary spectral resonance: the thicker the shape, the greater the resonance. All local cluster deformations dynamically affect the quality of sounds in all states, as sounds were designed using SDPs with high-level synthesis parameters exposed to receive the deformation data. Figure 3 shows a performance image with swarm visualization projected for the audience.

Fig. 3. Performance with large tabletop capacitive panel enabling hand-sized control regions. Visualization of swarms is projected on the performance surface from above and also projected for audience members.

Human Voice: Musical Goals and Features. Voice explores a poem and uses the recorded voice of the poet as the primary sound source. The compositional intent is to create emergent discourse through structure of call and response by constructing multiple voices of the poet as sound sources. Onsets and durations of sound sources emphasize temporal dynamics at phrase level, rather than the micro-temporal levels of timbre transformation as in Mutandrum. The number of sound sources and when they come and go is paramount, with the management of multiple voices derived from cluster division, merger, and movement, evoking musical idioms such as polyphony and antiphony. In contrast to Mutandrum, the use of timbre in Human Voice is subordinated. Sounds do not undergo major timbre transformations synchronized with cluster transformations. Timbre is applied with nuance to help distinguish multiple voices and to enhance the clarity of spoken texts. Local synchronization of image and sound is not emphasized by cluster deformation, but only at the points of cluster division and merger. These cluster phase transitions are consistently reflected by the introduction and termination of voice sources. The autonomous phase transition behavior of clusters is an important contributor to the musical texture. Cluster states also require close monitoring by the performer to defer unwanted phase transitions. To do this the performer applies a "shepherding" movement technique to prolong the current swarm state and achieve longer phrase structures (see "Melisma" in Table 3).

Table 3. Comparing Indirection Profiles of two compositions, *Mutandrum* and *Human Voice*. Comparison is drawn against the duration ranges of performance gestural articulation units (PGAU) and latency of indirection for each PGAU. Duration ranges of agent data types are presented in Table 1. Duration ranges of sound design patterns (SDP) are presented in Table 2.

PGAU	PROFILES in Mutandrum and Human Voice							
	PGAU duration range		Agent data type		SDP type		Maximum latency of indirection	
	Mut.	H.V.	Mut.	H.V.	Mut.	H.V.	Mut.	H.V.
Punctum	100 ms–500 ms	300 ms–1 s	AD 1, 2, 3	AD 6, 7, 8	SDP 1 & 2	SDP 4	500 ms	1.5 s
Brevis	300 ms–2 s	500 ms–2 s	AD 3 to 6	AD 7 & 8	SDP 1,2, 3	SDP 3 & 4	1 s	3 s
Longa	4 s–9 s	3 s–15 s	AD 4 to 8	AD 4, 5, 6	SDP 2,3,4	SDP 3,4,5	3 s	5 s
Melisma	8 s–13 s	5 s–60 s	AD 4, 5, 6	AD 1 to 5	SDP 2,3,5	SDP 3,4,5	4 s	6 s

Compositional choices in Human Voice reflect the physical affordances of a digital capacitive touch screen with a 16:9 ratio, 1920 × 1080 pixel resolution, and screen area of 21 × 12.5 in.. The resolution of 0.01 in. per pixel supports ten fingers' independent touch points capacity with arm arch range and wrist orientation supported by the performer's standing position. Figure 4 shows performance with ten-finger touch applied to swarm visualization projected for the audience. As spoken text is present throughout the piece, the compositional design focuses on textual antiphony and on polyphonic explorations. Therefore the strategy is to present these voices with intelligibility and clarity, avoiding extreme timbre and pitch deformation while applying subtle affects such as chorusing and simulated spatial characteristics such as sound source locations. To achieve this design objective the deformation relationship between cluster and sound is not as heightened as in Mutandrum. At all times the number of sound sources are subjected to the continuous tracking of four distinct levels of cluster bifurcation. Therefore in Human Voice, swarm bifurcation has a structural role in the musical progression.

Fig. 4. Performance of Human Voice with high-resolution capacitive touch screen, showing ten-finger control signal capacity

As an instrumental paradigm, there are many table top models. Touch introduces excitatory signals into the system. From the author's experience, performing Human Voice is reminiscent to the 12 silk string instrument called gayaguem, illustrated in Fig. 5. Of course, these have completely different tactile sensation and resistance; still the kinaesthetic address from a performer's perspective is highly compatible. Having performed gayageum, this author can report that cognitive plasticity of digital music instruments is possible with proper HCI engineering with adequate building blocks.

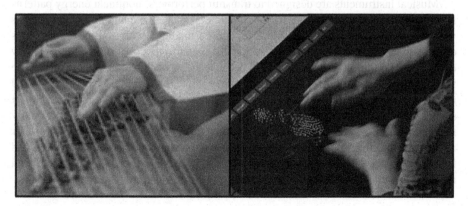

Fig. 5. Comparative illustration of a performer's kinesthetic orientation with the gayaguem (left) and swarm agents (right)

4.2   Design and Implementation of Model Based Indirection

The experimental system presents an interaction modality through which a performer inputs data to sound indirectly, based upon a model. Performer's actions on the touch screen engage swarm agents, influencing agents' collective emergent features, then control signals are transmitted from feature extracted data to parameterized sound synthesis engines. This pathway of indirection provides affordances for reciprocity between the performer and the swarm simulation. With traditional music instruments reciprocity is generated when a performer inputs excitatory energy into a resonating body, and the instrument amplifies and differentiates that energy to contribute the resulting sound quality. While learning to play music instruments entails learning to shape the excitatory input patterns, learning to play swarms in these works entails learning the model of introducing excitatory energy into sound engines by working with swarms through social engagement.

Designing indirection and engineering audio-visual presentation including process time is guided by sensitivity for intersensory asynchronies in perception, for example the Just Noticeable Different (JND) boundary of 50 ms for cross modal performance and permissible ranges. The compiled study from [48] reports optimal intersensory JND between audio and visual when audio is presented 50 ms before visual. Due to the brain's capacity for adaptively widening, when audio precedes visual the permissible JND ranges from 250 ms, when audio follows visual it is 150 ms [49, 50]. In another example, in Human Voice the most frequently used gesture articulation unit is longer than 500 ms in order to accommodate syllable durations ranging 240 ms to 340 ms.

The analogy of HCI direct manipulation [51] in music performance comes close to instruments like harp and drum, but is not ubiquitous. Musical instruments are physically fabricated complex systems refined through extensive conditioning and tuning. The response characteristics of an instrument are complex and nonlinear: to produce musical tones requires skillful manipulations. Sound is produced by microvariations at oscillatory level; a performer cannot directly control single oscillations or manipulate all conditions of instrumental components to shape an absolute result.

Musical instruments are designed to transmit performers' nonlinear energy patterns into the physical components of the instrument that shape the quality of sound. This is why a large class of musical instruments can be modeled with nonlinear oscillators coupled to passive linear systems [52, 53]. This scenario tests the limits of the analogy of direct manipulation adopted from HCI because the music instrument is already a case for indirection for resulting sound. An obvious example is a violin. The bow is a physical model that offers an indirection with a degree of freedom to generate more variety of sounds than afforded by bare fingers. And this indirection can be computationally modeled as bow pressure and angle, etc. to simulate the friction dynamics [54–56]. For a working definition, model based indirection is a technique to instrument an extended interactive pathway to optimize the relationship between performance input and resulting sounds, where the extension model engages a generative mechanism.

4.3 Performance Gestural Articulation Units (PGAU)

Table 3 presents a comparative analysis of indirection and resulting temporal dynamics in the two compositions. Indirection is observed with respect to the actions of a performer and the corresponding swarm data and resulting sound patterns. The table compares indirection across four types of hand movements, referred to as Performance Gestural Articulation Units (PGAU). In order of increasing duration and indirection the units are named after Gregorian notation, punctum, brevis, longa, and melisma. The nomenclature is adopted in reference to chant tradition where durations are context dependent with no absolute values. For a generalizable definition applicable to both human movements and computational model, PGAU can be defined as a context dependent unit of gesture with a recognizable pattern having onset and termination in varying duration within a limit. PGAU are applied to express a functional contribution to the temporal dynamics in situ of performance along with system constituents [47]. In this context, the constituents are swarms, SDPs and a performance score.

For each type of PGAU in the two compositions, Table 3 shows SDP models and agent data (from Tables 1 and 2). The two compositions adopt different combinations of agent data groups and SDPs for PGAU. The differences reflect the different sound sources and compositional structure in the two cases. As an example, Human Voice does not apply SDP1 and SDP2, which generate micro-variations of pitch, loudness, and timbre. This is because in Human Voice, these attributes are rendered by the recorded voice performance of a poet, and are preserved at the performance timescale rather than transformed. Timbre and loudness variation are applied using longer–duration SDPs.

PGAU is an expression unit of temporally defined hand gestures analogous to excitatory input of a music instrument. Similarly, impact from PGAU propagates through indirection dataflow in the system, accumulating data extraction time and sound processing time while inheriting the temporal definitions of the SDPs. These accumulations result in duration of indirection extending sound events beyond PGAU hand movement. Table 3 illustrates how PGAU engages simultaneously multiple agent data types and SDPs, generating multiple levels of indirection. Indirection built into the design is most easily observed in the latency of prolonged sound responses to PGAUs. The Maximum Latency of Indirection (Table 3) was comparatively observed in recorded performances of each composition, measured from the onsets of PGAUs to the response times in the sounds, also from the releases of PGAUs to the latent duration of lasting effects in the sounds. While a novice can play with this system, a performance skill deepens in part through mastering the relationship between PGAU, swarms, and sounds shadowing swarms through model based indirection.

5 Composing Structured Reciprocity

Each composition encodes association of temporal dynamics between swarms and sounds, as follows. For each section of the musical score an HIEC selection of swarm agent types has been assigned, and for each section of the music performance code SDPs have been developed to respond to agent behaviors. The reproducibility of these associations enables a performer's learning curve when encountering the predicted behaviors so that each composition can be rehearsable. Reciprocity is structured in a time window that represents concurrent presence of agent behaviors and SDPs. This structure is composed anticipating the efforts require to rehearse, to perform, and to listen. Emergent swarm behaviors generate control data for sounds' attributes that are too detailed for a performer to control directly. The performer rehearses the reliability of swarm behaviors and how to induce and prolong cluster phase transitions and steady states, generating sound control data required to render the musical score. Reciprocity emerges as a practice of shared control data generation in performance.

The following outlines the process end-to-end for encoding, activating, generating, and measuring reciprocity. Encoding: In the experimental system reciprocity is encoded in the temporal dynamics of the indirection model. This encoding combines the model of PGAU performance engagement, the swarm feature data extraction, and the temporal dynamics of the SDPs. Activating: Reciprocity is activated by the performer's PGAU prioritized for swarms' behavioral tendencies and the levels of sound transformation specified in the score. Generating: Reciprocity is generated by the requirements of the musical score and the performer's engagement with the swarm tendency "envelope"— the average rate a swarm recovers its native tendency following a PGAU intervention. Measuring: Reciprocity is measured by the performer in judging the need to induce changes in swarm behaviors with respect to the SDP. During the bidirectional process when the composer develops SDPs and swarm tendencies, the composer anticipates the performer's measure of reciprocity, as follows: (1) SDPs are computationally modeled to express the compositional idea; (2) swarms are designed to exhibit tendencies that are a good fit for expressive control of the SDPs; (3) swarm data feature extraction is tuned to recognize collective behaviors; (4) SDP mapping is fine tuned to reflect the variety of detail in the swarm data.

Swarms and sounds are scheduled by a series of initializations, some automated, some activated by the performer, as outlined in a performance score. Layers of SDPs respond concurrently to parallel data streams. Figure 6 synthesizes PGAUs with the durations of four sets of agent data types (AD1-4) and five types of SDPs (SDP1-5) from Tables 1, 2 and 3. The onset of a PGAU can transform multiple concurrent data streams. In Fig. 3, agent data streams AD1 and AD2 are updated roughly at 10 Hz while behaviors in AD3 and AD4 emerge over longer durations. The arrows at AD3 and AD4 in Fig. 6 indicate the potential for a performer to prolong those behaviors. Concurrently, SDP1 updates at about 5 Hz and SDP 2 updates at 2 to 4 Hz, while SDP3, 4 and 5 progress across longer durations. The arrows at SDP4 and 5 indicate the potential for a performer to further prolong PGAUs. Figure 6 across the top indicates maximum and minimum durations for PGAU types observed in performances of two compositions, to the duration limit of the figure.

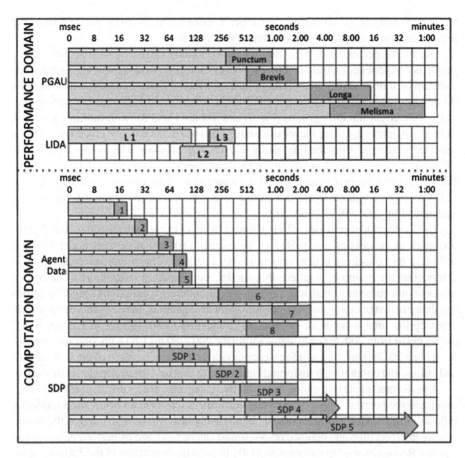

Fig. 6. Comparison of minimum and maximum duration ranges of agent data types, SDPs, PGAU types, and the LIDA model. The darker shaded areas are the valid range for each item. The duration scale left to right is Log2. Arrows on SDP4 and SP5 indicate potential prolongation.

For experimental analysis the LIDA model [36] provides a reference to measure the range of performer's engagement in reciprocity with respect to the system temporal dynamics. Figure 6 compares the duration of the LIDA cognitive cycle to durations of agent data types and SDPs, discussed in the next section. The layered profile in Fig. 6 illustrates a multi-temporal capacity for designing indirection, which is used to prioritize the data from selected swarm tendencies. The mapping from swarm to sound at multiple time scales formalizes the mappings from swarm emergent features to SDPs.

6   Discussion

Reciprocity structured by designed indirection in the signal path enables the integrity of the three agents of co-creation: swarms, composition, and performance. Designing indirection utilizes PGAU, swarms' behavioral tendencies, and SDP. Coherently designed, structured reciprocity leverages performer's associative memory for learning and refining performance skills with the interactive system.

During the performance with audiovisual continuity driven by swarm dynamics, a performer experiences a time window for action selection across evolving swarms and a stream of sounds. SDPs are building blocks for model based indirection that increase the degree of freedom and capacity for PGAU, to act in nested time windows with respect to the concurrent duration groups (Fig. 6 and Tables 1 and 3), with multiple layers of indirection extending from the swarm state. The swarm data at any given time will be reflected in sound during the time delay of each SDP window. The temporal extension of each indirection layer depends on the SDP parameters and swarm tendency envelope. For understanding performers' parallel engagement with multiple temporal layers, LIDA's single cognitive cycle provides a reference model to distinguish perception, understanding, and action selection.

The LIDA model provides a 260–390 ms cognitive cycle with an initial 200–280 ms unconscious processing comprised of perception (80–100 ms), then understanding, followed by conscious action selection (60–110 ms). The durations considered in composing for reciprocity reflect this model, commencing with short durations of sensorimotor engagements that do not require deliberation, followed by longer durations involving action planning and recognition of musical patterns. SDP1 events occur within a perception time window of 50–100 ms (compared to 80–100 ms in LIDA). SDP2 events occur from 200–500 ms, many within the 200–280 ms LIDA unconscious period. Roughly a 50–280 ms time windows encompass the basic perception of pitch, loudness, and pulses, and continuing transformation of sounds that have been already set in motion.

A performer's action decision falls into two categories at any given moment, PGAU onset and the purpose. Most of the time, performers intervene in bifurcation modes or influence the transformation modes of already launched events. SDP1 and SDP2 do not require interpretation and planned response and can be modified by performer's ongoing actions. Recognition of spatial cues in SDP3 falls on the borderline of the 390 ms cognitive cycle proposed in the LIDA model.

Agent data is detected in multiple time scales: 15–120 ms for AD1 and AD2 afford duration for sensorimotor response; 250 ms–3 s for AD3 and AD4 afford duration for recognition of evolving patterns and phase transitions. SDP4 can carry all of SDP1, 2, 3 in a single sound event and SDP5 can carry multiple sound events forming a larger phrase structure. SDP4 and SDP5 are programmed to host indirection with durations greater than the 390 ms action cycle. The duration required for action planning with SDP4 or SDP5 depends on the emerging complexity and temporal dynamics, but is approximately twice the minimum duration (500 ms) of SDP4, which allows at least two cognitive cycles for action planning.

To conclude: (1) Structured reciprocity helps optimize the use of evolutionary tendencies including their intuitive qualities, towards desired outcomes in interactive applications. The ongoing generative mechanism of the swarm model accompanies performers with a "visual metronome" to gauge and anticipate tendencies and emerging patterns. The intuitive quality of visualized swarm dynamics aids the performer's capacity to predict future states and to plan action repertoire towards future states of sounds. (2) Observational data from the case study lends quantitative guidance towards formalizing indirection for complex interactive scenarios. Model-based indirection provides performers with time latency needed for action planning. With indirection design, the goal is to engage swarms in the model of indirection, which facilitates the efficient use of data from swarms' inherent tendencies. The efficiency is achieved by consulting the swarms' generative mechanism to drive details of musical outcomes along with SDPs. The better the fit of inherent swarm tendencies, the closer the resulting association of visualized swarm dynamics with anticipated sounds.

Acknowledgements. The author wishes to thank Hiroki Sayama as a scientific collaborator, Robin Bargar as a producing partner, and Jeff Meyers, Arthur Peters and Kevin Bolander for supporting software development.

References

1. Galanter, P.: Computational aesthetic evaluation: past and future. In: McCormack, J., d'Inverno, M. (eds.) Computers and Creativity, pp. 255–293. Springer, Heidelberg (2012). https://doi.org/10.1007/978-3-642-31727-9_10
2. Boden, M., Edmonds, E.: What is generative art? Digit. Creat. **20**(1/2), 21–46 (2009)
3. Stiny, G., Gips, J.: Shape grammars and the generative specification of painting and sculpture. In: Freiman, C.V. (ed.) Information Processing 71, pp. 1460–1465. North Holland, Amsterdam (1972)
4. Romero, J.J., Machado, P.: The Art of Artificial Evolution. Springer, Berlin (2008)
5. Cope, D.: Computers and Musical Style. A-R Editions, Madison (1991)
6. Dubnov, S., Argamon, S., Burns, K. (eds.): The Structure of Style: Algorithmic Approaches to Understanding Manner and Meaning. Springer, Heidelberg (2010)
7. Todd, P.M.: A connectionist approach to algorithmic composition. Comput. Music J. **13**(4), 27–43 (1989)
8. Brooks, F., Hopkins, A., Neumann, P., Wright, W.: An experiment in musical composition. IRE Trans. Electron. Comput. **6**(1), 175–182 (1957)
9. Phon-Amnuaisuk, S., Law, E.H.H., Kuan, H.C.: Evolving music generation with SOM-fitness genetic programming. In: Giacobini, M. (ed.) EvoWorkshops 2007. LNCS, vol. 4448, pp. 557–566. Springer, Heidelberg (2007). https://doi.org/10.1007/978-3-540-71805-5_61
10. Law, E.H.H., Phon-Amnuaisuk, S.: Towards music fitness evaluation with the hierarchical SOM. In: Giacobini, M., et al. (eds.) EvoWorkshops 2008. LNCS, vol. 4974, pp. 443–452. Springer, Heidelberg (2008). https://doi.org/10.1007/978-3-540-78761-7_47
11. McDermott, J., Griffith, N.J.L., O'Neill, M.: Toward user-directed evolution of sound synthesis parameters. In: Rothlauf, F., et al. (eds.) EvoWorkshops 2005. LNCS, vol. 3449, pp. 517–526. Springer, Heidelberg (2005). https://doi.org/10.1007/978-3-540-32003-6_52
12. Mitchell, T.J., Pipe, A.G.: Convergence synthesis of dynamic frequency modulation tones using an evolution strategy. In: Rothlauf, F., et al. (eds.) EvoWorkshops 2005. LNCS, vol. 3449, pp. 533–538. Springer, Heidelberg (2005). https://doi.org/10.1007/978-3-540-32003-6_54
13. Magnus, C.: Evolutionary musique concrète. In: Rothlauf, F., et al. (eds.) EvoWorkshops 2006. LNCS, vol. 3907, pp. 688–695. Springer, Heidelberg (2006). https://doi.org/10.1007/11732242_65

14. Hazan, A., Ramirez, R., Maestre, E., Perez, A., Pertusa, A.: Modelling expressive performance: a regression tree approach based on strongly typed genetic programming. In: Rothlauf, F., et al. (eds.) EvoWorkshops 2006. LNCS, vol. 3907, pp. 676–687. Springer, Heidelberg (2006). https://doi.org/10.1007/11732242_64

15. Ramirez, R., Hazan, A., Marine, J., Serra, X.: Evolutionary computing for expressive music performance. In: Romero, J., Machado, P. (eds.) The Art of Artificial Evolution, pp. 123–144. Springer, Heidelberg (2008)

16. Bilotta, E., Pantano, P.: Artificial life music tells of complexity. In: Proceedings of Artificial Life Models for Musical Applications ECAL 2001 Workshop, Prague (2001)

17. Miranda, E., Kirke, A., Zhang, Q.: Artificial evolution of expressive performance of music: an imitative multi-agent systems approach. Comput. Music J. **34**(1), 80–96 (2010)

18. Todd, P.M., Werner, G.M.: Frankensteinian methods for evolutionary music composition. In: Griffith, N., Todd, P. (eds.) Musical Networks: Parallel Distributed Perception and Performance. MIT Press/Bradford Books, Cambridge (1998)

19. Unemi, T.: Simulated breeding–a framework of breeding artifacts on the computer. Kybernetes **32**(1/2), 203–220 (2003)

20. Takagi, H.: Interactive evolutionary computation: fusion of the capabilities of optimization and human evaluation. Proc. IEEE **89**(9), 1275–1296 (2001)

21. Sayama, H.: Decentralized control and interactive design methods for large-scale heterogeneous self-organizing swarms. In: Almeida e Costa, F., Rocha, L.M., Costa, E., Harvey, I., Coutinho, A. (eds.) ECAL 2007. LNCS (LNAI), vol. 4648, pp. 675–684. Springer, Heidelberg (2007). https://doi.org/10.1007/978-3-540-74913-4_68

22. David Murray-Rust, D., Smaill, A., Edwards, M.: MAMA: an architecture for interactive musical agents. In: Brewka, G., et al. (eds.) Proceedings of ECAI 2006. IOS Press (2006)

23. Huepe, C., Colasso, M., Cádiz, R.F.: Generating music from flocking dynamics. In: LaViers, A., Egerstedt, M. (eds.) Controls and Art, pp. 155–179. Springer, Cham (2014). https://doi.org/10.1007/978-3-319-03904-6_7

24. Blackwell, T.: Improvised music with swarms. In: Proceedings of the 2002 Congress on Evolutionary Computation, CEC 2002 (2002). https://doi.org/10.1109/cec.2002.1004458

25. Grace, L.D.: Music box: composing and performing visual music. In: Proceedings of the International Conference on Advances in Computer Entertainment Technology (ACE 2009), p. 445. ACM, New York (2009). https://doi.org/10.1145/1690388.1690493

26. Davis, T., Karamanlis, O.: Gestural control of sonic swarms: composing with grouped sound objects. In: Proceedings SMC 2007, 4th Sound and Music Computing Conference (2007)

27. Peignier, S., Abernot, J., Rigotti, C., Beslon, G.: EvoMove: evolutionary-based living musical companion. In: Proceedings of 14th European Conference on Artificial Life (2017)

28. Schacher, J., Bisig, D., Kocher, P.: The map and the flock: emergence in mapping with swarm algorithms. Comput. Music J. **38**(3), 49–63 (2014). https://doi.org/10.1162/COMJ_a_00256

29. Choi, I., Bargar, R.: A playable evolutionary interface for performance and social engagement. In: Camurri, A., Costa, C. (eds.) INTETAIN 2011. LNICST, vol. 78, pp. 170–182. Springer, Heidelberg (2012). https://doi.org/10.1007/978-3-642-30214-5_19

30. Bisig, D., Kocher, P.: Tools and abstractions for swarm based music and art. In: Proceedings of 38th Annual International Computer Music Conference, ICMC 2012, Ljubljana. ICMA (2012)

31. Ringer, A., Crossley-Holland, P.: Musical composition. In: Encyclopaedia Britannica (2008)

32. Choi, I.: A manifold interface for kinesthetic notation in high-dimensional systems. In: Battier, M., Wanderly, M. (eds.) Trends in Gestural Control of Music, Paris. IRCAM (2000)

33. Matell, M., Meck, W., Nicolelis, M.: Integration of behavior and timing: anatomically separate systems or distributed processing? In: Meck, W. (ed.) Functional and Neural Mechanisms of Interval Timing, pp. 371–391. CRC Press, Boca Raton (2003)
34. Buhusi, C.: Associative and temporal learning: new directions. Behav. Process. **101**, 1–3 (2014)
35. Choi, I.: Interactive exploration of a chaotic oscillator for generating musical signals in real-time concert performance. J. Franklin Inst. **331B**(6), 785–818 (1994)
36. Chua, L.: Local activity is the origin of complexity. Int. J. Bifurcat. Chaos **15**(11), 3435–3456 (2005)
37. Koelsch, S.: Toward a neural basis of music perception – a review and updated model. Front. Psychol. **2**, 110 (2011)
38. Zioga, I., Di Bernardi Luft, C., Bhattacharya, J.: Musical training shapes neural responses to melodic and prosodic expectation. Brain Res. **1650**, 267–282 (2016)
39. Ellis, C., Adams, T., Bochner, A.: Autoethnography: an overview. Forum Qual. Soc. Res. **12**(1), 10 (2010)
40. Ellingson, L., Ellis, C.: Autoethnography as constructionist project. In: Holstein, J.A., Gubrium, J.F. (eds.) Handbook of Constructionist Research, pp. 445–466. Guilford Press, New York (2008)
41. Ashby, W.R.: Variety, constraint, and the law of requisite variety. In: Modern Systems Research for the Behavioral Scientist. Aldine, Chicago (1968)
42. von Foerster, H.: On self-organizing systems and their environments. In: Observing Systems, Chap. 1. Intersystems, Seaside (1981)
43. Franklin, S., Patterson, F.: The LIDA architecture: adding new modes of learning to an intelligent, autonomous, software agent. In: IDPT 2006 Proceedings (Integrated Design and Process Technology). Society for Design and Process Science (2006)
44. Madl, T., Baars, B.J., Franklin, S.: The timing of the cognitive cycle. PLoS ONE **6**(4), e14803 (2011). https://doi.org/10.1371/journal.pone.0014803
45. Reynolds, C.: Flocks, herds and schools: a distributed behavioral model. In: SIGGRAPH 1987: Proceedings of the 14th Annual Conference on Computer Graphics and Interactive Techniques, pp. 25–34. Association for Computing Machinery (1987)
46. Choi, I., Bargar, R.: Sounds shadowing agents generating audible features from emergent behaviors. In: Sayama, H., et al. (eds.) Proceedings of the Fourteenth International Conference on the Synthesis and Simulation of Living Systems, pp. 726–733. MIT Press, Cambridge (2014)
47. Choi, I.: Interactive composition and performance framework with evolutionary computing. In: Proceedings of 43rd Annual International Computer Music Conference, Shanghai, pp. 351–356. ICMA (2017)
48. Keetels, M., Vroomen, J.: Perception of synchrony between the senses. In: Murray, M., Wallace, M. (eds.) The Neural Bases of Multisensory Processes, Chap. 9. CRC Press, Boca Raton (2012)
49. Besle, J., Fort, A., Delpuech, C., Giard, M.-H.: Bimodal speech: early suppressive visual effects in human auditory cortex. Eur. J. Neurosci. **20**(8), 2225–2234 (2004)
50. Flinker, A., Korzeniewska, A., Shestyuk, A.Y., Franaszczuk, P.J., Dronkers, N.F., Knight, R.T., Crone, N.E.: Redefining the role of Broca's area in speech. Proc. Natl. Acad. Sci. U.S.A. **112**(9), 2871–2875 (2015)
51. Shneiderman, B.: Direct manipulation: a step beyond programming languages. IEEE Comput. **16**(8), 57–69 (1983)
52. McIntyre, M.E., Schumacher, R.T., Woodhouse, J.: On the oscillations of musical instruments. J. Acoust. Soc. Am. **74**(5), 1325–1345 (1983)

53. Rodet, X.: Nonlinear oscillator models of musical instrument excitation. In: Proceedings of the International Computer Music Conference, San Francisco, pp. 412–413. ICMA (1992)
54. McIntyre, M.E., Woodhouse, J.: On the fundamentals of bowed-string dynamics. Acustica **43**, 93–108 (1979)
55. Woodhouse, J.: On the stability of bowed string motion. Acustica **80**, 58–72 (1994)
56. Debut, V., Antunes, J., Inácio, O.: Linear modal stability analysis of bowed-strings. J. Acoust. Soc. Am. **141**(3), 2107–2120 (2017)

Creating a Theatrical Experience on a Virtual Stage

Joe Geigel[✉]

Department of Computer Science, Rochester Institute of Technology,
Rochester, NY, USA
jmg@cs.rit.edu

Abstract. This paper describes the use of virtual and augmented reality, combined with motion capture technologies, to produce virtual theatre: live theatrical performance fully realized and experienced in a virtual space. The virtual theatre dance performance *Farewell to Dawn*, which was presented in Rochester, NY in December 2016, is used to illustrate and explore affordances of these technologies in terms the liveness, perspective, and social presence.

1 Introduction

In this paper, we describe a realization of virtual theatre, which we define as shared, live performance, experienced in a virtual space, with participants contributing from different physical locales. Using this definition, we see virtual theatre as a specialization of the more general term of *telematic art* [1], particularly suited to live theatre and making use of modern hardware and software that enable interaction, viewing, and immersion in shared virtual reality spaces.

Our goal is to produce a shared experience in the virtual world that mirrors that of theatre in a physical space. In contrast to theatrical productions that use make use of virtual elements to enhance physical theatre (e.g. virtual scenography [23]), we are concerned with performance that is realized, viewed, and experienced completely a the virtual world.

Since the advent of virtual reality, the use of virtual worlds for theatrical applications has been an active area of exploration. Stages in virtual worlds have housed productions of Shakespeares work [7,17,26], assisted in lighting and staging [13], been used to recreate historical theatre from the past [31], and served as rehearsal spaces for actors performing on a physical stage [25,27].

Theatre is, by its very nature, a collaborative art; an active and live interplay between actors and audience. In addition to the basic technical issues related to building a system that enables this kind of performance, a major challenge is to create a shared experience where each participant feels as if they play an active part in the collaborative process even though they may be in different physical spaces.

We look to answer the question: *What it is that makes live theatre such a unique experience?* and explore if one can recreate that feeling in a distributed scenario even though it is experienced from different physical locales.

© Springer International Publishing AG, part of Springer Nature 2018
A. D. Cheok et al. (Eds.): ACE 2017, LNCS 10714, pp. 713–725, 2018.
https://doi.org/10.1007/978-3-319-76270-8_49

In this paper, we use the virtual theatre production of *Farewell to Dawn*[1] which was presented in Rochester, NY in December 2016 as a testbed to explore our ideas.

The remainder of the paper is organized as follows. In Sect. 2, we discuss attributes that distinguish theatre from other forms of entertainment. This is followed by a description of *Farewell to Dawn*. The next section provides a discussion on how our performance relates to the attributes mentioned in Sect. 2. Finally, the paper finishes with conclusions and future work.

2   The Theatrical Experience in the Physical World

In the physical world, theatre presents a unique experience as compared to other forms of media based entertainment such as television or film. In this paper, we focus on three attributes that define this experience and use these as guiding principles to frame our discussion about theatre for the virtual stage.

Liveness. Liveness can be described as connection of experiencing an event, as it is happening [4]. Each live performance is unique and different from every other performance, even if well rehearsed. Mistakes can be made and small variations in performance are not only possible but most likely to occur.

Theatre is unique in this sense in comparison to recorded media like film and TV, as the mere process of recording or saving for later viewing removes the liveness of the experience. Even events that are streamed live (e.g. live simulcast of theatrical performances or live TV broadcasts) loose their sense of "liveness" as, though they are viewed as the event is happening, the performers have no sense of connection and engagement with the audience [28].

Perspective. Perspective refers to the realization that the experience of each participant will depend upon their position in the theatre from where they view and interact with the performance. The actor's perspective is surely different that of the audience, but even each audience member has his or her own seat in the auditorium making the point of view of each audience member unique from every other member. In addition, with theatre, an audience member is active observer. Unlike film where the perspective is carefully and creatively determined by the cinematographer, during a theatrical performance, the participant is in control of their point of view: where they wish to look, when they choose to look, or even whether they choose to look.

With theatre, the performance itself is the art that provides the entertainment [29]. Certainly, one can film a live performance, but in doing so, the audience perspective and point of view is fixed, determined by the positioning of the camera and controlled via the intentions of the camera operator. The determination of where the attention is placed at any given time during a performance is an integral component of film or video capture, thus taking this ability away from an audience member who may be viewing the same live performance in the theatre.

---

[1] http://www.cs.rit.edu/~jmg/f2d.

Social Presence. Theatre is inherently a dynamic social activity; it involves a group of people, assembling in a common space to tell or take in a performed story. Social presence refers to the extent to which people coexist and react to others in a given space [12]. Clearly, any interplay, whether explicit or subtle, between the actors and audience is unique to theatre and live performance. Social presence between audience members: the feeling of a shared experience of action simultaneously viewed in the same space; communication, both verbal and non-verbal between viewers; even the sense of proximity being seated next to a fellow theatre-goer, all add to the excitement of a live theatrical experience.

Fig. 1. View of the virtual stage for *Farewell to Dawn*, a virtual theatre performance. Actors controlling the avatars are shown in the insets.

3   Farewell to Dawn

Farewell to Dawn [3] is a live, mixed-reality dance performance that combines virtual and augmented reality with motion capture and fully realizes our concept of virtual theatre. The piece explores the voyage of two dancers from a physical space to a virtual stage and back, as the day passes before them. Originally developed and performed as a mixed-reality experience in April 2016, a complete virtual theatre version was presented at the MAGIC center at the Rochester Institute of Technology in December 2016. A still from the performance, with inset of the actors controlling the avatars on the stage, is shown in Fig. 1[2].

---

[2] A 360 video of the December 2016 performance can be found at https://youtu.be/ o5lO_7DFku0.

3.1   Physical Setup

The physical set up for *Farewell to Dawn* is illustrated in Fig. 2. The action takes place on a stage in a virtual space with the performers represented by stylized avatars controlled by human dancers in separate, physical, motion capture spaces. These dancers are equipped with augmented reality headgear, through which they can see the view of the virtual stage from their avatars perspective. Audience members view the performance from the perspective of a seat in the virtual theatre.

Technically, we adapt a distributed 3D gaming engine [6] to create the shared experience, allowing us the ability to create an application for experiencing the performance on a variety of different output devices. Motion capture is performed using a set of networked Microsoft Kinect sensors, two Kinect devices for each dancer.

3.2   Participant Experiences

Actor Presence. A major challenge with acting in distributed virtual spaces lies with the interface, as the default means of interacting in these worlds using a mouse and/or keyboard is unnatural and non-intuitive. The communication of emotion through body language and facial expression is paramount for the trained actor, dancer, or performance artist [16,25,34]. To address this, we utilize motion capture to provide a natural interface for actors in controlling their avatars. With regards to avatar motion in virtual worlds, theatre and the performing arts can not only be used as a guide for animating believable and expressive motion in virtual worlds, but can also be used as a gold standard in evaluation of such motion [20]. In particular, the use of nonverbal communication such as body language, and facial expressions are key elements in theatrical communication [22].

In theatrical expression, proxemics (the relationship between actors in the space they inhabit) [8] is as importance as the kinesics (posture, gesture, body motion) [2]. In our past work on virtual theatre [5,6], projections on a large screen or wall were used to give the actor a very rudimentary sense of where their avatar stood on the virtual stage. Very often, motion of the avatar on the stage was achieved with assistance from a stage manager who would be watching and interacting from a separate workstation. The lack of the ability of the actor to accurately assess where he/she stood in the virtual space relative to stage setting, props, and most importantly, other actors, greatly restricted their expressive capabilities. Thus, it is essential that the actor in the physical space be able to experience the virtual stage from the point of view of their avatar.

We use augmented reality (specifically via a Microsoft Hololens) for this purpose. Though it would be tempting to fully immerse the actor in the virtual space, we chose an augmented reality experience for the actor as it is essential, particularly in dance, that the dancer be aware of the physical space that they inhabit. Figure 3 shows one of the dancers in the motion capture space.

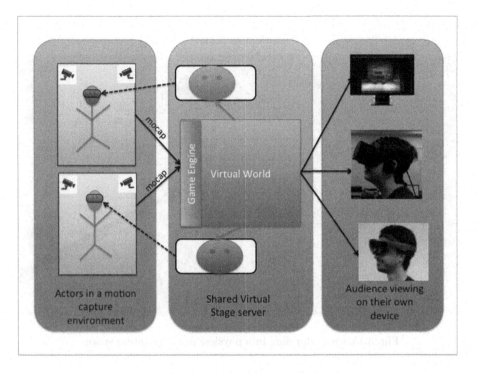

Fig. 2. Physical setup for *Farewell to Dawn*

The view of the stage as projected through the Hololens of one of the dancers is shown in Fig. 4. Though all participants share the same virtual space, the viewing experience can be customized for individual participants. For example, the dancers involved in the project found the particle representation of the avatar to be distracting, Thus, for the actor viewing app created for the Hololens, the avatar is represented more simply as a set of spheres; one sphere at each of the joints of the avatar.

Audience Perspectives. Audience members view the performance from the point of view of a seat in the virtual auditorium. Conceptually, individual audience members will do so from their own physical space using an immersive head mounted display. For the December performance, however, considering the limited number of head mounted devices available, we offered both an external experience, where audience members view the performance projected in a physical space (Fig. 5); and an immersive experience where the audience experiences the performance using an Oculus Rift.

Audience members are represented in the virtual space by futuristic heads whose orientation are adjusted based on the head motion of the person viewing the performance in the physical world as illustrated in Fig. 6.

Fig. 3. Actor performing in a physical motion capture space.

Fig. 4. View of the virtual stage for *Farewell to Dawn* from an actor's perspective as projected through a Hololens

Fig. 5. External audience viewing performance projected in a physical space.

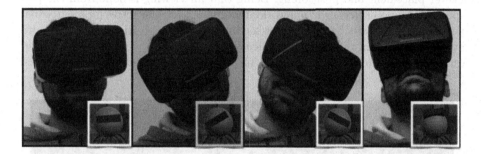

Fig. 6. Audience avatars in the virtual space which move based upon the head motion of the audience member watching in the physical space

4   Discussion

In this section, we discuss some the successes of *Farewell to Dawn*, particularly with respect to the attributes listed in Sect. 2. Though we did not conduct a formal user study, we present anecdotal observations as expressed by participants at the December performance.

4.1   Liveness

For audience members viewing the performance projected in a physical space (Fig. 5), a view of the dancers in the motion capture environment was projected on screens adjacent to the view of the action on the virtual stage. The correspondence between the motion of each dancer and their respective avatar during the performance was quite clear. Those viewing through the Oculus Rift did not have this "behind the scenes" view available to them. However, the general feeling was that the immersion afforded by the head mounted display increased the presence felt by these viewers, confirming studies previously reporting such connection [15] and contributing to sense of watching it live.

For the actors, the naturalness and intuitive interface of the motion capture environment made the performance feel like a live experience. Though it was the avatars that were performing on the virtual stage, the use of motion capture increased the sense of social embodiment [9] of each dancer with regards to the three aspects: self-location (experience of being inside the avatar body), agency (having full body motor control), and body ownership (self-attribution of the avatar body).

4.2   Perspective

Defining participant perspective involves setting both the position as well as the point of view of a user in the virtual space.

Theatre realized completely in virtual spaces provides extensive freedom of viewer placement and positioning. Being that all viewing is done from the perspective of a point in the virtual world, modifying the perspective for a particular participant can easily be achieved by setting the camera position to the appropriate position within the viewing application. This opens the door to some interesting new possibilities with regards to the means by which theatre in virtual

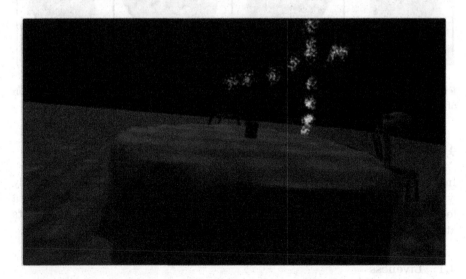

Fig. 7. View of Farewell to Dawn from the perspective of one sitting on the stage

spaces can be viewed and experienced by an audience member. Theatrical pieces such as *Draw Me Close* [21] and *To Be With Hamlet* [7] take advantage of this freedom to allow for new and unique audience perspectives.

In *Farewell to Dawn*, selected audience members were placed on the virtual stage allowing them to view the dance while seated amongst the tables and chairs of the cafe in front of where the avatars are performing, as shown in Fig. 7. This juxtaposition made many feel present at the cafe watching as one would on an actual city street (some to the extent that they were seen reaching out for the cup that was on the table).

4.3 Social Presence

Presence in virtual worlds is a rich and complex topic that can be explored from a variety of different perspectives [14]. With regards to virtual theatre, we consider social presence to relate to "presence as transportation" [14] where the participants not only feel transported to the virtual space, but also feel the presence of those around them in that space.

In the external viewing experience, the sense of co-presence amongst audience members naturally comes from the proximity and seating in the physical space. However, there is no social connection between the actors and the audience as there is no portal from the physical motion capture environment in which the actors are performing to the physical space where the audience is sitting.

Fig. 8. Audience members placed on the virtual stage. Audience members can view not only the dancers' avatars but also the motion of other audience members, giving a sense of shared co-presence.

In the immersive experience, co-presence is achieved thru the avatars of the audience members as well as the actors in the virtual space (Fig. 8). Multiuser virtual spaces have been shown to be successful in creating a sense of social presence [18] leading to what can be termed distributed liveness i.e. a sense of connectedness with other participants even though they may be in different physical spaces [33].

Finally, the sense of immersion provided by the head mounted display itself, combined with the proximity to the dancers in the virtual space, and the real time motion of the audience avatars, were reported to provide a further sense of connectedness with both the performers as well as fellow audience members.

4.4 Playback Options

Documentation of a theatrical performance has always presented a challenge as the mere act of recording is in direct contradiction with the "liveness" aspect that distinguishes live theatre [24]. Capture using video forces a fixed perspective and removes any sense of shared co-presence. A recent exciting trend in recording of theatre in VR (e.g. *Hereos: A Duet in Mixed Reality* [11] and *The Lion King VR Experience* [19]) makes use of 360° video presentation providing a unique perspective for the viewer. In these experiences, the viewer is given some control over their point of view, however, the perspective is still limited by the camera positioning as defined by the film maker.

With virtual theatre, since all of the action is realized within a 3D engine, "recording" of the performance can be achieved by saving time varying signals (avatar motion, lighting, staging) for playback later. In this case, the playback is a reconstruction of the performance, which can be experienced from any location in the virtual space. Though this approach does not address the absence of liveness, it does allow for the possibility of providing the correct perspective and creating social connectedness, at least amongst audience members when viewing a previously recorded performance.

5 Conclusions and Future Work

In this paper, we explored our vision of virtual theatre: enabling theatre on a virtual stage with participants in different physical locals, through the presentation of *Farewell to Dawn*, a virtual theatre dance performance. The presentation served two purposes: First, from a purely technical standpoint, it was a proof of concept of a hardware and software framework for enabling such a performance. Secondly, and more interestingly, it provided a means of exploration of the theatrical experience and determining how that same experience can be recreated using a virtual world.

Towards this goal, we have identified three characteristics of theatre: a sense of liveness, providing perspective, and facilitating social presence that must be achieved in the shared space while participants are separated physically.

Farewell to Dawn allowed for an initial exploration of these three characteristics. We are currently in the process of defining a followup performance piece that will consider these characteristics in more depth. Specifically, this new piece will include:

- **More realistic avatar models** – The use of a stylistic, "particles of light", representation for the avatars in *Farewell to Dawn* was both an artistic and functional choice as the particle system is quite forgiving of the sometimes noisy motion capture data provided by the Kinects. Moving forward, we would like to incorporate more realistic and more human characters to the virtual stage. New models will also include facial models capable of displaying facial expressions driven by facial motion capture systems; not only for actor avatars but for audience avatars as well.
- **Deliberate and intentional actor/audience interaction** – *Farewell to Dawn* presented a passive audience experience as there was no explicit interaction between actor and audience which is not uncommon for many theatrical situations. However, the next piece will force explicit and deliberate actor/audience interaction to test the effectiveness of social co-presence between the performers and the audience in the virtual space.
- **Formal measurement of participant engagement** – All reported observations of user experiences for *Farewell to Dawn* are purely anecdotal. For our next piece, we are planning to perform more formal data collection via questionnaires, and the use of affective sensors (e.g. Galvanic Skin Response and/or Pulse [10,32]) to assess participant engagement and presence.

This work has focused on the human experience during theatre: motion of the actors, the interplay between actors, the engagement of the audience. Looking forward, we would also like to experiment with other theatrical elements such as lighting, staging, and actor control and interaction with props and sets. The dynamic interplay of these elements with live music (e.g. [30]) would be an interesting direction in which to explore.

Acknowledgements. The author would like to thank the anonymous reviewers for their insights, suggestions, and pointers.

Farewell to Dawn is a collaborative effort between the Department of Computer Science, College of Imaging Arts and Science, and the MAGIC Center at RIT along with the Department of Theatre and Dance at Nazareth College. The author would like to extend a special thanks to Andy Phelps, Christopher Egert, and Jennifer Hinton from MAGIC, Heather Roffe from Nazareth, and all of the collaborators listed in the credits below.

This work is partially funded through a seed grant from the B. Thomas Golisano College of Computing an Information Sciences at RIT. Thanks to Anne Haake and Pengcheng Shi for their support.
Farewell to Dawn credits:
Dancers: Zhongyuan Fa, Anastasia Pembrook
Choreography: Zhongyuan Fa
Music: Hesham Fouad

Percussion: Peter Ferry
3D Stage Design: Stephen Cerqueira, Quincey Williams, Marla Schweppe
Virtual Stage System: Chirag Chandrakant Salian, Anna Dining, Victoria Mc Gowen,
Rasmi Mukula Kapuganti, Felipe Caputo, Joe Geigel
Videography: Anna Dining

References

1. Ascott, R.: Telematic Embrace: Visionary Theories of Art, Technology, and Consciousness. University of California Press, Berkeley (2007)
2. Birdwhistell, R.: Introduction to Kinesics: An Annotation System for Analysis of Body Motion and Gesture. Louisville University Press, Louisville (1952)
3. Caputo, F., Mc Gowen, V., Geigel, J., Cerqueira, S., Williams, Q., Schweppe, M., Fa, Z., Pembrook, A., Roffe, H.: Farewell to dawn: a mixed reality dance performance in a virtual space. In: ACM SIGGRAPH 2016 Posters (SIGGRAPH 2016), pp. 49:1–49:2. ACM, New York (2016)
4. Couldry, N.: Liveness, reality, and the mediated habitus from television to the mobile phone. Commun. Rev. **7**(4), 353–361 (2004)
5. Geigel, J., Schweppe, M.: Motion capture for realtime control of virtual actors in live, distributed, theatrical performances. In: Face and Gesture 2011, pp. 774–779, March 2011
6. Geigel, J., Schweppe, M., Huynh, D., Johnstone, B.: Adapting a virtual world for theatrical performance. Computer **44**(12), 33–38 (2011)
7. Gochfeld, D., Molina, J.: To be with hamlet. In: Di Federico, E., van Houte, N. (eds.) Mixed Reality and the Theatre of the Future: Fresh Perspectives on Arts and New Technologies, pp. 47–55. IETM, Brussels (2017). https://www.ietm.org/en/publications/fresh-perspectives-6-mixed-reality-and-the-theatre-of-the-future
8. Hall, E.T.: The Hidden Dimension. Doubleday and Company, New York (1966)
9. Kilteni, K., Groten, R., Slater, M.: The sense of embodiment in virtual reality. Presence Teleoperators Virtual Environ. **21**(4), 373–387 (2012)
10. Knapp, R.B., Jaimovich, J., Coghlan, N.: Measurement of motion and emotion during musical performance. In: 2009 3rd International Conference on Affective Computing and Intelligent Interaction and Workshops, pp. 1–5, September 2009
11. Laden, T.M.: Virtual reality and theater come together to a classic David Bowie tune, March 2017. https://creators.vice.com/en_us/article/8qbay3/david-bowie-virtual-reality-theater
12. Lee, K.M.: Presence, explicated. Commun. Theor. **14**(1), 27–50 (2004)
13. Lewis, M.: Bowen virtual theater. In: ACM SIGGRAPH 2003 Web Graphics (SIGGRAPH 2003), p. 1. ACM, New York (2003). http://doi.acm.org/10.1145/965333.965389
14. Lombard, M., Ditton, T.: At the heart of it all: the concept of presence. J. Comput. Mediated Commun. **3**(2), JCMC321 (1997)
15. Loomis, J.M.: Presence in virtual reality and everyday life: immersion within a world of representation. Presence Teleoperators Virtual Environ. **25**(2), 169–174 (2016)
16. Löytönen, T.: Emotions in the everyday life of a dance school: articulating unspoken values. Dance Res. J. **40**(1), 17–30 (2008)
17. Matsuba, S.N., Roehl, B.: Bottom, thou art translated: the making of VRML dream. IEEE Comput. Graph. Appl. **19**(2), 45–51 (1999)

18. Mennecke, B.E., Triplett, J.L., Hassall, L.M., Conde, Z.J., Heer, R.: An examination of a theory of embodied social presence in virtual worlds. Dec. Sci. **42**(2), 413–450 (2011)

19. Moynihan, T.: The lion king musical in VR is an incredible experience, November 2015. https://www.wired.com/2015/11/lion-king-vr-video/

20. Neff, M.: Lessons from the arts: what the performing arts literature can teach us about creating expressive character movement. In: Tanenbaum, J., El-Nasr, M.S., Nixon, M. (eds.) Nonverbal Communication in Virtual Worlds, pp. 123–148. ETC Press, Pittsburgh (2014). http://dl.acm.org/citation.cfm?id=2812748.2812758

21. Ohannessian, K.: Draw me close uses VR, props, and performance to evoke childhood, April 2017. https://uploadvr.com/draw-me-close-childhood/. Accessed 29 Apr 2017

22. Parker, J.R.: Theater as virtual reality. In: Tanenbaum, J., El-Nasr, M.S., Nixon, M. (eds.) Nonverbal Communication in Virtual Worlds, pp. 151–174. ETC Press, Pittsburgh (2014). http://dl.acm.org/citation.cfm?id=2812748.2812759

23. Reaney, M.: Virtual scenography: the actor, audience, computer interface. Theatr. Des. Technol. **32**, 36–43 (1996)

24. Reason, M.: Archive or memory? The detritus of live performance. New Theatr. Q. (NTQ) **19**(1), 82–89 (2003)

25. Reeve, C.: Presence in virtual theater. Presence **9**(2), 209–213 (2000)

26. Rowe, K.: Crowd-sourcing Shakespeare: screen work and screen play in second life. Shakespear. Stud. **38**, 58–67 (2010)

27. Slater, M., Howell, J., Steed, A., Pertaub, D.P., Garau, M.: Acting in virtual reality. In: Proceedings of the Third International Conference on Collaborative Virtual Environments (CVE 2000), pp. 103–110. ACM, New York (2000). http://doi.acm.org/10.1145/351006.351020

28. Smith, B.D.: Telematic composition. Ph.D. thesis, University of Illinois at Urbana-Champaign, Champaign (2011). aAI3503868

29. Sontag, S.: Film and theatre. Tulane Drama Rev. **11**(1), 24–37 (1966)

30. Stierman, C.: Kinotes: mapping musical scales to gestures in a kinect-based interface for musican expression. Unpublished doctoral dissertation, M.Sc thesis University of Amsterdam (2012)

31. Sutherland, T.: From (archival) page to (virtual) stage: the virtual vaudeville prototype. Am. Archivist **79**(2), 392–416 (2016)

32. Wang, C., Geelhoed, E.N., Stenton, P.P., Cesar, P.: Sensing a live audience. In: Proceedings of the SIGCHI Conference on Human Factors in Computing Systems (CHI 2014), pp. 1909–1912. ACM, New York (2014). http://doi.acm.org.ezproxy.rit.edu/10.1145/2556288.2557154

33. Webb, A.M., Wang, C., Kerne, A., Cesar, P.: Distributed liveness: understanding how new technologies transform performance experiences. In: Proceedings of the 19th ACM Conference on Computer-Supported Cooperative Work & Social Computing (CSCW 2016), pp. 432–437. ACM, New York (2016)

34. Wilson, G.D.: Psychology for Performing Artists. Whurr Publishers, London (2002)

Serious…ly! Just Kidding in Personalised Therapy Through Natural Interactions with Games

Rui Neves Madeira[1,3](✉) (iD), André Antunes[1,2] (iD), Octavian Postolache[2], and Nuno Correia[3]

[1] Escola Superior de Tecnologia de Setúbal, IPS, Setúbal, Portugal
{rui.madeira,andre.antunes}@estsetubal.ips.pt
[2] ISCTE-IUL and IT-IUL, Instituto Universitário de Lisboa, Lisbon, Portugal
opostolache@lx.it.pt
[3] NOVA LINCS, DI, Faculdade de Ciências e Tecnologia, UNL, Caparica, Portugal
nmc@fct.unl.pt

Abstract. Virtual Reality based rehabilitation is much based on sensing devices that capture and quantitatively assess the patients' movements to track their progress more accurately. There are a few commercially available and affordable sensors. Among them, Kinect is an important asset to the concept of Natural User Interfaces, which is gaining a wider space and great importance in gaming for therapy approaches. These solutions can create therapy environments that increase the motivation of patients to achieve successful completion of rehabilitation programs that can be very demanding. However, therapists still demand customisable tools towards particular groups of patients. This paper presents "just Physio kidding", which is a solution based on the use of serious games, natural user interfaces and personalisation to address both physiotherapy and cognitive stimulation therapy. Initially, it was designed for stroke patients and older adults on wheelchairs, then it was adapted to children with special needs. The paper details the game design, its underlying concept and platform, besides presenting the first user study with experts, which points out to the design of a personalised version.

Keywords: Natural user interface · NUI · Physiotherapy · Serious games
Cognitive stimulation · Cerebral palsy · Gamification · Kinect · Leap Motion
User study

1 Introduction

The main goal of rehabilitation is to give autonomy and quality of life to patients, helping them to achieve, or regain, the capacity they lack or have lost with age-related deterioration or after an illness, accident, etc. Usually, physiotherapy patients are submitted to repetitive exercise sessions of rehabilitation for several months, relying almost entirely on the therapists' supervision. Exercises should be monitored and evaluated on a regular basis to measure the patient's progress in treatment [1]. Therapists still require tools that, on the one hand, engage patients in the rehabilitation process, masking the repetitive exercises sessions, and, on the other hand, facilitate customisation by them towards a specific group of patients and personalisation according to each patient. Therefore,

© Springer International Publishing AG, part of Springer Nature 2018
A. D. Cheok et al. (Eds.): ACE 2017, LNCS 10714, pp. 726–745, 2018.
https://doi.org/10.1007/978-3-319-76270-8_50

technologies and projects that allow them to participate in the design of software to support the therapy sessions and rehabilitation process are of relevant importance to them.

The creation of solutions for rehabilitation using Virtual Reality (VR) technologies has expanded rapidly in the last years. VR-based rehabilitation is much based on sensing devices that capture and quantitatively assess the patients' movements to track their progress more accurately [2]. There are a few commercially available and affordable sensors whose impact on rehabilitation may be identical [3], which are Microsoft Kinect, Xtion Pro Live, Intel-Creative camera, and Leap Motion controller. Since these sensors are relatively recent, there are only a few clinical studies that used them, but motion capture using Kinect has become increasingly popular in physiotherapy and rehabilitation [3]. The Kinect represents the future of game interfaces in that it uses vision rather than "instrumenting" the user [4]. Thus, Kinect is an important asset to the concept of Natural User Interfaces (NUI), which is gaining a wider space and great importance across all fields, from gaming to therapy, and especially in gaming for therapy. NUI can be seen as the ability to interact with a machine using nothing but the human body, avoiding the use of visible control elements to the greatest possible extent to ensure a more natural control. Thus, Kinect has helped pave the way on how technology with a more natural user interaction can facilitate and complement many clinical applications [5].

If the VR and NUI-based tools are developed as serious games [6], or, at least, integrate game elements following the gamification concept [6], then the engaging qualities of the therapeutic programs would be improved [7]. Serious games are a valuable tool to present the same therapeutic exercise in a more appealingly way. It can help patients to exercise in a fun way, challenging their handicaps, both physical and cognitive, with tasks that demand the execution of therapeutic actions. The need to persuade the user to execute the exercises sessions is achieved by using voice, sound and visual effects, besides applying the usual game mechanics, such as points, leaderboards, and challenges.

This paper presents a work that explores the mix of gamification, serious games, and natural user interfaces, using the Kinect and the Leap Motion sensors, towards the design of a personalised solution named "just Physio kidding" (jPk). This software addresses both physiotherapy and cognitive stimulation therapy. Initially, it was designed for stroke patients and older adults on wheelchairs, then it was adapted to children with special needs. While primarily designed for upper limb rehabilitation, it can be used for full body tracking and therapy. The jPk game is offered as a component in a platform that supports games customisation by the therapists, allowing them to monitor in detail the performance of their patients. The jPk solution presents a two-fold answer to important needs of the therapists: (1) to engage patients through the use of games and NUI in the therapy approach; (2) and to support the therapists' supervision allowing them to customise the games and monitor the patients' data.

The focus of this paper is on detailing the game design, its mechanics and gameplay, and the underlying platform. Furthermore, it presents interesting and positive results of the first user study, which evaluated the first version of the prototype, indicating promising design paths as the inclusion of personalisation features.

2 Related Work

Being responsible for the therapeutic intervention, therapists try to seek and offer all the solutions available to help patients to gain the quality of life they need. The combination of serious games, mainly in the form of exergames, with NUI from VR technologies, can provide more motivation and engagement to patients while they are in rehabilitation activities [2]. Exergames have been successfully applied to the rehabilitation of people with motor impairments [8]. The motivation obtained with a game-based rehabilitation environment has the potential to make patients achieve successful completion of rehabilitation programs that can be dreary or very demanding [9], existing diverse projects helping patients to follow through with those otherwise often-repetitive therapy tasks [10, 11]. The engagement, effort and commitment to the rehabilitation process directly affect the effectiveness of long-term therapy, especially in the case of physiotherapy [12].

Concerning the sensors for NUI implementation, Microsoft Kinect (or Asus Xtion, which is not so much used in rehabilitation projects) is appropriate when full body motion is required, but the Leap Motion sensor is the most suitable option for hand tracking with individual fingers. Intel Creative camera, along with the newest version of Kinect, performs well for close range tracking [3]. Kinect is even considered the preferred console, compared with Nintendo Wii and PlayStation 3 Move, to be used for therapy exercises [3], which is due to its pervasiveness and more natural interface.

Kinect appears on several projects and solutions to control the games, provide feedback to patients, and even as a measuring tool [2, 13]. Kinerehab [14] is an application targeted to patients with motor disabilities. It uses the Kinect sensor to evaluate and estimate the biomechanics of fundamental movements. The game difficulty is often annotated by the therapists at the beginning of the therapy session. The research from Voxar labs also uses Kinect, linking its use in therapy (while monitoring the patient progress) to the user gaming experience, which is more of a focal point [15]. The authors wanted a rehabilitation system based on markerless interaction in a virtual reality environment. It is based on a game controlled by therapeutic movements, which is set by physiotherapists, inducing the user to do exercises correctly and capable of identifying whenever the patient is doing them correctly, warning him/her otherwise and also saving the statistics in a report for a further professional analysis. The authors conclude that the effectiveness of therapy goes up with the improvement of the gaming experience, which should be carefully designed. Their approach is very similar to ours.

In another work using Kinect [16], the researchers tested the use of games based on natural interaction, particularly full-body interaction, with a group of older adults with movement difficulties. They developed a game based on a series of pre-defined gestures: raise one arm, lifting both arms, clap, walking in place, say goodbye, among others. The set of movements was designed taking into account they could be performed with the participants seated. The results of this study indicated the participants had a good experience at the fun level, but low levels of difficulty and fatigue were obtained during the game execution. This approach and its results are in line with our previous work [17], which was the ignition for the jPk work. Other interesting projects use Kinect to assist therapists in the rehabilitation of older adults [18, 19]. Ma and Bechkoum developed a serious-game based therapy to stimulate physical exercises practice by stroke patients with upper limb motor disorders [20]. The system allows patients to interact in real-time with virtual objects to practice specific motor skills through diverse modalities.

Lange et al. used Kinect in a game-based rehabilitation task for balance training. Initial assessment of the prototype system with a set of participants with neurological injury demonstrated that the solution has potential in these cases [21]. Regarding the intervention with children, Luna-Oliva et al. [22] made a study providing evidence about the usefulness of Kinect Xbox 360 as a therapeutic modality for children with cerebral palsy (CP) in a school environment. The outcome measures showed improvements in different tests. A solution often followed consists in a game composed of some mini-games, which is the case with Liberi [23]. It was developed to help children with CP exercise more, in this case, pedalling on a recumbent bicycle to control characters in the minigames. The authors found the majority of the target group preferred to play action games, even though they had difficulties playing them. They proposed a set of usability guidelines [23], such as avoiding a fast pace, not requiring precision timing and not requiring multiple simultaneous inputs in order to mitigate some of their weak perform-ance. Along with the previous work, Chang et al. [24] showed that two adolescents with CP demonstrated high motivations for exercising with Kinect and improved their performance during the intervention. Still, in the target group of the children, the Superpop project allows them to execute therapeutic exercises masked by the art of popping bubbles [25]. The system can monitor the progress and allows the therapist to adjust the game, what is of interest to us. Once again, this project is using a well available technology to be able to move the therapy setting to children's homes while being able to monitor their progress. In another interesting research work, de Greef et al. aim to discern design guidelines that improve the efficacy, engagement and player persistence of serious motor skill games for mixed abilities [26]. They were creating Kinect-based games for children with special needs and trying to incorporate input from diverse stakeholders, such as parents, therapists, and children, during the iterative design process.

Planet 10 [27] is very interesting since a bio-medical sensor and treadmill are inte-grated and used as an alternative to Kinect in a first-person intergalactic space odyssey game for rehabilitation purposes. According to the authors, the game can be easily controlled with different types of equipment, such as Kinect. An interesting point is the fact that scenarios in the game were designed by using recommendations made by the therapist. The overall aim was to engage stroke patients in carrying out regular exercises. Finally, different projects are appearing with the integration of both Kinect and Leap Motion sensors in a complementary way for therapeutic purposes [28–30], which can work as a better solution to deal with the detection of hand and finger motions.

3   A Therapy Platform with Games Based on NUI

jPk relies on the Serious Game and NUI concepts in order to encourage physical exercise to combat both physical and cognitive deterioration. The main objective of this game is to help therapists to improve the quality and persistence of therapies, in a complement to their regular work, with or without their supervision in real-time.

Initially, a prototype of the game based on natural interactions was designed having in mind the rehabilitation of wheelchair-dependent patients, such as stroke patients and older adults, suffering from neuromuscular diseases, or other people with reduced mobility [17]. That first prototype was then shown to a panel composed of different therapists, with expertise in several rehabilitation areas, who evaluated it. Then, one of them, specialised in working with children with special needs, wanted to test it to find if its NUI system could work under the settings of her clinic. She believed the game design, the interaction design and its underlying principles were appropriate to her needs in the therapy sessions with the children.

3.1 A Prototype for Children with Special Needs

Very often, children with special needs have to exercise in the seated position, just like the patients on wheelchairs. Moreover, the set of upper-limb movements incorporated in the game design was versatile enough, configurable and corresponded to exercises of their therapy sessions. The set was designed to be customised to deal with the hemiplegia condition, which is usually the result of a stroke, characterized by one-half of a patient's body paralysis. Cerebral palsy can also affect one hemisphere, resulting in a limitation of functions, which does not necessarily cause paralysis but spasms [18, 19]. Hemiplegia is more severe than hemiparesis, wherein one-half of the body is weakened, but not paralysed. It was the case of the majority of the clinic's children. The therapist also wanted to replace the therapy sessions supported by the commercial exergames of the Nintendo Wii console with this customizable Kinect-based game.

Therefore, the second prototype is designed having in mind the therapy work in a clinic that deals with children with special needs, such as the cases of children with spinal muscular atrophy, developmental delay, or leukoencephalopathy, cerebral calcification, and cysts (LCC), besides the ones with CP. These have muscle weakness, reduced range of motion, and poor control over their movements, which pose additional difficulties and challenges with the finely controlled movement required by Kinect [8]. Thus, the Leap Motion sensor was integrated into the system. It was a new requirement since the clinic's patients exhibit different therapy needs that are directed to improve gross motor skills, at upper and lower limbs and torso, but also fine motor skills, at hands and fingers level.

3.2 The "just Physio kidding" Platform

The platform supports the therapeutic game, giving tools to the therapists to customise the game, monitor the patients' performance, and analyse their detailed data. It is comprised of six main components (Table 1), developed in C# under the .Net Framework, and uses the sensors' official SDKs and APIs.

All components and their applications share a common data access point, the web services client JPKM, which allows having a complete separation between logic and data (Fig. 1). The applications share a common data model that is implemented in a shared class library. Data is stored locally for each platform installation, since the system can be distributed across various therapy spaces, and a synchronisation with the platform's central database is performed at each local platform initialisation.

Table 1. Components of the platform.

Component	Description
JPK	**a desktop NUI-driven patient application (Game-based approach)**
JPKT	a desktop therapist application (allows NUI-based control)
JPKW	a therapist and administrator website
JPKM	shared models and web services client
JPKDATA	shared data models
JPKREST	RESTFul web services

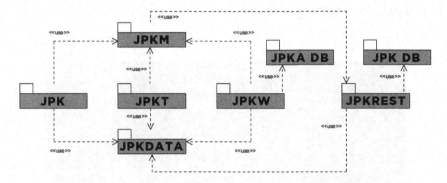

Fig. 1. The logical architecture diagram of "just Physio kidding".

The JPK and JPKT applications are both NUI-controlled (Kinect and Leap Motion). Voice synthesis and recognition are used since the applications respond to voice commands, in three provided languages, for navigation and action execution in the games (Fig. 2-left). Face recognition is implemented, with the user face being sampled at user registration and used to speed up the login process (Fig. 2-right).

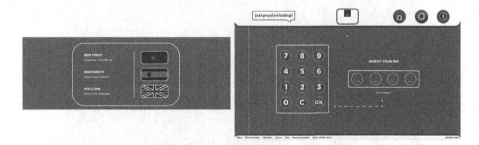

Fig. 2. UI design: (left) Initial screen to select language; (right) PIN insertion for login.

The platform's user interface (UI) is an original one, designed from scratch and taking into consideration the best practices in user interfaces, user experience and natural user interaction design. Along the design process, the particular needs of the jPk's end users were taken into account since several testing sessions have been conducted with the participation of children that are patients in the clinic.

The therapist plays an important role in this system since s/he is the user responsible for (1) configuring games according to the patient profile; (2) supervising patients' performance and progress. The patient has access to the NUI-based gaming component (JPK), but the therapist should use the NUI-based JPKT component (Fig. 3) to configure and schedule games, monitor her/his patients' sessions in loco, and analyse the data, both motion skills and gaming performance. The Web interface (JPKW) (Fig. 4) provides the therapist with remote access to the supervision tools, presenting additional features and more detailed statistical data. The executions of the exercises (movements in the games) can be analysed with the help of data charts and 3D visualisation of sampled patient's skeleton movements.

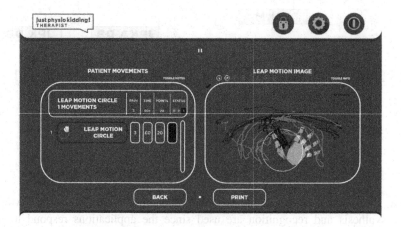

Fig. 3. JPKT: A patient's game movement analysis.

Fig. 4. JPKW: Game configuration.

3.3   Rationale and Game Mechanics

The implementation of the jPk system needed to take into account both the specific context being gamified and the qualities of the end-users [31], the children with special needs, in order to obtain the desired outcomes. It was required to provide a high motivation to the children to comply with crucial treatments and therapies. Therefore, there are four main differences concerning the previous version: a new user interface design, different games (more themes) that apply to children, incorporation of game movements addressing the fine motor skills of hands and fingers, and a first sketch of the integration of personalisation.

At the moment, the jPk platform includes four different games (called Challenges in the first version). They are available for autonomous execution by the patients, or their carers and therapists, through the Games button, but they can also be scheduled to the patient by the therapist. The first three games are Kinect-based only. The three come from the same basis regarding interaction design and gameplay, but each one of them presents its theme (Fig. 5): *eco*, *noir* and *Bill*. The Eco game's philosophy is based on the recycling theme, in which the user/patient has to collect waste materials and place them into the appropriate containers. The Noir theme is about a detective and objects that should be identified as clues to an important case under investigation. The third game has something to do with the Wild West and precious metals that have to be harvested, identified and put into the right railway wagon in order to be kept safe from the great evil enterprise. For each game, there are three groups of items and the corresponding containers. Objects from each items group share common identifying characteristics, like the colour or the material type, which suggest to the user where they should be placed.

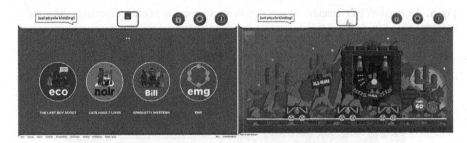

Fig. 5. Kinect-based games: (left) The games' screen; (right) Bill's scenario.

The fourth game is a multi-sensor game with a different design. This game uses both the Kinect and the Leap Motion sensors to track and validate the patient's performance of the movements. The user has to follow and reach objects that appear sequentially on screen, at pre-determined positions, and then execute hand/fingers movements on them.

Each game has its specific musical theme, which can be turned on/off for the gameplay. The games' data of authenticated users are sampled and recorded by the platform. It includes gameplay-specific data like the movement score, duration and status, but also

Kinect's data of the skeleton's joints and bones and Leap Motion's data of hands and fingers.

An important requirement for a solution such as jPk is that the patient must be aware of her/his presence in the game scenario, recognising her/himself to interact in some way with the game elements (Fig. 6). A character in the scene, preferably a humanoid character (as seen in other works [1]), would be great if the jPk game allowed. However, in this case, the representation of the patient/user's hands is the most appropriate approach, not colliding with the designed scene and the gameplay. Moreover, the user has at her/his disposal another visual aid of her/his interaction with the game, which is her/his silhouette appearing in a small window at the top of the centre of the screen.

Fig. 6. Noir game: UI elements towards patient's awareness of her/his presence in the game scenario.

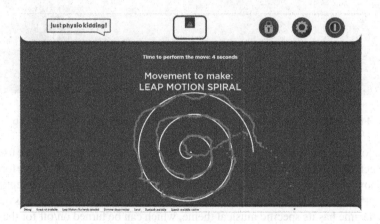

Fig. 7. JPK: Leap motion-based quest.

Regarding the game mechanics, the jPk game uses points, levels, leaderboards, badges, and challenges/quests, as tools to create a meaningful response [32]. The quests (see Fig. 7) are put to the patient as simpler games that are routines of movements created by the physiotherapist.

The quests are directed mainly for physiotherapy training/exercising that should be executed according to the results of the main games. Routines can be scheduled to integrate a global plan of rehabilitation exercises created by the therapist, who can, for instance, create and add routines to the system, supervise what her/his patients are doing, and analyse patients' progression in a particular routine.

3.4 Interaction Design

The use of unobtrusive sensors is essential since the use of natural user interfaces and interactions is a clear need for the project. The jPk team's therapists selected an initial set of primary movements of the upper-body, more specifically of the upper limb and torso, for balance training and motor coordination (Table 2). At the moment, all the interaction with the game is made at the upper limb and torso level. Depending on the movement, the required sensors are activated for interaction and data capturing.

Table 2. The set of primary movements captured by both sensors.

Sensor	Movement
Kinect	Weight transfer; Side reach; Anterior reach; Later reach; Torso rotation
Leap Motion	Hand supination, pronation, grab, pinch
	Finger stretching (for each finger), Thumb opposition
	Line, Circle, Triangle, Spiral and Saw shapes

The user interaction with the games must be done executing the required movements, which are encapsulated by the gameplay. Figure 8 shows the user interface used by the therapist to customise the game with the selection of movements towards the patient profile. The objects are placed on the screen at predetermined positions to require the execution of one or more primary movements in order to accomplish the action of reaching the object and dragging it to the appropriate container.

The game containers are positioned at the bottom of the screen, at left, centre and right locations (see Fig. 4). The required hand for a movement must be used for it to be recognised as valid. Game variations to the default game movements for each theme can be created using the therapist's applications JPKT/JPKW. The intended result for a game movement can be changed to be a simple reach of the object (touching it), instead of having to drag it. Other options are: keep touching the object for a few seconds (defined by the therapist for each patient); grabbing (closed hand) the object while dragging it; among others. For the fourth game, the interaction is made following the objects (Kinect-based) and executing a movement related to fine motor skills with each object when it is reached (Leap Motion-based).

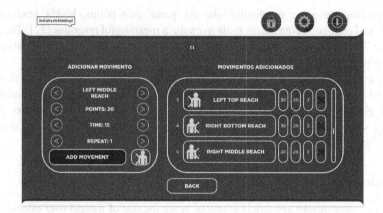

Fig. 8. JPKT: Configuring the set of movements for a new game.

3.5 Gameplay Basics

jPk implements a levelling system to inform the patient/user of her/his level of familiarity, and reward continued expertise and knowledge using the system. However, the levelling progression should be adapted to the patient to keep her/him engaged and motivated with the system, and rehabilitation program, as much as possible. Therapists can configure the games towards each one of her/his patients, defining profiles that take into account that each child presents very particular characteristics. The way engagement with the games works with one child may differ greatly from another child. It is important that the user experience within the game is reflected in a progressively nonlinear scoring and levelling system with a ranking to document progress benchmarks.

Therefore, the games can present several levels to the patient, based on different features, such as: (1) time limit on/off; (2) number of objects to caught; (3) objects appear on predefined limited zones; (4) only touch the objects, caught them and/or drag them to the containers; (5) background complexity. There is a difference between what we call the auto-game levels towards the flat and default configuration of the games and the profile-based levels. In the first case, at the end of every game level, the user is asked if s/he wants to keep playing, progressing automatically to a level that is similar to the level before, changing little regarding the objects positioning, time limit, and the number of objects. However, each subsequent level should necessarily be increasingly more difficult to attain. This rule also applied to the profile-based levels system, but in this case, the system tries to adapt the next level to the user expectations and therapeutic needs based on the current user profile. When a game is scheduled to a patient, it presents a particular configuration taking into account the user profile. The user's current profile may suggest to maintain or increase the movements' difficulty, working on the angle and reach amplitudes, besides changing the gameplay settings.

Thus, the scoring of a game and their quests (routines) is based on sum and mean values of the movements included in the game. The game result contains each game's movements status, a score, the duration level, a patient's pain level, the sum of the game's movements individual scores, the sum of all game's movements durations and the mean of the pain level for each movement. When a movement is considered accomplished, or its time limit is reached, the movement results are recorded and the next movement is invoked, until the game's end. The default scoring system for a game movement was designed to allow a coherent evaluation of the game results between games and users (Table 3). When the time limit of a game movement is reached without the patient getting a complete or intermediate successful movement, the result status will be 'Wrong' and the points gained will be 0. The status will be 'captured', and the points gained ten if the object is reached, captured (if required), but dragged into the wrong container (if dragging is required). If the patient executes a complete successful movement, then the result status will be 'Right' and the points gained will be 20.

Table 3. The scoring system for a game movement.

Game movement result	Points	Status
unsuccessful movement	0 points	Wrong
intermediate successful movement	10 points	Captured
complete successful movement	20 points	Right

Several result screens are displayed to the user after performing a routine or a game. The game results show the user the final game duration and score, besides a list containing all the movements included in the game, detailing them with the status, time and score values. The status is displayed with different colours, red, grey and green, referencing wrong, captured and right values. A personal leaderboard is displayed showing the final game score values for every execution of that type of game. The global game results are displayed, allowing the user to compare its progression with other users on that type of game. When personalisation is active, the displaying of these leaderboards and result screens is conditioned by the current user profile. For instance, if a user is currently positioned in a less competitive profile, the global results leaderboard will not be displayed.

The system awards users with badges and trophies as a means to reward the user for overcoming a specific action or task, providing a more friendly progression usage meter and promoting user engagement. The badges and trophies are grouped in the following categories: (1) Game usage badges; (2) Game trophies; (3) Global trophies.

In the first category, the user interaction with the system is measured to recognise usage benchmarks. These badges replace the previously awarded ones with updated versions. Each kind of routine and game has a unique badge that displays the number of times performed. The user wins one point in that badge each time s/he executes that game. Each user only has the badges of the games and routines s/he has executed so far. The badges have five variants depending on the user experience on that specific game or routine (Newbie, Rookie, Regular, Advanced, Expert). On the other hand, game trophies award the patient's performance in playing a specific game. The game execution trophies are based on gaming parameters such as the movement result status and the duration. The patient can acquire two trophies in a particular game: AccurateGame-Trophy - awarded when all game movements have a success status; QuickGameTrophy

- awarded when all individual game movements are performed in less time than their duration limit. Finally, the global trophies are relative to the global game results.

4 Evaluation

We drew on the knowledge of the therapist's team to evaluate the implemented prototype throughout the whole development process regarding: instructional objectives and strategies best suited for the target-rehabilitation; implementing the set of required movements of the upper-body; designing adequate engaging/motivating games for the target audience; and evaluating the overall effect of gameplay. It was very important to involve these stakeholders in the design process of the system, mainly to have their input towards what could be personalised in the future.

The user study has been divided into two phases. Initially, we wanted to test the prototype among health professionals, especially physiotherapists, who are the experts that should use the application with their patients. In the second phase, after implementing jPk, we tested it with the end users, which were the patients (children with special needs) and their therapists.

4.1 Phase 1 – The Rehabilitation Professionals

Regarding the first phase, the user tests were conducted with 18 voluntary participants (7 male and 11 female) aged 21 to 56 ($\bar{x} = 34.9$; $\sigma = 10.1$). Not all participants were physiotherapists. We had 2 physiotherapy students, one programmer of systems with similarities to jPk, one biomedical engineer that is involved with adaptive technologies for amputees. In terms of years of experience leading with the field of rehabilitation, participants presented values ranging from 0, the students, to 35, the oldest ($\bar{x} = 11.9$; $\sigma = 9.9$). The questionnaire was divided into three parts, each one with a set of statements that participants had to rate (using a seven-point Likert-type scale) at the end of the testing phase.

The first part (Table 4) was used to assess the prototype's usefulness and the appropriateness of the selected basic movements and the creation of routines based on them, besides assessing each one of the applications – NUI games and therapist application.

The questionnaire revealed very positive results regarding the user experience with jPk's applications. Participants felt that the chosen set of movements is suitable for the intended purpose of rehabilitation ($\bar{x} = 5.2$; $\sigma = 1.26$). Almost 80% of the participants rated S1 with a positive value. Only two participants rated it negatively. The results were even better ($\bar{x} = 6.3$; $\sigma = 0.96$) when they had to rate S2, with 55.56% of them giving the maximum value of 7. It seemed that only one of them had doubts about the usefulness of creating the routines, at least the way the research and development team designed them. It is clear that participants saw the existence of a challenge game with its mechanics based on the basic movements has being important to improve the rehabilitation process. The results of S3 are conclusive and leave no room for doubt ($\bar{x} = 6.8$; $\sigma = 0.43$). The panel of experts loved the idea of having a game based on an everyday life scenario, since one of the major issues they found in rehabilitation is the lack of motivation shown by patients for realizing repetitive exercises when they do not see anything related to everyday life tasks. The results of the first three statements proved that the experts really approved the ideas behind jPk, considering it very useful for the desired goal with its appropriate set of basic movements and the creation of quests.

Table 4. Questionnaire's part 1.

Statements
jPk's usefulness and appropriateness:
S1. The chosen set of movements is suitable for the intended purpose of rehabilitation.
S2. The creation of quests based on movements is suited to the intended purpose of rehabilitation.
S3. The existence of games with a gameplay based on the basic movements improves the rehabilitation process.
The NUI application (games) for the patient:
S4. The NUI application (which is composed of the quests/routines and the games) for the patient is suitable for the potential end users.
S5. The design of the patient's NUI application is appealing to the potential end users.
S6. The features of the patient's NUI application are suitable for the potential end users.
The application for the therapist:
S7. The application for the therapist is suitable for the potential end users.
S8. The design of the therapist's application is appealing to the potential end users.
S9. The features of the therapist's application are suitable for the potential end users.

About the NUI-based application for the patients, about a quarter of the participants showed some doubts (27.78% have rated with 4), although none of them has rated the statement "The NUI application for the patient is suitable for the potential end-users" negatively ($\bar{x} = 5.1$; $\sigma = 0.96$). Participants rated S4 positively (44.44% agreed, 16.67% much agreed and 11.11% strongly agreed). However, the results are not as confident as in the first three statements related to the global project concept since some participants thought the user would have to interact with the application interfaces only using gestures. This issue raises some doubts in the experts since it can be frustrating and demotivating for patients. However, participants rated very positively S5 considering that the main features are suitable for the potential end users ($\bar{x} = 5.5$; $\sigma = 0.86$). One participant rated it with only 3, but the rest gave positive ratings to S5 with 50% giving 6 out of 7 points. On the other hand, participants evaluated the design of the patient's NUI application as being really appealing to the potential end-users ($\bar{x} = 6.2$; $\sigma = 0.79$). They believe patients will feel very motivated to use jPk since the design is well done and enough interesting.

Finally, participants also evaluated the application for the therapist positively. According to them, this is a very important application since it allows therapists to feel in control of what happens with their patients in the jPk context. Participants considered the application for the therapist suitable for its potential end users ($\bar{x} = 5.2$; $\sigma = 1.48$), which can be exactly themselves. Only two of them rated negatively S7 with 2 points and 50% of them rated this statement with 6 points, which is very good. Moreover, the results of S8 are even better with only one participant rating it with a negative value (3, the highest) and two of them having some doubts (rated it with 4) regarding the design of the therapist's application ($\bar{x} = 5.7$; $\sigma = 1.19$). At last, the results obtained for S9 ($\bar{x} = 5.2$; $\sigma = 1.34$) are very close to those results for S7, although presenting a lower standard deviation. All participants except 3 gave positive ratings to S9, which means that overall they agreed with the features that the application offers. The combined result of S7, S8 and S9 proves that participants are very willing to use jPk, particularly the application to supervise their patients.

The second part of the questionnaire was intended for measuring the global usability of the jPk applications, so it was based on the Portuguese version of the System Usability Scale (SUS) [33], which is the most used questionnaire for measuring perceptions of usability, being technology independent. Therefore, we applied the 10 item questionnaire with seven response options instead of the usual five options (thus using a seven-point Likert-type scale, 1 – strongly disagree; 7 – strongly agree). Participants completed the questionnaire right after having used the prototype and before any debriefing or another discussion, following the advice of Brooke [34].

The SUS scores were calculated for each user (Fig. 9) with a mean ($\bar{x}$) value of 78.1 and a standard deviation (σ) of 10.5. Despite the wide usage of SUS, there has been little guidance on interpreting SUS scores, but it is known that the average SUS score is a 68 [35]. Therefore, the score obtained with our study is considered above average. Moreover, converting the raw score of 78.1 to a percentile rank through a normalising process [35] results in a rank around 80%, which means it has higher perceived usability than 80% of all products tested with SUS. It can be interpreted as a grade of a B. A score above 80.3 gets an A and this is also the point where users are more likely to be recommending the product to a friend or colleague [35]. Thus, jPk's score is very near it, which means it can get recommendations easily. Indeed, Fig. 9 shows that 9 of the participants got scores above 80, which means they are strong candidates to be recommending the jPk solution to others.

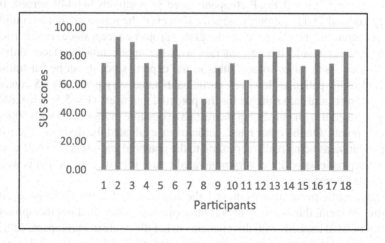

Fig. 9. Part 2 questionnaire's results (SUS scores) for each participant.

Finally, the third part of the questionnaire was directed to understand how the experts look into the smart adaptation, or personalisation, of the jPk games towards its end-users, particularly, the children. Personalisation is essential to pervasive healthcare environments, such as jPk, which focuses on a human-centred paradigm aiming to provide adaptive and personalised services to the users, according to the context. Once again, we applied the questionnaire (Table 5) using a seven-point Likert-type scale (1 – "strongly disagree"; 7 – "strongly agree").

Table 5. Questionnaire's part 3.

Statements
P3.S1. The jPk games automatically adapted to the patient profile will be more interesting for the rehabilitation process.
P3.S2. The jPk games can be easily adapted in the following ways:
P3.S2.a. The design of graphics.
P3.S2.b. Messages for the patient.
P3.S2.c. The level of difficulty of the quests/routines.
P3.S2.d. Selection of movements for the games.
P3.S2.e. Games (eco, Bill, noir) configuration.

Participants considered that applying the concept of personalisation to the games of jPk will be more interesting for rehabilitation purposes. Thus, one participant rated statement P3.S1 with a 5, two of them rated it with a 6 and the remaining gave a score of 7 points, resulting in a $\bar{x}$ of 6.8 and a σ of 0.55. Furthermore, Table 6 shows that all the aspects purposed by us to be taken into account in a future implementation of automatic adaptations have been very well received by participants. Particularly, the level of difficulty of the routines ($\bar{x} = 6.4$; $\sigma = 0.98$) and the games configuration ($\bar{x} = 6.7$; $\sigma = 0.59$) are clear winners for future adaptation towards patients profiles. These overall results demonstrate that the panel of experts are willing, even keen, to use systems such as jPk with personalisation features applied to them, which can enable a dynamically adaptation of therapeutics according to the patient performance, a better in-home rehabilitation procedures and remotely analysis, and more efficient progress monitoring and performance feedback.

Table 6. The results of questionnaire's part 3.

Statement	1 – strongly disagree	2	3	4	5	6	7 – strongly agree
P3.S2.a	0.0%	0.0%	0.0%	44.4%	16.7%	27.8%	11.1%
P3.S2.b	0.0%	0.0%	0.0%	11.1%	44.4%	27.8%	16.7%
P3.S2.c	0.0%	0.0%	5.6%	0.0%	0.0%	33.3%	61.1%
P3.S2.d	0.0%	0.0%	0.0%	0.0%	33.3%	44.4%	22.2%
P3.S2.e	0.0%	0.0%	0.0%	0.0%	5.6%	22.2%	72.2%

5 Conclusions and Future Work

This paper presented "just Physio kidding", which is focused on interactive and smart rehabilitation towards children with special needs, exploiting the Gamification and NUI concepts. We conducted a user study to evaluate our first prototype among a panel of experts, which were mainly physiotherapists. The results of the user study allowed us to conclude that not only these potential end-users, but the community in general, are receptive to this kind of applications, and a high number of them is not familiar with the use of NUI-based solutions in rehabilitation. Only a few of them have used NUI devices for rehabilitation, which makes this work a novelty to the Portuguese community. It is noteworthy that solutions used by a few of them were not specifically created for rehabilitation.

User tests with children and an acceptance evaluation with a physiotherapist were conducted in the clinic to align the development with the needs of the health professionals that cope with these "special patients" (Fig. 10). Although they have not yet been fully analysed, the results were positive, and it will be possible to present them soon.

Fig. 10. M (child with spinal muscular atrophy II) is playing and testing jPk games while being supported by the physiotherapist.

The jPk platform is a valuable tool for patients and therapists and will keep growing and trying to create new ways of promoting a better quality of life for its users. The panel of experts will be evaluating the system in further phases of development until we reach a stable final version of the product. In further studies, besides the qualitative but somewhat subjective questionnaires, it will be possible to present experiments based on concrete movements' metrics.

Acknowledgments. We thank clinic "Cresce com Amor" for providing the support needed for the tests with the end-users. Special thanks to therapist Ana Carolina Bernardo for her particular participation in the jPk design and tests supervision. This research is supported by Instituto de Telecomunicações, IT-IUL, at ISCTE-IUL, Lisbon, Portugal, and Fundação para Ciência e

Tecnologia under the project "TailorPhy - Smart Sensors and Tailored Environments for Physiotherapy" with the grant PTDC/DTP-DES/6776/2014.

References

1. d'Ornellas, M.C., Cargnin, D.J., Cervi Prado, A.L.: A thoroughly approach to upper limb rehabilitation using serious games for intensive group physical therapy or individual biofeedback training. In: Proceedings of the 2014 Brazilian Symposium on Computer Games and Digital Entertainment (SBGAMES 2014), pp. 140–147. IEEE, Washington (2014)
2. Chang, C.-Y., Lange, B., Zhang, M., Koenig, S., Requejo, P., Somboon, N., Sawchuk, A.A., Rizzo, A.A.: Towards pervasive physical rehabilitation using microsoft kinect. In: Proceedings of PervasiveHealth 2012, pp. 159–162. ICST, Brussels (2012)
3. Hondori, H.M., Khademi, M.: A review on technical and clinical impact of microsoft kinect on physical therapy and rehabilitation. J. Med. Eng. (2014)
4. Tanaka, K., Parker, J., Baradoy, G., Sheehan, D., Holash, J., Katz, L.: A comparison of exergaming interfaces for use in rehabilitation programs and research. Loading 6(9), 69–81 (2012)
5. De Gama, A., Fallavoillta, P., Teichrieb, V., Navab, N.: Motor rehabilitation using kinect: a systematic review. Games Health J. 4, 123–125 (2015)
6. Deterding, S., Sicart, M., Nacke, L., O'Hara, K., Dixon, D. Gamification: using game-design elements in non-gaming contexts. In: Proceedings of the CHI 2011 Extended Abstracts on Human Factors in Computing Systems (CHI EA 2011), pp. 2425–2428. ACM, New York (2011)
7. Waddington, J., Linehan, C., Gerling, K., Hicks, K., Hodgson, T.L.: Participatory design of therapeutic video games for young people with neurological vision impairment. In: Proceedings of CHI 2015, pp. 3533–3542. ACM, New York (2015)
8. Hernandez, H.A., Graham, T.C.N., Fehlings, D., Switzer, L., Ye, Z., Bellay, Q., Hamza, M.A., Savery, C., Stach, T.: Design of an exergaming station for children with cerebral palsy. In: Proceedings of CHI 2012, pp. 2619–2628. ACM, New York (2012)
9. Wiemeyer, J., Kliem, A.: Serious games in prevention and rehabilitation - a new panacea for elderly people? Eur. Rev. Aging Phys. Act. 9(1), 41–50 (2012)
10. Kato, P.M., Cole, S.W., Bradlyn, A.S., Pollock, B.H.: A video game improves behavioral outcomes in adolescents and young adults with cancer: a randomized trial. Pediatrics 122(2), 305–317 (2008)
11. Achtman, R.L., Green, C.S., Bavelier, D.: Video games as a tool to train visual skills. Restor. Neurol. Neurosci. 26(4–5), 435–446 (2008)
12. Sveistrup, H.: Motor rehabilitation using virtual reality. J. Neuroeng. Rehabil. 10, 1–10 (2004)
13. Clark, R.A., Pua, Y.-H., Bryant, A.L., Hunt, M.A.: Validity of the Microsoft Kinect for providing lateral trunk lean feedback during gait retraining. Gait Posture 38(4), 1064–1066 (2013)
14. Huang, J.D.: Kinerehab: a kinect-based system for physical rehabilitation: a pilot study for young adults with motor disabilities. In: Proceedings of ASSETS 2011, pp. 319–320. ACM (2011)
15. Freitas, D.Q., Da Gama, A., Figueiredo, L., Chaves, T.M., Marques-Oliveira, D., Teichrieb, V., Araújo, C.: Development and evaluation of a kinect based motor rehabilitation game. In: Proceedings of SBGames, pp. 144–153 (2012)

16. Gerling, K., Livingston, I., Nacke, L., Mandryk, R.: Full-body motion-based game interaction for older adults. In: Proceedings of the SIGCHI Conference on Human Factors in Computing Systems, pp. 1873–1882. ACM, Austin (2012)
17. Madeira, R.N., Costa, L., Postolache, O.: PhysioMate - Pervasive physical rehabilitation based on NUI and gamification. In: Proceedings of EPE 2014, pp. 612–616. IEEE (2014)
18. Maggiorini, D., Ripamonti, L.A., Zanon, E.: Supporting seniors rehabilitation through videogame technology: a distributed approach. In: Proceedings of the Second International Workshop on Games and Software Engineering: realizing User Engagement with Game Engineering Techniques (GAS 2012), pp. 16–22. IEEE Press, Piscataway (2012)
19. Marston, H.R., Smith, S.T.: Interactive Videogame Technologies to Support Independence in the Elderly: A Narrative Review. Games Health J. 1(2), 139–152 (2012)
20. Ma, M., Bechkoum, K.: Serious games for movement therapy after stroke. In: IEEE International Conference on Systems, Man and Cybernetics, pp. 872-877 (2008)
21. Lange, B., Chang, C., Suma, E., Newman, B., Rizzo, A.S., Bolas, M.: Development and evaluation of low cost game-based balance rehabilitation tool using the microsoft kinect sensor. In: International Conference of the Engineering in Medicine and Biology Society, pp. 1831–1834 (2011)
22. Luna-Oliva, L., Ortiz-Gutiérrez, R.M., Cano-de la Cuerda, R., Piédrola, R.M., Alguacil-Diego, I.M., Sánchez-Camarero, C., Martínez Culebras Mdel, C.: Kinect Xbox 360 as a therapeutic modality for children with cerebral palsy in a school environment: A preliminary study. J. NeuroRehabilitation 33(4), 513–521 (2013)
23. Hernandez, H.A., Ye, Z., Nicholas Graham, T.C., Fehlings, D., Switzer, L.: Designing action-based exergames for children with cerebral palsy. In: Proceedings of SIGCHI Conference on Human Factors in Computing Systems (CHI 2013), pp. 1261–1270. ACM, New York (2013)
24. Chang, Y.J., Han, W.Y., Tsai, Y.C.: A Kinect-based upper limb rehabilitation system to assist people with cerebral palsy. Res. Dev. Disabil. 34(11), 3654–3659 (2013)
25. Human-Automation Systems Lab at Georgia Tech. SuperPop Project develops game for children with motor skills impairments. http://www.engadget.com/gallery/superpop-project-at-georgia-tech/. Accessed 27 July 2017
26. de Greef, K., van der Spek, E.D., Bekker, T.: Designing Kinect games to train motor skills for mixed ability players. In: Proceedings of the 3rd European Conference on Gaming and Playful Interaction in Health Care (Games for Health 2013), pp. 197–205 (2013)
27. Patil, Y., Sarris, M., Gunter, M., Averette, L.: PLANET 10: a space odyssey. In: Proceedings of CHI PLAY Companion 2016, pp. 67–70. ACM, New York (2016)
28. Vinkler, M., Sochor, J.: Integrating motion tracking sensors to human-computer interaction with respect to specific user needs. In: Proceedings of CESCG 2014: The 18th Central European Seminar on Computer Graphics (2014)
29. Zhu, G., Cai, S., Ma, Y., Liu, E.: A series of leap motion-based matching games for enhancing the fine motor skills of children with autism. In: 2015 Proceedings of 15th International Conference on Advanced Learning Technologies, Hualien, pp. 430–431. IEEE (2015)
30. Penelle, B., Debeir, O.: Multi-sensor data fusion for hand tracking using kinect and leap motion. In: Proceedings of the 2014 Virtual Reality International Conference (VRIC 2014), 7 p. ACM, New York (2014). Article 22
31. Hamari, J., Koivisto, J., Sarsa, H.: Does gamification work? – A literature review of empirical studies on gamification. In: Proceedings of System Sciences 2014, pp. 3025–3034. IEEE (2014)
32. Zichermann, G., Cunningham, C.: Gamification by Design Implementing Game Mechanics in Web and Mobile Apps, p. 36. O'Reilly Media, Sebastopol (2011)

33. Martins, A.I., Rosa, A.F., Queirós, A., Silva, A., Rocha, N.P.: European Portuguese validation of the system usability scale (SUS). Procedia Comput. Sci. **67**, 293–300 (2015)
34. Brooke, J.: SUS: A 'quick and dirty' usability scale. In: Jordan, P.W., Thomas, B., Weerdmeester, B.A., McClelland, I.L. (eds.) Usability Evaluation in Industry, pp. 189–194. Taylor & Francis, London (1996)
35. Sauro, J.: A Practical Guide to the System Usability Scale: Background, Benchmarks, & Best Practices. Measuring Usability LLC, Denver (2011)

Building Virtual World for a Project Management Game – A Case Study

Akash Mohan[1]([✉]), Pranalika Arya[2], and Sandeep Athavale[1]

[1] Tata Consultancy Services Limited, Pune, India
{akash.mohan,athavale.sandeep}@tcs.com
[2] National Institute of Design, Gandhinagar, India
pranalikaarya@gmail.com

Abstract. Virtual worlds are becoming prevalent and find application in a variety of fields. While technology enables us to build virtual worlds which look more realistic, the scenarios that we encounter in the virtual world is often not sufficiently close to real world. Hence, there is a need to develop a method that helps designers build a virtual world that not only looks real but also feels real. Such a method will help in the design of virtual environment using elements from the real world, which significantly improves the authenticity and user experience.

We demonstrate such a method and an example of designing virtual world through a case study. We use software project management as the context and serious games as the medium in our case. We begin with an ontology for capturing the real-world elements of our context (such as time, space, task, people etc.). We then conduct a user study to identify and extract elements from the ontology that would help in representing the real world authentically in the virtual world. Further, we design a virtual world game based on the extracted elements. Finally, we do a post hoc analysis on whether the virtual world that we built was sufficiently authentic.

This paper presents a literature review, method to design an "authentic" virtual world and an illustration of design through the case study of software project management game.

Keywords: Virtual world · Serious game · Fidelity · Representation

1 Introduction

Virtual worlds are used for a variety of purposes including training, learning, gaming etc. The representations in a virtual world ranges from renderings of architectural design which is very close to reality to completely fantasized worlds in games where everything can be abstract and artificial. There is a range of other possibilities in between where the simulation draws a variable number of elements of reality. For example, simulations for the training of aircraft pilots, surgeons need high physical fidelity of objects they visualize and interact with but the lesser complexity of other objects which are around but irrelevant, whereas training environments for business managers may not need high

© Springer International Publishing AG, part of Springer Nature 2018
A. D. Cheok et al. (Eds.): ACE 2017, LNCS 10714, pp. 746–760, 2018.
https://doi.org/10.1007/978-3-319-76270-8_51

physical fidelity but more of functional fidelity like interactive characters, real-life scenarios etc.

Simulations are very useful for training physical and mental 'performance skills' but they may not be engaging while acquiring these skills. Serious games are playing an important role of presenting cognitive and behavioral learning in an engaging way [13]. On the continuum of reality to artificiality (refer Fig. 1), we see that games are completely artificial worlds. Serious games are a special case, which attempts to achieve a serious purpose through an artificial game world. Simulations are truthful representations of a real world in a virtual environment whereas gamification is applying game elements like scoring/rewarding, competition etc. for engagement and motivation in performing real-world tasks.

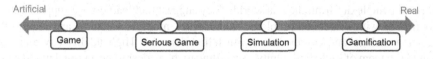

Fig. 1. The real-artificial continuum

The simulations and serious games extract "that" part of the real world which is necessary and sufficient to meet the purpose of creation of such virtual world. Representation of the entire world is neither necessary nor economical. Therefore, the important question is how much content or elements from the real world should be drawn down into the virtual world? Today this answer is left to the designer's abilities and also (rightly) driven by the constraints of budget and timelines. However, there is no established method that guides the designer in this translation from real to virtual world. The scope of this paper is to understand this translation of real-world elements to the serious game through a case study.

Here, we present a case study about building a prototype of a game for training software project managers. There have been few attempts already in creating virtual worlds for software project management learning [7, 10, 14]. However, the purpose of previous work is to understand the effectiveness of learning through this medium rather than how this medium should be designed in the first place.

In our case, we begin with the study of an ontology of real world, in the context of software project management organization. We then conduct multiple user studies to identify which elements of the ontology matter to the users. We then design a virtual world that represents these elements and integrates game features to create an engaging experience for the learner. We then conduct user testing of the prototype for perceived fidelity.

2   Literature on Dimensions of Virtual World

Practical learning implies acquiring the skills and thought processes needed to respond appropriately under pressure in various real-time situations. Good digital game-based platforms have the capability to draw learners into virtual environments that look and feel familiar and relevant and therefore likely to impart and extract real-time behaviors. According to Ambrose [3], digital games can be motivational because one can quickly see and understand the connection between the learning experience and their real-life work. Within an effective game-based learning environment, one can work toward a goal, choose actions and experience the consequences of those actions along the way. One can make mistakes in risk-free settings through experimentation, one can actively learn and practice the right way to do things. It possesses the potential of high engagement in practicing behaviors and thought processes that can easily be transferred from the simulated environment to real life over a longer period of time. However, the cost of creating such rich virtual worlds may be disproportionate to the expected benefits. Therefore, we search for literature that guides us in knowing how much to translate.

Westera et al. [19] argue that the virtual world for learning may not and does not need all complexity from the real world. They suggest that learners are supposed to be confronted with ill-defined problems, which allow multiple solutions and require the decision making and collaboration with fellow learners. High fidelity environments would rob them of such opportunity. According to them, designing a virtual world game involves specification of two fundamental dimensions of space and time. The space dimension covers the static configuration of the (virtual) game locations, including the associated objects, attributes, and relationships. The locations may be physical spaces such as room or road and abstract spaces such as a cell in a table. Players move within these spaces to interact with objects and people. Objects can again be physical such as a copier or phone or they can be abstract such as data. The time dimension covers the evolution and the state changes through the game. The state changes can occur due to events or due to decisions that players take. The authors talk about the social dimension of the game as the communication, co-operation, opposition or competition between players or characters therein. While the dimensions presented here are essential, we do not know why these 3 dimensions were selected from the possibility space. To make our point about the larger possibility space, we refer to Bronack et al. [6]. According to them, there are three critical attributes of effectively designing virtual worlds: Thematic design of space, Promotion of presence and Awareness of unique qualities of human behavior in the online social environment. Two of the three match with Westera et al. [19] but they bring a new one.

Westera et al. [19] also suggest few techniques to reduce representation complexity, for example - reducing the depth of state change sequences and increasing width. They also present a scenario generation toolkit to reduce development effort. However, there is no clear guidance on how a designer should proceed in selecting elements to be represented in the virtual world.

Further, we explore fidelity in the context of designing virtual world. The concept of fidelity in the context of the virtual world refers to how closely it is represented to the real world [2]. However, it is unclear as to what Fidelity refers to primarily, the level of functionality, the level of visual polish or the level of interactivity [11]. Thus, the uni-dimensional idea of fidelity as high and low might not be an appropriate classification, as an artifact could be well developed in one aspect, while not so developed in other aspects. We classify such artifacts as having Mixed-fidelity. There are two types of fidelity: Physical and Functional fidelity. Physical fidelity refers to factors like visual display, controls, audio, and physics models driving these variables. While functional fidelity includes the extent to which the game environment acts like the real world in terms of its response to player actions, thus encompassing the elements of game narrative and interactivity. Some researchers suggest that higher levels of fidelity can lead to better learning because the transfer of knowledge would be easier when the virtual world and the real world are close [13]. However, it is also observed that virtual worlds with very high visual fidelity fall into what is called the uncanny valley [5, 17], which wakes up our 'wardens of reality' causing a sudden drop in believability [18]. Smith [15] in his review of research related to simulations in the classroom concluded that the 'physical fidelity' of the simulation materials is less important than the extent to which the simulation promotes 'realistic problem-solving processes', a process Smith describes as the 'cognitive realism' of the task. It is also argued that virtual environments which aim for high visual fidelity risk undermining players' tolerance for inaccuracies or deviations in appearance and behavior [5].

We also look at the construct of authenticity. Barab et al. [4] suggest that since serious games provide an artificial view of the real world, it is important that this environment and associated tasks are authentic in order to evoke real-world experiences. Rooney et al. [13] suggest that even though high authenticity is desired, it can cause cognitive overload. They suggest that the key is to balance simplicity and authenticity. Similar to Smith [15], Herrington et al. [9] propose that physical verisimilitude to real situations is of less importance in learning than 'cognitive realism'. The learning environments they studied have varying degrees of fidelity to reality, but all have strong linkage to real-world professional practice, and to the 'cognitive realism' described by Smith [16]. They observe that the scenarios are not drawn in elaborate, resource intensive ways, but are built up through the creation and development of realistic and engaging ideas. Sometimes real-world tasks are not engaging and they need to be made engaging while keeping the truthfulness of cognitive effort.

The literature survey is in agreement of the need to reduce the real-world complexity/fidelity while representing in the virtual game world but stops short of suggesting a method to achieve the same.

3 Overview of Software Project Management

A project is a temporary endeavor undertaken to create a unique product or service. 'Temporary' means that every project has a definite beginning and definite end. 'Unique' means that the product or service is different in some distinguishing way from all similar products or services. Project Management is the application of knowledge, skills, tools, and techniques to project activities in order to meet or exceed stakeholder's needs and expectations from a project. This involves balancing competing demands among –(a) Scope, time, cost and quality and (b) Stakeholders with differing needs and expectations. Software Projects are like any other projects but with a heavy dependency on human effort as software is predominantly human crafted. In this study, we keep the scope of our discussion to development projects which follow a waterfall model.

To understand the range of concepts that represent the software project domain, we refer to the work of Abels et al. [1] who proposed PROMONT - A Project Management Ontology. It formalizes the typical elements used for project structuring (such as task, milestone, resource or checklist) shown in Table 1.

Table 1. Elements from a Project Management Ontology reproduced from [1]

Concept	Definition
Initiative	Any intention or endeavor, super ordinate concept for project, task and process
Project	A project is a structured approach to deliver a certain result. It consists of an amount of time, budget and resource restrictions and conditions and is usually divided into a set of tasks
Task	Project-specific initiative. May be divided into sub-tasks. May be implemented by the application of a process
Activity	Task that has been assigned to a specific resource. The assignment determines duration and costs of task execution
Phase	Subdivision of Project timing with specific objective. Often ends with a gate
Resource	Consumable or not-consumable good or entity. Resources are necessary to execute an initiative
Employee	Person working for an organizational unit. Subset of Resource
Machine	A non-consumable, non-human Resource
Calendar	A timetable showing the availability and workload of a resource during a period. Also used for a project overview calendar
Skill	Property and potential of a resource to satisfy a requirement for a task
Event	Occurrence of an action at a specific point in time. Has zero duration and may trigger tasks
Milestone	Event with significant meaning for project status
Gate	Milestone ending a phase. Usually associated with a formal review task
Risk	Possible source of shortcomings or failure in the project. Might be sanctioned
Objective	Desired outcome of an Initiative. Can be a physical product, a service or a document
Result	Actual outcome of an Initiative, Can be a physical product, a service or a document

These concepts are needed to design a virtual world that provide a reasonably authentic experience of the domain to the learners. The expected audience for this game are existing project managers or budding managers who want to learn navigation of software projects through its stages and events. They would learn managing scope, schedule, effort, tasks, and relationships through emerging situations as they navigate through the project and hone communication, negotiation, problem-solving, and decision-making skills on the way.

4   Virtual World Design Process

We followed our own 4-O (alphabet O) method for virtual world design. The 4 Os represent the 4 stages: Obtain, Observe, Outline, and Outcome as shown in Fig. 2. The details of the stages have been elaborated in the subsequent sections.

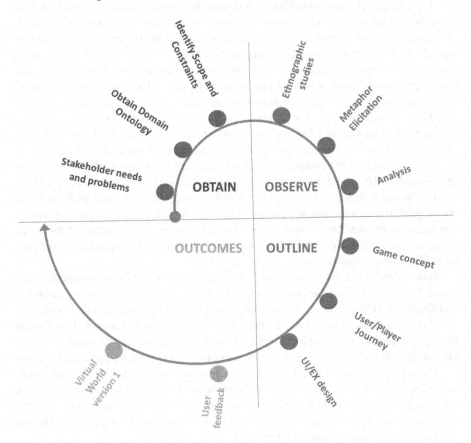

Fig. 2. The 4O Model for virtual world design

Why do we need a new method for designing virtual world? We reviewed existing models and found that existing research mostly discusses the macro aspects of designing (or high-level design) Virtual Worlds. For example, the 4D model elaborates to Discover, Define, Develop and Deliver/Deploy. While experienced designers expect methodologies to be 'liberal' or less restrictive, novice designers might require more support within each stage to enable them to complete the design. Also, it happens quite often that designers are put to develop virtual worlds in domains which they do not know for e.g. a space simulation. Though, we are aware the physics of the objects in space, the designer has limited knowledge on the problems faced by scientists and astronauts in space. In such cases, it becomes crucial to understand the world from the users.

Our model focusses on understanding the user's world through non-verbal means, to enable high authenticity of the game.

The 4O model is inspired from the 4D design thinking methodology or double diamond design process [8]. The 4D methodology divides a project into processes with four distinct stages: Discover, Design, Develop and Deploy. This methodology is used mostly by design practitioners. Firstly, it delves into understanding the problem, then designing a solution for it, which needs to be prototyped and tested immediately. Laying on the same principles, the 4O model was created. Like, in the 4D, first phase "Discover" starts from discovering the problem, here our first phase "Obtain" starts from obtaining and understanding the information of the problem and the domain. Unlike 4D model, the design doesn't start in second phase onwards, our 4O second phase "Observe" comprise of going to the users and understanding what they see. The third stage, Develop in 4D corresponds to Outline (or design a prototype in 4O) and finally the Deploy in 4D corresponds to measuring Outcomes stage in 4O. The difference in 4D and 4O is not much in the stages but more in the details. We describe each stage of 4O further.

The first stage of 4O comprises of **obtaining** the knowledge of the domain to be represented in the virtual world. This includes identifying the purpose and problems from the key stakeholders, a study of the domain through literature and finally defining the scope. To understand the domain in a systematic way, we suggest acquiring domain ontologies as the first step. Ontology is a formal naming and definition of the types, properties, and interrelationships of the entities that really or fundamentally exist for a particular domain of discourse.

This stage allows us to make a list of candidate elements to be represented in virtual world. The scope decisions are based on the stakeholder needs and constraints on budget and timelines. This narrows down the candidate list by eliminating certain branches.

This second stage comprises of **observing** users in their real world. This is done through conducting ethnographic interviews and analysing data. In ethnography - Metaphor elicitation and Laddering techniques can be used for extracting data from the users.

The reason we chose Metaphor elicitation as a method to gather data is that people use metaphors as tools to make sense of the world around them. Metaphors provide the constructs for our thinking, perceptions, and communication with one another. Metaphors give meaningful form to concepts and provide structure for experiences that are not highly structured by their own terms [6].

Metaphor elicitation or ZMET (Zaltman Metaphor Elicitation Techniques) [20] is a method which is commonly used to understand the conscious and unconscious thoughts by exploring people's non-literal metaphoric expression. Each user is given a topic/scenario and a set of visuals in the form of photos from an online repository, magazine etc. It is important to note that the master set visuals are often not related to the scenario under concern, this is done to elicit genuine responses. Then, the users are asked to select those visuals which they feel are related to the topic they are assigned. The conductor of the experiment tries to understand the reasons for the participant choosing that image. The relation between the images connects back with their real-life stories, experiences, from which we received insights.

The data we collected from interviews were in the form of personal experiences (or stories). Though the stories were insightful and authentic, we need structure to build a virtual world. Each story was broken down into the following components:

i.   Situations (the problem/scenarios experienced by the participants)
ii. Choices (taken by the participants to tackle the situations)
iii. Implications (Impact of the selected choices)
iv. Reasoning (of the choices, selected for particular problem/scenario)

Once the data has been mapped into this format, the crux of the game story emerges. The objects, people, physical space and events form the elements in the virtual world based on their frequency of occurrence in the situations. Based on the budget allocated for developing the virtual world, this list can be truncated and the elements implemented. For e.g. the designers might choose to select the top 50 or top 100 items on the list based on the required functional fidelity.

This third stage comprises of creating **Outline** of the design. This includes detailing the virtual world based on data collected in the 'observe' phase.

Making it a Game – The user journeys, interactions, challenges, factors that can cause boredom are identified and a game idea is conceptualized around these elements. The game goal, character roles, tasks, situations, choices are aligned with the real world. Elements of fantasy, curiosity, surprise are added.

UI ideation – The representation ideas are brainstormed and sketched, and various factors are detailed such as user journey, layout, information placement, and the UI and UX elements for the user.

The fourth and final, stage comprise of presenting and testing the **Outcomes** of the design. The intended outcomes are player engagement and meeting the purpose of learning. This is done through user testing of the concept. The users were shown UI design prototype and interviewed in structured and semi-structured format to understand how closely they rate the experience of a prototype with the reality.

User testing can indicate the fidelity perceived by users for overall experience as well as for each component. If the perceived fidelity is below the acceptable threshold that designer has set, more elements could be added.

5   Designing the Project Management Game - A Case Study

In this section, we describe how we used the 4O design process to design a prototype of a project management game, Foresight. Foresight is a simulation game intended to train novice managers to take decisions in real life scenarios.

5.1   Obtain

The first stage starts with obtaining information about the domain. Since we were designing a project management game, we started with the study of the workplace/task ontology by Mizoguchi et al. [12] where the authors mention generic ontology consisting of space, structure, things, time, events, people, function, and behavior. We found that these elements are fundamental considerations for designing the virtual world. We then applied the project management ontology [1] and elements in Table 1, to identify specific elements such as project, phases, tasks, milestone, employees, skills, resources and results. We also studied another viewpoint from the typical training content of managers and from there brought in elements such as scenarios, choices, decisions, and implications as another set of interest. We combined the elements from the above sources to make a list of elements to be represented in the virtual world.

We identified 3 aspects of project management to focus, Project delivery, Client Interaction and Social Interaction. The reason for selecting these topics was that these were the areas in which there would be the most number of challenging situations during the project. We also chose the topics in a way that it includes both people-task interaction and people-people interaction. We also restricted employee types of project managers and developers and so on.

5.2 Observe

The objective of this phase is to get a set of finite values to the above elements based on what the users mostly encounter. We found this through user interviews.

Firstly, the participants were selected and divided into groups, allocating each with one of these topics - Project delivery, Client Interaction, and Social Interaction. This meant, there were 3 groups and each group was assigned one topic. A participant from each group was given 2–3 magazines (visual based) and was asked to find visuals, which he/she can relate to the problem/scenario faced, with regards to the given topic. The participants were given some time for this activity. Once, they were done with it, we conducted the semi-structured interviews. These interviews were one on one, each lasting for about 40–50 min per participant.

The individual interviews started with Step 1, ice-breaking questions (which were common for all the 3 topics) and we also collected demographic information. This included their names, age, and role, number of years in the organization along with their perception of the organization, environment, and people. In step 2, a set of questions were framed, which were topic specific. The interaction with participants/subjects was not limited to these framed questions alone, but it also encompassed the subsequent questions, asked on the basis of the answers given by the participants during the interview itself.

After the above questions were answered by the participants, the step 3 involved asking the participants about the visuals, which he/she selected from the magazines, prior to the interview. The participants were asked the questions such as-

- What is the content of the image?
- What is the reason behind selecting the image?
- How does the image relate to the problem/scenario?
- Describe the problem/scenario in detail (their experiences, their story).
- What choices did he/she take to tackle the problem/scenario?
- What were the reasons and impact of taking such choices?
- How does he/she feel about those choices taken?

- What other choices would he/she take, to tackle the same problem/scenario?
- Mention any other problem/scenario, apart from the visuals.

With an extension to the above-mentioned reason for this method selection, the images helped the participants to re-collect their stories and experiences. The participants mentioned that the images helped them to refresh their memories regarding various situations faced in a real office environment. The answers given by the participants, helped us to extract a list of elements that they encounter and recollect in the real world. Since we collect data from multiple participants, we also know the frequency of each element and we could find out the ones that are commonly appearing.

Through analysis of elements from Obtain and Observe stages, we selected a list for our virtual world game. A sample is listed below and Fig. 3 depicts the important elements and their relationships.

- Workspace (desk, table, chair, tools, phone, laptop)
- Team members (age, gender, knowledge, emotional states, relationships)
- Tasks, Budget, Schedule
- Set of predefined events and emergent scenarios
- Activities (People perform tasks, people make decisions, people meet people)

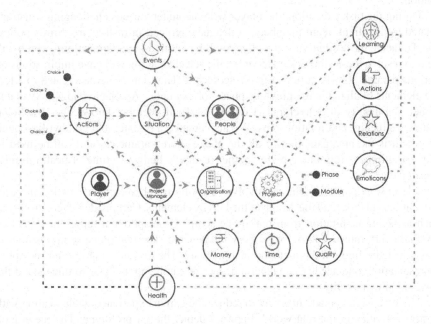

Fig. 3. Elements obtained from our analysis and their relation

Since we collected data from a limited number of people, we were able to include most of the elements that emerged from the study. However, this might not be possible all the time, especially when the scenario elicitation is conducted over considerably large sample size when a lot of elements will be generated.

5.3 Outline

The game storyline started to take its shape in this stage. It began with conceptualizing and defining the roles of the player. The player would be playing the role of project manager in the game. Liaising with delivery head, dealing with a client, forming a team for the project, delegating work to the team members, etc. would be some of his/her tasks to accomplish/perform. Fixed money and time would be given to the player in order to conduct the project. The player needs to achieve certain quality while executing the project work. Thus, the player needs to complete the project within the given limits and create required quality output while keeping the team morale good.

We use the study of PM BOK from the obtain phase to define the game story. The project is divided into 5 phases - Initiate, Plan, Execute, Monitor and Close. Each phase comprises of tasks such as meeting the client for understanding the requirements, reviewing the documentation work, coding etc., which the player needs to do. To execute all the tasks, the player will have to form his/her team. These team members (NPC or Non-playing characters) are available with certain information like age, physical health, work experience, personality, and skills. The player needs to invest money in building the team by carefully selecting these NPCs on the basis of the above-mentioned information.

During the task execution, the player will encounter various challenging situations related to the client, team members, colleagues, project, infrastructure, firm's policy, etc. To tackle these situations, the player will be entitled to certain actions, which will help to resolve these situations. However, the selected action will have implications on various parameters which reflect in the scorecard. The scorecard was created to affect the elements finalized in the previous phase for example - Available budget, Available Time, The quality of deliverable, Task status, Team member knowledge, emotional states, wellbeing, and relationships. We also created a transferable goodwill account. Goodwill is the amalgamation of all the above score parameters and can be used to transfer currency from one type to another (example budget to time or health to relationship etc.)

The next step within Outline involves creating rough sketches to define the user navigation and flow, and the design of the UI/UX elements. Certain ideas were discussed such as taking inspiration from real office setup or metaphorical representations like football court, music studio, exploratory kitchen, etc. The real office setup inspiration was selected ruling out the metaphorical pathway. The reason being that for metaphor representation, one needs to conduct a deeper research and analysis to understand the correlation with reality.

The UI design is made in a way to reduce the gap in experience while dealing with project activities in the real world. Figure 4 depict the UI prototype. The menu icon encompasses the prioritized navigation trend, for easy access and consists of the dashboard, task list, resources. The time and score are placed at the bottom panel since the user would need to view the time, calendar, and score most often. Hence, they are neither hidden nor placed in menu icon; instead, they remain constantly visible to the player. The Hint is purposely placed beside the score on right bottom corner for the intuitive feeling of the user to access it when needed and doesn't have to search for it. People and action panels are placed on the right middle section as a slider bar. The reason being, the slider bar would only flash on when the player needs to liaise with NPCs. The communication icons in people and action slider bar follow the flat design concept with icons representing the essence of each mode. Overall, the player needs to tackle the situation by clicking on the NPCs, action and communication mode as appropriate. Thus, the micro-interaction with each type of element would enhance the realistic experience for the user.

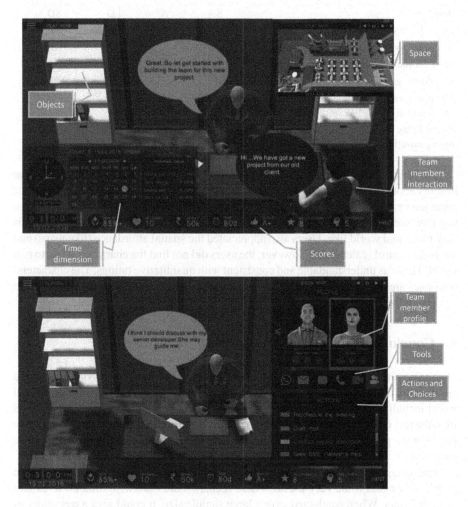

Fig. 4. Screenshots of the 'Foresight' game prototype with components

5.4 Outcomes

We conducted a survey to assess the usability and authenticity of the virtual world, and followed it with semi-structured interviews. There were 16 participants, who we identified to be potential users of the project management game. They were professionals who were managers or aspiring managers working in an IT services organization. We walked the participants through the prototype of the game. Table 2 summarizes the questions we posed and distribution of answers. In Table 2. the abbreviations in column (2–5) mean SA – Strongly Agree; A- Agree; D- Disagree; and SD- Strongly disagree.

Table 2. Distribution of answers given by participants in the post hoc survey

Item	SA	A	D	SD
I found it difficult to locate all the menu icons	0%	12.5%	0%	87.5%
I was able to understand the game with ease	62.5%	37.5%	0%	0%
Most people would understand the game easily	50%	43.75%	6.25%	0%
I found the game interface easy to understand	25%	75%	0%	0%
The game was very similar to the real office environment	43.75%	43.75%	12.5%	0%
I would play this game even if it is not mandated by organizational policy	75%	12.5%	6.25%	6.25%

The semi-structured interviews with the participants also gave us some qualitative insights about the prototype design. Users felt the actions, situations, and events in the game are very similar to their actions in real life office environment. Users did mention that new scenarios popping in the middle of the project, causes interruption, which is very much real world like. Users also appreciated the spatial affordance (like maps) and temporal control (calendars). However, the users did not find the characters close to real world. This was understandable and consistent with quantitative ratings. The characters' responses are also based on limited intelligence and hence looked unreal and they can be made better with a repository of behaviors if available to draw upon.

6 Conclusion and Future Work

The main contribution of our work is a method which helps to design virtual world in any domain. Our 4-O method taps into the macro and micro aspects of designing a virtual world including understanding, extraction, representation, and validation of elements from the real world with fidelity and complexity. Our case study of designing a prototype for software project management game provides a good test case for the method we proposed.

The metaphor elicitation technique as a strategy to collect real-life scenarios from people was found to be very useful. These scenarios are otherwise difficult to extract from the users. When conducted over a large sample size, it could give a repository of interesting and authentic real-life situations which could be used for building games, simulations etc. with high functional fidelity.

We acknowledge that Virtual world design is a space teeming with methods for designing, developing and evaluating, which makes it difficult to come up with a contribution which is non-overlapping on existing ones. Though, the current method might not be entirely "new", it is useful for novice designers for building virtual worlds.

Future work includes a rigorous assessment of prototypes for fidelity and usability by users and experts. Metaphor elicitation is an effective technique in collecting scenarios about real-life experiences, albeit a time taking one. Gamification and crowd-sourcing the scenario collection process (through ZMET) could help save effort and time. In the long term, we intend to develop the prototype into a game and study if the scenarios in the game actually evoke real-life response among players.

References

1. Abels, S., Ahlemann, F., Hahn, A., Hausmann, K., Strickmann, J.: PROMONT – a project management ontology as a reference for virtual project organizations. In: Meersman, R., Tari, Z., Herrero, P. (eds.) OTM 2006. LNCS, vol. 4277, pp. 813–823. Springer, Heidelberg (2006). https://doi.org/10.1007/11915034_105
2. Alexander, A.L., et al.: From gaming to training: A review of studies on fidelity, immersion, presence, and buy-in and their effects on transfer in PC-based simulations and games. DARWARS Training Impact Group (2005)
3. Ambrose, S.A.: How Learning Works: Seven Research-Based Principles for Smart Teaching. Jossey-Bass, San Francisco (2010)
4. Barab, S.A., et al.: Grounded constructions and how technology can help. TechTrends. **43**(2), 15–23 (1998)
5. Brenton, H., et al.: The uncanny valley: does it exist. In: 19th British HCI Group Annual Conference: Workshop on Human-Animated Character Interaction (2005)
6. Bronack, S., et al.: Designing virtual worlds to facilitate meaningful communication: issues, considerations, and lessons learned. Tech. Commun. **55**(3), 261–269 (2008)
7. Calderón, A., Ruiz, M.: Bringing real-life practice in software project management training through a simulation-based serious game. In: Proceedings of the 6th International Conference on Computer Supported Education (2014)
8. Council, D.: The 'double diamond' design process model (2005)
9. Herrington, J., et al.: Immersive learning technologies: realism and online authentic learning. J. Comput High. Educ. **19**(1), 80–99 (2007)
10. Lee, W.-L.: Spreadsheet based experiential learning environment for project management. In: Proceedings of the 2011 Winter Simulation Conference (WSC) (2011)
11. McCurdy, M., et al.: Breaking the fidelity barrier. In: Proceedings of the SIGCHI Conference on Human Factors in Computing Systems - CHI 06 (2006)
12. Mizoguchi, R., et al.: Task ontology for reuse of problem solving knowledge. In: Towards Very Large Knowledge Bases, pp. 46–59 (1995)
13. Rooney, P.: A theoretical framework for serious game design. Int. J. Game-Based Learn. **2**(4), 41–60 (2012)
14. Sadabadi, A.T.: A decision support system for game-based simulative environment of software development project management. Int J. Mach. Learn. Comput. **2**(2), 173–177 (2012)
15. Smith, P.E.: Simulating the classroom with media and computers: past efforts future possibilities. Simul. Gaming **18**(3), 395–413 (1987)
16. Smith, P.: Instructional simulation: research, theory, and a case study (1986)
17. Tinwell, A., Grimshaw, M.: Bridging the uncanny. In: Proceedings of the 13th International MindTrek Conference: Everyday Life in the Ubiquitous Era on - MindTrek 2009 (2009)

18. Wages, R., Grünvogel, S.M., Grützmacher, B.: How realistic is realism? considerations on the aesthetics of computer games. In: Rauterberg, M. (ed.) ICEC 2004. LNCS, vol. 3166, pp. 216–225. Springer, Heidelberg (2004). https://doi.org/10.1007/978-3-540-28643-1_28
19. Westera, W., et al.: Serious games for higher education: a framework for reducing design complexity. J. Comput. Assist. Learn. **24**(5), 420–432 (2008)
20. Zaltman, G., Coulter, R.H.: Seeing the voice of the consumer: metaphor-based advertising research. J. Advertising Res. **35**(4), 35–51 (1995)

Timebender: A Multiplayer Game Featuring Bullet Time Mechanics

Christoph Pressler and Helmut Hlavacs[✉]

Entertainment Computing Research Group, University of Vienna,
Währinger Straße 29, 1090 Vienna, Austria
helmut.hlavacs@univie.ac.at

Abstract. We first evaluate different ways of implementing bullet time into multiplayer online shooters and discuss their problems. We then show a new approach on how to implement slow motion elements into a multiplayer game. Players have a special ability which spawns spheres, called timebubbles, that grow around them and slow down everything in them. Players can use a bullet dodging mode inside these spheres to evade incoming bullets.

A game called Timebender was developed to test these new approaches and a user study was conducted to evaluate if the new approach works. The results show that the approach used by Timebender avoids the problems of other titles that include such mechanics.

Keywords: Game · Multiplayer · Online · Shooter · Bullet time
Slowmotion · Unity

1   Introduction

Over the last few decades the video game sector has grown and is now one of the biggest in the whole entertainment-industry. Big Projects like Grand Theft Auto 5 (Rockstar Games, 2013) create more revenue than many profitable movies. This is not a big surprise, considering the wide range of possibilities modern technologies have to offer for video games and the rapid speed in which they continue to advance. There can be no doubt that many different innovations in the coming years that will lead to further growth of the video game sector. Two of the most prominent developments of 2016 and 2017 are virtual reality and augmented reality, which both change the way the user interacts with games.

One of such advances, which has been used in the movie industry previously, is given by slow motion effects. While there are popular games that use such effects, e.g. the Max Payne [8] series from Rockstar Games, most of these are single player games. The few multiplayer games that do incorporate similar gameplay mechanics are either old or show deficiencies in other areas. In a single player shooter game the simplest solution would be to slow down the entire level. However, this is not a feasible approach in an online mutliplayer game, since it would mean that every player is slowed down once one player wants to halt time.

© Springer International Publishing AG, part of Springer Nature 2018
A. D. Cheok et al. (Eds.): ACE 2017, LNCS 10714, pp. 761–773, 2018.
https://doi.org/10.1007/978-3-319-76270-8_52

This would ruin the experience for the other players, as it would break the game flow [1,3].

There are different options on how to introduce slow motion elements to a multiplayer shooter. One, as already described, is to slow down time for the entire level. A second is to dynamically create a small arena where time is slowed down and only two players battle each other while the other players watch the battle.

Another problem that arises is the technical implementation of bullet time in multiplayer mode. For reasons already mentioned, it would be impractical to slow down the entire level. Consequently, there must be a system of different time zones in one single level. These time zones must be synchronized over the network.

The goals of our work are to design, implement and evaluate a multiplayer mode in an enjoyable game featuring slow motion effects, a.k.a., bullet time, without impeding players in their game flow. We describe the design considerations, the implementation of a simple multiplayer shooter incorporating them, and an evaluation with several test participants.

2 Related Work

As mentioned before, this is not the first project that adds slow motion elements to an ordinary shooter. In this chapter we present games which also implement time manipulation, as well as a dedicated game engine for multiplayer games that features it.

Max Payne 3 [8] (Rockstar Games, 2012) featured an online mutliplayer mode with integrated bullet time and is therefore one of the closest works thematically. The team behind the game chose to slow down time for every player that sees or is seen by the player that activates slow motion mode. While the player who uses the special ability that slows down time can reload and fire at the normal rate, players who are trapped in bullet time, but did not start it, have increased reloading and firing times. While this is a good approach, it comes with some drawbacks. The bullet time happens very suddenly and without any kind of warning. This can cause confusion and might feel unfair. While it is the intention of such an ability to gain an advantage over the other players, the reason it is beneficial should not be because the other players simply do not know what is happening.

Additionally, the authors of this work do not think that it is a good idea to just restrict the abilities of the other players, which happens here in the form of decreasing fire rate and reload speed. It would be more interesting and motivating for a player to create an intense, thrilling situation, a kind of duel where the player who uses the ability only has a tactical advantage but players within reach play under the same conditions [1,3].

Another problem created by this scenario is that players that are not in immediate reach are also affected by the bullet time. The problem is that, once a player has activated bullet time, every player they see and every player this player sees - repeatedly - is also affected by bullet time, even if they are in completely different areas of the map. This breaks the flows of players that are not interacting with the player that uses the ability and is therefore questionable [1, 3]. With Timebender we avoid the described problems. The time effect does not happen instantly and without warning. Instead a bubble forms around the player who used the ability. Although this *timebubble* grows fast, other players still realize what is happening and can act accordingly. Second, players within the described timebubble are slowed down equally, meaning that the player who used the ability does not gain any other advantages. The size of the bubble prevents players on the other side of the map to be affected by bullet time Fig. 2. Since bullets that enter the timebubble are slowed down as well, there is no advantage for players outside of the bubble.

TimeShift [9] is a game from Saber Interactive, released in 2007, that gives the player several time controlling abilities. While the players already had many different abilities in single player mode, the developers decided to change the skill set for the multiplayer mode. Since Timebender only employs multiplayer mode, we only concentrate on the multiplayer part of TimeShift. Unsurprisingly, the developers faced the same problems that the authors of this work faced. In an interview with the games-site "Gamespot" in 2007 Kyle Pschel, the senior producer on TimeShift, was asked in which ways time manipulation would work in multiplayer mode. His answer was:

> When we first started working with multiplayer, we talked about using the abilities just like in single-player, where you can slow, stop, or reverse the flow of time, while you and your weapons remain unaffected. But the problem in multiplayer is that while you're having the time of your life, the 15 other frozen players are helpless. Ultimately, it wasn't fun. [...] Each user's suit exports the time-shifting abilities to these chronos grenades that come in three flavors (slow, stop, and now reverse). [..] When it impacts, it expands into an approximately 10-foot sphere of temporal space controlled by the given power. [..] If your opponent fires a rocket and you throw down a slow grenade, the rocket will speed along until it enters the sphere [...] [4]

The team that made TimeShift concluded that freezing all players but one would not lead to an enjoyable game experience, so they decided to express the players' time manipulation abilities via grenades. The authors think this is a good approach towards the problems facing the developers. As in Timebender, a sphere marks the time distortion's region of influence. However, TimeShift packs the slow motion effect into a weapon that primarily should handicap other players. Since one goal of this work is to create fair duels in bullet time, integrating the effect into a weapon is not an option. The biggest difference to the integration of the slow motion effect in Timebender is that in Timebender the sphere expands around the player that initiates it, while in TimeShift the ability to manipulate time is in itself a weapon, since it appears in the form of a grenade. One of the ideas behind the game developed for this paper was to create a duel-like situation (comparable to some of the scenes of the film Matrix [12] (Village Roadshow Pictures, 1999)), which means that encapsulation of the ability into a grenade is not practical, since there would be no duel, but simply a restriction of possible movement for the opponent.

Although Superhot [10] features no multiplayer mode, it is the most recent game that gained public attention by integrating advanced time manipulation mechanics into a shooter. In this game, time only moves when the player moves, meaning that when the player is stationary time stands still as well. While this idea constitutes a novel approach and works well in single player mode, it would be very hard to integrate into multiplayer mode in a way that improves the gaming experience. The authors also thought about including this mechanic into a timebubble, so that the time in the timebubble moves as fast as the player that made the bubble. However, this would confuse players that are affected by the timebubble but did not create it and cause them to feel as if the controls are not working, since the game speed would change without any input made by them.

FizzX [7] is a real-time game engine that was built with time manipulation for networked games in mind. As FizzX is no game but a game engine. Nevertheless, the authors think it is very important to investigate other areas regarding time manipulation mechanics as well. FizzX records player states with an inbuilt "time manipulation module" so that every object has its own timeline. This enables developers to independently control the time-states of different objects/players. While this is a good solution for games that want to control every aspect of time, this is not necessary for Timebender, considering Timebender only includes a bullet time ability but no rewind function. This means developing the game like this game engine, with an own module just to save the player states, would be unnecessarily time consuming and add lag to the multiplayer mode.

3   Design Considerations

While developing Timebender, many different design choices had to be made. Before making the first real content we had to make sure that the concept behind the different parts of the game was finished, so that he had to revise as little as possible. For instance, it would be very time consuming to completely change the player model in one of the later phases of development since many components would change, or more precisely, would need to be changed.

Bullet Time. The most vital question regarding this project was how to implement bullet time mode. This question creates multiple follow up questions:

- What should it do?
  Very early during the creation process the authors decided to implement duel situations like those in the film Matrix [12], so that one player can dodge incoming bullets (cf. Fig. 1), since this enhances gameplay through providing more options for the player [11].
- Should bullet time handicap players and therefore be a weapon, or should it be something that only benefits the player using it?
  Since the last question introduced the goal of implementing advanced dodging mechanics, this question has already been answered. It should not be just a

weapon. Both players can dodge incoming bullets or shoot them, but no player has an actual gameplay advantage. The only advantage left is the surprise effect, in that bullet time will catch the other players unawares. The authors tried to eliminate the surprise factor by creating a transition. The slow motion effect starts small and gets bigger gradually, instead of just popping up.

– Who should be effected by bullet time?
This is another vital decision that greatly effects the game, offering many different possibilities. Basically there are two main options: Either everyone is effected, or just a small group of players. Since one of the goals is to a create duel situations, the first was not a viable solution, since everyone would feel the impact. The second variant, where just a small group of players is affected, can be realized in three different approaches. First, one could implement the same mechanics as mentioned in Max Payne 3 [8] in Sect. 2, but since the aim was to minimize the risk of slowing down the whole map, this idea was abandoned. Second, a real duel could be created dynamically by forging a stadium and moving every non-effected player into a spectator mode, so that only two players are fighting for a limited time span while the spectators observe. As this would break the game flow of the non-effected player, this idea was discarded as well, although it had the potential to create tense duels. In the end it was decided to create spheres, called *timebubbles*, which allow the time dilution effect to slowly expand. Players are not surprised and just a limited amount of players is effected. Figure 2 illustrates the maximum size of a timebubble.

– How should it be integrated into the game?
Another still open question was how to integrate the bullet time into the game. There were two possible solutions to this problem: The timebubble could either be initiated by an item the player utilized or an inherent ability of the characters. In order to keep the impact of luck to a minimum, the authors chose to make the creation of timebubbles an inherent ability. The question now was how to integrate this ability into the game. In order to emphasize the uniqueness of the time bubble ability, the path chosen was to limit the use of the ability to once per match. This way, players would have to think carefully and tactically about when to spend this once-per-match advantage.

The finished bullet time mode is a ability the player can use one single time. When the player uses this ability a green sphere spawns at the position of the player and grows over the duration of one second to reach its final size. Inside this sphere everything moves in slow motion, which leads to longer reloading times, meaning that every shot should be well considered.

Apart from all normal moving abilities the player can now activate a bullet dodging mode by using an assigned key. Once inside this new movement mode, the player not only walks forward and sideways, but also simultaneously bends his body into the walking direction. As soon as the player presses the assigned key again the movement mode returns to its normal state and the players upper body resets its position.

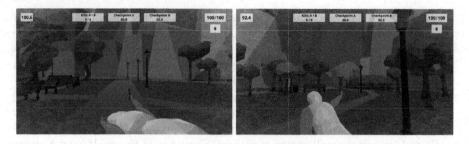

Fig. 1. These pictures illustrate how a player can bend his body.

Fig. 2. The red circle marks the size of the timebubble, the green point a player, the blue circle the size of a checkpoint. (Color figure online)

A timebubble also adds some visual effects to the scene. Bullets, which fly in slow motion inside the bubble, leave a white trail behind. Figure 3 shows this effect. Additionally, the screen looks like its frozen on the edges to further immerse players.

Game Mode. Another question that needs to be answered in the process of creating the game is which game modes should be supported. A single player mode was neither necessary nor doable in a reasonable amount of time, so it was clear from the beginning that this would be a multiplayer only title.

Multiplayer. There are many different ways to create a multiplayer shooter. Some examples would be bomb defusion, deathmatch (with or without teams) and capture the flag. Timbender implements team deathmatch, since both are common modes and most players know these concepts already. To restrain chaos, we decided on the formation of teams of players and added objectives to the game. Teams have to capture checkpoints in order to win. As a result, every player has a clear goal, which is an important aspect [6] in every game.

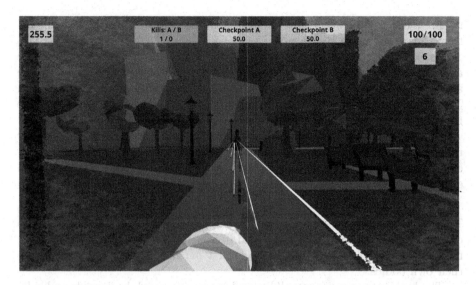

Fig. 3. This picture illustrates how the dodging mode can help to avoid bullets, as well as the visual effects inside a timebubble.

Winning Conditions. Each match ends after a fixed period of time. After the time has passed, the team with the most points wins. Possession of a checkpoint is worth one point. Teams can gain one additional point if they have a higher kill count, meaning that they have eliminated more players than the other team. If both teams have the same point sum the team with the higher kill count wins, if both also have an equal number of kills the team with the highest overall checkpoint value wins. Every checkpoint has a value between zero and one hundred. If the score is above 50 team one owns the checkpoint, if it is below 50 team two owns the checkpoint. The value of each checkpoint changes according to how many players of each team are present in it - for example, if a checkpoint contains two players of team one but only one player of team two, the checkpoint value will rise. If both teams have the same points, kills and checkpoint values the final result of the match is a draw.

3.1 The Player Model

One of the absolutely necessary components of every game is the player, which means that it is always a good idea to start with the creation of a player figure.

Apart from creating the player, there would also have been the alternative of downloading an already made asset from the Unity [13] Asset Store or some other source. On initial thought this saves a lot of time which would have to go into modelling and animating the player. However, this can deceive. The creation of a dodging-mode would require deep changes to the downloaded model, which would necessitate separate animation after all. Furthermore, it would be necessary to understand the details of the downloaded model, which would certainly require a decent amount of time. Hence the authors created a new player model from square one using Blender [2].

As expected, the bullet-dodging mode was more difficult to implement. Basic animations do not suffice here, as a player can move his body freely and there are no fixed moves. Conveniently, Unity [13] offers inverse kinematics support. This enables the developers to provide Unity [13] a bone and a position and the game engine automatically creates a fitting animation.

After the player model was imported the base controlling and shooter mechanics were implemented. Since there already exist many working shooters, most decisions that were made in this phase of development, were based on existing games.

Third Person Movement. Although a first person shooter would be easier to create, Timebender needed to be a third person shooter. The advanced dodging mechanics would not make any sense in first person, as players would not see their own bodies.

The basic movements are walking and running forward, backwards and sideways, along with jumping. Although implementing multiple weapons would be beneficial for Timebender, time did not suffice and as a result, only one basic weapon is available in the game. The authors chose a simple pistol, since this type of weapon can create the most exciting duels inside a timebubble. For example, if one would fire continuously with a machine gun inside a timebubble, it would be almost impossible to dodge incoming bullets.

Reloading and Shooting. A mechanic added late to the game was reloading. At the beginning of development the player did not need to reload the gun, which resulted in the problem that players were firing constantly at each other. This lead to unwanted scenarios, especially inside a timebubble. With the reloading mechanic in place, players have to think before they shoot. A weapon can only hold up to six bullets, meaning every shot counts, as reloading inside a timebubble is very time consuming.

Another element every shooter contains is a crosshair. While many games have a fixed crosshair at the center of the screen, we decided to create a dynamic crosshair, which means the crosshair is shown on top of the object that would be hit. After a certain distance, the crosshair is fixed to the spot, since otherwise it would be to small to spot.

Level Layout. One of the most important aspects of every shooter game in general is the level layout [1,5]. However, although this is very important, the main focus of this paper lies elsewhere. Nevertheless, the authors tried to create a scene where players can use the slow motion abilities in a useful way. There are only two chocking points on the map to increase playability [5], since the level is comprised of two open spaces with one checkpoint in the center of each (cf. Fig. 4).

This also means that there is only one choice the player, or whole team, has to make in the beginning - which checkpoint do they want to reach first? It benefits the game if the players do not have much choice in a multiplayer shooter [5]. After the beginning phase of each game battles mostly take place around the checkpoints.

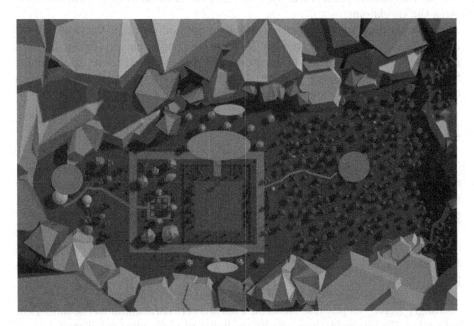

Fig. 4. The basic level layout: The orange spots mark checkpoints, blue spots mark the spawning points and pink spots mark the choking points. (Color figure online)

3.2 Bullet Time

Overview. As already mentioned, bullet time is integrated into the game by the use of timebubbles. A timebubble is a prefab that is spawned by the player. It is composed of a simple transparent sphere, a network identity for network synchronization and a script that handles its behaviour. Objects that can be slowed down must hold a custom script which implements an interface. This interface defines just one method that takes two arguments. One float that holds the factor by which everything slows down and one bool that indicates if slow motion should be activated or deactivated.

Every object that should work with slow motion must implement the interface. Once slow motion is activated, the object entering slow motion decides what to do. This enables developers to easily add slow motion functionality to other objects and change the behaviour for every object individually. For instance, the player controller simply multiplies all internal speed variables with the given float.

Time Sphere Script. The time sphere script manages the size of the timebubble as well as collisions with objects. The Unity [13] Start method, which gets called once at the beginning of a match, calculates all the information that is needed to scale the bubble. The game designer can set scaling time and end size in the editor and the script calculates the rest. Additionally, this script holds the current timebubble point status and can therefore calculate which team currently owns the checkpoint.

When an object enters the timebubble, a method checks if the other object implements the mentioned interface. If it does, the one method from the interface gets called, so that slow motion is either activated or deactivated. Additionally, this script holds all objects that are colliding at any given time, so that it can disable slow motion behaviour once it is destroyed.

4   Evaluation and Discussion

To evaluate if Timebender has met the set goals a user study with eleven participants, who had varying experience with games, was performed. Users played the game for half an hour and then filled out a questionnaire. After filling out they were asked what their main concerns were and what they liked best.

Since this produces qualitative attributes the authors had to use a metric scale for expressing opinion. It was decided to use a likert scale with four possible answers, which is used in nearly all fields research and well suited for this paper [14].

Each item in Table 1 had "Strongly Disagree", "Disagree", "Agree" and "Strongly Agree" as possible answers. This answers correspond to the numerical values 1–4. To interpret these results median and mode were calculated.

4.1   Interpretation of the Results

As you can see the participants agreed to every item, which means Timebender has met the intended goals. The technical execution of Timebender met the set requirements, the mutliplayer mode was as intuitive as planned and bullet time was well integrated into the game. Only the enhancement of gameplay, as well as the enjoyment of the game as a whole were statistically not answered with "strongly agree", but "agree".

This hints that, while the slow motion effect worked great, the shooter itself was not so much fun. This is most likely due to the limited development time. In the interviews that were conducted after playing the game, most players stated that it was too hard to hit enemies and that they felt like the bullets make no damage. Another complaint was that the dynamic crosshair was too small for screens that have a resolution below Full HD and that the contrast between the black crosshair and colorful background was to low. We also noticed during the playtests that player use bullet dodging mode only very rarely. This most likely happens because players are too concentrated and do not realize that they can use bullet dodging mode.

Table 1. This table shows which item corresponds to which goal as well as each median and mode.

Goal	Item	Median	Mode
Create a game that is enjoyable to play	Timebender is fun to play	3	3
	I would recommend Timebender to my friends	3	3
Create a game that uses state of the art technical components	Timebender is an up-to-date game	4	4
	Timebender runs smooth on my computer	4	4
Implement a multiplayer mode that is simple to understand and use	The multiplayer mode in Timebender is easy to understand	4	4
Implement bullet time in a way that makes sense	The bullet time does not feel out of place in Timebender	4	4
Implement a multiplayer mode that contains multiplayer related problems like lag which cause reduced playability	Lag is not noticable or just in an amount that does not downgrade my experience	4	4
Implement bullet time in a way that enhances gameplay	The bullet time improves my experience	3	3
	I like interacting with timebubbles	3	3
Implement bullet time in a way that does not break the gameflow for the players	The bullet time does not disturb me, even if someone else uses it	4	4
Implement bullet time in a way that does not handicap the player initiating it	Other players gain no advantage over me when I use bullet time	4	4

Nevertheless, Timebender has made progress in implementing bullet time in multiplayer. Players are never disturbed by bullet time, like in May Payne 3™ [8]. Additionally, players do not perceive slow motion as something negative, like in TimeShift™ [9] were slow motion appeared in the form of a grenade.

5 Conclusions and Future Work

This paper presented a new way to implement slow motion effects into a multiplayer online shooter. By spawning spheres that grow and alter time bullet time effects are introduced that do not disturb players. With integrating a bullet dodging mode gameplay is enhanced further and new gameplay styles get possible.

Assuming that players do not want a big advantage or disadvantage when using bullet time, the game Timebender did not handicap players when they interact with timebubbles. However, this also reduces the motivation for players to use their slow motion ability.

The implementation of slow motion effects are realized using an interface. This enables developers to quickly change the behaviour of objects individually and add behaviours to new objects.

A conducted user study shows that Timebender has met all goals. However, there is still much potential that is unexhausted. The audiovisual presentation of timebubbles can be improved drastically. Future work should also investigate ways to enhance bullet dodging, so that players are more willing to use such a mode. Without a doubt, the shooter elements of Timebender also could be improved immensely, but since the focus of this project lay on the slow motion effect, this is not as important as the other stated points.

References

1. Almeida, S., Veloso, A., Mealha, Ó., Roque, L., Moura, A.: A video game level analysis model proposal. In: 2012 16th International Conference on Information Visualisation, pp. 474–479, July 2012
2. Blender Foundation: Blender. Software (2015). https://www.blender.org/, version: 2.74
3. Gallacher, N.: Game audio - an investigation into the effect of audio on player immersion. Comput. Games J. **2**(2), 52–79 (2013). https://doi.org/10.1007/BF03392342
4. Gamespot: TimeShift Updated Q&A - Multiplayer. Web page, May 2007. https://www.gamespot.com/articles/timeshift-updated-qanda-multiplayer/1100-6170272/. Accessed 16 June 2017
5. Ølsted, P.T., Ma, B., Risi, S.: Interactive evolution of levels for a competitive multiplayer FPS. In: 2015 IEEE Congress on Evolutionary Computation (CEC), pp. 1527–1534, May 2015
6. Omar, H.M., Jaafar, A.: Heuristics evaluation in computer games. In: 2010 International Conference on Information Retrieval Knowledge Management (CAMP), pp. 188–193, March 2010
7. Ratti, S., Towle, C., Proulx, P., Shirmohammadi, S.: Fizzx: multiplayer time manipulation in networked games. In: 2009 8th Annual Workshop on Network and Systems Support for Games (NetGames), pp. 1–2, November 2009
8. Rockstar Games: Max Payne 3. Software, May 2012. http://www.rockstargames.com/maxpayne3/
9. Saber Interactive: TimeShift. Software, October 2007. http://saber3d.com/portfolio_page/timeshift/
10. SUPERHOT Team: Superhot. Software, February 2016. https://superhotgame.com/
11. Sweetser, P., Johnson, D.: Player-centered game environments: assessing player opinions, experiences, and issues. In: Rauterberg, M. (ed.) ICEC 2004. LNCS, vol. 3166, pp. 321–332. Springer, Heidelberg (2004). https://doi.org/10.1007/978-3-540-28643-1_40
12. The Wachowski Brothers: The Matrix (1999)

13. Unity Technologies: Unity. Software (2016). https://unity3d.com, version: 5.6
14. Yusoff, R., Janor, R.M.: A proposed metric scale for expressing opinion. In: 2012 International Conference on Statistics in Science, Business and Engineering (ICSSBE), pp. 1–6, September 2012

Move, Interact, Learn, Eat – A Toolbox
for Educational Location-Based Games

Leif Oppermann[1]([⊠]), Steffen Schaal[2], Manuela Eisenhardt[2],
Constantin Brosda[1], Heike Müller[3], and Silke Bartsch[3]

[1] Fraunhofer FIT, Schloss Birlinghoven, 53754 Sankt Augustin, Germany
leif.oppermann@fit.fraunhofer.de
[2] PH Ludwigsburg, Reuteallee 46, 71634 Ludwigsburg, Germany
schaal@ph-ludwigsburg.de
[3] PH Karlsruhe, Bismarckstr. 10, 76133 Karlsruhe, Germany
bartsch@ph-karlsruhe.de

Abstract. Educational location-based games provide a link between content
and its real-life relevance in a physical environment. Location-based activities
for authentic learning provide multiple opportunities, but educators still perceive
technological and organisational barriers. There is a need for easy-to-use tools to
facilitate the design of playful location-based mobile learning activities that can
be integrated into larger curriculums. In this project a transdisciplinary team
(educational experts in outdoor education, in nutrition and consumer education,
computer scientists) co-created an online authoring system for location-based
games, the MILE.designer. This authoring system provides several formats of
tasks that can easily be adapted and located intuitively using a simple map
interface. Several tasks can be combined into an educational geogame to be
provided for a native smartphone app, the MILE.explorer. The theoretical
background and the transdisciplinary development process are described, formative and summative evaluation results based on participatory observation and
on focus group discussions are presented and further implications discussed.

Keywords: Educational location-based game · Learning game design model
Online authoring system

1 Introduction

Adolescents today grow up with ubiquitous technology. Their Internet- and GPS-
enabled smartphones are the switchboards of their lifes. They like to play digital games
and spend about 200 min online on a typical weekday [1]. At the same time, they also
grow up in a consumer society and sometimes could know a little bit more about the
origin of our human nutrition and its relation to nature. Dreblow and Schönheit provide a
meta-review of studies about the consumer competency of adolescents [2]. They cite a
study with 3,000 participants aged 11–15, from which only 21% identified and correctly
answered the non-sense question *"which cows do only provide UHT milk"*. The same
group estimated that chicken laid 3.1 eggs a day on average; and only 31% of the
adolescents gave the correct answer to this. Although the authors' reflection highlights

© Springer International Publishing AG, part of Springer Nature 2018
A. D. Cheok et al. (Eds.): ACE 2017, LNCS 10714, pp. 774–794, 2018.
https://doi.org/10.1007/978-3-319-76270-8_53

that such results might say more about the distance between today's agricultural production and its consumers, and less about a specific consumer competency problem, they documented a pressing concern nevertheless. Our research question is derived from this: Can we utilize digital games on smartphones to influence the interest of youngsters about the origin of food?

Using pervasive technology for entertainment and other purposes has been well studied over the past two decades, especially since GPS became publicly available in the year 2000. Benford et al. stated that *"a new generation of entertainment technology takes computer games to the streets – and ultimately beyond"* [3, 4]. The use of mobile technology for applications in education and learning has also been equally well studied, e.g. with the early *Savannah* [5], where children playfully explore through GPS-enabled and networked technology what it is like to be lions that have to survive in the desert, or with Klopfer's broader work on *Augmented Learning* [6].

Most of these projects, especially in the research domain, have been developed by interdisciplinary teams, which is an accepted best practice. Chamberlin et al. [7] present a learning games design model that differentiates three phases of educational games development: pre-development, development, final stages.

1. Pre-development: A consortium of game developers and content experts start together with a broad educational objective before engaging in immersion: game developers learn about the content and the educational implementation, the content experts experience different already existing learning games. Finally, the consortium refines the objectives, prepares design documents and creates prototypes.
2. Development: The prototypes are stepwise improved using a multi-stage formative evaluation circle with the participation of the development consortium and the target users and relevant gatekeepers.
3. Final stages: Summative evaluations are conducted with the final game and a larger audience is involved. The results are used for a final revision of the learning game.

In this paper, the MILE project[1] (move-interact-learn-eat) is presented as an example for a collaborative, transdisciplinary development process that follows the above learning games design model. The resulting MILE toolbox consists of an authoring system combined with a mobile app to facilitate a template-based online creation of mobile, location-based games in the domain of nutrition and consumer sciences for adolescents. First, the domain and its theoretical background are outlined, leading to our own design framework. Then, the system and user experience are described, before the results of a formative study of the authoring system using participatory observation and focus group discussions are described and discussed.

---

[1] MILE is the name of a research project, funded by the Baden-Wuerttemberg State Ministry for Rural Areas and Consumer Protection (MLR). For more information on the project, visit www.mile-bw.de.

2 Related Work

The content for this paper is derived from nutrition and consumer sciences and employs mobile, location-based learning technology. Most young people in Western societies are merely eating as consumers with little knowledge about the origin of their food [8, 9]. But especially the awareness of cultural and natural resources of food production is an important objective of nutrition and consumer education [10, 11] as well as of an education for sustainable development [12]. At the same time, especially young people are intensive users of geo-enabled mobile phones and thus these devices with all their potential applications could be considered as mediators for authentic, location-based learning about food, food production and sustainability.

Mobile devices are personal assistants for most adolescents and adults today [1, 13] and their potential for lifelong, ubiquitous learning is undoubted [10, 14–18]. Beneath offering mobile learning opportunities smartphones allow for location-based learning activities that help to transform a physical space into a personally relevant place [19, 20]. Mobile devices have been successfully used in several domains to support knowledge acquisition [16, 21–24], motivation and interest [21, 25, 26], attitudes and awareness [27, 28] during location-based, authentic learning.

Authentic learning is focused on real-world problems and their solutions, it provides problem-based, collaborative, reflective activities and it is inherently multi-, trans- or interdisciplinary [29, 30]. During mobile, location-based activities learners are guided to different places that are relevant for the topic and that allocate opportunities to interact with the environment. Mobile devices such as smartphones and tablets then offer the place-specific information, they can be used to retain impressions (e.g. audio, photo, video), to share them and thus they allow different ways of direct and indirect communication. Learners are asked to apply this information and knowledge to solve tasks in the field instead of just consuming it [17]. The learners autonomously discover a site supported by an adequately structured mobile learning activity that can be - according to Ryan and Deci [31] - a way to promote self-determination in an educational setting.

Mobile games played on smartphones or tablets are popular amongst adolescents, the American Common Sense Census [13] shows that at least one third of the teens respectively every second tween plays every day. While gaming is mostly done in traditional, non-geo-enabled game designs, the hardware provides sensors that allow for different kinds of experiences. Location-based games, so called "geogames" [32], are played in the physical space and locomotion is part of the activities. Geogames combine location- and game based learning, the players' geographical position is part of the narrative and the game flow [33, 34]. Geogames are conceptually grounded in the theoretical framework of Digital Game-based Learning (DGBL) that combines playing as an active form of entertainment and knowledge acquisition [35–37]. It is intended to captivate the players' attention and to use the game-related enjoyment as a starting point for learning processes or to increase situational interest or topic-related awareness and attitudes [38].

The potential of mobile, location- and game-based learning activities for authentic learning is evident, but (technological) barriers for educational staff still exist [39–41].

Schlieder [32] as well as Pirker et al. [42] point out that general findings from game design research should be part of educational applications for location-based learning and playful learning experiences. This is a challenge for educators, educational designers and computer scientists to be solved collaboratively. On the one hand, several models and frameworks for educational game design already exist [43–47] and most of them highlight the need for transdisciplinary collaboration. On the other hand recent educational game design processes are reported to be difficult due to the experts' different academic background, theoretical foundation and finally to the specific language of the involved disciplines [45, 48].

Most technological barriers when building location-based experiences arise from the fact that the domain experts – in our case educationalists – are no computer scientists. They sense the possibilities offered by the new technology and would like to employ them, but lack all the detailed knowledge about the material of the technology in its early stages. A typical approach to tackle this problem is the use of authoring tools. While early prototype experiences were purpose-built and usually programmed and configured by the same set of people, the need to separate those roles soon arose. One particular approach is that of performance-led research in the wild [49] where artists and human-computer interaction researchers collaboratively designed, deployed and studied such experiences. Here, technological details would be shared amongst all roles, but ultimately solved by the tech experts. When content was configured by the artists/domain experts themselves, specific requirements for the supporting tools became evident with regards to on-location authoring [50] and using wireless positioning technology to pin content to specific locations [51, 52]. Oppermann and Slussareff [53] provide a comprehensive overview of seminal pervasive games, their characteristics and technical components, the underlying authoring concepts, as well as considerations for the design process and a link to learning theories.

Hull et al. [54] presented an early and complete solution for authoring location-based experiences for PDAs. Later work by Wetzel et al. [55] proposed separating these roles even further so as to have three roles: game programmer, game designer, and content contributor. This separation led to the use of content templates (called shapes) for a particular design that had to be filled with data to form a shape-instance called a "marble". This approach intrinsically leads to structured data which can be easily configured through authoring tools also by non-technicians. Resulting experiences spanned from a minimalistic geo-game called "Tidy City" [56], over a game for young families to accompany a touring exhibition about dwarfs [57], to an educational games suite for natural history museums [58]. Previous evidence from these experiences showed that content creators could work with such "scaffolding" tools; one particular writer stated that she "stopped using Word for writing the texts". The MILE toolbox has been built on the same principles.

3 The MILE Project

The MILE (Move-Interact-Learn-Eat) is an interdisciplinary project that aims to develop a research-based online platform and authoring system allowing multipliers and educators to create geogames for adolescents. They act as multipliers out of school to foster nutrition and consumer education with the key objectives focusing a food production and consumer behavior that yields on a deeper understanding of regionally and seasonally grown agricultural products, responsible and sustainable value chains in adolescents' everyday life. The MILE consortium consists of experts in the domain of nutrition and consumer sciences, biology and outdoor education as well as computer scientists. The MILE consortium adapted the learning games design model [7] to the purposes of location-based games considering previous findings related to location-based learning in environmental education [59].

3.1 Design Framework

The theoretical framework for the design of educational location-based games is grounded on an empirical model for environmental competence [60] that relates knowledge and attitudes to the tendency of environmental behavior. The authors conclude that a way to attain pro-environmentally competent people would be to increase knowledge and appreciation for nature (ibid., p. 17). Schaal et al. [38] expanded this model for mobile, location-based games in the context of biodiversity: According to them appreciation might be positively influenced by adding game-related enjoyment as well as situational interest by discovering content in an authentic, location-based game narrative.

The MILE framework was adapted to the demands of the nutrition and consumer science content (see detailed in [61]):

1. Attitudes, food preferences and daily routines are biographically developed factors [62] and they determine to a high extend consumer behaviors. In the MILE framework they are considered as personal prerequisites.
2. System knowledge about i.e. sustainable food production chains, action-related knowledge for responsible consumers' decisions and efficacy knowledge about the consequences of individuals' behavior determine the content of the MILE games.
3. Consumer behavior is considered to depend strongly on situational influences [63]. A first step towards situational interest is to foster situated, authentic learning and to respect psychological basic needs. Both could be facilitated using a mobile, location-based game [9, 64].
4. Enjoyment during the game experience could be a moderator for learning and a key for engagement in serious games [65, 66]. Tamborini et al. [67] describe the game enjoyment depending on the perception of competence and autonomy as well as on social relatedness while playing.

These four areas for the design of mobile, location-based MILE games are challenging and further hints are encountered provided by the computer interface. This fact might put off a relevant proportion of educators in the field setting up their own playful activities for adolescents learning about food and food production. Therefore, the MILE project also provided a five hours workshop format to introduce the MILE tools to the educators and to prepare them for the design of the MILE games. Additionally, a preliminary handbook was provided with a step-by-step description of the design process.

3.2   Experience Description

This experience description follows the ideal form of a guided staging of a MILE mission. Nevertheless, players are also invited to play the game on their own.

The players gather in front of a local café. They have been invited by an educator, who will guide them during the process and assist if needed. The educator informs the players about the day's program and requests them to download the native Android application "MILE.explorer" from the project's portal to their smartphones. Three players are sharing one smartphone and will solve the mission as a team. While downloading the appropriate educator created game they are informed that they will need to walk to different places in the surroundings to solve the tasks and collect points. As soon as the download finishes the multimedia introduction sets the frame for the upcoming mini games and with entering an arbitrary nickname they are ready to go.

On the main screen of the application they see a map with a number of different flags, some are in a nearby park, others are attached to a bakery and a supermarket. They decide to start with the nearest which is the bakery and click on the item, but a pop up tells them to get closer, so they walk in front of the bakery. Now they can open the mini game which asks them a multiple-choice question about the ingredients of a local bread with a photo of it. As this information is listed in the shop-window the player can answer it easily and receive 20 points for the correct answer. Now they proceed with walking and answering the other riddles. After 45 min of playing they have solved the last mini-game and a final screen asks them to come back to the café. They are excited so find out if the others have managed to solve all riddles and walk back.

3.3   System Overview

The MILE system is split into two parts: the MILE.designer for game creation and the MILE.explorer smartphone app for playing the game (see Fig. 1).

Fig. 1. The MILE system includes the MILE.designer for game creation and the MILE.explorer mobile application for playing the location based game

The **MILE.designer** is a web-based content management system especially developed for game design. Multiple educators can work together on one mission as the platform supports cooperative work. It serves the data for the MILE.explorer smartphone app. The educators are guided step by step through the mission creation process, from creating a new mission, adding mini-games, to publishing. The user interface is designed as simple as possible and with well-known features (e.g. numbered tabs for each step of game-design, Google Maps location selection by simple drag-and-drop). Each mission consists of an arbitrary series of mini-games. MILE missions follow a location-based seek'n'find game mechanics similar to a scavenger hunt. Ten different templates for location-based tasks are defined:

- Single-choice and multiple-choice quizzes
- GPS-single-choice quiz: the possible solutions are geo-referenced and to select a solution the player must go to this place
- Matching and sorting tasks for texts or images
- Free-text tasks
- Number estimation tasks
- Find-place-tasks: picking-up a riddle and finding a specific place which is not indicated on the game map
- Speeding task: after arriving at the task position, another point has to be reached in a given time

In addition to these mini games an introduction and ending can be edited. This sets up the frame for the mission and storytelling that allows the use of media as well. Creating a mini-game includes editing the question and answers depending on the type, assigning a circular geo fence using a map-editing tool to define the location and entering the number of associated points. The educator can choose to either use written text, images, audio or video to ask questions or give advices per mini-game. For the purpose of testing, the mission state can be set to test mode, in which it is only accessible for the educators. If the educator has finished editing and testing the mission it is added to the public directory of MILE games for the MILE.explorer.

The **MILE.explorer** is an Android smartphone App for playing the games created with the MILE.designer. Once downloaded from the official website, the user can browse through the list of published missions in the directory and download them one by one. These missions are classified by the pedagogical administrators of the MILE to allow easy access to full featured and tested missions. After downloading, the mission can be played offline so as to stage missions in remote areas. An e-mail registration is not required for users. They can start playing simply by choosing a nickname. After the introduction has been shown to the user, the main map becomes visible. The current position as well as all available mini-games are drawn as icons on the map. If the MILE.explorer is used with an active mobile network connection and the user opt-in, the educator can login in and see the live progress of their players during the current session with the number of mini-games played and their positions. The educator can then send messages to assist users even during the mission if needed.

4   Study

Stemming from design-based research [68–71], the general objective for the design of MILE games is twofold:

- On the one hand the MILE games should provide playful activities for adolescents to discover different food- and consume-related problems immediately in an authentic context and in an everyday life setting (e.g. food waste: what happens with unsold bread in the local bakeries - an interactive treasure hunt!). Therefore, the design process focuses on criteria for the creation of MILE games including adequately structured educational, location-based tasks at every distinct position.
- On the other hand, the MILE authoring system, the so-called MILE.Designer, should be an easy-to-use web-based interface that allows educators and multipliers to create intuitively location-based games for smartphones (see Fig. 1).

Consequently, the aims of this study target three elements of an educational design process acknowledging Chamberlin et al.'s learning games design model [13]:

- Identification of the tools' and systems' requirements respecting transdisciplinary assets from educators' and developers' perspectives (Sect. 4.1)
- Usability and goal-oriented design of MILE games: To what extend educators and multipliers are able to design MILE.Missions adequately with the provided authoring tools (Sect. 4.2)?
- The adolescents' perspective and summative evaluation: How do the players profit from playing a MILE.Mission in the context of nutrition and consumer science (Sect. 4.3)?

4.1   Iterative Development

This section describes the transdisciplinary design process, the development of the MILE authoring system.

Educator-Developer Workshops

Based on previous work [61] the educational experts identified the objectives and described the theoretical framework for the MILE project (outlined in the section above). The content fosters the adolescents' awareness of local food and food production, the educational methodology focuses on research for the creation of location-based learning tasks [59] and specific requirements are formulated. These were discussed with the computer scientist and the results were fixed in a requirements review (see Tables 1 and 2 for a summary).

Table 1. Requirements for the online authoring system for educators.

MILE.Designer
• Individual log-in
• Usability for step-by-step design process support
• Identification of points of interest and drag&drop-functionality to flag them in digital map
• Selection of different template-based task formats
• Upload of video, image, audio and text for the complete game and for each task to provide a game narrative

Table 2. Requirements for the mobile app for players.

MILE.Explorer
• Players select a MILE game and download it, all data are stored in the MILE app
• Player chose a nickname and either start a new game or continue an already existing one
• After starting the game, the game narrative and the rules are presented before presenting the game map with the players' recent GPS-position and with all task locations
• A task can be accomplished if the player reaches the specific location
• Every location-specific task is introduced (via video, audio, text and/or image), after the solution the player receives immediately a feedback and the rewards (e.g. points)
• After the player has finished all tasks a game narrative closes the game session and the sum of points are sent to the MILE platform to rank the result

It was also required that educators get extra information to support their supervision and coordination roles. They get real-time positions of players during a session (if mobile data is enabled) and can send text-messages to all players, e.g. for calling them back to the meeting point.

Usability Workshops with Target Users (Educators and Multipliers)
This section is dedicated to the usability of the authoring system and goal-oriented design of MILE games together with the educators and multipliers as target users. The first version of the MILE tools (MILE Designer and MILE app) was set up in March 2015. The formative evaluation was conducted in a three-step-procedure:

1. The first trials were set up in an educator-developer-team to assure a general functionality of the MILE Designer (iteration step I). The first MILE games were created collaboratively and field-tested. The educator-developer team consisted of two full professors (nutrition/home economics and nutrition- and consumer education, biology and biology education) and one graduated nutritional scientist from two universities of education, one computer scientist (group leader mixed and augmented reality) and two graduated developers from the same team. Furthermore, a target group representative (nutrition science educator) was involved at this first stage of development.
2. The MILE tools were revised and in early May 2015 the MILE tools were implemented into a focus group workshop and a moderate participant observation according to Kawulich [72] (iteration step II). The focus group was formed of six educational and computer science experts, four educators/multipliers in the field of nutrition science and four pre-service teacher students. Parts of the MILE consortium moderated the focus group workshop, the educational researchers within the consortium observed and documented the process. The results were used for the next iteration of the MILE tools.
3. End of May and June 2015 two workshops for educational multipliers and pre-service-teachers (N = 40) lead to further implications for the (a) format of introduction to the MILE tools and for the design of a (b) final version of the MILE tools (iteration step III).

In the focus group workshop (iteration step II) two procedures were used:

1. Think-pair-share: The participants (N = 14, see above) played a pre-defined MILE game and afterwards they created their own games in pairs with the MILE designer. Then the participants were asked to think about (a) the usability of the MILE app and the MILE designer, (b) the automated support during playing and during setting up the MILE game and (c) the support by the templates for location-based activities. The individual results were discussed in pairs, noted and finally shared in the focus group.
2. Structured, open-ended questions: Every participant was asked to give a written feed-back about (a) the game design, (b) the MILE game operation system, (c) the display and screen design of the MILE game, (d) the GPS services.

The workshop participants gave a structured feedback about (a) technological purposes of the MILE tools, (b) the usability of the tools and about (c) game-experience related perceptions.

The results of the focus group discussions and the open questionnaires (iteration step II) are outlined in Tables 3 and 4. The suggestions were used for a revision of the MILE tools, especially the game introduction via video improved the game flow. Furthermore, balancing the accuracy of GPS positioning and the battery runtime was a task for the developers. Despite of the preview mode all revisions were realized for the second iteration of the MILE tools.

Table 3. Feedback on game design in the mobile app MILE.Explorer from focus group participants (N = 14) in May 2015 (iteration step II).

Tool or field	Description
Game flow	• Seek'n'find game mechanics are highly appreciated • Combination of mobile game and location-based task is perceived to be fruitful and engaging • Different location-based tasks contribute to game enjoyment • Gratification by collecting points increases enjoyment, time constraints decrease engagement in location-based tasks • Narrative is important for game flow, video at the beginning and the end of the game are recommended
Functionality/usability	• Intuitive screen interface • Google maps and the landmarks are known from other activities • Positioning on the map and sensibility of the GPS function have to be improved • High differences of the reliability of the GPS positioning depending on devices • Help/support function is needed • Technical breakdowns
Location-based task	• Different formats of activities and engagement increase enjoyment • Explanation in text combined with audio/video is highly appreciated, but in (some) tasks has to be improved • Open text questions are interesting, but difficult to fill out correctly • Some tasks provide immediate feedback, should be given for every task • Landmarks partially overlap the map and hinder orientation

Table 4. Feedback on MILE.Designer from focus group participants (N = 14) in May 2015 (iteration step II).

Tool or field	Description
Functionality/usability	• Step-by-step and template-based design are highly appreciated is → design process comprehensible and goal-oriented also for inexperienced users • Usability of the MILE designer interface is easy-to-use • Developers' terms are sometimes not familiar to educators and should be explained or adapted • Pre-positioning of the single tasks' template landmarks should be not the same • Interactive preview mode in the MILE designer is needed
Educational use	• MILE designer allows the design of games suitable for formal and informal educational purposes • Design process could be also used for peer-to-peer activities

The subsequent workshops with educational multipliers and pre-service teachers showed that most of the technical purposes were revised successfully. Some complaints occurred considering the accuracy of the GPS positioning which differed dramatically between different devices. Thus it was recommended to use a diameter of the landmark of at least 20 m and to highlight in the educators' workshops for the prerequisites to reach adequate GPS accuracy. Furthermore it was highlighted to thoroughly pay attention to the explanation of the game mechanics, of the tasks and the gratification in the game as well as to identify relevant narratives specifically for the target group. The narrative and the rules, in the given examples, were highlighted to be clear and motivating. According to the German grading system (1 best, 6 worst grading) the participants graded the MILE tools as good (grade 1,96).

Central feedback of the workshop participants was that they enjoyed – again – the combination of tasks in the "real environment" and mobile gaming. The game narrative and the location-based tasks were perceived to be engaging and suitable for playful learning. They praised the easy-to-use of the MILE tools and highlighted the MILE games for the following educational activities: (i) perfect way for informal learning for adolescents, (ii) fits location-based activities in several domains, (iii) combines nutrition and physical activity in an ideal way.

4.2   Designing MILE Games – Development Phase

This section is dedicated to the analysis of MILE games designed by nutrition and consumer science educators, multipliers and pre-service teacher students. During the first development phase, 51 MILE games were designed covering various topics in the field of nutrition education, examples are displayed in Table 5.

Table 5. Examples of MILE games designed during the development phase

Game	Description
Luigi lost his ice cream recipe	Players discover prerequisites and quality criterions for artisanal icecream at different places at the city
Message from the earth	Players explore different places in a city offering sustainable, regional and seasonal food
The bread code	Players inquire the food production chain from crop to bread. The game mimics Dan Browns's "Da Vinci Code"

Table 6. Grade of location-awareness in a marble [73]

Grade	Description
0 – no location awareness	The marble could be solved in any other location. There is no interaction between the players and the location
1 – limited location-awareness	The location offers additional information on-site. The information could help the players to solve the marble, but is not specific for the site. There is limited interaction between the players and the location
2 – essential location-awareness	On-site examination of the location is essential for completing the marble, as the location provides critical information. Interaction between the players and the location is essential
3 – exclusive location-awareness	The location is the exclusive information necessary to solve the marble

Every game consists of several location-based tasks, so-called marbles, which were analyzed as single elements. Bartsch et al. [73] and Brosda et al. [74] identified the grade of location awareness (Table 6) and the use of audio (Table 7) as quality indicators for marbles as location-based tasks.

Table 7. Use of audio in a marble [74]

Purpose of audio	Description
Redundancy	Audio gives redundant information also provided as written text in the smartphone screen
Enrichment	Audio gives information not provided in the written text as enrichment
Complementarity	Audio gives complementary information to avoid split-attention effects and directs attention away from the screen to the environment

The results of both studies highlighted that although the educators, multipliers and teacher students had at least a one-day workshop to introduce them to the design of MILE games, their marbles met the requirements for fruitful location-based learning only to a marginal degree: The analysis revealed that only 3% respectively 26% of the marbles (out of N = 290) met grade 3 and 2 of location-awareness, only 11% (out of N = 257) marbles provided audio adequately. This could indicate that the technological affordances of designing MILE games are probably not the main concern anymore. It seems that much rather the educational requirements for successful experiential location-based learning are the crucial factors for the educators.

4.3   Implementation and Summative Evaluation

This section describes the results of the implementation phase of three selected MILE games with adolescent players in a school setting. The educator-developer-team selected three of the MILE games and revised the marbles if needed to provide best practice examples.

Sample and Methodology
110 secondary school students aged 12.5 ± 1.2 years (mean ± standard deviation) played one of the three MILE games during a field trip learning experience. In average a MILE game took 56 ± 5.8 min. A questionnaire and a digital concept mapping assessment were provided before and immediately after the MILE game within a pre-post-test-design (measures see Table 8).

Table 8. Measures in pre-post-test (scales based on [38])

Pretest	Posttest
Knowledge about sustainable, regional and seasonal food [75] Concept mapping assessment tool for smartphones: 6 terms and 5 relations Analysis of correspondence related to an expert concept map	
General interest in topics of nutrition and consumer science (6 items, Cronbachs α = .88) based on self-determination theory [31, 76]	**Situational interest in topics of nutrition and consumer science offered in the MILE games** (6 items, Cronbachs α = .89)
Nutrition- and consume-related attitudes and behavior (14 items, Cronbachs α = .86)	**Game-related enjoyment** (9 items, Cronbachs α = .89)
Socio-economic status, frequency of smartphone use, gender, school type, grades in maths and language	**Grading of the game experience according to the German school marks** (1 = brilliant, 6 = game failed)

5   Results

Grading of the Game Experience
Two thirds of the players graded the game experience as good or brilliant, the average school mark for the whole cohort was 2.50 ± 1.2. The grading of the three MILE games differed significantly (from grade 2.2 to 3.1, ANOVA $df = 2, F = 6.4, p < .005$) The MILE game "Message from the earth" was the best graded (grade 2.2 ± 1.1), dealing with food and consume-related sustainability issues. The MILE games were significantly better graded by students of high-stratification school (German *Gymnasium*, ANOVA $df = 2, F = 5.5, p < .005$) without any age or gender effect. Also the socio-economic status did not affect the grading of the MILE games (Table 9).

Table 9. Pearson correlation, two-sided (*p < .05, **p < .005, ***p < .001)

	Attitudes/behavior	Situational interest	Game enjoyment	Pre	Knowledge post	Gain
General interest	−.544***	.551***	.191*			
Attitudes/behavior		−.278**				
Situational interest			.615***			
Game enjoyment						
Pre knowledge					.266**	−.537***
Post knowledge						.671***

Relationships and Influencing Factors

The relationship between the variables and the influencing factors were first analyzed using a Pearson correlation matrix before conducting regression analyses.

The higher the general nutrition- and consumer-related attitudes and behavior was, the lower the players rated their general interest in nutrition and consumer topics before playing a MILE game. This means that those who do not have adequate attitudes and behaviors are strongly interested in playing a MILE game dealing with topics of nutrition and consumer sciences.

The pre-knowledge was, as often in educational studies, correlated to the post knowledge but the negative correlation between the pre knowledge and the knowledge gain was remarkable: Players starting with a low nutrition- and consumer-related knowledge profited most from playing a MILE game.

These correlations were used to be integrated into a regression model to reveal influencing factors (see Fig. 2). The regression analyses showed that the knowledge gain, as supposed within the correlations, was highest for those players who started before the MILE game with a low prior knowledge as well as with disadvantageous nutrition- and consume-related attitudes and a lower general interest in nutrition and consumer education topics.

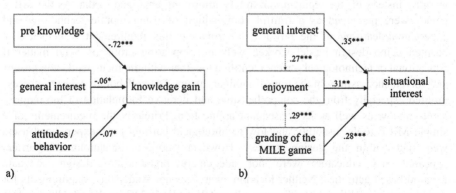

Fig. 2. Regression models (a) knowledge, (b) situational interest (β weights on the arrows, (*p < .05, **p < .005, ***p < .001)

As one goal of the MILE games is to increase situational interest in nutrition- and consume-related topics, it was an important dependent variable. Situational interest depends directly on the grading of the MILE game and on the general interest in nutrition and consumer topics. Furthermore, both variables moderate the game-related enjoyment which is also strongly influencing the situational interest. Therefore, increasing situational interest could be reached when providing playful and enjoyable activities like realized within the MILE games.

6   Discussion

Following the three-step model for educational games design, the results of the formative evaluation process indicated a successive improvement of the MILE tools and a high acceptance of the location-based games postulated by the educational multipliers in nutrition and consumer education.

The analysis of the implementation phase and the summative evaluation revealed that the adolescent players rated the MILE game experience positively, knowledge increased and situational interest rose successfully. Especially adolescents who were generally interested in nutrition topics with low prior knowledge were successfully addressed through the MILE games. This is an important finding, because the MILE games lasted just for more or less one hour, locomotion from one to another location took most of that time and therefore time-on-task was quite low. Nevertheless the players were strongly engaged in the MILE games and they significantly profited from the tasks provided during the games. This is in line with Iten and Petko's [77] conclusion that serious games should rather be engaging than just being fun. The participants' feedback from the focus group and the workshops showed that this requirement was already met and the last step of the learning game design model – the summative evaluation – points towards reaching that claim. In future research it would be important to include the MILE games in a comprehensive learning arrangement offering a preparatory phase as well as a classroom activity to get data about long-term effects and to compare it to educational settings without location-based games.

Anderson [78] highlights that educational technology should somehow transform learning instead of just replacing or simply improving analogue media. As the MILE games were perceived as a fruitful combination of using mobile technology and experiential learning in the physical environment this requirement was met. The adapted game design model worked well and appearing problems – no matter if educational or technological – were identified together with the focus/workshop groups and solved successfully in the transdisciplinary team. The collaborative design process profited especially from the comprehensible and iterative formulation of the requirements review as well as its consequent application. Primarily the requirements of a simple MILE tools' usability and low technological barriers for inexperienced users were met within the design process. However, more non-technological barriers appeared and educators were not adequately prepared to design adequate location-based activities: Neither location-awareness nor Anderson's requirements for digital medias' additional benefit were adequately addressed. Even though all educators and multipliers received at least a five hours workshop to experience a MILE game and to use the MILE tools, the educational benefit of well-designed location-based games was marginally realized. Therefore a stronger emphasis is needed not only on the technological part of MILE games but also on the educators' digital 21st century skills development [79, 80]. To better support the educators in creating MILE missions, a tutorial-style handbook [81] has since been published.

Grounded on the design based research approach the findings are specific for the design process of the MILE tools, they thus have to be interpreted carefully and their transferability might be limited [82]. But describing the general design process might notably help educators in other domains to set up location-based games efficiently and supports them in endeavours appearing during the design process [83].

7   Conclusion

Using location-based games might be a way to reach adolescents with a low degree of awareness about nutrition- and consumer-science education topics. The MILE project provides evidence – as a result of an in-tense educational design research process – that the MILE tools adequately address educators needs to design these games focusing on educational needs rather than on technological challenges. A further iteration step focuses on educators' skills development. On the one hand this has already been realized by the revision of the MILE handbook and by providing explanatory videos for the educational affordances designing MILE games. On the other hand the preparatory workshops for educators have to be modified to foster more intensively the educational rather than the technological aspects when designing location-based games for nutrition and consumer education.

Overall, we believe that our main hypothesis can be confirmed in that we can use digital games on smartphones to address and influence the interest of adolescents about the origin of food. Smartphones are of central importance for (not only) young people's media consumption today. Giving educators and multipliers the tools to reach them on this channel seems like the way forward. But it also has to be noted that this is mainly to answer the shifted media consumption patterns, and not to close an often cited, alleged gap between so-called "digital natives" and "digital naives". Nature magazine's July 2017 editorial headlined that "The digital native is a myth" [84], citing a recent work by Kirschner and Bruyckere [85] and a report by Jones and Shao [86]. Hence, it will be interesting to see how our approach to authoring educational location-based games will continue to work in practice and maybe even grow beyond its original region. Furthermore, as our study was limited to an initial use of location-based games, future research should also focus on long-term effects on learning and on the development of attitudes. We also believe that much work in the larger educational domain remains to be done and hope that future projects will pick up on our approach to integrating smartphone technology into curriculums. Therefore, the MILE tools are publicly available free of charge for educational purposes and we hope that other researchers and educators will use them for their future work.

Acknowledgments. We are grateful to all participating educators, students and educational multipliers participating in this study. Thanks must go to Andreas Taske for implementing the Android app and for tech support. Special thanks go to Lena Lapschansky for supporting this study and for collaboration in the research project. The project is funded by the Baden-Wuerttemberg State Ministry for Rural Areas and Consumer Protection (MLR) within the grant "Jugendliche und digitale Medien" from 12/2012–11/2016.

References

1. MPFS, JIM-Studie: Jugend, Information, (Multi-) Media. Basisstudie zum Medienumgang 12-bis 19-Jähriger in Deutschland. Medienpädagogischer Forschungsverbund Südwest, Stuttgart (2016)
2. Dreblow, M., Schönheit, I.: Konsumkompetenz von Jugendlichen. Ein Überblick über Kernaussagen aus aktuellen Jugendstudien. Verbraucherzentrale Bundesverband e. V. (vzbv), Berlin (2010)
3. Benford, S., Magerkurth, C., Ljungstrand, P.: Bridging the physical and digital in pervasive gaming. Commun. ACM **48**(3), 54–57 (2005)
4. Montola, M., Stenros, J., Waern, A.: Pervasive Games: Theory and Design. Morgan Kaufmann, San Francisco (2009)
5. Facer, K., Joiner, R., Stanton, D., Reid, J., Hull, R., Kirk, D.: Savannah: mobile gaming and learning? J. Comput. Assist. Learn. **20**(6), 399–409 (2004)
6. Klopfer, E.: Augmented Learning: Research and Design of Mobile Educational Games. MIT Press, Cambridge (2011)
7. Chamberlin, B., Trespalacios, J., Gallagher, R.: Bridging research and game development: a learning games design model. Educ. Technol. Use Des. Improv. Learn. Oppor. 151–171 (2014)
8. Bartsch, S.: Jugendesskultur: Bedeutungen des Essens für Jugendliche im Kontext Familie und Peergroup. In: Bundeszentrale für gesundheitliche Aufklärung (BZgA) (Hrsg.), Reihe Forschung und Praxis der Gesundheitsförderung, Köln, vol. 30 (2008)
9. Erhel, S., Jamet, E.: Digital game-based learning: impact of instructions and feedback on motivation and learning effectiveness. Comput. Educ. **67**, 156–167 (2013)
10. Hsiao, H.-S., Lin, C.-C., Feng, R.-T., Li, K.J.: Location based services for outdoor ecological learning system: design and implementation. Educ. Technol. Soc. **13**(4), 98–111 (2010)
11. Bartsch, S.: Subjektive Theorien von Studierenden zur Nachhaltigen Ernährung. Explorationsstudie. HiBiFo–Haushalt Bild. Forsch. **4**(4), 78–92 (2015)
12. Lucas, P.L., Kok, M.T., Nilsson, M., Alkemade, R.: Integrating biodiversity and ecosystem services in the post-2015 development agenda: goal structure, target areas and means of implementation. Sustainability **6**(1), 193–216 (2013)
13. Rideout, V., Pai, S., Saphir, M.: The Common Sense Census: Media Use by Tweens and Teens (2015)
14. Specht, M., Ebner, M., Löcker, C.: Mobiles und ubiquitäres lernen-technologien und didaktische aspekte. Lehrb. Für Lern. Lehren Mit Technol. (2013)
15. Brown, E.: Introduction to location-based mobile learning. Learning Sciences Research Institute, University of Nottingham (2010)
16. Pachler, N., Bachmair, B., Cook, J.: Mobile Learning: Structures, Agency. Practices. Springer, London (2009). https://doi.org/10.1007/978-1-4419-0585-7

17. Frohberg, D., Göth, C., Schwabe, G.: Mobile learning projects–a critical analysis of the state of the art. J. Comput. Assist. Learn. **25**(4), 307–331 (2009)
18. Clough, G., Jones, A.C., McAndrew, P., Scanlon, E.: Informal learning with PDAs and smartphones. J. Comput. Assist. Learn. **24**(5), 359–371 (2008)
19. Harrison, S., Dourish, P.: Re-Place-ing space: the roles of place and space in collaborative systems. In: CSCW, Boston (1996)
20. Dourish, P.: Re-space-ing place: place and space ten years on. In: Proceedings of the 2006 20th Anniversary Conference on Computer Supported Cooperative Work, pp. 299–308 (2006)
21. Ruchter, M., Klar, B., Geiger, W.: Comparing the effects of mobile computers and traditional approaches in environmental education. Comput. Educ. **54**(4), 1054–1067 (2010)
22. Chang, C.-S., Chen, T.-S., Hsu, W.-H.: The study on integrating WebQuest with mobile learning for environmental education. Comput. Educ. **57**(1), 1228–1239 (2011)
23. Huang, W.-H., Huang, W.-Y., Tschopp, J.: Sustaining iterative game playing processes in DGBL: the relationship between motivational processing and outcome processing. Comput. Educ. **55**(2), 789–797 (2010)
24. Shih, J.-L., Chuang, C.-W., Hwang, G.-J.: An inquiry-based mobile learning approach to enhancing social science learning effectiveness. J. Educ. Technol. Soc. **13**(4), 50–60 (2010)
25. Heimonen, T., et al.: Seek'N'Share: a platform for location-based collaborative mobile learning. In: Proceedings of the 12th International Conference on Mobile and Ubiquitous Multimedia, p. 38 (2013)
26. Lai, C.-H., Yang, J.-C., Chen, F.-C., Ho, C.-W., Chan, T.-W.: Affordances of mobile technologies for experiential learning: the interplay of technology and pedagogical practices. J. Comput. Assist. Learn. **23**(4), 326–337 (2007)
27. Uzunboylu, H., Cavus, N., Ercag, E.: Using mobile learning to increase environmental awareness. Comput. Educ. **52**(2), 381–389 (2009)
28. Schaal, S., Grübmeyer, S., Matt, M.: Outdoors and online-inquiry with mobile devices in preservice science teacher education. World J. Educ. Technol. **4**(2), 113–125 (2012)
29. Lave, J., Wenger, E.: Situated Learning: Legitimate Peripheral Participation. Cambridge University Press, Cambridge (1991)
30. Vanderbilt, C.: Anchored instruction and situated cognition revisited. Educ. Technol. **33**(3), 52–70 (1993)
31. Ryan, R.M., Deci, E.L.: Self-determination theory and the facilitation of intrinsic motivation, social development, and well-being. Am. Psychol. **55**(1), 68–78 (2000)
32. Schlieder, C.: Geogames–Gestaltungsaufgaben und geoinformatische Lösungsansätze. Inform.-Spektrum **37**(6), 567–574 (2014)
33. von Borries, F., Walz, S.P., Böttger, M.: Space Time Play. Birkhäuser, Basel (2007)
34. de Souza e Silva, A., Sutko, D.M.: Digital Cityscapes: Merging Digital and Urban Playspaces. Peter Lang, New York (2009)
35. Hamari, J., Keronen, L., Alha, K.: Why do people play games? A review of studies on adoption and use. In: 48th Hawaii International Conference on System Sciences (HICSS), pp. 3559–3568 (2015)
36. Kerres, M., Bormann, M.: Explizites Lernen in Serious Games: Zur Einbettung von Lernaufgaben in digitalen Spielwelten. Z. Für E-Learn. **4**, 23–34 (2009)
37. Prensky, M.: Digital Game-Based Learning, Paragon House edn. Paragon House Publication, St. Paul (2008)
38. Schaal, S., Schaal, S., Lude, A.: Digital Geogames to foster local biodiversity. Int. J. Transform. Res. **2**(2), 16–29 (2015)

39. Marfisi-Schottman, I., George, S.: Supporting teachers to design and use mobile collaborative learning games. In: International Conference on Mobile Learning, pp. 3–10 (2014)

40. Ketelhut, D.J., Schifter, C.C.: Teachers and game-based learning: improving understanding of how to increase efficacy of adoption. Comput. Educ. **56**(2), 539–546 (2011)

41. Wright, S., Parchoma, G.: Technologies for learning? An actor-network theory critique of 'affordances' in research on mobile learning. Res. Learn. Technol. **19**(3), 247–258 (2011)

42. Pirker, J., Gütl, C., Weiner, P., Garcia-Barrios, V.M., Tomintz, M.: Location-based mobile application creator creating educational mobile scavenger hunts. In: 2014 International Conference on Interactive Mobile Communication Technologies and Learning (IMCL), pp. 160–164 (2014)

43. Chamberlin, B., Trespalacios, J., Gallagher, R.: The learning games design model: immersion, collaboration, and outcomes-driven development. Int. J. Game Based Learn. (IJGBL) **2**(3), 87–110 (2012)

44. Ardito, C., Sintoris, C., Raptis, D., Yiannoutsou, N., Avouris, N., Costabile, M.F.: Design guidelines for location-based mobile games for learning. In: International Conference on Social Applications for Lifelong Learning, pp. 96–100 (2010)

45. Hirumi, A., Appelman, B., Rieber, L., Eck, R.V.: Preparing instructional designers for game-based learning: Part III. Game design as a collaborative process. TechTrends **54**(5), 38–45 (2010)

46. Baggetun, R.: MOTEL: a mobile learning framework for geo-tagging and explorations of sites for learning. Res. Pract. Technol. Enhanc. Learn. **4**(01), 83–107 (2009)

47. McMahon, M., Ojeda, C.: A model of immersion to guide the design of serious games. In: E-learn: World Conference on E-learning in Corporate, Government, Healthcare, and Higher Education, pp. 1833–1842 (2008)

48. Kirkley, J., Kirkley, S., Heneghan, J.: Building bridges between serious game design and instructional design. Des. Use Simul. Comput. Games Educ. **2**, 74 (2007)

49. Benford, S., et al.: Performance-led research in the wild. ACM Trans. Comput. Hum. Interact. **20**(3), 14:1–14:22 (2013)

50. Weal, M.J., et al.: Requirements for in-situ authoring of location based experiences. In: MobileHCI, Helsinki (2006)

51. Oppermann, L., Koleva, B., Benford, S., Jacobs, R., Watkins, M.: Fighting with jelly: user-centered development of a wireless infrastructure visualization tool for authoring location-aware experiences. In: Advances in Computer Entertainment Technology (ACE), Yokohama, pp. 322–329 (2008)

52. Oppermann, L., Broll, G., Capra, M., Benford, S.: Extending authoring tools for location-aware applications with an infrastructure visualization layer. In: Dourish, P., Friday, A. (eds.) UbiComp 2006. LNCS, vol. 4206, pp. 52–68. Springer, Heidelberg (2006). https://doi.org/10.1007/11853565_4

53. Oppermann, L., Slussareff, M.: Pervasive games. In: Dörner, R., Göbel, S., Kickmeier-Rust, M., Masuch, M., Zweig, K. (eds.) Entertainment Computing and Serious Games. LNCS, vol. 9970, pp. 475–520. Springer, Cham (2016). https://doi.org/10.1007/978-3-319-46152-6_18

54. Hull, R., Clayton, B., Melamed, T.: Rapid authoring of mediascapes. In: Davies, N., Mynatt, E.D., Siio, I. (eds.) UbiComp 2004. LNCS, vol. 3205, pp. 125–142. Springer, Heidelberg (2004). https://doi.org/10.1007/978-3-540-30119-6_8

55. Wetzel, R., Blum, L., Jurgelionis, A., Oppermann, L.: Shapes, marbles and pebbles: template-based content creation for location-based games. In: IADIS International Conference Game and Entertainment Technologies, Lisbon (2012)

56. Wetzel, R., Blum, L., Feng, F., Oppermann, L., Straeubig, M.: Tidy city: a location-based game for city exploration based on usercreated content. In: Mensch & Computer, Chemnitz, pp. 487–496 (2011)

57. Schröder, T.: Zwergenwelten. Fraunhofer-Mag. 4, 32–34 (2013)

58. Rojas, S.L., Oppermann, L., Blum, L., Wolpers, M.: Natural Europe educational games suite: using structured museum-data for creating mobile educational games. In: Proceedings of the 11th Conference on Advances in Computer Entertainment Technology, Funchal, pp. 6:1–6:6 (2014)

59. Schaal, S., Lude, A.: Using mobile devices in environmental education and education for sustainable development—comparing theory and practice in a nation wide survey. Sustainability 7(8), 10153–10170 (2015)

60. Roczen, N., Kaiser, F.G., Bogner, F.X., Wilson, M.: A competence model for environmental education. Environ. Behav. 46(8), 972–992 (2014)

61. Schaal, S., Bartsch, S.: Jugend im Web 2.0 - Spielorientiertes Lern- und Informationsangebot zur Herkunft unserer Nahrung im Projekt MILE. In: Dr.-Rainer-Wild-Stiftung (Hg.), Jugend und Ernährung - zwischen Fremd- und Selbstbestimmung, Heidelberg, pp. 147–164 (2015)

62. Bartsch, S., Methfessel, B.: Der subjektive Faktor. Bild. Einem Leb. Fach Haushalt Bild. Forsch. 3, 3–32 (2014)

63. Foxall, G.R., Yani-de-Soriano, M.M.: Situational influences on consumers' attitudes and behavior. J. Bus. Res. 58(4), 518–525 (2005)

64. Li, M.-C., Tsai, C.-C.: Game-based learning in science education: a review of relevant research. J. Sci. Educ. Technol. 22(6), 877–898 (2013)

65. Allen, L.K., Crossley, S.A., Snow, E.L., McNamara, D.S.: L2 writing practice: game enjoyment as a key to engagement. Lang. Learn. Technol. 18(2), 124–150 (2014)

66. Ke, F.: A qualitative meta-analysis of computer games as learning tools. Handb. Res. Eff. Electron. Gaming Educ. 1, 1–32 (2009)

67. Tamborini, R., Bowman, N.D., Eden, A., Grizzard, M., Organ, A.: Defining media enjoyment as the satisfaction of intrinsic needs. J. Commun. 60(4), 758–777 (2010)

68. Collins, A.: Toward a design science of education. In: Scanlon, E., O'Shea, T. (eds.) New Directions in Educational Technology. NATO ASI Series (Series F: Computer and Systems Sciences), vol. 96, pp. 15–22. Springer, Heidelberg (1992). https://doi.org/10.1007/978-3-642-77750-9_2

69. Design-Based Research Collective: Design-based research: an emerging paradigm for educational inquiry. Educ. Res. 5–8 (2003)

70. Barab, S., Squire, K.: Design-based research: putting a stake in the ground. J. Learn. Sci. 13(1), 1–14 (2004)

71. McKenney, S.: Conducting Educational Design Research. Routledge, New York (2012)

72. Kawulich, B.B.: Participant observation as a data collection method. In: Forum Qualitative Sozialforschung/Forum: Qualitative Social Research, vol. 6 (2005)

73. Bartsch, S., Müller, H., Oppermann, L., Schaal, S.: Using smartphones for tracing local food – location-based games on mobile devices in consumer and nutrition education. In: Bartsch, S., Lysaght, P. (eds.) Places of Food Production. Origin, Identity, Imagination, Frankfurt am Main, pp. 235–249 (2017)

74. Brosda, C., Bartsch, S., Oppermann, L., Schaal, S.: On the use of audio in the educational location based game platform MILE. In: Proceedings of the 18th International Conference on Human-Computer Interaction with Mobile Devices and Services Adjunct, Florence, pp. 1049–1054 (2016)

75. Schaal, S., Bogner, F.X., Girwidz, R.: Concept mapping assessment of media assisted learning in interdisciplinary science education. Res. Sci. Educ. 40(3), 339–352 (2010)

76. Ryan, R.M., Koestner, R., Deci, E.L.: Ego-involved persistence: when free-choice behavior is not intrinsically motivated. Motiv. Emot. **15**(3), 185–205 (1991)
77. Iten, N., Petko, D.: Learning with serious games: is fun playing the game a predictor of learning success? Br. J. Educ. Technol. **47**(1), 151–163 (2016)
78. Anderson, M.: Perfect ICT Every Lesson. Independent Thinking Press, an imprint of Crown House Publishing (2013)
79. Sardone, N.B., Devlin-Scherer, R.: Teacher candidate responses to digital games: 21st-century skills development. J. Res. Technol. Educ. **42**(4), 409–425 (2010)
80. Beetham, H., Sharpe, R.: Rethinking Pedagogy for a Digital Age: Designing for 21st Century Learning. Routledge, New York (2013)
81. Bartsch, S., Schaal, S., Oppermann, L., Lapschansky, L., Müller, H., Eisenhardt, M.: Mit dem Smartphone auf der Spur unseres Essens: Handbuch zur Erstellung mobiler, ortsbezogner Spielemissionen für die Ernährungs- und Verbraucherbildung. RabenStück Verlag (2017)
82. Anderson, T., Shattuck, J.: Design-based research: a decade of progress in education research? Educ. Res. **41**(1), 16–25 (2012)
83. Dede, C., Jass Ketelhut, D., Whitehouse, P., Breit, L., McCloskey, E.M.: A research agenda for online teacher professional development. J. Teach. Educ. **60**(1), 8–19 (2009)
84. The digital native is a myth (editorial). Nat. News, **547**(7664), 380 (2017)
85. Kirschner, P.A., De Bruyckere, P.: The myths of the digital native and the multitasker. Teach. Teach. Educ. **67**, 135–142 (2017)
86. Jones, C., Shao, B.: The net generation and digital natives: implications for higher education, 26 June 2011. https://www.heacademy.ac.uk/knowledge-hub/net-generation-and-digital-natives-implications-higher-education. Accessed 23 Oct 2017

Awkward Annie: Game-Based Assessment of English Pragmatic Skills

G. Tanner Jackson[1(⊠)], Lindsay Grace[2], Patricia Inglese[1],
Jennifer Wain[1], and Robert Hone[2]

[1] Educational Testing Service, Princeton, NJ 08541, USA
{gtjackson, pinglese, jwain}@ets.org
[2] American University, Washington, DC 20016, USA
{grace, hone}@american.edu

Abstract. This paper describes efforts related to the design, development, and evaluation of a game-based assessment called Awkward Annie. The Awkward Annie game focuses on English language pragmatic skills and represents a novel design that asks players to violate social norms by intentionally selecting the most inappropriate things to say to virtual colleagues. Awkward Annie was evaluated through two studies. Study 1 was a small-scale lab-based study with predominantly non-native English speakers (n = 36). Study 2 was a scaled up extension of the same design but with native English speakers on Amazon Mechanical Turk (n = 328). Both studies explored potential relations between user experience, understanding the play mechanics (i.e., being inappropriate), game performance, and English pragmatic ability. The studies also indicate cultural differences in players comfort with acting inappropriately. The results of these studies benefit both cross-cultural game design and the assessment of socio-pragmatics and pragmalinguistics. Additionally, this research advances the current state of assessment practices by investigating how games could potentially provide an alternative to traditional selected response testing.

Keywords: Educational games · English pragmatics · User experience

1 Introduction

1.1 Communication

The ability to effectively communicate in today's global environment is critical. Effective communication is complex and multimodal. While formal learning of a language provides the foundational knowledge of "what" to say, a more nuanced understanding of pragmatics, which relates to knowing "how", "where", and "when" to speak, largely relies on an understanding of the social and cultural norms which govern acceptable communication across contexts. Learning the subtleties of communication can be accomplished through direct instruction, conversational practice, and personal (immersed) experience; however, these experiences are often not offered in the traditional classroom environment and pragmatic competency through practice and experience alone can take years to refine [8, 11]. In addition, implementing these approaches in face-to-face settings can be costly and/or impractical (e.g., traveling to another country).

© Springer International Publishing AG, part of Springer Nature 2018
A. D. Cheok et al. (Eds.): ACE 2017, LNCS 10714, pp. 795–808, 2018.
https://doi.org/10.1007/978-3-319-76270-8_54

Advancement in technologies, specifically the use of digital games in education, now offer the distinct advantages of being experiential, engaging, and fun [6], while also being more cost-effective for larger scale distribution. Additionally, using an educational game for the instruction and assessment of pragmatics, provides the greatest potential for a low-stakes [12], safe environment where users have more opportunities to engage, experiment, learn [5], and fail without adverse consequences, than in higher-stakes real world conversational interactions. While there are a plethora of digital games designed to teach and assess vocabulary and more complex language use [4], our research indicates that the study presented here is one of the first to explore the use of digital game-based assessment to measure English language sociopragmatic proficiency. Subsequent paragraphs, however, are indented.

1.2 English Language Pragmatics

This project set out to design, implement and evaluate a game-based assessment (GBA) for measuring English language pragmatics. Pragmatics is an area of research that has seen increased interest over the past four decades in the fields of linguistics, applied linguistics, second language acquisition, and communicative studies due to its critical role in communicative language use [14]. Pragmatic ability can generally be defined as the appropriate use of language in a particular sociocultural context, or knowing what to say, how, to whom and when. Successful communication requires more than an ability to form grammatically accurate sentences; it involves an awareness of the socio-cultural environment, the interlocuters, and the context in any given communicative interaction. Leech [10] notably proposed two widely accepted sub-components of pragmatics, pragmalinguistics and sociolinguistics, which delve deeper into the specific knowledge and abilities associated with pragmatic awareness. Pragmalinguistics refers to the more linguistic components of language, such as the strategies and grammatical knowledge associated with language use. Sociopragmatics includes the knowledge of socially appropriate conventions and rules associated with a particular sociocultural context, situation or speech community. Examples of socio-pragmatic knowledge entail, for example, an understanding of social relationships, power distance, and degree of imposition. For instance, the pragmalinguistic components of the request "Can you bring me a cup of coffee?" include the use of modal verbs, questions, and direct language strategies, while sociopragmatic knowledge suggests that such a direct request would be more appropriate with a friend than a boss.

Pragmatic ability is considered to have a major role in successful communication [14] and a lack thereof has been known to cause communication breakdowns in the workplace [2] and create a negative impression of the speaker [18]. Despite its recognized importance and the possible high-stakes consequences associated with a lack of pragmatic ability, materials specifically targeting pragmatic instruction and assessment are limited. Therefore, recent efforts have focused on defining the construct of pragmatics [17] and developing materials that target pragmatic ability.

Pragmatic ability refers to 'the ability to control the complex interplay of language, language users, and language use contexts' [16]. Successful communication requires more than an ability to form grammatically accurate sentences; it involves an awareness of the socio-cultural environment, the interlocuters, and the context in any given communicative interaction. Some researchers have developed 3-D virtual world learning environments to investigate aspects of applied culture training (which includes aspects of pragmatics) and performance within predominantly military-like settings [15]. This, and other, work indicates that rich contextual and sociocultural input is needed to successfully assess pragmatic ability. This complex approach may be more feasible and appropriate to represent within an adaptive online virtual environment than through traditional text-based instructional materials [1]. To that effect, the GBA being developed for this project aims to represent some of the complexity of sociocultural interactions by providing the necessary contextual information (e.g., character backgrounds, power relationships, sociocultural environment) to assess pragmatic awareness within an engaging and interactive game design.

2 Game-Based Assessments

The Awkward Annie Game-Based Assessment (GBA) is a joint project between Institution 1 and Institution 2, shown in Fig. 1. Awkward Annie targets non-native English speaking adults and attempts to measure aspects of the pragmalinguistic and sociopragmatic dependencies between three social practices (greetings, small talk, requests) and how they interact with three social dimensions (social familiarity, power differences, and imposition size). These social practices and dimensions have been explored in previous work within the field and are aligned with practical applications that occur on a regular basis. Initial concepts for the GBA isolated these dimensions to better provide clear evidence on each dimension, however these streamlined approaches did not sufficiently allow for an exploration of the interdependencies across dimensions.

By factoring in the assessment evidence needs with the game design goals (investigating impact of design choices on engagement and enjoyment), the collaborative project team settled on a series of selected-response conversations situated within a light narrative context of an office work environment. This concept was developed through an Evidence Centered game Design approach (ECgD; [7]) and eventually evolved into Awkward Annie. The overall design of Awkward Annie provides a storyline where Awkward Annie, the player character, is a new employee starting a new job. This context was determined to provide an experiential environment rich in opportunity for conversations between diverse people with varying degrees of familiarity within a hierarchical setting (i.e., strangers and friends as colleagues and bosses), facilitating the assessment (and learning) of both pragmalinguistics and sociopragmatics [13].

To facilitate the storyline, conversations and response items at varying degrees of appropriateness were developed to evaluate the players' knowledge of the constructs. However, while being a prudent approach to assessment design, it was hypothesized that a game which focused on selecting the typical appropriate responses would be lacking from a game perspective, deficient in features that would be enjoyable and foster motivation, engagement and persistence through the game (i.e., it is what people do on a day-to-day basis).

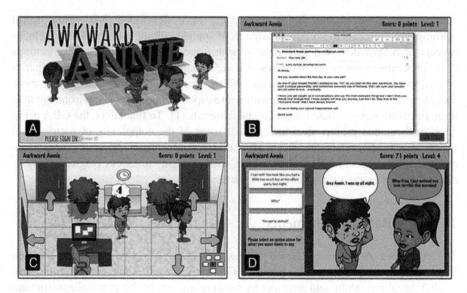

Fig. 1. (A) Intro screen, (B) Context and instruction, (C) Environment navigation, and (D) Conversation selection.

Instead, the game designers hypothesized that reversing the goal, where the game would require the player to select the most inappropriate response as opposed to the most appropriate, would improve the design from a game design perspective by allowing the player the enjoyment of being inappropriate, escaping from reality to interact in ways not permitted during real-life situations, and allowing for the development of playful and amusing conversations and Non-Player Character (NPC) reactions [3, 6, 20]. From a pragmatic literacy assessment perspective, this strategy assumes that the ability to identify the least appropriate response is indicative of knowing the most appropriate response (by the absence of its selection).

Thus, Awkward Annie is a GBA where the user is asked to play the role of "Awkward Annie" who is an inappropriate, but endearing character that completely fails at social interactions with her friends and colleagues. As part of this interaction, players must navigate through an office-like environment (see panel C in Fig. 1 and example rooms in Fig. 2) and engage in various conversations with a variety of NPCs including long-time friends, new acquaintances, same level colleagues, and higher status managers.

In each of these conversations the player is presented with 3 options (appropriate, mildly inappropriate, and most inappropriate) and must select the most inappropriate statements (panel D in Fig. 1). The degrees of statement inappropriateness were designed by pragmatics experts and refined through rounds of review by native speakers. Scores are provided for the three answer options and a minimum score must be reached in order for the player to successfully complete a given conversation. Conversations can be repeated as many times as are necessary to reach a successful outcome, and each conversation must be completed for the player to engage in subsequent conversations with a particular character. However, players can choose the order in which to interact with any of the available characters and can move between characters as they wish. When players succeed at selecting the awkward conversational statement they can watch as the NPCs find this behavior strange and rightly react to her ostentatious shenanigans, but (amazingly) continue to tolerate her behavior.

For each conversation, players are given a variety of dialogue choices that have varying levels of awkwardness. Sample in-game dialogue choices include (ordered from least to most social awkwardness for the given context)

Greeting to boss:

- "Good Morning"
- "Hey, it's Mikey the Muscle! How are you this Morning?"
- "There he is! The one who put the Man in Manager!"

Small talk with a peer:

- "It's like we just saw each other yesterday. Speaking of... have you been keeping up with The Bachelor?"
- "I know I just started here but I think the IT guy was just hitting on me!"
- "Since we are both new here, do you want to help me set up a speed dating night with our new coworkers?"

For each of the dialogue selections that a player makes, they are also given visual feedback and a score. The visual feedback includes a variety of non-player character responses, including visual character reactions (e.g., surprise, annoyance, confusion). The better the player performance, the larger the NPC response. Sample NPC reactions from the character, Mike, are shown in Fig. 2.

Fig. 2. Sample reactions by NPCs in the Awkward Annie game

3 Study 1

The purpose of Study 1 was to evaluate the Awkward Annie game prototype and identify relations between gameplay, English pragmatics ability (for the United States), and user experience. In other words, the research question for this study is, "How do aspects of gameplay relate to independent external measures of pragmatics and user experience?" This study of 36 adult working professionals was 61% female, had an age range of 21 to 65, and consisted of 10 native speakers and 26 non-native speakers.

3.1 Procedure

The study was conducted in a computer lab with small groups consisting of approximately 5–10 participants, lasted approximately one hour, and involved 3 self-paced phases: presurvey, gameplay, and postsurvey. The presurvey was used to collect demographic information as well as information regarding participants' education, use and application of the English language. During the gameplay phase, participants interacted with Awkward Annie. Upon finishing the game, they then completed a postsurvey related to their experience with the game and pragmatic ability.

Presurvey

Researchers provided participants with an ID number and password to log in and begin the presurvey, which took approximately 15 min. The presurvey included questions related to participants' gender, ethnicity, educational background, technology usage, as well as their use of and comfort with the English (and other) language(s). The final page of the presurvey presented an introduction to the Awkward Annie game mechanics, a map of the game environment, and directions on how to play.

Awkward Annie (v1.39)

After completing the presurvey, participants were then asked to complete the game at their own pace (typically 12–20 min) and were able to ask questions of the researcher when needed. The version of Awkward Annie used within the study (v1.39) focused on the adult workplace and included 18 total conversations with the automated characters, all of which must be successfully completed to end the game. Conversations were designed to simulate a combination of 1 or more social practices related to pragmatics (greetings, small talk, and requests). In this version of Awkward Annie each conversation consisted of 3 player decisions, and a minimum score of 10 was required to complete a given conversation. For each decision the response scores for appropriate, mildly inappropriate, and very inappropriate corresponded to 0, 3, and 5 points respectively. These point values were used to reward players for not selecting the appropriate option (0), but with slightly less weight being attributed to the more subjective task of discriminating between the mildly inappropriate (3) and highly inappropriate options (5).

Primary items tracked

Number of Conversation Attempts (# Convo): Within Awkward Annie, the number of conversations is a direct indicator of how many attempts (both successes and failures) users made while interacting with the various characters. Thus, higher numbers of total conversations indicates a larger number of failed conversations (i.e., users with more conversations required additional attempts to complete each conversation and the game overall).

Game Success (% Success): The percentage of game success is computed as the number of successful conversations divided by the total number of conversations, then multiplied by 100 to produce a percent. This variable is an indicator of how efficient players were at navigating the conversations and a higher percentage indicates more successful game play.

Average Conversation Score (Avg Score): The average conversation score is an indicator of how well players were able to discriminate between the 3 conversational options (appropriate, mildly inappropriate, and most inappropriate). A higher score indicates more successful discrimination between levels of appropriateness.

Postsurvey

After playing the game, participants took approximately 15–20 min to complete the postsurvey where they responded to 53 items related to their user experience and English language pragmatic skills. The user experience questions consisted of 26 likert scale items (1-strongly disagree, 6-strongly agree) focusing on positive aspects (e.g., "I was engaged while playing the game"), negative emotions (e.g., "I was frustrated while playing the game"), basic gameplay (e.g., "I understood how to play the game"), and general perceptions (e.g., "The characters reacted appropriately to my choices.").

3.2 Study 1 Results

Study 1 analyses focused on relations between measures of participants' performance (both game and postsurvey) and user experience. Initial analyses on the proportion of correct responses on the postsurvey revealed a range of pragmatic ability for these native and non-native English speakers (M = .49, SD = .07, range = .33). Similarly, there appears to be a range of ability across the game performance measures: # convos (M = 22.31, SD = 9.93, range = 47), % success (M = 88%, SD = 20%, range = 77%), and average score (M = 11.82, SD = 2.93, range = 11.63). The survey questions were on a scale from 1–7 (higher scores indicating stronger agreement) and showed a range of responses with predominantly positive ratings: had fun (Mode = 6, M = 5.19, SD = 1.35, range = 1–7), was engaged (Mode = 5, M = 4.42, SD = 1.03, range = 1–6), was frustrated (Mode = 1, M = 2.47, SD = 1.36, range = 1–5), understood how to play (Mode = 6, M = 5.47, SD = 1.424, range = 3–7), liked selecting awkward statements (Mode = 6, M = 5.36, SD = 1.55, range = 1–7), and reactions were appropriate (Mode = 6, M = 5.50, SD = 1.38, range = 2–7).

Subsequent analyses focused on identifying how gameplay performance related to the users' knowledge and experience (see Table 1 for correlations). It is important to note that this version of the game was designed for assessment purposes and not learning per se. Therefore, the study design and ensuing analyses were conducted to investigate the game as an assessment tool and not an intervention which would cause changes in knowledge or skills.

The initial study correlations in Table 1 are a subset of the larger 53 item survey, but the questions selected here represent the categories of individual differences which were found to be of particular interest (positive, negative, gameplay, and perceptions). These results provide some initial evidence that the gameplay metrics within Awkward Annie (i.e., # Convo, % Success, Avg Score) are capturing evidence related to players' pragmatic ability (post survey pragmatics % correct), but that performance within the game may be related to how well a player understood the underlying mechanic of selecting the most inappropriate conversation option (evidenced by the significant correlations with understanding play and English speaking ability). Additionally, the correlation between engagement and # Convos indicates that disengaged players had more failed conversations.

Table 1. Pearson correlations between study 1 performance, user experience, and individual differences (*p < .05; **p < .01).

Pearson correlations	Awkward Annie			Pragmatics	User experience	
	# Convo	% Success	Avg score	% Correct	I understood how to play	I selected statements to the best of my ability
% Success	−.937**	.—	.991**	.523**	.479**	.550**
Average score	−.916**	.991**	.—	.522**	.478**	.560**
Post test pragmatics % correct	−.536**	.523**	.522**	.—	.528**	.539**
I had fun	−.239	.253	.256	.318	.635**	.570**
I was engaged while playing the game	−.352*	.287	.282	.273	.370*	.226
I was frustrated while playing this game	.280	−.296	−.293	−.318	−.678**	−.477**
I understood how to play the game	−.465**	.479**	.478**	.528**	.—	.476**
I liked selecting the most awkward statements	−.180	.207	.210	.309	.528**	.580**
The characters reacted appropriately to my choices	−.215	.320	.337*	.261	.515**	.540**
How many hours per week (outside of work) do you spend using smart devices, including computers, iPads, smartphones?	−.131	.083	.091	.102	.164	.036
How would you describe your English speaking ability?	−.462**	.491**	.508**	.080	.108	.051
How much time do you spend communicating in English with members of the community outside of work?	−146	.184	.223	.364	.435*	.198

To investigate relations further, additional correlations focused on how game performance, understanding how to play, and the perceived quality of game choices players made (right columns in Table 1) relate to measures of performance (both game and postsurvey), user experience, and select individual differences. This second set of correlations provides some initial insight into factors which may be contributing to differences in the overall interaction (e.g., understanding how to play) as well as factors that may not be affecting performance (e.g., frequency of technology usage). In addition, a separate correlation found that the technology usage question within Table 1 was positively correlated with time spent communicating in English also within the table (r = .422, p < .05). By combining the results across these analyses a tentative conceptual representation can be formed that identifies the factors which seem to be contributing to the overall performance within the game and with the external measure of pragmatics.

Our preliminary understanding of these factors is that a non-native English speaker's confidence in and frequency of use speaking English relates both to how much they understand the Awkward Annie game and also how much they enjoy it. Understanding the game play of Awkward Annie not only relates to a more enjoyable experience, but it also positively relates to a person's performance within the game and on the external measure of pragmatics. Thus, understanding the novel mechanic of selecting the inappropriate conversation option may pose a difficulty for certain users and those same users are having difficulty with playing the game and applying pragmatics within the English language. We also found that people who perform well within the game tend to do well on the pragmatics postsurvey. Thus we are getting initial (and tentative) evidence that the game is capturing evidence of the target skills.

4 Study 2

The purpose of the second study was to conduct a scaled up replication of Study 1 effects and establish a baseline of behaviors with a larger sample of native English speakers. Thus, Study 2 used the same evaluation design, materials, and version of Awkward Annie from Study 1, with only slight modifications to shorten the Presurvey for native speakers. However, Study 2 was conducted completely online with 328 native English speaking adults through Amazon Mechanical Turk.

4.1 Study 2 Results

Similar to Study 1, initial analyses focused on identifying basic relations between English language pragmatics skills, game performance, and user experience. Analyses on the proportion of correct responses on the postsurvey revealed a range of pragmatic ability for these native English speakers (M = .77, SD = .08, range = .57). Although these native speakers have a significantly higher average on the pragmatics survey than the predominantly non-native speakers in Study 1, t(362) = 20.16, p < .001, there is still a range of ability to examine relations between the game, pragmatics ability, and user variables. Similarly, there appears to be at least a moderate range of ability across the game performance measures of # convos (M = 18.85, SD = 1.93, range = 21), % success (M = 96% SD = 7%, range = 53%), and average score (M = 13.09, SD = 1.08, range = 8.86). With this native English speaking population, it appears that game success (% success) is also significantly higher than in Study 1, t(361) = 5.00, p < .001. Thus, not surprisingly, being a native speaker of English does appear to be related to a significant in- crease in pragmatic ability. Despite this significant increase in performance, there is still a range of pragmatic abilities within the native population.

To examine relations in more detail, Pearson correlations (see Table 2) were conducted which yielded a significant positive relation between the postsurvey pragmatics performance and two of the game performance variables (% Success: r = .132, p = .017; Avg Score: r = .158, p = .004), and a marginal negative correlation with the number of conversations (# Convo: r = −.101, p = .067). These initial results indicate that the gameplay metrics within Awkward Annie are capturing aspects related to the range of players' pragmatic ability within this native speaking population.

Table 2. Pearson correlations between Study 2 performance, user experience, and individual differences (*p < .05; **p < .01).

Pearson correlations	Awkward Annie			Pragmatics	User experience	
	# Convo	% Sucess	Avg score	% Correct	I understood how to play	I selected statements to the best of my ability
% Success	−.967**	.—	.950**	.132*	.183**	.170**
Average score	−.922**	.950*	.—	.158**	.164**	.138**
Post test pragmatics % correct	−.101	.132*	.158**	.—	.056	−.023
I had fun	−.056	.055	.059	.024	.336**	.222**
I was engaged while playing the game	−.053	.048	.050	.068	.403**	.343**
I was frustrated while playing this game	.098	−.092	−.079	.011	−.281**	−.188**
I understood how to play the game	.198**	.183*	.164**	.056	.—	.548**
I selected statements to the best of my ability	−.149**	.170*	.138*	−.023	.548**	.—
I liked selecting the most awkward statements	−.107	.110*	.094	.080	.292**	.258**
The characters reacted appropriately to my choices	−.109*	.111*	.137*	.232**	.350**	.248**
How many hours per week (outside of work) do you spend using smart devices, including computers, iPads, smartphones?	−.013	.032	.006	.154**	−.057	−.002

Additional correlations examined how the two sources of performance metrics (3 from the game and 1 from the survey) and two critical user experience items related to particular user experience factors and frequency of technology use. Similar to Study 1, the user experience survey items were on a scale from 1–7 (higher scores indicating stronger agreement) and had a range of responses with predominantly positive ratings: had fun (Mode = 7, M = 5.95, SD = 1.24, range = 1–7), was engaged (Mode = 6, M = 5.46, SD = .88, range = 1–6), was frustrated (Mode = 1, M = 1.78, SD = 1.01, range = 1–6), understood how to play (Mode = 7, M = 6.61, SD = .70, range = 2–7), selected to best of ability (Mode = 7, M = 6.69, SD = .53, range = 4–7), liked selecting awkward statements (Mode = 7, M = 6.24, SD = 1.14, range = 1–7), and reactions were appropriate (Mode = 6, M = 6.04, SD = .92, range = 1–7).

Similar to Study 1 this set of correlations provides some initial insight into factors which may be contributing to differences in the overall interaction as well as those factors that may not be affecting game performance.

In contrast to Study 1, there were no significant correlations between the positive or negative user experience variables and gameplay performance (all p > .05). However, these positive and negative experiences were significantly related to both understanding how to play and the perceived ability to select correct statements. Thus, players who understood that they needed to be inappropriate also enjoyed the experience more, were less frustrated, and felt that they performed closer to the best of their ability.

There were no significant relations between a players' technology usage (frequency of using computers, comfort level with technology, frequency of playing video games) and their understanding of how to play the game or game performance (all p > .05). Thus, it appears that although the game mechanic of being inappropriate is somewhat out of the ordinary, that design did not appear to require significant technical expertise to engage.

Similar to Study 1, the current findings suggest that players' reported level of understanding how to play Awkward Annie relates to their user experience as well as both the perceived and actual game performance levels. People who understood that they were supposed to be awkward found the experience to be enjoyable. Conversely understanding or accepting the novel mechanic of selecting the inappropriate option may be somewhat difficult for certain users and those same people to have difficulty both playing and enjoying the game.

5   Conclusions

Overall, the Awkward Annie studies provided an operational conceptualization of (a portion of) English pragmatic ability which is aligned with existing literature [17], developed a game-based assessment which addresses these skills, conducted a pilot investigation of relevant factors for game and pragmatics performance with non-native English speakers, as well as collected a larger baseline sample of user data with native English speakers. These results indicate that Awkward Annie is successfully measuring aspects of English pragmatic ability, and that a variety of factors contribute to performance both within the game itself and on the external assessment of pragmatics skills. These results are informative for assessment purposes as the fairly unique approach to confirming the negative response (i.e., being inappropriate) does appear to be providing evidence of the desired skills, but may require additional scaffolding to ensure users fully understand the game intent. The findings are also relevant for the education and game-based research communities due to the novel design of the game and its associated successes and shortcomings.

In terms of the Awkward Annie GBA, revisions to certain key areas targeting the clarity of game navigation and pragmatically appropriate content will need to be addressed. It was evident that users will need further guidance and support to understand how to navigate the game and to follow the game's instructions. In particular, some non-native English speakers required additional clarification on the mechanics of the game (i.e., selecting the most inappropriate or awkward response was the correct answer). While this aligns with the initial study results, which demonstrated that higher levels of confidence in English language proficiency related positively to game performance, it still suggests a need for a tutorial or further feedback and support during game play. This also supports current efforts which aim to empirically address whether choosing the inappropriate (versus appropriate) response option is both an effective measure of pragmatic ability and an engaging form of game play. Additionally, the novelty, enjoyment, and impact of selecting (in)appropriate conversation options may be dependent upon the timescale of interaction (short or long) which has been suggested in prior research on educational games [9].

Another aspect of the game that will merit further refinement is the conversation options. Qualitative, offline feedback from the Study 1 suggested that users found it difficult to choose between the mildly inappropriate and most inappropriate responses, noting that both options were often awkward enough for either to be considered the "correct" choice.

It is also worth mentioning that the pragmatics content was developed in accordance with other research focusing on pragmatically appropriate language use and task difficulty [19]. However, without explicitly receiving instruction on pragmatically appropriate language in the American workplace, some participants (native and non-native English speakers alike) noted that the response options were often unclear. For example, one non-native speaker explained that since she was unfamiliar with inappropriate topics for small talk in the American culture, she tried to follow the sociocultural norms of her own Chinese culture and considered personal relationships as a more inappropriate topic than politics (see Fig. 3 for example of this dialogue). Although, this decision may lead to confusion on the part of the user, it is actually construct relevant for the assessment and an important dimension to capture within the gameplay.

In addition to culture specific references, the discrimination between options can be further compounded by the potential subjectivity associated with pragmatically appropriate language use. Thus, future work aims to further examine and norm the game content with a larger population of native English speakers so that distinctions between conversation options have stronger empirical support. Future studies are also planned that will explore the effect of selecting the inappropriate versus appropriate options to examine the potential effect on affective and performance variables.

Despite these potential limitations, the current work with Awkward Annie has illustrated the potential for the environment and provided initial support for this unique

Fig. 3. Example small talk conversation option, demonstrating two workplace inappropriate conversation topics, personal relationships (option 1) and politics (option 2).

and novel approach. This research advances the current state of assessment practices by investigating how games could potentially provide an alternative to traditional selected response testing. The initial study, with support from the Amazon Mechanical Turk follow-up study, has identified several key factors and constructs which may have significant impact on game design, game-based assessment practices, and measures of pragmatic ability.

References

1. Belz, J.A.: The role of computer mediation in the instruction and development of L2 pragmatic ability. Ann. Rev. Appl. Linguist. **27**, 45 (2007)
2. Clyne, M.: Inter-Cultural Communication at Work: Cultural Values in Discourse. Cambridge University Press, Cambridge, UK (1994)
3. Cole, H., Griffiths, M.D.: Social interactions in massively multi-player online role-playing gamers. Cyber Psychol. Behav. **10**(4), 575–583 (2007)
4. Cornillie, F., Thorne, S.L., Desmet, P.: ReCALL special issue: digital games for language learning: challenges and opportunities. ReCALL **24**(03), 243–256 (2012)
5. Garris, R., Ahlers, R., Driskell, J.E.: Games, motivation, and learning: a research and practice model. Simul. Gaming **33**(4), 441–467 (2002)
6. Gee, J.P.: What video games have to teach us about learning and literacy. Comput. Entertain. **1**(1), 20 (2003)
7. Hoffman, E., John, M., Makany, T.: How do game design frameworks align with learning and assessment design frameworks? Paper presented at the annual meeting for the National Council for Measurement in Education, Philadelphia, PA (2014)

8. Ishihara, N., Cohen, A.D.: Teaching and Learning Pragmatics: Where Language and Culture Meet. Pearson, Harlow (2010)
9. Jackson, G.T., McNamara, D.S.: Motivation and performance in a game-based intelligent tutoring system. J. Educ. Psychol. **105**, 1036–1049 (2013)
10. Leech, G.N.: Principles of Pragmatics. Longman, London, England (1983)
11. Limberg, H.: Principles for pragmatics teaching: apologies in the EFL classroom. ELT J. **69**(3), 275–285 (2015)
12. McDonald, K.K., Hannafin, R.D.: Using web-based computer games to meet the demands of today's high-stakes testing: a mixed method inquiry. J. Res. Technol. Educ. **35**(4), 459–472 (2003)
13. Pivec, M., Dziabenko, O., Schinnerl, I.: Game-based learning in universities and lifelong learning: "UniGame: social skills and knowledge training" game concept. J. Univ. Comput. Sci. **10**(1), 14–26 (2004)
14. Riddiford, N., Joe, A.: Tracking the development of sociopragmatic skills. TESOL Q. **44**(1), 195–205 (2010)
15. Surface, E.A., Dierdorff, E.C., Watson, A.M.: Special operations language training software measurement of effectiveness study: Tactical Iraqi study final report. Special Operations Forces Language Office, Tampa, FL, USA (2007)
16. Taguchi, N.: Longitudinal study of higher-order inferential ability in L2 English. In: Byrnes, H., Ortega, L. (eds.) The Longitudinal Study of Advanced L2 Capacities. Lawrence Erlbaum, Mahwah (2008)
17. Timpe-Laughlin, V., Wain, J., Schmidgall, J.: Defining and operationalizing the construct of pragmatic ability: Review and recommendations. ETS Research Report Series. Princeton, NJ. Educational Testing Service (2015)
18. Timpe, V.: Assessing Intercultural Language Learning. Peter Lang, Frankfurt aM (2013a)
19. Timpe, V.: The difficulty with difficulty: the issue of determining task difficulty in TBLA. J. Linguist. Lang. Teach. **4**(1), 13–28 (2013)
20. Yee, N.: Motivations for play in online games. Cyber Psychol. Behav. **9**(6), 772–775 (2006)

Using a Serious Game to Assess Spatial Memory in Children and Adults

Mauricio Loachamín-Valencia[1], M.-Carmen Juan[1]([⊠])[iD],
Magdalena Méndez-López[2], and Elena Pérez-Hernández[3]

[1] Instituto Universitario de Automática e Informática Industrial,
Universitat Politècnica de València, C/Camino de Vera, s/n, 46022 Valencia, Spain
{mrenan,mcarmen}@dsic.upv.es
[2] Departamento de Psicología y Sociología,
Universidad de Zaragoza, Zaragoza, Spain
mmendez@unizar.es
[3] Departamento de Psicología Evolutiva y de la Educación,
Universidad Autónoma de Madrid, Madrid, Spain
elena.perezh@uam.es

Abstract. Short-term spatial memory has traditionally been assessed using visual stimuli, but not auditory stimuli. In this paper, we design and test a serious game with auditory stimuli for assessing short-term spatial memory. The interaction is achieved by gestures (by raising your arms). The auditory stimuli are emitted by smart devices placed at different locations. A total of 70 participants (32 children and 38 adults) took part in the study. The outcomes obtained with our game were compared with traditional methods. The results indicated that the outcomes in the game for the adults were significantly greater than those obtained by the children. This result is consistent with the assumption that the ability of humans increases continuously during maturation. Correlations were found between our game and traditional methods, suggesting its validity for assessing spatial memory. The results indicate that both groups easily learn how to perform the task and are good at recalling the locations of sounds emitted from different positions. With regard to satisfaction with our game, the mean scores of the children were higher for nearly all of the questions. The mean scores for all of the questions, except one, were greater than 4 on a scale from 1 to 5. These results show the satisfaction of the participants with our game. The results suggest that our game promotes engagement and allows the assessment of spatial memory in an ecological way.

Keywords: Gamification · Serious game · Auditory · Short-term memory
Karotz · Color-depth sensor · Microsoft Kinect[TM] · Natural User Interface

1 Introduction

The terms gamification or serious games are commonly used interchangeably to refer to the use of games in non-game contexts. According to Deterding et al. [1], gamification refers to the use of design element characteristics for games in non-game contexts. The

© Springer International Publishing AG, part of Springer Nature 2018
A. D. Cheok et al. (Eds.): ACE 2017, LNCS 10714, pp. 809–829, 2018.
https://doi.org/10.1007/978-3-319-76270-8_55

underlying idea of serious games is to combine game playing with a serious purpose (i.e., cognitive testing) [2]. Several works have suggested that serious games help in the learning process when they are used in relevant contexts that engage learners (e.g., [3]). For example, serious games have also been previously used for individuals with autism for learning purposes [4]; as an assessment tool for cognition and performance in an activity of daily living (in their case, cooking); or for training of cognitive functions in older adults [5].

Psychological science is interested in the assessment of a human's ability to learn about spatial and auditory information in different situations and contexts. Memory can be divided into short-term memory and long-term memory, depending on whether the information to be stored is useful for a limited period of time or is relevant to be stored stably for any future need [6]. Spatial and auditory memories have the capacity to store representations of spatial and auditory stimuli, respectively. Spatial memory allows us to find a place that we have visited before, follow a route after consulting a map, or remember where we left our belongings, among other examples. The assessment of spatial memory contributes to the understanding of individual differences in behavior and helps to prevent and detect pathology [6]. From a psychological perspective, there has been research interest in the ability to learn spatial and auditory information. The reason is that they are significant processes in daily life. Spatial learning is associated with academic outcomes [7] and with the functional maturation of the frontal pole [8]. Auditory learning facilitates taking notes while listening, written expression, and oral expression [9]. Some learning and behavioral problems are related to impairments in these processes [10, 11]. Also, many learning experiences require considering auditory and spatial information simultaneously. Some examples are orientation in space and identification of people or objects. Since there are no procedures for assessing spatial learning for auditory stimuli, its implications for different types of learning remain unclear.

To our knowledge, the combination of Natural User Interfaces (NUI) and smart devices has not been explored for the assessment of cognitive processes, and especially for the assessment of spatial memory using auditory stimuli. We believe this combination promotes engagement and allows assessment in an ecological way. The development of new games for neuropsychological assessment represents an alternative for the evaluation of memory. These tools can be used for assessment as well as for training.

The objectives of our work are the following: to develop a game that is able to recognize gestures and integrate gesture recognition with smart devices; to obtain indicators of the participants' performance; to compare the performance obtained by using the game between the two groups of the study (i.e., children and adults); to compare the outcomes obtained on a questionnaire about perceptions and satisfaction and between the two groups.

A sample composed of adult participants is considered to determine the maximum performance with the game. We compare the performance between adults and children in order to determine whether or not the children achieve full competence in the game. Therefore, our research questions are the following: (RQ1) Is the new game a valid tool for assessing spatial memory? (RQ2) Are the performance outcomes obtained with the game between children and adults different? (RQ3) Is the level of satisfaction with the game between children and adults different?

In order to answer the research questions we proceed as follows: (RQ1) We observe the correlations between the outcomes obtained in the game and traditional tools; (RQ2) We check if there are statistically significant differences in the performance outcomes obtained with the game between children and adults; (RQ3) We check if there are statistically significant differences in the level of satisfaction between children and adults.

2 Background

2.1 Gesture Interaction

Human body motion and gesture recognition have received increasing attention (e.g., [12, 13]). Since the arms and, in particular, the hands are used to gesture and are a natural means of communication among humans, they are also of importance in Human-Computer Interaction. Arm-motion recognition has been achieved through sensor-based and vision-based techniques. For sensor-based recognition, different sensors have been used to capture the position and orientation of the arms (e.g., accelerometer [14], or sensors worn on the body [15]. The vision-based methods use images obtained through cameras/sensors, extract their characteristics, and analyze the actions performed by users. Recognition can be static or dynamic. Static gestures are time independent, whereas dynamic gestures are time dependent. The cameras/sensors can be of different types, color cameras (RGB), or color-depth cameras (RGB-D). Pisharady and Saerbeck, 2015 [13] reviewed conventional hand-gesture recognition using RGB cameras as well as recognition using RGB-D sensors. Pisharady and Saerbeck, 2015 [13] classified the techniques used for dynamic hand gesture recognition as: (a) Hidde Markov Models (e.g., [16]) and other statistical methods (e.g., [17]); (b) Artificial Neural Networks (e.g., [18]) and other learning based methods (e.g., [19]); (c) Eigenspace-based methods (e.g., [20]); (d) Curve fitting [21]; and (e) Dynamic programming [22]/Dynamic time warping (e.g., [23]). Depth sensors have already been used in computer vision for many years both commercial and non-commercial (e.g., [24]). An example of a non-commercial depth sensor is an IR Time-of-Flight Range Camera [24]. However, the appearance of low-cost, color-depth cameras/sensors led to a much more widespread use than their predecessors. Two of these sensors were Kinect^{TM} [25, 26] by Microsoft, and Xtion PRO LIVE by ASUS. Sensors of this type provide reliable tracking of human body postures and obtain the coordinates of a skeletal model. These coordinates can be used for human body motion and gesture recognition.

Low-cost, color-depth sensors have been used extensively for gesture interaction, and they have contributed to different areas. One of these areas is serious games. For example, Martín-SanJosé et al. [27] presented a game for learning historical ages. The researchers proposed a custom-built touch table and used the Microsoft Kinect^{TM} sensor for hand-gesture recognition. They used this table to compare a personalized, free-learning itinerary with a linear learning itinerary. Their results showed that there were no statistically significant differences between the two learning itineraries. In another game for the same purpose [28, 29], this same group used Kinect^{TM} for gesture interaction and autostereoscopic display for 3D perception. The interaction of the children was similar to the interaction that is used in our game. In their game, the children had to raise their hands to select the elements that appeared on the screen. In our case, the children also have to raise their hands. The main difference is that, in our case, the children did not have to select elements, just raise both arms. A similar proposal was also used for dental learning [30]. Homer et al. [31] determined the effects of interactivity in a Kinect-based literacy game for beginning readers. Those authors concluded that the activities in the game were not distracting. They were interesting and engaging activities for children, and they could support children's acquisition of language and literacy. Lin et al. [32] presented a game for a child to play blocks in a natural and intuitive way. They concluded that the users (children and adults) could fully immerse themselves in the game and construct a complicated structure easily. The game facilitated the learning experience.

With regard to how gesture interaction can assist in populations with special needs, one of the biggest contributions of low-cost, color-depth sensors is related to improvement in sign-language recognition. Sun et al. [33] proposed a discriminative exemplar coding for American sign-language recognition. Lee et al. [34] also proposed a system for Taiwanese sign-language recognition that showed a good recognition rate. The proposals demonstrated feasibility and effectiveness. Armin et al. [35] reviewed the potential offered by low-cost, color-depth sensors in the context of educational methods for teaching children with sensory disabilities. For example, a Kinect-based game could help blind children to learn the name of objects by establishing links between tactile information and sound information. The authors highlighted the usefulness of low-cost, color-depth sensors as an attractive learning technology.

There are also games for the physical training of motor skills in children with a developmental disorder using color-depth sensors (e.g. autism, attention deficit/hyperactivity disorder, etc.), e.g., [36]. One of these games consisted of moving a girl along a path by using the movement of a hand [36]. The girl was shown on a TV screen or projector. The game aimed to train children in an engaging way and tried to keep their attention during the session. The game was compared with a classical procedure. There were significant improvements in motor learning of students with motor difficulties when the developed game was used. Similarly, another game showed positive effects for motor rehabilitation of children with cerebral palsy [37].

2.2 Smart Devices

Smart devices, especially those with a human appearance, have contributed to the study of human learning. One of the most interesting examples of their contributions is related to the field of autism. Adolescents with a diagnosis of autism played a face-match card game using a humanoid robot [38]. They played in pairs with a partner of a similar age who had a physical impairment. The game consisted of a face match. There were three playing conditions to establish comparisons: playing with the robot; playing with a computerized touch-screen whiteboard; and playing with conventional cards. Although the results were variable, they showed the feasibility of using robots in a school setting. Humanoid robots were also used for verbal learning. Children could learn words for several real objects in their first language after watching a video of a robot naming them [39]. Even toddlers aged 18–24 months could learn several words from a robot [40]. Robots have also been considered for learning about geometry in preschool education [41]. Children interacted with a Linux-based robot in the context of an educational game. The results showed positive effects of the experience with the robot in the learning of geometry. In addition, the interaction with this robot contributed to the spatial learning of three-year-old children [42]. Timms [43] emphasized the importance of the physical embodiment of the devices used. However, other types of devices showed interesting findings. For example, children learned about natural environments with a handheld device shaped like a horn that was used during the exploration of a woodland [44]. The horn provided non-speech audio sounds related to ecological sounds and the children had to interpret their significance (e.g., a light sabre sound means photosynthesis). The learning experience stimulated creativity and imagination in the children.

To our knowledge, the only study that has used the Karotz robot was presented by de Graaf et al. [45]. De Graaf et al. [45] installed Karotz robots in the home of older people. The goal was to improve their health. The role of the Karotz robot was to work as a 'personal assistant' who was interested in their progress and gave recommendations, such as controlling their weight.

2.3   Assessment of Spatial Memory

The assessment of spatial memory using visual stimuli has been carried out using different types of applications. For example, ARSM Task [46, 47] is a mobile augmented reality game for assessing spatial memory in children. The game was tested in a room with a size of about 5 m^2. Real boxes were placed in the room. Inside the boxes were image targets and the virtual objects appeared on these image targets. The game consisted of 7 levels, in which the number of boxes and virtual objects to remember increased (in Level I, there were 2 boxes and 1 object to remember; in Level II, there were four boxes and 2 objects to remember, etc.). Juan et al. [46] found similarities in the results using ARSM Task and traditional methods. MnemoCity Task [48] had a virtual reality environment, with passive stereoscopy and natural interaction to evaluate spatial memory in children. The study compared two types of interaction: (1) a gamepad; (2) a steering wheel (with a built-in Wii Remote[TM] control) and Wii Balance Board[TM]. The steering wheel was used to determine the user's turns. The Wii Balance Board[TM] was used to determine the participant's speed. The virtual environment recreated a park in which some tables were placed. The elements that the user had to locate appeared on the tables. Rodríguez et al. [48] also obtained correlations between their MnemoCity Task and traditional methods. Cárdenas et al. [49] developed a virtual labyrinth to assess spatial memory in adults. In this virtual labyrinth, the participant had to remember the route in order to find the exit. In their study, two types of interaction were compared: a gamepad and a bicycle. Pedaling on the bike indicated the speed. The handlebar turns indicated the turns that the avatar had to make in the virtual world. The performance of the participants that was obtained with the labyrinth correlated with traditional methods.

There are several reasons for researchers to use gamification in the field of psychological assessment. The review of Lumsden et al. [50] described these reasons after considering empirical studies that tested the possibilities of games applied to the training or assessment of cognitive skills. These games were developed for processes such as executive functions and memory, combining different processes in certain cases. Lumsden et al. [50] mentioned some of the positive aspects that are related to the purpose of the assessment which include the following: the active involvement of the user and motivation; clearly determined goals; and the reduction of anxiety suffered during a testing session. This last aspect is very important for assessment in psychology, both for clinical and non-clinical populations.

Fig. 1. Karotz rabbit.

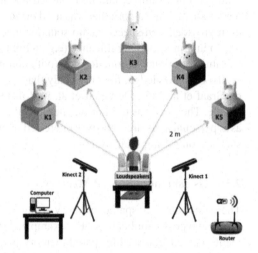

Fig. 2. Diagram of the game area.

3   Design and Development of the Game

3.1   Design of the Game

The game was designed to use Natural User Interfaces (NUI) and smart devices for managing auditory stimuli. For the NUI, the proposal was to use a low-cost, color-depth sensor to capture movements. We used Microsoft Kinect™, but other sensors could also be used. Karotz rabbits were proposed as smart devices. Figure 1 shows an image of a Karotz rabbit. The game was designed to test the users' ability to detect and localize auditory stimuli that are emitted in different positions of a game area (Fig. 2). The game consists of guessing the rabbit that emitted a sound. However, the rabbits are identical. The only difference is their performance (sounds and movements of their ears). Therefore, the player must concentrate on the rabbits' locations and memorize them. Some communication codes were identified and defined. When a player raises his/her arms in front of a rabbit, it means "Hello, I know you did it". The rabbits move their ears and turn on lights when they want to get the attention of the player (which means "Hello, I'm here.") or when they have understood the player's response (which means "Agreed!"). The children are told that they have to hear the response of the Karotz when they raise their arms in order to be sure that the Karotz has understood their action. If this response is not emitted, the children must repeat the action. Figure 3 shows a participant that is raising his arms in front of a Karotz rabbit.

Our game is framed in the short-term type of memory. We are interested in the ability of the participants to retrieve a sequence of locations of the auditory stimuli emitted. This sequence is also called "memory span", which represents the capacity of short-term storage to retain spatial items. We are interested in determining the maximum capacity of each participant in this type of memory span. A participant that did not retrieve a certain memory span in a certain number of attempts would not have been able to retrieve a longer memory span. Based on our experience, we have established that the number of attempts in our game in each level is 3.

Fig. 3. A participant raising his arms in front of a Karotz rabbit.

Fifteen children participated in a preliminary study to determine which gestures were easier for Kinect™ to recognize. It was determined that the most appropriate gesture for our game was to raise both arms at the same time in front of a Karotz. The identification was correct 95% of the time (when raising the arms and then lowering them immediately). To achieve 100% detection, the children were told to stand in front of a Karotz with their arms raised until they heard the message from the Karotz, which indicated that the Karotz had been selected ("Agreed!").

The area of the game for our study was defined to be around 5 m². Nevertheless, this area can be delimited within a room with larger dimensions. In our study, artificial turf was placed on the floor for guide paths, and a rug was used to indicate the initial position of the player. The walls were covered with wrapping paper to eliminate any spatial cues. The height of the Karotz rabbit was adjusted by placing cardboard boxes on the tables. Five Karotz rabbits were placed on tables with the following locations (see Fig. 2): Karotz rabbit 1 (−60°), Karotz rabbit 2 (−30°), Karotz rabbit 3 (0°), Karotz rabbit 4 (+30°), Karotz rabbit 5 (+60°). Each Karotz rabbit emits its assigned sound. The game included a total of 45 acoustic stimuli, which should be randomly emitted in different locations to avoid repetitions or established sequences. The game was defined to be composed of five different levels based on the number of stimuli presented in each trial (Fig. 4). Each level was defined to relate to a specific theme. The chosen themes were: nature, a party, a farm, a house, and a big city. Each level consists of 3 trials. The difference between levels lies in the number of sounds to be used in each trial, which will increase by 1 at each subsequent level. Specifically, the acoustic stimuli were distributed as follows: Level I (1 acoustic stimulus for each trial, 3 stimuli in total); Level II (2 acoustic stimuli for each trial, 6 stimuli in total); Level III (3 acoustic stimuli for each trial, 9 stimuli in total); Level IV (4 acoustic stimuli for each trial, 12 stimuli in total); and Level V (5 acoustic stimuli for each trial, 15 stimuli in total).

Each level has two phases: the search phase and the location phase. In the search phase, the user learns the sounds and their location. First, the user listens to the instructions through the loudspeakers. Then, the user listens to the continuous sound emitted by a Karotz and memorizes its location. While the sound is playing, the participant moves to stand in front of the Karotz that emits the sound and raises his/her arms to make the selection. The Karotz emits a message to indicate that it has understood the gesture. The user is told that he/she must listen to the message of the Karotz after raising his/her arms. If the Karotz does not emit such a message, the user must repeat the action.

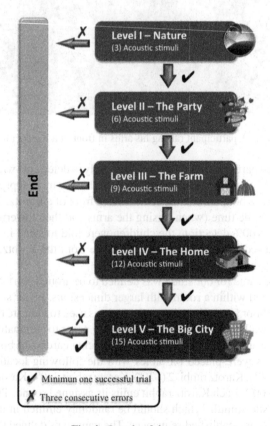

Fig. 4. Levels of the game.

The participant's spatial memory is evaluated in the location phase. First, the user listens to the instructions through the loudspeakers and also the sound that has to be located. In this phase, the user has to remember the location of the Karotz that emitted the stimulus (sound). The stimuli are only emitted once. The user has to move to the correct location and raise his/her arms in front of the Karotz in order to select it. Then he/she must return to the starting position. The game stores all of the answers (successes or failures).

A trial is successfully passed if all of the sounds are correctly located. If a sound is not correctly located, the trial has not been passed. If there is at least one successful test of the 3 trials of a given level, the user has passed that level and advances to the next level. The participant must perform the 3 trials of one level, regardless of whether he/she has successfully passed all of the stimuli of the first trial. If the user fails in all 3 trials at any level, the game ends. The game also ends when the participant completes level V.

3.2   Hardware and Software

We used two Microsoft Kinect™ v1 devices and five Karotz rabbits. The Kinect™ v1 devices include a RGB camera with a resolution of 640×480 pixels, an infrared camera, an infrared projector, and a multiarray microphone. The Karotz rabbits are shaped like a rabbit and are 30 cm tall (Fig. 1). They can connect to the Internet through a wireless access point. They have loudspeakers, a webcam, an LED-light (in their bellies), and they can move their ears. Their technical specifications are: 400 MHz ARM-CPU, 64 MB-RAM, 256 MB of storage, and a Linux operating system.

An HP computer with an Intel i5 processor and Windows 7 operating system was used. This computer had USB ports connected to a separate USB host controller. This allowed two Kinect™ devices to be used simultaneously. Additionally, this computer was used as the server. Two conventional loudspeakers were used to give instructions during the game. We used a wireless-G Router with WAN port for networking and accessing the Internet. This Internet access was required by the five Karotz rabbits and the computer.

The sounds were edited using Audacity 2.0.3 to ensure the loudness of 70 dB, frequency > 3000 Hz, 4-s duration, and stereo format. For the voice of the messages, the audio clips were recorded using Audacity 2.0.3, and they had identical characteristics to the sounds, except that the duration varied depending on the specific instructions or message.

Visual Basic 2008 Express Edition was used for the development of the system that manages the procedure during the game and the graphical interface for the supervisor. To program the Kinect™ device, we used Visual C++ 2010 Express Edition, Kinect SDK 1.8, OpenNI 2.0 SDK, and Nite. The system has three modules: (a) one to configure and manage the Karotz rabbits, their IPs, and the IP of the sounds server; (b) one to register the participant's information and for the evaluation process; and (c) one to manage the communication among the Karotz rabbits and the Kinect™ devices.

The system has a graphical interface that allows the supervisor to introduce the player's code, date of birth, and gender. The role of the supervisor is to supervise the task by observing the supervisor's interface, which offers information about the participant's progress. The supervisor does not control the rabbits. The supervisor can observe the performance carried out by the player (i.e., trials, successes, and failures (Fig. 5)).

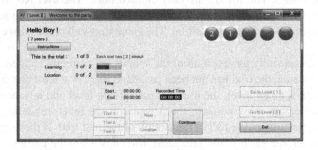

Fig. 5. Screen that displays the player's performance.

4   Study

4.1   Participants

A total of 70 participants were involved in our study. A total of 32 healthy children (16 girls, 16 boys) took part in this study, with ages ranging from 9 to 10 years old. The children were attending the fifth grade at a public school. Before carrying out the study, the parents of the participating children received written information about the aims and procedures of the study, and they signed a consent form to allow their children to participate. The children who participated received a diploma and a snack immediately after the test session. They were not informed about this reward until the end of the study.

A total of 38 healthy adults (19 women, 19 men) took part in the study, ranging in age between 18 and 28 years old ($M = 21.32$, $SD = 2.86$). The participants were recruited throughout the campus of a large public university. The students had the following education levels: vocational education (28.95%), undergraduate (44.74%), or graduate (26.31%). Before the study, all of the participants were informed in writing about the aims and procedures, and they signed an informed consent form. The participants received a diploma and a snack right after the test session, but they were not informed about the snack until they had completed the procedures of the study.

The study was conducted in accordance with the European Directive 2001/20/EC and the Helsinki Declaration for biomedical research involving humans. The Ethics Committee of the Universitat Politècnica de València (UPV) approved the research protocol.

4.2   Measurements

We assessed the participants' ability to recall auditory stimuli and their locations by registering their performance during the task. The database of the system recorded successes or failures in the detection and location of stimuli. Four variables based on performance during the task were stored. These variables were the following: Number of Correct Stimuli (NCS), Number of Correct Levels (NCL), Task Time (TT), Number of Errors (NE). NCS was the number of auditory icons that a participant could successfully locate. NCL was the sum of the number of levels correctly performed. TT was the total time in seconds that a participant spent to complete the task. Finally, NE was the sum of the number of errors that a participant could commit. In addition, we calculated the task score (TS) which is the sum of all auditory icons (of any block and Level) for which the participant correctly indicated the emitting rabbit. The TS allows us to determine the performance of the participants. The maximum possible task score was 45.

Visuospatial learning and auditory learning were also assessed in the participants by using traditional methods. We selected specific subtests that are included in the Test of Memory and Learning battery (TOMAL) [51]. The TOMAL battery assesses various domains of learning. We also selected subtests that are included in the EDAF test. The EDAF measures auditory and phonological discrimination [52]. We used the direct scores obtained in all of the subtests used.

We selected the TOMAL subtest for the assessment of visuospatial learning: Memory for Location (ML). This subtest consists of a spatial recall task of one or more large dots that appear within a square or rectangle. The participant is asked to identify the location of the dots within a grid. The range of the grid is 3×3 and 4×4 (with 9 locations and 16 locations, respectively). In order to assess immediate retrieval of auditory items, we used two verbal span subtests of the TOMAL battery: Digits Forward (DF) and Digits Backward (DB). The DF is a number recall task that measures low-level rote recall of a sequence of numbers. The DB task (a variation of the DF task) consists of a sequential recall of a sequence of numbers but in reverse order. For the assessment of auditory and phonological discrimination, we selected the EDAF subtest: Environmental Sound Discrimination (ESD). The ESD is a discrimination task about sounds of the environment that are played on a CD (i.e., baby's crying, traffic noise, etc.). We also measured the participants' everyday memory. We selected eight questions from the ECM-Questionnaire (ECM) for this purpose [53]. The skills are rated on a 4-point Likert scale ($1 = never$ to $4 = almost\ always$). The questions are "I have good spatial orientation, I get lost where I have often been before, I forget where I have put things, I recognize the places I have been before, I know how to go home, I remember where I store my things, I get lost in familiar places, I forget how to go to a place that I have already been explained how to get to". In the case of the child participants, their parents completed the Parent Report version of this questionnaire.

To assess the participants' perceptions and satisfaction with the game, we designed a Questionnaire (QS) based on the questionnaires of Lewis [54] and Lund [55] (Table 1). Items were selected from these two existing instruments based on their appropriateness for assessing learning, satisfaction, and interaction with the game, and the items were adapted to our studies. The participants responded to the items using a 5-point Likert scale ($1 = $ "strongly disagree" to $5 = $ "strongly agree").

Table 1. Questionnaire (QS).

Question ID	Question
Q1	It was easy to use this task
Q2	It was easy to learn to use this task
Q3	I would recommend it to a friend
Q4	Overall, I am satisfied with this task
Q5	The interactive interface is pleasant (body movements)
Q6	I like using the auditory interface (sounds)
Q7	Overall, this interaction was fun

4.3 Study Design

For the children, the test sessions took place from Monday to Friday between 9:00 and 14:00 over three weeks during the normal school year. For the adults, the study was carried out over two weeks, from Monday to Friday between 9:00 and 15:00. A supervisor guided the participants through the steps to follow during testing and helped them become familiar with the area of interaction. The supervisor did not interfere with the game performance unless the participants requested assistance or experienced a technical problem (system failure). At the end of the session, the supervisor administered the QS questionnaire to each participant.

4.4 Performance Outcomes Using the Game

Data from the children and adults were analyzed using the statistical open source toolkit *R* (www.r-project.org) with the *RStudio* IDE *Desktop* (www.rstudio.com). The normality of the data was analyzed based on Shapiro-Wilk and Anderson-Darling tests. The TS, NCS, NCL, and NE variables did not fit the normal distribution, so we applied the Mann-Whitney U test for unpaired data. The TT variable did fit the normal distribution, so an ANOVA test was used. The Mann-Whitney U test for unpaired data was used to determine the statistically significant differences for the QS questionnaire between children and adults.

The results showed that the group of children performed worse than the group of adults (see Table 2). The Task Score (TS) indicates statistically significant differences in favor of the adults (Fig. 6). The results of the comparisons indicate statistically significant differences for the variables related to successes (NCS and NCL) in favor of the adults. Also, the group of children committed a significantly higher number of errors (NE) and they spent more time on the game (TT) than the adults.

Table 2. Mann-Whitney U test analysis for TS, NCS, NCL, and NE variables. ANOVA for the TT variable.

Var.	Child $\mu \pm \sigma$	Adult $\mu \pm \sigma$	U	Z	p
TS	34.28 ± 11.35	43.68 ± 1.97	153.0	−5.465	<0.001*
NCS	34.28 ± 11.35	43.68 ± 1.97	153.0	−5.465	<0.001*
NCL	2.75 ± 1.27	4.29 ± 1.01	199.5	−4.988	<0.001*
NE	4.53 ± 0.98	4.08 ± 0.78	849.0	3.117	<0.001*
Var.	Child $\mu \pm \sigma$	Adult $\mu \pm \sigma$	d.f.	F	p
TT	610.2 ± 165.5	518.2 ± 52.7	1, 68	10.49	0.002*

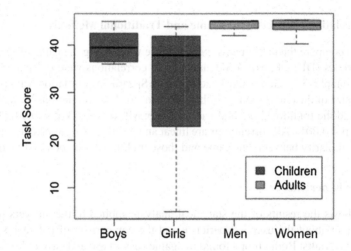

Fig. 6. Graph showing the outcomes for the TS variable.

4.5   Outcomes Using Traditional Methods

The outcomes obtained with the traditional methods were analyzed to determine whether or not there were differences between the two groups. Table 3 shows the results and statistics. The results showed that adults demonstrated significantly greater visuo-spatial learning (DB, DF, ML and ECM). For the discrimination of sounds, there were no statistically significant differences for the ESD variable.

Table 3. Mann-Whitney U test analysis for DB, ESD, and ECM. ANOVA for the DF and ML variables.

	Child $\mu \pm \sigma$	Adult $\mu \pm \sigma$	U	Z	p
DB	20.66 ± 8.43	36.74 ± 13.80	144.5	-5.47	<0.001*
ESD	14.34 ± 0.90	14.66 ± 0.53	510.0	-1.35	0.189
ECM	3.62 ± 2.77	11.11 ± 4.24	71.5	-6.34	<0.001*
	Child $\mu \pm \sigma$	Adult $\mu \pm \sigma$	d.f.	F	p
DF	8.12 ± 1.84	57.13 ± 14.86	1, 68	-18.52	<0.001*
ML	11.03 ± 6.15	19.05 ± 5.11	1, 68	-5.96	<0.001*

4.6   Correlations Between Our Game and Traditional Methods

In order to compare the participants' performance when using the game (TS) and traditional methods (DB, DF, ML, ESD, and ECM), correlations were calculated with the complete sample (32 children and 38 adults). The Spearman correlation was applied and the effect size of the correlation was obtained, rho (ρ). The correlations between the TS variable and the traditional method variables are: ML ($\rho = 0.43$, $p < 0.001*$) and DB ($\rho = 0.45$, $p < 0.001$). All correlations are linear and positive. These correlations demonstrate the similarity between our game and those traditional methods (ML and DB).

4.7   User Experience

Table 4 shows the results of the statistical analysis applied to the answers to the QS questionnaire about the users' experience and the comparison of the scores between children and adults. Both groups found the game easy to use and easy to learn (Q1 and Q2). The children were significantly more likely than the adults to recommend the game to their friends (Q3), and they were significantly more satisfied with the game (Q4). Both groups found the interface pleasant to use with regard to body movements (Q5) and the auditory interface (Q6). The children found the interface significantly more fun than the adults (Q7) (Table 4).

Table 4. Mann-Whitney U test analysis and r effect size for differences between children and adults on the QS questionnaire. '**' indicates significant difference at level $\alpha = 0.05$.

Q#.	Children	$\mu_{Ch} \pm \sigma_{Ch}$	Adults	$\mu_A \pm \sigma_A$	U	Z	p	r
1	[5]; [1]	4.44 ± 0.88	[4]; [1]	4.21 ± 0.70	748.5	1.832	0.069	0.219
2	[5]; [0]	4.81 ± 0.40	[5]; [0]	4.82 ± 0.39	606.0	-0.035	>0.99	0.004
3	[5]; [0]	4.53 ± 0.98	[4]; [1]	4.08 ± 0.78	849.0	3.117	<0.001**	0.373
4	[5]; [1]	4.62 ± 0.55	[4]; [1]	4.32 ± 0.62	772.0	2.182	0.035**	0.261
5	[4]; [2]	4.09 ± 1.06	[4]; [2]	3.89 ± 0.92	696.5	1.105	0.278	0.132
6	[4]; [1]	4.25 ± 0.80	[4]; [1]	4.29 ± 0.69	605.5	-0.032	0.997	0.004
7	[5]; [0]	4.78 ± 0.49	[4]; [1]	4.24 ± 0.54	918.5	4.162	<0.001**	0.497

Figure 7 shows graphically the mean scores for the QS questionnaire. The children gave a mean score of 4.55 ± 0.55 on the QS questionnaire, and the adults gave a mean score of 4.26 ± 0.47. These results and the observations of the supervisor indicate that both children and adults understood how to interact with the game and were able to learn and recall a sequence of auditory icons with their respective locations while moving.

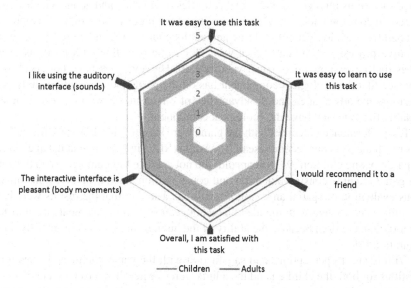

Fig. 7. Graph showing the mean scores for the questionnaire.

5 Discussion

Our game combines Natural User Interfaces (using gestures) with smart devices. The game was designed for the assessment of spatial memory by using auditory stimuli. Previous proposals for the assessment of spatial memory are centered on visual cues [46–49]. Traditional methods consider each skill separately [51–53]. However, our game combines auditory stimuli with real visual cues for the assessment of spatial memory.

A study involving 70 participants (32 children and 38 adults) was carried out. The participants played with our game, and traditional tests [51–53] were also administered. The results of the game were compared with the results obtained using traditional methods. Correlations were found between our game and traditional methods, indicating that our game has proven to be a valid tool for assessing spatial memory by using auditory stimuli for both children and adults. This result affirmatively answers our first research question (RQ1). These correlations are in line with previous works for assessing spatial memory (only based in visual cues) that also obtained correlations between their tasks and traditional methods [46–49]. This result is also in line with other previous works that have demonstrated that serious games have the potential to be used as assessment tools (e.g., [56]) or for diagnosis (e.g., [57]).

With regard to ecological validity, in neuropsychological assessment, ecological validity can be defined as the "functional and predictive relation between the participant's performance on a set of neuropsychological tests and the participant's performance in a variety of real-world settings" [58]. Therefore, the development of new games for neuropsychological assessment represents an important tool for early identification of atypical development or for assessment of memory as a cognitive function that is linked to various intellectual and social activities of children and adults. Games of this type could contribute to a better understanding of the influence of different variables on the cognitive development of children and adults. Our game can be used for assessing cognitive processes in an ecological way. Our game is in line with previous serious games that have shown ecological validity [59]. However, we have not checked the influence that the ecological component has on the participants. A future study could determine the advantages and disadvantages of our proposal with respect to another modality that does not have the ecological component.

The performance outcomes with the game were significantly lower for the children. This result answers our second research question (RQ2) indicating that the age range of the participating children (9–10 years old) did not achieve full competence in the game. The game requires constant attention and concentration since it involves the simultaneous evaluation of spatial and auditory abilities. The fact that the results were better for adults is consistent with the idea that adults can store more elements in short-term memory than children because the ability of the humans increases continuously during maturation [6].

With regard to perceptions and satisfaction with the game, the mean scores for all questions for both the children and the adults were greater than 4 (on a scale of 1 to 5). Only Q5 for the adults had a mean score of 3.89 ("Q5: The interactive interface is pleasant (body movements)"). Therefore, we can conclude that all of the participants found the game easy to learn and easy to use, they had a good time, and they have shown their satisfaction with the game. The analysis showed that the children scored significantly higher on questions Q3 (recommend the game to a friend), Q4 (satisfied with the game), and Q7 (fun). This result answers our third research question (RQ3) indicating that the children were significantly more satisfied with the game than the adults. Since the game seemed easy to use for both children and adults, they were able to concentrate on the tasks to be done rather than on the control mechanisms. The Karotz make sounds and move their ears and illuminate their central part, so the participants can consider them as pets or toys. This aspect could influence the greater fun experienced by the children. The use of multiple sensory modalities may influence participants' satisfaction. The communication of the participants with the Karotz raising their arms can be interpreted as a code of communication between equals, which can influence the attractiveness of the game. Many participants were accustomed to this type of interaction given the proliferation of games that use color-depth sensors, so this type of interaction seemed natural. From our point of view, all of this contributes to the immersion that our game induces and the motivation that the participants showed. The supervisor's observations corroborate our perception of immersion. The supervisor added that many participants did not realize that the Karotz rabbits were there and they even talked to the Karotz rabbits. However, we have not yet determined the influence that the physical appearance of the Karotz had on the children and their motivation for the activity. The study of this influence could be part of another work.

With regard to the interaction and selection of the Karotz, in this work the interaction has been achieved through gestures. However, the button that the Karotz have on top could be used, a natural language user interface could be used, the correct Karotz could be selected on a tablet, etc. As future work, we are studying the incorporation of other types of interaction and their comparison. However, the intention of our proposal is for the game to be used by blind people and the alternative interaction would also have to consider this population. Thus, pressing the button on the top of the Karotz or using a tablet would not be viable alternatives. Also, other types of robots that are currently on the market or that could appear in the future could be used to reproduce or improve our proposal.

6 Conclusion

Our game presents an alternative tool to assess both multimodal integration and learning of auditory and spatial information in children and adults. The game could be used for assessment and training of spatial memory. The game could help in the identification of alterations in spatial memory in both children and adults. In children, the game could help in the early identification of atypical development, children with Attention Deficit Hyperactivity Disorder, etc. In adults, the game could help in the identification of alterations in memory, such as Alzheimer's disease, other types of dementia with alterations of orientation, patients with sequelae after suffering a stroke or head trauma, etc.

As a computer-based game, our game facilitates the control of the presentation of stimuli and the recording of responses. We assume that a supervisor of this experience might make some mistakes due to distraction and/or tiredness, among other causes. The game could be enhanced by adding visual keys (lights in the bellies of the Karotz rabbits or movement of their ears). In this paper, we have compared children and adults, but other comparisons are also possible. For example, it would be interesting to compare the performance of children with normal vision and blind children or to use this new game with children with developmental disorders. Another study could focus on the suitability of the game for people with autism. In that study, it would be very interesting to determine if the appearance of the Karotz is especially suitable for this population.

Acknowledgments. This work was mainly funded by the Spanish Ministry of Economy and Competitiveness (MINECO) through the CHILDMNEMOS project (TIN2012-37381-C02-01) and cofinanced by the European Regional Development Fund (FEDER).

Other financial support was received from the Government of the Republic of Ecuador through the Scholarship Program of the Secretary of Higher Education, Science, Technology and Innovation (SENESCYT), the *Conselleria d'Educació, Investigació, Cultura i Esport* through the grant for consolidable research groups in favour of the Computer Graphics and Multimedia group of the ai2 (PI. Prof. M.-Carmen Juan; Ref. AICO/2017/041) (2017–2018), the Government of Aragon (Department of Industry and Innovation), and the European Social Fund for Aragon.

We would like to thank the following for their contributions: Jimena Bonilla; the users who participated in the study; and the reviewers for their valuable comments.

References

1. Deterding, S., Dixon, D., Khaled, R., Nacke, L.: From game design elements to gamefulness: defining "Gamification". In: Proceedings of the 15th International Academic MindTrek Conference: Envisioning Future Media Environments (MindTrek 2011), pp. 9–15. ACM, New York (2011)
2. Wiemeyer, J., Kliem, A.: Serious games in prevention and rehabilitation - a new panacea for elderly people? Eur. Rev. Aging Phys. Act. **9**, 41–50 (2012)
3. Catalano, C.E., Luccini, A.M., Mortara, M.: Best practices for effective design and evaluation of serious games. Int. J. Serious Games **1**, e1–e13 (2014)
4. Whyte, E.M., Smyth, J.M., Scherf, K.S.: Designing serious game interventions for individuals with Autism. J. Autism Dev. Disord. **45**, 3820–3831 (2015)
5. Kim, K.-W., Choi, Y., You, H., Na, D.L., Yoh, M.-S., Park, J.-K., Seo, J.-H., Ko, M.-H.: Effects of a serious game training on cognitive functions in older adults. J. Am. Geriatr. Soc. **63**, 603–605 (2015)
6. Lezak, M.D.: Neuropsychological Assessment. Oxford University Press, New York (1995)
7. Rourke, B.P.: Arithmetic disabilities, specific and otherwise: a neuropsychological perspective. J. Learn. Disabil. **26**, 214–226 (1993)
8. Arai, S., Okamoto, Y., Fujioka, T., Inohara, K., Ishitobi, M., Matsumura, Y., Jung, M., Kawamura, K., Takiguchi, S., Tomoda, A., Wada, Y., Hiratani, M., Matsuura, N., Kosaka, H.: Altered frontal pole development affects self-generated spatial working memory in ADHD. Brain Dev. **38**, 471–480 (2016)
9. Dehn, M.J.: Cognitive processing deficits. In: Morris, R.J., Mather, N. (eds.) Evidence-Based Interventions for Students with Learning and Behavioral Challenges, pp. 258–287. Routledge, New York and London (2008)
10. Graham, J.A., Heywood, S.: The effects of elimination of hand gestures and of verbal codability on speech performance. Eur. J. Soc. Psychol. **5**, 189–195 (1975)
11. Rauscher, F.H., Krauss, R.M., Chen, Y.: Gesture, speech, and lexical access: the role of lexical movements in speech production. Psychol. Sci. **7**, 226–231 (1996)
12. Khan, R.Z., Ibraheem, N.A.: Hand gesture recognition: a literature review. Int. J. Artif. Intell. Appl. **3**(4), 161–174 (2012)
13. Pisharady, P.K., Saerbeck, M.: Recent methods and databases in vision-based hand gesture recognition: a review. Comput. Vis. Image Underst. **141**, 152–165 (2015)
14. Agrawal, S., Constandache, I., Gaonkar, S., Choudhury, R.R., Caves, K., DeRuyter, F.: Using mobile phones to write in air. In: Proceedings of the 7th ACM International Conference on Mobile Systems, Applications, and Services, Washington, DC, USA, pp. 15–28 (2011)
15. Park, T., Lee, J., Hwang, I., Yoo, C., Nachman, L., Song, J.: Egesture: a collaborative architecture for energy-efficient gesture recognition with hand-worn sensor and mobile devices. In: Proceedings of the 9th ACM Conference on Embedded Networked Sensor Systems, pp. 260–273. ACM, Seattle (2011)
16. Beh, J., Han, D.K., Durasiwami, R., Ko, H.: Hidden Markov model on a unit hyper-sphere space for gesture trajectory recognition. Pattern Recognit. Lett. **36**, 144–153 (2014)
17. Suk, H.I., Sin, B.K., Lee, S.W.: Hand gesture recognition based on dynamic Bayesian network framework. Pattern Recognit. **43**(9), 3059–3072 (2010)

18. Yang, M.H., Ahuja, N., Tabb, M.: Extraction of 2D motion trajectories and its application to hand gesture recognition. IEEE Trans. Pattern Anal. Mach. Intell. **24**(8), 1061–1074 (2002)
19. Shen, X.H., Hua, G., Williams, L., Wu, Y.: Dynamic hand gesture recognition: an exemplar-based approach from motion divergence fields. Image Vis. Comput. **30**(3), 227–235 (2012)
20. Patwardhan, K.S., Roy, S.D.: Hand gesture modelling and recognition involving changing shapes and trajectories, using a predictive eigentracker. Pattern Recognit. Lett. **28**, 329–334 (2007)
21. Shin, M.C., Tsap, L.V., Goldgof, D.B.: Gesture recognition using Bezier curves for visualization navigation from registered 3-D data. Pattern Recognit. **37**(5), 1011–1024 (2004)
22. Kuremoto, T., Kinoshita, Y., Feng, L., Watanabe, S., Kobayashi, K., Obayashi, M.: A gesture recognition system with retina-v1 model and one-pass dynamic programming. Neurocomputing **116**, 291–300 (2012)
23. Corradini, A.: Dynamic time warping for off-line recognition of a small gesture vocabulary. In: Proceedings of the IEEE International Workshop on Computer Vision (ICCVW 2001), pp. 82–89. IEEE (2001)
24. Breuer, P., Eckes, C., Müller, S.: Hand gesture recognition with a novel IR time-of-flight range camera–a pilot study. In: Gagalowicz, A., Philips, W. (eds.) MIRAGE 2007. LNCS, vol. 4418, pp. 247–260. Springer, Heidelberg (2007). https://doi.org/ 10.1007/978-3-540-71457-6_23
25. Zhang, Z.: Microsoft Kinect sensor and its effect. IEEE Multi Med. **19**(2), 4–10 (2012)
26. Shotton, J., Fitzgibbon, A., Cook, M., Sharp, T., Finocchio, M., Moore, R., Kipman, A., Blake, A.: Real-time human pose recognition in parts from single depth images. In: The IEEE Computer Vision and Pattern Recognition, pp. 116–124. ACM, New York (2011)
27. Martín-SanJosé, J.F., Juan, M.C., Gil-Gómez, J.A., Rando, N.: Flexible learning itinerary vs. linear learning itinerary. Sci. Comput. Program. **88**, 3–21 (2014)
28. Martín-SanJosé, J.F., Juan, M.C., Torres, E., Vicent, M.J.: Playful interaction for learning collaboratively and individually. J. Ambient Intell. Smart Environ. **6**, 295–311 (2014)
29. Martín-SanJosé, J.F., Juan, M.C., Mollá, R., Vivó, R.: Advanced displays and natural user interfaces to support learning. Interact. Learn. Environ. **25**(1), 17–34 (2017)
30. Rodríguez-Andrés, D., Juan, M. C., Mollá, R., Méndez-López, M.: A 3D serious game for dental learning in higher education. In: Proceedings of the 17th IEEE International Conference on Advanced Learning Technologies (ICALT2017), pp. 111–115. IEEE (2017)
31. Homer, B., Kinzer, C., Plass, J., Letourneau, S., Hoffman, D., Bromley, M., Hayward, E., Turkay, S., Kornak, Y.: Moved to learn: the effects of interactivity in a Kinect-based literacy game for beginning readers. Comput. Educ. **74**, 37–49 (2014)
32. Lin, J., Sun, Q., Li, G., He, Y.: SnapBlocks: a snapping interface for assembling toy blocks with XBOX kinect. Multimed. Tools Appl. **73**, 2009–2032 (2014)
33. Sun, C., Zhang, T., Bao, B.K., Xu, C., Mei, T.: Discriminative exemplar coding for sign language recognition with Kinect. IEEE Trans. Cybern. **43**, 1418–1428 (2013)
34. Lee, G.C., Yeh, F.-H., Hsiao, Y.-H.: Kinect-based Taiwanese sign-language recognition system. Multimed. Tools Appl. **75**, 261–279 (2016)
35. Armin, K., Mehrana, Z., Fatemeh, D.: Using kinect in teaching children with hearing and visual impairment. In: Proceedings of the 4th International Conference on e-Learning and e-Teaching (ICELET 2013), pp. 86–90. IEEE (2013)
36. Retalis, S., Boloudakis, M., Altanis, G., Nikou, N.: Children with motor impairments play a kinect learning game: first findings from a pilot case in an authentic classroom environment. Interact. Des. Archit. **19**, 91–104 (2014)

37. Luna-Oliva, L., Ortiz-Gutiérrez, R.M., Cano-de la Cuerda, R., Piédrola, R.M., Alguacil-Diego, I.M., Sánchez-Camarero, C., Martínez Culebras, M.D.C.: Kinect Xbox 360 as a therapeutic modality for children with cerebral palsy in a school environment: a preliminary study. NeuroRehabilitation **33**, 513–521 (2013)

38. Jordan, K., King, M., Hellersteth, S., Wirén, A., Mulligan, H.: Feasibility of using a humanoid robot for enhancing attention and social skills in adolescents with autism spectrum disorder. Int. J. Rehabil. Res. **36**, 221–227 (2013)

39. Moriguchi, Y., Kanda, T., Ishiguro, H., Shimada, Y., Itakura, S.: Can young children learn words from a robot? Interact. Stud. **12**, 107–118 (2011)

40. Movellan, J.R., Eckhardt, M., Virnes, M., Rodriguez, A.: Sociable robot improves toddler vocabulary skills. In: Proceedings of the 4th ACM/IEEE International Conference on Human Robot Interaction, pp. 307–308. ACM, New York (2009)

41. Keren, G., Fridin, M.: Kindergarten social assistive robot (KindSAR) for children's geometric thinking and metacognitive development in preschool education: a pilot study. Comput. Hum. Behav. **35**, 400–412 (2014)

42. Keren, G., Ben-David, A., Fridin, M.: Kindergarten assistive robotics (KAR) as a tool for spatial cognition development in pre-school education. In: 2012 IEEE/RSJ International Conference on Intelligent Robots and Systems, pp. 1084–1089. IEEE (2012)

43. Timms, M.J.: Letting artificial intelligence in education out of the box: educational cobots and smart classrooms. Int. J. Artif. Intell. Educ. **26**, 701–712 (2016)

44. Randell, C., Price, S., Rogers, Y., Harris, E., Fitzpatrick, G.: The ambient horn: designing a novel audio-based learning experience. Pers. Ubiquitous Comput. **8**, 177–183 (2004)

45. de Graaf, M.M.A., Allouch, S.B., Klamer, T.: Sharing a life with Harvey: exploring the acceptance of and relationship-building with a social robot. Comput. Hum. Behav. **43**, 1–14 (2015)

46. Juan, M.-C., Mendez-Lopez, M., Perez-Hernandez, E., Albiol-Perez, S.: Augmented reality for the assessment of children's spatial memory in real settings. PLoS ONE **9**, e113751 (2014)

47. Mendez-Lopez, M., Perez-Hernandez, E., Juan, M.C.: Learning in the navigational space: age differences in a short-term memory for objects task. Learn. Individ. Differences **60**, 11–22 (2016)

48. Rodríguez-Andrés, D., Juan, M.-C., Méndez-López, M., Pérez-Hernández, E., Lluch, J.: MnemoCity task: assessment of children's spatial memory using stereoscopy and virtual environments. PLoS ONE **11**, e0161858 (2016)

49. Cárdenas-Delgado, S., Méndez-López, M., Juan, M.-C., Pérez-Hernández, E., Lluch, J., Vivó, R.: Using a virtual maze task to assess spatial short-term memory in adults. In: Proceedings of the International Conference on Computer Graphics Theory and Applications, pp. 46–57. Scitepress (2017)

50. Lumsden, J., Edwards, E.A., Lawrence, N.S., Coyle, D., Munafò, M.R.: Gamification of cognitive assessment and cognitive training: a systematic review of applications and efficacy. JMIR Serious Games **4**, e11 (2016)

51. Reynolds, C.R., Bigler, E.D.: TOMAL test of memory and learning: examiner's manual. Austin, TX: Pro-Ed [TOMAL Test de memoria y aprendizaje. Manual de interpretación (E. Goikoetxea, & Departamento I + D de TEA Ediciones, Adapters), (TEA Ediciones, Madrid)] (2001)

52. Brancal, M.F., Alcantud, F., Ferrer, A.M., Quiroga, M.E.: EDAF: Evaluación de la discriminación auditiva y fonológica. TEA Ediciones, Lebón, Madrid (2009)

53. Kamphaus, K.W., Perez-Hernandez, E., Sanchez-Sanchez, F.: Cuestionario de Evaluación Clínica de la Memoria. TEA Ediciones, Madrid (in press)

54. Lewis, J.R.: IBM computer usability satisfaction questionnaires: psychometric evaluation and instructions for use. Int. J. Hum. Comput. Interact. **7**(1), 57–78 (1995)
55. Lund, A.M.: Measuring usability with the USE questionnaire. Usability User Exp. Newslett. STC Usability SIG. **8**(2), 1–4 (2001)
56. Vallejo, V., Wyss, P., Chesham, A., Mitache, A.V., Müri, R.M., Mosimann, U.P., Nef, T.: Evaluation of a new serious game based multitasking assessment tool for cognition and activities of daily living: comparison with a real cooking task. Comput. Hum. Behav. **70**, 500–506 (2017)
57. Tarnanas, I., Tsolaki, M., Nef, T.M., Müri, R., Mosimann, U.P.: Can a novel computerized cognitive screening test provide additional information for early detection of Alzheimer's disease? Alzheimer's Dementia **10**, 790–798 (2014)
58. Spooner, D., Pachana, N.: Ecological validity in neuropsychological assessment: a case for greater consideration in research with neurologically intact populations. Arch. Clin. Neuropsychol. **21**, 327–337 (2006)
59. Tarnanas, I., Schlee, W., Tsolaki, M., Müri, R., Mosimann, U., Nef, T.: Ecological validity of virtual reality daily living activities screening for early dementia: longitudinal study. JMIR Serious Games **1**, e1 (2013)

Mafia Game Setting Research
Using Game Refinement Measurement

Shuo Xiong[1(✉)], Wenlin Li[2(✉)], Xinting Mao[1(✉)], and Hiroyuki Iida[1(✉)]

[1] Japan Advanced Institute of Science and Technology, Nomi, Japan
{xiongshuo,maoxinting,iida}@jaist.ac.jp
[2] Huazhong University of Science and Technology, Wuhan, China
liwenlin223@gmail.com

Abstract. This paper explores the game sophistication of a popular party game called Mafia or Werewolf. It focuses on the playing settings, i.e., the number of total players (say N) including citizen, mafia (m), sheriff (s) and doctor (d), denoted as $MFG(N, m, d, s)$. Computer simulations for a simple version of Mafia game are conducted to collect the data while game refinement measure is employed for the assessment. The results indicate several interesting observations. For example, the measure of game refinement reduces as the number of players increases. This implies that Mafia game would become boring as the number of players becomes too large. $MFG(N, m, s, d)$ can be played reasonably with $N \in \{14, 15, 16\}$, $m \in \{5, 6\}$, $s = 1$ and $d \in \{1, 2\}$. In particular, $MFG(15, 5, 1, 1)$ or $MFG(15, 6, 1, 2)$ is the best to play under the assumption that its game refinement measure is within the sophisticated zone. Moreover, the level of players affects the game balancing and game sophistication. For example, mafia would dominate citizens if all players are weak, which implies that the game sophistication would be reduced.

Keywords: Game refinement theory · Mafia game · Game theory

1 Introduction

Mafia game or Werewolf game is a popular party game, which can be played in a party or just on the Internet. There are two groups in a simple version: Mafia and citizens. There are several rounds to play and every round has a certain progress. The game ends when one of the groups is killed by the other group. As a popular multi-player game, Mafia game is a good research target because different settings can affect the game balancing [11]. For example, it is interesting to know about the appropriate number of players in a given multi-player game to maintain the attractiveness [14].

To our best knowledge, no one has investigated the comfortable settings of Mafia game. A computer simulation for Mafia game is conducted to collect the data such as the game length, whereas game refinement measurement is employed for the assessment. As a benchmark for this study we have chosen a

© Springer International Publishing AG, part of Springer Nature 2018
A. D. Cheok et al. (Eds.): ACE 2017, LNCS 10714, pp. 830–846, 2018.
https://doi.org/10.1007/978-3-319-76270-8_56

simplest version of Mafia game in which there are only Mafia group members and citizen group members including a Sheriff and a Doctor, but without any special characters and additional rules.

The structure of this paper is as follows. Section 2 presents the related works. The rules of simple Mafia game and our assessment methodology are described in Sect. 3. Simulation and data collection are presented in Sect. 4. Data analysis and discussion are given in Sect. 5. Finally, concluding remarks are given in Sect. 6.

2 Related Works

At the beginning, Mafia game was created for psychology research in 1970s [18]. Then it evolved into a party game for fun. Dmitry Davidoff is generally acknowledged as the game's creator. He dates the first game to spring 1987 at the Psychology Department of Moscow State University, spreading to classrooms, dorms, and summer camps of Moscow University, he developed the game to combine psychology research with his duties teaching high school students [10]. In 1998 the Kaliningrad Higher school of the Internal Affairs Ministry published the methodical textbook Nonverbal communications. Developing role-playing games "Mafia" and "Murderer" for a course on Visual psychodiagnostics, to teach various methods of reading body language and nonverbal signals. Therefore, Mafia game not only can make human feel relax, but also the game has certain strong academic meaning in the psychology and society communication.

Mafia game as an interesting research target from the multi-player game domain has been investigated from various perspectives. Basically we focus on four areas: psychology and game theory, artificial intelligence, team work strategy, and design of the game.

There are several works focused on the human behavior and the psychological aspects of playing a werewolf that used various features for determining whether a player is a werewolf. For example, they include a study that used each player utterances, utterance lengths, and the number of interruptions [8]; a study that used hand and head movements [3]; and a study that used the number of words in each utterance [15] to determine whether a player was a werewolf.

Braverman et al. [2] performed a theoretical study on Mafia game to find the optimal strategies for different groups and calculate the winning rate. They were interested in the best strategies for the different groups in such scenarios and in evaluating their relative power, then analyzed two variants that are with or without a Sheriff - which is also called a Detective - and found out the best strategy in the absence of a Sheriff, i.e., for the total number of players (say R) the number of Mafia members is $O(\sqrt{R})$, there will be an equal rate for each group to win. Conversely, when the number of Mafia members is linear in R, it is proved to be fair when there are Sheriffs in the game, which means that even a single Sheriff could change the qualitative behavior of the game.

There are other Mafia game studies that concentrated on other aspects than strategies. Katagami et al. [8] focused on the nonverbal information in Mafia game. They studied on how nonverbal information, like gestures and facial expressions, impacts the winning rate. After the investigation, they found out that nonverbal information is important for the victory of the game. Furthermore, Kobayashi et al. [9] developed a match system for humans with life-like agents. With this system, they tried to analyze nonverbal information from movies of games played by human to verify whether a life-like agent can give impressions like a human if they mount the analyzed movement on a life-like agent. They found that the movement which is felt doubtful is also doubtful even if a life-like agent expressed, though there was a difference in an impression that is influenced by the contents of utterances.

Furthermore, several audiovisual corpora containing dialogue data in the Mafia game were constructed to analyze group communication [6,13]. Hirata [5] constructed a behavioral model by obtaining behavioral information from play logs describing play between humans. The proposed model identifies an action selection probability to realize an agent that can behave like humans.

Later Bi [1] concentrated on a werewolf-side strategy called the "stealth werewolf" strategy with which each of the werewolf-side players (Mafia members) behaves like a citizen without showing their special roles. They limited some of the human-side strategies and they calculated the ϵ-Nash equilibrium of strategies for both sides under the limitation. They found out that this strategy is not friendly to the Mafia group.

From the game design's point of view, Revenant [4] created a custom game in Blizzard's StarCraft II which we call "SC2Mafia". Similar to other web-based Mafia games, SC2Mafia is inspired by the classic party game of the same name but features a faster pace and a wide range of different role options. The only requirement to play SC2Mafia is a copy of StarCraft II. People who have not purchased the game can also download StarCraft II Starter Edition, which has been made available by Blizzard for free. SC2Mafia features a strong player base and loyal community of users who are playing games at almost any time during the day. The most interesting feature in SC2Mafia game is that every player has his/her own special ability, and room number, e.g., Spy can wiretap the talking of Mafia or Triad group in night, Lookout can observe a player and see who "visited" them during a particular night, etc.

Generally, academic research approaches have been focusing mainly on the human behaviors, artificial intelligence or natural language processing. However, there are hardly any studies about Mafia game settings or the game balancing issue. As a base of the game, this paper will therefore propose a method to examine the balancing and sophisticated (or comfortable) settings of Mafia game.

3   Assessment Methodology

This section presents our assessment methodology for analyzing Mafia game in this study. It presents a simple version of Mafia game as a benchmark, whereas a short sketch of game progress model for Mafia game is given to apply the measure of game refinement for the assessment.

3.1   Simple Version of Mafia Game

We introduce the rules of a simple version of Mafia game (or "Werewolf" game). We need some participants collected in a circle, and a game coordinator assigns each player to one of the two groups: Mafia or Citizens. Citizens know only their own identity, whereas Mafia members know not only the identity of themselves but also of their fellows. The target is to defeat the other group. The game consists of two alternating phases – day and night. During the night the Mafia members make a decision to kill one of the Citizens. Then during the day time, all the players discuss together and vote for a possible mafia that they want to execute. There can also be some special characters of the Citizens who can use their skills to achieve the success, such as Sheriff (to investigate whether a player is mafia member or not at night) and Doctors (to save a killed character at night) [11].

There can be many variations of Mafia game. A typical modification of the game is to add characters with special skills as many as possible. For example, in the "Werewolf" game, besides Prophet (the same as Sheriff in Mafia) and Guarder (the same as Doctor in Mafia), a number of characters can be added, such as Hunter (when a hunter is killed, he can kill anyone of the alive characters for revenge), Witch (she has a poison to kill any character and a panacea to save a partner) and Twins (two citizens knowing the identity of each other) etc. "Werewolf" game also adds some event cards to adjust the game process, which makes the game more interesting [2].

Mafia game is played in a party to enjoy or just to kill time. Currently, there are two types of Mafia game – one is the traditional card game, in which players get together and pick cards to decide their roles. They also need to choose one person as the compere master, who has to control the game period such as to remind Mafia, Sheriff and Doctor to do their works. Another one is the Mafia video game in which players use computers to play. Players are assigned to their characters by the game system, and can use skills by pressing a simple button. The game system can also judge automatically which group is the winner. The most famous Mafia video game platform is the custom map in StarCraft II as shown in Fig. 1. Later we introduce the simple Mafia game in detail.

Notation 1. *$MFG(N, m, s, d)$ denotes a game of Mafia that has totally N players which consists of m Mafia group members and $N - m$ citizen group members including s sheriffs and d doctors. $MFG(N, m)$ simply stands for a game of Mafia that has totally N players including m Mafia group members and $N - m$ citizen group members.*

3.2   Methodology

Game refinement theory was established in 2004 by Iida et al. [7]. This theory gives a measure to quantify the sophistication of the game under consideration. It provides us with a deep insight into current games and we are therefore enabled to improve the quality of the game [12]. In game refinement theory, the game

Fig. 1. A screenshot of Mafia game map in StarCraft II

progress is divided into two elements. One is called game speed or scoring rate, while another one is game information progress with a focus on the game outcome. Game information progress presents the degree of certainty of a game's result in time or in steps. Finally, we use a physical model to get the second derivative of game [16], which we call game refinement value. Many games have been analyzed by this measure as shown in Table 1 [17]. Here GR stands for the measure of game refinement, where $GR = \frac{\sqrt{G}}{T}$ which is derived from the game information progress model. From the results, we conjecture the relation between the measure of game refinement and game sophistication, as stated below.

Table 1. Measures of game refinement for various types of games

	G	T	GR
Chess	35	80	0.074
Shogi	80	115	0.078
Go	250	208	0.076
Basketball	36.38	82.01	0.073
Soccer	2.64	22	0.073
Badminton	46.336	79.344	0.086
Table tennis	54.863	96.465	0.077
DotA ver 6.80	68.6	106.2	0.078
StarCraft II Terran	1.64	16	0.081
The king of the fighters 98	14.6	36.7	0.104

Conjecture 1. Sophisticated games have a common factor (i.e., same degree of informatical acceleration value, say 0.07–0.08) to feel engaged or excited regardless of different type of games.

Therefore, it is expected that Mafia game can be analyzed by this method. In Sect. 3.3, the detail of mathematical process will be described.

3.3 Game Progress Model of Mafia Game

Let us consider the game progress of Mafia game. In every day and night, players will use their skills and logic to kill citizens or execute the mafia member, while the number of players is reduced to a certain value, then game ends. Therefore, let K and L be the average number of players killed and average game length, respectively. If one knows the game information progress, for example, after the game, the game progress $x(t)$ will be given as a linear function of time t with $0 \leq t \leq L$ and $0 \leq x(t) \leq K$, as shown in Eq. (1).

$$x(t) = \frac{K}{L} t \tag{1}$$

However, the game information progress given by Eq. (1) is usually unknown during the in-game period. Hence, the game information progress is reasonably assumed to be exponential. This is because the game outcome is uncertain until the very end of game in many games. Hence, a realistic model of game information progress is given by Eq. (2).

$$x(t) = K(\frac{t}{L})^n \tag{2}$$

Here n stands for a constant parameter which is given based on the perspective of an observer in the game considered. Then the acceleration of game information progress is obtained by deriving Eq. (2) twice. Solving it at $t = L$, the equation becomes

$$x''(L) = \frac{Kn(n-1)}{L^n}t^{n-2} = \frac{K}{L^2}n(n-1)$$

Similarly, we get the game refinement value $GR = \frac{\sqrt{K}}{L}$. The average game length L is given by $L = QT$ where Q and T stands for the average number of survivals and the average number of turns, respectively. Thus, the final form of game refinement is given by $GR = \frac{\sqrt{K}}{QT}$.

4 Simulation and Data Collection

For the computer simulation, we need the details of the simple version of Mafia game, which are given below.

* The game needs N players and one more person to coordinate it.
* At the beginning, players are randomly divided into $(N - m)$ citizens and m mafia members.
* Mafia members know the identity of each other, while citizens know only the identity of themselves but do not know others.
* There are two alternating phases: day and night.

* During the day, there are two consecutive subphases:
  * Debate. Everyone still alive can say anything related to accusing or defending.
  * Vote. Everyone has a chance to vote for whom should be executed. The player who gets the highest number of votes is eliminated (in case of a tie, random again). The victims faction is revealed.
* During the night:
  * Sheriff decides whom he wants to inspect, then the game compere will tell Sheriff if the object who was inspected belongs to Mafia or citizens.
  * Mafia members jointly decide whom they want to kill.
  * Doctor decides whom he wants to save.
  * Game compere announces the night finished, and all the players open their eyes and are mentioned who has been killed or that nobody has been killed and that it was a peace night.
* Repeat the process. The game continues until there is only one group (either the citizens or mafia) left and that group wins.

We create a program to simulate the above process of Mafia game $MFG(N, m, 1, 1)$ where we assume that there is a sheriff and a doctor. Every round is divided into 4 parts – 1. Night citizens' strategy; 2. Night Mafia's strategy; 3. Day discussion; 4. Day vote. Then, we follow the Nash equilibrium strategy and the algorithm as below.

* Sheriff will check the identity of a specific target player at night, then write his identity in "last word". If he finds out the mafia member and can be alive until the next day, he will show his sheriff status and ask citizens to execute the mafia.
* Doctor will save himself at night, while he knows who is the sheriff. The doctor will always protect sheriff, unless he was killed.
* Mafia members will kill a player each night, because mafia members do not know whether the doctor is alive or not and his decision, even if they know who is sheriff, they still keep killing a player randomly. The detail of Nash equilibrium strategy is given in Fig. 2.
* Citizens will vote and execute a player at the day time. If sheriff has information, then they will vote somebody based on the sheriff's suggestion. Otherwise, they will vote a player (who was not investigated by sheriff) randomly. If several players have the same poll, randomly vote again until someone can be executed.
* All the players repeat this process, until one group wins the game.

Then, we use Python to create a simulation program to simulate the game process. For each case, the number of simulation runs is 10000, then the results are shown in Table 3. The pseudo code is given in Algorithm 1.

Algorithm 1. Nash equilibrium strategy to play simple Mafia game

---

```
 1: function ASSIGNMENT(N, m)
 2:     count(mafia)=m, count(sheriff)=1, count(doctor)=1, count(players)=n
 3:     Random(n,m);
 4:         N ← mafia, sheriff, doctor, citizen
 5: end function
 6: function INVESTIGATE(sheriff)
 7:     Random(left players)
 8:        if checked
 9:            return -1
10:        else
11:            get character of target player i
12:            i ← m,d,c
13:        return 0
14: end function
15: function KILL(mafia)
16:     Random(left players)
17:        if mafia member
18:            return -1
19:        else
20:            kill target player j
21:        return 0
22: end function
23: function SAVE(doctor)
24:     Random(left players)
25:        if Sheriff=1
26:            protect sheriff k
27:        else
28:        .   protect (left players) k
29:        return 0
30:        if j =!k
31:            n=n-1;
32: end function
33: function DISCUSSION(players)
34:     if i = m
35:         show sheriff's status
36:     else
37:         keep silence
38: end function
39: function VOTE(players)
40:     if i = 1
41:         vote i
42:     else
43:         vote N-i-sheriff
44:     n=n-1;
45:         return 0
46: end function
47: function MAIN(players)
48:     while m > \frac{n}{2}
49:         return 0
50:     else
51:         repeat
52: end function
```

Table 2. Nash equilibrium in Mafia game for Doctor and Mafia

Doctor	Mafia	
	Kill Sheriff	Kill randomly
Save Sheriff	$(1, 0)$	$(0 \leq v \leq 1, 0 \leq v \leq 1)$
Save randomly	$(0 \leq v \leq 1, 0 \leq v \leq 1)$	$(0 \leq v \leq 1, 0 \leq v \leq 1)$

5   Data Analysis and Discussion

In this section we analyze the data which are obtained by computer simulations and we discuss the results.

5.1   Data Analysis

In this study, the game refinement measure is employed for the assessment of game sophistication. However, game balance or fairness for both sides (citizens group and mafia group) is another important aspect. For example, Table 3 shows that the winning ratio of the citizens group is significantly low in $MFG(12, 6)$ while the winning ratio of the mafia group is also low in $MFG(12, 1)$. Therefore, we need to identify the balanceable setting.

Table 3. The results of simulation for $MFG(12, m)$

N	m	Citizens win	Rounds	Death	Mafia win	Rounds	Death
12	6	267	6.07	10.63	9733	1.12	1.22
12	5	3284	5.38	10.01	6716	3.44	5.82
12	4	5975	5.04	9.52	4025	4.64	8.21
12	3	7859	4.60	8.76	2141	5.36	9.63
12	2	9003	3.97	7.60	997	5.78	10.46
12	1	9578	2.91	5.58	422	6.07	11.00

Considering the game played by human with full of emotional behaviors, mafia members know each other and hence they have the information advantage over the citizens group, here we pick up the setting in which the wining ratio of the citizens group is a little higher than the mafia group, just like $MFG(12, 4)$ and $MFG(12, 3)$. We show, in Table 4, the results of simulations for various settings denoted by $MFG(12, m, s, d)$. The results indicate two remarks: (1) For the citizens group, sheriff is much more important than doctor from the viewpoint of game balancing, and (2) $MFG(12, 5, 1, 2)$ among four different settings is the best to play from the viewpoint of game balancing while minimizing the difference of winning ratio between citizens and mafia.

Table 4. The results of simulation for $MFG(12, m, s, d)$

Setting	Citizens win	Rounds	Death	Mafia win	Rounds	Death
MFG(12,5,1,2)	5216	5.21	9.86	4784	3.21	5.41
MFG(12,4,1,1)	6716	4.96	9.49	3284	4.49	7.93
MFG(12,3,0,1)	7722	4.44	8.88	2278	5.29	9.52
MFG(12,3,1,0)	2170	5.15	9.65	7830	5.05	8.97

Further simulations are conducted to find the comfortable settings based on the measure of game refinement and game balancing for various settings $MFG(N, m, s, d)$ with $8 \leq N \leq 20$. The average number of players killed (say K) is calculated for the setting $MFG(12, 5, 1, 2)$ as $K = \frac{5216*9.86+4784*5.41}{10000} = 7.73$. Similarly, the average number of turns or game length (say T) is obtained. Thus we can find the refinement value for each setting described in Table 5.

From Table 5 the following remarks are given.

Table 5. The results of simulation for various settings $MFG(N, m, s, d)$

Setting	Citizens win	Ave. death	Round	Ave. length	GR
MFG(20,9,4,4)	6635	13.20	7.61	76.09	0.0478
MFG(20,8,1,2)	5782	14.74	7.80	78.03	0.0492
MFG(19,7,1,1)	6532	15.12	7.83	74.40	0.0523
MFG(19,6,1,1)	7798	15.56	8.03	76.24	0.0517
MFG(18,7,1,2)	6347	13.56	7.17	64.55	0.0571
MFG(18,6,1,1)	6541	14.12	7.43	66.88	0.0562
MFG(17,7,1,2)	6938	13.27	6.89	58.58	0.0622
MFG(17,7,1,1)	5128	12.27	6.37	54.15	0.0647
MFG(16,6,1,2)	6980	12.22	6.46	51.72	0.0676
MFG(16,6,1,1)	5241	11.62	6.23	49.84	0.0684
MFG(15,6,1,2)	7548	11.95	6.21	46.61	0.0742
MFG(15,5,1,1)	7575	12.06	6.25	46.90	0.0740
MFG(14,5,1,2)	7612	10.72	5.67	39.66	0.0825
MFG(14,5,1,1)	5838	10.34	5.55	38.87	0.0827
MFG(13,6,1,2)	5117	8.35	4.38	28.45	0.1016
MFG(13,5,1,1)	6540	9.96	5.20	33.80	0.0934
MFG(12,5,1,2)	5292	7.75	4.27	25.59	0.1088
MFG(12,4,1,1)	6554	8.93	4.80	28.79	0.1038
MFG(11,4,1,1)	7269	8.51	4.46	24.54	0.1189
MFG(10,3,1,1)	7464	7.33	3.94	19.71	0.1373
MFG(9,4,2,1)	5424	5.74	3.27	14.69	0.1630
MFG(8,3,1,1)	5393	5.29	3.00	12.01	0.1916

Remark 1. The measure of game refinement would reduce as the number of players increases. This may imply that Mafia game would become boring as the number of players becomes too large.

Remark 2. $MFG(N, m, s, d)$ can be played reasonably with $N \in \{14, 15, 16\}$, $m \in \{5, 6\}$, $s = 1$ and $d \in \{1, 2\}$. In particular, $MFG(15, 5, 1, 1)$ or $MFG(15, 6, 1, 2)$ is the best to play under the assumption that its GR value is within the sophisticated zone 0.07-0.08.

Remark 2 suggests that the most suitable number of players is 15. It is interesting to note that for all the defeat setting in StarCrart II complex Mafia game map, the number of players also equals to 15, which we can see at the bottom right corner in the screenshot (see Fig. 2). Therefore, the game designers used their experience to set 15 players, which coincides with our research results.

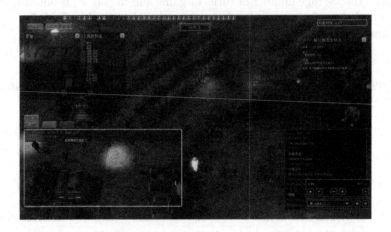

Fig. 2. A screenshot of StarCraft II

To observe the relation between the performance quality and game characteristics, further simulations are conducted using three different level of AIs: strong, fair and weak.

– The strong AI always follows the Nash equilibrium strategy as described in Algorithm 1.
– In the fair AI, doctor will protect randomly and mafia member will kill randomly. We change the save function in Algorithm 1.
– In the weak AI, doctor will protect randomly, mafia will kill randomly and sheriff will not show their identity. We change the save and discussion function in Algorithm 1.

Then, computer simulations are performed using these different AIs for the two settings: $MFG(15, 5, 1, 1)$ and $MFG(20, 9, 4, 4)$. The results are presented in Table 6.

Table 6. The results of simulation using different AIs for two settings

Setting	AI level	Citizens win	Death	Round	Length	GR
$MFG(15, 5, 1, 1)$	Strong	7575	12.06	6.25	46.90	0.0740
	Fair	7552	12.11	6.16	46.20	0.0753
	Weak	1781	10.34	7.93	59.49	0.0541
$MFG(20, 9, 4, 4)$	Strong	6635	13.20	7.61	76.09	0.0478
	Fair	4691	11.51	6.29	62.9	0.0554
	Weak	380	8.60	5.79	57.6	0.0509

Remark 3. The level of players affects the game balancing and game sophistication. For example, mafia would dominate citizens if all the players are weak, in case the game sophistication would be reduced, which implies that game would be boring.

5.2   Mafia Game and SC2Mafia Compared

The analysis of the simple version of Mafia game suggests that the number of players $N \in \{14, 15, 16\}$ will make players feel more enjoyable or comfortable, whereas the number of citizens $N - m \in \{9, 10\}$ will be a balanceable setting. Interestingly, this observation concerning the game setting can be seen in the SC2Mafia game. A short sketch of the SC2Mafia game features is outlined below [4].

* At the beginning, there are always 15 participants. Then, the host computer player chooses a rule or setting from system, or custom-defined.
* Every player has a "room number", some characters' skills are related to their room numbers, and all behaviours in the night period need to be pointed to a certain number (or a certain player).
* Not only Mafia and citizen group, but also Triad and some other neutral characters exist.
* Every player has a special skill. For example, there is a leader – Godfather – in Mafia group, whom Sheriff cannot investigate whether he belongs to Mafia or not. Moreover, Godfather is invincible at night, which means that he cannot be killed by Citizens or Triad characters' attack. Another example is Mass Murderer – a neutral character, who can perform a killing spree at someone's house every night, killing anyone who visits that player at night. Mass Murderer will win if he is the last player remained alive.

SC2Mafia is too complex and it is related with natural language processing, we cannot use program or coding to simulate all the situations in our research. Therefore, in this subsection, we just focus on a simple research question: How powerful is the Godfather? In order to solve it, we can use a program to simulate the winning ratio as Table 7.

Table 7. The results of simulation for Godfather case

Setting	Win for citizens	Average death	Average length	GR
Normal(15,5,1,1)	7531	12.05	46.94	0.0739
Normal(15,6,1,1)	5844	11.21	43.83	0.0764
Godfather(15,1+0,1,1)	7687	10.35	40.39	0.0802
Godfather(15,1+1,1,1)	5506	12.35	48.36	0.0727

From Table 7 two conclusion could be gotten:

1. Compared with the winning ratio, we believe 1 Godfather has same power as 5 normal Mafia killers. Therefore, while Mafia group has a Godfather, Citizens group needs to set more characters that has special abilities to keep balance.
2. While the total number of players is decided, changing the setting will not change the interesting level to a large degree if the setting is still in balance.

However, the research of SC2Mafia is not only limited to this issue, in order to analyze the different setting rules in SC2Mafia, we need to collect the human's replay of SC2Mafia and analyze the refinement values. Some classic balance setting rules can be followed as Table 8 shows.

Table 8. Some setting rules in SC2Mafia game

Name	Setting rules
Traditional	4 Mafia members 10 normal Citizens (1 doctor+1 Sheriff) 1 Neutral Benign
Little Italy	Godfather + 3 Mafia members 9 Specially Skill Citizens (emphasis on Town Protective) 1 Neutral Benign, 1 Neutral Evil
China Town	Dragon Head + 3 Triad members 9 Specially Skill Citizens (emphasis on Town Killing) 1 Neutral Benign, 1 Neutral Evil
Red & Blue	Godfather, Dragon Head, 3 Random (Mafia or Triad) 9 Specially Skill Citizens 1 Neutral Benign
Heresy	9 Specially Skill Citizens (1 Mason + 1 Mason Leader) 3 Original (1 Witch Doctor + 2 Cultist) 1 Neutral Killing, 1 Neutral Evil, 1 Neutral Benign
Blood Rust	Godfather + 1 Mafia member 2 Mass Murderers, 1 Neutral Benign 10 Specially Skill Citizens
Family Glory	Godfather + 2 Mafia members 1 Neutral Killing, 1 Neutral Evil, 1 Neutral Benign 9 Specially Skill Citizens

Except traditional mode, every player has a specially identity and skill during the game setting. Here we introduce several identities to enable readers to understand the SC2Mafia system well. We need to mention that, the types of character are not only limited as seen in the list, according to the game developed, more and more characters and rules setting will be created [4].

Citizen Group

- Bodyguard. Guard one player each night. If someone attacks a guarded player, both the attacker and the Bodyguard die instead of the guarded player.
- Bus Driver. Swap two players at night, making actions that target the first player instead target the second player.
- Detective. Track one person's activity each night.
- Doctor. Visit someone at night to save them if someone tries to kill them.
- Block someone's role at night, canceling their night abilities.
- Investigator. Check one player each night for that player's criminal record.
- Jailor. Jail and roleblock one player each night following a day where no lynch occurred. Speak anonymously with the jailed player at night, and optionally execute that player.
- Lookout. See everyone who visits his target each night.
- Mason Leader. May to try to convert one person to a Mason each night. This ability only works on Citizens. Also collaborates with the other Masons at night in the secret Mason chat.
- Mayor. May reveal himself during the day and thereafter, have additional votes
- Sheriff. Check one player each night for criminal activity.
- Spy. Hears what people say during chats at night (Mafia, Triad, Cultist, and Masons).
- Veteran. May go on alert during the night. If he goes on alert, will automatically kills any player who targets him that night.
- Vigilante. Kill one target at night.

Mafia/Triad

- Godfather/Dragon Head: The leader of Mafia/Triad. Kill one target at night, investigation immunization, invincible in night.
- Mafioso/Enforcer: The normal killer of Mafia/Triad. Kill one target at night.
- Consigliere/Administrator. Investigate one player each night
- Agent/Vanguard. See who one person visits and is visited by each night.
- Framer/Forger. Frame one player each night.
- Janitor/Incense Master. Sanitize one player each night.
- Disguiser/Informant. Kill a player and steal their identity. Consort/

Neutral

- Amnesiac. Convert to any role from the graveyard.

- Arsonist. Need to be the last person left alive. Either douse a person in gasoline or kill all previously doused targets at night. May also undouse himself by taking no action.
- Cultist. Wins if the Town, Mafia, and all other killing roles are dead or converted to Cultists. Speak together at night with other Cultists and attempt to convert a player to a cultist.
- Executioner. He need live to see his target lynched during the day, invincible in night. While his target was killed in night, Executioner will change to the Jester.
- Jester. Need die by being lynched during the day, the player who vote guilt will suicide in the next night. Annoy another player at night, indicating to that player that he was visited by a Jester.
- Judge. Need Survive and see Town loses the game. May call court during the day, stopping all discussion and forcing an anonymous ballot vote where the Judge has additional votes. Also, can speak to the entire town at night, anonymously.
- Mass Murderer. Need to be the last person left alive. Perform a killing spree at someone's house each night, killing anyone who visits that player at night, invincible in night.
- Serial Killer. Need to be the last person left alive. Kill one target at night, invincible in night.
- Survivor. Survive to the end of the game, regardless of whether or not the Town or Mafia win.
- Witch. Survive and see the town lose the game. Force one person to use their night ability on a target of the Witch's choice.
- Witch Doctor. Save a player, protecting him from death and converting him to the Cult if he was attacked that night. Also, may speak with the Cult at night in the Cultist night chat.

Then, we played the SC2Mafia to collect data. For each setting, we have 10 samples, also the research supported by Python simulation. Table 9 show the each parameter in SC2Mafia.

Table 9. The results of simulation for Godfather case

Setting	Average death	Average length	GR
Traditional	9.2	41.57	0.0730
Little Italy (15)	11.9	44.96	0.0767
China Town (15)	11.5	45.09	0.0752
Red & Blue (15)	12.6	51.68	0.0688
Heresy (15)	13.2	50.54	0.0719
Blood Rust (15)	8.4	44.27	0.0655
Family Glory (15)	10.7	41.56	0.0787

6   Concluding Remarks

The results of our computer simulations using a simple version of Mafia game show some interesting aspects of Mafia game and suggest the reasonable settings from the perspective of game sophistication, as summarized below. For the citizens group, sheriff is much more important than doctor from the viewpoint of game balancing. For $N = 12$, $MFG(12, m, s, d)$ is the best to play with $m = 5, s = 1, d = 2$ or $m = 4, s = 1, d = 1$ from the viewpoint of game balancing while minimizing the difference of winning ratio between two groups of mafia and citizens. The measure of game refinement would reduce as the number of players increases. This may imply that Mafia game would become boring as the number of players becomes too many. $MFG(N, m, s, d)$ can be played reasonably with $N \in \{14, 15, 16\}$, $m \in \{5, 6\}$, $s = 1$ and $d \in \{1, 2\}$. In particular, $MFG(15, 5, 1, 1)$ or $MFG(15, 6, 1, 2)$ is the best under the assumption that its GR value is within the sophisticated zone. Moreover, the level of players affects the game balancing and game sophistication. For example, mafia would dominate citizens if all players are weak, which implies that the game sophistication would be reduced.

In this paper, we also analyze the complicated versions of Mafia game in StarCrart II custom map (SC2Mafia). In SC2Mafia, there are many different balance settings with 15 participates, for each setting we collected human's data and support by Python simulation, then the refinement value of human almost closed to the pure AI simulation, what means while the total number of players was decided, the game exciting level and progress almost similar. Therefore, 15 or 16 participates could be considered as the most interesting setting by reasonable evidence. In the future, the more SC2Mafia related work will be researched, also we will focus on the real AI design in Mafia game.

Acknowledgements. This research is funded by a grant from the Japan Society for the Promotion of Science (JSPS), within the framework of the Grant-in-Aid for Challenging Exploratory Research and Grant-in-Aid for JSPS Fellow.

References

1. Bi, X., Tanaka, T.: Human-side strategies in the werewolf game against the stealth werewolf strategy. In: Plaat, A., Kosters, W., van den Herik, J. (eds.) CG 2016. LNCS, vol. 10068, pp. 93–102. Springer, Cham (2016). https://doi.org/10.1007/978-3-319-50935-8_9

2. Braverman, M., Etesami, O., Mossel, E.: Mafia: a theoretical study of players and coalitions in a partial information environment. Ann. Appl. Probab. **18**(3), 825–846 (2008)

3. Chittaranjan, G., Hung, H.: Are you awerewolf? Detecting deceptive roles and outcomes in a conversational role-playing game. In: IEEE International Conference on Acoustics Speech and Signal Processing, pp. 5334–5337 (2010)

4. Dark. Revenant. Starcraft ii mafia wiki. http://sc2mafia.wikia.com. Accessed 2017

5. Hirata, Y., Inaba, M., Takahashi, K., Toriumi, F., Osawa, H., Katagami, D., Shinoda, K.: Werewolf game modeling using action probabilities based on play log analysis. In: Plaat, A., Kosters, W., van den Herik, J. (eds.) CG 2016. LNCS, vol. 10068, pp. 103–114. Springer, Cham (2016). https://doi.org/10.1007/978-3-319-50935-8_10

6. Hung, H., Chittaranjan, G.: The idiap wolf corpus: exploring group behaviour in a competitive role-playing game. In: International Conference on Multimedia 2010, Firenze, Italy, October, pp. 879–882 (2010)

7. Iida, H., Takahara, K., Nagashima, J., Kajihara, Y., Hashimoto, T.: An application of game-refinement theory to Mah Jong. In: Rauterberg, M. (ed.) ICEC 2004. LNCS, vol. 3166, pp. 333–338. Springer, Heidelberg (2004). https://doi.org/10.1007/978-3-540-28643-1_41

8. Katagami, D., Takaku, S., Inaba, M., Osawa, H.: Investigation of the effects of nonverbal information on werewolf. In: IEEE International Conference on Fuzzy Systems, pp. 982–987 (2014)

9. Kobayashi, Y., Osawa, H., Inaba, M., Shinoda, K., Toriumi, F., Katagami, D.: Development of werewolf match system for human players mediated with lifelike agents. In: International Conference, pp. 205–207 (2014)

10. Markulis, P., Strang, D.: The game of the "in" & "out" groups. Dev. Bus. Simul. Experiential Learn. 43(1) (2016). https://journals.tdl.org/absel/index.php/absel/article/viewFile/3010/2958

11. Migdał, P.: A mathematical model of the mafia game. arXiv preprint arXiv:1009.1031 (2010)

12. Panumate, C., Xiong, S., Iida, H.: An approach to quantifying pokemon's entertainment impact with focus on battle. In: 2015 3rd International Conference on Applied Computing and Information Technology/2nd International Conference on Computational Science and Intelligence (ACIT-CSI), pp. 60–66. IEEE (2015)

13. Prévot, L., Yao, Y., Gingold, A., Bel, B., Chan, K.Y.J.: Toward a scary comparative corpus: the werewolf spoken corpus. In: SEMDIAL 2015 goDIAL, p. 204 (2015)

14. Ramadhan, A., Iida, H., Maulidevi, N.U.: Game refinement theory and multiplayer games: case study using UNO. In: The Seventh International Conference on Information, Process, and Knowledge Management, pp. 119–125 (2015)

15. Xia, F., Wang, H., Huang, J.: Deception detection via blob motion pattern analysis. In: Paiva, A.C.R., Prada, R., Picard, R.W. (eds.) ACII 2007. LNCS, vol. 4738, pp. 727–728. Springer, Heidelberg (2007). https://doi.org/10.1007/978-3-540-74889-2_70

16. Xiong, S., Tiwary, P.P., Iida, H.: Solving the sophistication-population paradox of game refinement theory. In: Wallner, G., Kriglstein, S., Hlavacs, H., Malaka, R., Lugmayr, A., Yang, H.-S. (eds.) ICEC 2016. LNCS, vol. 9926, pp. 266–271. Springer, Cham (2016). https://doi.org/10.1007/978-3-319-46100-7_28

17. Xiong, S., Zuo, L., Iida, H.: Quantifying engagement of electronic sports game. Adv. Soc. Behav. Sci. 5, 37–42 (2014)

18. Yao, E.: A theoretical study of mafia games. Mathematics (2008)

Exploring Patterns of Shared Control in Digital Multiplayer Games

Philipp Sykownik(✉) ⓘ, Katharina Emmerich, and Maic Masuch

Entertainment Computing Group, University of Duisburg-Essen,
Duisburg, Germany
{philipp.sykownik,katharina.emmerich,maic.masuch}@uni-due.de

Abstract. This paper investigates the concept of shared control to design for innovative and enjoyable multiplayer experiences. More research on collective control over a single game character could support the design of compelling social experiences and provides insights in how the social context affects individual player experience. Hence, this paper addresses two perspectives: game design and game user research. First, a classification of possibilities to implement shared control is presented. As a proof of concept the shared control game *Shairit* was developed. Furthermore, we present an empirical study researching the impact of player interdependency on player experience induced by different forms of shared control implemented in *Shairit*. Results indicate that varying degrees of player interdependency in shared control do not provide fundamentally different player experiences in terms of need satisfaction, social presence and enjoyment. Further, findings suggest that a loss of individual control and feedback should not be associated with negative experiences per se, but should rather be acknowledged as legitimate mechanics to induce enjoyment in a multiplayer setting.

Keywords: Shared control · Distributed control
Collaborative games · Team play · Interaction design
Player experience · Need satisfaction · Game design

1 Introduction

In 2014, the implementation of *Twitch Plays Pokémon* (TPP)[1] led to a striking social phenomenon in the context of digital multiplayer gaming. TPP was an interactive gaming stream of the popular game *Pokémon Red* on the streaming platform *Twitch*[2], which allowed all viewers to simultaneously control a single game instance by typing game commands into the integrated chat system (i.e. "up", "a").

This form of shared control was a great success: In sum 1,165,140 individual players actively participated in the project, and 9+ million were spectating

---

[1] http://twitchplayspokemon.org/ - 2017/07/30.
[2] https://www.twitch.tv/ - 2017/07/30.

© Springer International Publishing AG, part of Springer Nature 2018
A. D. Cheok et al. (Eds.): ACE 2017, LNCS 10714, pp. 847–867, 2018.
https://doi.org/10.1007/978-3-319-76270-8_57

with a peak of 121,000 individual comments being simultaneously entered.[3] The resulting gameplay was chaotic. A great number of conflicting commands was entered by players at every moment, whereas the game actually only processed and displayed one of them. Furthermore, the stream suffered from a delay of 30 s between the submission of a chat command and its eventual execution, thus probably preventing players from comprehending their contribution. The whole game design contradicts several basic game design principles regarding input processing and the provision of direct feedback (e.g. Chap. 8 in [1]).

Hence, the TPP phenomenon raises questions regarding the players' motivations and experiences. The sharing of control over a single game character constitutes an extreme situation in terms of interdependency between players. Thus, shared control could expand the list of interdependency subtypes recently examined by Borderie and Michinov in context of social flow experiences [4].

Common theories on player experience highlight the importance of feelings of competence, autonomy, and relatedness [20]. It can be assumed that sharing the control over a game leads to a reduced sense of autonomy and competence, thereby interfering with game enjoyment. However, the popularity of TPP implies the capability of shared control to induce highly interesting and motivating social experiences. This might be due to an increased feeling of relatedness. It is known that social aspects are a main motivation to play digital games [20,22] and that the social context of gaming affects the overall experience [5,6]. The social dynamics of shared control in TPP seem to be motivating enough for players to play a game that did not even react reliably on their input, indicating that social aspects may indeed suppress the impact of other player experience factors. Thus, an imbalance of player experience dimensions apparently does not necessarily impair game enjoyment. In general, more research on the interplay of social interaction and other dimensions is needed to explain which aspects are important for a positive experience. Hence, it is promising to further examine the concept of shared control in the context of digital games, player experience, and need satisfaction.

This paper contributes a systematic approach in this context. We provide a distinct terminology and a comprehensive classification to discuss different forms of shared control in digital games, revealing the wide range of design possibilities. Moreover, we present results of a study comparing different forms of shared control based on an exemplary implementation of a game with four different game modes. Those results provide insights into how shared control can influence need satisfaction and game enjoyment. Hence, our work informs researchers and game designers interested in designing compelling social experiences based on the shared control concept.

---

[3] https://blog.twitch.tv/tpp-victory-the-thundershock-heard-around-the-world-3128a5b1cdf5#.jkda9l2cm - 2017/07/30.

2   Game Enjoyment as Need Satisfaction

Ryan and colleagues [20] introduced a model that defines game motivation and enjoyment as the satisfaction of psychological needs based on their Self-Determination Theory (SDT). In the context of games, SDT assumes that players are intrinsically motivated to play games that provide satisfaction of their basic needs for competence, autonomy, and relatedness. In order to assess need satisfaction in games, they developed the Player Experience of Need Satisfaction questionnaire (PENS) [16]. Their approach was applied and validated in various studies [10,15,20,23], which account for its relevance in game research today. Recently, a review of the immersive experience questionnaire (IEQ), the game engagement questionnaire (GEQ), and the PENS was conducted, which are all three widely used and known instruments to assess player experience [7]. According to this recent analysis, PENS and other approaches are adequate to assess facets of player experience, even if they differ in advantages and disadvantages. After all, the trichotomy of competence, autonomy, and relatedness satisfaction is intuitively reflected in the discussion about TPP, as its shared control mechanic seems to impair competence and autonomy, but enhances relatedness satisfaction. Because of this intuitive matching, SDT and PENS are used in this paper to guide an initial investigation of player experience induced by shared control.

According to Ryan and colleagues [20] games provide feelings of competence, if players get opportunities to attain new skills by overcoming optimal challenges and receive positive feedback on their actions. Optimal challenges are difficult to overcome, but nevertheless possible to master. Additionally, they comprise a clear goal definition, thus players exactly know what they try to achieve. Games provide a feeling of autonomy, if they make players feels as they are acting volitionally, i.e. the in-game actions they conduct are in line with their inner selfs and values. This feeling is not necessarily based on the number of choices a game offers, but on its potential to generate commitment and volitional engagement for the actions a player can take [17]. To foster feelings of relatedness, games have to provide individual players with moments of relevance, in which they have the opportunity to acknowledge, support, and impact each other. Experience of relatedness is not only supposed to refer to human players, but can also be experienced during the interaction with single player games that provide non-player characters [17].

3   Towards a Classification of Shared Control

Shared control can intuitively be understood as a game control mode, in which players collectively control one single game character. However, the possibilities to implement shared control are manifold. Therefore, we argue for a more precise definition and suggest a systematic categorization of shared control patterns based on the review of commercial games and related literature.

Shared Characters belong to design patterns for collaboration [21]. This game mechanic allows players to distribute control over several characters among each other. *Lego Star Wars*[4], for example, provides a pool of several characters, between which players can actively switch, as long as the desired character is not controlled by someone else. Thus, players have to collaboratively coordinate who should control which character. An example that illustrates how sharing a single character simultaneously can be realized is the game *Octodad: Deadliest Catch*[5]. It makes up to four players collectively control the main character of the game by distributing control over its extremities among players. In contrast, the more recent arcade racing game *Trackmania Turbo*[6] allows two players to control speed and direction of the same car simultaneously. Based on the latter two examples shared control can be related to the notion of *Concurrent Timing* by Harris et al. [8]. Thus it would be a subtype of synchronized actions that allows players to simultaneously control their respective in-game actions in context of an interdependent task. Although Harris et al.'s types of synchronized actions can be used to conceptually describe shared control, it seems not applicable to define distinctive forms of shared control, since it does not account for the different ways multiple players can be represented in the game (eg. sharing one representation vs. alternating between representations). In conclusion, shared control does not necessarily refer only to the sharing of control in terms of performed actions, but also to a sharing of a player representation, and how the two aspects relate to each other.

It is important to note that not all games are avatar-based like *Octodad* and represent players as a personalized entity like a character. *Trackmania Turbo* provides no character as player representation and games like *Tetris*[7] do not have any explicit player representation at all. Since it should not be important what type of player representation is collectively controlled, a neutral term should be used to prevent discussion on shared control from being biased against a specific type of player representation. In sum, a classification of shared control should account for aspects of player actions and player representations, and be independent from a specific type of player representation.

A term that ensures independence from types of representation is *Locus of Manipulation* (LoM). An LoM is defined as the "in-game position of the player's ability to assert control over the game-world" [2]. In other words, any perceptible in-game instance that proves a player's manipulation of the game world.

Regarding the aspect of sharing control over in-game actions Loparev et al.'s [11] work provides an initial distinction of basic shared control principles. With *WeGame* they introduced a middleware solution that allows players to play existing single player games collectively in a co-located setting [11]. It included an alternation of control corresponding to traditional gamepad passing, as well as simultaneous control that allows players to simultaneously control a shared character.

---

[4] (Traveller's Tales, 2011).
[5] (Young Horses Inc., 2014).
[6] (Nadeo, 2016).
[7] (Nintendo, 1985).

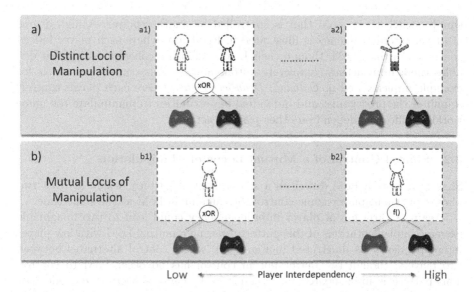

Low ◄─────── Player Interdependency ────► High

Fig. 1. Types of shared control: (a) Two players share two distinct LoM. (b) Two players share a mutual LoM. (a1) Sharing control of distinct LoM through control alternation. (a2) Sharing control of distinct LoM that establish a coherent entity. (b1) Sharing control of a mutual LoM by control alternation. (b2) Simultaneous control of a mutual LoM through input processing function.

Based on the distinction between alternating and simultaneous control and the concept of LoM, Fig. 1 illustrates a classification of shared control. Hence, shared control is basically defined either as the sharing of distinct LoM, or as the sharing of a mutual LoM (Fig. 1a, b). Within these two types, several variations are imaginable that differ in the degree of player interdependency (Fig. 1a1, a2, b1, b2). The classification is further described in the following.

3.1 Shared Control of Distinct Loci of Manipulation

Sharing the control of distinct LoM describes a pattern where each player of a multiplayer game controls at least one LoM that is not simultaneously controlled by another player at any point in time. At the same time players switch between those shared LoM, or are at least highly dependent from each other because they establish a coherent entity.

Further, by varying player interdependency, two specific implementations of sharing distinct LoM are imaginable as the extremes of a continuous dimension. Figure 1(a1) illustrates the lower end of this continuum, a pattern that is implemented for example in *Lego Star Wars*, where each player controls a distinct character, with the possibility to switch between various shared characters. This reflects a low degree of player interdependency, since players are able to manipulate the game world rather autonomously through their individual LoM. Nevertheless they are not completely autonomous, because they cannot simply switch to an LoM that is controlled by another player. A high degree of player interdependency is illustrated in Fig. 1(a2), where each player indeed controls a distinct LoM, though their LoM establish a coherent entity that disables them from acting completely autonomously. This control pattern is for example implemented in *Octodad: Deadliest Catch*, where each player controls a limb of the protagonist and individual opportunities to manipulate the game world significantly depend on other player's actions.

3.2   Shared Control of a Mutual Locus of Manipulation

Sharing a mutual LoM describes a shared control pattern, where at least two players of a multiplayer game control the same main LoM at the same time.

Again, a variation of player interdependency could lead to two imaginable extreme implementations of this pattern: sharing a mutual LoM with low player interdependency as illustrated in Fig. 1(b1), where control alternates between two players, though the player not in control has no other LoM to control. This pattern is implemented for example in *WeGame's Sequential* mode [11]. Figure 1(b2) illustrates a high degree of player interdependency, where players simultaneously control a mutual LoM. Their collective manipulation depends on a specific processing function that defines how the individual parts of collective input are represented in the final manipulation. For example, in *Trackmania* the direction of player input is averaged, resulting in a combined direction. Actually, several combinations of input directions would then lead to no change of direction at all. In contrast, *WeGame's Legion* mode weighted individual player input based on similarity to other player's input. Hence, its processing function calculated a final command that does not equally represent all incoming inputs.

3.3   Player Interdependence in Shared Control

As visualized in Fig. 1, the degree of player interdependency allows for an unspecified number of variations to design shared control that are not further specified in this paper. Though, several examples of general approaches to vary player interdependency are provided. Generally, hybrid forms of sharing distinct and mutual LoM are imaginable and for example implemented in *WeGame's Legion* [11] mode which allows players to dynamically change the set of distinct LoM (distinct abilities of a character) they want to control. Thus, some players may collectively control for example the movement (mutually shared LoM), whereas others control the usage of a certain special ability (another mutually controlled LoM that is distinct from the movement). Additionally, certain features of shared control allow for further variation, as for example the alternation of control could be varied by the sequence (random vs. fixed, depending, or dynamic factors), the frequency of alternation, and the use of feedback mechanics (visualizing the duration of control). Correspondingly, simultaneous forms of shared control could differ between their input processing, transparency of individual contribution, and the enforcement of collective input.

4   Shairit - A Shared Control Game

The shared control game *Shairit* was developed to systematically evaluate shared control of a mutual LoM as it was implemented in TPP. Furthermore, it extends *WeGame* [11], by implementing variations of alternating and simultaneous control. *Shairit* includes four control modes, which can be categorized as sharing control over a mutual LoM with various degrees of player interdependency. It was developed to examine whether different implementations of shared control work as an entertaining game in a small group setting and to initially investigate player experience in terms of enjoyment, need satisfaction and facets of sociality.

Shairit is a four-player collaborative local multiplayer game, whereby its game modes mainly differ in the implemented control mechanic. Players share the control over a single LoM that is represented as a sphere (see Fig. 2). The four modes include two modes with alternating control and two modes with simultaneous control. Throughout 13 levels players have to collect several orbs by navigating the sphere. The source of conflict arises from different types of cubes that have to be used or bypassed to reach the orbs. Obstacle cubes are, as the name implies, obstacles players have to navigate around. They are static and can neither be moved, nor jumped on. Push cubes can be pushed by colliding with them. Jump cubes (Fig. 2) can be jumped on. Death cubes (see Fig. 2) are either static or patrol between waypoints. When players collide with them, the actual level's progress is reset and the LoM will respawn at the starting position. Death cubes can be moved by pushing push cubes against them. The game is controlled by *Xbox One/360* gamepads, utilizing only two or three input modalities of it, depending on the control mode. Players navigate the sphere with the left analog stick and jump by pressing "A". The shoulder button is used to conduct special actions in two of the four modes.

4.1   Alternating Control Modes

In the alternating control modes, LoM control alternates between players, what reflects the pattern shown in Fig. 1(b1).

Low Player Interdependency Mode. In the Alternating Control mode with low player interdependency (Alternating-Low), control over the sphere alternates every five seconds between players in a fixed sequence. To conduct a seamless transition, players could try to imitate the inputs of the active player. To indicate which player has control over the LoM, player-specific icons appear above the sphere (see Fig. 2). Interdependency is assumed to be low, because individual actions do not directly affect each other.

High Player Interdependency Mode. The Alternating Control mode with high player interdependency (Alternating-High) alternates control in randomized order every five seconds. Due to the randomizing, players cannot simply internalize control alternation and consequently should pay more attention to

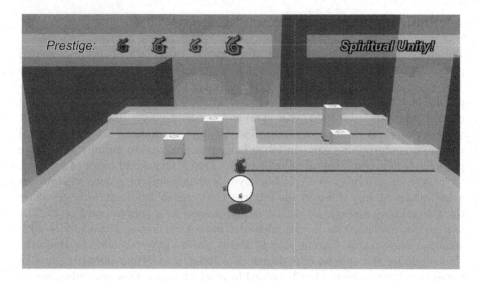

Fig. 2. In *Shairit* players have to collect turquoise orbs. Screenshot shows the Alternating Control mode with high player interdependency. To reach the orb in the back of this level players have to get over the yellow death cubes by jumping from jump cube to jump cube

play the game seamlessly. Furthermore, interdependency is increased by a voting system. It allows players that are not in control, to vote for the currently controlling player by pressing the gamepad's shoulder button. If the active player receives votes from all others, he is granted another time frame of control, in which players can vote again. Thus, the mode allows players to manipulate the control sequence. As in Alternating-Low mode, icons above the sphere visualize which player currently has control. Additionally, it indicates the remaining control time by slowly vanishing (see Fig. 2). Furthermore, players are provided with individual and group feedback on the similarity between their inputs during a control alternation, which is called prestige. It shall enhance player communication and is visualized on the top border of Fig. 2, with individual prestige on the left and group prestige on the right side.

4.2 Simultaneous Control Modes

In the simultaneous control modes, players simultaneously control a shared LoM, what reflects the pattern shown in Fig. 1(b2).

Low Player Interdependency Mode. In the Simultaneous Control mode with low player interdependency (Simultaneous-Low), players can navigate the sphere simultaneously. Their input values are averaged each frame and processed into a combined movement direction. This input processing can lead to situations, where diametrical inputs do not result in movement at all. Player interdependency is assumed to be rather low (but higher than in the alternating control modes), because the mode does not require collective contribution to win the game. Theoretically a single player could play alone, without other players' contribution. Thus, collective input actually increases the difficulty.

High Player Interdependency Mode. Simultaneous Control mode with high player interdependency (Simultaneous-High) allows players to simultaneously navigate the sphere, but requires collective input to overcome certain obstacles in the game. This is caused by a certain input processing function that increases movement speed for each player that conducts input. Thus, if only one player is conducting input, the sphere is moving with just one fourth of its maximum speed. Consequently, this mechanic is assumed to induce high player interdependency. Further, players are provided with individual and group feedback as in Alternating-High mode (see Fig. 2). Here, the individual prestige increases or decreases based on similarity between player inputs. If a certain threshold is reached, pressing the shoulder button consumes individual prestige and grants exclusive control for five seconds, indicated by an icon above the sphere. This mechanics shall foster discussion on strategic use of prestige and thereby increase player interdependency.

5 Evaluation

The game *Shairit* was used to systematically evaluate player experience induced by different implementations of shared control. Additionally, we wanted to explore, if game enjoyment may be caused by different facets of player experience depending on the played mode. Therefore, our investigation was guided by the following two questions:

(1) Do various shared control modes induce different player experiences in terms of enjoyment, need satisfaction or social presence?
(2) Do various shared control modes cause different associations between game enjoyment and other facets of the player experience?

5.1 Study Design

To answer our research questions, we used a between-subject design with four study conditions in accordance with the four game modes of *Shairit*. Hence, the form of shared control serves as independent variable. As dependent variables, we assessed diverse dimensions of player experience including enjoyment, need satisfaction, and social presence.

Procedure and Measures. The study was conducted under controlled conditions in a laboratory at the university. As the game is designed for four players, participants were required to participate as groups of four people. Participants could either directly register as groups of acquainted people, or as singles that were organized to form a quartet by the examiner. All groups were randomly assigned to one of the four study conditions.

First, participants were asked to individually complete a pre-play questionnaire that assessed demographic data as well as their experience with digital games ("no experience at all" (1) to "highly experienced" (5)), and their familiarity ("stranger" (1) to "close friend" (5)) with each other as potential confounding variables. After that, the examiner explained the game's objective, rules and control principle. Then participants had to play all 13 levels successively. The game was projected on a wall via beamer and players sat on a sofa during play, using wireless *Xbox One* gamepads to control the game. As such, the laboratory provides a rather homelike atmosphere for the multiplayer setting. The examiner sat in the back and did not interfere in gameplay unless being asked direct questions. If progress in a level stagnated for more than five minutes, the examiner offered the opportunity to skip the current level. On average, the game was completed in about 20 min and only few groups had to skip the most difficult level. Conclusively, participants completed a post-play questionnaire that assessed their player experience in terms of enjoyment, need satisfaction, and social presence.

As a measure of enjoyment and intrinsic motivation the corresponding sub-scale of the Intrinsic Motivation Inventory (IMI) [19] was applied. The IMI was identified as a widely used instrument to measure game enjoyment [12]. Additionally, is was chosen because the notion of intrinsic motivation is directly linked to the satisfaction of psychological needs, i.e. need satisfaction leads to the emergence of intrinsic motivation to engage in playing games [3,13,14]. The sub-scale consists of seven items that have to be rated on a 7-point Likert scale (e.g. "I enjoyed playing *Shairit* very much"). PENS Accordingly, the PENS [16] was applied to assess levels of psychological need satisfaction. On three sub-scales it refers to the satisfaction of *competence* (PENS-C), *autonomy* (PENS-A), and *relatedness* (PENS-R). Furthermore, the sub-scale *intuitive control* (PENS-IC) was included in the study, because it seemed adequate to evaluate how far shared control as a control pattern is perceived as intuitive. The PENS asks participants to reflect on their player experience when playing *Shairit* and to rate all items on a 7-point Likert scale.

Finally, the experience of social presence and the perceived quality of the social interaction between team mates was assessed by the Cooperative Social Presence (CSP) sub-scale of the Competitive and Cooperative Presence in Gaming Questionnaire (CCPIG) [9][8]. It is designed for the evaluation of collaborative digital games and is divided into the two dimensions *perceived team cohesion* and *team involvement*. Team cohesion represents the level of perceived effectiveness and successful collaboration of the team. Team involvement refers to the degree of involvement, investment and dependency in a team. The questionnaire asks respondents to indicate their agreement with each statement on a 5-point Likert scale.

---

[8] The CCPIG can be found at: https://www.sites.google.com/site/ccpigq/downloads - 2017/07/30.

Table 1. Mean values and standard deviations regarding age, gender, familiarity, and game expertise among condition groups.

	Alternating-Low ($N = 24$) M (SD)	Alternating-High ($N = 32$) M (SD)	Simultaneous-Low ($N = 19$) M (SD)	Simultaneous-High ($N = 19$) M (SD)
Age	25.38 (3.29)	21.03 (2.62)	22.11 (3.07)	25.32 (3.73)
Gender	14 male 8 female	4 male 27 female	8 male 11 female	14 male 5 female
Familiarity	2.83 (1.53)	3.56 (1.31)	2.79 (1.44)	2.95 (1.25)
Expertise*	3.71 (1.04)	2.31 (0.93)	2.95 (1.18)	4.00 (1.00)

* Significant differences between certain groups were found.

5.2   Results

In sum 96 subjects (24 groups) participated in the study. However, data of two participants was excluded from the analysis due to incomplete data sets. Hence, the final sample includes 94 participants (40 male, 52 female, 2 prefer not to say). Age of participants ranges from 18 to 33 years ($M = 23.22$, $SD = 3.67$). Participants were students recruited at the university, who received certification of participating required for certain lectures. The distribution of participants among groups and corresponding mean scores of their attributes age, gender, game expertise, and familiarity is presented in Table 1. The distribution of male and female participants among the conditions is notably unequal and will be considered when controlling for potential confounding effects of game expertise and familiarity. For all following analyses, preconditions for parametric procedures were tested in advance. In case of violated assumptions of normality or homogeneity of variances, corresponding non-parametric tests were applied. If relevant, further assumptions of methods are specified in the following.

Differences Between Conditions. In order to test if groups differ in terms of player experience (research question 1), analyses were conducted to compare mean values regarding enjoyment, need satisfaction, and social presence. Mean values can be found in Table 2.

In general, scores for enjoyment (IMI) tend to be rather high in all groups. A Kruskal-Wallis test shows no significant difference between groups ($\chi^2(3, N = 94) = 5.017$, $p = .16$).

Mean scores for perceived competence are all moderately high and highest in the Simultaneous-High condition. Autonomy means are also moderately high except for a medium score in the Alternating-Low condition. Scores for relatedness are rather moderate, and high in Simultaneous-High mode. To test the significance of these group differences in need satisfaction, analyses of variance were conducted. Results indicate that the type of game mode had no main effect on perceived competence ($F(3, 90) = 1.36$, $p = .26$), autonomy ($F(3, 90) = 1.94$, $p = .13$), or relatedness ($F(3, 90) = 1.48$, $p = .23$).

Table 2. Mean values and standard deviations regarding all investigated dependent variables in the four study conditions.

	Alternating-Low (N = 24) M (SD)	Alternating-High (N = 32) M (SD)	Simultaneous-Low (N = 19) M (SD)	Simultaneous-High (N = 19) M (SD)
IMI	5.35 (1.19)	5.208 (1.29)	4.63 (1.60)	5.58 (1.20)
PENS-C	4.46 (1.56)	4.13 (1.68)	4.25 (1.49)	5.00 (1.35)
PENS-A	3.43 (1.19)	4.08 (1.23)	4.02 (1.45)	4.32 (1.34)
PENS-R	3.96 (0.97)	3.98 (1.15)	3.40 (1.35)	4.12 (1.16)
PENS-IC*	6.01 (1.12)	5.76 (1.04)	6.18 (0.75)	6.53 (0.60)
CSP-TC*	4.10 (0.57)	4.28 (0.63)	3.73 (0.82)	4.31 (0.47)
CSP-TI	4.23 (0.49)	4.27 (0.44)	3.66 (0.93)	4.23 (0.45)

* Significant differences between certain groups were found.

Social aspects were investigated by comparing scores for perceived team cohesion and team involvement. Mean scores for both are lowest in the Simultaneous-Low condition, as compared to rather high means in the other three conditions. A Kruskal-Wallis test partly validates this descriptive impression and reveals a significant difference between groups in terms of team cohesion ($\chi^2(3, N = 94) = 8.34$, $p = .04$). Based on a Bonferroni post hoc analysis participants perceived a significantly lower degree of team cohesion in the Simultaneous-Low condition compared to the Alternating-High condition ($z = -2.674$, $p = .045$). Contrarily, a Welch ANOVA shows no main effect of game mode on perceived team involvement ($F(3, 43.55) = 2.37$, $p = .084$).

Control was perceived as highly intuitive in each mode, as illustrated in Table 2. Only control of the Alternating-High mode tended to be rated as less intuitive compared to other modes. A Kruskal-Wallis test was calculated to compare measures of intuitive control between groups. The test indicates that there is an overall significant difference ($\chi^2(3, N = 94) = 9.21$, $p = .027$). Post hoc Dunn-Bonferroni tests reveal that players experienced higher intuitive controls in Simultaneous-High condition than in Alternating-High ($z = 3.02$, $p = .015$). All other pairwise comparisons are not significant.

Controlling for Game Expertise and Familiarity. Game expertise and familiarity of players might have affected perceived need satisfaction and the social experience. To investigate whether these aspects have influenced the analysis of group differences, we included them in our analysis as potential confounding variables. Hence, we tested for preconditions and assumptions of an analysis of covariance. For both variables, we analyzed group differences and associations with dependent variables in each group.

In terms of mean familiarity, differences between groups are not significant according to a Kruskall-Wallis test ($\chi^2(3, N = 94) = 5.204$, $p = .16$). To check for a potential confounding effect, associations between familiarity and the dependent variables were investigated based on scatterplots and Pearson's r. We assumed a linear relationship, if scatterplots and correlation coefficients indicated a linear association. Familiarity is only significantly correlated with relatedness in the Simultaneous-High condition ($r = .486, n = 19$, $p = .035$) and with team cohesion in the Alternating-Low condition ($r = .623, n = 24$, $p = .001$). Since a systematic linear relationship between familiarity and the dependent variables in all conditions is a main precondition for the analysis of covariance, it can be concluded that familiarity seems to have no general confounding effect on the dependent variables in our study.

The distribution of gender and game expertise among the four study groups is rather uneven as indicated by mean values (cf. Table 2). Both aspects seem to be closely related. An independent samples T-test reveals a significant difference between male and female participants in terms of game expertise ($t(90) = 8.61$ $p < .001$), indicating that men had more experience with digital games ($M = 4.05, SD = .845$) than women ($M = 2.4, SD = .955$) in our sample. Correspondingly, a one-way analysis of variances shows a general significant difference between the four study conditions regarding the reported expertise ($F(3, 90) = 14.06$, $p < .001$). Dunn-Bonferroni post hoc tests indicate that participants in the Alternating-High condition, which also is the group with the smallest number of male players (4 males, 27 females), reported significantly less game expertise ($M = 2.31$) than participants in the Alternating-Low ($M = 3.71$, $p < .001$) and in the Simultaneous-High condition ($M = 4$, $p < .001$), which are the two groups that contained considerably more male than female players. To control for potential confounding effects of game experience on our dependent variables, correlations between game expertise and those variables were examined. Pearson's r values and scatterplots show only two significant correlations: game expertise is positively correlated with competence in the Alternating-High ($r = .381, n = 32$, $p = .032$) and the Simultaneous-Low condition ($r = .545, n = 19$, $p = .016$). Thus, the assumption of a linear relationship between the potential covariate game expertise and the dependent variables in each condition is violated. Accordingly, no further analysis of covariance for game expertise was conducted, as no confounding effect is indicated.

Associations Between Enjoyment and Facets of Player Experience. To address our second research question, we calculated correlations between IMI scores and the other dependent variables in order to gain insights into what specific dimensions of game experience account for the degree of enjoyment.

For reasons of clarity Table 3 summarizes Pearson's r coefficients of relationships between IMI scores and the other dependent variables for each condition. The perceived level of need satisfaction was positively associated with enjoyment in almost every combination. Only in the Simultaneous-High condition relatedness was not correlated with the IMI scores. Measures for social presence were positively associated with enjoyment in the Simultaneous-Low condition. Additionally, team cohesion was found to be positively correlated with IMI scores in the Alternating-Low, and Team Involvement in the Simultaneous-High condition.

Table 3. Significant Associations between IMI and other Dimensions of Player Experience for each Mode

	Alternating-Low ($N = 24$)	Alternating-High ($N = 32$)	Simultaneous-Low ($N = 19$)	Simultaneous-High ($N = 19$)
IMI with	r	r	r	r
PENS-C	.709**	.538*	.535*	.719**
PENS-A	.651**	.352*	.785**	.81**
PENS-R	.656**	.391*	.538*	.306
CSP-TC	.455*	.048	.622**	.321
CSP-TI	.402	-.047	.640**	.576**

* Correlation is significant at the .05 level (2-tailed)
** Correlation is significant at the .01 level (2-tailed).

6   Discussion

Generally, playing *Shairit* proved to be an entertaining experience. This conclusion is justified by the reported high enjoyment scores as well as by observations made during gameplay. Consequently, shared control can provide an enjoyable experience not only as an extension for existing single player games [11], but also as a core mechanic.

6.1   Differences in Player Experience

The shared control modes of *Shairit* provide high levels of enjoyment and, furthermore, do not differ significantly from each other in terms of player experience. Therefore, the implemented patterns of shared control seem to induce an entertaining player experience equally well, what qualifies each of them as a recommendable multiplayer game mechanic. Further, we suppose, that the entertainment value of *Shairit* is indeed based on the interdependency between players introduced by the sharing of control, as *Shairit*'s entire game design is focused on the requirement of coordinating the collective control or the alternation of individual control. Hence, there are no other game mechanics that could be additional sources of game enjoyment (e.g., special abilities, story, customizing). Even the prestige and voting systems in two of the modes are tightly bound to the shared control mechanic.

Surprisingly, players reported high perceived intuitiveness of control for all game modes. This is surprising, because we assumed, that especially in the simultaneous modes players could be confused by the input processing, as these modes reduce comprehensibility of individual influence. However, perceived intuitiveness was not lower compared to alternating control. Hence, the loss of individual control did not impair ease of control, but rather seems to be acknowledged as an essential part of the game challenge by players, as intended. Moreover, it has to be noted that—despite the novel input processing—*Shairit* features a rather simple input interface that only requires players to control the analog stick and one or two buttons. Differences regarding perceived intuitiveness of control between Alternating-High and Simultaneous-High are probably caused by differences in game expertise: Simultaneous-High had higher values in both, game expertise and intuitive control. Participants who are used to video game controls may have had less struggle to adapt to the novel input scheme compared to rather inexperienced participants.

We did not find any significant differences regarding need satisfaction between game modes. Hence, the variation of the shared control pattern (alternating control vs. simultaneous control) does not affect the overall player experience induced by the game in terms of need satisfaction. Given that the alternating control modes allow for individual exclusive control like common games without shared control do, our findings invalidate our initial concern that loosing exclusivity of control automatically undermines perceived autonomy and competence experiences. On the contrary, a detailed look at the results reveals that *Shairit* tends to provide moderately high levels of competence and autonomy satisfaction, independent of the control pattern. Maybe these needs were not primarily addressed by the game itself, but rather by the social processes induced by it. For instance, it can be a source of competence and autonomy satisfaction if a player takes on a leading role in team coordination, something that was previously reported by Rozendaal et al. [18].

Thus, a lack of in-game mechanics that foster individual feelings of competence and autonomy might be compensated by social processes. Additionally, team success and the impression of team competence is supposed to influence the individual experience of competence. Thus, being successful as a team in a highly interdependent task may contribute to the impression of one's own competence. Interestingly, scores of relatedness satisfaction tended to be lower than scores of competence and autonomy. This contradicts the initial assumption, that the social experience plays a more essential role in shared control than individual feelings of competence or autonomy.

For a more in-depth investigation of the social dynamics during gameplay we also compared feelings of cooperative social presence. In sum, the scores for team cohesion and team involvement were high in all groups and support the assumption that team related experiences are an essential part of the player experience in shared control games. Nevertheless, team cohesion was significantly lower in the Simultaneous-Low mode than in the Alternating-High mode. This difference can be explained by looking at the items of the corresponding team cohesion scale. Team cohesion includes aspects of effective team communication, goal-sharing, commitment to work together, and feeling like a part of a team. By comparing the control mechanics of the two modes, it becomes apparent that the Simultaneous-Low mode does not require players to work together, or to participate at all. Players do not have to communicate with each other or be equally committed to the game's goal in order to succeed. In contrast, in all other game modes progress is negatively affected if individual players decide against participation. Given that team cohesion was rather high in all other modes, we assumed that the Simultaneous-Low mode in general tended to foster less feelings of team cohesion. Although no significant difference was found regarding the degree of team involvement, a detailed look at the means and standard deviations of team cohesion and involvement reveals that both dimensions tend to be experienced in a similar manner. Probably, issues of the data distribution (violations of normality and variance homogeneity assumptions) and the resultant use of different tests caused one dimension to differ significantly and the other not. This inconsistency should be addressed in future evaluations of the modes, especially because the difference in team involvement would have been significant at the .10 level. Support for assuming that team involvement could actually differ in the same way as team cohesion may be found in its operationalization. Since it reflects the individually experienced cognitive investment to and dependency from one's team mates, we would again argue, that the Simultaneous-Low mode failed to foster such experience as sufficiently as the other modes, due to the fact that it does not enforce cooperation at all. In conclusion, comparing items for relatedness and the CSP scales indicates, that they represent different qualities of sociality in games. Relatedness is supposed to assess the building of emotional relationships. In contrast, CSP scales focus more on the functional aspects of relationship building with regard to the game's goals and challenges. Consequently, we suggest to consider both instruments to gain a more comprehensive insight into the social dynamics during gameplay.

Although the variation of control mode did not lead to statistically significant differences in the majority of assessed player experience dimensions, mean score tendencies offer interesting starting points for further research. In the Simultaneous-High mode players experienced a high degree of competence. Whereas competence could be intuitively expected to be satisfied in modes with individual control that allows players to easily comprehend their contribution and success, one may ask what aspects may induce such high competence satisfaction during simultaneous control. One potential source was already described above in reference to Rozendaal and colleagues [18]. In addition one could also ask why competence satisfaction is not higher in modes of alternating control. An initial assumption is that competence satisfaction could have been partly impaired in these modes because not only individual success, but also failure is recognizable for each player. This could lead to reprehensive behavior among player, as observed by Loparev and colleagues [11]: Their *WeGame* offered a mechanic that visualizes individual input during collective control and occasionally caused more experienced players blaming others. Similarly, it seems suspicious that players of the Alternating-Low mode tended to experience less autonomy compared to the other modes.

We expected it to provide more autonomy satisfaction than modes with simultaneous control due to its opportunities for individual goal achievement. Thus, the question is, why does it not? One initial thought is that an enforced loss of exclusive control (every time control alternates) has significant negative consequences for autonomy satisfaction that other beneficial aspects of the mode can not compensate. Further, in this mode players know that they are responsible for progress on a regular basis. Thus, inexperienced players may anticipate feelings of guilt on a regular basis, because they know to be confronted with situations they fear. In contrast, the voting system in the Alternating-High mode maybe compensated those negative consequences by allowing players to influence the control alternation.

In sum it is notable that the Simultaneous-High mode tended to induce the highest scores regarding nearly every examined facet, indicating that it may be well balanced in terms of potential advantages and disadvantages for either sociality aspects or individual-centric experiences. Additionally, compared to the other modes it probably represents the most consequent implementation of shared control. Thus, results validate the value of this interaction pattern, even if it seems unintuitive at first glance. In conclusion we emphasize that the complex interplay of specific degrees of input enforcement, exclusivity of control, and visibility of individual contribution is supposed to shape the social player experience and is worthwhile to be investigated in future analyses.

6.2 Familiarity and Game Expertise

In our evaluation we controlled for degrees of familiarity and game expertise. We were interested in whether they systematically influence potential main effects of our experimental manipulation on player experience. Since the degree of familiarity probably determines the quality of social interaction between players, we expected familiarity to impact the extent to which our game fosters social player experience. Interestingly, our results did not indicate a systematic confounding effect of familiarity. However, significant correlations between familiarity and relatedness, as well as familiarity and team cohesion in some modes indicate that strangers and friends may experience different qualities of sociality in certain control modes.

Probably most surprising is the lack of association between familiarity and enjoyment, which emphasizes that shared control sufficiently induces an entertaining experience independent of group composition in terms of interpersonal relationships.

Besides familiarity, we assessed game expertise because we expected it to represent players' experience with diverse game mechanics. We assumed that it may determine to what extent they are able and willing to adapt to novel interaction patterns. Hence, participants with more expertise are supposed to adapt faster to the game context than inexperienced players, allowing them to experience higher need satisfaction, particularly in terms of competence.

Game expertise significantly differed between some groups. This may be related to the unequal distribution of male and female participants, who differed in their reported game expertise. Nevertheless, inconsistent associations between game expertise and player experience contradict a systematic influence of game expertise on potential main effects of our experimental manipulation. In fact, game expertise was only found to be positively associated with competence satisfaction in the Alternating-High and the Simultaneous-Low condition. Those correlations can be intuitively interpreted. Since in the Alternating-High mode players could vote for other players, it is reasonable to expect less experienced players voting for more experienced players in order to overcome difficult passages. Accordingly, more experienced players would have increased time of control and thus more opportunities to feel competent. Similarly, in the Simultaneous-Low mode experienced players could simply take over control if a challenge becomes too hard (while the other players do not provide any input). Hence, despite not systematically influencing need satisfaction in our different shared control settings, associations between game expertise and competence in certain modes indicate that game expertise may influence competence satisfaction if opportunities to withdraw from or to overtake control are provided. Since game expertise was not associated with enjoyment, neither, the evaluated shared control patterns seem to be enjoyable for experienced and inexperienced players likewise.

6.3   Associations Between Enjoyment and Facets of Player Experience

In accordance with SDT [20], psychological need satisfaction was associated with enjoyment in almost every mode of *Shairit*. This implies that individual experiences of competence and autonomy may be essential for a positive player experience, even if a game is intended to rely mainly on sociality aspects. Interestingly, facets of sociality were inconsistently associated with game enjoyment across conditions in our study, indicating that game enjoyment of shared control may not depend on qualities of social interactions per se. This is surprising, as we expected that the experience of a game that heavily relies on team coordination and communication would automatically benefit from emotional, cognitive, and behavioral engagement of team members. The Simultaneous-Low mode, which does not require players to work together, was the only mode in which variables of sociality were associated with enjoyment. This indicates that players enjoy this mode, if they explicitly decide to work together, despite not being forced to do so. The lower the experience of mutual engagement in this mode, the less enjoyable is the experience. Independence of enjoyment from team cohesion or team involvement in other modes may reflect that even if the team is not working together in a cohesive and effective way, the experience of *Shairit* is still enjoyable for the individual. Indeed, observations of gameplay indicate that an essential part of the fun arises from moments of failed team coordination. Nevertheless, a comprehensive analysis of predictors for enjoyment of shared control is needed to adequately interpret associations between facets of player experience.

6.4   Limitations

Some limitations have to be mentioned regarding the experimental evaluation of *Shairit*. Since our study groups were unequal in size, the validity of our statistical analysis may not be optimal. We accounted for that in specific cases by choosing adequate test statistics, but lastly analysis would benefit from equal sample sizes.

Though familiarity and expertise did not have a confounding effect in our study, we still suggest to consider them as potential influences that have to be controlled for and further examined in future studies. Studies focusing their effects should include a systematic manipulation of those variables by deliberately assembling player groups beforehand to test different constellations of players and compare their experiences and interactions. Moreover, we recommend to think about more sophisticated ways of assessing players' familiarity and expertise. As it was not the focus of our study, we measured both aspects by simply asking players to rate their game expertise and familiarity with their co-players on a custom scale. These subjective scales may have been interpreted very differently by participants (e.g., "close friend" might mean different things to different people). In sum, subjective assessment and unsystematic distribution of experienced and inexperienced as well as familiar and unfamiliar participants could have affected our findings.

Regarding the conceptualization of *Shairit* it has to be noted that the game design is based on intuitive considerations and, thus, still has to be further validated in terms of induced experience of interdependency. Moreover, we investigated shared control in just one game. Whereas this bespoke setting allowed us to implement different types of shared control and investigate them under controlled conditions, findings are limited to similar game concepts. It has to be considered that other game genres may trigger different forms of social interaction and offer distinct design spaces that require other implementations of shared control to create a good game. Given the fundamental differences between shared control and traditional game control, we decided not to include a control condition in our analysis (comparing shared control to a common individual control pattern). Nevertheless, comparability of the two concepts can be further examined.

7   Conclusion

Sharing the control of interactive environments is an experience people seldom have in reality. As the evaluation of our shared control game *Shairit* has proven, it sufficiently provides an entertaining experience. Hence, our work illustrates the potential of shared control patterns for developing innovative, compelling, and highly social games. To support game designers and researchers alike, we additionally provided a comprehensive classification of types of shared control, that is supposed to guide and expand game design approaches of future collaborative multiplayer games.

The different implementations of shared control evaluated in our study provided equally high levels of enjoyment and need satisfaction.

Furthermore, not only sociality aspects but also more individual experiences like perceived competence and autonomy were identified as essential aspects of enjoying local shared control. Nevertheless, future research is needed to investigate the interrelation between enforced interdependencies and the comprehensibility of individual contributions, as well as their impact on player experience. Insights will help to better understand how shared control can benefit or harm individual enjoyment. This paper contributes to this research by presenting interesting findings of a comprehensive multiplayer study. Conclusively, understanding the experience of shared control not only informs game designers interested in designing compelling social experiences but also contributes to the fundamental understanding of how people enjoy playing together in groups.

References

1. Adams, E.: Fundamentals of Game Design, 2nd edn. New Riders, Berkeley (2010)
2. Bayliss, P.: Beings in the game-world: characters, avatars, and players. In: Gibbs, M. (ed.) Proceedings of the 4th Australasian Conference on Interactive Entertainment. RMIT University, Melbourne, Australia (2007)
3. Birk, M.V., Toker, D., Mandryk, R.L., Conati, C.: Modeling motivation in a social network game using player-centric traits and personality traits. In: Ricci, F., Bontcheva, K., Conlan, O., Lawless, S. (eds.) UMAP 2015. LNCS, vol. 9146, pp. 18–30. Springer, Cham (2015). https://doi.org/10.1007/978-3-319-20267-9_2
4. Borderie, J., Michinov, N.: Identifying social forms of flow in multiuser video games. In: Kowert, R., Quandt, T. (eds.) New perspectives on the social aspects of digital gaming, pp. 32–45. Routledge Advances in Game Studies (2017). https://www.researchgate.net/publication/316001626_Identifying_social_forms_of_flow_in_multiuser_video_games
5. De Kort, Y.A., Ijsselsteijn, W.A.: People, places, and play: player experience in a socio-spatial context. Comput. Entertainment **6**(2), 1 (2008)
6. De Kort, Y.A., Ijsselsteijn, W.A., Poels, K.: Digital games as social presence technology: development of the social presence in gaming questionnaire (SPGQ). In: Moreno, L. (ed.) Presence 2007, pp. 195–203. Starlab, Barcelona (2007)
7. Denisova, A., Nordin, A.I., Cairns, P.: The convergence of player experience questionnaires. In: Cox, A., Toups, Z.O., Mandryk, R.L., Cairns, P., vanden Abeele, V., Johnson, D. (eds.) Proceedings of the 2016 Annual Symposium on Computer-Human Interaction in Play - CHI PLAY 2016, pp. 33–37. ACM Press, New York (2016)
8. Harris, J., Hancock, M., Scott, S.D.: Leveraging asymmetries in multiplayer games. In: Cox, A., Toups, Z.O., Mandryk, R.L., Cairns, P., vanden Abeele, V., Johnson, D. (eds.) Proceedings of the 2016 Annual Symposium on Computer-Human Interaction in Play - CHI PLAY 2016. pp. 350–361. ACM Press, New York (2016)
9. Hudson, M., Cairns, P.: Measuring social presence in team-based digital games. In: Riva, G., Waterworth, J., Murray, D. (eds.) Interacting with Presence, pp. 83–101. Psychology, De Gruyter Open, Warsaw (2014)
10. Johnson, D., Gardner, J.: Personality, motivation and video games. In: Brereton, M., Viller, S., Kraal, B. (eds.) The 22nd Conference of the Computer-Human Interaction Special Interest Group of Australia, p. 276 (2010)
11. Loparev, A., Lasecki, W.S., Murray, K.I., Bigham, J.P.: Introducing shared character control to existing video games. In: Proceedings of Foundations of Digital Games 2014 (2014)
12. Mekler, E.D., Bopp, J.A., Tuch, A.N., Opwis, K.: A systematic review of quantitative studies on the enjoyment of digital entertainment games. In: Jones, M., Palanque, P., Schmidt, A., Grossman, T. (eds.) Proceedings of the 32nd Annual ACM Conference on Human Factors in Computing Systems, pp. 927–936 (2014)
13. Peng, W., Lin, J.H., Pfeiffer, K.A., Winn, B.: Need satisfaction supportive game features as motivational determinants: an experimental study of a self-determination theory guided exergame. Media Psychol. **15**(2), 175–196 (2012)
14. Przybylski, A.K., Rigby, C.S., Ryan, R.M.: A motivational model of video game engagement. Rev. General Psychol. **14**(2), 154–166 (2010)
15. Rieger, D., Wulf, T., Kneer, J., Frischlich, L., Bente, G.: The winner takes it all: the effect of in-game success and need satisfaction on mood repair and enjoyment. Comput. Hum. Behav. **39**, 281–286 (2014)

16. Rigby, S., Ryan, R.: The player experience of need satisfaction (PENS): an applied model and methodology for understanding key components of the player experience (2007)
17. Rigby, S., Ryan, R.M.: Glued to Games: How Video Games Draw us in and Hold us Spellbound. New directions in media, Praeger (2011)
18. Rozendaal, M.C., Braat, B.A.L., Wensveen, S.A.G.: Exploring sociality and engagement in play through game-control distribution. AI Soc. **25**(2), 193–201 (2010)
19. Ryan, R.M., Mims, V., Koestner, R.: Relation of reward contingency and interpersonal context to intrinsic motivation: a review and test using cognitive evaluation theory. J. Pers. Soc. Psychol. **45**(4), 736 (1983). http://psycnet.apa.org/journals/psp/45/4/736.pdf
20. Ryan, R.M., Rigby, C.S., Przybylski, A.: The motivational pull of video games: a self-determination theory approach. Motiv. Emot. **30**(4), 344–360 (2006)
21. Seif El-Nasr, M., Aghabeigi, B., Milam, D., Erfani, M., Lameman, B., Maygoli, H., Mah, S.: Understanding and evaluating cooperative games. In: CHI 2010 - We Are CHI, p. 253. ACM, New York (2010)
22. Yee, N.: Motivations for play in online games. Cyberpsychology Behav. **9**(6), 772–775 (2006). The impact of the Internet, multimedia and virtual reality on behavior and society
23. Yildirim, I.G.: Time pressure as video game design element and basic need satisfaction. In: Kaye, J., Druin, A., Lampe, C., Morris, D., Hourcade, J.P. (eds.) The 2016 CHI Conference Extended Abstracts, pp. 2005–2011 (2016)

RAIL: A Domain-Specific Language for Generating NPC Behaviors in Action/Adventure Game

Meng Zhu[✉] and Alf Inge Wang

Norwegian University of Science and Technology,
Sem Sælandsvei 7-9, 7491 Trondheim, Norway
{zhumeng,alfw}@idi.ntnu.no

Abstract. Domain-Specific Modeling (DSM) has shown its effectiveness of improving software productivity in many software domains [1], where Domain Specific Language (DSL) plays a key role. Also in the domain of video games, researchers have proposed various DSLs for developing different aspects of several game genres. This paper presents a DSL named RAIL for generating Non-Playable Character (NPC) behaviors in Action/Adventure Games. Our DSL borrows concepts from State Machines and adds some features to better suit the target domain. Further, we have implemented a tool-chain for RAIL using the Eclipse language workbench, and the tool-chain has been integrated with the level editor of the Torque2D game engine. To evaluate the DSL, we developed a prototype game and collected data regarding the development time and code lines. The results showed that RAIL significantly improves the productivity of developing NPC behaviors in the target game with a reasonable associated cost. In addition, the integration of the RAIL and the Torque 2D tool-chains provides a smooth development workflow.

Keywords: Game development · Domain specific language · NPC behavior

1 Introduction

Domain-Specific Modeling (DSM) is an emerging software development methodology, which uses modeling languages specifically developed for a relatively narrow domain to model the problems within the domain. Further, either the solution is generated from the models, or the models are executable as (part of) the solution itself. In DSM, the Domain-Specific Language (DSL) plays a key role, which raises the language concepts to a higher abstraction level than General Purpose Languages (GPL) such as Java or UML, thus making the modeled solution simpler than using GPL.

Games are difficult to develop [2], and DSM can potentially reduce the complexity and cost of the development activities. DSM has shown its usefulness in developing software for many application domains [1], and we believe it also has special advantages for game domain, such as: higher abstraction level of models helps communication between technical and non-technical people in the cross-disciplinary team; DSLs use problem domain concepts thus allow game designers to implement gameplay without going through programmers; and DSM enables fast prototyping which is important in

© Springer International Publishing AG, part of Springer Nature 2018
A. D. Cheok et al. (Eds.): ACE 2017, LNCS 10714, pp. 868–881, 2018.
https://doi.org/10.1007/978-3-319-76270-8_58

game development. Researchers have proposed some approaches adapting DSM to computer game domain, such as [3–5].

Note that "computer game" is a broad software domain, ranging from simple card games to massively multiplayer online games. It is impractical to create a DSL that supports *all* computer games simply because the number of language concepts will explode. Most of the existing DSM approaches have narrowed down the target domain to one game genre, e.g. Tower Defense [4] and 2D Platformer [6]. Some approaches further narrow down the scope to a game family or even a single game project, e.g. [7, 8]. Our DSL presented in this paper also targets specifically the Action/Adventure game genre. Moreover, it only focuses on the NPC behavior part of the entire game, which further narrows down the scope of the DSL.

Our DSL is named Reactive AI Language (RAIL), and it has borrowed the basic concepts from State Machines with some additional domain-specific features. We have implemented a tool chain for RAIL and integrated the tool chain with Torque 2D game engine. To evaluate the DSL and the tool chain, a prototype was developed and data on development effort was collected. The results showed that RAIL significantly improved the productivity in developing the prototype with an acceptable associated cost, and the integration of the RAIL and Torque 2D tool chains offers a smooth workflow.

The rest of the paper is organized as follows: Sect. 2 discusses related work; Sect. 3 presents the essential concepts of RAIL; Sect. 4 describes the design and implementation of RAIL and its tool chain; Sect. 5 presents the prototype to validate RAIL and discuss the results. Section 6 concludes the paper.

2   Related Work

Researchers have been exploring the potentials of DSM in game development in the recent years, and more and more model-driven approaches have been proposed in literature, such as [3, 16–19]. The major differences of the RAIL-based approach from the related work are on the target domain and the game engine-interoperability.

Some existing approaches ignore the game engine while they tend to generate code directly based on the OS or some kinds of graphics SDK, for example [20, 21]. Without the support from game engines, is it hard to support scalable game development. Other approaches use run-time game engines as domain frameworks, such as [22, 23] use Microsoft XNA, and [24] uses the Corona SDK. Some approaches further modify game engines to promote them to a domain framework as suggested in [25], such as [25–30]. However, the game engine tools (world editor for example) have been ignored, thus they failed to take the full advantage of the game engines. The RAIL-based approach emphasizes the cooperation of game engine tools and MDD tools, making the non-technical game developers easier to work with, which is an important contribution of our work. Pleuß and Hußmann's approach [31–33] is the closest to our approach. They integrate MDD with authoring tools, more specifically Adobe Flash. In their approach, two kinds of artifacts are generated: script code (ActionScript) and media objects (FLA files). The script code implements the game logic and the media objects can be edited with Adobe Flash tool. Our paper discusses the integration with commercial game engines instead of general media tools, which further reduces the gap between MDD and commercial game development.

Regarding the target domain, many game genres have been explored by model-driven game development community, e.g. Platformer [6], RPG [34], Point & Click Adventure [5], and Pervasive Games [35]. Our approach focused on Action/Adventure which is not addressed in related work to our best knowledge. More importantly, we not only defined the genre of the target games, but also specified which part of the game is to be modeled. The target domain definition is therefore more systematic than most of the existing work.

State machines have been used as basis in several existing DSLs. E.g. it was used in [33] for modeling UI interaction, in [3] for modeling entity behaviors. [36] extends the general State Machine with adding domain-specific features such as hierarchical structure, parallel structure, and multi-interaction node for modeling narrative aspects of games. Our modification to the state machine is mainly adding trigger concept, which was proved effective in our prototyping.

3   RAIL: The Essential Concepts

RAIL is a behavioral DSL aiming at modeling the high-level AI of characters in action/adventure games. The behaviors to be modeled follow an event-reaction pattern, for example, the behavior of the Ghost (enemy actor) in Pac-Man (Namco, 1980). The Ghost behavior can be regarded as a state machine: The default state of the Ghosts is Patrol, where they randomly move around the map. If they receive an event that the player comes close, they will enter the Chase state, where they try to catch the player by running to him. While the player obtains a power-up anytime, he will have limited time to eat the Ghost. When the Ghosts receive the event about this, they will enter the Flee state and try their best to run away from the player.

We can identify some major concepts from the above description:

- AI Pattern: A specific kind of characters usually follows a behavioral pattern, determining what they are going to do when a given event is received in different conditions. We use the AI Pattern concept to denote such patterns, and each character in the target game is "controlled" by one AI Pattern.
- AI Pattern State: A specific event can trigger different behaviors for the same character when it is in different conditions. The "AI Pattern State" concept is the abstraction of the condition of the NPC at a moment. Typical examples of state include "chase" and "flee" in Pac-Man.
- Action: a meaningful character behavior consists of a sequence of moves, and each move completes a basic task. We use Action to denote the basic moves. Examples of Actions include "move to a location", "flee from the player", etc.
- Event: The action of characters is triggered by an event or an event composite, e.g. "the player enters vision", "the player becomes invisible", "the light is off". An event can trigger an action, and/or other events, and the event-action chain is the building block for complex behaviors.

RAIL is intended to support the modeling of the reactive AI in terms of the above concepts. Note that RAIL is built on top of the previous introduced concepts, while the internal details of the concepts is out of the language scope. E.g. given the Action "Walk to a place", it can be used as a building block in models, but how a NPC walk to a location involves a lot of low-level technologies such as path-finding, animation playback, which will not be modeled with RAIL. In another word, the problem domain of RAIL is restricted to the high-level AI of Action/Adventure games, and low-level technologies still must be implemented using traditional methods. Although the target domain sounds narrow, it is still valuable for practical development, because the high-level behavior is game-specific, and it is very difficult or even impossible to generalize it for various games. Implementation of the high-level behavior thus must be done in each individual project, which can take much of development resources. To address this problem, game engines provide scripting languages with some domain-specific support; for example, Unreal script supports the "state" concept at the language level. However, RAIL as a dedicated DSL can further raise the abstraction level and make the solution even simpler.

4 DSL Design and Implementation

The abstract syntax and static semantics of RAIL are defined with a meta-model, which is specified using the Ecore meta-language provided by Eclipse Modeling Framework (EMF). We use the tree-view as the concrete syntax for RAIL, whose implementation, i.e. a RAIL model editor can be generated almost directly from EMF tools. Moreover, a code generator has been created using Acceleo, which is an eclipse based tool for code generation. Finally, the above RAIL tools are integrated with Torque2D game engine following the Engine Cooperative Game Modeling(ECGM) methodology [9]. ECGM is a model-driven game development methodology which emphasizes the interoperability of game engine tools and model-driven tools through model-transformations. We will detail the design and implementation of RAIL in the rest of this section.

4.1 RAIL Meta-Model

Figure 1 shows an excerpt of the RAIL meta-model, and some low-level details are omitted to fit it the page format.

The top-level RAIL construct is Game, which is the container of all AIPatterns in a game. Each computer game to be modeled should have one and only one instance of Game. AIPattern is the central construct of RAIL models that corresponds to the AI Pattern concept as described earlier. Modeling with RAIL is mainly about creating various AIPattern instances, each of which defines a kind of NPC behavior. AIPattern is stateful, meaning that the reactions of NPCs to events are influenced by the state that the NPC is in at a moment. Here we borrowed concepts from state machines. The State construct denotes the state of AI Patterns. Each AIPattern possesses a group of States, but an AIPattern can only have one "Active State" at a given moment, and the initial Active State is the "default" state. A special case of AIPattern is that it has only one

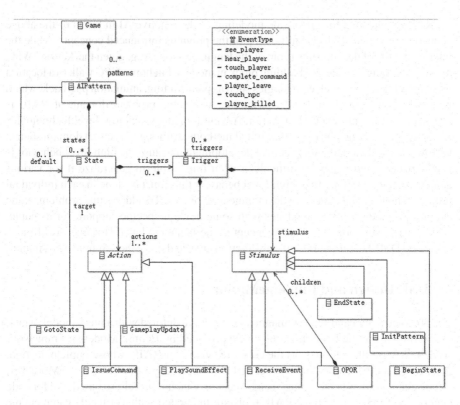

Fig. 1. RAIL Meta-model

state, then the state can be omitted and the Triggers (described later) will be directly connected to the AIPattern.

A State has a group of triggers, which defines the actions to be performed in reaction to a stimulus that is typically an event or a composite of events. For example, a trigger can be:

Event("*See Player*") - > Action("*Move to The Player*")
Example 1

or be more complex as:

Event("*See Player*") OR Event("*Hear Player*") - > Action("*Alert Alliance*") AND Action("*Move to The Player*")
Example 2

The Event construct can be further elaborated with vision events, input events, AI interactive events, etc. The stimulus can also be something other than the Events, for example, state change, pattern initialization, and a group of basic stimuli connected with logic operations.

The Action construct encapsulates the actual actions to be performed by the AI pattern as the result of the stimulus. A common kind of actions is the IssueCommand, which will in effect send a specific command to the NPC controlled by the AI pattern, such as "Move to A Location", "Attack A Target", and "Look at A Place". Another kind of action is the Pattern Controller, which provides a way to manipulate the AIPattern at run-time, e.g. "Go to State" action sets the current State of the AI pattern to the one specified in the Action parameters.

The Triggers cannot only connect to States, but also directly associate with AIPatterns, and then they become "Default Triggers". The Default Triggers will take effect in any State, and if they conflict with the State-owned triggers, they have the priority.

RAIL is a DSL similar to a State Machine, which is a widely used design pattern [10] in gameplay programming. RAIL borrowed some concepts from the state machine, and made some important modifications to better fit it to the game modeling domain, such as:

- Defined domain-specific constructs to describe game domain concepts, such as *Actions* and *Events*.
- Provided *Trigger* concept, which can represent the reaction-based behaviors in a natural way.
- Supported global behavioral rules that will take effect in any state.
- Supported compact version of *AIPattern* with no state.

Note that RAIL is not intended to be a unified solution for modeling the gameplay of all the action/adventure games. Instead, it should be customized for each game families or even a single game project. But the high-level structure of the language, i.e. the constructs showed in Fig. 1 should be reused without major modifications.

4.2 Tool Chain Implementation

The concrete syntax of RAIL is based on a tree-view. We choose this form because the AIPattern-State-Trigger-Action/Event hierarchy naturally follows a tree structure. Figure 2 shows a RAIL model example within the Eclipse-based model editor.

With the Eclipse Modelling Framework (EMF), the model editor can be automatically generated from the meta-model. The code of the generated model editor is in java, and is deployed as an Eclipse plug-in, so that the tool is integrated with the Eclipse IDE. The java code can be modified for customization purposes, for example, changing the appearance of the language constructs, and optimizing the user interface. The default concrete syntax that the generated model editor provides is the Tree View, which is a perfect match for the structure of RAIL.

The code generator, on the other hand, requires much more work to create. There exist various frameworks on the Eclipse platform for code generation, such as Xtend and ATL. We chose Acceleo (https://eclipse.org/acceleo/). Acceleo provides a template language for creating code generators following the template and meta-model approach [11]. The code generator for RAIL was then implemented as a couple of templates, which took RAIL models as input and generated code in Torque script for Torque 2D game engine that we will discuss in next section. The code generation templates can be created and executed in the Eclipse platform since Acceleo is an Eclipse plug-in.

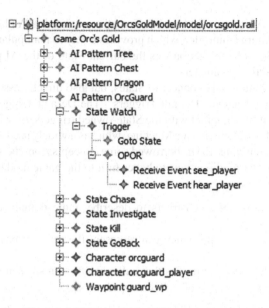

Fig. 2. A RAIL model in eclipse-based editor

4.3   Integration of RAIL with Torque 2D Engine

Torque 2D is a commercial game engine developed by GarageGames (www.garage-games.com), which supports developing various genres of 2D games. Torque 2D provides a script language called "Torque Script" for developing game-specific code, which has a C-style syntax plus some object-based features. Moreover, Torque 2D engine comes with a powerful world editor: The Torque Game Builder (TGB). TGB organizes the game world through scenes (levels), and the scenes can be created in a WYSIWYG way.

There are mainly two steps in the process of integrating RAIL with Torque 2D: (1) raise the abstraction level of Torque 2D, and (2) implement the generator for script code and world data.

1. Raise the Abstraction Level of Torque 2D

Since RAIL was designed only for modeling high-level AI of Action/Adventure games, it targets a narrower domain and lies on a higher abstraction level than Torque 2D APIs. An abstraction layer must be implemented on top of the Torque 2D APIs to promote Torque 2D to a suitable domain framework [8].

The abstraction layer was implemented as a Torque Script library, where several concepts were implemented using an Object-Oriented approach. Character is the core module of the abstraction layer. Character simulates the creature or the machinery in a game that can perceive surroundings and react to the environment. Character is both an event source and an event handler: Character detects other objects at every frame, using the perception simulation algorithm, and generates corresponding perception events.

The events are sent to the AI layer (modeled with RAIL) as the input for decision-making. On the other hand, a Character is also responsible for performing the commands sent from the AI layer, like move and attack. Other modules of the abstraction layer including input handling, event management, and global rules, which will not be discussed in detail in this paper.

2. Generate Code and World Editor Data for Torque 2D

To integrate RAIL tools with Torque 2D engine tools, two Acceleo projects were created: (1) Torque Script generator, and (2) TGB data generator.

Each RAIL model includes multiple AIPatterns, each of which defines a specific type of NPC such as neutral NPC, enemy soldier, and boss. The Torque Script generator generates a Torque Script class for each pattern, and a couple of member functions for the states and triggers possessed by the pattern.

The Torque Script code must be associated with the graphical objects in the TGB, and the code-object relationships were built automatically through a TGB data generator. The generator is also developed with Acceleo as templates, and the format of the generated data complies with the TGB extension protocol. The TGB uses an object palette to manage available scene objects. For each kind of scene object, e.g. a picture, or a sprite animation, there is a visual object in the palette. The TGB extension protocol allows adding customized object prototypes to the palette of the world editor. We create one pattern object prototype in the TGB palette for each AIPattern in the RAIL model. Therefore, the AIPattern is visualized in the TGB as a graphical object like other built-in scene objects. When creating game scenes, designers access the AIPattern through the graphical objects in the TGB palette without knowing the existence of the generated code.

4.4 Tool Chain Architecture

Figure 3 shows the tool chain architecture of RAIL. The dotted line between Pattern A in the object palette and Pattern A in C Script Code implies the association automatically built by the tool chain. If a user wants to connect Pattern A modeled with RAIL to character A in a level, he or she can drag Pattern A from the TGB palette to somewhere near the character in the level. The pattern will automatically link to the nearest character, and the association is built by the generated code as well as the domain framework. Figure 4 shows an example of using AIPattern in the TGB and the RAIL Editor.

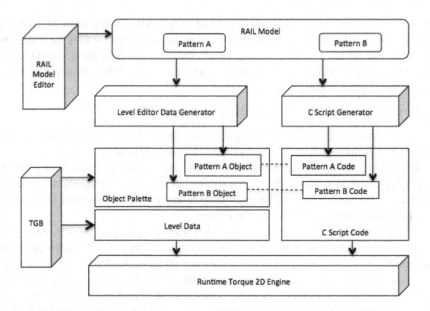

Fig. 3. The Tool chain architecture for RAIL modeling with torque 2D

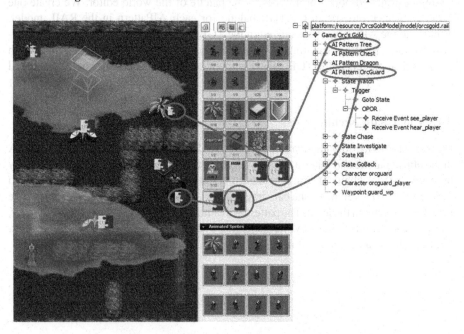

Fig. 4. Use AIPattern in TGB and RAIL editor

5   Orc's Gold: A Prototype Game

To evaluate the RAIL as a game development tool, a prototype game was developed. The game is a 2D action/adventure game named *Orc's Gold*. The game concept is that a player controls a human character who should steal gold chests from orc's camps. The chests are guarded by orc guards and dragons, and they will try to kill the player if possible. The player can walk or run. When he is running, he moves faster than the orc guards so he can take the chests by wisely using the advantage of speed. If a player successfully steals all the gold chests on the map, he wins the game. Figure 5 shows a screenshot of *Orc's Gold*.

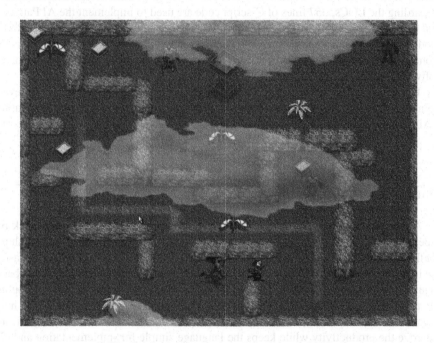

Fig. 5. An In-Game screenshot of *Orc's Gold*

The game uses four AIPatterns to control the characters, which are Orc Guard, Dragon, Chest and Tree. The trees are purely decorative objects that almost have nothing to do with the gameplay, but they will play a "swing" animation when a player touches them. To evaluate the productivity impact of RAIL modeling, the four patterns were implemented by the first author using two methods: the manual coding method and the DSM method. The time used and Lines of Code (LOC) developed for the two methods are summarized in Table 1, from which we see that the domain framework including the low-level AI, input handling and other low-level mechanics took more time and lines of code to develop than the high-level AI Patterns. However, the domain framework is on a low abstraction level and less relevant to specific gameplay, it is reusable for future AI Patterns and even in future games.

Table 1. Comparison of manual coding and DSM in developing *Orc's Gold*

Method	Time used (Hours)		LOCs written	
	Domain framework	AI patterns	Domain framework	AI patterns
Manual coding	20.5	**9.5**	1741	**357**
MDGD with RAIL		**0.7**		**0**

The time spent on the AI Pattern development is 9.5 h with the traditional manual coding method, and it is dramatically reduced to 0.7 h with the RAIL-based method. Regarding the LOCs, 357 lines of C-script code are used to implement the AI Patterns, and with MDGD method, all the AI Pattern code is automatically generated from a RAIL model, and no manual coding is needed. There is a significant productivity improvement from using RAIL, and the result is also in line with the reports of DSM from other software domains such as [12–14].

The benefits of DSM are not free, and the initial investment must be made for developing the DSL and the corresponding tools [15]. The time and LOCs used in creating RAIL and its tool chain are presented in Table 2.

Table 2. Cost of developing RAIL and its tool-chain

	Time (Hours)	LOCs
RAIL and its tool-chain	4.5	278

As it was discussed in [15], the initial investment on DSM can be paid back by repetitively use of the DSL and the tools created, and by lowering the technical threshold for the developers. The more products and variants created with the DSL tools, the faster the investment is paid back. In the RAIL case, interestingly the investment is paid back in just one product: if we add the cost of developing RAIL tools to the cost of developing the prototype, the total cost is still lower than the manual coding method. This may because of two reasons: (1) the RAIL lies on a proper abstraction level that can significant improve the productivity while keeps the language simple for implementation and (2) the use of EMF and Acceleo framework significantly improved the productivity of developing the DSL tools.

By analyzing the logic of the generated code and the manually written code, the performance of them is expected to be equivalent, because the algorithms and the mechanics implemented with two methods are identical. The results of a simple profiling also support the impression.

The RAIL-based modeling method also improves modifiability of the software. For instance, since the C-script does not fully support object-oriented programming, the manual code sometimes has duplicated parts spreading among several modules, and when the duplicated code needs to be changed, the same modifications must be done several times on different modules. This is an error-prone task. Thanks to the language features provided by Acceleo, the problem can be solved at the code generation level in RAIL-based modeling: the duplicated parts of the generated code can be generated from one code-generator module, and modifying the module will result in the modifications on all the generated modules with the duplicated parts. Generally, the language for writing code generator provides an extra means to compensate the drawbacks of the target language for modularizing the generated code well.

Modern game engines have provided various visual programming tools such as Unreal Kismet. Comparing to these tools, RAIL-based development requires less software engineering skills from the users, because the language concepts are closer to the game domain instead of the programming domain.

6 Conclusion

RAIL as a **domain-specific** language can specify behavioral aspects of Action/Adventure games. Prototyping Orc's Gold showed that RAIL and its tools can significantly reduce the time and code lines needed. Moreover, the cooperation of engine tools and MDGD tools offers an efficient workflow, which is benefit from the ECGM methodology [9].

The initial investment of model-driven development is of general concern. RAIL maximizes the interoperability of MDD and game engines, which can reduce the requirements to the MDD tools. The use of language workbench, i.e. EMF and Acceleo also significantly reduced the initial investment in the practical aspects. The case study showed that the initial investment on the meta-model and code generator for RAIL was acceptable, and it was paid back in just one project. Moreover, the tools can be used for creating many more patterns for extending Orcs´Gold to a real game, and even be able to be reused in other 2D action/adventure games.

Splitting the low-level AI and the high-level AI is necessary in game modeling. Script languages or GPLs are appropriate for implementing low-level AI, because they were just created for solving the problems on this abstraction level. The case study showed that low-level AI costs a lot of development effort, and this may raise a question that if RAIL has solved the difficult problems. But the low-level AI is reusable among patterns, even reusable among games, so the cost does not scale with the project complexity. The part of game that RAIL addressed can scale, which is more time-consuming in a real game project.

Further work includes extending RAIL to support larger scale games, and more game architectures, e.g. client-server, and applying it in more prototypes/games to get valuable feedback.

References

1. Kelly, S., Tolvanen, J.-P.: Domain-Specific Modeling: Enabling Full Code Generation. Wiley, Hoboken (2008)
2. Blow, J.: Game development: harder than you think. Queue **1**(10), 28 (2004)
3. Hernandez, F.E., Ortega, F.R.: Eberos GML2D: a graphical domain-specific language for modeling 2D video games. In: Proceedings of the 10th Workshop on Domain-Specific Modeling, Reno, Nevada (2010)

4. Sanchez, K., Garces, K., Casallas, R.: A DSL for rapid prototyping of cross-platform tower defense games. In: 10th Colombian Computing Conference, 10CCC 2015, 21 September 2015–25 September 2015. Institute of Electrical and Electronics Engineers Inc., Bogota (2015)
5. Walter, R., Masuch, M.: How to integrate domain-specific languages into the game development process. In: Proceedings of the 8th International Conference on Advances in Computer Entertainment Technology. ACM (2011)
6. Reyno, E.M., Carsi Cubel, J.: Automatic prototyping in model-driven game development. Comput. Entertain. 7(2), 29 (2009)
7. Van Hoecke, S., Samyn, K., Deglorie, G., Janssens, O., Lambert, P., Van de Walle, R.: Enabling control of 3D visuals, scenarios and non-linear gameplay in serious game development through model-driven authoring. In: Vaz de Carvalho, C., Escudeiro, P., Coelho, A. (eds.) Serious Games, Interaction, and Simulation. LNICST, vol. 161, pp. 103–110. Springer, Cham (2016). https://doi.org/10.1007/978-3-319-29060-7_16
8. Maier, S., Volk, D.: Facilitating language-oriented game development by the help of language workbenches. In: Proceedings of the 2008 Conference on Future Play: Research, Play, Share. ACM (2008)
9. Zhu, M., Wang, A.I., Trætteberg, H.: Engine- cooperative game modeling (ECGM): bridge model-driven game development and game engine tool-chains. In: ACE2016 the 13th International Conference on Advances in Computer 2016, Osaka, Japan
10. Gamma, E., et al.: Design Patterns: Elements of Reusable Object-Oriented Software. Pearson Education, Upper Saddle River (1994)
11. Stahl, T., Voelter, M., Czarnecki, K.: Model-Driven Software Development: Technology, Engineering, Management. Wiley, Chichester (2006)
12. Kieburtz, R.B., et al.: A software engineering experiment in software component generation. In: Proceedings of the 18th International Conference on Software Engineering. IEEE Computer Society (1996)
13. Weiss, D.M.: Software Product-Line Engineering: a Family-Based Software Development Process. Addison-Wesley Longman Publishing Co., Inc., Boston (1999)
14. Kelly, S., Tolvanen, J.-P.: Visual domain-specific modeling: benefits and experiences of using metaCASE tools. In: International Workshop on Model Engineering, at ECOOP (2000)
15. Kelly, S., Tolvanen, J.-P.: Domain-Specific Modeling Enabling Full Code Generation. Wiley, Hoboken (2008)
16. Furtado, A.W., Santos, A.L.: Using domain-specific modeling towards computer games development industrialization. In: The 6th OOPSLA Workshop on Domain-Specific Modeling (DSM06). Citeseer (2006)
17. Guana, V., Stroulia, E.: Phydsl: a code-generation environment for 2d physics-based games. In: 2014 IEEE Games, Entertainment, and Media Conference (IEEE GEM) (2014)
18. Matallaoui, A., Herzig, P., Zarnekow, R.: Model-driven serious game development integration of the gamification modeling language GaML with unity. In: 48th Annual Hawaii International Conference on System Sciences, HICSS 2015, January 5, 2015–January 8, 2015. IEEE Computer Society, Kauai (2015)
19. Reyno, E.M., Cubel, J.A.C.: Model-driven game development: 2D platform game prototyping. In: 9th International Conference on Intelligent Games and Simulation, GAME-ON 2008, 17 November 2008–19 November 2008. EUROSIS, Valencia (2008)
20. Reyno, E.M., et al.: Automatic prototyping in model-driven game development. Comput. Entertain. 7(2), 1–9 (2009)

21. Reyno, E.M., Cubel, J.A.C.: Model-driven game development: 2D platform game prototyping. In: Game-On 2008, 9th International Conference on Intelligent Games and Simulation, EUROSIS (2008)

22. Hernandez, F.E., Ortega, F.R.: Eberos GML2D: a graphical domain-specific language for modeling 2D video games. In: Proceedings of the 10th Workshop on Domain-Specific Modeling, p. 1. ACM, Reno (2010)

23. Walter, R., Masuch, M.: How to integrate domain-specific languages into the game development process. In: Proceedings of the 8th International Conference on Advances in Computer Entertainment Technology, pp. 1–8. ACM, Lisbon (2011)

24. Marques, E., et al.: The RPG DSL: a case study of language engineering using MDD for generating RPG games for mobile phones. In: Proceedings of the 2012 Workshop on Domain-Specific Modeling, pp. 13–18. ACM, Tucson (2012)

25. Furtado, A.W.B., et al.: Improving digital game development with software product lines. IEEE Softw. **28**(5), 30–37 (2011)

26. Furtado, A.W.B., Santos, A.L.M.: Using domain-specific modeling towards computer games development industrialization. In: 6th OOPSLA Workshop on Domain-Specific Modeling (DSM 2006) (2006)

27. Furtado, A.W.B., Santos, A.L.M.: Extending visual studio .NET as a software factory for computer games development in the .NET platform. In: 2nd International Conference on Innovative Views of .NET Technologies (IVNET06) (2007)

28. Furtado, A.W.B., Santos, A.L.M., Ramalho, G.L.: A computer games software factory and edutainment platform for Microsoft .NET. In: SB Games 2007 (2007)

29. Furtado, A.W.B., Santos, A.L.M., Ramalho, G.L.: SharpLudus revisited: from ad hoc and monolithic digital game DSLs to effectively customized DSM approaches. In: Proceedings of the Compilation of the Co-located Workshops on DSM 2011, TMC 2011, AGERE! 2011, AOOPES 2011, NEAT 2011, & VMIL 2011, pp. 57–62. ACM, Portland (2011)

30. Sarinho, V.T., et al.: A generative programming approach for game development. In: 2009 VIII Brazilian Symposium on Games and Digital Entertainment (SBGAMES) (2009)

31. Pleuß, A., Hußmann, H.: Integrating authoring tools into model-driven development of interactive multimedia applications. In: Jacko, Julie A. (ed.) HCI 2007. LNCS, vol. 4550, pp. 1168–1177. Springer, Heidelberg (2007). https://doi.org/10.1007/978-3-540-73105-4_127

32. Pleuss, A.: MML: a language for modeling interactive multimedia applications. In: Seventh IEEE International Symposium on Multimedia (2005)

33. Pleuß, A.: Modeling the user interface of multimedia applications. In: Briand, L., Williams, C. (eds.) MODELS 2005. LNCS, vol. 3713, pp. 676–690. Springer, Heidelberg (2005). https://doi.org/10.1007/11557432_50

34. Cutumisu, M., et al.: Generating ambient behaviors in computer role-playing games. IEEE Intell. Syst. **21**(5), 19–27 (2006)

35. Guo, H., et al.: Realcoins: a case study of enhanced model driven development for pervasive games. Int. J. Multimed. Ubiquitous Eng. **10**(5), 395–411 (2015)

36. Marchiori, E.J., et al.: A visual language for the creation of narrative educational games. J. Vis. Lang. Comput. **22**(6), 443–452 (2011)

Speech Emotion Recognition Based on a Recurrent Neural Network Classification Model

Rubén D. Fonnegra(ID) and Gloria M. Díaz(✉)(ID)

Instituto Tecnológico Metropolitano, Medellín, Colombia
{rubenfonnegra,gloriadiaz}@itm.edu.co
http://www.itm.edu.co/

Abstract. Affective computing is still one of the most active areas of study for developing best human-machine interactions. Specifically, speech emotion recognition is widely used, due to its implementation feasibility. In this paper, we investigate the discriminative capabilities of recurrent neural networks in human emotion analysis from low-level acoustic descriptors extracted from speech signals. The proposed approach starts extracting 1580 features from the audio signal using the well-known OpenSmile toolbox. These features are then used as input to a recurrent Long Short-Term Memory (LSTM) neural network, which is trained for deciding the emotion content of the evaluated utterance. Performance evaluation was conducted by two experiments: a gender independent and a gender-dependent classification. Experimental results show that the proposed approach achieves 92% emotion recognition accuracy in the gender independent experiment, which outperforms previous works using the same experimental data. In the gender-dependent experiment, accuracy was 94.3% and 84.4% for men and women, respectively.

Keywords: Speech emotion recognition · Audio signals
Deep learning

1 Introduction

Emotion recognition concerns to describing the high-level affective content of an utterance from the low-level acoustic signal produced by a speaker. This has been a growing field of study that had shown be useful in large variety of applications in diverse areas related to the human-computer interaction (HCI) [1,2] such as behavior and mood analysis, which uses it for improving the user experience in both video games interaction and entertainment fields [3,4]; the emotional advertising, that attempts to identify the emotions generated by information given in advertisement to attract the largest number of users attention [5]; among others.

Although several kinds of signals, including electroencephalography [6] and facial expressions [7], have been studied for recognizing speaker emotions, speech

© Springer International Publishing AG, part of Springer Nature 2018
A. D. Cheok et al. (Eds.): ACE 2017, LNCS 10714, pp. 882–892, 2018.
https://doi.org/10.1007/978-3-319-76270-8_59

acoustic signals continue being one of the most used due to the feasibility of implementing end-user systems that only requires a microphone for capturing the input signals. Nevertheless, speech-based emotion recognition is still a challenging task, due to the natural intra and inter-variability of subject voices. To leading with those challenges several feature extractors have been proposed, among of them, INTERSPEECH 2010 paralinguistic challenge features have been considered as representative descriptors reflecting paralinguistic information assessment [8]. Those are a set of quantitative features that describe intensity, speaking variations, envelope and vocalization changes; which had shown to be one of the most feasible approaches for characterizing audio signals [8–11].

On the other hand, the use of Deep Learning had shown increasing use due to the development of dedicated and high-performance processors which make faster training neural network based algorithms. Recently, novel techniques for pattern recognition in speech signals using Deep Learning approaches have been proposed, either as feature extraction approaches [12,13] or as classification models that use conventional acoustic descriptors [14]. Thus, Deep Belief Network and Autoencoders architectures have been used to create higher representations from low-level descriptors [15]; while Extreme Learning Machines, Multilayer Perceptrons and Long Short Term Memory (LSTM) models have been used as classification models [15–18]. In spite of these techniques propose a novel data interpretation, overall accuracy has not outperform other state-of-the-art techniques such as kernel based classification models.

In this work, a classification approach based on a recurrent deep learning model namely LSTM is proposed for recognizing the emotion of an utterance from the voice audio signal. For doing so, signals are initially processed for extracting state-of-the-art low-level features, which are then used as inputs of a deep neural network that performs a recurrent analysis of the signals for deciding the actual emotion between six possibilities i.e. anger, fear, disgust, happiness, surprise and sadness. This paper is organized as follows, the proposed approach and the database used for evaluation are described in the Sect. 3, the Sect. 4 presents the results reported by the proposed model and the performance comparison with some relevant state-of-the-art works. Finally, conclusions and future work are discussed in the Sect. 5.

2   Previous Works

As was mentioned above, development of speech emotion recognition systems (SER) has been a widely active field in the last years. Several strategies had been proposed, either using audio speech signals alone or fusing it with other information such as provided by visual expressions and physiological signals [6,7]. A complete revision of those proposals can be found in [19].

With the aim to provide a performance comparison baseline, this section describes those works, recently published, which report results using the same public dataset used herein for evaluating the proposed approach, i.e., eNTER-FACE'05 database (see Sect. 3.4). In [14] a transfer learning model is proposed, in which 16 low-level descriptors (LLDs) and 12 functionals audio features are extracted using the openEAR toolkit. A transfer learning model, which includes autoencoders based technique for feature transfer, maps a general structure of input characteristics by moving them from source to target to train a support vector machine (SVM). The main drawback of this model is that it is highly dependent on training reconstruction of data for knowledge transfer. An SVM learning model was also used in [20] to differentiate between the six different emotions included in the eNTERFACE database, but the feature vector was composed of 7 short time-based features and three long-time based features extracted from the speech audio signals using JAudio toolkit. Reported results achieve an accuracy of 0.7857. Likewise, in [12] a sparse local discriminant canonical correlation analysis for multimodal information fusion was presented. In the case of audio emotion recognition, authors propose to apply a feature extraction stage to convert time domain signals into spectrograms with a 20 ms window and 10 ms overlap. The spectrograms are processed using the Principal Components Analysis (PCA) method to obtain 60 components, which are then considered as inputs of a sparse autoencoder (400 units) to create a subspace representation, which is also used to train an SVM model. This approach improves previous results, achieving an accuracy of 0.74. Additionally, in [13] an audio emotion recognition system based on extreme learning machine (ELM) is proposed. Initially, a signal processing stage extracts multi-directional regression features (MDR) by pre-emphasize audio signals and frame them using hamming windows. Then, Fourier transform based spectral analysis and filter is applied using 24 Mel-scale Frequencies, obtaining 24 values per frame. At this point, a four-directional three-point linear regression is carried out to extract 96 features. The features are processed by an ELM classifier that achieves an overall accuracy of 0.6404.

On the other hand, a speech emotion recognition system based on a recurrent deep learning strategy was recently described in [18]. As our proposed method, this approach uses low-level features for representing the voice audio signal and an LSTM architecture for classifying it. However, the feature description model is focused on the analysis of utterances where emotions can reach their highest expression peak, besides that suppress silence in sentences, or non-expressive words. That is to say, that only verbal features are used for characterizing the signal. This approach reaches an accuracy of 63.5% in an imbalanced database, by which results are not comparable.

3   Materials and Methods

Figure 1 illustrates the proposed approach for identifying emotions from audio low-level signal cues produced by a speaker, which is composed of two main stages: training and recognition stages. Likewise, both training and recognition stages are composed of two modules, in the first module, the voice signal is described by a total of 1580 features that are extracted using the OpenSmile toolbox [21]. As was proposed in [22], these features result from split the input

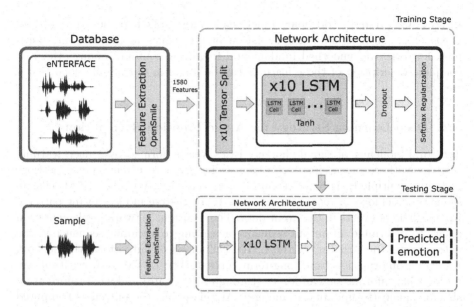

Fig. 1. Overview of the proposed approach for identifying emotions from speech signals.

signal into 10 fragments, each of which is described by 158 low-level features, respectively. Then, in the second module, a recurrent neural network is implemented as a classification model able to recognizing between six different emotions: anger, fear, disgust, happiness, surprise, or sadness. So, the output will be the predicted emotion according to an input into the network.

3.1   Feature Extraction

Due to the main characteristic of speech signals, which is data changes across time; a temporal modeling of data was considered as processing and feature extraction stage. As was proposed by [22], the input audio signal is split into 10 segments with similar sampling size. Then, each segment is processed by the OpenSmile extractor, which generates a vector of 158 low-level features, corresponding to the well known INTERSPEECH 2010 Paralinguistic challenge features [8]. Thus, the whole signal is described by 1580 features. The idea of using INTERSPEECH 2010 features is considering not only linguistic information from audio signals but also identify non-verbal patterns which could tell an emotion.

The extracted features correspond to a set of 34 low-level descriptors (LLDs), with its corresponding delta coefficients namely: loudness raised to a power of 0.3, Mel Frequency Cepstral coefficients (MFCCs), logarithmic power of Mel-frequency bands, 8 line spectral pair frequencies from 8 linear prediction coding (LPC) coefficients, envelope of fundamental frequency contour, voicing probability of fundamental frequency, maximum and minimum value absolute positions, contour mean, slope of the contour linear approximation and, offset of the contour linear approximation. Besides, a set of 21 functionals were applied to 68

LLDs (1428), and 19 additional functionals were applied to the 4 pitch-based LLDs (152), such as standard deviation of the values in the contour, skewness, kurtosis, the smoothed fundamental frequency contour, among others. A complete description of those features can be found in OpenSmile documentation [21].

3.2   Deep Learning Strategy for Audio Emotion Recognition

Temporal modeling of signal characteristics was performed by a deep learning strategy with recurrent instance analysis; i.e. by a recurrent neural network including multiple Long Short-Term Memory cells (LSTM). The LSTM cells are structures included in recurrent networks that preserve most relevant patterns from a chain of events in the input data. The recurrent network implementation allows to determine an output sequence according to an input sequence in the network, and the structure of the LSTM cell allows to outperform the network by storing information from long-term context. The LSTM network itself can decide what information can forget (through forget gate) and what information should remain (to update parameters). At this point, the output is computed taking into account the input after to parameters updating. Optimization, based on gradient descendent algorithm, allows to minimize the error of LSTM cells in time through sequences. This characteristic is considered in this work to learn temporal changes in the features extracted from the audio signals.

A general LSTM architecture is described in [23]; and an example of an LSTM cell is shown in Fig. 2. The network consists of 10 LSTM cells (the number of input signal splits), where every LSTM cell is connected to the next, consecutively. This architecture allows to perform an analysis of characteristics for each signal segment in the same amount of batches (10 batches). The learning rate of the network was set to 0.001 and the activation function of the recurrent cells was hyperbolic tangent (Tanh). To avoid overfitting, we included a dropout function layer after the output of recurrent LSTM cells. Additionally, a softmax regularization was applied into the output layer to establish probabilistic density function of the classes. On the other hand, due to the parameter considerations of the algorithm to avoid divergence and maximizing performance, the selected optimizer parameter was Adaptive Moment Estimation (Adam), which is fully described in Subsect. 3.3.

3.3   Adaptive Moment Estimation (Adam) Optimizer

The network parameters of the architecture described in Subsect. 3.2 were optimized during the training stage by a stochastic gradient descendant based algorithm named Adaptive Moment Estimation (Adam) optimizer [24]. Adam optimization is a momentum based learning algorithm (mean and variance), which allows adaptive single parameter tuning (such as Adagrad and RMSprop) but considering gradients initialization and small decaying rates. These considerations significantly improve parameters optimization to increase accuracy and to

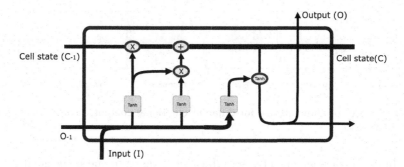

Fig. 2. General structure of the Recurrent LSTM network

avoid divergence during the training stage. Adam moment estimation and optimization rules are described by the Eqs. (1), (2) and (3) respectively, where the optimizer constant values were set to $\beta_1 = 0.9, \beta_2 = 0.999, \alpha = 0.001, \varepsilon = 10^{-8}$ (being α = Learning rate) during training.

$$m_t = \beta_1 m_{t-1} + (1 - \beta_1)g_t \tag{1}$$

$$v_t = \beta_2 v_{t-1} + (1 - \beta_2)g_t^2 \tag{2}$$

$$\theta_{t+1} = \theta_t - \frac{\alpha}{\sqrt{v_t} + \epsilon} m_t \tag{3}$$

3.4 The eNTERFACE'05 Database

The proposed approach was evaluated with a public, available and widely used dataset i.e. the eNTERFACE'05 database [25], which allows to compare the obtained results with state-of-the-art. This is a bimodal database that contains video and audio signals of subjects expressing affective sentences in English language. 43 different non-professional actors (35 men and 13 women) coming from 14 different countries were asked to express emotions through specific sentences (5 sentences) for six different emotions (anger, fear, disgust, happiness, surprise, and sadness). So, the database is composed of a total of 1290 bimodal samples, corresponding to five videos (one per sentence) for six different emotion (five samples per emotion) taken from 43 subjects. Data were herein preprocessed separating audio signals from video frames, to remain only the audio signals. Figure 3 shows graphics of some sample signals from the database, in which the different emotional content is illustrated.

4 Experimental Results

4.1 Experimental Setup

In this work, we carried out two different experiment to evaluate the performance of the proposed approach: a gender-dependent case and a gender-independent

Fig. 3. Samples of audio signals for different emotional content, taken from eNTER-FACE database

case. In the gender-dependent case, subjects belonging to one single gender (only males or females) were considered, while in the gender-independent case, subjects belonging to both genders (males and females) were mixed-up. In both cases, we use an iterative 5-folding cross-validation approach aiming to compare results with previous works [22,26]. In this way, in the gender-independent case, a total of 1260 samples were considered, which were split into 1008 samples for training and 252 for testing; to the male-dependent case, we considered 792 samples as training set and 198 as testing set (990 samples in total) and; for female-dependent case, we considered 216 samples as training set and 54 samples as testing set (270 samples in total). Cross-validation algorithm was carried out with 1000 iterations, where each fold was statistically stratified for keeping data normally distribution. The model performance was evaluated using confusion matrices and overall accuracy, which was estimated according to Eq. (4).

$$Accuracy = \frac{Correct\ predictions\ emotions\ (hits)}{Amount\ of\ samples} \tag{4}$$

4.2 Gender-Independent Emotion Recognition Results

Table 1 shows the confusion matrix reported by the proposed model to the gender independent experiment. As can be observed, highest accuracy is obtained to the surprise emotion. However, other emotions such as anger, happiness, and sadness reach more than to 90% accuracy. On the other hand, disgust has reached lowest results with 83.8% accuracy, being confused with surprise and anger, principally.

Table 1. Confusion matrix for audio emotion recognition in gender-independent case

Emotion	Predictions					
	Anger	Disgust	Fear	Happiness	Sadness	Surprise
Anger	**0.933**	0.004	0.004	0.004	0.009	0.042
Disgust	0.038	**0.838**	0.004	0.028	0.023	0.066
Fear	0.023	0.019	**0.890**	0.028	0.023	0.014
Happiness	0.033	0.023	0.004	**0.900**	0.004	0.033
Sadness	0.0	0.023	0.0	0.0	**0.942**	0.033
Surprise	0.019	0.004	0.0	0.004	0.014	**0.957**

Finally, fear recognition shown an accuracy of 89%, which is not a significantly low value. In comparison with [26], our method improves performance for recognition of all emotions. Concerning to [22], emotions such as fear (+0.14), happiness (+0.02), sadness (+0.02) and surprise (+0.07) have significantly improved performance, while anger achieves similar performance (−0.007). Additionally, the general accuracy was of 0.920, which outperforms s state-of-the-art proposals. Table 2 shows the performance comparison in terms of general accuracy between state-of-the-art methods and the proposed approach.

Table 2. Performance comparison of the proposed approach with previous state-of-the-art works

Reference	Accuracy rate
Deng et al. [14]	0.591
Hossain et al. [13]	0.640
Dobrivsek et al. [26]	0.725
Fu et al. [12]	0.740
Yan et al. [22]	0.763
Porial et al. [20]	0.785
Our strategy	**0.920**

4.3   Gender-Dependent Emotion Recognition

Due to the variety of subjects, we evaluate gender dependent case emotion recognition. The accuracy obtained in the male-dependent case shows a better accuracy than the obtained in gender-independent case (94.3%). While, this performance measure decrease in the female-dependent evaluation, achieving an accuracy of 84.4%, which not differs from performance obtain in state-of-the-art (87.4%). Tables 3 and 4 show results obtained for male and female, respectively. We consider that emotion recognition in the female can be improved including new samples (81% of data = males and 19% of data = females).

Table 3. Confusion matrix for audio emotion recognition in male participants

Emotion	Predictions					
	Anger	Disgust	Fear	Happiness	Sadness	Surprise
Anger	**0.933**	0.006	0.0	0.036	0.012	0.012
Disgust	0.012	**0.957**	0.012	0.0	0.012	0.006
Fear	0.006	0.012	**0.915**	0.012	0.024	0.030
Happiness	0.018	0.006	0.006	**0.969**	0.0	0.0
Sadness	0.018	0.006	0.006	0.006	**0.963**	0.0
Surprise	0.006	0.036	0.018	0.024	0.0	**0.915**

Table 4. Confusion matrix for audio emotion recognition in female participants

Emotion	Predictions					
	Anger	Disgust	Fear	Happiness	Sadness	Surprise
Anger	**0.822**	0.022	0.088	0.022	0.0	0.044
Disgust	0.0	**0.933**	0.0	0.0	0.0	0.066
Fear	0.111	0.044	**0.800**	0.022	0.022	0.0
Happiness	0.044	0.022	0.0	**0.777**	0.0	0.155
Sadness	0.0	0.044	0.0	0.0	**0.888**	0.0
Surprise	0.022	0.022	0.022	0.022	0.044	**0.866**

5   Conclusions and Future Work

In this paper, we proposed an audio-based emotion recognition, which implements a Long Short Term Memory (LSTM) deep network architecture as a classification model able to distinguish between six different emotions (anger, disgust, fear, happiness, sadness, and surprise). Audio signals were featured using the OpenSmile feature extractor, which had shown be one of the most feasible descriptors of voice signals.

Performance evaluation was carried out using the public well-known eNTER-FACE'05 database, which allowed to compare results with state-of-the-art methods. From the results, the proposed approach accuracy outperform all the previous works that reported results to this dataset, showing that the combination of acoustic features and deep learning models is a feasible approach for recognizing emotions of an utterance produced by a speaker.

Experimental results showed the best performance for discriminating emotions in male cases (94%) respect to the female cases (84.4%), which could be caused by the small number of samples used for training the classification model. For which, an evaluation with a larger database is desirable and will be performed in a future work.

As future work, we suggest combining the proposed approach with video analysis techniques in order to improve emotion recognition accuracy from bimodal signals.

References

1. Corneanu, C.A., Simón, M.O., Cohn, J.F., Guerrero, S.E.: Survey on rgb, 3d, thermal, and multimodal approaches for facial expression recognition: history, trends, and affect-related applications. IEEE Trans. Pattern Anal. Mach. Intell. **38**(8), 1548–1568 (2016)
2. Zhou, X., Shen, W.: Research on interactive device ergonomics designed for elderly users in the human-computer interaction. Int. J. Smart Home **10**(2), 49–62 (2016)
3. Balducci, F., Grana, C., Cucchiara, R.: Affective level design for a role-playing videogame evaluated by a brain-computer interface and machine learning methods. Vis. Comput. **33**(4), 413–427 (2017)

4. Bartsch, A., Hartmann, T.: The role of cognitive and affective challenge in enter-tainment experience. Commun. Res. **44**(1), 29–53 (2017)
5. Consoli, D.: A new concept of marketing: the emotional marketing. BRAND Broad Res. Account. Negot. Distrib. **1**(1), 52–59 (2010)
6. Lin, Y.P., Wang, C.H., Jung, T.P., Wu, T.L., Jeng, S.K., Duann, J.R., Chen, J.H.: Eeg-based emotion recognition in music listening. IEEE Trans. Biomed. Eng. **57**(7), 1798–1806 (2010)
7. Wegbreit, E., Weissman, A.B., Cushman, G.K., Puzia, M.E., Kim, K.L., Leiben-luft, E., Dickstein, D.P.: Facial emotion recognition in childhood-onset bipolar i disorder: an evaluation of developmental differences between youths and adults. Bipolar Disord. **17**(5), 471–485 (2015)
8. Schuller, B.W., Steidl, S., Batliner, A., Burkhardt, F., Devillers, L., Müller, C.A., Narayanan, S.S., et al.: The interspeech 2010 paralinguistic challenge. In: Inter-speech, vol. 2010, pp. 2795–2798 (2010)
9. Kaya, H., Salah, A.A., Karpov, A., Frolova, O., Grigorev, A., Lyakso, E.: Emo-tion, age, and gender classification in children's speech by humans and machines. Comput. Speech Lang. **46**(Suppl. C), 268–283 (2017)
10. Zhang, Y., Liu, J., Hu, J., Xie, X., Huang, S.: Social personality evaluation based on prosodic and acoustic features. In: Proceedings of the 2017 International Con-ference on Machine Learning and Soft Computing, pp. 214–218. ACM (2017)
11. Jassim, W.A., Paramesran, R., Harte, N.: Speech emotion classification using com-bined neurogram and interspeech 2010 paralinguistic challenge features. IET Signal Process. **11**(5), 587–595 (2017)
12. Fu, J., Mao, Q., Tu, J., Zhan, Y.: Multimodal shared features learning for emotion recognition by enhanced sparse local discriminative canonical correlation analysis. Multimed. Syst., 1–11 (2017). https://doi.org/10.1007/s00530-017-0547-8
13. Hossain, M.S., Muhammad, G.: Audio-visual emotion recognition using multi-directional regression and ridgelet transform. J. Multimodal User Interfac. **10**(4), 325–333 (2016)
14. Deng, J., Zhang, Z., Marchi, E., Schuller, B.: Sparse autoencoder-based feature transfer learning for speech emotion recognition. In: 2013 Humaine Association Conference on Affective Computing and Intelligent Interaction (ACII), pp. 511–516. IEEE (2013)
15. Schmidt, E.M., Kim, Y.E.: Learning emotion-based acoustic features with deep belief networks. In: 2011 IEEE Workshop on Applications of Signal Processing to Audio and Acoustics (WASPAA), pp. 65–68, October 2011
16. Han, K., Yu, D., Tashev, I.: Speech emotion recognition using deep neural network and extreme learning machine. In: Interspeech, pp. 223–227 (2014)
17. Cibau, N.E., Albornoz, E.M., Rufiner, H.L.: Speech emotion recognition using a deep autoencoder. An. XV Reun. Proces. Inf. Control **16**, 934–939 (2013)
18. Mirsamadi, S., Barsoum, E., Zhang, C.: Automatic speech emotion recognition using recurrent neural networks with local attention. In: 2017 IEEE International Conference on Acoustics, Speech and Signal Processing (ICASSP), pp. 2227–2231. IEEE (2017)
19. Alva, M.Y., Nachamai, M., Paulose, J.: A comprehensive survey on features and methods for speech emotion detection. In: 2015 IEEE International Conference on Electrical, Computer and Communication Technologies (ICECCT), pp. 1–6. IEEE (2015)
20. Poria, S., Cambria, E., Hussain, A., Huang, G.B.: Towards an intelligent framework for multimodal affective data analysis. Neural Netw. **63**, 104–116 (2015)

21. Eyben, F., Wöllmer, M., Schuller, B.: Opensmile: the munich versatile and fast open-source audio feature extractor. In: Proceedings of the 18th ACM international conference on Multimedia, pp. 1459–1462. ACM (2010)
22. Yan, J., Zheng, W., Xu, Q., Lu, G., Li, H., Wang, B.: Sparse kernel reduced-rank regression for bimodal emotion recognition from facial expression and speech. IEEE Trans. Multimed. **18**(7), 1319–1329 (2016)
23. Hochreiter, S., Schmidhuber, J.: Long short-term memory. Neural Comput. **9**(8), 1735–1780 (1997)
24. Kingma, D., Ba, J.: Adam: a method for stochastic optimization. arXiv preprint arXiv:1412.6980 (2014)
25. Martin, O., Kotsia, I., Macq, B., Pitas, I.: The enterface'05 audio-visual emotion database. In: 22nd International Conference on Data Engineering Workshops, 2006, Proceedings, p. 8. IEEE (2006)
26. Dobrišek, S., Gajšek, R., Mihelič, F., Pavešić, N., Štruc, V.: Towards efficient multimodal emotion recognition. Int. J. Adv. Rob. Syst. **10**(1), 53 (2013)

Author Index

Aakster, Yacintha 84
Álvarez, Nahum 360
Ando, Shunnosuke 626
Anjos, Ivo 430
Antunes, André 726
Arya, Pranalika 746
Ascensão, Mariana 430
Ashby, Simone 557
Athavale, Sandeep 746
Azhar, Azhri 462

Backlund, Per 508
Bala, Paulo 32
Banalzwaa, Mohammed Rabea Taleb 462
Bartsch, Silke 774
Bevilacqua, Fernando 508
Bielawski, Kevin Stanley 462
Born, Felix 46
Broekhuijsen, Mendel 406
Brosda, Constantin 774
Brückner, Stefan 415
Bulygin, Denis 608

Camilleri, Elizabeth 202
Casas, Sergio 293
Cavaco, Sofia 430
Centieiro, Pedro 318
Cesar, Pablo 488
Cheok, Adrian David 462
Chisik, Yoram 117
Choi, Insook 689
Clavero Jiménez, Marta 239
Coelho, António 219, 278
Correia, Nuno 726
Cruz, Marco 318

Damen, Koen 406
de Boer, Victor 637
de Kock, Suzanne 543
Dias, A. Eduardo 318
Díaz, Gloria M. 882
Dickinson, Patrick 187
Dionísio, Mara 32

Doi, Mayuka 368
dos Santos Faria, Ana Lucia 117
Drachen, Anders 531
Dzardanova, Elena 1

Eisenhardt, Manuela 774
Emmerich, Katharina 847
Englezos, Konstantinos 128
Engström, Henrik 508

Fonnegra, Rubén D. 882
Fukayama, Satoru 671
Fukusato, Tsukasa 153
Furukawa, Kiyoshi 139
Furukawa, Shoichi 153

Garcês Costa, Diana Leonor 117
García-Pereira, Inma 293
Gardeli, Anna 128
Gavalas, Damianos 1
Geigel, Joe 713
Gerling, Kathrin 187
Gimeno, Jesús 293
Gómez Maureira, Marcello A. 202, 239, 543
Goto, Masataka 671
Gowen, Carl 187
Grace, Lindsay 795
Grilo, Margarida 430
Guimarães, Isabel 430

Hagen, Kristoffer 384
Hakulinen, Jaakko 567
Hanna, Julian 557
Hara, Kenta 653
Hara, Takenori 66
Hasegawa, Shoichi 614
Hicks, Kieran 187
Hirayama, Shiho 66
Hitchens, Michael 531
Hlavacs, Helmut 761
Høivik, Torbjørn 384
Hone, Robert 795

Ichikawa, Kazuko   66
Iida, Hiroyuki   830
Ikeda, Kohei   470
Inglese, Patricia   795
Ishikawa, Hiroyo   172
Itaya, Akari   339
Iwamoto, Naoya   653

Jackson, G. Tanner   795
Jacob, João   219, 278
James, Amanda M. S.   239
Jansen, Josien   637
Juan, M.-Carmen   809

Kade, Daniel   14
Kajimoto, Hiroyuki   261
Kakitsuka, Ryo   653
Kaneko, Kunitake   172
Kaplan, Oral   272
Karunanayaka, Kasun   462
Kasapakis, Vlasios   1
Katayose, Haruhiro   626
Kato, Hirokazu   272
Kato, Takuya   653
Keskinen, Tuuli   567
Kitahara, Tetsuro   339
Kniestedt, Isabelle   202, 239
Kodama, Sachiko   311
Koge, Masahiro   261
Kohori, Tomoko   66
Koizumi, Naoya   470
Kono, Yasuyuki   588
Konstantinova, Ksenia   608
Kurabayashi, Shuichi   415
Kurihara, Kazutaka   339

Lentelink, Stefan   84
Li, Wenlin   830
Lindell, Rikard   14
Linehan, Conor   187
Loachamín-Valencia, Mauricio   809
Lopes, Ana   219, 278
López Ibáñez, Manuel   360

Madeira, Rui Neves   726
Magalhães, João   430
Mäkelä, Ville   567
Mao, Xinting   830

Markopoulos, Panos   406
Masuch, Maic   46, 847
Matos, Sónia   557
Matsumoto, Hiroko   66
Matsuura, Yu   311
Mavroudi, Dimitra   128
McCutcheon, Christopher   531
Méndez-López, Magdalena   809
Minakuchi, Misturu   601
Mitake, Hironori   614
Miyashita, Homei   368
Mohan, Akash   746
Mondou, Damien   103
Morishima, Shigeo   153, 653
Moteir, Ibrahim Gamal Mahmoud   462
Müller, Heike   774
Muramatsu, Michiko   66
Musabirov, Ilya   608

Nack, Frank   488, 637
Naemura, Takeshi   470
Naganuma, Hiroyuki   66
Nagao, Katashi   339
Nakamura, Takuto   261
Nisi, Valentina   32
Nóbrega, Rui   219, 278
Nunes, Nuno   32

Oakley, Ian   32
Ochiai, Yoichi   451
Ohmura, Hidefumi   139
Oishi, Erika   261
Okopny, Paul   608
Olsen, Gaute Meek   384
Oppermann, Leif   774
Osone, Hiroyuki   451
Özcan, Oğuzhan   14

Panza, Alice   488
Peinado, Federico   61, 360
Peñas, Gabriel   61
Pérez-Hernández, Elena   809
Plopski, Alexander   272
Portalés, Cristina   293
Postolache, Octavian   726
Pressler, Christoph   761
Prigent, Armelle   103

Rahman, Nur Ellyza Abd   462
Redi, Judith A.   488
Revel, Arnaud   103
Rodrigues, Ricardo   557
Rodrigues, Rui   219, 278
Röggla, Thomas   488
Romão, Teresa   318

Saarinen, Santeri   567
Sandor, Christian   272
Sato, Yukiko   415
Schaal, Steffen   774
Shibayama, Takuro   139
Shirzadian, Najereh   488
Shum, Hubert P. H.   653
Stavrakis, Modestos   128
Stratis, Manolis   128
Sugasawara, Shunsuke   588
Sykownik, Philipp   847

Takahashi, Tatsuji   139
Taketomi, Takafumi   272
Tjon-A-Pauw, Ana-Liza   637
Treepong, Bantita   614
Tsuchida, Shuhei   671
Turunen, Markku   567

Uchiyama, Hiroko   66
Uemura, Aiko   339
Ürey, Hakan   14

van Delden, Robby   84
van Leiden, Fabienne   406
Vera, Lucía   293
Vosinakis, Spyros   128

Wain, Jennifer   795
Wang, Alf Inge   384, 868
Waragai, Ikumi   415
Wibulpolprasert, Panut   614

Xiong, Shuo   830

Yamaguchi, Shugo   153
Yamamoto, Goshiro   272
Yamano, Masayuki   66
Yoshida, Takatoshi   451
Yoshitake, Yasuhide   272

Zhu, Meng   868
Zürn, Xenia   406

Printed in the United States
By Bookmasters